The Globaliz... of W...

The Globalization of World Politics

An introduction to international relations

Second Edition

Edited by

John Baylis and Steve Smith

OXFORD
UNIVERSITY PRESS

OXFORD

UNIVERSITY PRESS

Great Clarendon Street, Oxford OX2 6DP

Oxford University Press is a department of the University of Oxford.
It furthers the University's objective of excellence in research, scholarship,
and education by publishing worldwide in

Oxford New York

Athens Auckland Bangkok Bogotá Buenos Aires Cape Town
Chennai Dar es Salaam Delhi Florence Hong Kong Istanbul Karachi
Kolkata Kuala Lumpur Madrid Melbourne Mexico City Mumbai Nairobi
Paris São Paulo Shanghai Singapore Taipei Tokyo Toronto Warsaw

with associated companies in Berlin Ibadan

Oxford is a registered trade mark of Oxford University Press
in the UK and in certain other countries

Published in the United States
by Oxford University Press Inc., New York

Editorial arrangement © John Baylis and Steve Smith 2001
The individual chapters © the several contributors 2001

British Library Cataloguing in Publication Data

Data available

Library of Congress Cataloging in Publication Data

Data available

ISBN 0-19-878263-2

10 9 8 7 6 5 4 3 2

Typeset by RefineCatch Limited, Bungay, Suffolk
Printed and bound in Great Britain by
Bath Press Ltd., Bath, Avon

Editors' preface

The first edition of this book proved to be much more successful than either of the editors expected. We hoped that a text that combined history, theory, structure, and process, together with contemporary international issues, would prove popular with students and their teachers. What we did not expect was that the book would be adopted as a major text in such a short time in a wide range of international/world politics courses in thirty-three countries, including the United States, United Kingdom, Australia, Canada, Denmark, Sweden, Finland, Germany, France, Spain, Belgium, South Africa, Japan, Brazil, and India. We have also been greatly heartened by all the very helpful comments we have received from teachers in many of these countries. Some of these were solicited by our publishers and some have been sent to us quite independently. The overwhelming judgement has been that the book 'works' in the contemporary teaching environment. Teachers liked the combination of history and theory, in particular, and students found the chapters interesting, easy to understand and, to use a hackneyed phrase, 'user-friendly'. We also received some very useful suggestions on how the book could be made even better.

In the light of these comments we decided to use much the same structure and format for the second edition, while at the same time bringing the text up to date and adding some new material which we, and a number of our reviewers, felt had been neglected in the first edition. In modifying the structure the main change is that we have added a fifth section containing two new chapters on 'Globalization in the future'. We have done this to strengthen the globalization theme (which has also been enhanced in the rewriting of all the chapters) and to provide a more effective conclusion to the book. We have also added a number of other new chapters. In Part One, the history has been brought up to date with a chapter on 'International history since 1989' and in Part Four we have added a chapter on 'The communications and Internet revolution' to highlight the importance of contemporary global communications. The chapters on 'International political economy in the age of globalization' and 'Regionalism and integration' (now 'European and regional integration') have been completely rewritten by different contributors while a new chapter in Part Two on 'Contemporary mainstream approaches' has been added. Another chapter in Section Two entitled 'New approaches to international theory' has undergone significant rewriting and is now titled 'Reflectivist and constructivist approaches to international theory'. Readers of the first edition will also note that we have modified the titles of a number of chapters: 'Marxist theories of international relations' (in place of 'World system theory') and 'The United Nations and international order' (rather than 'International organization').

Finally, we have added more links to the Web at the end of chapters (again to emphasize the globalization theme), which we hope will encourage students to use the new, exciting technology available to them, to further their studies and acquire new transferable skills—so essential in the new (globalized) world we live in!

Acknowledgements

We would like to thank all those who sent us or OUP comments on the strengths and weaknesses of the first edition: we hope that they can see that we have tried to deal with all the suggestions we received. We would also like to thank the nine anonymous referees who commented in detail for OUP on the first edition. Special thanks are also due to Jan Jindy Pettman and Steve Lamy who gave us page-by-page suggestions for improvements. We would like to give our very warm and sincere thanks to Patricia Owens who did the editorial work on this second edition: she was a superbly efficient editorial assistant, and we both owe her a lot. This second edition is much stronger because of her professionalism and hard work. Thanks also go to Donia Richards for her secretarial work on this edition. Finally, we want to thank Angela Griffin at OUP for all her support, encouragement, and involvement in this project.

Steve Smith and John Baylis

Aberystwyth
January 2001

A Companion Website accompanies The Globalization of World Politics Second Edition

Students and teachers are invited to the book's Companion Website at:

www.oup.com/uk/best.textbooks/politics/globalization2e

Drawn up by Patricia Owens (University of Aberystwyth), this substantial site contains a range of material for lecturers and students:

Web links
A list of useful annotated web addresses to help with further reading and research (organized by chapter)

Data
Extra figures, tables, maps, and useful data relating to each chapter in the book (organized by chapter)

Glossary
Comprehensive A–Z dictionary of key IR terms

Review questions
Further questions, with varying degrees of difficulty, relating to each chapter in the book (organized by chapter)

PowerPoint
A full PowerPoint lecture series—fully customizable (organized by chapter)

IR Theory in Practice site
Interactive case studies to demonstrate the difference (and similarities) between the IR theory highlighted in the book and to show how theoretical concepts illuminate recent developments in world politics.

Contents

Part One The historical context

Part Two Theories of world politics

Part Five Globalization in the future

Detailed contents

List of figures

List of boxes

List of tables

About the contributors

Jonathan Aronson is Director and Professor of the School of International Relations at the University of Southern California. He also is a Professor in the Annenberg School for Communication. Aronson is a specialist on international trade and international communications policy and has written on issues related to international finance, trade in services, and international intellectual property. His books include: *Managing the World Economy: The Consequences of International Corporate Alliances* (Council on Foreign Relations) and *When Countries Talk: International Trade in Telecommunications Services* (Ballinger). Aronson is a member of the Council on Foreign Relations, the Pacific Council on International Policy, and the Asia Society.

John Baylis is a Professor and Head of the Department of Politics and International Relations at the University of Wales, Swansea. He was formerly Dean of Social Sciences at the University of Wales, Aberystwyth. His publications include: *Dilemmas of World Politics*, ed. with N. J. Rengger (Oxford University Press, 1992), *The Diplomacy of Pragmatism: Britain and the Formation of NATO* (Macmillan, 1993), and *Ambiguity and Deterrence: British Nuclear Strategy 1945–1964* (Oxford University Press, 1995) and *Anglo-American Relations Since 1939: The Enduring Alliance* (Manchester University Press, 1998).

Alex J. Bellamy is Lecturer in Defence Studies, King's College London, at the Joint Services Command and Staff College. He has written widely on the conflicts in former Yugoslavia. His articles include, 'Reconsidering Rambouillet', in *Contemporary Security Policy* 22 (1) 2001 and 'Human Wrongs in Kosovo 1974–99' in *International Journal of Human Rights* 4 (2) 2000. He is currently working on projects on Croatian nationalism, democratic control of the armed forces in the Balkans, and the war in Kosovo.

Chris Brown is Professor of International Relations at the London School of Economics. He is the author of *International Relations Theory: New Normative Approaches* (Harvester Wheatsheaf, 1992), and *Understanding International Relations* (Macmillan, 1997 and 2001), editor of *Political Restructuring in Europe* (Routledge, 1994), and the author of some three dozen articles and chapters in international political theory. His collection of *Texts in International Relations from the Greeks to the First World War*, co-edited with Terry Nardin and N. J. Rengger, will be published by Cambridge University Press in 2001.

Susan L. Carruthers is Senior Lecturer in the Department of International Politics, University of Wales, Aberystwyth. She is an international historian, specializing in communications and culture. She is the author of *Winning Hearts and Minds: British Governments and Colonial Counterinsurgency, 1944–60* (Leicester University Press, 1995), and co-editor of *War, Culture and the Media* (Flick Books, 1996). Her most recent book is *The Media at War: Communication and Conflict in the Twentieth Century* (Macmillan, 1999).

Thomas Christiansen is Director of the Jean Monnet Centre and Lecturer in European Studies in the Department of International Politics, University of Wales, Aberystwyth. Among his latest publications are *Committee Governance in the European Union*, ed. with

E. Kirchner (Manchester University Press, 2000) and *The Social Construction of Europe*, ed. with K. E. Jørgensen and A. Wiener (Sage, 2001). A book on the European Commission is in preparation.

Ian Clark is a Professor at the Department of International Politics at Aberystwyth after many years at the University of Cambridge. He has teaching and research interests that combine international history with the theory of international relations. He has also written extensively on the history of nuclear strategy and on the ethics of war. His publications include *Limited Nuclear War* (1982), *Waging War: A Philosophical Introduction* (1988), *The Hierarchy of States* (1989), and two books on the history of British nuclear policy. He co-edited *Classical Theories of International Relations* (1996). His recent work has been on globalization. This has resulted in two books from Oxford University Press, *Globalization and Fragmentation: International Relations in the Twentieth Century* (1997) and *Globalization and International Relations Theory* (1999).

Michael Cox is Professor of International Politics at the University of Wales, Aberystwyth. An Associate Research Fellow at Chatham House since 1994, and appointed editor of the *Review of International Studies* in 1998, he is the author and editor of over ten books including most recently *E. H. Carr: A Critical Appraisal* (Palgrave, 2000), *A Farewell to Arms? From Long War to Long Peace in Northern Ireland* (Manchester University Press, 2000), and *American Democracy Promotion: Impulses, Impacts and Strategies* (Oxford University Press, 2000).

Richard Crockatt is Reader in American History at the University of East Anglia where he also teaches international relations. He is author of *The Fifty Years War: The United States and the Soviet Union in World Politics, 1941–1991* (Routledge, 1995), and editor of *British Documents on Foreign Affairs, 1940–1945* (University Publications of America, forthcoming).

Tim Dunne is Senior Lecturer in International Politics at the University of Wales, Aberystwyth. His book *Inventing International Society: A History of the English School* was published by Macmillan in 1998. In addition, he has co-edited three collections for Cambridge University Press: *The Eighty Years Crisis: International Relations 1919–1999*, *Human Rights in Global Politics*, and *The Interregnum: Controversies in World Politics 1989–1999*. He is an associate editor of the *Review of International Studies* and the *International Journal of Human Rights*. Currently, he is working on a manuscript on International Society for Polity.

Owen Greene is Senior Lecturer in International Relations and Security Studies at the Department of Peace Studies, Bradford University. He trained in mathematics and physics, and researched in theoretical physics for several years before turning to international relations. He is author or co-author of ten books and over 150 other research works on international environmental issues and international security problems. His recent work has focused on the development, implementation, and effectiveness of international regimes, particularly in the areas of climate change, ozone depletion, regional sea pollution, and the significance of monitoring, transparency, and review processes.

Fred Halliday is Professor of International Relations at the London School of Economics. His books include *Revolution and World Politics, The Rise and Fall of the Sixth Great*

Power (1999), *Nation and Religion in the Middle East* (2000) and *The World at 2000. Perils and Promises* (2000).

Stephen Hobden is a Lecturer in the Department of International Politics, University of Wales, Aberystwyth. His research and teaching interests are theories of large-scale social change, the international politics of Latin America, and the international drug trade. He is currently working on a book on the history of the trade in illegal drugs.

Darryl Howlett is a Senior Lecturer in International Relations at the University of Southampton. His most recent publications are: with John Simpson 'Nuclear Proliferation: The Evolving Policy Debate', in Stuart Croft and Terry Terriff (eds.), *Critical Reflections on Security and Change*, (Frank Cass, 2000); and with Tanya Ogilvie-White, John Simpson, and Emily Taylor, *Nuclear Weapons Policy at the Crossroads* (Royal Institute for International Affairs, 2000, distributed in the United States by the Brookings Institution, Washington, DC).

Robert Jackson is a Professor at the University of British Columbia. His publications include: *The Global Covenant: Human Conduct in a World of States (Oxford University Press, 2000); (ed.), Sovereignty at the Millennium* (Political Studies, Special Issue, July 1999); co-author with Georg Sorensen, *Introduction to International Relations* (Oxford University Press, 1999); *Quasi-States* (Cambridge University Press, 1990); and with A. James (eds.), *States in a Changing World* (Clarendon Press, 1993). He is completing a book entitled *Sovereignty: Evolution of an Idea.*

Richard Wyn Jones is Senior Lecturer in International Politics at the University of Wales, Aberystwyth where he has special responsibility for teaching through the medium of the Welsh language. He is author of *Security, Strategy and Critical Theory* (Lynne Rienner, 1999) and editor of *Critical Theory and World Politics* (Lynne Rienner, 2000).

Steven L. Lamy is an Associate Professor in the University of Southern California's School of International Relations. His areas of expertise include international relations theory, foreign policy analysis, the foreign policies of Western advanced industrial states, and teaching and curriculum development in international relations. Dr Lamy has published over thirty articles and book chapters in these areas and has edited a book on contemporary international issues. His current work is on the domestic sources of foreign policy in European states.

Andrew Linklater is the Woodrow Wilson Professor of International Politics at the University of Wales, Aberystwyth. His most recent book is *The Transformation of Political Community: Ethical Foundations of the Post-Westphalian Era* which was published by Polity Press in 1998. His current research focuses on linkages between historical sociology and international relations.

Richard Little is Professor in the Department of International Politics at the University of Bristol. He is a former editor of the *Review of International Studies*. His latest book, co-authored with Barry Buzan is *International Systems in World History: Remaking the Study of International Relations* (Oxford University Press, 2000).

Simon Murden is a Lecturer in the Department of Politics, University of Plymouth. He specializes in the politics of culture and hegemony, and has particular expertise in Middle Eastern politics and security studies. He is the author of *Emergent Regional*

Powers and International Relations in the Gulf, 1988–1991 (Ithaca Press, 1995) and is currently writing a volume entitled *Islam in the New Hegemony* for Lynne Rienner.

Jan Jindy Pettman is Director of the Centre for Women's Studies at the Australian National University, and co-editor of the *International Feminist Journal of Politics*. Her current research focuses on gender, globalization and labour migration, and the gendered politics of identity. She is the author of *Worlding Women: A Feminist International Politics* (Routledge, 1996).

Brian C. Schmidt is lecturer in the Department of International Politics at the University of Wales, Aberystwyth. His research interests are in International Relations Theory and Disciplinary History. He is the author of *The Political Discourse of Anarchy: A Disciplinary History of International Relations* (SUNY Press, 1998).

Jan Aart Scholte is Reader in International Studies at the University of Warwick. He is author of *International Relations of Social Change* (Open University Press, 1993) and *Globalization: A Critical Introduction* (Macmillan, 2000) as well as co-author of *Contesting Global Governance: Multilateral Economic Institutions and Global Social Movements* (Cambridge University Press, 2000) and co-editor of *Civil Society and Global Finance* (United Nations University Press, forthcoming 2001).

Len Scott is a Senior Lecturer in the Department of International Politics, University of Wales, Aberystwyth where he specializes in international history and intelligence studies. His recent publications include *Macmillan, Kennedy and the Cuban Missile Crisis: Political, Military and Intelligence Aspects* (Macmillan, 1999) and, with Stephen Twigge, *Planning Armageddon: Britain, the United States and the Command of Nuclear Forces, 1945–1964* (Harwood Academic Press, 2000).

Steve Smith is a Professor in the Department of International Politics, and Pro Vice Chancellor (Academic Affairs) at the University of Wales, Aberystwyth. He specializes in international political theory. His latest publications include *International Relations Theory Today*, ed. with Ken Booth (Polity Press, 1995) and *International Theory: Positivism and Beyond*, ed. with Ken Booth and Marysia Zalewski (Cambridge University Press, 1996).

Paul Taylor is Professor of International Relations at the London School of Economics and Political Science (LSE), where he specializes in international organization, particularly the economic and social arrangements of the United Nations and the politics of the institutions of the European Union. He published *International Organization in the Modern World* (Pinter, 1993) and *The European Union in the 1990s* (Oxford University Press, 1996). He has edited and contributed to a number of books on international organization, especially with A. J. R. Groom, most recently on the *United Nations at the Millennium* (Continuum, 2000).

Caroline Thomas is Professor in the Politics Department at Southampton University. Her recent publications include *Global Governance, Development and Human Security* (Pluto Press, 2000) and A. Taylor and C. Thomas (eds.) *Global Trade and Global Social Issues* (Routledge, 1999).

Peter Willetts is Professor of Global Politics at City University. He has written extensively on international organizations, including editing two books on NGOs, *Pressure*

Groups in the Global System (Pinter, 1982) and *'The Conscience of the World': The Influence of Non-Governmental Organizations in the UN System* (Hurst, 1996).

Nicholas J. Wheeler is Senior Lecturer in the Department of International Politics at the University of Wales, Aberystwyth. He has written widely on human rights and humanitarian intervention and is the author of *Saving Strangers: Humanitarian Intervention in International Society* (Oxford University Press, 2000).

Brian White is Professor of International Relations at Staffordshire University and a Visiting Professor at the University of Toulouse. He is the author of *Britain, Detente and Changing East-West Relations* (Routledge, 1992) and *Understanding European Foreign Policy* (Macmillan, 2000). He also co-edited and contributed to *British Foreign Policy: Tradition, Change and Transformation* (Unwin Hyman, 1988), *Understanding Foreign Policy: The Foreign Policy Systems Approach* (Elgar, 1989), and *Issues in World Politics* (Macmillan, 1997; 2nd edn. forthcoming).

Ngaire Woods is Fellow and Lecturer in Politics and International Relations at University College, Oxford University. She has written extensively on international institutions and globalization, including *The Political Economy of Globalization* (Macmillan, 2000), *Inequality, Globalization and World Politics* (with Andrew Hurrell: Oxford University Press, 1999), *Explaining International Relations since 1945* (Oxford University Press, 1986), and numerous journal articles on the reform of global economic institutions. She is presently completing a book on the politics of the IMF and World Bank.

Introduction

Steve Smith and John Baylis

THE aim of this book is to provide the reader with an overview of contemporary world politics. The title of the book is not accidental; first, we want to introduce you to world politics, as distinct from international politics or international relations; second, many think that the contemporary, post-cold war world is distinctly different from previous periods because of globalization. We think that it is especially difficult to explain world politics in such an era because globalization is a particularly controversial term. It is controversial because there is considerable dispute over just what it means to talk of this being an era of globalization, and whether that means that the main features of world politics are any different to those of previous eras. In this Introduction we want to explain how we propose to deal with the concept of globalization and offer you some arguments in favour of seeing it as an important new development in world politics and also some arguments against such a view.

Before turning to look at globalization in order to set the scene for the chapters that follow, we want to do two things. We will first say something about the various terms used to describe global politics, and then we will spend some time looking at the main ways in which global politics has been explained up to the late 1990s. We need to do both of these things because our aim in this Introduction is not to put forward one view of how to think about globalization, agreed by all the contributors to this volume; rather we want to give the reader a context within which to read the chapters that follow and that means giving a variety of views on globalization and how to think about it. Our central concern is to point out that the main theoretical accounts of world politics all see globalization differently; some treat it as nothing more than a temporary phase in human history, and one which does not mean that we need to rethink how we understand world politics; others see it as but the latest manifestation of the growth of Western capitalism and modernization; and others see it as representing a fundamental transformation of world politics, one that requires new ways of understanding. The contributors to this book hold no one agreed view, and in fact there are representatives of all the responses just mentioned. From what we have said so far you should note that there are three main aims of this book:

- To offer an overview of world politics in an era of globalization.

- To summarize the main theoretical approaches available to explain contemporary world politics.
- To provide the material necessary to answer

the question of whether globalization marks a fundamental transformation in world politics.

From international politics to world politics

Why does the main title of this book refer to world politics rather than international politics or inter-national relations? These are the traditional names used to describe the kinds of interactions and processes that are the concern of this book. Indeed, you could look at the table of contents of many other introductory books and find a similar listing of main topics dealt with, yet often these books would have either international relations or international polit-ics as their main title. Furthermore, the discipline that studies these issues is nearly always called Inter-national Politics or International Relations. Our rea-son for choosing the phrase 'world politics' is that we think it is more inclusive than either of the alterna-tive terms. It is meant to denote the fact that our interest is in the politics and political patterns in the world, and not only those between nation-states (as the term international politics implies). Thus, we are interested in relations between organizations that may or may not be states (such as, for example, multinational companies, terrorist groups or human rights non-governmental organizations (NGOs); these are all known as transnational actors). Simi-larly, the term 'international relations' seems too exclusive; of course, it does represent a widening of

our concern from simply the political relations between nation-states, but it still restricts our focus to *inter-national* relations, whereas we think that rela-tions between, say, cities and other governments or international organizations can be equally import-ant to what states do. So we prefer to characterize the relations we are interested in as those of world polit-ics, with the important proviso that we do not want the reader to define politics too narrowly. You will see this issue arising time and time again in the chap-ters that follow, since many contributors want to define politics very widely. One obvious example concerns the relationship between politics and eco-nomics; there is clearly an overlap, and a lot of bar-gaining power goes to him or her that can persuade others that the existing distribution of resources is 'simply' economic rather than a political issue. So, we want you to think about politics very loosely for the time being, and several of the chapters will describe as political, features of the contemporary world that you may not have previously thought of as such. Our focus, then, is with the patterns of polit-ical relations, defined broadly, that characterize the contemporary world. Many will be between states, but many, perhaps most, will not.

Theories of world politics

The basic problem facing anyone trying to under-stand contemporary world politics is that there is so much material to look at that it is difficult to know which things matter and which do not. Where on earth would you start if you wanted to explain the most important political processes? Whenever indi-

viduals are faced with such a problem they have to resort to **theories**, whether they are aware of them or not. A theory is not simply some grand formal model with hypotheses and assumptions; rather **a theory is some kind of simplifying device that allows you to decide which facts matter and which do not**. A good analogy is with sunglasses with different coloured lenses; put on the red pair and the world looks red, put on the yellow pair and it looks yellow. The world is not any different, it just looks different. Well, so it is with theories. Shortly we are going to summarize the three main theoretical views that have dominated the study of world politics, so you will get an idea of which 'colours' they paint world politics. But before we do so, please note that we do not think that theory is an option. It is not as if you can say that you do not want to bother with a theory, all you want to do is to look at the 'facts'. We believe that this is simply impossible, since the only way in which you can decide which of the millions of possible facts to look at is by adhering to some simplifying device which tells you which ones matter the most. We think of theory as such a simplifying device. Note also that you may well not be aware of your theory, it may just be the view of the world that you have inherited from family, peer group, or the media. It may just seem common sense to you and not at all anything complicated like a theory. But we fervently believe that all that is happening in such a case is that your theoretical assumptions are **implicit** rather than **explicit**, and we prefer to try and be as explicit as possible when it comes to thinking about world politics; otherwise we may be looking at the world through the equivalent of red sunglasses without even being aware that we are wearing them.

People have tried to make sense of world politics for centuries, and especially so since the separate academic discipline of International Politics was formed in 1919 when the Department of International Politics was set up at Aberystwyth. Interestingly, the man who set up that Department, a Welsh industrialist called David Davies, saw its purpose as being to help prevent war. By studying international politics scientifically, academics could find the causes of the world's main political problems and put forward solutions to help politicians solve them. For the next twenty years, the discipline was marked by such a commitment to change the world. This is known as a **normative** position, with the task of academic study being one of making the world a better place. Its opponents characterized it as **Idealism**, in that it had a view of how the world ought to be and tried to assist events to turn out that way. In its place its opponents preferred an approach they called **Realism**, which, rather unsurprisingly stressed seeing the world as it really is rather than how we would like it to be. And, the world as it really is is not seen by realists as a very pleasant place; human beings are at best selfish and probably much worse. Notions such as the perfectibility of human beings and the possibility of an improvement of world politics seem far-fetched. This debate between Idealism and Realism has continued to the present day, but it is fair to say that Realism has tended to have the upper hand. This is mainly because it appears to accord more with common sense than does Idealism, especially when the media bombard us daily with images of how awful humans can be to one another. Having said which we would like you to think about whether such a realist view is as neutral as it is common-sensical? After all, if we teach world politics to generations of students and tell them that people are selfish, then doesn't that become common-sense and don't they, when they go off into the media or to work for government departments or the military or even when they talk to their kids over the dinner table, simply repeat what they have been taught and, if in positions of power, act accordingly? We will leave you to think about this as you read the rest of this book; for now we would like to keep the issue open and simply point out that we are not convinced that Realism is as objective or non-normative as it is portrayed as being.

What is certainly true is that Realism has been the dominant way of explaining world politics in the last one hundred years. What we are now going to do is to summarize the main assumptions underlying Realism and then do the same for its two main rivals as theories of world politics, **Liberalism** and **Marxism**. These three theories will be discussed in much more detail in Part Two of this book, along with a chapter dealing with the most recent approaches that seek to explain contemporary world politics. They will also be reflected in the other three parts that comprise the book. In Part One we look at the **historical** background to the contemporary world. In Part Three we will look at the main **structures and processes** of contemporary world politics. In Part Four we will deal with some of the main **issues** in the globalized world. So although we will not go into much depth now about these theories, we do need to give you a flavour of their main themes since we want, after summarizing them, to say something about how each might think about globalization.

Realism and world politics

For realists the main actors on the world stage are **states**, which are legally sovereign actors. **Sovereignty** means that there is no actor above the state that can compel it to act in specific ways. Other actors such as multinational corporations or international organizations all have to work within the framework of inter-state relations. As for what propels states to act as they do, realists see human nature as centrally important. For realists, human nature is fixed and crucially it is selfish. To think otherwise is to make a mistake, and it was such a mistake that the realists accused the idealists of making. As a result, world politics (or more accurately for realists international politics) represents a struggle for **power** between states each trying to maximize their national interests. Such order as exists in world politics is the result of the workings of a mechanism known as the **balance of power**, whereby states act so as to prevent any one state dominating. Thus world politics is all about bargaining and alliances, with diplomacy a key mechanism for balancing various national interests, but finally the most important tool available for implementing states' foreign policies is military force. Ultimately, since there is no sovereign body above the states that make up the international political system, world politics is a **self-help system** in which states must rely on their own military resources to achieve their ends. Often these ends can be achieved through co-operation, but the potential for conflict is ever-present. In recent years, an important variant of Realism, known as Neo-Realism, has developed. This view stresses the importance of the **structure** of the international political system in affecting the behaviour of all states; thus during the cold war there were two main powers dominating the international system and this led to certain rules of behaviour; now that the cold war has ended the structure of world politics is said to be moving towards multipolarity, which for neo-realists will involve very different rules of the game.

Liberalism and world politics

Liberals have a different view of world politics, and like realists, have a long tradition. Earlier we mentioned Idealism, and this was really one rather extreme version of Liberalism. There are many variants of Liberalism (or, as it is often known, pluralism) as you will see when you read the chapter on it in Part Two, but the main themes that run through liberal thought are that human beings are perfectible, that democracy is necessary for that perfectibility to develop, and that ideas matter. Behind all this lies a belief in **progress**. Accordingly, liberals reject the realist notion that war is the natural condition of world politics. They also question the idea that the state is the main actor on the world political stage, although they do not deny that it is important. But they do see multinational corporations, transnational actors such as terrorist groups, and international organizations as central actors in some issue-areas of world politics. In those issue-areas in which the state acts, they tend to think of the state not as a unitary or united actor but as a set of bureaucracies each with its own interests. Therefore there can be no such thing as a **national** interest, since it merely represents the result of whatever bureaucratic organizations dominate the domestic decision-making process. In relations between states, liberals stress the possibilities for **co-operation**, and the key issue becomes devising international settings in which co-operation can be best achieved. The picture of world politics that results from the liberal view is of a complex system of bargaining between many different types of actors. Military force is still important but the liberal agenda is not as restricted as is the realist one. Liberals see national interests in much more than military terms, and stress the importance of economic, environmental, and technological issues. Order in world politics emerges not from a balance of power but from the interactions between many layers of governing arrangements, comprising laws, agreed norms, international **regimes**, and institutional rules. Fundamentally, liberals do not think that sovereignty is as important in practice as realists think it is in theory. States may be legally sovereign, but in practice they have to negotiate with all sorts of other actors, with the result that their freedom to act as they might wish is seriously curtailed. Interdependence between states is a critically important feature of world politics.

Marxist theories and world politics

The third main theoretical position we want to mention, **Marxist theory** is also known as **Structuralism** or **World-System theory**, which immediately gives you clues as to its main assumptions. We want to point out that Marxist theory has been historically the least influential of the three theories we are discussing, and it has less in common with either Realism or Liberalism than they do with each other. For Marxist theory, the most important feature of world politics is that they take place within a world capitalist economy. In this world economy the most important actors are not states but classes, and the behaviour of all other actors is ultimately explicable by class forces. Thus states, multinational corporations, and even international organizations represent the dominant class interest in the world economic system. Marxist theorists differ over how much leeway actors such as states have, but all agree

that the world economy severely constrains the freedom of manœuvre of states. Rather than world politics being an arena of conflict between national interests or an arena with many different issue-areas, Marxist theorists conceive of world politics as the setting in which **class conflicts** are played out. As for order in world politics, Marxist theorists think of it primarily in economic rather than in military terms. The key feature of the international economy is the division of the world into core, semi-periphery, and periphery areas. Within the semi-periphery and the periphery there exist cores which are tied into the capitalist world economy, whilst within even the core area there are peripheral economic areas. In all of this what matters is the dominance of the power not of states but of **international capitalism**, and it is these forces that ultimately determine the main political patterns in world politics. Sovereignty is not anything like as important for Marxist theorists as it is for realists since it refers to political and legal matters, whereas the most important feature of world politics is the degree of economic autonomy, and here Marxist theorists see all states as having to play by the rules of the international capitalist economy.

The three theories and globalization

These three theoretical perspectives together have tended to be the main theories that have been used to understand world politics. In the 1980s it became common to talk of there being an **inter-paradigm** debate; that is to say that the three theories (known as paradigms after the influential philosopher of natural science, Thomas Kuhn) were in competition, and that the 'truth' about world politics lay in the debate between them. At first sight each seems to be particularly good at explaining some aspects of world politics better than the others, and an obvious temptation would be to try and combine them into some overall account. But we need to warn you that this is not the easy option it may seem. This is because the three theories are not so much different views of the same world, but are instead **three views of different worlds**. Let us explain this briefly:

whilst it is clear that each of the three focuses on different aspects of world politics (Realism on the power relations between states, Liberalism on a much wider set of interactions between states and non-state actors, and Marxist theory on the patterns of the world economy) each is saying more than this. Each view is claiming that it is picking out **the most important features** of world politics and that it offers a **better account** than do the rival theories. Thus, the three approaches are really in competition with one another; and, whilst you can certainly choose between them it is not so easy to add bits from one to the others. For example, if you are a Marxist theorist, you think that state behaviour is ultimately determined by class forces; forces that the realist does not think affect state behaviour. In other words these three theories are really versions of what world politics is like rather than partial pictures of it. They do not agree on what the 'it' is!

We now need to be clear that we do not think that any one of these theories has all the answers when it comes to explaining world politics in an era of globalization. In fact each sees globalization differently. We do not want to tell you which theory seems best, since the purpose of this book is to give you a variety of conceptual lenses through which you might want to look at globalization. All we will do is to say a few words about how each theory might respond to globalization. We will then go on to say something about the rise of globalization and offer some ideas on its strengths and weaknesses as a description of contemporary world politics.

1. For realists, globalization does not alter the most significant feature of world politics, namely the territorial division of the world into nation-states. Whilst the increased interconnectedness between economies and societies might make them more dependent on one another, the same cannot be said about the states-system. Here, states retain sovereignty, and globalization does not render obsolete the struggle for political power between states. Nor does it undermine the importance of the threat of the use of force, or the importance of the balance of power. Globalization, then, may affect our social, economic, and cultural lives, but it does not transcend the international political system of states.

2. For liberals, the picture looks very different. They tend to see globalization as the end product of a long-running transformation of world politics. For them, globalization fundamentally undermines realist accounts of world politics since it shows that states are no longer as central actors as they once were. In their place are a myriad of actors, of differing importance according to the issue-area concerned. Liberals are particularly interested in the revolution in technology and communications represented by globalization. This economically and technologically led increased interconnectedness between societies results in a very different pattern of world political relations from that which has gone before. States are no longer sealed units, if ever they were, and as a result the world looks more like a cobweb of relations than like the state model of Realism or the class model of Marxist theory.

3. For Marxist theorists, globalization is a bit of a sham. It is nothing particularly new, and is really only the latest stage in the development of international capitalism. It does not mark a qualitative shift in world politics, and nor does it render all our existing theories and concepts redundant. Above all it is a Western-led phenomenon which basically simply furthers the development of international capitalism. Rather than make the world more alike, it further deepens the existing divide between the core, semi-periphery, and the periphery.

By the end of the book we hope you will work out which of these theories (if any) best explains globalization. We spend a lot of time in Part Two outlining these theories in more detail so as to give you much more of an idea of the main ideas involved. But the central point we want to make here is to reinforce our comment earlier that theories do not portray 'the' truth. In other words, the theories we have mentioned will see globalization differently because they have a **prior** view of what is most important in world politics. Therefore the option is not available of simply answering the tempting question of which theory has the 'truest' or 'correct' view of globalization.

Globalization and its precursors

The focus of this book is globalization, and as we have already said our concern is with offering you an overview of world politics in a globalized era. **By globalization we simply mean the process of increasing interconnectedness between societies such that events in one part of the world more and more have effects on peoples and societies far away.** A globalized world is one in which political, economic, cultural, and social events become more and more interconnected, and also one in which they have more impact. In other words, societies are affected more and more extensively and more and more deeply by events of other societies. These events can conveniently be divided into three types, **social**, **economic**, and **political**. In each case, the world seems to be 'shrinking', and people are increasingly aware of this. The World Wide Web is but the most graphic example of this, since it allows you to sit at home and have instant communication with web sites around the world. Electronic mail has also transformed communications in a way that the two editors of this book would not have envisaged ten years ago. But these are only the most obvious examples. Others would include: worldwide television communications, global newspapers, international social movements such as Amnesty or Greenpeace, global franchises such as McDonalds, Coca Cola, and Pizza Hut, the global economy (go and look in your nearest supermarket and work out the number of countries' products represented there), and global risks such as pollution, AIDS, etc. There are, of course, many other examples, but we are sure that you get the picture. It is this pattern of events that seems to have changed the nature of world politics from what it was just a few years ago. The important point to stress is that it is not just that the world has changed but that the changes are qualitative and not merely quantitative; a strong case can be made that a 'new' world political system has emerged as a result of globalization.

Having said which, we want to point out that globalization is not some entirely new phenomenon in world history; indeed, as we will note later on, many argue that it is merely a new name for a long-term feature. Whilst we want to leave it to you to judge whether in its current manifestation it represents a new phase in world history or merely a continuation of processes that have been around for a long time, we do want to note that there have been several precursors to globalization. In other words, globalization bears a marked similarity to at least nine features of world politics discussed by writers before the contemporary period. We will now note these briefly.

First, globalization has many features in common with the **theory of modernization** (see Modelski 1972 and Morse 1976). According to these writers, industrialization brings into existence a whole new set of contacts between societies, and changes the political, economic, and social processes that characterized the pre-modernized world. Crucially, industrialization alters the nature of the state, both widening its responsibilities and weakening its control over outcomes. The result is that the old power-politics model of international relations becomes outmoded. Force becomes less usable, states have to negotiate with other actors to achieve their goals, and the very identity of the state as an actor is called into question. In many respects it seems that modernization is part of the globalization process, differing only in that it applied more to the developed world and involved nothing like as extensive a set of transactions.

Second, there are clear similarities with the arguments of influential writers such as Walt Rostow (1960) who argued that **economic growth** followed a pattern in all economies as they went through industrialization. Their economies developed in the shadow of more 'developed' economies until they reached the stage where they were capable of self-sustained economic growth. What this has in common with globalization is that Rostow saw a clear pattern to economic development, one marked by stages which all economies would follow as they adopted capitalist policies. There was an automaticity to history that globalization theory tends also to rely on.

Third, there was the important literature emerging

out of the Liberal paradigm discussed above. Specifically there were very influential works on the nature of **economic interdependence** (Cooper 1968), the role of transnational actors (Keohane and Nye 1971) and the resulting cobweb model of world politics (Mansbach, Ferguson, and Lampert 1976). Much of this literature anticipates the main theoretical themes of globalization, although again it tends to be applied much more to the developed world than is the case with globalization.

Fourth, there are notable similarities between the picture of the world painted by globalization and that portrayed in Marshall McLuhan's influential work on the **'global village'** (1964). According to McLuhan, advances in electronic communications resulted in a world where we could see in real time events that were occurring in distant parts of the world. For McLuhan, the main effects of this development were that time and space become compressed to such an extent that everything loses its traditional identity. As a result, the old groupings of political, economic, and social organization simply do not work any more. Without doubt, McLuhan's work significantly anticipates some of the main themes of globalization, although it should be noted that he was talking primarily about the communications revolution, whereas the globalization literature tends to be much more extensive.

Fifth, there are significant overlaps between some of the main themes of globalization and the work of writers such as John Burton (1972), who spoke of the emergence of a **'world society'**. According to Burton, the old states-system was becoming outmoded, as increasingly significant interactions took place between non-state actors. It was Burton who coined the phrase of the 'cobweb' model of world politics. The central message here was that the most important patterns in world politics were those created by trade, communications, language, ideology, etc., along with the more traditional focus on the political relations between states.

Sixth, in the 1960s, 1970s, and 1980s, there was the visionary work of those associated with the **World Order Models Project** (WOMP), which was an organization set up in 1968 to promote the development of alternatives to the inter-state system which would result in the elimination of war. What is most interesting about their many studies (see, for example, Mendlovitz (1975), and Falk (1975; 1995b)), is that they focused on the questions of global government that today are central to much work going on under the name of globalization. For WOMPers (as they were known), the unit of analysis is the individual, and the level of analysis is the global. Interestingly by the mid-1990s WOMP had become much wider in its focus, concentrating on the world's most vulnerable people and the environment.

Seventh, there are important parallels between some of the ideas of globalization and the thoughts of those who argued for the existence of an **international society**. Prominent amongst these was Hedley Bull (1977), who pointed to the development over the centuries of a set of agreed norms and common understandings between state leaders, such that they effectively formed a society rather than merely an international system. However, although Bull was perturbed by the emergence of what he called the 'new medievalism', in which a series of sub-national and inter-national organizations vied with the state for authority, he did not feel that the nation-state was about to be replaced by the development of a world society.

Eighth, globalization theory has several points in common with the infamous argument of Francis Fukuyama (1992) about the **'end of history'**. Fukuyama's main claim is that the power of the economic market is resulting in liberal democracy replacing all other types of government. Though he recognizes that there are other types of political regimes to challenge liberal democracy, he does not think that any of the alternatives such as communism, fascism, or Islam will be able to deliver the economic goods in the way that liberal democracy can. In this sense there is a direction to history and that direction is towards the expansion of the economic market throughout the world.

Finally, there are very marked similarities between some of the political aspects of globalization and long-standing ideas of liberal progress. These have most recently been expressed in the **'liberal peace' theory** of writers such as Bruce Russett (1993) and Michael Doyle (1983a and 1983b), although they go back centuries to writers such as Immanuel Kant. The main idea is that liberal democracies do not fight one another, and although of course there can be dispute as to what is a liberal democracy, adherents to this view claim quite plausibly that there is no case where two democracies have ever gone to war. The reason they claim this is that public accountability is so central in democratic systems that publics will not allow leaders easily to engage in wars with other democratic nations. Again the main link with globalization is the assumption that there is progress to history, and that this is making it far more difficult to start wars.

Globalization: myth or reality?

Our final task in this Introduction is to offer you a summary of the main arguments for and against globalization. We do not expect you to decide where you stand on the issue at this stage, but we think that we have to give you some of the main arguments so that you can keep them in mind as you read the rest of this book. Because the arguments for globalization being an important new phase of world politics have been rehearsed above, and also because they are most effectively summarized in the chapter that follows, we will spend a little more time on the criticisms. The main arguments in favour of globalization comprising a new era of world politics are:

1. The pace of **economic transformation** is so great that it has created a new world politics. States are no longer closed units and they cannot control their economies. The world economy is more interdependent than ever, with trade and finances ever expanding.

2. **Communications** have fundamentally revolutionized the way we deal with the rest of the world. We now live in a world where events in one location can be immediately observed on the other side of the world. Electronic communications alter our notions of the social groups we work and live in.

3. There is now, more than ever before, a **global culture**, so that most urban areas resemble one another. The world shares a common culture, much of it emanating from Hollywood.

4. The world is becoming more **homogeneous**. Differences between peoples are diminishing.

5. **Time and space seem to be collapsing**. Our old ideas of geographical space and of chronological time are undermined by the speed of modern communications and media.

6. There is emerging a **global polity**, with transnational social and political movements and the beginnings of a transfer of allegiance from the state to sub-state, transnational, and international bodies.

7. A **cosmopolitan culture** is developing. People are beginning to 'think globally and act locally'.

8. A **risk culture** is emerging with people realizing both that the main risks that face them are global (pollution and AIDS) and that states are unable to deal with the problems.

However, just as there are powerful reasons for seeing globalization as a new stage in world politics, often allied to the view that globalization is progressive, that is to say that it improves the lives of people, there are also arguments that suggest the opposite. Some of the main ones are given below.

1. One obvious objection to the globalization thesis is that it is merely a buzz-word to denote the latest phase of capitalism. In a very powerful critique of the globalization theory, Hirst and Thompson (1996) argue that one effect of the globalization thesis is that it makes it appear as if national governments are powerless in the face of global trends. This ends up paralysing governmental attempts to subject global economic forces to control and regulation. Believing that most globalization theory lacks historical depth they point out that it paints the current situation as **more unique than it is** and also as more firmly entrenched than it might in fact be. Current trends may well be reversible. They conclude that

the more extreme versions of globalization are 'a myth', and they support this claim with five main conclusions from their study of the contemporary world economy (2–3): **First**, the present internationalized economy is not unique in history. In some respects they say it is less open than the international economy was between 1870 and 1914. **Second**, they find that 'genuinely' transnational companies are relatively rare, most are national companies trading internationally. There is no trend towards the development of international companies. **Third**, there is no shift of finance and capital from the developed to the underdeveloped worlds. Direct investment is highly concentrated amongst the countries of the developed world. **Fourth**, the world economy is not global, rather trade, investment, and financial flows are concentrated in and between three blocks—Europe, North America, and Japan. **Finally**, they argue that this group of three blocks could, if they co-ordinated policies, regulate global economic markets and forces. Note that Hirst and Thompson are only looking at economic theories of globalization, and many of the main accounts deal with factors such as communications and culture more than economics; nonetheless, theirs is a very powerful critique of one of the main planks of the more extreme globalization thesis, with their central criticism being that seeing the global economy as something beyond our control both misleads us and prevents us from developing policies to control the national economy. All too often we are told that our economy must obey 'the global market', but Hirst and Thompson believe that this is a myth.

2. Another obvious objection is that globalization is very **uneven in its effects**. At times it sounds very much like a Western theory applicable only to a small part of humankind. To pretend that even a small minority of the world's population can connect to the World Wide Web is clearly an exaggeration when in reality most people on the planet have probably never made a telephone call in their lives. In other words, globalization only applies to the developed world. In the rest of the world, there is nothing like the degree of globalization. We are in danger of overestimating the extent and the depth of globalization.

3. A related objection is that globalization may well be simply **the latest stage of Western imperialism**. It is the old modernization theory discussed above in new guise. The forces that are being globalized are conveniently those found in the Western world. What about non-Western values? Where do they fit into this emerging global world? The worry is that they do not fit in at all, and what is being celebrated in globalization is the triumph of a Western world view, at the expense of the world views of other cultures.

4. Critics have also noted that there are very considerable **losers** as the world becomes more globalized. This is because it represents the success of liberal capitalism in an economically divided world. Perhaps one outcome is that globalization allows the more efficient exploitation of less well-off nations, and all in the name of openness. The technologies accompanying globalization are technologies that automatically benefit the richest economies in the world, and allow their interests to override local ones. So, not only is globalization imperialist it is also exploitative.

5. We also need to make the straightforward point that not all globalized forces are necessarily '**good**' ones. Globalization makes it easier for drug cartels and terrorists to operate, and the World Wide Web's anarchy raises crucial questions of censorship and preventing access to certain kinds of material.

6. Turning to the so-called **global governance** aspects of globalization, the main worry here is who are the transnational social movements responsible and democratically accountable to? If IBM or Shell becomes more and more powerful in the world, does this not raise the issue of how accountable are they to democratic control? David Held has made a strong case for the development of what he calls 'cosmopolitan democracy' (1995), but this has clearly defined legal and democratic features. The worry is that most of the emerging powerful actors in a globalized

world precisely are NOT accountable. This argument also applies to seemingly 'good' global actors such as Amnesty International and Greenpeace.

7. Finally, there seems to us to be **a paradox** at the heart of the globalization thesis. On the one hand it is usually portrayed as the triumph of Western, market-led values, but how do we then explain the tremendous economic success that some national economies have had in the globalized world? We are thinking here in the main of the so-called 'Tigers' of Asia, countries such as Singapore, Taiwan, Malaysia, and Korea, which have enjoyed some of the highest growth rates in the international economy, but subscribe to very different 'Asian' values. These nations emphatically reject Western values, and yet they have had enormous economic success. The paradox then is whether these countries can continue to modernize so successfully without adopting Western values. If they can, then what does this do to one of the main themes of globalization, namely the argument that globalization represents the spreading across the globe of a set of values? If these countries do continue to follow their own roads towards economic and social modernization, then we must anticipate future disputes between 'Western' and 'Asian' values over issues like human rights, gender, and religion.

We hope that these arguments for and against globalization will cause you to think deeply about the utility of the concept of globalization in explaining contemporary world politics. The chapters that follow do not take a common stance for or against globalization. We will end by posing some questions that we would like you to keep in mind as you read the remaining chapters:

- Is globalization a new phenomenon in world politics?
- Which theory discussed above best explains globalization?
- Is globalization a positive or a negative development?
- Is globalization merely the latest stage of capitalist development?
- Does globalization make the state obsolete?
- Does globalization make the world more or less democratic?
- Is globalization merely Western imperialism in a new guise?
- Does globalization make war less likely?

We hope that this introduction and the chapters that follow help you to answer these questions, and that this book as a whole provides you with a good overview of the politics of the contemporary world. Whether or not you conclude that globalization is a new phase in world politics, and whether you think it is a positive or a negative development we will now leave you to decide.

GUIDE TO FURTHER READING

There are several good introductory guides to globalization. The most comprehensive discussion is found in D. Held *et al.*, *Global Transformations* (Cambridge: Polity Press, 1999). See also D. Held and A. McGrew (eds.), *Global Transformations Reader* (Cambridge: Polity Press, 2000). M. Waters, *Globalization* (London: Routledge, 1995) is a clear overview, written by a sociologist. J. A. Scholte, *International Relations of Social Change* (Buckingham: Open University Press, 1993) is an extremely clear and comprehensive introduction to the social relations aspects of globalization. His latest book *Globalization: A Critical Introduction* (London: Macmillan, 2000) offers an excellent overview. A. McGrew and P. Lewis, *Global Politics* (Cambridge: Polity Press, 1992) is a good collection of essays about global politics and contains some very relevant chapters on the relationship between the three theories discussed above and globalization. R. Robertson, *Globalization: Social Theory and Global Culture* (London: Sage, 1992) is a very widely cited survey of the relations between globalization and global culture. J. N. Rosenau and E.-D. Czempiel, *Governance without Government* (Cambridge: Cambridge University Press, 1992) is a good collection of essays dealing with the political aspects of globalization. J. N. Rosenau, *Turbulence in World Politics* (Princeton: Princeton University Press, 1990) and J. A. Camilleri and J. Falk, *The End of Sovereignty* (Aldershot: Edward Elgar, 1992) are both very good at looking at the main trends in world politics at the beginning of the 1990s. Excellent critiques of the globalization thesis are R. Falk, *Predatory Globalization: A Critique* (Cambridge : Polity Press, 1999), L. Weiss, *The Myth of the Powerless State* (Cambridge: Polity Press, 1998), and P. Hirst and G. Thompson, *Globalization in Question*, 2nd edn. (Cambridge: Polity Press, 2000).

1 The globalization of world politics

Jan Aart Scholte

READER'S GUIDE

This opening chapter considers the implications of globalization for the states-system and for the nature of governance more generally. Its first section elaborates a general definition of globalization. The second section describes how globalization has been shifting world politics away from the Westphalian system and its central premise of sovereign statehood. The third section reviews four shifts in the character of governance in connection with globalization: (*a*) the growth of transborder links between substate authorities; (*b*) the expansion of suprastate law and institutions; (*c*) increased private-sector involvement in global regulation; and (*d*) the spread of global civil society. The chapter ends by arguing that current trends in governance under conditions of globalization have worrying implications for democracy.

Introduction: a globalizing world

When a new word becomes popular, it is often because it captures an important change that is taking place in the world. A new idea is needed to describe a new condition. For example, when the philosopher Jeremy Bentham coined the term 'international' in the 1780s, it caught hold because it highlighted a deepening reality of his day, namely, the rise of nation-states and of cross-border transactions between them. People had not spoken of 'international relations' before this time, since humanity had not previously been organized into national communities governed by territorial states.

Two hundred years later, starting in the 1980s, talk of 'globalization' became rife. The term quickly entered standard vocabulary—not only in academic circles, but also among journalists, politicians, business people, advertisers, and entertainers. Broadly equivalent notions emerged roughly simultaneously across many languages. 'Globalization' in English has been paralleled, for example, by *Quanqiuhua* in Chinese, *globalizzazione* in Italian, *глобализация* in Russian, and *jatyanthareekaranaya* in Sinhalese. It has become common to speak of global markets, global communications, global conferences, global threats, and so on. During the late twentieth century students of International Relations and other disciplines began to examine questions of global (as distinct from international) governance, global environmental change, global gender relations, global political economy, and more.

It is true that ideas of globality were circulating well before 1980. English-speakers have regularly used the adjective 'global' to designate 'the whole world' since the end of the nineteenth century. (Previously the word had mainly meant 'spherical'.) The terms 'globalize' and 'globalism' were introduced in a little-read book published in 1944, while the noun 'globalization' entered a dictionary for the first time in 1961 (Reiser and Davies 1944: 212, 219; Webster 1961). Nevertheless, although global-speak had this long gestation period, it did not become part of the vocabulary of everyday life until recent decades. For example, hardly any titles of books and articles published before 1975 include references to global-ness, whereas today the concept has become pervasive.

Globalization: a definition

Should we conclude that, as was the case with the word 'international' two centuries ago, the recent proliferation of references to globalization signals that an important change is taking place in world affairs? If so, what is the nature of this change more precisely? Critics have rightly objected that the term 'globalization' is often used vaguely and inconsistently. Can we formulate a clear and helpful notion?

At least five general usages of the word 'globalization' can be distinguished. For example, the word has often been taken to mean **internationalization**, that is, an intensification of cross-border interactions and interdependence between countries. A second usage has treated globalization as **liberalization**, that is, a process of removing government-imposed restrictions on movements between countries in order to create an 'open', 'integrated' world economy. A third conception has viewed globalization in terms of **universalization**, that is, the spread of various objects and experiences to people at all corners of the earth. Fourth, many people (especially critics of cultural imperialism) have defined globalization as **westernization**, especially in an Americanized form. Still others have identified globalization as **deterritorialization**, that is, a shift in geography whereby territorial places, territorial distances and territorial borders lose some of their previously overriding influence. These five conceptions overlap to some extent, but their respective emphases are significantly different.

The present chapter adopts the fifth type of approach and draws a sharp distinction between 'global' relations and 'international' relations. People have frequently employed the notions 'globalization' and 'internationalization' interchangeably. Yet if the concepts refer to the same conditions, then talk of 'globalization' is redundant. Current debates about globalization would in this case merely rehash the same arguments that realists, liberalists, and Marxists rehearsed twenty, sixty, and even a hundred and more years ago. The survey of theories in Part Two of this book would then include nothing that might not equally have been written in an International Relations textbook of the 1930s or the 1970s.

However, a significant change has been unfolding in the world roughly since the 1960s, and the term 'globalization' characterizes it well. As the word is used here, globalization refers to **processes whereby** many social relations become relatively delinked from territorial geography, so that human lives are increasingly played out in the world as a single place. (See related conceptions in Box 1.1.) Social relations—that is, the countless and complex ways that people interact with and affect each other—are more and more being conducted and organized on the basis of a planetary unit. By the same token, country locations and in particular the boundaries between territorial states are in some important senses becoming less central to our lives. Globalization is thus an ongoing trend whereby the world has—in many respects and at a generally accelerating rate—become one relatively borderless social sphere. Territorial spaces remain significant, to be sure, but the geography of world politics is now no longer reducible to territoriality.

Globalization needs in this light to be distinguished from internationalization. As the construction of that term indicates, 'internationalization' refers to a process of intensifying connections between national domains. As a result of internationalization, countries may come to have wide-ranging and deep effects on each other, but they remain distinct and separate places. In international relations, countries are divided from each other by clearly marked frontiers as well as by the substantial time that is generally required to cover the distance between their respective territories. To put the difference in a nutshell, the international realm is a patchwork of bordered countries, while the global sphere is a web of transborder networks. Whereas international links (for example, trade in cocoa) require people to cross considerable distances in comparatively long time intervals, global connections (for example, satellite newscasts) are effectively distance-less and instantaneous. Global phenomena can extend across the world at the same time and can move between places in no time; in this sense they have a **supraterritorial** and **transworld** character. While the patterns of 'international' interdependence are strongly influenced by national-state divisions, the lines of 'global' interconnections often have little correspondence to territorial boundaries. International and global relations can coexist, of course, and indeed the contemporary world is at the same time both internationalized and globalizing.

Box 1.1 Globalization: making the world a single place

'Globalization refers to all those processes by which the peoples of the world are incorporated into a single world society, global society.'

(Martin Albrow 1990)

'Globalization can . . . be defined as the intensification of worldwide social relations which link distant localities in such a way that local happenings are shaped by events occurring many miles away and vice versa.'

(Anthony Giddens 1990)

'*Die Globalisierung* . . . global networking that has welded together previously disparate and isolated communities on this planet into mutual dependence and unity of "one world".'

(Emanuel Richter, translated from German)

'The characteristics of the globalization trend include the internationalizing of production, the new international division of labor, new migratory movements from South to North, the new competitive environment that accelerates these processes, and the internationalizing of the state . . . making states into agencies of the globalizing world.'

(Robert Cox 1994)

'The world is becoming a global shopping mall in which ideas and products are available everywhere at the same time.'

(Rosabeth Moss Kanter 1995)

'Globalization is what we in the Third World have for several centuries called colonization.'

(Martin Khor 1995)

'Globalization can be thought of as a process (or set of processes) which embodies a transformation of the spatial organization of social relations and transactions.'

(David Held *et al.* 1999)

Aspects of globalization

The distinctiveness of global spaces will perhaps become more clear if we take a quick survey of some of their various manifestations in our lives. In terms of **communications**, for example, globalization has been occurring through the growth of computer networks, telephony, electronic mass media, and the like. Such technologies permit persons to have nearly immediate contact with each other, irrespective of their location on earth and regardless of the state borders that might lie between them. Hence a fax will reach a destination across the ocean almost as quickly as a receiver next door.

In respect of **organizations**, globalization has been transpiring through the proliferation and growth of companies, associations, and regulatory agencies that operate as transborder networks. Bodies such as Nissan Corporation, Save the Children, and the World Intellectual Property Organization treat the whole planet as their field of activity and regard humanity at large as their actual or potential clients.

Ecologically, globalization has been taking place through such phenomena as planetary climate change (or 'global warming'), stratospheric ozone depletion, and a decline in Earth's biological diversity. None of these environmental developments can be isolated in one or the other country; they have arisen in, and affect, the world as a single place.

In respect of **production**, so-called 'global factories' have expanded in sectors like motorcars and microelectronics. Here the various stages of manufacture (for example, research and development, processing of materials, preparation of components, assembly of parts, finishing, and quality control) are not confined within a national economy, but link up across several countries in a single production line. Concurrently, globalization has been unfolding in respect of money and finance, with the emergence of round-the-clock round-the-world stock and bond markets, the spread of globally recognized credit cards, the increasing use of currencies like the US dollar, the yen, and the euro all over the world, and so on.

Meanwhile the **military** sphere has seen the advent of global weaponry. Intercontinental ballistic missiles and spy satellites, for instance, have in certain respects turned the world as a whole into a single realm of battle. Although the Gulf War of 1990–1 was fought on the ground in Iraq and Kuwait, it equally involved satellite remote sensing, supersonic bombing raids, electronic transborder payments to fund the operations, a propaganda struggle in the global mass media, and a transworld coalition against the Baghdad government legitimated through a global governance agency, the United Nations.

Globalization has also encompassed many **norms** that govern our lives, including thousands of technical standards and (purportedly) universal human rights. These and an ever-increasing number of other rules have acquired a supraterritorial rather than a country-specific character.

Finally, globalization has been evident in **everyday thinking**. People living at the start of the twenty-first century are aware of the world as a single place to an extent that earlier generations were not. Perhaps the greatest spur to this shift in consciousness came in 1966, with the production of the first photographs taken from outer space showing planet Earth as one location.

Taking the preceding observations in sum, we see that globalization has had very wide-ranging scope. Indeed, the process has in some way touched every aspect of social relations. The radio brings reports from Buenos Aires and Beijing straight to our breakfast tables. Swings on the global financial markets make and break our fortunes, sometimes from one day to the next. We drink Coca-Cola, munch a Big Mac, wear jeans, listen to the latest hit singles, and watch the newest video releases simultaneously with millions upon millions of other people all over the planet. Our car adds to the greenhouse effect together with the bus in Bombay. Via the Internet, the worldwide network of computer networks, our office can be in immediate contact with Warsaw or Washington. Suprastate regimes like the European Union are largely determining our food prices, while soldiers from our national army are joining troops from multiple other states in a single UN peacekeeping operation. Our contributions to Oxfam translate overnight into relief work in Rwanda. These sorts of circumstances did not exist when our parents were children, and there is at present every indication that our children will experience globality even more intensely than we currently do. Today we live not only in a country; in very direct and immediate senses we also live in the world as a single place.

History

It is hard to determine a specific moment when globalization started or to describe exact stages of its historical development. Questions of origins and periodization are notoriously imprecise and contentious. History shows no obvious and precise watersheds on which everyone will agree. Researchers have variously dated the onset of globalization from the dawn of human intercontinental migration (Gamble 1994), or from the start of the modern era (Robertson 1992: 58–9), or from the late nineteenth century (Chase-Dunn 1989: 2), or from the 1950s (Rosenau 1990), or from the 1970s (Harvey 1989). However, if we conceive of globalization as the rise of supraterritoriality, then its chronology lies in a combination of several of these positions. (See Box 1.2 for a suggestive chronology of globalization.)

Writers like Robertson and Chase-Dunn are right that early signs of globalization appeared a century and more ago, although to a much smaller extent and at a far slower pace. For example, telegraphic communication commenced in the 1840s. Several global social movements (feminism) and regulatory bodies (the Universal Postal Union) emerged later in the nineteenth century. Intercontinental short-wave radio programmes multiplied in the 1920s. Intergovernmental meetings on transboundary pollution were held as early as the 1930s.

On the other hand, globalization did not figure continually, comprehensively, intensely, and with rapidly increasing frequency in the lives of a large proportion of humanity until around the 1960s. Indeed, almost all of the illustrations of globalization given above relate only to the second half of the twentieth century, and not before. Worldwide direct dialling was not available before the 1980s, for example. It is only since the 1960s that the world has acquired most of the late 1990s figures of 850 million telephone connection points, 1.1 billion television receivers, 60,000 transborder corporations, 16,500 transborder citizens associations, US$1.5 trillion in foreign exchange transactions every day, and nearly 1.5 billion passengers per year on scheduled airline flights. **Fully fledged globalization—a process with such weight that it requires us to make fundamental adjustments to our understanding of world politics—is a fairly new development.**

Qualifications

Having established that globalization is a major and on the whole relatively recent turn in world history, we need to sober our judgements by expressing a number of cautions concerning its extent, depth, causes, and consequences. Unfortunately, many discussions of globalization suffer from oversimplifications, exaggerations, and wishful thinking. As a result of such intellectual sloppiness, certain sceptics have gone to an opposite extreme and dismissed notions of globalization as mythology (Hirst and Thompson 1999: 2). The following five qualifications respond to the critiques of globalism and point towards a more nuanced understanding.

First, **globalization has not been experienced everywhere to the same extent.** On the whole, the decreased importance of territorial geography has gone markedly further in North America, the Pacific Rim, and Western Europe than in Sub-Saharan Africa and Central Asia. Phenomena like global companies and electronic mail have been mainly concentrated in the so-called North of the world. In addition, globalization has generally affected city dwellers, professional people, and younger generations relatively more than other groups, although the process has left no one completely untouched. The point about globalization is not that certain conditions come to exist in all places and for all people to the same degree. Rather, it means that many things happen in the contemporary world largely irrespective of territorial distances and borders.

Second, **globalization is not the straightforward process of cultural homogenization** that some accounts would have us believe. True, the transcendence of territorial geography by electronic mass media and the like has helped to give worldwide currency to a host of objects, ideas, standards, and habits. However, globalization has by no means brought an end to cultural diversity. For instance, different audiences interpret a global film differently, and a global product may be used differently in different places in accordance with specific local needs and customs. Moreover, the experience of having the whole world converge on one's home turf has prompted many people defensively to reassert their cultural distinctiveness, in some cases even more insistently than ever. In this way globalization

Box 1.2 Some key events in the history of globalization

500s BC	emergence of the first world religions
1522	first circumnavigation of the earth
1700s	Enlightenment thinkers posit a trend toward the social unification of the world
1851	first world's fair (in London)
1852	establishment of the first foreign manufacturing subsidiary
1865	creation of the first global regulatory agency (the International Telegraph Union)
1866	first permanent transoceanic telegraph cable comes into service
1884	introduction of transworld co-ordination of clocks (in relation to Greenwich Mean Time)
1891	first transborder telephone calls (between London and Paris)
1919	initiation of the first scheduled transborder airline services
1920	inauguration of the League of Nations
1929	institution of the first offshore finance arrangements (in Luxembourg)*
1930	first global radio broadcast (the speech of George V opening the London Naval Conference, relayed simultaneously to 242 stations across six continents)
1945	formation of the United Nations Organization
1946	construction of the first digital computer
1949	introduction of package holidays sets the stage for large-scale global tourism
1954	establishment of the first export processing zone (in Ireland)
1954	launch of the 'Marlboro cowboy', a future global icon
1955	first McDonald's restaurant
1956	first transoceanic telephone cable link
1957	advent of intercontinental ballistic missiles
1957	issuance of the first eurocurrency loan (by a Soviet bank, in US dollars, on the London market)*
1960	Marshall McLuhan coins the phrase 'global village'
1962	launch of the first communications satellite
1963	introduction of direct dialling of transborder telephone calls
1963	issuance of the first eurobond (by a borrower in Italy, in US dollars, on the London market)*
1966	first photographs of planet Earth from outer space
1969	construction of the first wide-body passenger jet (the Boeing 747)
1969	creation of the first multi-site computer network (the ARPANET of the US military)
1971	establishment of the first wholly electronic stock exchange (the US-based NASDAQ system)
1972	first global ecological conference (the United Nations Conference on the Human Environment)
1974	US Government eliminates foreign exchange controls on current account transactions (other states follow in later years)
1976	launch of the first direct broadcast satellite (i.e. transmitting to rooftop dishes)
1977	first commercial use of fibre-optic cables, vastly increasing capacities of telecommunications
1977	creation of the SWIFT system for electronic interbank fund transfers worldwide
1987	appearance of a near-complete 'ozone hole' over Antarctica, heightening global ecological awareness
1987	stock-market crash on Wall Street spreads world-wide overnight
1991	introduction of the World Wide Web
1997	completion of a continuous round-the-world fibre-optic cable link
1999–2000	upsurge of 'anti-globalization' protests against global economic institutions

* The terms 'offshore', 'eurocurrencies', and 'eurobonds' are further clarified in Chapter 24 on Global Trade and Finance.

has contributed to a proliferation of national, ethnic, and religious revivalist movements since the 1960s (Scholte 2000: Ch. 7). So globalization involves a complex mix of concurrent tendencies towards cultural convergence on the one hand and increased inter-group differentiation on the other.

Third, **globalization has not eliminated the significance of territoriality** in world politics. Yes, the process has introduced additional dimensions of geography to social relations, with the arrival of cyberspace, communication via electromagnetic waves, and so on. However, this does not mean that the old geography of latitudes, longitudes, and altitudes no longer matters in the contemporary world. For example, territorial place obviously remains important in respect of the location of natural resources, feelings of national identity, and much more. Territorial distance retains significant restraining and buffering effects when it comes to things like terrestrial travel and merchandise trade. Meanwhile the frontiers of territorial states continue to inhibit migration and smuggling, even if border guards can do nothing to stop missile attacks or electronic money transfers. Hence globalization has not brought the end of territorial geography, but rather has created a new supraterritorial space alongside, and interrelated with, the old territorial spaces. The 'map' of world affairs has gained an additional dimension and consequently has become more complicated.

Fourth, **globalization cannot be understood in terms of a single driving force**. For instance, the process is not reducible to an American or Western plot. Nor is it simply the inevitable outcome of capitalism, or the preordained end-result of the Industrial Revolution, or the consequence of a modern secular quest for universal truth. There is probably something to all of these arguments about causes—and others, too—but each thesis by itself offers at best only a partial insight. A fuller explanation of globalization needs to consider a complex and fluctuating mix of forces, some of which are mutually reinforcing and some of which are contradictory.

Fifth, and perhaps most importantly, **globaliza-**tion is not a panacea. Some liberalist accounts have heralded the coming of a 'borderless world' as the dawn of universal equality, prosperity, peace, and freedom (Ohmae 1990). Regrettably, evidence of the past several decades has sooner pointed to contrary outcomes. For one thing, people have—depending on their age, class, gender, nationality, race, religion, and other social categories—generally had unequal access to, unequal voices in, and unequal benefits from globalization. Poverty is still rampant in the contemporary globalizing world. Human-induced ecological degradation has never been worse. Although a third world war has thus far been avoided, thirty-five major armed conflicts (those involving over 1,000 deaths per year) were underway as of 1993 (Weiss *et al.* 1994: 18). Nor has globalization proved to be a formula for democracy (as will be detailed later) or an answer to problems of alienation. Clearly there is no automatic link between globalization and emancipation.

Nevertheless, to acknowledge the above limitations to change is not to say that nothing has changed in world politics as a result of globalization. Although some commentators are prone to exaggerate its extent, a substantial, wide-ranging and deeply penetrating shift in the spatial character of world politics has been unfolding in recent decades. In this light globalization most definitely warrants the mass of attention that it has attracted.

Key points

- Globalization refers to a process—still ongoing—through which the world has in many respects been becoming a single place.

- Globalization has in one way or another encompassed every sphere of social life.

- Although considerable groundwork for globalization was laid in earlier times, the fully-fledged trend dates roughly from the 1960s.

- Many accounts of globalization suffer from oversimplifications, exaggerations, and wishful thinking.

Globalization and the states-system

Discussions of globalization often involve explorations of far-reaching historical change. Researchers are asking whether, as the world becomes a single place, it also becomes a fundamentally different kind of place. For example, might the declining importance of territorial distance and borders trigger significant changes in prevailing modes of production? Might globalization shift the way that people construct their senses of identity and community so that, for instance, they become less (or perhaps more) nationalistic? Might the process alter relationships between human beings and the natural environment? Might globalization change the way people formulate knowledge of the world, for example, encouraging a resurgence of religious belief? Might globalization transform structures of governance, that is, the ways rules are made and authority is exercised?

In response to such questions, commentators have variously linked globalization to the rise of the **information society**, the onset of **late capitalism**, the advent of **post-modernity**, the demise of communism, and even **the end of history** (see Box 1.3). In these accounts globalization is depicted as a transition phase between epochs of history. The present chapter is not the place to evaluate these larger claims and draw overall conclusions about the implications of globalization for social change. I attempt this broader analysis elsewhere (Scholte 2000: Part II). The rest of this chapter only offers some general reflections on the implications of globalization for the states-system and wider patterns of governance.

The Westphalian order

Before the onset of intensified globalization several decades ago, world politics was chiefly organized on the basis of the so-called Westphalian system. The name is derived from the Peace of Westphalia (1648), which contains an early official statement of the core principles that came to dominate world affairs during the subsequent three hundred years. The Westphalian system was a states-system. In the nineteenth and twentieth centuries, as states increasingly took the form of nation-states, people came to refer to 'international' as well as interstate relations and frequently described the Westphalian order as 'the international system'.

The Westphalian system was a framework of governance. That is, it provided a general way to formulate, implement, monitor and enforce social rules. At the core of this mode of governance stood the principles of statehood and sovereignty. Statehood meant that the world was divided into territorial parcels, each of which was ruled by a separate government. This modern state was a centralized, formally organized public authority apparatus that enjoyed a legal (and mostly effective) monopoly over the means of armed violence in the area of its jurisdiction. The Westphalian state was moreover sovereign, that is, it exercised comprehensive, supreme, unqualified, and exclusive control over its designated territorial domain. **Comprehensive** rule meant that, in principle, the sovereign state had jurisdiction over all affairs in the country. **Supreme** rule meant that, recognizing no superior authority, the sovereign state had the final say in respect of its territorial realm. **Unqualified** rule meant that, although Westphalian times witnessed periodic invasions and occasional debates about possible duties of humanitarian intervention, on the whole the state's right of total authority over its territory was treated as sacrosanct by other states. Finally, **exclusive** rule meant that sovereign states did not share competences in regard to their respective domestic jurisdictions. There was no 'joint sovereignty' amongst states; 'pooled sovereignty' was a contradiction in terms.

It must be stressed that the Westphalian order was a historical phenomenon. In other words, the system of sovereign states was a particular framework of governance that arose at a specific time owing to the peculiar circumstances of a certain period. Sovereign statehood is not a timeless, natural condition. Politics operated without this organizing principle prior to the seventeenth century,

---

Box 1.3 **Key concepts of contemporary social change that are often associated with globalization**

Information society

A number of social theorists have argued since the early 1970s that contemporary society is experiencing a major shift in the focus of production. Whereas previously economic activity revolved around agriculture and manufacturing, in the newly emerging circumstances—including in particular those of globalization—information and knowledge are said to constitute the principal sources of wealth. Computers, mass media and telecommunications are allegedly becoming the most important assets in the economy, taking precedence over land, labour, industrial plant, and money. Instead of referring to an 'information society', some commentators advance similar arguments in terms of 'the information age', 'post-industrial society', 'the services economy', or 'the knowledge society'.

Late capitalism

Both Marxists and others have invoked this phrase to suggest that contemporary history has brought changes in the institutions and processes of capitalism (see Ch. 10). Like theorists of information society, some authors highlight a shift in the focus of surplus accumulation away from older industries to economies of data, signs, and images. Others emphasize the rise of global companies, or moves towards decentralized corporate management, or the emergence of a neo-imperialism vis-à-vis the so-called 'Third World', and so on. Some writers have made points of this kind while speaking of 'the end of organized capitalism' or even 'post-capitalist society' rather than 'late capitalism'.

Post-modernity

Along with globalization, 'post-modernity' and 'post-modernism' rank amongst the prominent buzzwords of contemporary social theory (see Ch. 11). Like globalization, their meaning can be quite elusive. Notions of the post-modern usually suggest some kind of crisis in, or departure from, the circumstances of modernity. For example, many commentators associate post-modernity with a demise of foundational knowledge. From this perspective, the post-modern condition involves the loss of the modern, rationalist, positivist conviction that we can, via science, establish fixed and universal truths and meanings. Ideas of post-modernity often also refer to intensified preoccupations in contemporary society with questions of identity. The post-modern individual has a 'fractured self' with multiple and fluctuating senses of being and belonging (for instance, in terms of nationality, gender, race, and sexuality). Many authors furthermore discuss post-modernity with reference to experiences of rapid change and ephemerality in a world dominated by mass media and consumerism. Post-modernists in International Relations in addition frequently highlight an end to the certainties of territoriality and sovereign statehood that once dominated the theory and practice of world politics. In each of these and other ways, post-modernity introduces increased uncertainty, insecurity, and disorder into social life. Note, however, that other commentators question such claims and suggest that recent historical developments involve an extension rather than a transcendence of modernity. They prefer to describe present-day circumstances in terms of 'high modernity', 'late modernity', or 'hypermodernity'.

The end of history

This thesis gained widespread attention in the early 1990s through the pen of Francis Fukuyama, a former official of the US Department of State. Fukuyama (1992) argued that the demise of communist regimes heralded a world-wide triumph of liberal democracy over all rival forms of governance. Since, in his view, liberal democracy was free of fundamental internal contradictions and answered the deepest human longings, its triumph marked the end of social evolution.

---

and there is no reason why world history could not once again carry on without a system of sovereign states.

The end of sovereignty

In fact, it can be argued that, largely owing to globalization, the Westphalian system is already past history. The state apparatus survives, and indeed is in some respects larger, stronger, and more intrusive in social life than ever before. However, the core Westphalian norm of sovereignty is no longer operative; nor can it be retrieved in the present globalizing world. The concept of sovereignty continues to be important in political rhetoric, especially for people who seek to slow and reverse reductions of national self-determination in the face of globalization. However, both juridically and practically, state regulatory capacities have ceased to meet the criteria of sovereignty as it was traditionally conceived.

State sovereignty is premised on territorialist geography. In order for governments to exercise total and exclusive authority over a specified territorial domain, events must occur at territorial locations, and jurisdictions must be separated by clearly demarcated territorial borders that officials can keep under strict surveillance. Yet when, with globalization, social relations acquire a host of supraterritorial qualities, and borders are transcended with a deluge of electronic and other flows, crucial preconditions for effective sovereignty no longer prevail. (See Fig. 1.1.)

On the one hand, a number of material developments have undercut state sovereignty. A state today is quite unable by itself to control phenomena like global companies, satellite remote sensing, global ecological problems, and global stock and bond trading. None of these conditions can be tied to a bounded territorial space over which a state might endeavour to exercise full control. Computer data transmissions, nuclear fallout, and telephone calls do not halt at frontier checkpoints. Global mass media have detracted from the state's dominion over language and education. In the face of huge offshore bank deposits and massive transworld electronic money transfers, states have also lost sole ownership of another former hallmark of sovereignty, the national currency.

Alongside these material changes, globalization has also loosened some important cultural and psychological underpinnings of sovereignty. For example, as a result of the growth of transborder networks, many people have acquired loyalties that supplement and in some cases even override feelings of national solidarity that previously lent legitimacy to state sovereignty. With the help of global conferences, global telecommunications, and so on, significant supraterritorial bonds have been cemented in women's movements, among a transnational managerial class, in lesbian and gay circles, among disabled persons, and in thousands of computer-mediated communities formed through newsgroups and chat rooms on the Internet. At the same time, globalization has also, as already mentioned, often reinvigorated more localized loyalties, for example, among indigenous peoples and other substate ethnic groups. In addition, many people in the contemporary globalizing world have become increasingly ready to give values such as economic growth, human rights, and ecological integrity a higher priority than state sovereignty and the associated norm of national self-determination.

States have affected the manner and rate at which they have lost sovereignty in the face of globalization, but they have not had the option to retain

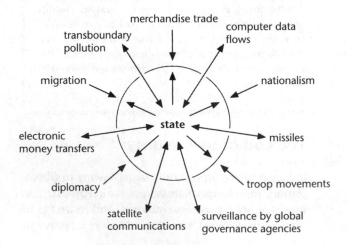

Fig. 1.1 The state in a globalizing world

comprehensive, supreme, unqualified, exclusive rule over their respective territorial jurisdictions. Even the Chinese government, which has been particularly insistent on perpetuating a sovereignty-centred world order, put 'global interdependence' at the heart of its Ten-Year Economic Blueprint for the 1990s. Of course there were violations of sovereignty under the Westphalian system, too, but at that time the norm was at least hypothetically realizable. A state could, by strengthening its institutions and instruments, graduate from mere legal sovereignty to effective sovereignty. In contrast, under conditions of contemporary globalization, governance in terms of supreme and exclusive territorial state authority has become utterly impracticable. No amount of institution building and unilateral legislation will allow a state to achieve absolute control of its realm. Indeed, many new post-colonial states—established during the recent time of large-scale globalization— have never been sovereign.

The persistence of the state

Yet although globalization has brought an end to sovereignty, it has not augured the demise of the state. On the contrary, with the exception of a few implosions of government (for instance, in Somalia and Afghanistan), the state has proved to be highly robust in contemporary history. Even the turbulence attending the collapse of communist rule yielded only certain changes to state borders. As a structure of governance the state has remained intact in the countries of Eastern Europe and the former Soviet Union.

Indeed, most states have during the time of globalization actually enlarged their payroll, budget, scope of activities, and surveillance capacities. For the moment there is little sign that globalization is leading either to a centralized, sovereign world government, as liberal universalists have long predicted and advocated, or to anarchical governance through local communities, as promoted by some radical ecologists. Hence globalists forecast the demise of the territorial state at their peril. Neither they nor the state-centric realists have it right. Globalization is not dissolving the state, but it has not left it untouched either. The challenge for students of politics is to determine how the growth of supra-territorial social spaces is altering the activities and role of the state in contemporary history. Three general shifts can be briefly mentioned here. (For further elaboration see Scholte 1997.)

First, under the influence of globalization **the constituencies of the state have been changing**. The sovereign state normally promoted domestic interests and acted as a protective barrier against external intrusions. In contrast, the post-sovereign state often advances transborder as well as national causes. For example, the Iranian state during the 1980s gave extensive support to transworld Islamicism. More generally, contemporary states have frequently served the interests of global capital in addition to (and sometimes to the detriment of) national capital.

Second, large-scale globalization has arguably constrained states to engage in **more frequent and more intensive multilateral consultations**. To take one prominent example, major states have met regularly since the mid-1970s as the so-called Group of 7 (or 8 if one includes Russia) to exchange views and where possible co-ordinate policy, particularly on macroeconomic matters. Concurrently, leading officials from finance ministries and central banks have developed extensive interchanges through the so-called Group of 10. Much transgovernmental consultation has also grown between other ministries, for example, of trade or the environment. In addition to ad hoc exchanges, much multilateralism has become institutionalized in permanent regional and transworld organizations, as discussed in the next section.

Third, accelerated globalization since the 1960s may have **reduced the chances of major interstate war**. It is striking that most contemporary warfare takes the form of internal insurrection against a national government rather than armed conflict between states. Although it is too early to draw definitive conclusions on this point, the expansion of global interests would seem to be substantially reducing incentives for states to embark on territorial conquest. Interstate warfare generally advances little purpose for—and sooner positively harms—global capitalism, global environmental management, global tourism, and so on.

Key points

- Globalization is connected to a number of potentially far-reaching changes in world order.
- Globalization has presented a fundamental challenge to the Westphalian states-system and its central principle of state sovereignty.

- Although globalization has brought the demise of sovereignty, it is by no means dissolving the state.
- The post-sovereign state may well behave differently from its Westphalian predecessor.

Post-sovereign governance

If world politics is no longer based on the core principle of sovereign statehood, how is governance being conducted in the contemporary globalizing world? Preceding paragraphs have stressed that the state is still very much in the picture, although its capacities, orientations, and activities have changed with the decline of sovereignty. At the same time, however, other parties besides the state have also acquired important roles in processes of governance. Their efforts to shape rules and norms sometimes complement the actions of states, but on other occasions they may compete with and possibly override the initiatives of national governments. In any case, governance is today far from reducible to the state and interstate relations. Regulatory activities in world politics now also involve substate institutions, suprastate organs, market agencies and civil society organizations.

Substate global governance

One new turn in present times of globalization has been the growth of direct transborder links between substate authorities, who have consequently taken a substantial number of policy initiatives that bypass central governments. For example, various provinces of Canada and China, as well as most of the US federal states, now have their own 'diplomatic' missions abroad that operate relatively independently from their respective national embassies. In Europe some fifty substate regional governments in seventeen countries maintain direct contacts through the Assembly of European Regions, the European

Union's Committee of the Regions, and several other such bodies created since the 1970s.

At a municipal level, too, considerable transborder co-operation has developed between local authorities on matters such as pollution control, crime prevention, disarmament, and development co-operation. Some of this collaboration has been institutionalized in bodies such as the World Association of Major Metropolises, founded in 1985, and the International Council for Local Environmental Initiatives, started in 1990. This development is hardly surprising, particularly in regard to large urban centres. Global capital flows, air corridors, and telecommunications webs often connect cities like Bangkok and Frankfurt as much to each other as to their respective national hinterlands.

Suprastate global governance

At the same time that globalization has encouraged some shift in governance 'downwards' to provincial and municipal governments, numerous other competences have moved 'upwards' to suprastate authorities. Permanent multilateral institutions are by no means new to recent decades, but their number, size, scope, and impact has greatly expanded with contemporary accelerated globalization.

For one thing, suprastate **regional** governance arrangements have proliferated and grown (albeit to differing degrees) in every part of the world. In total well over a hundred such agreements have been concluded since 1945, the largest numbers during the 1970s and 1990s. The furthest developed regional organization, the European Union (EU), has issued over 20,000 regulatory measures (see Ch. 23).

At the same time new and pre-existent **transworld** bodies like the United Nations (UN) (see Ch. 16) and the Bank for International Settlements (BIS) have also seen their tasks enlarged. Indeed, in the light of their increased initiative and influence, what used to be called 'international organizations' might now suitably be designated 'global governance agencies'. In other words, far more now occurs in these quarters than the 'intergovernmental' consultation and co-ordination for which the older institutions were originally established.

The growth of suprastate regulation covers a very wide spectrum, only part of which can be mentioned here. In the field of **macroeconomic policy**, for example, the Organization for Economic Co-operation and Development (OECD) has since the 1960s issued influential guidelines on a whole host of matters, including new information technologies, environmental problems, taxation, and transborder corporations. Since 1979 the International Monetary Fund (IMF) and the World Bank have supplemented their already significant stabilization and development functions with far-reaching structural adjustment programmes in almost 100 countries. The IMF has also conducted detailed annual policy surveillance of all of its member states. The World Trade Organization (WTO), established in 1995, covers a much wider range of activities with substantially greater powers than its forerunner, the General Agreement on Tariffs and Trade. (See further Ch. 24.)

As for other fields of policy, suprastate agencies like the UN, the Organization of African Unity (OAU), and the Organization for Security and Co-operation in Europe (OSCE) have acquired much-increased prominence in respect of **conflict management**. Suprastate governance has also greatly expanded in the area of **human rights** (see Ch. 28), including an unprecedented number of multinational humanitarian interventions since the 1990s. Although the idea of human rights goes back centuries, most formalized global law on the subject has emerged since 1960. Beginning with the UN Conference on the Human Environment in 1972, a proliferation of global meetings, legal instruments, and institutions have addressed ecological degradation throughout the world (see Ch. 18). In regard

to electronic media, the handbook of technical standards established by the International Telecommunication Union (ITU) now runs to some 10,000 pages. As these examples indicate, rulers and citizens alike have increasingly recognized that the territorial governance offered by states cannot by itself provide adequate management of supraterritorial activities linked to contemporary information, communications and weapons technologies, global ecological changes, global markets, and so on.

Of course significant limitations to suprastate governance remain. Official regional and transworld regulation is still considerably underdeveloped in various fields, including competition policy, financial markets, labour standards, gender equity and arms control, for example. In addition, most suprastate governance institutions have been inadequately staffed and chronically underfinanced. Poor co-ordination between transworld agencies and the frequent absence of effective enforcement mechanisms have further undermined the reputation of global law. Nevertheless, suprastate regulation has become sufficiently widespread and effective that it forms an important part of governance in today's globalizing world.

Marketized global governance

The present review of contemporary governance would be incomplete if it only covered official agencies at substate, state, and suprastate levels. Not all regulation in the globalizing world of recent decades has emanated from the public sector. Market institutions, too, have played an important role in global governance, often stepping in where public-sector agencies have left gaps.

The construction and implementation of rules by private-sector bodies has gone especially far in respect of global financial markets, where limited effective official governance has developed. With regard to global securities trading, for example, standard procedures and codes of conduct have emanated mainly from industry bodies like the International Federation of Stock Exchanges (founded in 1961) and the International Securities Market Association (1969), as well as from the semi-official International Organization of Securities

Commissions (1984). Meanwhile bond-rating agencies such as Moody's Investors Service and Standard & Poor's have effectively filled a regulatory role in global credit markets (Sinclair 1994). In addition, commercial banks have taken considerable initiative alongside official agencies like the IMF in managing (some would say mismanaging) the recurrent financial crises of debt-ridden countries in the South since 1982.

Global policy initiatives by the private sector have ranged beyond the financial markets, too. For example, the World Economic Forum (WEF), founded in 1971, now unites some 900 major companies under the motto of 'entrepreneurship in the global public interest'. Among its many initiatives, the Forum has undertaken conciliation attempts in several major interstate conflicts, including the Arab–Israeli dispute. The WEF was also instrumental in launching the Uruguay Round of world trade negotiations that resulted in the creation of the WTO. Scores of corporate endowments have also become active in global policy-making. Two prominent examples are the Ford Foundation (which has been especially influential in the field of development aid since the 1960s) and the Soros Foundations (which have been major promoters of liberal democracy in the former Soviet bloc). Set up in 1991, a World Business Council for Sustainable Development has injected a corporate input into global environmental management. There have even been proposals to create a permanent 'Chamber of Companies' in the United Nations alongside the General Assembly of states. Clearly, contemporary global governance is not an affair of the public sector alone.

Global civil society

Market institutions are not the only actors outside the public sector that have contributed to governance in the contemporary globalizing world. Notable initiative has also come from a non-official, nonprofit 'third sector' of global civil society. Here citizens have mobilized in voluntary associations to shape policies and the deeper structures of social relations (like militarism or capitalism, for example) that those policies reflect. These civic groups are global both insofar as they address transworld prob-

lems and in the sense that they pursue their causes by exploiting the circumstances of globalization (air travel, computer networks, global laws, and so on). As noted earlier, precursors of today's transborder civic organizations date back to the nineteenth century; however, contemporary activities involve far larger numbers of people, greater institutional resources, and bigger impacts.

Global civic associations show enormous diversity. For one thing, they address an extremely wide spectrum of issues, from aboriginal rights to HIV/ AIDS. They also hold extremely divergent visions of the world that they wish to fashion, drawing inspiration variously from liberalism, anarchism, neofascism, a host of traditional and new religions, and much else. Some of the movements are global in the sense that they work through transworld networks, like Development Alternatives with Women for a New Era (DAWN). In contrast, others 'think globally and act locally', that is, they hold a global orientation while operating at a grassroots level. Some groups campaign in isolation, while others pursue their aims through large coalitions. Illustrating the latter approach, the Pesticides Action Network has encompassed some 350 groups in over fifty countries. Civil society activity includes both sporadic amateur improvisations (such as many student protests) and long-term professionalized and institutionalized programmes (of the kind sustained by Greenpeace and Christian Aid). Finally, global civic groups have embraced a variety of strategies. Some activists have seen fit to work with official agencies and the business sector, while others have regarded any collaboration with 'the establishment' as an unacceptable compromise of their principles.

Although global civic associations have often suffered from shortages of resources and divisive internal disputes, they can exert considerable influence in contemporary governance. Among other things, these movements have contributed substantially to policy innovation in areas such as ecological sustainability, human rights protection, disaster relief, welfare provision, and community improvement. By 1990 most of the major global governance agencies had set up offices for liaison with what they generally call non-governmental organizations, or 'NGOs' (see Ch. 17). Many civic associations have played important roles both in advising the official

Box 1.4 HIV/AIDS: a case study in global governance

Acquired immunodeficiency sydrome (AIDS) was first identified in 1981. In an era of globalization, when several hundred million passengers take transborder flights each year, the number of recorded cases of AIDS grew to 150,000 worldwide in 1988 and over 400,000 at the end of 1991. By 2000 some 34 million people across the world carried HIV, the virus believed to cause the disease, so that, in the absence of curative therapies, millions more AIDS cases are in prospect.

HIV/AIDS has attracted global attention as no previous transborder epidemic. The plight quickly became the focus of global panic, global conferences, global support groups, global policies, and global commemoration with an annual World AIDS Day on 1 December. It was soon recognized that, in the words of a former Prime Minister of France, 'AIDS will be conquered everywhere or it will not be conquered at all'.

The global campaign against AIDS has involved a very wide range of governance agencies. For their part, states have activated their public health systems, both individually and through regular intergovernmental consultations. At the same time, local authorities have created various support facilities for patients and their carers. Meanwhile suprastate bodies have taken initiatives such as the AIDS Task Force of the European Union and the Global Programme on AIDS of the World Health Organization. Some global companies like Benetton have sponsored public service advertising to combat the spread of the disease. The International Red Cross and other nonprofit associations involved in patient care have maintained regular transboundary communication and co-ordination. At the grassroots, afflicted individuals have formed a Global Network of People Living with HIV and AIDS. No such multifaceted attempt at extensive global regulation met, say, the worldwide influenza epidemic of 1918–19, let alone the intercontinental bubonic plague of the fourteenth century.

institutions and in helping to implement their policies. Indeed, bodies like the World Bank and the Office of the United Nations High Commissioner for Refugees have sometimes become quite dependent on NGO assistance. Thousands of civic organizations have attended the various UN-sponsored global issue conferences held since the 1970s, where these groups have lobbied officials and influenced the resultant programmes of action. Such scenarios illustrate an emergent new politics, whereby civil society groups channel many of their efforts to reshape national and local government policies through suprastate regulatory agencies.

In this and other ways, many activists in global civil society have aimed—and to some extent succeeded—not only to change policies, but also to reconstruct the very nature of politics. Their initiatives have frequently challenged prevailing concepts, procedures, and tactics of political action. For example, a number of these associations have adopted nonhierarchical modes of decision-taking, and in general they have included women to a greater extent than occurs in official and commercial channels. The expansion of global civil society has helped to make popular participation in world politics far more direct and extensive than in Westphalian days, when citizen involvement tended to mean no more than a vote in national elections to determine which political party would conduct the state's foreign policy.

Key points

- Globalization has encouraged increased direct transborder collaboration between provincial and municipal governments.

- Globalization has brought a major expansion of suprastate regulation by regional and transworld governance agencies.

- The private sector has taken an active role in contemporary governance, for example, through market-based supervisory agencies, foundations, and advisory councils.

- With great diversity of organizational form, issue-focus, and tactics, global civil society has injected considerable dynamism and innovation into contemporary world politics.

The challenge of global democracy

We have now seen that globalization has encouraged a shift in governance away from a single focus on the states-system to a multilayered complex of rule-making and order creation where no location is sovereign. Politics now lacks a clear centre of command and control of the kind previously provided by the Westphalian state. In addition, considerable initiative in regulatory processes is now found outside public-sector bodies, namely, in market agents and civil society. What do these developments imply for democracy?

Democracy — rule by the people — is widely regarded to be the central legitimating ethic of modern governance. Although definitions of democracy, and the mechanisms to achieve it, have shown considerable diversity between countries and time periods, there is a broad and fairly solid consensus in today's world that good governance requires democratic governance. Hence before closing this chapter it is appropriate to ask a crucial normative question, namely, what is happening to democracy in the contemporary globalizing world?

At first glance globalization would seem to offer possibilities for enhancing democracy. As we saw earlier, globalization has been unravelling state sovereignty, and there is a fundamental tension between sovereignty and democracy. Sovereignty involves comprehensive, supreme, unqualified, and exclusive power, whereas democracy is generally presumed to rest on limited, dispersed, conditional, and collective power. Even where governments are popularly elected, there remains a potentially dangerous concentration of power in the state. To this extent the removal of sovereignty ought, in principle, to present opportunities for increasing democracy.

Regrettably, however, globalization has thus far more usually made things worse. Contemporary post-sovereign governance is strewn with democratic deficits. The state, global governance agencies, the market, and global civic associations have all suffered from shortfalls in respect of popular participation and access, consultation and debate, inclusion and representativeness, transparency and accountability.

Globalization and the democratic state

Some enthusiasts have assumed that globalization and democratization would be two sides of the same coin. Adopting this perspective, many liberalists have celebrated a worldwide wind of democratic change in recent decades with the collapse of *apartheid*, communism, and other one-party systems. However, multiparty competition has not by itself provided a guarantee for greater popular participation in, and control of, the state. Countless governments have continued habitually to violate human rights in the current time of globalization. Meanwhile even those states that receive top ratings from Amnesty International have rarely consulted their populations specifically on global policies. For example, citizens have almost never had any significant say in a state's decision whether or not to adopt an IMF structural adjustment programme. Moreover, even were the state fully to involve its citizens in these matters, national governments have often, as we have seen, had limited control over global flows. To this extent the state does not, by itself, offer sufficient means to secure the collective will in relation to global capital, global ecological problems, and so on. Democratically run government has to be supplemented by other instruments and institutions.

Suprastate governance and democracy

Unfortunately, regional and transworld governance agencies have not so far come even close to providing the necessary further guarantees of democracy. To begin with, affected publics have had very little direct involvement in these institutions. Most meetings of the World Bank Board of Governors, the EU Council of Ministers, the UN Security Council, and other such decision-taking bodies are held behind closed doors. Moreover, most of the world's citizens are completely ignorant of the *modus operandi* of these bodies. The organizations are largely realms of 'technopolitics', where accountants, chemists, economists, engineers, lawyers, managers, and other 'experts' are largely exempted from democratic scrutiny. When their policies have unhappy consequences—as in the case of the detrimental welfare effects of many structural adjustment policies, for instance—the agencies concerned are not held formally and publicly accountable.

It can be argued that suprastate bodies are indirectly representative, insofar as state delegations are in attendance to speak for the various national populations of the world. However, most states have pretty dubious democratic credentials. Moreover, the rule of one-state-one-vote that prevails in many global organs means that, formally at least, Andorra and India have an equal say. Elsewhere, the reservation of permanent membership and veto powers in the Security Council to five states is democratically unjustifiable. So, too, are quota-based votes in the IMF and World Bank, where one-quarter of the member states control three-quarters of the votes.

The undemocratic character of suprastate governance agencies has been increasingly acknowledged in recent years. In the case of the European Union, some (limited) steps have been taken since the late 1970s to increase popular access and direct participation in policy processes. In 1992 the Maastricht Treaty prescribed *inter alia* that the European Commission should consult more widely and that the popularly elected European Parliament should gain increased competences. The EU and many other suprastate organizations have moved towards greater public disclosure of information concerning their operations, including via the Internet. In addition, the IMF and the World Bank have inaugurated modest programmes of policy evaluation by external panels. However, on the whole, steps to enhance democracy in suprastate governance have thus far shown little sign of moving out of the slow lane.

Global market democracy?

Other worrying reductions of democracy have resulted from the previously described marketization of governance. True, champions of *laissez-faire* claim that the 'free market' enlarges the scope for popular participation and control. From this optimistic perspective, global democracy is achieved when consumers and capitalists (rather than citizens) vote with their pocketbooks (rather than their ballots) for the best value for money (rather than the maximization of human potential) in a global market (rather than a territorial state).

However, this vision presumes that money and material comforts are the be-all and end-all of politics. Traditional democratic concerns with human dignity and equal opportunity are subordinated to obsessions with managerial efficiency and product quality. In market democracy accountability means the boardroom's responsibility to shareholders and the company's responsibility to the customer. Yet in practice shareholders rarely effect principled changes in corporate policies, and consumers are often captives of oligopoly. Most disturbingly, of course, access and participation in market-based governance mechanisms are determined primarily by wealth and income. One needs capital to become a shareholder. Very few people receive invitations to attend meetings of bodies like the World Economic Forum, and almost all of the participants come from a narrow and highly privileged circle.

Global civil society and democracy

Other commentators have looked to civil society as the way to secure democracy in the contemporary globalizing world. It is certainly the case that transborder civic activism has shown impressive growth in recent decades. In particular, globalization has provided opportunities for women, disabled persons, lesbians and gay men, and indigenous peoples to mobilize to a degree that was generally unavailable to them in Westphalian world politics.

However, these gains for democracy need to be kept in perspective and set against other profoundly undemocratic features of contemporary global civil society. For one thing, only a very small proportion of the world's people has been directly involved in these initiatives. The vast dispossessed majority of humanity has lacked the funds, the language skills (or translation facilities), access to the Internet, and other resources on which the influence of global civic associations depends. As a result, this activism has for the most part remained the preserve of a narrow, disproportionately white, and overwhelmingly middle-class population residing chiefly in North America and Western Europe. In spite of some increase, fewer than 15 per cent of the NGOs with consultative status at the UN are based in the so-called South. Moreover, in the South as well as the North, many NGOs are self-elected and follow no formal procedures to ensure transparency of their operations and accountability towards those whom they claim to serve.

In sum, then, democracy is in a precarious position across all areas of contemporary governance. In the present-day globalizing world, the construction and implementation of rules occurs mainly through élite competition rather than through representative, let alone participatory, democracy. At the moment it is unclear whether and how democracy can be adequately realized in a more global world. Hence imaginative rethinking of democracy is arguably the prime task facing political theory today.

Key points

- Globalization makes it impossible to achieve democracy solely through the state.

- Suprastate governance agencies suffer from severe democratic deficits.

- Global governance through market channels implies deep inequalities and the rule of efficiency over democracy.

- Global civil society, too, often has shaky democratic credentials.

Conclusion

This opening chapter, like the rest of the book, indicates that globalization has changed, and continues to change, the nature of world politics. The character of those changes is much debated. Analysts are deeply divided when it comes to definitions, measurements, chronologies, explanations, prognoses, and normative assessments of globalization. Indeed, many researchers on the subject will disagree with much of the argument put forward in this chapter. However, it is clear that we today face some different issues and dynamics of world affairs. It will not do to study 'international relations' in the way of earlier generations of students.

To recapitulate, I have suggested that contemporary history is witnessing a significant shift in the spatial character of politics. In addition to the old geography of territorial places, distances, and borders, we now have an extensive supraterritorial dimension in which certain circumstances are effectively placeless (they can occur anywhere on earth), distanceless (they can cross the planet in no time), and borderless (they can unfold relatively unhindered by state frontiers).

The accelerated spread of global relations since the middle of the twentieth century has had a number of important implications for patterns of governance. On the one hand, globalization has rendered the old core principle of sovereign statehood unworkable, although national governments continue to play a key role in the regulation of social life. On the other hand, globalization has encouraged the growth of a number of other sites of governance, including transborder relations between substate authorities, suprastate regimes, regulatory initiatives by market institutions, and the campaigns of global civil society.

Thus students of International Relations today need to explore world politics with a broader conception of governance. We cannot, following the traditional pattern, automatically take the state and the states-system as the starting point of investigation. Nor can we assume, complacently, that old models of sovereignty and democracy will provide good governance in a globalizing world. Assuring democracy in post-sovereign governance is a key challenge for politics in the twenty-first century.

QUESTIONS

1 How is globalization distinct from internationalization?

2 How new is the phenomenon of globalization?

3 Specify some misconceptions that are commonly associated with the idea of globalization.

4 What are the driving forces behind globalization?

5 What is meant by state sovereignty?

6 How has globalization eroded sovereign statehood?

7 Why does the state persist in the contemporary era of globalization?

8 Assess the relationship between globalization and war.

9 Discuss recent advances in, and continuing limitations of, suprastate law.

10 Illustrate how private-sector bodies contribute to governance of global relations.

11 How are global civic associations involved in contemporary governance?

12 Evaluate the implications of globalization for democracy.

GUIDE TO FURTHER READING

Bull, H., *The Anarchical Society: A Study of Order in World Politics* (London: Macmillan, 1977). This classic study of intemational relations theory explores the emergence, subsequent evolution, and future prospects of the states-system.

Carlsson, I. *et al.*, *Our Global Neighbourhood* (Oxford: Oxford University Press, 1995). This report of the Commission on Global Governance (a group of academics, activists, and statespersons from around the world) surveys the development of transworld regulation, especially through the United Nations system. It highlights various shortcomings in present arrangements and makes a number of suggestions for institutional reform.

Cutler, A. C. *et al.* (eds.), *Private Authority and International Affairs* (New York: SUNY Press, 1999). This volume explores the involvement in contemporary governance of regulatory institutions created by business.

Edwards, M., and Gaventa, J. (eds.), *Global Citizen Action: Perspectives and Challenges* (Boulder, Colo.: Westview Press, 2001). This book brings together leading researchers on and practitioners in global civil society. The chapters present both case studies of global citizen action and general lessons of experience.

Held, D., McGrew, A., Goldblatt, D., and Perraton, J., *Global Transformations: Politics, Economics and Culture* (Cambridge: Polity Press, 1999). This major study of the history of globalization includes extensive examinations of military issues, global trade, global finance, global production, migration, global communications and environmental problems.

Hirst, P., and Thompson, G., *Globalization in Question: The International Economy and the Possibilities of Governance* (Cambridge: Polity Press, 1999, 2nd edn.). This book argues against globalist presumptions that globalization is new, irreversible, and beyond state control.

Kofman, E., and Youngs, G. (eds.), *Globalization: Theory and Practice* (London: Pinter, 2001, 2nd edn.). The essays in this book develop insights about globalization that are gained from cross-disciplinary dialogue between International Relations and Geography. Insofar as globalization involves a transformation of the spatial aspects of social life, it is a subject on which geographers have much of interest to say.

Peterson, V. S., and Runyan, A. S., *Global Gender Issues* (Boulder, Colo.: Westview Press, 1999 2nd edn.). This textbook highlights a number of important but often neglected ways that gender relations (i.e. social constructions of femininity and masculinity) are involved in globalization.

Sakamoto, Y. (ed.), *Global Transformation: Challenges to the State System* (Tokyo: United Nations University Press, 1994). Academics from different parts of the world give their perspectives on changing contours of contemporary world politics.

Scholte, J. A., *Globalization: A Critical Introduction* (Basingstoke: Palgrave, 2000). This text develops at greater length the concerns of the above chapter: namely, definitions of globalization; the consequences of contemporary globalization for governance; and the challenges of democracy in a globalizing world.

Sklair, L., *The Transnational Capitalist Class* (Oxford: Blackwell, 2001). This investigation of globalization focuses on the role of transnational corporations, a global capitalist class, and a global culture of consumerism.

Waters, M., *Globalization* (London: Routledge, 1995). This introductory sociology text offers a concise survey of theories of globalization and also reviews the economic, political, and cultural repercussions of the process.

WEB LINKS

www.csgr.org   Website of the Centre for the Study of Globalization and Regionalization at the University of Warwick, the main research centre on globalization of the (UK) Economic and Social Research Council.

www.focusweb.org   Website of Focus on the Global South, a regional institute of research and advocacy on globalization from a Southern perspective.

www.un.org   Central website of the United Nations system.

www.weforum.org   Website of the World Economic Forum, a leading source of reports and comments on globalization from a business perspective.

Part One

The historical context

In this part of the book, we want to provide you with a historical context within which to make sense of globalization. We have two main aims: **first**, we want to introduce you to the main aspects of international history and we will do this by giving you an increasingly more chronologically concentrated set of chapters. We start with an overview of international society from its origins in Ancient Greece through to the twentieth century. We think that you need to have some basic understanding of the main developments in the history of world politics, as well as some kind of context for thinking about the contemporary period of world history. This is followed by two chapters that look at the main themes of twentieth-century history, one dealing with the period before the Second World War, the other dealing with the period after it. We then have a chapter that is specifically concerned with the period since the late 1980s, and that concentrates on the most significant historical development of that period, namely the end of the cold war. Our final chapter looks at developments within international history since 1990. We want these chapters to give you a lot of historical information which will be of interest in its own right, but our **second** aim is to draw to your attention the main themes of international history so that you can develop a deeper understanding of the issues, both theoretical and empirical that are dealt with in the remaining four sections of this book. As such we think that an overview of international history gives you a context within which to begin thinking about globalization: is it a new phenomenon that fundamentally changes the main patterns of international history or are there precedents for it that make it seem less revolutionary?

2 The evolution of international society

Robert H. Jackson

READER'S GUIDE

This chapter discusses the idea of international society and some of its historical manifestations. The starting point is human beings organized into geographically separate political communities and the horizontal relations of conflict and co-operation that ensue from their joint political existences. International society should be understood as a distinctive institutional response to accommodate that reality of political coexistence. It has assumed different forms from ancient times to the present era but it also discloses common features the most important being a relationship of independence between political communities, usually conceived as states.

Origins and definitions

In order to understand the contemporary world and the significance of globalization we need to consider the evolution of international society. The historical origin of international relations can only be a matter of speculation. But, speaking conceptually, it was a time when people began to settle down on the land and form themselves into separate territory-based political communities. Each group faced the inescapable problem of co-existing with neighbour-ing groups whom they could not ignore or avoid because they were right there next door. Each group also had to deal with groups that were farther away but still capable of affecting them. Their geographical contiguity must have come to be regarded as a zone of political proximity if not a frontier or border of some kind. (The institution of formally demarcated international boundaries is of course a much later invention of the modern European society of states.) Where contact occurred it must have involved activities such as competition, disputes, threats, intimidation, intervention, invasion, conquest, and other belligerent interactions. But it also must have involved dialogue, collaboration, exchange, communication, recognition, and similar non-belligerent relations.

That social reality of group relations on a horizontal plane could be considered, figuratively speaking, as the core problem of international relations, which is built on a fundamental distinction between our collective selves and other collective selves in a territorial world of many such collective selves in contact with each other. If there were no horizontal lines of territorial division between 'we' and 'they' there could still be human societies: perhaps isolated political communities, perhaps roaming or marauding groups, perhaps a vertical society such as an empire, possibly even a cosmopolitan world society of all humankind devoid of fundamental group differentiation, or some other social formation or arrangement. But there could not be international relations in the usual meaning of the term. In short, international relations as historically and conventionally understood are relations of territorially based and delimited political groups.

We now begin to arrive at a definition of 'international society'. As already indicated, it stands for relations between politically organized human groupings which occupy distinctive territories and enjoy and exercise a measure of independence from each other. International society can thus be conceived as a society of political communities which are not under any higher political authority. In the language of international relations such detached communities are referred to as states which are usually conceptualized as consisting of (1) a permanent population (2) occupying a defined territory (3) under a central government (4) which is independent of all other governments of a similar kind (Brownlie 1979). That condition of constitutional or political independence is ordinarily spoken of as state sovereignty (James 1986: 25). Hedley Bull (1977: 8) sums up the foundation of the subject: 'The

---

Box 2.1 **Key concepts**

coexistence: the doctrine of live and let live between political communities, or states.

territory: a portion of the earth's surface appropriated by a political community, or state.

state sovereignty: a state's characteristic being politically independent of all other states.

suzerain state: a state which dominates and subordinates neighbouring states, without taking them over.

empire: a state which possesses both a home territory and foreign territories: an imperial state.

theocracy: a state based on religion.

hegemony: power and control exercised by a leading state over other states.

reason of state: the practical application of the doctrine of realism and virtually synonymous with it.

balance of power: a doctrine and an arrangement whereby the power of one state (or group of states) is checked by the countervailing power of other states.

national security: a fundamental value in the foreign policy of states.

society of states: an association of sovereign states based on their common interests, values, and norms.

international law: the formal rules of conduct that states acknowledge or contract between themselves.

international order: a shared value and condition of stability and predictability in the relations of states.

non-discrimination: a doctrine of equal treatment between states.

self-determination: the right of a political community or state to become a sovereign state.

right of self-defence: a state's right to wage war in its own defence.

world society: the society produced by globalization.

global covenant: the rules, values, and norms which govern the global society of states.

> ## Box 2.2 The earliest records of 'international society'
>
> There are recorded formal agreements among ancient city-states which date as far back as 2400 BC, alliances dating to 1390 BC, and envoys as early as 653 BC (Barber 1979: 8–9).

starting point of international relations is the existence of states, or independent political communities, each of which possesses a government and asserts sovereignty in relation to a particular portion of the earth's surface and a particular segment of the human population.'

Hedley Bull (1977: 13) offers the following definition of international society: 'A society of states (or international society) exists when a group of states, conscious of certain common interests and common values, form a society in the sense that they conceive themselves to be bound by a common set of rules in their relations with one another, and share in the working of common institutions.' International society is basically a pluralistic or 'liberal' political arrangement. The core value is the political opportunity of people to enjoy a geographically separate group existence free from unsolicited interference from neighbouring groups and other outsiders. Independence is the core value in a cluster of important international values, including self-determination, non-intervention, right of self-defence, and the like. The basic institutional arrangement which embodies and expresses those values is state sovereignty.

One of the most noteworthy and characteristic arrangements between sovereign states is diplomacy which obviously is intended primarily to facilitate and smooth their relations. Of course diplomatic arrangements have been expressed differently from one time or place to the next: diplomacy in ancient Greece was not the same as diplomacy in Renaissance Italy which was different again from the classical diplomacy of the eighteenth century or the global diplomacy of the twentieth century (Nicolson 1954). Another arrangement is international law, which is a more recent innovation dating back only as far as the sixteenth and seventeenth centuries

when the first recognizable international legal texts were written that sought to document the rather novel legal practices of what at that time were recently discerned entities known as sovereign states. Other such arrangements include recognition, reciprocity, the laws of war, international conferences, and much else. In the past century an increasingly important arrangement is the large and extensive complex of international organizations—universal, regional and functional—by means of which much of the business of international relations is nowadays conducted.

One point deserves particular emphasis so that the idea and expression of international society is understood in its proper historical context. Vertical or hierarchical relations between political groups are a historical commonplace throughout most of the world as far back as recorded history can take us. Political empire is the prevalent form of group relations. Horizontal relations between political groups is comparatively rare. The ancient Greeks constructed an international society which survived for several centuries in a surrounding political environment of various hegemonic empires, including Persia, Macedonia, and the Roman empire. At that time there were also great empires and suzerain-state systems beyond Europe and the Middle East, including the Chinese empire which was the greatest of them all and which lasted for millennia, albeit in different dynastic incarnations.

Empire was the prevalent mode of large-scale political group relations in Western Europe throughout the era of the Roman empire and that of its successor, medieval Christendom, which lasted until about the sixteenth century. In the late Middle Ages (1300–1500) the Renaissance Italians constructed and operated a small regional international society based on the city states of northern and central Italy. The first modern international society based on large-scale territorial states came into existence a little later in north-western Europe out of which the contemporary global international society has evolved (see chronology below). But empires continued to exist in Europe and many other parts of the world down to the twentieth century. Eastern Europe was dominated by empires until the end of the First World War. Although Europeans created a society of states among themselves which was the very definition of political modernity, at the very same time they constructed vast empires to rule non-European political communities in the rest of the world. International society is thus uncommon in history even though it has become globalized in the twentieth century and now prevails in every continent.

Key points

- International society is an association of member states who not only interact across international borders but also share common purposes, organizations, and standards of conduct.

- There are different historical versions of international society the most important of which is the contemporary global international society.

- In understanding international society it is important to keep in mind contrasting group relations, such as empires, which are far more common historically.

- Political independence is the core value of international society.

Ancient Greece and Renaissance Italy

In an important survey Adam Watson (1992) identifies, among others, the independent city-states of Classical Greece, the states-system of Renaissance Italy, the anti-hegemonial Peace of Westphalia, the Concert of Europe, the globalization of the European states-system, the era of the two superpowers, and the contemporary international society. So we are dealing with a large historical subject of which only a few highlights can be examined in this chapter.

In this section I shall briefly discuss two incipient and important forerunners of the idea and institution of international society: ancient Greece and Renaissance Italy. The first historical manifestation of an international society is ancient Greece, then known as Hellas, which was a geographical area and a cultural unity but not a single political entity or state. Hellenic international society comprised a large number of city-states based geographically on

the lower Balkan Peninsula and the many islands in the surrounding Aegean, Adriatic, and Mediterranean seas. The Hellenes thought of themselves as sharing a common ancestry, language, religion, and way of life, all of which distinguished them from neighbours whom they regarded as 'barbarians'—those who did not speak Greek—of whom the Persians were the defining case (Wight 1977: 46–7; 85). Athens was the most famous of the Greek city-states but there were also many others, such as Sparta and Corinth, which taken together formed the first international society in Western history. It is important to emphasize, then, that ancient Greece was not a state: the Greeks referred to themselves as Hellenes. Hellenic international society consisted of city-states which were more or less independent of each other but shared a common culture that was essential to their cohesion as an international society. Furthermore, as indicated, the ancient Greeks sharply distinguished Hellas from neighbouring non-Greek 'barbarians', such as the Persians, with whom they had political relations but no cultural affinities or political association.

There were extensive and elaborate relations between the city-states of Hellas. Their religion, customs, traditions, and politics were similar even though each city-state had its own identity, ceremonies, cults, oracles, and political arrangements. The Oracle at Delphi was consulted as a source of

Box 2.3 Approximate chronology of international society

500–100 BC	Ancient Greek or Hellenic
1300–1500	Renaissance Italian
1500–1650	Early modern European
1650–1950	European cum Western
1950–	Global

authority in disputes between city-states. The ancient Greeks evolved a special political vocabulary that included 'reconciliation', 'truce', 'convention', 'alliance', 'coalition', 'arbitration', 'treaty', 'peace', among other translated words. They had a concept of neutrality which was expressed by a word that translates 'to stay quiet' (Nicolson 1954: 3–14). They did not possess an institution of diplomacy based on resident ambassadors which was an invention of the Italian Renaissance. They nevertheless developed a comparable institution, known as proxeny, which served the same basic function and involved local residents from other Greek cities (Wight 1977: 53–6).

Whether there existed an international society as defined above by Hedley Bull, of which the Greek cities were self-consciously members, is less clear and more controversial. The ancient Greeks did not articulate a body of international law because they could not conceive of the polis—the city-state political communities in which they lived—as having rights and obligations in relation to other city-states on some basis of rough equality (Wight 1977: 51) The ancient Greek city-states were politically self-contained even though they were based on a common culture and religion; they were not part of a larger political association consisting, for example, of a common body of international law. Their international society, to the extent that it existed, was cultural–religious rather than legal–political.

Even though the ancient Greeks had no explicit conception of international law as such, they did nevertheless recognize that certain principles ordained by the gods or dictated by practical reality should govern the conduct of international affairs between the city-states of Hellas. Treaties were under the special custody of Zeus, the all-powerful ruler of gods and men, and it was considered an offence to break a treaty without a recognized justification, or to abandon an ally in the middle of a military campaign. According to Harold Nicolson (1954: 5), among the ancient Greeks 'there seems . . . to have existed a religious sanction, mitigating the unrestrained barbarities of war and analogous to our Geneva Convention'. That analogy might be misplaced because the Geneva Conventions are an elaborate and explicit body of international law. But narrow expediency and strict opportunism in both war and foreign policy were considered wrong: it was

immoral to engage in a surprise military attack; atrocities were associated with the conduct expected of barbarians but not Greeks. Some states, such as Sparta, were censured for their diplomatic unreliability. And apart from the laws and customs which obtained among the cities of Hellas, according to Nicolson (p. 10) the Greeks did dimly recognize the existence of certain standards of conduct which applied to all mankind, civilized and barbarian alike.

These practices obviously come close to Hedley Bull's concept and so it is not surprising that ancient Greece is often seen as the first significant international society in the Western tradition. But it should again be emphasized that the Greeks did not operate with a concept of equal sovereignty. Some states clearly were more equal than others: there were a few major powers, such as Athens and Sparta, and many lesser powers who often became entangled in their rivalries, coalitions, and wars. Minor states were not the equals of major powers. That is made clear by Thucydides in his account of the Peloponnesian war (431–404 BC) between Athens and Sparta which polarized Greek international society. In a famous dialogue the people of Melos, a small city-state, appeal for justice from the powerful Athenians, who have presented them with an ultimatum. But the Athenians spurn this appeal with the response that justice between states depends on equality of power: 'the strong do what they have the power to do and the weak accept what they have to accept . . . This is the safe rule—to stand up to one's equals, to behave with deference towards one's superiors, and to treat one's inferiors with moderation'. (Thucydides, trans. Warner 1972: 402; 407). Here is the classic statement of the political ethics of Realism in the Western tradition (see Ch. 6).

Hellas was finally overwhelmed by imperial Macedonia, which was a continental state based on the Balkan peninsula. Even the greatest power in the ancient Greek world, Athens, lacked the power to withstand the Macedonian bid for supremacy over the Hellenes. That ushered in an age of hierarchy and empire in the relations of political communities in that part of the world. The Romans, who eventually displaced the Macedonians, developed an even greater empire in the course of conquering, occupying, and ruling most of Europe and a large part of the Middle East and North Africa. Although the Romans recognized a primitive law of nations (jus gentium) it was not an express law for independent or sovereign states. Rome was the only sovereign and its relations with all other political communities in its domain were imperial rather than international. Instead of dialogue and conciliation between independent states, under the Roman imperium there was only the alternative of obedience or revolt.

After a long period of decline the (Western) empire at Rome disintegrated in the fourth century AD under the impact of 'barbarian' assaults from the imperial peripheries. It was eventually succeeded by a theocracy—that is, a government based on organized religion, in this case Latin Christendom which was one of two successor empires to that of Rome. The (Eastern) empire at Constantinople—which also was a theocracy—was not overthrown but lived on for another thousand years in the incarnation of Greek—i.e. Orthodox—Christianity (Byzantium). It was finally destroyed in the mid-fifteenth century by the Ottoman Turks, a rising Muslim imperial state. In North Africa the Roman empire was eventually succeeded, after the passing of several centuries, by rising Islamic states; that same area came to be dominated much later by the Ottoman empire. The Middle Ages were thus an age of empire, and the relations and conflicts of different empires, and not an age of international society based on sovereign states.

Medieval Europe in the West, which lasted for about a thousand years from the year 500 until about 1500, has been called a Respublica Christiana: a universal society based on a joint structure of religious authority (sacerdotium) and political authority (regnum) which gave at least minimal unity and cohesion to Europeans whatever their language and wherever their homeland happened to be (Wight 1977: 47). That at least was the formal arrangement acknowledged in medieval political theory (Gierke 1987: 13) In practice, of course, medieval Europe was fragmented along feudal lines at both the regional and local level of society. Medieval Europeans had a customary political loyalty to their immediate feudal superiors in those numerous local communities in which the vast majority lived out their lives. Their loyalty to the king (or in other words the secular state) was weak. Medieval Europeans as a whole nevertheless did have a customary religious obedience to the (Western) Church which was an over-arching hierarchy of bishops and priests headed by the Bishop of Rome, the Pope. The Pope could also assert, and occasionally he did assert, his vocation as judge in disputes between secular rulers. Even as late as the start of the early modern period (1500–1650) the Pope was still revered in many parts of Europe and periodically he performed the role of a mediator between sovereign rulers, as when Pope Innocent IV settled the division of the newly discovered American continent and surrounding oceans between Spain and Portugal.

In the course of time, however, the European kings beat down the feudal barons and challenged the Pope and in that way they became state defenders against internal disorder and external intervention or threat. This political transformation is perfectly summarized by Martin Wight (1986: 25): 'The common man's inner circle of loyalty expanded, his outer circle of loyalty shrank, and the two met and coincided in a doubly definite circle between, where loyalty before had been vague. Thus the modern state came into existence; a narrower and at the same time a stronger unit of loyalty than medieval Christendom.' The medieval ecclesiastical–political order began to unravel during the sixteenth century under the impact of the Protestant Reformation and the new political theology of Martin Luther which enhanced the authority of kings and the legitimacy of their kingdoms. By that time the papacy itself had long since become a state and indeed a significant power: one among several rival Italian powers (Burckhardt 1958: 120–42). The Renaissance papacy, infamous for nepotism and corruption, nevertheless went on to contribute innovations in diplomacy, such as resident ambassadors and rules for the diplomatic corps at Rome. It is one of the curious paradoxes of European history that the papacy acted not only to resist and undermine but also to foster the institution and expansion of early modern international society.

The second noteworthy historical experiment in the evolution of international society involved the small states of the Italian Renaissance which were the first to break free from the medieval empire and flourished in northern Italy between the fourteenth and the sixteenth centuries. The Renaissance was an enlightenment in the arts and sciences launched by the recovery of ancient learning, particularly that of

Greece and Rome, which had been kept alive by Arabic scholars in the Muslim world during the Middle Ages. In inventing the Renaissance the Italians also invented the modern independent state, or stato, of which the most prominent examples were Venice, Florence, Milan, and the Papal states. They were usually based on a city and its environs— although they sometimes extended farther afield, as in the case of the Venetian republic which occupied extensive territories along the northern and eastern Adriatic Sea. By instituting their own free-standing political systems the new Italian men of the stato were of course defying and breaking free from medieval religious–political authority (Burckhardt 1958: 26–44). The republic of Venice, the predominant trading state of that era, brought many diplomatic practices and institutions of international society to Europe having acquired them from their political and trading relations with Byzantium. The Venetian republic set the standard for other Italian states, later for France and Spain, and eventually for Europe as a whole (Nicolson 1954: 24).

The conviction that the interests of the state and the conduct of statecraft must be guided by a separate political ethics was given a free rein by the Italians. That Realist kind of political thinking based on what we would term 'power politics' and the 'national interest' came to be known as reason of state and later as realpolitik in which the morality of the state and the ethics of statecraft is distinguished from universal religious ethics or common morality and is elevated above them (Vincent 1982: 74). The Italian city-states did nevertheless institute among themselves for about a century (1420–1527) a social order based on diplomatic dialogue. The Renaissance Italians also had an acute insight into the importance of the balance of power for maintaining international order among themselves. But the agreements they made were all too often based on expediency, which was an inadequate foundation for the development of a permanent international society among themselves. It also encouraged intervention by external powers in the support of one Italian state (or combination of states) against another, which eventually destroyed the society of Italian states and put in its place a system of foreign domination from across the Alps.

In the end the Italian city-states were too small, too weak, and too divided to defend themselves against the far larger territorial states which were being politically engineered by ambitious rulers in Western Europe. France or Spain by themselves were as large as all the Italian states put together. The Italian states were thus confronted by a new and altogether more dangerous external challenge to their independence than had ever come from among themselves. They might have resisted the new territorial states more effectively had they been able to unite politically and militarily into one large territorial state of their own. Machiavelli (1965) called for a united Italy in the early years of the sixteenth century, and devoted much thought to how it might be brought about not only politically but also militarily in a book on the art of war. But Italian rulers were unable or unwilling to do that probably owing to the exceptionally well-entrenched rivalries between their various city-states and the extent of their personal or dynastic ambitions. In the sixteenth century they were overwhelmed by the Austro-Spanish Habsburgs and the French whose long hegemony over the Italian peninsula did not finally end until the mid-nineteenth century.

Box 2.4 Renaissance theories of statecraft

Statecraft was theorized by Machiavelli (1469–1527), particularly in his classic study of The Prince, as an instrumental foreign policy outlook in which political virtue was equated with astuteness in the development and employment of state power, and political vice was a naïve (i.e. Christian) faith in justice. Honour, glory, fortune, necessity, and above all virtue—in the strictly secular sense of adroit statecraft—are central ideas for Machiavelli and other Renaissance political commentators (such as Francesco Guicciardini the political historian of Florence). These ideas form an important part of what has come to be known as the classical theory of realism (Angelo 1969: ch. 7).

Key points

- Two forerunner international societies were ancient Greece and Renaissance Italy.

- Two empires which contrasted with these international societies and also served as a historical bridge between them were the Roman empire and its direct Christian successor in the West, the medieval Respublica Christiana.

- Greek international society was based on the polis and Hellenic culture.

- Italian international society was based on the stato and the strong urban identities and rivalries of Renaissance Italians.

- These small international societies were eventually overwhelmed by neighbouring hegemonic powers.

European international society

Medieval cathedrals took many years, sometimes centuries, to reach their final form: similarly, the classical European international society which began to be constructed as early as the sixteenth and seventeenth centuries was only completed in the eighteenth and nineteenth. The modern territorial state upon which it was based was a derivative of the Italian Renaissance and the Protestant Reformation. The rulers of the new European states took their cue from the Italians and, as a result, the arts and sciences of the Renaissance, including the art of statecraft, spread to all of Western Europe. The political theology of Martin Luther—with its 'impulse towards disengaging political elements from religious modes of thought' (Wolin 1960: 143)—also disengaged the political legitimacy of the state from the religious sanction of the medieval Respublica Christiana. Machiavelli and Luther are important architects of the modern society of states.

In the modern era secular politics, and particularly the politics of the state and the art of statecraft, was liberated from the moral inhibitions and religious constraints of the medieval Christian world. The sovereign state now shaped the relations of the main political groupings of Europe, and those relations were now recognizable international relations. Many European rulers were ambitious to expand their territories, while many others were anxious to defend their realms against external encroachments. As a result international rivalries developed which often resulted in wars and the enlargement of some countries at the expense of others. At various times

France, Spain, Austria, England, Holland, Denmark, Sweden, Poland, Prussia, Russia, and other states of the new European international society were at war. Some wars were spawned by the Protestant Reformation which profoundly divided the European Christian population in the sixteenth and seventeenth centuries. But other wars (increasingly a majority) were provoked by the mere existence of independent states whose rulers resorted to war as a principal means of defending their interests, pursuing their ambitions, and, if possible, expanding their territorial holdings. War became an international institution for resolving conflicts between sovereign states.

The Catholic Habsburgs, who controlled a sprawling dynastic state which comprised extensive disjointed territories in Austria, Spain, the Netherlands, Italy, Bohemia, Hungary, and other parts of Western and Eastern Europe, tried—in the name of the Respublica Christiana—to impose their imperium on a Europe that was fracturing into religious-cum-political communities, some Catholic and some Protestant, under the impact of the Protestant Reformation and the Catholic Counter-Reformation. That bid for European supremacy led to the devastating Thirty Years War (1618–48) in which the Habsburgs were defeated and peace treaties were negotiated at Westphalia in 1648 (Wedgwood 1992). That was not the first gamble for political mastery in Europe and it would not be the last. But after 1648 the language of international justification would gradually change, away from Christian unity and religious orthodoxy and towards international diver-

THE EVOLUTION OF INTERNATIONAL SOCIETY

sity based on a secular society of sovereign states. The treaties of Westphalia and those of Utrecht (1713) still referred to the Respublica Christiana, but they were the last to do that. For what had come into historical existence in the meantime was a secular European society of states in which overarching political and religious authority was no longer in existence in any substantive sense.

The Reformation and Counter-Reformation conflicts made it clear by the mid-seventeenth century that Protestant states and Catholic states must coexist. The fundamental problem of their relations was thus recognized to be political and not religious. The war itself was not fought along religious lines: it was fought along political–territorial lines with some Catholic states—most notably France—aligned with Protestant states such as Sweden in an alliance against the Catholic Habsburgs. The anti-Habsburg alliance also demonstrated the doctrine of the balance of power: the organization of a coalition of states whose joint military power is intended to operate as a counterweight against bids for political hegemony and empire. The doctrine of reason of state took precedence over any residual obligation to support Respublica Christiana which was now seen in many quarters as merely the ideology of one side in the conflict. That secular move away from religious legitimacy has been a cornerstone of international society ever since. The treaties of Westphalia formally recognized the existence of separate sovereignties in one international society. Religion was no longer a legal ground for intervention or war among European states. The settlement thus created a new international covenant based on state sovereignty which displaced the medieval idea of Respublica Christiana. The seeds of state sovereignty and non-intervention that those seventeenth-century statespeople planted would eventually evolve into the Charter of the United Nations, the Geneva Conventions, and other contemporary bodies of international law.

The procedural starting point of modern European international society, speaking very generally, is thus usually identified with the Peace of Westphalia. That at least is the conventional view. Martin Wight (1977: 150–2) argues, somewhat to the contrary, that Westphalia is the coming of age but not the coming into existence of European international society, the

> ### Box 2.5 **Westphalian international society**
>
> Westphalian international society was based on three principles. The first principle was rex est imperator in regno suo (the king is emperor in his own realm). This norm specifies that sovereigns are not subject to any higher political authority. Every king is independent and equal to every other king. The second principle was cujus regio, ejus religio (the ruler determines the religion of his realm). This norm specifies that outsiders have no right to intervene in a sovereign jurisdiction on religious grounds. The third principle was the balance of power: that was intended to prevent any hegemon from arising and dominating everybody else.

> ### Box 2.6 **Grotius and international law**
>
> The emerging idea of international law was spelled out by Hugo Grotius, a Dutch Protestant diplomat and philosopher, whose Laws of War and Peace (1625) provided an intellectual foundation for the subject that was enormously influential and is still regarded as a founding text. Grotius hoped to restrict war and expand peace by clarifying standards of conduct which were insulated against all religious doctrines and could therefore govern the relations of all independent states, Protestant and Catholic alike.

beginnings of which he traces to the Council of Constance (1415) which, in effect, transformed the papacy into a quasi-secular political power with its own territory. F. H. Hinsley (1967: 153) argues, on the other side, that modern international society only fully emerged in the eighteenth century, because prior to that time the Respublica Christiana was still in existence. But however we choose to look at it, the multinational treaties of Westphalia, and those which came after, were conceived as the foundation of secular international law or what came to be known as the 'public law of Europe' (Hinsley 1967: 168).

Adam Watson (1992: ch. 17) captures the Westphalian moment very aptly: 'the charter of a Europe permanently organized on an anti-hegemonial principle.' That European society of states had several prominent characteristics which can be summarized.

- First, it consisted of member states whose political independence and juridical equality was acknowledged by international law.
- Second, every member state was legitimate in the eyes of all other members.
- Third, the relations between sovereign states were managed, increasingly, by a professional corps of diplomats and conducted by means of an organized multilateral system of diplomatic communication.
- Fourth, the religion of international society was still Christian but that was increasingly indistinguishable from the culture which was European.
- Finally, a balance of power between member states was conceived which was intended to prevent any one state from making a bid for hegemony.

The anti-hegemonial notion of a countervailing alliance of major powers aimed at preserving the freedom of all member states and maintaining the pluralist European society of states as a whole was only worked out by trial and error and fully theorized much later. The greatest historical threat to the European balance of power before the twentieth century was posed by Napoleon's bid for continental hegemony (1795–1815). British and later American foreign policy can be read as historical lessons in attempting to preserve or restore the balance of power. In the eighteenth and nineteenth centuries Britain often played the role of the defender of the balance of power by adding military (especially naval) weight to the coalition which formed against the hegemon, most notably in the case of post-revolutionary Napoleonic France. The United States played a similar role in the Second World War against Nazi Germany and Imperial Japan, and in the cold war against Communist Russia. Insofar as both Britain and the United States accepted and indeed defended the principles of international society against contrary revolutionary ideologies, they could not themselves be regarded as hegemons in the classical political meaning of the term.

In sum: the first fully articulated conception of the theory and practice of international society as an explicit covenant with a legal and political foundation is worked out in Europe among its sovereign states. Edmund Burke, with his eye on the alleged threat posed to monarchical and dynastic Europe by republican and revolutionary France, went so far as to refer to eighteenth-century Europe as 'virtually one great state having the same basis of general law, with some diversity of provincial customs and local establishments'. Burke saw European international society as based on two fundamental principles: a 'law of neighbourhood'—recognition of neighbouring states and respect for their independence—and 'rules of prudence'—the responsibility of statespeople not only to safeguard the national interest but also preserve international society (Raffety 1928: 156–61). Similar ideas were expressed by many European publicists of the day and there is little doubt that modern international society is rooted in the political culture and political thought of the European peoples.

Key points

- The Peace of Westphalia was the first explicit expression of a European society of states which served as a precedent for all subsequent developments of international society.
- That international society displaced and succeeded the medieval Respublica Christiana.
- It was the external aspect of the development of modern secular states which had to find an orderly and legitimate way to conduct mutual relations without submitting to either superior authority or hegemonic domination from abroad.
- It was the first completely explicit international society with its own diplomatic institutions, formal body of law, and enunciated practices of prudential statecraft, including the balance of power.

The globalization of international society

The spread of European political control beyond Europe which began in the late fifteenth century and only came to an end in the early twentieth century proved to be an expansion not only of European imperialism but also, later, of international society (Bull and Watson). The history of modern Europe is—in very significant part—a history of political and economic rivalry and particularly war between sovereign states. European rivalries were conducted wherever European ambitions and power could be projected—i.e. eventually on a global scale. European states entered into competitions with each other to penetrate and control economically desirable and militarily useful areas in other parts of the world. Until the nineteenth century large-scale wars were fought by those states outside Europe. Non-European territories and populations came under the control of European governments by conquest or occupation, and were sometimes transferred from one European state to another as happened in the case of French Canada which the British annexed at the end of their successful Seven Years War with France (1756–63). However, a 'remarkable achievement' of the nineteenth-century Concert of Europe—a balance of power coalition originally formed by the great powers that defeated Napoleon (Britain, Austria, Prussia, and Russia)—was their avoidance of war in the course of their competitive expansion outside Europe—in marked contrast to 'the incessant acts of war against each other overseas in previous centuries' (Watson 1992: 272). International law, diplomacy, and the balance of power thus came to be applied around the world and not only in Europe or the West. By the late nineteenth century even isolated and previously inaccessible continents, like the interior of Africa, were under the jurisdiction and manipulation of European powers.

Not every non-Western country fell under the political control of a Western imperial state. But those countries which escaped were still obliged to accept international law and follow the diplomatic practices of international society. The Ottoman empire (Turkey), which geographically and ethnically was a partly European state, had for centuries been in close contact with European states but had never accepted the conduct requirements of international society. Instead, the Ottomans insisted on treating European states on their own Islamic terms. Although for several centuries the Ottoman empire regularly intervened in Europe with the aim, usually, of undercutting their Habsburg enemies, they held aloof from the conventions of Christian and later European international society with regard to which, as Moslems, they considered themselves superior. At the height of their power between the mid-fifteenth century and the turn of the seventeenth century the Ottomans were able to dictate terms to European states. By the mid-nineteenth century, however, they had long been in decline and were obliged by what were now clearly superior European powers to accept international law and other dictates of Western states. Japan elected to do the same a little later although without the same compulsion and humiliation. Japan successfully acquired the persona and substance of a modern power and by the early twentieth century had defeated the Russian empire in a major war and had become a colonial power herself. China was subjected to extensive territorial encroachments by European states, the United States, and Japan, and did not acquire full membership in international society until 1945 at which time China became a permanent member of the UN Security Council. Most other non-Western political systems were not able to resist Western imperialism and lost their independence as a result. That proved to be the case throughout South Asia, South-East Asia, most of the Middle East, and virtually all of Africa, the Caribbean, and the Pacific.

The second stage of the globalization of international society was via reactive nationalism and anticolonialism. In that reaction indigenous political leaders made claims for decolonization and independence based on European and American ideas of self-determination. That involved a further claim for subsequent equal membership of a universal international society open to all cultures and civilizations without discrimination (Jackson 1990). That 'revolt against the West', as Hedley Bull put it,

> ## Box 2.7 The right of self-determination
>
> The principle of legitimacy that sanctioned decolonization was spelled out in the celebrated 1960 UN General Assembly Declaration on the Granting of Independence to Colonial Countries and Peoples (Resolution 1514) which declared not only that 'all peoples have the right to self-determination' and thus membership of international society but also that 'the further continuation of colonialism . . . is a crime which constitutes a violation of the Charter of the United Nations'.

was the main vehicle by which international society expanded after the Second World War. In a short period of some twenty years, beginning with the independence of India and Pakistan in 1947, most colonies in Asia and Africa became sovereign states and full members of the United Nations. European decolonization in the Third World more than tripled the membership of the society of states from about 50 to over 160.

The final act of European decolonization which completed the globalization of international society was the dissolution of the Soviet Union at the end of the cold war. Here self-determination was based not on overseas colonies but, rather, on the internal borders of the former Russian (Tsarist) empire which the communists took over and preserved after their revolution in 1917. Those old Russian imperial frontiers thus became new international boundaries. The dissolution of the Soviet Union together with the simultaneous breakup of Yugoslavia, Ethiopia, and Czechoslovakia expanded the membership of international society to well over 180. Today, for the first time in world history, there is one continuous international society of global extent—without any intervening gaps of isolated aboriginal government or imposed colonial jurisdiction and also without any external hegemons—based on local territorial sovereignty and a common set of rules the most important of which are embodied by the United Nations Charter.

Key points

- Through their rivalries and wars European states developed the military organization and technology to project their power on a global scale and few non-European political systems could block their expansion.

- European international law, diplomacy, and the balance of power came to be applied around the world.

- Indigenous non-Western nationalists eventually went into revolt and claimed a right of self-determination which led to decolonization and the expansion of international society.

- That was followed by a further expansion after the cold war brought about by the disintegration of the Soviet Union and several other communist states.

- Today, for the first time in history, there is one inclusive international society of global extent.

Problems of global international society

The core values and norms of the contemporary global society of states are international peace and security, state sovereignty, self-determination, non-intervention, non-discrimination and generally the sanctity, integrity, and inviolability of all existing states regardless of their level of development, form of government, political ideology, pattern of culture or any other domestic characteristic or condition. We can speak of these values and norms as embodying and expressing the global covenant of contemporary international society. This social framework exists fundamentally to validate and underwrite the sovereignty of the member states of global international society. State sovereignty, arguably the main pillar, is universally affirmed.

But this global construct also involves problems and predicaments some of which are unprecedented in the history of international society. Only the most important can be discussed briefly as a conclusion to this chapter.

First, there is a noteworthy absence of a common underlying culture to support global international society which cuts across all the major cultures and civilizations. There is no cultural support, comparable to Christianity or European civilization which helped to sustain European cum Western international society. Perhaps the norms and values of free markets, human rights, liberal democracy, and the rule of law can provide that support. They are avowed and generally observed by the vanguard developed states of the present day, such as the members of the OECD. But the fact remains that other important members of international society, such as many states of East Asia and many Islamic states, dispute some of these norms and values. Russia may yet revert to that position too.

Second, if the global covenant is going to be supported in the future, that support is likely to be widely forthcoming only if its core norms and values respond to the interests and concerns of the vast majority if not all the members of contemporary international society. That probably requires that they be divorced or at least distanced from the norms and values of any particular culture, including that of the West. All members still clearly and publicly avow the above-noted core norms and values of international society most of which are incorporated into regional international organizations, such as the Charter of the Organization for African Unity (Brownlie 1971: 2–8).

Third, the regional diversity of contemporary global international society is far more pronounced than that of European international society or any other previous society of states. That is conducive to international pluralism based on groupings of states, such as South-East Asia, Western Europe, Latin America, or Africa, which share a geographical region and may also have cultural affinities and an interconnected economic life. To accommodate successfully that regional–cultural pluralism the global covenant cannot be encumbered with intrusive norms and values of a particular culture, including those of the Western democracies.

Fourth, since 1945 there has been a definite freezing and sanctifying of international boundaries as the globe has been enclosed by local sovereign jurisdiction based on self-determination. That has evidently discouraged states from engaging in acts of aggression or armed intervention in other states with a view to territorial expansion which were not uncommon practices of historical European international society between the members of which recurrent wars were fought over territory and other issues. However, that has also created a barrier to the formation of new jurisdictions by effectively prohibiting a reshuffling of certain territorial jurisdictions of international society in response to changing socio-political identities and consequent demands for national self-determination, such as witnessed in Croatia and Bosnia-Herzegovina.

Fifth, the doctrine of non-intervention has created an inversion of the traditional security dilemma in many states, particularly post-colonial and post-communist states. In those states the security threat is more likely to come from within: the prevailing pattern of warfare is internal rather than international (Holsti 1996). In more than a few sub-Saharan African countries, for example, the main security threat comes from armed rebels or from the government, or both, which often hold citizens hostage in what are referred to as failed or collapsed states (Zartman 1995). The doctrine of non-intervention makes it difficult if not impossible for international society to address the problem. It is also difficult to institute some kind of international trusteeship for obviously failed states, such as Somalia, owing to the fact that the institution and law of trusteeship which currently exists is designed for colonies and not for independent countries. International society currently has no generally accepted procedures for dealing with the problem of failed states.

Sixth, the current global international society, although based on formally equal state sovereignty, in fact contains huge substantive inequalities between member states, particularly between the rich OECD states and the poorest Asian and African Third World States. That socio-economic disparity has led to an unprecedented theory and practice of international aid in which rich states are called upon to help ameliorate poverty in poor states. That has changed the ethos of international society: the traditional ethos was national self-reliance and reciprocity; the new ethos when it comes to poor states is international benevolence and non-reciprocity. International material assistance is still largely voluntary, but poor states and their advocates have endeavoured to make it obligatory for rich states to devote a certain share of their GNP to international aid. Global international society contains a normative asymmetry of non-reciprocal rights and responsibilities which previous international societies of more or less equally developed states did not contain.

Seventh, global international society is perhaps evolving into a world society, both organizationally and normatively, which differs significantly in several important respects from previous international societies. It involves cosmopolitan norms, such as human rights, which sanctify and indemnify human beings regardless of their citizenship. It involves global norms, such as environmental protection, which place new responsibilities, legal as well as moral, on sovereign states, particularly those states with the greatest capacity to cause pollution. It involves the rebirth of minorities, the awakening of aboriginal groups, and the rise of gender in world politics. And it involves a rapidly expanding role for non-governmental organizations (NGOs), such as Greenpeace or Amnesty International, which are assuming growing importance in world politics. NGOs have always existed, of course, but they are more prominent today than they have been since the sovereign state gained ascendancy over all other political and social groups in the seventeenth century.

Finally, this tendency for international society to evolve into a world society raises important questions about the continuing primacy of state sovereignty. Many of these issues are raised in other chapters in this book and cannot be dealt with at length here. Suffice it to say, by way of conclusion, that state sovereignty has been a defining characteristic of international politics for 350 years. However, state sovereignty is not a static institution. On the contrary, it is a dynamic institution and it continues to evolve. For example, at one time dynastic families held state sovereignty, but today it is the collective entitlement of entire national populations. At one time sovereign states had a right to initiate aggressive war in pursuit of their self-defined interests, but that right has been denied and extinguished in the twentieth century. At one time sovereign states could control foreign populated territory as colonial dependencies. That right has also been extinguished. Many other examples of state sovereignty as a dynamic, evolving institution could also be given. But perhaps these examples are sufficient to make us sceptical about claims that world politics is moving beyond state sovereignty. It is far more likely that state sovereignty is evolving yet again.

However, it must be emphasized that historical change is ongoing, the dust is swirling all about, and it will be some time before anyone can get a clear view of this fundamentally important issue. But if I had to bet on the shape of world politics at the end of the twenty-first century my money would be on the prognosis that our great grandchildren will be living in a world which is still defined fundamentally by state sovereignty and probably even by existing states on the map. But I would not bet that sovereign states then will be the same institutions that they are today. History will see to that.

Box 2.8 UN Charter of Economic Rights and Duties of States

'Every State has the right to benefit from the advances and developments in science and technology . . . Every State has the duty to co-operate in promoting . . . the welfare and living standards of all peoples, in particular those of developing countries . . . International co-operation for development is the shared goal and common duty of all States . . . developed countries should grant generalised preferential, non-reciprocal and non-discriminatory treatment to developing countries . . . ' (Charter of the Economic Rights and Duties of States, UN General Assembly, 1974).

Key points

- Today international society is a global social framework of shared norms and values based on state sovereignty.
- An important manifestation of that social framework is the UN Charter.

- But those shared norms and values have provoked unprecedented problems and predicaments of contemporary world politics.
- There is a current debate about the future of state sovereignty and thus also about the future of the contemporary global international society.

QUESTIONS

1 What does international society tell us about the political values and inclinations of human beings around the world?

2 What is the core value of international society?

3 Briefly discuss and evaluate Hedley Bull's concept of international society.

4 Compare the international society of ancient Greece with that of Renaissance Italy.

5 Discuss the Peace of Westphalia as a new stage in the evolution of international society.

6 Why has an originally European society of states been generally accepted around the world?

7 Can a global international society which contains both extremely rich members and extremely poor members be viable over the longer term?

8 Is global international society part of the solution or part of the problem when it comes to the issue of failed states?

9 Does international society based on state sovereignty have any future?

GUIDE TO FURTHER READING

Watson, Adam, *The Evolution of International Society* (London: Routledge, 1992). The definitive study of the history of various international societies and rival or related empires.

Bull, Hedley, and Watson, Adam (eds.), *The Expansion of International Society* (Oxford: Clarendon Press, 1984). The only elaborate account of the historical expansion of European society to the rest of the world.

Armstrong, David, *Revolution and World Order* (Oxford: Clarendon, 1993). An important study of revolutionary states in international society.

Hamilton, K., and Langhorne, R., *The Practice of Diplomacy* (London: Routledge, 1995). An excellent history of the evolution of the idea and institution of diplomacy.

Stern, Geoffrey, *The Structure of International Society* (London: Pinter, 1995). An outstanding recent textbook on international society.

Lyons, Gene M., and Mastanduno, Michael (eds.), *Beyond Westphalia?* (Baltimore and London: Johns Hopkins University Press, 1995). A recent exploration of the question whether international society is evolving beyond a society of sovereign states.

WEB LINKS

www.hyperhistory.com/online_n2/History_n2/a.html

www.fsmiths.com

www.hartford-hwp,com/gateway/index.html

www.wsu.edu:8080/~dee/GREECE/GREECE.HTM

3 International history 1900–1945

Susan L. Carruthers

READER'S GUIDE

This chapter seeks to draw out and suggest explanations for the key transformations in international relations between 1900 and 1945. These years were marked by massive upheaval. Within 45 years, the world experienced two Total Wars, a global economic slump, and the ending of four major empires, with Tsarist Russia being overthrown by a Bolshevik Revolution. This chapter identifies turmoil within Europe, and its eclipse as the arbiter of international affairs, as the most significant feature of the first half of the twentieth century. By 1945, Europe was shattered by its long crisis. The continent was divided between two newly emergent superpowers—the United States and the USSR, both of which had primarily concentrated on their own internal development in the inter-war years. How do we account for the decline of Europe? The chapter looks both at developments within the continent and further afield: what role did the US and the USSR play between the wars, and how did Japan rise to prominence in the Far East? The chapter concludes with an examination of the historical controversy surrounding the origins of the Second World War, which dramatically brought about Europe's collapse.

Introduction

The year 1900 forms a convenient, but not necessarily the most helpful, starting point for an analysis of **modern** international history. Eric Hobsbawm has suggested that the twentieth century really only began in 1914, with a cataclysmic war which swept away the nineteenth-century status quo, whereby a handful of European states dominated the affairs of the world (Hobsbawm 1994: 3). Before the First World War, Europe had not experienced a major war involving most of its dominant states for a century. The world had **never** experienced a conflict that enmeshed so many different countries and peoples. Not only was this war truly a 'world war', but it was also the century's first '**Total War**', during which the major protagonists mobilized virtually their whole populations, male and female alike—whether as soldiers at the front line or as workers on the 'Home Front'.

The consequences of the First World War were enormous. After over four years of war, the diplomats and political leaders who gathered at Versailles in 1919 to forge a peace settlement were adamant that their endeavours must not just resolve the immediate post-war issues (what to do with the vanquished countries, especially Germany, and with the Austro-Hungarian and Ottoman empires which had collapsed during the war) but also make war impossible in the future. 'Never again' was the overwhelming popular sentiment. And yet only twenty years after the **Treaty of Versailles**, another world war was under way—this one even more global in its reach than the first. The years 1900–45 thus mark the most destructive period in human history. Not only did human beings kill one another in greater numbers than in any other span of four decades, but they also found more barbaric methods of doing so: from the Nazi genocide of six million Jews carried out in the concentration camps, to America's dropping of atomic bombs on the Japanese cities of Hiroshima and Nagasaki in August 1945.

The world of 1945 was almost unrecognizable from that of 1900 (as Boxes 3.1 and 3.2 suggest). The story of these years is, overwhelmingly, one of disintegration. A series of empires collapsed in Austro-Hungary, Turkey, and Russia in the course of World War I. Imperial China, long subject to foreign incursions, also slid into prolonged civil war. The international economy collapsed after the **Wall Street Crash** of 1929. And, partly as a result of the

---

Box 3.1 Key features of the world in 1900

European states dominate the global pattern of international relations

- 1 in 4 of the world's population lives in Europe (approximately 400m. of a 1600m. total)
- the European 'great powers' (Britain, France, Italy, Germany, Austria-Hungary, and Russia) have a concentration of military power, as well as dominating world trade

Colonial empires of European states (especially Britain and France, but also Belgium, the Netherlands, and Portugal) cover much of the world

- approximately 500m. people live under European colonial rule
- search for colonies continues; especially Germany in Africa, and Tsarist Russia in Asia

Several territorial empires in a protracted state of collapse

- the Habsburg empire (covering Austro-Hungary and much of central Europe and the Balkans)
- the Ottoman empire (centred on Turkey, and encompassing much of the Middle East and the Balkans)
- Tsarist Russia
- Imperial China

Global capitalist economy

- in 1900 centred primarily on the UK, as the world's largest imperial and trading power, but increasingly under threat
- rapid industrial expansion in North America
- Japan modernizing and industrializing

> ## Box 3.2 **Key features of the world in 1945**
>
> **Prominence of the US and USSR**
>
> US first nuclear superpower, after explosion of atomic bombs on Hiroshima and Nagasaki, August 1945
>
> US emerges from World War II as major creditor nation, and centre of the international economy
>
> USSR in economic ruin after war, but Red Army occupies all Eastern and much of Central Europe, to Berlin and beyond
>
> **Collapse of Europe**
>
> • rapidly divided between East and West; Germany split until 1989
>
> • national economies in ruin; large debts owing to US
>
> • European colonial empires undermined by war; by Japanese overrunning of colonies in South-East Asia
>
> **Growing nationalism in the colonial empires**
>
> • wartime 'Atlantic Charter' makes commitment to national self determination
>
> • India seeking independence (achieved in 1947)
>
> • Ho Chi Minh declares Vietnam an independent republic in 1945
>
> **Civil war in China**
>
> • ended with victory of Mao and establishment of the Peoples Republic of China in 1949
>
> • together with the population of the USSR, one-third of the world now lives under communist rule

ensuing Depression, democracies crumbled in the 1930s, while extreme right-wing dictatorships flourished in Germany, Italy, Spain, Japan, and many countries of Latin America. The culmination of these turbulent years, which with hindsight we call the 'inter-war period', was another Total War which left few of the world's citizens entirely untouched.

The most globally significant transformation during the first half of the twentieth century was Europe's effective collapse as pre-eminent continent. A world dominated in 1900 by a small group of economically prosperous and populous European states, whose empires encompassed much of the globe, by 1945 had been replaced by one in which the major arbiters of international affairs were the two new 'superpowers'—the United States of America and the Soviet Union. Europe, at least temporarily, was in a state of ruin and indebtedness, with Eastern and Central Europe lying under Soviet occupation. The Second World War further intensified Europe's disintegration. But in fact that war only accentuated a process several decades old. Many historians would argue that the Second World War was essentially a continuation of the First. Europe was not so much suffering a '**Twenty Year Crisis**' (E. H. Carr's description of the period 1919–39 (Carr 1939)) as undergoing a '**Thirty-Year War**', whose roots stretched back to the 1870s.

The origins of World War One

Why did Europe lose its predominant place in the world in the years between 1900 and 1945? The answer lies partly in Europe itself and partly beyond. European states fought viciously with one another on their own soil. However, the continent which had given birth to the Industrial Revolution, and had formed the hub of global financial activity, also faced economic challenges from rapidly industrializing states—most obviously the United States. Similarly, in the Far East, Japan underwent rapid expansion in the early twentieth century, posing a significant economic and military challenge to the

European powers' trading and colonial interests in East Asia.

We will consider global economic developments in due course, but first we will examine the **internal roots** of Europe's instability. These are frequently dated back to the 1870s, when the continent's relative tranquillity following the Napoleonic Wars was disturbed by the creation of a single, unified German nation-state.

Germany's bid for world power status

The unified Germany's territorial ambitions rapidly became apparent. Although Bismarck himself had cautioned against further German expansionism, his successors were less circumspect, and sought to assert German parity with the other great powers by acquiring the most important badge of great power status—an overseas empire. **Imperial disputes** were thus an important contributory factor to the outbreak of war in 1914, and in Marxist accounts of the war's origins were allotted causal primacy. Certainly, Britain was not keen to see its own position as the world's most powerful trading nation overshadowed by Germany, with whom it was now engaged in fierce naval rivalry. France had equally compelling reasons to fear German expansion. The opening years of the twentieth century thus saw a hitherto unlikely alliance of Britain, France, and Tsarist Russia merging in an attempt to halt Germany's determined search for territory and markets. Germans, however, saw themselves not as the aggressors but rather as the victims of an imperial system which operated entirely to their disadvantage: Britain and France dominated Africa, Asia, and the Middle East; Russia, Japan, and Britain competed in China, while the US held sway in Latin America. Between them, these powers appeared to have carved up the international market to their exclusive satisfaction. Gaining colonies was thus not solely a matter of prestige or status but was regarded as an economic imperative for Germany. The main areas of contention were **North Africa**, where clashes occurred with France and Britain over Morocco in 1906 and in 1911, and the **Middle East**, as Germany sought to build a railway from Berlin to Baghdad.

The European colonial powers had, however, clashed over imperial issues before. Consequently, many historians regard these disputes alone as insufficient to explain the war which broke out in July 1914. The evaluation of various explanatory factors continues to generate much historiographical debate. Some historians concur with, others dispute, the verdict of the war's victors—that 'war guilt' belonged to Germany alone. The most famous explication of this view was Fritz Fischer's *Griff nach der Weltmacht* (*Bid for World Power*), published in 1961, which emphasized the extent of Germany's annexationist aims in the war, arguing that the German government deliberately went to war in their pursuit. Others have insisted that a general war came about more by accident than design, partly due to the way in which military plans had been drawn up. German strategy, devised by Count Alfred von Schlieffen, was designed to counter the prospect of Germany fighting a war on two fronts against France and Russia. His plan therefore envisaged a decisive blow against France before German troops turned to the tardily mobilized Russians. Thus the **'Schlieffen plan'** served to widen the war rapidly, once the opening shots had been fired. Those opening shots were fired, not by Germany, but in Sarajevo at Archduke Franz Ferdinand (the heir to the throne of the Austro-Hungarian empire) by a Serb nationalist. This assassination should alert us to other deep-seated origins of Europe's crisis, and ultimately of the war itself.

The 'Eastern Question'

Besides the 'German problem' the other main source of instability in late nineteenth- and early twentieth-century Europe was the so-called 'Eastern Question', which arose from the slow collapse of the Ottoman empire. The European great powers each took considerable interest in how the power vacuum that was spreading from the Balkans to the Middle East would be filled. But the peoples over whom the Ottoman dynasty had ruled were also keen to assert, in the **age of nationalism**, their right to self-rule. In the Balkans, rival national groups clashed in a series of wars, with the backing of various European great powers. Consequently, the Tsarist Russian empire (although itself in a state of terminal collapse) refused to watch

---

Box 3.3 **The 'German problem'**

Germany before unification

- Until 1871, 'Germany' did not exist in anything like the shape we know it today.

- 'Germany' was a collection of twenty-five states, ranging in size from small principalities to the economically and militarily assertive Prussia with a population of some 30m. (Bavaria, the second largest, contained 5.5m.)

- Some ethnic Germans lived under the sovereignty of other states; as in Alsace-Lorraine, which was part of France, and Schleswig-Holstein, ruled by Denmark.

Unification

- The bringing together of these states, and the annexation of 'foreign' lands containing ethnic Germans, was the work of the Prussian Chancellor Otto von Bismarck.

- Three wars were fought to secure German unification, and to ensure that Prussia predominated to Austria's exclusion: against Denmark (1864) over Schleswig-Holstein; Austria-Hungary (1866), and France (1870) over Alsace-Lorraine.

Germany after unification

- For the first time in modern history, the centre of Europe was dominated by a single, vast state.

- Germany's population of nearly 67m. (by 1913) was second in size only to the Russian empire.

- Germany underwent rapid industrialization. Germany's coal, iron, and steel production (in the 1870s well below the UK's) outstripped Britain's by 1914

- From 1871 to 1914, the value of Germany's agricultural output doubled; industrial production quadrupled and overseas trade more than tripled.

- With such great reserves of territory, population, military, and industrial strength, Germany had the capacity—and the inclination, many believed—for outward expansion. The birth of a unified Germany thus constituted the birth of 'the German problem', as far as other European states were concerned, by fundamentally disrupting the **balance of power** in Europe. Other states were accordingly disposed to enter into alliances in order to prevent Germany from using its central geo-strategic location and economic resources to achieve further territorial enlargement.

---

impassively while Austro-Hungary threatened Russia's fellow Slavs in Serbia after the assassination of Franz Ferdinand in June 1914. What might have been a localized incident quickly sparked a general war. The complicated alliance system built up over the previous two decades rapidly ensured that Austria-Hungary and Germany, on the one side, confronted Britain, France, and Russia on the other. The ensuing war was to last for over four years. Much of it was marked by a military stalemate—most vividly, and horrifically, epitomized by the trench-warfare which decimated a generation of young French, British, and German men.

Key points

- Europe's long-term instability can be traced back to the creation of a unified Germany in the 1870s, which disrupted the balance of power.

- The European powers clashed over imperial issues in the late nineteenth and early twentieth centuries, as Germany sought colonies and markets.

- A number of European dynasties were in a state of collapse, leaving open the question of what territorial and constitutional arrangements would replace these empires when they finally disintegrated.

- At the same time, nationalism was growing, particularly in the Balkans and Central Europe, with nationalist movements asserting their claims to statehood in the decaying Ottoman and Austro-Hungarian empires.

- A combination of imperial, nationalist, and economic tension ultimately resulted in the First World War.

Peace-making, 1919: the Versailles settlement

Post-war problems

When the war finally ended, the peacemakers who gathered at Versailles in 1919 confronted a daunting set of problems. The war left millions of individual casualties, either through death, injury or the loss of homes and livelihoods. The teetering Austro-Hungarian and Ottoman empires were also victims of the war, while a Bolshevik revolution had overthrown the Tsarist regime in Russia. Had anyone really **won** the war? Certainly the victors' economies, no less than those of the vanquished, were depleted by the strain of four years of Total War. On all sides, the combatants had sought to pursue this war until their enemies were utterly defeated. Total War demanded Total Victory, but the cost of totally defeating an enemy was near ruination of one's own state. The domestic ruin facing France in particular, on whose soil much of the fighting had occurred, added a punitive dimension to the peacemakers' agenda: how could reparations (money, goods, or raw materials) be extracted from Germany to finance domestic reconstruction? How, most critically, could the peacemakers ensure that Germany did not seek to dominate Europe ever again?

It should come as no surprise, given both the intractability of Europe's problems and the diversity of the victorious coalition, that the peacemakers failed to agree amongst themselves on the shape of the post-war order. The principal European victors, Britain and France, concurred over German responsibility for the war, which justified a harsh settlement, but they differed over its terms. However, the guiding force at Versailles was not one (or more) of the European powers, but the President of the United States.

President Wilson's 'Fourteen Points'

America had joined the war in its latter stages, and its President provided a set of principles which he intended should shape the subsequent peace. How was war to be avoided? Woodrow Wilson's 'Fourteen Points' called for a new approach to international diplomacy: 'open covenants, openly arrived at', would replace the old-style secret diplomacy which produced various private inter-state deals over who would gain what territory after the First World War. Wilson also believed that the avoidance of war could be furthered by creating an international organization, based on the principle of **'collective security'** (see Ch. 12). His scheme for a **League of Nations** was premised on the 'peace-loving' member states regarding any threat to the international peace—any violation of the sovereignty of one member by another state—as an act of aggression which ultimately threatened them all, and therefore had to be responded to collectively. Ideally, however, the very existence of the League would serve to ensure that aggressive states desisted from expansionist actions. The League was thus one of the distinctive features of the post-1919 world: the first formalized attempt to create an international body designed to mediate disputes with permanent structures and a codified Charter. Despite its ignominious failure to take assertive action against Japanese, Italian, and German aggression in the 1930s, the League provided a model for the United Nations Organization in 1945.

Self-determination: the creation of new states

Just as significant as Wilson's insistence on an international collective security body was his commitment to the principle of **'national self-determination'**. Wilson was an opponent of imperialism, and believed passionately in the right of distinct national groups to govern themselves by being accorded sovereignty over their own territory. To each nation a state: this was Wilson's ideal. However, in practice, the nationalities of those parts of Europe where empires had recently crumbled—especially the Balkans, and Central and Eastern Europe—were not neatly parcelled into distinct territorial areas. The peacemakers therefore faced a difficult task of drawing the boundaries of the new

Box 3.4 Wilson's 'Fourteen Points': a summary

1. Open covenants of peace, openly arrived at; international diplomacy to be carried on publicly.

2. Absolute freedom of navigation on the seas.

3. The removal, as far as possible, of all economic barriers.

4. Disarmament undertaken, and guaranteed, by states to the lowest point consistent with domestic safety

5. A free, open-minded, and impartial adjustment of all colonial claims, based on the principle that the interests of the population concerned must have equal weight with the equitable claims of the government whose title is to be determined.

6. The evacuation of all Russian territory and settlement of questions affecting Russia.

7. Belgium must be evacuated and restored.

8. French territory to be evacuated and restored, and Alsace-Lorraine to be returned to French rule.

9. Italian frontiers to be adjusted along clearly recognizable lines of nationality.

10. The peoples of Austria-Hungary to be given the opportunity for autonomous development.

11. Romania, Serbia, and Montenegro to be evacuated; Serbia to be given access to the sea; and international guarantees of the independence and territorial integrity of the Balkan states to be made.

12. The Turkish portions of the Ottoman empire to be assured a secure sovereignty; other nationalities to be allowed to develop autonomously; the Dardanelles to be permanently open to shipping.

13. An independent Polish state to be established, with free and secure access to the sea.

14. A general association of nations to be formed to afford mutual guarantees of political independence and territorial integrity to all states.

---

it as 'Czecho-Germano-Polono-Magyaro-Rutheno-Romano- Slovakia'.

Wilson's insistence on self-determination, given messy human realities, generated as many contradictions as it solved: sixty million people being awarded a state of their own while another twenty-five million were transformed into minorities within these imperfect nation-states. Not surprisingly, the new states in Southern, Eastern, and Central Europe—Hungary, Yugoslavia, Rumania, Bulgaria, Czechoslovakia, Poland—suffered serious problems. They had to contend not only with ethnic cleavages but also with weak economies and fledgling political institutions. Why, given the problems of boundary-drawing, and the weakness of the resulting states (leaving Germany surrounded by relatively defence-less neighbours), did the peacemakers demur to Wilson's insistence on self-determination? The answer lies in the West European powers' preoccupation with a new threat. At Versailles, the peace-makers certainly feared a possible future resurgence of Germany. Perhaps equally vividly, however, they were haunted by the spectre of Bolshevism spreading from Lenin's newly created Union of Soviet Socialist Republics (USSR) into Western Europe. Lenin, after all, explicitly stated that the Soviet revolution was but the start of a world revolution—an historical inevitability which the Moscow-led Communist International (**Comintern**) was dedicated to hastening. Moreover, the war seemed to have provided the ideal breeding ground for communist parties in Western Europe, which the Soviets could infiltrate and use as vehicles of world revolution.

Fear of Bolshevism thus explains British and French politicians' enthusiasm for self-determination. After all, these new states were virtually bound to be anti-Soviet since they were largely created from land formerly belonging to Russia: Finland, the Baltic Republics, Poland, and Rumania. They were the ideal 'quarantine belt' for the USSR. But they did not address the threat which Germany posed to European security: thus the interwar era saw another period of alliance-building and treaty-signing, as France and Britain (and Italy, after 1925) extended guarantees to various Eastern and Central European states, promising action if their boundaries were violated by an aggressor.

states of Europe, some of which had never existed before. Often the boundaries reflected uneasy compromises: for example, Czechoslovakia, a state for the first time in 1919, was composed of so many national groups that Mussolini scornfully referred to

The future of Germany

In many ways the territorial settlement which Versailles established stored up problems for the future, not least in its reshaping of Germany. When the peacemakers came to determine Germany's fate, they did not apply the principal of self-determination rigidly. Largely at French insistence, France regained the lost province of Alsace-Lorraine and occupied the Saar—the key industrial area on Germany's western flank—in order to extract coal, steel, and iron. French troops also occupied the Rhineland, to ensure that Germany remained demilitarized, as the treaty insisted. Additionally, German politicians (and much of the population) resented the inclusion of Germans in the reconstituted Poland. Poland had not existed as an independent state since the eighteenth century, but now it divided the vast bulk of Germany from East Prussia. This anomalous situation resulted from the peacemakers' determination that Poland should have an outlet to the sea at the port of Danzig (or Gdansk). Where was Danzig's right to self-determination, Germans demanded?

The territorial arrangements of 1919, under which Germany lost 13 per cent of her land and nearly seven million people, angered many Germans, providing a potent grievance for Hitler's National Socialists to manipulate in the 1930s. But what perhaps hurt even more was the inscription of German 'war guilt' into the treaty.

'War guilt' and reparations

The victors included the 'war guilt' clause largely in order to justify the extraction of swingeing reparations from Germany. Popular pressure in Britain and France encouraged the peacemakers to 'squeeze the German lemon until the pips squeak', a line most vigorously pursued by the French premier, Georges Clemenceau. The British Prime Minister, Lloyd George, also agreed that reparations should be exacted from Germany, though not at such a punitive level as France sought. The issue of exactly **how much** Germany should pay in reparations was in fact never settled at Versailles. Unable to agree, the allies left the matter to a Reparations Commission

(and ultimately, the sum was scaled ever downwards).

While it is easy to understand why the economic dismemberment of Germany appealed to these leaders—punishing Germany was electorally popular, and also seemed to guarantee future German inability to launch all-out wars—the wisdom of such a move was questionable. It was indeed called into question almost before the ink had dried on the treaty. In 1919, a women's international congress in Zurich predicted that the settlement would 'create all over Europe discords and animositites which can only lead to future wars . . .' (Pettman, 1996: 109). In the same year, if from a rather different perspective, the eminent British economist, John Maynard Keynes (an adviser to the British delegation at Versailles) produced an influential indictment of the treaty entitled *The Economic Consequences of the Peace*. Keynes propounded a compelling thesis: economic ruination of Germany—the result of punitive reparations—would prevent the recovery of Europe as a whole. Germany was the motor of the European economic engine. In punishing Germany, the Allies were effectively prolonging their own wartime privations.

To sum up, then, as the French general Foch acutely predicted after the signing of the treaty, Versailles would not bring peace, only an armistice for twenty years. It had solved none of Europe's fundamental problems. In economic terms, it was (if one followed Keynes's reasoning) too hard on Germany, and consequently on Europe as a whole. The interwar years thus saw Europe's economic position decline further relative to that of the United States, which emerged from the war as the net beneficiary, being owed huge sums by Britain and France, which Wilson insisted they repay. In its territorial arrangements, and the selective application of Wilsonian principles, the peace was also arguably too severe on Germany. (This was certainly the argument many Germans advanced, most vehemently under Hitler's regime.) Moreover, a growing number of non-Germans had some sympathy with the view that Versailles bequeathed Germany legitimate grievances: this in part explains the policy of **appeasement** pursued by British governments in the 1930s. But, according to another line of reasoning (expounded by, amongst others, the historian A. J. P.

Fig. 3.1 Europe after the First World War
Map reproduced from Keylor (1992: 93)

Taylor), the real problem with Versailles was that it was **not hard enough**. The 'German problem' was unresolved, insofar as Germany still remained the largest unitary state in the heart of Europe. Moreover, Germany's potential to wage war again had not been absolutely destroyed. However viewed—whether as too punitive or insufficiently so—the Treaty of Versailles was almost bound to fail, not least in the absence of any major power absolutely committed to upholding it.

Key points

- Many of the terms of the peace treaties concluded following World War I (referred to as the Versailles settlement) were shaped by the 'Fourteen Points' supplied by American President, Woodrow Wilson.

- Future wars were to be deterred by the League of Nations, which would take collective action against aggressor states.

- A series of new states was created in the Balkans and Eastern and Central Europe, where the Ottoman and Austro-Hungarian empires had collapsed.

- Germany was found 'guilty' of having begun the war: Germany lost land to Poland; Alsace-Lorraine was returned to France; Germany was to be disarmed, with France occupying the Rhineland as a security zone; and reparations were to be repaid to the victorious powers.

- Many critics found fault with the settlement, either because it was too hard, or not hard enough, on Germany.

The global economic slump, 1929–1933

In the 1920s America came to assume the pivotal position in the global economy that Britain had occupied prior to 1914. By 1929, the US produced 42 per cent of the world's industrial output, with Germany, Britain, and France together accounting for only 28 per cent (Hobsbawm 1994: 97). Initially, the vibrancy of the US economy provided the illusion that the world economy had survived the rigours of World War I relatively intact, albeit with the US replacing Britain as the new key financier. The survival of the pre-1914 system transpired to be an illusion, as the war had irreparably damaged the globalized world economy evolving since the time of the Industrial Revolution. The Wall Street stock-market crash of 29 October 1929, and its aftermath, starkly revealed the illusory nature of post-war economic regeneration. Soon no one could be in doubt that the world financial system was in convulsion.

The underlying causes of 'the largest global earthquake ever to be measured on the economic historians' Richter Scale—the Great Inter-War Depression' (Hobsbawm 1994: 86) continue to be disputed, and

cannot be rehearsed at any length here. Beyond dispute, however, is the truly global impact of the Depression. The after-shocks of the stock market crash around the world illustrate the degree to which states in the interwar years were not entirely autonomous entities, determining their own fates in isolation. Rather they were at the mercy of profound economic forces over which national governments had less control than policy-makers and industrialists doubtless liked to imagine. Globalization, in economic terms, was a potent reality—as the events of 1929 brought home with distressing vividness.

The results of **the Depression** in America and Europe are familiar enough to Western readers. Western Europe depended on American loans in various forms, so when they dried up America's Depression was duplicated in Europe. Its symptoms included spiralling inflation and a collapse of consumer demand in the leading industrial countries which led to a decline in manufacturing industry. This in turn meant massive unemployment. In the era before social welfare provision was seen as part of

Box 3.5 **The US and the USSR between the wars**

One reason why the 1919 peace settlement did not last, it is often argued, was the failure of any major power, particularly the US, to sponsor it. After the Second World War, the US and the USSR emerged as 'superpowers', and their mutual hostility—the cold war—dominated the world for forty years. Why were both relatively inactive on the international scene in the twenty years after the First World War?

The USSR

Nov. 1917   The **Bolshevik Revolution** brought a Marxist-Leninist regime to power in the former Tsarist empire.

Mar. 1918   Lenin concluded a **separate peace treaty** with Germany (in which one-fourth of Russian territory and a third of its population were surrendered), in order to concentrate on consolidating the revolution.

1918–20   Before consolidation could occur, **Civil War** broke out. Trotsky's Red Army quelled the counter-revolutionary forces of the White Russians, who were aided by interventions from France, Britain, Japan, and the US.

1924   Josef Stalin came to power, following Lenin's death, and concentrated on building '**socialism in one country**'.

1929   The first **Five-Year Plan** for the Soviet economy was introduced, and Stalin stepped up the pace of state planning of industry, together with the collectivization of agriculture.

1936–8   Stalin undertook the **Great Purge** of the enemies of his dictatorship.

Aug. 1939   Stalin signed a **non-aggression pact with Nazi Germany**. This suggests how small a role ideology now played in Soviet foreign policy (although Stalin did not altogether abandon the USSR's support for communist parties around the world). Instead Soviet security concerns were uppermost, and the Pact promised the USSR land in the Baltic, in return for Soviet acquiescence towards Hilter's march into Poland.

The US

Mar. 1920   The US **Senate refused to ratify the Treaty of Versailles**, concluding a separate peace with Germany in 1921 which did not include the 'war guilt' clause, or the terms of the League of Nations. The US had thus embarked upon an essentially isolationist foreign policy, which it pursued until the Japanese attack on Pearl Harbor. However, the US government did remain concerned with, and involved in, a number of international issues, particularly those relating to disarmament and security—not least in the Pacific, a traditional area of US concern, where Japan was in the ascendant.

1921–2   The Washington Disarmament Conference was notable for the manner in which it dealt with Japan's growing power in the Pacific. The relative strength of the navies of the US, UK, Japan, France, and Italy was fixed in a ratio of 5 : 5 : 3 : 1.75 : 1.75. The sovereignty of China was also affirmed, and an 'Open Door' policy of trade with China maintained.

1931   The US government's concern with Japanese aggression against China was evident in its response to the **Manchurian crisis**, beginning in 1931, when Japanese forces occupied an ever greater part of the North Chinese province of Manchuria. Although not a member of the League of Nations, the US did offer to assist its efforts to establish the origins of the crisis. However, the US stopped far short of actually using—or encouraging the League to use—force to reverse Japan's aggression.

Throughout the inter-war years, America's primary influence on the world lay not so much in the diplomatic sphere, as in the realm of economics, where the US economy was emerging as the world's strongest. US capital helped rebuild Germany, with loans enabling Germany to make reparations to Britain and France, who could then repay their own debts to the US.

Table 3.1 Major wartime and post-war foreign loans of US government (in millions of dollars)

Recipient nation	Pre-Armistice (cash)	Post-Armistice (cash & supplies)	Total indebtedness
Great Britain	3696.0	581.0	4277.0
France	1970.0	1434.8	3404.8
Italy	1031.0	617.0	1648.0
Russia	187.7	4.9	192.6
Belgium	171.8	207.3	379.1

Source; Harold Moulton and Leo Pasvolsky, *War Debts and World Prosperity* (1932: 426), and Thomas A. Bailey, *A Diplomatic History of the American People* (1974: 657).

the state's duty to its citizens (an era ushered in by World War II in most parts of Western Europe and America), unemployment meant utter destitution and grinding poverty for millions. Even for those who remained employed, hyper-inflation—and in some countries the complete collapse of currencies—led to the overnight elimination of savings, and to paper money becoming virtually worthless, as in Weimar Germany.

Perhaps less well known in Europe or America are the results of the Depression elsewhere in the world. Every country that participated in international trade was affected—whether they were independent states (as in Latin America) or colonial territories under the rule of Western European powers. The precipitous drop in the western world's demand for goods and crops did not just mean unemployment for workers in factories in the West. It also spelt ruin for the producers of raw materials from which consumer goods were manufactured. To take but one example, Japanese silk farmers suddenly found their livelihoods ruined as Americans ceased to buy silk stockings in the Depression of the early 1930s. Similarly growers of crops farmed in what we now know as the Developing World (or Third World), which were sold to the developed world, found that the prices they received for their commodities plummeted. Brazil's coffee growers attempted to prevent the coffee price from collapsing by selling it to Brazilian railway companies as an alternative fuel to coal.

In economic terms, the result of the Depression was that the globalization of the world economy stuttered as states attempted to reverse the process. Rather than a global free trade system continuing to develop (as it had from the Industrial Revolution up to 1914), the major capitalist states now sought to isolate their national economies as far as possible from the vagaries of the international market. Free trade was abandoned in favour of protectionist policies, whereby states attempted to make their economies as self-sufficient as possible. High tariff barriers were erected to dissuade domestic manufacturers from importing foreign goods. As a result the volume of international trade fell sharply. America led the way in protectionism, being in the fortunate position of needing other countries' products less than did Britain, for example, and many other industrialized states.

The economic crisis of the 1930s was accompanied by profound political upheavals. We might question whether, without the Depression, Hitler would have found such fertile soil for Nazism in Germany. Although it is overly reductionistic to argue that the Depression alone accounts for Hitler's accession to power in 1933, nevertheless the human costs of economic collapse certainly made extremist political solutions appear attractive during the 1930s. Having secured power in Germany, Hitler proceeded to encourage Nazi movements on Germany's borders, especially in Austria and Czechoslovakia. Meanwhile, Mussolini completed the construction of the 'Fascist State' in Italy in the 1930s, while in Spain Franco ultimately defeated the Popular Front ranged against him. But the emergence of more radicalized (and often also racialized) forms of politics was not simply a European phenomenon. Several Latin American regimes toppled during the 1930s, to be replaced with new ones of either a pronounced left- or right-wing complexion. In the colonized world, nationalist movements were also given a powerful impetus by the Depression. In India, for example, Gandhi mobilized a mass campaign of civil disobedience against British rule, while in French Indo-China, Ho Chi Minh's communist nationalists embarked on the long road to independence which would ultimately entail protracted wars with both France and America after 1945.

Key points

- Since the Industrial Revolution, global capitalist economy had been developing, with an expanding level of world trade.

- The First World War disrupted this development, with a profound negative impact on the international economic system, which was initially masked by the vibrancy of the US economy in the 1920s.

- In 1929, the Wall Street stock-market crash induced a world depression, illustrating the degree to which national economics were affected by international economic forces.

- Depressions in many countries around the world resulted in extremist political movements gaining strength, many of which were of an extreme right-wing nature.

The origins of World War Two in Asia and the Pacific

Europeans sometimes display a tendency to regard World War Two as primarily a European phenomenon. In fact, war was already under way in Asia before September 1939. So to understand how conflicts in Asia and Europe merged into a 'world war' (albeit with distinct 'theatres'), we must clearly examine interwar developments in Asia, particularly in Japan and China.

In some respects Japan's position in Asia during the first decades of the twentieth century was akin to Germany's in Europe. After unification, Germany underwent rapid modernization and industrialization. It had sought an enlarged empire, challenging those of France and Britain in the years prior to 1914. Germany emerged from the First World War aggrieved at the treatment meted out by the victors and determined to reverse key aspects of the Versailles Settlement—a 'revisionism' heightened by the catastrophic consequences of the Depression. Under an extreme right-wing regime, Germany sought a solution to its problems through outward expansion, and found its path eased by the weakness of the states geographically closest to it. Much of this could also be said of Japan.

Japan and the 'Meiji Restoration'

During the reign of Emperor Meiji (from around 1868 to 1912), Japan's rulers fostered rapid industrialization, borrowing a model from Western Europe and North America. This was accompanied by a modernization of Japanese society and political life: the feudal agricultural system was abolished; the army was reorganized and conscription introduced, heralding the disintegration of the Samurai caste; education and foreign travel were encouraged; and a new parliamentary system was implemented. Like Germany's, Japan's rulers in the late nineteenth century developed imperialistic inclinations. Unlike Germany, Japan did not naturally possess within its own frontiers an abundance of the raw materials for industrialization. Both, however, shared a belief that their population was growing so rapidly that the populace would soon outstrip the state's geographical and financial capacity to support it. Thus Hitler sought *Lebensraum* (living space) for the German people in Central and Eastern Europe, while Japan looked towards China as the most suitable sphere for expansion.

Japanese expansion in China

Just as Germany profited from the decline of its imperial neighbours (in Austria-Hungary, Turkey, and Russia), Japan's expansionism was likewise eased by the state of near-extinction in which China languished. China, once a great dynastic empire, by the late nineteenth century had almost ceased to function as a state. The last emperor was toppled in 1911, and China slid into a protracted state of civil war. As provincial warlords fought one another, the Nationalist Guomindang movement under Sun Yat Sen (and latterly Chiang Kai Shek) clashed with Mao Zedong's Chinese Communist Party, which ultimately triumphed in 1949. Such internal chaos, and the absence of strong central government, provided fresh opportunities for foreign 'profiteers'. China had long been infiltrated by outside powers, anxious for a share of its 'exotic' goods—tea, spices, opium, silk—and to trade with the world's most populous state. Britain in the nineteenth and early twentieth century had the most extensive China trade, but Tsarist Russia was also heavily involved in railway-building in northern China. Japan took particular interest in the region of Manchuria, and clashed with Russia during 1904–5 in a war which marked the first major defeat in modern times of a European power by an Asian state. Japan's position in China was strengthened still further as a result of the First World War, during which Japan fought against Germany, using the opportunity to secure Germany's Chinese possessions.

Although Japan had opposed Germany, both felt dissatisfied by the terms of the Versailles settlement. Japan had tried, and failed, to have the principle of racial equality written into the terms of the treaties. That the Western powers were indeed racially prejudiced against the Japanese seemed to be confirmed by America's 1924 immigration legislation, which virtually prevented further Japanese immigration into the US. The Japanese government also felt that the country had not received adequate territory in recognition of its part in the war. As the 1920s progressed, Tokyo additionally protested against the way in which America and Britain sought, through the **Washington treaties**, both to limit Japan's naval construction and to prevent China falling more effectively under Japanese domination.

Some Japanese policy-makers remained committed to an internationalist policy during the 1920s. In particular they believed that Japan should behave as a responsible member of the international community, and take an active role in the League of Nations. But increasingly the army gained prominence in Japanese political life. The officer class (especially that part of it stationed in northern China following Japan's victory in the 1904–5 war with Russia) pressed ever more forcibly for Japanese expansion in China. Japan's experience of social upheaval strengthened the appeal of militarism. In the late 1920s, Japan suffered from two destabilizing tremors, one literal, the other figurative. The Great Kanto Earthquake of 1923 resulted in nearly 100,000 deaths and the destruction of about 2,000,000 homes. The volcanic eruption seemed to symbolize the volatility of Japanese society during a period of rapid modernization. The second, metaphorical, great tremor to hit Japanese society was the Depression. As in Europe, the socio-economic conditions of Japan's depression provided fertile soil for right-wing extremism. Outward expansionism looked even more attractive, and Japanese political and military leaders increasingly talked of establishing a 'co-prosperity sphere' in Asia. This phrase was a euphemism for Japanese economic hegemony (if not outright rule) over various neighbouring states. Such imperialistic aspirations were fuelled by rising Japanese nationalism, the ideological foundation of which was Shintoism: a belief in the divinity and infallibility of the emperor, to whom each citizen owed personal allegiance.

The Manchurian crisis and after

Japan's foreign policy thus became increasingly assertive. The 'Manchurian crisis' of 1931 demonstrated this, and is sometimes regarded as the opening shot of the Second World War. Japan used a minor skirmish between Japanese soldiers and Chinese 'bandits' as a pretext to occupy a greater portion of Manchuria. Despite Chinese protests to the League of Nations, Japan was unrepentant, and by 1932 had established a puppet state in the whole of Manchuria, called **Manchuguo**. The League's response to the first blatant act of aggression by one

Box 3.6 The origins of the war in the Pacific: a chronology

18 Sept. 1930	Mukden incident in Manchuria between Japanese troops and Chinese 'bandits'. Marks the start of Japan's conquest of Manchuria.	7 July 1937	Outbreak of war between Japan and China.
24 Feb. 1933	League of Nations adopts the Lytton Report, which recommends international mediation in the dispute between Japan and China, and urges League members not to recognize the Japanese puppet state in Manchuria (Manchuguo), but does not seek to impose sanctions on Japan.	6 Nov. 1937	Italy joins the Anti-Comintern Pact.
		14 June 1939	Japan begins a blockade of the Chinese city of Tientsin.
		26 July 1939	America retracts 1911 trade treaty with Japan.
		30 Aug. 1940	Japan occupies northern Indo-China.
		13 April 1941	Japan signs neutrality pact with USSR.
27 March 1933	Japan announces her withdrawal from the League.	21 July 1941	Vichy France permits Japan to occupy the whole of Indo-China.
29 Dec. 1934	Japan denounces the 1922 Washington naval treaty.	26 July 1941	America freezes Japanese assets.
15 Jan. 1936	Japan withdraws from London naval conference.	7 Dec. 1941	Japan attacks the US Navy at Pearl Harbor.
25 Nov. 1936	Germany and Japan sign the Anti-Comintern Pact.	8 Dec. 1941	Britain and America declare war on Japan.
		11 Dec. 1941	Germany and Italy declare war on the US.

of its member states against another was insipid: a Commission under the British Earl Lytton was dispatched to investigate the initial Sino-Japanese incident which had sparked the crisis. Its Report was a year in the making, and even then recommended moderation—urging both non-recognition of Manchuguo and international mediation of Japan and China's differences, but not any forcible action against Japan for its violation of international law.

Would Hitler's aggression in Europe and Mussolini's in East Africa (where he tried to capture Abyssinia, the last independent African state) have been deterred had the League acted decisively over Manchuria? The answer seems almost certainly not. Neither dictator had much regard for the niceties of international law, and most historians agree that both had long-term territorial ambitions which would scarcely have been deflected by a firmer League response to the Manchurian crisis. However, the League's abject failure to check Japanese aggres-

sion did perhaps help create a permissive atmosphere, which emboldened the European dictators to disrespect international law in the expectation that they would not incur international sanctions. Certainly, in East Asia, Japan's rulers were not deterred from further aggression by the upshot of the Manchurian crisis. The puppet state of Manchuguo continued to exist until the end of the Second World War, and the fact that most states chose not to recognize its existence made little odds to the Japanese government, and doubtless was of small comfort to the Manchurians themselves.

By 1937, Japan was involved in full-scale war with China, and this too lasted until 1945. But Japan's mounting incursions into neighbours' territory—the so-called **'New Order'** in East Asia—were not altogether ignored by the Western powers. In 1939, the US government cancelled its 1911 trade agreement with Japan, thus restricting the latter's ability to import raw materials necessary to its war machine. Not surprisingly, relations between the two states deteriorated rapidly and dramatically, culminating in Japan's bombing of the US navy at Pearl Harbor in December 1941. As a result, Britain and the US declared war on Japan on 8 December, while Germany and Italy reciprocated with a declaration of war on the USA three days later. The Second World War was now unquestionably global in scope. However, for many months there had been no doubt as to where the main lines of division lay in Asia, nor that an axis was emerging between Japan, Germany, and Italy. A Three-Power Pact was concluded in 1940, which was transformed into a military alliance in 1942. Thus while the German army overran huge swathes of continental Europe, Japan occupied large parts of Asia hitherto colonized by European states. The Dutch East Indies and French Indo-China fell to Japan, just as Holland and France lay under Nazi rule. And although Britain itself repelled German invasion, the same was not true of its South-East Asian colonies, Burma, Ceylon, and Malaya.

Key points

- From 1868 onwards, Japan underwent a rapid period of industrialization and modernization, with profound social, economic, and political consequences.
- To find new markets, raw materials, and land for Japan's growing population, Japan began to expand into northern China, whilst China was in a protracted state of civil war.
- Japan, although it fought against Germany during World War I, emerged from that war similarly dissatisfied with the post-war settlement.
- Between 1931 and 1933, Japan consolidated its hold over Manchuria, establishing a puppet state, 'Manchuguo': the League of Nations' response to the most blatant act of aggression it had thus far faced was minimal.
- By 1937, Japan was at war with China, which caused worsening relations with the US—ultimately leading to Japan's attack on Pearl Harbor.

The path to war in Europe

As the crisis in the Far East deepened during the 1930s, Europe lurched from one crisis to the next: Italy's invasion of Abyssinia (Ethiopia); Germany's remilitarization of the Rhineland; civil war in Spain; Germany's expansion into Austria, then Czechoslovakia, followed by Poland, at which point Britain and France declared war on Germany in September 1939.

The controversy over the origins of the Second World War

It was suggested earlier in this chapter that in many ways the Second World War was a continuation of the First: another manifestation of Europe's deep-rooted instability, and a reflection of the imbalance of power which had existed on the continent ever since the unification of Germany. However, many

historians would argue that besides the profound structural forces which were at work undermining the stability of Europe, human agency also played a role in bringing about the Second World War. Indeed, to tell the story of the origins of that war without reference to Hitler, would be akin to telling the story of Adam and Eve without the serpent. To many (historians or otherwise), the Second World War was, quite simply, 'Hitler's war', which he planned, and which was the conscious result of his determination to achieve world mastery. This was also the verdict of the post-war Nuremberg trials of Nazi war criminals.

However, the origins of the Second World War have been—perhaps surprisingly—a matter of considerable historiographical dispute. While most historians agree that responsibility for the war rests with Hitler and Nazi Germany, they have differed over whether Hitler actually **planned** the war, and what the extent of his territorial ambitions was—mastery of Europe, or German hegemony of the world? Did Hitler have a timetable for the expansionist ambitions he had set out in his autobiography-cum-manifesto *Mein Kampf*? Had he decided, by 1937, to take Czechoslovakia and then Poland, before turning to Western Europe, as a document (entitled the Hossbach Memorandum) used in the Nuremberg tribunal seemed to suggest? Did he think he could expand German power in Europe **without** causing a major war? Or did he believe that a Total War was inevitable, but did not foresee this coming about until the 1940s, when the German economy would be fully mobilized for such a war? All these questions have been posed by historians, and divergent answers given (Robertson 1971; Finney 1997).

The most controversial treatment of the war's origins by a serious historian remains A. J. P. Taylor's *The Origins of the Second World War*, first published in 1961 to a barrage of criticism. The cause of the furore was Taylor's suggestion that Hitler essentially resembled any other European statesman. Nazi ideology—though responsible for the 'evil of the gas chambers' —did not suffice to explain the war. Hitler, like his Weimar predecessors, had merely sought to enhance Germany's position after the Versailles settlement, and to reverse its unfavourable, and unfair, aspects. Far from having a timetable for expansion, and general war, Hitler was an opportunist, who capitalized on the blunders of others, and the opportunities afforded him by the appeasers in Britain and France. War in September 1939 caught Hitler essentially by surprise. Although Taylor later claimed in his autobiography that his view of Hitler as blunderer and opportunist had become the new orthodoxy, this is something of an exaggeration (Taylor 1983: 299). It is probably truer to say that most historians believe that Hitler had a long-term fixity of purpose—expansion in Europe, if not further afield—coupled with a short-term flexibility in his tactics and timing. Certainly, most reject Taylor's contention that Nazi ideology had nothing whatever to do with the Second World War.

The rise of fascism and Nazism in Europe

A. J. P. Taylor aside, most academic historians regard Nazi and fascist ideology as essential to understanding both the origins and practices of the war. Fuelled by popular dissatisfaction with the 1919 settlement, extreme right-wing movements arose in the 1920s and 1930s. These fed on the social, economic, and political instabilities engendered by World War I. Italy had never really achieved stable central government despite unification in the nineteenth century. Although fascist mythology claimed that Mussolini seized power with his '**March on Rome**', in reality he was invited to form a parliament by the king and conservative politicians in 1922, because the traditional right-wing parties had failed to form a stable government. Far from marching on Rome, he was brought to the capital by special train. Once Prime Minister, Mussolini set about conducting a 'fascist revolution' in Italian life, which no doubt horrified at least some of those responsible for bringing him to power.

As many historians and political theorists have pointed out, 'fascism' evades easy definition—arguably so incoherent as not to constitute a political philosophy at all. As practised in Italy, it entailed the establishment of a type of state popularly termed '**totalitarian**' (especially after 1945), in which almost all aspects of its citizens' lives were subject to invasive regulation. In the sphere of employment, trade unions were abolished and 'corporations' of employers and employees established, overseen by fascist bureaucrats. Whatever the legitimation in terms of harmonious labour relations, 'corporatism' in practice ensured that the interests of big business prevailed over those of organized labour. In politics, opposition parties were eliminated, and a personality cult was built around the figure of Mussolini, 'Il Duce'. Social life was heavily imbued with fascist ideology—from women's institutes, to football clubs and youth leagues.

Fascist precepts also influenced foreign policy, although there was some continuity of purpose between Mussolini and his predecessors. Fascism glorified violence and struggle, within society and between states, as natural and heroic. War was the ultimate test not only of individual 'manhood' but of a state's maturity and position in the international hierarchy. Mussolini was thus committed to over-turning that part of the Versailles settlement which had subtracted territory from Italy in the Adriatic. In addition, he strove to expand his 'New Roman Empire' into North Africa, by war if necessary. The obvious target was Abyssinia—the last remaining independent state in Africa—and in 1935, Italian troops moved to seize control of the country from Haile Selassie. This became a more protracted cam-paign than Mussolini had probably envisaged. Its most obvious beneficiary was not Il Duce himself, but Adolf Hitler, who used the cover of Mussolini's North African adventure to proceed with his own plans for dismantling the 1919 settlement in Europe.

Hitler came to power in Germany over a decade after Mussolini's accession in Italy. After years of street-fighting and rabble-rousing in beer cellars, Hit-ler's National Socialist party achieved success at the German polls in 1933. Once in power as Reich Chancellor, Hitler—like Mussolini—moved to con-solidate the grip of his party over both the organs of the state, and the German people as a whole. Nazis assumed power in central and local government; the state directed industry, and controlled the German mass media. Opposition parties were abolished, and dissent stifled, either by physical punishment or the fear of it. Hitler's particular targets of detestation— the Jews, gypsies, and homosexuals—were sent in ever increasing numbers to concentration camps. No aspect of German life was left untouched by the Nazi party and ideology. Even the most intimate aspects of private life—relating to reproduction and childrearing—were subordinated to the imperatives of the Third Reich. German women were accordingly exhorted to produce genetically pure children for the greater good of the Reich.

In this regard, as in others, Nazism closely re-sembled Italian fascism: Mussolini also insisting that 'Maternity is the patriotism of women' (Mazower 1999: 82). But Nazism exhibited distinct, and more virulent, strains, especially in its genocidal anti-Semitism. At the heart of Hitler's world view was his racist belief in the superiority of the pure German people—the Aryan race. Not only did he believe that Germany had been unfairly robbed of land and people in 1919, but his territorial aims went far beyond mere rectification of the wrongs of Versailles. In pursuit of more *lebensraum* (living space), Aryan Germans must fufil racial and historical destiny, by expanding eastwards (the *drang nach osten*), at the expense of the slavonic *untermenschen* ('sub-humans') who inhabited Eastern Europe, and the Soviet Union in particular. Hitler's world view thus rested on a debased Social Darwinism, in which the 'fittest' race was compelled to expand at the expense of its genetically inferior neighbours.

From appeasement to war

The Nazis made no secret of their territorial ambi-tions; *Mein Kampf* spelt out Hitler's racial views and expansionist plans quite explicitly. Why, therefore, did the governments of Britain and France not do more to prevent Hitler from realizing these plans? Why was Hitler allowed to remilitarize the Rhine-land, annex Austria, and invade Czechoslovakia before the Allies confronted him over his incursion into Poland in September 1939? Why, in short, was Hitler appeased for so long?

The policy of **appeasement** pursued by the West-ern powers throughout much of the 1930s has received considerable scholarly attention, and remains a potent source of historical analogies for politicians. The first generation of post-war histor-ians was extremely (if understandably) harsh in its verdict on the appeasers: Chamberlain and his French counterparts were the '**Guilty Men of Munich**'. By cravenly appeasing Hitler, the leaders of France and Britain simply fed his appetite, and emboldened the Führer to believe that he could suc-cessfully carry off ever more audacious violations of the Treaty of Versailles.

A number of subsequent historians have been somewhat kinder to the 'appeasers'. Certainly we should not underestimate the magnitude of the domestic and international crises confronting West European policy-makers and diplomats in the 1930s. Japan's violations of Chinese sovereignty were a source of concern in the Far East. Events in Asia thus provided a convenient cover for Hitler to leave the Geneva disarmament conference and the League in 1933, and to begin the process of German rearmament. Germany also profited from Italy's invasion of Abyssinia, and was a far from reliable ally to Mussolini during the ensuing war there. Although Mussolini announced the formation of a '**Rome–Berlin Axis**' between Germany and Italy in November 1936, in fact, Hitler had sent some arms to Haile Selassie's beleagured forces in Abyssinia—precisely to protract the war, enabling Germany to tear more gaping holes in the fabric of the Versailles settlement, while British and French attention was still focused on north-east Africa. As the League grappled with the issue of whether or not to apply sanctions to Italy over Abyssinia, civil war broke out in Spain. The ideological fissures in Europe were now unmistakable.

British and French politicians accordingly faced the daunting scenario of war on three fronts: in the Pacific (against Japan); the Mediterranean (against Italy), and Central Europe (against Germany). Neither Britain nor France was prepared militarily for such an eventuality. Nor, for much of the 1930s, did a majority of British and French citizens appear to favour going to war to prevent or reverse acts of aggression. There were after all pressing domestic issues to be attended to: the Depression had created chronic unemployment and poverty. Moreover, the memory of World War I was still vivid, and this made politicians, mindful of the publics they served, cautious about embarking on military solutions to international problems. Appeasement, some historians would thus argue, was in certain respects a justifiable attempt to 'buy time'. It enabled British and French rearmament to proceed, and public opinion to be mobilized, so that if Germany did have to be challenged militarily, and Hitler's pose as a 'man of peace' was proved a sham, then at least a serious military effort could be mounted against him.

However, this more charitable interpretation of appeasement might be criticized on the grounds that it credits the appeasers with considerable foresight—with seeking a breathing-space which would enable them, ultimately, to wage more effective war against Hitler, whereas in fact they tended to believe that by giving in to his demands, the Führer would cease to make them. Chamberlain not only accepted that Germany did have some legitimate grievances but additionally regarded Hitler in the same light as other statesmen. The British premier therefore assumed that differences between European statesmen could be ironed out through negotiation and compromise, as all essentially wanted peace. This underestimation of Nazi intentions consequently enabled Hitler to launch a spectacular series of assaults on the Versailles settlement with impunity. He reoccupied the Rhineland in 1936, with surprisingly little response from France. He encouraged Nazi movements in Austria, and pressurized the Austrian chancellor Schuschnigg to include Nazis in his government. Then in March 1938 he dispatched German troops over the border to secure the 'unification' of Austria with Germany (*Anschluss*). Czechoslovakia was next. Here, Hitler again deployed as legitimation the fact that Germany had been wronged in 1919, when three and a half million Germans of the Sudetenland had been incorporated within the new Czech state. German troop movements against Czechoslovakia began in May 1938. While British and French leaders were clearly alarmed by this development, they nevertheless continued to appease Hitler, and indeed the high-point of the policy was the now notorious **Munich conference** of September 1938. At Munich, the British and French premiers agreed to German occupation of the Sudetenland, but offered a guarantee (with Italy and Germany) of the borders of the remaining Czech state. Hitler also promised Chamberlain that their two countries would 'never go to war with one another again'—the famous piece of paper which Chamberlain claimed would secure '**peace for our time**'.

As we know, it did not. In March 1939, Germany invaded the remainder of Czechoslovakia, and Britain and France ignored their pledges made at Munich, with Chamberlain having decided some months earlier that Czechoslovakia was indefensible. However, in the wake of Germany's effective occupation of all Central Europe, the Western powers showered guarantees on the remaining free states of Eastern Europe and the Balkans. Why this sudden diplomatic revolution? The answer seems to be that appeasement no longer appeared morally defensible once Hitler's ambitions had clearly outstripped revision of German grievances outstanding from 1919. By sending German troops into Prague, Hitler revealed that his territorial greed was not just

---

Box 3.7 The origins of World War Two in Europe: a chronology

30 Oct. 1922	Mussolini becomes Prime Minister of Italy.	22 Sept. 1938	Chamberlain and Hitler meet at Godesburg.
30 Jan. 1933	Hitler becomes Chancellor of Germany.	29/30 Sept. 1938	Munich Conference.
14 Oct. 1933	Germany leaves the Geneva disarmament conference and walks out of the League of Nations.	28 March 1939	End of Spanish Civil War.
		31 March 1939	Britain and France extend a guarantee to Poland that they will defend Poland's territorial integrity from German attack, after Germany occupies the remainder of Czechoslovakia.
14/15 June 1934	Hitler and Mussolini meet in Venice.		
25 July 1934	Murder of Austrian Chancellor, Dollfuss, by Austrian Nazis.		
16 March 1935	Germany reintroduces conscription.	17 April 1939	USSR proposes alliance to Britain and France.
3 Oct. 1935	Italy invades Abyssinia/Ethiopia.	22 May 1939	Pact of Steel signed between Italy and Germany.
11 Oct. 1935	League decides to impose sanctions against Italy.	12 Aug. 1939	Britain and France begin military talks with USSR.
7 March 1936	Germany reoccupies the Rhineland (which the Treaty of Versailles had established as a demilitarized zone).	23 Aug. 1939	Stalin signs Nazi–Soviet Pact.
		25 Aug. 1939	Britain signs treaty with Poland.
9 May 1936	Italy annexes Abyssinia.	1 Sept. 1939	Germany invades Poland; Italy remains neutral.
17 July 1936	Civil war breaks out in Spain between Franco's fascist forces and the communist/socialist/syndicalist Popular Front.	3 Sept. 1939	Britain and France declare war on Germany.
1 Nov. 1936	Mussolini announces the existence of the Rome–Berlin Axis.	17 Sept. 1939	USSR invades Poland.
		30 Nov. 1939	USSR invades Finland.
11 Dec. 1937	Italy leaves the League of Nations.	9 April 1940	Germany invades Denmark and Norway.
13 March 1938	Austria united with Germany (*Anschluss*).	10 June 1940	Italy enters the war.
20 May 1938	Rumours of German troop movements against Czechoslovakia.	22 June 1940	France signs armistice with Germany.
15 Sept. 1938	British PM Chamberlain meets Hitler at Berchtesgaden.	22 June 1941	Germany invades USSR.
		8 Dec. 1941	US enters the war.

---

for 'Germanic' lands. Why assume that he would be satisfied with Czechoslovakia? Poland, the Low Countries, and France all now appeared in imminent danger of German expansionism. Fearing for their own territorial integrity, the leaders of Britain and France thus determined to go to war with Hitler over Poland in September 1939. The Czechs might have been sacrificed on the altar of appeasement, but the Poles would not suffer the same fate without a fight.

Key points

- The origins of the Second World War have been the subject of particular historiographical controversy. Historians still dispute how far Hitler actually planned the war; whether he foresaw the extent of the war that began in 1939; and how ambitious Nazi territorial expansionism actually was (European hegemony or world domination?).

- Fascism and Nazism, as practised in Italy and Germany, led to a complete reordering of those societies, eliminating any notion of a private sphere. In foreign policy terms, ambitious territorial plans were mapped which went far beyond the revision of aspects of the Treaty of Versailles.

- Confronted with numerous international crises—in China, Abyssinia, and Europe—policy-makers in Britain and France adopted a policy of appeasing Hitler.

- Once Germany occupied Prague in March 1939, appeasement was abandoned, and Britain and France declared war on Germany once it invaded Poland in September 1939.

Conclusion

This chapter has emphasized the protracted crisis which existed in Europe since the late nineteenth century, and which was manifest in the two Total Wars that engulfed Europe and the wider world in the first half of the twentieth century. The First World War left many European states economically ruined, and with political structures weakened. Indeed, a number of empires based in Europe collapsed during the war—those of Austro-Hungary, Turkey, and Tsarist Russia. The war also profoundly disrupted the growth of an effectively functioning international capitalist economy. Although this consequence of the war was initially masked by the buoyancy of the American economy, when the latter collapsed in October 1929, a general Depression soon spread thereafter to all parts of the world which had been engaged in international trade. The Depression thus reveals not only the economic interconnectedness of the interwar world, but the degree to which the formerly predominant European economies (particularly Britain's) had been eclipsed by America.

But the threat to the primacy of Europe did not spring from American economic growth alone. Japan was an emergent force in East Asia, which had undergone rapid industrialization, and, by the 1930s, was embarking on a search for territory in China, and beyond. And within Europe, post-war conditions and popular dissatisfaction with the Treaty of Versailles encouraged extremist political movements, most notably fascism in Italy (and Spain) and Nazism in Germany. Both Mussolini and Hitler set out to enlarge the boundaries of their states, and even if Hitler did not plan the type of war which ultimately broke out in September 1939, there is no doubt that he was prepared to risk war in order to achieve his ambitions.

The Second World War, as the next chapter explores, had profound global consequences. It saw an unlikely alliance of Britain, America, and the USSR come together to fight the Axis powers of Japan, Italy, and Germany. But this alliance was not to survive the onset of peace, and had shown signs of severe strain even as the war progressed. Indeed one might argue that the cold war was emerging while the World War was still being fought. Thus some revisionist historians, most notably the American Gar Alperovitz, suggest that America's dropping of the atomic bombs on Hiroshima and Nagasaki was actually the first shot of the cold war—the bombs being aimed less at persuading Japan to surrender (which it was about to do in any case) than at intimidating the Soviet Union with a show of American might. Whatever the merits of this argument, certainly the two superpowers, having emerged from their interwar isolationism, found it impossible to agree on the shape of the post-war world. America wanted a world based on free markets and liberalization. The Soviets wanted if not the spread of communism world wide, as many Americans feared, then at least a 'security zone' of satellite states in Eastern Europe. The post-war stalemate resulted in the division of Europe into two camps for the next forty-five years, and the temporary solution of the 'German problem' with the division of Germany into two separate states.

The war profoundly affected the map of Europe. It also radically reshaped Europe's position in the world. The two superpowers were now predominant, as was evident from the degree of physical and economic influence they exercised over their respective 'satellites', in Europe and beyond. Moreover, the war dramatically undercut the power and prestige of the European imperial powers in their colonies. In Asia, the British, French, and Dutch found many of their territories overrun by the Japanese, and the colonial powers' attempts to regain control after the war were largely short-lived. In a world dominated by two superpowers who professed anti-colonial credentials, and following a war that had encouraged nationalist movements, imperialism increasingly appeared anachronistic. The era of European domination of the world was over.

Viewed at such distance it is no surprise, then, that the first half of the last century should seem overwhelmingly fragmented and fissiparous: marked by imperial dissolutions, the emergence of violently exclusive nationalisms, and global economic collapse. Yet, in seeming paradox, these years also bear signs of increasing globalization, with the development of certain boundary-collapsing modes of communication, commerce and transport whose growth accelerated rapidly after 1945. By the end of the 1920s, the USSR had already pioneered international radio broadcasting, soon to be joined by the BBC's External Services (later its World Service). While French companies pioneered the newsreel as a visual catalogue of current affairs and curios, Hollywood movies enjoyed growing popularity with European audiences—so much so that Hitler ultimately debarred them from German cinemas, while privately relishing screenings of Disney cartoons and *Gone With the Wind*. Likewise, certain states (notably the Soviet Union and Nazi Germany) took alarm at the enthusiasm with which their citizens greeted such racially and politically transgressive imports as American jazz and swing music.

The ability to traverse the globe with greater ease and speed was not confined to cultural and consumer products alone. Individuals with disposable income and surplus leisure time could themselves travel to foreign destinations ever more readily. Then as now, the world's shrinkage was most enthusiastically heralded by those enjoying expanded opportunities that let them experience globalization, first-hand, as time-saving and horizon-widening. Only in the latter part of the twentieth century did the processes of **global** interconnectedness acquire a coinage, and more querulous critics. But such interconnectivity was certainly palpable during the twentieth century's earliest decades—whether to a bourgeois Briton enjoying one of Mr Thomas Cook's earliest package tours, or a Brazilian farmer struggling to cope with the collapsed price of coffee.

QUESTIONS

1 In what ways did Europe dominate international politics at the start of the twentieth century?

2 Why was Germany regarded as a 'problem' after its unification in 1871?

3 What factors resulted in the outbreak of World War I in 1914?

4 What were the main weaknesses with the post-war peace settlement?

5 Was Germany treated unfairly by the Treaty of Versailles?

6 Why were the US and the USSR not more active in international politics between the First and Second World Wars?

7 Why did the Wall Street stock-market crash of October 1929 have such profound international consequences?

8 In what ways was Japan a 'threat' to the European great powers during the first half of the twentieth century?

9 Is it fair to regard the Second World War as 'Hitler's War'?

10 What were the weaknesses with the policy of appeasement?

11 How far was the Second World War responsible for Western Europe's eclipse by other powers?

GUIDE TO FURTHER READING

General

Hobsbawm, E., *Age of Extremes: The Short Twentieth Century 1914–91* (London: Michael Joseph, 1994). This is an extremely readable and thought-provoking look at the century which Hobsbawm regards as beginning in 1914.

Keylor, W., *The Twentieth Century World: An International History* (New York: Oxford University Press, 1992). This book provides an excellent overview of the entire century, with lengthy sections of the period up to 1945. Economic factors are dealt with particularly well.

Mazower, M., *Dark Continent: Europe's Twentieth Century* (London: Penguin, 1999). An incisive and provocative history of Europe in the twentieth century, synthesizing a great deal of material with engaging verve.

Ross, G., *The Great Powers and the Decline of the European States System, 1914–45* (London: Longmans, 1983). A short, but detailed, diplomatic history, outlining the collapse of the 'states system' comprised by the European Great Powers, and containing useful chronologies.

World War I and after

Henig, R., *Versailles and After, 1919–33* (London: Methuen, 1984). A pamphlet setting out the main terms of the post-war peace settlement.

Joll, J., *The Origins of the First World War* (London: Longmans, 1984). A useful synthesis of the debate on the origins of the war.

World War II

Iriye, A., *The Origins of the Second World War in Asia and the Pacific* (London: Longmans, 1987). In the same series as Joll's book, this volume examines the growth of Japanese imperialism and the onset of the war.

Finney, P., *The Origins of the Second World War* (London: Arnold, 1997). A recent assemblage of key articles, covering the range of historiographical debates over the origins of the Second World War, interpretations of the nature of the 'dictatorships', and appraisals of appeasement.

Robertson, E. M. (ed.), *The Origins of the Second World War: Historical Interpretations* (London: Macmillan, 1971). A useful collection of articles illustrating the extent of the row over Taylor's thesis; including a vicious exchange between Taylor and his chief opponent, Hugh Trevor-Roper.

Taylor, A. J. P., *The Origins of the Second World War* (Harmondsworth: Penguin, 1961). This book sparked a huge controversy on account of Taylor's claim that Hitler—an ordinary European statesman—blundered into the war. Taylor also has much to say about Versailles and appeasement.

4 International history 1945–1990

Len Scott

READER'S GUIDE

This chapter examines some of the principal developments in international politics from 1945 to 1990. Fundamental changes in politics, technology and ideology took place in this period, with enormous consequences for world affairs. The onset of the cold war, the creation of nuclear weapons, and the end of European imperialism are the principal developments explored in the chapter. Since 1945 world politics has been greatly influenced by the conflict between the United States and the Soviet Union, each of which emerged as 'superpowers'. The ideological, political, and military interests of these two states and their allies, extended around the globe. How far, and in what ways, conflict in Europe, Asia, and elsewhere was promoted or prevented by the cold war are central questions. Similarly, how the process of decolonization became intermingled with cold war conflicts is a central issue in understanding many wars and conflicts in the 'Third World'. Finally, how dangerous was the nuclear confrontation between East and West? Did nuclear weapons keep the peace between the superpowers or did they provoke conflict and risk global catastrophe? The chapter raises these questions, and explores the relationship between nuclear weapons development and phases in East–West relations, first with *détente*, and then with the deterioration of Soviet–American relations in the 1980s.

Introduction

The Second World War was global in scope and total in nature. It helped bring about fundamental changes in world politics after 1945. Before 1939 Europe had been the arbiter of world affairs, and both the Soviet Union and the United States remained, for different reasons, preoccupied with internal development at the expense of any significant global role. The war brought the Soviets and the Americans militarily and politically deep into Europe, and helped transform their relations with each other. This transformation was soon reflected in their relations outside Europe where various confrontations developed. Like the Second World War, the cold war had its origins in Europe, but quickly spread, with enormous consequences for countries and peoples around the world.

After 1945 European power was increasingly in eclipse, although this was not always apparent to those who held power or to their supporters. The economic plight of the wartime belligerents, including those Western European countries who had emerged as victors, was nevertheless increasingly and transparently obvious, as was the growing realization of the military and economic potential of the United States and the Soviet Union. Both countries emerged as 'superpowers', combining global political objectives with military capabilities that included weapons of mass destruction and the means to deliver them over intercontinental distances. In Europe, the military involvement of the superpowers soon took the form of enduring political commitments, notwithstanding early American intentions to withdraw and demobilize their troops after 1945. European political, economic, and military weakness contrasted with the appearance of Soviet strength and the growing Western perception of malign Soviet intent. The onset of the cold war in Europe marked the collapse of the wartime alliance between the UK, the USSR, and the USA. How far this alliance had been a marriage of convenience, and how far its breakdown was inevitable after 1945 remain crucial and contentious issues. What is beyond doubt is that the legacies of the Second World War provided a heavy burden for succeeding generations. Arguably the most notable, and certainly the most dramatic, legacy was the atomic bomb, built at enormous cost and driven by fear that Nazi Germany might win this first nuclear arms race, with terrifying consequences. After 1945 nuclear weapons presented unprecedented challenges to world politics and to the leaders responsible for conducting post-war diplomacy. The cold war provided context and pretext for the growth of nuclear arsenals which threatened the very existence of humankind, and which have continued (and continued to spread) beyond the end of the cold war and the East–West confrontation.

Since 1945 world politics has been transformed in a variety of ways. These changes reflected political, technological, and ideological developments, of which three are examined in this chapter: (1) The End of Empire: the withdrawal of European countries from their empires in Africa and Asia; (2) The cold war: the political and military confrontation between the United States and the Soviet Union; (3) The Bomb: the development of the atomic bomb and the hydrogen bomb, and the means of their delivery. There have of course been other important changes, and indeed equally important continuities, some of which are explored in other chapters. The transformation of the international political economy and the creation of the United Nations are among several key developments. Nevertheless, the three principal changes outlined above provide a framework for exploring events and trends which have shaped the post-war world.

End of empire

The collapse of imperialism in the twentieth century was a fundamental change in world politics. It reflected and contributed to the decreasing importance of Europe as the arbiter of world affairs. The belief that national self-determination should be a guiding principle in international politics marked a transformation of attitudes and values. During the age of imperialism political status had accrued to imperial powers. After 1945 imperialism was viewed with growing international hostility. Colonialism and the United Nations Charter were increasingly recognized as incompatible, though independence was often slow and sometimes marked by prolonged conflict and war. The cold war often complicated and hindered the transition to independence. Various factors influenced the process of decolonization: the attitude of the colonial power; the ideology and strategy of the anti-imperialist forces; and the role of external powers. Political, economic, and military factors played various roles in shaping the timing and nature of the transfer of power. Different imperial powers and newly emerging independent states had different experiences of withdrawal from empire. Three of the principal European experiences of withdrawal from empire are discussed below.

Britain

In 1945 the British empire extended across the globe. Between 1947 and 1980 forty-nine territories were granted their independence. There was debate within Britain over Britain's imperial role, which can be traced back to the nineteenth century, but after 1945 growing recognition of the justice of **self-determination** combined with realization of the strength of nationalism brought about a reappraisal of policy. Withdrawal from India, the 'Jewel in the Crown' of the empire, in 1947 was the most dramatic, and in (most) British eyes, successful, act of decolonization, and one which paved the way for the creation of the world's largest democracy. How far the ensuing hostility between India and Pakistan was avoidable, and how far it reflected previous British efforts to divide and rule, remains a matter for debate. What is clear is that India was something of an exception in the early post-war years, and that successive British governments were reluctant to rush toward decolonization. The key period for the British empire in Africa, came toward the end of the 1950s and early 1960s, symbolized by Prime Minister Harold Macmillan's speech in South Africa in 1960 when he warned his hosts of the **'wind of change'** blowing through their continent.

The transition from empire was on the whole peaceful, and led to the creation of democratic and stable states. There were some conflicts with indigenous revolutionary elements, notably in Kenya (1952–6) and Malaya (1948–60), but these were of limited scale and in Malaya, an effective counter-insurgency policy was pursued. From the European perspective, the British experience was more successful than the French. In Rhodesia/Zimbabwe, however, the transition to 'one person one vote' and black majority rule, was prevented by a

Table 4.1 Principal acts of European decolonization 1945–1980

Country	Colonial state	Year of independence
India	Britain	1947
Pakistan	Britain	1947
Burma	Britain	1948
Indonesia	Holland	1949
Ghana	Britain	1957
Malaya	Britain	1957
French African colonies	France	1960
Zaire	Belgium	1960
Algeria	France	1962
Kenya	Britain	1963
Guinea-Bissau	Portugal	1974
Mozambique	Portugal	1975
Cape Verde	Portugal	1975
Sao Tome	Portugal	1975
Angola	Portugal	1975
Zimbabwe	Britain	1980

Box 4.1 **Key concepts**

Superpower: term used to describe the United States and the Soviet Union after 1945, denoting their global political involvements and military capabilities, including in particular their nuclear arsenals.

'Wind of change': reference by British Prime Minister Harold Macmillan in a speech in South Africa in 1960 to the political changes taking place across Africa heralding the end of European imperialism.

Apartheid: system of racial segregation introduced in South Africa in 1948, designed to ensure white minority domination.

Hegemony: political (and/or economic) domination of a region, usually by a superpower.

Truman doctrine: statement made by President Harry Truman in March 1947 that it 'must be the policy of the United States to support free people who are resisting attempted subjugation by armed minorities or by outside pressures'. Intended to persuade Congress to support limited aid to Turkey and Greece the doctrine came to underpin the policy of containment and American economic and political support for its allies.

Containment: American political strategy for resisting perceived Soviet expansion, first publicly espoused by an American diplomat, George Kennan, in 1947. Containment became a powerful factor in American policy towards the Soviet Union for the next forty years.

North Atlantic Treaty Organization (NATO): organization established by treaty in April 1949 comprising 12 (later 16) countries from Western Europe and North America. The most important aspect of the NATO alliance was the American commitment to the defence of Western Europe.

Détente: relaxation of tension between East and West; Soviet–American *détente* lasted from the late 1960s to the late 1970s, and was characterized by negotiations and nuclear arms control agreements.

Rapprochement: re-establishment of more friendly relations between the People's Republic of China and the United States in the early 1970s.

Ostpolitik: The West German government's 'Eastern Policy' of the mid to late 1960s, designed to develop relations between West Germany and members of the Warsaw Pact.

Glasnost: policy of greater openness pursued by Soviet President Mikhail Gorbachev from 1985, involving greater toleration of internal dissent and criticism.

Perestroika: policy of restructuring, pursued by Gorbachev in tandem with *Glasnost*, and intended to modernise the Soviet political and economic system.

Sinatra doctrine: statement by the Soviet foreign ministry in October 1989 that countries of Eastern Europe were 'doing it their way' (a reference to Frank Sinatra's song 'I did it my way') and which marked the end of the Brezhnev doctrine and Soviet hegemony in Eastern Europe.

Brezhnev doctrine: declaration by Soviet premier Leonid Brezhnev in November 1968 that members of the Warsaw pact would enjoy only 'limited sovereignty' in their political development.

Mutually Assured Destruction (MAD): condition in which both superpowers possessed the capacity to destroy their adversary even after being attacked first with nuclear weapons.

---

white minority prepared to disregard both the British government and world opinion. This minority was aided and abetted by the South African government. Under **apartheid**, after 1948, the South Africans engaged in what many saw as the racial equivalent of imperialism. South Africa also practised a more traditional form of imperialism in its occupation of Namibia, and exercised an important influence in post-colonial/cold war struggles in Angola and Mozambique.

Britain, like France, sought to ensure that independence was granted on terms advantageous to the colonial power, even where the decision to leave often reflected the judgement that the cost of fighting the nationalists was too great. Britain and France sought to maximize their interests by economic and political frameworks designed to serve their advantage. The British Commonwealth and the French Union in Africa were the main instruments of this, though the British Commonwealth developed its own identity, and frequently voiced views and concerns at variance with those of the British government. In the 1980s for example the Commonwealth played a major part in the campaigns against apartheid South Africa, bringing it into conflict with the Thatcher government in Britain.

France

The British experience of decolonization stood in contrast to that of the French. France had been occupied during the Second World War, and successive governments sought to preserve French prestige in international affairs by maintaining her imperial status. In Indo-China after 1945 the French attempted to preserve their colonial role, only withdrawing after prolonged guerrilla war and military defeat at the hands of the Vietnamese revolutionary forces, the Viet Minh, led by Ho Chi Minh. In Africa, the picture was different. The wind of change also blew through French Africa, and under President Charles de Gaulle, France withdrew from empire, while attempting to preserve its influence by means of the French Union and later the French Community. In Algeria, however, the French refused to leave. Algeria was regarded by many French people to be part of France itself. The resulting war, from 1954 to 1962, led to up to 45,000 deaths, and France itself was brought to the edge of civil war.

Portugal

The last European empire in Africa was that of Portugal, and when the military dictatorship was overthrown in Lisbon, withdrawal from empire followed swiftly. The transition to independence occurred with relative ease in Guinea-Bissau, Cape Verde, and Sao Tome, but in Mozambique and Angola the anti-colonial struggle was already giving way to conflict among the different anti-colonial groups. These organizations received support from various external powers (America, the Soviet Union, Cuba, and South Africa) which helped arm and finance them. The pattern of resulting conflict reflected a complex of anti-colonial, tribal, and ideological allegiances. In Angola Cuban troops supported the MPLA who were

opposed by invading South African forces, while the United States provided various types of assistance, including sophisticated weapons, to the anti-communist UNITA. Cold war perspectives and antagonisms thus fuelled regional instability, while prolongation and escalation of the conflict exacerbated global Soviet–American tensions (see below).

The consequences for the populations concerned were continuing civil war and, eventually, in the case of Mozambique, famine and mass starvation. How far political and ideological divisions, and how far tribal factors were responsible for conflict is one question, and one that was to be asked of many newly emergent African states. Indeed, in general, how far tribal divisions were created or made worse by the imperial powers is an important question in examining the political stability of the newly independent states. Equally important is how capable the new political leaderships in these societies were in tackling their political and economic problems.

Legacies and consequences: nationalism or communism?

The pattern of decolonization in Africa was thus diverse, reflecting the attitudes of the colonial powers, the nature of the local nationalist or revolutionary movements, and in some cases the involvement of external states, including the main cold war protagonists. In Asia, the relationship between nationalism and revolutionary Marxism was a potent force. In Malaya the British defeated an insurgent communist movement (1948–1960). In Indo-China the French failed to do likewise (1946–1954). For the Vietnamese, centuries of foreign oppression—Chinese, Japanese, French—soon focused on a new 'imperialist' adversary, the United States. For the Americans, early reluctance to support European imperialism gave way to incremental and covert involvement, and from 1965, growing open commitment to the newly created state of South Vietnam. The American aim of containing communism was soon applied to the conflicts of Indo-China. Chinese and Soviet support for North Vietnam and the Viet Cong (the communist guerrillas) were part of the cold war context of the war. The United States, however, failed to devise limited war objectives with a political strategy for defeating these forces. North Vietnamese success in revolutionary warfare eventually led Washington to search for 'peace with honour' once political objectives could not be achieved, and 'victory' was no longer possible. The Viet Cong's *Tet* (Vietnamese New Year) offensive in 1968 marked a decisive event in the war, though it was not until 1973 that American forces were finally withdrawn, two years before South Vietnam was defeated.

The global trend towards decolonization has been a key development since 1945, but one frequently offset by local circumstances. Some countries have lost their independence since 1945, such as Tibet, invaded by China in 1950, and East Timor, invaded by Indonesia in 1975. Yet, while imperialism has generally withered, other forms of domination or **hegemony** have arisen. The notion of hegemony has been used as criticism of the behaviour of the superpowers, most notably with Soviet hegemony in Eastern Europe, and American hegemony in Central America. European retreat from empire did not result in isolationism: Britain, and particularly France, sought to intervene, both overtly and covertly, in post-colonial affairs using a variety of methods including economic development assistance.

Key points

- Different European powers had different attitudes to decolonization after 1945: some, such as the British, decided to leave while others wished to preserve their Empires, in part (the French) or whole (the Portuguese).

- European powers adopted different attitudes to different regions/countries; e.g. British withdrawal from Asia came much more quickly after 1945 than from Africa.

- The process of decolonization was relatively peaceful in many cases; it led to revolutionary wars in others (Algeria, Malaya and Angola), depending on the attitudes of the colonial power and the nationalist movements.

- The struggle for independence/national liberation became embroiled in cold war conflicts when the superpowers and/or their allies became involved, e.g. Vietnam.

- Whether decolonization was judged successful depends, in part, on whose perspective you adopt—that of the European power or the independence movement.

The cold war

The rise of the United States as a world power after 1945 was of paramount importance in international politics. Its conflict with the Soviet Union provided one of the crucial dynamics in world affairs, and one which affected—directly or indirectly—every part of the globe. In the West, historians have debated, with vigour and acrimony, who was responsible for the collapse of the wartime relationship between the United States and the Soviet Union. The rise of the Soviet Union as a global power after 1945 is equally crucial in understanding international affairs in this period. Relations between the Union of Soviet Socialist Republics (USSR) and its Eastern European 'allies', with the People's Republic of China (PRC), and with various revolutionary movements and governments in the 'third world', have been vital issues in world

politics, as well as key factors in Soviet–American affairs.

Discerning phases in East–West relations casts light on key characteristics of the cold war. How such phases are defined is a matter of debate. The issue of when the cold war began, for example, is closely bound up with the question of who (if anyone) was responsible. Some historians date the origins of the cold war back to the 'Russian revolution' of 1917, while most focus on various events between 1945 and 1950. Whether the cold war was inevitable, whether it was the consequence of mistakes and misperceptions by political leaders, or whether it was the response of courageous Western leaders to malign and aggressive Soviet intent, are central issues in debates about the origins of the cold war, and its subsequent development. Hitherto, these debates have drawn from Western archives and sources, and are often focused on Western actions and reactions. With the end of the cold war greater evidence is appearing about Soviet actions, and how Moscow perceived the issues. The following sets out various key phases of the cold war (with which not all historians would agree), but which help identify key features and changes in East–West relations after 1945.

1945–1953: Onset of the cold war

The onset of the cold war in Europe reflected failure to implement the principles agreed at the wartime conferences of Yalta and Potsdam. The future of Germany, and of various Central and Eastern European countries, notably Poland, were issues of growing tension between the former wartime allies. Reconciling the principles of national self-determination with perceptions of national security was a formidable task. In the West there was a growing feeling that Soviet policy towards Eastern Europe was guided not by historic concern with security but by ideological expansion. In March 1947 the Truman administration sought to justify limited aid to Turkey and Greece with a rhetoric designed to arouse awareness of Soviet ambitions, and a declaration that America would support those threatened by Soviet subversion or expansion. **The Truman doctrine** and the associated policy of **containment** expressed the self-image of the United States as inherently defensive, and was underpinned by the Marshall Plan for European economic recovery, proclaimed in June 1947, which was essential to the economic rebuilding of Western Europe. In Eastern Europe democratic socialist and other anti-communist forces were systematically undermined and eliminated as Marxist-Leninist regimes loyal to Moscow were installed. The only exception was in Yugoslavia, where the Marxist leader, Marshal Tito, consolidated his position while maintaining independence from Moscow. Subsequently Tito's Yugoslavia was to play an important role in the 'Third World's' Non-Aligned Movement.

The first major confrontation of the cold war took place over Berlin in 1948. The former German capital had been left deep in the heart of the Soviet zone of occupation, and in June 1948 Stalin sought to resolve its status by severing road and rail communications. West Berlin's population and political autonomy were kept alive by a massive airlift. Stalin ended the blockade in May 1949. The crisis also saw the deployment of American long-range bombers in Britain, officially described as 'atomic-capable', though none were actually armed with nuclear weapons. The American military deployment was followed by the political commitment enshrined in the **North Atlantic Treaty Organisation (NATO)** treaty signed in April 1949. The key principle of the treaty—that an attack on one member would be treated as an attack on all—accorded with the principle of collective self-defence enshrined in Article 51 of the United Nations Charter. In practice, the cornerstone of the alliance was the commitment of the United States to defend Western Europe. In reality, this meant the willingness of the United States to use nuclear weapons to deter Soviet 'aggression'. For the Soviet Union 'political encirclement' soon entailed a growing military, and specifically nuclear, threat.

While the origins of the cold war were in Europe, events and conflicts in Asia and elsewhere also played a key part. In 1949 the thirty-year-long Chinese civil war ended in victory for the communists under Mao Zedong. This had a major impact on Asian affairs and on perceptions in both Moscow and Washington. In 1950 the North Korean attack on South Korea was interpreted as part of a general communist offensive, and a test case for American resolve and the will of the United Nations to withstand aggression. The resulting American and UN commitment, followed in October 1950 by Chinese involvement, led to a war lasting three years and in which over three million people died before pre-war borders were restored. North and South Korea themselves remained locked in seemingly perpetual hostility, even after the end of the cold war.

1953–1969: Conflict, confrontation, and compromise

One consequence of the Korean war was the build-up of American conventional forces in Western Europe, in case communist aggression in Asia was a feint to detract from the real intent in Europe. The idea that communism was a monolithic political entity controlled from Moscow became an enduring American fixation, not shared in London and elsewhere. Western Europeans nevertheless depended on the United States for military security and this dependence deepened as the cold war confrontation in Europe was consolidated. The rearmament of the Federal Republic of Germany in 1954 precipitated the creation of the Warsaw Pact in 1955. The military build-up continued apace, with unprecedented concentrations of conventional and moreover nuclear forces. By the 1960s there were some 7,000 nuclear weapons in Western Europe alone. NATO deployed these nuclear weapons to offset Soviet conventional superiority, while Soviet 'theatre nuclear' forces in Europe compensated for overall American nuclear superiority. Towards the end of the 1950s the United States also deployed nuclear missiles in Europe.

The death of Stalin in 1953 was an important event, and had significant consequences for the USSR, at home and abroad. Stalin's eventual successor, Nikita Khrushchev, strove to modernize Soviet society, but helped unleash reformist tendencies in Eastern Europe. While Polish reformism was controlled, the position in Hungary threatened Soviet hegemony, and in 1956 Soviet intervention brought bloodshed to the streets of Budapest, and international condemnation on Moscow. The Soviet intervention coincided with an attack on Egypt by Britain, France, and Israel, precipitated by General Nasser's seizure of the Suez canal. The British government's actions provoked fierce domestic and international criticism, and the most serious rift in the 'special relationship' between Britain and the United States. The Eisenhower administration was strongly opposed to the actions of its allies, and in the face of what were effectively US economic sanctions, the British abandoned the operation (and their support for the French and Israelis). International opprobrium at the Soviet action in Budapest was lessened and deflected by what many saw as the final spasms of European imperialism.

Khruschev's policy towards the West was a mixture of seeking coexistence while pursuing confrontation. Soviet support for movements of national liberation aroused fears in the West of a global communist challenge and further strengthened American determination to support friends and subvert enemies in the 'Third World'. American commitments to liberal democracy and national self-determination were mediated by cold war perspectives, as well as by perceptions of American economic and political interest. Crises over Berlin in 1961 and Cuba in 1962 (see Box 4.2) marked the most dangerous moments of the cold war. In both there was risk of direct military confrontation, and certainly in October 1962 the possibility of nuclear war. How close the world came to Armageddon during the Cuban missile crisis and exactly why peace

Box 4.2 The Cuban missile crisis

In October 1962 the United States discovered that, contrary to public and private assurances, the Soviet leadership had secretly deployed nuclear missiles in Cuba. President Kennedy responded by imposing a partial blockade or 'quarantine' of the island, and US nuclear forces moved to unprecedented states of alert. The superpowers stood 'eyeball to eyeball', and most historians believe that this was the moment during the cold war when the risk of nuclear war was at its greatest. Indeed, recent evidence suggests that the risk of inadvertent nuclear war, arising from a concatenation of misperceptions, insubordinate actions, and organizational failures, may well have been greater than has been realized. The diplomatic impasse was resolved six days after Kennedy announced the 'quarantine' of Cuba, when Nikita Khruschev undertook to withdraw the missiles in return for assurances that the United States would not invade Cuba. It has also now emerged that President Kennedy provided a secret undertaking to remove equivalent NATO nuclear missiles from Europe.

Table 4.2 Cold war crises

1948–9	Berlin	USSR/US/UK
1954–5	Taiwan straits crisis	US/PRC
1961	Berlin	USSR/US/NATO
1962	Cuba	USSR/US/Cuba
1973	Arab/Israeli war	Egypt/Israel/Syria/US/USSR
1983	Exercise Able Archer	USSR/US/NATO

was preserved remain matters of great debate among historians and surviving officials.

The events of 1962 were followed by a more stable period of coexistence and competition. Nuclear arsenals continued to grow and both superpowers continued to support friends and subvert enemies. At the same time as America's commitment in Vietnam was deepening, Soviet–Chinese relations were deteriorating. Indeed, by 1969 China and the USSR fought a minor border war over a territorial dispute. Despite these tensions, the foundations for what became known as *détente* were laid between the USSR and USA, and for what became known as *rapprochement* between China and the United States. *Détente* in Europe had its origins in the *Ostpolitik* of the German Socialist Chancellor, Willy Brandt, and resulted in agreements that recognized the peculiar status of Berlin, and the sovereignty of East Germany. Soviet–American *détente* had its roots in mutual recognition of the need to avoid nuclear crises, and in the economic and military incentives in avoiding an unconstrained arms race. Both Washington and Moscow also looked towards Beijing in making their 'bilateral' calculations.

1969–1979: The rise and fall of *détente*

The period known as *détente* represented an attempt by both superpowers to manage their relations with each other within a framework of negotiations and agreements. In the West *détente* was associated with the political leadership of President Richard Nixon and his adviser Henry Kissinger, who were also instrumental in Sino–American *rapprochement*. This new phase in Soviet–American relations did not mark an end to political conflict as each side sought to pursue various political goals, some of which were to prove increasingly incompatible with the aspirations of the other superpower. Both sides maintained support for friendly regimes and movements, and this came at a time when various political upheavals were taking place in the 'Third World' (see Table 4.3). How far the superpowers were able to control their friends and how far they were entangled by their commitments was underlined in 1973 when the Arab–Israeli war embroiled both the US and the USSR in what became a potentially dangerous confrontation.

In Washington, Soviet support for revolutionary movements in the 'Third World' was seen as evidence of duplicity. Some Americans claim that Moscow's support for revolutionary forces in Ethiopia in 1975 killed *détente*. Others cite the Soviet role in Angola in 1978. Furthermore, the perception that the USSR was using arms control agreements to gain military advantage was linked to Soviet behaviour in the 'Third World'. Growing Soviet military superiority was reflected in growing Soviet influence, it was argued. The view from Moscow was different, reflecting different assumptions about the scope and purpose of *détente*. Other events were also seen to weaken American influence. The overthrow of the Shah of Iran in 1979, resulted in the loss of an important Western ally in the region, though the militant Islamic government was as hostile to the USSR as to the USA.

December 1979 marked a point of transition in East–West affairs. NATO agreed to deploy land-based Cruise and Pershing II missiles in Europe if negotiations with the Soviets did not reduce what NATO saw as a serious imbalance. Later in the month, Soviet armed forces intervened in Afghanistan to support their revolutionary allies. The USSR was bitterly condemned in the West and in the 'Third World' for its actions, and soon became committed to a protracted and bloody struggle which many compared to the American war in Vietnam. In the United States the impact on the Carter administration was to change the President's view of the Soviet Union. Republican and other critics had increasingly used foreign and defence policy issues to attack the Carter Presidency. Perceptions of the cold war and of American weakness permeated domestic politics. And in 1980 Ronald Reagan was elected President, committed to a more confrontational approach with the Soviets in arms control, 'Third World' conflicts, and East–West relations in general.

1979–86: 'The second cold war'

The resulting period of tension and confrontation between the superpowers has been described as the **'second cold war'** and compared to the early period

Table 4.3 Revolutionary upheavals in the 'Third World', 1974–1980

Ethiopia	Overthrow of Haile Selassie	Sept. 1974
Cambodia	Khmer Rouge takes Phnom Penh	April 1975
Vietnam	North Vietnam/Viet Cong take Saigon	April 1975
Laos	Pathet Lao takes over state	May 1975
Guinea-Bissau	Independence from Portugal	Sept. 1974
Mozambique	Independence from Portugal	June 1975
Cape Verde	Independence from Portugal	July 1975
Sao Tome	Independence from Portugal	July 1975
Angola	Independence from Portugal	Nov. 1975
Afghanistan	Military coup in Afghanistan	April 1978
Iran	Ayatollah Khomeini installed in power	Feb. 1979
Grenada	New Jewel Movement takes power	March 1979
Nicaragua	Sandinistas take Managua	July 1979
Zimbabwe	Independence from Britain	April 1980

Source: Halliday F. (1986) *The Making of the Second Cold War* (Verso) 92.

of confrontation and tension between 1946 and 1953. In Western Europe and the Soviet Union there was real fear of nuclear war. Much of this was a reaction to the rhetoric and policies of the Reagan administration. American statements on nuclear weapons (see below) and military intervention in Grenada in 1983 and against Libya in 1986 were seen as evidence of a new belligerence. Reagan's policy towards Central America, and support for the rebel *Contras* in Nicaragua, was a source of controversy within the United States and internationally. In 1986 the International Court of Justice found the United States guilty of violating international law for the CIA's covert attacks on Nicaraguan harbours.

The Reagan administration's use of military power was nonetheless limited: the rhetoric and the perception were at variance with the reality. Some operations ended in humiliating failure, notably in the Lebanon in 1983. Nevertheless, there is evidence that the Soviet leadership took very seriously the words (and deeds) of the Reagan administration and believed that the US leadership was planning a nuclear first strike. In 1983 Soviet air defences shot down a South Korean civilian airliner in Soviet airspace. The American reaction and the imminent deployment of US nuclear missiles in Europe created a climate of great tension in East–West relations. And in November 1983 Soviet intelligence misinterpreted a NATO training exercise (codenamed *Able Archer*)

and led the Soviet leadership to believe that NATO was preparing to attack them. How close the world came to a serious nuclear confrontation in 1983 is not yet clear.

Throughout the early 1980s the Soviets were handicapped by a succession of ageing political leaders (Brezhnev, Andropov, and Chernenko) whose ill-health further inhibited Soviet responses to the American challenge and the American threat. This changed dramatically after Mikhail Gorbachev became President in 1985. Gorbachev's 'new thinking' in foreign policy and his domestic reforms created a revolution both in the USSR's foreign relations and within Soviet society. At home the policies of *glasnost* (or openness) and *perestroika* (or restructuring) unleashed nationalist and other forces which, to Gorbachev's dismay, were to destroy the Union of Soviet Socialist Republics.

Gorbachev's aim in foreign policy was to transform relations with the United States and Western Europe (on the latter, for example, see Box 4.3). His domestic reforms were also a catalyst for change in Eastern Europe, though unlike Khrushchev, Gorbachev was not prepared to respond with force or coercion. When confronted with revolt in Eastern Europe, Gorbachev's foreign ministry declared that countries of Eastern Europe were 'doing it their way' and invoked Frank Sinatra's song 'I did it my way' to mark the end of the **Brezhnev doctrine** which had

> ## Box 4.3 Mikhail Gorbachev's 1987 vision of European security
>
> 'We are firmly opposed to the division of the continent into military blocs facing each other, against the accumulation of military arsenals in Europe, against everything that is the source of the threat of war. In the spirit of the new thinking we advanced the idea of the "common European home" . . . [with] the recognition of a certain integral whole, although the states in question belong to different social systems and are members of opposing military-political blocs ranged against each other.'

limited Eastern European sovereignty and political development. The **Sinatra doctrine** meant that Eastern Europeans were now allowed to 'do it their way'. Throughout Eastern Europe Moscow-aligned regimes gave way to democracies, in what for the most part was a peaceful as well as speedy transition (see Chapter 5). Most dramatically, Germany became united and East Germany (the German Democratic Republic) disappeared.

Gorbachev's policy toward the West used agreements on nuclear weapons as a means of building trust, and demonstrating the serious and radical nature of his purpose. However, despite similar radical agreements on conventional forces in Europe (culminating in the Paris agreement of 1990), the end of the cold war marked success in nuclear arms control rather than the beginning of nuclear disarmament. The histories of the cold war and of the bomb are very closely connected, but while the cold war is now over, nuclear weapons are still very much in existence.

Key points

- There are disagreements about when the cold war started, why, and who was responsible.

- The cold war began in Europe with the failure to implement the agreements reached at Potsdam and Yalta.

- Distinct phases can be seen in East–West relations during which tension and the risk of direct confrontation grew and receded.

- Some civil and regional wars were intensified and prolonged by superpower involvement; others may have been prevented or shortened.

- The end of the cold war has not resulted in the abolition of nuclear weapons.

The bomb

Using the bomb in 1945

Nuclear weapons preceded and post-dated the cold war. The Western allies developed the atomic bomb in the war against Nazi Germany and Imperial Japan, and intended to use the weapon in much the same way as they had used strategic bombing against German and Japanese cities. The destruction of the Japanese cities of Hiroshima and Nagasaki was of great significance in post-war affairs, but, as Table 4.4 shows, the scale of the casualties and the extent of the devastation were not exceptional. The precise importance of Hiroshima and Nagasaki in post-war affairs remains a matter of continuing controversy. Aside from the moral issues involved in attacking civilian populations, the destruction of the two cities has generated fierce debate, particularly among American historians, about why the bomb was dropped. Gar Alperovitz in his celebrated book *Atomic Diplomacy*, first published in 1965, claimed that as President Truman knew that Japan was defeated his real reason for dropping the bomb was to coerce the Soviet Union to serve post-war American interests in Europe and Asia. Such claims generated angry and dismissive responses from other historians. Ensuing debates have benefited from

Table 4.4 Second World War estimated casualties

Hiroshima (6 August 1945): 70–80,000 'prompt'; 140,000 by end 1945; 200,000 by 1950

Nagasaki: (9 August 1945): 30–40,000 'prompt'; 70,000 by end 1945; 140,000 by 1950

Tokyo (9 March 1945): 100,000 +

Dresden (13–15 February 1945): 60–135,000

Coventry (14 November 1940): 568

Leningrad (siege 1941–4): 1,000,000 +

Sources: R. Rhodes, *The Making of the Atomic Bomb* (Harmondsworth: Penguin, 1986); Committee for the Compilation of Materials, *Damage Caused by the Atomic Bombs in Hiroshima and Nagasaki, Hiroshima and Nagasaki: The Physical, Medical, and Social Effects of the Atomic Bombings* (London: Hutchinson, 1981); M. Gilbert, *Churchill: A Life* (London: Heinemann, 1991).

more historical evidence, though this has only partially resolved the controversies. Inasmuch as a consensus now exists among historians it is that Truman's decision reflected various considerations. Debate remains about how far Truman dropped the bomb simply to end the war and how far other factors, including the coercion of the Soviet Union in post-war affairs, entered his calculations.

Whether Hiroshima and Nagasaki should have been destroyed nevertheless remains a matter for debate. So too is the question of what were the effects of their destruction. Whether the use of nuclear weapons demonstrated the awesome power of such weapons to post-war decision-makers and thereby inhibited their use, or whether by accelerating the development of the Soviet atomic bomb Hiroshima speeded up or even started the nuclear arms race are questions to consider.

Towards the global battlefield

The bomb that was dropped on Hiroshima was equivalent in destructive power to 12,500 tons of TNT. In 1952 the United States exploded a thermonuclear or hydrogen bomb, equivalent to 10,400,000 tons of TNT. Subsequent nuclear weapons were measured in this new megaton range, each capable of destroying the largest of cities in a single explosion. Equally significant was the development of the means to deliver them. In 1945 the American bomber that destroyed Hiroshima took some six

hours to cross the Pacific and reach its target. Initially the United States did not possess bombers that had the range to reach the USSR from the USA, and used British and other bases to hold at risk Soviet targets. Both superpowers developed long-range bombers, and then ballistic missiles that could target the other superpower each other from their own territory. In 1957 the USSR tested an Intercontinental Ballistic Missile (ICBM) and later that year launched a satellite, *Sputnik*, into space using such a missile. In 1960 the United States began deploying ballistic missiles on submarines. (For details of the technological arms race see Table 4.5)

By then the world was potentially a global battlefield in which both superpowers could strike each other's territory from their own, and in no more than the 30–40 minutes it took a ballistic missile to travel from one continent to the other. The global dimension was increased by the emergence of other nuclear weapon states—Britain in 1952, France in 1960, and China in 1964. In the 1950s there was growing concern at the spread or **proliferation** of nuclear weapons and in the 1960s a nuclear Non-Proliferation Treaty (NPT) was negotiated in which those states which had nuclear weapons committed themselves to halt the arms race, while those states who did not have nuclear weapons promised not to develop them. Despite the apparent success of the

Table 4.5 The nuclear technology race

Weapon	Date of testing or Deployment	
	USA	USSR
Atomic bomb	1945	1949
Intercontinental bomber	1948	1955
Jet bomber	1951	1954
Hydrogen bomb	1952	1953
Intercontinental Ballistic Missile	1958	1957
Submarine Launched Ballistic Missile	1960	1964
Anti-Ballistic Missile	1974	1966
Multiple Independently targetable Re-entry Vehicle	1970	1975

Source: R. McNamara, *Blundering into Disaster* (London: Bloomsbury, 1987), 60.

Table 4.6 The arms race: American and Soviet nuclear bombs and warheads
1945–1990

	1945	1950	1955	1960	1965	1970	1975	1980	1985	1990
USA	2	450	4,750	6,068	5,550	4,000	8,500	10,100	11,200	9,680
USSR	0	0	20	300	600	1,800	2,800	6,000	9,900	10,999

Sources: R. McNamara, *Blundering into Disaster* (London: Bloomsbury, 1987) 154–5; International Institute for Strategic Studies, *The Military Balance 1990–1991* (IISS, 1991). Soviet figures given here are based on Western estimates.

NPT agreement several states are known to have developed nuclear weapons (Israel, India, Pakistan, and apartheid South Africa) and others have invested considerable effort in doing so (Iraq and North Korea). There is also disquieting evidence that India and Pakistan came close to a nuclear confrontation in 1990.

Both the Soviet Union and United States also made some attempt to develop weapons that could shoot down incoming ballistic missiles and thereby provide defence against nuclear attack. These anti-ballistic missiles (ABMs) were technologically ineffective and both sides continued to rely on offensive nuclear weapons for their security. In 1972 an agreement was concluded which limited ABM defences to a token level. However in 1983 President Reagan cast doubt on the principles of this agreement by launching the Strategic Defense Initiative (SDI) (see below).

The growth in Soviet and American arsenals is often characterized as an arms race, though how far perception of the adversary and how far internal political and bureaucratic pressures caused the growth of nuclear arsenals is a matter for debate. For the United States, commitments to its NATO allies also provided pressures and opportunities to develop and deploy shorter-range ('tactical' and 'theatre') nuclear weapons. At the strategic (or long-range) level qualitative change was as significant as quantitative change. In particular, the fear that one side would have sufficient weapons of sufficient accuracy to destroy the other side's nuclear arsenal became a mutual fear. Robert Oppenheimer, one of the scientists who created the American atomic bomb, characterized the atomic age as like two scorpions trapped in a glass jar. The scorpions have no means of escape and no alternative but to threaten that which it would be suicidal to carry out. Yet the logic of what became known in the West as **Mutually Assured Destruction (MAD)** depended upon each side being able to destroy their adversary after being attacked. For much of the cold war both sides feared that the other was moving, or believed it was moving, to a position of meaningful superiority. What is clear is that ideas of MAD were of only limited relevance to the military force structures and strategies adopted by the superpowers.

The situation was further complicated by the differences in the attitude of the two superpowers. The Soviet Union was confronted first by a situation of American monopoly, and then by enduring US superiority. This was coupled with political encirclement and growing antagonism with a nuclear armed China. From the American side misperception of Soviet nuclear strength in 1950s was allied with concern about Soviet political ambitions. This was further complicated by US military and political commitments, especially to NATO, and its determination to use nuclear weapons against, and thereby to deter, Soviet aggression towards Western Europe. Even if a nuclear war could never be won, the policies and strategies of both superpowers, and of NATO, can be seen to be ambiguous on these critical issues.

Rise and fall of *détente*: fall and rise of arms control

How far the arms race was the result of mutual misperceptions, how far the unavoidable outcome of irreconcilable political differences are central questions. Some influential Americans believed that the Soviets were bent on world domination, which the

Table 4.7 Principal arms control and disarmament agreements

Country	Colonial state	Signed	Parties
Geneva protocol	Chemical weapons: bans use	1925	100+
Limited Test Ban Treaty	Bans atmospheric, underwater, outer-space nuclear tests	1963	100+
Nuclear Non-Proliferation Treaty	Limits spread of nuclear weapons	1968	100+
Biological Weapons Convention	Bans production/use	1972	80+
SALT I	Limits strategic arms*	1972	US/USSR
ABM Treaty	Limits anti-ballistic missiles	1972	US/USSR
SALT II	Limits strategic arms*	1979	US/USSR
Intermediate Nuclear Forces Treaty	Bans two categories of land-based missiles	1987	US/USSR
START1	Reduces strategic arms*	1990	US/USSR

* Strategic arms are long-range weapons
Source: adapted from Harvard Nuclear Study Group, 'Arms Control and Disarmament: What Can and Can't be Done', in F. Holroyd (ed.), *Thinking About Nuclear Weapons* (Open University, 1985), 96.

communist rhetoric of world revolution certainly encouraged. What is clear is that nuclear weapons provided the context and pretext for their more dangerous confrontations, most notably when the Soviet Union deployed nuclear missiles in Cuba in 1962. It is also clear that when political confrontation gave way to Soviet–American *détente*, agreements on nuclear weapons became the most tangible achievement of *détente*. Yet, just as *détente* was a way of managing East–West conflict, and did not resolve the basis of disagreement, so too, arms control was a means of regulating the growth of nuclear arsenals, not of eliminating them (see Table 4.6). On the other hand, critics argued, arms control served to legitimize the existence and growth of nuclear arsenals. Disarmament meant getting rid of weapons. While arms control was sometimes presented as a first step to disarmament it was more generally recognized as a means of managing nuclear weapons.

Yet just as *détente* collapsed in the 1970s, the achievements of the SALT (Strategic Arms Limitation Talks) process gave way to renewed conflict and debate over nuclear weapons. In the West, critics of *détente* and arms control argued that the Soviets were acquiring nuclear superiority. Some of these critics also urged that the United States should now pursue policies and strategies based on the idea that victory in nuclear war was possible. The election of Ronald Reagan to the American Presidency in 1980 was a watershed in Soviet–American relations. The period of the 'Second Cold War' marked a new phase in the political and nuclear relationship between East and West. One issue which Reagan inherited, and which loomed large in the breakdown of relations between East and West, was nuclear missiles in Europe. NATO's decision to deploy land-based missiles capable of striking Soviet territory, precipitated a period of great tension in relations between NATO and the USSR, and political friction within NATO. Reagan's own incautious public remarks reinforced perceptions that he was as ill-informed as he was dangerous in matters nuclear, though some of his arms policies were consistent with those of his predecessor, Jimmy Carter. On arms control Reagan was disinterested in agreements that would freeze the status quo for the sake of getting an agreement, and Soviet and American negotiators proved unable to make progress in talks on long-range and intermediate-range weapons. One particular initiative had significant consequences for arms control and for the USA's relations both with the Soviets and its allies. The **Strategic Defense Initiative** (SDI), quickly dubbed 'Star Wars', was a research programme designed to explore the feasibility of space-based defences against ballistic missiles. The Soviets appear to have taken SDI very seriously, and claimed that President Reagan's real purpose was to regain the nuclear monopoly of the 1950s. The technological advances claimed by SDI proponents did not materialize, however, and the programme was reduced and marginalized. A second debate has now emerged concerning possible limited US national as well as theatre defence against ballistic missiles, and has focused on concerns about the proliferation of weapons of mass destruction and the ballistic missiles capable of delivering them.

The advent of Mikhail Gorbachev paved the way for agreements on nuclear and conventional forces, which helped ease the tensions that had characterized the early 1980s. In 1987 Gorbachev travelled to America to sign the Intermediate Nuclear Forces (INF) Treaty banning intermediate-range nuclear missiles, including Cruise and Pershing II. This agreement was heralded as a triumph for the Soviet President, but NATO leaders, including Thatcher and Reagan argued that it was vindication of the policies pursued by NATO since 1979. The INF treaty was concluded more quickly than a new agreement on cutting strategic nuclear weapons, in part because of Soviet views on SDI. And it was Reagan's successor, George Bush, who concluded a Strategic Arms Reductions Treaty (START) agreement, which reduced long-range nuclear weapons (though only back to the level they had been in the early 1980s). By the time that a follow-on START-2 agreement was reached in 1992, the USSR had disintegrated. The collapse of the USSR meant that four nuclear weapons states were now created (Russia, Kazakhstan, Belarus, and Ukraine). Nevertheless, all the new states made clear their commitments to the treaty and to the new cordial relations with the West, which marked the end of the cold war. On the other hand, the disintegration of the Soviet Union has raised fears about the spread of nuclear technologies (and nuclear technologists). Moreover, the continuing proliferation of nuclear weapons raises the prospect of regional arms races and crises, such as when India and Pakistan are believed to have come close to nuclear confrontation in 1990. The end of the cold war may have reduced some nuclear problems. It may well have increased others. It has certainly not solved the problem of nuclear weapons.

Key points

- There remains a debate about the use of the bomb in 1945, and the effect that this had on the cold war.

- Nuclear weapons have been an important factor in the cold war. How far the arms race has had a momentum of its own is a matter of debate.

- Agreements on limiting and controlling the growth of nuclear arsenals have played an important role in Soviet–American (and East–West) relations.

- States with nuclear weapons have agreed on the desirability of preventing the spread of nuclear weapons to other states.

- Various international crises have occurred in which there has been the risk of nuclear war. Judging how close we came to nuclear war at these times remains a matter of debate.

Conclusion

The changes that have taken place in world politics since 1945 have been enormous. Assessing their significance raises many complex issues about the nature of international history and international relations. The question of who won the cold war, and how, and with what implications, are matters on which fierce controversy has been generated. Several points are emphasized in this conclusion concerning the relationship between the three trends explored in the chapter (end of empire, cold war, and the bomb). The period of history since 1945 has witnessed the end of European empires constructed before, and in the early part of, the twentieth century, and has also witnessed the rise and fall of the cold war. The end of the cold war has also been followed by the demise of one of the two principal protagonists in that conflict, the Union of Soviet Socialist Republics. The relationship between the end of empire and cold war conflicts in the 'Third World' is a close though problematic one. In some cases cold war involvement of the superpowers helped bring about change. In others, where the superpowers became directly involved it resulted in the escalation and prolongation of the conflict. Marxist ideology in various forms provided inspiration to many 'Third World' liberation movements, but provocation to the United States and others. The example of Vietnam is most obvious in these respects, but in a range of anti-colonial struggles the cold war played a major part. Precisely how the cold war influenced decolonization is best assessed on a case by case basis. One key issue is how far the values and objectives of revolutionary leaders and their movements were nationalist rather than Marxist. It is claimed that both Ho Chi Minh in Vietnam and Fidel Castro in Cuba were primarily nationalists who could have been won over to the West, but turned to Moscow and to communism in the face of American and Western hostility. The divisions between the USSR and the People's Republic of China also demonstrate the diverging trends within the practice of Marxism. In several instances conflict between communists became as bitter as conflict between communists and capitalists.

Similarly, the relationship between the cold war and the history of nuclear weapons is a close though problematic one. Some historians contend that the use of atomic weapons by the United States played a decisive part in the origins of the cold war. Others would see the paranoia created by the threat of total annihilation to be central to understanding Soviet defence and foreign policy: the unprecedented threat of devastation provides the key to understanding the mutual hostility and fear of both sets of leaders in the nuclear age. It is also argued that without nuclear weapons direct Soviet–American conflict would have been much more likely, and that had nuclear weapons not acted as a deterrent then war in Europe would have been much more likely. On the other hand there are those who contend that nuclear weapons have played a relatively limited role in East–West relations, and that in political terms their importance is exaggerated.

Nuclear weapons have been a focus for political agreement, and during *détente* nuclear arms agreements acted as the currency of international politics. How far and why nuclear weapons have helped keep the peace (if indeed they have) raises very important questions not only for assessing the cold war but for contemplating the proliferation of nuclear and other weapons of mass destruction into the twenty-first century. How close we came to nuclear war in 1961 (Berlin) or 1962 (Cuba) or 1973 (Arab–Israeli war) or 1983 (Exercise 'Able Archer') and what lessons might be learned from these events are crucial questions for historians and policy-makers alike. One central issue is how far cold war perspectives and the involvement of nuclear-armed superpowers imposed stability in regions where previous instability had led to war and conflict. The cold war may have led to unprecedented concentrations of military and nuclear forces in Europe, but this was a period characterized by stability and great economic prosperity, certainly in the West. How far this stability was bought at the risk of an ever-present danger of nuclear confrontation is a question historians are still exploring and debating.

Both the cold war and the age of empire are over, though across the globe their legacies, good and bad, seen and unseen, persist. The age of 'the bomb', and of other weapons of mass destruction (chemical and biological) continues. How far the clash of communist and liberal/capitalist ideologies helped facilitate and/or retard the process of globalization is a matter for debate. Despite the limitations of the human imagination the global consequences of nuclear war remain all too real. The accident at the Soviet nuclear reactor at Chernobyl in 1986 showed that radioactivity knows no boundaries. In the 1980s some scientists suggested that a only a fraction of the world's nuclear weapons exploded over a fraction of the world's cities could bring an end to life itself in the northern hemisphere. While the threat of strategic nuclear war has receded the global problem of nuclear weapons remains a common and urgent concern as humanity addresses the next millennium.

QUESTIONS

1 Was Harry Truman to blame for the collapse of the wartime alliance after 1945 and the onset of the cold war?

2 Why did the United States become involved in wars in Asia after 1945? Illustrate your answer by reference to either the Korean or Vietnam wars.

3 Did *détente* succeed?

4 Should Ronald Reagan or Mikhail Gorbachev claim the greater credit for the ending of the cold war?

5 Why did France try to remain an imperial power in Indo-China and Algeria?

6 What were the consequences of the collapse of the Portuguese empire in Africa?

7 Were the British successful at decolonization after 1945?

8 Compare and contrast the end of Empire in Africa with that in Asia after 1945.

9 Why were atomic bombs dropped on Hiroshima and Nagasaki?

10 Did nuclear weapons help prevent war in Europe after 1945?

11 How close did we come to nuclear war during either the Berlin crisis (1961) or the Cuban missile crisis (1962)?

12 What role did nuclear weapons play in Soviet–American relations during the 1980s?

GUIDE TO FURTHER READING

General

Calvocoressi, P., *World Politics since 1945* (London: Longman, 1991). Provides a comprehensive survey of the major developments in world politics from 1945 to 1990, including analysis of the relationship between the superpower confrontation and the 'Third World'.

Dunbabin, J. P. D., *International Politics since 1945*, i, *The Cold War: The Great Powers and their Allies*, and ii, *The Post-Imperial Age: The Great Powers and the Wider World* (London: Longman, 1994). This 2-volume work provides an analytical account of the principal events and developments in international politics since 1945. Vol. 1 focuses on the superpower conflict and the role of Europe in the cold war; vol. 2 covers decolonization, regional issues, and the new challenges facing the international system in later decades.

The cold war

Gaddis, J., *Russia, The Soviet Union and the United States: An Interpretative History* (New York: McGraw-Hill, 1990). Provides an overview of relations between Russia, then the Soviet Union, and the United States, and examines the different phases of the relationship, including the origins, dynamics, and end of the cold war.

Halliday, F., *The Making of the Second Cold War* (London: Verso, 2nd edn. 1986). Explores the phase in the cold war of Soviet–American antagonism, 1979–85, and places this in a broader thematic and historical analysis of the cold war.

The bomb

Lebow, R. N., and Stein, J. G., *We All Lost the Cold War* (Princeton: Princeton University Press, 1994). Provides a revisionist interpretation of the cold war which reassesses the role and risks of nuclear deterrence by detailed examination of two case studies: the Cuban missile crisis and the Arab–Israeli war of 1973.

Newhouse, J., *The Nuclear Age* (London: Michael Joseph, 1989). Provides a history of nuclear weapons which examines the technological and political dimensions of the arms race, from the use of the bomb at Hiroshima to the debates and issues of the 1980s.

Bird, K., and Lifschultz, L. (eds.), *Hiroshima's Shadow* (Stony Creek, Conn.: The Pamphleteer's Press, 1998). A wide-ranging collection of articles on the destruction of Hiroshima and Nagasaki, which provide comprehensive coverage of the military, political, ethical, and historiographical issues and debates about the use of atomic weapons in 1945.

Decolonization

Law, D. A., *Eclipse of Empire* (Cambridge: Cambridge University Press, 1993). This provides a detailed analysis of the British withdrawal from empire, and draws comparisons with other experiences such as the French in Africa and the Dutch in Indonesia.

WEB LINKS

http://cwihp.si.edu   Woodrow Wilson International Center for Scholars: Cold War International History Project.

5 The end of the cold war

Richard Crockatt

READER'S GUIDE

The end of the cold war represented a turning point in the structures of international politics, in the roles and functions of nation-states, and in international organizations. The chief cause of the end of the cold war was the collapse of communism in the Soviet Union and Eastern Europe. This had deep internal roots in the history of Soviet bloc societies but a full explanation of the end of the cold war must include examination of external pressures, particularly the policies of the United States, and growing relative economic disadvantage experienced by the Soviet bloc over the post-war period. Close attention is given in this chapter to the policies and personality of Mikhail Gorbachev but due emphasis is also given to historical and systemic factors in the international environment. Opinions on the implications of the end of the cold war have been varied and often conflicting, but by the turn of the millennium it was evident that the issue of globalization had replaced the characteristic cold war concerns with superpower bipolarity, the nuclear arms race, and ideology.

Introduction

Historical events do not come with labels upon them, telling us precisely how important they are. Only the passage of time can do that, and it may take years. Communist Chinese Prime Minister Chou En Lai is reported to have said, in reply to a question about the significance of the French Revolution, that 'it's too soon to tell'. Nevertheless, some events are sufficiently momentous in their immediate effects for us to be able to say with confidence that something important has happened, even if full explanations are as yet unattainable.

The events of 1989–91, from the collapse of the Iron Curtain to the dismantling of the Soviet Union in December 1991, represent a turning point in three respects. **First**, they marked the end of the broadly bipolar structure, based on US–Soviet rivalry, which the international system had assumed since the late 1940s.

A **second** set of important changes took place at the level of the nation-state. Former communist states experienced serious problems of transition, ranging from economic collapse, which affected them all, to (in the case of the Soviet Union, Czechoslovakia, and most explosively Yugoslavia) the disintegration of the state itself. Even those states which maintained communist systems, such as China, North Korea, and Cuba, faced enormous challenges, since they had to accommodate themselves to positions of increased marginality. Yet those states not in the throes of post-communist transition were also forced to redefine their national interests and roles in the light of the radical change in the international balance of power. This applied as much to large states such as the United States, whose policies had been premised on the Soviet threat, as to small states in the Third World which had been to a greater or lesser degree 'client' states of the superpowers. The general point is that the end of the cold war enforced a redefinition of national interests on all states and in some cases a reshaping of the states themselves.

The **third** important indicator of change in the end of the cold war lay in new or modified roles for international organizations. Most obviously the ending of the virtually automatic split in the United Nations (UN) Security Council along cold war lines, which had found the United Sates and the Soviet Union routinely using the veto against each other's proposals, released the potential for the UN to work as a genuinely collective body. The novel possibility of consensus on major issues in the Security Council did not ensure that the UN would act decisively or with authority—it was still a creature of the states which composed it and they continued to guard their national sovereignties—but it did remove one obstacle to collective decision-making and one which had crippled the UN during the cold war (see Ch. 17).

The end of the cold war also had an impact on various multilateral treaty organizations. The Warsaw Pact (or Warsaw Treaty Organization) was disbanded, while the North Atlantic Treaty Organization (NATO) struggled to reconceive itself in a context in which European security as a whole was being redefined. Questions too were raised about possible roles for other existing European security organizations such as the Western European Union (WEU) and the Conference on Security and Co-operation in Europe (CSCE). The European Union (EU) debated expansion of its membership to include nations from Eastern Europe. However tentative these gestures, however unrealized the ambition to create a new European and a new international order, the end of the cold war forced such questions on to the agenda (see Ch. 20).

In short, the end of the cold war saw radical change at the system level, at the level of the nation-state, and in international organizations. Domestic politics also underwent transformation, most obviously in those nations which overthrew communism but also in the United States, where to a considerable extent moral and cultural issues (such as drugs) displaced the ideological and security issues characteristic of the cold war agenda.

Before examining the causes and consequences of these transformations, two preliminary points must be made. The first has to do with what is meant by the term 'cold war'. It has been used in two distinct senses: first, in a narrow sense to refer to the years between the Truman doctrine (1947) and the Krushchev thaw of the mid-1950s, during which virtually unrelieved antagonism existed between the superpowers. To the extent that the open antagonisms of these years were reproduced later in, for example, the Kennedy years and the first Reagan administration, then the term cold war is also applied to these instances. The term refers to a certain kind of **behaviour**, characterized by open ideological confrontation. Such periods of cold war alternated with periods of *détente* (1953–60, 1969–75, 1985–9), during which negotiations and tension reduction were firmly on the agenda.

The second meaning of 'cold war', and the one which is adopted here, has to do with the **structure** rather than the behaviour of East–West relations. To the extent that key elements of that structure remained continuous throughout the post-war period, then cold war refers to the whole period from the late 1940s to the late 1980s. Viewed from this perspective, *détente* was part of the cold war rather than a departure from it, in that while there was behavioural change in periods of *détente*, the fundamental structure of US–Soviet relations remained constant. When we talk of the end of the cold war we therefore mean the end of that structural condition which was defined by political and military rivalry between the United States and the Soviet Union, ideological antagonism between capitalism and communism, the division of Europe, and the extension of conflict at the centre to the periphery of the international system.

A second preliminary point involves the relationship between the collapse of communism and the end of the cold war. On the face of it, they are one and the same thing. The **great game** of US–Soviet conflict ended when one of the competitors gave up the fight. However, while it is true that communism's demise was the proximate cause of the end of the cold war, it is wrong to suggest that it is to be wholly explained in these terms. In what follows we shall analyse the end of the cold war with reference to three sets of factors: (1) internal developments in the Soviet bloc; (2) external forces in the form of Western policies towards the Soviet bloc; and (3) the changing relative position of the Soviet

bloc with respect to the West. This will be followed by a discussion of the immediate global consequences of the end of the cold war. The chapter will end with some inevitably tentative ideas about possible futures.

Key points

- The end of the cold war was a major historical turning point as measured by changes in the international system, the nation-state, and international organizations.

- The term 'cold war' can refer both to the behavioural characteristics of US–Soviet relations, which fluctuated over the period 1945–89, or to the basic structure of their relations, which remained constant.

- The key structural elements of the cold war are political and military (above all nuclear) rivalry between the United States and the Soviet Union, ideological conflict between capitalism and communism, the division of Europe, and the extension of superpower conflict to the Third World.

- The collapse of communism was the proximate cause of the end of the cold war but does not explain all aspects of the transformation of international politics since 1989.

Internal factors: the collapse of communism in the Soviet Union

Structural problems in the Soviet system

Among the most striking features of communism's collapse was its suddenness, a surprise as much to most Western experts on the Soviet Union and Eastern Europe as to political leaders and the public. One Western Soviet expert, whose views are fairly representative, wrote in a study published in 1986, that 'it

is unlikely that the [Soviet] state is now, or will be in the late 1980s, in danger of social or political disintegration. Thus we must study the factors which made the regime stable in the post-Stalin era and are still at work at the present' (Bialer 1986: 19). It is true that revolutionary change by its nature contains a large element of the incalculable. Institutional inertia, social customs, and psychological habit ensure that systems can maintain their outer shapes long after they have begun to decay internally. Perhaps the most useful general observation on the causes of revolution remains that of the French political philosopher Alexis de Tocqueville: that 'the most dangerous moment for a bad government is generally that in which it sets about reform' (Tocqueville 1933: 186). This model, generalized as it is, is a useful starting point for an understanding of Mikhail Gorbachev's revolutionary period in power.

Gorbachev's accession to power in March 1985 was itself an event of considerable significance. He was the first General Secretary of the Soviet Communist Party to have reached maturity after the Second World War. He had little adult experience of the Stalinist period and was less beholden to the Stalinist legacy than his predecessors. He had been appointed to the ruling Politburo as recently as 1978 towards the end of the **era of stagnation** under Brezhnev. In projecting a new dynamism as a representative of the rising class of educated professionals, he presented a striking contrast to the ageing and intellectually stultified leaders of the Brezhnev period. His path to leadership was not immediate on Brezhnev's death. Following the latter's death in 1982 an interregnum ensued during which first Yuri Andropov and then Konstantin Chernenko were appointed and died in each case within little more than a year in office. The passing of the old guard, combined with Gorbachev's power base among advocates of change, which enabled him to make key changes in personnel, conveyed the sense that Gorbachev was inaugurating a new era in Soviet history.

Crucially, however, it was evidently not his intention to dismantle the Soviet Union. His widely read political credo, *Perestroika* (1988), was firmly anti-Stalinist but not anti-socialist. 'Through *perestroika* and *glasnost*,' he wrote, 'the ideals of socialism will gain fresh impetus'; and they would do so through a return to the ideals of Lenin, who 'lives on in the minds and hearts of millions of people' (Gorbachev 1988: 131; 25). Indeed the sense of renewal which Gorbachev projected did not seem to presage the end of the cold war. On the contrary, it was felt by many on the Right in the United States that a reinvigorated Soviet Union would present a more severe challenge to the West than the old sclerotic leadership.

How, then, are we to explain the transformation of the next few years? We can usefully distinguish between long-term and short-term causes. The chief

Box 5.1 Change in the Soviet Union

1985 March	On the death of Konstantin Chernenko, Mikhail Gorbachev becomes General Secretary of the Soviet Communist Party
1987	Publication of Gorbachev's book *Perestroika*.
1988 April	The Soviet Union undertakes to withdraw troops from Afghanistan by February 1989; in October Gorbachev becomes President of the USSR, replacing Andrei Gromyko.
1989 March	Elections held for the Congress of People's Deputies
1990 March	Congress of People's Deputies abolishes the leading role of the Communist Party; Lithuania declares independence from the USSR.
1991 Aug.	Coup against Gorbachev.
1991 Dec.	USSR ceases to exist and CIS (Commonwealth of Independent States) comes into being.

long-term problem was economic, though arguably it had political roots, in that economic policies and practices were dictated by political ideology. Structural weaknesses were built into the system of the command economy which relied on inflexible central planning, rewarded gross output of goods rather than productivity, and offered disincentives to innovation in management and production techniques. In place of a market relation between consumer demand and supply, from the late 1920s the centre dictated what kinds of goods should be produced and at what prices, according pre-eminence to heavy industrial production with a view to forced-marching the Soviet economy into the twentieth century. Arguably, this approach succeeded up to a point; the Soviet Union's ability to withstand Germany's onslaught in 1941 and ultimately to defeat the Third Reich owed a good deal to the brutal pace at which Stalin pushed the Soviet economy and the Soviet people in the 1930s. Such success came at

enormous human cost and at the cost of entrenching the primacy of heavy industry in Soviet economic thinking far beyond the point of utility. That
point was reached somewhere in the 1970s when the
computer and automation revolution overtook the
West but virtually bypassed the Soviet Union except
in the military sector. Even there the Soviet Union
found it hard to keep pace with the West (Dibb 1988:
266). Furthermore, agriculture was a notoriously
weak sector of the Soviet economy. In agriculture, as
in industry, central planning stifled productivity and
promoted inflexible practices.

These problems were **systemic** and of long standing. If so, why was the Soviet Union able to survive
so long and why did these problems become critical
in the 1980s? The answers to both questions have
political as well as economic components. Survival
was possible economically because, as mentioned
above, the Soviet economy performed well in certain
fields such as the production of heavy industrial
goods and military equipment. It also had large
reserves of oil which could be sold for hard currency.
Politically, the legacy of discipline and repression
supplied by the Communist Party served to stifle
dissent and more positively to promote an ethos of
collective sacrifice such as is undertaken by governments in wartime. Indeed, the Soviet system could
be described as essentially a war economy. As for the
question of why conditions became critical in the
1980s, economically, as we have seen, the failure to
modernize in line with the West was of paramount
importance. Furthermore, a serious decline in harvests in the late 1970s and a slow-down in production in some key industries suggested a general climate of economic stagnation. Commentary also
began to appear in the West during the early 1980s
on a decline in general health in the Soviet Union,
rising death rates and infant mortality rates
(Hobsbawm 1994: 472).

The effects of Gorbachev's reforms: *glasnost* and political restructuring

However, even these problems might not have been
critical, given the capacity of the Soviet system to
sustain itself despite handicaps. It took specific ini-

tiatives by Gorbachev to turn these systemic problems into a systemic crisis. The first of these initiatives was the decision to permit dissemination of
knowledge about the realities of Soviet life (*glasnost*
or 'openness'), the second and third were political
and economic restructuring (*perestroika*). Elements
of these programmes had been present in previous
reform efforts in the Soviet Union, for example during the Khrushchev period. If there was one element
which differentiated Gorbachev's approach from
that of his predecessors it was his conviction that
consent rather than coercion should, as far as
possible, guide implementation of these changes.

Glasnost was in one sense the old communist tradition of self-criticism writ large. The difference was
that *glasnost* was less purely ritualistic, less hedged
around with restrictions, and more open-ended than
the usual forms of self-criticism which took place in
the pages of *Pravda* and similar publications.
Designed to purify and cleanse rather than destroy,
to serve as a means of gaining public support for
Gorbachev's reforms rather than as a vehicle for
attacks on the system itself, *glasnost* quickly
exceeded the bounds set for it. Once controls on the
press, radio, television, and the film industry were
loosened, control of public opinion began to slip
from Gorbachev's grasp. (Indeed only now could
one begin to speak of public opinion in the Soviet
Union.) Freedom of expression gave a voice to those

Box 5.2 **Internal causes of the collapse of Soviet communism**

Long-term causes

- structural weaknesses in the economy, including:
- inflexible central planning system
- inability to modernize
- inefficiency and absence of incentives in agricultural production

Short-term causes

- economic stagnation in the 1970s and 1980s
- poor harvests in the late 1970s and early 1980s
- Gorbachev's political and economic reforms

who opposed Gorbachev as well as to those who wanted to go farther and faster than he did. While *glasnost* did not of itself create opposition parties, the logic of *glasnost* was ultimately to undermine the fundamental principle of the Party's leading role. Although the Party's privileged position, guaranteed by Article 6 of the Soviet Constitution, was not abolished until 1990, a sequence of reforms, culminating in major changes proposed at the 19th Party Congress in June 1988, effected a fundamental shift in the balance of political forces with the Soviet state. Perhaps it would be truer to say that in these reforms Gorbachev was acknowledging the existence of a newly emerging civil society distinct from the interest of the Communist Party and the government.

Gorbachev's major proposal was for a new legislature, only one-third of whose delegates would be reserved for the Communist Party and its affiliated organizations. The other delegates to the Congress of People's Deputies, as the new body was known, would be directly elected on the basis of popular choice. At a stroke, following the elections of 1989, the political system was transformed by the entry into public life of a mass of new participants, a large proportion of whom were not beholden to the Communist Party. Indeed huge numbers of Communist candidates were defeated. The first meeting of the Congress in May 1989 has been described as 'the most momentous event in the Soviet Union since the 1917 Revolution'. There took place 'a whirlwind of free debate that scattered every known communist taboo' (Roxburgh 1991: 135).

The other major element of political restructuring was the creation of an executive presidency, a post for which Gorbachev insisted he be allowed to stand unopposed. His aim was to maintain a grip on the direction of change, but it was inevitable that his critics, and even some of his supporters, should note the irony of a leader who preached democracy but claimed the right to stand above it himself. Arguably, however, Gorbachev's pursuit of reform from the top down, self-serving though it was, was both very much in the Russian/Soviet tradition and understandable in a country which was subject to growing splits. The erosion of the integrative force of the Communist Party transformed the dynamics of the political institutions at the centre but also threatened the structure of the Soviet Union itself.

> ## Box 5.3 Essentials of *glasnost* and *perestroika*
>
> ### Essentials of *glasnost* (openness)
>
> - promotion of principle of freedom to criticize
> - loosening of controls on media and publishing
> - freedom of worship
>
> ### Essentials of *perestroika* (restructuring)
>
> - new legislature, two-thirds of which was to be elected on the basis of popular choice (i.e. allowing non-communists to be elected).
> - creation of an executive presidency.
> - ending of the 'leading role' of the Communist Party.
> - Enterprise Law, allowing state enterprises to sell part of their product on the open market.
> - Joint Ventures Law, allowing foreign companies to own Soviet enterprises.

The collapse of the Soviet empire

A multi-ethnic, multilingual entity, composed of fifteen 'autonomous' republics and numerous subunits within them, the Soviet Union was in all but name an empire, held together by powerful central institutions, pressure for ideological conformity, and the threat of force. The Communist Party played a key role in each of these areas and the erosion of the Party's power released aspirations for freedom which had been suppressed but not destroyed by seventy years of Soviet rule. Demands for independence came in particular from the Baltic republics, Estonia, Latvia, and Lithuania, and from Georgia, but the power of example supplied by these movements affected virtually all the Soviet republics. A more tangled and bloody conflict arose in Azerbaijan, resulting from the desire of Armenians in Ngorny Karabakh (an Armenian region administered by Azerbaijan) for incorporation into the Soviet Republic of Armenia.

For the purposes of understanding the collapse of Soviet rule **two** points are important about these events:

1. The 'nationalities question' was evidently a blind spot of Mikhail Gorbachev's. He was noticeably unsympathetic to their demands and, though keen to maintain his credibility as a liberal by claiming that the more violent attempts to suppress nationalism in the republics had been undertaken without his orders, he insisted that Moscow could not countenance secession.

2. However, when faced with the reality of secessionist actions (above all in the Baltic republics), he was unwilling in practice to use the full force of Soviet military power to suppress them. The result was that Gorbachev succeeded in alienating both liberals, who argued that Russia should not stand in the way of independence movements, and conservatives, who saw in Gorbachev's concessions to nationalism a betrayal of the integrity of the Soviet Union.

During 1990 and 1991 Gorbachev oscillated between trying to satisfy conservatives and liberals. To the former he promised suppression of nationalism by force. Swinging to the latter in the early months of 1991, he announced a proposal for a new 'Union treaty' which would devolve power substantially to the Soviet republics. It was this move which provoked conservatives to mount the coup of August 1991, during which Gorbachev was held for several days in the Crimea, while Boris Yeltsin defied the coup plotters in Moscow and thus laid the basis for his subsequent career as President of Russia. The coup's failure did not, contrary to Gorbachev's hopes and expectations, restore his position and status in the eyes of the Soviet people, not least because it was felt that Gorbachev's indulgence of the Right had helped to make the coup attempt possible. Furthermore, Gorbachev seemed unaware of how far public opinion had moved under the stimulus of the movement he had set in motion. In a press conference on his return to Moscow after the coup, he continued to defend the Communist Party. He seemed clearly yesterday's man. Within a few months the logic of *perestroika* and nationalism was followed through with the dismantling of the Soviet Union and its replacement by a loose Confederation of Independent States (CIS).

Economic restructuring

Economic restructuring in a sense cannot be separated from politics since, as was suggested above, under the Soviet system economics like all areas of social life was subject to a political and ideologically derived rationale. Nevertheless, economic initiatives were important in their own right under Gorbachev, in that their goal was precisely to effect a separation of the economic from the political, or at least to go some way in that direction. Real changes began in 1987 with the legalization (within clearly specified limits) of private farming and business co-operatives. A year later the Enterprise Law granted limited freedom to managers of state enterprises to sell a proportion of their products on the open market rather than, as had been the practice, having to sell all of it to the government (Goldman 1992: 111–17).

In all these measures there was a partial move towards a free market or, more precisely, an attempt to straddle the gap between the stifling command economy and an incentive-led market system. In the sphere of foreign economic policy, a new law on Joint Ventures allowed foreign companies ownership of enterprises in the Soviet Union (initially 49 per cent and then, following amendment in 1990, 100 per cent). This was a huge innovation for an economy which had generally sought to insulate itself from capitalism. Such trade as had taken place with the West had been tightly controlled by the Ministry of Foreign Trade. Now individual companies could make their own arrangements (Hough 1988: 66–72).

The effect of these economic changes was catastrophic. The reforms managed to cut the ground from under the old system without putting in its place viable new economic mechanisms. State planning was in abeyance but there was no fully operating market mechanism in its place; price levels were inconsistent, some reflecting the input of government subsidies and some reflecting what consumers would pay. Inflation, shortages, and declining production were the harvest of five years of *perestroika* and *glasnost*. To these could be added rising crime rates, a sense of social disarray, and a general feeling of uncertainty about the future. By the time Gorbachev left office in 1991 much of the exhilaration which had attended the liberation from communist oppression had been expended. Destructuring perhaps inevitably proved easier than restructuring. That this was to remain a continuing problem is evident in the efforts of Gorbachev's successor, Boris Yeltsin, to make the transition to a market economy during 1992–3 by means of 'shock therapy', the result of which was rampant inflation (Phillips 2000: 123–8).

Key points

- The suddenness of the collapse of communism defied the predictions of experts.
- Gorbachev's accession to power represented the advent of a new generation in the Soviet leadership, though Gorbachev gave little indication early on that he would break the mould of Soviet politics.

- The Soviet Union suffered from systemic economic problems which were compounded in the 1980s by poor harvests and a failure to meet the challenge of the computer revolution.
- *Glasnost* began with relaxation of censorship which Gorbachev hoped to be able to control, but the process soon eluded his grasp as something approaching a genuine public opinion emerged.
- A combination of *glasnost* and political restructuring undermined the role of the Communist Party and ultimately the Soviet Union itself which by the end of 1991 had dissolved into separate republics.
- Economic restructuring had the effect of destroying the rationale of the old system without putting viable new mechanisms in its place.

The collapse of communism in Eastern Europe

The collapse of communism in Eastern Europe, marked most graphically by the destruction of the Berlin Wall in November 1989, was intimately related to events in the Soviet Union but also had roots of its own. The nations of Eastern Europe had experienced only forty years of communist rule as opposed to the seventy of the Soviet Union and in all cases except Yugoslavia had had communism imposed on them rather than choosing it themselves. The suddenness of communist collapse in Eastern Europe, the relative ease with which citizens shed the habits of forty years, suggests that those habits were to a considerable extent a matter of form. One important force which had held them in place since the late 1940s was the threat of Soviet intervention to reimpose orthodoxy should Eastern Europeans stray from the path set down for them. **Two** things therefore need explaining:

1. The sources of opposition in Eastern Europe to communist rule.
2. The Soviet Union's decision not to intervene to

check the uprisings which took place in the summer and autumn of 1989.

The legacy of protest in Eastern Europe

After Stalin's draconian imposition of Soviet rule between 1947 and 1953 Khrushchev had acknowledged the principle of separate paths to socialism, though within strict limits. In practice this meant that where socialism and the integrity of the bloc itself seemed at risk, as in the popular uprisings in Hungary in 1956 and Czechoslovakia in 1968, Moscow would act uncompromisingly. The crushing of the Czechoslovak revolt in August 1968 was justified on the principle of **'limited sovereignty'** for Eastern bloc nations (also known as the **Brezhnev doctrine**). Where, as in Poland in 1956 and 1980–1, indigenous leaders could be found to enforce Moscow's will, direct intervention could be avoided.

Box 5.4 Revolutions in Eastern Europe

1988

May   Janos Kadar replaced as General Secretary of the Czechoslovak Communist Party.

1989

Jan.   Hungarian parliament permits independent parties.

April   Ban on Solidarity in Poland repealed.

June   Elections in Poland won overwhelmingly by Solidarity candidates.

July   Solidarity invited by General Jaruselski to form coalition government.

Sept.   Hungary allows East German refugees to cross into Austria.

Oct.   Hungary adopts new constitution which guarantees multiparty democracy. East German leader Erich Honecker resigns and is replaced by Egon Krenz.

Nov.   3rd: Czechoslovakia opens border for Easteners seeking to go to the West. 10th: Berlin Wall dismantled; General Secretary of the Bulgarian Community Party, Zhivkov, resigns. 24th: Czechoslovak leadership resigns.

Dec.   6th: East German government resigns. 22nd: Ceausescu overthrown in Romania and executed (on the 25th).

Where, however, as in Romania and Albania, communism developed distinctively national forms but within the framework of rigid dictatorships, Moscow was prepared to tolerate, or at least grudgingly accept, a greater or lesser degree of detachment from Moscow. In the case of Albania, a small nation with no border with the Soviet Union, this went as far as alignment with China in the growing split between the Soviet Union and China. Romania under Ceausescu maintained a somewhat ambiguous relationship with Moscow and the Warsaw Pact, not unlike France's with NATO: political and military independence within the framework of broad bloc alignment. In short, the Eastern bloc was more diverse and potentially more fragile than the word 'bloc' would suggest.

In accounting for the events of 1989 it would be hard to overestimate the importance of the rise of **Solidarity** in Poland in 1980. Poland had always been critical to Moscow both because of its strategic position on the Soviet border and because of the legacy of hatred between the Poles and the Russians. Formed in the shipyards of Gdansk as a union of workers, Solidarity quickly assumed the status of a quasi-political body independent of the Communist Party, its membership comprising one-third of the Polish people. It called for a referendum on Polish membership of the WTO and on the principle of one-party rule. With alarm bells ringing furiously in Moscow, Soviet military intervention was forestalled only by the insertion of a new Polish leader, General Jaruselski, who was willing to do Moscow's bidding by declaring martial law and banning Solidarity. However, the difference from earlier instances of suppression of opposition was that Solidarity continued a thriving underground existence during the 1980s, while the Catholic Church carried on public opposition along lines laid down by Solidarity. Dissidence thus achieved momentum and extended beyond small groups of intellectuals.

Beyond Poland, though events were less dramatic, dissidence also had a history and gained some new stimulus from the development of organizations designed to monitor compliance of Eastern bloc governments with the human rights provisions of the Helsinki Accords, agreed at the Conference on Security and Co-operation in Europe (1975). Particularly important was **Charter 77** in Czechoslovakia. A similar group existed in Moscow itself. Though these organizations were hounded by the authorities, their members imprisoned and in some cases deported, they attracted enormous attention in the West and exerted some leverage over Soviet bloc governments. They were after all simply demanding that their governments make good the promises they had made on human rights in signing the Helsinki Accords. In this way the *détente* agreements proved to have important subterranean effects in the Soviet bloc.

Flowing directly from this point, and of crucial significance in accounting for the timing of the collapse of communism in Eastern Europe, was the demonstration effect of *glasnost* and *perestroika* in the Soviet Union. After 1985, above all in Poland and Hungary, while dissidents demanded the same—indeed more—from their governments as Gorbachev was giving to the Soviet people, the Eastern European leaderships were bereft of the instrument they had always been able to rely on in the past—the threat of Soviet intervention. By the middle of 1988 the opposition in Hungary had forced the removal of the Communist Party leader, Janos Kadar. In January 1989 General Jaruselski was forced to repeal the ban on Solidarity and hold elections. In the elections, which were won decisively by Solidarity, Jaruselski found himself being urged by Gorbachev to accede to a Solidarity-led government (Gati 1990: 167; Dawisha 1990: 155).

Gorbachev and the end of the Brezhnev doctrine

Why did Gorbachev abandon the **Brezhnev doctrine**? Doubtless there were many reasons, but the chief one was probably the recognition that suppression of change in Eastern Europe would have been totally inconsistent with his domestic reforms in the Soviet Union. His credibility at home, which was fragile enough once the economy began to fail, required that he endorse similar policies in the Soviet Union's 'internal empire', though it is doubtful that he foresaw the radically destabilizing effect which such changes would have on the governments of Eastern Europe. If reform in the Soviet Union was led from the top, at least initially, in Eastern Europe it had a popular base which immediately threatened the communist leaderships and created a revolutionary situation.

A further reason for Gorbachev's reluctance to enforce the Brezhnev doctrine was that he had made much in his speeches and writings of his vision of a **common European home** which would bring to an end the division of Europe. Again one wonders whether he foresaw that this would entail the end of communism; it is more likely that he envisaged a reformed and reinvigorated communist system pursuing moderate policies of genuinely peaceful coexistence with the West, expanded trade, and greatly increased contacts across the board. In any event, the logic of his non-interventionist position was to preclude direct Soviet control over the processes of change in Eastern Europe.

There were foreign policy considerations too in the policy of **laissez-faire** towards Eastern Europe. Retrenchment, in the form of withdrawal from the costly, increasingly unpopular, and futile intervention in Afghanistan (1979), was the order of the day rather than new ventures. Revision of military policy in line with **new thinking** in foreign policy generally (treated below in greater detail) ruled out the kind of aggressive and interventionist policies which had characterized the later Brezhnev years. Finally, Gorbachev could hardly expect to maintain good relations with the West, achieve arms agreements and improved trade terms if he was seen to be engaging in the suppression of freedom in Eastern Europe.

It was in these circumstances that governmental authority decayed in Poland and Hungary during the early months of 1989 and finally collapsed in all of Eastern Europe by the end of the year. Collapse was initiated by the removal of the security fence between Austria and Hungary, allowing thousands of East Germans to pass over the border and through to West Germany during September. Suddenly, with Hungary's connivance in this flight from East to West, the illusion of communism, which had been sustained by the Iron Curtain, evaporated. Efforts to check the process of collapse in East Germany, then Czechoslovakia and Bulgaria, by bringing in new leaders proved futile. Changes of personnel only delayed the inevitable briefly. The Berlin Wall was breached by demonstrators in November, opening up the possibility, which had been unthinkable for close to a generation, of German unification. In Czechoslovakia, in the face of massive popular protest, the government fell in November and Vaclav Havel, playwright and dissident, was elected President. Only in Romania did violence take place, as President Ceausescu's security police undertook a savage and short-lived attempt to defend his rule and destroy the popular opposition. By the end of December Ceausescu and his wife had been captured and executed. Only in Albania did communism linger on, but there too during 1990 the old leadership fell to the inexorable logic of events.

The manner of communist collapse in Eastern Europe suggested that their systems were both rigid and brittle and that they had relied on the ultimate threat of Soviet force to maintain their shapes. With that threat removed, the stimulus to change which had always been present was able to express itself.

Key points

• The end of communism in Eastern Europe was sudden but protest against communist rule was nothing new.

• The Soviet Union had always been forced to acknowledge the existence of national differences and desires for autonomy among Eastern European nations and had tried to maintain a balance between maintaining the integrity of the Soviet bloc and allowing some diversity.

• The Polish union Solidarity illustrated the deep currents of dissent, whose momentum was maintained even after the banning of the organization in 1981.

• A catalyst for the revolutionary process was Gorbachev's abandonment of the Brezhnev doctrine of limited sovereignty for Eastern Europe.

• Failure of the attempts by Eastern European leaders to stem the tide of revolution in 1989 by installing new personnel illustrated the degree to which the crisis of communism was systemic.

External factors: relations with the United States

Debate about US policy and the end of the cold war

Debate about who or what was responsible for ending the cold war began as soon as it had happened and quickly generated a large literature (see Hogan 1992). It became an issue in the US presidential election of 1992 (Kennan 1992; Pipes 1992). The Republican Party's claim, stripped to essentials, was that President Reagan's tough stance towards the Soviet Union, especially his refusal to compromise on the development of the Strategic Defense Initiative (SDI), had been decisive in forcing the Soviet Union to the negotiating table and subsequently bringing about the fall of communism itself. The United States had proved that it was prepared to outspend the Soviet Union, particularly in nuclear arms, thereby forcing the Soviet Union either to match the West and bankrupt itself or come to terms and negotiate real reductions in nuclear arms. Gorbachev chose the latter course, signalled by his signing of

the Intermediate Nuclear Forces (INF) Treaty in December 1987, by his unilateral reduction in conventional forces announced at the UN in 1988, and by progress towards the Strategic Arms Reduction Treaty (START) I, signed in 1991. Without these agreements, Gorbachev could not hope to fund his domestic renewal plans. Ultimately, it was argued, Reagan's policies, which built on the legacy of Truman's containment, brought Gorbachev and the Soviet Union to its knees.

There were **two** responses to this argument:

The **first** was to say, as did Raymond Garthoff, author of the most substantial analysis of the end of the cold war, *The Great Transition*, that the West did not win the cold war through geopolitical containment and military deterrence. Still less was the cold war won by the Reagan military build-up. Instead ' "victory" came when a new generation of Soviet leaders realized how badly their system at home and their policies abroad had failed. What containment did do was to successfully preclude any temptation by Moscow to advance Soviet

Box 5.5 **US–Soviet summitry 1985–1991**

1985 Nov.	Geneva Summit (Gorbachev–Reagan)
1986 Oct.	Reykjavik Summit (Gorbachev–Reagan)
1987 Dec.	Washington Summit (Gorbachev–Reagan) at which INF (Intermediate Nuclear Forces) Treaty is signed
1988 May-June	Moscow Summit (Gorbachev–Reagan)
1989 Dec.	Malta Summit (Gorbachev–Bush)
1990 May	Washington Summit (Gorbachev–Bush)
1991 July	START (Strategic Arms Reduction) Treaty signed in Moscow (Gorbachev–Bush)

Soviet–American diplomacy 1985–1991

It must be emphasized at the outset that Soviet–American relations did not change overnight on the accession of Gorbachev. On the American side deep scepticism prevailed towards Gorbachev until as late as autumn 1989. Despite the signature of the INF Treaty in December 1987, which was the first arms reduction as opposed to arms control treaty of the cold war period, progress was slow in other areas. Reagan was evidently inclined to reach arms agreements but not at the cost of what he considered to be essential elements of security. Bush took no initiatives towards the Soviet Union during the first nine months of his presidency (January–September 1989). Bush's Secretary of Defense, Richard Cheyney, remarked in May 1989 that he felt Gorbachev could easily fail with *perestroika* and be overthrown by hardliners. It was therefore dangerous to put much trust in Gorbachev (*Guardian* 3 May 1989: 26). Bush indicated that he did not share these views but they were evidently common in some government circles. It was only with the collapse of communism in Eastern Europe that the entire structure of East–West relations can be said to have changed.

Nevertheless, there was a qualitative difference in US–Soviet relations in the period between 1985 and 1989 as compared with the years which preceded it. As recently as 1983 Reagan had labelled the Soviet Union an evil empire. (Nor, incidentally, did he abandon this view, however much he moderated his public rhetoric later.) Furthermore, among his chief foreign policy priorities during his first term as president were a massive nuclear and conventional arms build-up and support for groups in the Third World—most notably the Contras in Nicaragua and the Mujaheddin in Afghanistan—which were opposing Soviet power or governments of what were taken to be Soviet client states. The Soviet Union for its part was heavily embroiled in Afghanistan and was assuming an intransigent stand on the issue of intermediate and theatre nuclear forces in Europe. The latter years of the Carter administration and Reagan's first term indeed represented what has been called the **second cold war** (Halliday 1983).

One important stimulus for change was the new

hegemony by military means' (Garthoff 1994: 753).

The **second** response to the Western triumphalist argument is the claim that Reagan's policies not only did not end the cold war but actually delayed its end. 'The Carter–Reagan build-up did not defeat the Soviet Union,' wrote Richard Ned Lebow and Janet Gross Stein, 'on the contrary it prolonged the cold war. Gorbachev's determination to reform an economy crippled in part by defense spending urged by special interests, but far more by structural rigidities, fuelled his persistent search for an accommodation with the West. That persistence, not SDI, ended the Cold War' (Lebow and Stein 1994: 37).

These two responses have in common a conviction that internal factors were primarily responsible for the end of the cold war. Neither discounts external pressures but they interpret them quite differently.

Was Reaganism of no account in the collapse of communism, as Garthoff claims, or was it an active hindrance, as Lebow and Stein argue? We can evaluate the significance of external pressures by looking at the record of diplomacy between 1985 and 1991.

philosophy of foreign affairs which Gorbachev brought to bear on US–Soviet relations. **New thinking** in foreign policy meant in the first place acknowledging that in an age of weapons of mass destruction, against which there was no reliable defence, security could not be achieved by amassing more and more weapons. Achieving security was a political rather than a military task and could be undertaken only in co-operation between the contending parties. Recognition of **common security** interest, of interdependence, and of common global challenges replaced the traditional Soviet assumption of the inevitability of conflict between capitalism and communism. Associated with this revision of Soviet orthodoxy was the military doctrine of **reasonable sufficiency** which involved an explicit renunciation of aggressive motives and enabled the Soviet leadership for the first time to contemplate asymmetrical cuts in troops and weaponry. Without this change in philosophy the INF Treaty could not have been signed, since it involved the abandonment of principles—such as the insistence that the British and French nuclear deterrents be considered in conjunction with American weapons—which had been integral to the Soviet negotiating position since the 1960s.

In other areas of foreign policy too concession seemed the order of the day. In August 1989 it was announced that Soviet troops would be withdrawn from Afghanistan. During the following year in a speech to the United Nations Gorbachev restated his new foreign policy doctrines and added a commitment to nuclear disarmament by the year 2000 and a unilateral reduction of Soviet armed forces by 500,000 (White 1990: 159–61; Oberdorfer 1992: 316–19). There can be little doubt, first, that Gorbachev had indeed abandoned principles and practices which had been integral to Soviet policy until the 1980s and, second, that these concessions were responsible in large part for the sea-change in US–Soviet relations during these years.

It seems clear also that Reagan's refusal to move on SDI and other issues faced Gorbachev with the choice of either failing to reach any agreement or making concessions in order to reach agreements. Even if, as some claim, Reagan's intransigence initially delayed agreements, Gorbachev seems to have calculated that the further forward he went with domestic *perestroika* the less flexibility he had in foreign policy. To that extent, Reagan's maintenance of a hard line on key issues did have the effect of forcing concessions from the Soviet Union.

That is not the whole story, however. Movement was not all one way, nor did all the advantage in these agreements lie with the United States. On the critical question, for example, of Gorbachev's decision not to make Soviet agreement to the INF Treaty conditional on abandonment of SDI, Gorbachev evidently recognized that SDI was a politically contentious issue in the United States and that he had more to gain by moderating his position. This proved to be the case, since following signature of the INF Treaty the American Congress moved to limit funds for SDI. Furthermore, the issue of verification of the Treaty was as problematic for the American military as for the Soviet military, both of whom harboured deep suspicions of intrusive verification regimes. Most significant, however, was the character of Ronald Reagan, whose stance on nuclear weapons was more complex and contradictory than his most aggressive public statements would suggest.

We have to reckon with a Reagan who came close at the Reykjavik summit of 1986 to agreeing with Gorbachev to the establishment of a nuclear-free world, who regarded SDI, with evident sincerity, as a wholly peaceful (because **defensive**) initiative which would render offensive weapons redundant once both sides were supplied with it, and who above all, again with evident sincerity, had a visceral hatred of nuclear weapons and an equally strong desire to be rid of them. Reagan had never really subscribed to the theory of nuclear deterrence and its associated concept of Mutually Assured Destruction (MAD). On a visit to the US nuclear command centre in 1980 he had been shocked to discover that the centre could be destroyed by a direct hit from a Soviet missile. Hence his determination to promote the development of SDI. In short, like many on the left, but for quite different reasons, Reagan had emancipated himself to a degree from inherited nuclear doctrines. He was not prepared to give ground unilaterally or put American security at risk. Indeed he had shown during his first term that he was willing to commit vast new sums of money to American defence. However, he was in many respects bolder in seeking arms agreements (or more foolhardy, as some of his critics suggested) than many of his advisers who had been schooled in the orthodoxy of nuclear deterrence. Besides, it was easier for a known conservative to reach agreements with the Soviet Union than for a liberal. Richard Nixon's promotion of *détente* was another example. Since there could be no doubt about their Americanism and commitment to anti-communism, they had a freedom to reach accommodations with the Soviet Union which would have been the object of deep suspicion if they had been made by liberals.

The conclusion must be that, while the main story is of Soviet concessions to the United States, there was some movement on the American side too. Reagan's signature of the INF Treaty was not without political risks. The Treaty encountered considerable opposition from conservatives in the United States and from some European leaders too who felt that it represented a reduced American commitment to the nuclear defence of Europe. The departure from the Reagan administration during his second term of well-known foreign policy 'hawks'—among them Defense Secretary Weinberger and Assistant Secretary of Defense Richard Perle—demonstrates a mellowing of policy towards the Soviet Union as compared with the years 1981–5. There was thus an element of interaction between the Reagan administration and the new leadership in the Soviet Union, which casts doubt on those explanations of the end of the cold war which see it as a simple either-or:

either Reagan's policies were the catalyst or Gorbachev's policies were wholly responsible.

Key points

- Opinion about the American role in ending the cold war has tended to polarize: either the Reagan hard line forced the Soviet Union to its knees or Reagan's policies were immaterial or actually served to prolong the cold war.

- Soviet–American relations did not change overnight with the advent of Gorbachev. The United States responded cautiously to his initiatives.

- Gorbachev's new thinking in foreign policy overthrew the conventional wisdom of Soviet foreign policy.

- Gorbachev's concessions, which helped to produce the INF Treaty and generally improve the climate of Soviet–American relations, were promoted initially in a controlled fashion but tended to become more unilateral and sweeping as the pace of domestic reform quickened.

- The story is not simply one of Soviet concessions. The United States made some significant movement too, indicating that a polarized interpretation of the end of the cold war is too simple and schematic.

The interaction between internal and external environments

Isolation of the communist system from the global capitalist system

The end of the cold war is not to be explained only in terms of specific decisions or policies of the superpowers. There are some factors which are given in the underlying conditions of the relationship between East and West. The most important of these

was the isolation of the Soviet Union and the communist bloc from the modernizing current of capitalism. Initially, communist doctrine had held that the success of the Bolshevik Revolution could only be guaranteed by the spread of revolution, preferably throughout the world but in any event to the developed nations of Europe. When this did not happen in the years immediately following 1917 Stalin invented the doctrine of socialism in one country to justify the restriction of the Revolution to Russia. The subsequent extension of communism to Eastern Europe, China, North Korea, and Cuba after the Second World War was in theory a stepping-stone to world revolution but in practice the advance of communism coincided with the expansion of world capitalism in what Eric Hobsbawm has called 'the golden years' (Hobsbawm 1994). The clash of these two processes, of course, gave the cold war its global character during and after the 1950s (see Ch. 4).

For our purposes the most important feature of these developments was the continued separation of the communist and capitalist blocs, a symbol of which was the Soviet Union's refusal to participate in the US Marshall Plan for post-war reconstruction (1948–52). The Soviet Union believed, with justification, that the conditions for participation demanded by the United States, which involved opening the Soviet bloc to Western investment and hence to Western economic and political leverage, would undermine the autonomy of the Soviet system and leave it at a disadvantage with respect to the West. Nor did the decision to undertake separate development initially seem to harm the Soviet bloc. During the 1950s Soviet growth rates actually exceeded those of all the capitalist nations except West Germany and Japan (Munting 1982: 132, 137; Van der Wee 1987: 50). Clearly this was from a low starting point and barely hid structural weaknesses in industrial production and agriculture. Nevertheless, the gross figures were impressive, and the launch of Sputnik in 1957 ahead of the US space satellite programme appeared to suggest considerable dynamism in the Soviet economy, sufficient at least to offer a real military threat to the West. Khrushchev announced in 1960 that he expected the Soviet economy to out-produce the United States within ten years and there were many in the West across the political spectrum who believed him.

From the perspective of the end of the cold war, the West's anxiety in the 1950s and early 1960s looks misplaced. We know that Soviet growth rates slowed in the 1960s and fell sharply in the 1970s and 1980s, and that the Soviet leadership's motive for détente with the West in the 1970s was in part to gain imports of 'high tech' goods in recognition of the Soviet Union's increasing backwardness. The key conclusion to be drawn is that the Soviet bloc suffered not merely from low levels of growth and productivity in absolute terms but from increasing **relative** disadvantage with respect to the West. The world was changing around the Soviet bloc, bearing out Trotsky's prediction (considered heretical by Stalin in the late 1920s) that a Soviet island of communism could not survive in a capitalist sea.

Crucially too, Soviet bloc efforts to develop fuller trade links, greater travel opportunities and cultural exchanges with the West exposed the vulnerability of communism to Western economic and cultural influence rather than strengthening it. Economically this was manifested in the debts owed by such nations as Poland and Hungary to Western banks. Culturally, citizens of Eastern Europe were increasingly able to make comparisons between their own lives and those lived in the West. West German TV, for example, was widely viewed in East Germany and Czechoslovakia; Radio Free Europe and similar stations beamed their programmes to the Eastern bloc. One must also take account of the growth of the trans-European peace movement in the 1970s, which linked anti-nuclear and pro-democracy forces on both sides of the Iron Curtain. While there is dispute about how far such pressures influenced government policies in the West, it is plausible to assume that they helped to generate the ferment in Eastern Europe (Thompson 1990; Kaldor 1995). In short, isolationism and economic autarky (separate development in isolation from world trade), which had arguably fostered growth and ideological cohesion in the Eastern bloc in the early post-war period, later became a liability and was ultimately impossible to sustain.

It is helpful to view the cold war as having been composed of two distinct but overlapping systems:

1. A **cold war system** which was defined by US–Soviet antagonism, the nuclear stand-off, and the extension of these central conflicts to the periphery of the international system.

2. The **global capitalist system** which was defined by the expansion of production and trade and growing economic interdependence.

The Soviet Union's existence was defined and limited by the cold war, while the United States was a full, indeed the chief, participant in the growth of world capitalism. However great the United States' economic problems from the 1970s onwards—and they were considerable—they were not such as to produce the disabling crisis of political legitimacy experienced by the Soviet Union. One way of putting this is to say that the United States was never wholly consumed by the cold war, politically or economically. By contrast, the Soviet Union, limited as it was by ideology and history to a debilitating isolationism, was unable to meet the challenge posed by the globalization of the capitalist political economy and Western consumer culture (Crockatt 1995: 370–1).

Key points

- The causes of the end of the cold war are to be found not only in internal and external conditions considered separately but in the interaction between the two.

- The separation of the communist bloc from capitalism, though not apparently disadvantageous to communism until the 1970s, left it at an increasing relative disadvantage to the capitalist West.

- Growing consciousness of relative disadvantage was a factor in the collapse of communism.

Conclusion

The end of the cold war removed more or less at a stroke the **structural** and **ideological** conditions which underlay superpower conflict over the previous forty years. This in itself seemed to promise a general relaxation of tension and a reduction in the threat of major, especially nuclear, war. To the extent that superpower conflict lay behind regional conflicts in various parts of the world, then the end of the cold war held out the possibility of resolution of these conflicts. On the most optimistic reading, conditions were now present for a new world order in which American power, in concert with other members of the UN Security Council, would serve as a global stabilizer. One writer, expressing the triumphalism which characterized some early American reactions to the end of the cold war, talked of a 'unipolar moment' (Krauthammer 1990–1). The Gulf War of 1991 was taken by some to be the model for a new type of collective international action in which the UN, with strong US backing, would act as its founders had intended as a genuine collective security organization. Beyond this, the end of the cold war would bring a 'peace dividend' both financial and political. Nations could now afford to expend fewer resources on military and foreign policy, and devote it to domestic growth.

At the opposite extreme was the view that the cold war had served to stabilize international politics, that indeed it had fostered the **long peace** of the post-war years, defined as the absence of war between the major powers (Gaddis 1986). From this perspective the end of the cold war was therefore a destabilizing event, however much one might welcome the collapse of communism. The most pessimistic predictions were of chaos and violence in the successor states of the Soviet Union and Eastern Europe, as long-suppressed national and ethnic forces achieved expression, and a general rise in global instability (Mearsheimer 1990).

There is little point in attempting to draw up a simple balance sheet between these two positions, since both optimists and pessimists could find evidence to support their contentions. Each new development in international politics contained potentially positive and negative tendencies and events moved swiftly in the decade following the end of the cold war. It is more appropriate to ask how the end of the cold war affected the broad environment in which international conflict took place. More specifically, what principles of order, if any, now underpinned the international system?

In the immediate aftermath of the end of the cold war, analysts tended to focus on the disappearance of cold war structures and agendas. Ideas about possible futures of the international system, as outlined above, were initially either vague or reflective of assumptions born in the cold war. As the dust settled from the cold war, however, a number of possible ways of describing the new realities, not all of them mutually exclusive, emerged. Some envisaged multipolarity based either on three major economic blocs—North America, especially after the signing of the North American Free Trade Association (NAFTA) in 1993, the European Union, and East Asia—or on a larger number of dominant powers (Rusi 1997; Kegley and Wittkopf 1999) while others favoured 'unipolarity', based on the dominance of the United States in the international system. George Bush's 'new world order' promised a Wilsonian scheme of internationalism, based (like Woodrow Wilson's) on the assumption of strong American backing for mechanisms for settling international disputes, preventing aggression, securing international justice. If this concept lasted for only a short time, it was because it was so closely associated with prosecution of the Gulf War. The ambiguous outcome of the war, which raised a host of questions about the motives and effects of the UN-backed coalition's intervention in Iraq and left Saddam Hussein in power, failed to substantiate the claims made for the 'new world order'. Nevertheless, discussion of developments in global 'governance', at the core of which lay the UN and its associated institutions, suggested an increasing role for internationalist ideas and institutions (Halliday 1999: 121–4).

Undoubtedly, as the new millennium approached, the most discussed paradigm for the post-cold war international order was 'globalization'. Its attractiveness lay in its ability to encompass at once **processes**, especially transnational exchanges of information, goods, and finance, and **structures**, including those based on relations between non-governmental organizations as well as nation-states. Furthermore, globalization could be shown to have had a history and to that extent it could be employed to link the period of cold war with what preceded it and followed it (Clark 1997). Finally, globalization could be linked to the central question of the role of the United States in the post-cold war world since the United States was the most globalizing of all world powers in the extent of its economic, cultural, political and military reach.

In the early 1990s, estimates of the United States varied greatly. Despite the prevalence of 'triumphalists' such as Charles Krauthammer (1990–1) and Francis Fukuyama (1992), the influence of 'declinists' such as Paul Kennedy (1998) remained strong

and he was joined by other interpreters from across the political spectrum, including Samuel Huntington (1993 and 1996). To many observers, 'winning the cold war' did not remove the challenges to American power from rival economies such as Japan's or (in Huntington's interpretation) from cultural antagonists in the form of the Muslim world. In the second half of the 1990s, however, the combination of crisis in the Asian economies and a sustained boom in the United States economy led to a revised assessment of the United States and of its role in international politics. While some observers asked 'whatever happened to the Pacific century?' (Foot and Walter 1999) others noted that the 'American century' (announced in 1941 by Henry Luce) was far from over. Whether the American century was to be praised or deplored was scarcely the issue, wrote one American scholar of the left. The fact was that 'American standards of all kinds are the standard of globalization' (Cumings 1999: 294).

Given the potential speed of chance in international politics, it could not be assumed that this state of affairs would continue indefinitely, not least because globalization inspired opposition as well as endorsement. Indeed, as long as globalization proceeded, it was likely that fragmentation and other countervailing processes would also exert some force (Clark 1997). As for the cold war, it seemed now firmly to be part of history.

Key points

- The end of the cold war offered grounds for both pessimistic and optimistic speculation.

- Both the above approaches could find evidence for their contentions in the varied and conflicting tendencies in post-cold war international developments.

- The novelty of the post-cold war international system lay not in the existence of instability and conflict but in the environment in which conflict took place.

- In the aftermath of the cold war, globalization and the future of the United States were considered by many scholars to be closely linked, though countervailing processes to both could be expected to develop.

Box 5.6 Key concepts

Brezhnev doctrine: the idea of 'limited sovereignty' for Soviet bloc nations, which was used to justify the crushing of the reform movement in Czechoslovakia in 1968.

Civil society: the network of social institutions and practices (economic relationships, family and kinship groups, religious and other social affiliations) which underlie strictly political institutions. For democratic theorists the voluntary character of the above associations is taken to be essential to the workings of democratic politics.

Common European home: Gorbachev's concept (associated with his New Thinking in foreign policy) of the essential unity of Europe and of the need to overcome the 'artificiality and temporariness of the bloc-to-bloc confrontation and the archaic nature of the "iron curtain"'.

Evil empire: Reagan's term, used in a speech of 1983, to describe the Soviet Union.

New thinking: the general label given by Gorbachev to his reforms in domestic and foreign policy.

Pax Americana: Latin phrase (literally American peace, adapted from Pax Romana) implying a global peace dictated by American power.

Reasonable sufficiency: Gorbachev's term (associated with his New Thinking in foreign policy) for a defence policy which relied on the minimum necessary level of weaponry consistent with national security, and designed to overcome the spiralling dynamics of the nuclear arms race.

Separate paths to socialism: Khrushchev's acknowledgement of the existence of diversity in the Soviet bloc and of the validity (within strict limits) of separate routes to the common socialist goal.

Socialism in one country: Stalin's term used to justify the Soviet Union's departure from the orthodox Marxist view that socialism in the Soviet Union could succeed only in conjunction with socialist revolutions in advanced industrial nations.

QUESTIONS

1 Does an examination of the end of the cold war help in understanding how systemic change occurs in world politics?

2 What do you think Gorbachev hoped to achieve through *glasnost* and *perestroika*?

3 What are the connections between change in the Soviet Union and the revolutions in Eastern Europe?

4 Why did changes of leadership in Eastern Europe in the summer and autumn of 1989 fail to stem the collapse of communism?

5 Can you find ways, other than those presented in this chapter, of conceptualizing the relationship between external and internal causes of the collapse of communism in the Soviet Union?

6 Did the West 'win' the cold war?

7 What role, if any, did the Reagan administration play in bringing about the end of the cold war?

8 Why did experts by and large fail to anticipate the collapse of communism?

9 Is the post-cold war international system more unstable than the cold war international system?

10 What ordering principles, if any, operate in post-cold war international politics?

11 Can communism be regarded as a victim of the 'globalization of world politics'?

GUIDE TO FURTHER READING

The fullest international history of the end of the cold war is R. Garthoff, *The Great Transition: American-Soviet Relations and the End of the Cold War* (Washington, DC: Brookings Institution, 1994) but D. Oberdorfer, *The Turn: From the Cold War to a New Era* (New York: Touchstone Books, 1992) is a highly intelligent, readable, and comprehensive journalistic account. Michael Beschloss and Strobe Talbott, *At the Highest Levels: The Inside Story of the End of the Cold War* (Boston: Little Brown, 1993) gives a blow-by-blow account of the high politics of the years 1989–91. A range of viewpoints is contained in M. Hogan (ed.), *The End of the Cold War: Its Meaning and Implications* (Cambridge: Cambridge University Press, 1992). Long perspectives can be gained from E. Hobsbawm, *Age of Extremes: The Short Twentieth Century, 1914–1991* (London: Michael Joseph, 1994) who presents the end of the cold war in the light of the twentieth century as a whole, and R. Crockatt, *The Fifty Years War: The United States and the Soviet Union in World Politics* (London: Routledge, 1995) who covers US–Soviet relations from 1941 to 1991.

On the collapse of communism in the Soviet Union a good place to start is with two books by journalists: A. Roxburgh, *The Second Russian Revolution* (London: BBC Publications, 1991) and David Remnick, *Lenin's Tomb: The Last Days of the Soviet Empire* (London: Viking, 1993). M. Goldman, *What Went Wrong with Perestroika* (1992) is good on economic issues. A comprehensive and scholarly account is Mike Bowker, *Russian Foreign Policy and the End of the Cold War* (Aldershot: Dartmouth Publishing Company 1997). Eastern European developments are well covered in C. Gati, *The Bloc that Failed: Soviet-East European Relations in Transition* (Bloomington: Indiana University Press, 1990), K. Dawisha, *Eastern Europe, Gorbachev and Reform: The Great Challenge* (Cambridge: Cambridge University Press, 1990). On the American side see John L. Gaddis, *The United States and the End of the Cold War: Implications, Reconsiderations, Provocations* (New York: Oxford University Press, 1992).

WEB LINKS

http://cwihp.si.edu   The Cold War International History Project disseminates new information and perspectives on the history of the cold war.

6 International history since 1989

Michael Cox

READER'S GUIDE

This chapter examines the main historical trends in the period following the end of the cold war in 1989 and the collapse of the USSR two years later in 1991. It begins with a simple historian's warning—that the world may have changed much less than some analysts seem to believe—before going on to look at the different ways in which writers from three schools of thought (liberal, realist, and radical) have sought to understand the dynamics and the contradictions of the international system after communism. It then tries to relate these very different 'grand' theories to the real world by looking at the following developments: the triumph of capitalism as a world organizing principle, the renewal of US hegemony, the decline of post-communist Russia, the rise of China, the Asian-Pacific crisis, the limits of European power and the still enormous gap that exists between the relatively rich North and the still very poor South. It concludes with a brief discussion around the question: whatever happened to war after the cold war?

Introduction

The images which stick in our mind most reveal a lot about the way we think: and perhaps no image or images sticks in our mind as much as those inspired by the events of 1989 when official communism collapsed in Eastern Europe, to be followed two years later by the collapse of the USSR. These extraordin- ary and most unanticipated upheavals not only changed the world as we had hitherto known it, but made possible the creation of what seemed to be a new **international system**. Historians will no doubt continue to dispute why the cold war came to an end—was it American pressure that caused the demise of Soviet power, or did the Soviet system confront insoluble problems of its own? Many will also continue to ask why the so-called experts failed to predict some of the most fundamental shifts in the whole of the twentieth century. But there is no disputing the simple fact that in the space of two to three years all of our standard signposts were either uprooted or turned round to point the other way. Little wonder there was so much confusion and disarray—as well as a good deal of optimism too—about the collapse of the bipolar world we had lived in for the better part of forty years.

In this chapter we shall try to make sense of history after 1989 not by citing one event after another, but rather by looking for the main trends. This should not only allow us to think more conceptually about what happened after the cold war, but to reflect about the future as well—something which social scientists and students of world politics have rarely managed to do with any great degree of success. Let us begin however with two words of warning.

The first is that while the world is now a very different place to what it was when there were two superpowers espousing two sets of clearly opposed ideologies, there are important ways in which the world might be said not to have changed very much at all. The international system may have altered dramatically because of what took place in 1989 and after; but that does not mean the world order that

has come into existence bears no resemblance at all to what existed before (see Ch. 30). Indeed, a number of historians (possibly the majority) would insist that much less has changed than many commentators have suggested. America after all still remains very powerful; Europe continues along the path of integration; the **North–South divide** has not disappeared; and wars continue to blight the new international landscape. Even the international institutions we rely on to manage our global affairs are very much the same: NATO, the International Monetary Fund, the World Bank, and the various European bodies based in Brussels and Strasbourg, were established long before the cold war came to an end, and continue to play a vital role.

This leads us to file a second warning: that although some of the world's key problems might appear to be the product of new times, several—the Gulf War, state breakdown in Yugoslavia, nuclear proliferation and the continuing disintegration of Afghanistan—are very much connected to the end of the cold war and the consequences thereof. Thus when analysts suggest that we live in a **post-cold war era**, they do not mean this just in terms of chronological time but imply something else as well: that many (though not all) of the unsolved dilemmas facing humanity can themselves be traced back to what transpired because of 1989. To this extent, the world is still very much a prisoner of the past, and we might suggest that it is the complex interaction between the past and the present, between the problematic legacy of history and new emerging forces that are shaping our international system. This is what makes the study of the post-cold war years so interesting, so difficult to understand, and even harder to predict.

Box 6.1 **Getting it right: getting it wrong**

'Who called the East Asian crisis? Or the collapse of the Soviet Union? Yugoslavia's demise or Mexico's crash? Japan's swift transformation from global economic powerhouse to financial wreck? No one. A theory's value is proportional to its predictive power. As these examples illustrate, the theories we bank to interpret world affairs, or that heads of governments and corporations use to guide their decisions, sometimes fall flat. Indeed, the flood of events that have caught the experts by surprise in recent years has heightened awareness about the poverty of the theoretical apparatus at our disposal'.

(Moises Nam, Editor, *Foreign Policy* (Spring 1998), 9).

Key points

- Most experts failed to anticipate the end of the cold war.
- There is no agreed view about why the cold war came to an end.
- The world after 1989 may be less different than certain pundits assume.
- Many of the world's new problems can be traced back to the end of the cold war.

Competing visions of the post-cold war world

The complexity of the post-cold war period is perhaps best understood if we take a look at the very different, and entirely credible ways in which different writers from different ideological and cultural backgrounds have tried to understand—and in some ways anticipate—the main features of the modern era. As we shall see, the big picture theorists basically fall into three distinct camps: **liberal optimists** who see enormous potential in the new world in the making and look forward to much better times ahead (see Ch. 8); **hard-nosed realists** who feel that the world is still as dangerous as it was before, if not more so (see Ch. 7); and **radicals** who insist that the international order remains as unequal and as exploitative as ever (see Ch. 10). Here we attempt to make no qualitative judgement about the intrinsic worth of these different visions; only to summarize them.

Liberal optimists

If we are to treat liberalism as an explanatory theory seriously, perhaps the best place to start is with one of the most influential liberal theories of the post-cold war world—that advanced by a former US State Department official, Francis Fukuyama. An expert on the Third World with a penchant for philosophical speculation, Fukayama shot to fame in the late 1980s. His basic thesis—advanced with a great sense of timing in the middle of 1989—consisted of a rather simple but highly important set of assertions. These can be summarized thus: (*a*) that 'history' since the French Revolution had been driven by a core dynamic conflict between the forces supporting collectivism and those endorsing the ideals of 'bourgeois' individualism; (*b*) that with the Russian Revolution of 1917 the balance clearly tilted towards the former; (*c*) by the late 1970s however the balance began to tilt the other way as the various efforts at economic planning in the Third World started to show signs of fatigue; already before the fall of communism therefore the socialist project was in trouble; (*d*) this became manifest when Gorbachev assumed office in the USSR in 1985 and began to challenge traditional Soviet ways of thinking about

the world in general and the role of the market in particular; and (*e*) it became clearer still when Gorbachev finally decided to abandon Eastern Europe and the peoples of these countries opted for 'bourgeois' **democracy and market economics**—thus ending the division of Europe on terms entirely favourable to the West. This, according to Fukuyama, represented a huge victory for the forces of individualism, marking what he termed the 'end' of one phase in 'history', and the beginning of another where liberal economic values would prevail globally. Political life might now be less exciting than in the past. There would, he agreed, be no great conflict between powerful contending ideological currents about ends. Politics would become about means. But that was the way things were and would continue to be for the foreseeable future—perhaps for ever. All other options had been tried and failed. There was now no alternative to liberal capitalism.

Fukuyama's optimistic assessments about the inevitability of the market were paralleled by a series of equally upbeat political statements about the potential for peace in the post-cold war age. Ironically these assumed their sharpest political form soon after Iraq invaded Kuwait in 1990. President George Bush then used the occasion to outline his own particular vision and declared to both houses of Congress that the threat posed by Saddam to the Middle East opened up the very real possibility of building a 'new world order' based on a combination of US military power, collective action by all the major powers, and an enhanced role for the United Nations. Bush's optimistic rhetoric (and following Bush, Clinton's) also drew inspiration from a number of academic theories about the world—theories which became increasingly popular and influential after 1989. Building upon the collapse of communism, but drawing intellectual sustenance from other, longer-term trends, the conclusion they arrived at was that the international system could look forward to less dangerous times.

In its specifics, the liberal political thesis advanced the following three hypotheses:

1. In a world where liberal democracy was rapidly

Box 6.2 The triumph of liberalism?

'The twentieth century saw the developed world descend into a paroxysm of ideological violence, as liberalism contended first with the remnants of absolutism, then bolshevism and fascism, and finally an updated Marxism that threatened to lead to the ultimate apocalypse of nuclear war. But the century that began full of self-confidence in the ultimate triumph of Western liberal democracy seems at its close to be returning full circle to where it started: not to an "end of ideology" or a convergence between capitalism and socialism, but to an unabashed victory of economic and political liberalism'.

(Francis Fukuyama, 'The End of History?', *National Interest*, Summer 1989)

becoming the norm, there was less likelihood of war—not because democracies never went to war (they had done so, after all, in 1914 and again in 1939), but rather because democracies did not go to war with one another; and because the number of democracies had grown exponentially since the early 1970s—accelerating after 1989 and 1991 to include most of the countries of the old Soviet bloc—it followed that peace was now far more likely than war.

2. Those who accepted this thesis also tended to have great faith in international institutions and their pacifying role. The modern world, according to a number of liberal theorists like John Ikenberry, was especially rich in multilateral institutions—the United Nations, the North Atlantic Treaty Organization, the International Monetary Fund, the World Bank, and the European Union, being perhaps the most significant. Naturally enough, these served the particular interests of the various nation-states. But they also performed the larger function of binding different states together and getting them to abide by similar, non-conflictual norms, so contributing to the cause of peace.

3. Underpinning both of these arguments was a final point concerning the operation of the modern international economy (see Ch. 13). Liberals agreed there was still a good deal of economic competition between the different countries. Globalization to this extent had not done away with the political space known as the nation-state. On the other hand, as world trade grew, as the financial ties between different geographical zones deepened, and countries invested more heavily in each other's economy (as indeed happened throughout the 1990s) then each state would develop a powerful set of material incentives to get on with their neighbours (see Ch. 24). The possibility of war remained, but in an increasingly integrated world economic system, the likelihood of it actually occurring would diminish rapidly. Globalization therefore was not merely an economic imperative, but served an important security role as well.

Key points

- Francis Fukuyama's concept of an 'end of history' refers not to the end of historical time, but to the final victory of liberal values over their ideological rivals.

- Liberal optimism about the post-cold war era seeks to locate that optimism within a larger, empirically-verifiable theory about the modern world.

- This theory rests on three concrete arguments: one about the pacific character of democracies, another about the integrative role played by multilateral institutions, and a third about the benign security consequences of global capitalism.

Realist warnings

If liberals looked forward to a more peaceful and prosperous world, other scholars and popular commentators painted an altogether bleaker picture of the international system in formation. Not for them visions of security, stability, and economic order but rather chaos, conflict, and disintegration. This pessimistic vision drew its inspiration from three sources: a particular reading of the classics of Realism like Thucydides, Machiavelli, and Hobbes; lessons

Box 6.3 Why Realism is right

'There is much well worth criticizing in the classically realist theory of the international relations and what was once eponymously called statecraft; many of us have bored first-year tutorials with our skilful skewering of the balance-of-power theory, the concept of power, and—of course—the national interest. The problem is that with our intellectual rigour, all too often we correct the grammar but forget the plot. Flawed though the principal texts of classical realism may be, when compared with our contemporary would-be master-mistress-works, they have an overriding virtue. To risk the vernacular; they got the big things right enough.'

(Colin Gray, 'Clausewitz rules OK?', *Review of International Studies*, December 1999, 162)

drawn from the cold war; and what it saw happening after the cold war in collapsing countries like ex-Yugoslavia and declining regions such as sub-Saharan Africa. The conclusion that they then arrived at was as simple, as it was stark: the world was not facing such a rosy future.

Three influential realists have helped shape the debate about the post-cold war period: let us briefly sum up their views below.

John Mearsheimer goes 'back to the future'

Mearsheimer is a professor of political science in the University of Chicago. A military historian by training and a realist by theoretical inclination, Mearsheimer took issue with what he felt was the simple-minded triumphalism that swept the United States following the end of the cold war. In his view this new found optimism was premised upon a major misreading of history in general and the cold war in particular. In his opinion the cold war—far from making the world a more dangerous place—had actually made it much safer after 1945. It thus followed that the new international order would be less stable rather than more as a result of what had happened in Eastern Europe after 1989. He spelt out the reasons why in one of the most cited articles of the post-cold war period. Published in the major American journal *International Security* in the summer of 1990, his 'Back to the Future: Instability in Europe

after the Cold War' spawned a furious debate that has not yet come to an end.

Mearsheimer's pessimism was based, first, on his analysis of the structure of the international system during the cold war. His thesis was neither original nor outstanding, but it was one with which other realists readily concurred. Bipolarity, he argued, had produced stability and order after the Second World War: its collapse therefore could only generate new problems—further nuclear proliferation being perhaps the most dangerous (see Ch. 19). Mearsheimer also felt that the division of Europe and Germany after 1946 had contributed to a new continental order; hence the unification of both was likely to introduce **uncertainty**. Finally, he believed (along with many others) that with the collapse of communism in the East, old ethnic hatreds would once again resurface and thrust the continent back into the chaos and the bloodshed that had marked its none-too-happy history between the two world wars. As the Balkans descended into barbarity after 1990, Mearsheimer's gloomy prognosis about Europe (or at least one part of it) going 'back to the future' looked prescient indeed.

Samuel Huntington and 'the clash of civilizations'

Perhaps an even more influential scholar than Meirsheimer, was the American political scientist based at Harvard, Samuel Huntington. A serious figure in many debates over a number of years, Huntington was part leading academic and part policy adviser to several US administrations—and had occupied this influential space since the late 1950s. Close to those in power and keen to use his influence to shape the policy debate in the United States as it unfolded after 1989, Huntington's warnings about the future direction world politics might take were read at the time as indicative of at least one strand of tough-minded opinion in the US policy-making elite. His views however (like those of Mearsheimer) carried far beyond the US and helped shape the way many analysts began to think about the character of conflict in the post-communist era. Some in fact suspected, or feared, that the Huntington thesis was not merely a reflection of the world 'out there', but instead an attempt by the US to find, even invent, a new and useful enemy that would give it a role and provide justification for its continued **hegemony** in a post-Soviet world.

At the heart of Huntington's argument was a powerful refutation of the liberal argument that the world now faced more tranquil times. Not so, opined Huntington: the cold war clash of secular economic ideologies might have come to a conclusion, but this did not mean the end of conflict as such. This, he insisted, would simply assume a new form—and this form he argued would be 'civilizational' in character. This would be the latest phase in what he termed the evolution in conflict in the modern world. However, instead of this occurring within a pre-existing set of Western norms—even communism he accepted was a secular political ideology that had arisen under Western conditions—it would be between the 'West' and those other countries and regions in the world that did not adhere to such values as respect for the individual, human rights, democracy, and secularism. Identity and culture thus lay at the heart of the new antagonisms according to Huntington; and it was this that would be the new fault line in the post-cold war world, pitting those nations in Western Europe and the US that embodied one form of 'civilization' against those in the Middle East, China, and Asia (even post-communist Russia) where the value systems were profoundly different (see Ch. 28). Nor was there much the West could do to avoid this clash. The differences between civilizations after all were real and they were important. They were not an invention of the West, or even of Samuel Huntington for that matter. Huntington indeed made it clear that he did not actually advocate such a conflict. He simply felt that these profound oppositions existed—witness, he said, the ongoing struggle between militant Islam and the liberal democracies, and the very real tensions that existed between the more traditional value system in the countries of Asia and those in the more developed West. These were proof enough of difference, and until the West recognized this reality, it would be unable to deal with it wisely.

Robert Kaplan and 'the coming anarchy'

If Mearsheimer's argument drew inspiration from his study of the cold war in Europe, and Huntington's from his analysis of the changing character of conflict through historical time, Robert D. Kaplan's derived succour from his observations about those parts of the world experiencing collapse and disintegration. His argument formed the third central challenge to liberal optimism in the 1990s. 'The Coming Anarchy' was first published in the influential magazine, *Atlantic Monthly* in 1994. Building upon the work of other writers, Kaplan's vision of the future was perhaps the least sustained empirically but without question the most frightening of our three gloomy readings of the post-cold war era—unsurprisingly so given his core working assumption that economic and human collapse in parts of Africa were as relevant to understanding the future character of world politics, as the Balkans were a hundred years ago, prior to the two Balkan wars and the outbreak of World War I in 1914.

The picture drawn of the new world by Kaplan was bleak—even desperate. In his world, the real world he felt, old structures and traditional certainties were rapidly dissolving producing chaos and misery, notably (but not only) in countries like Sierra Leone and Zaire in West Africa where life for ordinary people had become virtually intolerable. Meanwhile, in other parts of the world, old-fashioned conflicts between ideologies such as communism and capitalism were giving way to less easily regulated—and possibly more fundamental—clashes over resources such as water, cropland forests, and even fish. Scarcer resources in turn were placing an even greater strain on several of the poorer countries in the world, countries whose populations were increasing at an alarming rate, and where few mechanisms existed for settling disputes peacefully. Of course, not all of the countries of the world were experiencing such horrors, as Kaplan readily admitted. In fact, according to Kaplan, the world was rapidly dividing after the cold war into those areas and regions whose inhabitants in the main were 'healthy, well fed and pampered by technology' and those whose people were condemned to a Hobbesian life where conditions were 'nasty, brutish and short'. However, the have-nots would not stay put and would soon come hammering on the doors of the more prosperous zones fuelling even more tensions in a world without meaning or welfare for the vast majority.

Key points

- Realists are not realists because they are 'realistic', but rather because they have what they believe is a more coherent analysis about the way states have always operated—and operate now.

- Mearsheimer's argument about going 'back to the future' is built upon the basic realist argument that the cold war system of bipolarity led to a 'long peace' that might now be undermined by its dissolution.

- Huntington's thesis about the 'clash of civilizations' takes as its starting-point the inevitability of conflict as a historically proven fact, and goes on to argue that the next key conflicts in the world will not be economic or ideological but cultural.

- Kaplan's 'coming anarchy' builds on the experience of what he terms the 'dying regions' of the world—like parts of Africa—and asserts that the West ignores what is happening in these areas at its risk.

Radical alternatives

Though radical politics lost much of its edge following the collapse of communism—indeed one of the key trends of the post-cold war period has been the virtual disappearance of serious left-wing parties advocating **anti-capitalist solutions**—radical theory continued to flourish, though on the margins of mainstream international relations rather than at its heart (see Ch. 10). Much of this theory has been written under the broad umbrella of that subsection of the discipline known as international political economy, though quite a lot gradually seeped into the subject from other areas like environmental politics, feminist theory, and development studies. Some of the most influential, however, derived from the work of important individuals who grew up intellectually outside academic international relations. We discuss two of the most significant of these below.

Noam Chomsky and the power of criticism

One such lone voice has been the brilliant American linguistic theorist Noam Chomsky of the Massachussetts Institute of Technology. Marginalized in his own country—he once referred to himself as a dissident in the land of the deaf and the blind—Chomsky has been a radical voice in what he regards as an American academic wilderness peopled by those either too spineless or too dependent to attack the status quo. Yet from his position on the edges of the mainstream, Chomsky has managed to influence and inspire many younger scholars. A best-selling writer who refuses to keep quiet, Chomsky has painted an impressionistic but powerful picture of the modern world. Chomsky's analysis might be summed up thus:

1. The basic character of the international system post-1989 may have altered in outward appearance, but in essence it has changed very little: it still remains divided between the rich powerful states and the highly dependent ones in the Third World.

2. Far from representing a force for good in the world the United States is an imperial and expansionary power, whose principle aim in the post-cold war period has been to make the world safe for the multinationals.

3. The purpose of modern elite democracy and US democracy promotion, is not to empower ordinary people around the world, but to reduce political choice. Indeed, if anything, the US is actually afraid of real democracy and would soon undermine it if it did not advance its own material and strategic interests.

4. The reach of the American state globally is matched by its ability to 'manufacture consent' at home, thus ensuring that few people seriously question what is being done abroad in their name.

5. We should beware the new humanitarian interventionism sometimes practised by the West after 1989: it is only old-style imperialism wearing new ideological clothes.

Robert Cox and the political economy of hegemony

A very different sort of radical theorist is Robert Cox, a Canadian who worked for twenty-five years at the International Labour Office, before moving to Columbia University in New York, and then York

> ### Box 6.4 Noam Chomsky takes at a sceptical look at 'humanitarian intervention' after the cold war
>
> 'From a contrasting perspective, the "new inter-ventionism" is replaying an old record. It is an updated variant of traditional practices that were impeded in a bipolar world system that allowed some space for nonalignment—a concept that effectively vanishes when one of the two poles disappears. The Soviet Union and to some extent China, set limits on the actions of the Western powers in their traditional domains, not only by virtue of the military deterrent, but also because of their occasional willingness, however opportunistic, to lend support to targets of Western subversion and aggression. With the Soviet deterrent in decline, the cold war victors are more free to exercise their will under the cloak of good intentions but in pursuit of interests that have a very familiar ring outside the realm of enlightenment.'
>
> (Noam Chomsky, *The New Military Humanism* (Monroe, Me: Common Courage Press, 1999), 11)

University in Canada. Like Chomsky, Cox's work developed apart from the mainstream and from what he later termed 'the dominant currents of thought in international relations'. However, unlike Chomsky, Cox did manage to build up quite a large following in international relations from the early 1980s onwards (see Ch. 10). Influenced by several different writers himself—Vico, Sorel, Weber, Polanyi, Braudel, Antonio Gramsci, and E. H. Carr being perhaps the most significant—Cox went on to shape the outlook of other influential writers like Stephen Gill, Kees van der Pijl, and Craig Murphy.

Though much of Cox's most important work appeared before the end of the cold war, he still has much to say about the nature of world order after the collapse of what he once termed 'real socialism'. In schematic terms it could be summarized in the following way:

1. The 'new' world order must be understood historically or it cannot be understood at all, and that the essential transformation in world politics occurred not in 1989 or even 1991 but following the crisis of the mid-1970s. At this point there was a decisive shift from Keynesian growth policies to financially determined neo-liberalism. Ever since, the international system as a whole has been operating under the strict discipline of a neo-liberal economic agenda—set not by any one country, but by a transnational elite.

2. The ideologies and structures built up in the post-war period basically remain the same. The concept of the national security state, intelligence and surveillance systems, and co-option of subordinate states under the umbrella of larger ones—none of these things altered in any fundamental way as a result of the end of the cold war.

3. The so-called 'new world order' is far from stable: the unplanned dynamics of capital accumulation, global financial deregulation, the increasing number of economic losers and the end of the cold war itself, makes the international system anything but secure: and while working class revolution in the traditional Marxist sense is most unlikely, the possibility of new emancipatory challenges to globalization remains on the political agenda (see Ch. 10).

Key points

- Some of the more significant radical writers on world politics developed their ideas outside of—and in opposition to—mainstream international relations.

- Noam Chomsky is a famous best-selling author in the United States whose critique of what he terms the 'American empire' takes as its point of intellectual departure the notion that in the new world order very little has changed: the powerful and the powerful states still remain hegemonic.

- Robert Cox has a more established reputation in the field of international political economy, but like Chomsky believes that the structures of power established in the post-war period remain in place.

Global trends in the post-cold war era

This brief summary of the ways in which different authors have attempted to make sense of the post-cold war world should not only be useful in its own right, but also alert us to an issue that any serious historian is bound to confront when seeking to make sense about the world after communism: that to understand this world we not only need to know the bare facts but we have to make sense of these facts—and one very important way of doing this is by thinking in large-scale ways. These different visions tell us something else as well: that there may be no single overarching theory adequate to explain the way the world now operates. To this extent we might think of our various grand pictures not in terms of their correctness, but rather as more, or less, useful instruments that help us explain the very different, quite contradictory, facets of the modern period. The issue then is not whether liberals, realists, or radicals have a firmer grasp of a given single reality, but what part of that reality they better explain. Nobody after all has a monopoly on that thing we call 'truth'. And no serious engagement with the post-cold war period should assume that the 'truth' is easy to grasp. It is not. Indeed, it is significant that when other writers on the post-cold war period have attempted to 'think big' about the subject, they too have employed working categories that try to capture the sheer complexity (duality even) of our era. Thus Max Singer and Aaron Wildavsky (1993) writing about what they term the 'real world order' after 1989 conclude that there is not a single 'zone' but two: in one (mainly the advanced capitalist countries) there is peace and relative prosperity, and in the other (primarily in the old Third World and the former Soviet bloc) there is turmoil. The American historian, John Gaddis, has devised a similar typology and refers to the world as being the product of two competing forces—one integrative and the other disintegrative. Harvey Staar has adopted a very similar approach and significantly entitles one of his more recent studies *Anarchy, Order and Integration* (Staar 1999), in this way indicating that the international system is not only a highly complex place, but that even those factors which make for stability and prosperity in one

part of it, may lead to quite different consequences in another.

It is within this larger framework that we shall now attempt to situate the dominant developments in the post-cold war world. No doubt there are others, and without doubt there may be some not mentioned below that might take on greater significance in the future. But as historians we have to sift through the evidence and attempt to distinguish between what is important and what we deem to be less important. This thematic approach may not satisfy all tastes. Some might prefer a more straightforward chronological approach. But the facts, as E. H. Carr once pointed out, do not speak for themselves. We have to try and make some sense of them, and one important way of doing so is to look for the main trends. To 'lump' history together, as John Gaddis noted, is just as important and useful than always trying to 'split' it.

The triumph of capitalism

A standard history of the post-cold war era could easily begin, and more often than not does, with a war—the Gulf War—followed by another conflict, the one that led to the break-up of Yugoslavia and the death of hundreds of thousands of people; it would then continue with the genocide in Rwanda, go on to mention the fall of the Russian President Boris Yeltsin, take note of the NATO war to 'liberate' Kosovo, and probably conclude with the historic meeting between the two Korean leaders in 2000. These, after all, were headline events that captured the public imagination, and will no doubt be written about at great length by future historians of the period. There is nothing wrong with such an approach—except it misses what will almost certainly turn out to be the single most important trend of the post-communist era: the triumph of capitalism as a world system, one that transformed the lives of most of humanity for better or worse, swept away all barriers to the operation of the market around the world (often with devastating social

---

Box 6.5 William Greider describes the 'manic logic of one world capitalism'

'The logic of commerce and capital has overpowered the inertia of politics and launched an epoch of great social transformations. Settled facts of material life are being revised for rich and poor nations alike. Social understandings that were formed by the hard political struggles of the twentieth century are put in doubt. Old verities about the rank ordering of nations are revised and a new map of the world is gradually being drawn. These great changes sweep over the affairs of mere governments and destabilize the established political orders in both advanced and primitive societies. Everything seems new, and strange. Nothing seems certain.'

(William Greider, *One World Ready or Not* (Harmondsworth: Penguin, 1998), 11)

---

consequences), and transformed the character of international politics.

Indeed, if we think of the cold war as an ongoing competition between different economic systems, where in one private property dominated and in the other the means of production were nationalized, then we can better understand the real significance of what really happened in 1989. For what transpired, in essence, was not simply the withdrawal of Soviet power from Eastern Europe or even the subsequent collapse of the Warsaw Pact and the **reunification of Germany**—all important changes in themselves—but rather the end of a competition between alternative economic systems and the victory of one of them over the other. Moreover, what occurred in Poland, Czechoslvakia, and Hungary and the like had an enormous demonstration effect on the rest of the world, signalling to those who might have thought otherwise that there was now no alternative to the market. Then, when in 1991, the USSR finally disintegrated and withdrew its support from its diminishing number of allies around the world (Cuba and Vietnam in particular) it put increased pressure on these regimes to change as well. Little wonder the West felt it had won the cold war.

The move from a bifurcated, two-world order in which the market only operated in some countries, to one in which it was operating in all (or nearly all), had immense and long-lasting consequences.

Perhaps the most important was to give enormous new powers to those financial bodies, notably the International Monetary Fund and the World Bank who were now delegated the critically important tasks of helping transform the previously planned economic systems and turning them into functioning market economies. The programme of (often painful) change they advocated was basically the same everywhere: privatization of the means of production, deregulation of all economic activity, encouragement of competition, balanced budgets, strict financial adherence to goals set by those who adhered to the orthodox neo-liberal economic agenda being set in Washington, and integration into the wider world capitalist economy (see Ch. 13). Though the formula was not specifically American, by the early 1990s it had become known, quite simply, as '**Washington Consensus**', to be blamed by some for having produced unnecessary hardship in the less developed countries and disaster in post-communist Russia, and by others for having transformed once 'basket case' countries into shining examples of economic efficiency.

If one result of the global triumph of the market was to increase the power of those institutions assigned the job of managing capitalism as an international system, another was to change the ways in which countries tended to determine their foreign policy goals. It would be an exaggeration to say that during the cold war foreign policy was basically about military security, and that in the new era it was primarily concerned with economics, but there is something to the argument. In fact, what we see throughout the advanced capitalist countries during the 1990s is an interesting trend, whereby on the one hand governments begin to reduce the vast amounts being spent on the military, and on the other start thinking far more seriously about how to make their economies lean and efficient in an increasingly tough environment. At the same time, government departments whose primary purpose was to help national companies win markets abroad tended to move up the bureaucratic ladder, while those viewed as having a less important economic function tended to move down. Even intelligence agencies found themselves under increasing pressure after the cold war to define a new role for themselves, and whilst they continued to carry out their 'normal' assignments of specifying traditional threats to national security, some of them did start to take on new missions, one of which was to help their countries compete more effectively.

Inevitably, in this age of geo-economics, the character of politics—domestic and international—changed out of all recognition. During the cold war, after all, politics in the West had largely been defined by the larger strategic relationship with the 'other', the Soviet Union. Now, with the end of the cold war, and the subsequent collapse of the USSR, the focus shifted towards the global world economy and how countries might survive and prosper within it. Inevitably, this had a huge impact on the way people lived, thought, and entertained themselves—on what we might generically call 'culture'. Even the heroes of popular literature changed in the process. Thus whereas in the days of the superpower stand-off the most respected individual was the brave warrior or the wily spy—witness here the cult of the soldier and the popularity of the Bond movies—now the new men (and women) of distinction were the entrepreneurs and the new get-rich whizz-kids of the computer world. The way people worked changed too as they adjusted to the new environment. Certainly, they had to work much harder and realized they had to, for if their company failed to compete globally, then what followed was as inevitable as it was bound to be painful. Nothing was sacrosanct in the new international economy where globalization did not just seem to describe the way world operated, but in a very important sense was deployed by governments as well to spur on people and firms to ever greater efforts.

Capitalism in its new post-communist manifestation thus assumed an increasingly intensive form, where little thought appeared to be given to human welfare and social cohesion, and everything seemed to revolve around profit and the balance sheet. Naturally enough, the system did have its radical critics who could justifiably point to the growth of inequality and insecurity in the advanced capitalist countries, and hunger and crippling debt in the less developed parts of the world (see Ch. 26). The system was also prone to great fluctuation and many feared that at some point it was bound to meet its nemesis,

as some thought it had done during the great financial crisis of 1997 and 1998. Even some of those who were the beneficiaries of the new economic order, like the financier George Soros, were concerned about the consequences of this new 'unfettered capitalism' and urged governments to intervene more often and more effectively to protect society from its ravages. Others went further still and in the so-called 'Battle of Seattle' in 1999 took their protest against the logic of globalization to the streets.

The critics, however, faced two fairly obvious problems. The first, and most obvious, was that they could propose nothing more by way of an alternative, other than a more humane and possibly more regulated form of the same. The second, and more serious problem, was that whatever its flaws and weaknesses, the new capitalism did at least produce the goods: in fact, it overproduced them. It also created enormous prosperity (even if wealth was concentrated in a few hands), generated fantastic technological changes that were transforming and in ways improving the lives of ordinary people, and in its new globalized form was rapidly undermining some of the more traditional reasons why nations used to go to war. To this extent the liberals were right. The new 'turbo-charged capitalism' may well have been ruthless, as the American journalist William Greider pointed out in his popular *One World Ready or Not*. It was undoubtedly uncontrollable. However, it did have its progressive side. It also remained extraordinarily innovative, and as long as it continued to be so, would remain—as one cynic rather nicely put it—the 'only game in town'. As Susan Strange observed in her normally pithy way, perhaps in the end the system would go on, not because it worked perfectly, or even well, but because of the difficulty of finding, and building, something very much different or better.

Key points

- The existence of communism limited the geographic range of capitalism; its rollback has therefore led to a rapid spread of market principles around the whole world.

- The short-hand term used to define global economic policy during the 1990s was the

'Washington consensus', describing a strict set of economic criteria that all countries had to adhere to, whatever the welfare consequences.

- There has been a detectable trend in the advanced capitalist countries towards a more economically-driven foreign policy.

- The critics of capitalism make a powerful case, but thus far have been unable to provide a serious economic alternative to the market.

The United States—the new hegemony

If a triumphant capitalism was one result of the end of the cold war, another was a resurgence of American self-confidence—so much so that by the beginning of the new millennium pundits were confidently predicting that the new century would be even more 'American' than the old one. This was a development that few had foretold, and hardly anybody had anticipated in the late 1980s, when all the talk then had been about US decline and the inability of the United States to compete effectively in the world economy. Indeed, one of the best-selling books of the late Reagan years (written by the English historian, Paul Kennedy) predicted a fairly bleak future and warned US leaders that the nation faced what all other empires had confronted before (Kennedy 1998): an erosion in its global position that would over time turn the United States from a superpower into what Richard Rosecrance of the University of California had earlier called an 'ordinary country'. And though the US still had many assets, probably more than any of its nearest rivals, ultimately it could not avoid its fate.

Of course, talk of America's imminent demise turned out to be most premature (some indeed wondered whether it had ever been true). There were many reasons why, but the first and most immediate was the **Gulf War** and the overwhelming defeat of Saddam Hussein by a hugely impressive display of American military firepower. To many, at least, it now looked as if America was right back on top. George Bush was certainly keen to point out to those willing to listen that US victory in the Gulf had not only kicked the so-called 'Vietnam Syndrome', but

Box 6.6 Whatever happened to American decline?

'At the inception of the twenty-first century, books on "the American century" proliferate monthly if not daily. We now have *The American Century Dictionary*, *The American Century Thesaurus*, and even *The American Century Cookbook*; perhaps the American baseball cap or cologne is not far behind . . . If this intoxicating optimism is commonplace today, it would have seemed demented just a few short years ago: back then scholars and popular pundits who are supposed to know the occult science of international affairs were full of dread about American decline and Japanese and German advance. The American century looked like an accountably short one.'

(Bruce Cumings, 'Still the American Century', *Review of International Studies*, 25 (December 1999), 271)

was the best answer possible to those who only a couple of years previously had been predicting an erosion of American influence. When this major event was followed only a few months later by the disintegration of the USSR, it looked as if the US was quite literally 'riding high' on top of the world. At a stroke almost, the United States now found itself in a position of unrivalled dominance in a unipolar world where its reach seemed unlimited and its freedom of manoeuvre unprecedented.

Yet the worries persisted. The economy under Bush grew only slowly while the financial deficit (that is the difference between what the US spent and what it raised in taxes) showed no signs of diminishing. These concerns did not persist for long however, and while Bush's successor, Bill Clinton, appeared to have no great interest in foreign policy, he was especially keen to get the economy right. Under his brash political leadership, US fortunes began to soar. The facts, for once, seemed to speak for themselves. Between 1992 and 2000 the US experienced the longest boom of the post-war period, during which the value of US stocks doubled and then doubled again, unemployment dropped dramatically as tens of millions of new jobs were created, and the American deficit finally disappeared. By the end of the decade there were few speaking as they had been only ten years earlier of US economic frailty or an American inability to compete effectively.

But it was not economics alone that made Americans increasingly self-confident as the decade wore on. American soft power in the shape of popular culture, styles of dress, even American fast food appeared to have an irresistible appeal to many ordinary people around the globe. Moreover, this particular form of influence was underwritten by a determined and quite conscious American effort to retain its primacy. The rest of the world in turn continued to look to America for political and military leadership—something that became all too apparent during the long-drawn-out carnage in Bosnia where it was decisive American intervention (after European and UN dithering) that finally brought that particular phase of the conflict in former Yugoslavia to an end (see Ch. 22). It was not insignificant, and did not go unnoticed, that the Treaty which finally brought the **war in Bosnia** to a conclusion in November 1995 was not signed in Paris, London or Brussels, but in the small American town of Dayton, Ohio.

These events alone would not have made the difference they did, however, unless there existed certain fundamentals (what international relations theorists term 'structural power') that made the US the key, indispensable factor in world politics. A combination of military prowess and relatively high levels of military expenditure certainly constituted one of these props. One calculation was that by the end of the 1990s the US was spending as much on national security as the rest of the world put together. Another key asset was its intelligence-gathering capabilities, critical—indeed essential— during any war. Then there was the almighty dollar, the only national currency that was recognized by all countries. Finally, the US, and the US alone, had crucial global reach that extended across the Pacific and the Atlantic, into Central and Latin America, and deep into the heart of the Middle East and South Asia. In each of these vital regions, the United States continued to act as referee and player, often compelling others to seek agreement. Thus there would have been no peace process between **Israel and the Palestinians**, (fragile though it was), without the United States. It was American mediation between Pakistan and India that defused tension between these two

nuclear powers on at least two critical occasions. And it is inconceivable that without an American presence in South Korea, the leaders of both North and South could have entered into negotiation in 2000 after nearly fifty years of bitter cold war.

Inevitably, with this awesome power at its disposal, there was some concern that the United States would not use its formidable assets wisely or well. Some even feared a new assertive and aggressive phase in American foreign policy, a worry expressed with some feeling at the time of the Gulf War. The larger criticism though was not that the US would be tempted to act in an imperial fashion, but rather that it would act unilaterally; and it did so on numerous occasions, often bypassing the United Nations when it did not do its bidding while refusing to join the international bodies like the **World Court** if they limited its range of choice. Of equal concern was the US refusal sometimes to act at all. Its initial decision not to get drawn into the Bosnian imbroglio, and its subsequent refusal to do anything in Rwanda as the killings intensified, were at least two examples of America, 'the reluctant superpower', unwilling to deploy its forces in countries where US public opinion would not support such action. This did not make the United States isolationist. Indeed, throughout the 1990s it 'intervened' in all sorts of ways, from getting involved in the Northern Ireland peace process to bringing about the enlargement of NATO after 1994. Nor was it a disinterested player. With its stake in the global economy and several security guarantees to many countries in the world, it could not afford to be. However, in the new era, it would make a very clear distinction indeed between those areas where it had a vital interest, and those where it did not. This, if nothing else, distinguished its foreign policy in the post-cold war era to its grand strategy before 1991, when it was virtually impossible to draw such neat conceptual distinctions between countries it would defend against communism and those it would not.

Key points

- In the late 1980s there were many writers like Paul Kennedy who argued that the United States was in decline.

- This once fashionable view is no longer accepted by the majority of commentators. A combination of factors including the collapse of the USSR, the long economic boom in America itself, and what international relations writers define as 'structural power', still makes the United States dominant.
- The major problem facing US foreign policy after the cold war is not isolationism but unilateralism and often indifference to those areas of the world where it perceives it has no vital interest.

Russia—reform or decline?

While the United States prospered in a world increasingly organized along economic lines consonant with American interests and values, post-communist Russia lurched from one near-fatal crisis to another throughout the 1990s. This was not how things were meant to be immediately after the break-up of the USSR and the election of the then popular Boris Yeltsin. According to the prevalent Western line of the time, Russia, with a good deal of political support from its new-found allies in the Clinton White House, and even more direct financial assistance from the IMF, would emerge at some time in the future as a stable democratic entity with a functioning capitalist economy. The transition from authoritarian communism and planning would not be painless. Nor would it be without its ups and downs. But at the end of the day, Russia would become what the reformers liked to refer to as a 'normal country'.

That at least was the theory. The actual outcome was rather different and in the years following Yeltsin's election, Russian industrial production dropped by nearly 40 per cent, over 80 per cent of Russians experienced a reduction in their living standards, health care disintegrated, life expectancy fell along with the birth rate, and morale overall collapsed. A significant number of Russians clearly did not care for the new order (if that is what it can be called) and registered their protest either by repeatedly expressing nostalgia for the good old days under Soviet rule, or by supporting the newly formed Russian Communist Party led by Gennadi Zyuganov. Significantly, the only people who seemed to benefit

from what some critics came to refer to as Russian 'criminal capitalism' were the new super-rich, the overwhelming majority of whom were simply members of the old Soviet elite who had used their position of privilege under the previous order to enrich themselves under the new one. Nor, in the end, did the political process even lead to the election of a truly democratic President. In December 1999, Boris Yeltsin finally resigned from office: three months later the Russian people elected a former KGB officer—Vladimir Putin—a man with little interest in **human rights** (see Ch. 28) even less in democratic norms, and who came to power after having waged a brutal war of ethnic destruction in the republic of Chechnya.

How do we explain this crisis, and what are its implications for the rest of the world? Let us deal with each question in turn.

At least two reasons have been suggested by analysts to explain the failure of Russia to make the transition. One, interestingly enough, concerns the sort of advice provided by the West itself. Russia, according to this thesis, had the misfortune to enter the world order in 1991 at a time when market triumphalism was in the ascendant. Irresponsible policies, which had little to do with Russian conditions and everything with what some felt was neo-liberal hubris, were foisted on the country. Predictably, the results of this irresponsible intervention were ruinous. This version of events, inevitably, has been challenged by both the **IMF and Russian reformers** themselves. The real failure, they argue, was not the medicine but the failure to apply it properly. Thus what had worked in countries like Poland and the Czech republic—so-called shock therapy—was not implemented in Russia. Russia thus drifted and suffered the consequences of having abandoned planning without then going for the market. As an IMF official is reported to have remarked, 'Russia had its chance and it blew it'.

Whichever of the different explanations we favour, the fact remains that the situation in Russia post-USSR was always going to be extremely challenging. With over seventy years experience of communism, an imperial past, a vast military-industrial complex now with little purpose, and no democratic tradition worth speaking of, Russia was, in many ways, an improbable candidate for liberal democratic capitalism. Indeed, at a very early stage, it was evident to observers abroad that events within the country were not unfolding as planned. In December 1993, for instance, the US woke up to discover that nearly one quarter of all Russians had voted for the extreme nationalist, Vladimir Zhironovsky, someone who advocated the reconstruction of the former USSR (by force if needs be) and the reacquisition of Alaska! Five years later, policymakers then had to come to terms with a more material crisis when the Russian **financial system collapsed**, in the process wiping out the savings of many aspiring middle-class Russians. And less than two years on, it had to accept the decision of the Russian people when they elected a leader who had only a few years earlier been warning that America had a sinister plan of reducing Russia to the level of a Third World dependency.

Given these many problems the West had to be prepared to take the long view. The United States especially stressed that one simply had to keep faith with Russia, even if Russia at times did things of which it disapproved. Better a constructive relationship with an errant ally, it was reasoned, than a return to the days of the cold war. Even Putin's election did not provoke much of a response. US Secretary of State, Madelaine Albright, was unambiguously clear: Putin, she insisted, would be judged by his actions in the here and now, not by his associations and words of the past. British Prime Minister Blair adopted exactly the same outlook. Putin, he agreed, was not perfect but he had at least been elected. Moreover, he promised to bring order to Russia and to pursue a pro-Western foreign policy—reasons enough to give him a chance.

Realism rather than idealism thus shaped the Western response to Russia, one born firstly out of a need to manage Russia's still huge nuclear arsenal, second by Russia's geographical position at the heart of the Eurasian subcontinent, and finally by its permanent membership of the UN Security Council where it had the power to veto, or support, any American initiative. There was, in addition, a more basic material consideration. Russia may have been in crisis with little chance of becoming an advanced market economy in the near future; however, it still possessed important natural assets such as oil and gold. After nearly ten years of trying to get to the market (with Western support) it also owed the West several billion dollars. Lastly, there was always the very real danger that things could get worse. Hopefully, the consequences of this could be contained. However, in an age of porous borders this was most unlikely. Faced with such a daunting prospect (theoretical though it may have seemed to some) the West was thus more than happy to turn a blind eye to Russian actions in **Chechnya**, and prepared to do business with Putin. Even under conditions of globalization, there were still some very big states facing some very real problems—and if these threatened to disturb the peace or upset world order, then the West's attitude towards them was just as likely to be guided by a desire for stability as by democratic niceties. In the meantime the more cynical could at least console themselves with the thought that even if reform had not managed to improve life for ordinary Russians, it had, if nothing else, made Russia much weaker. As one observer remarked, better a collapsing Russia than a unified, capable Soviet Union.

Box 6.7 Russia's ruin

'Only a few years ago, American policy-makers were confidently predicting that a regimen of privatization and market reform would in due course transform Russia into a stable and prosperous democracy . . . Today all that has passed away. Far from fulfilling their promise of a better life, the US-sponsored reforms of the 1990s have left many, if not most Russians worse off. For this state of affairs many Russians today blame the Western aid and advice they had received. Some indeed believe that the United States set out deliberately to destroy their economy.'

(Janine R. Wedel, 'Tainted Transactions', *The National Interest*, 59 (Spring 2000), 23)

Key points

- The attempt to build a popular functioning market economy in Russia thus far has been unsuccessful.
- However, there is too much at stake for the West to now abandon Russia—in spite of human rights

abuses in Chechnya and the election of Vladimir Putin, a former KGB officer, to the office of President.

• Even if economic reform has been unable to restore Russia, because Russia is now so weak it does not represent a serious problem internationally.

China—Asian tiger: regional threat

When analysts talk of an end to the cold war taking place in 1989, they are normally referring to the course of events in Eastern and Central Europe. But in the same year in which communist authority collapsed on the European continent, it was being reaffirmed in China. The two processes were intimately connected. Indeed, there is every likelihood that if Gorbachev had decided to crack down in Poland or East Germany, the Chinese Communist Party might have been persuaded to act with less severity itself. But seeing the destruction of state authority in the other socialist countries convinced leaders in Beijing that unless it took swift action, they too might go the same way. Out of such brutal calculations was born the massacre of **Tiananmen Square** in June 1989—a decisive, effective, and bloody action that sent a clear and simple message to those who cared to listen that in spite (and perhaps even because) of economic reform, there would be no tinkering with the fundamentals of the Chinese political system.

The modern history of China begins therefore when a number of Western pundits like Fukuyama were talking rather too easily about it coming to an end. China thereafter remained what the American foreign policy guru, Zbigniew Brzezinski, rather aptly termed 'unfinished business', a hybrid system with strong residues of communist ideology articulated by a powerful party bureaucracy, an inefficient but still important state sector combined with, and coexisting uneasily alongside, dynamic capitalist entrepreneurship driven by foreign investment—much of it overseas Chinese and most of it located in the special economic zones in the coastal provinces of the East and South-East. Many experts took the view that this combination of opposites—communism and commercialism—was basically not viable over the longer term. Others felt that the two could not only exist side by side, but that the success of one actually presupposed the other, and that China's great strides forward economically would have been inconceivable without a powerful state holding the ring. Either way, this peculiar form of 'market Stalinism' or what some have termed 'Leninism with capitalist characteristics', did not easily fit into simple pre-existing socio-economic categories.

Historically, the origins of this hybrid can be traced back to the 1970s and the twin decisions taken then to open up relations with the United States and integrate at least parts of China into the global economy—largely as a way of offsetting the power of the former USSR, but also as a means of renovating China's moribund economic system. At around the same time, China took the equally momentous decision to privatize agriculture, thus laying the foundation for a great upsurge of economic activity in the Chinese countryside. In purely economic terms the results of these changes were striking, and by the 1990s China (ironically) had become one of the great success stories of international capitalism. But marketization and globalization were not neutral, and as China grew closer to the West economically, it found itself under growing pressure to abide by international political norms. The dynamics of the new capitalism also led to a tide of rising expectations amongst an increasingly large Chinese middle class. Not only that: the wider needs of a booming and modern market economy demanded more information—always a dangerous commodity in a tightly controlled political system—as well as more contact with the outside world, a process that Chinese leaders seemed to find as difficult to control as it was potentially destabilizing.

If one consequence of economic reform was to produce massive (and some felt potentially explosive) changes within China itself, another was to increase its weight within the international system. For many years a nuclear-have and a permanent member of the UN Security Council, China in the 1990s became a major factor in regional politics and an aspiring power in its own right. This not only caused quite a stir in Asia-Pacific but generated one of the great foreign policy debates in the United States. To many in the region, of course, China continues to be viewed as the number one problem—an increasingly assertive presence that has threatened to take over the disputed Spratley Islands as well as undermine the independence of Taiwan. China has even warned that if Taiwan made any attempt to establish itself as a sovereign country independent of China, it would not stand idly by. Nor, it seems, would the United States, where at least some analysts have seen all this not just as some internal Chinese problem, but a symptom of something else: a classic rising power that one day would come into conflict with the only nation that stood in its way—the United States. One commentator, Nicholas Kristoff of *The New York Times* has even compared China in 2000 to the Germany of old—resentful, ruthless and expansionary with a growing military capability to match its ambitions. This is not an unpopular view in certain circles. Indeed, there are those who feel that a combination of history, geography, and capabilities makes China a natural threat to the region and therefore an adversary of the US.

This rather gloomy prognosis has not been entirely repudiated by critics. Nonetheless, the official position adopted by both George Bush senior and Democrat Clinton (though things could change under the more conservative Bush junior) was that while modern China may have had its differences with the United States, co-operation was still possible. The record (they said) spoke for itself. Thus China, it was pointed out, did not exercise its veto to halt UN actions against Iraq in 1990 and 1991. Nor did it block the Security Council's approval of the international protectorate over Kosovo. It peacefully reacquired Hong Kong from the British. It approved the deployment of UN peace-keepers to East Timor. And it acted very responsibly during the Asia financial crisis of 1998. In short, over most issues—Taiwan being the obvious exception—China's international conduct at least had been relatively restrained. Nor was this all according to those who advocated engagement rather than containment. China was also a huge market for American goods, a massive market for the region and potentially one of the biggest markets in the world! Moreover, as China continued to engage with the world market it was bound to evolve, and the only consequence of treating it as an enemy would be to make it into one, and so delay, rather than accelerate, any progressive change in its internal character.

The great policy debate about China, was, in effect, part of a much deeper discussion—one that had preceded the end of the cold war but became more intense after its end; and this revolved around a simple but fundamental question: namely, what impact was rapid market change and global economic integration likely to have upon the functioning of political systems in general and repressive polities in particular? Inevitably, the supporters for capitalism saw only positive political outcomes arguing (possibly with some justification) that once the market genie had been let out of the bottle there could be no putting it back in again. Others were always more sceptical, feeling that this was little more than a fancy rationalization used by Western governments and their multinational allies to justify doing business with dictators and dictatorships like China. Only time would tell who was right. Meanwhile, out there in the 'real world', Western policy-makers could see only economic opportunities. Moreover, if they didn't take them, then their competitors would. A vast China market comprising a billion consumers beckoned; new orders were there to be won and vast investments made as China

---

Box 6.8 China rising

'For those with an interest in thinking strategically about modern international affairs, there is no more important challenge than to understand the nature and implications of a rising China. As this reality dawns on the public policy community, the debate has often been simplistic. The exchange seems to be between those who assert that China will soon rise to be the world's largest economy and those who argue that it cannot sustain current levels of growth. Some suggest that China will muddle through difficulties, while others suggest it faces a major crisis of governance. It is argued by some that China can only be wrapped in the warm embrace of "engagement", whereas others stress the need to "contain" Chinese power. While the issues raised by these clusters of questions are undoubtedly important, the debates about their accuracy have rarely been sufficiently sophisticated.'

(Gerald Segal and David S. G. Goodman quoted in their (edited) volume, *China Rising* (London: Routledge, 1997), 1)

continued in its headlong rush towards market modernity. And there was no time to lose. It was these very material considerations, rather than liberal concerns about free speech and human rights, that were likely to determine the West's attitude towards China in an era of geo-economics.

Key points

- China's rise in the 1990s has been on the basis of an economic system that is an almost unique blend of capitalism and communism.

- Policy-makers in the United States in particular are more concerned about the great business opportunities in China than they are about political freedom.

- However, over time, many predict that market reform and China's integration in the global economy will lead to irreversible political change.

- Meanwhile, many in the Asia-Pacific region regard China as the number one threat.

Whatever happened to the Pacific Century?

The image of China rising in the wake of Soviet collapse has to be set within a larger context, and for the greater part of the 1980s and 1990s this was one of an expanding Asia-Pacific region with Japan at its epicentre and the other economic 'tigers' like South Korea, Thailand, and Indonesia following closely behind in its wake. And as the region as a whole prospered, many commentators—probably the vast majority—began to reflect on what this meant for

---

Box 6.9 The trouble with Asian tigers

'Like revolution, financial mayhem is a major historical event. In the post-cold war era, and particularly in East Asia, where geoeconomy has largely displaced geopolitics as the major agent of change.'

(François Godemont, *The Downsizing of Asia* (London: Routledge, 1999), 1)

---

the international system as a whole. The answer seemed obvious: a new Pacific age was dawning that would not only bring unheard of prosperity to this once backward part of the world (one of the few in the post-war period to escape from underdevelopment) but over time challenge European and American pre-eminence. Japan in particular became the subject of much wild analysis as its economy boomed and its trade surpluses with the rest of the world grew. Hardly a day went by when one 'expert' or another did not engage in some fairly fanciful observations about either the peculiar work habits of the Japanese, or the even more bizarre character of its protected economic system that threatened to out-produce its competitors and lay the foundation for a new Japanese hegemony in the twenty-first century. In this way Japan, the model Asian democracy of the cold war years, which had relinquished all claims to great power status, that had willingly subordinated itself in security terms to the United States, that had even had a clause inserted into its Constitution preventing it from deploying Japanese troops abroad, which had quite consciously turned itself into a semi-sovereign state more interested in producing cars and tape decks than battleships and guns, was now portrayed as a potential threat. It must all have seemed quite galling.

The speed with which these various truths and half-truths, myths, and semi-educated speculations about Japan and the region collapsed, is one of the great stories of the 1990s. But like many great events, when the bubble burst and history began to destroy established views and undermine fixed preconceptions, so preoccupied were most analysts with the idea of a new Pacific Century, that when the crash finally came in the second half of the decade, all eyes were looking the other way. What followed must have seemed utterly bewildering. Certainly, hardly anybody of note (with a few exceptions) foresaw the chain of events that unravelled after 2 July 1997, the day when Thailand's government gave up the struggle to defend the parity of its own currency, the baht, against the dollar. Within a few months the contagion had spread, and by the end of the year it was calculated that the wave of financial and monetary destruction had destroyed somewhere close to $700bn. of capital. To all intents and purposes, by the middle of 1997, the region's economy had more or less ground to a halt. This was not the first bust experienced by the booming Asia Pacific. Nor did it prove fatal. However, it was without doubt the biggest economic collapse in the area's turbulent history, one that undermined local business confidence and set off a chain reaction globally that for a time appeared to threaten the very survival of the international financial system as a whole. For a very brief moment the edifice of post-cold war global capitalism looked as if it was gazing over a very steep precipice.

The several post-mortems held on the crash have not arrived at a settled consensus, and opinion has veered wildly between what Richard Higgot has called 'domesticist explanations' that stress cronyism, inadequate banking supervision, and lack of transparency, to 'internationalist' ones that point to excessive deregulation in global financial markets, the extent of economic integration in the modern world economy where shocks in one country can have an enormous and speedy impact in others, and the end of the cold war and the failure of the United States to take remedial action early enough to prop up an area no longer threatened by communism. No doubt that particular discussion will run and run. More important (and more measurable) though have been the consequences. One has been to shake old political norms to the core. In some countries this simply led to a change in government; in others a questioning of the normal rules of the political game. It assumed its most acute form however in Indonesia—significantly the region's worst hit economy—where the thirty-five year old military dictatorship finally went under in 1998. But this was not all. The crisis also undermined the glamour and attractiveness of the once highly esteemed Asian way to prosperity, and after 1997 one tended to hear far fewer lengthy perorations from local elites about the superiority of the Asian system and its accompanying set of authoritarian values. The crisis thus had the unintended outcome of strengthening the champions of the Anglo-Saxon liberal model with its greater stress on individualism, choice, and anarchic competition, while delivering what many saw as a fatal blow to the Asian model with its emphasis on community, tradition, hierarchy, and consensus.

The consequences of the crash therefore were huge and over the space of a few years transformed the region, bringing economic hardship and misery in its wake. Even in one of the countries that suffered less than some others—South Korea—the fall-out was extremely high. The crisis there was as fast in coming as it was brutal in its results. In October 1997, unemployment in South Korea stood at only 2.7 per cent; by March 1998 it had risen to 8.5 per cent. Prices also rose dramatically, sometimes by over 300 per cent, thus threatening the livelihood of even those who remained in full-time employment. Elsewhere (with the possible exception of Singapore) the consequences were even grimmer with downsizing becoming the norm in economies forced to come to terms with the deepest recession in the region's recent history.

Perhaps the most important spin-off of the crisis however was less regional than global; and while it might be overly dramatic to suggest that what happened in Asia Pacific (with its knock-on effects elsewhere) undermined the case for free trade, open markets, and financial deregulation, it did deal the old 'Washington Consensus' a severe blow from which it never really fully recovered. It also achieved something as well: reassured those who had earlier worried that the American century was about to be eclipsed by the rise of Asia Pacific or overtaken by Japan and the Japanese model of capitalism. The panic was over, and on the eve of the new millennium there were few policy-makers back in Washington fretting about the demise of US influence, or losing sleep because of the Japanese economic challenge. In the battle of economic models, the one made in America seemed to stand unrivalled in 2000. The post-cold war fear that the United States would soon be surpassed by better and differently organized competitors stretched out along the Pacific Rim appeared to have passed into history.

Key points

- Until the second half of the 1990s the accepted wisdom was that Asia-Pacific had achieved economic take-off: many even predicted a new 'Pacific Century'.

- The Asian economic crisis that began in 1997 has

led to a massive shake-out and profound social and political consequences.

- The crisis also had a major impact on the stability of the world financial system.

- The collapse of the idea of a new Pacific Century has only confirmed US hegemony.

- US policy-makers no longer worry about Japan as an economic rival and the Japanese model of capitalism.

Europe—integration, expansion, and paralysis

During the twentieth century Europe has been one of the great testing grounds for theories of international relations. Thus out of the carnage of the First World War was born that greatest of all expressions of liberal faith in international institutions, the League of Nations. Created in a flush of post-war optimism, the League represented a laboratory on a large-scale for what many—including E. H. Carr—later regarded as a deeply flawed utopian experiment in organized collective security that was bound to fail. The collapse of the inter-war system followed in quick order by the cold war not only seemed to put pay to such idealism, but also appeared to confirm one of the basic truths of Realism: namely, that in the real world of opposing nation-states, the only thing standing between the European states-system and the breakdown of order, were not fine words or legal documents condemning aggression—these after all had not stopped Italy, Germany, or Japan—but raw military power and the willingness to deploy this to deter expansion. The rebirth of Western Europe after 1947 provided what many then saw as a refutation of this position. The speedy rapprochement between France and Germany, and the creation of a zone of democratic peace were, it was now argued, powerful confirmation of the liberal thesis that states were not fixed things bound to collide, but rather active entities able to negotiate a new set of co-operative relationships. Liberalism also worked economically and one of its most significant triumphs—it was suggested—was the creation of a zone of prosperity in the West that by 1989 had totally exposed the economic pretensions of Soviet-style communism in the East. In this way, the theory of Liberalism, when translated into practice, did more than military pressure, and possibly even more than the Atlantic Alliance, in winning the cold war and so overcoming the division of Europe.

Far from settling the great debate between realists and liberals, the birth of a new Europe only seemed to provide new empirical evidence which the two sides could deploy in order to confirm their own particular truth claims. There was very little give, and even less take in the debate which ensued. Thus whereas liberals emphasized the central importance of a non-military organization like the European Union in helping stabilize the continent after 1989, realists pointed to NATO. Realists insisted that the disaster in former Yugoslavia—as Mearsheimer might have predicted—only confirmed their thesis that the end of the cold war would bring chaos in its wake. Liberals meanwhile emphasized the important ways in which institutions like the Council of Europe and the **Organization for Security and Co-operation** in Europe had helped establish new democratic norms, thus laying the foundation-stone for better times ahead. And while realists stressed that we had to prepare for the worst because the worst was always likely to happens, liberals took an altogether more sanguine view, arguing that the history of the post-cold war decade (ex-Yugoslavia aside) proved that Europe as a whole was bound for peace rather than war, further integration rather than economic conflict, and increased co-operation rather than hostility (see Ch. 18).

At least four important events shaped the course of European history during the first decade of the post-cold war period: German unification, European integration, the war in the former Yugoslavia, and the decision to expand NATO. Let us deal briefly with each.

German unification

German unification was neither welcomed by the other European powers, who worried about its impact on the peace, nor much looked forward to by many in West Germany who feared the economic costs of unity were bound to outweigh the alleged political benefits. The first set of concerns proved groundless: the second did not. Indeed, if anything, people seriously underestimated the price that

Germany as a whole would have to pay. The shock was especially sharp in the early 1990s as factory after factory closed down in the East, causing large-scale unemployment there and thrusting Western Germany into its deepest recession of the entire post-war period. True, by 1996, some of the gloom had lifted. However, it had not been dispelled, and as Germany entered the twenty-first century, the human costs and output losses associated with the economic collapse of the old command economy, had left a profound mark that would take many years to overcome.

The short-term pain endured by Germany should not however obscure our understanding of the historical significance of unification: Germany, in the end, still remained one of the more obvious international 'winners' of the 1990s. After all, as a result of what happened in 1989, it was transformed from a divided nation, effectively controlled by the two superpowers, into a more independent actor. In the process, it also became the key country, as well as the largest, in Europe as a whole. Moreover, it was now (and would remain for the foreseeable future) the central actor in the emerging economies of East and Central Europe. It had also developed a significant economic presence in countries like Poland, the Czech Republic, and Hungary. Russia meanwhile looked to it for most of its bilateral aid. And it had become America's new 'special relation' across the Atlantic. These were not insignificant gains.

European integration

If the birth of a new Germany was one of the most immediate consequences of 1989, a more long-term result was to accelerate the process of European integration. The two processes were closely connected. If German unification did pose a problem—as even the most sanguine of analysts recognized at the time—then an answer had to be found. However, the solution, it was reasoned, was not to attack unification as such, or whip up hysteria based on a series of outdated stereotypes about the aggressive 'Germans' (the atavistic position adopted by Mrs Thatcher for instance), but to integrate the country ever more deeply into Europe. Integration, not containment, was thus seen in continental Europe at least as the modern answer to the new German Question. This was certainly the position adopted by France. It was

also the view of the Americans. The new Europe demanded what US Secretary of State James Baker referred to in 1990 as a new 'security architecture'. This would comprise several old institutions—including the European Community—playing an expanded role right across the continent. The EC could not play its part however unless, and until, it became more integrated: partly to make it a more effective player in Eastern Europe, but also because a Germany fully locked into a more integrated Community was likely to be more in harmony with its neighbours than a Germany that was not.

Inevitably, the logic of economic integration generated new and bold demands for a wider conception of Europe, one that would not only possess its own currency (later launched as the Euro) but its own common foreign and security policy as well. This was perhaps a bridge too far: indeed, it soon became plain that while Europe was fast becoming a serious economic player in global terms (one with the largest GNP in the world) it remained a political pygmy unable to act in international politics. Europe thus presented a dual image. In trade and economics, and in dealing with the emerging economies of Central Europe, it gave every appearance of being a strong and dynamic force. But in the realms of security and diplomacy—what is sometimes talked of as 'high politics'—it was basically paralysed. The extent of this paralysis soon became obvious when the former Yugoslavia began to implode—our third area of concern.

The war in former Yugoslavia

The disintegration of Yugoslavia—the most ethnically diverse but politically most plural of the former communist countries of East-Central Europe—is a tragic story that many have interpreted as morally emblematic of our time with its parade of 'good guys' on one side—normally the Bosnian Muslims and sometimes the Croats—and its line-up of political ogres and monsters on the other, invariably the Serbs, the Yugoslav army, and key Serb leaders like Slobodan Milosevic and Radovan Karadzic. The bare facts are by now well known. In September 1990 Slovenia declared its independence; this was followed a few months later by a Croatian decision to do the same. In February 1992, a referendum was then held to decide the fate of Bosnia-Hercegovina, and even though the Bosnian Serbs (comprising nearly 36 per cent of the electorate) boycotted the election, the Bosnian Muslims and Croats voted in favour of leaving Yugoslavia and forming a new state. Thereafter this most tragic of post-cold war European conflicts unfolded with great speed and intensity, exacting an appalling price in terms of lives lost, peoples displaced, and property destroyed. Finally, on 22 December 1995, a US-brokered peace deal was signed by the warring parties at Dayton. Unfortunately, this left unresolved a number of key issues, one being Kosovo which remained under Serbian rule. The status of Kosovo, however, was finally resolved in 1999 after an extensive air war conducted by NATO against Serbia, following which Kosovo was made into a formal protectorate under the protection of the West (see Ch. 22).

What happened in the former Yugoslavia has been variously interpreted as a war of civilizations between Muslim and Christians (a view favoured by those influenced by the work of Samuel Huntington), the inevitable consequence of Balkan history, the by-product of the collapse of communism and the end of the cold war in one particularly diverse part of Europe, and a monument to Western indifference and the West's refusal to intervene early enough or decisively enough to prevent ethnic cleansing in a part of the world where it did not have—or said it did not have—a vital interest. Certainly, the role of the West has come under intense scrutiny and neither the EU (who were early handed the responsibility of dealing with the situation) nor the UN, come out of the whole thing with very much

credit. The war also exposed deep divisions on the European side, with some countries being much more in favour of self-determination and the break-up of Yugoslavia than others. Germany in particular appeared to act with what some saw as almost total indifference towards the concerns of its allies when it insisted on recognizing Bosnian independence—a move which some felt at the time (and have argued since) only exacerbated the situation rather than calming it down.

The expansion of NATO

If the third Balkan War exposed the pretensions of the Europeans, it also served to highlight the still central role played by the United States in the new European order. And, if we are looking for continuities in history, then one of the most obvious is the extent to which Europe after the cold war remained every bit as dependent on the US for its security as it had been before. By the same token, if one action speaks louder than a thousand words, then one of the most critical actions in Europe after 1989 was the American decision to expand NATO and offer up full membership to three former enemies: Poland, the Czech Republic, and Hungary. The supreme irony was that this had never been Washington's intention in the immediate aftermath of 1989. However, a combination of events— Zhironovsky's showing in the 1993 elections in Russia, domestic pressure upon Clinton from his Republican opponents at home, and what the Americans saw as the abject failure of the Europeans to provide a European answer to a European problem in ex-Yugoslavia—convinced the US that it really had no alternative. Thus in 1994, the decision was taken in principle; and on 12 March 1999, Madelaine Albright formally welcomed NATO's new Central European members into the Alliance. A critically important corner had been turned confirming what many had always wanted, some had not anticipated, and a few vehemently resented: a strong American presence in Europe. With or without a Soviet threat, the US remained the number one power on the continent—by invitation.

Box 6.10 A new European security architecture?

'Twice this century, America sent its young men to Europe to fight and often die, for Europe's freedom. It is worth remembering that on neither occasion was communism or the Soviet Union the enemy. The demise of both will not result in a loss of common commitment since that predated the cold war and will live on after it. The United States continues to need Europe as much as Europe needs the United States.'

(Malcolm Rifkind in *NATO Review*, 2 (March 1995), 8)

Key points

- Europe has been, and remains in the post-cold war era a major testing-ground for liberal and realist international relations theories.

- The key question facing Europe after 1989 has been how to manage the process of German unification.

- The expansion and integration of the European economic space has not been accompanied by a parallel development of a Common Foreign and Security Policy.

- The collapse of Yugoslavia was a major test which the European Union failed to pass.

Still the North: still the South

Often the most significant facts about the international system are those sometimes least talked about by the discipline of international relations—at least that used to be the case during the cold war when most academics were almost completely fixated (and in some ways legitimately so) on the strategic dimensions of the superpower relationship and the impact which the conflict more generally was having upon the different regions of the world. The world, from this point of view, mattered not for its own sake, but in terms of the part it played in the larger drama involving the two principle actors, the United States and the USSR. Nowhere was this more true than in the 'Third World', a vague and loose term conceived in the 1950s, which if nothing else did at least have the advantage from the point of view of the other two worlds (the democratic and capitalist, and the communist and planned), of putting the less developed countries in their rightful place at the end of the political and economic line.

Several factors have led some analysts at least to doubt the very utility of the term, 'Third World'. The most obvious perhaps has been the collapse of what might generically be termed the Third World project of achieving independent economic development outside of the world market system. This retreat began in the early 1980s and continued thereafter as one country after another, from Mexico to India, decided to abandon the policies of economic aut-

archy and adopt the type of market-led strategies most favoured in the West. Another reason for dispensing with the term was the end of the cold war itself. This not only undermined the cause of non-alignment, but rendered illogical the whole idea of a Third World—a concept that only made sense in an international system where there were two other poles and not just one. There was a third objection: that the term was far too broad, including countries as different as Botswana and Argentina, continents as diverse as Africa and Latin America, and regions as far apart economically and culturally as the oil-rich Middle East and the oil-dependent Asian sub-continent. Many analysts therefore (though not all) drew the not unreasonable conclusion that the concept ought to be abandoned altogether.

Getting rid of the concept however did not change the basic conditions under which the vast majority of the world's people continued to live in the 1990s; and while different commentators would identify very different reasons, it would involve denial on an unprecedented scale not to recognize the simple fact that the world still remains divided between a relatively rich 'North' within which the overwhelming bulk of the world's economic activity takes place, and a very poor 'South' where it does not (see Ch. 26). To this extent, the end of the cold war and the collapse of communism has changed very little. Indeed, according to many critics it might have made it a good deal worse: first, by bringing the less-developed countries more completely under the control of the West and its various economic institutions; second, by leading to a reduction in foreign aid; and, finally, by making it increasingly difficult for some 'Third World' states to exploit the superpower rivalry to their own advantage. The cold war may have produced much misery in a number of the more backward countries (think here of its impact in places like Angola, Mozambique, and Afghanistan). On the other hand, some were especially adept at manipulating the old East–West rivalry to their own advantage.

The triumph of capitalism therefore did not necessarily lead to an improvement in the lives of billions of people, a point made not just by radicals critical of the status quo, but also by those who insist that after the failure of planning, capitalism stands alone as the only feasible way rationally of organizing a modern economy. One such observer is the famous Peruvian economist Hernando de Soto. Admired by many on the right, and listened to by several governments (many of whom he advises) de Soto's message—delivered in great style in his best-selling study, *The Mystery of Capital* published in 2000—is a blunt one. 'The hour of capitalism's triumph' he has argued, is also 'its hour of crisis'. After ten years of reform, restructuring and dancing to the 'economic tune' of the experts at the IMF, the masses are still waiting. Communism has been seen off, he accepts, and possibly for good. But its demise has not for the most part seen a viable capitalism kick-started in those parts of the world where it was not already well established. The 'new world order' thus looks very much like the old one with North America, Europe, and parts of Asia still in economic command. Everything has changed, or so it seems, but the fundamentals remain the same.

De Soto's bleak message that capitalism has triumphed in the 'West' but failed nearly everywhere else, is not one likely to be greeted with universal approval by those more optimistic than he. Their argument is not without some foundation. The West, they point out, has tried to improve things and in some instances succeeded. For example, it has linked economic reform and structural adjustment to what it has termed 'good governance'. In many places—the Middle East and Southern Africa being good examples—the end of the cold war has also created a new context that has made possible the settlement of long-standing disputes. In other regions too, like Central America, it made some form of negotiated peace feasible. Vietnam and Cambodia have also come in from the cold. Moreover, there are winners in the 'South', as well as losers. India for example is now experiencing a boom of sorts, while Mexico is rapidly altering as a result of foreign investment. It is not all doom and gloom.

But it is difficult to be too sanguine. In sub-Saharan Africa after all, a number of states have simply imploded from within, while in others—such as Ethiopia and Eritrea—long-standing disputes inherited from the old world continue. Nor should we assume that these problems—amongst the many others facing the 'Third World'—can be kept outside the citadels of power and wealth. Poor people frequently move, and invariably their point of destination is Western Europe and the United States. They also grow drugs which then find their way inside the walls of the West, often wreaking havoc on their inner cities. And if things become too desperate, they sometimes revolt (as they did in Chiapas in Mexico) and commit acts of 'terrorism'. Uneven development in the world economy will always come back to haunt us all.

Box 6.11 Still the North–South divide

'Today across the world, 1.3 billion people live on less than one dollar a day; 3 billion live on under two dollars a day; 3 billion have no access to clean water; 3 billion have no access to sanitation; 2 billion have no access to electricity. We talk of financial crises while in Jakarta, in Moscow, in sub-Saharan Africa, in the slums of India and in the barrios of Latin America, the human pain of poverty is all around us.'

(James D. Wolfensohn of the World Bank, quoted in *The Reality of Aid 2000* (London: Earthscan, 2000), 10)

Key points

- Many experts now question the use of the term 'Third World'.

- In the 1990s, poverty remains a reality for the majority of people.

- The end of the cold war has produced contradictory results in the less-developed countries.

- The political tensions caused by underdevelopment cannot be isolated from the advanced countries.

Conclusion: a farewell to arms?

If the study of international relations has been inspired by the horrors of war and the possibilities of peace, then it should come as no surprise to discover that in 1989—as before in 1918 and again in 1945—many people, expert and lay-person alike, looked forward to more peaceful times. Indeed, one of the oft-expressed hopes was that with the end of the cold war and a reduction in the tensions normally associated with the superpower conflict, the world would become (as liberals expected) a more settled and less dangerous place. Some went even further and predicted that in a world without ideological division, the 'swords' of war would now be able to be turned into the proverbial 'plough-shares', and that the vast amounts of money that had once been expended on weapons would be used for more peaceful and more socially useful purposes. There was even a great deal of talk in the immediate aftermath of the end of the cold war that vast 'peace dividends' would be paid out—dividends it was argued that could either be redeployed to help the needy, or reinvested to make the economies of the world more productive and efficient.

How should we now judge such optimism? As the liberal rantings of the deluded or a reasonable forecast of what actually happened? The answer, quite simply, is neither. As always the truth is complex, and nowhere more so—as we have seen throughout this chapter—when it comes to assessing the future of war and the likelihood of peace in the modern world.

Let us begin with the good news, and the best news of all perhaps is that nuclear war is now far less of a probability between the United States and post-communist Russia, than it ever was between the US and the former USSR. True, nuclear weapons have not been abolished; we may even be living in the 'second nuclear age' as one realist has suggested. But nuclear war is still far less likely to happen. Moreover, there have been what the experts call 'nuclear rollback' in a number of countries including Brazil, South Africa, Ukraine, Kazakhstan, and Belarus. To this extent, the international effort to control the spread of nuclear weapons has been relatively suc-cessful. Spending on the military has gone down too since the end of the cold war—by quite substantial amounts in many cases. Finally, casualty levels from conventional wars have actually fallen, or remained more or less the same.

Now for the bad news: and the first piece is that some states seem determined either to remain or to become nuclear capable—the two most significant examples being India and Pakistan, who in May 1998 both conducted important nuclear tests. A number of other countries like Iraq and North Korea have also been trying (thus far without success) to develop nuclear weapons of their own. Wars have also increased in number—especially in Europe and Africa. Their character has also changed and wars now tend to be fought within collapsing states for the control of specific areas rather than between states. This is presumably why the victims of war are increasingly likely to be civilians rather than soldiers. Finally, though spending on arms has gone down, it still remains very high around the world; the arms trade also continues to flourish and will go on doing so no doubt as long as there are sellers of such weapons making a profit and buyers willing to purchase them.

But of even more significance, perhaps, is that the major states still continue to act, think, and plan as if war is still a possibility. The character of the wars

---

Box 6.12 New wars

'Today the international security environment is far more complex than it was in the cold war era of bipolarity. The radically diminished threat of a world war has been replaced by the reality of intra-state conflicts which undermine stability security at the domestic and regional levels. A serious challenge for the international system is the increasing number of weak or even failed states and their inability to control developments on their own territory . . .'

(Adam Daniel Rotfeld in *SIPRI Yearbook 1998* (Oxford: Oxford University Press, 1998), 1)

they are planning to fight are certainly different to those they planned to fight before 1989 when there was a stalemate in Europe. They also do not plan to fight each other, but rather those countries like Iraq and North Korea referred to in the jargon as 'rogue states'. But the planning goes on, to the extent that the United States is now seriously contemplating creating a defensive nuclear shield to protect it from any likely attack from those they deem to be enemies. Realists of course would argue that such planning, and indeed planning for war more generally, are simply the prudent actions taken by statesmen and women living in the real world rather than academic ivory towers. Moreover, that by planning for the worst, the worst might never happen. That, they say, is the lesson of twentieth-century history. Their various opponents might draw rather different conclusions. Wars don't just happen they believe; nor are they just facts of life. Rather they are the results of mind-sets and beliefs, and as long as there are those who think we have to plan for the worst, then the worst will almost certainly happen. That is also a lesson we might draw from that thing we call 'history'.

Key points

- Many hoped there would be peace after the end of the cold war.
- The end of the cold war made nuclear war less likely and reduced military spending.
- The end of the cold war also increased the number of wars and led to a proportionate rise in civilian casualties.

QUESTIONS

1 Why do you think international relations has had such difficulties in anticipating major events?

2 Have liberal theorists been too optimistic and realists too pessimistic about the world after the cold war?

3 Has radical theory anything to tell us about the course of international history since 1989?

4 If capitalism has triumphed since the end of the cold war, why does it still have its critics?

5 Why did so many writers seem to get American decline wrong?

6 What are the main reasons for the failure of reform in Russia and should the West be worried about it?

7 Should US policy-makers aim to engage with China or contain it?

8 Whatever happened to the Pacific Century?

9 Outline the main issues facing Europe after the cold war.

10 Has capitalism failed the poor?

11 Is the world a safer or more dangerous place since the end of the cold war?

GUIDE TO FURTHER READING

Michael Cox, Ken Booth and Tim Dunne (eds.), *The Interregnum: Controversies in World Politics, 1989–1999* (Cambridge: Cambridge University Press, 1999) provides a wide-ranging survey of most of the key issues and problems facing the international system after the cold war.

Michael Cox, G. John Ikenberry, and Takashi Inoguchi (eds.), *American Democracy Promotion: Impulses, Strategies, and Impacts* (Oxford: Oxford University Press, 2000) looks at a critically important and neglected facet of US foreign policy.

Ken Booth (ed.), *Statecraft and Security: The Cold War and Beyond* (Cambridge: Cambridge University Press, 1998) brings together a number of well-known experts who reflect widely on the 'real world'.

Noam Chomsky, *World Orders, Old and New* (London: Pluto Press, 1994) is a refreshing and iconoclastic look at the international system by the 'old man' of American radicalism.

William Greider, *One World Ready or Not: the Manic Logic of Global Capitalism* (Harmondsworth: Penguin Books, 1997) is a racy but highly readable account which argues there is a fundamental instability at the heart of the new global economy.

Ethan Kapstein and Michael Mastanduno (eds.), *Unipolar Politics: Realism and State Strategies After the Cold War* (New York: Columbia University Press, 1999) is an empirically rooted attempt to show that the struggle for power between states did not stop when the cold war ended.

Patrick O'Meara, Howard D. Mehlinger, and Matthew Krain (eds.), *Globalization and the Challenges of a New Century* (Bloomington: Indiana University Press, 2000) is a very useful collection of many well-known essays about global order and disorder.

François Godement, *The Downsizing of Asia* (London: Routledge, 1999) provides a lively and critical view of the Asian crash and its consequences.

Daniel Burstein and Arne de Keijzer, *Big Dragon—The Future of China* (New York: Simon & Schuster, 1998) in spite of the title is a relatively balanced account of China.

Mary Kaldor and Basker Vashee (eds.), *New Wars* (London: Pinter Press, 1997) reminds us that armed conflict still kills, maims, and displaces hundreds of thousands of people in the poorer countries of the world.

Part Two

Theories of world politics

In this part of the book we introduce you to the main theories that try to explain world politics. We have two main aims: **first**, we want you to be able to grasp the main themes of the theories that have been most influential in explaining world politics. To this end, we have included in this section chapters on the three main theoretical perspectives on world politics: Realism, Liberalism, and Marxism. Of these, Realism has been by far the most influential theory but, as we mentioned in the Introduction, it has also attracted fierce criticism for being an ideology masquerading as an objective theory. Most of the history of international relations theory has seen a dispute between Realism and its two main rivals, with the debate between Realism and Liberalism being the most long-standing and well-developed. For this reason we have a chapter on contemporary mainstream debates between neo-realists and neo-liberals. We then want to introduce you to other recent theoretical work in world politics, thereby giving you an up-to-date survey of the reflectivist and constructivist theoretical literature. So, by the end of this section we hope that you will be able to understand the main themes of the various theories and be able to assess their comparative strengths and weaknesses. Our **second** aim is to give you the overview of theory that you need to be able to assess the significance of globalization for our understanding of world politics. After reading these chapters on theory we hope that you will be in a better position to see how these theories of world politics might interpret globalization in different ways. We feel that you should then be able both to decide for yourself which interpretation you find most convincing and what kind of evidence you might find in the remaining sections of the book to enable you to be able to work out just how much globalization marks a new distinct stage in world politics, requiring new theories, or whether it is simply a fad or fashion which might alter the surface of world politics but not its main underlying features.

Part Two

Theories of world politics

7 Realism

Tim Dunne and Brian C. Schmidt

READER'S GUIDE

Realism is the dominant theory of International Relations. Why? Because it provides the most powerful explanation for the state of war which is the regular condition of life in the international system. This is the bold claim made by realists in defence of their tradition, a claim which will be critically examined in this chapter. The second section will ask whether there is one Realism or a variety of Realism*s*? The argument presented below suggests that despite important differences, particularly between historical realism and structural realism, it is possible to identify a shared core which all realists subscribe to. Section three outlines these common elements: self-help, statism, and survival. In the final section, we will return to the question how far Realism is relevant for explaining or understanding *our* world? Although it leaves many areas of the globalization of world politics uncharted, Realism's emphasis upon material forces such as state power remains an important dimension of international relations after the cold war.

Introduction: the timeless wisdom of Realism

The story of Realism most often begins with a mythical tale of the idealist or utopian writers of the inter-war period (1919–39). Writing in the aftermath of World War One, the 'idealists', a term that realist writers have retrospectively imposed on the inter-war scholars, focused much of their attention on understanding the cause of war so as to find a remedy for its existence. Yet according to the realists, the inter-war scholars' approach was flawed in a number of respects. They, for example, ignored the role of power, overestimated the degree to which human beings were rational, mistakenly believed that nation-states shared a set of common interests, and were overly passionate in their belief in the capacity of humankind to overcome the scourge of war. The outbreak of World War Two in 1939 confirmed, for the realists at least, the inadequacies of the inter-war idealists' approach to studying international politics.

A new approach, one based on the timeless insights of Realism, rose from the ashes of the discredited idealist approach.[1] Histories of the academic field of International Relations describe a Great Debate that took place in the late 1930s and early 1940s between the inter-war idealists and a new generation of realist writers, which included E. H. Carr, Hans J. Morgenthau, Reinhold Niebuhr, Frederick Schuman, George Kennan, and others, who all emphasized the ubiquity of power and the competitive nature of politics among nations. The standard account of the Great Debate is that the realists emerged victorious, and the rest of the International Relations story is, in many respects, a footnote to Realism.[2] It is important to note, however, that at its inception, there was a need for Realism to define itself against an alleged 'idealist' position. From 1939 to the present, leading theorists and policy-makers have continued to view the world through realist lenses. The prescriptions it offered were particularly well suited to the United States' rise to become the global hegemon (or leader). Realism taught American leaders to focus on interests rather than ideology, to seek peace through strength, and to recognize that great powers can coexist even if they have antithetical values and beliefs. The fact that Realism offers something of a 'manual' for maximizing the interests of the state in a hostile environment explains in part why it remains 'the central tradition in the study of world politics' (Keohane 1989a: 36). This also helps to explain why alternative perspectives (see Ch. 11) must of necessity engage with, and attempt to go beyond, Realism.

The theory of Realism that became dominant after World War Two, which we will describe as modern realism (1939–79), is often claimed to rest on an older, classical tradition of thought. The very idea of the timeless wisdom of Realism suggests that modern realism has a number of intellectual antecedents, which we will call classical realism (up to the twentieth century). Indeed, many contemporary realist writers often claim to be part of an ancient tradition of thought that includes such illustrious figures as Thucydides (c. 460–406 BC), Niccolo Machiavelli (1469–1527), Thomas Hobbes (1588–1679), and Jean-Jacques Rousseau (1712–78). The insights that classical realism offered on the way in which state leaders should conduct themselves in the realm of international politics are often grouped under the doctrine of *raison d'état*, or reason of state. Together, writers associated with *raison d'état* are seen as providing a set of maxims to leaders on how to conduct their foreign affairs so as to ensure the security of the state. Many successful leaders of the nineteenth and twentieth century have claimed to follow the timeless principles of classical realism.

According to the historian Friedrich Meinecke, '*Raison d'état* is the fundamental principle of international conduct, the State's First Law of Motion. It tells the statesman what he must do to preserve the health and strength of the State' (Meinecke 1957: 1). Most importantly, the state, which is identified as the key actor in international politics, must pursue power, and it is the duty of the statesperson to calculate rationally the most appropriate steps that should be taken so as to perpetuate the life of the state in a hostile and threatening environment. For realists of all stripes, the survival of the state can never be guaranteed, because the use of force culminating in war is a legitimate instrument of statecraft. As we will see, the assumption that the state is the principal actor coupled with the view that the environment in which states inhabit is a perilous place help to define the essential core of Realism. There is, however, one issue in particular that theorists associated with *raison d'état*, and classical realism more generally, were concerned with; that is, the role, if any, that morals and ethics occupy in international politics.

Realists are sceptical of the idea that universal moral principles exist and, therefore, warn state leaders against sacrificing their own self-interests in order to adhere to some indeterminate notion of 'ethical' conduct. Moreover, realists argue that the need for survival requires state leaders to distance themselves from traditional morality which attaches a positive value to caution, piety, and the greater good of humankind as a whole. Machiavelli argued that these principles were positively harmful if adhered to by state leaders. It was imperative that state leaders learned a different kind of morality which accorded not to traditional Christian virtues but to political necessity and prudence. Proponents of *raison d'état* often speak of a **dual moral standard**: one moral standard for individual citizens living inside the state and a different standard for the state in its external relations with other states. Justification for the two moral standards stems from the fact that the condition of international politics often make it necessary for state leaders to act in a manner (for example, cheating, lying, killing) that would be entirely unacceptable for the individual. But before we reach the conclusion that Realism is completely immoral, it is important to add that proponents of *raison d'état* argue that the state itself represents a moral force, for it is the existence of the state that creates the possibility for an ethical political community to exist domestically. Thus preserving the life of the state and the ethical community it envelops becomes a moral duty of the statesperson.

Although the advanced student might be able to detect some subtle differences, it is fair to say that there is a significant degree of continuity between classical and modern realism. Indeed, the three core elements that we identify with Realism—**statism**, **survival**, and **self-help**—are present in the work of a classical realist such as Thucydides and a modern realist such as Hans J. Morgenthau. We argue that these 'three Ss' constitute the corners of the realist triangle. While we will expand on the meaning of these 'three Ss' later in the chapter, it is important to be clear at the outset what these terms signify.

Realism identifies the group as the fundamental unit of political analysis. During earlier times, such as when Thucydides and Machiavelli were writing, the basic unit was the *polis* or city-state, but since the Treaty of Westphalia (1648) realists consider the sovereign state as the principle actor in international politics. This is often referred to as the state-centric assumption of Realism. Statism is the term given to the idea of the state as the legitimate representative of the collective will of the people. The legitimacy of the state is what enables it to exercise authority internally as manifest, for example, in the making and enforcement of law. Yet outside the boundaries of the state, realists argue that a condition of

anarchy exists. By anarchy what is most often meant is that international politics takes place in an arena that has no overarching central authority above the individual collection of sovereign states. Thus rather than necessarily denoting complete chaos and lawlessness, the concept of anarchy is used by realists to emphasize the point that the international realm is distinguished by the lack of a central authority. As we will see, realists draw a variety of conclusions about the effect that anarchy has on shaping the basic character of international politics.

Following from this, realists draw a sharp distinction between domestic and international politics. Thus while Hans J. Morgenthau argues that 'international politics, like all politics, is a struggle for power,' he goes to great lengths to demonstrate the qualitatively different result this struggle has on international politics as compared to domestic politics (Morgenthau [1948]1955: 25). One major factor that realists argue sets international politics apart from domestic politics is that while the latter is able to constrain and channel the power-seeking ambitions of individuals in a less violent direction (for example, the pursuit of wealth), the former is much less able to do so. For realists, it is self-evident that the incidence of violence is greater at the international than the domestic level. A prominent explanation that realists provide for this difference in behaviour relates to the different organizational **structure** of domestic and international politics. Realists argue that the basic structure of international politics is one of anarchy in that each of the independent sovereign states consider themselves to be their own highest authority and do not recognize a higher power above them. Conversely, domestic politics is often described as a hierarchic structure in which different political actors stand in various relations of super- and subordination.

It is largely on the basis of how realists depict the international environment that they conclude that the first priority for state leaders is to ensure the survival of their state. Under anarchy, the survival of the state cannot be guaranteed. Realists correctly assume that all states wish to perpetuate their existence. Looking back at history, however, realists note that the actions of some states resulted in other states losing their existence (look at the results that Germany achieved at the beginning of World War II).

This is partly explained in light of the power differentials of states. Intuitively, states with more power stand a better chance of surviving than states with less power. **Power** is crucial to the realist lexicon and traditionally has been defined narrowly in military strategic terms. It is the ability to get what you want either through the threat or use of force. Yet irrespective of how much power a state may possess, the core **national interest** of all states must be survival. While states obviously have various interests, such as economic, environmental, and humanitarian, if their existence was to be jeopardized, then these other interests would not stand a chance of ever being realized. Like the pursuit of power, the promotion of the national interest is an iron law of necessity.

Self-help is the principle of action in an anarchical system where there is no global government. According to Realism, each state actor is responsible for ensuring their own well-being and survival. Unlike domestic politics where a range of institutions and mechanisms seek to ensure the welfare of the individual citizen, these are either non-existent or extremely weak in the international realm. Realists do not believe it is prudent for a state to entrust its safety and survival on another actor or international institution such as the League of Nations or the United Nations. For as Machiavelli recognized, today's friend can quickly become tomorrow's enemy. States, in short, should not depend on others for their own security. Moreover, realists once again turn to the historical record and note the unfortunate fate of Ethiopia under the League of Nations and Kuwait under the United Nations and conclude that states should ultimately rely on themselves for security.

You may at this point be asking what options are available to states to ensure their own security. Consistent with the principle of self-help, if a state feels threatened it should seek to augment its own power capabilities by engaging, for example, in a military arms build-up. Yet this may prove to be insufficient for a number of smaller states who feel threatened by a much larger state. This brings us to one of the crucial mechanisms that realists throughout the ages have considered to be essential to preserving the liberty of states—the **balance of power**. Although various meanings have been attributed to the concept of

the balance of power, the most common definition holds that if the survival of a state or a number of weaker states is threatened by a hegemonic state or coalition of stronger states, they should join forces, establish a formal alliance, and seek to preserve their own independence by checking the power of the opposing side. The mechanism of the balance of power seeks to ensure an equilibrium of power in which case no one state or coalition of states is in a position to dominate all the others. The cold war competition between the East and West, as institutionalized through the formal alliance system of the Warsaw Pact and the North Atlantic Treaty Organization (NATO), provides a prominent example of the balance of power mechanism in action.

Before continuing to engage with realist thought in more detail, let us remind ourselves that the story of the discipline of International Relations, like all texts, is open to multiple readings. Moreover, the final chapters have yet to be written. An interesting thought experiment is to ask whether Realism will have the last word. When 'the end of the world as we know it' is upon us, and the conclusion to the 'book' of International Relations is being hastily drafted, will it be written by a realist? Many contemporary theorists would argue that the discipline's centre of gravity is already shifting away from Realism towards a new kind of Liberalism, a theory more appropriate for the post-cold war era perhaps. Other more radical voices argue that what is needed is nothing less than a transformation in our political imagination, in terms of widening our sense of community beyond the confines of the sovereign state which realists (and some Liberal thinkers) take for granted (see Ch. 29). This is especially the case in light of the arguments that some proponents of globalization are making about the state being transcended by global economic forces. Although the chapter does not have the space to do justice to these critical arguments, the 'headlines' are presented in Box 7.3 in the hope that the reader will consult them in their original form.

By way of a response to the critics, it is worth reminding them that the death-knell of Realism has been sounded a number of times already, by the scientific approach in the 1960s and transnationalism in the 1970s, only to see the resurgence of a more robust form of Realism in the late 1970s and 1980s (commonly termed 'neo-realism'). In this respect Realism shares with Conservatism (its ideological godfather) the recognition that a theory without the means to change is without the means of its own preservation. The question of Realism's resilience touches upon one of its central claims, namely, that it is the embodiment of laws of international politics which remain true across time (history) and space (geopolitics). This argument is made by a leading contemporary realist, Robert Gilpin, who cast doubt on 'whether or not twentieth-century students of international relations know anything that Thucydides and his fifth-century BC compatriots did not know about the behaviour of states' (1981: 227–8).

Thucydides was the historian of the Peloponnesian War, a conflict between two great powers in the ancient Greek world, Athens and Sparta. Thucydides' work has been admired by subsequent generations of realists for the insights he raised about many of the perennial issues of international politics. Thucydides' explanation of the underlying cause of the war—'the growth of Athenian power and the fear which this caused in Sparta' (1.23)—is considered to be a classic example of the impact that the anarchical structure of international politics has on the behaviour of state actors. On this reading, Thucydides makes it clear that Sparta's national interest, like that of all states, was survival, and the changing distribution of power represented a direct threat to its existence. Sparta was, therefore, compelled by necessity to go to war in order to forestall being vanquished by Athens. Thucydides also makes it clear that Athens felt equally compelled to pursue power in order to preserve the empire it had acquired. The famous Athenian leader, Pericles, claimed to be acting on the basis of the most fundamental of human motivations: ambition, fear, and self-interest.

One of the significant episodes of the war between Athens and Sparta is known as the 'Melian dialogue' and represents a fascinating illustration of a number of key realist principles. Case Study 1 (Box 7.1) reconstructs the dialogue between the Athenian leaders who arrived on the island of Melos to assert their right of conquest over the islanders, and the response this provoked.

In short, what the Athenians are asserting over the Melians is the logic of power politics. Because of their vastly superior military force, they are able to present a *fait accompli* to the Melians: either submit peacefully or be exterminated. The Melians for their part try and 'buck' the logic of power politics, appealing in turn with arguments grounded in justice, God, and their allies the Spartans. As the dialogue makes clear, the Melians were forced to submit to the realist iron law that 'the strong do what they have the power to do and the weak accept what they have to accept'. Later realists would concur with Thucydides' suggestion that the logic of power politics has universal applicability. Instead of Athens and Melos, we could just as easily substitute, for example, Nazi Germany and Czechoslovakia in 1939, the Soviet Union and Hungary in 1956, or Indonesia and East Timor in 1975. In each case, the weaker state had to submit to the will of the stronger. Power trumps morality, and the threat or use of force triumphs over legal principles such as the right to independence (sovereignty). There are also alternative readings of Thucydides that highlight what happens when states act purely on the basis of self-interest without any consideration of moral and ethical principles. After all, Athens suffers epic defeat even while following the timeless tenets of Realism.

The question whether Realism does embody 'timeless truths' about politics will be returned to in the conclusion of the chapter. Could a scholar who understood the history of international conflict in the fifth century BC really apply the same conceptual tools to global politics at the end of the second millennium? In the following section we will begin to unravel Realism in order to reveal the way in which the tradition has evolved over the last twenty-five centuries. After considering the main tributaries which flow into the realist stream of thinking, the third section will attempt to disinter a 'core' of realist principles to which all realists could subscribe.

Key points

- Realism has been the dominant theory of world politics since the beginning of academic International Relations.

- Outside of the academy, Realism has a much longer history. Scepticism about the capacity of human reason to deliver moral progress resonates

Box 7.1 Case Study 1: The Melian dialogue—Realism and the preparation for war

ATHENIANS. Then we on our side will use no fine phrases saying, for example, that we have a right to our empire because we defeated the Persians . . . And we ask you on your side not to imagine that you will influence us by saying that you, though a colony of Sparta, have not joined Sparta in the war, or that you have never done us any harm . . . you know as well as we do that, when these matters are discussed by practical people, **the standard of justice depends on the equality of power to compel and that in fact the strong do what they have the power to do and the weak accept what they have to accept**.

MELIANS. Then in our view (since you force us to leave justice out of account and to confine ourselves to self-interest) . . . you should not destroy a principle that is to the general good of all men—namely, that in the case of all who fall into danger there should be such a thing as fair play and just dealing.

ATHENIANS. We do not want any trouble in bringing you into our empire, and we want you to be spared for the good both of yourselves and of ourselves.

MELIANS. And how could it be just as good for us to be the slaves as for you to be the masters?

ATHENIANS. You, by giving in, would save yourselves from disaster; we by not destroying you, would be able to profit from you.

MELIANS. So you do not agree to our being neutral, friends instead of enemies, but allies of neither side?

ATHENIANS. No . . . if we were on friendly terms with you, our subjects would regard that as a sign of weakness in us, whereas your hatred is evidence of our power . . . . So that **by conquering you we shall increase not only the size but the security of our empire**.

MELIANS. But do you think there is no security for you in what we suggest? For here again, since you will not let us mention justice, but tell us to give in to your interests, we, too, must tell you what our interests are and, if yours and ours happen to coincide, we must try to persuade you of the fact. Is it not certain that you will make enemies of all states who are at present neutral, when they see what is happening here and naturally conclude that in course of time you will attack them too? . . . Yet we know that in war, fortune sometimes makes the odds more level.

ATHENIANS. Hope, that comforter in danger!

MELIANS. We trust that the gods will give us fortune as good as yours, because we are standing for what is right against what is wrong; and as for what we lack in power, we trust that it will be made up for by our alliance with the Spartans, who are bound, if for no other reason, then for honour's sake, and because we are their kinsman, to come to our help.

ATHENIANS. So far as the favour of the gods is concerned, we think we have as much right to that as you have. . . . Our opinion of the gods and our knowledge of men lead us to conclude that **it is a general and necessary law of nature to rule whatever one can**. This is not a law that we made ourselves, nor were we the first to act upon it when it was made. We found it already in existence, and we shall leave it to exist forever among those who come after us. We are merely acting in accordance with it, and we know that you or anybody else with the same power as ours would be acting in precisely the same way. And therefore, so far as the gods are concerned, we see no good reason why we should fear to be at a disadvantage. But with regard to your views about Sparta and your confidence that she, out of a sense of honour, will come to your aid, we must say that we congratulate you on your simplicity but do not envy you your folly . . . of all people we know the Spartans are most conspicuous for believing that what they like doing is honourable and what suits their interests is just.

MELIANS. But this is the very point where we can feel most sure. Their own self-interest will make them refuse to betray their own colonists, the Melians.

ATHENIANS. You seem to forget that if one follows one's self-interest one wants to be safe, whereas **the path of justice and honour involves one in danger** . . . . Do not be led astray by a false sense of honour. . . . You, if you take the right view, will be careful to avoid this. And, when you are allowed to choose between war and safety, you will not be so insensitively arrogant as to make the wrong choice. You will see that there is nothing disgraceful in giving way to the greatest city in Hellas when she is offering you such reasonable terms—alliance on a tribute-paying basis and liberty to enjoy your own property. **This is the safe rule—to stand up to one's equals, to behave with deference to one's superiors, and to treat one's inferiors with moderation**.

MELIANS. Our decision, Athenians, is just the same as it was at first. We are not prepared to give up in a short moment the liberty which out city has enjoyed from its foundation for 700 years.

ATHENIANS. You seem to us . . . to see uncertainties as realities, simply because you would like them to be so.

(This is an edited extract from Thucydides, *The Peloponnesian War*, trans. Rex Warner (London: Penguin Classics, 1954), 360–5) through the work of classical political theorists such as Thucydides, Machiavelli, Hobbes, and Rousseau.

- In 'The Melian dialogue', one of the episodes of the Peloponnesian War, Thucydides uses the words of the Athenians to highlight the realist view of a number of key concepts such as self-interest, alliances, balance of power, capabilities, and insecurity. The people of Melos respond in

idealist verse, appealing to justice, fairness, luck, the gods, and in the final instance, to common interests.

- At the end of the millennium, Realism continues to attract academicians and inform policy-makers, although the passing of the cold war has seen a revival in the fortunes of Liberalism, and a variety of more critical approaches grouped under the banner of post-positivism.

One Realism, or many?

The intellectual exercise of articulating a unified theory of Realism has been criticized by writers who are both sympathetic and critical of the tradition (Doyle 1997; M. J. Smith 1986). In the words of a leading critic of Realism, 'there is no single tradition of political realism, but rather a knot of historically constituted tensions, contradictions and evasions' (Walker 1993: 106). Consistent with the argument that there is not one Realism, but many, is the attempt to delineate different types of Realism. The most simple distinction is a form of periodization that we introduced in the preceding section: classical realism (up to the twentieth century), modern realism (1939–79), and neo-realism (1979 onwards). These different periods do not, however, overcome the problem of diversity. For example, not all classical realists agree on the causes of war, or whether the balance of power is a natural state or one that must be created.

An alternative form of classification is thematic (a summary of the varieties of realism outlined below is contained in Table 7.1). One of the most convincing of these is R. B. J. Walker's distinction between historical realism and structural realism (1993: 108–22) which the following classification builds on.[3] Machiavelli is the leading classical exponent of **historical realism** in that he recognized the difficulties of devising universal maxims of state conduct that could be used at all times and places to ensure the survival of the state. Machiavelli recognized the flux of political life and appreciated the point that change is a continuous process. Therefore he warned

state leaders always to hedge their bets and, rather than propounding timeless truths, Machiavelli offered what can be termed 'situation-bound knowledge' that always had to take the immediate context into consideration. E. H. Carr is the modern Machiavelli, advocating a foreign policy which recognizes the interplay of power and morality, consent and coercion, and force and appeasement. Carr concluded that the fundamental problem of international politics was how to foster peaceful change in the relations between satisfied and non-satisfied powers without the need to resort to war.

The **structural realism** lineage begins with Thucydides' representation of power politics as a law of human behaviour. The drive for power and the will to dominate are held to be fundamental aspects of human nature. The behaviour of the state as a self-seeking egoist is understood to be merely a reflection of the characteristics of the people that comprise the state. It is human nature that explains why international politics is necessarily power politics. This reduction of Realism to a condition of human nature is one which frequently reappears in the leading works of the realist canon, most famously in the work of the high priest of post-war Realism, Hans J. Morgenthau. It can usefully be thought of as a 'structural' theory—**structural realism I**—because human nature is viewed by realists as the determining structure, one which stands outside of history and cannot be transcended. Morgenthau notes, 'politics, like society in general, is governed by objective laws that have their roots in human nature' (Morgenthau

[1948]1955: 4). The important point for Morgenthau is, first, to recognize that these laws exist and second, to devise the most appropriate policies that are consistent with the basic fact that human beings are flawed creatures. For both Thucydides and Morgenthau, the essential continuity of the power-seeking behaviour of states is rooted in the biological drives of human beings.

The more frequent use of the term 'structural' in the literature—**structural realism II**[4]—is to denote the form of realist argument which attributes the cause of conflict to the anarchic structure of the international system. This form of structural realism is most often associated with Kenneth Waltz's landmark book, *Theory of International Politics* (1979). According to Waltz, anarchy prevents states from entering into co-operative agreements to end the state of war. The condition of anarchy—that is, the fact that there is no 'higher power' to ensure the peace among sovereign·states—is often viewed as synonymous to a state of war. By the state of war, structural realists do not intend to convey the impression that large-scale war is a daily occurrence in international politics, but rather the possibility that a particular state may resort to force indicates that the outbreak of war is always a likely scenario in an anarchical environment. Thus, the structure of the system can drive states to war even if state leaders desire peace (Butterfield 1951: 21). Structural realists insist that the type of state, for example a democracy or totalitarian state, or the personality of the leader is less important in accounting for the phenomena of war than the fact that action takes place within the context of an anarchical realm. But as a number of scholars have pointed out, contemporary realists like Waltz who have tried to construct a realist theory without relying on an assumption about human nature often 'smuggle' into their idea of a 'system' behavioural assumptions about states as competitive and egoistic entities. Moreover, in the work of contemporary structural realists, these traits appear to be prior to the interactions of states as though they existed before the game of power politics began.

The fourth and final type of realism develops out of a reading of Thomas Hobbes. Although his great work *Leviathan* is often cited by realists for its graphically pessimistic portrayal of human nature, Hobbes can more usefully be deployed in support of **liberal realism**. His analogy between individuals in a state of nature and sovereigns in a state of war suggests a kind of permanent cold war where states are constantly living in fear of being attacked. But crucially, Hobbes believed that states are less vulnerable than individuals in the state of nature, and are therefore able to coexist with other sovereigns. As elementary rules of coexistence are formulated, such as the principles of sovereignty and non-intervention, the anarchical system becomes an anarchical society, and Realism metamorphoses into a form of liberal realism. This liberal wing of realism has appealed in particular to British international relations theorists, who have, as John Vincent put it, 'flattered Hobbes by imitating him' (1981: 96–101).[5]

Given the varieties of Realism that exist, it is hardly surprising that the overall coherence of Realism as a tradition of inquiry into international relations has been questioned (Forde 1992: 62). The answer to the question of 'coherence' is, of course, contingent upon how strict the criteria are for judging the continuities which underpin a particular theory. Here it is perhaps a mistake to understand traditions as a single stream of thought, handed down in a neatly wrapped package from one generation of realists to another. Instead it is preferable to think of living traditions like Realism as the embodiment of both continuities and conflicts. For this reason it is important for students to read realists in their historical and political contexts, to try and understand the world they were speaking to and the forces they were reacting against.

While recognizing the danger of imposing a 'mythology of coherence' (Skinner 1988: 39) on the various theorists and practitioners identified with Realism, there are good reasons for attempting to identify a shared core of propositions which all realists subscribe to (see section below, 'The essential Realism'). In the first instance, there is virtue in simplicity; complex ideas can be filtered, leaving a residual substance which may not conform to any one of the ingredients but is nevertheless a virtual representation of all of them. A second reason for attempting to arrive at a composite Realism is that, despite the different strands running through the tradition, there is a sense in which all realists share a common set of propositions. These will be considered in the third section of this chapter.

Table 7.1 A taxonomy of realisms

Type of Realism	Key thinkers (classical and modern)	Key texts	'Big idea'
Structural realism I (Human Nature)	Thucydides (c.430–400 BC)	*The Peloponnesian War*	International politics is driven by an endless struggle for power which has its roots in human nature. Justice, law, and society have either no place or are circumscribed.
	Morgenthau (1948)	*Politics Among Nations*	
Historical or practical realism	Machiavelli (1532)	*The Prince*	Political realism recognizes that principles are subordinated to policies; the ultimate skill of the state leader is to accept, and adapt to, the changing power political configurations in world politics.
	Carr (1939)	*The Twenty Years' Crisis 1919–1939*	
Structural realism II (international system)	Rousseau (c.1750)	*The State of War*	It is not human nature, but the anarchical system which fosters fear, jealousy, suspicion, and insecurity. Conflict can emerge even if the actors have benign intent towards each other.
	Waltz (1979)	*Theory of International Politics*	
Liberal realism	Hobbes (1651)	*Leviathan*	The international anarchy can be cushioned by states who have the capability to deter other states from aggression, and who are able to construct elementary rules for their coexistence.
	Bull (1977)	*The Anarchical Society*	

Key points

- There is a lack of consensus in the literature as to whether we can meaningfully speak about Realism as a single coherent theory.

- There are good reasons for delineating different types of Realism. The most important cleavage is between those who see Realism as a licence to take any course of action necessary to ensure political survival (historical realists) and those who see it as a permanent condition of conflict or the preparation for future conflicts (structural realists).

- Structural realism divides into two wings: those writers who emphasize human nature as the structure (structural realism I) and those who believe that anarchy is the structure which shapes and shoves the behaviour of states (structural realism II).

- At the margins of Realism we find a form of liberal realism which rejects the pessimistic picture of historical and structural realists, believing that the state of war can be mitigated by the management of power by the leading states in the system and the development of practices such as diplomacy and customary international law.

- The question whether it is legitimate to speak of a coherent tradition of political realism touches upon an important debate conducted by historians of ideas. Most classical realists did not consider themselves to be adherents of a particular tradition, for this reason Realism, like all other traditions, is something of an invention.

- Once we admit to a variety of realisms, we are in danger of exaggerating the particular characteristics of each thinker and the context within which they wrote, at a cost of gleaning a better understanding of Realism as a whole.

The essential Realism

The previous paragraphs have argued that Realism is a theoretical broad church, embracing a variety of authors and texts. Despite the numerous denominations, we argue that all realists subscribe to the following 'three Ss': statism, survival, self-help.[6] Each of these elements is considered in more detail in the subsections below.

Statism

For realists, the state is the main actor and sovereignty is its distinguishing trait. The meaning of the sovereign state is inextricably bound up with the use of force. In terms of its internal dimension, to illustrate this relationship between violence and the state we need to look no further than Max Weber's famous definition of the state as 'the monopoly of the legitimate use of physical force within a given territory'.[7] Within this territorial space, **sovereignty** means that the state has supreme authority to make and enforce laws. This is the basis of the unwritten contract between individuals and the state. According to Hobbes, for example, we trade our liberty in return for a guarantee of security. Once security has been established, civil society can begin. But in the absence of security, there can be no art, no culture, no society. All these finer aspects of social life are secondary in importance. The first move, then, for the realist is to organize power domestically. In this respect, 'every state is fundamentally a Machstaat' or power state (Donelan 1990: 25). Only after power has been organized, can community begin.

Realist international theory appears to operate according to the assumption that, domestically, the problem of order and security is solved. The presence of a sovereign authority domestically implies that individuals need not worry about their own security, since this is provided for them in the form of a system of law, police protection, prisons, and other coercive measures. This allows members of the political community living 'inside' the state to pursue the good life. However, on the 'outside', in the relations among independent sovereign states, insecurities, dangers, and threats to the very existence of the state loom large. Realists largely explain this on the basis that the very condition for order and security—namely, the existence of a sovereign—is missing from the international realm. Yet it is worthwhile to evaluate critically the assumptions that are being made here. Is it really the case that you always feel secure inside your own state? Is a central authority a prerequisite for peace and order? Is the inside/outside distinction that realists draw between peace and security on the one hand, and violence and insecurity on the other hand defensible?

Realists claim that in anarchy, states compete with other states for security, markets, influence, and so on. And the nature of the competition is often viewed in zero-sum terms; in other words, more for one actor means less for another. This competitive logic of power politics makes agreement on universal principles difficult, apart from the principle of non-intervention in the internal affairs of other sovereign states. This international legal aspect of sovereignty functions as a 'no trespass sign' placed on the border between states. But even this principle, designed to facilitate coexistence, is suspended by realists who argue that in practice non-intervention does not apply in relations between great powers and their 'near abroad'.

Given that the first move of the state is to organize power domestically, and the second is to accumulate **power** internationally, it is self-evidently important to consider in more depth what realists mean by their ubiquitous fusion of politics with power. It is one thing to say that international politics is a struggle for power, but this merely begs the question of what realists mean by power. Morgenthau offers the following definition of power: 'man's control over the minds and actions of other men' ([1948]1955: 26). There are two important points that realists make about the elusive concept of power. First, power is a relational concept; one does not exercise power in a vacuum, but in relation to another entity. Second, power is a relative concept; calculations need to be made not only about one's own power capabilities, but about the power that other state actors possess. Yet the task of accurately assessing the power of states is infinitely complex, and often is reduced to counting the number of troops, tanks, aircraft, and naval ships a country possesses in the belief that this translates in the ability to get other actors to do something they would not otherwise do. There have been, however, a number of criticisms made of classical and modern Realism's over-reliance on this one-dimensional view of power.

There are two important exceptions to this tendency. First, the more liberal wing of realism has long noted the importance of more subtle understanding of power as prestige; in other words, the ability to get what you want without either the threat or the use of force but through diplomatic influence or authority. Second, E. H. Carr grafted economic and ideological dimensions onto the traditional realist equation of power 'equals' military force. Despite these revisions, Realism has been purchased at a discount precisely because its currency, power, has remained under-theorized and inconsistently used. Simply by asserting that states seek power provides no answer to crucial questions. Why do states struggle for power? Why is the accumulation of power, as Morgenthau argued, 'always the immediate aim'? Surely power is a means to an end rather than an end in itself?

Contemporary structural realists have in recent years sought to bring more conceptual clarity to bear on the meaning of power in the realist discourse. Kenneth Waltz tries to overcome the problem by shifting the focus from power to **capabilities**. He suggests that capabilities can be ranked according to their strength in the following areas: 'size of population and territory, resource endowment, economic capability, military strength, political stability and competence' (1979: 131). The difficulty here is that resource strength does not always lead to military victory. For example, in the 1967 Six Day War between Israel and Egypt, Jordan, and Syria, the distribution of resources clearly favoured the Arab coalition and yet the supposedly weaker side annihilated its enemies' forces and seized their territory. The definition of power as capabilities is even less successful at explaining the relative economic success of Japan over China. A more sophisticated understanding of power would focus on the ability of a state to control

or influence its environment in situations that are not necessarily conflictual.

An additional weakness with the realist treatment of power concerns its exclusive focus upon state power. For realists, states are the only actors that really 'count'. Transnational corporations, international organizations, and religious denominations, like all other ideologies, rise and fall but the state is the one permanent feature in the landscape of modern global politics. Moreover, it is not clear that these non-state actors are autonomous from state power, whether this be Italy in the case of the papacy or the US in the case of corporations like Microsoft. The extent to which non-state actors bear the imprint of a statist identity is further endorsed by the fact that these actors have to make their way in an international system whose rules are made by states. There is no better example of this than the importance of American hegemonic power 'underwriting' the Bretton Woods trading system which has set the framework for international economic relations in the post–1945 period. The motivation for this was not altruism on the part of the US but the rational calculation that it had more to gain from managing the international system than to lose by refusing to exercise leadership. Moreover, realists argue that an open, free-trade economic system, such as what was established at Bretton Woods, depends on the existence of a hegemon who is willing to shoulder the financial burdens of managing the system. This realist argument, popularly known as **hegemonic stability theory**, maintains that international economic order is dependent on the existence of a dominant state.

Survival

The second principle which unites most realists of all persuasions is the assertion that, in international politics, the pre-eminent goal is **survival**. Although there is an ambiguity in the works of the realists as to whether the accumulation of power is an end in itself, one would think that there is no dissenting from the argument that the ultimate concern of states is for security. Survival is held to be a precondition for attaining all other goals, whether these involve conquest or merely independence. According to Waltz, 'beyond the survival motive, the aims of states may be endlessly varied' (1979: 91). Yet a recent controversy among realists has arisen over the question of whether states are in fact principally security or power maximizers. This controversy pits *defensive* against *offensive* realists, and has a number of significant implications for how we view the prospects of international security and co-operation. Defensive realists such as Waltz and Joseph Grieco (1997) argue that states have security as their principal interest and therefore only seek the requisite amount of power to ensure their own survival. According to this view, states are profoundly defensive actors and will not seek to gain greater amounts of power if that means jeopardizing their own security. Offensive realism, as put forth by John Mearsheimer (1994/5), argues that the ultimate goal of all states is to achieve a hegemonic position in the international system. States, according to this view, always desire more power and are willing, if the opportunity arises, to alter the existing distribution of power even if such an action may jeopardize their own security. In terms of survival, defensive realists hold that the existence of status quo powers lessens the competition for power while offensive realists argue that the competition is always keen because revisionist states and aspiring hegemons are always willing to take risks with the aim of improving their position in the international system.

Niccolo Machiavelli tried to make a 'science' out of his reflections on the art of survival. His short and engaging book, *The Prince*, was written with the explicit intention of codifying a set of maxims which will enable leaders to maintain their hold on power. Machiavelli derived these maxims from his experience as a diplomat and his studies of ancient history. For instance, he was full of admiration for the Roman empire which annexed all potential enemies through conquest and imperial domination. Ergo, the lesson that Princes or Sovereigns must be prepared to break their promises if it is in their interests, and to conquer neighbouring states before they (inevitably) attack you. There are a number of ethical and practical difficulties associated with Machiavelli's recommendations, particularly when relating these to contemporary international politics. Indeed, it is the perceived moral bankruptcy of Realism which has provoked a number of the most influential criticisms of the theory, summarized in Box 7.3.

In important respects, we find two related Machiavellian themes recurring in the writings of modern realists, both of which derive from the idea that the realm of international politics requires different moral and political rules than those which apply in domestic politics. The task of understanding the real nature of international politics, and the need to protect the state at all costs (even if this may mean the sacrifice of one's own citizens) places a heavy burden on the shoulders of state leaders. In the words of Henry Kissinger, the academic realist who became Secretary of State during the Nixon Presidency, 'a nation's survival is its first and ultimate responsibility; it cannot be compromised or put to risk' (1977: 204). Their guide must be an ethic of responsibility: the careful weighing up of consequences; the realization that individual acts of an immoral kind might have to be taken for the greater good. By way of an example, think of the ways in which governments frequently suspend the legal and political rights of 'suspected terrorists' in view of the threat they pose to 'national security'. A realist would argue that letting a suspected terrorist out of prison because there is insufficient evidence for prosecution would be an irresponsible act which might jeopardize the lives of innocent civilians. An ethic of responsibility is frequently used as a justification for breaking the laws of war, as in the case of the United States decision to drop nuclear bombs on Hiroshima and Nagasaki in 1945. The principle difficulty with the realist formulation of an 'ethics of responsibility' is that, whilst instructing leaders to consider the consequences of their actions, it does not provide a guide to how state leaders should weigh the consequences (M. J. Smith 1986: 51).

Not only does Realism provide an alternative moral code for state leaders, it suggests a wider objection to the whole enterprise of bringing ethics into international politics. Starting from the assumption that each state has its own particular values and beliefs, realists argue that the state is the supreme good and there can be no community beyond borders. Without a common culture, and common institutions, the idea of an 'international community', so frequently articulated by journalists, is seriously premature. E. H. Carr turned scepticism about moral universals into a 'critical weapon' which he wielded in order to reveal how the supposedly universal principles adumbrated by the Great Powers (such as the virtue of free trade or self-determination) were really 'unconscious reflexions of national policy' (Carr 1946: 87). This moral relativism has generated a substantial body of criticism, particularly from liberal theorists: if all values are relative, how can we judge the actions of state-leaders? Are there not some policies which are wrong irrespective of which states commit them, such as torture or the denial of civil rights? Whilst the intuitive answer to these questions is 'yes', the argument gets more murky when other states with non-Western cultures argue that what we call 'torture' they call a 'rite of passage' (as in the case of female genital mutilation in certain African states). Moreover, many developing states argue that civil rights undermine social cohesion by privileging the individual's rights over the collective good. A realist would therefore see the pursuit of human rights in foreign policy as the imposition of one state's moral principles on another (Morgenthau 1978: 4).

Self-help

Kenneth Waltz's path-breaking work *Theory of International Politics* brought to the realist tradition a deeper understanding of the **international system** within which states coexist. Unlike many other realists, Waltz argued that international politics was not unique because of the regularity of war and conflict, since this was as familiar in domestic politics. The key difference between domestic and international orders lies in their **structure**. In the domestic polity, citizens do not have to defend themselves. In the international system, there is no higher authority to prevent and counter the use of force. Security can therefore only be realized through **self-help**. In an anarchic structure, 'self-help is necessarily the principle of action' (Waltz 1979: 111). But in the course of providing for one's own security, the state in question will automatically be fuelling the insecurity of other states.

The term given to this spiral of insecurity is the **security dilemma**.[8] According to Wheeler and Booth, security dilemmas exist 'when the military preparations of one state create an unresolvable uncertainty in the mind of another as to whether those preparations are for "defensive" purposes only (to enhance its security in an uncertain world) or whether they are for offensive purposes (to change the status quo to its advantage)' (1992: 30). This scenario suggests that one state's quest for security is often another state's source of insecurity. States find it very difficult to trust one another and often view the intentions of others in a negative light. Thus the military preparations of one state are likely to be matched by neighbouring states. The irony is that at the end of the day, states often feel no more secure than before they undertook measures to enhance their own security.

Is there any escape from the security dilemma? There is a divergence in the realist camp between structural realists who believe the security dilemma to be a perennial condition of international politics, and historical realists who believe that, even in a self-help system, the dilemma can be mitigated. The principle mechanism by which it may be mitigated is through the operation of the balance of power. Maintaining a balance of power therefore became a central objective in the foreign policies of the Great Powers; this idea of a contrived balance is well illustrated by the British foreign office memorandum quoted in Box 7.2.

In a self-help system, structural realists argue that the balance of power will emerge even in the absence of a conscious policy to maintain the balance (i.e. prudent statecraft). Waltz argues that balances of power result irrespective of the intentions of any particular state. In an anarchical system populated by states who seek to perpetuate themselves, alliances will be formed that seek to check and balance the power against threatening states. A fortuitous balance will be established through the interactions of states in the same way that an equilibrium is established between firms and consumers in a free economic market (according to classical liberal economic theory). Liberal realists are more likely to emphasize the crucial role state leaders and diplomats play in maintaining the balance of power. In other words, the balance of power is not natural or inevitable, it must be constructed.

All varieties of Realism are united in the view that the balance of power is not a stable condition.

Box 7.2 British foreign policy and the balance of power

History shows that the danger threatening the independence of this or that nation has generally arisen, at least in part, out of the momentary predominance of a neighbouring State at once militarily powerful, economically efficient, and ambitious to extend its frontiers or spread its influence . . . The only check on the abuse of political predominance derived from such a position has always consisted in the opposition of an equally formidable rival, or a combination of several countries forming leagues of defence. The equilibrium established by such a grouping of forces is technically known as the balance of power, and it has become almost an historical truism to identify England's secular policy with the maintenance of this balance by throwing her weight now in this scale and now in that, but ever on the side opposed to the political dictatorship of the strongest single State or group at a given time.

Memorandum by Sir Eyre Crowe on the Present State of British Relations with France and Germany, 1 January 1907
(Viotti and Kauppi 1993: 50).

Whether it is the contrived balance of the Concert of Europe in the early nineteenth century, or the more fortuitous balance of the cold war, balances of power are broken—either through war or peaceful change—and new balances emerge. What the perennial collapsing of the balance of power demonstrates is that states are at best able to mitigate the worst consequences of the security dilemma but are not able to escape it. The reason for this terminal condition is the absence of trust in international relations.

Historically realists have illustrated the lack of trust among states by reference to the parable of the 'stag hunt'. In *Man, the State and War*, Kenneth Waltz revisits Rousseau's parable:

Assume that five men who have acquired a rudimentary ability to speak and to understand each other happen to come together at a time when all of them suffer from hunger. The hunger of each will be satisfied by the fifth part of a stag, so they 'agree' to co-operate in a project to trap one. But also the hunger of any one of them will be satisfied by a hare, so,

as a hare comes within reach, one of them grabs it. The defector obtains the means of satisfying his hunger but in doing so permits the stag to escape. His immediate interest prevails over consideration for his fellows.   (1959: 167–8)

Waltz argues that the metaphor of the stag hunt provides not only a justification for the establishment of government, but a basis for understanding the problem of co-ordinating the interests of the individual versus the interests of the common good, and the pay-off between short-term interests and long-term interests.   In the self-help system of international politics, the logic of self-interest mitigates against the provision of collective goods such as 'security' or 'free trade'. In the case of the latter, according to the theory of comparative advantage, all states would be wealthier in a world that allowed freedom of goods and services across borders. But individual states, or groups of states like the European Union, can increase their wealth by pursuing protectionist policies providing other states do not respond in kind. Of course the logical outcome is for the remaining states to become protectionist, international trade collapses, and a world recession reduces the wealth of each state.

The contemporary liberal solution to this problem of collective action in self-help systems is through the construction of regimes (see Ch. 14). In other words, by establishing patterns of rules, norms and procedures, such as those embodied in the World Trade Organization (WTO), states are likely to be more confident that other states will comply with the rules and that defectors will be punished. Contemporary structural realists agree with liberals that regimes can facilitate co-operation under certain circumstances, although realists believe that in a self-help system co-operation is 'harder to achieve, more difficult to maintain, and more dependent on state power' (Grieco, in Baldwin 1993: 302). One reason for this is that structural realists argue that states are more concerned about relative than absolute gains. Thus the question is not whether all will be better off through co-operation, but rather who will likely gain more than another. It is because of this concern with relative gains issues that realists argue that co-operation is difficult to achieve in a self-help system (see Ch. 9).

A more thoroughgoing challenge to the way in which realists have set up the problem of collective action in a self-help system comes from constructivsm (see Ch. 11).[9] Although this is a complex argument, the key move in the critique is to argue that anarchy need not imply a self-help system. Historically, anarchy has accommodated varieties of inter-state practices. In the eighteenth century, philosophers and lawyers portrayed the European states-system as a commonwealth, a family of nations, with common laws and customs. In the twentieth century, the decentralized international system has witnessed a diverse pattern of interactions, from a literal state of war to brief periods of collective security to examples of regional integration. Only the first of these three conditions could be described in terms of self-help. As Alexander Wendt puts it: 'Self-help presupposes self-interest; it does not explain it. Anarchy is what states make of it' (1994: 388).

✗ Key points

- **Statism** is the centrepiece of Realism. This involves two claims. First, for the theorist, the state is the pre-eminent actor and all other actors in world politics are of lesser significance. Second, state 'sovereignty' signifies the existence of an independent political community, one which has juridical authority over its territory.

- **Key criticism**: Statism is flawed both on empirical (challenges to state power from 'above' and 'below') and normative grounds (the inability of sovereign states to respond to collective global problems such as famine, environmental degradation, and human rights abuses).

- **Survival**: The primary objective of all states is survival; this is the supreme national interest to which all political leaders must adhere. All other goals such as economic prosperity are secondary (or 'low politics'). In order to preserve the security of their state, leaders must adopt an ethical code which judges actions according to the outcome rather than in terms of a judgement about whether the individual act is right or wrong. If there are any moral universals for political realists, these can only be concretized in particular communities.

- **Key criticism**: Are there no limits to what actions a state can take in the name of necessity?

- **Self-help**: No other state can be relied upon to guarantee your survival. In international politics, the structure of the system does not permit friendship, trust, and honour; only a perennial condition of uncertainty generated by the absence of a global government. Coexistence is achieved through the maintenance of the balance of power, and limited co-operation is possible in interactions where the realist state stands to gain more than other states.

- **Key criticism**: Self-help is not an inevitable consequence of the absence of a world government; self-help is the game which states have chosen to play. Moreover, there are historical and contemporary examples where states have preferred collective security systems, or forms of regional integration, in preference to self-help.

Conclusion: Realism and the globalization of world politics

The chapter opened by considering the often repeated realist claim that the pattern of international politics—wars interrupted for periods characterized by the preparation for future wars—have remained constant over the preceding twenty-five centuries. Realists have consistently held that the continuities in international relations are more important than the changes, but many find this to be problematic in the present age of globalization. In the concluding paragraphs below, we will briefly evaluate whether Realism can speak to our world, or has become, as its critics suggest, an anachronistic theory.

Box 7.3 What the critics say

R. ASHLEY: Structural realists portray the structure of the international system as though there is only one structure (that of power) and its existence is independent of states (rather than constructed by them). For this reason, contemporary structural realism is a static, conservative theory (1984).

C. BEITZ: The analogy between individuals in a state of nature and states in international anarchy is misplaced for four reasons. States are not the only actors; the power of states is massively unequal; states are not independent of each other; patterns of co-operation exist (even if motivated by self-interest) despite the absence of a global government capable of enforcing rule (1979).

K. BOOTH: Realism cannot speak to our world. Survival for the majority of individuals in global politics is threatened not by armies of 'foreign' states but more often by their own governments, or more broadly, structures of global capitalism which produce and reproduce the daily round of 'human wrongs' such as malnutrition, death from preventable diseases, slavery, prostitution, and exploitation (1995b).

C. BROWN: The strongest argument against Realism's moral scepticism is that states employ a moral language of rights and duties in their relations with each other (1992).

J. BURTON: Interactions of states is only one of many levels of interaction in world society. Rather than an image of states as billiard balls impacting on each other at random, Burton argues we should think about international relations as a 'cobweb model' of interactions and linkages between multiple actors (firms, individuals, groups, etc.) (1990).

R. COX: Realism is problem-solving theory. It accepts the prevailing order, and seeks only to isolate aspects of the system in order to understand how it works. The idea of theory serving an emancipatory purpose—i.e. contemplating alternative world orders—is not in the structural realist's vocabulary (1986).

F. HALLIDAY: The realist conception of the state in international politics (where states are equal, they are in control of their territory, they coincide with nations, and represent their peoples) is very unrealistic. A more adequate interpretation of the state is provided by sociology, which makes an analytical distinction between the state and society, the state and government, and the state and nation (1994).

M. HOLLIS and S. SMITH: Realism assumes that the methods of the natural sciences can be employed to explain the social world (of which international relations is

part). Realism can therefore be equated with a form of positivism which seeks to uncover causal laws that can both explain and predict the occurrence of events in world politics (1990).

F. KRATOCHWIL: Contrary to the expectations of contemporary structural realism, the end of the cold war was not brought about by any radical shift in the distribution of power in the international system, and moreover, this shift occurred without a major war (1993).

A. LINKLATER: We must go beyond the structural realist emphasis upon constraints, and the liberal realist predilection for order, in order to develop an emancipatory form of theory which seeks to deepen the sense of solidarity, and widen the bonds of community in global politics (1990b).

V. SPIKE PETERSON: The realist emphasis upon national security is contradictory for women, since it masks over 'women's systemic insecurity'. Taking feminism seriously requires a radical rethink of the way in which security is framed by a form of sovereignty which legitimizes violence against women and gendered divisions of resources and identities (1992).

J. ROSENBERG: Realism is a conservative ideology. Fundamental to this conservatism is the autonomy realists accord to the international realm. 'The borders and landscapes of this environment are set and policed by the twin concepts of sovereignty and anarchy' (1994: 30).

M. J. SMITH: Despite the argument that values should not impact objective policy formulation, Realism too often appears as nothing more than the (traditional) values and beliefs of the author in question, leaving the suspicion that it is conservative intuitionism masquerading as an international political theory (1986).

C. SYLVESTER: From Machiavelli to the early twenty-first century, the qualities 'men' have ascribed to 'women'—such as irrationality, intuition, temptation—have been regarded as a danger to international affairs. For this reason, historical realists argue that statecraft should remain 'mancraft' (1994).

J. VASQUEZ: A statistical analysis of International Relations literature in the 1950s and 1960s underscores the dominance of the realist paradigm in terms of the overwhelming reliance on the core assumptions of Realism. However, although Realism dominated the field, it did not adequately explain international politics from a social science perspective. For example, of 7,044 realist hypotheses tested in the field, only 157 of these fail to be falsified (1998: 149).

It has often been argued that the end of the cold war dealt a fatal blow for Realism. Despite its supporters' faith in the capacity of Realism to predict changes in the international system, most contemporary structural realists predicted the continuity of a stable bipolar (or two superpowers) system well into the twenty-first century (Waltz 1979: 210). It would therefore appear that the peaceful conclusion of the cold war, which represents one of the most significant changes in the contemporary international system, raises some serious problems for Realism. Critics of structural realism were right in objecting to its inability to theorize changes in the international system, and some questioned whether the reign of Realism might not be coming to an end. (Although, in fairness to Realism, none of the other paradigms of international politics managed to predict the disintegration of the cold war system with the clarity of many Central and East European intellectuals and dissidents.) Yet various realists have provided explanations to account for the end of the cold war and do not find the events that culminated in the collapse of the Soviet Union to represent a major anomaly for realism, see Case Study 2 (Box 7.4).

Moreover, the understandable idealism which greeted the end of the Soviet empire has become more muted in the last few years as the world has witnessed some of the most horrific conflicts of the twentieth century. In the former Yugoslavia we have seen war crimes committed by all of the protagonists, crimes that Europe thought had been banished by the defeat of Nazism. Whilst it would be too strong to claim that the Balkan war was a realist war (because of the multiplicity of complex causes) its origins in the fear engendered by the collapse of the Yugoslav state allied to the contagion of a form of nationalism defined by the fiction of a pure ethnic identity, bear a resemblance to an atavistic realism of blood and belonging. War in Africa, rising tensions between India and Pakistan, conflict in the Middle East, and concern about the intentions of China continue to confirm the relevance of Realism. There seems little doubt that realist ideas will be drawn upon in the future by state leaders who believe the use of force is the only instrument left to insure their survival.

This is not to suggest that Realism is only useful as

> **Box 7.4 Case study 2: After the cold war—Realism's eternal return?**
>
> • Leading non-realist theorists have argued that the end of the cold war represents a failure for Realism in general, and neo- or structural realism in particular. Why? First, Waltz's 1979 book *Theory of International Politics* aligns structural realism with positivism, and the objective of all positivist theories is to predict. Despite this clear scientific objective, most realists were unwilling to specify when and how the international system was going to change although Waltz believed it was likely to last well into the twenty-first century. This in itself suggests that Realism is a conservative theory, privileging an explanation of continuity over theorizing alternative future orders.
>
> • While realists could claim that all branches of IR theory were caught out by the collapse of bipolarity at the end of the 1980s, there is a second and more weighty criticism of Realism and that concerns its failure to *explain* the end of the cold war. The most common realist reply is to argue that a state in decline will try to reverse this process by curtailing its external commitments. In other words, the Soviet Union retreated, and in this sense, was defeated. The problem here is that, when they did make general predictions, contemporary realists expected the opposite.
>
> • Again, we find that Realism lends itself to any number of possible consequences. Realism can lend itself to an expansionist foreign policy or to appeasement; to a retreat from empire or to expanding the frontier for security reasons. The ambiguity of this point is put very succinctly by John Vazquez (in his excellent critique of neo-realism and the end of the cold war): 'The great virtue of realism is that it can explain almost any foreign policy event. Its great defect is that it tends to do this after the fact, rather than before' (Vazquez, 1998: 324).

a guide to understanding the origins and settlement of wars. It will continue to serve as a critical weapon for revealing the interplay of national interests beneath the rhetoric of universalist sentiments. There is no more powerful example of this than Realism's potential to deconstruct a Marxist or a Liberal progressivist view of history which sees the gradual triumphing of European ideas and values

Box 7.5 Key concepts in realist thought

anarchy Does not imply chaos, but the absence of political authority.

anarchic system The 'ordering principle' of international politics, and that which defines its structure.

balance of power Refers to an equilibrium between states; historical realists regard it as the product of diplomacy (contrived balance) whereas structural realists regard the system as having a tendency towards a natural equilibrium (fortuitous balance).

capabilities Population and size of territory, resources, economic strength, military capability, and competence (Waltz 1979:131)

dual moral standards The idea that there are two principles or standards of right and wrong: one for the individual citizen and different one for the state.

ethic of responsibility For historical realists, an ethic of responsibility is the limits of ethics in international politics; it involves the weighing up of consequences and the realization that positive outcomes may result from amoral actions.

idealism Holds that ideas have important causal effect on events in international politics, and that ideas can change. Referred to by realists as utopianism since it underestimates the logic of power politics and the constraints this imposes upon political action.

interdependence A condition where the actions of one state impact upon other states (can be strategic interdependence or economic). Realists equate interdependence with vulnerability.

hegemony The influence a great power is able to establish on other states in the system; extent of influence ranges from leadership to dominance.

hegemonic stability theory A realist based explanation for co-operation that argues that a dominant state is required to ensure a liberal, free-trade international political economy.

international system A set of interrelated parts connected to form a whole. Systems have defining principles such as hierarchy (in domestic politics and anarchy (in international politics).

national interest Invoked by realists and state leaders to signify that which is most important to the state—survival being at the top of the list.

power The ability to control outcomes e.g. state A is able to get state B to act in a way which maximizes the interests of A.

self-help In an anarchical environment, states cannot assume other states will come to their defence even if they are allies.

sovereignty The state has supreme authority domestically and independence internationally

state A legal territorial entity composed of a stable population and a government; it possesses a monopoly over the legitimate use of force; its sovereignty is recognized by other states in the international system.

statism The ideology which supports the organization of humankind into particular communities; the values and beliefs of that community are protected and sustained by the state.

state of war The conditions (often described by classical realists) where there is no actual conflict, but a permanent cold war that could become a 'hot' war at any time.

structure In the philosophy of the social sciences a structure is something which exists independently of the actor (e.g. social class) but is an important determinant in the nature of the action (e.g. revolution). For contemporary structural realists, the number of great powers in the international system constitutes the structure.

survival The first priority for state leaders, emphasized by historical realists such as Machiavelli, Meinecke, and Weber.

throughout the world. A realist has no problem understanding aspects of the globalization of world politics—indeed structural realists could claim to have theorized more completely the nature of the international system than any other paradigm on offer. What is interesting about a realist theory of globalization is the acceptance of the militarization of the international system, and the patterns of political control and domination which extend beyond borders (such as hegemonic control or spheres of influence), but a concomitant rejection of the idea that globalization is accompanied by a deepening sense of community. From Rousseau to Waltz, realists have argued that interdependence brought about through intimate contact with modernity is as likely to breed 'mutual vulnerability' as peace and prosperity. And while questioning the extent to which the world has become 'interdependent', realists insist that the state is not going to be eclipsed by global forces operating either below or above the nation-state.

There are good reasons for thinking that the twenty-first century will be a realist century. The Western sense of immortality, fuelled by the Enlightenment discoveries of reason and democracy, was dealt a fatal blow by the Holocaust. Despite the efforts of federalists to rekindle the idealist flame, Europe continues to be divided by interests and not united by a common good. Outside of Europe and North America, many of the assumptions which underpinned the post-war international order, particularly those associated with human rights, are increasingly being seen as nothing more than a Western idea backed by economic dollars and military 'divisions'. As the axis of world politics shifts to the Asia-Pacific region, this model of democratic individualism which the liberal West has tried to export to the rest of the world is being revealed as culturally contingent and economically retarded. This comes as no surprise to realists who understand that words are weapons and that internationalist ideas are the continuation of statism by other means. Here we find an alliance between Realism and many non-Western states' leaders who recognize that values are shared within particular communities and not between them, that knowledge is contingent and not grounded in universal reason, that global cultures are fragmented and contested. Rather than transforming global politics in its own image, as liberalism has sought to do in this century, the West may need to become more realist in order to survive the next.

QUESTIONS

1   How does the Melian dialogue represent key concepts such as self-interest, the balance of power, alliances, capabilities, empires and justice?

2   Do you think there is one Realism, or many?

3   Do you know more about international relations than an Athenian student during The Peloponnesian War?

4   Is the practice of international politics realist? How does Realism inform state practice? Through what channels or processes does it shape foreign policy?

5   Do realists confuse a description of war and conflict, for an explanation of why it occurs?

6   How can the security dilemma be escaped or mitigated?

7   Is Realism any more than the ideology of powerful, satisfied states?

8   How far do the critics of Realism overlook the extent to which the theory is grounded in an ethical defence of the state?

9   How would realists try to explain the continuing instability in the Balkans? Do you find their arguments convincing?

10 Will the West have to learn to be more realist, and not less, if its civilization is to survive in the twenty-first century?

GUIDE TO FURTHER READING

The most comprehensive book on twentieth-century Realism is Michael Joseph Smith, *Realist Thought from Weber to Kissinger* (Baton Rouge: Louisiana State University Press, 1986). For an effective single chapter survey, particularly on structural realism, see Martin Hollis and Steve Smith, *Explaining and Understanding International Relations* (Oxford: Clarendon, 1990), chapter 5. The Paul Viotti and Mark Kauppi, *International Relations Theory: Realism, Pluralism, Globalism* (New York: Macmillan, 1993) textbook has an extensive treatment of Realism in chapter 2, including important excerpts from the classical precursors.

The best single work on historical realism is N. Machiavelli, *The Prince*, ed. Q. Skinner (Cambridge: Cambridge University Press, 1988). E. H. Carr, *The Twenty Years' Crisis 1919–1939: An Introduction to the Study of International Relations* (London: Macmillan, 1946) is a hugely important and thought-provoking work which brings historical Realism into the twentieth century, see especially chapters 5 and 6. The bible for liberal realism is Hedley Bull, *The Anarchical Society: A Study of Order in World Politics* (London: Macmillan, 1977). Structural realism I, with its emphasis upon laws of human nature, is exemplified in Hans J. Morgenthau, *Politics among Nations: The Struggle for Power and Peace* (New York: Knopf, 1978), chapter 1. Kenneth Waltz, *Theory of International Politics* (Reading, Mass.: Addison-Wesley, 1979) is the exemplar for structural Realism II, see in particular, chapters 1 and 6. Alongside this work, the student should consult Robert Keohane, *Neorealism and its Critics* (New York: Columbia University Press, 1986). This collection of essays includes key chapters by Waltz, an interesting defence of Realism by Robert Gilpin, and powerful critiques by Richard Ashley, Robert Cox, and J. G. Ruggie. A more recent collection which takes the debate further is David A. Baldwin, *Neorealism and Neoliberalism: The Contemporary Debate* (New York: Columbia University Press, 1993). For the more penetrating constructivist challenge to Realism, see A. Wendt in *International Organization*, 46:2 (1992), 395–421; and *American Political Science Review*, 88:2 (1994), 384–96.

NOTES

1. Realism, *realpolitik*, and *raison d'état* are broadly interchangeable. In this chapter, Realism with an upper case 'R' will be used to signify the general tradition. When discussing particular realists, or types of realism (such as historical realism), lower case 'r' will be used.

2. A number of critical histories of the field of International Relations have recently challenged the notion that the inter-war period was essentially 'idealist' in character. Both Peter Wilson (1998) and Brian C. Schmidt (1998) argue that it is simply a myth that an idealist paradigm dominated the study of international relations during the interwar period of the field's history.

3. The other 'critical' distinction is made by Richard Ashley who contrasts the 'practical realism' of Machiavelli and Carr with the 'technical realism' of Gilpin and Waltz (1981: 221).

4. What we have termed 'structural realism II' is often referred to in the literature as Neo-Realism. Robert Keohane argues that Neo-Realism differs from earlier forms of Realism 'in that it does not rest on the presumed iniquity of the human race' (1989b: 40). Although Keohane is right to note the shift in causation from human nature to anarchy, he is wrong to believe that this is anything other than a change from one kind of structure to another (hence the use in the chapter of 'structural realism I' and 'II').

5. The extent to which British liberal realism, found in the work of Martin Wight and Hedley Bull constitues a break from Realism, is a matter of some debate in the literature. For contrasting answers, compare Booth (1995*b*) and Dunne (1998). This is not to suggest that the category liberal realism does not also apply to certain American thinkers, notably Herz (1981).

6. There are a number of similar versions of this idea of a 'shared core' to Realism in the literature. Keohane distils the core into: state as actor, state as rational, state as power maximizer (Keohane 1989*b*: 39) and (Gilpin 1986: 304–5) are two examples among many.

7. M. J. Smith, 23. Weber is rightly regarded by Smith as the theorist who has shaped twentieth-century realist thought, principally because of his fusion of politics with power.

8. It is important to note that not all conflict results from the security dilemma (since both parties have benign intent); historically, more conflicts have been caused through predator states.

9. Alex Wendt defines constructivism in the following terms: 'Constructivism is a structural theory of the international system which makes the following core claims (1) states are the principal units of analysis for international political theory; (2) the key structures in the states system are intersubjective, rather than material; and (3) state identities and interests are in important part constructed by these social structures, rather than given exogenously to the system by human nature or domestic politics' (1994: 385).

8 Liberalism

Tim Dunne

READER'S GUIDE

The practice of international relations has not been accommodating to Liberalism. Whereas the domestic political realm in many states has witnessed an impressive degree of progress, with institutions providing for order *and* justice, the international realm in the era of the modern states system has been characterized by a precarious order and the *absence* of justice. In the introductory section, the chapter will address this dilemma of Liberalism's false promise as well as considering the moments in history when Liberalism has impacted significantly on the theory and practice of international relations. Like all grand theory, Liberalism is an aggregation of a number of different ideas. Section two seeks to uncover the most important variations on the Liberal theme, beginning with the visionary liberal internationalism of the Enlightenment, through to the liberal idealism of the inter-war period, and ending with the liberal institutionalism which became popular in the immediate post-war years. This discussion begs two important questions, dealt with in section three. What has become of these three historic elements in liberal thinking on international relations? And how have contemporary writers situated in these various strands sought to cope with globalization? The final section summarizes the arguments that have gone before, as well as reflecting more broadly on the fate of liberalism in international relations at the end of the millennium.

Introduction

Although Realism is regarded as the dominant theory of international relations, Liberalism[1] has a strong claim to being the historic alternative. Rather like political parties, Realism is the 'natural' party of government and Liberalism is the leader of the opposition, whose main function is to hound the talking heads of power politics for their remorseless pessimism. And like historic parties of 'opposition', Liberalism has occasionally found itself in the ascendancy, when its ideas and values set the agenda for international relations. In the twentieth century, Liberal thinking influenced policy-making élites and public opinion in a number of Western states after the First World War, an era often referred to in academic International Relations as **Idealism**. There was a brief resurgence of liberal sentiment at the end of World War II, with the birth of the United Nations, although these flames of hope were soon extinguished by the return of cold war power politics. The end of the cold war has seen a resurgence of Liberalism as Western state leaders proclaimed a 'New World Order' and liberal intellectuals provided theoretical justifications for the inherent supremacy of Liberalism over all other competing ideologies.

One of the most respected contemporary theorists in the field, Stanley Hoffmann, once famously wrote that 'international affairs have been the nemesis of liberalism'. 'The essence of liberalism', Hoffmann continues, 'is self-restraint, moderation, compromise and peace' whereas 'the essence of international politics is exactly the opposite: troubled peace, at best, or the state of war' (Hoffmann 1987: 396). This explanation comes as no surprise to realists, who argue that there can be no progress, no law, and no justice, where there is no common power. The fact that historically international politics has not been hospitable to liberal ideas should not be interpreted as a surrender by liberals to the logic of power politics. Liberals argue that power politics itself is the product of ideas, and crucially, ideas can change. So, even if the world hasn't been accommodating to liberalism to date, this does not mean that it cannot be made into a liberal world order. Given this disposition, it is not surprising that Liberalism is described in the literature as the 'tradition of optimism' (Clark 1989: 49–66).

While the belief in the possibility of progress is one identifier of a liberal approach to politics, there are other general propositions that unite the various strands of liberalism. Perhaps the appropriate way to begin this discussion is with a three-dimensional definition. Liberalism is an ideology whose central concern is the liberty of the individual; liberals see the establishment of the state as a necessary part of preserving liberty either from harm by other individuals or by states; the state must always be the servant of the collective will, not the master, and democratic institutions are the means of guaranteeing this. Here it is important to note that Liberalism is primarily a theory of government, one that seeks to reconcile order (security) and justice (equality) within a particular community. But as we will see in the course of the chapter, many advocates of this tradition have recognized that providing order and justice on the 'inside' may not be possible without reform of the 'outside'. The argument being made here is a crucial one. As long as states continue to exist in relation to one another as individuals did in the state of nature, the liberal project of providing peace and progress will forever be undermined.

As is often the case with general theories of international politics, we quite quickly move from identifying assumptions shared by all liberals to the realization that there are fundamental disagreements. As Box 8.1 demonstrates, liberals offer radically different answers to what they take to be the pre-eminent dilemma in international relations, namely, why wars occur: are they caused by imperialism, the balance of power, or undemocratic regimes? Furthermore, liberals diverge on whether peace is the goal of world politics, or order? And how should this be established, through collective security, commerce, or world government? Finally, liberals are divided on the issue of how liberal states should respond to non-liberal states (or civilizations), by conquest, conversion, or toleration?

Box 8.1 Liberalism and the causes of war, determinants of peace

One of the most useful analytical tools for thinking about differences between individual thinkers or particular variations on a broad theme such as Liberalism, is to differentiate between levels of analysis. For example, Kenneth Waltz's *Man, The State and War* examined the causes of conflict operating at the level of the individual, the state, and the international system itself. The table below turns Waltz on his head, as it were, in order to show how different liberal thinkers have provided competing explanations (across the three levels of analysis) for the causes of war and the determinants of peace.

'Images' of Liberalism	Public figure/ period	Causes of conflict	Determinants of peace
First image: (Human nature)	Richard Cobden (mid-19th c.)	Interventions by governments domestically and internationally disturbing the natural order	Individual liberty, free trade, prosperity, interdependence
Second image: (The state)	Woodrow Wilson (early 20th c.)	Undemocratic nature of international politics; especially foreign policy and the balance of power	National self-determination; open governments responsive to public opinion; **collective security**
Third image: (The structure of the system)	J. A. Hobson (early 20th c.)	The balance of power system	A **world government**, with powers to mediate and enforce decisions

Key points

- Liberalism is fundamentally anchored around the liberty of the individual. Domestic and international institutions are to be judged according to whether they further this aim. But note that this basic principle allows for significant variations, for example, those who believe that freedom needs to be constrained for the greater good.

- From the eighteenth century onwards, Liberalism has exerted a strong influence on the practice of world politics.

- The high-water mark of liberal thinking in international relations was reached in the inter-war period in the work of idealists who believed that warfare was an unnecessary and outmoded way of settling disputes between states.

- In view of the significant divergences within the liberal tradition—on issues such as human nature, the causes of wars, and the relative importance different kinds of liberals place on the individual, the state, and international institutions in delivering progress—it is perhaps more appropriate to think of not one Liberalism, but contending liberalisms.

Varieties of Liberalism

Liberal thinking on international relations can be dimly perceived in the various plans for peace articulated by philosophers (and theologians) from the sixteenth century onwards. Such thinkers rejected the idea that conflict was a natural condition for relations between states, one which could only be tamed by the careful management of power through balance of power policies and the construction of alliances against the state which threatened international order. In 1517 Erasmus first iterated a familiar liberal theme; war is unprofitable. To overcome it, the kings and princes of Europe must desire peace, and perform kind gestures in relations with fellow sovereigns in the expectation that these will be reciprocated. Other early liberal thinkers placed an emphasis upon the need for institutional structures to constrain international 'outlaws'. Towards the end of the seventeenth century, William Penn advocated a 'Diet' (or Parliament) of Europe. Indeed, there are some remarkable parallels between Penn's ideas and the institutions of the European Union today. Penn envisaged that the number of delegates to the Parliament should be proportional to the power of the state, and that legislation required a kind of 'qualified majority voting', or as Penn put it, the support of 75 per cent of the delegates.

These broad sketches of ideas from some of the progenitors of liberal thinking in international relations show how, from Penn's plans for a 'Diet' in 1693 to the Treaty on European Union in 1992, there are common themes underlying Liberalism; in this instance, the theme is the importance of submitting the separate 'wills' of individual states to a general will agreed by states acting collectively (see, for example, Kant's 'third definitive article' in Box 8.2. Yet it would be wrong to suggest that the development of liberal thinking on international affairs has been linear. Indeed, it is often possible to portray current political differences in terms of contrasting liberal principles. To return to the Treaty on European Union mentioned above, the debate which raged in many European countries could be presented as one in which the liberal principle of integration was challenged by another liberal principle of the right of states to retain sovereignty over key aspects of social and economic policies.

How should we understand this relationship between autonomy and **integration** which is embodied in Liberalism? One way might be to apply a historical approach, providing detailed accounts of the contexts with which various philosophers, politicians and international lawyers contributed to the elaboration of key liberal values and beliefs. Although the contextual approach has merit it tends to downplay the dialogue between past and present, closing off the parallels between Immanuel Kant (an eighteenth-century philosopher-king from Konigsberg) and Francis Fukuyama (the late twentieth-century political thinker and former employee of the US State Department). An alternative method, which is favoured in this chapter, is to lay bare the variety of liberalisms thematically rather than historically.[2] To this end, the following section identifies three patterns of thought as the principal constituents of Liberalism: **liberal internationalism**, **idealism**, and **liberal institutionalism**.

As Box 8.2 demonstrates, many of the great liberal figures such as Immanuel Kant believed that human potentiality can only be realized through the transformation of individual attitudes as well as the binding of states together into some kind of federation. In this sense, Kant combines a commitment to international institutions (embodied in both idealists and liberal institutionalists) as well as the liberal internationalists' belief that democratic forms of government are inherently superior. Like Kant, the thinking of many other great liberal thinkers reaches beyond the boundaries of any single category. For this reason it is important not to use the categories as labels for particular thinkers, but as representations of a discernible strand in the history of liberal thinking on international relations.

Liberal internationalism

Immanuel Kant and Jeremy Bentham were two of the leading liberal internationalists of the Enlightenment. Both were reacting to the barbarity of international relations, or what Kant graphically described as 'the lawless state of savagery', at a time when domestic politics was at the cusp of a new age of rights, citizenship, and constitutionalism. Their abhorrence of the lawless savagery led them individually to elaborate plans for 'perpetual peace'. Although written over two centuries ago, these manifestos contain the seeds of key liberal internationalist ideas, in particular, the belief that reason could deliver freedom and justice in international relations. For Kant the imperative to achieve perpetual peace required the transformation of individual consciousness, republican constitutionalism and a federal contract between states to abolish war (rather than to regulate it as liberal

Box 8.2   Immanuel Kant's 'Perpetual Peace: A Philosophical Sketch'

First Definitive Article: *The Civil Constitution of Every State shall be Republican*

'If, as is inevitably the case under this constitution, the consent of the citizens is required to decide whether or not war is to be declared, it is very natural that they will have great hesitation in embarking on so dangerous an enterprise . . . . But under a constitution where the subject is not a citizen, and which is therefore not republican, it is the simplest thing in the world to go to war. For the head of state is not a fellow citizen, but the owner of the state, and a war will not force him to make the slightest sacrifice so far as his banquets, hunts, pleasure palaces and court festivals are concerned . . . ' (Kant 1991: 99–102)

Second Definitive Article: *The Right of Nations shall be based on a Federation of Free States*

'Each nation, for the sake of its own security, can and ought to demand of the others that they should enter along with it into a constitution, similar to a civil one, within which the rights of each could be secured . . . . But

peace can neither be inaugurated nor secured without a general agreement between the nations; thus a particular kind of league, which we will call a *pacific federation* is required. It would be different from *a peace treaty* in that the latter terminates *one* war, whereas the former would seek to end *all wars* for good . . . . It can be shown that this idea of *federalism*, extending gradually to encompass all states and thus leading to perpetual peace, is practicable and has objective reality' (Kant 1991: 102–5).

Third Definitive Article: *Cosmopolitan Right shall be limited to Conditions of Universal Hospitality*

'The peoples of the earth have thus entered in varying degrees into a universal community, and it has developed to the point where a violation of rights in one part of the world is felt *everywhere*. The idea of a cosmopolitan right is therefore not fantastic and overstrained; it is a necessary complement to the unwritten code of political and international right, transforming it into a universal right of humanity' (Kant 1991: 105–8).

realists such as Hugo Grotius had argued). This federation can be likened to a permanent peace treaty, rather than a 'superstate' actor or world government.

Jeremy Bentham tried to address the specific problem of the tendency among states to resort to war as a means of settling international disputes. 'But, establish a common tribunal', Bentham argued, and 'the necessity for war no longer follows from a difference of opinion' (Luard 1992: 416). Like many liberal thinkers after him, Bentham showed that federal states such as the German Diet, the American Confederation, and the Swiss League were able to transform their identity from one based on conflicting interests to a more peaceful federation. As Bentham famously argued, 'between the interests of nations there is nowhere any real conflict'. Note that these plans for a permanent peace imply an extension of the social contract between individuals in domestic society to states in the international system, in other words, subjecting the states to a system of legal rights and duties. But crucially, liberal internationalists—unlike the idealists of the inter-war period—believed

that a law-governed international society could emerge without a **world government**.

The idea of a natural order underpinning human society is the cornerstone of liberal internationalism. For the clearest statement of this position, we must turn to the Scottish political economist and moral philosopher, Adam Smith. By pursuing their own self-interest, individuals are inadvertently promoting the public good. The mechanism which intervenes between the motives of the individual and 'ends' of society as a whole, is what Smith referred to as 'an invisible hand'. Although Smith believed that the natural harmony between individual and state did not extend to a harmony between states (Wyatt-Walter 1996: 28) this is precisely what was emphasized by liberal internationalists in the nineteenth century like Richard Cobden. In common with many key figures in the Liberal tradition, Cobden was a political activist as well as a writer and commentator on public affairs. He was an eloquent opponent of the exercise of arbitrary power by governments the world over. 'The progress of freedom', he compellingly argued, 'depends more upon the maintenance of peace, the spread of commerce, and the diffusion of education, than upon the labours of cabinets and foreign offices' (Hill 1996: 114). For Cobden, politics was too important to be left to politicians.

It was primarily this liberal idea of a natural 'harmony of interests' in international political and economic relations which E. H. Carr attacked in his polemical work *The Twenty Years' Crisis*. Although Carr's book remains one of the most stimulating in the field, one 'which leaves us nowhere to hide' (Booth 1995b: 123), it could be argued that Carr incorrectly targets idealists of the interwar period as the object of his attack instead of the liberal internationalists of the nineteenth century. As we will see in the following section, rather than relying on a natural harmony to deliver peace, idealists fervently believed that a new international order had to be constructed, one which was managed by an international organization. This line of argument represents a significant shift from the nineteenth-century **liberal internationalism** to the **idealist** movement in the early part of the twentieth century.

Idealism

Like liberal internationalism, the era of **idealism** (from the early 1900s through to the late 1930s) was motivated by the desire to prevent war. However, many idealists were sceptical that *laissez faire* economic principles, like free trade, would deliver peace. Idealists, like J. A. Hobson, argued that imperialism—the subjugation of foreign peoples and their resources—was becoming the primary cause of conflict in international politics. For Hobson, imperialism resulted from underconsumption within developed capitalist societies. This led capitalists to search for higher profits overseas, which became a competitive dynamic between states and the catalyst for militarism, leading to war. Here we see a departure from the liberal internationalist argument that capitalism was inherently pacific. The fact that Britain and Germany had highly interdependent economies before the Great War (1914–18), seemed to confirm the fatal flaw in the liberal internationalist association of **interdependence** with peace. From the turn of the century, the

contradictions within European civilization, of progress and exemplarism on the one hand and the harnessing of industrial power for military purposes on the other, could no longer be contained. Europe stumbled into a horrific war killing fifteen million people. The war not only brought an end to three empires it was also a contributing factor to the Russian Revolution of 1917.

The First World War shifted liberal thinking towards a recognition that peace is not a natural condition but is one which must be constructed. In a powerful critique of the idea that peace and prosperity were part of a latent natural order, the publicist and author Leonard Woolf argued that peace and prosperity required 'consciously devised machinery' (Luard 1992: 465). But perhaps the most famous advocate of an international authority for the management of international relations was Woodrow Wilson. According to the US President, peace could only be secured with the creation of an international institution to regulate the international anarchy. Security could not be left to secret bilateral diplomatic deals and a blind faith in the balance of power. Like domestic society, international society must have a system of governance which has democratic procedures for coping with disputes, and an international force which could be mobilized if negotiations failed. In this sense, liberal idealism rests on a **domestic analogy** (Suganami 1989: 94–113).

In his famous 'fourteen points' speech, addressed to Congress in January 1918, Wilson argued that 'a general association of nations must be formed' to preserve the coming peace (see Box 8.3). The League of Nations, was of course, the general association which idealists willed into existence. For the League to be effective, it had to have the military power to deter aggression and, when necessary, to use a preponderance of power to enforce its will. This was the idea behind the **collective security** system which was central to the League of Nations. Collective security refers to an arrangement where 'each state in the system accepts that the security of one is the concern of all, and agrees to join in a collective response to aggression' (Roberts and Kingsbury 1993: 30). It can be contrasted with an alliance system of security, where a number of states join together usually as a response to a specific external threat (sometimes known as collective defence). In

Box 8.3 Woodrow Wilson's 'Fourteen Points' and the realism of idealism

1. Open covenants openly arrived at.

2. Freedom of the seas alike in peace and war.

3. The removal of all economic barriers to trade . . .

4. Reduction of national armaments.

5. A readjustment of all colonial claims . . .

6. The evacuation of Russian territory and the independent determination by Russia of her own political development and national policy.

7. The evacuation and restoration of Belgium.

8. The evacuation and restoration of France and the return of Alsace-Lorraine.

9. A readjustment of the frontiers of Italy along national lines.

10. Self-determination for the peoples of Austria–Hungary.

11. A redrawing of the boundaries of the Balkan states along historically established lines of nationality.

12. Self-determination for the peoples under Turkish rule . . .

13. The independence of Poland with free access to the sea guaranteed by international covenant.

14. The formation of a general association of nations under specific covenants for the purpose of affording mutual guarantees of political independence and territorial integrity to great and small states alike.

These '14 points' contain many idealist principles, in particular the importance of self-determination from colonial rule as well as the need for an international organization to maintain peace and security. But a close reading not just of the 14 points, but of the political context of the time, suggests that there was more than a twist of realism to the idealist principles articulated by Woodrow Wilson. This comes through strongly in the following passage. 'As a number of historians have shown, Wilson advanced his Fourteen Points for many reasons, but one, obviously, was a shrewd appreciation that liberal democracy was the best antidote to Bolshevism and reaction in a world turned upside down by global war. Even his support for self-determination was as much a strategic ploy as a moral demand. As the record reveals, the ultimate purpose of the slogan was not to free all nations, but rather to undermine the remaining empires on the European continent and win America friends in east and central Europe. Wilson understood, even if his later realist critics did not, the power of values and norms in international relations' (Cox, 2000: 6–7).

the case of the League of Nations, Article 16 noted the obligation that, in the event of war, all member states must cease normal relations with the offending state, impose sanctions, and if necessary, commit their armed forces to the disposal of the League Council should the use of force be required to restore the status quo.

The experience of the League of Nations was a disaster. Whilst the moral rhetoric at the creation of the League was decidedly idealist, in practice states remained imprisoned by self-interest. There is no better example of this than the United States' decision not to join the institution it had created. With the Soviet Union outside the system for ideological reasons, the League of Nations quickly became a talking shop for the 'satisfied' powers. Hitler's decision in March 1936 to reoccupy the Rhineland, a designated demilitarized zone according to the

terms of the Treaty of Versailles, effectively pulled the plug on the League's life-support system (it had been put on the 'critical' list following the Manchurian crisis in 1931 and the Ethiopian crisis in 1935). Indeed, throughout the 1930s, the term crisis had become the most familiar one in international affairs.

Although the League of Nations was the principal organ of the idealist inter-war order, it is important to note other ideas which dominated liberal thinking in the early part of the twentieth century. Education became a vital addition to the liberal agenda, hence the origins of the study of International Relations as a discipline in Aberystwyth in 1919 with the founding of the Woodrow Wilson professorship. One of the tasks of the Wilson Professor was to promote the League of Nations as well as contributing to 'the truer understanding of civilizations other than our own' (John *et al.* 1972: 86). It is this self-consciously **normative** approach to the discipline of International Relations, the belief that scholarship is about what ought to be and not just what is, that sets the idealists apart from the institutionalists who were to carry the torch of liberalism through the early post-1945 period.

Outside of the military–security issue area, liberal ideas made an important contribution to global politics even during the cold war. The principle of self-determination, championed by liberal internationalists for centuries, signalled the end of empire. The protection of individuals from human rights abuses was enshrined in the three key standard setting documents: the 1948 Universal Declaration, the Covenant on Economic, Social, and Cultural Rights, and the Covenant on Civil and Political Rights. Even the more radical calls in the mid-1970s for a 'New International Economic Order' emanating from poorer post-colonial states contained within it the kernel of a liberal defence of justice as fairness. The problem of the uneven distribution of wealth and power between the 'developed' and the 'developing' world is one which has been championed by a succession of liberal state-leaders, from the 1980 Brandt Report (named after the former West German Chancellor Willy Brandt) to the 1995 report by the Commission on Global Governance, chaired by Ingvar Carlson (then Swedish Prime Minister) and Shridath Ramphal (former Secretary-General of the Commonwealth).

Liberal institutionalism

According to the history of the discipline of International Relations, the collapse of the League of Nations signified the end of **idealism**. There is no doubt that the language of **liberal institutionalism** was less avowedly **normative**; how could anyone assume progress after Auschwitz? Yet certain fundamental tenets remained. Even in the early 1940s, there was a recognition of the need to replace the League with another international institution with responsibility for international peace and security. Only this time, in the case of the United Nations there was an awareness among the framers of the Charter of the need for a consensus between the

Great Powers in order for enforcement action to be taken, hence the veto system (Article 27 of the UN Charter) which allowed any of the five permanent members of the Security Council the power of veto. This revision constituted an important modification to the classical model of collective security (Roberts 1996: 315). With the ideological polarity of the cold war, the UN procedures for collective security were still-born (as either of the superpowers and their allies would veto any action proposed by the other).[3] It was not until the end of the cold war that a collective security system was operationalized, following the invasion of Kuwait by Iraq on 2 August 1990 (see Box 8.4.)

An important argument by liberal institutionalists in the early post-war period concerned the state's inability to cope with modernization. David Mitrany, a pioneer **integration** theorist, argued that transnational co-operation was required in order to resolve common problems (Mitrany 1943). His core concept was **ramification**, meaning the likelihood that co-operation in one sector would lead governments to extend the range of collaboration across other sectors. As states become more embedded in an **integration** process, the 'cost' of withdrawing from co-operative ventures increases.

This argument about the positive benefits from transnational co-operation is one which lies at the core of **liberal institutionalism** (and remains central to neo-liberal institutionalists, as noted in the following section). For writers such as Haas, international and regional institutions were a necessary counterpart to sovereign states whose capacity to deliver welfare goals was decreasing (1968: 154–8). The work of liberal institutionalists like Mitrany and Haas, provided an important impetus to closer co-operation between European states, initially through the creation of the European Coal and Steel Community in 1952. Consistent with Mitrany's hypothesis, co-operation in the energy sector provided governments with the confidence to undertake the more ambitious plan for a European Economic Community enshrined in the Treaty of Rome in 1956.

By the late 1960s and early 1970s, a new generation of scholars (particularly in the US) influenced by the European integration literature, began to examine in greater analytical depth the impact of modernization on the states system.[4] In particular,

Box 8.4 Case study 1: The Gulf War and collective security

Iraq had always argued that the sovereign state of Kuwait was an artificial creation of the imperial powers. When this political motive was allied to an economic imperative, caused primarily by the accumulated war debts following the eight-year war with Iran, the annexation of Kuwait seemed to be a solution to Iraq's problems. The Iraqi President, Saddam Hussein, also assumed that the West would not use force to defend Kuwait, a miscalculation which was fuelled by the memory of the support the West had given Iraq during the Iran–Iraq war (the so-called 'fundamentalism' of Iran was considered to be a graver threat to international order than the extreme nationalism of the Iraqi regime).

The invasion of Kuwait on 2 August 1990 led to a series of UN resolutions calling for Iraq to withdraw unconditionally. Economic sanctions were applied whilst the US-led coalition of international forces gathered in Saudi Arabia. Operation 'Desert Storm' crushed the Iraqi resistance in a matter of six weeks (16 January to 28 February 1991). The Gulf War had certainly revived the UN doctrine of collective security, although a number of doubts remained about the underlying motivations for the war and the way in which it was fought (for instance, the coalition of national armies was controlled by the US rather than by a UN military command as envisaged in the Charter). President Bush declared that the war was about more than one small country, it was about a 'big idea; **a new world order'**. The content of this new world order was 'peaceful settlement of disputes, solidarity against aggression, reduced and controlled arsenals, and just treatment of all peoples'.

they rejected the state-centric view of the world adopted by both traditional realists and behaviouralists. World politics, according to liberal institutionalists (or pluralists as they are often referred to) were no longer an exclusive arena for states, as it had been for the first three hundred years of the Westphalian states system. In one of the central texts of this genre, Robert Keohane and Joseph Nye argued that the centrality of other actors, such as interest groups, transnational corporations and international non-governmental organizations, had to be taken into consideration (1972). Here the overriding image of international relations is one of a cobweb of diverse actors linked through multiple channels of interaction.

Although the phenomenon of **transnationalism** was an important addition to the International Relations theorists' vocabulary, it remained underdeveloped as a theoretical concept. Perhaps the most important contribution of **pluralism** was its elaboration of **interdependence**. Due to the expansion of capitalism and the emergence of a global culture, pluralists recognized a growing interconnectedness between states which brought with it a shared responsibility for the environment. The following passage sums up this position neatly:

We are all now caught up in a complex systemic web of interactions such that changes in one part of the system have direct and indirect consequences for the rest of the system.   (Little 1996: 77)

Clearly absolute state autonomy, so keenly entrenched in the minds of state leaders, was being circumscribed by interdependence. Moreover, this process is irreversible (Morse 1976: 97). Unlike realists however, liberal institutionalists believe that the decline of state autonomy is not necessarily regrettable, rather, they see transnationalism and interdependence as phenomena which must be managed.

Key points

- **Liberal internationalism**: The strand in liberal thinking which holds that the natural order has been corrupted by undemocratic state leaders and out-dated policies such as the balance of power. Prescriptively, liberal internationalists believe that contact between the peoples of the world, through commerce or travel, will facilitate a more pacific form of international relations.

- **Idealism**: Although there are important continuities between liberal internationalism and idealism, such as the belief in the power of world public opinion to tame the interests of states, idealism is distinct in that it believes in the importance of constructing an international order. For idealists, as opposed to internationalists, the freedom of states is part of the problem of international relations and not part of the solution. Two requirements follow from their diagnosis. The first is the need for explicitly normative thinking: how to promote peace and build a better world. Second, states must be part of an international organization, and be bound by its rules and norms.

- Central to **idealism** was the formation of an international organization to facilitate peaceful change, disarmament, arbitration, and (where necessary) enforcement. The League of Nations was founded in 1920 but its collective security system failed to prevent the descent into world war in the 1930s. The victor states in the wartime alliance against Nazi Germany pushed for a new international institution to represent the society of states and resist aggression. The United Nations Charter was signed in June 1945 by fifty states in San Francisco. It represented a departure from the League in two important respects. Membership was near universal, and the great powers were able to prevent any enforcement action from taking place which might be contrary to their interests.

- **Liberal institutionalism**: The third figure in the pattern of Liberalism. In the 1940s, liberal institutionalists turned to international institutions to carry out a number of functions the state could not perform. This was the catalyst for integration theory in Europe and pluralism in the United States. By the early 1970s, pluralism had mounted a significant challenge to realism. It focused on new actors (transnational corporations, non-governmental organizations) and new patterns of interaction (interdependence, integration).

Three liberal responses to globalization

The previous section has delineated three elements in the history of liberal thinking on international relations. Below, the chapter will bring this conversation between contending liberalisms up to date, hence the prefix 'neo' attached to each variant. Although the underlying arguments within each element remain constant, there have been discernible shifts in the political purposes to which those arguments have been utilized.

Neo-liberal internationalism

One of the 'big ideas' in the theory and practice of international relations in the 1990s is known as 'the democratic peace thesis'. The kernel of this argument, which can be traced back to Kant's philosophical sketch on Perpetual Peace, is that liberal states do not go to war with other liberal states. In this sense, liberal states have created what Michael Doyle has termed, a 'separate peace'. Although liberal states are pacific in relation to other liberal states, Doyle recognizes that liberal democracies are as aggressive as any other type of state in their relations with authoritarian regimes and stateless peoples (Doyle 1995b: 100).

Although the empirical evidence seems to support the democratic peace thesis, it is important to bear in mind the limitations of the argument. In the first instance, for the theory to be compelling, supporters of the 'democratic peace thesis' must provide an explanation as to why war has become unthinkable between liberal states. Over two centuries ago, Kant argued that if the decision to use force was taken by the people, rather than by the prince, then the frequency of conflicts would be drastically reduced. But logically this argument implies a lower frequency of conflicts between liberal and non-liberal states, and this has proven to be contrary to the historical evidence. An alternative explanation for the 'democratic peace thesis' might be that liberal states tend to be wealthy, and therefore have less to gain (and more to lose) by engaging in conflicts than poorer authoritarian states. Perhaps the most convincing explanation of all is the simple fact that liberal states tend to be in relations of amity with other liberal states. War between Canada and the US is unthinkable, perhaps not because of their liberal democratic constitutions, but because they are friends (Wendt, 199: 298–99). Indeed, war between states with contrasting political and economic systems may also be unthinkable because they have a history of friendly relations. An example here is Mexico and Cuba, who although claiming a common revolutionary tradition nevertheless embrace antithetical economic ideologies.

Irrespective of the scholarly search for an answer to the reasons why liberal democratic states are more peaceful, it is important to note the political consequences of this hypothesis. In 1989 Francis Fukuyama wrote an article entitled 'The End of History' which celebrated the triumph of liberalism over all other ideologies, contending that liberal states were more stable internally and more peaceful in their international relations (Fukuyama 1989: 3–18). Whilst restating a familiar liberal internationalist theme, albeit with a Hegelian spin, Fukuyama's article and subsequent book served the political purpose of underlining the superiority of American values, thereby providing legitimacy to those who sought to 'export' liberalism. It was no longer a case of liberalism in one country, as it had appeared to some realists during the cold war, but rather liberalism for all countries.

What instruments are available to states to spread liberal values and widen the zone of peace? There are a wide range of options open to Western states in their attempt to globalize liberalism. At one end of the spectrum, the collapse of state structures (for example, in Somalia or Yugoslavia) prompts many liberals to call for forcible humanitarian intervention. But as critics from the realist 'right' and critical theory 'left' often argue, intervention even for liberal reasons often exacerbates the problem. Since the question of humanitarian intervention is dealt with in detail in Chapter 22 the paragraphs below will focus on the non-military instruments at the disposal of state leaders and international institutions for promoting liberal values in global politics.

At the political level, the powerful states in the international system are able to use institutional leverage as a means of embedding formerly non-liberal states into the liberal world order. The EU has done this extensively in its relations with former communist states of Central and Eastern Europe. The 'bargain' can be seen in terms of material rewards (access to the single market and structural adjustment funds) in return for accepting western values in the economic and political/social spheres. Increasingly, the US has used a combination of punitive and rewarding strategies to spread liberal ideas in previously illiberal parts of the world (see Box 8.5).

Box 8.5 Defending and extending the liberal zone of peace

Contemporary liberal internationalists believe history proves that liberal states act peacefully towards one another. Yet this empirical law does not tell liberal states how to behave towards non-liberal states. Should they try to convert them, thereby bringing them into the zone of peace, or should they pursue a more defensive strategy? The former has not been successful in the past, and in a world of many nuclear weapons states, crusading could be suicidal. For this reason, Michael Doyle suggests a dual-track approach.

- The first track is preserving the liberal community which means forging strong alliances with other like-minded states and defending itself against illiberal regimes. This may require liberal states to include in their foreign policy strategies like the balance of power in order to contain authoritarian states.

- The second track is more expansionist and aims to extend the liberal zone by a variety of economic and diplomatic instruments. He categorizes these in terms of 'inspiration' (hoping peoples living in non-democratic regimes will struggle for their liberty), 'instigation' (peace-building and economic restructuring) and 'intervention' (legitimate if the majority of a polity is demonstrating widespread disaffection with their government and / or their basic rights are being systematically violated).

Doyle concludes by warning liberals against assuming that the march of liberalism will continue unabated. It is in our hands, he argues, whether the international system becomes more pacific and stable, or whether antagonisms deepen. We must be willing to pay the price—in institutional costs and development aid—to increase the prospects for a peaceful future. This might be cheap when compared with the alternative of dealing with hostile and unstable authoritarian states (Doyle, 1999).

In relations with the Third World, where there are fewer prospects for exerting regional institutional leverage, the most effective tool has been conditionality: the policies developing countries must pursue in return for economic benefits such as loans or investment. More recently, **conditionality** has expanded from the requirement to liberalize and privatize the economic sector, to include targets on 'good governance', and compliance to human rights norms. While proponents might claim some successes, its reception in Asia has been contested. The rapid economic development of some Asian states has made them economically less dependent on Western aid or expertise, and at the same time they have become increasingly critical of the liberal internationalist assumption that liberal values are universally shared. The Australian dilemma, illustrated in Case Study 2 (Box 8.6) between promoting human rights in the Asia-Pacific region without damaging its economic and security interests, might serve as a microcosm for future relations between a weaker West and a potential economic colossus like China.

The attempt by Western states to globalize liberalism has highlighted a number of endemic weaknesses in the neo-liberal internationalist position.[5] First, from an intellectual point of view, theorists like Doyle and Fukuyama are complacent about the degree to which their own society is indeed liberal and prone to overestimate the number of stable liberal democracies in the world. Second, a defeat for Stalinist-style communism does not mean that liberalism has triumphed over all other ideologies. Social democracy remains an important ideology in Northern Europe, and a variety of forms of non-liberal consitutionalism exist, for example, in Asia and to a lesser extent in Japan. Third, Western states have done little to remove the suspicion among radicals in their own countries and public opinion in South-East Asia, that the project of spreading liberal values is a convenient fiction for promoting the commercial interests of Western firms. Finally, the neo-liberal internationalist agenda of the 1990s highlights the often conflicting principles which underpin liberalism. Promoting economic liberalization, particularly in economically impoverished countries, frequently comes into conflict with the norms of democracy and human rights. Two examples illustrate this dilemma. First, the more the West becomes involved in the organization of developing states' political and economic infrastructure, the less those states are able to be accountable to their domestic constituencies, thereby cutting through the link between the government and the people which is so central to modern liberal forms of representative democracy (Hurrell and Woods 1995: 463). Second, in order to qualify for Western aid and loans, states are often required to meet harsh economic criteria requiring cuts in many welfare programmes; the example of the poorest children in parts of Africa having to pay for primary school education (Booth and Dunne, 1999: 310)– which is their right according to the Universal Declaration of Human Rights—is a stark reminder of the fact that economic liberalism and political liberalism are frequently opposed.

Neo-idealism

Like the Idealists of the inter-war period, neo-idealists have a good deal in common with liberal internationalism: both share a commitment to democratic forms of government, and both believe that interdependence breeds peace. That said, neo-idealists believe that peace and justice are not natural conditions, they are the product of deliberate design. Moreover, the processes of globalization have added to the enormity of this task. Encouraging or even coercing non-liberal states to become more democratic is only part of what is required in order to bring about a truly liberal world order. Consistent with the original idealists, neo-idealists argue that reform needs to take place at the international level: like states themselves, international institutions need to be made more democratic.[6] Similarly, neo-idealists believe that global social movements must be brought into the decision-making structures, since these are often closer to ordinary people than their own governments. In addition to tackling the global 'democratic deficit', neo-idealists are more prone to point to the dark side of globalization than liberal internationalists. These arguments are discussed in greater length below.

Liberal internationalists tend to use the term globalization in positive ways, as though we lived in a global village, signifying economic and moral

Box 8.6 Case study 2: Promoting liberal values in an illiberal region — The Australian dilemma*

How can Australia, with its broadly Western liberal values, be accepted by northern neighbours such as Indonesia, Malaysia, Thailand, and the Philippines? Is it enough that the countries of the region share common interests (in trade and maintaining a stable order) or are there cultural barriers to co-operation? The case of Australian–Indonesian relations is a fascinating example of the conundrum over what happens when the fault-lines between civilizations come to the surface. Decades of diplomatic indifference were brought to an end in 1988, when the two Foreign Ministers began negotiating the Timor Gap Zone of Co-operation Treaty, outlining agreed boundaries for mineral exploitation in the Timor Sea. Undoubtedly the normalization of bilateral relations with Indonesia is beneficial for trade and security. However, Indonesia has one of the worst human rights records in world politics: democracy is not part of its political culture, political protests are put down with excessive violence, and the operations of the Indonesian Army are guided by the goal of imposing order through terror.

The brutality of the Indonesian army towards East Timor in particular has received widespread condemnation ever since the occupation of that part of the island in 1975. Slow but important steps towards democratization in the late 1990s presented the rest of the world with an opportunity to pressurize the Indonesian Government into holding a referendum on whether the East Timorese wanted independence or a continuation of the status quo. This strategy bore fruit, and when given the chance, on 30 August 1999, the people of East Timor voted overwhelmingly for independence (despite significant levels of intimidation). The ensuing campaign of terror indicated that Indonesia's pledge to ensure peace and security in the province was not being fulfilled; moreover, there was mounting evidence that the Indonesian Army was funding the militia groups. Australia responded to this crisis robustly, calling for an interim international peacekeeping force. Indonesia was initially reluctant to accept such a force, especially one led by an 'outsider' in the region. Days of lobbying by key state leaders and international financial institutions—Indonesia is in receipt of massive loans following the collapse of its currency in 1997/8—forced Indonesia to capitulate. On 20th September 1999, the first troops of 'Operation Stabilize' arrived in East Timor and began the process of restoring peace and security in the newly independent state.

What implications does this case hold for understanding the defence of human rights? The case is a fascinating one for the reason that Asia has always militantly defended its right to determine its own affairs; according to the 'ASEAN way' sovereignty is not thought to be something that should be compromised in the way that many smaller European states accept (even encourage). Yet here we had an Australian-led force, with a robust mandate, defending the right of the East Timorese to democracy and self-determination. Ten years earlier, most commentators would have regarded such a scenario as completely implausible. How then did it become possible? One set of reasons concerns the changing standard of what counts as acceptable behaviour in international society. The balance between sovereignty and human rights has tipped significantly in favour of the latter in times of crisis. Moreover, even those governments less prone to crusading for human rights, find themselves being forced to defend them. This is exactly the position that Australia found itself in. Although it was the Labor governments of the Hawke–Keating–Evans era who lent considerable support to the pursuit of human rights norms in international relations, it was their right-wing successor who risked soldiers lives in pursuit of those ends. Arguably, the fact that the Prime Minister, John Howard, and the Minister for Foreign Affairs and Trade, Alexander Downer, *did not* aggressively pursue human rights in foreign policy might have made them seem more acceptable to the region. What is clear is that had Australia rationally calculated its interests in a realist manner, it would not have advocated the need for an interventionary force. This was bound to antagonize the Government in Jakarta who Australia needs good relations with for reasons of trade and security. How, then, was it able to placate both Indonesia and the wider region? Perhaps the best argument is that Australia was able to present itself as a 'bridging power' between the political cultures of Europe and North America and those of its Asian neighbours. Mindful of the concerns of many Asian states, Australia focused its attention on security the support of ASEAN countries such as Thailand and the Philippines as a means of convincing Indonesia of the operation's legitimacy (Dunne, Hill, and Hanson: 2000).

* In this case study the collective noun 'Australia' is used in the knowledge that there are multiple identities in Australian political culture. The referent, therefore, is the Australian government/state.

interconnectedness. Yet for more radical neo-idealists, the world seems more like a scene from the film *Blade Runner* with post-modern technologies coexisting with ethical anarchy and urban decay. Neo-idealists like Richard Falk recognize that globalization and community are frequently at odds with each other. 'This tension between the ethical imperatives of the global neighbourhood and the dynamics of economic globalisation', he argues, is 'an evasion that has been characteristic of all post-Wilsonian variants of liberal internationalism' (1995*a*: 573). In this sense, neo-liberal internationalism has fallen prey to the neo-liberal consensus which minimizes the role of the public sector in providing for welfare, and elevates the market as the appropriate mechanism for allocating resources, investment, and employment opportunities. Although the globalization of liberalism has improved the per capita income of the vast majority of the world's population, the rate of increase among the powerful states has been far greater. According to the United Nations Development Programme the share of global income of the richest fifth of the world's population is 72 times greater than the poorest fifth. The average daily income of these 'have-nots' is less than $1 a day.[7]

Neo-idealists offer a radically different set of prescriptions to liberal internationalists. At the level of international institutions, writers such as David Held, Norberto Bobbio, and Danielle Archibugi (Archibugi and Held 1995) among others, believe that global politics must be democratized. Held's diagnosis begins by revealing the inadequacies of the 'Westphalian order' (or the modern states-system which is conventionally dated from the middle of the seventeenth century). During the latter stages of this period, we have witnessed rapid democratization with a number of states, but this has not been accompanied by democratization of the society of states (Held 1993). This task is increasingly urgent given the current levels of interconnectedness, since 'national' governments are no longer in control of the forces which shape their citizens' lives (for example, the decision by one state to permit deforestation has environmental consequences for all states). After 1945, the UN Charter set limits to the sovereignty of states by recognizing the rights of individuals in a whole series of human rights conventions. But even if the UN had lived up to its Charter in the post–1945 period, it would still have left the building blocks of the Westphalian order largely intact, namely: the hierarchy between great powers and the rest (symbolized by the permanent membership of the Security Council); massive inequalities of wealth between states; and a minimal role for non-state actors to influence decision-making in international relations.

In place of the Westphalian and UN models, Held outlines a '**cosmopolitan model of democracy**'. This requires, in the first instance, the creation of regional parliaments and the extension of the authority of such regional bodies (like the European Union) which are already in existence. Second, human rights conventions must be entrenched in national parliaments and monitored by a new International Court of Human Rights. Third, reform of the UN, or the replacement of it, with a genuinely democratic and accountable global parliament. Without appearing to be too sanguine about the prospects for the realization of the **cosmopolitan model of democracy**, Held is nevertheless adamant that if democracy is to thrive, it must penetrate the institutions and regimes which manage global politics.

Neo-idealism emphasizes not just macro-institutional democratic reform, but also democratization at the 'grass-roots'. Radical liberals like Richard Falk argue that global civil society has emancipatory potential. The evolution of international humanitarian law, and the extent to which these laws are complied with, is largely down to the millions of individuals who are active supporters of human rights groups like Amnesty International and Human Rights Watch (Falk 1995*b*: 164). Similarly, global protest movements have been largely responsible for the heightened global sensitivity to environmental degradation. This emphasis by neo-idealists on what Falk calls 'globalization from below' is an important antidote to mainstream liberalism's somewhat status quo oriented world view which sanctifies market forces, and seeks only piecemeal reform of international institutions such as the UN.

Neo-liberal institutionalism

In the 1980s, pluralism metamorphosed into **neo-liberal institutionalism**.[8] One of the problems with the former 'label' is that few of the thinkers actually identified themselves with the movement. By contrast, liberal institutionalism has attracted some of the most prolific and influential thinkers in the field, and has become the new orthodoxy in a number of key North American schools of International Relations. In addition to a high degree of self-identification on the part of contemporary liberal institutionalists, the second important revision to the earlier pluralism can be identified in the far more focused research agenda of liberal internationalism. The third and most substantive revision to **pluralism** concerns the shift back towards a state-centric approach to world politics (a shift signalled by Keohane and Nye in 1977).

The core principles of neo-liberal institutionalism can be distilled into the following four principles.

- **Actor**: Liberal institutionalists take for granted the state as a legitimate representation of society. Although emphasizing the importance of non-state actors in his early pluralist work, Robert Keohane's understanding of neo-liberal institutionalism admits that non-state actors are subordinate to states (Keohane 1989*a*: 8).

- **Structure**: Liberals broadly accept the structural condition of anarchy in the international system, but crucially, anarchy does not mean co-operation between states is impossible, as the existence (and proliferation) of **international regimes** demonstrates. In short, regimes and international institutions can mitigate anarchy by reducing verification costs, reinforcing reciprocity, and making defection from norms easier to punish (see Chapter 14).

- **Process**: Integration at the regional and global level is increasing. Here the future direction of the European Union is considered to be a vital test case for neo-liberal institutionalism.

- **Motivation**: States will enter into co-operative relations even if another state will gain more from the interaction, in other words, 'absolute gains' are more important for liberal institutionalists than 'relative gains' (emphasized by neo-realists).

It is vital to bear in mind the context out of which

neo-liberal institutionalism developed. Leading neo-liberal institutionalists such as Axelrod, Keohane, and Oye, developed their ideas in response to Kenneth Waltz's theory of neo-realism outlined in his 1979 work *Theory of International Politics*. Moreover, this response was from within the mainstream as opposed to the radical critical theory challenge from the margins which also developed in the 1980s (Ashley 1984; Cox 1981). Given this context, it is not surprising that **neo-liberal institutionalism** often seems closer to contemporary realism than to the tradition of liberal thinking about international relations.

As the analysis of **neo-idealism** demonstrates, radical liberals do not take the state for granted. Legitimacy is not something that states possess by right, but something which has to be earned through humane government and democratic procedures. Moreover, early liberal institutionalists, such as Mitrany and Haas, were sceptical about whether states could deliver liberal goals of order and justice even if they had the will. Accordingly, they prescribed devolving power down to local government/regional assemblies or up to supra-state organizations or world government.

Apart from a considerable divergence between the complacent statism of neo-liberal institutionalism, and the scepticism towards the state shown by early liberal institutionalists, there is one other significant demarcation between **neo-liberal institutionalism** and the other two elements in liberal thinking. Both **liberal internationalism** and **idealism** were wider ranging, more critical, and above all, more *political* than contemporary neo-liberal institutionalism (Long, 1996). (For a much more in depth analysis of neo-liberal institutionalism, see Chapter 9). In his defence, Keohane is justly critical of the naïve assumption of classical liberal internationalists that commerce breeds peace. A free trade system, according to Keohane, provides incentives for co-operation but does not guarantee it. Here he is making an important distinction between co-operation and harmony. 'Co-operation is not automatic', Keohane argues, 'but requires planning and negotiation' (1989: 11). On this point, we see an interesting overlap between the inter-war idealists and neo-liberal institutionalism. However, the fact that both camps see co-operation as the handiwork of individuals and institutions (as opposed to being part of a natural order) should not blind us to the point that Keohane et al see the role of institutions as regulating interests rather than transforming identities, as neo-idealists believe.

Key points

- The research agenda of **neo-liberal internationalism** is dominated by the debate about liberal states: how far the liberal zone of peace extends, why relations within it are peaceful, and what pattern is likely to evolve in relations between liberal states and authoritarian regimes? Crucially, in the post-cold war era, neo-liberal internationalists have lent their voices in support of Western (particularly American) attempts to use the levers of foreign policy to put pressure on authoritarian states to liberalize.

- Neo-idealists have responded to globalization by calling for a double democratization of both international institutions and domestic state structures. Radical **neo-idealism** is critical of mainstream liberalism's devotion to 'globalization from above' which marginalizes the possibility of change from below through the practices of global civil society.

- The most conventional of all contemporary liberalisms is **neo-liberal institutionalism**. At the centre of their research programme is how to initiate and maintain co-operation under conditions of anarchy. This task is facilitated by the creation of regimes. Notice that neo-liberal institutionalists share with realists the assumption that states are the most significant actors, and that the international environment is anarchic. Their accounts diverge, however, on the prospects for achieving sustained patterns of co-operation under anarchy

Conclusion and postscript: the crisis of Liberalism

There is something of a crisis in contemporary liberal thinking on international relations. The euphoria with which liberals greeted the end of the cold war in 1989 has to a large extent been dissipated; the great caravan of humanity, kick-started with the revolutions of 1989, is once again coming to a spluttering halt. Successive post-cold war conflicts, in Afghanistan, Liberia, Chechnya, Somalia, Burundi, and Rwanda (to name a few) remind us that in many parts of the world, the conditions which fuelled these tensions in the cold war period remain in place; for example, the geopolitical rivalry to grant massive arms transfers to states involved in 'civil' wars.

The audit of global politics at the beginning of the twenty-first century, from a liberal point of view, begins to take on a much darker hue when the wars of the former Yugoslavia are included. Unlike the tragedies of Rwanda and Burundi, the conflicts in Bosnia and Kosovo took place on the doorstep of the liberal zone. How could the national hatreds exhib-

ited by all the warring parties take root once again in Western soil? Liberal internationalists like Michael Ignatieff despaired that acts of ethnic cleansing had returned to haunt Europe fifty years after the Holocaust. After all, it was the **Enlightenment** which provided a vocabulary for articulating liberal ideas such as human rights and humanitarian law. 'What made the Balkan wars so shocking' argued Ignatieff, 'was how little these universals were respected in their home continent' (1995).

In the remaining paragraphs, by way of a response to Ignatieff, I suggest two explanations for the growing disenchantment with Liberalism. First, as we have seen throughout the chapter, Liberalism does not have a single voice; moreover, competing liberal arguments can often be used to defend different positions. The imperative to intervene in the wars of the former Yugoslavia, advocated by Ignatieff and other liberal internationalists, is backed up by the cosmopolitan liberal principle of the equal worth of all individuals: a sentiment captured by the words of

Box 8.7 Key concepts of Liberalism

Collective security

Refers to an arrangement where 'each state in the system accepts that the security of one is the concern of all, and agrees to join in a collective response to aggression' (Roberts and Kingsbury, 1993: 30).

Conditionality

The way in which states or international institutions impose conditions upon developing countries in advance of distributing economic benefits.

Cosmopolitan model of democracy

Associated with David Held, and other neo-idealists, a cosmopolitan model of democracy requires the following: the creation of regional parliaments and the extension of the authority of such regional bodies (like the European Union) which are already in existence; human rights conventions must be entrenched in national parliaments and monitored by a new International Court of Human Rights; the UN must be replaced with a genuinely democratic and accountable global parliament.

Democratic peace

A central plank of liberal internationalist thought, the democratic peace thesis holds that war has become unthinkable between liberal states.

Democracy promotion

The strategy adopted by leading Western states and institutions—particularly the US—to use instruments of foreign and economic policy to spread liberal values. Advocates make an explicit linkage between the mutually reinforcing effects of democratisation and open markets.

Enlightenment

Associated with rationalist thinkers of the eighteenth century. Key ideas (which some would argue remain mottoes for our age) include: secularism, progress, reason, science, knowledge, and freedom. The motto of the Enlightenment is: 'Sapere aude! Have courage to use your own understanding' (Reiss 1991: 54).

Idealism

Idealists seek to apply liberal thinking in domestic politics to international relations, in other words, institutionalize the rule of law. This reasoning is known as the domestic analogy. According to idealists in the early twentieth century, there were two principal requirements for a new world order. First: state leaders, intellectuals, and public opinion had to believe that progress was possible. Second: an international organization had to be created to facilitate peaceful change, disarmament, arbitration, and (where necessary) enforcement. The League of Nations was founded in 1920 but its collective security system failed to prevent the descent into world war in the 1930s.

Integration

A process of ever closer union between states, in a regional or international context. The process often begins by co-operation to solve technical problems, referred to by Mitrany as ramification.

Interdependence

A condition where states (or peoples) are affected by decisions taken by others; for example, a decision to raise interest rates in Germany automatically exerts upward pressure on interest rates in other European states. Interdependence can be symmetric, i.e. both sets of actors are affected equally, or it can be asymmetric, where the impact varies between actors.

Liberalism

An ideology whose central concern is the liberty of the individual. For most liberals, the establishment of the state is necessary to preserve individual liberty from being destroyed or harmed by other individuals or by other states. But the state must always be the servant of the collective will and not (as in the case of Realism) the master.

Liberal institutionalism

In the 1940s, liberals turned to international institutions to carry out a number of functions the state could not perform. This was the catalyst for integration theory in Europe and pluralism in the United States. By the early 1970s, pluralism had mounted a significant challenge to realism. It focused on new actors (transnational corporations, non-governmental organizations) and new patterns of interaction (interdependence, integration).

Liberal internationalism

The strand in liberal thinking which holds that the natural order has been corrupted by undemocratic state leaders and outdated policies such as the balance of power. Prescriptively, liberal internationalists believe that contact between the peoples of the world, through commerce or travel, will facilitate a more pacific form of international relations. Key concept of liberal internationalism: the idea of a harmony of interests.

Box 8.7 **continued**

Normative

The belief that theories should be concerned with what ought to be, rather than merely diagnosing what is. Norm creation refers to the setting of standards in international relations which governments (and other actors) ought to meet.

Pluralism

An umbrella term, borrowed from American political science, used to signify International Relations theorists who

rejected the realist view of the primacy of the state and the coherence of the state-as-actor.

World government

Associated in particular with those idealists who believe that peace can never be achieved in a world divided into separate sovereign states. Just as the state of nature in civil society was abolished by governments, the state of war in international society must be ended by the establishment of a world government.

---

the poet John Donne, 'any man's death diminishes me, because I am involved in Mankind'. But other liberals, of a more communitarian persuasion, argue that our obligations to all of humankind are less significant than our duties to citizens of our own state. On this line of argument, the tragedy in Bosnia may diminish us all, but this is not a sufficient reason to risk the lives of our fellow citizens in defence of abstract moral universals. How can Liberalism be our guide when, from different perspectives, it can support intervention and non-intervention? Hoffmann is surely right to argue that the case of degenerating states reveals how sovereignty, democracy, national self-determination, and human rights 'are four norms in conflict and a source of complete liberal disarray' (1995: 169).

A deeper reason for the crisis in Liberalism, and one which is prompted by Ignatieff's argument, is that it is bound up with an increasingly discredited Enlightenment view of the world (Laidi, 1998). Contrary to the hopes of liberal internationalists, the application of reason and science to politics has not

brought communities together. Indeed, it has arguably shown the fragmented nature of the political community, which is regularly expressed in terms of ethnic, linguistic, or religious differences. Critics of Liberalism from the left and right view the very idea of 'moral universals' as dangerous. Communitarian-minded liberals worry that the universalizing mission of liberal values such as democracy, capitalism, and secularism, undermine the traditions and practices of non-Western cultures (Gray 1995: 146). Radical critics are also suspicious of the motives for promoting liberal values. The Marxist writer Immanuel Wallerstein has a nice way of putting this in terms of universalism as 'a "gift" of the powerful to the weak' which places them in a double-bind: 'to refuse the gift is to lose; to accept the gift is to lose' (in Brown, 1999). The key question for Liberalism at the dawn of a new century is whether it can reinvent itself as a non-universalizing, non-Westernizing political idea, which preserves the traditional liberal value of human solidarity without undermining cultural diversity.

QUESTIONS

1 Do you agree with Stanley Hoffmann that international affairs are 'inhospitable' to Liberalism? What arguments might one draw upon to support or refute this proposition?

2 Was the language of international morality, used by idealists, a way of masking over the interests of Britain and France in maintaining their dominance of the post-World War I international system?

3 Are democracies more peaceful than authoritarian states? If so, why?

4 Should liberal states promote their values abroad? If so, by what means?

5 How much progress (if any) has there been in liberal internationalist thinking since Kant?

6 Which element of Liberalism best explains the development of the European Union, (neo)liberal institutionalism or (neo)idealism?

7 Are all forms of Liberalism premissed on an optimistic view of human nature?

8 Evaluate the success of Australia's foreign policy towards Indonesia and the Asia-Pacific Region? Has it been a good liberal citizen in the region?

9 What do neo-liberal institutionalists have in common with idealists? At what point do their accounts of international relations diverge?

10 Given the different strands in liberal thinking, can we meaningfully talk about a coherent liberal tradition?

GUIDE TO FURTHER READING

Excellent general discussions of Liberalism include the following: S. Hoffmann, *Janus and Minerva* (Boulder, Colo.: Westview, 1987), 394–436; M. J. Smith, (1992), 'Liberalism and International Reform', in T. Nardin and D. Mapel (eds.), *Traditions of International Ethics* (Cambridge: Cambridge University Press, 1992). Useful short extracts from classical liberal thinkers are contained in E. Luard (ed.), *Basic Texts in International Relations* (London: Macmillan, 1992). Two recent edited collections have much to say about Liberalism and how liberal states should conduct international relations: M. Cox, G. J. Ikenberry, and T. Inoguchi (eds.), *American Democracy Promotion: Impulses, Strategies and Impacts* (Oxford: Oxford University Press, 2000), 1–17, and T. V. Paul and J. A. Hall, *International Order and the Future of World Politics* (Cambridge: Cambridge University Press, 1999). For thought-provoking critiques of Liberalism as a theory of politics and society, see John Gray, *Enlightenment's Wake: Politics and Culture at the Close of the Modern Age* (London: Routledge, 1995) and Z. Laidi, *A World Without Meaning: The Crisis of Meaning in International Politics*, trans. J. Burham and J. Coulon (London: Routledge, 1998). Critical essays on Liberalism in international relations can be found in the 'Millennium Special Issue', *The Globalization of Liberalism?* 24: 3 (1995); and Michael Cox, Ken Booth, and Tim Dunne (eds.), *The Interregnum: Controversies in World Politics 1989–1999* (Cambridge: Cambridge University Press, 1999).

NOTES

1. Upper case 'Liberalism' signifies the broad Liberal tradition in international thought, whereas lower case 'liberalism' signifies a particular kind of liberal thinking, or an individual liberal thinker. International Relations refers to the academic discipline, and international relations refers to the practices of international actors.

2. For an alternative system of classifying liberalisms, see Doyle (1995).

3. Between 1945 and 1990, there were 232 resolutions vetoed, between 1990 and 1994, there were only 4 vetoes.

4. Arguably, pluralism is an inadequate term in view of its usage in political philosophy to denote a form of liberalism which privileges difference over universalism.

5. For an excellent discussion of the 'crisis of liberal internationalism', see Hoffmann (1995).

6. The link between the inter-war idealists, and the work of writers who I have termed 'neo-idealist' is brought out well by Luigi Bonanate (1995).

7. 'Ten Years of Human Development', *Human Development Report* 1999, the United Nations Development Programme, www.undp.org.

8. Often referred to in the literature as either neo-liberal institutionalism (Keohane 1989) or simply neo-liberalism.

Contemporary mainstream approaches: neo-realism and neo-liberalism

Steven L. Lamy

READER'S GUIDE

This chapter reviews the core assumptions of neo-realism and neo-liberalism and it explores the debate between these intellectual siblings that has dominated mainstream academic scholarship in international relations in the United States. Realism and neo-realism and to some extent, neo-liberalism, have also had a profound impact on US foreign policy. Neo-realists dominate the world of security studies and neo-liberals focus on political economy and more recently on issues like human rights and the environment. These theories do not offer starkly contrasting images of the world. Neo-realists state that they are concerned with issues of survival. They claim that neo-liberals are too optimistic about the possibilities for co-operation among states. Neo-liberals counter with claims that all states have mutual interests and can gain from co-operation. Both are normative theories of a sort, biased towards the state, the capitalist market, and the status quo. The processes of globalization have forced neo-realists and neo-liberals to consider similar issues and address new challenges to international order. In the introduction, I discuss the various versions of neo-liberalism and neo-realism and ask the reader to consider how theory shapes our image of the world. Each theory represents an attempt by scholars to offer a better explanation for the behaviour of states and describe the nature of international politics. Similarly, the more policy-relevant versions of these theories prescribe competing policy agendas. The next section of the chapter reviews three versions of neo-realism: Waltz's structural realism;

Grieco's neo-realism or modern realism with its focus on absolute and relative gains; and, thirdly, what security scholars call offensive and defensive realism or neo-realism. The third section of the chapter reviews the assumptions of neo-liberal and neo-liberal institutionalist perspectives. The fourth section focuses on the 'neo-neo-debate'. This is a debate that many US scholars think is the most important intellectual issue in international relations today. Many other scholars see it as not much of a debate at all. It is a debate about refining common assumptions and about the future role and effectiveness of international institutions and the possibilities of co-operation. However, it is not a debate between mainstream and critical perspectives. It is a debate between 'rule-makers' and it leaves out the voices on the margins or the 'rule-takers'. In the fifth section of the chapter, I review how neo-realists and neo-liberal thinkers react to the processes of globalization. The chapter concludes with a suggestion that we are only seeing part of the world if we limit our studies to the neo perspectives and the neo-neo debate. A neo-neo agenda is not a global agenda and it offers a myopic view of human relations, the state, and the international system. Yet, these theories remain dominant in US academic and policy communities and, therefore, it is important that they are understood.

Introduction

The debate between neo-realists and neo-liberals has dominated mainstream international relations scholarship in the United States since the mid-1980s. Two of the major US journals in the field, *International Organization* and *International Security*, are dominated by articles that address the relative merits of each theory and its value in explaining the world of international politics. Neo-realism and neo-liberalism are the progeny of realism and liberalism, respectively. They are more than theories; they are paradigms or conceptual frameworks that define a field of study, limit our conception of reality, and define an agenda for research and policy-making. As previous chapters on liberalism and realism have suggested, there are many versions and interpretations of each paradigm or theory. Some realists are more 'hard-line' on issues such as defence or participation in international agreements, while other realists take more accommodating positions on these same issues. Tim Dunne's chapter on liberalism provides a useful description of the varieties of this theory, and this chapter will explore those that have the greatest impact on academic discourse in the United

States and on the people who develop US foreign policy. This chapter will also show the considerable differences in how the scholarly and policy world define and use the labels, neo-realism and neo-liberalism.

For most academics, neo-realism refers to Kenneth Waltz's *Theory of International Politics* (1979). Waltz's theory emphasizes the importance of the structure of the international system and its role as the primary determinant of state behaviour. Yet, most scholars and policy-makers use neo-realism to describe a recent or updated version of realism. Recently, in the area of security studies, some scholars use the terms offensive and defensive realism when discussing the current version of realism or neo-realism.

In the academic world, neo-liberal generally refers to neo-liberal institutionalism or what is now called institutional theory by those writing in this theoretical domain. However, in the policy world, neo-liberalism means something different. A neo-liberal foreign policy promotes free trade or open markets and western democratic values and institutions. Most of the leading Western states have joined the

US-led chorus, calling for the 'enlargement' of the community of democratic and capitalist nation-states. There is no other game in town, the financial and political institutions created after the Second World War have survived and these provide the foundation for current political and economic power arrangements. These are institutions created by policy-makers who embrace neo-liberal or realist/neo-realist assumptions about the world.

In reality, neo-liberal foreign policies tend not to be as wedded to the ideals of democratic peace, free trade, and open borders. National interests take precedence over morality and universal ideals and, much to the dismay of traditional realists, economic interests are given priority over geopolitical ones.

For students beginning their study of International Relations, these labels and contending definitions can be confusing and frustrating. Yet, as you have learned in your reading of previous chapters in this volume, understanding these perspectives and theories is the only way you can hope to understand and explain how leaders and citizens alike see the world and respond to issues and events. This understanding may be more important when discussing neo-realism and neo-liberalism because they represent dominant perspectives in the policy world and in the US academic community.

There are clear differences between neo-realism and neo-liberalism; however, these differences should not be exaggerated. Robert Keohane (Baldwin 1993), a neo-liberal institutionalist, has stated that neo-liberal institutionalism borrows equally from realism and liberalism. Both theories represent status-quo perspectives and are what Robert Cox calls problem-solving theories (see Chs. 10 and 11). This means that both neo-realism and neo-liberalism address issues and problems that could disrupt the status quo, namely, the issues of security, conflict, and co-operation.

Neither theory advances prescriptions for major reform or radical transformation of the international system. Rather, they are system maintainer theories, meaning that adherents are generally satisfied with the current international system and its actors, values, and power arrangements. These theories address different sets of issues. In general, neo-realist theory focuses on issues of military security and war.

Neo-liberal theorists focus on issues of co-operation, international political economy and, most recently, the environment. For neo-liberal institutionalists, the core question for research is how to promote and support co-operation in an anarchic and competitive international system. For neo-realists, the core research question is how to survive in this system.

A review of the assumptions of each theory and an analysis of the contending positions in the so-called neos debate and a discussion of how neo-liberals and neo-realists react to the processes of globalization follows.

Key points

- The neo-neo debate has been the dominant focus in international relations theory scholarship in the US for the last 10–15 years.

- More than just theories, neo-realism and neo-liberalism represent paradigms or conceptual frameworks that shape individuals' images of the world and influence research priorities and policy debates and choices.

- There are several versions of neo-realism or neo-liberalism.

- Neo-liberalism in the academic world refers most often to neo-liberal institutionalism. In the policy world, neo-liberalism is identified with the promotion of capitalism and Western democratic values and institutions.

- Rational choice approaches and game theory have been integrated into neo-realist and neo-liberal theory to explain policy choices and the behaviour of states in conflict and co-operative situations. These present more rigorous and scientific versions of the theories.

- Neo-realist and neo-liberal theories are status-quo oriented problem-solving theories. They share many assumptions about actors, values, issues and power arrangements in the international system. Neo-realists and neo-liberals study different worlds. Neo-realists study security issues and are concerned with issues of power and survival. Neo-liberals study political economy and focus on co-operation and institutions.

Neo-realism

Kenneth Waltz's theory of **structural realism** is only one version of neo-realism. A second group of neo-realists, represented by the scholarly contributions of Joseph Grieco (1988*a* and 1988*b*), have integrated Waltz's ideas with the ideas of more traditional realists such as Hans Morgenthau, Raymond Aron, Stanley Hoffmann, and Robert Gilpin to construct a contemporary or **modern realist** profile. A third version of neo-realism is found in security studies. Here scholars talk about **offensive** and **defensive realists**. These versions of neo-realism are briefly reviewed in the next few pages.

Structural realism

Waltz's neo-realism is distinctive from traditional or classical realism in a number of ways. **First**, realism is primarily an inductive theory. For example, Hans Morgenthau would explain international politics by looking at the actions and interactions of the states in the system. Thus, the decision by Pakistan and India to test nuclear weapons would be explained by looking at the influence of military leaders in both states and the long-standing differences compounded by their geographic proximity. All of these explanations are unit or bottom-up explanations. Neo-realists, such as Waltz, do not deny the importance of unit-level explanations; however, they believe that the effects of structure must be considered. According to Waltz, structure is defined by the ordering principle of the international system, which is anarchy, and the distribution of capabilities across units, which are states. Waltz also assumes that there is no differentiation of function between different units.

The structure of the international system shapes all foreign policy choices. For a neo-realist, a better explanation for India and Pakistan's nuclear testing would be anarchy or the lack of a common power or central authority to enforce rules and maintain order in the system. In a competitive system, this condition creates a need for weapons to survive. Additionally, in an anarchic system, states with greater power tend to have greater influence.

A **second** difference between traditional realists and Waltz's neo-realism is found in their view of power. To realists, power is an end in itself. Hans Morgenthau describes the realist view:

The main signpost that helps political realism to find its way through the landscape of international politics is the concept of interest defined in terms of power.... We assume that statesmen think and act in terms of interest defined as power, and the evidence of history bears that assumption out. (1962: 5)

Although traditional realists recognize different elements of power (for example, economic resources, and technology), military power is considered the most obvious element of a state's power. Waltz would not agree with those who say that military force is not as essential as it once was as a tool of statecraft. As recent conflicts in the Balkans, Russia, the Middle East, Africa, and Asia suggest, many leaders still believe that they can resolve their differences with force.

For neo-realists, power is more than the accumulation of military resources and the ability to use this power to coerce and control other states in the system. Waltz and other neo-realists see power as the combined capabilities of a state. States are differentiated in the system by their power and not by their function. Power gives a state a place or position in the international system and that shapes the state's behaviour. During the cold war, the US and the USSR were positioned as the only two super powers. Neo-realists would say that such positioning explains the similarities in their behaviour. The distribution of power and any dramatic changes in that distribution of power help to explain the structure of the international system. Specifically, states will seek to maintain their position or placement in the system. The end of the cold war and the disintegration of the Soviet empire upset the balance of power and, in the eyes of many neo-realists, increased uncertainty and instability in the international system. Waltz concurs with traditional realists when he states that the central mechanism for order in the system is balance of power. The renewed emphasis on the importance of the UN and NATO and their interventions in crisis areas around the world, may be indicative of the major powers' current search for order in the international system. Waltz would challenge neo-liberal institutionalists who believe that we can manage the processes of globalization by merely building effective international institutions. He would argue that their effectiveness depends on the support of major powers.

A **third** difference between realism and Waltz's neo-realism is each one's view on how states react to the condition of anarchy. To realists, anarchy is a condition of the system, and states react to it according to their size, location, domestic politics, and leadership qualities. In contrast, neo-realists suggest that anarchy defines the system. Further, all states are functionally similar units, meaning that they all experience the same constraints presented by anarchy and strive to maintain their position in the system. Neo-realists explain any differences in policy by differences in power or capabilities. Both Belgium and China recognize that one of the constraints of anarchy is the need for security to protect their national interests. Leaders in these countries may select different policy paths to achieve that security. A small country such as Belgium, with limited resources, responds to anarchy and the resulting security dilemma by joining alliances and taking an activist role in regional and international organizations, seeking to control the arms race. China, a major power and a large country, would most likely pursue a unilateral strategy of increasing military strength to protect and secure their interests.

Relative and absolute gains

Joseph Grieco (1988*a*) is one of several realist/neo-realist scholars who focuses on the concepts of relative and absolute gains. Grieco claims that states are interested in increasing their power and influence (absolute gains) and, thus, will co-operate with other states or actors in the system to increase their capabilities. However, Grieco claims that states are also concerned with how much power and influence other states might achieve (relative gains) in any co-operative endeavour. This situation can be used to show a key difference between neo-liberals and neo-

realists. Neo-liberals claim that co-operation does not work when states fail to follow the rules and 'cheat' to secure their national interests. Neo-realists claim that there are two barriers to international co-operation: cheating and the relative gains of other actors. Further, when states fail to comply with rules that encourage co-operation, other states may abandon multilateral activity and act unilaterally.

The likelihood of states abandoning international co-operative efforts is increased if participants see other states gaining more from the arrangement. If states agree to a ban on the production and use of landmines, all of the signatories to the treaty will be concerned about compliance. Institutions will be established to enforce the treaty. Neo-realists argue that leaders must be vigilant for cheaters and must focus on those states that could gain a military advantage when this weapon system is removed. In some security situations, landmines may be the only effective deterrent against a neighbouring state with superior land forces. In this situation, the relative gains issue is one of survival. In a world of uncertainty and competition, the fundamental

---

Box 9.1 **Core assumptions of neo-realists**

- States and other actors interact in an anarchic environment. This means that there is no central authority to enforce rules and norms or protect the interests of the larger global community.

- The structure of the system is a major determinant of actor behaviour.

- States are self-interest oriented, and an anarchic and competitive system pushes them to favour self-help over co-operative behaviour.

- States are rational actors, selecting strategies to maximize benefits and minimize losses.

- The most critical problem presented by anarchy is survival.

- States see all other states as potential enemies and threats to their national security. This distrust and fear creates a security dilemma, and this motivates the policies of most states.

question, according to Grieco and others who share his view of neo-realism, is not whether all parties gain from the co-operation; but, who will gain more if we co-operate?

Security studies and neo-realism

Recently, security studies scholars, primarily in the US, have suggested a more nuanced version of a realism that reflects their interests in understanding the nature of the security threats presented by the international system and the strategy options states must pursue to survive and prosper in the system. These two versions of neo-realism, offensive and defensive realism (many scholars in this area prefer to be called modern realists and not neo-realists) is more policy relevant than Waltz and Grieco's version of neo-realism and, thus, may be seen as more prescriptive than the other versions (Jervis 1999).

Offensive neo-realists appear to accept most of Waltz's ideas and a good portion of the assumptions of traditional realism. Defensive neo-realists suggest that our assumptions of relations with other states depend on whether they are friends or enemies. When dealing with friends such as the European Union, the assumptions governing US leaders are more akin to those promoted by neo-liberals. However, there is little difference between defensive and offensive neo-realists when they are dealing with expansionary or pariah states or traditional enemies.

John Mearsheimer (1990, 1994/5), an offensive realist in security studies, suggests that relative power and not absolute power is most important to states. He would suggest that leaders of countries should pursue security policies that weaken their potential enemies and increase their power relative to all others. To offensive neo-realists, international relations is a prisoner's dilemma game. In this era of globalization, the incompatibility of states' goals and interests enhances the competitive nature of an anarchic system and makes conflict as inevitable as co-operation. Thus, talk of reducing military budgets at the end of the cold war was considered by offensive neo-realists to be pure folly. Leaders must always be prepared for an expansionary state that will challenge the global order. Moreover, if the major powers begin a campaign of disarmament and reduce their power relative to other states, they are simply inviting these expansionary states to attack.

Defensive neo-realists, Robert Jervis (1999) and Jack Snyder (1991) claim that most leaders understand that the costs of war clearly outweigh the benefits. The use of military force for conquest and expansion is a security strategy that most leaders reject in this age of complex interdependence and globalization. War remains a tool of statecraft for some; however, most wars are seen by citizens and leaders alike to be caused by irrational or dysfunctional forces within a society, such as excessive militarism or ethnonationalism.

Defensive neo-realists are often confused with neo-liberals. Although they have some sympathy for the neo-liberal argument that war can be avoided by creating security institutions (for example, alliances or arms control treaties) that diminish the security dilemma and provide mutual security for participating states, they do not see institutions as the most effective way to prevent all wars. Defensive neo-realists share some of the pessimism of offensive neo-realists. Most believe that conflict is simply unavoidable in some situations. First, aggressive and expansionary states do exist and they challenge world order and, second, simply in pursuit of their national interests, some states may make conflict with others unavoidable.

Defensive neo-realists are more optimistic than are offensive neo-realists; however, they are considerably less optimistic than neo-liberals for several reasons (Jervis 1999). First, defensive neo-realists see conflict as unnecessary only in a subset of situations (for example, economic relations). Second, leaders can never be certain that an aggressive move by a state (for example, support for a revolutionary movement in a neighbouring state) is an expansionary action intended to challenge the existing order or simply a preventive policy aimed at protecting their security. Third, defensive realists challenge the neo-liberal view that it is relatively easy to find areas where national interests might converge and become the basis for co-operation and institution building. Although they recognize that areas of common or mutual interests exist, defensive neo-realists are concerned about noncompliance or cheating by states especially in security policy areas.

Key points

- Kenneth Waltz's structural realism has had a major impact on scholars in International Relations. Waltz claims that the structure of the international system is the key factor in shaping the behaviour of states. Waltz's neo-realism also expands our view of power and capabilities; however, he agrees with traditional realists when he states that major powers still determine the nature of the international system.

- Structural realists minimize the importance of national attributes as determinants of a state's foreign policy behaviour. To these neo-realists, all states are functionally similar units, experiencing the same constraints presented by anarchy.

- Structural realists accept many assumptions of traditional realism. They believe that force remains an important and effective tool of statecraft and balance of power is still the central mechanism for order in the system.

- Joseph Grieco represents a group of neo-realists or modern realists who are critical of neo-liberal institutionalists who claim states are mainly interested in absolute gains. Grieco claims that all states are interested in both absolute and relative gains. How gains are distributed is an important issue. Thus, there are two barriers to international co-operation, fear of those who might not follow the rules and the relative gains of others.

- Scholars in security studies present two versions of neo-realism or modern realism. Offensive neo-realists emphasize the importance of relative power. Like traditional realists, they believe that conflict is inevitable in the international system and leaders must always be wary of expansionary powers. Defensive realists are often confused with neo-liberal institutionalists. They recognize the costs of war and assume that it usually results from irrational forces in a society. However, they admit that expansionary states willing to use military force make it impossible to live in a world without weapons. Co-operation is possible, but, it is more likely to succeed in relations with friendly states.

Neo-liberalism

As the previous chapter on liberalism indicates, there are a number of versions of the theory and all have their progeny in contemporary neo-liberal debates. David Baldwin (1993) identified four varieties of liberalism that influence contemporary international relations: commercial, republican, sociological, and liberal institutionalism.

The first, **commercial liberalism**, advocates free trade and a market or capitalist economy as the way towards peace and prosperity. Today, this view is promoted by global financial institutions, most of the major trading states, and multinational corporations. **Republican liberalism** states that democratic states are more inclined to respect the rights of their citizens and are less likely to go to war with their democratic neighbours. In current scholarship, this view is presented as democratic peace theory.

These two forms of liberalism, commercial and republican, have been combined to form the core foreign policy goals of many of the world's major powers. This neo-liberal internationalism is promoted by the US and its G-8 partners, the UK, France, Germany, and Japan, in trade, aid, and security policies.

In **sociological liberalism**, the notion of community and the process of interdependence are important elements. As transnational activities increase, people in distant lands are linked and their governments become more interdependent. As a result, it becomes more difficult and more costly for states to act unilaterally and to avoid co-operation with neighbours. The cost of war or other deviant behaviour increases for all states and, eventually, a peaceful international community is built. Many of the assumptions of sociological liberalism are represented in the current globalization literature dealing with popular culture and civil society. Much of the globalization literature suggests that it is a transnational process and that it builds communities of scholars, producers, consumers, musicians, artists, activists, and others, who transcend the boundaries of states.

Liberal institutionalism or **neo-liberal institutionalism** is considered by many scholars to present the most convincing challenge to realist and neo-realist thinking. The roots of this version of neo-liberalism are found in the functional integration scholarship of the 1940s and the 1950s and regional integration studies of the 1960s. These studies suggest that the way towards peace and prosperity is to have independent states pool their resources and even surrender some of their sovereignty to create integrated communities to promote economic growth or respond to regional problems (see Ch. 23). The European Union is one such institution that began as regional community for encouraging multilateral co-operation in the production of coal and steel. Proponents of integration and community building were motivated to challenge dominant realist thinking because of the experiences of the two world wars. Rooted in liberal thinking, integration theories promoted after the Second World War were less idealistic and more pragmatic than the liberal internationalism that dominated policy debates after the First World War.

The third generation of liberal institutional scholarship was the transnationalism and complex interdependence of the 1970s (Keohane and Nye 1972, 1977). Theorists in these camps presented arguments that suggested that the world had become more pluralistic in terms of actors involved in international interactions and that these actors had become more dependent on each other. Complex interdependence presented a world with four characteristics: (1) increasing linkages among states and non-state actors; (2) a new agenda of international issues with no distinction between low and high politics; (3) a recognition of multiple channels for interaction among actors across national boundaries; and (4) the decline of the efficacy of military force as a tool of statecraft. Complex interdependence scholars would suggest that globalization represents an increase in linkages and channels for interaction, as well as in the number of interconnections.

Neo-liberal institutionalism or institutional theory shares many of the assumptions of neo-realism; however, its adherents claim that neo-realists focus excessively on conflict and competition and minimize the chances for co-operation even in an anarchic international system. Neo-liberal institutionalists see 'institutions' as the mediator and the means to achieve co-operation among actors in the system. Currently, neo-liberal institutionalists are focusing their research on issues of global governance and the creation and maintenance of institutions associated with managing the processes of globalization.

The core assumptions of neo-liberal institutionalists include:

- States are key actors in international relations, but not the only significant actors. States are rational

---

Box 9.2 Neo-liberal views on institutions and regimes

- **Institutions** are seen as persistent and as connected sets of rules and practices that prescribe roles, constrain activity, and shape the expectations of actors. Institutions may include organizations, bureaucratic agencies, treaties and agreements, and informal practices that states accept as binding. The balance of power in the international system is an example of an institution.

  Adapted from Haas, Keohane, and Levy in Institutions for the Earth (1993: 4–5).

- **Regimes** are social institutions that are based on agreed rules, norms, principles, and decision-making procedures. These govern the interactions of various state and non-state actors in issue areas such as the environment or human rights. The global market in coffee, for example, is governed by a variety of treaties, trade agreements, scientific and research protocols, market protocols, and the interests of producers, consumers, and distributors. States organize these interests and consider the practices, rules, and procedures to create a governing arrangement or regime that controls the production of coffee, monitors its distribution, and ultimately determines the price for consumers.

  (Adapted from Young 1997: 6).

or instrumental actors, always seeking to maximize their interests in all issue areas.

- In this competitive environment, states seek to maximize absolute gains through co-operation. Rational behaviour leads states to see value in co-operative behaviour. States are less concerned with gains or advantages achieved by other states in co-operative arrangements.

- The greatest obstacle to successful co-operation is non-compliance or cheating by states.

- Co-operation is never without problems, but states will shift loyalty and resources to institutions if these are seen as mutually beneficial and if they provide states with increasing opportunities to secure their international interests.

The neo-liberal institutional perspective is more relevant in issue areas where states have mutual interests. For example, most world leaders believe that we will all benefit from an open trade system, and many support trade rules that protect the environment. Institutions have been created to manage international behaviour in both areas. The neo-liberal view may have less relevance in areas in which states have no mutual interests. Thus, co-operation in military or national security areas, where someone's gain is perceived as someone else's loss (a zero-sum perspective) may be more difficult to achieve.

Key points

- Contemporary neo-liberalism has been shaped by the assumptions of commercial, republican, sociological, and institutional liberalism.

- Commercial and republican liberalism provide the foundation for current neo-liberal thinking in Western governments. These countries promote free trade and democracy in their foreign policy programmes.

Box 9.3 **The main features of the neo-realist/neo-liberal debate**

1. Both agree that the international system is anarchic. Neo-realists say that anarchy puts more constraints on foreign policy and that neo-liberals minimize the importance of survival as the goal of each state. Neo-liberals claim that neo-realists minimize the importance of international interdependence, globalization, and the regimes created to manage these interactions.

2. Neo-realists believe that international co-operation will not happen unless states make it happen. They feel that it is hard to achieve, difficult to maintain, and dependent on state power. Neo-liberals believe that co-operation is easy to achieve in areas where states have mutual interests.

3. Neo-liberals think that actors with common interests try to maximize absolute gains. Neo-realists claim that neo-liberals overlook the importance of relative gains. Neo-liberals want to maximize the total amount of gains for all parties involved, whereas the neo-realists believe that the fundamental goal of states in co-operative relationships is to prevent others from gaining more.

4. Neo-realists state that anarchy requires states to be preoccupied with relative power, security, and survival in a competitive international system. Neo-liberals are more concerned with economic welfare or international political economy issues and other non-military issue areas such as international environmental concerns.

5. Neo-realists emphasize the capabilities (power) of states over the intentions and interests of states. Capabilities are essential for security and independence. Neo-realists claim that uncertainty about the intentions of other states forces states to focus on their capabilities. Neo-liberals emphasize intentions and preferences.

6. Neo-liberals see institutions and regimes as significant forces in international relations. Neo-realists state that neo-liberals exaggerate the impact of regimes and institutions on state behavior. Neo-liberals claim that they facilitate co-operation, and neo-realists say that they do not mitigate the constraining effects of anarchy on co-operation.

(Adapted from Baldwin 1993: 4–8)

- Neo-liberal institutionalism, the other side of the neo-neo debate, is rooted in the functional integration theoretical work of the 1950s and 60s and the complex interdependence and transnational studies literature of the 1970s and 80s.

- Neo-liberal institutionalists see institutions as the mediator and the means to achieve co-operation in the international system. Regimes and institutions help govern a competitive and anarchic international system and they encourage, and at times require, multilateralism and co-operation as a means of securing national interests.

- Neo-liberal institutionalists recognize that co-operation may be harder to achieve in areas where leaders perceive they have no mutual interests.

- Neo-liberals believe that states co-operate to achieve absolute gains and the greatest obstacle to co-operation is 'cheating' or non-compliance by other states.

The neo-neo debate

By now it should be clear that the neos debate is not particularly contentious, nor is the intellectual difference between the two theories significant. As was suggested earlier in the chapter, neo-realists and neo-liberals share an epistemology; they focus on similar questions and agree on a number of assumptions about man, the state, and the international system. A summary of the major points of contention is presented in Box 9.3.

If anything, the current neo-liberal institutionalist literature appears to try hard to prove that they are a part of the neo-realist/realist family. As Robert Jervis (1999: 43) states, there is not much of a gap between the two theories. As evidence of this, he quotes Robert Keohane and Lisa Martin: 'for better or worse institutional theory is a half-sibling of neo-realism.'

The following reviews key aspects of this debate. With regard to anarchy, both theories share several assumptions. First, they agree that anarchy means that there is no common authority to enforce any rules or laws constraining the behaviour of states or other actors. Neo-liberal institutionalists and neo-realists agree that anarchy encourages states to act unilaterally and to promote self-help behaviour. The condition of anarchy also makes co-operation more difficult to achieve. However, neo-realists tend to be more pessimistic and see the world as much more competitive and conflictive. To most neo-realists, international relations is a struggle for survival, and in every interaction, there is a chance of a loss of power to a future competitor or enemy. For neo-liberal institutionalists, international relations is competitive; however, the opportunities for co-operation in areas of mutual interest may mitigate the effects of anarchy.

Some scholars suggest that the real difference between the neos is that they study different worlds. The neo-liberal institutionalists focus their scholarship on political economy, the environment and human rights issues. Neo-liberals work in what we once called the low politics arena, issues related to human security and the good life. Their assumptions work better in these issue areas.

Neo-realists tend to dominate the security studies area. They study issues of international security or what was once called the high politics issues. Many neo-realists assume that what distinguishes the study of international relations from political science is the emphasis on issues of survival. Moreover, high politics issues are the real issues, and the low politics of economic welfare and other good life issues are seen as less than international relations mainstream issues.

For neo-liberal institutionalists, foreign policy is now about managing complex interdependence and the various processes of globalization. It is also about responding to problems that threaten the economic well being, if not the survival, of people around the world. Foreign policy leaders must find ways to manage financial markets so that the gap between rich and poor does not become insurmountable. These same leaders must find ways to deal with toxic waste dumping that threaten clean water supplies in developing states. The anodyne for neo-liberal institutionalists is to create institutions to manage issue areas where states have mutual interests. Creating, maintaining, and further empowering these institutions is the future of foreign policy for neo-liberal institutionalists.

Neo-realists take a more state-centric view of foreign policy. They recognize international relations as a world of co-operation and conflict. However, close to their traditional realist roots, neo-realists see foreign policy dominated by issues of national security and survival. The most effective tool of statecraft is still force or the threat of force and, even in these times of globalization, states must continue to look after their own interests. All states, in the language of the neo-realists, are egoistic value maximizers.

Neo-realists accept the existence of institutions and regimes (see Box 9.2) and recognize their role as tools or instruments of statecraft. From a neo-realist view, states work to establish these regimes and institutions if they serve their interests (absolute gain), and they continue to support these same regimes and institutions if the co-operative activities promoted by the institution do not unfairly advantage (relative gains) other states. Neo-realists also would agree that institutions can shape the content and direction of foreign policy in certain issue areas and when the issue at hand is not central to the security interests of a given state.

Neo-liberals agree that once established, institutions can do more than shape or influence the foreign policy of states. Institutions can promote a foreign policy agenda by providing critical information and expertise. Institutions also may facilitate policy-making and encourage more co-operation at local, national, and international levels. They often serve as a catalyst for coalition building among state and non-state actors. Recent work on environmental institutions suggests that they can promote changes in national policies and actually encourage both national and international policies that address environmental problems (Haas, Keohane, and Levy 1993).

A major issue of contention in the debate is the notion that institutions have become significant in international relations. Further, they can make a difference by helping to resolve global and regional problems and encourage co-operation rather than conflict. Neo-liberal institutionalists expect an increase in the number of institutions and an increase in co-operative behaviour. They predict that these institutions will have a greater role in managing the processes of globalization and that states will come to the point where they realize that acting unilaterally or limiting co-operative behaviour will not lead to the resolution or management of critical global problems. Ultimately, neo-liberal institutionalists claim that the significance of these institutions as players in the game of international politics will increase substantially.

Neo-realists recognize that that these institutions are likely to become more significant in areas of mutual interest, where national security interests are not at stake. However, the emphasis that states place on relative gains will limit the growth of institutions and will always make co-operation difficult. For neo-realists, the important question is not will we all gain from this co-operation, but, who will gain more?

What is left out of the debate?

One could argue that the neo-neo debate leaves out a great number of issues. Perhaps with a purpose, it narrows the agenda of international relations. It is not a debate about some of the most critical questions like 'Why war?' or 'Why inequality in the international system?' Remember this is a debate that occurs within the mainstream of international relations scholarship. Neo-realists and neo-liberal institutionalists agree on the questions; they simply offer different responses. Some important issues are left out and assumptions about international politics may be overlooked. As a student of international relations, you should be able to identify the strengths and weaknesses of a theory. Let us consider three possible areas for discussion: the role of domestic politics, learning, and political globalization.

Both theories assume that states are value maximizers and that anarchy constrains the behaviour of states. But, what about domestic forces that might promote a more co-operative strategy to address moral or ethical issues? Neo-realist assumptions suggest a sameness in foreign policy that may not be true. How do we account for the moral dimensions of foreign policy such as development assistance given to poor states who have no strategic or economic value to the donor? Or how do we explain domestic interests that promote isolationist policies in the US at a time when system changes would suggest international activism might result in both absolute and relative gains? We may need to challenge Waltz and ask if the internal make-up of a state matters. All politics is now glocal (global and local) and neo-realists especially, but also neo-liberals, must pay attention to what goes on inside a state. Issues of political culture, identity, and domestic political games must be considered.

We must assume that leaders and citizens alike learn something from their experiences. The lessons of two world wars prompted Europeans to set aside issues of sovereignty and nationalism and build an economic community. Although some neo-liberal institutionalists recognize the importance of learning, in general neither theory explores the possibility that states will learn and may shift from a traditional self-interest perspective to an emphasis on common interests. There may be a momentum to co-operation and institution building that both theories underestimate. Can we assume that institutions and co-operation have had some impact on conditions of anarchy?

Both neo-realist and neo-liberals neglect the fact the political activities may be shifting away from the state. A number of scholars have suggested that one of the most significant outcomes of globalization is the emergence of global or transnational political advocacy networks (Keck and Sikkink 1998). Institutions promoted primarily by these advocacy networks have had a major impact on human rights issues such as child labour and security. The recent campaign against the further use of landmines was initiated outside the state and challenged power centres, namely the military and military industries, within states. How will these successful transnational political campaigns affect neo-liberal and neo-realist thinking?

Key points

- The neo-neo debate is not a debate between two polar opposite worldviews. They share an epistemology, focus on similar questions and they agree on a number of assumptions about international politics. This is an intra-paradigm debate.

- Neo-liberal institutionalists and neo-realists study different worlds of international politics. Neo-realists focus on security and military issues—the high politics issue area. Neo-liberal institutionalists focus on political economy, environmental issues, and lately, human rights issues. These issues have been called the low politics issue agenda.

- Neo-realists explain that all states must be concerned with the absolute and relative gains that result from international agreements and co-operative efforts. Neo-liberal institutionalists are less concerned about relative gains and consider that all will benefit from absolute gains.

- Neo-realists are more cautious about co-operation and remind us the world is still a competitive place where self-interest rules.

- Neo-liberal institutionalists believe that states and other actors can be persuaded to co-operate if they are convinced that all states will comply with rules and co-operation will result in absolute gains.

- This debate does not discuss many important issues that challenge some of the core assumptions of each theory. For example, neo-realism cannot explain foreign policy behaviour that challenges the norm of national interest over human interests. Neither theory addresses the impact of learning on the foreign policy behaviour of states.

- Globalization has contributed to a shift in political activity away from the state. Transnational social movements have forced states to address critical international issues and in several situations that have supported the establishment of institutions that promote further co-operation and, fundamentally challenge the power of states.

Neo-liberals and neo-realists on globalization

As I suggested earlier in this chapter, most neo-realists do not think that globalization changes the game of international politics much at all. States might require more resources and expertise to maintain their sovereignty, but neo-realists think most evidence suggests that states are increasing their expenditures and their jurisdictions over a wide variety of areas. Ultimately, we still all look to the state to solve the problems we face, and the state still has a monopoly over the legal use of coercive power. Most neo-realists assume that conditions of anarchy and competition accentuate the concerns for absolute and relative gains. As Waltz (See Box 9.4) suggested in a recent article on the topic: 'The terms of political, economic and military competition are set by the larger units of the international political system' (Waltz 2000: 53).

States remain the primary actors and the only actors with enough power to control or manage the processes of globalization. What neo-realists are most concerned with are the new security challenges presented by globalization. Two examples follow.

Neo-realists are concerned with the uneven nature of economic globalization. Inequality in the international system may be the greatest security threat in the future. People without food are inclined to seek change, and often that change will be violent. Global economic forces often look for the lowest common denominator in terms of labour costs, safety, and environmental rules. This could create two security problems for states. First, the push and pull of globalization and the search for the lowest common denominator could lead to the loss of key industries and resources that are important for national security. Second, economic globalization can accentuate existing differences in societies, creating instability in strategic regions, thereby challenging world order.

Most neo-realists would claim that forces of globalization challenge sovereignty; however, states have not lost their authority and control. Yet, globalization has had a significant impact on domestic politics and the existing power structures. Transnational social movements (TSMOS) and global advocacy networks have successfully shifted many political issues away from the state. For example, some neo-realists are concerned that the power and security of the state are being undermined by political movements seeking to force states to make new rules that control the use of nuclear and conventional weapons. These movements deftly use the press, the Internet, and activist networks to challenge many of the core assumptions of the dominant realist/neo-realist policy perspective. Realists and neo-realists tend to favour elitist models of decision-making, especially in security areas. Some neo-realists have expressed concern that globalization might contrib-

---

Box 9.4 Waltz on globalization

Kenneth Waltz, a prominent structural realist/neo-realist, accepts that globalization presents new challenges for national leaders; however, he denies that the state is being pushed aside by new global actors. According to Waltz, globalization is the fad of the 1990s. It is exaggerated and much of the world has been left out of the process. Globalization is made in America, that is, current institutions and rules that sustain and promote the global economy are under American control. The state has not lost power; in fact, the state has expanded its functions and its control over societies and economies at home and abroad. Waltz claims that states adapt to new environments and transform their power and authority to respond to new policy issues. Ultimately, he states, international politics is still *inter-national*. Waltz makes a strong case against those who argue that states are less important than corporations, markets, or other non-state actors. Waltz argues that no other actor can match the state in terms of its capabilities and successes: 'States perform essential political, social and economic functions, and no other organization rivals them in these respects. They foster the institutions that make internal peace and prosperity possible' (Waltz 2000: 51).

What matters most in shaping international politics are the capabilities of states and not globalization.

(Adapted from Waltz 2000: 46–56)

ute to an unwanted democratization of politics in critical security areas (see Ch. 12). Their concern is that expertise will be overwhelmed by public emotions.

Most of the discussion of globalization among neo-liberals falls into two categories: (1) a free market commercial neo-liberalism that dominates policy circles throughout the world and (2) academic neo-liberal institutionalism that promotes regimes and institutions as the most effective means of managing the globalization process.

The end of the cold war was the end of the Soviet experiment in command economics and it left capitalism and free market ideas with few challengers in international economic institutions and national governments. Free market neo-liberals believe that governments should not fight globalization or attempt to slow it down. These neo-liberals want minimal government interference in the national or global market. From this perspective, institutions should promote rules and norms that keep the market open and discourage states who attempt to interfere with market forces. Other more social democratic neo-liberals support institutions and regimes that manage the economic processes of globalization as a means to prevent the uneven flow of capital and other resources that might widen the gap between rich and poor states.

Recent demonstrations against global economic institutions in the US and Europe suggest that there are many who feel that the market is anything but fair. People marching in the streets of London and Seattle called for global institutions that provide economic well-being for all and for reformed institutions that promote social justice, ecological balance, and human rights (see Box 9.5). The critics of economic globalization state that governments will have to extend their jurisdictions and intervene more extensively in the market to address these concerns, as well as open the market and all of its

---

Box 9.5 Neo-liberalism and its current critics

Critical voices

'Free trade theorists claimed that the *rising tide will lift all boats*, providing broad economic benefits to all levels of society. The evidence so far clearly shows that it lifts only yachts.' (Barker and Mander 1999: 4).

Critics of the World Trade Organization (WTO) and economic globalization are primarily concerned with the centralization of the world's political and economic institutions. The critics see the WTO as an undemocratic organization that represents the interests of global corporations. In December 1999, representatives from over 1,000 organizations, from 80+ countries, took to the streets in Seattle, Washington, to protest WTO rulings against national trade laws or regulations that consider issues related to health, the environment, and human rights. The WTO has consistently ruled against governments that pass legislation that impede the free flow of goods, services, and capital. Critics have called for an open decision-making process and they want their political leaders to pressure the officials who govern the global economic institutions (for example, WTO, IMF, and the World Bank), to consider more than market factors in their decision-making.

Neo-liberal defenders

The benefits of globalization are clear to neo-liberal free market advocates, and they believe that those who fight against these processes suffer from globalphobia. First, the more global the economy, the more manufacturers or producers in a given country can take advantage of commodities, production processes, and markets in other countries. Second, globalization encourages the diffusion of knowledge and technology, which increases the opportunities for economic growth worldwide. Most neo-liberals have incredible faith in the market and believe that globalization will encourage further economic integration among public and private actors in the economy. Economic integration is seen in giant corporations in Europe merging with their US counterparts. Neo-liberals predict that the globalization momentum will increase due to the declining costs of transportation and communications. Distance is disappearing.

(Adapted from Burtless *et al.* 1998)

opportunities to those people now left out. Given the current neo-liberal thinking, this kind of radical change is unlikely.

Key points

- Neo-realists think that states are still the principle actors in international politics. Globalization challenges some areas of state authority and control; but, politics is still inter-national.

- Neo-realists are concerned about new security challenges resulting from uneven globalization, namely, inequality and conflict.

- Globalization provides opportunities and resources for transnational social movements that challenge the authority of states in various policy areas. Neo-realists are not supportive of any movement that seeks to open critical security issues to public debate.

- Free market neo-liberals believe globalization is a positive force. Eventually, all states will benefit from the economic growth promoted by the forces of globalization. They believe that states should not fight globalization or attempt to control it with unwanted political interventions.

- Some neo-liberals believe that states should intervene to promote capitalism with a human face or a market that is more sensitive to the needs and interests of all the people. New institutions can be created and older ones reformed to prevent the uneven flow of capital, promote environmental sustainability, and protect the rights of citizens.

Conclusion: narrowing the agenda of international relations

Neo-realism and neo-liberal institutionalism are status quo rationalist theories. They are theories firmly embraced by mainstream scholars and by key decision-makers in many countries. There are some differences between these theories; however, these differences are minor compared to the issues that divide reflectivist and rationalist theories and critical and problem-solving theories (see Ch.11).

In scholarly communities, neo-realism generally represents an attempt to make realism more theoretically rigorous. Waltz's emphasis on system structure and its impact on the behaviour of states leads one to conclude that international relations is not explained by looking inside the state. Neo-realists who reduce international politics to micro-economic rational choice or instrumental thinking also minimize the idiosyncratic attributes of individual decision-makers and the different cultural and historical factors that shape politics within a state. These more scientific and parsimonious versions of neo-realism offer researchers some powerful explanations of state behaviour. However, do these explanations offer a complete picture of a given event or a policy choice? Does neo-realist scholarship narrow the research agenda? Recently, neo-realist scholars were criticized for their inability to explain the end of the cold war and other major transformations in the international system. Neo-realists minimize the importance of culture, traditions, and identity—all factors that shaped the emergence of new communities that helped to transform the Soviet empire.

Contributions by neo-realists in security studies have had a significant impact on the policy community. Both defensive and offensive neo-realists claim that the world remains competitive and uncertain and the structure of the international system makes power politics the dominant policy paradigm. This fits with the interests and belief systems of most military strategists and foreign policy decision-makers in positions of power in the world today. This continues the realist tradition that has dominated international politics for centuries and it suggests that the criticisms of the realist/neo-realist tradition may be limited to the academic world. However, critical perspectives, inside and outside the academic world, are causing some realists/neo-realists to re-examine their assumptions about how this world works. Certainly, defensive neo-realists represent a group of scholars and potential policy advisers who understand the importance of multilateralism and the need to build effective institutions to prevent arms races that might lead to war. There is some change, but the agenda remains state-centric and focused on military security issues.

Neo-liberalism, whether the policy variety or the academic neo-liberal institutionalism, is a rejection of the more utopian or cosmopolitan versions of liberalism. US foreign policy since the end of the cold war has involved a careful use of power to spread an American version of liberal democracy: peace through trade, investment, and commerce. In the last few years, US foreign policy has promoted business and markets over human rights, the environment, and social justice. Washington's brand of neo-liberalism has been endorsed by many of the world's major powers and smaller trading states. The dominant philosophy of statecraft has become a form of 'pragmatic meliorism' with markets and Western democratic institutions as the chosen means for improving our lives. Again, we see a narrowing of choices and a narrowing of the issues and ideas that define our study of international politics.

Neo-liberal institutionalism with its focus on co-operation, institutions, and regimes, may offer the broadest agenda of issues and ideas for scholars and policy-makers. Neo-liberal institutionalists are now asking if institutions matter in a variety of issue areas. Scholars are asking important questions about the impact of international regimes and institutions on domestic politics and the ability of institutions to promote rules and norms that encourage environmental sustainability, human rights, and economic development. It is interesting that many neo-liberal institutionalists in the US find it necessary to emphasize their intellectual relationship with neo-realists and ignore their connections with the English School (see Ch. 8) and more cosmopolitan versions of liberalism (see Ch. 29). The emphasis on the shared assumptions with neo-realism, presents a further narrowing of the agenda of international politics. A neo-liberal institutional perspective that focuses on the nature of international society or community and the importance of institutions as promoters of norms and values may be more appropriate for understanding and explaining contemporary international politics.

Every theory leaves something out. No theories can claim to offer a picture of the world that is complete. No theory has exclusive claims to the truth. Theories in international politics offer insights into the behaviour of states. Realists and neo-realists give great insights into power, conflict, and the politics of survival. However, neo-realism does not help us understand the impact of economic interdependence on state behaviour or the potential effects of institutions and regimes on domestic politics. Here is where neo-liberal institutionalism helps us construct a picture of international politics. Theories empower some actors and policy strategies and dismiss others. Neo-realism and neo-liberal institutionalism are theories that address status quo issues and consider questions about how to keep the system operating. These theories do not raise questions about the dominant belief system or the distribution of power and how these may be connected to conditions of poverty and violence. As you continue your studies in international politics, be critical of the theories being presented. Which theories explain the most? Which theory helps you make sense of this world? What does your theory leave out? Who or what perspective does the theory empower? Who or what view of the world is left out?

QUESTIONS

1 What are the similarities between traditional realism and neo-realism?

2 What are the intellectual foundations of neo-liberal institutionalism?

3 What assumptions about international politics are shared by neo-liberals and neo-realists? What are the significant differences between these two theories?

4 How do you react to those who say that the neo-neo debate is not much of a debate at all? Is this merely an academic debate or has this discussion had any influence on foreign policy?

5 Do you think globalization will have any impact on neo-realist and neo-liberal thinking? Are either theories useful in trying to explain and understand the globalization process?

6 What are defensive and offensive neo-realists? How important are these theories to military strategists?

7 What is the difference between relative and absolute gains? What role do these concepts play in neo-realist thinking? Neo-liberal thinking?

8 How might the proliferation of institutions in various policy areas influence the foreign policy process in major, middle, and small states? Do you think these institutions will mitigate the effects of anarchy as neo-liberals claim?

9 Why do you think neo-realism and neo-liberalism maintain such dominance in US International Relations scholarship?

10 If we study international politics as defined by neo-realists and neo-liberal institutionalists, what are the issues and controversies we would focus on? What is left out of our study of international politics?

GUIDE TO FURTHER READING

General surveys with excellent coverage of the neo-realist and neo-liberal perspectives:

Burchill, S., Linklater, A., *et al.*, *Theories of International Relations* (Basingstoke: Macmillan, 1996). This collection of essays is particularly good on liberal internationalism and neo-realism.

Doyle, Michael, *Ways of War and Peace* (New York: W. W. Norton, 1997). Discusses the antecedents to neo-realism and neo-liberalism. Excellent sections on Hobbes and structural realism and varieties of liberalism.

Halliday, F., *Rethinking International Relations* (Vancouver: University of British Columbia Press, 1994). Lively and honest analysis of the current theoretical debates.

Luard, E.(ed.), *Basic Texts in International Relations* (New York: St Martins, 1997). An excellent collection of classical, modern, and contemporary essays in international relations presented in three sections: the nature of man; the state; and the international system.

For the more advanced student of International Relations:

Smith, S., Booth, K., and Zalewski, M. (eds.), *International Relations Theory and Beyond* (Cambridge: Cambridge University Press, 1996). Excellent on critical theory and challenges to rationalist approaches.

For more information on the neo-liberal/neo-realist debate:

Baldwin, D. (ed.), *Neorealism and Neoliberalism: The Contemporary Debate* (New York: Columbia University Press, 1993). Includes reflections on the debate section with articles by Grieco and Keohane.

Kegley, C. (ed.), *Controversies in International Relations Theory: Realism and the Neoliberal Challenge* (New York: St. Martins, 1995). The first part of the text includes excellent chapters by Waltz, Holsti, Doyle, and Grieco.

Doyle, M., and Ikenberry, G. J. (eds.), *New Thinking in International Relations Theory* (Boulder, Colo.: Westview Press, 1997). The chapters by Grieco on realism and world politics and Weber on institutions and change are very useful.

Security and neo-realism:

Brown, M. E., Lynn-Jones, S. M., and Miller, S. E. (eds.), *The Perils of Anarchy: Contemporary Realism and International Security* (Cambridge, Mass.: MIT Press, 1995). A collection of essays from *International Security*.

Snyder, J., *Myths of Empire: Domestic Politics and International Ambition* (Ithaca, NY: Cornell University Press, 1991). A defensive realist view of war and expansion or overextension. An excellent use of case studies to test competing explanations of overextension.

Neo-liberalism and neo-liberal institutionalism:

Kahler, M. (ed.), *Liberalization and Foreign Policy* (New York: Columbia University Press, 1997). Excellent essays on political and economic liberalization and their impact on foreign policy.

Milner, H., *Interests, Institutions, and Information* (Princeton: Princeton University Press, 1997). Explores how two-level games influence international co-operation. The reader is introduced to how neo-liberals use rational choice approaches to explain state behaviour.

Haas, P., Keohane, R., and Levy, M. (eds.), *Institutions for the Earth* (Cambridge, Mass.: MIT Press, 1993). An excellent collection of case studies asking if institutions have any impact on international, regional, and domestic environmental policies.

10 Marxist theories of International Relations

Stephen Hobden and Richard Wyn Jones

READER'S GUIDE

This chapter will introduce, outline, and assess the Marxist contribution to the study of International Relations. Having identified a number of core features common to Marxist approaches, the chapter discusses four strands within contemporary Marxism which make particularly significant contributions to our understanding of world politics: world-system theory; Gramscianism; critical theory; and New Marxism. The chapter argues that no analysis of globalization is complete without an input from Marxist theory. Indeed, Marx can be depicted as the *first* theorist of globalization, and from the perspective of Marxism, the features often pointed to as evidence of globalization are hardly novel, but are rather the modern manifestations of long-term tendencies within the development of capitalism.

Introduction: the continuing relevance of Marxism

With the end of the cold war, the collapse of Communist party rule in Russia and throughout Eastern Europe, and the global truimph of 'free market' capitalism, it became commonplace to assume that the ideas of Marx, and his numerous disciples, could be safely consigned to the dustbin of history. The 'great experiment' had clearly failed. While Communist parties retained power in China, Vietnam, and Cuba,

The authors would like to acknowledge the advice and assistance of Michael Cox and Adam Morton.

they did not now constitute a threat to the hegemony of the global capitalist system. Rather, in order to try and retain power, these parties were themselves being forced to submit to the apparently unassailable logic of 'the market' by aping many of the central features of contemporary capitalist societies. The example of North Korea, where a communist government has tried to maintain a particularly brutal and idiosyncratic form of central control over its economy and society, credible reports of mass famine served only to confirm the perception that communism no longer offered a viable or attractive alternative. One of the key lessons of the twentieth century, therefore, would appear to be that Marxist thought leads only to a historical dead end. The future is liberal and capitalist.

Yet despite this, Marx, and Marxist thought more generally, refuses to go away. The end of the Soviet experiment, and the apparent lack of a credible alternative to capitalism may have led to a crisis in Marxism, but ten years later there appears to be something of a renaissance. There are probably two reasons why this renaissance is occurring, and why Marxists walk with a renewed spring in their step.

First, for many Marxists the communist experiment in the Soviet Union and in its east European client states, had become a major embarrassment. In the decades immediately after the October Revolution, most had felt an allegiance to the Soviet Union as the first 'Workers' State', subsequently, however, this loyalty had been stretched beyond breaking point by the depravities of Stalinism, and by Soviet behaviour in its post-Second World War satellites in Eastern Europe. 'Actually existing socialism' was plainly not the communist utopia that many dreamed of and that Marx had apparently promised. Some Marxists were openly critical of the Soviet Union. Others just kept quiet and hoped that the situation, and human rights record, would improve.

The break-up of the Eastern Bloc and the demise of the Soviet Union has in a sense wiped the slate clean. It has reopened the possibility of being able to argue in favour of Marx's ideas without having to defend the actions of governments who justify their behaviour with reference to them. Moreover, the disappearance of the Soviet Union, has encouraged an appreciation of Marx's work less encumbered by the baggage of Marxism-Leninism as a state ideology. The significance of this is underlined when it is realized that many of the concepts and practices that are often taken as being axiomatic of Marxism, do not in fact figure in Marx's writings: these include the 'vanguard party', 'democratic centralism', and the centrally directed 'command economy'.

Second, and perhaps more importantly, Marx's social theory still retains formidable analytical purchase on the world we inhabit. The vast bulk of his theoretical efforts consisted of a painstaking analysis of capitalism as a mode of production (key Marxist terminology is defined in Box 10.1), and the basic elements of his account have not been bettered.

Box 10.1 A glossary of Marxist terms

Capitalism: The capitalist mode of production, in Marx's analysis, involved a specific set of social relations that were particular to a specific historical period. For Marx there were three main characteristics of capitalism. (1) Everything involved in production (e.g. raw materials, machines, labour involved in the creation of commodities, and the commodities themselves) is given an exchange value, and all can be exchanged, one for the other. In essence, under capitalism everything has its price, including people's working time. (2) Everything that is needed to undertake production (i.e. the factories, and the raw materials) is owned by one class—the capitalists. (3) Workers are 'free', but in order to survive must sell their labour to the capitalist class in order to survive, and because the capitalist class own the *means of production*, and control the *relations of production*, they also control the profit that results from the labour of workers.

Means (or forces) of production: These are the elements that combine in the production process. They include labour as well as the tools and technology available during any given historical period.

Relations of production: Relations of production link and organize the means of production in the production process. They involve both the technical and institutional relationships necessary to allow the production process to proceed, as well as the broader structures that govern the control of the means of production, and control of the end-product(s) of that process. Private property and wage labour are two of the key features of the relations of production in capitalist society.

Indeed, with the ever-increasing penetration of the market mechanism into all aspects of life, it is arguable that Marx's forensic examination of both the extraordinary dynamism and inherent contradictions of capitalism is even more relevant now than in his own time. There is certainly much in his writings that is extraordinarily prescient. A particular strength of Marx's work is his analysis of crisis. Orthodox accounts of capitalism suggest that free markets will move towards equilibrium and will be inherently stable. Our day-to-day lived experience suggests otherwise. The 1987 stock market crash and the Asian financial crisis of the late 1990s demonstrate that global capitalism continues to be rocked by massive convulsions which have enormous implications for the lives of individuals around the globe. On Marx's account, such convulsions, and their baleful human consequences, are an inherent and inescapable part of the very system itself.

But while much of Marx's analysis of capitalism has stood the test of time, history has treated other elements of his ideas less kindly. His belief that capitalism would be superseded, just as previous modes of production such as feudalism had been, and moreover, would be superseded by socialism, has proven to be at the very least premature. And as has already been mentioned, attempts to date to construct alternative societies based on Marxist ideas have been less than successful. Nevertheless, much of the conceptual armoury developed by Marx in his analysis of capitalism still retains an enormous utility in a world increasingly dominated by free markets.

Compared to Realism and Liberalism, Marxist thought presents a rather unfamiliar view of international relations. Whilst the former portray world politics in ways which resonate with those presented in the foreign news pages of our newspapers and magazines, Marxist theories aim to expose a deeper, underlying—indeed hidden—truth. This is that the familiar events of world politics—wars, treaties, international aid operations, etc.—all occur within structures which have an enormous influence on those events. These are the structures of a global capitalist system. Thus, Marxists would argue, any attempt to understand world politics must be based on a broader understanding of the processes which operate within global capitalism.

In addition to presenting a rather unfamiliar view

of world politics, Marxist theories are also discomforting, for they argue that the effects of global capitalism are to ensure that the powerful and wealthy continue to prosper at the expense of the powerless and the poor. We are all aware that there is gross inequality in the world. Statistics concerning the human costs of poverty are truly numbing in their awfulness (see Box 10.2). Approximately a third

---

Box 10.2 Indicators of world inequality

- One-fifth of the world's population are living in extreme poverty.

- 70 per cent of the world's poor and two-thirds of the world's illiterates are women.

- One-third of the world's children are undernourished.

- Half the world's population lacks regular access to the most essential drugs.

- 100 million children live or work on the street.

- In 1998 the 48 least developed countries attracted less than $US3 billion in direct foreign investment—0.4 per cent of the global total.

- The combined wealth of the world's 200 richest people reached $US1 trillion in 1999; the combined income of 582 million people living in the 43 least developed countries is $US146 billion

- More than 30,000 children die a day from easily preventable diseases.

- Since 1980 more than $US1.3 trillion has been transferred from less developed countries to more developed countries in debt interest payments—yet the size of the total debt has not decreased.

- Each year the developing world pays the West nine times more in debt repayments than it receives in aid.

- In 1996 Comic Relief in the UK raised £26 million in the world's biggest telethon. This is roughly what Africa pays out in debt in one day.

- To achieve universal provision of basic services in developing countries would cost $80 billion per year.

(Sources: World Health Organization, United Nations, World Bank, Jubilee 2000)

of the world's population use up the vast bulk of the world's resources with the rest having to make-do as best they can. Indeed, according to the 1996 United Nations Human Development Report, the total wealth of the world's 358 billionaires is equal to the combined incomes of the poorest 45 per cent of the world's population. Marxist theorists argue that the relative prosperity of the few is dependent on the destitution of the many. In Marx's own words, 'Accumulation of wealth at one pole is, therefore, at the same time accumulation of misery, agony of toil, slavery, ignorance, brutality at the opposite pole.'

In the next section we will outline some of the central features of the Marxist approach—or **historical materialism** as it is often known. Following on from this, subsequent sections will explore some of the most important strands in contemporary Marx-inspired thinking about world politics. We should note, however, that given the richness and variety of Marxist thinking about world politics, the account

that follows is inevitably destined to be partial and to some extent arbitrary. Our aim in the following is to provide a route map that we hope will encourage readers themselves further to explore the work of Marx and of those who have built on the foundations he laid.

Key points

- Marx's work retains its relevance despite the collapse of Communist party rule in the former Soviet Union.

- Of particular importance is Marx's analysis of capitalism, which has yet to be bettered.

- Marxist analyses of international relations aim to reveal the hidden workings of global capitalism. These hidden workings provide the context in which international events occur.

The essential elements of Marxist theories of world politics

In his inaugural address to the Working Men's International Association in London in 1864, Karl Marx told his audience that history had 'taught the working classes the duty to master (for) themselves the mysteries of international politics'. However, despite the fact that Marx himself wrote copiously about international affairs, most of this writing was journalistic in character. He did not incorporate the international dimension into his theoretical mapping of the contours of capitalism. Given the vast scope of Marx's work, this 'omission' should perhaps not surprise us. The sheer scale of the theoretical enterprise in which he was engaged, as well as the nature of his own methodology, inevitably meant that Marx's work would be contingent and unfinished. That said, since his death many of those who have taken inspiration from Marx's approach have attempted to apply his theoretical insights to international relations.

Given that Marx was an enormously prolific writer, and given also that his ideas developed and changed over time in significant ways, it is not surprising that his legacy has been open to numerous—and often contradictory—interpretations. In addition, real-world developments have also led some of those influenced by Marx to revise his ideas in the light of experience. Hence a variety of different schools of thought have emerged which either claim Marx as a direct inspiration, or whose work can be linked to Marx's legacy. This chapter will focus on four strands of contemporary Marxist thought that have all made major contributions to thinking about world politics. These are world-system theory, Gramscianism, critical theory, and New Marxism. But before we move to discuss what is distinctive about these approaches, it is important that we first examine the essential elements of commonality that lie between them.

First, all the theorists discussed in this chapter share with Marx the view that the social world should be analysed as a **totality**. For them the academic division of the social world into different areas of enquiry—history, philosophy, economics, political science, sociology, international relations, etc.—is both arbitrary and unhelpful. Rather, none can be understood without knowledge of the others: the social world had to be studied as a whole. Given the scale and complexity of the social world, this entreaty clearly makes great demands of the analyst. In his *magnum opus*, volume one of *Capital*, Marx's methodological solution was to start with the simplest of social relations and then proceed to build them up into a more and more complex picture. But however the need to address the totality of relationships in a social world is operationalized, there can be no doubt that for Marxist theorists, the disciplinary boundaries that characterize the contemporary social sciences need to be transcended if we are to generate a proper understanding of the dynamics of world politics.

Another key element of Marxist thought, which serves further to underline this concern with interconnection and context, is the **materialist conception of history**. The central contention here is that processes of historical change are ultimately a reflection of the economic development of society. That is, economic development is effectively the motor of history. The central dynamic that Marx identifies is tension between the **means of production** and **relations of production** that together form the **economic base** of a given society. As the means of production develop, for example through technological advancement, previous relations of production become outmoded, and indeed become fetters restricting the most effective utilization of the new productive capacity. This in turn leads to a process of social change whereby relations of production are transformed in order to better accommodate the new configuration of means.

Developments in the economic base act as a catalyst for the broader transformation of society as a whole. This is because, as Marx argues in a 'Preface' to his *Contribution to the Critique of Political Economy*, 'the mode of production of material life conditions the social, political and intellectual life process in general'. Thus the legal, political, and cultural institutions and practices of a given society, reflect and reinforce—in a more or less mediated form—the pattern of power and control in the economy. It follows logically, therefore, that change in the economic base ultimately leads to change in the 'legal and political **superstructure**'. (For a diagrammatical representation of the **base–superstructure model** see Fig. 10.1).

Class plays a key role in Marxist analysis. In contrast to liberals who believe that there is an essential harmony of interest between various social groups, Marxists hold that society is systematically prone to class conflict. Indeed in the *Communist Manifesto*, which Marx co-authored with Engels, it is argued that 'the history of all hitherto existing societies is the history of class struggle'. In capitalist society, the main axis of conflict is between the bourgeoisie (the capitalist) and proletariat (the workers).

Despite his commitment to rigorous scholarship, Marx did not think it either possible or desirable for the analyst to remain a detached or neutral observer to this great clash between capital and labour. Rather, in one of his most frequently cited comments, he argued that 'philosophers have only interpreted the world in various ways; the point, however, is to change it'. Marx was committed to the cause of **emancipation**. It is clear from Marx's own work, however, that this commitment is emphatically NOT a justification for the uncritical acceptance of some party-line, or an excuse to dogmatically

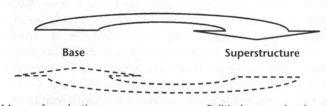

Base   Superstructure

Means of production   Political system, legal system,
↔ relations of production   culture etc.

Fig. 10.1 The base–superstructure model

ignore facts which cast doubt on some long-cherished belief. Marx insisted on the deployment of solid evidence in order to support (and refute) arguments, and indeed pioneered the use of official statistics in social science writing. Nonetheless, Marx was not interested in developing an understanding of the dynamics of capitalist society simply for the sake of it. Rather he expected such an understanding to make it easier to overthrow the prevailing order and replace it with a communist society—a society in which wage labour and private property are abolished and social relations transformed.

It is important to emphasize that the essential elements of Marxist thought all-too-briefly discussed in this section, are also essentially contested. That is, they are subject to much discussion and disagreement even among those contemporary writers who have been influenced by Marxist writings. There is disagreement as to how these ideas and concepts should be interpreted and how they should be operationalized. Analysts also differ over which elements of Marxist thought are most relevant, which have been proven to be mistaken, and which should now be considered as outmoded or in need of radical overhaul. So, for example, while proponents of the four strands of contemporary Marxism discussed in the following sections would all share classical Marx's commitment to emancipation, few would share Marx's apparent belief that the replacement of capitalism by socialism is inevitable. Moreover, there are substantial differences between them in terms of their attitudes to the legacy of Marx's ideas. The work of the New Marxists draws far more directly on Marx's original ideas than the work of the Critical Theorists. Indeed the latter would probably be more comfortable as being viewed as post-Marxists rather than straightforward Marxists. But even for them, as the very term post-Marxism suggests, the ideas of Marx remain a basic point of departure.

Having considered what unites different Marxist approaches to the study of international relations, we will now turn to the task of examing their distinguishing features, as well as their major claims and contributions.

Key points

- Marx himself provided little in terms of a theoretical analysis of International Relations.

- His ideas have been interpreted and appropriated in a number of different and contradictory ways resulting in a number of competing schools of Marxism.

- Underlying these different schools are several common elements that can be traced back to Marx's writings.

World-system theory

The origins of world-system theory

The origins of world-system theory can be traced back to the first systematic attempt to apply the ideas of Marx to the international sphere, that is to the critique of imperialism advanced by such thinkers as Hobson, Luxemburg, Bukharin, and Hilferding and Lenin at the start of the twentieth century (see Brewer 1990). Without doubt, the most well-known and influential work to emerge from this debate is the pamphlet written by Lenin, and published in 1917, called *Imperialism, the Highest Stage of Capital-* *ism.* Lenin's ideas represented both a development on and a departure from those of Marx. It was a development on Marx in that Lenin accepted Marx's basic thesis that it is the economic mode of production that ultimately determines broader social and political relations: a relationship usually summarized via the famous base–superstructure model. Lenin also accepted Marx's contention that history can only be correctly understood in terms of class conflict.

However, Lenin argued that the character of capitalism had changed somewhat since Marx published the first volume of *Capital* in 1867. Capitalism had entered a new stage—indeed, its highest and final stage—with the development of **monopoly capitalism**. Under monopoly capitalism, a two-tier structure had developed within the world-economy with a dominant **core** exploiting a less-developed **periphery**. Such a structure dramatically complicates Marx's view of a simple divergence of interests between the proletariat and bourgeoisie. With the development of a core and periphery, there was no longer an automatic harmony of interests between all workers. The bourgeoisie in the core countries could use profits derived from exploiting the periphery to improve the lot of their own proletariat. In other words, the capitalists of the core could pacify—or bluntly, buy off—their own working class through the further exploitation of the periphery. Thus, according to Lenin's analysis, the structural division between the core and periphery determines the nature of the relationship between the bourgeoisie and proletariat of each country.

Even this rather simplistic summary of Lenin's theory of imperialism should alert us to two important features of the world-system approach to the understanding of world politics. The first is that all politics, international and domestic, takes place within the framework of a capitalist world-economy. The second is the contention that states are not the only important actors in world politics, rather social classes are also very significant. Moreover, it is the location of these states and classes within the structure of the capitalist world-economy that constrains their behaviour and determines patterns of interaction and domination between them.

Lenin's views were developed by the Latin American dependency school, the writers of which developed the notion of core and periphery in greater depth. In particular the work of Raul Prebisch was especially significant. He argued that countries in the periphery were suffering as a result of what he called 'the declining terms of trade'. Put simply he suggested that the price of manufactured goods increased more rapidly than that of raw materials. So, for example, year by year it requires more tons of coffee to pay for a refrigerator. As a result of their reliance on primary goods, each year countries of the periphery are becoming poorer relative to the core. These arguments were developed further by writers such as André Gunder Frank, and Henrique Fernando Cardoso. It is from the framework developed by such writers that contemporary world-system theory can be seen to have emerged.

The key features of Wallerstein's world-system theory

In order to outline the key features of world-system theory, we shall concentrate on the work of perhaps its most prominent protagonist, Immanuel Wallerstein.

For Wallerstein the dominant form of social organization has been what he calls 'world-systems'. History has witnessed two types of world-system: **world-empires**, and **world-economies**. The main distinction between a world-empire and a world-economy relates to how decisions about resource distribution—crudely, who gets what—are made. In a world-empire a centralized political system uses its power to redistribute resources from peripheral areas to the central core area. In the Roman empire this took the form of the payment of 'tributes' by the outlying provinces back to the Roman heartland. By contrast, in a world-economy there is no single centre of political authority, but rather we find multiple competing centres of power. Resources are not distributed by central decree but rather through the medium of a **market**. However, although the mechanism for resource distribution is different, the net effect of both types of system is the same, and that is the transfer of resources from the periphery to the core.

The modern world-system is an example of a world-economy. According to Wallerstein this system emerged in Europe at around the turn of the sixteenth century. It subsequently expanded to bring about the current situation where there is no corner of the globe which is not thoroughly implicated within it. The driving force behind this seemingly relentless process of expansion and incorporation has been the 'ceaseless accumulation of capital': or, in a nutshell, capitalism. Thus the modern world-system is above all else a capitalist system—it is this which provides its central dynamic.

Wallerstein defines capitalism as 'a system of production for sale in a market for profit and appropri-

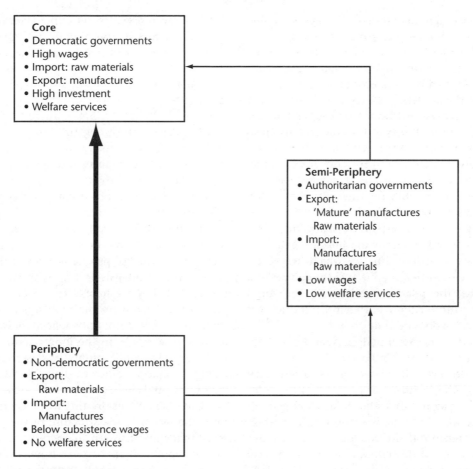

Fig. 10.2 Interrelationships in the world economy

ation of this profit on the basis of individual or collective ownership' (1979: 66). He argues that within
the context of this system, specific institutions are
continually being created and recreated. This state of
flux not only extends to what are normally considered to be narrowly economic institutions such as
particular companies or even industries. It is equally
true for what are often thought to be permanent,
even primordial institutions, such as the family unit,
ethnic groups, and states. According to Wallerstein,
none of these are timeless—none remain the same.
To claim otherwise is to adopt an **ahistoric** attitude,
that is, to fail to understand that the characteristics
of social institutions are historically specific. For
Wallerstein all social institutions, large and small, are
continually adapting and changing within the context of a dynamic world-system. Furthermore, and

crucially, it is not only the elements within the system which change. Wallerstein argues that the system itself is historically bounded. It had a beginning,
has a middle, and will have an end.

The modern world-system has features which can
be described in terms of space and time. The **spatial**
dimension focuses on the differing economic roles
played by different regions within the world-
economy. To the core–periphery distinction, posited
by Lenin and developed by Dependency theorists,
Wallerstein has (somewhat controversially) added
another economic zone in his description of the
world-economy, an intermediate **semi-periphery**.
According to Wallerstein, the semi-peripheral zone
has an intermediate role within the world-system
displaying certain features characteristic of the core
and others characteristic of the periphery. For

example, although penetrated by core economic interests, the semi-periphery has its own relatively vibrant indigenously owned industrial base (see Fig. 10.2). Because of this hybrid nature, the semi-periphery plays important economic and political roles within the modern world-system. In particular, it provides a source of labour that counteracts any upward pressure on wages in the core and also provides a new home for those industries that can no longer function profitably in the core (for example, car assembly and textiles). The semi-periphery also plays a vital role in stabilizing the political structure of the world-system.

According to world-system theorists, the three zones of the world-economy are linked together in an exploitative relationship in which wealth is drained away from the periphery to the centre. As a consequence, the relative positions of the zones become ever more deeply entrenched: the rich get richer whilst the poor become poorer.

Together, the core, semi-periphery, and periphery make up the spatial dimension of the world-economy. However, described in isolation they provide a rather static portrayal of the world-system. In order to understand the dynamics of their interaction over time we must turn our attention to the **temporal** dimensions of Wallerstein's description of the world-economy. These are cyclical rhythms, secular trends, contradictions and crisis. It is these, when combined with the spatial dimensions, which determine the historical trajectory of the system.

The first temporal dimension, **cyclical rhythms**, is concerned with the tendency of the capitalist world-economy to go through recurrent periods of expansion and subsequent contraction, or more colloquially, boom and bust. Whatever the underlying processes responsible for these waves of growth and depression, it is important to note that each cycle does not simply return the system to the point from which it started. Rather, if we plot the end-point of each wave we discover the **secular trends** within the system. Secular trends refers to the long-term growth or contraction of the world economy.

The third temporal feature of the world-system is **contradictions**. These arise because of 'constraints imposed by systemic structures which make one set of behavior optimal for actors in the short run and a different, even opposite, set of behavior optimal for the same actors in the middle run' (1991a: 261). These constraints can best be explained and understood by examining what Wallerstein regards as one of the main contradictions confronting the capitalist system, the crisis of underconsumption.

In the short term it is in the interests of capitalists to maximize profits through driving down the wages of the producers, i.e. their workers. However, to realize their profits, capitalists need to sell the products that their workers produce to consumers who are willing and able to buy them. The contradiction arises from the fact that the workers (the producers) are also the potential consumers, and the more that wage levels are driven down in the quest to maximize profits, the less purchasing-power the workers enjoy. Thus, capitalists end up with shelves full of things that they are unable to sell and no way of getting their hands on the profits. So, although in the short term it might be beneficial for capitalists to depress wage levels, in the longer term this might well lead to a fall in profits because wage earners would be able to purchase fewer goods: in other words, it would create a crisis of underconsumption. Thus, contradictions in the world-economy arise from the fact that the structure of the system can mean that apparently sensible actions by individuals can, in combination or over time, result in very different—and possibly unwelcome—outcomes from the ones originally intended.

In everyday language we tend to use the word **crisis** to dramatize even relatively minor problems. However, in the context of the world-system, Wallerstein wishes to reserve the term to refer to a very specific temporal occurrence. For him, a crisis constitutes a unique set of circumstances that can only be manifested once in the lifetime of a world-system. It occurs when the contradictions, the secular trends and the cyclical rhythms at work within that system combine in such a way as to mean that the system cannot continue to reproduce itself. Thus, a crisis within a particular world-system heralds its end and replacement by another system.

Wallerstein's view is that the current world-system is now in such a crisis (see Wallerstein 1996), which will involve its demise and replacement by another system. Interestingly, Wallerstein argues that it is in a period of crisis that the actors within a world-system have most freedom of action. When a system is operating smoothly behaviour is very much determined by the nature of its structure. However, when the system enters a period of terminal decline—its period of crisis—the structures lose much of their power and individual or collective action becomes far more meaningful. This argument is particularly significant because Wallerstein regards a crisis as a period of uncertainty where any number of outcomes are possible. The present crisis could result in the development of a system which gives rise to a more emancipated society, or in a system that is even less palatable than our own. Through our actions, we can help determine the outcome.

Recent developments in world-system theory

Wallerstein's work has come under considerable criticism, both from Marxists and non-Marxists. Various other writers have built on the frame-work established by Wallerstein. Indeed, world-system theory is now a flourishing sub-field of both Marxism and international relations theory.

Other world-system theorists have made distinctive contributions to the literature. Christopher Chase-Dunn, for example, lays much more emphasis on the role of the inter-state system than Wallerstein. He argues that the capitalist mode of production has a single logic in which both politico-military and exploitative economic relations play key roles. In a sense he attempts to bridge the gap between Wallerstein's work and that of the New Marxists (discussed in a subsequent section), by placing much more of an emphasis on production in the world-economy and how this influences its development and future trajectory (see Chase-Dunn 1998).

Frank and Gills argue that Wallerstein's view of the world-capitalist system as a European phenomenon that has spread throughout the world, is mistaken and Eurocentric. In contrast, Frank and Gills hold that the European world-system is an offshoot of a much older world-system based on the Middle East (Frank and Gills 1996). Their work builds on that of Janet Abu-Lughod. She has challenged Wallerstein's account of the emergence of the modern world-system in the sixteenth century arguing that, during the medieval period, Europe was a peripheral area to a world-economy centred on the Middle East (Abu-Lughold 1989). Frank and Gills argue that the current world-system can be traced back well beyond medieval times, and that in fact key features can be traced back for 5000 years.

Key points

- World-system theory can be seen as a direct development of Lenin's work on imperialism and the Latin American dependency school.

- Immanuel Wallerstein and his work on the modern world-system is a key contribution to this school.

- Wallerstein's work has been developed by a number of other writers who have built on his initial foundational work.

Gramscianism

In this section we discuss the strand of Marxist theory that has emerged from the work of the Italian Marxist Antonio Gramsci. Gramsci's work has become particularly influential in the study of International Political Economy, where a neo-Gramscian or 'Italian' school is flourishing. Here we will discuss Gramsci's legacy, and the work of Robert W. Cox, a contemporary theorist who has been instrumental in introducing his work to an International Relations audience.

Antonio Gramsci

Antonio Gramsci (1891–1937) was a Sardinian and one of the founding members of the Italian Communist party. He was jailed in 1926 for his political activities, and spent the remainder of his life in prison, suffering the most appalling privations under a regime personally supervised by Mussolini. Although he is regarded by many as the most creative Marxist thinker of the twentieth century, he produced no single, integrated theoretical treatise. Rather his intellectual legacy has been transmitted primarily through his remarkable *Prison Notebooks*. As their title suggests, these are a collection of notes and some longer essays which Gramsci produced during his long period in captivity. They contain reflections not only on political theory, but also on a wide range of other subjects including economics, philosophy, history, and literary criticism. Given the circumstances under which they were written, where, with failing health, Gramsci had to work without access to books, and had to write in code in order to confuse the prison censor, it is not surprising that the ideas contained in the *Notebooks* are somewhat fragmentary and are sometimes opaque. They are suggestive rather than definitive statements, and as such open to a range of different interpretations.

The key question which animated Gramsci's theoretical work was why had it proven to be so difficult to promote revolution in Western Europe? Marx, after all, had predicted that revolution, and the transition to socialism, would occur first in the most advanced capitalist societies. But, in the event, it was the Bolsheviks of comparatively backward Russia that had made the first 'breakthrough' while all the subsequent efforts by putative revolutionaries in Western and Central Europe to emulate their success had ended in failure. The history of the early twentieth century seemed to suggest, therefore, that there was a flaw in classic Marxist analysis. But where had they gone wrong?

Gramsci's answer to this question revolves around his use of the concept of **hegemony**. Hegemony is a term widely used in International Relations theory, most frequently in order to describe the most powerful state in the international system, or the dominant state in a particular region. So, for example, the

United Kingdom is regarded as having been the hegemonic power in the international system of the nineteenth century, while India is widely viewed as the current regional hegemon in South Asia. Gramsci's use of hegemony is also related to his understanding of power, but it reflects a conceptualization of power that is broader and richer than that usually encountered in the work of contemporary realists.

Gramsci adopts Machiavelli's view of power as a centaur, half beast, half man: a mixture of coercion and consent. In understanding how the prevailing order was maintained, Marxists had concentrated almost exclusively on the coercive practices and capabilities of the state, an institution that Engels once described as 'nothing but a machine for the oppression of one class by another'. On this understanding, it was simply coercion, or the fear of coercion, that kept the exploited and alienated majority in society from rising up and overthrowing the system that was the cause of their suffering. Gramsci recognized that while this characterization may have held true in less developed societies, such as pre-revolutionary Russia, it was not the case in the more developed countries of the West. Here the system was maintained not merely by coercion, but also through consent.

Consent, on Gramsci's reading, is created and re-created by the hegemony of the ruling stratum in society. It is this hegemony that allows the moral, political, and cultural values of the dominant group to become widely dispersed throughout society and to be accepted by subordinate groups and classes as their own. Indeed, according to Gramsci's analysis, dominant ideologies become sedimented in society to the extent that they take on the status of unquestioned 'common sense'. All this takes place through the institutions of **civil society**. Civil society is the network of institutions and practices in society that enjoy some autonomy from the state, and through which groups and individuals organize, represent and express themselves to each other and to the state. These include, for example, the media, the education system, churches, voluntary organizations, etc.

Several important implications flow from this analysis. The first is that Marxist theory needs to take superstructural phenomena seriously, because while the structure of society may ultimately be a reflection of social relations of production in the economic base, the nature of relations in the super-structure are of great relevance in determining how susceptible that society is to change and transform-ation. Gramsci used the term **historic bloc** to describe the mutually reinforcing and reciprocal relationships between the socio-economic relations (base) and political and cultural practices (super-structure) that *together* underpin a given order. Its use serves as a reminder that for Gramsci and Gram-scians, to reduce analysis to the narrow consider-ation of economic relationships, on the one hand, or solely to politics and ideas on the other, is deeply mistaken. It is the interaction that matters.

Another crucial implication is for political prac-tice. If the hegemony of the ruling class or stratum is a key element in the perpetuation of its dominance, then society can only be transformed if that hege-monic position is successfully challenged. This entails a **counter hegemonic** struggle in civil soci-ety, in which the prevailing hegemony is under-mined, allowing an alternative historic bloc to be constructed.

Gramsci's writing reflects a particular time and a particular, and in many ways unique, set of circum-stances. This has led several writers to question the broader applicability of his ideas. Their central argument is that Gramsci was primarily concerned with a specific national society, that is Italy, rather than the analysis of international circumstances more generally, and that his thinking was relevant to a particular historical epoch, and cannot therefore be regarded as a source of 'transhistorical' concepts (see Burnham 1991; Germain and Kenny 1998). We would suggest, however, that a careful analysis of the *Prison Notebooks* reveals that Gramsci was indeed attempting to develop a conceptual framework that, while certainly not claiming universal, timeless val-idity, would certainly be applicable to other soci-eties. Furthermore, and as his analysis of Italian soci-ety demonstrates, he was very well aware of the sig-nificance of developments in the international sphere. But the most important test, of course, is how useful ideas and concepts derived from Gram-sci's work prove to be when they are removed from their original context and applied to other issues and problems? It is to this that we now turn our attention.

Robert Cox—the analysis of 'world order'

The person who has done most to introduce Gramsci to the study of world politics is the Canadian scholar Robert W. Cox. He has developed a Gramscian approach that involves both a critique of prevailing theories of International Relations and International Political Economy and the development of an alter-native framework for the analysis of world politics.

To explain Cox's ideas we would like to begin by discussing one particular sentence in his seminal 1981 article 'Social Forces, States, and World Orders: Beyond International Relations Theory'. The sen-tence, which has become one of the most often-quoted lines in all of contemporary International Relations theory, reads as follows: 'Theory is always *for* some one, and *for* some purpose' (1981: 128). It expresses a world-view that follows logically from the Gramscian, and broader Marxist position, that has been explored in this chapter. If ideas and values are (ultimately) a reflection of a particular set of social relations, and are transformed as those rela-tions are themselves transformed, then this suggests that all knowledge (of the social world at least) must reflect a certain context, a certain time, a certain space. Knowledge, in other words, cannot be object-ive and timeless in the sense that some contempor-ary realists, for example, would like to claim.

One key implication of this is that there can be no simple separation between facts and values. Whether consciously or not, all theorists inevitably bring their values to bear on their analysis. This leads Cox to suggest that we need to look closely at those theories, those ideas, those analyses that claim to be objective or value free, and ask who or what is it for, and what purpose does it serve? He subjects Realism, and in particular its contemporary variant neo-realism to a thoroughgoing critique in these grounds. According to Cox, these theories are for—or serve the interests of—those who prosper under the prevailing order, that is the inhabitants of the developed states, and in particular the ruling elites. Their purpose, whether consciously or not, is to reinforce and legitimate the status quo. They do this by making the current con-figuration of International Relations appear natural and immutable. When realists (falsely) claim to be describing the world as it is, as it has been, and as it always will be, what they are in fact doing is reinforcing the ruling hegemony in the current world order.

Cox contrasts **problem-solving theory**, that is theory which accepts the parameters of the present order, and thus helps legitimate an unjust and deeply iniquitous system, with **critical theory**. Critical theory attempts to challenge the prevailing order by seeking out, analysing and, where possible, assisting social processes that can potentially lead to emancipatory change (see Ch. 11).

One way in which theory can contribute to these emancipatory goals is by developing a theoretical understanding of world orders that grasps both the sources of stability in a given system, and also the dynamics of processes of transformation. In this context, Cox draws upon Gramsci's notion of hegemony and transposes it to the international realm, arguing that hegemony is as important for maintaining stability and continuity here as it is at the domestic level. According to Cox, successive dominant powers in the international system have shaped a world order that suits their interests, and have done so not only as a result of their coercive capabilities, but also because they have managed to generate broad consent for that order even among those who are disadvantaged by it.

For the two hegemons that Cox analyses (the United Kingdom and the United States) the ruling, hegemonic idea has been 'free trade'. The claim that this system benefits everybody has been so widely accepted that it has attained 'common sense' status. Yet the reality is that while 'free trade' is very much in the interests of the hegemon (which, as the most efficient producer in the global economy, can produce goods which are competitive in all markets, so long as they have access to them), its benefits for peripheral states and regions are far less apparent. Indeed many would argue that 'free trade' is a hin-

drance to their economic and social development. The degree to which a state can successfully produce and reproduce its hegemony is an indication of the extent of its power. The success of the United States in gaining worldwide acceptance for neo-liberalism suggests just how dominant the current hegemon has become (see Box 10.3).

But despite the dominance of the present world order, Cox does not expect it to remain unchallenged. Rather he maintains Marx's view that capitalism is an inherently unstable system, riven by inescapable contradictions. Inevitable economic crises will act as a catalyst for the emergence of counter-hegemonic movements. The success of such movements is however far from assured. In this sense, thinkers like Cox face the future on the basis of a dictum popularized by Gramsci, that is, combining 'pessimism of the intellect' with 'optimism of the will'.

Key points

- Drawing upon the work of Antonio Gramsci for inspiration, writers within an 'Italian' school of international relations have made a considerable contribution to thinking about world politics.

- Gramsci shifted the focus of Marxist analysis more towards superstructural phenomena. In particular he explored the processes by which consent for a particular social and political system was produced and reproduced through the operation of hegemony. Hegemony allows the ideas and ideologies of the ruling stratum to become widely dispersed, and widely accepted, throughout society.

- Thinkers such as Robert W. Cox have attempted to 'internationalize' Gramsci's thought by transposing several of his key concepts, most notably hegemony, to the global context.

Box 10.3 The politics of neo-liberalism

A very good example of the hegemonic power of the United States, many Marxists would argue, is the success that it has had in getting neo-liberal policies accepted as the norm throughout the world. The set of policies most closely associated with the neo-liberal project (in particular reduction of state spending, currency devaluation, privatization, and the promotion of free markets) are, revealingly, known as the 'Washington consensus'. Many would argue that these are 'common sense' policies and that those Third World countries that have adopted them have merely realized that such economic policies best reflect their interests. However, Marxists would argue that an analysis of the self-interest of the hegemon, and the use of coercive power, provide a more convincing explanation of why such policies have been adopted.

The adoption of neo-liberal policies by Third World countries has had a number of implications. Spending on health and education have been reduced, they have been forced to rely more on the export of raw materials, and their markets have been saturated with manufactured goods from the industrialized world. It doesn't take a conspiracy theorist to suggest that these neo-liberal polices are in the interests of capitalists in the developed world. There are three main areas where the adoption of neo-liberal policies in the Third World is in the direct interest of the developed world. First there is the area of free trade. Without entering into arguments about the benefits of free trade, it will always be in the interest of the hegemon to promote free trade—this is because, assuming it is the most efficient producer, its goods will be cheaper anywhere in the world. It is only if countries put up barriers to trade, to protect their own production, that the hegemon's products will be more expensive. Second there is the area of raw materials. If Third World countries are going to compete in a free trade situation the usual result is that they become more reliant on the export of raw materials (because their industrial products cannot compete in a free trade situation with those of the developed world). Again this is in the interest of the hegemon, as increases in

the supply of raw material exports mean that the price falls. Additionally where Third World countries have devalued their currency as part of a neo-liberal package the price of their exported raw materials goes down. Finally, when Third World governments have privatized industries, investors from North America and Europe have frequently been able to snap up airlines, telecommunications companies, and oil industries at bargain prices. Duncan Green (1995) gives an eloquent description of the impacts of neo-liberalism on Latin American counties.

If neo-liberal policies appear to have such negative results for Third World countries why have they been so widely adopted? This is where the coercive element comes in. Through the 1970s and 1980s and continuing to today there has been a major debt crisis between the Third World and the West. This debt crisis came about primarily as a result of excessive and unwise lending by Western banks. Third World countries were unable to pay off the interest on these debts, let alone the debt itself. They turned to the major global financial institutions such as the International Monetary Fund for assistance. Although the IMF is a part of the United Nations it is heavily controlled by Western countries, in particular the United States. For example, the United States has 18 per cent of the votes, while Mozambique has only 0.07 per cent. In total the 10 most industrialized countries have over 50 per cent of the votes. For Third World countries, the price of getting assistance was that they would implement neo-liberal policies. Only once these were implemented, and only on condition that the policies were maintained, would the IMF agree to provide aid to continue with debt repayment.

Hence Marxists would argue that a deeper analysis of the adoption of neo-liberal policies is required. Such an analysis would suggest that the global acceptance of neo-liberalism is very much in the interests of the developed world and has involved a large degree of coercion. That such policies seem 'natural' and 'common sense' is an indication of the hegemonic power of the United States.

Critical theory

Critical theory has been an enormously influential school of thought in fields of academic endeavour that range from aesthetics and psychoanalysis, to sociology and ethics. Nevertheless, it is only relatively recently that its influence has begun to be felt on the discipline of International Relations. There are, without doubt, many overlaps between critical theory and Gramscian approaches to the study of world politics. Most obviously, of course, there is the overlap in terminology. As we have seen in the previous section, Robert W. Cox refers to his own Gramsci-influenced approach as critical theory. Moreover, both Gramscianism and critical theory have their roots in Western Europe of the 1920s and 1930s—a place and a time in which Marxism was forced to come to terms not only with the failure of a series of attempted revolutionary uprisings, but also the rise of fascism. Indeed, both critical theory and Gramscianism grew out of attempts from within the Marxist tradition to understand why the optimism of an earlier generation who had believed in the inevitability of emancipatory transformation, had proven to be so disastrously misplaced. We would certainly argue, therefore, that it is a mistake to draw too strong a dividing line between both schools of thought. Indeed, it is understandable that many commentators regard them as to all intents and purposes, identical.

Nevertheless, there are differences between them. Contemporary critical theory and Gramscian thoughts about International Relations draw upon the ideas of different thinkers, with differing intellectual concerns. In addition, there is a clear difference in focus between the two strands, with those influenced by Gramsci tending to be much more concerned with issues relating to the subfield of international political economy than critical theorists. Critical theorists, on the other hand, have involved themselves with questions concerning international society and security. In this section, therefore, we will briefly introduce critical theory and the thought of one of its main proponents in the field of International Relations, Andrew Linklater. We would urge the reader to read what we have to say in conjunction with the section on critical theory in Chapter 11, 'Reflectivist and constructivist approaches to international theory'.

Critical theory has developed out of the work of the **Frankfurt School**. This was an extraordinarily talented group of thinkers who began to work with each other in the 1920s and 1930s. As left-wing German Jews, the members of the school were forced into exile by the Nazis' rise to power in the early 1930s, and much of their most creative work was produced after they had successfully sought refuge in the United States. At the end of the Second World War some returned to Germany while others remained in the United States. The leading lights of the first generation of the Frankfurt School included **Max Horkheimer**, **Theodor Adorno** and **Herbert Marcuse**. A subsequent generation has taken up the legacy of these thinkers and developed it in important and innovative ways. The best known is **Jürgen Habermas**, who is regarded by many as the most influential of all contemporary social theorists. Given the vast scope of critical theory writing, we can do no more here than introduce some of the key features.

The first point to note is that their intellectual concerns are rather different from most other Marxists in that they have not been much interested in the further development of analysis of the economic base of society. They have instead concentrated on questions relating to culture, bureaucracy, the social basis and nature of authoritarianism, and the structure of the family, and on exploring such concepts as reason and rationality, theories of knowledge, etc. Frankfurt School theorists have been particularly innovative in terms of their analysis of the role of the media, and what they have famously termed the 'culture industry'. In other words, in classical Marxist terms, the focus of critical theory is almost entirely superstructural.

Another key feature is that critical theorists have been highly dubious as to whether the proletariat in contemporary society does in fact embody the potential for emancipatory transformation in the way that Marx had believed. Rather, with the rise of mass culture and the increasing commodification of every element of social life, Frankfurt School thinkers have argued that the working class has simply been absorbed by the system and no longer represents a threat to it. This, to use Marcuse's famous phrase, is a 'one-dimensional' society to which the vast majority simply cannot begin to conceive an alternative.

Critical theorists have made some of their most important contributions through their explorations of the meaning of **emancipation**. Emancipation, as we have seen, is a key concern of Marxist thinkers, but the meaning that they give to the term is often very unclear and deeply ambiguous. Emancipation clearly means different things to different people. In addition, the historical record is unfortunately replete with examples of unspeakably barbaric behaviour being justified in the name of emancipation, of which imperialism and Stalinism are but two. Critical theorists have given sustained consideration to what human capacities and capabilities are being invoked in calls for emancipation, and, on this basis, sketching the contours of a more emancipated world. Two interesting themes have emerged from these deliberations.

For the first generation of critical theorists, emancipation had to be conceived of in terms of a **reconciliation with nature**. This formulation is in stark contrast with more traditional Marxist approaches which have equated emancipation with the process of humanity gaining ever greater mastery over nature. Marx spoke of the desirability of moving 'from the age of necessity to an age of freedom', which meant in part moving from a period where men and women were dominated by, and in thrall to, natural processes, to a period in which they enjoyed dominion. Horkheimer, Adorno, and Marcuse argued, however, that humanity's increased domination over nature had been bought at a very heavy price. This is because the kind of mind-set that is required for conquering nature slips all too easily into the domination of other human beings. It also leads to the hollowing out of some of the finest sensibilities of which humankind is capable. Nothing is valued in and for itself, but is viewed solely in terms of instrumental calculation.

It must be admitted that these critical theorists were extremely vague about what reconciliation might mean in practice. Although one might reasonably argue that simply formulating the problem in this way is actually a major contribution in its own right as it forces us to think about familiar things in a very different light. The contemporary German sociologist **Ulrich Beck**, has pursued a similar theme with his discussion of 'ecological enlightenment'. The ideas of the Frankfurt School on this issue also chime with sections of the contemporary Green movement.

The second strand of thought arises from the work of a more recent generation of critical theorists, and in particular the work of Habermas, with his stress on the centrality of communication and dialogue to processes of emancipation. In contrast to classical Marxists who locate the potential for emancipation in the economic base of society—that is the realm of production—Habermas argues that the promise of a better society lies in the realm of communication. Setting aside the various twists and turns of his argument, Habermas's central point as far as political practice is concerned is that the route to emancipation lies through **radical democracy**. That is, a system in which the widest possible participation is encouraged not only in word (as is the case in many Western democracies) but also in deed, by actively identifying barriers to participation—be they social, economic or cultural—and overcoming them. For Habermas and his many followers, participation is not to be confined within the borders of a particular sovereign state. Rights and obligations extend beyond state frontiers. This, of course, leads him directly to the concerns of International Relations, and it is striking that Habermas's recent writings have begun to focus on the international realm. However, thus far, the most systematic attempt to think through some of the key issues in world politics from a recognizably Habermasian perspective has been made by **Andrew Linklater**.

Andrew Linklater is one of the most distinguished contemporary International Relations theorists, and certainly the most significant critical theorist writing in the field. He has used some of the key principles and precepts developed in Habermas's work in order to argue that emancipation in the realm of international relations should be understood in terms of the expansion of the moral boundaries of a political community (see Ch. 29). In other words, he equates emancipation with a process in which the borders of the sovereign state lose their ethical and moral significance.

Since the establishment of the present international system—an event which is usually traced back to 1648 and the signing of the Treaty of Westphalia—state borders have acted as an ethical boundary. They denote the furthest extent of our sense of duty and obligation, or at best, the point where our sense of duty and obligation is radically transformed, only proceeding further in a very attenuated form. For critical theorists, this situation is simply indefensible. The goal is therefore to move towards a situation in which citizens share the same duties and obligations towards non-citizens as they do towards their fellow citizens.

To arrive at such a situation would, of course, entail a wholesale transformation of the present insitutions of governance—a transformation which most of us would find very unlikely at present. But an important element of the critical theory method is to identify—and, if possible, nurture—tendencies that exist within the present conjuncture that point in the direction of emancipation. The technical term for this is **immanent critique**. On this basis, Linklater identifies the development of the European Union as representing a progressive, or emancipatory tendency in contemporary world politics. It suggests that an important part of the international system is entering a **post-Westphalian era** in which the sovereign state, which has for so long claimed an exclusive hold on its citizens, is beginning to lose some of its pre-eminence. Given the notorious pessimism of the thinkers of the Frankfurt School, the guarded optimism of Linklater in this context is indeed striking.

Key points

- Critical theory has its roots in the work of the Frankfurt School, a group of thinkers including Max Horkheimer, Theodor Adorno, Herbert Marcuse, and Jürgen Habermas.

- Among they key concerns of critical theorists is emancipation, and, in particular, the human capacities and capabilities appealed to in calls for emancipatory action.

- Several different understandings of emancipation have emerged from the critical theory tradition. The first generation of the Frankfurt School equated emancipation with a reconciliation with nature. Habermas has argued that emancipatory potential lies in the realm of communication and that radical democracy is the way in which that potential can be unlocked.

- Andrew Linklater has developed on critical theory themes to argue in favour of the expansion of the moral boundaries of the political community and has pointed to the European Union as an example of a post-Westphalian institution of governance.

New Marxism

In our exploration of world-system theory, Gramscianism, and critical theory, we have been discussing thinkers whose engagement with Marx's ideas has been mediated through the work of early or midtwentieth-century interpreters. In this section, by contrast, we examine the work of writers who derive their ideas more directly from Marx's own writings. These New Marxists have returned to the fundamental tenets of Marxist thought and sought to reappropriate ideas that they regard as having been neglected or somehow misinterpreted by subsequent generations. On this basis they have sought both to criticize other developments within Marxism, and to make their own original theoretical contributions to the understanding of contemporary trends. In this section we will introduce the work of two writers associated with this strand of Marxist thought: Bill Warren, a trenchant critic of dependency and world-system approaches; and Justin Rosenberg, who has used key elements of Marx's writings to critique realist approaches to International Relations and to suggest how an alternative to Realism might be developed.

Bill Warren—imperialism and the rise of Third World capitalism

It is often forgotten that Marx's analysis of capitalism was far more than some simplistic, one-sided condemnation. In addition to pointing forcefully to the inhumanity of capitalist society, Marx was also keenly aware of its great dynamism. As is clear from the *Communist Manifesto*, for example, Marx regarded capitalism as a **necessary** stage in human development. Through its development of the productive capacities of society, capitalism both lays the economic foundation upon which an emancipated society can subsequently be built, and generates the intense class struggle which is the necessary catalyst for such a transformation. As a result of this view, Marx argued that the introduction of capitalism by the colonial powers into the colonies should be regarded as a positive development. Just as capitalism had ended the 'folly of feudalism' in Britain and other European countries, so its progressive characteristics would overthrow backward modes of production throughout the world. This would not be a cost-free or painless process. Marx noted that it was 'sickening . . . to human feeling to witness these myriad of industrious patriarchal and inoffensive social organisations disorganised and dissolved into their units, thrown into a sea of woes, and their individual members losing at the same time their ancient form of civilisation'. However, while the resulting human misery was to be bitterly regretted, it was unavoidable and historically necessary. Capitalism was a phase of world history that had to be endured if a socialist order was to emerge in the longer term.

As we saw in the last section, Lenin did not so much reject Marx's view, as argue that the character of capitalism had changed by the start of the twentieth century. As a result capitalism could no longer be regarded as playing a progressive role—indeed for the colonies it was deeply regressive. It was regressive, not only in the sense that it was not developing the productive base of what has come to be known as

the Third World in the way that Marx had expected, but also because the profits that it was possible to extract through the exploitation of the colonies allowed capitalists to deflect the revolutionary potential of the working classes in the developed core states. For Lenin, therefore, imperialism represented the phase where capitalism definitively ceased to play any progressive function—imperialism was both 'the highest stage of capitalism' and its final stage. This view became the standard Marxist and neo-Marxist position through much of the twentieth century.

The British Marxist, Bill Warren, rejected this view. In his book *Imperialism: Pioneer of Capitalism* he argued that Lenin had been both empirically and theoretically mistaken. In contrast, he argued that the line argued by Marx remained essentially valid. Capitalism, according to Warren, was fulfilling its historic role in the periphery by rapidly developing the means of production and, crucially for a future transition to socialism, facilitating the emergence of an urban working class. Imperialism should therefore be seen as 'the pioneer of capitalism' rather than its 'highest stage'.

To back up his view Warren examined in depth the development of capitalism in a range of Third World countries. Colonialism, he argued, had brought about a marked improvement in material welfare throughout the world. This improvement took three main forms—better health care, better education, and greater access to consumer goods. Each of these was crucial in laying the foundations for the long-term development of productive forces. In terms of health care, Warren notes that throughout the colonial world, life expectancy increased and child mortality decreased, resulting in large increases in population. Likewise with education, Warren argued that in Third World countries the percentage of the population attending primary, secondary, and, in particular, tertiary levels of education was higher than it had been in Europe at an equivalent level of development. So, for example, the Third World secondary school enrolment rate of 20 per cent, achieved in 1970, had only been reached in the developed world between 1930 and 1950. Finally, provision of consumer goods increased enormously during the colonial period, stimulating a large increase in domestic production.

Furthermore, Warren argues that in the post-colonial era there has been an enormous increase in the wealth and productive capacity of Third World countries. This process has, of course, been uneven, and there have been winners and losers, but such irregularities are inherent in capitalist development. In particular growth rates in the Third World have increased significantly during the post-Second World War era. Warren argues that they compare favourably with growth rates in Europe during the eighteenth and nineteenth centuries—an equivalent period in terms of the level of industrial development.

Overall, Warren suggests that the picture of North–South relations depicted by dependency theorists and world-systems theorists is an incomplete one. Certainly the introduction of capitalism throughout the world has had its costs, but it is not leading to the 'development of underdevelopment' as many have argued. Making direct reference to Marx, Warren argues that we should not be anti-capitalist in those situations where capitalist development is increasing levels of productivity and making material improvements to living standards—these are part of capitalism's historic mission as a precursor to a transition to socialism.

Warren's argument is clearly a contentious one. Evidence provided by, for example, World Bank reports, indicates a growing immiseration of much of the Third World. Nonetheless, in one important sense he could be viewed as being essentially correct. Imperialism was not the 'highest stage' of capitalism as Lenin had claimed, it was rather 'the pioneer' by which the capitalist mode of production expanded from its European heartland throughout the globe—leading directly to the globalized capitalist world of today.

Justin Rosenberg—capitalism and global social relations

Warren rejected the belief held by most neo-Marxists during the twentieth century that exposure to capitalism has been detrimental for much of the Third World. He argued that this view ignored a key insight in Marx's thought, namely that capitalism provides for rapid social transformation. The work of Justin Rosenberg also suggests that theorists of international relations have much to gain from a direct engagement with Marx's ideas. In contrast to Warren however, the focus of Rosenberg's analysis is the character of the international system and its relationship to the changing nature of social relations.

Rosenberg's starting point is a critique of realist International Relations theory. His particular objection is to Realism's claim to provide an ahistorical, essentially timeless account of international relations. In marked contrast, Rosenberg argues that we need a theory that allows the development of a historical account of how international relations have developed. He analyses the differences in the character of international relations between the Greek and Italian city-states. A touchstone of realist theory is the similarity between these two historical cases. Rosenberg, however, describes the alleged resemblances between these two eras as a 'gigantic optical illusion'. Instead his analysis suggests that the character of the international system in each of these periods was completely different. In addition, he charges that attempts to provide an explanation of historical outcomes during these periods working purely from the inter-state level is not feasible (as, for example, in realist accounts of the Peloponnesian War). Finally, Rosenberg argues that realist attempts to portray international systems as autonomous, entirely political realms, founder because in the Greek and Italian examples this external autonomy was based on the character of internal—and in each case different—sets of social relations.

As an alternative, Rosenberg argues for the development of a theory of international relations that is sensitive to the changing character of world poltics. This theory must also recognize that international relations are part of a broader pattern of social relations. His starting point is Marx's observation that

it is always the direct relationship of the owners of the conditions of production to the direct producers . . . which reveals the innermost secret, the hidden basis of the entire social structure, and with it the political form of the relation of sovereignty and dependence, in short, the corresponding specific form of the state.

In other words, the character of the relations of production permeate the whole of society—right up to, *and including*, relations between states. The form of the state will be different under different modes of production, and as a result the characteristics of inter-state relations will also vary. Hence if we want to understand the way that international relations operate in any particular era, our starting point has to be an examination of the mode of production, and in particular the relations of production. Changes in the character of international relations can thus only be understood by examining the social relations that provide their fundamental underpinnings. Thus if we wish to understand the change between international relations in Ancient Greece and international relations in the feudal era, for example, then we need to analyse the change in social relations between these two eras.

Turning to the contemporary era, Rosenberg argues that two of the core concepts in realist theorizing, sovereignty and anarchy, can fruitfully be re-evaluated in the light of Marx's method. Indeed, for Rosenberg, both sovereignty and anarchy reflect particular features of the capitalist era. Sovereignty reflects the way in which the state has become separated from the production process under capitalism, with its role becoming purely 'political'. Although states are involved in the regulation of production, they tend not to be directly embroiled in the process of surplus extraction. In all previous eras, by contrast, states were involved directly in production. But with the separation of sovereign territorial governance and production, capitalist enterprises are now able to operate internationally with much greater autonomy from state control. The current situation is therefore a novel and very significant development in social arrangements.

Likewise, Rosenberg suggests that a Marxist approach facilitates a rethinking of that other keystone of realist thought, anarchy. Rosenberg argues that a theory of anarchy is contained within Marx's analysis of capitalism. This posits that anarchy is a key feature of capitalist production. All wage-earners and capitalists, after all, exist in a condition of competition with each other. In Marx's own words, 'in the society where the capitalist mode of production prevails, anarchy in the social division of labour and despotism in the manufacturing division of labour

mutually condition each other.' The conclusion drawn by Rosenberg is that anarchy is a condition of capitalist relations and not a set of circumstances confined to international relations: it is inherent in social relations within the capitalist mode of production rather than a transhistorical feature of relations between states.

Both Warren and Rosenberg argue that a 'return' to Marx provides us with invaluable intellectual resources for thinking about world politics. Warren's work is primarily a challenge to the Dependency and World-System theory approaches. His key argument is that they have tended to overlook a key element of Marx's thinking, that is the capacity of capitalism to produce rapid and progressive social change. Through his empirical analysis he seeks to establish that a key tenet of much Marxian theorizing about world politics—namely 'the development of underdevelopment'—is in fact incorrect. To the contrary he points to wide-scale improvements in the Third World during the twentieth century, both in terms of economic growth and social welfare. Rosenberg builds on Marx's work in order both to criticize prevailing orthodoxies in international relations theory and to develop an alternative theoretical position. He deploys Marx's key insight that the character of social relations reflects underlying relations of production in order to analyse how international systems change over time.

Key points

- New Marxism is characterized by a direct (re)appropriation of the concepts and categories developed by Marx.

- Warren deploys Marx's analysis of capitalism and colonialism to criticize some of the central ideas of dependency and world-system theorists.

- Rosenberg uses Marx's ideas to criticize realist theories of international relations and to develop an alternative approach which seeks to understand historical change in world politics as a reflection of transformations in the prevailing relations of production.

Marxist theories of International Relations and globalization

In this chapter, we have attempted to outline some of the fundamental tenets of Marxist thinking, and to introduce four contemporary strands of thought that have in different ways attempted to build on these principles and precepts in order to develop an understanding of world politics. In this concluding section we will discuss how Marxist theorists, in general, view the phenomenon of globalization.

As was outlined in the first chapter of this book, globalization is the name given to the process whereby social transactions of all kinds increasingly take place without account for national or state boundaries, with the result that the world has become 'one relatively borderless social sphere'. The particular trends pointed to as typifying globalization include: the growing integration of national economies; a growing awareness of ecological interdependence; the proliferation of companies, social movements, and intergovernmental agencies operating on a global scale; and a communications revolution which has aided the development of a global consciousness.

Marxist theorists would certainly not seek to deny that these developments are taking place, nor would they deny their importance, but they would reject any notion that they are somehow novel. Rather, in the words of Chase-Dunn, they are 'continuations of trends that have long accompanied the expansion of capitalism' (1994: 97). Marx and Engels were clearly aware not only of the global scope of capitalism, but also of its potential for social transformation. In a particularly prescient section of the *Communist Manifesto*, for example, they argue that:

The bourgeoisie has through its exploitation of the world market given a cosmopolitan character to production and consumption in every country.... All old-established national industries have been destroyed or are daily being destroyed. They are dislodged by new industries, whose introduction becomes a life and death question for all civilised nations, by industries that no longer work up indigenous raw material, but raw material drawn from the remotest zones; industries whose products are consumed, not only at home, but in every quarter of the globe.... National one-sidedness and narrow-mindedness become more and more impossible, and from the numerous local literatures, there arises a world literature.

According to Marxist theorists, the globe has long been dominated by a single integrated economic and political entity—a global capitalist system—which has gradually incorporated all of humanity within its grasp. Within this system, all elements have always been interrelated and interdependent. 'National economies' have long been integrated to such an extent that their very nature has been dependent on their position within a capitalist world-economy. The only thing 'new' is an increased awareness of these linkages. Similarly, ecological processes have always ignored state-boundaries, even if it is only recently that growing environmental degradation has finally allowed this fact to permeate into public consciousness.

The growth of multinational corporations certainly does not signify any major change in the structure of the modern capitalist system. Rather, they form part of a long-term trend towards the further integration of the global economy. Neither is international contact between those movements who oppose the prevailing political and economic order a new development. In fact, as even the most cursory examination of the historical record will amply attest, such movements, be they socialist, nationalist, or ecological in character, have always drawn inspiration from, and forged links with, similar groups in other countries. Finally, the much-vaunted communications revolution is the latest manifestation of a long-term trend under capitalism whereby space and time are becoming increasingly compressed.

Whilst the intensity of cross-border flows may be increasing, this does not necessarily signify the fundamental change in the nature of world politics proclaimed by so many of those who argue that we have entered an era of globalization. Marxist theorists insist that the only way to discover how significant contemporary developments really are is to view them in the context of the deeper structural processes at work. When this is done, we may well discover indications that important changes are afoot. Many Marxists, for example, regard the delegitimation of the sovereign-state as a very important contemporary development. However, the essential first step in generating any understanding of those trends regarded as evidence of globalization must be to map-out the contours of global capitalism itself. If we fail to do so, we will inevitably fail to gauge the real significance of the changes which are occurring.

Another danger of adopting an ahistoric and uncritical attitude to globalization is that it can blind us to the way in which reference to globalization is increasingly becoming part of the ideological armoury of elites within the contemporary world. Globalization is now regularly cited as a reason to promote measures to reduce workers' rights and lessen other constraints on business. Many politicians and business leaders argue that unless businesses are allowed to function without constraints, they will not be able to compete in a globalizing economy.

Such ideological justifications for policies which favour the interests of business can only be countered through a broader understanding of the relationship between the political and the economic structures of capitalism. As we have seen, the understanding proffered by the Marxist theorists suggests that there is nothing natural or inevitable about a world order based on a global market. The current organization of global capitalism is in a constant state of change and crisis. Therefore, rather than accept the inevitability of the present order, the task facing us is to lay the foundations for a new way of organizing society—a global society which is more just and more humane than our own.

Key points

- Marxists are rather sceptical about the emphasis currently being placed on the notion of globalization.

- Rather than being a recent phenomenon they see the recent manifestations of globalization as being part of long-term trends in the development of capitalism.

- Furthermore the notion of globalization is increasingly being used as an ideological tool to justify reductions in workers rights and welfare provision.

QUESTIONS

1 How would you account for the continuing vitality of Marxist thought?

2 How did Lenin's approach to international relations differ from that of Marx?

3 How useful is Wallerstein's notion of a semi-periphery?

4 Assess Warren's criticisms of world-system theory.

5 Evaluate Rosenberg's contribution to Marxist International Relations theory.

6 In what ways does Gramsci's notion of hegemony differ from that employed by realist International Relations writers?

7 How has Linklater developed critical theory for an International Relations audience?

8 How do Marxist theorists view the notion of 'globalization'?

9 What do you regard as the main contribution of Marxist theory to our understanding of world politics?

GUIDE TO FURTHER READING

In order to develop an understanding of the basic elements of Marx's ideas, and the origins of Marxism in general, we strongly suggest that you start by reading Marx and Engels' *Communist Manifesto*. Numerous editions are available, some of which are very reasonably priced. Despite having been first published in 1848, the Manifesto remains a very powerful statement, whose impact has scarcely been dulled by the passage of time. The more ambitious may then wish to tackle *Capital*, volume one of which is the most readable by some distance, and the only one that was completed in Marx's lifetime. Again many different editions are available. C. J Arthur has produced a helpful 'Student's Edition' that sensitively abridges the text and supplies a useful introduction (*Capital: Student Edition*, London: Lawrence & Wishart, 1992).

On Marx himself, Francis Wheen's recent biography, simply titled *Karl Marx* (London: Fourth Estate, 1999), has been rightly praised for its liveliness and lightness of touch. It is both enjoyable and highly informative and can be wholeheartedly recommended. There are also a number of short introductions to Marx's ideas available. P. Singer's *Marx* (Oxford: Oxford University Press, 1985) is especially worthwhile. Leszek Kolawoski's imposing three-volume survey, *The Main Currents of Marxism* (Oxford: Oxford University Press, 1978), provides an overview of the whole Marxist tradition. Although some of his judgements can be questioned—he is, for example, notably unsympathetic to the Frankfurt School—it remains a landmark study. For those of a more historical bent, Perry Anderson's *Passages from Antiquity to Feudalism* and *Lineages of the Absolutist State* (both: London: New Left Books, 1974) are a stunning demonstration of the analytical power of the Marxist approach. While undoubtedly challenging, both are well worth the investment of time and energy.

On Marxism and International Relations, see the excellent discussion by John Hobson in *The State and International Relations* (Cambridge: Cambridge, University Press, 2000), ch. 4. Michael Cox's article 'Rebels without a Cause? Radical Theorists and the World System after the Cold War', *New Political Economy* 3: 3 (1998), 445–60, provides a wide-ranging and notably accessible overview of contemporary Marxist writing about international relations. Andrew Gamble, *Timewalkers: The Prehistory of Global Colonisation*, (Cambridge, Mass.: Harvard University Press, 1999) also discusses the fate of Marxist approaches to International Relations after the cold war.

The most complete account of the world-system approach to the study of International Relations is to be found in the work of Immanuel Wallerstein. If you have the time and energy the three volumes of *The Modern World-System*, are well worth studying (San Diego: Academic Press, 1974, 1980, 1989). Shorter summaries of Wallerstein's approach to world-system theorizing can be found in: (S. Hobden, *Internatinal Relations and Historical Sociology: Breaking down Boundaries* (London: Routledge, 1998), ch. 7; T. R. Shannon, *An Introduction to the World System Perspective* (Boulder, Colo.: Westview, 1996); and I. Wallerstein, 'The Inter-State Structure of the Modern World-System', in S. Smith, K. Booth, and M. Zalewski (eds.), *International Theory: Positivism and Beyond* (Cambridge: Cambridge University Press, 1996). For an excellent introduction to the various contemporary writers within world-system theory see Denemark *et al.*, *World System History* (London: Routledge, 2000).

Stephen Gill's edited volume *Gramsci, Historical Materialism and International Relations* (Cambridge: Cambridge University Press, 1993) draws together an important series of essays on Gramscian approaches to the study of world politics. The best introduction to Robert Cox's work is the 1996 volume, Robert Cox with Timothy J. Sinclair, *Approaches to World Order* (Cambridge: Cambridge University Press), which reproduces most of his key essays including the seminal 1981 article 'Social Forces, States, and World Orders: Beyond International Relations Theory'. For a brief and very useful survey of Gramscian approaches see also A. Morton, 'On Gramsci', *Politics*, 19:1 (1999), 1–8. Those interested in discovering more about Gramsci's life and ideas should read Giuseppe Friori's deeply moving biography, *Antonio Gramsci: Life of a Revolutionary*, trans. Tom Nairn (London: Verso, 1990).

The first three chapters of Richard Wyn Jones, *Security, Strategy and Critical Theory* (Boulder, Colo.: Lynn Rienner, 1999), provide an introduction to, and overview of, some of the key intellectual concerns of the Frankfurt School. All three of Andrew Linklater's books can be highly recommended: *Men and Citizens in the Theory of International Relations* and *Beyond Realism and Marxism: Critical Theory and International Relations* (both London: Macmillan, 1990); and *The Transformation of Political Community* (Cambridge: Polity Press, 1998). Also very useful is his essay on the 'The Achievements of Critical Theory', in Smith, Booth, and Zalewski (1996). The collection *Critical Theory and World Politics* (Boulder, Colo.: Lynne Rienner, 2000), edited by Richard Wyn Jones, brings together the key critical theorists in International Relations as well as Gramscians such as Robert Cox. This book also contains two important critiques of critical theory by Chris Brown and Alexander Wendt. On New Marxism, see B. Warren, *Imperialism: Pioneer of Capitalism* (London: New Left Books, 1980), and J. Rosenberg *The Empire of Civil Society: A Critique of the Realist Theory of International Relations* (London: Verso, 1994). In addition, the recently established journal *Historical Materialism* provides a forum for New Marxist writing.

WEB LINKS

www.csf.colorado.edu/mirrors/marxists.org/archive/marx/index.htm   *The Marx and Engels Internet Archive*: A large collection of works (including the *Communist Manifesto*), letters and images relating to Marx and Engels.

www.yorku.ca/socreg   *The Socialist Register*: An annual academic socialist journal. Edited by Leo Panitch and Colin Leys. Site includes links to selected articles from current and past volumes.

www.monthlyreview.org   *The Monthly Review*: Long-established Marxist journal from the US, edited by Paul Sweezy, Harry Magdoff and Ellen Meiksins Wood.

www.newleftreview.com   *The New Left Review*: A leading Marxist theoretical journal. Founded in 1960, NLR has been called 'the flagship of the Western intellectual left'.

www.cruznet.net/~marcus/gramsci-links.html   *Gramsci Links Archive*: Includes links to a variety of Gramsci-related sites—including 'Gramsci at the Movies' (a selection of reviews from a Gramscian perspective)!

www.uta.edu/huma/illuminations   *Illuminations: The Critical Theory Web Site*: Firmly based in Frankfurt School thought, this site maintains a collection of articles, excerpts, and chapters from many contemporary writers of and about critical theory.

11 Reflectivist and constructivist approaches to international theory

Steve Smith

READER'S GUIDE

This chapter summarizes the main alternatives to rationalist theories of international relations within the context of a framework for thinking about contemporary international relations theory. Following on from the preceding four chapters which looked at the three main theories of international relations and the current debate between neo-realism and neo-liberalism, this chapter outlines the distinctions between those theories that are explanatory and those that are constitutive, and between theories that are foundationalist and those that are non-foundationalist. Explanatory/foundationalist theories are termed rationalist (and these include the theories dealt with in the preceding four chapters). Constitutive/non-foundationalist theories come in two main versions, a group of them are termed reflectivist, and the other main approach is known as social constructivism; these theories are the main concern of this chapter. Most of the chapter looks at the leading influential contemporary reflectivist theories. These do not share the main assumptions of rationalist theories, and instead see theories as constituting the social world. The main theories dealt with are: normative theory, feminist theory, critical theory, historical sociology and post-modernism. The chapter then looks at social constructivism, which is an attempt to bridge the gap between rationalist and reflectivist theories. The chapter provides a clear context for thinking about these new approaches, and poses the question of whether social constructivism is really a bridge between rationalist and reflectivist theories.

Introduction

The four previous chapters have given you overviews of the three dominant theories of international relations (realism, liberalism, and structuralism) originally discussed in the Introduction of this book, and the contemporary debate between the two leading mainstream theories, **neo-realism** and **neo-liberalism**. These three approaches have dominated the discipline for the last fifty years, and the debate between adherents of them has defined the areas of disagreement in international theory. The resulting **'inter-paradigm debate'** has been extremely influential in thinking about international relations, with generations of students told that the debate between the various elements effectively exhausts the kinds of questions that can be asked about international relations. The problem has been that the inter-paradigm debate by no means covers the range of issues that any contemporary theory of world politics needs to deal with. Instead it ends up being a rather conservative political move because it gives the impression of open-mindedness and intellectual pluralism; whereas, in fact, as Tim Dunne and Brian Schmidt have pointed out, of the three theories involved in the inter-paradigm debate one, realism, has tended to be dominant, with its contest with liberalism being the central theme of what debate has existed in international theory. It is important to note that one major factor supporting the dominance of realism has been that it seems to portray the world we commonsensically understand. Thus alternative views can be dismissed as **normative** or **value-laden**, to be negatively compared with the **objectivity** of realism. These two thoughts (the common-sense relevance of realism and its objectivity) lead us to what has changed in recent years to subvert the dominance of realism.

In the last decade or so this picture has changed dramatically in two ways. First there has been, as Steve Lamy outlines in Chapter 9, a major debate between **neo-realism** and **neo-liberalism**, known as the **neo-neo** debate or the **neo-neo synthesis**, and this has been covered in detail in that chapter. The second change has been the appearance of a range of new approaches being developed to explain world politics. In part this reflects a changing world, as the end of the cold war system significantly reduced the creditability of realism, especially in its neo-realist guise where the stability of the bi-polar system was seen as a continuing feature of world politics; as that bi-polarity dramatically disappeared, so too did the explanatory power of the theory that most relied on it, neo-realism. But this was not by any means the only reason for the rise of new approaches. There are three other obvious reasons: first, there were other changes underway in world politics that made the development of new approaches important, and here I am thinking mainly of the kinds of features discussed previously under the heading of **globalization**. Whatever the explanatory power of realism, it did not seem very good at dealing with the rise of non-state actors, social movements, radically expanding transactions, and the like. In short, new approaches were needed to explain these parts of world politics, even if realism was still good at dealing with the power politics aspects. Second, there were major developments underway in other academic disciplines, especially in the social sciences generally, but also in the philosophy of science and social science that attacked the underlying methodological (i.e. how to undertake study) assumption of realism, a position known as **positivism** (we will discuss this below); in its place a whole host of alternative ways of thinking about the social sciences were being proposed, and International Relations simply caught the bug. Third, realism's dominance was called into question by a resurgence of its historical main competitor, liberalism, in the form of **neo-liberal institutionalism**, as discussed in Chapter 8, with this debate now comprising the mainstream of the discipline. Meanwhile, whilst those in the mainstream were engaged in this debate, a series of alternative approaches were being proposed as being more relevant to world politics at the turn of the millennium.

Key points

- Realism, liberalism, and structuralism together comprised the **inter-paradigm debate** of the 1980s, with realism dominant amongst the three theories.

- The **inter-paradigm debate** despite promising intellectual openness ended up naturalizing the dominance of realism by pretending that there was real debate, whereas 'common-sense' and the seeming 'objectivity' of realism did the work.

- The dominance of realism has in recent years been undermined by three sets of developments: first, **globalization** has brought a host of other features of world politics to centre-stage; second, **positivism**, the underlying methodological assumption of realism, has been significantly undermined by developments in the social sciences and in philosophy; third, **neo-liberal institutionalism** has become increasingly important in challenging realism in the mainstream literature, with the resulting debate, the **neo-neo synthesis** dominating the mainstream literature.

Explanatory/constitutive theories and foundational/anti-foundational theories

In order to understand the current situation with regards to international theory I want to introduce two distinctions that might help you see the differences between the theories that we are going to look at below. The terms can be a little unsettling, but they are merely convenient words for discussing what in fact are fairly straightforward ideas. The first distinction is between **explanatory** and **constitutive** theory. An explanatory theory is one that sees the world as something external to our theories of it; in contrast a constitutive theory is one that thinks our theories actually help construct the world. Whilst this is a distinction adopted in both scientific and non-scientific disciplines, a minute's thought should make you realize why it is more appealing in the non-scientific world: the reason of course is that in a very obvious way our theories about the world in which we live make us act in certain ways, and thereby may make the theories we hold become self-confirming. If for example we think that individuals are naturally aggressive then we are likely to adopt a different posture towards them than if we think they are naturally peaceful. However, you should not regard this claim as self-evidently true, since it assumes that our ability to think and reason makes us able to determine our choices, i.e. that we have

free will rather than having our 'choices' determined behind our backs as it were. What if our human nature is such that we desire certain things 'naturally', and that our language and seemingly 'free choices' are simply our rationalizations for our needs? This is only the opening stage of a very complex, but fascinating, debate about what it is to be human, and you will find it dealt with in a number of texts should you wish to follow up on it (see, for example, Hollis and Smith, 1990). The upshot of it, whichever position you eventually adopt, is that there is a genuine debate between those theories that think of the social world as like the natural world, and those theories that see our language and concepts as helping create that reality. Theories that think that the natural and the social worlds are the same are known as **naturalist** theories.

In International Relations, the more structural realist and structuralist theories dealt with in Chapters 7 and 10 tend to be explanatory theories, which see the task of theory as being to report on a world that is external to our theories; their concern is to uncover **regularities** in human behaviour and thereby explain the social world in much the same way as a natural scientist might explain the physical world. By contrast, nearly all the approaches developed in the last decade or so tend to be constitutive theories, and interestingly the same is true of some liberal thought. For these theories, theory is not external to the things it is trying to explain, and instead may construct how we think about the world. Or, to put it another way, our theories define what we see as the external world. Thus the very concepts we use to think about the world help to make that world what it is (think about the concepts that matter in your own life, such as happiness, love, wealth, status, etc.). To make my position clear I believe our theories of the social world constitute that world; I say this not so that you should believe it, but only so that you can see where my biases might lie in what follows.

The **foundational/anti-foundational** distinction refers to the simple-sounding issue of whether our beliefs about the world can be tested or evaluated against any neutral or objective procedures. This is a distinction central to the branch of the philosophy of social science known as **epistemology** (simply defined as the study of how we can claim to know something). A foundationalist position is one that thinks that all truth claims (i.e. about some feature of the world) can be judged true or false. An anti-foundationalist thinks that truth claims cannot be so judged since there are never neutral grounds for so doing; instead each theory will define what counts as the facts and so there will be no neutral position available to determine between rival claims. Think for example of a Marxist and a Conservative arguing about the 'true' state of the economy, or of an Islamic Fundamentalist and a Radical Feminist discussing the 'true' status of women in Muslim societies. Foundationalists look for what are termed **meta-theoretical** (or above any particular theory) grounds for choosing between truth claims; anti-foundationalists think that there are no such positions available, and that believing there to be some is itself simply a reflection of an adherence to a particular view of epistemology.

In many senses most of the new approaches to international theory are much less wedded to foundationalism than were the traditional theories that comprised the inter-paradigm debate. Thus, **post-modernism**, some **feminist theory**, and much **normative theory** would tend towards anti-foundationalism, although the **neo-neo debate**, his-torical sociology, and critical theory would tend towards foundationalism; interestingly, **social constructivism** wishes to portray itself as occupying the middle ground, a claim we will investigate later in this chapter. On the whole, and as a rough guide, explanatory theories tend to be foundational while constitutive theories tend to be anti-foundational. The point at this stage is not to construct some checklist, nor to get you thinking about the differences as much as it is to draw your attention to the role that these assumptions about the nature of knowledge have on the theories that we are going to discuss. The central point I want to make in this section is that the two distinctions mentioned in this section were never really discussed in the literature of international relations. The last decade has seen these underlying assumptions brought more and more into the open and the most important effect of this has been to undermine realism's claim to be delivering **the** truth.

Each of the distinctions has been brought into the open because of a massively important reversal in the way in which social scientists have thought about their ways of constructing knowledge. Until the late 1980s most social scientists in International Relations tended to be **positivists**; since then positivism has been under attack. Positivism is best defined as a view of how to create knowledge that relies on four main assumptions: first a belief in the unity of science, i.e. that the same methodologies apply in both the scientific and non-scientific worlds. Second, there is a distinction between facts and values, with facts being neutral between theories. Thirdly, that the social world, like the natural one, has regularities, and that these can be 'discovered' by our theories in much the same way as a scientist does in looking for the regularities in nature. Finally, that the way to determine the truth of statements is by appeal to these neutral facts; this is known as an **empiricist** epistemology.

It is the rejection of these assumptions that has characterized the debate in international theory in the last decade. Yosef Lapid (1989) has termed this 'a post-positivist era'. In simple terms, traditional international theory was dominated by the four kinds of positivistic assumptions noted above. Since the late 1980s, the new approaches that have emerged have tended to question these same assumptions. The resulting map of international theory at the turn of the millennium is one that has three main features: first the continuing dominance of the three theories that together made up the inter-paradigm debate, this can be termed the **rationalist** position, and is epitomized by the **neo-neo debate**; second, the emergence of non-positivistic theories, which together can be termed the **reflectivist** position, and epitomized by the **post-modernist, critical theory, historical sociology, normative theory**, and much **feminist work** to be discussed below; and third, the development of an approach that tries to speak to both rationalist and reflectivist positions, and this is the position, associated mainly with the work of Alexander Wendt (see especially 1992, 1999) and known as **social constructivism**. Figure 11.1 illustrates the resulting configuration of the theories at the turn of the millennium.

Note that this is a very rough representation of how the various theories can be categorized. It is misleading in some respects since, as the previous four chapters have shown, there are quite different versions of the three main theories and some of these are less rationalistic than others. Similarly, some of the approaches classified as 'reflectivist' are markedly less so than others; for example historical sociology tends to adopt similar theoretical methods as do rationalist approaches, although it tends to reject the central unit of rationalism, the state, hence its classification as a reflectivist approach. Having said which the classification is broadly illustrative of the theoretical landscape, and you might best think of it as a useful starting point for thinking about the differences between the theories involved. As you learn

more and more about them you will see how rough and ready a picture this is, but it is as good a categorization as any other. But so as to show you some of the complexities involved, think about quite what the reflectivist approaches are reflectivist about: for feminists it is gender, for normative theories it is values, for post-modernists it is the construction of knowledge, for historical sociologists it is the state/class relationship, and for critical theorists it is the knowledge/power relationship. There are similarities but there are important differences.

Key points

- Theories can be distinguished according to whether they are **explanatory** or **constitutive** and whether they are **foundational** or **anti-foundational**. As a rough guide, explanatory theories are foundational and constitutive theories are anti-foundational.

- The three main theories comprising the **inter-paradigm debate** were based on a set of positivist assumptions, namely that a denial of the idea that social science theories can use the same methodologies as theories of the natural sciences, that facts and values can be distinguished, that neutral facts can act as arbiters between rival truth claims, and that the social world has regularities which theories can 'discover'.

- Since the late 1980s there has been a rejection of **positivism**, with the main new approaches tending more towards **constitutive and anti-foundational** assumptions.

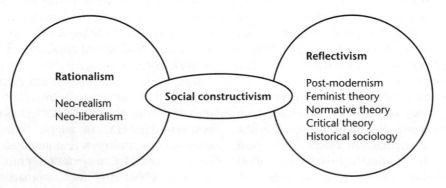

Fig. 11.1 International theory in the late 1990s

- The current theoretical situation is one in which there are three main positions: first, **rationalist** theories that are essentially the latest versions of the **realist** and **liberal** theories dealt with in previous chapters; second, **reflectivist** theories that are **post-positivist**; and thirdly **social constructivist** theories that try and bridge the gap between the first two sets.

Reflectivist theories

Before looking at the main **reflectivist** theories, I need to make two important points. The first concerns the title 'reflectivist'. Frankly there is no agreed label for these theories, and you will see many different ones in the literature. The most popular of these are 'radical', 'alternative', 'post-positivist', and even simply 'new'. I have chosen to use the phrase 'reflectivist' for one main reason, this is the term used within the mainstream US literature to categorize these approaches in a way that explicitly differentiates them from the 'rationalist' mainstream. This does not mean that I accept the label, only that it allows me to end this chapter by looking at the ways in which the mainstream distinguishes between reflectivist and social constructivist approaches. The second point I want to make is that reflectivist approaches differ considerably from one another, and indeed there is little that they share; the one thing that they do share, however, is a rejection of the core assumptions of **rationalist** theories, assumptions that you will find discussed in detail in the preceding four chapters and in the section on explanatory theory immediately above, and of course come into play when the mainstream makes the distinction between reflectivist and social constructivist approaches. I will now look at the main reflectivist theories and you will see that they have relatively little in common other than a rejection of rationalist accounts!

Normative theory

One of the most interesting developments in international theory in the last decade has been the re-emergence of **normative theory** as a focus of international theory. For decades this work was out of fashion as the mainstream of the discipline fell under the spell of **positivism**. Remember that the main claims of positivism included the thought that there was a clear division between 'facts' and 'values'. What this meant was that it was simply not scholarly to spend too much time on debates about what the world should look like. Instead what was preferred was a concern with the way things were. There are two basic problems with this position: first, that it is a very narrow definition of what politics is about, since for thousands of years students of politics have been fascinated with the search for 'the good life', with the strengths and weaknesses of specific ways of life and of certain forms of political arrangement. Thus, defining politics as limited to the empirical domain is a very restricting move, and you may well think a political one (i.e. a move designed to support certain, that is the existing, political arrangements); after all, if all we can do is to discuss **how** things operate and not **why**, then this naturalizes existing power divisions. So, when I have power the study of politics should be restricted to how it operates; if you raise the question of whether I should have power, then if I can dismiss this as 'value-laden' or 'normative' this immediately delegitimizes your work.

A second problem with the marginalizing of normative work is the rather serious objection that **all** theories reflect values, the only question being whether or not the values are hidden or not. An example is the one given in the previous paragraph; if I can tell you that things just 'are the way they are', then this clearly represents my views of what the social world is like and which features of it are fixed and which are not. In my view, as the author of this chapter, all theories have values running throughout their analysis, from what they choose to focus on as

Box 11.1 **Chris Brown's view of normative theory**

By normative international relations theory is meant that body of work which addresses the moral dimension of international relations and the wider questions of meaning and interpretation generated by the discipline. At its most basic it addresses the ethical nature of the relations between communities/states, whether in the context of the old agenda, which focused on violence and war, or the new(er) agenda, which mixes these traditional concerns with the modern demand for international distributive justice.

Source: Brown (1992: 3–4)

the 'facts' to be explained, through the methods they use to study these 'facts', down to the policy-prescriptions they suggest. Thus it is not that normative theory is odd, or optional; rather all theories have normative assumptions and implications, but in most cases these are hidden.

In the last decade or so, then, there has been a major resurgence of normative theory about world politics. Probably the best survey of this literature is by Chris Brown (1992). For his view of what normative theory is see Box 11.1. In his book he sets up his survey by outlining two main normative positions about world politics, **cosmopolitanism** and **communitarianism**. Cosmopolitanism is the view that the central focus of any normative theory of world politics should concentrate either on **humanity as a whole** or on **individuals**; on the other hand, communitarianism maintains that the appropriate focus is the **political community** (the state). What this distinction means is that the terms of the debate are whether there is a basis for rights and obligations between states in world politics or whether the bearers of these rights and obligations are individuals, either as individuals, or as a whole, in the sense of meaning humanity. For example do states have the right to hold large nuclear stockpiles to defend themselves if these weapons could potentially wipe out humanity? Or, is it acceptable for some cultures to perform 'female circumcision' because 'that is their way of doing things' or are there rights that the women concerned have that are

more important than the rights of the state to make its own decisions? This leads us into complex questions about intervention and human rights, but you can quickly see how massive normative debates might ensue from these and related issues.

In the bulk of his book, Brown uses the distinction between cosmopolitanism and communitarianism to examine three main focal points of normative international theory: the moral value to be assigned to state autonomy, the ethics of inter-state violence (**Just War Theory**), and the issue of international justice with specific regard to the obligations that the richer states of the world have to poorer countries. As you can imagine, cosmopolitans and communitarians have rather different views on these issues. To take the first question, cosmopolitanism clearly rejects the notion that states have a right to autonomy if that autonomy allows the state to undertake behaviour that conflicts with the moral rights of either humanity as a whole or of individuals; communitarianism on the other hand opposes any restrictions on autonomy that do not arise out of the community itself. Similarly, cosmopolitanists and communitarians will differ over when it is right for states to intervene in the affairs of others and over how we should evaluate calls for a more just distribution of economic resources. Particularly influential theorists on the first question have been Beitz (1979), Frost (1996), and Nardin (1983); for the second question the main writer has been Walzer (1977); and for the third question the key writers have been Rawls (1971) and Barry (1989). A particularly good overview of the main debates can be found in Cochran (1999).

Normative questions have become more 'policy relevant' in the last few years as governments have felt the need to justify their positions in moral terms. This has led to a renewed interest in normative theory and an increasing dissatisfaction with theories that (proudly) claim to be non-normative or 'realistic'. Particularly powerful examples of this new normative agenda are the debates over humanitarian intervention (see Ch. 22) and the British government's search for an ethical foreign policy. Each of these examples has led to explicit discussions about the 'right' moral stance to take, for example over the wars in former Yugoslavia, or over Western intervention in, say, Rwanda or Somalia. In this sense, normative theory is more obviously relevant to foreign policy than for several generations; and please note the consequence, which is that those theorists who claim that theory should NOT be normative may be unable to debate central issues of foreign policy.

Key points

- **Normative theory** was out of fashion for decades because of the dominance of **positivism**, which portrayed it as 'value-laden' and 'unscientific'.

- In the last decade or so there has been a resurgence of interest in normative theory. Thereby connecting international theory with the main debates that have been going on in the discipline of Politics. It is now more widely accepted that **all theories have normative assumptions either explicitly or implicitly.**

- The key distinction in normative theory is between **cosmopolitanism** and **communitarianism.** The former sees the bearers of rights and obligations as individuals; the latter sees them as being the state.

- **Chris Brown** identifies three main areas of debate in contemporary normative theory: the **autonomy of the state**, the **ethics of the use of force**, and **international justice.**

- In the last decade, normative issues have become more relevant to debates about foreign policy, for example in discussions of **ethical foreign policy** or how to respond to calls for **humanitarian intervention.**

Feminist theory

Chapter 27 will deal in some detail with the main varieties of feminist theory, and I do not wish to repeat that summary here. What I want to do instead is to give you a simple overview of the four main types of feminist theory before spending most time looking at one variant of it. I want to be clear, however, that the variant I am going to spend most time on, **feminist standpoint theory**, is not necessarily my 'preferred' variant of feminism. I look at it simply because Chapter 27, on gender, does a comprehen-

sive job of showing the great strength of one of the other variants, **liberal feminism;** the section below on **post-modernism** overlaps with what I would want to say about a third variant, **feminist post-modernism;** and the final variant, **socialist/Marxist feminism** has much in common with some of the material on **Marxism** discussed in Chapter 10.

Feminist work on world politics has only become common since the mid-1980s. It originally developed in work on the politics of development and in peace research, but by the late 1980s a first wave of feminism, **liberal feminism**, was posing the question of 'where were the women in world politics'. Note that the term 'liberal' has to be treated with care in this context: it decidedly does NOT mean quite the same thing as is meant by the same phrase in the chapter on liberalism (Ch. 8). All that the term liberal means in the context of feminism is that it starts from the notion that the key units of society are individuals and that these individuals have rights; thus, liberal feminists argue that the same rights should be granted to women as have traditionally been granted to men. Thus to ask 'where are the women' was a very radical political act, precisely because they were not written about in the main texts, and thus appeared invisible. Then writers such as Cynthia Enloe (1989, 1993, 2000) began to show just how involved were women in world politics. In her first two books on this subject (1989, 1993) she looked at the roles women actually occupied in world politics. It was not that they were not there but that they in fact played central roles, either as cheap factory labour, as prostitutes around military bases, or as the wives of diplomats. The point is that the conventional picture painted by the traditional international theory deemed these activities as less important than the actions of statesmen (sic). Enloe was intent on showing just how critically important were the activities of women to the functioning of the international economic and political systems, of how much power it took for international politics to keep functioning as it has done. In her most recent book (Enloe 2000), she looks at the ways in which militarization has affected the lives of women around the world. Taking women seriously therefore made a difference to the standard view of world politics. This has been called the 'add women and stir' version of feminism. Accordingly, liberal feminists look at the ways in which women are excluded from power and from playing a full part in political activity; being restricted instead to roles critically important for the functioning of things, but that are not usually deemed to be important for theories of world politics. Fundamentally, liberal feminists want the same rights and opportunities that are available to men, extended to women, although using Enloe as an example of a liberal feminist writer is problematic because she also has socialist and even standpoint leanings. Nonetheless, her starting point is very much a liberal feminist starting point, even if she does then go on to show the structures that cause women to appear in world politics where they do.

A second strand of feminist theory is **socialist/Marxist feminism**. As the name implies the influence here is Marxism, with its insistence on the role of material, primarily economic, forces in determining the lives of women. For Marxist feminism, the cause of women's inequality is to be found in the capitalist system; overthrowing capitalism is the necessary route for the achievement of the equal treatment of women. Socialist feminism, noting that the oppression of women occurred in pre-capitalist societies, and continues in socialist societies, differs from Marxist feminism in that it introduces a second central material cause in determining women's unequal treatment, namely the patriarchal system of male dominance. For Marxist feminists, then, capitalism is the primary oppressor, for socialist feminists it is capitalism plus patriarchy. For socialist/Marxist feminists, then, the focus of a theory of world politics would be on the patterns by which the world capitalist system and the patriarchal system of power lead to women being systematically disadvantaged compared to men. As you can well imagine, this approach is especially insightful when it comes to looking at the nature of the world economy and the differential advantages and disadvantages of it that apply to women.

The third variant of feminist theory I want to mention is **post-modernist** feminism. As the name implies this is a series of theoretical works that bring together post-modern work on identity with a focus on gender. Here, in distinction to other variants of feminism, the concern is with gender, and not women. Gender refers to the social construction of differences between men and women, and for post-modern feminists the key issue is what kind of social roles for men and women are constructed by the structures and processes of world politics. In other words, what kind of 'men' are required to serve in armies? Note the recent fierce debates about both women and homosexual men and women serving in the armed forces. How, to put it simply, has world politics led to certain kinds of 'men' and 'women' being produced? This is a radical question, one which we cannot go into here, but although it seems so very far removed from the main theories of world politics, and thereby you might be tempted to ignore it, please reflect on the thought that what you may be as a man or a woman may not be 'natural'; instead it may be that what it means to be a man or woman in your society when you read this is very different to its meaning for other readers.

The final version of feminist theory I want to mention, and in fact the version I want to highlight, is **standpoint feminism** (Zalewski 1993*a*). This variant developed out of **radical** feminism, which basically claims that the world has been dominated by men and by their ideas. Accordingly, radical feminists proposed that the experiences of women had been ignored, except where they have been unfavourably compared to male experiences. The aim then is to re-describe reality according to a female view. In the work of influential feminist theorists such as Sandra Harding (1986), this approach gets developed into standpoint feminism, which is an attempt to develop a female version of reality. Since knowledge to date has been male knowledge, the result has been only a partial understanding of the world. Standpoint feminists want to improve on that understanding by incorporating female perspectives. This is a controversial move in feminism since it assumes that there is such a thing as **a** feminist view of the world (as distinct from a variety of female views according to their social/economic/cultural/sexual locations). It also runs the risk of essentializing and fixing the views and nature of women, by saying that **this** is how women see the world. Nonetheless despite these dangers of standpoint feminism, it has been very influential in showing just how male-dominated are the main theories of world politics. For an extremely convincing example of how standpoint feminists look at world politics, see Box 11.2, which is J. Ann Tickner's reformulation of the famous

'Six principles of political realism' developed by the 'godfather' of realism, Hans Morgenthau. In each case you will see how Tickner shows how the seemingly 'objective' rules of Morgenthau in fact reflect male values and definitions of reality, rather than female ones. You will then see how she reformulates these same rules according to female rather than male characteristics.

I want to conclude this section by noting that although I have chosen to call this 'feminist theory' this is both deliberate and misleading. It is deliberate because I want to focus on the roles that women occupy in world politics, that is to say I want to be women-centred. It is misleading because the question of the role of women has to be understood within the context of the changing roles of masculinity and femininity; in other words, the focus should more accurately be on **gender** rather than on women. Thus much of the most interesting work that is going on in this area (and Enloe typifies it) is concerned with the gendered effects of world politics. A good overview of the literature on gender and world politics can be found in the recent book by Jill Steans (1998); similarly there are important works on what is known as **men's studies** (see Seidler, 1989, Brittan, 1989, Connell, 1995, Carver, 1996; for a feminist discussion see Zalewski and Parpart (eds.), 1998). But I didn't use gender in this chapter because I did not want a discussion of the role of women to merely end up focusing on men and their roles in world politics.

Key points

- There are four main variants of feminist theory, **liberal**, **Marxist/socialist**, **post-modern**, and **standpoint feminisms**.

- **Liberal** feminism looks at the roles women play in world politics and asks why they are marginalized. It wants the same opportunities afforded to women as are afforded to men.

- **Marxist/socialist** feminists focus on the **international capitalist system**. Marxist feminists see the oppression of women as a by-product of capitalism, whereas socialist feminists see both capitalism and **patriarchy** as the structures to be overcome if women are to have any hope of equality.

- **Post-modernist** feminists are concerned with gender as opposed to the position of women as such. They enquire into the ways in which **masculinity** and **femininity** get constructed, and are especially interested in how world politics constructs certain types of 'men' and 'women'.

- **Standpoint** feminists, such as **J. Ann Tickner** want to correct the male dominance of our knowledge of the world. Tickner does this be re-describing the six 'objective' principles of international politics developed by **Hans Morgenthau** according to a female version of the world.

- The focus of this chapter is on **feminism**, but this should be understood within the context of **gender**, which includes how both masculinity and femininity are constructed by world politics.

Critical theory

Critical theory has a long intellectual tradition, being a development out of Marxist thought dating from at least the 1920s when it developed out the work of the **Frankfurt School**. It has significant overlaps with **Marxism**, but has become particularly influential in international theory since the early 1980s. The most influential figures have been Andrew Linklater (1990*a*, 1998) and Robert Cox (1996).

I am going to base my comments on critical theory on a very good survey of **critical theory** by Mark Hoffman (1987). Hoffman notes that it was first articulated in detail by Max Horkheimer in a 1937 article. Horkheimer was concerned to change society and he thought that the theories to achieve this could not be developed in the way that natural science develops theories. Social scientists could not be like natural scientists in the sense of being independent from and disinterested in their subject matter; they were part of the society they were studying. In a major contribution to thinking about the nature of the social sciences, Horkheimer argued that there was a close connection between knowledge and power. He thought that in the social sciences the most important forces for change were social forces, and not some 'independent' logic of the things being explained. At this point, Horkheimer differentiates

Box 11.2 J. Ann Tickner's reformulation of Hans Morgenthau's principles of political realism

Morgenthau's six principles

1. Politics, like society in general, is governed by objective laws that have their roots in human nature which is unchanging: therefore it is possible to develop a rational theory that reflects these objective laws.

2. The main signpost of political realism is the concept of interest defined in terms of power which infuses rational order into the subject matter of politics, and thus makes the theoretical understanding of politics possible. Political realism stresses the rational, objective, and unemotional.

3. Realism assumes that interest defined as power is an objective category which in universally valid but not with a meaning that is fixed once and for all. Power is the control of man over man.

4. Political realism is aware of the moral significance of political action. It is also aware of the tension between the moral command and the requirements of successful political action.

5. Political realism refuses to identify the moral aspirations of a particular nation with the moral laws that govern the universe. It is the concept of interest defined in terms of power that saves us from moral excess and political folly.

6. The political realist maintains the autonomy of the political sphere. He asks 'How does this policy affect the power of the nation?' Political realism is based on a pluralistic conception of human nature. A man who is nothing but 'political man' would be a beast, for he would be completely lacking in moral restraints. But, in order to develop an autonomous theory of political behaviour, 'political man' must be abstracted from other aspects of human nature.

Tickner's six principles

1. A feminist perspective believes that objectivity, as it is culturally defined, is associated with masculinity. Therefore supposedly 'objective' laws of human nature are based on a partial masculine view of human nature. Human nature is both masculine and feminine: it contains elements of social reproduction and development as well as political domination. Dynamic objectivity offers us a more connected view of objectivity with less potential for domination.

2. A feminist perspective believes that the national interest is multi-dimensional and contextually contingent. Therefore it cannot be defined solely in terms of power. In the contemporary world the national interest demands co-operative rather than zero-sum solutions to a set of interdependent global problems which include nuclear war, economic well-being, and environmental degradation.

3. Power cannot be infused with meaning that is universally valid. Power as domination and control privileges masculinity and ignores the possibility of collective empowerment, another aspect of power often associated with femininity.

4. A feminist perspective rejects the possibility of separating moral command from political action. All political action has moral significance. The realist agenda for maximizing order through power and control prioritizes the moral command of order over those of justice and the satisfaction of basic needs necessary to ensure social reproduction.

5. While recognizing that the moral aspirations of particular nations cannot be equated with universal moral principles, a feminist perspective seeks to find common moral elements in human aspirations which could become the basis for de-escalating international conflict and building international community.

6. A feminist perspective denies the validity of the autonomy of the political. Since autonomy is associated with masculinity in Western culture, disciplinary efforts to construct a world view which does not rest on a pluralistic conception of human nature are partial and masculine. Building boundaries around a narrowly defined political realm defines political in a way that excludes the concerns and contributions of women.

Source: Tickner (1988: 430–1, 437–8).

between 'traditional' and 'critical' theory: traditional theory sees the world as a set of facts waiting to be discovered through the use of science. We have seen this view earlier when we discussed **positivism**, and Horkheimer's target is indeed the application of positivism to the social sciences. He argued that traditional theorists were wrong to argue that the 'fact' waiting to be discovered could be perceived independently of the social framework in which perception occurs. But the situation was worse than that because Horkheimer argued that traditional theory encouraged the increasing manipulation of human lives. It saw the social world as an area for control and domination, just like nature, and therefore was indifferent to the possibilities of human emancipation.

In its place Horkheimer proposed the adoption of **critical theory.** As Hoffman notes, critical theory did not see facts in the same way as did traditional theory. For critical theorists, facts are the products of specific social and historical frameworks. By realizing that theories are embedded in these frameworks allows critical theorists to reflect on the interests served by any particular theory. The explicit aim of critical theory is to advance human emancipation, and this means that theory is openly **normative**, with a role to play in political debate. This of course is the opposite to the view of theory proposed by traditional or **positivist** theory, in which theory is meant to be neutral and concerned only with uncovering pre-existing facts or regularities in an independent external world. In the post-war period the leading exponent of critical theory has been Jürgen Habermas, whose most influential claim has been his notion of the **ideal speech situation**, whereby individuals would exhibit **communicative competence** to lead to a rational consensus in political debate. Such a situation would lead to the development of an emancipatory politics. This is often known as a situation of **discourse ethics.**

In international theory the first major critical theory contribution was by **Robert Cox** (1981, in his 1996: ch. 6). Cox's article was enormously influential because it was written in part as an attack on the main assumptions of **neo-realism**, which he criticizes most effectively because of its hidden **normative** commitments. Rather than being an 'objective' theory, neo-realism is exposed by Cox as having a series of views about what states should pursue in their foreign policies, namely neo-realist rationality. It also is revealed as a partial theory which defines the state in a specific (and non-economic) way, and rules out of its purview a set of other political relations. In short, Cox argues that neo-realism typifies what Horkheimer meant by traditional theory: Cox calls it **problem-solving theory**, which 'takes the world as it finds it, with the prevailing social and power relationships and the institutions into which they are organized, as the given framework for action. The general aim of problem solving is to make these relationships and institutions work smoothly by dealing effectively with particular sources of trouble . . . the general pattern of institutions and relationships is not called into question' (1996: 88). The effect then is to **reify** and **legitimize** the existing order. Problem-solving theory therefore works to make the existing distribution of power seem natural. But, Cox points out, in a famous quote, despite this, **'Theory is always *for* someone and *for* some purpose'** (1996: 87). Theories see the world from specific social and political positions and are not independent. There is, he says, **'no such thing as theory in itself, divorced from a standpoint in time and space.** When any theory so represents itself, it is the more important to examine it as ideology, and to lay bare its **concealed** perspective' (1996: 87).

In contrast, Cox proposes that international theory should be **critical theory**. Hoffman has very clearly summarized Cox's ideas about critical theory, and they are reprinted in Box 11.3. Particularly interesting is the view of reality (ontology) adopted by critical theorists. Echoing the themes of many of the other **reflectivist** approaches, Cox notes that social structures are **intersubjective**, meaning that they are socially constructed. Thus although they do not have the same status for positivists as things like trees and buildings, the structures for a critical theorist have very similar effects. Therefore Cox focuses on how the 'givens' of traditional theory, such as 'individuals' or 'states' are produced by certain historical and social forces. Thus a state is not, contra neo-realism, always a state; states differ enormously throughout history and they are very different things at different times. For Cox, then, the state is not the given of international theory that

---

Box 11.3 Robert Cox's critical theory

1. It stands apart from the prevailing order of the world and asks how that order came about; it is a reflective appraisal of the framework that problem-solving takes as given.

2. It contemplates the social and political complex as a whole and seeks to understand the process of change within both the whole and its parts.

3. It entails a theory of history, understanding history as a process of continuous change and transformation.

4. It questions the origins and legitimacy of social and political institutions and how and whether they are changing; it seeks to determine what elements are universal to world order and what elements are historically contingent.

5. It contains problem-solving theory and has a concern with both technical and practical cognitive knowledge interests and constantly adjusts its concepts in light of the changing subject it seeks to understand.

6. It contains a normative, utopian element in favour of a social and political order different from the prevailing order that also recognizes the constraints placed on possible alternative world order by historical processes: the potential for transformation exists within the prevailing order but it is also constrained by the historical forces that created that order.

7. It is a guide for strategic action, for bringing about an alternative order.

Source: Hoffman (1987: 237–8).

---

neo-realism sees it as. Instead the state emerges out of social forces, as do other social structures. Cox is particularly interested in how these social structures can be transcended and overcome, hence his focus on the nature of **hegemony**.

Since Cox's introduction of critical theory into international theory, there have been a number of very significant contributions from other critical theorists. I am not going to summarize these, since I do not have the space, but two particularly interesting examples are the contributions of Andrew Linklater (1990, 1998) and the development of **critical**

security studies, based on the work of writers such as Ken Booth (1991) and Richard Wyn Jones (1995, 1999). For a good summary of the work of these, and other, critical theorists see Devetak (1996*a*). Central to all these writers is a concern with how the present order has evolved. Thus critical theory is not limited to an examination of the inter-state system but, rather, focuses on all the main examples of power and domination. This makes it particularly suited for contemporary world politics because it does not treat the state as the 'natural' actor and instead is concerned with all the features of domination in a globalized world.

Key points

- **Critical theory** has its roots in Marxism, and developed out of the **Frankfurt School** in the 1920s. Its most influential proponent since 1945 has been **Jürgen Habermas**.

- In an influential 1937 article one of the founders of critical theory, **Max Horkheimer**, distinguished between **traditional** and **critical** theory.

- **Robert Cox** writes of the difference between **problem-solving** and **critical theory**. The former takes the world as given and reifies existing distributions of power. The latter enquires into how the current distribution of power came into existence.

- Cox argues that **theory is always for someone and for some purpose**, and that **there is no such thing as theory in itself**.

- Critical theory sees **social structures as real in their effects**, whereas they would not by seen as real by positivism since they cannot be directly observed.

- There are many other contributions of critical theory; particularly important are the works of **Linklater** and of those working in the area of **critical security studies**.

Historical sociology

Just as critical theory problematizes the state and refuses to see it as some kind of given in world politics, so does **historical sociology**. Indeed the main theme of historical sociology is an interest in the ways in which societies develop through history. In this sense it is concerned with the underlying structures that shape the institutions and organizations that human society is arranged into. Historical sociology has a long history. Dennis Smith, in his excellent introduction to the approach, argues that we are currently on the crest of the second wave of historical sociology, the first wave starting in the middle of the eighteenth century and running until the 1920s when interest in the approach declined. The first wave was a response to the great events of the eighteenth century, such as the American and French revolutions as well as the processes of industrialization and nation building. The second wave has been of particular interest to international theory, because the key writers, Michael Mann, Theda Skocpol, Immanuel Wallerstein, Charles Tilly, and John Hall, have all to a greater or lesser extent focused their explanations of the development of societies on the relationship between the domestic and the international. Tilly has neatly summarized this interest with the statement that 'states made war but war made the state'. In short, the central feature of historical sociology has been an interest in how the structures that we take for granted (as 'natural') are the products of a set of complex social processes.

Thus, whereas **neo-realism** takes the state as a given, historical sociology asks how specific kinds of states have been produced by the various forces at work in domestic and international societies. I am going to look at two examples of this, one by **Charles Tilly**, the other by **Michael Mann**. The point to keep in mind is that these writers show just how complex is the state as an organization, thereby undermining the rather simple view of the state found in neo-realist writings. Also note that historical sociologists fundamentally undermine the thought that a state is a state is a state. States differ and they are not functionally similar as neo-realism portrays them as being. Furthermore, historical sociologists show that there can be no simple distinction between international and domestic societies. They are inevitably interlinked and therefore it is inaccurate to claim, as does neo-realism, that they can be separated. There is no such thing as 'an international system' that is self-contained and thereby able to exert decisive

influence on the behaviour of states; but of course this is exactly what Waltz wants to argue. Finally, note that historical sociology shows that the state is created by international and domestic forces, and that the international is itself a determinant of the nature of the state; that thought looks particularly relevant to the debate on globalization, since, as we discussed in the Introduction, one of its dominant themes is that the international economic system places demands on states such that only certain kinds of states can prosper.

Charles Tilly's work is particularly interesting because it is a clear example of how complex an entity is the state. In his 1990 book, *Coercion, Capital and European States, AD 900–1990*, Tilly poses the following main question: 'What accounts for the great variation over time and space in the kinds of states that have prevailed in Europe since AD 990, and why did European states eventually converge on different variants of the national state?' (1990: 5). The answer that he gives is that the national state eventually dominated because of its role in fighting wars. Distinguishing between capital-intensive and coercion-intensive regimes (or economic power-based and military power-based systems), Tilly notes that three types of states resulted from the combinations of these forms of power, tribute-making empires, systems of fragmented sovereignty (city-states), and national states. These states were the result of the different class structures that resulted from the concentrations of capital and coercion. Broadly speaking, coercion-intensive regimes had fewer cities and more agricultural class systems than did capital-intensive systems, which led to the development of classes representing commercial and trading interests. Where capital accumulation was high relative to the ability of the state to coerce its citizens, then city-states developed; on the other hand where there was coercion but not capital accumulation, then tribute-making empires developed. As Dennis Smith notes (1991: 83), each of these is a form of indirect rule, requiring the ruler to rely on the co-operation of relatively autonomous local powers. But with the rise in the scale of war, the result was that national states started to acquire a decisive advantage over the other kinds of state organizations. This was because national states could afford large armies and could respond to the demands of the classes representing both agricultural and commercial interests.

Through about a 350-year period starting around 1500, national states became the norm as they were the only states that could afford the military means to fight the kind of large-scale wars that were occurring. States, in other words, became transformed by war; Tilly notes that the three types of states noted above all converged on one version of the state, so now that is seen as the norm. Yet, in contrast to neo-realism, Tilly notes that the state has not been of one form throughout its history. His work shows how different types of states have existed throughout history, all with different combinations of class structures and modes of operating. And, crucially, **it is war that explains the convergence of these types of states into the national state form**. War plays this central role because it is through preparing for war that states gain their powers as they have to build up an infrastructure of taxation, supply, and administration. The national state thus acquires more and more power over its population by its involvement in war, and therefore could dominate other state forms because they were more efficient than either tribute-gathering empires or city-states in this process.

The second example of historical sociology is the work of Michael Mann. Mann is involved in a four-volume study of the sources of social power dealing with the whole of human history! (The first two volumes have appeared dealing with the period up to 1914, see his (1986) and (1993).) This is an enormously ambitious project, and is aimed at showing just how states have taken the forms that they have. In this sense it is similar to the work of Tilly, but the major innovation of Mann's work is that he has developed a sophisticated account of the forms of power that combine to form certain types of states. This is his IEMP model (standing for Ideological, Economic, Military and Political forms of power). Given that the first two volumes come to nearly 1400 pages, I am not going to summarize his work! Suffice to say that his painstaking study of the ways in which the various forms of power have combined in specific historical circumstances constitutes a major contribution to our thinking of how states have come into existence and about how they have related to the international political system. What I have done is to summarize his argument in Box 11.4.

I hope that this brief summary of historical sociology gives you an idea of its potential to shed light on how the state has taken the form that it has throughout history. It should make you think that the version of the state presented by **neo-realism** is very simple, but note also that there is a surprising overlap between the focus of neo-realism on war and the focus of historical sociology on how states, classes and war interact.

Key points

- **Historical sociology** has a long history, having been a subject of study for several centuries. Its central focus is with **how societies develop the forms that they do**.

- Contemporary historical sociology is concerned above all with how the state has developed since the Middle Ages. It is basically a study of the **interactions between states, classes, capitalism, and war.**

- **Charles Tilly** looks at how the three main kinds of state forms that existed at the end of the Middle Ages eventually converged on one form, namely the **national state**. He argues that the decisive reason was the ability of the national state to **fight wars**.

- **Michael Mann** has developed a powerful model of the sources of state power, known as the **IEMP Model**. This helps him show how the various forms of state have taken the forms that they have.

- **Historical sociology** undercuts **neo-realism** because it shows that the state is not one functionally similar organization, but instead has altered over time. But, like neo-realism, it too is interested in war and therefore the two approaches have quite a bit in common.

Post-modernism

Post-modernism has been a particularly influential theoretical development throughout all the social sciences in the last twenty years. It reached inter-

Box 11.4 Mann's IEMP model of power organization

Mann differentiates between three aspects of power:

1. Between distributive power and collective power, where distributive power is the power of *a* over *b* (for *a* to acquire more distributive power, *b* must lose some), and collective power is the joint power of actors (where *a* and *b* can co-operate to exploit nature or another actor, *c*).

2. Power may be extensive or intensive. Extensive power can organize large numbers of people over far-flung territories. Intensive power mobilizes a high level of commitment from participants.

3. Power may be authoritative or diffused. Authoritative power comprises willed commands by an actor and conscious obedience by subordinates. It is found most typically in military and political power organizations. Diffused power is not directly commanded; it spreads in a relatively spontaneous, unconscious, and decentred way. People are constrained to act in different ways but not by command of any particular person or organization. Diffused power is found most typically in ideological and economic power organizations.

Mann argues that the most effective exercise of power combines all these three elements. He argues that there are four sources of social power which together may determine the overall structure of societies. The four are

1. Ideological power derives from the human need to find ultimate meaning in life, to share norms and values, and to participate in aesthetic and ritualpractices. Control over ideology brings general social power.

2. Economic power derives from the need to extract, transform, distribute, and consume the resources of nature. It is peculiarly powerful because it combines intensive co-operation with extensive circuits of distribution, exchange, and consumption. This provides a stable blend of intensive and extensive power and normally of authoritative and diffused power.

3. Military power is the social organization of physical force. It derives from the necessity of organized defence and the utility of aggression. Military power has both intensive and extensive aspects, and it can also organize people over large areas. Those who monopolize it can wield a degree of general social power.

4. Political power derives from the usefulness of territorial and centralized regulation. Political power means state power. It is essentially authoritative, commanded, and willed from a centre.

The struggle to control ideological, economic, military, and political power organizations provides the central drama of social development. Societies are structured primarily by entwined ideological, economic, military, and political power.

Source: Mann (1993: 6–10)

national theory in the mid-1980s, but could only have been said to have arrived in the last few years. It is fair to say that it is probably as popular a theoretical approach as any of the **reflectivist** theories discussed in this chapter. As Richard Devetak comments in his extremely useful summary of post-modernism, part of the difficulty is defining precisely what post-modernism is (1996*b*: 179). Frankly, there is far more to debate on this question of defining post-modernism than there is space for in this entire book! One useful definition is by Jean-François Lyotard, who writes that: 'Simplifying to the extreme, I define *postmodern* as incredulity towards metanarratives' (1984: xxiv). The key word

here is 'metanarrative', by which is meant a theory that asserts it has clear foundations for making knowledge claims (to use the jargon, it involves a foundational epistemology). What he means by this is that post-modernism is essentially concerned with deconstructing, and dis-trusting any account of human life that claims to have direct access to 'the truth'. Thus, Freudian psychoanalysis, Marxism, standpoint feminism, for example, are all deemed suspect because they claim to have uncovered some truth about the world. Post-modernists are also unhappy with critical theory, since they believe that it too is just another metanarrative.

Devetak helpfully analyses the key themes of post-modernism. I will look at two of the themes he discusses, the power–knowledge relationship, and the textual strategies used by post-modernists. Post-modern work on the **power–knowledge** relationship has been most influenced by the works of **Michel Foucault**. Central to Foucault's work has been a concern with the relationship between power and knowledge; note that this is also a key concern of **critical theorists**. Foucault is opposed to the notion (dominant in **rationalist** theories) that knowledge is immune from the workings of power. As noted above, this is a key assumption of **positivism**. Instead, Foucault argues that power in fact **produces knowledge**. All power requires knowledge and all knowledge relies on and reinforces existing power relations. Thus there is no such thing as 'truth', existing outside of power. To paraphrase Foucault, how can history have a truth if truth has a history? Truth is not something external to social settings, but is instead part of them. Accordingly, post-modernists want to look at what power relations are supported by 'truths' and knowledge-practices. Post-modern international theorists have used this insight to examine the 'truths' of international relations theory to see how the concepts and knowledge claims that dominate the discipline in fact are highly contingent on specific power relations. Two recent examples are the work of Cynthia Weber (1995) and Jens Bartelson (1995) on the concept of sovereignty. In both cases the concept of sovereignty is revealed to be both historically variable, despite the attempts of mainstream scholars to imbue it artificially with a fixed meaning, and is itself caught up in the practice of sovereignty by producing the discourse about it.

How do post-modernists study history in the light of this relationship between power and knowledge? Foucault's answer is the approach known as **genealogy**. In 11.5, I summarize a very good summary of this approach by Richard Ashley (1987), which gives you the main themes of a genealogical approach. The central message of genealogy is that there is no such thing as truth, only regimes of truth. These reflect the ways in which, through history both power and truth develop together in a mutually sustaining relationship. What this means is that statements about the social world are only 'true' within specific **discourses**. Accordingly, post-modernism is

concerned with how some discourses and therefore some truths dominate others. Here, of course is exactly where power comes in. It is for this reason that post-modernists are opposed to any metanarratives, since they imply that there are conditions for establishing the truth or falsity of knowledge claims that are not the product of any discourse, and thereby not the products of power.

Devetak's second theme of post-modernism concerns the **textual strategies** it uses. This is very complicated, but the main claim is that, following **Derrida**, the very way in which we construct the social world is textual. For Derrida (1976) the world is constituted like a text in the sense that interpreting the world reflects the concepts and structures of language, what he terms the textual interplay at work. Derrida has two main ways of exposing these textual interplays, **deconstruction** and **double reading**. Deconstruction is based on the idea that seemingly stable and natural concepts and relations within language are in fact artificial constructs, arranged hierarchically in that in the case of opposites in language one term is always privileged over the other. Therefore, deconstruction is a way of showing how all theories and discourses rely on artificial stabilities produced by the use of seemingly objective and natural oppositions in language (rich/poor, good/bad, powerful/powerless, right/wrong). Double reading is Derrida's way of showing how these stabilizations operate by subjecting the text to two readings, the first is a repetition of the dominant reading to show how it achieves its coherence, the second points to the internal tensions within a text that result from the use of seemingly natural stabilizations. The aim is not to come to a 'correct' or even 'one' reading of a text, but instead to show how there is always more than one reading of any text. In international theory, **Richard Ashley** (1988) has performed exactly such a double reading of the concept of anarchy by providing first a reading of the anarchy problematique according to the traditional literature, and then a second reading that shows how the seemingly natural opposition between anarchy and sovereignty that does the work in the first reading is in fact a false opposition. By radically disrupting the first reading Ashley shows just how arbitrary is the 'truth' of the traditional assumptions made about anarchy and the kind of logic of state action that it requires. In a

Box 11.5 Foucault's notion of genealogy

First, adopting a genealogical attitude involves a radical shift in one's analytical focus. It involves a shift away from an interest in uncovering the structures of history and towards an interest in understanding the movement and clashes of historical practices that would impose or resist structure. . . . with this shift . . . social enquiry is increasingly disposed to find its focus in the posing of 'how' questions, not 'what' questions. How . . . are structures of history produced, differentiated, reified, and transformed? How . . . are fields of practice pried open, bounded and secured? How . . . are regions of silence established?

Second, having refused any notion of universal truth or deep identities transcending differences, a genealogical attitude is disposed to comprehend all history, including the production of order, in terms of the endless power political clash of multiple wills. Only a single drama is ever staged in this non-place, the endlessly repeated play of dominations. Practices . . . are to be understood to contain their own strategies, their own political technologies . . . for the disciplining of plural historical practices in the production of historical modes of domination.

Third, a genealogical attitude disposes one to be especially attentive to the historical emergence, bounding, conquest, and administration of social spaces . . . one might think, for example, of divisions of territory and populations among nation states . . . one might also think of the separation of spheres of politics and economics, the distinction between high and low politics, the differentiation of public and private spaces, the line of demarcation between domestic and international, the disciplinary division between science and philosophy, the boundary between the social and the natural, or the separation of the normal and legitimate from the abnormal and crim-

inal . . . a genealogical posture entails a readiness to approach a field of practice historically, as an historically emergent and always contested product of multiple practices . . . as such, a field of practice . . . is seen as a field of clashes, a battlefield . . . one is supposed to look for the strategies, techniques, and rituals of power by which multiple themes, concepts, narratives, and practices are excluded, silenced, dispersed, recombined, or given new or reverse emphases, thereby to privilege some elements over others, impose boundaries, and discipline practice in a manner producing just this normalised division of practical space.

Fourth, what goes for the production and disciplining of social space goes also for the production and disciplining of subjects. From a genealogical standpoint there are no subjects, no fully formed identical egos, having an existence prior to practice and then implicated in power political struggles. Like fields of practice, subjects emerge in history . . . as such, the subject is itself a site of political power contest and ceaselessly so.

Fifth, a genealogical posture does not sustain an interest in those noble enterprises—such as philosophy, religion, positive social science, or the utopian political crusade—that would embark on searches for the hidden essences, the universal truths, the profound insights into the secret identity that transcends difference . . . from a genealogical standpoint . . . they are instead resituated right on the surface of political life. They are seen as political practice intimately engaged in the interpretation, production, and normalisation of modes of imposed order, modes of domination. They are seen as means by which practices are disciplined and domination advances in history.

Source: Ashley (1987: 409–11)

similar move **Rob Walker** (1993) looks at the construction of the tradition of **realism** and shows how this is only possible by ignoring the major nuances and complexities within the thoughts of the key thinkers of this tradition, such as Machiavelli and Hobbes. As a final example, **David Campbell** has, in three books (1992, 1993, 1998), applied postmodern theory to empirical examples in world politics, such as the construction of US foreign policy, the Gulf War, and the Bosnian conflict.

As you can imagine, such a theoretical position

has been very controversial in the literature. Many members of the mainstream think that postmodernism has nothing to say about the 'real' world, and that it is merely playing with words. However, it seems clear to me that post-modernism is in fact taking apart the very concepts and methods of our thinking. It helps us think about the conditions under which we are able to theorize about world politics; and to many, post-modernism is the most appropriate theory for a globalized world.

Key points

- **Lyotard** defines **post-modernism** as **incredulity towards metanarratives**, meaning that it denies the possibility of foundations for establishing the truth of statements existing outside of a **discourse**.

- **Foucault** focuses on the **power–knowledge relationship** which sees the two as mutually constituted. It implies that there can be no truth outside of **regimes of truth**. How can history have a truth if truth has a history?

- **Foucault** proposes a **genealogical** approach to look at history, and this approach uncovers how certain regimes of truth have dominated others.

- **Derrida** argues that the world is like a text in that it cannot simply be grasped, but has to be interpreted. He looks at how texts are constructed, and proposes two main tools to enable us to see how arbitrary are the seemingly 'natural' oppositions of language. These are **deconstruction** and **double reading**.

- **Post-modern** approaches are attacked by the mainstream for being too theoretical and not enough concerned with the 'real' world; but postmodernists reply that in the social world there is no such thing as the 'real' world in the sense of a reality that is not interpreted by us.

Bridging the gap: social constructivism

This development in international relations theory promises much, since its great appeal is that it claims to sit precisely at the intersection **between rationalist and reflectivist approaches**. Its proponents say that it can be this middle way because it deals with the same features of world politics as are central to both the **neo-realist** and the **neo-liberal** components of **rationalism**, and yet is centrally concerned with both the meanings actors give to their actions and the identity of these actors, each of which is a central theme of **reflectivist** approaches. The three main proponents of this view are Kratochwil (1989), Onuf (1989) and Wendt (1992, 1999), although a particularly influential collection is that edited by Katzenstein (1996). I am going to concentrate on Wendt simply because his work has been enormously influential in developing the **social constructivist** position. His 1992 article 'Anarchy is what States Make of It: The Social Construction of Power Politics' has probably been cited in the professional literature more than any other article in the last decade. Its title also neatly sums up exactly what is the central claim of social constructivism. Similarly, his 1999 book *Social Theory of International Politics* is the most developed statement of the social constructivist position. I will here concentrate on his 1992 article, since this contains the core elements of his argument, and does so without getting into the considerable philosophical depth that is found in his 1999 book. However, let me be absolutely clear at the outset, I do not think that social constructivism can deliver what it claims, but equally I am sure that it promises to be one of the most important theoretical developments of recent decades (for a discussion of this see Smith, 2000); the reason is that if it could deliver what it promises then it would be the dominant theory in the discipline, since it could relate to all other approaches on their own terms, whereas at the moment there is virtually no contact between **rationalist** and **reflectivist** theories since they do not share the same view of how to build knowledge. If Wendt is right then social constructivists can debate the effects of anarchy and the relative/absolute gains issue with the **rationalists**, and at the same time discuss with post-modernists, feminists, historical sociologists, critical theorists, and normative theorists the meanings attached to action and, crucially, the processes by which the identities of the actors are formed.

Before we get into Wendt's argument, look at the contents of Box 11.6, which is a quote from the then President of the International Studies Association

Box 11.6 Robert Keohane's view of the rationalist–reflectivist debate

My chief argument in this essay is that students of international institutions should direct their attention to the relative merits of two approaches, the rationalistic, and the reflective. Until we understand the strengths and weaknesses of each, we will be unable to design research strategies that are sufficiently multifaceted to encompass our subject-matter, and our empirical work will suffer accordingly . . . indeed, the greatest weakness of the reflective school lies not in deficiencies in their critical arguments but in the lack of a clear reflective program that could be employed by students of world politics. Waltzian neo-realism has such a research program; so does neo-liberal institutionalism . . . until the reflective scholars or others sympathetic to their arguments have delineated such a research program and shown in particular studies that it can illuminate important issues of world politics they will remain on the margins of the field, largely invisible to the preponderance of empirical researchers . . . reflective approaches are less well specified as theories: their advocates have been more adept at pointing out what is omitted in rationalistic theory than in developing theories of their own with *a priori* content. Supporters of this research program need to develop testable theories, and to be explicit about their scope . . . above all, students of world politics who are sympathetic to this position need to carry out systematic empirical investigations, guided by their ideas. Without such detailed studies, it will be impossible to evaluate their research program. Eventually, we may hope for a synthesis between the rationalistic and reflective approaches.

Source: Keohane (1989a: 161, 173–4).

(ISA, which is the main, US-based, professional organization for teachers and researchers of International Relations), Robert Keohane. The quote comes from his presidential address to the ISA in 1988: I hope that you can see what Keohane is saying here—he is arguing that unless the reflectivists can develop 'testable hypotheses' then they will be marginalized in the study of world politics. The central thing to note is that this challenge is one made according to the rules for generating knowledge that rationalists accept **but that reflectivists do not accept**. This soon can get very complicated, but the straightforward version of it is that the challenge issued by Keohane is essentially a **positivist** one, and it is precisely positivism that the reflectivists reject. Not surprisingly, rationalists and reflectivists do not tend to talk to one another very much since they do not share a common language. Exactly the identities that rationalists take as given become the starting point for the research project of the reflectivists; accordingly, their version of the key issues in world politics are nothing like those of the rationalists. There really is very little contact between the two positions and they resemble rival camps, publishing in different journals and going to different conferences. I say all of this simply to indicate just how much is at stake if Wendt and the constructivists can indeed bridge the gap between rationalists and reflectivists. They, and neither the rationalists nor the reflectivists would be at the centre of the discipline. Or to put it another way, constructivists would be the acceptable face of rationalism for reflectivists and the acceptable face of reflectivism for rationalists!! If Wendt can establish that his position is capable of serving as the point of contact then he will have created a theoretical synthesis of the various, previously incompatible, positions of the discipline. Wendt's central claim is shown in Box 11.7.

I want to run through his argument by summarizing it in a number of points. As I read it his argument progresses in the following way:

1. He sees the **neo-realist/neo-liberal** debate as central to International Relations theory, and being concerned with the issue of whether state action is influenced more by system structure (neo-realism) or by the processes, interactions, and learning of institutions (neo-liberalism). (391)

2. Both **neo-realism** and **neo-liberalism** are **rationalist** theories, based on rational choice theory and taking the identities and interests of actors as given; for rationalists, processes such as those of institutions affect the behaviour but not the identities and interests of actors. For both theories, the actors are self-interested states. (391–2)

3. There exist social theories that do not take interests and identities as given, and these are known as **reflectivist** or **constructivist** theories, and,

> ### Box 11.7 Wendt's view of the social constructivist project
>
> My objective in this article is to build a bridge between these two traditions (rationalism and reflectivism) . . . by developing a constructivist argument . . . on behalf of the liberal claim that international institutions can transform state identities and interests . . . my strategy for building this bridge would be to argue against the neo-realist claim that self-help is given by anarchic structure exogenously to process . . . I argue that self-help and power politics do not follow logically or causally from anarchy, and if today we find ourselves in a self-help world this is due to process, not structure. There is no 'logic' of anarchy apart from the practices that create and instantiate one structure of identities and interests rather than another; structure has no existence or causal powers apart from process. Self-help and power politics are institutions, not essential features of anarchy. *Anarchy is what states make of it.*
>
> Source: Wendt (1992: 394–5).

whatever their differences, they all focus on how inter-subjective practices between actors result in identities and interests being formed in the processes of interaction rather than being formed prior to interaction. We are what we are by how we interact rather than being what we are regardless of how we interact. (393–4)

4. Whereas **neo-realists** treat the self-help nature of anarchy as **the** logic of the system, Wendt argues that collective meanings define the structures, which organize our actions, and actors acquire their interests and identities by participating in such collective meanings. Identities and interests are relational and are defined as we define situations. Institutions are relatively stable sets of identities and interests. Self-help is one such institution, and is therefore not the only way of combining definitions of identities and interests in a condition of anarchy. (395–9)

5. Wendt thinks that we assume too much if we think that states have given identities and interests prior to interaction. There **is no such thing as an automatic security dilemma for states**; such

a claim, or one that says that states are in the situation of individuals in Rousseau's famous 'stag-hunt', presupposes that states have acquired selfish interests and identities prior to their interactions. Instead, self-help emerges only out of interaction between states. (400–4)

6. If states find themselves in a self-help situation then this is because their practices made it that way, and if the practices change then so will the inter-subjective knowledge that constitutes the system. This does not imply, however, that self-help, like any other social system, can be easily changed, since once constituted it becomes a social fact that reinforces certain forms of behaviour and punishes others, and it becomes part of the self-identity of actors. Inter-subjective understandings therefore may be self-perpetuating. (405–11)

7. The fact that specific formations of interests and identities may be self-perpetuating does not mean that they cannot be changed. Wendt gives three examples of alternatives to the self-help version of international relations that he has painted. These are by practices of sovereignty, by an evolution of co-operation and by critical strategic practice. (412–22)

8. The future research agenda for international relations should be to look at the relationship between what actors **do** and what they **are**. In other words the discipline should look at how state actors define social structures such as the international system. Wendt thinks that this is where neo-liberals and reflectivists can work together to offer an account of international relations that competes with the neo-realist account by enquiring into how specific empirical practices relate to the creation and re-creation of identities and interests. (422–5)

In other words, the identities and interests that rationalists take as given and which they see as resulting in the international politics we observe are not in fact given but are things we have created. Having created them we could create them otherwise; it would be difficult because we have all internalized the 'way the world is', but we could make it otherwise.

Now, this is a very powerful argument, but I want to argue that it will not serve as the bridge between **rationalists** and **reflectivists** in the way that Wendt hopes. There are five reasons for this.

The first is that Wendt is in fact not really anything like as much of a constructivist as he implies, and certainly not enough to satisfy **reflectivists**. This is because he defines interests and identities very narrowly. Post-modernists, as we have seen, certainly want to say something much more radical about identity than does Wendt. At the end of the day I think that Wendt is firmly on the rationalist side of the divide, and that he is not really a reflectivist. Thus his version of constructivism is defined from this perspective. He is in fact a very 'thin' constructivist, and not the kind of 'thick' or 'deep' constructivist that we find amongst the reflectivists.

Second, Wendt certainly accepts that the most important actors in world politics are states, and that their dominance will continue. Indeed, he is clear that his research project resembles that of neo-realism: 'to that extent, I am a statist and a realist' (424). As you will quickly see, this is much more restricted a definition of world politics than the one that the reflectivists would want to propose.

Third, although Wendt says he wants to bring together neo-liberals and reflectivists (constructivists), it is clear to me that he is not bringing together two groups that share the same view of how to construct knowledge; to put it simply, the **rationalists** are essentially **positivists** and the **reflectivists** are essentially **post-positivists**. The latter have a very different idea of how to construct knowledge to that held by the former. In plain language, they cannot be combined together because they have mutually exclusive assumptions.

Fourth, Wendt's structures (institutions) are really rather specific kinds of structures. Unlike materialist theories such as Marxism or Feminism, they are composed of ideas. This means that he sees social structures as very 'light' things, comprising the ideas that actors have in their heads. Yet many other social theories would want to argue that social structures reflect strong material interests. Note that there is no place in his account for structures such as capitalism or patriarchy. In other words, many theorists think that ideational structures (Wendt's only form of structure) reflect underlying material interests; we

think certain things because it is in our interests to do so. The central point here is that his structures are not material enough, being composed only of ideas.

Finally, Wendt thinks that identities are created in the process of interaction, but critics point out that we do not come to interactions without some pre-existing identity. Rather than our identities being created via interaction our identities are in part prior to that interaction. Think for example of your identity as a woman or a man; although it is clear that some aspects of this are constructed in the ways in which you relate to others via interaction, it is equally the case that some aspects of your identity exist prior to any given interaction. This means that your identity will cause you to construct the other parties to interaction in certain ways. There is never a first encounter. Again, note that this is really saying that his idea of identity is a very light or thin one.

All of these points make me think that Wendt does not quite pull it off. The main reason is that despite his genuine interest in both sets of theories he is, when pushed, revealed as a rationalist, and is actually more of a realist that he initially claims to be. Thus he is not in fact sitting between the rationalists and reflectivists, trying to bring them together, but is in fact on one side of the fence trying to talk to those on the other side; but being on the rationalist side of the fence means that although he uses many of the same terms and concepts as reflectivists, he defines them **rather more narrowly and from the opposite position in the debate about how to construct theories**. But please note that many think that he does manage to bring the two approaches together, and you will want to make up your own mind.

Key points

- **Social constructivism** offers the prospect of bridging the gap between **rationalist** and **reflectivist** theories.

- There are many constructivists but the best example is **Alexander Wendt** whose version of constructivism is summarized in his 1992 article 'Anarchy is what states make of it' and developed more fully in his 1999 book *Social Theory of International Politics*.

- Wendt's attempt is important because **Robert Keohane** pointed out that unless the reflectivists could come up with a research programme then they would remain on the margins of the discipline. Wendt offers such a research programme because he promises to bring neo-liberals and reflectivists together.

- Wendt's key claim is that international anarchy is not fixed, and does not automatically involve the self-interested state behaviour that rationalists see as built into the system. Instead he thinks that anarchy could take on several different forms because the selfish identities and interests assumed by rationalists are in fact the products of interaction and are not prior to it.

- There are several important objections to Wendt's argument. The main ones are that he is really a rationalist and a realist, so that he is not in fact bringing together rationalism and reflectivism, but is instead defining constructivism in a very narrow way, one that is acceptable to rationalists, but which would not be accepted by reflectivists who want a far deeper definition of identity and interest than he provides. Moreover, Wendt sees states as the 'givens' of world politics, but why should this be so instead of classes or companies or ethnicities or genders? Finally, note that his view of identity is an ideational one, whereas many argue that material interests determine our ideas and therefore our ideational structures. In short, his account is really much more traditional and rationalist than at first seems to be the case.

Conclusion

In this chapter I have tried to summarize the main alternatives to the dominant **rationalist** mainstream of international theory. I looked at a range of **reflectivist** theories and then examined the main features of **social constructivism**. I think that you will see that all of these approaches offer very different accounts of world politics to that offered by the rationalist mainstream. My hope is that you will think through just how each of these theories explains world politics in this age of **globalization**. Each has clear strengths, and probably the best place for you to start thinking about which is most useful is for you to cast your mind back to the Introduction and to Chapter 1; in each of these chapters we made a lot of points about globalization, and in the Introduction in particular we highlighted some pluses and minuses of globalization. Crucially, you now need to think about which of the theoretical perspectives discussed in this chapter gives you the best overview of the globalized world we have been discussing.

The **rationalist** perspective, and particularly the **neo-neo synthesis**, as discussed in Chapter 9, dominates the professional literature in the discipline of International Relations. That is the theoretical debate you will find in most of the journals, particularly the US-based ones. It focuses on the kinds of international political relations that concern many Western governments, particularly the debate about the future security structure of the international system. It is also very strong at looking at economic foreign policy, as the discussions on the relative gains/absolute gains issue suggests. But do you think that it is wide enough a perspective to capture what are to you the most important features of world politics? You might think on the one hand that we need theories that define the political realm rather more widely, so as to take in identity, economics, ethnicity, culture, and the like. On the other hand you might think that the most important features of world politics remain those that have dominated for the last two thousand years, namely the problems of war and peace, and of international stability. If you think this then you will probably prefer the rationalist theoretical agenda, and you will certainly do so if you think that these problems are 'natural', that is to say that they are features outside our control in the same way as the concerns of the natural scientist relate to a 'real' world that exists whatever we think about it.

Reflectivist theories obviously differ enormously with regards to what they are reflective about. As noted above they are really very different, but I put them together in one category because they are all rejecting the central concerns of rationalism. Do you think that any one of them gives you a better understanding of the main features of world politics than that provided by the rationalist mainstream? Or do you think that they are not really dealing with what are 'obviously' the most important features of world politics? The real problem with reflectivist theories is that they do not add up to one theoretical position in the way that the rationalist theories do. In some important ways, if you are a feminist then you do not necessarily agree with post-modernists or critical theorists. More fundamentally still, you cannot be **both** a critical theorist and a post-modernist! In short, the collection of theories gathered together under the reflectivist label have a set of mutually exclusive assumptions and there is no easy way to see the theories being combined. Some combinations are possible (a feminist post-modernism, or a normative critical theory) but the one thing that is clearly correct is that the whole lot cannot be added together to form one theoretical agenda in the way that the neo-neo debate serves on the rationalist side. Moreover, the reflectivists do not have the same idea of how to construct knowledge as the rationalists, and therefore they are unable to respond to Keohane's challenge for them to come up with testable hypotheses to compare with those provided by the rationalist position. This means that the prospect of a rationalist–reflectivist debate is very low. The two sides simply see world politics in very different ways. Which side (or which subdivision) do you think explains world politics most effectively?

All of this makes **social constructivism** particularly attractive since it offers the prospect of a *via media*, a third way that represents a synthesis between rationalism and reflectivism. As discussed above, this position, most clearly associated with Wendt, looks very promising to many. Wendt's recent (1999) book has attracted considerable attention for precisely this reason. But I also noted the problems associated with Wendt's position. Centrally, there is the difficulty that he is not really a reflectivist at all, but, rather, is a rationalist (and a statist, and a positivist, and a realist!), and either his

attempt to bridge the gap is always going to be unsuccessful because he is actually not sitting between the two positions, but instead is on one side, or maybe he is not trying to find a middle way at all; perhaps instead he is trying to find an alternative to rationalism that rationalists can still relate to and which they can debate with. Certainly this is how many mainstream scholars see social constructivism, as something very different to reflectivism and I now want to say something about this difference.

Earlier I quoted Robert Keohane's view of the need for reflectivist approaches to develop testable theories; let me now mention two more recent statements of the differences between social constructivism and reflectivist approaches, both published in 1998. In his review of the state of the field, Stephen Walt has argued that although realism remains the dominant theory of international politics, the key debate in international relations theory has been, and continues to be, that between realism and liberalism. He then notes that there is a third approach, which he sees as the main alternative to these two. Yet Walt does not have reflectivist approaches in mind; rather he sees the alternative as social constructivism, which he defines in such a way as to cover nearly all the concerns that are central to reflectivist approaches. He criticizes reflectivist writers for not offering alternatives to the mainstream, but instead remaining 'a self-consciously dissident minority' (Walt, 1998: 32). Note just how much this view delegitimizes reflectivist work and how it polices the boundaries of the discipline. My second example is the article by Peter Katzenstein, Robert Keohane, and Stephen Krasner in which they review the last fifty years of international relations theory. They claim that the current situation is one where the main debate is that between rationalism and constructivism: 'rationalism . . . and constructivism now provide the major points of contestation for international relations scholarship' (Katzenstein, Keohane, and Krasner, 1998: 646). In contrast they have little time for what they term **post-modern** work (basically what I have here defined as reflectivist work); 'post-modernism denies . . . the use of evidence to adjudicate between truth claims . . . [it] falls clearly outside of the social science enterprise, and in IR research it risks becoming self-referential and disengaged from the world, protests to the contrary notwithstanding' (Katzenstein, Keohane and Krasner, 1998, 678). The key point I want you to bear in mind here is that rationalists are saying that reflectivist work is not 'proper' or 'legitimate' social science. It cannot therefore be published in the main journals because it lies outside the social science enterprise. This is a very important claim, one that of course reflectivists will deny, pointing out that the rationalists have a very restricted and very North American view of what social science is. But I hope you can see how undermining it must be if you are told not only that your questions and answers are wrong, but that you are not scholarly and professional.

In conclusion, then, I want you to think about whether social constructivism is the way forward for international theory. Do you think that constructivism can serve as the middle way between rationalism and reflectivism, or are their views of how to construct knowledge so different that they cannot be combined? The trouble of course is that it sounds eminently sensible to say that the two positions of rationalism and reflectivism need to be combined, and the focus of the neo-liberals on institutions and learning makes it possible to see a way of linking up with reflectivists who focus on identity and the construction of actors. But this poses the ultimate question in social theory, namely whether there are always going to be two ways of theorizing the social world: one an inside account focusing on the meanings that actors attach to their actions; the other an outsider account, which sees the beliefs of actors as the product of material interests. I cannot pretend to answer that question, and this is not because of the space available in this chapter; rather this is such a hotly disputed question in all the social sciences that the only honest thing to do is to say that there is no easy or definitive answer. What I will say is that the answer to it will depend in part on how you see the social world and on what kinds of features of world politics matter to you.

I hope that this chapter has given you a good overview of the main alternatives to rationalist international theory. My chief hope is that you will take from what I have written the thought that there is no one theory of world politics that is right simply because it deals with the **truth**. I also hope that you will be sceptical any time any theorist tells you that s/he is dealing with 'reality' or with 'how the world really is'; since I think that this is where the values of the theorist (or lecturer, or chapter writer!) can be smuggled in through the back door. I think that world politics in an era of globalization is very complex and there are a variety of theories that try and account for different parts of that complexity. You should work out which theories both explain best the things you are concerned with and also offer you the chance to reflect on their own assumptions. One thing is for sure: there are enough theories to choose between and they paint very different world politics. Which theory paints the picture that you feel best captures the most salient features of world politics?

QUESTIONS

1 Why do the post-positivist theories reject positivism?

2 What does it mean to say that the main difference between theories is whether they are explanatory or constitutive?

3 Do you agree with Robert Keohane when he says that the reflectivist approaches need to develop testable hypotheses, to compete with those provided by rationalism, if reflectivism is to be taken seriously as a theoretical approach?

4 Is normative theory anything more than an optional extra for the study of world politics?

5 Do you find J. Ann Tickner's reformulation of Hans Morgenthau's six principles of realism a convincing demonstration of the need to include female perspectives on world politics?

6 Do you agree with Robert Cox that theory is always for someone and for some purpose?

7 What are the main implications of historical sociology for the study of world politics?

8 What might adopting a genealogical approach, such as that proposed by Richard Ashley, do for our understanding of world politics?

9 Do you think that Alexander Wendt's social constructivism succeeds in bridging the gap between rationalism and reflectivism?

10 Which of the main alternatives discussed in this chapter do you think offers the best account of world politics? Why?

11 Is social constructivism a middle way between rationalist and reflectivist approaches?

12 Are reflectivist approaches part of the social science enterprise?

GUIDE TO FURTHER READING

There are many books dealing with contemporary international theory. A very good survey is provided by Burchill and Linklater, *Theories of International Relations* (Basingstoke: Macmillan, 1996). Another very good survey is that of P. R. Viotti and M. V. Kauppi, *International Relations Theory: Realism, Pluralism, Globalism*, 2nd edn. (New York: Macmillan, 1993). For two sets of essays on contemporary theory see K. Booth and S. Smith (eds.) *International Relations Theory Today* (Cambridge: Polity Press, 1995), and S. Smith, K. Booth, and M. Zalewski (eds.), *International Theory: Positivism and Beyond* (Cambridge: Cambridge University Press, 1996). On reflectivist approaches, see, for normative theory, C. Brown, *International Relations Theory: New Normative Approaches* (Hemel Hempstead: Harvester Wheatsheaf, 1992) and M. Frost *Ethics in International Relations: A Constitutive Theory* (Cambridge: Cambridge University Press, 1996); for feminist theory see M. Zalewski 'Feminist Theory and International Relations', in M. Bowker and R. Brown (eds.), *From Cold War to Collapse* (Cambridge: Cambridge University Press, 1993), C. Enloe, *Bananas, Beaches and Bases: Making Feminist Sense of International Politics* (London: Pandora, 1989) and *The Morning After: Sexual Politics at the End of the Cold War* (Berkeley: California University Press, 1993), and J. J. Pettman, *Worlding Women: A Feminist International Politics* (St Leonards: Allen & Unwin, 1996); for critical theory see R. Cox with T. Sinclair, *Approaches to World Order* (Cambridge: Cambridge University Press, 1996), and A. Linklater, *Beyond Realism and Marxism* (London: Macmillan, 1990) and *The Transformation of Community* (Cambridge: Polity Press, 1998); for historical sociology see Michael Mann, *The Sources of Social Power*, vols. 1 and 2 (Cambridge: Cambridge University Press, 1986 and 1993), and D. Smith, *The Rise of Historical Sociology* (Cambridge: Polity Press, 1991); for post-modernism, see R. B. J. Walker, *Inside/Outside: International Relations as Political Theory* (Cambridge: Cambridge University Press, 1993) and J. George, *Discourses of Global Politics* (Boulder, Colo.: Lynne Rienner, 1994), and D. Campbell, *Writing Security: United States Foreign Policy and the Politics of Identity* (Manchester: Manchester University Press, 1992), *Politics without Principle: Sovereignty, Ethics and the Narratives of the Gulf War* (Boulder, Colo.: Lynne Rienner, 1993), and *National Deconstruction: Violence, Identity and Justice in Bosnia* (Minneapolis: University of Minnesota Press, 1998). On social constructivism see A. Wendt, 'Anarchy is What States Make of it', *International Organization*, 46: 2 (1992), and *Social Theory of International Politics* (Cambridge: Cambridge University Press, 1999), F. Kratochwil, *Rules, Norms, and Decisions* (Cambridge: Cambridge University Press, 1989, P. Katzenstein (ed.), *The Culture of National Security: Norms and Identity in World Politics* (New York: Columbia University Press, 1996), and N. Onuf, *A World of our Making: Rules and Rule in Social Theory and International Relations* (Columbia: University of South Carolina Press, 1989).

Part Three

Structures and processes

In this section of the book we want to introduce you to the main underlying structures and processes in contemporary world politics. There is obviously going to be some overlap between this section and the next, since the division between structures and processes, and international issues is largely one of perspective. For us, the difference is that by structures and processes we mean relatively stable features of world politics that are more enduring and constant than are the issues dealt with in the next section. Again we have two aims in this section: **first**, we want you to get a good overview of some of the most important structures and processes in world politics at the end of the twentieth century. We therefore have chosen a series of ways of thinking about world politics that draw attention to these underlying features. Again, note that we realize that what is a structure and what is a process is largely a matter of debate, but it may help to say that together these provide the setting in which the issues dealt with in the next part of the book have to be played out. All of the features examined in this section of the book will be important for the resolution of the issues we deal with in the next section, since they comprise both the main structures of world politics that these issues have to face and the main processes that will determine their fate. Our **second** aim is that these structures and processes will help you to think about globalization by forcing you to ask again whether or not it is a qualitatively different form of world politics than hitherto. Does globalization require or represent an overthrow of the structures and processes that have been central in world politics to date?

Part Three

Structures and processes

12 International and global security in the post-cold war era

John Baylis

READER'S GUIDE

This chapter focuses on two central arguments about the effects of the end of the cold war on international security. The first argument suggests that very little of substance has changed: international relations is likely to be as violent in the future as it has been in the past. The second argument suggests that co-operation as well as competition has been a feature of international politics in the past and the post-cold war era has opened up an opportunity for an even more benign system of international and global security to develop. In the context of this debate the chapter begins by looking at traditional realist and more contemporary neo-realist perspectives on international security. Refinements of the neo-realist perspective (which reflect a more optimistic view of future international security) are then considered under the headings of 'contingent realism', 'mature anarchy', 'liberal institutionalism', and 'democratic peace'. Other perspectives are developed under the headings of 'collective security', 'constructivist' theory, critical security theory, feminist approaches, 'post-modernist' approaches, and 'globalist views'. The chapter ends by considering the continuing tension between national and international security and suggests that, despite the important changes associated with the processes of globalization, it remains too early to make a definitive judgement about whether a fundamentally different paradigm of international politics is emerging, or whether it is possible for such a transformation to occur. Globalization is affecting security in a number of important ways, but there are also many traditional issues and concerns.

Introduction

Students of international politics deal with some of the most profound questions it is possible to consider. Amongst the most important of these is whether international security is possible to achieve in the kind of world in which we live. For much of the intellectual history of the subject a debate has raged between **realists** and **idealists**, who have been respectively pessimistic and optimistic in their response to this central question in the international politics field (see Ch. 7). In the post-World War I period idealism claimed widespread support as the League of Nations seemed to offer some hope for greater international order. In contrast, during the cold war which developed after 1945, realism became the dominant school of thought. War and violent conflict were seen as perennial features of inter-state relations stretching back through human history. With the end of the cold war, however, the debate has been renewed and intensified. For some, the end of the intense ideological confrontation between East and West was a major turning point in international history, ushering in a new paradigm in which inter-state violence would gradually become a thing of the past and new communitarian values would bring greater co-operation between individuals and human collectivities of various kinds (including states). This reflected more optimistic views about the development of a peaceful global society. For others, however, realism remained the best approach to thinking about international security. In their view, very little of substance had changed as a result of the events of 1989. The end of the cold war had brought a new, more co-operative era between the superpowers into existence, but it was likely to be temporary as states continued to compete and force remained the ultimate arbiter of international disputes.

This chapter focuses on this debate, highlighting the different strands of thinking within these two optimistic and pessimistic schools of thought. Before this can be done, however, it is necessary to consider what is meant by 'security' and to probe the relationship between **national security** and **international security**. Attention will then shift to traditional ways of thinking about national security and the influence which these ideas have had on contemporary thinking. This will be followed by a survey of alternative ideas and approaches which have emerged in the literature in recent years. The conclusion will then provide an assessment of these ideas before returning to the central question of whether or not greater international security is more, or less, likely in the new century.

What is meant by the concept of security?

Most writers agree that security is a 'contested concept'. There is a consensus that it implies freedom from threats to core values (for both individuals and groups) but there is a major disagreement about whether the main focus of enquiry should be on 'individual', 'national', or 'international' security. For much of the cold war period most writing on the subject was dominated by the idea of national security, which was largely defined in militarized terms. The main area of interest for both academics and statesmen tended to be on the military capabilities that their own states should develop to deal with the threats that faced them. More recently, however, this idea of security has been criticized for being **ethnocentric** (culturally biased) and too narrowly defined. Instead a number of contemporary writers have argued for an expanded conception of security outward from the limits of parochial national security to include a range of other considerations. Barry Buzan, in his study, *People, States and Fear*, argues for a view of security which includes political, economic, societal, environmental as well as military aspects and which is also defined in broader international terms (see Box 12.2). This involves states overcoming 'excessively self-referenced security policies' and thinking instead about the security interests of their neighbours (Buzan 1983: 214–42). Buzan's work raises interesting and important questions about whether national and international security considerations can be compatible and whether states, given the nature of the international system, are capable of thinking in more co-operative international and global terms.

This focus on the tension between national and international security is not accepted by all writers on security. There are those who argue that the emphasis on the state and inter-state relations ignores the fundamental changes which have been taking place in world politics especially in the aftermath of the cold war. For some, the dual processes of integration and fragmentation which characterize the contemporary world mean that much more attention should be given to 'societal security'. According to this view, growing integration in regions like Europe is undermining the classical political order based on nation-states, leaving nations exposed within larger political frameworks (like the EU). At the same time the fragmentation of various states, like the Soviet Union and Yugoslavia, has created new problems of boundaries, minorities, and organizing ideologies which are causing increasing regional instability (Waever *et al.* 1993: 196). This has led to the argument that ethno-national groups, rather than states, should become the centre of attention for security analysts.

At the same time, there are other commentators

Box 12.1 Notions of 'security'

'A nation is secure to the extent to which it is not in danger of having to sacrifice core values if it wishes to avoid war, and is able, if challenged, to maintain them by victory in such a war.'

(Walter Lippmann)

'Security, in any objective sense, measures the absence of threats to acquired values and in a subjective sense, the absence of fear that such values will be attacked.'

(Arnold Wolfers)

'In the case of security, the discussion is about the pursuit of freedom from threat. When this discussion is in the context of the international system, security is about the ability of states and societies to maintain their independent identity and their functional integrity.'

(Barry Buzan)

'Stable security can only be achieved by people and groups if they do not deprive others of it; this can be achieved if security is conceived as a process of emancipation.'

(Booth and Wheeler)

---

who argue that the stress on national and international security is less appropriate because of the emergence of an embryonic global society in the 1990s. Like the 'societal security' theorists they point to the fragmentation of the nation-state but they argue that more attention should be given, not to society at the ethno-national level, but to global society. These writers argue that one of the most important trends at the end of the twentieth century is the broad process of globalization which is taking place. They accept that this process brings new risks and dangers. These include the risks associated with such things as a breakdown of the global monetary system, global warming, and the dangers of nuclear accidents. These threats to security, on a planetary level, are viewed as being largely outside the control of nation-states. Only the development of a global community, they believe, can deal with this adequately. At the same time, there are other writers on globalization who stress the transformation of the state (rather than its demise) and the new security agenda facing the state in the early years of the new century.

Box 12.2 Different dimensions of international security

At the political level there has been a growing recognition that systems of government and ideologies have a powerful influence not only on domestic stability but also on international security. Authoritarian governments often seek to divert attention away from problems at home by pursuing foreign adventures. This appears to have been one of the major reasons for the Malvinas/Falklands war in 1982 between Argentina and Britain. The contemporary trend towards the fragmentation of states also poses wider security problems. This has been evident with the disintegration of the Soviet Union and Yugoslavia in the 1990s and could become a major problem if the Chinese Communist party began to lose effective control in the years ahead.

Population growth and problems over access to resources and markets has also led to greater attention being given to economic security issues. Deprivation and poverty are not only a source of internal conflict but can also spill over into tension between states. An example of this can be seen in the late 1980s in relations between Senegal and Mauritania. Disputes over agricultural land, together with population pressures gave rise to the expulsion of minority groups and ethnic violence in the Senegal River Valley bordering on Mauritania. The dispute did not lead to war between the two states but considerable diplomatic tensions were generated, demonstrating the growing importance of economic interdependence and the potential for conflict which can be created as a result.

Economic pressures can also encourage social tensions within states which can have implications for international security. In recent years large migration movements between states has produced group-identity conflicts. One of the most serious has been the migration from Bangladesh to north-east India. In the last twenty years the population of Assam has risen from 7 million to 22 million people causing major social changes which have altered the balance of political power between religious and ethnic groups in the state. This resulted in intergroup conflict which has caused difficulties between India and Bangladesh.

Many of the economic and social sources of insecurity in the contemporary world are linked to environmental scarcity. As Thomas Homer-Dixon has shown, scarcities of cropland, water, forests and fish, together with atmospheric changes such as global warming have an important impact on international security. Control over oil was a major cause of the Gulf War in 1991 and tension over the control of water resources in the occupied West Bank has helped heighten tension between Arabs and Jews in Israel complicating the efforts to achieve a durable peace settlement in the region.

(Homer-Dixon 1994: 18)

The traditional approach to national security

As Chapter 2 has shown, from the Treaty of Westphalia in 1648 onwards states have been regarded as by far the most powerful actors in the international system. They have been 'the universal standard of political legitimacy' with no higher authority to regulate their relations with each other. This has meant that security has been seen as the priority obligation of state governments. They have taken the view that there is no alternative but to seek their own protection in what has been described as a **self-help** world.

In the historical debate about how best to achieve national security writers like Hobbes, Machiavelli, and Rousseau tended to paint a rather pessimistic picture of the implications of state sovereignty. The international system was viewed as a rather brutal arena in which states would seek to achieve their own security at the expense of their neighbours. Interstate relations were seen as a struggle for power as states constantly attempted to take advantage of each other. According to this view **permanent peace** was unlikely to be achieved. All that states could do was to try and balance the power of other states to prevent any one from achieving overall hegemony. This was a view which was shared by writers, like E. H. Carr and Hans Morgenthau, who developed what became known as the realist school of thought in the aftermath of World War II.

This largely pessimistic view of international relations is shared by many contemporary writers like Kenneth Waltz and John Mearsheimer. The pessimism of these **neo-realists** rests on a number of key assumptions they make about the way the international system works (see Ch. 7).

Key neo-realist assumptions

- The international system is **anarchic**. They do not mean by this that it is necessarily chaotic. Rather, anarchy implies that there is no central authority capable of controlling state behaviour.

- States claiming sovereignty will inevitably develop **offensive military capabilities** to defend themselves and extend their power. As such they are potentially dangerous to each other.

- **Uncertainty**, leading to **a lack of trust**, is inherent in the international system. States can never be sure of the intentions of their neighbours and, therefore, they must always be on their guard.

- States will want to maintain their independence and sovereignty, and, as a result, **survival** will be the most basic driving force influencing their behaviour.

- Although states are rational, there will always be **room for miscalculation**. In a world of imperfect information, potential antagonists will always have an incentive to misrepresent their own capabilities to keep their opponents guessing. This may lead to mistakes about 'real' state interests.

Taken together, neo-realists argue that these assumptions produce a tendency for states to act aggressively towards each other.

According to this view, national security, or insecurity, is largely the result of the structure of the international system (this is why these writers are sometimes called 'structural realists'). The structure of anarchy is seen as being highly durable. The implication of this is that international politics in the future is likely to be as violent as international politics in the past. In an important article entitled 'Back to the Future' written in 1990 John Mearsheimer argued that the end of the cold war was likely to

usher in a return to the traditional multilateral balance of power politics of the past in which extreme nationalism and ethnic rivalries would lead to widespread **instability** and **conflict**. Mearsheimer viewed the cold war as a period of peace and stability brought about by the bipolar structure of power which prevailed. With the collapse of this system, he argued there would be a return to the kind of great power rivalries which had blighted international relations since the seventeenth century.

For neo-realist writers, like Mearsheimer, international politics may not be characterized by constant wars but there is nevertheless a relentless security competition which takes place, with war, like rain, always a possibility. It is accepted that co-operation among states can and does occur, but such co-operation has its limits. It is 'constrained by the dominating logic of security competition, which no amount of co-operation can eliminate' (Mearsheimer 1994/5: 9). Genuine long-lasting peace, or a world where states do not compete for power, therefore, is very unlikely to be achieved.

The 'security dilemma'

This view that war is a constant historical feature of international politics and is unlikely to disappear is based on the notion that states face what has been described as a **security dilemma** from which it is largely impossible to escape. The idea of a security dilemma was first clearly articulated in the 1950s by John Herz. It was, he said: 'a structural notion in which the self-help attempts of states to look after their security needs, tend regardless of intention to lead to rising insecurity for others as each interprets its own measures as defensive and the measures of others as potentially threatening' (Herz 1950: 157).

According to this view, in a self-help environment, like the international system, states are faced with an 'unresolveable uncertainty' about the military preparations made by other states. Are they designed simply for their own defence or are they part of a more aggressive design? Because the uncertainty is unresolveable, states are likely to remain mistrustful of each other. In turn, if mistrust is mutual, 'a dynamic "action–reaction" cycle may well result, which will take the fears of both to higher levels'. Insecurity will breed further insecurity, with the ever-present potential for war breaking out (Wheeler and Booth 1992: 29–31).

At the root of the security dilemma, therefore, are mistrust and fear. Even when states are believed to be benign in their intentions there is always the recognition that intentions can change. Being overly trusting opens up the prospects of being taken advantage of, with potentially disastrous consequences. This constant fear, according to Butterfield, creates an awful tragedy which afflicts international relations. 'Behind the great conflicts of mankind', he argues, there 'is a terrible predicament which lies at the heart of the story'. Writing in the 1950s Butterfield argued that there was no sign that mankind was capable of overcoming this 'irreducible dilemma' (Butterfield 1951: 20).

The difficulties of co-operation between states

For most contemporary neo-realist writers there is little prospect of a significant change in the nature of security in the post-cold war world. Pointing to the Gulf War, the violent disintegration of the former Yugoslavia and parts of the former Soviet Union, it is argued that we continue to live in a world of mistrust and constant security competition. Co-operation between states occurs, but it is difficult to achieve and even more difficult to sustain. There are two main factors, it is suggested, which continue to make co-operation difficult, even after the changes of 1989. The first is the prospect of cheating; the second is the concern which states have about what are called **relative-gains**.

> ## Box 12.3 A statesman's view of the 'security dilemma'
>
> 'The distinction between preparations made with the intention of going to war and precautions against attack is a true distinction, clear and definite in the minds of those who build up armaments. But it is a distinction that is not obvious or certain to others. Each Government, therefore, while resenting any suggestion that its own measures are anything more than for defence, regards similar measures of another government as preparation to attack.'
>
> (Lord Grey)

The problem of cheating

Writers like Waltz and Mearsheimer do not deny that states often co-operate or that in the post-cold war era there are even greater opportunities than in the past for states to work together. They argue, however, that there are distinct limits to this co-operation because states have always been, and remain, fearful that others will cheat on any agreements reached and attempt to gain advantages over them. This risk is regarded as being particularly important, given the nature of modern military technology which can bring about very rapid shifts in the balance of power between states. 'Such a development', Mearsheimer has argued, 'could create a window of opportunity for the cheating side to inflict a decisive defeat on the victim state' (Mearsheimer 1994/5: 20). States realize that this is the case and although they join alliances and sign arms control agreements, they remain cautious and aware of the need to provide for their own national security in the last resort. This is one of the reasons why, despite the Strategic Arms Reduction Agreements of the early 1990s and the extension of the Non-Proliferation Treaty in 1995, the nuclear powers continue to maintain some of their nuclear weapons.

The problem of relative-gains

Co-operation is also inhibited, according to many neo-realist writers, because states tend to be concerned with 'relative-gains', rather than 'absolute gains'. Instead of being interested in co-operation because it will benefit both partners, states, they suggest, always have to be aware of how much they are gaining compared with the state they are co-operating with. Because all states will be attempting to maximize their gains in a competitive, mistrustful, and uncertain international environment, co-operation will always be very difficult to achieve and hard to maintain.

Such a view of the problems of co-operation in the post-cold war world are not, however, shared by all writers, even within the neo-realist school. There is a wide body of opinion amongst scholars (and politicians) that the traditional or 'standard' neo-realist view of international relations should be modified or even replaced. Opposition to 'standard' neo-realism takes a wide variety of different forms. To illustrate alternative ways of thinking about international security in the 1990s eight different approaches will be considered. Despite the differences which exist between writers in these fields they all share a common view that greater international security in the future is possible through co-operation. Indeed, many of them argue that international security in the latter years of the twentieth century is undergoing significant changes which could bring greater opportunities for peace.

The opportunities for co-operation between states

'Contingent realism'

Contrary to the views of those neo-realists (like Waltz and Mearsheimer) who are pessimistic about co-operation between states in the post-cold war world, there are other neo-realist writers who present a rather more optimistic assessment. According to Charles Glaser, 'contrary to the conventional wisdom, the strong general propensity of adversaries to compete is not an inevitable logical consequence of structural realism's basic assumptions' (Glaser 1994/ 5: 51). Glaser accepts much of the analysis and assumptions of structural realism, but he argues that there are a wide range of conditions in which adversaries can best achieve their security goals through co-operative policies, rather than competitive ones. In such circumstances states will choose to co-operate rather than to compete. Security is therefore seen to be 'contingent' on the circumstances prevailing at the time.

Contingent realists argue that **standard** structural realism is flawed for **three** main reasons.

1. They reject the competition-bias inherent in the theory. Because international relations is characterized by self-help behaviour does not necessarily mean, they argue, that states are damned to perpetual competition which will result in war.

Faced with the uncertainties associated with being involved in an arms race, like that of the 1970s and 1980s, for example, states preferred to co-operate. There were distinct advantages in working together to reduce the risks and uncertainty in this period rather than engaging in relentless competition which characterized most of the cold war years.

2. A second, and related argument is that standard structural realism is flawed because of its emphasis on 'relative-gains'. States often pursue co-operation, it is argued, precisely because of the dangers of seeking relative advantages. As the security dilemma literature suggests, it is often best in security terms to accept rough parity rather than seek maximum gains which will spark off another round of the arms race leading to less security for all in the longer term.

3. The third flaw in the standard argument, according to contingent realists, is that the emphasis on cheating is overdone. Cheating is a problem which poses risks, but so does arms racing. Schelling and Halperin have argued that 'it cannot be assumed that an agreement that leaves some possibility of cheating is unacceptable or that cheating would necessarily result in strategically

---

Box 12.4 **Key concepts**

'A **security community** is a group of people which has become "integrated". By integration we mean the attainment, within a territory, of a "sense of community" and of institutions and practices strong enough and widespread enough to assure . . . dependable expectations of "peaceful change" among its population. By a "sense of community" we mean a belief . . . that common social problems must and can be resolved by processes of "peaceful change".'

(Karl Deutsch)

'**Security regimes** occur when a group of states cooperate to manage their disputes and avoid war by seeking to mute the security dilemma both by their own actions and by their assumptions about the behaviour of others.'

(Robert Jervis)

'A **security complex** involves a group of states whose primary security concerns link together sufficiently closely that their national securities cannot realistically be considered apart from one another.'

(Barry Buzan)

'Acceptance of **common security** as the organizing principle for efforts to reduce the risk of war, limit arms, and move towards disarmament, means, in principle, that cooperation will replace confrontation in resolving conflicts of interest. This is not to say that differences among nations should be expected to disappear . . . The task is only to ensure that these conflicts do not come to be expressed in acts of war, or in preparations for war. It means that nations must come to understand that the maintenance of world peace must be given a higher priority than the assertion of their own ideological or political positions.'

(*Palme Report* 1992)

---

important gains'. The risks involved in arms control may be preferable to the risks involved in arms racing. Contingent realists argue that this is often ignored by writers like Waltz and Mearsheimer. This was clearly the view of the superpowers in the late 1980s and early 1990s when a wide range of agreements were signed including the INF Treaty and the START I and II Treaties (see Ch. 19).

The main thrust of the argument is that there is no need to be overly pessimistic about international security in the aftermath of the cold war.

Key points

- 'Contingent realists' regard themselves as 'structural realists' or 'neo-realists'.

- They believe standard 'neo-realism' is flawed for three main reasons: they reject the competition bias in the theory; they do not accept that states are only motivated by 'relative gains'; they believe the emphasis on cheating is exaggerated.

- 'Contingent realists' tend to be more optimistic about co-operation between states than traditional 'neo-realists'.

Mature anarchy

The view that it is possible to ameliorate (if not necessarily to transcend) the security dilemma through greater co-operation between states is also shared by other writers who would describe themselves as 'neo-realists' or 'structural realists'. Barry Buzan has argued that one of the interesting and important features of the 1980s and 1990s is the gradual emergence of a rather more 'mature anarchy' in which states recognize the intense dangers of continuing to compete aggressively in a nuclear world. While accepting the tendency of states to focus on their own narrow parochial security interests, Buzan argues that there is a growing recognition amongst the more 'mature' states in the international system that there are good (security) reasons for taking into account the interests of their neighbours when making their own policies. States, he suggests, are increasingly internalizing 'the understanding that national securities are interdependent and that excessively self-referenced security policies, whatever their jingoistic attractions, are ultimately self-defeating' (Buzan 1983: 208). He cites the Nordic countries as providing an example of a group of states that have moved, through 'a maturing process', from fierce military rivalry to a security community. Buzan accepts that such an evolutionary process for international society as a whole is likely to be slow and uneven in its achievements. A change away from the preoccupation with national security towards a greater emphasis on international security, however, is, in his view, at least possible, and certainly desirable.

It could be argued that this is exactly what has happened in Western Europe over the past fifty years. After centuries of hostile relations between France and Germany, as well as between other Western European states, a new sense of 'community' was established with the Treaty of Rome which turned former enemies into close allies. Unlike the past these states no longer consider using violence or coercion to resolve their differences. Disagreements still occur but there is a consensus within the European Union that these will always be resolved peacefully by political means. Supporters of the concept of 'mature anarchy' argue that this ongoing 'civilizing' process in Europe can be extended further to achieve a wider security community by embracing other regions with whom economic and political co-operation is increasingly taking place.

Key points

- Supporters of the concept of 'mature anarchy' also accept that **structure** is a key element in determining state behaviour.

- There is, however, a trend towards 'mature anarchy', especially in Europe, which focuses on the growing importance of international security considerations.

- This is occurring because more states in the contemporary world are recognizing that their own security is interdependent with the security of other states.

- The more this happens the greater the chances of dampening down the security dilemma.

Liberal institutionalism

One of the main characteristics of the standard neo-realist approach to international security is the belief that international institutions do not have a very important part to play in the prevention of war. Institutions are seen as being the product of state interests and the constraints which are imposed by the international system itself. It is these interests and constraints which shape the decisions on whether to co-operate or compete rather than the institutions to which they belong.

Such views have been challenged by both statesmen and a number of international relations specialists, particularly following the end of the cold war. The British Foreign Secretary, Douglas Hurd, for example made the case in June 1992 that institutions themselves had played, and continued to play, a crucial role in **enhancing security**, particularly in Europe. He argued that the West had developed 'a set of international institutions which have proved their worth for one set of problems'. He went on to argue that the great challenge of the post-cold war era was to adapt these institutions to deal with the new circumstances which prevailed. (Hurd, quoted in Mearsheimer 1994/5).

This view reflected a belief, widely shared among Western statesmen that a framework of complementary, mutually reinforcing institutions—the EU, NATO, WEU, and the Organization for Security and Co-operation in Europe (OSCE)—could be developed to promote a more durable and stable European security system for the post-cold war era. For many observers such an approach has considerable potential in achieving peace in other regions of the world as well. ASEAN is often cited as an institution which has an important role to play in helping to maintain stability in South-East Asia. Similarly the Organization of African States plays a part in helping to resolve differences between African states.

This is a view which is also shared by a distinctive group of academic writers which developed during the 1980s and early 1990s. These writers all share a conviction that the developing pattern of **institutionalized co-operation** between states opens up unprecedented opportunities to achieve greater international security in the years ahead. Although the past may have been characterized by constant wars and conflict, important changes are taking place in international relations at the beginning of the twenty-first century which create the opportunity to dampen down the traditional security competition between states.

This approach, known as liberal institutionalism, operates largely within the realist framework, but argues that international institutions are much more important in helping to achieve co-operation and stability than 'structural realists' realize (see Ch. 9). According to Keohane and Martin (1995: 42) 'institutions can provide information, reduce transaction costs, make commitments more credible, establish focal points for coordination and, in general, facilitate the operation of reciprocity'. Supporters of these ideas point to the importance of European economic and political institutions in overcoming the traditional hostility of European states. They also point to the developments within the European Union and NATO in the post-cold war era to demonstrate that by investing major resources states themselves clearly believe in the importance of institutions. According to this line of argument, if states were influenced only by narrow calculations of power, the EU and NATO would have withered away at the end of the cold war. In fact, the reverse has happened. Both retain their vitality at the beginning of the new century and are engaged in a process of expansion. This is not to say that institutions can prevent wars from occurring, but they can help to mitigate the fears of cheating and alleviate fears which sometimes arise from unequal gains from co-operation.

As such, it is suggested that in a world constrained by state power and divergent interests, international institutions operating on the basis of reciprocity at least will be a component of any lasting peace. In other words, international institutions themselves are unlikely to eradicate war from the international system but they can play a part in helping to achieve greater co-operation between states. This was reflected in Prime Minister Margaret Thatcher's call in 1990 to 'bring the new democracies of Eastern Europe into closer association with the institutions of Western Europe'. Despite some scepticism about the European Community, she argued that the EC had reconciled antagonisms within Western Europe in the post-Second World War period and it could be used to overcome divisions between East and West in Europe in the post-cold war period.

Key points

- Neo-realists reject the significance of international institutions in helping many to achieve peace and security.

- Contemporary politicians and academics, who write under the label of liberal institutionalism, however, see institutions as an important mechanism for achieving international security.

- Liberal institutionalists accept many of the assumptions of realism about the continuing importance of military power in international relations but argue that institutions can provide a framework for co-operation which can help to overcome the dangers of security competition between states.

Democratic peace theory

Another 'liberal' approach to international security has gathered momentum in the post-cold war world. This centres on the argument that democratic states tend not to fight other democratic states. Democracy, therefore, is seen as a major source of peace (see Ch. 8). As with 'liberal institutionalism', this is a notion which has received wide support in Western political and academic circles. In his State of the Union Address in 1994 President Bill Clinton went out of his way to point to the absence of war between democracies as a justification for American policies of promoting a process of democratization around the world. Support for this view can be seen in the Western policy of promoting democracy in Eastern and Central Europe following the end of the cold war and opening up the possibility of these states joining the European Union.

'Democratic peace' theory has been largely associated with the writings of Michael Doyle and Bruce Russett. In the same way that contemporary realists have been influenced by the work of Hobbes, Rousseau, and Machiavelli, Doyle points to the importance of the insights contained in Immanuel Kant's

1795 essay, *Perpetual Peace*. Doyle contends that democratic representation, an ideological commitment to human rights, and transnational interdependence provide an explanation for the 'peace-prone' tendencies of democratic states. (Doyle 1995*a*: 180–4) Equally, the absence of these attributes, he argues, provides a reason why non-democratic states tend to be 'war-prone'. Without these domestic values and restraints the logic of power replaces the liberal logic of accommodation.

Supporters of democratic peace ideas, as a way of promoting international security in the post-cold war era, do not only argue that wars between democracies are rare or non-existent. They also contend that democracies are more likely to settle mutual conflicts of interest short of the threat or use of any military force. It is accepted that conflicts of interest will, and do, arise between democratic states, but shared norms and institutional constraints mean that democracies rarely escalate those disputes to the point where they threaten to use military force against each other, or actually use force at all. Much more than other states, they settle their disagreement by mediation, negotiation, or other forms of peaceful diplomacy. One of the benefits of democracy, according to Doyle, is that differences will be managed long before they become violent disputes in the public arena. There is clearly a close link here with the arguments put forward by supporters of the concept of 'mature anarchy', discussed above.

These democratic peace arguments are not designed to reject realism completely but to suggest that liberal democracies do make rather more of a difference in international politics than realist writers accept. Bruce Russett has argued that there is no need to jettison the insights of realism which tell us that power and strategic considerations affect states' decisions to fight each other. But neither should one deny the limitations of those insights, and their inability to explain many of the instances when liberal states have chosen not to fight or to threaten one another. For Russett the danger resides in 'vulgar realism's' vision of war of all against all, 'in which the threat that other states pose is unaffected by their internal norms and institutions' (Russett 1995: 175).

Russett argues that democratic values are not the only influence permitting states to avoid war; power and strategic influences undoubtedly affect the calculations of all states, including democracies. And sometimes these strategic considerations can be predominant. Shared democracy, however, he believes, is important in international affairs and should not be ignored in any attempt to dampen down the security dilemma and achieve greater security. He is not saying that shared democratic values by themselves will eliminate all wars but, like liberal institutionalists, he argues that such values will contribute to a more peaceful world.

Key points

- Democratic peace theory emerged in the 1980s. The main argument was that the spread of democracy would lead to greater international security.

- Democratic peace theory is based on a Kantian logic emphasizing three elements—republican democratic representation, an ideological commitment to human rights, and transnational interdependence.

- Wars between democracies are seen as being rare and they are believed to settle mutual conflicts of interest without the threat or use of force more often than non-democratic states.

- Supporters of democratic peace ideas do not reject the insights of realism, but they reject 'vulgar realisms' preoccupation with the idea of war of all against all. They argue that internal norms and institutions matter.

Ideas of collective security

There are other approaches to contemporary international security which take realpolitik and power calculations seriously but which also argue that domestic politics, beliefs, and norms must also be included as important determinants of state behaviour. One such approach is that associated with collective security ideas. Proponents of collective security argue that although military force remains an important characteristic of international life, there are nevertheless realistic opportunities to move beyond the self-help world of realism, especially after the end of the cold war. They reject the idea that state behaviour is simply the product of the structure of the international system. Ideas, it is argued, are also important.

According to Charles and Clifford Kupchan, under collective security, states agree to abide by certain norms and rules to maintain stability, and when necessary, band together to stop aggression (C. and C. Kupchan 1995). Defined in these terms collective security involves a recognition by states that to enhance their security they must agree to three main principles in their inter-state relations.

- **First**, they must renounce the use of military force to alter the status quo and agree instead to settle all of their disputes peacefully. Changes will be possible in international relations, but ought to be achieved by negotiation rather than force.

- **Second**, they must broaden their conception of national interest to take in the interests of the international community as a whole. This means that when a troublemaker appears in the system, all of the responsible states automatically and collectively confront the aggressor with overwhelming military power.

- **Third**, and most importantly states must overcome the fear which dominates world politics and learn to trust each other. Such a system of security, as Inis Claude has argued, depends on states entrusting 'their destinies to collective security'.

Supporters of collective security as a way forward to achieving greater international security accept that their ideas are not a panacea for preventing war. They argue, however, that by setting up collective security institutions some of the worst excesses of the perennial competition between states can be avoided. According to this view, 'regulated, institutionalized balancing is preferable to unregulated balancing under anarchy' (C. and C. Kupchan 1995). Collective security is seen as a way of providing a more effective mechanism for balancing against an aggressor. By facing potential aggressors with preponderance, collective security arrangements are designed to provide deterrence and more effective action if deterrence breaks down.

It is also argued that collective security institutions contribute to the task of creating a more benign international system. They help create greater confidence so that states can concentrate their energies and resources on their own domestic welfare rather than on non-productive, excessive national security arrangements. Proponents argue that there are profound advantages to institutionalizing a security system that promises to deepen the accord among states rather than letting a self-help system take its course and simply hoping that great power conflict will not re-emerge. The aim, as with liberal institutionalism and democratic peace ideas, is to ameliorate security competition between states by reducing the possibility that unintended spirals of hostility will escalate into war.

Supporters of these ideas argue that although collective security arrangements, like the League of Nations, have failed in the past there is no iron law which says they must fail in the future. The post-cold war era they believe has created a more conducive international environment in which greater opportunities exist than in the past for states to share similar values and interests. This is particularly so in Europe with the spread of democratic values and the collapse of confrontation politics between East and West. These conditions provide the essential foundations for the successful functioning of a collective security system. Supporters also point to the Gulf War in 1991 as an example of effective collective security action in the post-cold war period (for a critique of collective security ideas see Box 12.6).

Key points

- Collective security theorists take power seriously but argue that it is possible to move beyond the self-help world of realism

- Collective security is based on three main conditions—that states must renounce the use of military force to alter the status quo; that they must broaden their view of national interest to take in the interests of the international community; and that states must overcome their fear and learn to trust each other.

- Collective security aims to create a more effective system of 'regulated institutionalized balancing' rather than relying on the unregulated balancing which takes place under anarchy.

- Collective security is believed to contribute to the creation of a more benign international system.

- Despite past failures, supporters argue that there is an opportunity to try collective security again with more success in the post-cold war world.

Alternative views on international and global security

'Social constructivist' theory

The notion that international relations are not only affected by power politics but also by ideas is also shared by writers who describe themselves as 'social constructivist theorists'. According to this view, the fundamental structures of international politics are **social** rather than strictly **material**. This leads social constructivists to argue that changing the way we **think** about international relations can bring a fundamental shift towards greater international security (see Ch. 11).

At one level, social constructivists, like Alexander Wendt, share many of the major realist assumptions about international politics. They accept that states are the key referent in the study of international politics and international security; that international politics is anarchic; that states often have offensive capabilities; that states cannot be absolutely certain of the intentions of other states; that states have a fundamental wish to survive; and that states attempt to behave rationally. They also see themselves as structuralists; that is to say they believe that the interests of individual states are in an important sense constructed by the structure of the international system.

However, social constructivists think about international politics in a very different way to neo-realists. The latter tend to view structure as being made up only of a distribution of material capabilities. On the other hand, they think that structure is the product of social relationships. Social structures, they argue, are made up of elements, such as **shared knowledge**, **material resources** and **practices**. This means that social structures are defined, in part, by shared understandings, expectations, or knowledge. As an example of this, Alexander Wendt argues that the security dilemma is a social structure composed of **inter-subjective understandings** in which states are so distrustful that they make worst-case assumptions about each other's intentions, and, as a result, define their interests in 'self-help' terms (Wendt 1992). In contrast, a security community is a rather different social structure, composed of shared knowledge in which states trust one another to resolve disputes without war.

The emphasis on the structure of shared knowledge is important in social constructivist thinking. Social structures include material things, like tanks and economic resources, but these only acquire **meaning** through the structure of shared knowledge in which they are embedded. The idea of power politics, or **realpolitik**, has meaning to the extent that states accept the idea as a basic rule of international politics. According to social constructivist writers, power politics is an idea which does affect the way states behave, but it does not describe all interstate behaviour. States are also influenced by other ideas, such as the rule of law and the importance of institutional co-operation and restraint. In his study, 'Anarchy is What States Make of it', Wendt argues that security dilemmas and wars are the result of self-fulfilling prophecies. The 'logic of reciprocity' means that states acquire a shared knowledge about the meaning of power and act accordingly. Equally, he argues, policies of reassurance can also help to bring about a structure of shared knowledge which can help to move states towards a more peaceful security community (see Wendt 1999).

Although social constructivists argue that security

dilemmas are not acts of god, they differ over whether they can be escaped. For some, the fact that structures are socially constructed does not necessarily mean that they can be changed. This is reflected in Wendt's comment that 'sometimes social structures so constrain action that transformative strategies are impossible' (Wendt 1995: 80). Many social constructivist writers, however, are more optimistic. They point to the changes in ideas introduced by Gorbachev during the second half of the 1980s which led to a shared knowledge about the end of the cold war. Once both sides accepted the cold war was over, it really was over. According to this view, understanding the crucial role of social structure is important in developing policies and processes of interaction which will lead towards co-operation rather than conflict. For the optimists, there is sufficient 'slack' in the international system which allows states to pursue policies of peaceful social change rather than engage in a perpetual competitive struggle for power. If there are opportunities for promoting social change most social constructivists believe it would be irresponsible not to pursue such policies.

Key points

- Social constructivist thinkers base their ideas on two main assumptions; (1) that the fundamental structures of international politics are socially constructed and (2) that changing the way we think about international relations can help to bring about greater international security.

- Social constructivist thinkers accept many of the assumptions of neo-realism, but they reject the view that 'structure' consists only of material capabilities. They stress the importance of social structure defined in terms of shared knowledge and practices as well as material capabilities.

- Social constructivist argue that material things aquire meaning only through the structure of shared knowledge in which they are embedded.

- Power politics and realpolitik emphasized by realists is seen as being derived from shared knowledge which is self-fulfilling.

- Social constructivists can be pessimistic or opti-

mistic about changing international relations and achieving international security.

'Critical security' theorists and 'feminist' approaches

Despite the differences between social constructivists and realists about the relationship between ideas and material factors they agree on the central role of the state in debates about international security. There are other theorists, however, who believe that the state has been given too much prominence. Both critical security theorists and feminist writers wish to de-emphasize the role of the state and reconceptualize security in a different way.

Robert Cox draws a distinction between **problem-solving theories** and **critical theories**. Problem-solving theorists work within the prevailing system. The take 'the existing social and political relations and institutions as starting points for analysis and then see how the problems arising from these can be solved and ameliorated' (Smith 2000). In contrast, critical theorists focus their attention on the way these existing relationships and institutions emerged and what might be done to change them (see Chs. 10 and 11). For critical security theorists states should not be the centre of analysis because they are not only extremely diverse in character but they are also often part of the problem of insecurity in the international system. They can be providers of security, but they can also be a source of threat to their own people. According to this view, therefore, attention should be focused on the individual rather than the state. With this as their main referent, writers like Booth and Wyn Jones, argue that security can best be assured through **human emancipation**, defined in terms of 'freeing people, as individuals and groups, from the social, physical, economic, political, and other constraints that stop them from carrying out what they would freely choose to do'. This focus on emancipation is designed to provide 'a theory of progress', 'a politics of hope' and a guide to 'a politics of resistance' (Booth 1999). Critics point to the vagueness of the concept of 'emancipation' and the difficulty of 'individual-based' theories to analyse international and global security (See Rengger, 2000).

Feminist writers also challenge the traditional

emphasis on the central role of the state in studies of international security. While there are significant differences between feminist theorists, (including critical theory and post-modernist/post-structuralist perspectives) all share the view that works on international politics in general, and international security in particular, have been written from a 'masculine' point of view (see Chs. 11 and 27). In her work Ann Tickner argues that women have 'seldom been recognised by the security literature' despite the fact that conflicts affect women, as much, if not more, than men. The vast majority of casualties and refugees in war are women and children and, as the recent war in Bosnia confirms, the rape of women is often used as a tool of war (Tickner 1995). Feminist writers argue that if gender is brought more explicitly into the study of security, not only will new issues and alternative perspectives be added to the security agenda, but the result will be a fundamentally different view of the nature of international security. According to Jill Steans: 'Rethinking security . . . involves thinking about militarism and patriarchy, mal-development and environmental degradation. It involves thinking about the relationship between poverty, debt and population growth. It involves thinking about resources and how they are distributed' (Steans 1998. See also Smith 2000).

Key points

- Critical security theorists argue that too much emphasis is given by most approaches to the state.

- Some critical security theorists wish to shift the main referent to the individual and suggest that 'emancipation' is the key to greater domestic and international security.

- Feminist writers argue that gender tends to be left out of the literature on international security, despite the impact of war on women.

- Feminist writers also argue that bringing gender issues back in, will result in a reconceptualization of the study of international security.

Post-modernist views

Recent years have seen the emergence of post-modernist approaches to international relations which has produced a somewhat distinctive perspective towards international security (see Ch. 11). Post-modernist writers share the view that ideas matter, but they also see discourse—how people talk about international politics and security—as an important driving force that shapes the way states behave. For writers like Richard Ashley realism is one of the central problems of international insecurity (Ashley 1984). This is because realism is a **discourse of power** and rule which has been dominant in international politics in the past and which has encouraged security competition between states. According to John Vasquez, power politics is an image of the world that encourages behaviour that helps bring about war. As such the attempt to balance power is itself part of the very behaviour that leads to war. According to Vasquez (1983), alliances do not produce peace, but lead to war. The aim, for many post-modernists, therefore, is to replace the discourse of realism with a 'communitarian discourse' that emphasizes peace and harmony. The idea is that once the 'software' program of realism that people carry around in their heads has been replaced by a new 'software' program based on communitarian norms, individuals, states, and regions will learn to co-operate with each other and global politics will become more peaceful.

One of the central differences between realism and post-modernism is their very different **epistemologies** (ideas about knowledge). John Mearsheimer has noted that, whereas realists see a fixed and knowable world, post-modernists see the possibility of 'endless interpretations of the world around them . . . there are no constants, no fixed meanings, no secure grounds, no profound secrets, no final structures or limits of history . . . there is only interpretation . . . History itself is grasped as a series of interpretations imposed upon interpretations— none primary, all arbitrary' (Mearsheimer 1994: 42–3). This emphasis on the basis of knowledge as subjective rather than objective leads post-modernists to emphasize the importance of **normative values**. Realism is viewed not only as a statist ideology, largely out of touch with the globalizing tendencies which are occurring in world politics but also as a dangerous discourse which is the main obstacle to efforts to establish a new and more peaceful hegemonic discourse. This is because it purports to provide a universal view of how the world is organized and what states have to do if they wish to survive. Post-modernists reject what they see as the 'preposterous certainty' of realism. In their view the enormous complexity and indeterminacy of human behaviour, across all its cultural, religious, historical and linguistic variations means that there can be no single interpretation of global reality. The problem with realism according to this view, is that by reducing the complexities of world politics to a single rigidly ordered framework of understanding, alternative interpretations and approaches to international security are ruled out. If the world is thought of in terms of anarchy then 'power politics' will be seen as the solution to the problem of insecurity. On the other hand, if anarchy and power politics are not seen as being an endemic feature of global history then other more peaceful approaches to security might be tried. This has led post-modernist writers to try and reconceptualize the debate about global security by opening up new questions which have been ignored or marginalized. Jim George has argued that in the new post-cold war strategic discourse 'attention . . . has been focused on the growing sense of insecurity concerning state involvement in military-industrial affairs and the perilous state of the global economy. Questioned, too, has been the fate of those around the world rendered insecure by lives lived at the margins of existence yet unaccounted for in the statistics on military spending and strategic calculation' (George 1994). George argues that such questions require a new communitarian discourse about security.

Post-modernist writers believe that it is not only essential to replace realism with a communitarian discourse but it is an achievable objective. Because experts, and especially academic writers, have an important role to play in influencing 'the flow of ideas about world politics' it is vital for them to play their part in the process of transforming language and discourse about international politics. The whole nature of global politics can be transformed, and the traditional security dilemma can be overcome, if post-modern **epistemic communities** play their part in spreading communitarian ideals (see Box 12.5).

Box 12.5 Pursuing the 'politics of resistance'

As people around the planet have illustrated in recent times, given the opportunities to understand the processes by which they are constituted (as, for example, subjects in an objective world of anarchical power politics) it is possible to change power relations and overturn irreducible 'realities'. In these circumstances it becomes possible also to say no, to ask why, to understand how. A range of resistances can flow from this. People can, for example, resist the damages of extreme nationalism, the illusory certainty of nuclear deterrence theory, the transformation of global life into the construction of otherness; they can help prevent their social and environmental structures being destroyed in the name of, for example, economic rationalism; they can oppose racism and sexism and the exploitation of the marginalized and 'different'; and they can insist on participating in decisions that define and determine their life opportunities and the fate of those brutalized by dominant regimes of stability and order 'out there' in the real world. In this way, a politics of resistance is possible that 'extend(s) processes of democratization into realms where it has never been tried: into the home, into the workplace, into processes of cultural production'

(Jim George)

Key points

- Post-modernists emphasize the importance of ideas and discourse in thinking about international security.

- Post-modernists aim to replace the 'discourse of realism' with a 'communitarian discourse'.

- Realist and post-modernist approaches have very different epistemologies.

- Post-modernists try to reconceptualize the debate about global security by looking at new questions which have been ignored by traditional approaches.

- There is a belief amongst post-modernist writers that the nature of international politics can be changed if 'epistemic communities' help to spread communitarian ideals.

Globalist views of international security

The opportunity to pursue changes in the international system is shared by scholars who point to new trends which are already taking place in world politics. In the past the state has been the centre of thinking about international relations. This state-centric view, however, is now increasingly challenged. Writers from the **global society** school of thought argue that at the begining of the twenty-first century the process of globalization (which has been developing for centuries) has accelerated to the point 'where the clear outlines of a global society' are now evident. The emergence of a global economic system, global communications, and the elements of a global culture have helped to provide a wide network of social relationships which **transcend state frontiers** and encompass people all over the world. This has led to the growing obsolescence of territorial wars between the great powers. At the same time, so the argument goes, new risks associated with the environment, poverty, and weapons of mass destruction are facing humanity, just at a time when the nation-state is in crisis.

Supporters of the 'global society' school accept that globalization, is an uneven and contradictory process. The end of the cold war has been characterized not only by an increasing global awareness and the creation of a range of global social movements but also by the fragmentation of nation-states. This has been most obvious amongst the former communist states, especially the Soviet Union, Yugoslavia, and Czechoslovakia. Much the same pressures, however, have been felt in Western democratic societies with key institutions like the monarchy, the churches, and the family under increasing pressure. This has created what Martin Shaw has described as 'a crisis of Western civil society'. With the end of East–West confrontation, Shaw (1994: 170) argues that 'the ideological cement of Western civil society has dissolved'. As a result, whole communities, including 'villages and towns, ethnic groupings, their ways of life, traditions and forms of social organization—are threatened, along with the lives and well-being of individuals' (Shaw 1994: 172).

The result of this 'fracture of statehood' has been a movement away from conflicts between the great powers to new forms of insecurity caused by nationalistic, ethnic, and religious rivalries within states and across state boundaries. This has been reflected in the brutal civil wars that have been fought in Bosnia, Russia, Somalia, Rwanda, Yemen, and Kosovo during the 1990s. Mary Kaldor has described these conflicts as '**new wars**' which can only be understood in the context of globalization. The intensification of interconnectedness, she argues, has meant that ideological and/or territorial cleavages of an earlier era have increasingly been supplanted by an emerging political cleavage between … cosmopolitanism, based on inclusive, multicultural values and the politics of particularist identities' (Kaldor 1999: 6). The cleavage between those who are part of the global processes and those who are excluded, give rise to wars which are characterized by 'population expulsion through various means such as mass killing, forcible resettlement, as well as a range of political, psychological and economic techniques of intimidation' (Kaldor 1999: 8).

Such conflicts pose a critical problem for the international community of whether to intervene in the domestic affairs of sovereign states to safeguard minority rights and individual human rights (see Chs. 22 and 28). This dilemma, according to global society theorists, reflects the historic transformation of human society which is taking place at the beginning of the twenty-first century. Although states continue to limp along, many global theorists argue, it is now increasingly necessary to think of the security of individuals and of groups within the emergent global society. The traditional focus on national or state security (and sovereignty) no longer reflects the radical changes which are taking place. What is needed, according to this school of thought, is a new politics of global responsibility, designed to address issues of global inequality, poverty, and environmental stress, as well as of human rights, minority rights, democracy, and individual and group security, which cut hugely across dominant interests on a world scale as well as within just about every state (see Chs. 18 and 26). Thinking in such globalist, rather than national or international terms, supporters argue, will lead to more effective action (including intervention where necessary) to deal with the risks to security which exist in the world community at present.

The globalist society approach to security is based on what Anthony Giddens (1990: 154–8) calls utopian realism. According to this view it is 'realistic' to envisage the radical transformation of international politics as we have known it in the past. Indeed such a transformation, it is argued, is already taking place. Given the trends towards globalization it is realistic to envisage the expansion of the regional 'security communities' which are already in existence into a broader security community. Shaw (1994) in his book *Global Society and International Relations* argues that it is possible to see emerging a gigantic northern security community. He sees this as stretching from North America and Western Europe to the major states of the former USSR and Eastern Europe and to Japan, the newly industrializing states of East Asia, and Australia. He also sees other powers, including China, India, Egypt, and South Africa, being involved in regional extensions of this community. At the root of such a vision is a process of **global communications** which can help to create a new consensus on norms and beliefs which, in turn, can help to create a new cosmopolitan global security order.

Not all writers on globalization, however, accept the analysis of the global society school. There are those who argue that while the state is being transformed (both from within and without) by the processes of globalization, it remains a key referent in the contemporary debate about security. This is one of the central arguments in Ian Clark's study of *Globalization and International Relations Theory*. Clark argues that : 'What globalization can bring to bear on the topic of security is an awareness of widespread systemic developments without any resulting need to downplay the role of the state, or assume its obsolescence. The question that has to be addressed by the student of contemporary security is not whether security should be reconceptualised around individuals or societies as alternatives to the state, but how the practice of states is being reconfigured to take account of new concerns with human rights and societal identity' (Clark 1999: 125). What is interesting for Clark is the way that security is being reshaped by globalization and the changes that this is creating for the security agenda of states. In particular, as states become less able to provide what they have traditionally provided, he argues that domestic bargains, about what citizens are prepared

to sacrifice for the state, are being renegotiated. This is reflected in the type of security activities in which states are prepared to engage, and in the extent to which they are prepared to pursue them unilaterally. According to this view of globalization states are not withering away but are being transformed as they struggle to deal with the range of new challenges (including those of security) that face them (see Ch. 30). Such a view also casts doubts about how likely it is that the diffusion of gobal norms will create the kind of consensus necessary for the creation of a global society capable of bringing greater peace and security in the world. (See Box 12.6)

Box 12.6 Reflections on war in the twenty-first century

'The end of the cold war in 1989 did not, and will not, in and of itself, result in an end to conflict. We see evidence of the truth of that statement on all sides. The Iraqi invasion of Kuwait, the civil war in the former Yugoslavia, the turmoil in northern Iraq, the tension between India and Pakistan, the unstable relations between North and South Korea, and the conflicts across the face of Sub-Saharan Africa in Somalia, Sudan, Rwanda, Burundi, Zaire, Sierra Leone, and Liberia. These all make clear that the world of the future will not be without conflict, conflict between disparate groups within nations and conflicts extending across national borders. Racial, religious, and ethnic tensions will remain. Nationalism will be a powerful force across the globe. Political revolutions will erupt as societies advance. Historic disputes over political boundaries will endure. And economic disparities among and within nations will increase as technology and education spread unevenly around the world. The underlying causes of Third World conflict that existed long before the cold war began remain now that it has ended. They will be compounded by potential strife among states of the former Soviet Union and by continuing tensions in the Middle East. It is just such tensions that in the past fifty years have contributed to 125 wars causing forty million deaths.'

(Robert S. McNamara, 'Reflecting on War in the Twenty-First Century: The Context for Nuclear Abolition', in John Baylis and Robert O'Neill (eds.), *Alternative Nuclear Futures: The Role of Nuclear Weapons in the Post-Cold War World* (Oxford: Oxford University Press, 1999), 167–82).

Key points

- Supporters of the 'global society school' argue that the end of the twentieth century witnessed an accelerating process of globalization.

- Globalization can be seen in the fields of economic development, communications, and culture. Global social movements are also a response to new risks associated with the environment, poverty, and weapons of mass destruction.

- Globalization is occurring at a time when the fragmentation of the nation-state is taking place, encouraged in particular by the end of the cold war.

- The 'fracture of statehood' is giving rise to new kinds of conflict within states rather than between states which the state system cannot deal with. This has helped encourage an emerging politics of global responsibility.

- Globalism is also encouraged by the spread of regional security communities and the development of a growing consensus on norms and beliefs.

- There are disputes about whether globalization will contribute to the weakening of the state or simply to its transformation, and over whether a global society can be created which will usher in a new period of peace and security.

The continuing tensions between national, international, and global security

At the centre of the contemporary debate about global and international security dealt with above is the issue of continuity and change. This involves questions about how the past is to be interpreted and whether international politics is in fact undergoing a dramatic change as a result of the processes of globalization. There are also questions about how far these changes represent a fundamental transformation of world politics and whether it is possible to create a global system characterized by long-term peace and security. For realists, the empirical historical record is interpreted as providing a justification for their views that international politics always has been characterized by security competition and frequent wars, and the chances are that this pattern will continue into the future. For them there was no paradigmatic shift in 1989; nothing really has changed. East–West relations may be more peaceful, at present, but the potential for a resumption of great power conflict remains and conflicts, like the ones in the former Yugoslavia and the Gulf War in the early 1990s, demonstrate the continuing importance of security competition between states as well as non-state groups. This reflects the tendency by realists to reject the argument that it is possible to change the practice of power politics by achieving a universal consensus in favour of 'new thinking' or a communitarian discourse based on more peaceful norms and beliefs. The chances of ideas like collective security being widely adopted, according to this view, are almost negligible (see Box 12.7).

Realists also reject the contention raised by some of their critics that the state is becoming less central as regional and global considerations loom larger. The continuing primacy of the state is seen as a firm reality for the foreseeable future. Even in Europe where a large group of states are steadily integrating their political economies, it is argued that this will simply result in a larger entity forced to play a state-like role in the international system. This leads many realists to argue that, whatever the attraction of trying to develop an international or global security strategy, states are still likely in the future to define their security interests largely in national terms.

There is, however, a growing awareness, even amongst realists, that the twin processes of globalization and fragmentation do mean that more

Box 12.7 **The problems with collective security**

John Mearsheimer has argued that collective security is inescapably flawed. There are nine main reasons, he suggests, why it is likely to fail:

1. States often find it difficult, if not impossible, to distinguish between the 'aggressor' and the 'victim' in international conflicts.

2. Collective security assumes that all aggression is wrong, whereas there may be circumstances where conquest is warranted against a threatening neighbour.

3. Because some states are especially friendly for historical or ideological reasons they will be unlikely to join a coalition against their friends.

4. Historical enmity between states may complicate the effective working of a collective security system.

5. Because sovereign states have a tendency to pass the

buck in paying the price of dealing with aggression there is often difficulty in distributing the burden equitably.

6. Difficulties arise in securing a rapid response to aggression because of the unwillingness to engage in pre-crisis contingency planning.

7. States are often reluctant to join a coalition because collective action is likely to transform a local conflict into an international conflict.

8. Democracies are reluctant to make an automatic commitment to join collective action because of state sovereignty.

9. Collective security implies a contradiction in the way military force is viewed. It is seen as abhorrent and yet states must be willing to use it against an aggressor.

(Mearsheimer 1994/5)

---

attention has to be given to the security agenda within and beyond the state. This has given rise to increasing interest in the concept of **societal security** mentioned earlier. Writers like Ole Waever, Barry Buzan, Morten Kelstrup, and Pierre Lemaitre have argued that giving more attention to 'society' (defined in ethno-national terms) does not diminish the importance of national security. It puts 'more of the "national" back into "national security". It also opens up that area between the state and full regional integration which is neglected by traditional analysis' (Waever *et al.* 1993: 196).

There is no doubt, however, that national security is being challenged by the forces of globalization, some of which have a positive effect, bringing states into greater contact with each other. As Bretherton has argued the intensification of global connectedness associated with economic globalization, eco-

logical interdependence, and the threats posed by weapons of mass destruction, means that 'co-operation between states is more than ever necessary' (Bretherton and Ponton 1996: 100–1). It has also been argued that increased multilateralism caused by globalization helps 'to facilitate dialogue at the elite level between states, providing significant gains for global security' (Lawler 1995: 56–7). At the same time, however, globalization also appears to be having negative effects on international security. It is often associated with rapid social change, increased economic inequality and challenges to cultural identity which contribute to conflicts within, and between, states. This ambivalent effect of globalization, in turn, reinforces the search for national security, and at the same time leads states to seek greater multilateral and global solutions as they are less able to provide security for their citizens.

Conclusions

What conclusions can we come to from this analysis of different views about international and global security in the late 1990s? In the twenty-first century strategic calculations and power are likely to remain a vitally important ingredient of state behaviour. The structure of the international system, whether defined in material or social terms, continues to be a major influence on inter-state relations particularly in the way that they regard their security interests. This does not mean, however, that states always have to define their national security interests in narrow terms. Neither does it preclude important changes in international security as ideas, discourse, and global developments modify the processes of interaction which characterize world politics.

The spread of democratic states and democratic values, together with a justifiable conviction, by Western statesmen in particular, that liberal institutions have an important role to play in moderating the traditional security dilemma, are helping to develop a more mature anarchy in the 1990s. Ideas of co-operative or common security (in which states take account of the security interests of their neighbours) are beginning to have a significant impact on security policies in Europe and in other parts of the world. Under the umbrella of co-operative security thinking, security communities and security regimes are being developed (see Box 12.4). This can be seen in the developments which have taken place in the European Union, the OSCE and NATO, as well as the relations between Nordic countries and between ASEAN states in South East Asia. Security regimes like the Non-Proliferation Treaty of 1968 (which was extended indefinitely in 1995) reflect the way that states facing global dangers often do accept norms and rules of behaviour that help to overcome the dangers of competition.

These developments in both the **theory and practice of security** involve, in some respects, something of a shift from the traditional preoccupation with national security to a growing recognition of the importance of international and global security considerations as well as the humanitarian implications of intra-state conflicts (see Ch. 22). In part, this may be the result of a shift in the discourse about security in the 1980s and 1990s (as critical theorists contend) but of equal, if not greater, significance is the changing geopolitical, economic and technological circumstances of the period and an acceptance that many national security objectives can only be achieved through broader co-operative action. Strategic calculations (which have a symbiotic relationship with the discourse on security) in some important respects are pushing states increasingly towards greater co-operation.

It must be said, however, that despite this trend, it is not universal and there remains a continuing tension between national, international, and global security interests which cannot be ignored. As Buzan (1983: 214–42) has argued 'the national security imperative of minimising vulnerabilities sits unhappily with the risks of international agreement, and the prospects for international agreement are weakened by the power–security dilemma effects of a national security strategy'.

An example of the practical importance of the contradiction which this tension causes can be seen from the debates which have taken place about nuclear deterrence since the end of the cold war. On one level, it has been recognized that as a 'threat-based' strategy, nuclear deterrence is a major impediment to the development of a 'co-operative security' system between East and West. This, together with the growing recognition of the global threat posed by weapons of mass destruction, has led to a wide range of policies designed to play down the significance of nuclear weapons and to reverse the arms race. The whole process of denuclearization inherent in the START I and II Treaties, the INF Treaty, the extension of the Non-Proliferation Treaty, the Comprehensive Test Ban Agreement, ongoing negotiations on a cut-off of fissile material production, the decision by the US and Russia to stop targeting each other, and the new NATO strategic concept, all reflect a determination by national governments to try and enhance international security by establishing and reinforcing global norms which de-emphasize the role of nuclear weapons in their security policies.

At another level, however, the nuclear powers continue to enhance qualitatively their nuclear capabilities (through computer simulation and other techniques) and following the 1998 nuclear tests by India and Pakistan fears re-emerged about the prospects of further nuclear proliferation. US interest in deploying a National Missile Defense (NMD) system against 'rogue' states and opposition by both the Russians and the Chinese also indicates that national security interests remain of critical importance at the beginning of the new century. Even though nuclear weapons have been pushed more into the background, they continue to exist and the nuclear states continue to maintain nuclear deterrent strategies. What this means is that states possessing nuclear weapons (both declared and undeclared) continue to pose an implicit threat to existing or potential adversaries simply through their continuing possession of nuclear weapons. The result is that states pursue the objective of greater co-operation which requires trust, while at the same time hedging their bets by maintaining national military capabilities which reflect a lack of trust and an uncertainty that co-operative security can ultimately succeed in overcoming the security dilemma completely. This reflects the contemporary lack of consensus generally about fully accepting co-operative security ideas as the foundation of national security.

In the early years of the twenty-first century, therefore, despite important changes which are taking place in world politics, the traditional **ambiguity** about international security remains. In many ways the world is a much safer place to live in as a result of the end of the cold war and the removal of nuclear confrontation as a central element in East–West relations. The spread of democratic and communitarian values, some of the processes of globalization and the generally co-operative effects of international institutions have played an important part in dampening down the competitive aspects of the security dilemma between states. These significant trends, however, are offset to a certain extent by evidence of the continuing importance of military force as an arbiter of disputes both between and particularly within states. Conventional arms races continue in

different regions of the world, nuclear, chemical, and biological weapons still provide a powerful influence on the security calculations of many states, crazy and ambitious politicians remain at the head of some governments, and cultural differences, as well as diverse values and the tensions inherent in globalization itself prevent the emergence of global agreement on a wide range of important issues (see Ch. 21). Societal insecurity is also increasingly evident as the forces of fragmentation and integration destabilize traditional identities and thereby complicate relationships within and between states.

As a result, it remains much too soon to conclude that a paradigmatic shift is taking place in international politics and global security in the aftermath of the cold war or that such a permanent shift is possible. Undoubtedly, as many other chapters in this book indicate, new and positive developments are taking place in the world in which we live which suggest that the future of world politics does not have to be like the past. At the same time, the empirical historical evidence suggests caution. Periods of more co-operative inter-state (and inter-group) relations have often led to a false dawn and an unwarranted euphoria that 'perpetual peace' was about to break out. The structure of the international system provides an important constraint on the way that individuals, states, or international institutions behave. So does the predominance of realist attitudes towards international and global security amongst many of the world's political leaders (see Ch. 7). This is not to argue that there is no room for peaceful change or that new ideas and discourses about international relations are unimportant in helping to shape choices that have to be made. Opportunities to develop greater international and global security will always exist. In a world of continuing diversity, mistrust, and uncertainly, however, it is likely that the search for a more co-operative global society is likely to remain in conflict with the powerful pressures which exist for states, and wider communities, to look after their own national and regional security against threats from without and within. Whether and how international and global security can be achieved still remains, as Herbert Butterfield once argued, 'the hardest nut of all' for students and practitioners of international politics to crack.

QUESTIONS

1 Why is security a 'contested concept'?

2 Why do traditional realist writers focus on national security?

3 What do neo-realist writers mean by 'structure'?

4 What is meant by the 'security dilemma'?

5 Why do states find it difficult to co-operate?

6 What do you understand by the terms 'contingent realism' and 'mature anarchy'?

7 Do you find 'liberal institutionalism' convincing?

8 Why might democratic states be more peaceful?

9 Why do you think collective security arrangements failed in the past?

10 How do 'constructivist', 'critical security' theory, and 'feminist' views about international security differ from those of 'neo-realists'?

11 Do you think ideas and discourse influence the way states behave?

12 Is the tension between national and global security resolvable?

GUIDE TO FURTHER READING

B. Buzan's *People, States and Fear* (London: Harvester, 1983) provides an excellent starting point for the study of national and international security. The book is written largely from a neo-realist perspective.

Michael Joseph Smith's study of *Realist Thought from Weber to Kissinger* (Baton Rouge: Louisiana State University Press, 1986) covers the development of what has been described as classical realism and discusses some of the major thinkers in the field. Kenneth Waltz provides an overview of neo-realism in his article 'Realist Thinking and Neorealist Theory', in the *Journal of International Affairs*, 44:1 (1990).

For a very interesting alternative view see Alexander Wendt, 'Anarchy is What States Make of it: The Social Construction of Power Politics', in *International Organization*, 46:2 (1992). This article gives a very useful analysis of the 'Constructivist' perspective. See also Alexander Wendt, *Social Theory of International Politics* (Cambridge: Cambridge University Press, 1999). A very useful broader evaluation of different theoretical positions is contained in N. J. Rengger, *International Relations, Political Theory and the Problem of Order: Beyond International Relations Theory?* (London: Routledge, 2000)

In their study *Identity, Migration and the New Security Agenda in Europe* (London: Pinter, 1993) Ole Waever, Barry Buzan, Morten Kelstrup, and Pierre Lemaitre develop the new concept of 'Societal Security'. This provides an original perspective for studying the kind of non-state aspects of security which have affected Europe in the post-cold war period.

Very useful discussions about the changing nature of security can be found in Ronnie D. Lipschutz (ed.), *On Security* (New York: Columbia University Press, 1995), C. Bretherton and G. Ponton (eds.), *Global Politics: An Introduction* (Oxford, Blackwell, 1996); T. Terriff, S. Croft, L. James, and P. Morgan, *Security Studies Today* (Cambridge: Polity Press, 1999); K. Krause and M. C. Williams, (eds.), *Critical Security Studies: Concepts and Cases* (London: UCL Press, 1997);

and S. Lawson (ed.), *The New Agenda for Global Security: Cooperating for Peace and Beyond* (St Leonards: Allen and Unwin,1995).

For a discussion of different theoretical approaches to security and some of the contemporary debates about security studies see Steve Smith, 'The Increasing Insecurity of Security Studies: Conceptualising Security in the Last Twenty years', *Contemporary Security Policy*, 20:3 (Dec. 1999).

WEB LINKS

The Internet provides a wide range of information on international security. The best guide to the use of the Internet on this subject is William M. Arkin, *The Internet and Strategic Studies* (The Center for Strategic Education, the Paul Nitze School of Advanced International Studies, Johns Hopkins University, 1998). Arkin has also produced *The US Military Online: A Directory for Internet Access to the Department of Defense* (Brassey's, 1998) and a nuclear homepage for the National Resources Defense Council (NRDC), 'The Internet and the Bomb: A Research Guide to Policy and Information about Nuclear Weapons' (1997, **www.nrdc.org/nrcdpro/nuclear**). The CNN documentary site **www.cnn.com/specials/cold war** covers every aspect of the cold war conflict and its eventual ending. **www.islandnet.com/~emerald/vpc/readings/ nukeuse.htm#list** covers the sixteen main nuclear crises during the cold war. **www.the-times.co.uk/onlinespecials/wordonline** provides a very useful archive for students interested in issues relating to international and global conflict. Also go to **www.sosig.ac.uk/roads/ subject-listing/World-cat/conflictsec.html** for the international conflict and security page of the Social Science Information Gateway, an invaluable resource for on-line information.

13 International political economy in an age of globalization

Ngaire Woods

READER'S GUIDE

This chapter examines what drives actors and explains events in the international economy. The first section outlines the history of the post-war economy. The history helps to explain why and how international political economy (IPE) has become so central to the study of international relations (section two). Amidst the many actors, processes and events in the recent history of the world economy, it is not obvious where one might begin to analyse IPE. This task is made easier by three traditional approaches to IPE which outline for us specific actors, processes, and levels of analysis. These are the liberal, mercantilist, and Marxist traditions which are outlined in section three. More recently, IPE has become divided by an argument about the uses (and abuses) of 'rational choice' analysis. What 'rational choice' means and the argument about how it should be used are both explored in section four. These perspectives and tools for studying IPE are then applied to help us to make sense of globalization and its impact on the world economy. Section five defines globalization and examines two core questions it poses for IPE. Is globalization diminishing

I would like to acknowledge the very helpful comments of Tim Barton (OUP), and Benno Teschke on the earlier draft of this chapter.

the role of states in the world economy? What explains the very different kinds of impact globalization has on different kinds of states? Globalization poses new challenges for all states (and other actors) in the world economy. It is often assumed that international institutions and organizations will manage these challenges. In the final section of the chapter we return to the theories of IPE in order to answer the question: what role can we expect institutions to play in managing globalization?

Introduction

International political economy (IPE) is about the interplay of economics and politics in world affairs. The core question of IPE is: what drives and explains events in the world economy? For some people this comes down to a battle of 'states versus markets'. However, this is misleading. The 'markets' of the world economy are not like local street bazaars in which all items can be openly and competitively traded and exchanged. Equally, politicians cannot rule the global economy much as they might like to.

World markets and countries, local firms, and multi-national corporations which trade and invest within them are all shaped by layers of rules, norms, laws, organizations, and even habits. Political scientists like to call all these features of the system 'institutions'. International political economy tries to explain what creates and perpetuates institutions and what impact institutions have on the world economy.

The post-war world economy

The institutions and framework of the world economy have their roots in the planning for a new economic order which took place during the last phase of the second world war. In 1944, policy-makers gathered at **Bretton Woods** in the United States to consider how to resolve two very serious problems. First, they needed to ensure that the Great Depression of the 1930s would not happen again. In other words, they had to find ways to ensure a stable global monetary system and an open world trading system (see Box 13.1). Second, they needed to rebuild the war-torn economies of Europe.

At Bretton Woods three institutions were planned in order to promote a **new world economic order** (see boxes 13.2 and 13.4). The International Monetary Fund was created to ensure a stable exchange rate regime and the provision of emergency assistance to countries facing a temporary crisis in their balance of payments regime. The International Bank for Reconstruction and Development (IBRD and later called the World Bank) was created to facilitate private investment and reconstruction in Europe. The Bank was also charged with assisting 'development' in other countries, a mandate which later became the main reason for its existence. Finally, the **General Agreement on Trade and Tariffs** (GATT) was signed in 1947 and became a forum for negotiations on trade liberalization.

The 1944 plans for the world economy, however, were soon postponed when in 1945 the United States made its first priority the containment of the Soviet Union. Fearing the rise of communism in war-ravaged Europe, the United States took a far more direct role than planned in reconstructing Europe and managing the world economy. The US announced the **Marshall Plan** in 1947 which

Box 13.1 Planning the post-war economy and avoiding another Great Depression

The Great Depression had been greatly exacerbated, if not caused, by 'beggar thy neighbour' economic policies. In the late 1920s and 1930s, governments all over the world tried to protect themselves from economic crisis by putting up trade barriers and devaluing their currencies. Each country believed that by doing this they would somehow manage to keep their economy afloat while all around them neighbouring economies sank. The Great Depression demonstrated that this did not work. At the end of the war, the challenge was to create a system which would prevent this, in particular by ensuring:

- a stable exchange rate system

- a reserve asset or unit of account (such as the gold standard)

- international capital flows could be controlled

- the availability of short-term loans to countries facing a temporary balance of payments crisis

- rules to keep economies open to trade

Box 13.2 The Bretton Woods institutions: the IMF and the World Bank

Both the IMF and the World Bank were established in 1946 after wartime negotiations held at Bretton Woods in the United States with headquarters (opposite one another) in Washington DC. **The IMF** was created to promote international monetary co-operation and resolve the interwar economic problems (see Box 13.1), although several of these functions ended when the Bretton Woods system broke down in 1971 (see Box 13.3). The IMF now has a membership of 183 countries each of whom contributes a quota of resources to the organization (proportionate to the size of their economy) which also determines their percentage of voting rights and the amount of resources to which they can have automatic access. Since the 1980s, the IMF has become an institution offering financial and technical assistance to developing and transition economies. The terms on which countries receive assistance include the government having to commit to undertake specific 'conditions' or policy reforms, called 'conditionality'. (see **www.imf.org**). What we now call the **World Bank** started out as the International Bank for Reconstruction and Development (IBRD), an agency to foster reconstruction in war-torn Europe as well as development in the rest of the world. It has since become the world's largest source of development assistance, providing nearly $16 billion in loans annually to eligible member countries, through the IBRD, the International Development Association (IDA), the International Finance Corporation (IFC) and the Multilateral Guarantee Agency (MIGA). As with the IMF, the World Bank requires members to whom it lends to undertake specific reforms within their economy. Most recently this has included requiring borrowing governments to demonstrate their commitment to reducing poverty within their countries. With the exception of IDA (which is funded by donations), the World Bank's resources come from its issue of bonds in the capital markets. These bonds are backed up by guarantees provided by the governments who belong to the institution (See **www.worldbank.org**).

directed massive financial aid to Europe and permitted the US to set conditions on it. The planned gold standard was replaced by the dollar standard which the US managed directly, backing the dollar with gold. Unsurprisingly, by the time the IMF, the World Bank, and the GATT began to function in the 1950s, they were distinctly Western bloc organizations which depended heavily on the United States.

US support for the Bretton Woods system began to change when weaknesses emerged in the US economy. After 1965 the US widened its costly military involvement in Vietnam, and also started to spend more money on public education and urban redevelopment programmes in the United States (President Johnson's 'Great Society' programmes), and all this without raising taxes. The damage was dramatic. As prices rose within the US economy, the competitiveness of US goods and services in the world economy dropped. Likewise, confidence in the US dollar plummeted. Firms and countries turned away from the dollar and the US capacity to back its

currency with gold was brought into question. Meanwhile, other countries in the world economy were enhancing their position. European allies were

Box 13.3 The 'Bretton Woods system' and its breakdown

What was the 'Bretton Woods system'?

At the Bretton Woods Conference in 1944 it was agreed that all countries' currencies would be fixed at a certain value. They became fixed to the dollar, and the US government promised to convert all dollars to gold at $35 per ounce. In other words, exchange rates were anchored to a dollar–gold standard. In the Bretton Woods system, any country wanting to change the value of its currency had to apply to the IMF for permission. The result was very stable and unchanging exchange rates.

What was the 'breakdown' of the system?

In August 1971 the US government announced that it was suspending the convertibility of the dollar to gold at $35 per ounce. This removed gold from the dollar–gold standard and paved the way for major currencies to 'float' instead of staying at fixed values. The US also announced in August 1971 that it was adding a 10 percent surcharge on import duties (to improve trade balance by curtailing imports which were flooding into the US, and to try to stem the outflow of dollars to the rest of the world), hence

also turning back the Bretton Woods ideal of maintaining open trade in times of economic difficulty.

Was this a sign of declining US hegemony?

Over a decade after the breakdown of the Bretton Woods system, leading academics debated whether the change reflected a loss in US power, or was indeed an exercise of its power. For some, the breakdown of the system was an exercise of US leadership: 'the US hegemon smashed the BW system in order to increase its own freedom of economic and political action' (Gowa 1983). Others argued that the US had lost its capacity to maintain the system, but explained that a regime could nevertheless survive without the hegemon (Keohane 1984). At the heart of the debate was a disagreement about whether co-operation in the international political economy depends upon one state being both capable and willing to set and enforce the rules of the game, with powers to abrogate and adjust those same rules. This debate about the nature of cooperation continues today in competing explanations of international institutions (see last section of this chapter).

---

benefiting from the growing and deepening economic integration in Europe. By the late 1960s, the development of the EEC provided a springboard for European policy-makers to diverge from US positions, such as over NATO military exercises and support for the gold standard. In Asia, the phenomenal success of export-led growth in Japan and in newly industrializing countries such as South Korea and Taiwan created a new challenge to US trade competitiveness, and a new agenda for trade negotiations.

Facing these pressures, the United States changed the rules of the international monetary system in 1971. The government announced that it would no longer convert dollars to gold at $35 per ounce, and that it was imposing a 10 per cent surcharge on import duties (to improve trade balance by curtailing imports which were flooding into the US, and to try to stem the outflow of dollars to the rest of the world). These actions broke the Bretton Woods system. This was not the only change in the world economy in the 1970s.

In the 1970s, the period of high growth enjoyed

after the second world war came to an abrupt end, leaving very high inflation. Further compounding the problem, the first oil crisis in 1973 plunged the world economy into **stagflation** (a combination of economic stagnation or low growth and high inflation). In the monetary system, the role of the IMF collapsed when the Bretton Woods system broke down in 1971 and the major industrialized countries failed to find a way to co-ordinate their exchange rate policies within the IMF framework. Instead, the major currencies floated and industrialized countries began to discuss monetary issues among themselves in groups such as the 'Group of Seven' (comprising the United States, Japan, Germany, the United Kingdom, France, Italy, and Canada) which first met in 1975.

In the trading system, co-operation had steadily grown in negotiations under the auspices of the GATT (see Box 13.4). However, in the 1970s, the gains which had been made in reducing tariff barriers especially among industrialized countries were reversed by policies of **new protectionism**. As each country grappled with stagflation, many introduced new forms of barriers (or 'non-tariff barriers'), in particular to keep out the new competitive imports from successful developing countries. An egregious example of the new protectionism was the Multifiber Arrangement of 1973 which placed restrictions on all textile and apparel imports from developing countries, blatantly violating the GATT principle of non-discrimination.

The new protectionism in industrialized countries

Box 13.4 The post-war trading system, the GATT, and the WTO

The General Agreement on Trade and Tariffs (GATT) was an interim agreement signed in 1947 in the expectation that it would be superseded by an international trade organization. A permanent trade organization was not created until 1994, and so for four decades the interim GATT continued to exist as an arrangement among 'contracting parties' backed up by a very small secretariat based in Geneva and a minuscule budget. In essence the GATT was a forum for trade negotiations, with numerous rounds of talks culminating in the very successful Kennedy Round of 1962–1967 where breakthroughs were made in the reduction of trade barriers among industrialized countries. However, when protectionism flourished in the 1970s, the GATT proved powerless to restrain powerful members such as the United States and European countries from restricting trade (e.g. Multifiber Arrangement 1974 restricting textile imports) and abusing the many exceptions and safeguards written into the agreement. The GATT also functioned as a forum for dispute settlement (i.e. upholding trade rules), however, it was both slow and impotent in this regard, constrained by the need for consensus on any decision regarding disputes. The GATT was replaced by the World Trade Organization as a result of agreements forged in the last round of GATT talks, the Uruguay Round (1986–94). Established on 1 January 1995, the WTO's functions include: administering WTO trade agreements; forum for trade negotiations; handling trade disputes; monitoring national trade policies; technical assistance and training for developing countries; cooperation with other international organizations. It is located in Geneva with a secretariat staff of 500 (see **www.wto.org**).

---

further fuelled the anger of developing countries who in the 1970s launched a concerted campaign in the United Nations General Assembly for a **New International Economic Order** (NIEO). The determination of developing countries to alter the rules of the game was further bolstered by the success of OPEC oil-producing developing countries in raising oil prices in 1973. The agenda of the NIEO covered trade, aid, investment, the international monetary and financial system, and institutional reform. Developing countries sought better representation in international economic institutions, a fairer trading system, more aid, the regulation of foreign investment, the protection of economic sovereignty, and reforms to ensure a more stable and equitable financial and monetary system.

The NIEO campaign was unsuccessful for several reasons. The United Nations General Assembly (UNGA) was an obvious institution for developing countries to choose in making their case since, unlike the IMF or World Bank, it offers every country one vote. However the UNGA had no power to implement the agenda of the developing countries. Furthermore, although many industrialized countries were sympathetic to the developing countries' case in the 1970s, these governments did not act on the agenda in the 1970s and by the 1980s a new set of governments with a distinctly less sympathetic ideology had come to power in the United States, the United Kingdom, and Western Germany.

The 1980s opened with a shift in US economic policy. In 1979 the US Federal Reserve dramatically raised interest rates. This action was taken to stem inflation by contracting economic activity in the United States. However, the reverberations in the rest of the world economy were immediate and extensive. During the 1960s and 1970s US and European policies had facilitated the rapid growth of **global capital markets** and financial flows. In the 1970s these flows were further buoyed by the investments of oil-producers who needed to find outlets for the vast profits made from the oil price rise of 1973. The money found its way to governments in developing countries who were offered loans at knock-down prices. The rise in interest rates in 1979 was an abrupt wake-up call to both borrowers and creditors (many of whom were US-based banks), who suddenly realized that many of the loans could not be repaid. The IMF was immediately called in to prevent any developing country defaulting on these loans, since it was feared that such a default would causes a global financial crisis.

The **debt crisis** meant that the IMF's role in the world economy became largely that of ensuring that indebted countries undertook 'structural adjustment' in their economies. **Structural adjustment** meant immediate measures to reduce inflation, government expenditure, and the role of the government in the economy, including trade liberalization, privatization, and deregulation. These 'neoliberal' policies were in marked contrast to the Keynesian analysis which had prevailed until the 1980s during the decades of growth in the world economy. **Keynesians** (named after economist John Maynard Keynes) believe that governments should play an active and interventionist role in the economy in order to ensure both growth and equity. By contrast, the new 'neoliberalism' sought to roll back the state and the role of government, leaving decisions about allocation, production and distribution in the economy to the market. By the late 1980s the term **Washington consensus** was being used, sometimes pejoratively to imply that these policies were mainly a reflection of US interests.

By the end of the cold war, the institutions created in 1944 still existed but their role in the world economy was very different to that which had been planned at Bretton Woods. The World Bank had become a development agency making loans to developing countries. The GATT had failed to stem the new protectionism of the 1970s and to meet the aspirations of developing countries, but trade negotiations undertaken in the 1980s (the final GATT round) created a new **World Trade Organization** (WTO) which could better enforce trade rules. The IMF had lost its role at the heart of the international monetary and financial system created at Bretton

Woods but had gained a new role with the debt crisis of the 1980s. Meanwhile, the policy challenges associated with these changes, along with globalization and increasing interdependence meant that IPE became central to the study of international relations.

Key points:

- Immediately after the Second World War international institutions were created to facilitate co-operation in the world economy and to ensure countries did not pursue the kinds of beggar-thy-neighbour policies which had contributed to the **Great Depression**.

- The onset of the cold war postponed the operation of these institutions, as the United States stepped in directly to manage the reconstruction of Europe and the international monetary system based on the dollar.

- The **Bretton Woods** system of managed exchange rates and capital flows operated until its breakdown in 1971 when the US announced it would no longer convert the dollar to gold.

- The 1970s were marked by a lack of international economic co-operation among the industrialized countries who floated their exchange rates and indulged in new forms of **trade protectionism**.

- Developing countries' dissatisfaction with the international system came to a head in the 1970s when they pushed unsuccessfully for a new international economic order.

- The debt crisis in the 1980s thrust the IMF into a new role, causing its work to overlap with that of the World Bank.

- Trade negotiations in the 1980s produced a new world trade organization.

The rise of IPE in the study of international relations

Until the 1970s, IPE was a rather neglected subject. Although a lively debate about the causes of under-development and inequality among nations was being undertaken by scholars in the Marxian tradition, this rarely permeated into the central concerns of mainstream international relations. Rather, as described in Chapter 4, the political and strategic challenges of the cold war consumed industrialized and developing countries alike, with the latter confronting decolonization and need to build post-colonial state structures.

By the early 1970s, international relations began to change as the events outlined above forced policy-makers and scholars alike to pay more attention to economic affairs. The power and predominance of the United States had been unquestioned in the Western alliance from the end of the Second World War, until the Vietnam debacle and economic strain began to erode **US hegemony** in the late 1960s. Suddenly economic relations seemed to present obstacles and constraints to foreign and domestic policy alike.

In the academic study of international relations, the challenge posed by the growing economic interdependence of countries, in particular for the United States, was analysed in a seminal 1968 book by Richard Cooper who wrote of the need for greater co-ordination and co-operation among states in a world in which every nation's balance of payments was becoming vulnerable to a greater number of shocks and disturbances. This work was soon elaborated by Professor Cooper's Harvard colleagues Robert Keohane and Joseph Nye whose second study of economic interdependence and its implications for international relations became a core text in the subject (Keohane and Nye 1977). These works all suggested that a new era of international relations was dawning. In particular, they proposed that international relations could no longer be conceived as a geo-strategic competition among states. Economic issues, new channels of communication, and new patterns of co-operation were all giving rise to a new world politics in which international political economy and international institutions would play a crucial role. The description aptly described the new diplomacy of détente emerging from the 1972 superpower summit.

Another kind of summit diplomacy which also took place in the 1970s was that between **North** (the industrialized countries) and **South** (developing countries). These negotiations were underpinned by a different kind of thinking and scholarship about IPE. The developing countries' push for reform of the international economic system reflected **dependency theory** and structuralist theories of international economic relations which highlighted negative aspects of interdependence. In particular, these theorists were concerned to identify aspects of the international economy and institutions which impeded the possibilities of development in the South. Their central concern was to answer why so many countries within the world economy remained under-developed, in spite of the promises of modernization and global growth. The most sympathetic official 'Northern' answer to these concerns was voiced in the **Brandt Report** 1980, the findings of a group of high-level policy-makers who had been asked to examine how and why the international community should respond to the challenges of interdependence and development.

Since the 1970s, international political economy has continued to advance as a core subject of international relations. As will be discussed below, globalization and its causes and effects on states and international co-operation and institutions has become a defining feature of international relations. Furthermore, the **end of the cold war** ended many of the geo-strategic aspirations and influence the West had enjoyed. The challenge of integrating the former Eastern bloc countries into the world system was soon defined primarily as one of economic transformation and integration. Equally, an explosion of tribal, religious, and ethnic conflict on the edges of Europe (in the former Yugoslavia) as well as in Africa (such as in Rwanda), in Asia (such as in Indonesia), and in the Middle East forced analysts more closely to examine the links between poverty, economic stagnation, and the indebtedness of countries on the one hand, and intra-state conflict on the other.

Box 13.5 The rise of IPE in international relations

1965   US government expenditure increases as America's involvement in Vietnam widens and expenditure on the 'Great Society' programmes at home commence.

1968   Cooper's *The Economics of Interdependence* is published.

1969   US multinational corporations produce approximately $140 billion worth of goods i.e. more than any single economy except the USA and USSR; many of the largest place over half their total assets abroad, earning more than half their total earnings overseas.

1971   President Nixon suspends the convertibility of the US dollar into gold (which leads to the floating of major currencies in 1973).

1972   US–USSR Summit fuels hopes for new economic opportunities afforded by *détente;*

President Nixon's visit to China;

European Economic Community further strengthened by accession of UK, Ireland, and Denmark.

1973   OPEC's oil embargo increases price of energy and bolsters developing countries' aspirations to use commodity power.

1973   Tokyo Round of GATT trade talks takes place as Japan and newly industrializing countries emerge as major competitors in world trade, sparking a new protectionism in industrialized countries.

1974   Developing countries push for a New International Economic Order in the General Assembly of the United Nations, including greater control over multinational corporations; and reform of global economic institutions.

1977   Keohane and Nye's *Power and Interdependence: World Politics in Transition* is published.

Finally, the end of the cold war thrust international institutions into the limelight. The United Nations, the IMF, the World Bank, and the newly created World Trade Organization all became an important focus of study and attention, providing further grist to the mill of IPE scholars concerned with examining the causes, determinants, and impact of international institutions and cooperation among states in economic affairs.

Key Points:

- The rise of IPE as a prominent subject in international relations was due in part to the decline in US economic preponderance and the challenge to traditional notions of power and security posed by the US failure in Vietnam.

- The rise in importance of IPE was also associated with new economic challenges in the 1970s, including the OPEC oil price rise and the developing countries' push for a NIEO which highlighted theories focusing on the nature and structure of the world economy.

- The economic challenges of both the end of the cold war and globalization have further underlined the centrality of IPE in the study of international relations.

Traditional approaches to IPE: liberal, mercantilist, and Marxian

There are several competing explanations for the nature of the institutions and system described above. A slightly old-fashioned way to describe the competing approaches to IPE is to divide the subject into liberal, mercantilist, and Marxist traditions. These labels still usefully describe different economic traditions each of which has a particular moral and analytical slant on global economic relations.

The liberal tradition

The liberal tradition is the **free market** one in which the role of voluntary exchange and markets is emphasized both as efficient and as morally desirable. The assumption is that free trade and the free movement of capital will ensure that investment flows to where it is most profitable to invest (hence, for example, flowing into underdeveloped areas where maximal gains might be made). Free trade is crucial for it permits countries to benefit from their comparative advantages. In other words, each country can exploit its own natural advantages, resources, and endowments and gain from specialization. The economy is oiled by freely exchangeable currencies and open markets which create a global system of prices which, like an **invisible hand**, ensures an efficient and equitable distribution of goods and services across the world economy. Order in the global economy is a fairly minimal one. The optimal role of governments and institutions is to ensure the smooth and relatively unfettered operation of markets. It is assumed that governments face a wide range of choices in the world system and likewise vis-à-vis their own societies and populations. This means that governments who fail to pursue 'good' economic policies do so because decision-makers are either too corrupt or too ignorant of the correct economic choices they might make.

The mercantilist tradition

The mercantilist tradition stands in stark contrast to the liberal one. Mercantilists share the presumptions of **realists** in international relations. They do not focus on individual policy-makers and their policy choices but rather assume that the world economy is an arena of **competition among states** seeking to maximize relative strength and power. Simply put, the international system is like a jungle in which each state has to do what it can to survive. For this reason, the aim of every state must be to maximize its wealth and independence. States will seek to do this by ensuring their self-sufficiency in key strategic industries and commodities, and by using trade protectionism (tariffs and other limits on exports and imports), subsidies, and selective investments in the domestic economy. Obviously, within this system some states have more power and capability than others. The most powerful states define the rules and limits of the system: through hegemony, alliances, and **balances of power**. Indeed, stability and order will only be achieved where one state can play the role of hegemon, or in other words, is willing and able to create, maintain and enforce basic rules. Amidst this, the economic policies of any one government will always be subservient to its quest to secure the external and internal sovereignty of the state.

The Marxian tradition

The Marxian tradition also sees the world economy as an arena of competition, but not among states. Capitalism is the driving force in the world economy. Using Marx's language, this means that world economic relations are best conceived as a **class struggle** between the 'oppressor and the oppressed'. The oppressors or capitalists are those who own the 'means of production' (trade and industry). The oppressed are the working class. The struggle

---

Box 13.6 Traditional perspectives on IPE

Liberal

The world economic has potential to be a seamless global marketplace in which free trade and the free movement of capital shape the policies of governments and economic actors. Order would be achieved by the 'invisible hand' of competition in the global marketplace.

Mercantilist

As an arena of inter-state competition, the world economy is one in which states seek to maximize their wealth and independence vis-à-vis other states. Order is achieved only where there is a balance of power or hegemony.

Marxist

The world economy is best described as an arena of capitalist competition in which classes (capitalists and workers) and social groups are in constant conflict. Capitalists (and the states they are based in) are driven by the search for profits, and order is achieved only where they succeed in exacting the submission of all others.

---

between the two arises because capitalists seek to increase their profits and this requires them to exploit ever more harshly the working class. In international relations this description of 'class relations' within a capitalist system has been applied to describe relations between the **core** (industrialized countries) and **periphery** (developing countries), and the unequal exchange which occurs between the two. **Dependency theorists** (who have focused mainly on Latin America) describe the ways classes and groups in the 'core' link to the 'periphery'. Underdevelopment and poverty in so many countries is explained as the result of economic, social, and political structures within countries which have been deeply influenced by their international economic relations. The global capitalist order within which these societies have emerged is, after all, a global capitalist order which reflects the interests of those who own the means of production.

It becomes clear in contrasting these traditions of thinking about international economic relations that each focuses on different actors and driving forces in the world economy, and that each has a different conception of what 'order' means and what is necessary to achieve it.

Comparing the different traditions also highlights three different **levels of analysis**: the structure of the international system (be that international capitalism or the configuration of power among states in the system) the nature of a particular government or

competition within its institutions, and the role of interest groups and societal forces within a country. At each of these levels of analysis we need to ask: what drives the actors concerned and therefore how might we explain their preferences, actions and the outcomes which result? In answering this question we enter into more methodological preoccupations which today divide the study of IPE.

Key points

- The labels liberal, mercantilist, and Marxian usefully describe three different analytical and moral starting points for the study of global economic relations.

- The liberal (or neo-liberal) perspective presents global economic order as the result of the relatively unfettered operation of markets, guided by rational individual policy-makers.

- Mercantilists describe the world economy as an arena for inter-state competition for power.

- Marxian analyses focus on the structure of the world capitalist economy, proposing that state and government choices simply reflect the preferences of those who own the means of production.

- The three traditional perspectives usefully highlight different actors, different processes, and different 'levels of analysis' in the study of IPE.

New approaches to IPE

IPE is divided by the different normative concerns and analytical questions which are highlighted by the traditions outlined above. Equally, the discipline is now subject to a lively **methodological debate** about how scholars might best explain policies and outcomes in IPE. In essence this debate is about whether you can assume what states' (and other actors') preferences and interests are. If you can, then rational choice (or 'neo-utilitarian') approaches to IPE make sense. However, if you open up the question as to why and how states and other actors come to have particular preferences, then you are pushed towards approaches now often labelled 'social constructivism'.

What is 'rational choice' or neo-utilitarianism?

In the United States, the study of IPE has become dominated by a 'rational choice' or neo-utilitarian approach. This borrows economic concepts to explain politics. Instead of exploring the ideas, personalities, ideologies, or historical traditions which lie behind policies and institutions, rational choice focuses on the **incentive structure** faced by those making decisions. It is assumed that actors' interests and preferences are known or fixed and that actors can make strategic choices as to how best to promote their interests. The term 'rational choice' is a useful one to describe this approach since it proposes that even though a particular policy may seem stupid or wrong, it may well have been rational. 'Rational' in this sense means that for the actor or group concerned, this was the optimal choice given the specific incentives and institutional constraints and opportunities that existed at the time (see Ch. 9).

The rational choice approach can be applied to any one of the several levels of analysis highlighted above: to individual decision-makers, to interest groups, to sectors in the economy, to parts of the government bureaucracy, or indeed to states in their interactions with other states. Let us examine two different applications of rational choice.

Political economy: the application of rational choice to groups within the state

Rational choice has been applied to interest groups and their influence on IPE in what has been called a **political economy approach**. This approach has its roots in explanations of trade policy which focus on interest groups. More recent applications have attempted to explain why countries adapt in particular ways to changes in the world economy. The analysis proceeds on the assumption that governments and their policies are important but that the policies and preferences of governments reflect the actions of specific interest groups within the economy. These groups may emerge along class or sectoral lines, indeed, the assumptions of rational choice are applied to explain how particular groups within the economy emerge and what their goals and policy preferences are. Furthermore, rational choice provides a framework for understanding the coalitions these groups enter into and their interactions with other institutions. For example, in explaining developing country responses to the debt crisis of the 1980s, a political economy approach starts out by examining the effect of **economic shocks** such as high interest rates and structural adjustment on interest groups. By demonstrating that the power of some interests (such as those working in the export sector) has increased and the power of others (such as those working in industries relying on diminishing state subsidies) has diminished, the approach proffers an explanation for radical shifts in government policies.

Institutionalism: the application of rational choice to states

A different application of rational choice lies in the **institutionalist approach** to IPE (about which more is said in the last section). This approach applies the assumptions of rational choice to states in their interaction with other states. Drawing on theories of **delegation and agency**, it offers an explanation as to why institutions exist and for what purposes. The core assumption is that states create international institutions and delegate power to them in order to maximize utility within the constraints of world markets and world politics. Frequently this comes down to the need to resolve collective-action problems. For example, states realize that they cannot achieve their goals in areas such as trade or environment, unless all other states also embark upon a particular course of action. Hence, institutions are created to ensure that there is no defection or free-riding, and the collective goal is achieved.

Social constructivism

In contrast to rational choice analysis, other approaches to international political economy assume that policies within the world economy are affected by **historical** and **sociological factors**. Much more attention is paid to the ways in which actors formulate preferences, as well as to the processes by which decisions are made and implemented (see Ch. 11). In other words, rather than assuming that a state or decision-maker's preferences reflect rational choices within given constraints and opportunities, analysts in a broader tradition of IPE, examine the beliefs, roles, traditions, ideologies and patterns of influence which shape preferences, behaviour and outcomes. More will be said below about social constructivism in general. Let us focus here on one particular variant.

The neo-Gramscian approach: a radical variant

One strand of thinking about how and why actors have particular preferences draws on the ideas and insights of Italian political theorist Antonio Gramsci to highlight the role of **politics**, **law**, **culture**, and **knowledge** generally in shaping the preferences and policies of actors. The starting point here is that interests, actions, and behaviour in the world economy all take place within a structure of ideas, culture, and knowledge. We cannot simply assume that the preferences of actors within the system reflect objectively definable competing 'interests'. Rather, the way actors understand their own preferences will depend heavily upon prevailing beliefs and patterns of thinking in the world

economy, many of which are embodied in institutions. The question this poses is: whose interests and ideas are embodied in the rules and norms of the system?

For neo-Gramscians the answer to the question 'in whose interest' lies in **hegemony**. The dominant power within the system will achieve goals not just through coercion but equally by ensuring the consent of other actors within the system. This means that dominant powers will promulgate institutions, ideologies and ideas all of which help to persuade other actors that their best interests converge with those of the dominant power. For example, neo-Gramscians interpret the dominance of neo-liberalism since the 1980s as a reflection of US interests in the global economy, successfully projected through structures of knowledge (it became the dominant paradigm in top research universities), through institutions (such as the IMF which became forceful proponents of neo-liberal policy prescriptions), and through broader cultural beliefs and understandings (the very language of 'free' market contrasting with restricted or repressive regimes).

New approaches to IPE highlight a powerful debate within the subject about whether we should treat states' interests and preferences as given or fixed. We return to this question in the final section of this chapter. There we will examine why states form institutions and what role such institutions might play in managing globalization. First, though we need to establish what is globalization in the world economy and what are its implications.

Key points:

- Rational choice explains outcomes in IPE as the result of actors' choices which are assumed always to be rationally power- or utility-maximizing within given particular incentives and institutional constraints.

- Political economy applies rational choice to sub-state actors such as coalitions, interest groups, and bureaucrats in order to explain outcomes in a state's foreign economic policy.

- Institutionalists apply rational choice to states in their interactions with other states in order to

Box 13.7 Examples of new approaches to IPE

Institutionalist

Institutionalists regard the world economy as an arena of inter-state co-operation. They see the core actors as governments and the institutions to whom they delegate power and the key driving forces as rational choice at the level of the state motivated by the potential gains from co-operation. For institutionalists the key condition for order is the existence of international institutions which permit co-operation to continue.

Political economy

For political economists the world economy is characterized by competition among vested interests within different kinds of states and the core actors are interest groups formed within the domestic economies of the states. The key driving force is rational choice at the level of groups within the domestic economy responding to changes in the international economy. Political economists are not concerned with theorizing about the conditions necessary for international order.

Neo-Gramscians

Neo-Gramscians see the world economy as an overarching structure of knowledge, ideas, and institutions which reflects the interests of dominant actors and within which competition takes place. They regard the structure of the system itself as vital in understanding the identities and preferences of the actors. For neo-Gramscians the key driving force of the system is capitalist competition, which is then constrained by the need of the powerful to gain the consent of the less powerful. Neo-Gramscians view simple dominance by one state as an insufficient condition for international order. Instead, they believe that hegemony requires control over the structures of knowledge and ideas as well.

explain international cooperation in economic affairs.

- Constructivist approaches pay more attention to how governments, states, and other actors construct their preferences, highlighting the role of identities, beliefs, traditions, and values in this process.

- Neo-Gramscians highlight that actors define and pursue their interests within a structure of ideas, culture, and knowledge which itself is shaped by hegemonic powers.

The globalization debate in international political economy

The nature and impact of globalization is the subject of profound debate within IPE (as within other areas of international relations discussed in this book). The term globalization is used to refer to at least three different sets of forces processes in the world economy. **Internationalization** describes the increase in economic transactions across borders which has been taking place since the turn of the century but which some argue has undergone a quantitative leap in recent decades. **The technological revolution** is a second aspect of globalization, describing the effect of new electronic communication which permits firms and other actors to operate globally with much less regard for location, distance, and borders. Finally, **liberalization** describes the policies undertaken by states which have made a new global economy possible. This includes both the rules and institutions created by powerful states to facilitate a new scale of transnational economic activity in certain sectors (but by no means all) of the world economy. It also includes the policies of smaller and less powerful states in the system who, by liberalizing trade, investment, and production, have integrated into the world economy.

In IPE several competing claims are made about globalization. For example, while some scholars argue that globalization is nothing new, others posit that globalization is dramatically diminishing the role of the state (see Ch. 1). Still others claim that globalization is exacerbating inequalities and giving rise to a more unequal and unjust world. To make sense of these different arguments and the evidence adduced to support them, it is worth thinking about the approaches to IPE covered in previous sections, for they help to identify key differences in emphasis which give rise to conflicting interpretations of globalization. For example, sceptics who deny that globalization is transforming world politics tend to focus on the 'internationalization' element of globalization (see Box 13.8). They can then draw upon evidence which throws into doubt whether the number

---

> ## Box 13.8 **Three aspects of globalization**
>
> - Internationalization describes the increase in transactions among states reflected in flows of trade, investment, and capital (cf the argument that these flows have not increased as much as is claimed: UNDP 1997). The processes of internationalization have been facilitated and are shaped by inter-state agreements on trade, investment, and capital, as well as by domestic policies permitting the private sector to transact abroad.
>
> - The technological revolution refers to the way modern communications (Internet, satellite communications, high-tech computers) made possible by technological advances have made distance and location less important factors not just for government (including at local and regional levels) but equally in the calculations of other actors such as firms' investment decisions or in the activities of social movements.
>
> - Liberalization describes government policies which reduce the role of the state in the economy such as through the dismantling of trade tariffs and barriers, the deregulation and opening of the financial sector to foreign investors, and the privatization of state enterprises.

of transactions taking place among states has indeed risen (UNDP 1997), and make the argument that there is 'nothing new' in the growing interdependence of states. By contrast, **liberal enthusiasts** of globalization focus on technological innovation and the non-political' 'objective' forces which are shrinking the world economy. They argue that this is creating a less political, more efficient, more unified world order. Their optimism and emphasis is rejected by critics who focus on liberalization and the role of states' policies in shaping globalization. These critics highlight the role of powerful states in setting the rules of the new globalized international economy, and their increasing influence over less powerful states.

In the next section the debate between sceptics and enthusiasts is examined in asking whether globalization is eroding the sovereignty and power of the state. The subsequent section examines the differences in the impact of globalization on strong and weak states.

Is globalization diminishing the role of the state in the world economy?

The globalists

'A global economy is emerging' claim those who depict a world in which multinational trade, production, investment, and financing moves in and out of countries ever more easily. The 'globalists' tell us that as a result, governments and **states are losing** their capacity to **control** economic interactions. This is partly because the quantity and rapidity of flows make it more difficult for governments to regulate trade, investment, or capital. Equally important is the fact that firms and investors can more easily take their business elsewhere puts new constraints on governments trying to retain and encourage investment. The argument here is that **footloose modern businesses** will simply exit from a country if a government does not pursue liberalizing policies which foster corporate profitability and flexibility. For this reason governments are under pressure to reduce taxes and to cut back state expenditure on health,

education, pensions, and so forth. When it comes to regulating international business, governments are permitting investors themselves to set the rules and these private actors are doing so though new private international networks and self-regulatory agencies. In sum, states are losing power in a global economic order in which state borders and governments are less influential. This eventuality is, of course, embraced by those interpreting it from a 'liberal' (see Box 13.6) starting point.

The sceptics

Countering the 'global economy' view are a variety of sceptics who highlight flaws in the argument and the evidence proposed by those who argue that the state is losing power. The proposition that states are under pressure to cut taxes and reduce expenditure is attacked by scholars who examine data of industrialized countries and demonstrate that the evidence does not back up this claim. Nor does the evidence suggest that MNEs relocate investment to areas where there are lower wages and lower taxes. Rather contemporary research into actual patterns of MNE investment discloses that in the new knowledge-intensive economy, factors such as the availability of skilled and semi-skilled labour, good infrastructure and proximity to market are crucial ingredients to choices of location. The conclusion drawn from this evidence is that the **role of states is not eroding**. To the contrary, states and government still have a very important and substantial role to play in a successful economy.

New constraints on states

While sceptics knock holes in some of the arguments about the erosion of state power in the face of global multinational enterprises, other aspects of globalization do constrain all states. In particular, the fact that billions of dollars can flood in—or out—of a country overnight sets a new constraint on monetary policy and opens up **new vulnerabilities** in the financial sectors of all countries. In other words governments have to be very careful in managing interest rates and **managing or floating exchange rates**. Equally they need robust domestic banking and financial

---

Box 13.9 **The globalists**

'The nation state has become an unnatural, even dysfunctional, unit for organizing human activity and managing economic endeavour in a borderless world. It represents no genuine, shared community of economic interest; it defines no meaningful flows of economic activity'.

Kenichi Ohmae, *The Borderless World: Power and Strategy in the Interlinked Economy* (London: Harper Collins, 1990, rep. 1994), 24.

Box 13.10 The sceptics

'the closer we looked the shallower and more unfounded became the claims of the more radical globalists. In particular, we began to be disturbed by three facts: first, the absence of a commonly accepted model of the new global economy and how it differs from previous sates of the international economy; second . . . the tendency casually to cite examples of internationalization of sectors and processes as if they were evidence of the growth of an economy dominated by autonomous global market forces; and third, the lack of historical depth, the tendency to portray current changes as both unique and without precedent and firmly set to persist long into the future'

Paul Hirst and Grahame Thompson, *Globalization in Question* (Cambridge: Polity Press, 1996), 2.

systems to weather the onslaught or recession of a tidal wave of capital. The punishment for poor policy is instantaneous and devastating. Furthermore, as the **Asian financial crisis** of 1997 (see Box 13.11) showed, it is not only the culprit country who bears the punishment. The financial crisis in Asia highlighted the potential vulnerability of all countries to massive inflows and outflows of capital. It also underlined that some states suffer the impact of globalization more than others.

The impact of globalization on different kinds of states

The Asian crisis highlights that states have different capacities to respond to globalization. Even though all states in the region were affected by the crisis,

Box 13.11 The Asian financial crisis

In 1997 a financial crisis spread rapidly throughout Asia. It began in March of that year when difficulties in Thailand's financial institutions sparked a tremendous outflow of capital from the country. As capital fled, the Thai currency was weakened, forcing the government to float (after which the currency depreciated by 15–20 per cent). Within weeks the crisis in Thailand spread to Indonesia, Malaysia, and the Philippines in what the IMF referred to as a 'currency meltdown'. By the end of 1997 Thailand, Indonesia, and Korea had all been forced to turn to the IMF to negotiate access to funds in return for agreement to abide by tough conditions setting out reforms they had to promise to undertake within their economies. Meanwhile, the Malaysian government undertook its own policies of adjustment and imposed capital controls in order to stem the damaging effects of capital mobility. Scholars are still debating the relative advantages and disadvantages of these strategies. A vigorous debate has focused in particular on whether the IMF was right to impose tough conditions, with some arguing that in so doing it exacerbated a deep recession in the region.

The debate about the IMF's intervention in the Asian financial crisis

The IMF applied heavy conditions to the Asian countries on the grounds that the causes of the crisis were 'mainly domestic': 'these countries became victims of their own

success' . . . which . . . 'led domestic and foreign investors to underestimate the countries' economic weaknesses'. 'The fundamental policy shortcomings' . . . of policymakers in these countries included permitting a 'buildup of overheating pressures','pegged exchange regimes', and 'weak management and poor control of risks, lax enforcement of prudential rules and inadequate supervision' in the financial system.

(IMF, *World Economic Outlook*, 1998, 3)

Critics argued that the IMF applied the wrong policies: 'the particular set of models that the IMF uses have been inappropriate in many situations, e.g. in the crisis in East Asia, it is clear that their forecasts concerning the countries affected by the crisis were badly misguided.'

(Joseph Stiglitz in Christopher Gilbert and David Vines (eds.), *The World Bank: Policies and Structure*, Cambridge: Cambridge University Press, 2000)

And that the IMF had no right to impose these kinds of conditions: 'The legitimate political institutions of the country should determine the nation's economic structure and the nature of its institutions. A nation's desperate need for short-term financial help does not give the IMF the moral right to substitute its technical judgements for the outcomes of the nation's political process'.

(Marty Feldstein, 'Refocusing the IMF', *Foreign Affairs* 77 (1998), 24).

their responses suggested that some enjoyed more choice or 'sovereignty' than others. Indonesia, Thailand and Korea turned to the IMF for assistance conditional on a raft of policies mostly defined in Washington DC. Meanwhile Malaysia formulated its own policies of adjustment and imposed policies such as capital controls which were greatly disapproved of in Washington DC. Although globalists and sceptics treat all states as equal in their arguments about globalization, it is worth questioning this.

One way to think about the impact of globalization is to distinguish between **strong states** and **weak states**. At the extreme end strong states are those which shape the rules and institutions which have made a global economy possible: we have already seen the way US policies shaped the creation, implementation, and breakdown of the Bretton Woods system. A more general description of strong states is that they can control—to some degree—the nature and speed of their integration into the world economy. Into this category we might place not only relatively strong industrialized countries, but also developing countries such as Brazil, Malaysia, China, Iraq, and Iran. In all of these cases globalization is having a powerful effect, as is evidenced by the restructuring of national and private industries in industrialized countries, the past decade of economic liberalization in Brazil, and in a radically different way, through international coercive interventions in Iraq. Yet at the same time, in each of these countries there are **high protective barriers** in important sectors of the economy, and serious debate about capital controls and the regulation of international capital. The capacity of these countries to control their integration into the world economy is doubtless related to their size, resources, geostrategic advantages, and economic strength. However, interestingly, it seems also to be related to their national ideology and the domestic power of the state. One thing that all 'strong states' have in common is that they guard with equal ferocity their independence in economic policy, foreign policy, human rights and security issues.

'Weak states' by contrast suffer from a lack of choice in their international economic relations. They have little or no influence in the creation and enforcement of rules in the system and they have exercised little control over their own integration into the world economy. For example, in the aftermath of the debt crisis of the 1980s, many 'weak states' opened up their economies, liberalized and deregulated, more as a result of coercive liberalization than of democratic policy choice. In the 1990s, this continued with what an international economist called **forced harmonization**, whereby, for instance, in the case of trade negotiations on intellectual property, developing countries were coerced into an agreement which transfers 'billions of dollars' worth of monopoly profits from poor countries to rich countries under the guise of protecting the property rights of inventors' (Rodrik, 1999).

Distinguishing among states according to their capacity to shape and respond to globalization is vital in analysing the impact on IPE. The example of the international financial system demonstrates that some states, in particular the United States, are rule-makers in the world economy, while less powerful states are rule-takers.

Key points:

- Globalization poses some new constraints for all states, including the most powerful. In particular, the emergence of global capital markets means that all governments have to be cautious in their choice of exchange rate and interest rate policies.

- On other issues of economic policy, wealthier and more powerful countries are less constrained by globalization than is portrayed by the globalists. This is because the firms and investors whom governments are keen to attract are not solely concerned with levels of taxation and wages. They are equally concerned with factors such as the skills of the workforce, the provision of infrastructure, and proximity to markets.

- At the international level the more powerful states in the system get to set (and enforce) many of the rules of the new global economy.

- Weaker states in the system not only must accept and abide by rules set by others, but also have little capacity to manage their integration into the world economy. These states do not enjoy much sovereignty or independence of policy choice in the global economy.

International institutions in the globalizing world economy

We have seen that globalization is increasing interdependence among states, it is also increased global interconnectedness, and the capacity of some states to influence others. The **Asian financial crisis** exhibited all three of these changes. The countries of Asia had 'liberalized' into global capital markets (with much encouragement from the United States and other industrialized countries) and soon became recipients of large inflows of short-term capital. As soon as confidence in Thailand faltered, reactions were instantaneously transmitted to investors (through the new communications networks). The subsequent debacle of 1997 demonstrated how quickly, easily and devastatingly a financial crisis in one country can spill over into others.

The management of the Asian financial crisis led some policy-makers to call for stronger, more effective international institutions, including a capacity to ensure better information and monitoring, deeper co-operation, and regulation in the world economy. At the same time however, others argued that the crisis revealed the problems and flaws of existing international institutions and the bias or interests which they reflect (see box 13.11). These positions echo a larger debate in IPE about the nature and impact of institutions in the world economy. This debate is important in helping us to determine what role international institutions might play in managing the new problems and challenges arising from globalization.

Competing accounts of institutions echo the differences in approaches to IPE already discussed in later sections (and see Ch. 14). Institutionalists (or neo-liberal institutionalists, as Chapter 9 refers to them) tell us that states will create institutions in order better to achieve gains through policy coordination and co-operation. However, several preconditions are necessary for this to occur. These conditions include: the existence of mutual interests that make joint gains from co-operation possible; a long-term relationship among a relatively small number of actors; and reciprocity according to

agreed-upon standards of appropriate behaviour. Under these conditions, institutionalists argue that states will agree to be bound by certain rules, norms, or decisions of international organizations. This does not mean that the most powerful states in the system will always obey the rules. Rather, institutions affect international politics because they open up new reasons to co-operate, they permit states to define their interests in a more co-operative way, they foster negotiations among states as well as compliance with mutually agreed rules and standards.

The institutionalist account offers reasons for a certain kind of optimism about the role international institutions will play in managing globalization. Institutions will smooth over many gaps and failures in the operation of markets, and serve to ensure that states make genuinely rational and optimizing decisions to co-operate. Globalization will be managed by existing institutions and organizations and indeed, new institutions will probably also emerge. Globalization managed in this way will ensure that the world economy moves more towards the **liberal** model (see Box 13.6) and that both strong and weak states benefit. Although there have been many protests about international organizations (see Box 13.12), these are the result of people misunderstanding the advantages of free trade and free movements of capital in the world economy.

Realists (and neo-realists in particular) disagree with institutionalists. Realists reject the idea that institutions emerge primarily as a solution to universal problems or market failures. They argue that international institutions and organizations will always reflect the interests of dominant states within the system. When these states wish to co-ordinate policies with others, they will create institutions. Once created, however, these institutions will not (as the institutionalists argue) transform the way states define and pursue their interests. Institutions will be effective only for as long as they do not diminish the power of dominant states vis-à-vis other states.

Let us consider what this means in practice. Take a

Box 13.12 Anti-globalization protests against international organizations

The WTO ministerial conference in Seattle, November 1999 (the day before):

'They are pouring into Seattle this weekend in vans and on buses, by air and on foot—the college students and the church groups, the environmental campaigners, the Teamsters, Ralph Nader, Chinese dissidents and the man who became a hero in France for defacing a McDonald's. All of them say they are outraged at the growing power of a group few even heard about five years ago, the World Trade Organization. And so, with tens of thousands massing, they are planning to turn what initially sounded like the yawner of all international meetings—a gathering of trade ministers from 135 countries to start the "Millennium Round" of trade liberalization talks—into the Woodstock of the era of globalization.'

(New York Times, 28 Nov. 1999)

The IMF and World Bank annual meeting in September 2000:

'Dozens of anticapitalism protesters and police were injured today as violent clashes erupted near the Prague Congress Centre where the International Monetary Fund and World Bank are holding their annual meeting. Eyewitnesses said that protesters threw stones, bottles and at least three petrol bombs at a police cordon 300m from the conference centre.'

(The Times, 26 Sep. 2000)

state deciding whether to sign up to a new trade agreement or support the decision of an international organization. The institutionalists argue that policy-makers will consider the **absolute gains** to be made from the agreement, including the potential longer-term gains such as advancing a more stable and credible system of rules. The neo-realists by contrast, argue that policy-makers will primarily be concerned with **relative gains**. In other words, they will ask, 'Do we gain more from this than other states?' (rather than, 'Do we gain from this?'). If other states stand to gain more, then the advantages of signing up are outweighed by the fact that the power of the state will be diminished vis-à-vis other states (see Ch. 9).

For realists, co-operation and institutions are heavily constrained by underlying calculations about power. Having signed an agreement or created an international organization, a powerful state will not necessarily be bound by it. Indeed, if it got in the way of the state's interests (defined in realist terms), a powerful state will simply sweep the institution aside. The implications for globalization and its impact on weak states are rather grim. International institutions, including organizations such as the IMF, the World Bank, and the WTO, will manage globalization but in the interests of their most powerful members. Institutions will only accommodate the needs and interests of weaker states where in so doing they do not diminish the dominant position of powerful states. From a realist perspective, it follows that **anti-globalization protesters in Seattle and Prague** were right to argue that the international institutions do not work for the interests of poor and developing countries. However, the realists are equally certain that such protests will have little impact.

This interpretation of international institutions is rebutted not only by institutionalists, but by those who delve into the ways ideas, beliefs, and interactions shape the behaviour of states. In an earlier section, we explored the **neo-Gramscian approach**, let us now introduce the broader constructivist approach which has been mentioned in other chapters of this book (see Ch. 11).

Constructivists reject the idea that institutions reflect the 'rational' calculations of states either within inter-state competition (realists) or as part of a calculation of longer-term economic advantage and benefits from co-operation (institutionalists). In fact what constructivists reject is the idea that states' interests are objectively definable and fixed. Instead, they argue that any one state's interests are affected by its **identity** as a state and that both its interests and identity are influenced by a **social structure of interactions**, **normative ideas**, and beliefs. If we cannot assume that states have a particular identity or interest prior to their interactions, then the institutionalists are wrong to assume that institutions emerge as rational responses to the needs of markets, trade, finance, and the like. Equally, the realists are wrong to assume that institutions can only be reflections of power politics. To quote constructivist Alex

Box 13.13 **The debate about institutions**

	Institutionalist (or 'neo-liberal institutionalist')	Realist (or 'neo-realist')	Constructivist
Under what conditions will states create international institutions?	For mutual gains (rationally calculated by states).	Only where relative position vis-à-vis other states is not adversely affected.	Institutions arise as a reflection of the identities and interests of states and groups which are themselves forged through interaction.
What impact do institutions have on international relations?	Expands the possible gains to be made from co-operation.	Facilitate the co-ordination of policies and actions but only insofar as this does not alter the balance of power among states.	Reinforce particular patterns of interaction, and reflect new ones.
The implications for globalization	Institutions can manage globalization to ensure a transitioin to a more 'liberal' economy (see Box 13.6).	Institutions will 'manage' globalization in the interests of dominant and powerful states.	Changing patterns of interaction and discourse will reflect in institutional reponses to globalization.

Wendt 'anarchy is what states make of it' (see Ch. 11). In other words, identities and interests are more fluid and changing than realists permit. Through their interactions and discourse, states change and these changes can reflect in institutions.

Constructivism and the neo-Gramscian approach highlight actors and processes involved in globalization which are neglected in realist and institutionalist accounts and have important ramifications for institutions. For example, the protesters against the WTO, the IMF, and the World Bank can be construed as part of an ongoing dialogue which affects states in several ways. The international attention to these issues places them on the agenda of international meetings and organizations, it also puts pressures on political leaders and encourages interest groups and pressures to form within the state. As a result the beliefs, ideas and conceptions of interest in international relations change and this can shift the attention, nature and functions of international institutions. On this view, globalization is not just a process affecting and managed by states. **Several**

other actors are involved, both within and across societies, including international institutions which play a dynamic role. The governance or management of globalization is shaped by a mixture of interests, beliefs and values about how the world works and how it ought to be. The existing institutions doubtless reflect the interests of powerful states, however, these interests are the products of the way states interact and are subject to reinterpretation and change.

Key points:

- Institutionalists argue that international institutions will play an important and positive role in ensuring that globalization results in widely spread benefits in the world economy.

- Realists and neo-realists reject the institutionalist argument on the grounds that it does not account for the unwillingness of states ever to sacrifice power relative to other states.

- Constructivists pay more attention to how governments, states and other actors construct their preferences, highlighting the role that state identities, dominant beliefs, and ongoing debates and contestation plays in this process.

Conclusions

Globalization increases the challenges faced by all actors in the world economy: states, firms, transnational actors, and international organizations. Strong states are trying to shape institutions to manage financial crises, powerful NGOs, and globalizing firms. Weak states are trying to survive increasingly precarious and changeable economic circumstances. Common to all states is the search for greater stability and predictability, although governments disagree over how and where this should be achieved. One layer of governance this chapter has not examined is that of regional organizations and institutions (see Ch. 21). The fact that in recent years virtually every state in the world has joined at least one regional trade grouping underscores the search for new ways to manage globalization. At the same time, regionalism highlights the scepticism of many states about international institutions, and their fears that institutions are too dominated by powerful states, or unlikely to constrain them. The result is an emerging multi-layered governance in the world economy. At each level (international, regional, and state) the core issues debated in this chapter arise. These include: whose interests are served by the institution? What forces are shaping it? Who has access to it? Whose values does it reflect? Globalization casts a spotlight on these arrangements since the transformations occurring in the world economy are being powerfully shaped by them.

Questions:

1 In what ways did the Bretton Woods framework for the post-war economy try to avoid the economic problems of the inter-war years?

2 What was the 'breakdown in the Bretton Woods system'?

3 Did a loss of US hegemony cause the breakdown of the Bretton Woods system?

4 Are there any issues on which mercantilists agree with liberals?

5 What is different about the Marxian and mercantilist depictions of power in the international economy?

6 Does rational choice theory explain more about outcomes than actors' preferences?

7 At what levels of analysis is rational choice applied in IPE?

8 In what way do neo-Gramscians invoke structure in their explanation of IPE?

9 What are the different processes referred to by the term globalization?

10 Why do sceptics doubt that globalization is transforming IPE?

11 What vulnerabilities faced by states in the globalizing economy did the Asian financial crisis demonstrate?

12 How can we explain the different impact globalization has on different states?

13 How and why do institutionalists argue that institutions change the behaviour of states?

14 For whom might the realist account of institutions and globalization be cheerful reading?

15 Why might social constructivists pay more attention to anti-globalization protests than either realists or institutionalists?

GUIDE TO FURTHER READING

Cox, Robert W. (ed.), *The New Realism: Perspectives on Multilateralism and World Order* (New York: St Martin's, 1997), essays which present and put into context critical, neo-Gramscian and neo-Marxian analyses of international political economy.

Held, David, Anthony McGrew, David Goldblatt, and Jonathan Perrator, *Global Transformations: Politics, Economics and Culture* (Cambridge: Polity Press, 1999), a vital resource book on the empirical evidence of globalization in all aspects of international relations.

Helleiner, Eric, *States and the Reemergence of Global Finance: from Bretton Woods to the 1990s* (Ithaca: Cornell University Press, 1994), an excellent account of the ways in which the policies of states have shaped the emergence of the international financial system.

Frieden, Jeffrey and David A. Lake (eds), *International Political Economy: Perspectives on Global Power and Wealth* (New York: St. Martin's Press, 2000), introduces core texts from each approach to international political economy with very useful editors' introductions.

Gilpin, Robert, *Global Political Economy* (New Jersey: Princeton University Press, 2001), presents a realist account of globalization and its impact on national policies and domestic economies, as well as an overview of developments in trade, finance, and money in the world economy.

Katzenstein, Peter, Robert Keohane, and Stephen Krasner, 'International Organization and the State of World Politics', *International Organization* (Autumn 1998), an excellent review article of key developments in the study of international relations and international political economy.

Odell, John S., *Negotiating the World Economy* (Cornell University Press, 2000), focuses on trade negotiations and highlights the effects of changing market conditions, negotiator beliefs and biases, and domestic politics on strategies and outcomes.

Rodrik, Dani, *The New Global Economy and Developing Countries: Making Openness Work* (Washington DC: Overseas Development Council, 1999), good critical anaysis of the advantages and disadvantages of globalization for developing countries.

Strange, Susan, *Mad Money* (Manchester University Press, 1998), a very readable somewhat idiosyncratic tour of contemporary policy and academic debates about the international financial system.

14 International regimes

Richard Little

READER'S GUIDE

Liberal institutionalists and realists are engaged in a major debate about the role played by regimes—delineated areas of rule-governed activity—in the international system. Both schools acknowledge that although the international system is anarchic (without a ruler) in structure, it has never been anomic (without rules). Interest in regimes surfaced in the 1970s along with concern about the ability of the United States to sustain the economic regimes formed after the Second World War. What are the essential features of regimes? There is no straightforward answer to this question, and the chapter uses a definition, typology, and examples to reveal their complex character. Under what circumstances do regimes come into existence? This question forms the nub of the debate. Although liberal institutionalists and realists use very similar tools of analysis—drawing on microeconomics and game theory—they arrive at very different conclusions. Are the conclusions compatible? The question remains contested.

Introduction

An important dimension of globalization has been the establishment of worldwide regimes to foster rule-governed activity within the international system. Although international rule-governed activity predates the emergence of the modern state it is only during the course of the twentieth century that regimes can be regarded as a global phenomenon, with states becoming enmeshed in increasingly complex sets of rules and institutions which regulate international relations around the world. There is

I am grateful to the editors for their comments and for the discussion of the chapter by the members of the International Politics Research Group at the Department of Politics, University of Bristol.

now no area of international intercourse devoid of regimes, where states are not circumscribed, to some extent or other, by the existence of mutually accepted sets of rules. Indeed, many regimes are so firmly embedded in the system that they are almost taken for granted. Most people do not consider it at all surprising, for example, that we can put a letter in a post-box, and be confident that it will be delivered anywhere in the world from the Antarctic to Zimbabwe, or that we can get on an aeroplane and expect to fly unmolested to our destination at any point across the globe. Only when something goes drastically wrong, as, for example, in 1983, when the Soviet Defence Forces shot down the civilian South Korean airliner, KAL 007, killing all 269 persons on board, is our attention drawn to the fact that international relations are, in practice, extensively regulated by complex regimes negotiated and policed by states.

It may seem unremarkable, at first sight, that states have established regimes to ensure that mail gets delivered anywhere in the world and that aircraft can fly safely from one country to another. The advantages of such regimes appear so obvious that it would be more remarkable if such regimes had not been put in place. However, the existence of these regimes becomes rather more surprising when it is acknowledged how much controversy can surround the formation of regimes, how contentious established regimes can prove to be, and how frequently attempts to form regimes can fail. It is because the use of regimes to promote everything from arms control to the enhancement of global economic welfare seems to be so self-evidently beneficial, that the difficulty of securing regimes requires some explanation. Sadly, there is no agreed answer. Although few doubt that regimes are an important feature of the contemporary international system, as this chapter aims to demonstrate, theorists in the field of international relations are deeply divided about how and why regimes are formed and maintained.

The concept of a regime is relatively recent, coming into common parlance in the 1970s. But students of international relations have been interested in rules regulating the behaviour of states since the origins of the state system. The contemporary focus on regimes, therefore, needs to be seen as the current phase in a long, essentially European tradition, that can be traced back at least to the time of Hugo Gro-

tius (1583–1645), the Dutch jurist, who is often identified as 'the father of international law'. Despite the length of this tradition, the status of international law has always been questioned within jurisprudence, that branch of legal studies investigating the theoretical or philosophical foundations of the law. It is argued by a significant school of thought that a legal system can only be established and enforced within the centralized structures provided by the state. Although this view has been contested, it is by no means obvious how law is formulated and maintained within the anarchic or decentralized structures of the international system. Indeed, the impression has sometimes been given that the international system is essentially **anomic**—devoid of agreed rules and norms. And this impression has been reinforced by the popular association of **anarchy** with a breakdown of order, rather than with a system lacking a centralized structure of government.

The problematic status of rules in the anarchic international system was largely overlooked, however, in the era after 1919, when the institutionalized study of international relations was established. In the wake of the traumatic First World War there was a widespread hope that states would now be willing to establish world order on the basis of international law, although little thought was given to whether there was any theoretical justification for such optimism. In any event, the hope was dashed when international law was so flagrantly violated during the 1930s. The approach came to be dismissed as idealistic; and after the Second World War, few accepted any longer that order in the international system could rest on international law. Moreover, theorists were preoccupied with working out the implications of moving from a multipolar system into the bipolar nuclear era.

By the 1970s, however, a series of global developments, to be discussed below, encouraged theorists in International Relations to return to the long-established theoretical concern with the role of rules in the international system. This new breed of theorists, primarily American, in the first instance, were and remain self-consciously interested in developing International Relations as a social science. They have spawned an enormous literature (Levy 1995), with research, now no longer confined to the United

States (Rittberger 1993), that is becoming increasingly complex and diverse.

It is argued in this chapter that regime theorists are located within two broad schools of thought: liberalism and realism (see Chs. 7 and 8). Although Hasenclever, Mayer and Rittberger (1997; 2000) see this division as an oversimplification, it does allow us to trace the broad parameters of the debate precipitated by the attempts to understand regimes. The chapter also aims to illustrate that in the attempt to accommodate the growth of regimes both realism and liberalism have had to move beyond their traditional frames of reference.

Realism is considered to have been in the past sceptical or uninterested in international law, while regime theorists in the liberal camp, identified as liberal institutionalists, have accepted key assumptions made by neo-realists, and these, along with their social science credentials, are considered to have moved them beyond the established liberal tradition (see Ch. 9). But despite the shared theoretical assumptions, liberal institutionalists and realists adhere to very different assessments of regimes (see Box 14.1). Liberal institionalists focus on the way that regimes allow states to overcome the obstacles to **collaboration** imposed by the anarchic structure of the international system. Realists, by contrast, are interested in the way that states use their power capabilities in situations requiring **co-ordination** to

influence the nature of regimes and the way that the costs and benefits derived from regime formation are divided up. Only after studying the two approaches can we assess to what extent these different approaches can be rendered compatible. Collaboration and co-ordination are seen to constitute different approaches to co-operation.

Why did IR theorists begin to focus on regime formation in the 1970s? One factor was the growing awareness that, at least in the context of the West, the United States had played the role of **hegemon** during and after the Second World War. The term derives from the Greek, meaning leader, and it was argued that the United States had been able to play this role because of its preponderance of power in the international system. During this era, the United States, because of its hegemonic position, had been able to establish and maintain a complex array of economic regimes in the West; the regimes had played a vital role in the growing prosperity which had taken place after the Second World War. By the 1970s, however, partly because of the economic success in Europe and Japan, and partly because of the disastrous policy in Vietnam, the capacity of the United States to maintain its hegemonic status was put in doubt. It is unsurprising that an interest in regimes coincided with this development.

Liberal institutionalists and realists both reacted to this development, but in very different ways. Liberal

---

Box 14.1 Liberal institutional v. realist approaches to the analysis of regimes

Common assumptions

1. States operate in an anarchic international system
2. States are rational and unitary actors
3. States are the units responsible for establishing regimes
4. Regimes are established on the basis of co-operation in the international system
5. Regimes promote international order

Competing assessments

Liberal institutionalists

1. Regimes enable states to collaborate
2. Regimes promote the common good
3. Regimes flourish best when promoted and maintained by a benign hegemon
4. Regimes promote globalization and a liberal world order

Realists

1. Regimes enable states to co-ordinate
2. Regimes generate differential benefits for states
3. Power is the central feature of regime formation and survival
4. The nature of world order depends on the underlying principles and norms of regimes

institutionalists were concerned about the possibil ity that at a point in time when the need for regimes was becoming increasingly urgent, the loss of hegemonic status by the United States could mean that it would be increasingly difficult to establish these regimes. Realists argued, by contrast, that if the United States did lose its hegemonic status, then there would be a shift in the balance of power and the liberal principles governing the regimes established by the United States would start to be challenged more effectively by Third World states wanting a new set of regimes established on the basis of different norms and principles. Although their analysis pointed in different directions, both liberal institutionalists and realists acknowledged the need for a more sophisticated theoretical understanding of regimes.

Key points

- Regimes represent an important feature of globalization.
- There is a growing number of global regimes being formed.
- The term, and social science approaches to, regimes is recent but fits into a long-standing tradition of thought about international law.
- The onset of detente, loss of hegemonic status by the US, and the growing awareness of environmental problems sensitized social scientists to the need for a theory of regimes.
- Liberal institutionalists and realists have developed competing approaches to the analysis of regimes.

The nature of regimes

Before presenting the theoretical approaches to regimes developed by the liberal institutionalists and the realists, it is necessary to present their common conceptualization of an international regime in more detail and illustrate the conceptualization with an examination of some of the major areas of world politics now regulated by regimes.

Conceptualizing regimes

Although it may be helpful in the first instance to think of regimes as rule governed behaviour, a more complex conceptualization has been developed by theorists working in the field of international relations. This conceptualization can be captured by a definition and typology of regimes.

Defining regimes

Although there are many definitions of a regime, they all take a similar form and the one that has become most widely used was formulated in the early 1980s by Stephen Krasner. It very effectively encapulates the complexity of the phenomenon (see Box 14.2). Krasner's definition reveals that a regime is more than a set of rules; it presupposes quite a high level of institutionalization. Indeed, regime theorists have been criticized for doing no more than introducing new terminology to characterize the familiar idea of an international organization. Regime theorists acknowledge that international organizations can be embraced by regime theory, but they insist that their approach encompasses much more. The parameters of regime theory can be demonstrated by examining a simple typology of regimes.

Classifying regimes

One simple but useful classification, establishes a typology of regimes along two dimensions (Levy 1995). The vertical dimension highlights the formality of a regime (see Box 14.3). A regime can be associated with a highly formalized agreement or even the emergence of an international organization. But, at the other extreme, a regime can come into existence

Box 14.2 Defining regimes

Regimes are identified by Krasner (1983: 2) as *'sets of implicit or explicit principles, norms, rules, and decision making procedures around which actors' expectations converge in a given area of international relations'*.

An example of a regime

This is a complex definition and it needs to be unpacked. Krasner has done this, by drawing on the General Agreement on Trade and Tariffs (GATT) for illustrative purposes. The GATT was initially an agreement drawn up in 1947 and reflected the belief of its signatories that it was necessary to establish an organization which would be responsible for the regulation of international trade. In fact, it proved impossible to establish such an organization at that time, and the GATT acted as a substitute. It was given a secretariat and a general director responsible for carrying out the preparatory work for a series of conferences where the signatories of the GATT met and reached agreements intended to foster international trade. In 1994, after the Uruguay Round of negotiations, it was agreed that it was now time to move beyond GATT and establish a formal World Trade Organization as originally intended. Krasner was writing before this development took place, but it does not affect the utility of the GATT as an illustration of what is meant by a regime.

The four defining elements of a regime

1. **Principles** are represented by coherent bodies of theoretical statements about how the world works. GATT operated on the basis of liberal principles which assert that global welfare will be maximized by free trade.
2. **Norms** specify general standards of behaviour, and identify the rights and obligations of states. So, in the case of the GATT, the basic norm is that tariffs and nontariff barriers should be reduced and eventually eliminated. Together, norms and principles define the essential character of a regime and these cannot be changed without transforming the nature of the regime.
3. **Rules** operate at a lower level of generality to principles and norms, and they are often designed to reconcile conflicts which may exist between the principles and norms. Third World states, for example, wanted rules which differentiated between developed and underdeveloped countries.
4. **Decision-making procedures** identify specific prescriptions for behaviour, the system of voting, for example, which will regularly change as a regime is consolidated and extended. The rules and procedures governing the GATT, for example, underwent substantial modification during its history. Indeed, the purpose of the successive conferences was to change the rules and decision-making procedures (Krasner, 1985: 4–5).

in the absence of any formal agreements. Historically, informal agreements between states have been established on the basis of precedence. The horizontal axis then focuses on the extent to which states expect or anticipate that their behaviour will be constrained by their accession to an implicit or explicit set of agreements.

If there are no formal agreements, and no convergence in the expectation that rules will be adhered to, then it is clear that there is **no regime** in existence. On the other hand, even in the absence of formal rules, there can be an expectation that informal rules will be observed, suggesting the existence of a **tacit regime**. By contrast, it is also possible to identify situations where formal rules have been brought into existence, without any expectation that they will be observed, indicating the existence of a **dead-letter regime**. Finally, there are **full-blown regimes**, where there is a high expectation that formal rules will be observed (see Box 14.3). Examples of these different types of regimes will be given in the next section. This is not the only way that regimes can be classified. It is possible, for example, to classify them on a geographical basis: **bilateral**, **regional**, and **global**.

Globalization and international regimes

During the course of the nineteenth and twentieth centuries the advancement of technology made it possible for more and more people to come into increasingly close contact across the globe. Worldwide communication is now instantaneous in many areas of activity. Not every aspect of this

Box 14.3 A typology of regimes

Convergence of expectations

Low	High	Formality
No regimes	Tacit regimes	Low
Dead-letter regimes	Full-blown regimes	High

This is not the only way that regimes can be classified. It is possible, for example, to classify them on a geographical basis: **bilateral**, **regional**, and **global**.

Source: Adapted from Levy (1995).

globalization of world politics is beneficial however. Technology has made it possible to see and talk to people on the other side of the globe and to fill the supermarkets, at least those in the wealthy sectors of the global economy, with increasingly exotic commodities from all round the world. But it has also made it possible to build weapons with the potential to wreak global devastation and to pollute the atmosphere with chemicals that could possibly have irreversible and certainly very dangerous global consequences. Our impact on the world we inhabit is both frightening and exciting. But either way it is becoming increasingly apparent that if we are all to benefit rather than suffer from globalization, it is essential to manage the process. No one thinks that this task will be easy; pessimists doubt that it is even possible. Regime theorists, on the other hand, see grounds for optimism. They believe that survival depends upon our capacity to regulate global activity by means of regimes; and, as we demonstrate in this section, although not in any comprehensive fashion, the evidence indicates that states can establish regimes across a wide range of activities.

Security regimes

Although security regimes are primarily a twentieth century phenomenon, permitting states to escape from the security dilemma (see Ch. 12), it is possible to identify earlier examples. The Concert of Europe, for instance, constitutes a regime formed by the conservative states of post-Napoleonic Europe to counter future revolution and conflict. At the same time, on the other side of the Atlantic, the British and Americans established the Rush Bagot agreement in 1817 to demilitarize the Great Lakes. But whereas the tacit regime in Europe began to decay soon after it was formed, the full-blown bilateral regime in North America became steadily stronger until eventually, the long border between Canada and the United States was permanently demilitarized.

Regular attempts to establish full-blown security regimes, however, only started to proliferate during the twentieth century, particularly after the onset of the cold war. But the effectiveness of these regimes has often been questioned. Jervis (1983*b*), for example, argued that some of the major regimes, such as SALT 1 (1972) and SALT 2 (1979) designed to bring the arms race between the United States and the Soviet Union under control, were effectively dead-letter regimes. Despite the prolonged negotiations and detailed agreements, there was no evidence that they brought the arms race under control, because neither superpower expected the other to desist from developing new weapons technology.

Nevertheless, there are arms control agreements which do seem to have established fragile security regimes. The Partial Test Ban Agreement of 1963, has undoubtedly encouraged a prohibition of atmospheric testing. And the 1968 Nonproliferation Agreement continues to act as a restraint on any increase in the number of nuclear weapons states. The agreement has been signed by over 170 states— the vast majority of states in the international system. Although fragile, the regime enjoys a very broad measure of support, so that any state breaching the agreement will confront widespread opposition.

Environmental regimes

As scientists have become increasingly aware of the damage being done to the global environment, so the importance attached to the need to establish environmental regimes has steadily risen. Oil pollution, global warming, and damage to the ozone layer are the issues which have attracted most public attention, but regimes have been established in a wide range of areas in the attempt to protect the global environment. For example, international conventions to save endangered plant and animal species can be traced back to the 1970s, and a comprehensive Convention on Biological Diversity came into force in December 1993. There have also been attempts since the mid-1980s to regulate the international movement of hazardous waste material, with the Basle Convention establishing a complete ban in March 1993 on the shipping of hazardous waste from countries in the developed world to countries in the underdeveloped world.

Despite the wide range of agreements intended to protect the global environment, it is unlikely that many will consolidate into full-blown regimes. Instead, there is a perennial danger that they will degenerate into dead-letter regimes. Even agreements which do prove to be effective may not turn out to have solved the original problem. For example, attempts to deal with the ozone layer can be traced back to 1977 when the United Nations Environment Programme established a Co-ordinating Committee to deal with the ozone layer. With the accumulating evidence about the damage being caused by pollution, concerned states eventually agreed to implement the Montreal Protocol in 1989 which put forward a raft of measures to protect the ozone layer. Despite the rapid implementation of these measures, scientific evidence in 1996 indicated that the situation was continuing to deteriorate. The initial measures were proving to be inadequate and it was clear that the rules established in the original regime would need to be extended. Even more depressing for environmentalists was the 1995 conference on climate change which met in Berlin. Although the problem of global warming was addressed, it proved impossible to agree on measures which might deal with the issue.

Communication regimes

Prior to the nineteenth century, the most significant areas of international communication regulated by regimes were concerned with shipping and postal services. With further developments in technology

however, the need for regimes extended to the international regulation of aircraft and telecommunications. Collectively, the resulting network of regimes can be seen to provide an essential part of the infrastructure underpinning the modern international economy. Without this infrastructure, international trade, foreign investment, and the worldwide monetary system could not be sustained.

The need for a regime governing shipping can be traced back to the technological developments in ship building in the sixteenth century that permitted in subsequent centuries an extraordinary expansion of international trade. This expansion could not have gone on, however, without the consolidation of a tacit regime ensuring, among other things, the freedom of movement for shipping on the high seas and the right of innocent passage through territorial waters under the sovereign jurisdiction of maritime states. The bulk of international trade continues to be transported by sea and these central norms remain in place. However, key rules operating under these norms have undergone change. In the third United Nations Conference on the Law of the Sea (UNCLOS) which went on from 1973 to 1982, for example, territorial waters were extended from three to twelve miles, but this new rule left the underlying norm about innocent passage undisturbed.

During the nineteenth and twentieth centuries a range of organizations have emerged to manage and strengthen the regimes which secure international communications. In 1863 the major industrial states came together to establish a standardized system for postal communication and this was formalized with the establishment of the Universal Postal Union in 1874. In 1865, the International Telegraph Union came into existence to regulate telegraphic communication and this evolved into the International Telecommunications Union in 1932 to cope with the increasingly complex technological developments in communications. Finally it is worth making reference to a range of organizations which have helped to maintain the regimes which operate in the areas of shipping and aircraft. The International Maritime Organization and the International Civil Aviation Organization, for example, are both specialized agencies of the United Nations and are responsible for the emergence of a large number of conventions which reinforce the regimes which can be observed in these crucial areas of international transport.

Economic regimes

It is often argued that the regimes in the economic arena are more firmly entrenched than in any other. As already noted, however, the international economy could not function in the absence of the infrastructure provided by the communication regimes. The two sets of regimes are inextricably interlinked. Indeed, over the last decade, as the regimes governing the international economy have become ever more firmly established, the underlying liberal principles governing these regimes have started to impinge on the communication regimes. This development is reflected in the growing attempts to open postal services, telecommunications, and national airlines to greater competition. This development will lead to a modification of the basic principle underlying these regimes which in the past has always favoured state control over the rules regulating these activities (Zacher and Sutton 1996).

It is not possible to provide even a brief survey of the complex economic regimes established in the era after the Second World War. But it is worth noting that they reflect the determined effort made by the United States, in particular, to consolidate a set of regimes built upon liberal principles. In particular, the United States wished to establish a trading regime established on free trade principles and, as we have seen, the GATT was established to achieve this goal. At the same time, however, the United States also recognized that trade requires stable domestic economies and a stable monetary system to flourish. A range of international organizations, such as the International Monetary Fund and the International Bank of Reconstruction and Development were established after 1945 to promote an environment where trade could flourish. Although there were fears that the economic regimes established by the United States would collapse as weaknesses in its own economy became apparent in the late 1960s, the economic regimes brought into existence after 1945 have proved to be surprisingly resilient.

Key points

- Regime theory is an attempt initiated in the 1970s by social scientists to account for the existence of rule-governed behaviour in the anarchic international system.

- Regimes have been defined by principles, norms, rules, and decision-making procedures.

- Regimes can be classified in terms of the formality of the underlying agreements and the degree of expectation that the agreements will be observed. Full-blown, tacit, and dead-letter regimes can be identified.

- Regimes now help to regulate international relations in many spheres of activity.

Competing theories of regime formation

Both liberal institutionalists and realists acknowledge that regimes are an important feature of contemporary international relations and they also start from the same theoretical premise that a regime represents the response of rational actors operating within the anarchic structure of the international system (see Ch. 9). But despite this common starting point, realists and liberal institionalists go on to make very different theoretical assessments of regimes.

The liberal institutional approach

Liberal institutionalists work from the premise that regimes are needed to overcome the problems generated by the anarchic structure of the international system. They have drawn on a number of theoretical ideas developed outside of international relations in an attempt to understand why anarchy inhibits collaboration and the ways in which the resulting obstacles might be overcome.

Impediments to regime formation

To develop a theoretical understanding of why the anarchic structure of the international system impedes regime formation, liberal institutionalists have turned to **microeconomics** and **game theory** for assistance. Microeconomists study the behaviour of economic units operating under the conditions of perfect competition found, in theory, within the market place. An analogy is drawn by liberal institutionalists between the economic market and the international system because both are constituted by anarchic structures. But, paradoxically, whereas for liberal institutionalists the anarchic structure of the international system poses a significant problem, for microeconomists, the absence of any centralized institutions constitutes the main asset of the market place. Unrestrained by external interference, rational economic units pursue competitive and self-interested strategies which result in goods being bought and sold at what microeconomic theory demonstrates is the optimum price, generating the best possible outcome for all the units operating within the market.

This benign image of the economic market might seem to generate very little insight for liberal institutionalists. But the microeconomic approach becomes more relevant when attention is turned to the concept of **market failure**. Although microeconomists insist that an unrestrained market provides the most effective mechanism for the production of economic goods, it is accepted that the market is not effective when it comes to the production of '**public goods**' like roads and hospitals. Indeed it is also acknowledged that there are circumstances when unrestrained competition can result in the production of what might be called '**public bads**'— the obvious example being pollution. Microeconomists argue that suboptimum outcomes, like the underprovision of public goods or the proliferation of public bads, is not the result of irrationality. Suboptimum outcomes emerge in circumstances when economic actors need to collaborate rather than compete. And under these circumstances, the market, which promotes competition, is not an appropriate mechanism for dealing with the situation. When market failure occurs, therefore, microeconomists accept that it is necessary to find an alternative mechanism to the market—one that generates collaboration rather than competition. The principal mechanism, often only accepted with reluctance, takes the form of state intervention. The state can, when necessary, intervene into the marketplace and require economic actors to collaborate rather than compete. So, for example, when rivers have become polluted as the result of industrial waste, the state can pass legislation which requires all the relevant economic actors to produce alternative outlets for the industrial waste which is polluting the rivers. Microeconomists circumvent the problem of market failure, therefore, by means of structural transformation. The anarchic structure of the market gives way to the hierarchical structure of the state.

Within the international system, of course, no global equivalent of the state exists to enact legislation compelling sovereign states to subscribe to a common policy. As a consequence, at least from the perspective of the microeconomist, it is unsurprising to find widespread evidence of global problems persisting because of the failure of sovereign states to collaborate and implement collective solutions. Global pollution, resource depletion, arms races, and trade barriers are seen by liberal institutionalists to constitute global problems arising from market failure—where states have preferred to compete rather than to collaborate. On the other hand, the existence of regimes indicates that collaboration is certainly possible within the anarchic arena. Anarchy does not preclude collaboration; it simply makes it difficult to achieve. The microeconomic approach, drawing on game theory, has helped to explain why.

The existence of collaborative as well as competitive strategies generates a much more complex situation than found in the purely competitive market setting. For instance, if a motorist fails to stop at an intersection, then whether or not an accident occurs will depend upon the behaviour of the motorists approaching the intersection on the other road. Most motorists, fortunately, adopt a cautious, co-operative strategy and so accidents at intersections are not a frequent occurrence. But in such cases of **strategic interaction**, the outcome, as the example illustrates, is determined by the interplay of decisions reached by independent actors. No single actor can dictate the outcome. **Game theory**, a branch of mathematics, has developed a very extensive study of strategic interaction, and liberal institutionalists, while generally avoiding the mathematics, have drawn on some of the conceptual apparatus developed by game theorists in order to enhance their theoretical appreciation of the factors which inhibit collaboration in an anarchic setting.

Theory building requires an analyst to distil the essential elements of the situation under scrutiny. Game theory is particularly parsimonious. The focus is on the interaction between two actors, each with only two possible strategies—one co-operative and the other competitive—which can be followed: strategic interaction, therefore, involves four possible outcomes. The strategies chosen are based on **rational** calculation. Rational actors, according to game theorists, (1) evaluate outcomes, (2) produce a preference ranking, and then (3) choose the best option available. These are the essential elements of rationality. What social scientists have realized is that they can use the very simple conceptual apparatus involving rational two-person games to model a wide range of social situations. The games are considered to distil the essential elements of situations that in reality are much more complex. By stripping away the detail, it becomes easier to understand the underlying dynamics of the situation. So, for example, it is argued that all examples of market failure can be modelled by the game known as Prisoners' Dilemma (see Box 14.4).

The logic associated with the Prisoners' Dilemma is seen by liberal institutionalists to account for why a wide range of irrational oucomes in the international arena can be explained in rational terms. It explains why states have persisted in overfishing the seas, in polluting the atmosphere, in selling arms to undesirable regimes, and promoting policies which inhibit trade. All represent cases of market failure, with states choosing to pursue competitive rather than collaborative strategies. They fail to pursue collaborative strategies because they expect the other members of the anarchic system to pursue competitive strategies. It would be irrational for one state to require its fishing industry to observe a fishing quota, for example, if it is believed that the fishing industries in other states are intending to disregard the quota. As a consequence, states avoid a Pareto optimal outcome and driven by rational calculation to pursue a strategy which, through strategic interaction leads to a suboptimal outcome.

If the Prisoners' Dilemma game does accurately map this situation, however, then it not only explains why anarchy inhibits collaboration, but it also indicates that states acknowledge the advantages of collaboration. They are only inhibited from moving to collaborative strategies by their expectation that other states will defect. The Prisoners' Dilemma demonstrates the importance of identifying a mechanism which will convince all the actors that there is no danger of defection. Liberal institutionalists believe that the establishment of regimes provides evidence that mechanisms of this kind must exist.

The facilitation of regime formation

Two different routes have been followed by liberal institutionalists in their attempt to explain the emergence of regimes. First they have drawn on the work of microeconomists who have insisted that state intervention is not the only mechanism available to produce public goods. It is suggested that if there is a dominant or hegemonic actor operating within the market, then that actor may well be prepared to sustain the cost of producing a public good (Olson 1965). The liberal institutionalists have had no difficulty extending this line of argument to the international arena. During the course of the nineteenth century, for example, a regime was established which outlawed the international traffic of slaves. States agreed to observe the humanitarian principle which underpinned this regime because they expected other states to do so. The expectation emerged because it was recognized that Great Britain intended to police the regime and possessed the naval capacity to do so. The regime was consolidated, therefore, because of Britain's hegemonic status within the international system.

As already indicated, it is widely accepted that the economic regimes established after the Second

Box 14.4 The game of Prisoners' Dilemma

The Prisoners' Dilemma scenario

The governor of a prison once had two prisoners whom he could not hang without a voluntary confession of at least one. Accordingly, he summoned one prisoner and offered him his freedom and a sum of money if he would confess at least a day before the second prisoner did so, so that an indictment could be prepared and so that the second prisoner could be hanged. If the latter should confess at least a day before him, however, the first prisoner was told, then the prisoner would be freed and rewarded and he would be hanged. "And what if we both should confess on the same day, your Excellency?" asked the first prisoner. 'Then you each will keep your life but will get ten years in prison'. 'And if neither of us should confess, your Excellency?' 'Then both of you will be set free—without any reward, of course. But will you bet your neck that your fellow prisoner—that crook—will not hurry to confess and pocket the reward? Now go back to your solitary cell and think about your answer until tomorrow.' The second prisoner in his interview was told the same, and each man spent the night alone considering his dilemma. (Deutsch, 1968, 120).

The two actors are confronted with two possible strategies, generating a situation with four possible outcomes. Being rational, the prisoners can place these outcomes on a preference ranking. The matrix below reveals the preference rankings for the two prisoners. Both prisoners will pursue the strategy which will optimize their position in the light of the strategies available to the other prisoner. To avoid being hanged, both prisoners will confess and end up in prison for ten years, thereby demonstrating how individual rationality leads to collective irrationality. The suboptimal outcome could only be avoided if the two prisoners possessed a mechanism which allowed them to collaborate.

In this figure, cell numerals refer to ordinally ranked preferences: 4 = best, 1 = worst. The first number in each cell refers to A's preference and the second number refers to B's preference.

		A Silent	A Confess*
B	Silent	3, 3‡	4, 1
B	Confess*	1, 4	2, 2†

* Dominant strategy: both players have dominant rather than contingent strategies. A strategy becomes dominant if it is preferable to the alternative strategy no matter which strategy the other player adopts.

† Denotes an equilibrium outcome.

‡ A Pareto Optimal Outcome: Vilfredo Pareto (1848–1923) was an Italian sociologist and economist who developed a criterion for identifying when an exchange between two parties has reached its most efficient or optimum point. He argued, in essence, that the point is reached when one party is better off and the other party is no worse off than before the exchange took place. An implication of this optimum is discussed later.

World War owe their existence to the presence of the United States as a hegemonic power. But when liberal institutionalist examined the consequences of hegemonic decline, they concluded that there is no reason to suppose that established regimes would cease to exist. Although the Prisoners' Dilemma indicated that market failures occur because in an anarchic system there is an expectation that states will compete rather than collaborate, once states have moved away from the suboptimum outcome resulting from mutually competitive strategies, then there is no incentive to defect from the mutually collaborative strategies and return to the suboptimum outcome. Even in the absence of a hegemon, therefore, liberal institutionalists argue that established regimes should persist (Keohane 1984).

The second route explored by the liberal institutionalists has reinforced this conclusion. It is argued that the Prisoners' Dilemma exaggerates the difficulty of generating collaboration within the anarchic international system. The Prisoners' Dilemma presupposes that the game is only played once. But, in reality, because situations persist over time, it is more appropriate to think of the game being played over and over again. The 'shadow of the future' looms over the players, affecting their strategic calculations. Because the game will be played on future occasions, it becomes worthwhile taking a risk and pursuing a collaborative strategy in order to produce the optimum outcome. If all states can be persuaded to do the same, then there will be little incentive to defect in the future, because if one state defects, then, 'tit for tat', all the others will follow. Accepting this line of argument, then, the major mechanism for establishing and maintaining a regime is not the existence of a hegemon, but the principle of **reciprocity**. Liberal institutionalists, therefore, have increasingly come to focus on factors that will strengthen reciprocity within the system. Inspection and surveillance facilities become very important to ensure that states are operating within the parameters of a regime. The establishment of satellite surveillance, for example, was a significant factor in encouraging the United States and the Soviet Union to reach arms control agreements. Attention has also been drawn to the importance of scientific knowledge. States are unwilling to restrict their activities on the basis of speculation and respond much more effectively when scientists start to agree about the significance of their findings. With states becoming ever more open and the constant expansion in scientific understanding, so the international environment will become increasingly 'information rich'. It is this trend, liberal institutionalist argue, that will do most to facilitate regime-building in the future (Keohane 1984)

The realist approach

From a liberal institutionalist perspective, realism has little to contribute to the understanding of regimes. The traditional realist emphasis on the inherently competitive nature of the international system is seen to inhibit rather than facilitate any explanation of how and why states collaborate to achieve the mutually advantageous benefits derived from the establishment of regimes. Indeed, the growth of regimes would seem to confirm that the realist perspective is becoming increasingly anachronistic. Unsurprisingly, realists contest such an evaluation. Two problems are identified with the liberal institutional approach. First, realists attack the liberal institutional assumption that the activities of a hegemon in the international system can be compared to the role of the state when dealing with cases

of market failure. Second, realists deny that regimes emerge as the result of states endeavouring to overcome the pressure to compete under conditions of anarchy. Regimes form, realists argue, in situations when uncoordinated strategies can interact to produce suboptimum outcomes. So from the realist perspective, the influence of microeconomics has encouraged the liberal institutionalists to advance an unsound assessment of regime formation. There is an irony here, because it was the neorealists (Waltz 1979) who first drew the analogy between the market and the international system. The common starting point, however, can lead in very different directions.

Power and regimes

Realists, like liberal institutionalists, were very aware in the 1970s and 1980s that the hegemonic status of the United States was being questioned. But they did not conclude that this development might lead to an anomic world. Instead, they focused on Third World demands for a new set of principles and norms to underpin the regimes associated with the world economy. Existing regimes were seen to work against the interests of Third World states, opening them up to unfair competition and malign economic forces. Realists took the case presented by the Third World seriously, but argued that the principles and norms demanded by the Third World would only come into operation if the balance of power moved against the West (Tucker 1977; Krasner 1985). This line of analysis runs directly counter to the image presented by the liberal institutionalists of the United States as a benign benefactor, underwriting a set of regimes which allowed the members of the anarchic international system to escape from a suboptimum outcome and into a position of Pareto optimality. In its place, it was necessary to view the United States as a hegemon using its power to sustain a regime which promoted its own long-term interests. Closer inspection of the liberal institutional position reveals a tacit support for the way that public goods have been defined by governments in the West. It may appear axiomatic to liberal institutionalists that states should wish to promote economic regimes built on liberal norms and principles. And the same argument applies to the promotion of human rights, the elimination of pollution, and all the other goals advanced by liberals in the West. But this position disregards the fact that it is by no means universally agreed that liberal norms and principles should be underpinning the regimes that are emerging in the international system.

From the realist perspective, therefore, the United States helped to ensure that regimes were underpinned by a particular set of principles and norms. But a full appreciation of the realist's position also requires the recognition that a hegemon can effectively veto the formation of a regime. For example, in 1972, when the United States launched its first remote sensing satellite, the event caused concern amongst a large range of countries. These satellites have the capacity to gather important and sensitive commercial and strategic data about countries all around the world. Not only can the satellites identify where military equipment is located, but they can also identify the size of a crop yield and the location of minerals. There were several attempts to establish a regime which would limit the right of states to acquire data without the permission of the state under surveillance (Brown *et al.* 1977). Many states have considered that they would benefit from such a regime. But because the balance of power was tilted in favour of the states which possessed these satellites and they were clear that such a regime would not work to their benefit they vetoed the proposed regime.

Regimes and co-ordination

As it stands, the realist account of regimes is incomplete, because it fails to explain why states adhere to the principles and norms underlying a regime which they oppose. In accounting for this anomaly, realists, like liberal institutionalists, resort to game theory. Realists insist, however, that states wishing to form a regime confront the problem of co-ordination, as illustrated by the Battle of the Sexes (see Box 14.6), not collaboration, as illustrated by the Prisoners' Dilemma. Here the problem is not associated with the danger of defection to a competitive strategy, but the possibility of failing to co-ordinate strategies, with the consequence that a mutually desired goal is unintentionally missed.

Co-ordination problems are very familiar to strategic thinkers. Schelling (1960) illustrates the problem with the example of a couple getting separated in a department store. Both wish to get back together again, but there is a danger that they will wait for each other in different places; situations of this kind generate a co-ordination problem. In the absence of communication, solving co-ordination problems can be difficult, even impossible. But with the aid of communication, a solution can be very straightforward and uncontroversial. For example, while communication between an aircraft and an air traffic control centre can occur in any mutually agreed language, it is obviously unacceptable for the pilot and the air traffic controller not to be able to speak a common language. Under the rules of the International Civil Aviation Organization, every international pilot and some personnel in every air traffic control centre must be able to speak English. This is a highly stable equilibrium and the rule undoubtedly contributes to air safety. But it is only one of a large body of rules which form the regime that regulates international civil aviation. It has major training implications and it is not an issue that can be constantly renegotiated. It needs to be embodied in a stable regime that all the involved parties can treat as a constant.

The decision to choose English under these circumstances may have been relatively uncontroversial, but it does not follow that a common aversion to certain outcomes (a pilot speaking only German and the air traffic controller speaking only Japanese) will necessarily generate a common interest in a particular outcome (everyone speaking English). There is little doubt that the French would have preferred their language to English; and, of course, English has no intrinsic merit over French in this context. And this is the main lesson to be learned from the Battle of the Sexes game—there can be more than one outcome reflecting a Pareto optimum. Indeed, there can be many positions that represent a Pareto optimum and they can then be located on what is referred to as the Pareto frontier (see Box 14.5). So in the context of civil aviation, every spoken language can be located on the frontier because, in principle, any language could be chosen, provided that everyone spoke it. And the use of any common language is preferable to the alternative which would arise in the

Box 14.5 The Battle of the Sexes and Pareto's frontier

The Battle of the Sexes

The scenario of this game envisages a couple who have just fallen in love and decide to go on holiday together. The problem is that one wants to go hiking in the mountains and the other wants to visit art galleries and museums in the city. But both much prefer to be with their partner than to go on holiday alone. When mapped onto a matrix, two stable equilibriums emerge from the scenario.

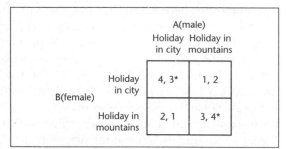

In this figure, cell numerals refer to ordinally ranked preferences: 4 = best, 1 = worst. The first number in each cell refers to A's preference and the second number refers to B's preference.

* Denotes an equilibrium outcome and a Pareto optimal strategy.

The Pareto frontier

Wishing to reach a compromise, the couple might decide to split their week's holiday, spending time in the city and in the mountains. Since the two extreme positions represent a Pareto optimum, so too must all the possible combinations and these can be mapped to form a Pareto frontier.

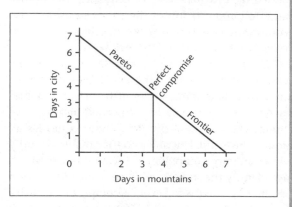

event of a failure to co-ordinate and identify a common language.

Realists argue that this line of analysis helps us to understand why states might conform to a regime while wishing to change the underlying principles. The explanation is that the states are already operating on the Pareto frontier. They observe the regime because they are operating in a co-ordination situation, and a failure to co-ordinate will move them into a less advantageous situation. The French can rail against the use of English in the civil aviation context, but they have no alternative but to persist with the policy. The same argument applies to Third World states; they wish to trade with the West, while preferring to do so on more advantageous terms. The application of new trade principles would represent another point on the Pareto frontier. But, as yet, because the balance of power continues to favour the West, there are few signs that new economic principles more favourable to the Third World are likely to emerge.

The situation is somewhat different in the area of communication regimes. All forms of electronic communication use electromagnetic waves which are emitted along an electromagnetic spectrum. Co-ordination here is essential, because interference occurs if more than one user adopts the same frequency of the spectrum at the same time over the same area. It is not possible, therefore, for states to operate on a unilateral basis and the establishment of a regime was essential. Moreover, because the electromagnetic spectrum is a limited resource, principles and rules for partitioning the resource had to be determined. In the first instance, states agreed that the spectrum should be allocated on the basis of need. But by 1980 this principle had resulted in the Soviet Union and the United States claiming half of the available frequencies and 90 per cent of the spectrum was allocated to provide benefits for 10 per cent of the world's population (Krasner 1985). It is unsurprising to find this outcome being challenged by developing states which argued that part of the spectrum should be reserved for future use. More surprisingly, this new principle has been accepted. But realists argue that this is not the result of altruism on the part of the developed world. It is a consequence of the fact that developing states can interfere with the signals of neighbouring countries. This gave them access to a power lever which they otherwise would not have possessed (Krasner 1991). Through the use of power, the developing states have managed to move in a more favourable direction along the Pareto frontier. By contrast, they have had little say over the allocation of geosynchronous orbits which are the most efficient locations for broadcasting satellites. Here too co-ordination is required, but only amongst those states already in a position to launch the satellite. So a different balance of power is involved.

Key points

- The market is used by liberal institutionalists as an analogy for the anarchic international system.

- In a market /international setting, public goods get underproduced and public bads get overproduced.

- Liberal institutionalists draw on the Prisoners' Dilemma game to account for the structural impediments to regime formation.

- A hegemon, 'the shadow of the future', and an information-rich environment promote collaboration and an escape route from Prisoners' Dilemmas.

- Realists argue that liberal institutionalists ignore the importance of power when examining regimes.

- Realists draw on the 'Battle of the Sexes' to illuminate the nature of co-ordination and its link to power in an anarchic setting.

Conclusion

Although liberal institutionalists and realists acknowledge that regimes are an important feature of the international system, and draw on identical tools of analysis, they reach very different conclusions about the circumstances in which regimes emerge. For liberal institutionalists, the need for regimes arises because there is always a danger in the anarchic international system that competitive strategies will trump co-operative strategies. Their analysis, therefore, focuses on ways of deterring competitive strategies that are otherwise seen to be the rational response within an anarchically structured system. By contrast, and paradoxically, given conventional assessments, realists link the emergence of regimes to situations where there is a mutual desire to co-operate, but where anarchy generates a problem of co-ordination. Again, in contrast to liberal institutionalists, realists assume that there is no incentive to defect once co-ordination has taken place.

The two approaches also adhere to divergent conceptions of power. For liberal institutionalists, power may be used by a hegemon to pressure other states to collaborate and conform to a regime. But it is also acknowledged that states can establish and maintain regimes in the absence of hegemonic power. Collaborative strategies are pursued and maintained because of the 'shadow of the future'—a mutual recognition that if any state defects from a regime, it will result in mass defection on a 'tit for tat' basis and states moving from an optimum to a suboptimum outcome. There seems little doubt that 'lead' states do establish regimes in the expectation that other states will follow. For example, in 1987, twenty-two states signed the Montreal Protocol agreeing to reduce CFC gases—which erode the ozone layer—by 50 per cent by 1998. But in 1990, the timetable was accelerated and the signatories expanded to eighty-one, all agreeing to eliminate all CFCs by 2000.

For realists, on the other hand, power is seen to play a crucial role, not as a threat to discipline states

---

Box 14.6 **Key concepts**

- **Anarchy:** a system operating in the absence of any central government.

- **Anomie:** a system operating in the absence of norms or rules.

- **'Battle of the Sexes':** a scenario in game theory illustrating the need for a co-ordination strategy.

- **Collaboration:** a form of co-operation requiring parties not to defect from a mutually desirable strategy for an individually preferable strategy.

- **Co-operation:** is required in any situation where parties must act together in order to achieve a mutually acceptable outcome.

- **Co-ordination:** a form of co-operation requiring parties to pursue a common strategy in order to avoid the mutually undesirable outcome arising from the pursuit of divergent strategies.

- **Exponential growth:** a situation where the rate of growth is not constant or linear but increases over time.

- **Game theory:** a branch of mathematics which explores strategic interaction.

- **Hegemony:** a system regulated by a dominant leader.

- **Microeconomics:** the branch of economics studying the behaviour of the firm in a market setting.

- **Market failure:** results from the inability of the market to produce goods which require collaborative strategies

- **'Prisoners' Dilemma':** a scenario in game theory illustrating the need for a collaboration strategy.

- **Public goods:** goods which can only be produced by a collective decision, and cannot, therefore, be produced in the market place.

- **Public bads:** the negative consequences which can arise when actors fail to collaborate.

- **Rationality:** reflected in the ability of individuals to rank order their preferences and choose the best available preference.

- **Reciprocity:** reflects a 'tit for tat' strategy, only co-operating if others do likewise.

- **Regimes:** sets of implicit or explicit principles, norms, rules, and decision-making procedures around which actors' expectations converge in a given area of international relations.

- **'Shadow of the future':** a metaphor indicating that decision-makers are conscious of the future when making decisions.

- **Strategic interaction:** occurs when an outcome is the product of decisions arrived at independently.

---

caught defecting from a collaborative agreement, but in the bargaining process—to determine the shape of a regime around which all states will co-ordinate their actions. For realists, the conflict over economic regimes reveals most clearly the importance of the role played by power in the establishment of regimes. It is the rich and powerful states in the North that have primarily determined the shape of these economic regimes. Third World states have had no alternative but to accept the regimes because of the need to engage in trade. By contrast, there have been massive violations of the human rights regimes that have emerged since the end of the Second World War. These dead-letter regimes have failed to become full-blown regimes, according to realists, because there is no co-ordination involved. States can unilaterally violate human rights regimes without paying the automatic penalty incurred in co-ordination situations.

Stein (1983) who introduced the distinction between collaborative and co-ordination games into the regime literature never assumed, however, that they represented mutually incompatible approaches to regime formation. It could be argued, therefore, that the debate between the liberal institutionalists and the realists can be resolved by empirical investigation. Do decision-makers who are responsible for establishing regimes see themselves in a 'Prisoners' Dilemma' or a 'Battle of the Sexes'? Liberal institutionalists insist that the former represents the characteristic situation, whereas realists focus on the latter. Although it is not possible to foreclose on this question, it is possible that the two types of games can be viewed in sequential terms. States may escape from the Prisoners' Dilemma by agreeing to collaborate, only to find that they then enter a Battle of the Sexes when the details come to be worked out.

QUESTIONS

1 What are the defining elements of a regime?

2 Is a regime the same as an organization?

3 Why did the study of international regimes develop in the 1970s?

4 What characteristic features do the realist and liberal institutionalist approaches to regime analysis share?

5 How has microeconomics influenced the liberal institutionalist approach to regimes?

6 What is meant by rationality in the context of game theory?

7 What are the main implications of strategic interaction?

8 What are the implications of the Prisoners' Dilemma game for regime analysis?

9 What major mechanisms do liberal institutionalists advance to promote regime formation?

10 How does the realist approach to regime analysis differ from the liberal institutional approach?

11 What does the Battle of the Sexes game tell us about the role of power in regime formation?

12 What does operating at the Pareto frontier mean in the context of regime theory?

GUIDE TO FURTHER READING

Brown, S. *et al.*, *Regimes for the Ocean, Outer Space and the Weather* (Washington, DC: Brookings Institution, 1997) An early attempt to examine areas which need to be regulated by regimes.

Hasenclever, A., Mayer, P., and Rittberger, V., *Theories of International Regimes* (Cambridge: Cambridge University Press, 1997). Argues that in addition to realism that focuses on power, and neoliberalism that focuses on interests, cognitivism, focusing on ideas, now forms a third school of thought in the regime literature.

Keohane, R. O., *After Hegemony: Cooperation and Discord in the World Political Economy* (Princeton: Princeton University Press, 1984). One of the most influential liberal institutional texts on the theory underlying regime formation.

Keohane, R. O., and Nye, J. S., *Power and Interdependence* (Boston: Little Brown, 1977). Examines the role of regimes in an interdependent world, advancing four models to account for regime change.

Krasner, S. D. (ed.), *International Regimes* (Ithaca, NY: Cornell University Press, 1983). A seminal text setting out the main theoretical issues.

—— *Structural Conflict: The Third World Against Global Liberalism* (Berkeley: University of California Press, 1985). This is one of the major realist texts. It explores North–South disputes over regimes.

Oye, K. A. (ed.), *Cooperation Under Anarchy* (Princeton: Princeton University Press, 1986). An influential set of theoretical essays on how co-operation takes place under anarchic conditions.

Rittberger, V. (ed.), *Regime Theory and International Relations* (Oxford: Clarendon Press, 1993). This important book examines regime theory from European and American perspectives.

Zacher, M. W., with B. A. Sutton, *Governing Global Networks: International Regimes for Transportation and Communications* (Cambridge: Cambridge University Press, 1996). A liberal institutional account of regimes, arguing that they are based on mutual interests, and not the dictates of the most powerful states.

15 Diplomacy

Brian White

READER'S GUIDE

This chapter identifies diplomacy as a key process of communication and negotiation in world politics and as an important foreign policy instrument used by global actors. The first section focuses on problems of definition moving from general to more specific meanings of this term. The second section looks more historically at different stages in the development of modern diplomacy—from 'traditional' to 'new'; from cold war to post-cold war. Each historical system is compared by reference to their common and divergent structures, processes and agenda. The third section looks at diplomacy as used by global actors as a means of achieving their foreign policy objectives. The chapter concludes by arguing that the context and forms of diplomacy have changed but it remains a highly relevant process in contemporary world politics and a useful instrument for a wide range of global actors.

What is diplomacy?

Diplomacy is one of those infuriatingly vague terms that can have different meanings depending upon user and usage. We can begin to make sense of it in relation to two major perspectives on world politics that might be labelled 'macro' (the big picture) and 'micro' (the small picture). The macro perspective tries to make sense of world politics as a whole. What are its constituent parts? How do they all fit together? The micro perspective tries to explain world politics from the different but complementary perspective of the actors involved in world politics. Traditionally, the micro perspective has focused on states and the governments that act on their behalf in world politics. But, as we shall see, this conventional state-centred focus is no longer adequate to cover the range of actors involved and the different processes that feature in a globalized system of world politics.

The conscientious reader will be able to find uses of this term that are so general that 'diplomacy' appears to be synonymous with 'world politics' or 'foreign policy' as a whole. You will find references to, for example, **great power diplomacy**, **summit diplomacy**, or **development diplomacy** which—particularly in media reports—appear to describe a process that is much wider than a specific discussion of one facet of diplomacy. Links between international relations and international history—often referred to as diplomatic history—help to reinforce this notion of interchangeability of terms. Similarly, references to, for example, 'British diplomacy', 'Russian diplomacy' or 'South African diplomacy' often suggest that the writer is referring not just to diplomacy as such but to British, Russian, or South African foreign policy as a whole.

Uses of the term diplomacy in such general ways are a potentially misleading shorthand, but at least they alert us to the fact that diplomacy is central both to an understanding of a global system of world politics and to the foreign policies of states and other actors on the international stage. From the 'macro' perspective of world politics, diplomacy refers to a **process of communications** that is central to the workings of the global system. Indeed, if world politics is characterized simply by the tension between conflict and co-operation, diplomacy, together with war, can be said to represent its defining institutions. If conflict and co-operation are placed at two ends of a spectrum (see Fig. 15.1) diplomacy can be located at the co-operation end representing forms of interaction that focus on the **resolution of conflict by dialogue and negotiation.** Diplomacy therefore is fundamentally related to attempts to manage and to create order within a global system, the object being to prevent conflict spilling over into war. This chapter characterizes the essential features of the diplomatic process.

Box 15.1 **Diplomacy in world politics**

Diplomacy in world politics refers to a communications process between international actors that seeks through negotiation to resolve conflict short of war. This process has been refined, institutionalized and professionalized over many centuries.

Box 15.2 **Diplomacy and foreign policy**

Diplomacy in foreign policy refers to the use of diplomacy as a policy instrument possibly in association with other instruments such as military force to enable an international actor to achieve its policy objectives.

From the 'micro' perspective of international actors like states, an understanding of diplomacy provides revealing insights into the behaviour of the actors themselves in the global system. From this perspective, however, diplomacy can be identified as a **policy instrument rather than a global process.** All actors have goals or ends towards which their foreign policy behaviour is directed. In order to achieve ends, actors clearly need means—often called policy instruments. Diplomacy provides one instrument that international actors use to implement their foreign policy. It may be used directly ('pure' diplomacy) with other parties or as a means of communicating the use or threatened use of other instruments ('mixed' diplomacy). A second function of this chapter is to characterize the essential features of diplomacy as a policy instrument.

World politics

Conflict	Co-operation
War	Diplomacy

Fig. 15.1 World politics

Diplomacy and world politics

Diplomacy as a communications process between political entities has existed for literally thousands of years. The earliest diplomatic document in our possession, discovered in the 1970s, is a letter inscribed on a tablet which has been dated some time around 2500 BC. It was sent from a kingdom called Ebla near the Mediterranean coast in what we would call the Middle East to the kingdom of Hamazi in what is now Northern Iran. It was carried by a messenger who made a round trip of almost 2,000 kilometres. In this one brief message, as Cohen (1995: 3) notes,

we have evidence of a fully-fledged diplomatic system: a working relationship between two distant kingdoms; the use of an emissary to convey a letter over a long distance; protocol, including the concept of equal status, an understood medium of communication, and a conventional form of address; a domestic organization for making and implementing foreign policy; an archive; a set of normative expectations about right and proper behaviour; a sense of . . . fellowship or brotherhod; trade or reciprocal gift-giving via envoys.

Traditional diplomacy

While the conventions and machinery of diplomacy have evolved over a long historical period—the city-states in Ancient Greece, for example, introduced a

diplomatic system that had many remarkably modern features—our global diplomatic system has its origins in fifteenth-century Italy where permanent embassies were first established (Hamilton and Langhorne 1995: chs. 1, 2). A 'traditional' diplomatic system developed thereafter which had some distinctive features. These can be usefully summarized under the headings of structure, process, and agenda—broadly relating to who was involved in diplomacy, how diplomatic activity was organized, and the substance of diplomacy. This framework will help us to compare traditional diplomacy with diplomatic systems that preceded it and those that followed.

Structure

Traditional diplomacy can be distinguished from its predecessors in the ancient and medieval worlds primarily because it constituted a communications process between recognizably modern states rather than between other forms of political organization like, for example, the Catholic Church. As relations between states expanded, political leaders (usually monarchs) found it increasingly necessary to negotiate with each other on a regular basis. But, given the distances involved, negotiations had to be indirect and diplomats were sent abroad for this purpose. If diplomacy as a state-based activity is central to the structure of traditional diplomacy, diplomatic agents acting on behalf of states later became institutionalized and eventually professionalized.

By institutionalized, we mean that particular institutions emerged which had diplomacy as their main function and diplomacy ceased to be an irregular activity undertaken by *ad hoc* representatives. As already noted, the Italian city-states were the first to establish permanent, resident missions or embassies abroad and other states in Europe soon followed their lead. The advantages of permanent representation abroad included practicality and continuity. Embassies became an important embodiment of state interests and a network of permanent embassies later became linked to specialized foreign departments established within home states. The

---

Box 15.3 **The Ebla-Hamazi tablet**

Thus says Ibubu, the director of the king's palace, to the messenger: 'You are my brother and I am your brother. As a brother I will grant whatever you desire, and you will grant whatever I desire. Give me good mercenaries (or, work-animals). Please send them. You are my brother and I am your brother. Ten beams of box-wood, two sledges of box-wood I, Ibubu have given the messenger (for you). Irkab-Damu, king of Ebla, is brother of Zizi, king of Hamazi, and Zizi, king of Hamazi, is brother of Irkab-Damu, king of Ebla'. Thus Tia-II, the scribe, has written. For the messenger of Zizi. (Reverse) Delivered.

(Cohen 1995: 3)

institutionalization of diplomacy with a dedicated workforce of diplomats at home and abroad was followed by the professionalization of diplomacy as an occupation.

Processes

In the traditional system, diplomacy was organized largely on a bilateral (two-party) basis and usually undertaken in secrecy. When two states developed a relationship of mutual importance, it became normal to exchange permanent embassies and to conduct diplomacy through those embassies on a state-to-state basis. Unless one state forced the other to accept a position, mutual agreement was the only means of achieving a settlement of any disputes. Limiting the relationship to two parties, of course, made it easier to keep any negotiations secret, although there were other good reasons in terms of the negotiating process itself for maintaining as much secrecy as possible. No good card or chess player reveals his or her 'hand' or strategy in advance, and diplomatic negotiations are similar to these games in important respects.

The traditional process of diplomacy also drew upon rules and procedures for behaviour from earlier diplomatic systems. From the fifteenth century onwards, **diplomacy became not just a regular process but also a regularized process.** Procedural rules known as diplomatic protocol were developed which included rather ostentatious ceremonies and also more practical procedures relating to such things as the order in which a treaty is signed by the parties involved in a negotiation. A series of rights, privileges, and immunities became attached both to diplomats and diplomatic activities.

These derived from two principles. The first essentially practical consideration was that diplomats should be able to conduct their business without fear or hindrance. The popular phrase, 'don't shoot the messenger!' not only suggests the need to safeguard the messenger who does not deserve to be blamed for the content of the message carried, but also indicates the importance of safeguarding the whole system of communications between international actors. The second principle was derived from the idea that the ambassador in particular is the direct representative of a sovereign monarch and, therefore, should be treated with the same consideration that a monarch would receive. This idea of representation was expanded to include the controversial idea of extra-territoriality which in this context simply means that the resident embassy abroad is regarded as part of the territory of the home state and subject to the laws of that state and, likewise, that the resident diplomatic staff are subject only to the laws of the home state.

Agenda

Traditional diplomacy can be characterized finally by its agenda—what issues did diplomats negotiate about? The important point to note here is that the agenda of traditional diplomacy was narrow certainly by comparison with later periods. Not only was the agenda set by the relatively under-developed state of bilateral relations but, more importantly, the preoccupations of diplomacy reflected the preoccupations of political leaders themselves.

For hundreds of years, foreign policy was seen as the exclusive province of monarchs and their advisers and, not surprisingly, personal ambitions—the acquisition of territory perhaps, or another throne—together with more general issues of war and peace constituted the most important issues on the diplomatic agenda. In a highly personalized structure, diplomats in essence were sent abroad by one monarch to win over another. Less desirable aspects of diplomacy occasionally surfaced as diplomats came under pressure to 'get a result' whatever the means employed. This prompted at least one cynical definition of a diplomat as 'an honest man sent abroad to lie on behalf of his country' (a remark usually credited to Henry Wotton, an Elizabethan diplomat). In general, however, it was quickly discovered that honesty rather than deceit is more likely to be effective in achieving objectives, whatever short-term gains might be made by more duplicitous behaviour. Traditional diplomacy reached its most developed form and was arguably most effective as a system for ordering international relations in nineteenth-century Europe. This is the period known, in a classic piece of overstatement, as the 'century of peace' in Europe.

New diplomacy

However successful traditional diplomacy may have been in promoting stability, order, and peace in nineteenth-century Europe, its failure to prevent World War I and, for some indeed, its role in actually causing that war, led to a widespread belief that a new form of diplomacy was needed. Though this was commonly referred to after World War I as the 'new' diplomacy, elements of this allegedly new form of diplomacy were already in evidence in the nineteenth century if not before, and there was a long transition period between traditional forms and the new system of diplomacy that evolved in the first half of the twentieth century. What was identifiably new about the 'new' diplomacy emerged from two important ideas (see Hamilton and Langhorne 1995: 137).

First, there was a demand that diplomacy should be more open to **public scrutiny and control**. This demand related less to a public involvement in the process than in the provision of information to the public about agreements reached. This focused attention on two interlinked elements of traditional diplomacy that were now seen to be problematic; excessive secrecy and the fact that diplomats were normally members of a closed social elite—the aristocracy. The **second** idea related to the importance of establishing **an international organization**—which initially took the form of the League of Nations after World War I—that would act both as an international forum for the peaceful settlement of disputes and as a deterrent against another world war by the threat of collective action against potential aggressors. Historically then the new diplomacy represented the widespread hope for a new start after 1918.

Structure

The structure of the new diplomacy remained similar in form to traditional diplomacy to the extent that states and governments remained the major actors in this system and were represented internationally by what was now a well-established network of permanent embassies abroad attached to foreign departments at home. There are two important changes to note, however, that have implications not only for the structure but also for the processes

and the issues that characterized the new diplomacy. First, **states were no longer the only actors** involved. Increasingly, they had to share the international stage with other actors such as international organizations who were also engaged in diplomacy. These organizations were of two types, intergovernmental (with governments only as members) and non-governmental (with private individuals and groups as members).

The second important change to note is that governments themselves were beginning to change in terms of the scope of their activities and the extent to which they sought to regulate the lives of their citizens. Where once they had simply provided for the physical security of their citizens they now had a **broader concern** with their social and economic well-being. Thus, the twentieth century saw an important change from the so-called **'nightwatchman state'** to the **'welfare state'**. This has implications for the range of issues that states needed to negotiate about in their international activity.

Processes

The changing interests of states as international actors and the growing number of non-state actors involved changed the nature of the new diplomacy as a process of negotiation. Most obviously, it made diplomacy a more complex activity involving more and different actors. States continued to negotiate bilaterally with each other on a state-to-state basis, but groups of states typically negotiated multilaterally through the auspices of intergovernmental organizations like the League of Nations and its successor the United Nations and, increasingly, with the growing range of non-governmental organizations which sought to influence inter state behaviour to achieve their own objectives. Again, it must be stressed that multilateral diplomacy was not strictly new in the sense that what had been called conference diplomacy between the Great Powers had been an important feature of nineteenth-century European diplomacy. Nor did multilateral diplomacy replace bilateral diplomacy. But, to the extent that it was more difficult to keep secret a process involving so many different actors, it is fair to say that the new diplomacy was a more open process than its predecessor.

Agenda

The agenda of the new diplomacy contained a number of new issues as well as a reinforced emphasis on military security. The avoidance of war now became a priority as the 'new' diplomats sought to make World War I 'the war to end all wars', but diplomatic activity also began to focus more on economic, social, and welfare issues relating to material well-being. These became known as **'low politics'** issues in contrast to the **'high politics'** issues associated with the traditional diplomatic agenda. These new issues not only reflected the wider interests and responsibilities of governments but also the often narrowly focused interests of non-state actors.

The other distinctive feature of the new agenda is that it increasingly featured **highly specialized issues** that raised question marks about the adequacy of the training given to diplomats. If the specialization required of new diplomats challenged their competence, their distinctive role was also challenged by two other trends: the direct role political leaders themselves often played in diplomacy and the growing tendency of political leaders in the interwar period to appoint personal envoys to represent them. Clearly, professional diplomats were no longer the only 'players' involved in the new diplomatic 'game' and they enjoyed far less autonomy than traditional diplomats had enjoyed in earlier periods.

Cold war diplomacy

Many of the characteristics of the new diplomacy continued to evolve in the period after World War II, indeed multilateralism and an increasingly specialized agenda contained issues like the environment, technology and arms control. In terms of changing structures and processes, a host of new states joined an already complex array of state and non-state actors as the former colonies of the European powers gained their independence. The fact that these new states were unfamiliar with the established rules and principles of diplomacy led to the first important attempt to give them the status of international law, notably in the 1961 Vienna Convention on Diplomatic Relations (see Berridge 1995: 20–31).

The term **'cold war diplomacy'** refers to some very specific aspects of diplomacy that emerged after World War II. From the late 1940s until the end of the 1980s, world politics was dominated by the ideological confrontation between the United States and the Soviet Union. Each superpower supported by a network of allies sought to undermine and 'defeat' the other by all means short of a real or a 'hot war'—hence the 'cold war' description of this confrontational system. The diplomatic activity associated with 'East–West' confrontation had a single dramatic focus—**the absolute necessity of avoiding a global, nuclear conflict** that could destroy the international system. The most important types of cold war diplomacy, nuclear, crisis, and summit diplomacy are defined in Box 15.4.

There was nothing new about nuclear diplomacy to the extent that states have always hoped that the size of their military forces would help to persuade or dissuade potential adversaries. The distinctiveness of nuclear diplomacy, however, is the extent to which both sides of the East–West divide relied upon their nuclear weapons in political and psychological terms to achieve their objectives, but also sought to avoid triggering a nuclear war. Given the destructive nature of nuclear weapons, however, there were unprecedented risks attached to this type of diplomacy and crises frequently emerged as a

---

Box 15.4 Types of cold war diplomacy

Nuclear diplomacy: refers to the interactions between states that possess nuclear weapons where one or more states threatens to use them either to dissuade an opponent from undertaking an action or to persuade them to call a halt to some action that has begun. The former is also known as **deterrence** and the latter as **compellence** or **coercive diplomacy**.

Crisis diplomacy: refers to the delicate communications and negotiations involved in a crisis. A **crisis** may be defined as a short, intense period in which the possibility of (nuclear) war is perceived to increase dramatically.

Summit diplomacy: refers to a direct meeting between heads of government (of the superpowers in particular) to resolve major problems. The 'summit' became a regular mode of contact during the cold war.

Diplomacy after the cold war

The end of the cold war represented a dramatic change in the international context within which diplomacy is conducted. The end of the ideological East–West conflict and the demise of the Soviet Union raised popular expectations about what might now be achieved by diplomacy and negotiation. The successful ousting of the invading Iraqi forces from Kuwait in 1991 by a US-led military coalition sanctioned by a UN resolution appeared to provide a model for the future. But optimism was soon replaced by a realization that the end of the cold war may have resolved some problems but other problems had merely been hidden from view during

result, which in turn required a particular diplomatic response. The successful resolution of the most serious nuclear crisis in October 1962 over Soviet missiles in Cuba led political leaders and analysts to look for clues about behaviour in that crisis that might provide principles of crisis management (see Richardson 1994: ch. 3).

But there are problems with the notion of 'crisis management'—as Richardson's extended comment explains (see Box 15.5)—and many analysts including Richardson now prefer the more traditional term 'crisis diplomacy'. From this perspective, the most important outcome of the Cuban missile crisis was not a checklist of guidelines for future crisis management but the agreement to set up a 'hot line'—a direct communications link between Moscow and Washington—that would maximize the chances of negotiating a direct settlement between the principal parties. Another form of direct communication was the summit meeting between the superpowers pioneered by the Geneva summit in 1955. Initially, summit meetings had symbolic value only but, by the 1970s, they had become a useful forum for negotiating tangible agreements which contributed to a reduction of East–West tensions. By the mid-1980s, a series of superpower summits played a significant role in bringing the cold war to an end.

the cold war period. The failure of diplomacy to resolve the breakdown of order in the Balkans (see Box 15.6) illustrates the intractable nature of many post-cold war problems on the international agenda.

At the beginning of the twenty-first century, diplomacy at the level of world politics can be characterized in two ways. First, diplomacy is now genuinely global in scope. Gone are the East–West ideological divisions that excluded a large number of states from 'normal' diplomatic intercourse during the cold war period. A good illustration of this is the extent to which 'North–South' dimensions of international diplomacy were obscured by the East–West focus. From a cold war perspective, developing states were the object of superpower attention only in so far as they might be tempted to side with one or the other. Problems of poverty and development were effectively sidelined. Since the end of the cold war, however, the specific concerns of development diplomacy (see Box 15.7) have occupied a much higher profile position in global diplomacy. Second, contemporary diplomacy can also be characterized as complex and fragmented. In terms of the analytical categories used here, there are multiple actors involved, complex multilateral as well as bilateral processes at work, and the substance of global diplomacy covers a wider agenda of issues than ever before.

Key points

- Diplomacy is a key concept in world politics. It refers to a process of communication and negotiation between states and other international actors.

- Diplomacy began in the ancient world but took on a recognizably modern form from the fifteenth century onwards with the establishment of the permanent embassy.

Box 15.7 Developmental diplomacy

Development diplomacy: refers to 'the process whereby third world countries attempt to negotiate improvements in their position in the international political economy. These negotiations largely take the form of bargaining with Western industrialised countries'.

(Williams 1994: 46).

- By the end of the nineteenth century all states had a network of embassies abroad linked to foreign departments at home. Diplomacy had also become an established profession.

- World War I was a 'watershed' in the history of diplomacy. The perceived failure of diplomacy to prevent this war led to a demand for a 'new' diplomacy that would be less secretive and more subject to democratic control. The outbreak of World War II revealed the limits of the 'new' diplomacy.

- Cold war diplomacy relates to the period after World War II when international relations were dominated by a global confrontation between the superpowers and their allies. The imperative need to avoid a nuclear war but also to 'win' the cold war produced a very delicate, dangerous form of diplomacy.

- The end of the cold war produced a new mood of optimism that diplomacy could resolve all major international problems. Such optimism quickly dissipated when a host of new problems and old problems in a new guise emerged.

- Post-cold war diplomacy is a global process but it is also fragmented by different sets of actors, processes and issues.

Diplomacy and foreign policy

As we noted in the introduction, diplomacy not only helps us to understand the nature of world politics as a whole but, from a different perspective, **it also reveals much about the behaviour of the actors in a global system of world politics**. The focus of this second major section is the relationship between diplomacy and the foreign policies of states. While this section will generalize from the experience of developed states, it should be apparent from the discussion so far in this chapter that developed states are not the only state actors in the system. The role of diplomacy in the behaviour of developing states and other non-state actors will also be discussed as well as new processes of negotiation that have evolved in a globalized system.

The making and the implementation of foreign policy

We need first to locate diplomacy within the foreign policy process of states. There are two major stages in that process—the making and the implementation (or the carrying out) of policy. A simple view suggests that the making of foreign policy is the exclusive business of government. So important is foreign policy to the achievement of the 'national interests' of the state that the most senior members of government will oversee and control the policy process. Having made the key decisions, they then hand them over to their foreign departments for implementation. Diplomacy is one of a set of instruments through which decisions are implemented, policy activated, and policy objectives— also established by the political leadership— achieved.

This is a reassuring picture in that, while the difficulties of successful implementation are underplayed, it does suggest that it is the politicians who establish the policy objectives and make the important decisions. If they are elected, this suggests the possibility of democratic control of foreign policy— in principle at least. The foreign policy bureaucracy, not elected of course, plays a subordinate, non-political, essentially instrumental role. This picture, however, is an idealized one, unlikely to match the realities of the process, particularly in developed states with their highly bureaucratized systems of government. As we shall see in the next section, the making and the implementation of foreign policy cannot be so easily split. The two stages can be separated for analysis but in practice they are parts of a continuous and interactive process.

Diplomacy as policy instrument

There is a specialized section of every government devoted to foreign policy. This usually takes the institutionalized form of a foreign department with a dedicated staff. In Britain, for example, the relevant department is the Foreign and Commonwealth Office and, in the United States, the Department of State performs the same function. The specialized staff are known respectively as the Diplomatic Service and Foreign Service Officers. **Every foreign department is linked to a network of embassies abroad and this constitutes the diplomatic machinery of government**. If we identify the main functions performed by this 'machine', it will become apparent that they relate not only to the implementation but also to the actual making of foreign policy. **Diplomacy as a government activity then refers not only to a particular policy instrument but also to the whole process of policy-making and implementation**.

As listed in Box 15.8, there are five major functions performed by the diplomatic machine. The first two of these functions are essential to the making of foreign policy. Information and data are the raw materials of foreign policy and it is part of the job of diplomats abroad to gather information and report back to the political leadership via the foreign department at home. Information relevant to policy-making can be gathered from both formal and informal sources. The formal sources include the local media and government reports. Informal

---

Box 15.8 Functions of the diplomatic machine

- Information gathering
- Policy advice
- Representation
- Negotiation
- Consular services

---

sources include personal contacts among the local political elite and the rest of the diplomatic corps—other states' diplomatic representatives based in that location. Given the expanded agenda of modern foreign policy, the scope and range of information required by government for policy-making purposes has increased dramatically. As much of this information is specialized, it is normal for trained representatives called attaches to be attached (as their name suggests) to the larger embassies. These may include commercial, military, scientific or cultural attaches, or some relevant mix of experts depending upon the precise nature of the relationship between the parties.

It is difficult in practice to separate the function of information gathering and political reporting from the expectation that diplomats will offer policy advice to government. Part of the purpose of having permanent representatives abroad is that they develop a familiarity with the country in which they are based and are able to use this together with other skills and experience to interpret data and to 'put a gloss' on their reports. They make assessments about likely developments and also make reports on the reception home government policies have received or are likely to receive. The distinction between giving advice and making policy is often blurred. The information and advice given by diplomats will certainly limit the perceived options available and may effectively structure the choices of the political leadership.

If diplomats contribute to policy-making by providing information and advice, the diplomatic machinery provides an important policy instrument relevant to policy implementation through the functions of representation, negotiation and consular services. Embassies not only represent the government abroad, they also represent the wider interests of the home state which go beyond the narrowly political realm. The ambassador and his/her staff will attempt to maintain good relations with the host state, to network with local elites, to be present at relevant ceremonial occasions and events where home interests need to be promoted—at trade fairs, for example. The status and size of the embassy provides a symbolic representation of the importance attached to relations with the host country. Increasing or decreasing the number of diplomats can be used politically to signal the current state of a relationship, or to indicate problems, as the cases in Box 15.9 illustrate.

Negotiation is perhaps the single most important function of the diplomatic machine. This covers a variety of activities from simple consultation—known as an 'exchange of views'—to detailed negotiations on a specific issue. Professional diplomats may take the lead on negotiations or they may play a supportive role if political leaders themselves or other envoys are involved. Whenever states require the agreement of other states or third parties, diplomacy is the technique used to secure that agreement.

Box 15.9 Diplomacy by expulsions

In May 1996, the British government both initiated and was on the receiving end of diplomatic actions designed to signal displeasure. In the first case, the Russian government required the removal of four British diplomats in the Moscow embassy who had allegedly been involved in espionage. In a 'tit for tat' response, preserving honour on both sides, the British government then required four Russian diplomats in London to be sent home. In a second, unrelated case, the British government expelled three Sudanese diplomats in response to a United Nations Security Council resolution to impose diplomatic and travel sanctions on Sudan because of concerns over complicity by the Sudanese military regime in acts of terrorism. In addition to the expulsions, the remaining Sudanese diplomats were required to give prior notice of trips outside London and entry visas were denied to members of the Sudanese government and military.

The ability to persuade other parties is central to the art of diplomacy. On some issues, persuasion itself may suffice. But not infrequently, some pressure may be required and the parties involved may then agree to compromise and to adjust their original positions. Pressure may take various forms including the imposition of time limits on the negotiation, seeking to isolate the other party diplomatically or, in extreme circumstances, threatening to break off diplomatic relations.

The final function of the machine, the provision of consular services, has two elements of which the second is more directly related to diplomacy as a policy instrument. The first type of consular activity involves action to support and protect home citizens abroad. This work, together with the processing of immigration applications from host citizens may be handled separately from embassy work. The second type of consular work is dedicated to commercial work, supporting trade relations with the host state. This type of work has increased dramatically in recent years and embassies are often evaluated in part at least in terms of their ability to boost home export promotion and trade activity generally.

The relationship between diplomacy and other policy instruments

We have established that diplomacy is an important policy instrument in its own right. Persuasion or 'pure diplomacy' may be sufficient to achieve a state's policy objectives abroad. Typically, however, diplomacy is linked to other policy instruments to produce what is called 'mixed diplomacy'. Here, diplomacy becomes a communications channel through which the use or threatened use of other instruments is transmitted to other parties. States learned long ago that persuasion is often more successful if 'sticks' and/or 'carrots' are attached. There are three other types of policy instrument that may be used in various ways either as potential rewards or punishments in the attempt to secure compliant behaviour in another party.

First, military force may be threatened or deployed to give 'muscle' to a negotiation. Diplo-macy and military force, often in combination, have been used by states for so many centuries that they may be regarded as the traditional instruments of foreign policy. The growing costs of warfare, how-ever, have led developed states at least to look for alternative instruments to strengthen their hand in negotiations. A second instrument, economic measures, is not new—trade diplomacy also has a long history. But trade and aid have been used increasingly since World War II to influence the outcome of negotiations. Both trade and aid can be threatened or used as a stick or as a carrot in the sense that either can be offered or withheld. The third instrument is the most recent in term of regular usage and can be labelled subversion. Where the other instruments are used to target governments directly, subversion is rather different in that it is focused on particular groups within other states with the object of undermining or overthrowing the government of that state. Subversion may include a variety of techniques including propaganda, intelligence activities, and assisting rebel groups (see Box 15.10). Given that secrecy normally surrounds these activities—if they are to be effective—

> ### Box 15.10 Diplomacy by subversion
>
> In September 1970, Salvador Allende was elected President of Chile, the first democratically elected Marxist leader. The United States government decided thereafter to use all means short of military invasion to bring down the Allende government for ideological reasons. A combination of diplomatic, economic, and subversion instruments were used to support a policy of destabilization. Chile was isolated diplomatically from the international community. US influence with international banks was used to withhold economic loans and the Chilean economy was thrown into chaos. Trade in its principal export, copper, was effectively paralysed. Some $8 million was made available to the US Central Intelligence Agency (CIA) for clandestine interference in Chile which was used to fund the activities of opposition political parties and paramilitary groups hostile to Allende. The Allende government was finally ousted by a coup in September 1973 and Allende himself was killed. (See Hersh 1983: chs. 21, 22.)

subversion is not strictly speaking part of the diplomatic process.

The effectiveness of mixed diplomacy in achieving policy objectives depends upon a variety of factors including the nature of the objective sought, the availability of relevant instruments, the nature of the 'mix' used, the costs attached to the use of particular instruments, and so on. In terms of selection, diplomacy continues to occupy a favoured position because it has certain comparative advantages—even though it may need to be supplemented by other instruments to be effective. First, diplomatic resources are readily available. All states and other actors have at least some capacity to communicate with other parties. Second, diplomacy has relatively few costs directly associated with it. While the use of other instruments may be regarded as politically unacceptable in certain circumstances—military force in particular—diplomacy, as Hocking and Smith suggest, is widely regarded as legitimate 'because of its association with negotiation and conciliation, which are valued as norms of international behaviour' (Hocking and Smith 1990: 205).

Diplomacy and developing states

The discussion in the previous sections has assumed that all states are similar with respect to diplomacy and foreign policy. There are however, important differences between developed and developing states which must qualify some of the generalizations we have made about 'states'. In particular, developing states are handicapped as effective international actors by having relatively underdeveloped diplomatic machines and by a restricted range of policy instruments. They tend to have a patchy system of representation abroad and limited resources available for policy analysis. They also have a limited range of policy instruments for bargaining with other actors and for implementing decisions made. For many developing states, the use of international organizations at both regional and global levels is crucial to compensate for weaknesses in national capabilities. We should note here the special role of the United Nations as a forum in which all developing states are represented and where they can attempt to co-ordinate their common interests and maximize their impact on world politics.

The management of multilateral diplomacy

We have focused on diplomacy as an instrument of state behaviour, whether we are talking about developed or developing states. Indeed, diplomacy used to be called 'statecraft' to emphasize the traditional dominance of states as international actors. However, even the most powerful states are no longer the only significant international actors in a global diplomatic system. Bilateral state-to-state diplomacy remains an important structural feature of that system but it has been increasingly supplemented by multilateral forms of diplomacy with a mixture of state and non-state actors involved. What forms do multilateral diplomacy take and how do actors seek to manage these complex relationships?

International organizations tend to act diplomatically in very much the same way as states. They may not have the extensive diplomatic apparatus performing a wide range of functions that are characteristic of developed states, but all have at least a rudimentary diplomatic machinery—whether they are intergovernmental organizations like the UN or nongovernmental organizations like the major multinational corporations. They can communicate their interests and deploy their resources to influence the outcome of negotiations. Indeed, many of these actors have a greater ability to influence the diplomatic process at a global level than smaller states. At a regional level, complex multilateral types of diplomacy have evolved which have reached their most developed form in Europe and can be illustrated by looking at foreign or external policy-making in the European Union (see Box 15.11).

The demands of multilateral diplomacy today impose constraints upon the ability of all actors to control outcomes. This is not only because it is a diverse and complex process with multiple actors negotiating about a wider range of issues than ever before. The international context within which those negotiations take place has also been radically transformed by levels of interconnectedness or interdependence between societies and the effect of the revolution in communications technology which has transformed diplomacy as process and as instrument. The result is that diplomacy has become

Box 15.11 **External diplomacy in the European Union**

The European Union is arguably a unique multilateral actor in world politics to the extent that state and non-state actors within the Union combine in different ways to act diplomatically on the international stage. The precise combination of actors and the associated policy processes depend largely upon the nature of the issue. There are three major types of EU foreign policy. Foreign policy 'proper', referred to in Euro-jargon as the 'Common Foreign and Security Policy' of the Union can be described as an intergovernmental process, largely though not exclusively controlled by the fifteen member states. Foreign economic policy or 'external relations', on the other hand, can be described as more of a transnational process with EU institutions like the European Commission playing a major role. In trade diplomacy, for example, the Commission acts on behalf of the member states though agreements with third parties need to be agreed by the Council of Ministers representing the member states. Finally, all fifteen member states continue to pursue their own individual diplomatic activities though over time their foreign policies have become increasingly 'Europeanized'—adapted to conform to a common EU policy.

less of a traditional art form with a premium on negotiating skills and 'winning' and more of a management process with actors seeking to reach agreements through a process of adjustment.

Key points

- Diplomacy plays a key role in the foreign policies of states and other international actors.

- A diplomatic 'machinery' (minimally a foreign department and overseas representation) may be highly developed or rudimentary depending upon the actor but it performs important functions in the making and the implementation of foreign policy.

- Diplomacy involves persuading other actors to do (or not to do) what you want (don't want) them to do. To be effective, ('pure') diplomacy may need to be supplemented by other instruments, but negotiating skills are central to the art of diplomacy.

- Diplomacy combined with other instruments (military, economic, subversion) is called mixed diplomacy. Here, diplomacy becomes a communications channel through which the use or threatened use of other instruments is transmitted to other parties.

- Diplomacy usually has comparative advantages over other instruments in terms of availability and cost.

- In complex, multilateral negotiations, diplomacy has become less an art form and more a management process reflecting high levels of interdependence between societies.

Conclusion

This chapter has tried to demonstrate that diplomacy is neither a vague concept nor does it describe international activity that is of interest only to diplomatic historians. As an international process and a policy instrument, diplomacy preceded the modern states-system. It then played a central role in the operation of that system for hundreds of years. Today, adapted to the demands of the contemporary global system, diplomacy continues to make an important contribution to co-operation and order in that system. But diplomacy is no panacea. It cannot guarantee international co-operation but, given goodwill on all sides, it can provide the means to make it happen through dialogue and negotiation. The problem now is that diplomatic systems have become so complex that a range of management skills beyond those deployed by the traditional diplomat is essential.

QUESTIONS

1 What is the difference between diplomacy as a 'process' and diplomacy as an 'instrument'?

2 What are the essential elements of 'traditional' diplomacy?

3 What was 'new' about the 'new diplomacy'?

4 What is the difference between the 'nightwatchman state' and the 'welfare state' and why is this difference important to the diplomatic agenda?

5 What was distinctive about 'cold war diplomacy'?

6 What is 'development diplomacy'?

7 What is the difference between 'crisis management' and 'crisis diplomacy'?

8 What is the foreign policy 'machine'? What functions does it perform?

9 What is the difference between 'pure' and 'mixed' diplomacy?

10 What factors contribute to the successful use of diplomacy?

11 What are the characteristics of multilateral diplomacy in a global system of world politics in terms of actors, processes, and issues?

GUIDE TO FURTHER READING

Barston, R. P., *Modern Diplomacy* (London: Longmans, 1988). Rather dated now perhaps but still a useful summary of diplomacy as a policy instrument of states. It is a textbook aimed specifically at undergraduates with little prior knowledge of diplomacy.

Berridge, G. R., *Diplomacy: Theory and Practice* (Hemel Hempstead: Harvester Wheatsheaf, 1995). This textbook is aimed at graduate students but it contains digestible material for undergraduates on forms of diplomacy and the negotiating process.

Hamilton, K., and Langhorne, R., *The Practice of Diplomacy* (London: Routledge, 1995). This scholarly book analyses the evolution and development of the modern diplomatic system. It is excellent on historical detail and the changing context of diplomacy.

Hocking, B. (ed.), *Foreign Ministries: Change and Adaptation* (Basingstoke: Macmillan, 1999). This is a useful, up to date, comparative study which analyses how effectively foreign ministries and the diplomatic machinery of states have adapted to the challenges of operating in a fragmented, multilateral policy environment.

Richardson, J. L., *Crisis Diplomacy: The Great Powers Since the Mid-Nineteenth Century* (Cambridge: Cambridge University Press, 1994). The most comprehensive book on crisis diplomacy published to date. It considers a wide range of case studies from the pre-nuclear as well as the nuclear era and contains an important critique of 'crisis management'.

Watson, A., *Diplomacy: The Dialogue Between States* (London: Methuen, 1982). A 'classic' book on diplomacy written by a former practitioner. It makes a strong case for the continuing relevance of diplomacy to solving the problems of world politics. It still offers important insights into the world of the diplomat.

16 The United Nations and international order

Paul Taylor

READER'S GUIDE

The United Nations is made up of a group of international institutions, which includes the central system, the specialized agencies, such as the World Health Organization (WHO), and the International Labour Organization (ILO), and the so called Funds and Programmes, which include institutions like the United Nations Children's Emergency Fund (UNICEF) and the United Nations Development Programme (UNDP). This chapter argues that the work of these institutions and their role in international society have altered since the late 1980s. They have taken on an increasing range of functions, but they have also become much more involved within states, often without the immediate consent of the host governments. This development reflects changes in views about the relationship between what happens within states and what happens between them. But it also means that justice for individuals is increasingly seen as a concomitant of international order—serious deficiencies in human rights, or in economic welfare, can lead to international tension and contribute to inter-state conflict. This development has led to challenges to traditional views about intervention within states, and the way in which they justify their sovereignty. The chapter concludes with a typology of the traditional functions of the United Nations, the more recent functions, and the problems that are in the way of carrying out both older and new functions more effectively. The student will need to turn to the bibliography to find detailed accounts of the items under these three headings. This chapter is concerned primarily with the relationship between the changing functions and international order, rather than the details of the functions themselves.

A brief history of the United Nations

The United Nations was established at the end of the Second World War as a result of initiatives taken by the governments of the states which had led the war against Germany and Japan, namely Britain, the United States, and the Soviet Union. They were determined to build upon the experience of the League of Nations from the interwar period, but to correct the problems that had been found with the earlier organization. In this they were joined by fifty-one other states at the beginning, including France and China, and over the years, since then, maintained near universal membership. By the mid-1990s there were nearly 200 member states. 'By a perverse paradox, the United Nations, identified in so many minds with internationalism, presided over the global triumph of the idea of the sovereign state.'[1]

Its main purpose was to maintain international peace and security, in the sense of dissuading states from attacking each other, and to organize countermeasures if this happened. But the founding document of the United Nations, the Charter, also referred to the needs and interests of peoples. In the Preamble it was asserted that: 'We the peoples of the United Nations [are] determined to reaffirm faith in fundamental human rights, in the dignity and worth of the human person, in the equal rights of men and women and of nations large and small.' In Article 1, para. 2 the founders said they were determined to develop 'friendly relations among nations based on respect for the principle of equal rights and self-determination of peoples and to take other appropriate measures to strengthen universal peace'. Peoples as well as states figured in the Charter.

The arrangements of the United Nations could be understood as developments from those of the League of Nations. In the League there had been no clear division of responsibilities between the main executive committee (the League Council), and the League Assembly in which all states were represented. In contrast in the United Nations, the Security Council, made up initially of eleven states, and then, after 1965, of fifteen states, was firmly given main responsibility for maintaining international peace and security. Decisions were to be by a majority of nine out of the fifteen, and each of the five permanent members, namely the US, Britain, France, the Soviet Union (later Russia), and China, could exercise a veto. The convention emerged that abstention by a permanent member would not be regarded as a veto. In the League there was no mechanism for co-ordinating military or economic actions against miscreant states, which was one reason for the League's weakness, as states feared that they would be vulnerable if they had to act individually and separately in response to League Council recommendations. In contrast, in the United Nations, there was to be an army set up by agreement between the Security Council and consenting states, to be commanded by the Military Staff Committee of Chiefs of Staff of the Permanent Members of the Security Council. The Security Council could demand member compliance under Article 25.

Security was the main concern of the United Nations proper, the so-called *central system*, based in New York, and within that the **Security Council**. But other institutions were set up alongside the Security Council, which were also developments from the arrangements of the League. There was to be an assembly of representatives of all members, called the **General Assembly**, which was now to agree its resolutions, in the main, by majority vote: the League Assembly had followed a rule of unanimity. Both institutions evolved more practical formulae, such as consensus and agreement without vote on the initiative of the Assembly President. But as the General Assembly's decisions were not necessarily unanimous, they were regarded as recommendations, rather than as binding decisions, with a small number of exceptions, such as the vote on the budget in its Fifth Committee. This was a binding decision taken by majority vote. The General Assembly was precluded from acting when a question was on the agenda of the Security Council, though in 1950, through the General Assembly's Uniting for Peace Resolution, a procedure was introduced by which an item could be transferred from the Council to the Assembly if the former had been unable to act. In addition to the Fifth Committee the Assembly had five other Committees of the Whole which could act on specific questions, such as legal, economic, and social.

The central system also included the **Secretariat**, headed by the Secretary-General, which was given responsibility for the administration of the activities of the central system, such as servicing the meetings of the Security Council and the General Assembly. It also carried out, on the recommendation of the other bodies, a number of research functions, and some quasi-management functions, amongst which the support of peacekeeping activities had become especially important by the mid-1990s. But its role was primarily bureaucratic and it lacked the political power, and the right of initiative of, say, the Commission of the European Union (Taylor 1996a). The one exception to this was the power of the Secretary-General himself, under Article 99 of the Charter, to bring situations that were likely to lead to a breakdown of international peace and security to the attention of the Security Council. This article, which at first sight appeared innocuous, was the legal basis for the remarkable expansion of the diplomatic role of the Secretary-General, compared with that of his League predecessors. Because of it he was empowered to become involved in a large range of areas, including economic and social problems, and humanitarian crises, which could be loosely interpreted as carrying a threat to peace.

The Secretariat and the General Assembly also had functions, alongside another institution in the central system—the **Economic and Social Council (ECOSOC)**—for overseeing the activities of a large number of other international institutions which formed what came to be called the United Nations system. In addition to the central system the latter was made up of two main kinds of institutions, namely the **Specialized Agencies** and the **Funds and Programmes** (see Box 16.1). The former included such well-known institutions as the World Health Organization (WHO), the International Labour Organization (ILO), and the Food and Agriculture Organization (FAO), which had their own constitutions, regularly assessed budgets, executive heads, and assemblies of state representatives. They were self-contained constitutionally, financially, and politically, and not subject to direct UN control. The Funds and Programmes were much closer to the central system, in the sense that their management arrangements were subject to direct General Assembly supervision, could be modified by Assembly resolution, and most importantly, were largely funded on a voluntary basis. Overall, they were a response to the failure to co-ordinate social and economic activities which did not fall clearly into the sphere of responsibility of any one of the Agencies, and therefore they emerged because of changes in global economic and social circumstances after the setting up of the Agencies. A number of new issues also came onto the agenda, such as the rights and interests of women, which was just one of the issues taken up in a number of global conferences. (A conference on the rights and interests of women took place at Beijing in September 1995)[2] The most important of the Funds and Programmes were the United Nations Development Programme (UNDP), The United Nations Fund for Population Activities (UNFPA), The World Food Progamme (WFP), and the United Nations International Children's Emergency Fund (UNICEF) (see Box 16.1).

The founders of the Charter had tried to improve on the mechanisms of the League for overseeing the economic and social institutions. The League had attributed responsibility for this to its Assembly, but the founders of the UN agreed to establish a smaller body, ECOSOC (54 members), to carry out this more specialized function. This body was appointed by, and responsible to, the General Assembly. These changes in the UN, compared with the League, were a consequence of thinking in more functionalist terms, by setting up organizations to deal with specific economic and social problems, but they did not

Box 16.1 The structure of the United Nations system

The central system

The Security Council of 15 members

The Economic and Social Council of 54 members

The General Assembly of representatives of member states

The Secretariat of the United Nations under the Secretary General

The funds and programmes

The United nations Development Programme (UNDP)

The United Nations Children's Emergency Fund (UNICEF)

The United Nations Conference on Trade and Development (UNCTAD)

The World Food Programme (WFP)

And many others

The specialized agencies

The World Health Organization (WHO)

The Food and Agriculture Organization (FAO)

The International Labour Organization (ILO)

The United Nations Industrial Development Organization (UNIDO)

The United Nations Educational Scientific and Cultural Organization (UNESCO)

And many others

Note 1: The funds and programmes depend mainly on voluntary contributions, and are more closely supervised by the central system, especially after A/48/162 in 1993 (see box 14.3).

Note 2: The agencies are constitutionally independent of the central system—they report to the ECOSOC, but cannot be instructed by it or by the General Assembly. They also have separate assessed budgets and their own assemblies and executives.

give ECOSOC the necessary powers to manage effectively.[3] It was only empowered under articles 61–66 of the Charter to issue recommendations to the Agencies, and to receive reports from them. In consequence the history of the UN's economic and social organizations was one of searching for ways of achieving effective management. The United Nations system, therefore, became multicentred and constantly concerned with the problems of co-ordination, as it was made up of a large number of constitutionally distinct institutions which had a strong urge to go their separate ways (see Taylor 1995).

The arrangements laid out in Chapter VII of the Charter for tackling an aggressor were never introduced, as in the late 1940s no agreement about the UN force on the terms of the Charter could be obtained. There followed a series of improvisations which included, first, an enforcement procedure under which the Security Council agreed a mandate for an agent to act on its behalf, as in Korea in the early 1950s and the Gulf War in the early 1990s, when action was undertaken principally by the United States and its allies. Second was classical

peace-keeping, which involved the establishment, usually by the Security Council, of a UN force under UN command to be placed between the parties to a dispute after a cease-fire. Such a force would only use its weapons to defend itself, would be established with the consent of the host state, and would not include forces from the major powers. This mechanism was first used, in the strict sense of peacekeeping, in November 1956, when a force was introduced into Egypt to facilitate the exodus of the British and French forces from the Suez canal area, and then to stand between Egyptian and Israeli forces. (The first force was the exception in that it was established by a General Assembly resolution.) After that date there was a steady flow of such forces, and a great expansion in their number after the end of the cold war in the late 1980s. There was also a relaxation of the basic rules which led to a number of problems (see Mayall 1996).

Third, after the late 1980s, the UN increasingly became involved in maintaining international order by helping to solve problems of disorder within states. Other parts of the United Nations system, the Specialized Agencies, and the Funds and

Programmes, as well as a wide range of other inter-governmental and non-governmental organizations, got more involved in work which was seen as related to the maintenance of international order. The security function had been the primary function and it still was. But, whereas during the cold war it was interpreted as being concerned with the interests of states in a narrow sense, resisting aggression and defending frontiers, afterwards a wider interpretation emerged. The meaning of the interests of states was broadened so that they got mixed up with the interests of peoples. This ambiguity was, of course, in the Charter, but it had been concealed by the cold war. This is a theme that runs throughout this chapter.

Three aspects are discussed. First is the development of new ways of maintaining international order, especially those which, after the end of the cold war, involved a more direct involvement of the international organization within the state. Second is the problem of reconciling the granting of a wider range of competences to the United Nations, and other international institutions, with the sovereignty of states. And third, the chapter concludes with a typology of the traditional and evolving roles of the United Nations, and the ways of improving its contribution.

Key points

- The United Nations was set up to preserve peace between states after the Second World War.
- In a number of ways it reflected lessons learned from its predecessor, the League of Nations.
- The central system was only a part of the United Nations system.

Problems within the state and problems between states

According to an essay by Hedley Bull, **order** among states, and **justice** within them, were often mutually exclusive: pursuing the one tended to exclude the other (Bull 1977). But by the late 1990s there had been changes in the relationship between these two key concepts which the practice of the UN both reflected and encouraged: there were standards which the state was expected to meet which included the provision of a minimum acceptable quality of economic and social justice.

One reason for this was an increasing objection to the classical realist argument that what went on within states was no concern of any outsider. It was entirely appropriate for the international community to make the attempt to put right violations of individual rights, since the cosmopolitan moral community was indivisible: individuals throughout the world had rights in common and owed obligations to each other. Such rights were increasingly interpreted as meaning both individual political and civil rights, as well as the right to basic provisions like food, water, health care, and accommodation. Although the efforts of the United Nations, and other international organizations, were entirely inadequate in this regard, the principle of their involvement in order to promote these rights was increasingly accepted.

But it was also understood that violations of individuals' rights were a major cause of disturbances in relations between states: a lack of internal justice risked international disorder. In consequence there was increasing challenge to the traditional injunction on the behaviour of diplomats that they should ignore the internal affairs of the states with which they dealt in order to preserve international stability. There was increasing unease with a dual standard of tolerance among states at the expense of intolerance within them. There was still some mileage in the old ways but the change in the moral climate was evident. The United Nations reinforced the perception that pursuing justice for individuals was an aspect of national interest. Thus in 1996 the US Administration's view that action in support of justice in Bosnia-Herzegovina was a part of US national interest, and not a betrayal of it, was attributable in part to the actions of the UN and the expectations it generated. The organization was a constant reminder to Americans of the positive relationship between order and justice, and it was in consequence heartily disliked by American right-wing anti-internationalists.[4] If there was a clear-cut conflict between perceptions of national interest and the pursuit of justice the former had priority, but more frequently the choice could not be put in such stark terms.

In an increasing number of cases states' contributions to activities such as **peacekeeping**, or **humanitarian intervention**, were defended in terms of national interest. Indeed both the moral injunction to be involved and the link with national interest were reinforced: states like Canada accepted an obligation to develop their capacity for peacekeeping, which was the moral course, but one which could also be justified as a reflection of national interest. Canada gained status in the international community through such contributions, and because of it could punch above that country's weight in the United Nations. The Japanese also responded to moral pressure founded in hard national interest when they contributed substantially to defraying the cost of British involvement in the Gulf War. This extraordinary act could only be explained in terms of the synthesis of morality and interest. Reputation in the United Nations context had become for some states an important national good. The Japanese wanted to be a good citizen in that context because it would help their case for becoming a permanent member of the Security Council.

An analogy is suggestive: not attempting to stop your neighbour from killing his wife when you have the capacity to do so is morally repugnant. But it may also be in your interest to act if not doing so leads to a weakening of the legal order, and a fall in property values in the neighbourhood! Conversely acting morally may also improve your personal standing and help get you elected to the District Council. Moral acts and national interest became interrelated when success within a common organization became a value: the sense of what was common had moved to the point of often making it difficult to disentangle moral motives and national interests. In this the UN had achieved status well ahead of the League of Nations: it was a club within which success mattered, a development which might be attributed to the changing sense of social space in the international community. Changes in communications, and the technology for moving items and people around the world, increasingly made denying the existence of a global neighbourhood look eccentric.

Key points

- It became more difficult for states, and diplomats, to accept that what happened within states was of no concern to anyone else.

- It became more common for governments to see active membership in the United Nations as serving their national interest as well as being right.

- The ending of the cold war had helped to promote this attitude.

The United Nations and conditions within states

But this had not always been the case. In the past the United Nations helped to promote the traditional view of the primacy of international order over justice in two major ways. The cold war stand-off

between the East and the West alerted member states to the danger of raising questions about the conditions of the sovereignty of states. Jean Kirkpatrick's notorious essay, which recommended tolerating

---

Box 16.2 **Key concepts**

Accountability: the state of being obliged to explain and justify an act or acts to another.

Competence: the right to act in a given area. Such a right may be extended by a government to an international organization, but this does not mean that ultimate responsibility has been transferred, but only that the international organization is permitted to act on the state's behalf.

Funds and programmes: institutions which are subject to the supervision of the General Assembly and which depend upon voluntary funding by states and other donors.

Justice: fair or morally defensible treatment for individuals, in the light of standards of human rights or economic or social well-being. In this chapter the term is interpreted broadly to include satisfactory standards with regard to human rights and economic conditions, such as adequate food, housing, and health care.

Intergovernmental and non-governmental organizations: see Box 17.12.

Intervention: when there is direct involvement within a state by an outside actor to achieve an outcome preferred by the intervening agency without the consent of the host state. In this chapter the word 'intervention' is placed in inverted commas when it is unclear whether consent has been given. Otherwise the word *involvement* is used.

Involvement: when an outsider, such as an international organization, acts within a state with or without the consent of that state.

Order: when relationships between actors, such as states, are stable, predictable, controlled, and not characterized by violence, turbulence, or chaos.

Recognition: the act, at present carried out by governments individually and separately, of acknowledging the status of another entity as a legal person, thus granting it a licence to act in international society, and to enter into contracts with its members. At present recognition is symbolized by establishing diplomatic relations, exchanging ambassadors, and accepting the other's membership in the United Nations.

Sovereignty: a condition necessary in states in that they are not subject to any higher authority. The government of a sovereign state is ultimately responsible for its citizens. In practice sovereignty has often been conditional. Internally governments have been subject to conventional standards, and externally conditions may mean that governments are more or less free to act independently. A sovereign government is free to choose within the framework of these conventions and standards.

Specialized agencies: international institutions which have a special relationship with the central system of the United Nations but which are constitutionally independent, having their own assessed budgets, executive heads and committees, and assemblies of the representatives of all state members.

---

obnoxious dictatorships in Latin America in order to fight communism, was at least a reasonable report of what the situation in fact was: unsavoury right-wing regimes in Latin America were tolerated by the US because they were anti-Soviet, and interfering in the other's sphere by East or West risked escalation of conflict.[5] Indeed interfering in one's own sphere risked creating opportunities for the other side. Ending the cold war reduced the risk that any promotion of justice could become a context of superpower rivalry. China was the chief heir to the tradition of cold war thinking, and any return to superpower bipolarity, with China replacing the Soviet Union, would revive this reason for hesitating about justice.

The UN also reflected the claims of colonies to become states, and elevated the right to statehood above any of the tests of viability, such as the existence of a nation, adequate economic performance, defensibility, or a prospect for achieving justice for citizens. This unconditional right to independence was enunciated in the December 1960 General Assembly Declaration on the Granting of Independence to Colonial Countries and Peoples, which was approved by a vote of 90 in favour, none against and 9 abstentions. In the subsequent phases of decolonization this often suited the ex-imperial powers, such as Britain, which became more anxious to be rid of them (Drower 1992). There emerged a convention that the claims of elites in the putative states could be a sufficient indication of popular enthusiasm, even when the elites were crooks and the claims misleading. There were few attempts to test this through such devices as a pre-independence referendum.

Charles Beitz was one of the first to question such insouciance on the part of the imperial states when he concluded, in defiance of political correctness in the 1970s, that statehood should not be unconditional: attention had to be given to the situation of individuals after independence, and such considerations could mean that independence in existing circumstances was unacceptable: the majority of individuals would be worse off (Beitz 1979). Michael Waltzer and Terry Nardin produced aguments that led to similar conclusions: states were conditional entities in that their right to exist should be dependent on a criterion of performance with regard to the interests of their citizens (Walzer 1977; Nardin 1983). Such writings surely helped to alter the moral content of diplomacy.

The clash between the principles of justice and the principles of national interest was of course never a continuous one. It appeared occasionally as a reaction to the harsh reality of international society. The skill of the diplomat who wished to pursue a moral foreign policy was to avoid situations in which the harsh choice had to be made, because it would inevitably have to be made in favour of the national interest.[6] But the United Nations in its new role provided an alternative to this stark choice. The international agency could be expected to salve the national conscience by doing something about the moral failures which national interest required the diplomat to ignore. The moment of choice increasingly became the moment of revelation: it launched the next moral crusade which states found increasingly difficult to ignore. For some by the late 1990s the United Nations had become the dynamic of the cosmopolitan commmunity as envisaged by Kant. Conscience needed an agent and the United Nations was it.

The new relationship between order and justice was, therefore, very much a product of particular circumstances: the end of the cold war, the end of the period of state-building and the specific conditions attached to decolonization, and, of course, the attachment of new expectations and the placing of new demands on the United Nations. The latter was not a trivial point. The fact that the United Nations achieved a degree of success indicated that with more effort and more resources it could do better. The question of commitment to the UN was, therefore, not just a question of commitment to an ideal, but rather of making as sure as possible that something that had worked could work better. The world had never got to this point before. After the failure to achieve what had been attempted there could be no easy return to the old standards of attainment: the world would forever have higher expectations, even if these were doomed to continuing disappointment.

Key points

- The cold war and the decolonization process discouraged more active involvement by the United Nations within states.

- Scholars involved with international theory questioned the previous orthodoxy that individuals in new states were necessarily better off after independence.

- The United Nations became a focus of the global conscience.

The United Nations and maintaining international order

In the mid-1990s the word **governance** was often used with reference to international organizations but there was no agreement about what was meant by this concept. In this chapter it will be seen as an indication of a step towards *legitimate* global *government* which is illuminated by reference to the distinction between order and justice. Use of the word governance in the later 1990s reflected the view that there were some international institutions, like the UN, which had acquired some but not all of the functions of legitimate government. One measure of the development of *legitimate* government was an ongoing concern with justice for individuals within the state. This meant more involvement with the performance of specific tasks, such as economic development or the promotion of higher levels of public health, but it extended beyond that to a system of international mechanisms for continuously monitoring the performance of the states with regard to their citizens, for repeating continuously the tests that were temporarily abandoned in the 1960 Declaration, and for promoting action, with or without government agreement, to correct any failures. 'Governance is not just the province of the state. Rather it is a function that can be performed by a wide variety of public and private, state and non-state, national and international institutions and practices.' 'But the governing powers, international, national and regional, need to be "sutured" together into a relatively well-integrated system' (Hirst and Thompson 1996: 183–4). The state inevitably played a key part in that process, but the role of the United Nations was also of increasing importance. Whether such action was effective, and what happened if governments resisted the attempt, were different questions which are discussed later. In the final section of the chapter the improvement of the UN's role in global governance in this sense is considered.

The theme of the chapter is thus clarified. Any discussion of the United Nations and International Order has to refer to the work of the United Nations with regard to issues which impinged upon justice in a broader sense, as well as that which more directly affected relations between states. It was about human rights, refugee problems, and humanitarian crisis, as well as about Chapter VII activities and peace-keeping. Change in the kind of international order which the United Nations reflected and promoted might also be more clearly understood in this approach. The perception was that what happened *within* states had now to be linked with what happened *between* them.

The United Nations became concerned with the question of international order in three major ways.

First, it was increasingly concerned, not just with the order of the international system, but with the promotion of internal standards within states. Increasingly it dealt with human rights infringements, administrative and economic collapse—rescuing failing states—and helped with elections and with providing humanitarian assistance (see Ch. 28). The nature of the activity was, however, secondary to the primary purpose which might be called *regime restoration*: when the state was endangered, not because of challenges to its sovereignty from without, but because its internal arrangements did not meet the standards expected, the UN claimed the right to act.

Second, it was concerned with what was traditionally the central principle of international order, and of the work of the United Nations and the League before it, namely the promotion of international peace and security through resisting aggression between states. It was in this defending the rights of states in international society. These rights, which were analogous with the primary national interests of states, were increasingly embodied in formal contracts between states. Interests had become rights and principles. The right to security was central to the United Nations, but so were the two other major rights: the right to protect the cultural life of the peoples within states, and the right to an adequate standard of economic provision. The definition of aggression had accordingly been expanded to include attempts to deny these rights.

The involvement of the United Nations in protection was clearly illustrated by the few actions of enforcement, such as the action in Kuwait in the early 1990s and the much earlier involvement in Korea. That such action did not strictly follow the rules of the Charter, contained in Chapter VII, was irrelevant to the principle: in both cases the sanction of the global organization was essential even though the action was carried out by an agent rather than the principal. These two cases should not be construed as the only measure of the United Nations success in this area; the organization embodied a general injunction on behaviour which could be measured by the rule as well as by the breach.

A **third** way in which the UN had become involved in the promotion of order was when sovereignty was contested by rival groups of citizens, often in civil war. The organization was then involved in the process of legitimizing states, either by recreating existing states through the reconciliation of warring internal groups, or by assisting with the dissolution of older states and creating new ones. It was useful to distinguish between the process of overcoming internal problems within existing states, where sovereignty was *not* contested—and restoring the conditions of their sovereignty—on the one hand, and helping with the resolution of disputes between internal groups which had demanded the right to set up separate states—where sovereignty was contested—on the other. At the time of writing it was still not clear which of these outcomes would arise in the most recent example of action mandated through the UN, that of Kosovo in 1999 and after. In the latter case the official doctrine was to protect the sovereignty of Serbia by keeping Kosovo within it, but there were many pressures in favour of independence.

Key points

- The United Nations had become involved in a multilayered system of governance sometimes working with states, sometimes alongside them, and sometimes apart from them.

- Global governance involved a stronger role for international organization in maintaining standards for individuals within states.

- By the mid-1990s the UN had become involved in maintaining international order in three main ways: concern with order within states, with resisting aggression between states, and by attempting to resolve disputes within states.

The United Nations and intervention within states

A difficulty in carrying out the new tasks was that it appeared to run counter to the doctrine of non-intervention. Intervention was traditionally defined as a deliberate incursion into a state without its consent by some outside agency, in order to change the functioning, policies, and goals of its government and achieve effects which favoured the intervening agency (Vincent 1974). One of the changes which was indicative of the changing role of the United Nations was that the traditional ways of justifying intervention without consent had been questioned. The point was not that this had led to the frequent use of the new justifications but rather that it indicated an anxiety about the increasing range, and changing nature, of involvements within states.[7]

Such involvements might be unopposed, or not detected, as well as positively accepted, but have the same effects as non-consensual intervention: to alter the working and output of government to suit an external actor. But very few involvements took place in defiance of the opposition of the host government. Kosovo was unique in that it was an exception to this rule. It was arguably the first occasion on which international forces had been used in the face of the defiance of a sovereign state to protect humanitarian standards. A key issue, therefore, was whether there was an increasing preparedness to intervene within states by the UN in this broader sense. A positive response would be a measure of movement towards global governance. Sovereignty was regarded as central to the system of states. It implied that they were equally members of international society, and were each equal with regard to international law. Sovereignty also implied that states recognized no higher authority than themselves, and that there was no superior jurisdiction; the governments of states had exclusive jurisdiction within their own frontiers, a principle which was enshrined in Article 2 (7) of the United Nations Charter. Intervention in the traditional sense was therefore necessarily always in opposition to the principles of international society, and it could only be tolerated as an exception to the rule.

But in earlier periods states had indeed intervened in each other's business and thought they had a right to do so in a number of situations. The American government refused to accept any curtailment of their right to intervene in the internal affairs of other states in their hemisphere until 1933, when they conceded the point at the seventh International Conference of American States, a position which was very similar to the Brezhnev doctrine of the 1970s, which held that the Soviet Union had the right to intervene in the member states of the socialist commonwealth to protect the principles of socialism.

Much earlier the British had insisted in their relations with other states on the abolition of slavery: they intervened to make sure that this had been done, in that they stopped ships on the high seas, and imposed it as a condition in treaties (Bethell 1970). There had also been a number of occasions when states had tried to bind other states to respect certain principles in their internal affairs. A number of states in Eastern Europe were bound to respect the rights of minorities within their frontiers by the agreements made at the Berlin Conference of 1878 by the Great Powers: they included Hungary and Bulgaria. At the end of the First World War the settlements had similarly imposed conditions on the new states to guarantee the rights of minorities within their frontiers (Claude 1955). In practice intervention was a common feature of international politics, often for good cause.

In the 1980s and 1990s the view was more fre-quently expressed that there should be a return to the earlier period, but this time with a greater determination and a wider range of instruments to protect generally accepted standards. The United Nations could be heir to the earlier aberrations but this time the principle of non-intervention would be challenged on behalf of universal, rather than particular values. To the extent that values were universal the right to intervene by the instrument of global governance would be justified. It was pointed out that the Charter had not merely asserted the rights of states, but also the rights of peoples: statehood could be interpreted as being conditional upon respect for such rights. For instance the Preamble held that the organization was 'to reaffirm faith in fundamental human rights', and Article 1(3) asserted the obligation to 'achieve international co-operation . . . in promoting and encouraging respect for human rights and fundamental freedoms for all'. There was ample evidence in the Charter to justify the view that extreme transgression of human rights could itself be a justification for intervention by the international community. Kosovo and thinking among international lawyers suggested that this might be accepted in the future.

There were a few examples of this view in the early 1990s: the clearest was probably Security Council Resolution 688 which sanctioned the creation of the Safe Havens in Iraq at the end of the Gulf War, which were intended to protect the Kurds against Saddam Hussein. The allies committed themselves to defend the Kurds and to provide them with humanitarian assistance. In the major pronouncements of the United Nations General Assembly on humanitarian assistance, for example, A/43/131 and A/46/182 there was reference to the primary responsibility of the target states for dealing with complex crises within their frontiers, although A/46/182 implied some relaxation of this in its precise wording: it held that 'The sovereignty, territorial integrity and national unity of States must be fully respected in accordance with the Charter of the United Nations. In this context, humanitarian assistance *should* be provided with the consent of the affected country and *in principle* on the basis of an appeal by the affected country' (italics added). The use of the phrase 'in principle', and the normative ' should', implied that there could be occasions when government approval was not possible, but where intervention was nevertheless necessary. This would appear to have been the case with the Kosovo action.

There was disagreement about whether the existing procedures of the United Nations, relying in particular on the approval of the Security Council, were adequate for the authorization of such novel forms of intervention, or whether further safeguards were necessary, such as a two-thirds majority in the General Assembly, and the supervision of the International Court of Justice.[8] It should be stressed though that the Security Council usually had not given explicit approval, but used circumlocutions such as 'all necessary means' as in SC678 which sanctioned the action against Iraq in 1990. It is suggested that in Kosovo this was also the case. The Permanent members, at least, understood that SC1203 meant that there could be action by states through NATO. But a stronger form of action would involve a new practice of explicit authorization. There was the irony here that in order to protect the interests of states a strengthening of the governance of international society might be appropriate: the erosion of the strict interpretation of Article 2(7) of the UN Charter depended upon the creation of countervailing procedures in the global organization. There could be no question of individual states, or particular groups of states, compromising the absolute prohibition on intervention. But the 'interventions' were proposed in order to strengthen rather than weaken states as the primary actors in international society.

The number of occasions remained, however, very limited when there was appeal to a principle involving the rights of individuals in the target territories. Well-known interventions, such as that of India in East Pakistan in 1971, Tanzania in the Uganda of Idi Amin, or of the United States in Panama, were justified by reference to the need to protect the citizens of the *invading* states, and their right of self-defence, both of which were ancient justifications of intervention under international law. The justification of the action in Kosovo also included a view of the security interests of the main participants, but it also included a clear humanitarian element.

Even Security Council Resolution 688 in 1991, referred to above, was somewhat ambiguous as Saddam Hussein's consent to the operation was

Box 16.3 Selected documents relevant to the changing role of the United Nations system

Development of the Economic and Social Organizations

A/32/197 The first major General Assembly Resolution on reform of the economic and social organizations, Dec. 1977.

A/48/162 A major step towards reform of the economic and social organization of the United Nations, especially the Economic and Social Council, Dec.1993.

Development of the UN's Role in Maintaining International Peace and Security

SC Res. 678, Nov., 1990, sanctioned the use of force against Saddam Hussein.

SC Res. 743 Feb. 1992, established UNPROFOR in Croatia.

SC Res. 770, 13 Aug. 1992, created UNPROFOR2 in Bosnia-Herzegovina.

SC 816, Apr. 1993 enforced the no-fly zone over Bosnia in that it permitted NATO war planes to intercept Bosnian Serb planes in the zones.

Development of Humanitarian Action through the UN

SC Res. 688, Apr., 1991 which sanctioned intervention in Iraq at the end of the Gulf war to protect the Kurds in north Iraq, and the Shia Muslims in the south, against the regime of Saddam Hussein.

SC Res. 733, 23 Jan. 1992, first sanctioned UN involvement in Somalia. A/46/182, 14 Apr. 1992, which is the major document on the development of the machinery for humanitarian assistance.

SC Res. 808, July 1993, which set up an *ad hoc* war tribunal with regard to war crimes in ex-Yugoslavia.

SC Res. 794, 3 Dec. 1992, which sanctioned the American move into Somalia; by that stage the central government of Somalia had ceased to exist in the eyes of the majority of states, or at least in the eyes of the member states of the Security Council which approved the resolution unanimously.

Note: documents may now be accessed through the Internet using Netscape or Spry Mosaic.

implied in a series of six-monthly agreements which covered its terms, known as a Memoradum(s) of Understanding (Taylor and Groom 1992). Perhaps it was better described as near-non-consensual intervention! On other occasions, such as that of the Security Council Resolution which first sanctioned UN involvement in Somalia, Resolution 733 which was adopted on 23 January 1992, action was in response to a request by Somalia, even though the government of that country was near expiry. The basis for that intervention was in fact Chapter VII of the Charter, and not humanitarian need. In resolution 794, which authorized the United States to dispatch 30,000 troops to 'establish a secure environment for Humanitarian Relief Operations in Somalia as soon as possible', approved unanimously on 3 December 1992 the explicit consent of the Somalia authorities was not mentioned, but by that time any pretence that such existed could be abandoned.

Key points

- New justifications for intervention in states were being considered by the early 1990s.

- But most operations of the United Nations were justified in the traditional way: there was a threat to international peace and security.

- But any relaxation of the traditional prohibition on intervention had to be treated very cautiously, and new methods of approval in the UN could be advisable if this happened.

The United Nations and forms of involvement within states

But there were other ways of dealing with the problem of how to act within states without the consent of the host government. The range of ways by which involvement could be contrived, to achieve the purposes usually attributed to intervention, was much wider than was usually appreciated. A small number of international organizations such as UNICEF and the ICRC were not required by their founding agreements, or the rules which governed their operations to obtain the formal consent of governments for such involvement. They naturally preferred this, but assumed that they could work on a territory unless expressly forbidden from doing so. In Cambodia UNICEF and ICRC had established a presence during the Vietnamese occupation and operated throughout the area in a low-key way. The publicity generated by reports of massive starvation there by the journalist John Pilger, who had the support of OXFAM, not only led to serious quarrels between OXFAM and the other participating organizations, but provoked the Vietnamese government to restrict aid to the area it occupied. Eventually aid had to be delivered to the Khmer Rouge area in the north-west of the country, where the people were no less deserving, from Thailand (Black 1992: esp. 219–21).

Non-governmental organizations were more likely to succeed in 'intervening' without positive approval than intergovernmental organizations, because of their ingenuity and flexibility in devising entry strategies. They were less sensitive to political constraints, for example, they were less constrained by anxiety about appearing to be partial if there was a dispute within a state. They were also less fearful of losing government funding, as they were financed to a significant degree by private voluntary contributions, and were more prepared to accept risks in the security of their staff. Non-governmental organizations had become major players both in humanitarian assistance and in development by the late 1980s. They often commanded large budgets and had very effective and skilled management (Seaman 1996: 17–32; also Willetts 1996).

The intergovernmental organizations of the UN system were more likely to be constrained by the fear of appearing to be partial in the event of civil war within states, even at the expense of failing to provide humanitarian relief, because of their equation of sovereignty with neutrality regarding internal affairs. This was the reason for the very slow UN involvement in Somalia in 1991–2. Their preference for working through governments, even those that were feeble or in disgrace, and their preference for information provided by governments over that from non-governmental organizations, was a response to the same constraints. They were also subject to rather stricter rules about the security of their staff than were non-governmental organizations.

But once present both NGOs and IGOs were capable of pursuing strategies of greater or lesser involvement with host governments. The government's response could vary from active hostility, which would be a situation quite close to non-consensual intervention, to one of reluctant tolerance. General Assembly Resolution 46\182 stated that 'the affected state has the primary role in the initiation, organization, co-ordination and implementation of humanitarian assistance within its territory'. But there were cases where this principle did not seem to have been followed. For instance, the Kenyan authorities felt that their own Drought Recovery Programme had been dealt with in a fairly cavalier way in the SEPHA consolidated appeal in 1992. The Kenyans had drawn up an appeal in close consultation with the agencies involved, so that when the programme was launched in October 1992 they were confident that it had the full backing of the UN. But subsequently 'they felt uncertain about how far funds contributed to SEPHA would be used for the DRP'—to use the tactful words of a report written by an official (see Taylor 1996b).

There was a wide range of forms of relationship between the UN institutions and host state governments in the various states in which they had become involved, in Africa, Central America, and elsewhere. These are evident in the provision of humanitarian assistance and increasingly in the development process. The traditional view of sovereignty would lead to a relative indifference to the character of the regime except in extremis. But a government could be objectionable to the point that to work with it, even in some areas of humanitarian assistance, would be to defend the indefensible.

There was the problem of how this judgement was to be made: in practice working in such circumstances, when that had the highest priority, would probably be left to non-governmental organizations, and to the few intergovernmental organizations that were willing and able to evade the regime. Simply being there had its uses: a presence would increase the chance of attracting the attention of the international community to a regime's shortcomings.

Working with acceptable regimes on what appeared to be a manageable crisis occured through the UNDP system and in particular the Resident Co-ordinator; but if there was a collapse of such a magnitude as to constitute a complex emergency, and if the government was discredited, then a different mechanism would be indicated, brought afresh into the country. The worse the crisis, and the greater the scale of necessary humanitarian assistance, the more important it was to make a judgement about a regime's acceptability, and to start afresh.

The difficulty in sanctioning any relaxation in the principle of non-intervention should not, however, be underestimated. There could be occasions when states might be particularly fearful of intervention, such as if an army engaged in counter-insurrection activities was accused of gross violations of human rights. The government of India was particularly concerned about any relaxation of the principle, and it was not difficult to think of reasons for this position: the Indian army was vulnerable to accusations of infringements of human rights in various parts of the country, such as Kashmir. Conversely newly independent states were likely to be suspicious of what appeared to be the granting of a licence to Western developed states to intervene in their affairs: the unfortunate reference by the then British Foreign Secretary Douglas Hurd to the possible need for a new kind of imperialism, meaning the taking over by the United Nations of territories where orderly government had collapsed—in a way reminiscent of the trusteeship system—could not have dampened such fears.[9]

In summary there could be a rather fundamentalist interpretation of Article 2(7) of the United Nations Charter, that there could be no intervention within a state without the express consent of the government of that state: the implication appeared to be that no form of behaviour of a sovereign government within its own frontiers was a matter of concern to outsiders. This position was probably most frequently seen in the arguments favoured by the government of mainland China. This position might be compared with the other traditional view, namely that intervention within a country to promote human rights was only capable of justification on the basis of a threat to international peace and security. Evidence of this could be the appearance of significant numbers of refugees, or the judgement that other states might intervene militarily.

In the hands of liberal lawyers this condition appeared flexible enough to justify intervention to defend human rights whenever it seemed prudent. The gradual expansion of the interpretation of Article 99, which gave the Secretary-General the right to bring a threatening crisis situation to the attention of the Security Council, illustrates this point. By the mid-1990s developments such as humanitarian crisis, or the movement of refugees were interpreted as constituting such a threat. Hard-liners, however, had a different view of the condition in Article 2(7): though the Chinese did not dispute the general principle, and could not if they were to remain members of the United Nations, they saw it more as a way of defeating any proposal to intervene. Liberals saw it as a bridge to action, hard-liners as a way of creating barriers by denying there was a threat to international peace and security wherever possible.

Another possibility was for intervention to take place on humanitarian grounds alone, to protect human rights. This possibility had entered the agenda by the late 1990s, but it had been seldom used. But it should not be forgotten that the members of the United Nations system, and other international organizations, were capable of evading the formal objections of governments to intervention. They could become involved in the absence of positive opposition. They could also pursue policies and act in ways that were not directly approved by governments which had allowed them entry, but which could affect the way in which that government worked and the conditions of its survival. They could get under the skin of sovereignty in order to promote sovereignty.

Key points

- Involvement in states did not necessarily depend on actual governmental approval.

- Organizations could act independently of governments once present, and some organizations, such as non-governmental organizations were skilful at establishing a presence without positive government consent.

Sovereignty and the competence of international organization

Sovereignty could be interpreted as being ultimately responsible—the buck stops with the sovereign. Having a role, and doing something, involved being granted a competence, and was not the same as being ultimately responsible. In recent years the analytical distinction between these two questions was more frequently reflected in the practice of states and international organizations: the question of which body was ultimately responsible was increasingly separated from that of which body was allowed competence.[10]

New problems in the way of legitimizing states by granting them sovereignty were matched by new problems about deciding what states should be able to do in order to remain sovereign. The exercise of functions such as control of foreign policy and defence used to be regarded as being central to sovereignty, and could not be allocated to other centres. But the member states of the European Union in the late 1990s could accept that the Union should have a role in their harmonized foreign policy, and that it might increase its involvement in the common defence. There was a majority for this among the Union's citizens. This was an astonishing development which seemed to remove the dilemma, discussed *inter alia* by Rousseau, that responsibility for maintaining the peace could not be allocated to a higher, federal authority without fatally damaging the entity which it was designed to protect, namely the state itself.[11]

The dilemma was avoided by insisting that *ultimate* responsibility remained with the states as they retained reserve powers, including the power to recover the competences. Public opinion and governments could accept the transfer of responsibility for foreign policy and defence without necessarily thinking of this as an infringement of sovereignty: as long as the reserve power was kept.

The expectation was that the chances of the reserve powers being utilized would be progressively reduced. The hierarchy of issues, with defence and foreign policy being regarded as high politics, and questions such as trade policy as low politics, would be compressed. Outside the European Union it was unusual for issues of foreign policy or defence to involve another supranational authority. But it was common for other questions, especially in the economic, social, and other technical areas, previously regarded as essential to the exercise of national sovereignty, to be handled elsewhere in whole or in part. In all these areas questions tended to move from the category of the special to that of the routine. But paradoxically the state's survival rested on the assumption that this transfer could not be guaranteed: the competences could still be recalled in principle even if this in practice was unlikely.

The trick with regard to justice and national interest was to avoid situations where a choice had to be made, because the national interest had to come first. The trick with regard to the extension of competence in areas which were earlier regarded as essential to sovereignty was to avoid situations in which the reserve powers would have be used. The crisis points in international politics would be, for example, when national interest and morality were in conflict; when a policy competence had to be renationalized; or when a state's ability to provide for the welfare of its citizens was in doubt. The test of successful statescraft was to avoid these dilemmas. The skilled diplomat would increasingly require a sophisticated grasp of paradox. The discussion so far permits a particular arrangement of the functions of the UN in the late 1990s. A distinction could be made between those functions which were more immediately concerned with questions of justice in the larger sense and those which were primarily about the older notion of order. The latter might be called traditional UN roles, reflecting the classical principles of international society. The former reflected the new principles, and involved new forms of UN involvement within the states which occurred mainly since the end of the cold war. The possibility of a third list was implied in the discussion, and is added below: it is made up of the difficulties in the way of more effective governance of the international system. There was an injunction to do better many of the things that had been tried. How might this be achieved?

Key points

- Competences were increasingly granted by states to international organizations to carry out tasks previously reserved to national governments.
- This meant that the conditions of sovereignty had changed, but not that the state was under threat.
- The new arrangements were to strengthen not weaken the state.

A typology of the roles of the United Nations in 2000

In this section the main roles of the United Nations system will be discussed briefly. Obviously in the late 1990s a number of them were the concern of a range of international organizations in addition to the United Nations. There was a considerable literature about each of them, and the purpose of this essay is not with any one of them but with the arrangement and interpretation of the whole. There are a large number of more detailed accounts available to the reader.

A. Peace and security between states

These are roles regarding the maintenance of international order in the traditional sense of promoting peace and security between states.

Traditional peace-enforcement. This was the role derived from Chapter VII of the Charter, but different in its mode of execution, as seen in operations such as that in Korea and the Gulf War. The operations were carried out through an agent, usually the US and allies, with a Security Council Mandate, rather than under UN command as stipulated in Chapter VII.

Traditional peacekeeping. This was peacekeeping as illustrated by the UN Emergency Force sent to Egypt after the Suez crisis in November 1956. The force was made up of lightly armed forces, using weapons only if attacked, located with the consent of the host state, under UN Secretary-General control, and excluding forces from the Security Council's permaments members.

Development in co-operation with governments. In this case Specialized Agencies, and other international organizations such as the World Bank, worked with governments. After the late 1960s the ideal form of such development was working through the United Nations Development Pro-gramme (UNDP) in co-operation with the host government, but this system was plagued with problems up to the time of writing. Co-ordination through UNDP proved difficult and the Agencies and Bank tended to have their own projects.

Social and technical functions in co-operation with governments. This covered the range of social and technical functions carried out by the Agencies, Funds, and Programmes in co-operation with governments, for instance, public health improvement and disease control through the World Health Organization, agricultural development through the Food and Agriculture Organization, and promoting industrial development tnrough the United Nations Conference on Trade and Development (UNCTAD) and the United Nations Industrial Development Organization (UNIDO).

Human rights monitoring and standard setting. The wide range of conventions and machinery related to human rights, focused upon standard-setting, monitoring, and generating modest pressures to comply.

The above were all aspects of the traditional functioning of the United Nations and were compatible with the hard doctrine of exclusive domestic jurisdiction: international organizations entered states only with their consent and worked with them once admitted on terms dictated by the government. Such methods were not abandoned but new approaches emerged especially after the late 1980s.

B. Justice within states

(The new forms of involvement were concerned with constructing and amending the state, so that it became more successful as a state, and less likely to be a source of disruption of the international order. This was a new form of international relations.)

Humanitarian assistance. In reconstructing states which had experienced major humanitarian crises, and the collapse of administrative and political structures, the United Nations had taken on a kind of modified trusteeship role. It helped create well-founded states, and, in a sense, issued certificates of legitimacy to new regimes, which was what it purported to do when it helped set up and supervise elections in Namibia, Cambodia, and Angola, and acted to ensure proper respect for human rights in El Salvador. This revealed an irony in the position of the United Nations with regard to sovereignty and Article 2(7) of the UN Charter in the late 1990s. A more flexible view of sovereignty was sought in order to facilitate more effective humanitarian assistance. At first sight, as the Secretary-General admitted this appeared to be a licence for the richer states to act as a world policeman and to trample on the interests of the weaker and less developed states (BBC Radio 4 programme, *The Thin Blue Line*, Sunday 25 April 1993). But the underlying purpose of the UN activities was to make states stronger not weaker: to make the world safe for sovereignty. It was recognized that the Geneva Conventions, and international law regarding human rights, rested on the sovereignty of states. It was the states that sanctioned them and which were responsible for upholding them. States that were properly constituted, in respecting human rights, and in promoting human welfare effectively, were more likely to be strong and stable pillars of such a system.

A **new development agenda**, involving project management alongside, but not with governments, emerged. Although the World Bank and the IMF were required to work with governments, since the end of the 1980s an increasing amount of development work was being conducted through non-governmental organizations and multinational companies, as well as UN agencies, which was not necessarily under the close supervision of the host governnment. This was like the work of the Commission of the EU with regard to the regions in Mediterranean countries—frequently bypassing national governments, and promoting development and a development agenda independently of them in direct links between the international and subnational actors. The role of the UNDP in Palestine in the late 1990s was analogous: the organization was the recipient of large quantities of official and non-official development money which it administered in Palestine to further the rehabilitation of that territory and its people, and it worked alongside the Palestinian authorities rather than under them.

The rehabilitation of states after crisis: this involved such activities as setting up administrations, training administrators and police forces. A considerable range of resources were deployed to serve these purposes in Cambodia and in Namibia, and Kosovo as well as in a large number of other 'states'. This function was that of state building or rehabilitation. It was also the chief legitimator of new regimes, in that it was regularly involved in the monitoring of elections, in effect conferring a licence of statehood.

New peace-keeping functions had developed, involving a wider range of uses for the military under UN command: such new uses included the provision of humanitarian assistance, land-mine clearance, weapon cleansing, as well as the promotion of ground rules, however feebly, in civil war. This would include the monitoring of war crimes, and the identification of the malefactors as with the Serbs in Bosnia-Herzegovina, and pronouncing on legitimate and illegitimate courses of action such as where to place various types of weapon, and which targets were non-acceptable. For example, UN agencies—not the Security Council—condemned an Israeli strike on a UN-protected compound in Lebanon in May 1996.

Human rights promotion and enforcement: international organization, including the United Nations, had become gradually more involved in the active defence of human rights and the charging of individuals accused of serious breaches, as with war crimes. The War Crimes Tribunal set up at the Hague in 1995 illustrated this.

Firmer standards over a wide range of issues were also promoted by international organizations with some degree of success. These included standards of environmental protection, such as protecting endangered species, biodiversity, and pollution control, as well as more effective population control. Large-scale Special Conferences became a feature of this work (Taylor and Groom 1989). This was not to say that by 2000 such standards were non-contentious—far from it—but they were being more firmly enunciated, and more widely accepted. Technical imperatives were conceivable.

The arms register. The United Nations had also set up a system for registering the flow of arms around the world: who was selling what to whom? There had also been the slow development of more sophisticated techniques for monitoring the development of crises, through noting troop movements, and recording areas of possible crop failure. The frontiers of states were increasingly permeable in ways not dreamed of by John Herz in the early 1960s (Hertz 1962) and this was one of the pillars of international accountability.

C. The problems of global governance in the early twenty-first century

The UN system had acquired many of the functions of governance but was deficient with regard to the necessary instruments, and in consequence fell short of successfully performing the new roles. What were the deficiencies?

There were continuing problems of co-ordination and planning, which were to be found in the management of the economic and social activities of the UN as well as in the performance of the expanded range of peacekeeping functions. These were extensively discussed in the literature and by 1996 had culminated in GA Resolution 48/162 of December 1994.

There were problems of coping with sovereignty and the need for neutrality, which in terms of UN activity were related problems. Sovereignty was still a problem with regard to the UN's becoming involved in grave crises within the state.

The financial problem. The United Nations system with regard to the regular budget and the peacekeeping fund had a serious financial shortfall, mainly because of the nonpayment by the United States of assessed contributions for the regular and peacekeeping budgets. The sum owed was around $3 billion and this was obviously a major source of practical and operational difficulties throughout the United Nations system.

There were problems of executive competence and legitimacy. As the functions of the system expanded the problems of the executive became more apparent. First there was a problem of representation. A number of states became increasingly unhappy about the restricted membership of the Security Council, but also complained about the membership of the executive committees of other organizations in the UN system. A second problem, from the point of view of effective governance, concerned the resolutions of the Security Council. There were three aspects of this. First, the Security Council was not obliged to seek the consistency of its resolutions with previous treaties, which remained valid and had not been abrogated. There was no instrument in the system which ensured that new resolutions were consistent with the existing body of treaty rules and agreements. For instance its recognition of the Republic of Cyprus, and non-recognition of the Turkish Republic of North Cyprus, was arguably inconsistent with the existing, valid treaties between Greece, Turkey, and Britain which guaranteed the bicommunality of Cyprus, a principle that had been unilaterally countermanded by 'Greek' Cyprus (Ertekun 1984). Second, there was no instrument whereby new Security Council resolutions would be required to be consistent with earlier Security Council resolutions. Frequently there were inconsistencies. Indeed in other parts of the UN system, such as the Committee on Disarmament, resolutions were approved which were inconsistent with what had been agreed previously. In instances such as these there were no procedures for ensuring that resolutions prompted the emergence of an internally consistent system of international laws. Third, the Security Council was not subject to any requirement for technical consistency in the sense that it was not subject to a rule requiring means to be appropriate to ends. It frequently passed resolutions without providing for the means for attaining the stated goals. The classic case of this in the 1990s was the setting up of the safe areas in ex-Yugoslavia, without providing the resources for their defence, or for their demilitarization.

The UN lacked mechanisms for judicial review and supervision. The European Union was less a victim of the kinds of problem discussed in the preceding paragraphs because it possessed two instruments which were designed to establish the coherent development and internal consistency of its internal mechanisms and laws: the Commission was enjoined to achieve such consistency, as was the European Court of Justice. Similarly all the EU's institutions including the Council of Ministers, made up of governmental representatives, were subject to the law of the Community and the supervision of the European Court of Justice. But in the UN system the International Court of Justice (ICJ) had no superior jurisdiction. The next logical step was to make the UN's institutions subject to the jurisdiction of the ICJ, on the analogy of the EU. A parallel measure was sought by the Secretary-General in the mid-1990s: the right to seek directly the view of the ICJ about, *inter alia*, the legality of courses of action proposed by the UN institutions.

The problem of information and analysis: the capacity of the UN to collect and interpet information needed further enhancement. In the first phase of the development of international institutions charged with maintaining international peace and security, the security function was that of a fire brigade. The League Council, according to the Covenant, was not a permament institution, but was to meet when a crisis had arisen. In a second phase, in the United Nations, the fire brigade was on permanent stand-by as the Security Council was a permanent institution which could be called on to act at short notice. In the third phase the security mechanisms of the organization were altered to facilitate an enhanced capacity to adopt an interpositional function between warring parties within states. At the same time enforcement procedures with regard to inter-state disputes developed along lines which were not foreseen by the founders, in that it became increasingly apparent that the United Nations could not take on such a role in itself. It would always need to rely on an agent of enforcement, such as an *ad hoc* coalition of states, a particular state, such as the US, or on a defence organization like NATO. In a fourth phase, visible by the late 1980s, the range of information and analysis had been improved, but needed further improvement, so that the best intelligence available from states would also be available to the UN; at the same time, the UN would have its own independent mechanisms as a way of validating what it had obtained from elsewhere. The fourth phase would be that of the global watch, taking the UN into ongoing monitoring of likely crisis situations, rather than the traditional role of responding when they occured.

Conclusions

In the late 1990s and early twenty-first century the system functions of the UN included the crucial function of acting as a trigger to set in train the processes appropriate to the upholding of the rules of the system. Over the previous half-century or so these rules had become increasingly numerous and specific, covering an increasing range of the activities of relations between states. Not only were they concerned with commerce, and the protection of the rights of states, but also with the rights of individuals. The biggest change of all was probably the latter one, with a number of conventions defining transgressions against the individual person, and beginning to set up remedies if they are demonstrated. But obtaining the agreement of governments to the principles of individual rights was but the first step. It was necessary to find ways of instituting the remedies and of triggering the actions of the relevant instruments. As within states, this was not merely a legal matter: it was also necessary to have an instrument to trigger action when a law had been transgressed. There was in this process an absolute need for an instrument which appeared to embody in some sense the collective will—as with police acting in the name of the collectivity in a stable democracy—which achieved consistency, and was impartial and reliable.

The closest to that in the international system in the late 1990s remained the executive committee of the UN, the Security Council, and it was striking that even the largest states tended to prefer to get its authorization for any action they proposed, as with the US intervention in Haiti. Regarding Kosovo, the active states were all concerned to demonstrate that they were acting justly according to the Charter and the relevant Security Council resolutions. A number of adjustments in the working methods of the Security Council in this context had been discussed in the literature, and had been proposed by governments: special procedures might be needed to reinforce the impression that the decisions taken represented the collective will. These included stronger qualified majorities in the Council, and a concurrent vote by a qualified or simple majority in the General Assembly. But the normal pattern was for Security Council involvement and it was to that body that even the more powerful states had come to seek authorization. As has been pointed out the Security Council did not give explicit authorization for the Kosovo action, but in the past it had also rarely done so, and a reading of the relevant Resolutions and related acts gives enough evidence to support the view that they could be construed as giving authorization.

Other ways of establishing the value of the UN stressed the role of what could be called the evolving civil society of governments. It had become the legitimizer of international agreements, including that SC 1244 which marked the end of the NATO bombing of the Serb military in Kosovo. In the late 1990s there was, however, a debate about the limits of the role of the UN which served to distinguish between a range of system functions and their location. The United States had tried to get support for a new strategic concept for NATO in 1998–9: US Secretary of State Madelaine Albright, proposed that NATO should act in lieu of the UN as an agent for global stability, partly because of the unpopularity of

the organization with some groups of Americans, partly because NATO was an effective organization which was in search of a role for itself at the end of the cold war, and partly because in 1996 Congress approved an act requiring the Administration to get its approval for each and every future US involvement in peacekeeping operations. But the US preference was rebuffed. At the NATO Council meeting in March 1999 the US was greatly disappointed by the refusal of other NATO members to accept the new US view of the NATO role. They asserted that the UN should have priority, and that NATO should not have a general sweeper role.

But this US initiative should be seen as an attempt to relocate a function of the international community, namely the executing of the various tasks linked with the maintenance of international peace and security, rather than an attempt to deny the UN the role of mandate giver. It went along with a number of other developments that were also noticeable in the mid- to late 1990s, such as the increasing use of local or regional organizations to carry out that function in some parts of the world, in particular in Africa, and indeed an increasing preparedness to work with non-governmental organizations to achieve UN approved goals. But it was important to note that those goals were UN approved. US officials and the military wanted the approval of a significant coalition if they could, and the UN mandate was an acceptable even desirable example.

It could be argued therefore—though it was too early to be sure—that different functions were now being distinguished and relocated. An operational function was being located more frequently in other organizations; but the function of overseeing and approving stayed with the UN Security Council, and it was the latter which was primarily responsible for legitimizing ensuing accords, and was the primary forum of their negotiation. The authority of the UN and the key position of the Security Council as the generator of mandates, the overseer of security maintenance operations, and the granter of legitimacy, was defended.

The context of the UN was also one in which governments acquired status in the system. They had come to regard success in that context as a criterion of success as states. Being accepted as a candidate for high office in the UN, for instance by membership of its key committees, and the performing of key roles in the system, had come to be regarded as legitimizing their autonomy.

There had been a qualitative change in the international civil society of governments which had two related elements. First was the gradual accumulation of institutional contexts in which governments were involved, and second was the gradual identification of an international moral order to which governments were under continuous pressure to react. Indeed it was now, for the first time, possible to construct a typology of the characters of governments in relation to this moral order. There were governments which were conformist; there were those which were missionary; which were creational, or vocational; and, of course, there were those which were reformist or revolutionary. For those governments which were positive about the international moral order, regardless of their orientation, the United Nations system was a key element in legitimizing that order. But this disposition was reinforced by the increasingly dense institutional context. Involvement through diplomats in that context was routine and increasingly was the mechanism through which governments derived their self-esteem.

For an increasing number of states there had indeed been a switch in the balance between internal resources and external performance in the sense that the external performance and pattern of involvement generated added value to—rather than consuming—internal resources. That British performance and status in the United Nations was a multiplier not a consumer of British diplomatic leverage was an obvious example, but the increasing density of the international institutional context meant that was likely to be true to a greater or lesser degree for all states. Diplomats had become not merely the instruments of state policy, and consumers of national power resources, but also actual generators of national merit. How they stood in the dense institutional context was a key element in government's judgement of itself and in the way it was judged by others in the system. Hence office holding, initiative taking, providing personnel, and norm policing were seen as having value because they added—in traditional terms—to the self-esteem and power of the state. The UN was a natural beneficiary of this and developments in peacekeeping including the Kosovo experience did not damage this role.

In this way the development of the international civil society had generated in governments ways of seeing their own worth and the worth of others which were similar to the ways in which individuals evaluated themselves, and were evaluated, in stable national orders. Measures of achievement and of status are socially determined: without the roles ascribed by society the state would lose its worth. This was a consequence of the two developments mentioned: reaching a particular stage in the increasing density of the institutional context, and a degree of consensus about the appropriate international moral order, or international community. In these two contexts the United Nations system was key, and that was one reason why states were overwhelmingly agreed that although the reform of the United Nations might be appropriate, no risks should be taken with regard to its survival. They agreed that the Charter should not be renegotiated, and the essential character of the system of agencies, funds, and programmes should not, and indeed, could not be altered. The Kosovo experience had by no means undermined this view, or damaged the view that the UN performed an essential system role in international society.

In this chapter the nature of the changes in the role of the United Nations with regard to the maintenance of international order have been reviewed, and on the basis of the discussion under this heading a typology of traditional and new functions was constructed. This typology was revealing in that it highlighted ways of improving the governance of the society of states which could be carried out through the United Nations. These improvements carried forward alterations that had already entered the agenda; a start had been made in their direction. However badly the new functions were performed, there were now new expectations. Finding adequate means for the better governance of international society could take a long time, but a return to the status quo ante was unlikely. But the new world, dimly glimpsed, was not a world without states. It was one in which states were promoted and protected more effectively. But the conditions of their sovereignty had altered.

QUESTIONS

1 How does the United Nations try to maintain international order?

2 Why have more states decided to support the work of the United Nations?

3 How far have traditional restraints with regard to intervention within states been relaxed?

4 What are the major new roles taken on by international organizations like the UN since the late 1980s?

5 What problems have been in the way of the UN carrying out its expanded roles more effectively?

6 Does allowing international organizations to do more undermine the sovereignty of states?

7 Why was there greater opposition to developing the international accountibilty of states during the cold war?

8 What lessons about the present role and future of the UN might be drawn from the Kosovo experience?

GUIDE TO FURTHER READING

Introductory surveys

Archer, Clive, *International Organisations*, 2nd edn. (London: Routledge, 1992). A useful, succinct survey of the range of international institutions in terms of their main purpose and nature.

Armstrong, David, *The Rise of the International Organisation: A Short History* (London: Macmillan, 1982). An account of the development of international institutions. Useful on their origins and the reasons for their appearance from the last century to the present.

Bennett, A. LeRoy, *International Organisations: Principles and Issues*, 5th edn. (Englewood Cliffs, NJ: Prentice Hall, 1991). A massive and detailed account of the universe of international institutions. Very strong as an empirical text on the range of international institutions and their work.

Taylor, Paul, and Groom, A. J. R. (eds.), *The United Nations at the Millennium* (London: Continuum, 2000). A detailed account of the institutions of the central United Nations system with chapters on the General Assembly, the Security Council, the Economic and Social Council, and others.

More advanced overviews

Barston, R. P., *Modern Diplomacy* (London: Longmans, 1988). A stimulating account of diplomatic processes in the modern age with frequent reference to the United Nations system.

Claude, Inis L., Jr., *Swords into Plowshares: The Progress and Problems of International Organization*, 4th edn. (New York: Random House, 1984). The classic text on international institutions at work. All the major themes, but particularly concerned with their role in war and peace.

Roberts, Adam, and Kingsbury, Benedict (eds.), *United Nations, Divided World: The UN's Roles in*

International Relations, 2nd edn. (Oxford: Clarendon Press, 1993). A collection of readings from practitioners and academics. Very important on the issues concerning the UN in the early twenty-first century.

Weiss, Thomas G., Forsythe, David P., and Coate, Roger A., *The United Nations and Changing World Politics*, 2nd edn. (Boulder, Colo.: Westview Press, 1997). A very good overview of the problems facing the UN in the early twenty-first century by leading US scholars.

On particular themes

Boutros Boutros-Ghali, *An Agenda for Peace* (New York: UN, 1992). The report from the Secretary-General which became a primary reference for all those concerned with the UN's role on the maintenance of international peace and security.

Brundtland, Gro Harlem, *et al.* (The Brundtland Report), *Our Common Future: Report of the World Commission on Environment and Development* (Oxford: Oxford University Press, 1987). A major study on problems concerning the environment and approaches to it.

James, Alan, *Peacekeeping in International Politics* (Basingstoke: Macmillan, 1990). The leading overview on peace-keeping.

Williams, Douglas, *The Specialised Agencies and the United Nations: The System in Crisis* (London: Hurst, 1987). This is still a highly relevant, and readable account of the work of the Specialized Agencies. The key text on the Agencies and still relevant.

Lyons, Gene M., and Mastanduno, Michael (eds.), *Beyond Westphalia: State Sovereignty and International Intervention* (Baltimore: Johns Hopkins University Press, 1995). A collection of readings on the key themes especially sovereignty.

White, Nigel D., *Keeping the Peace: the UN and the Maintenance of International Peace and Security*, 2nd edn. (Manchester: Manchester University Press, 1997). A useful account of the problems and achievements of the UN with regard to peacekeping

Theoretical Work

Groom, A. J. R., and Taylor, Paul, *Frameworks for International Cooperation* (London: Pinter, 1990). A comprehensive text on the theories applicable to the work of international institutions.

Jacobson, Harold K., *Networks of Interdependence: International Organizations and the Global Political System*, 2nd edn. (New York: Knopf, 1984). A theoretically informed look at the way international institutions responded to the increasing interdependence of states.

Taylor, Paul, *International Organization in the Modern World* (London: Pinter, 1995). A comparative approach to global and regional institutions.

Individual and national perspectives

Jensen, Erik, and Fisher, Thomas (eds.), *The United Kingdom—The United Nations* (London: Macmillan, 1990). The only developed account of Britain's relationship with the UN.

Parsons, Sir Anthony, *From Cold War to Hot Peace: UN Interventions 1947–1995* (Harmondsworth: Penguin Books, 1995). A readable and insightful account of the UN's involvement in civil wars by a highly placed British diplomat. A profound work.

Urquhart, Sir Brian, *A Life in Peace and War* (New York: Harper and Row, 1991). A highly readable autobiography of a man who for many years was Britain's senior member of the UN secretariat.

WEB LINKS

www.un.org   is the UN main website

www.unsystem.org   for all parts of the UN system including all Agencies, Funds and Programmes

www.unausa.org   for the UN Association of the USA

www.globalpolicy.org   Global Policy Forum

www.isn.ethz.ch   for the International Relations and Security Network

NOTES

1. See the excellent introduction to the development of the security functions of the United Nations in Roberts (1996: 283–308).

2. For an account of the involvement of the United Nations system in this issue, and others on the new Agenda, see Felix Dodds, (ed.), *The Way Forward: Beyond Agenda 21* (London: Earthscan, 1997).

3. For an interpretation of Functionalism see Claude (1971).

4. For an account of the diplomacy leading up to the agreements at Dayton in 1996 see Spyros Economides and Paul Taylor, 'Former Yugoslavia', in James Mayall (ed.), *The New Interventionism, 1991–1994* (Cambridge: Cambridge University Press, 1996).

5. See discussion of this issue, and reference to the Kirkpatrick essay, in Forsythe (1988: 259–60).

6. This is one of the arguments in Vincent (1986).

7. See the excellent collection of essays on intervention in Lyons and Mastanduno (1995).

8. See Development Studies Association, evidence to the Foreign Affairs Select Committee of the House of Commons, titled *The United Nations Humanitarian Response*, Nov. 1992.

9. This issue was discussed in oral evidence to the House of Commons Foreign Affairs Select Committee by Sir John Thomson and Sir Crispin Tickell, as reported in *The Expanding Role of the United Nations and its Implications* . . . (HMSO, 17 Feb. 1993), 175–6 and *passim*.

10. See the excellent discussion of the issues raised here, including recognition by the UN, in Dugard (1987).

11. This issue is discussed by the author in *The European Union in the 1990s* (Oxford University Press, 1996).

17 Transnational actors and international organizations in global politics

Peter Willetts

READER'S GUIDE

The subject of International Relations originally covered simply the relations between states, for example Britain's relations with India. Economic bodies and social groups, such as banks, industrial companies, students, environmentalists, and women's organizations, were given secondary status as non-state actors. This two-tier approach has been challenged, particularly by the effects of globalization. First, ambiguities in the meaning given to 'a state', and its mismatch with the contemporary world, result in it not being a useful concept. Greater clarity is obtained by analysing intergovernmental and inter-society relations, with no presumption that one sector is more important than the other. Second, we can recognize governments are losing sovereignty when faced with the economic activities of transnational companies and the violent threat from criminals and guerrillas. Third, non-governmental organizations (NGOs) engage in such a web of global relations, including participation in diplomacy, that governments have lost their political independence. We conclude that events in any area of global policy-making have to be understood in terms of complex systems, containing governments, companies, and NGOs interacting in a variety of international organizations.

Introduction

In diplomacy, international law, journalism, and academic analysis, it is widely assumed that international relations consists of the relations between coherent units called **states**. This chapter will argue that better understanding of political change is obtained by analysing the relations between governments and many other actors from each country. Global politics also includes companies and non-governmental organizations. (We will see below that this is a technical term. It does not cover all actors other than governments. In particular it excludes commercial bodies.) While there are less than 200 governments in the global system, there are approximately

- 60,000 major transnational companies (TNCs), such as Shell, Barclays Bank, Coca Cola, Ford, Microsoft, or Nestlé, with these parent companies having more than 500,000 foreign affiliates;

- 10,000 single-country non-governmental organizations (NGOs), such as Freedom House (USA), Médecins sans Frontières (France), Population Concern (UK), Sierra Club (USA), or the Women's Environmental Network (UK), who have significant international activities;

- 250 intergovernmental organizations (IGOs), such as the UN, NATO, the European Union, or the International Coffee Organization; and

- 5,800 international non-governmental organizations (INGOs), such as Amnesty International, the Baptist World Alliance, the International Chamber of Shipping, or the International Red Cross, plus a similar number of less-well-established international caucuses and networks of NGOs.

All these actors play a regular part in global politics and interact with the governments. In addition, even though they are considered not to be legitimate participants in the system, guerrilla groups and criminal gangs have some impact. Very many more companies and NGOs only operate in a single country, but have the potential to expand into other countries.[1]

Nobody can deny the number of these organizations and the range of their activities. The controversial questions are whether the non-state world has significance in its own right and whether it makes any difference to the analysis of inter-state relations. It is possible to *define* international relations as covering the relations between states. This is known as the state-centric approach, or **Realism**. Then it is only a tautology (true by definition) to say that non-state actors are of secondary importance. A more open-ended approach, known as **Pluralism**, is based on the assumption that all types of actors can affect political outcomes. It is an unacceptable analytical bias to decide, before research starts, that only states have any influence. Some state-centric writers acknowledge this point in a highly restrictive manner: 'non-state actors need to be taken into account just as and when they influence what goes on between states—and not otherwise' (James 1993: 270). This position appears to be reasonable for the study of subjects like UN peacekeeping, but it is arbitrary to make the claim for all subjects. Given that governments are important primarily because they assert the right to exercise authority over society, a suitable reply to James is 'governments need to be taken into account just as and when they influence what goes on among NGOs and not otherwise'. Until the evidence indicates otherwise, we must assume that governments and NGOs interact with each other, along with companies and international organizations. Who actually determines outcomes will vary from issue to issue.

The importance of words: from 'non-state' actors to transnational actors

Some preliminary comments about the vocabulary of International Relations are necessary. The very words, **non-state actors**, imply that states are dominant and other actors are secondary. There is ambiguity, because it is unclear whether intergovernmental organizations are regarded as inter-state or

Box 17.1 **Key concepts**

Realism: the theoretical approach that analyses all international relations as the relations of states engaged in the pursuit of power. Realism cannot accommodate any non-state actors within its analysis.

Neo-realism: the modification of the Realist approach that occurred in the early 1970s, by recognizing that economic resources—in addition to military capabilities—are a basis for exercising influence. The most significant change was in abandoning the concept of a single international system in favour of there being many issue-specific systems, each characterized by their own power structure. Thus Saudi Arabia may be the most powerful state in the politics of oil, while Brazil is the most powerful in the politics of rainforests. (See also Box 17.12.)

Pluralism: the theoretical approach that considers all organized groups as being potential political actors and analyses the processes by which actors mobilize support to achieve policy goals. Pluralism can encompass non-governmental organizations, companies, and international organizations. Elsewhere in this book, this approach is also referred to as Liberalism. The author of this chapter prefers the term Pluralism, as he does not accept the assumption that theory necessarily has a normative component.

State: the one word is used to refer to three distinct concepts:

1. In international law, a **state** is an entity that is recognized to exist when a government is in control of a community of people within a defined territory. It is comparable to the idea in domestic law of a company being a legal person.

2. In the study of international politics, each state is a **country**. It is a community of people who interact in the same political system and who have some common values.

3. In philosophy and sociology, the state consists of the apparatus of **government**, in its broadest sense, covering the executive, the legislature, the administration, the judiciary, the armed forces, and the police.

Sovereignty: the condition of a state being free from any higher legal authority. It is related to, but distinct from, the condition of a government being free from any external political constraints. Thus, during the cold war, many small states were sovereign, without their governments being politically independent.

Non-state actor: a term widely used to mean any actor that is not a government. Often it is not clear whether the term is being used to cover bodies such as the United Nations. Ambiguity is best avoided by referring separately to two categories, transnational actors and international organizations.

Nation: a group of people who recognize each other as sharing a common identity, with a focus on a homeland. This identity does not have to be acknowledged by other political groups for it to exist.

Nation-state: would exist if nearly all the members of a single nation were organized in a single state, without any other national communities being present. Although the term is widely used, no such entities exist.

Transnational actor: any non-governmental actor from one country that has relations with any actor from another country or with an international organization.

---

non-state organizations. It is also confusing to put into a single category actors that have very different structures, different resources, and different ways of influencing politics. So, from now on the term, 'non-state', will be abandoned.

An alternative word, **transnational**, has been coined by academics in order to assert forcefully that international relations are not limited to governments. Unfortunately, diplomats use the word transnational to mean a company, while other non-profit-making, non-violent groups are called NGOs. The differences can be handled by using 'trans-national' in the academic sense, to cover any private actor, and making it plain whether a company or another type of transnational actor is being discussed. On this basis, a summary of the different categories of participants in global politics from each country is given in the chart (Fig. 17.1).

It is still quite common to find analyses of international relations that concentrate primarily on the governments, give some attention to intergovernmental organizations and ignore the transnational actors. Even in fields such as environmental politics, where it is widely accepted that governments inter-

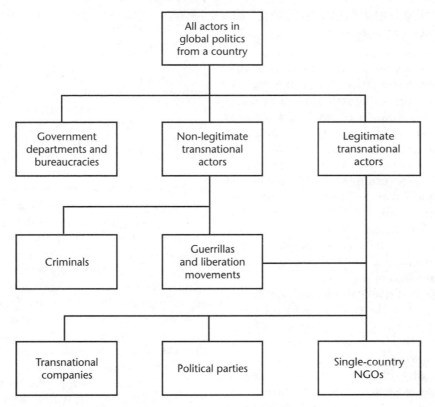

Fig. 17.1 Classification of global political actors
The bottom three categories all form international NGOs.

act intensely with UN agencies, commercial companies, and environmental pressure groups, it is sometimes taken for granted that governments are dominant (see for example Hurrell and Kingsbury 1992, or even Porter and Brown 1991: 35). The only way such bias towards the real world can be understood is in terms of the theoretical bias of orthodox analysis.

This chapter will first consider how assumptions made about 'states' inhibit analysis of transnational actors and international organizations. Then the nature of the different types of actors will be outlined. Finally, the case will be argued for always considering the activities of a diverse range of political actors.

Problems with the state-centric approach

The great advantage of the state-centric approach is that the bewildering complexity of world politics is reduced to the relative simplicity of the interactions of less than two hundred supposedly similar units.

However, there are *four* major problems that suggest the benefits of simplification have been gained at the cost of the picture being distorted and blurred.

1. Ambiguity between different meanings of a 'state'

Writers who refer to the state often fail to use the term consistently and lack intellectual rigour by merging three concepts. The **state** as a legal person is a highly abstract fiction. This is easily confused with the concrete concept of a **country**, with a distinct political system of people sharing common values. Then there is a very dissimilar concept of a state as the apparatus of **government**. Unfortunately, no standard method exists to handle the ambiguity. From now on, this chapter will use the word, state, to indicate the abstract legal concept, while country and government will be used to analyse political behaviour. Conventional ambiguous usage will be indicated by inverted commas.

With the legal and political-community concepts, *civil society is part of the state*, whereas for philosophers and sociologists focusing on the state as government *civil society is separate from the state*. Thus, in international law or when the state means the whole country, there is very little room to acknowledge the existence of distinct transnational actors. Alternatively, when the state means the government and does not encompass society, we can investigate both intergovernmental relations and the inter-society relations of transnational actors.

2. The lack of similarity between countries

The second problem is that defining all 'states' in the same way and giving them all the same legal status implies they are all essentially the same type of unit. If we consider the countries of the world, it is plain that they are not remotely similar. Orthodox analysis does acknowledge differences in size between 'the superpowers' and middle and small 'powers'. Nevertheless this does not suggest that at the end of the cold war the United States economy was twice the size of the Soviet Union's economy, nor that at the end of the twentieth century the US economy was nine times China's, 55 times Saudi Arabia's, more than 1,000 times Ethiopia's and 78,000 times greater than Kiribati's. In terms of population, the

divergences are even greater. The small island countries of the Caribbean and the Pacific with populations measured in tens of thousands are not comparable entities to ordinary small countries, let alone China or India: they are truly 'micro-states'. Alternatively, comparing the governments of the world reveals a diverse range of democracies, feudal regimes, ethnic oligarchies, economic oligarchies, populist regimes, theocracies, military dictatorships, and idiosyncratic combinations. The only thing that the countries have in common is the general recognition of their right to have their own government. They are legally equal and politically very different.

The consequence of admitting the differences in size is to make it obvious that the largest transnational actors are considerably larger than many of the countries. The 50 largest transnational industrial companies each have an annual sales revenue greater than the GNP of 132 members of the United Nations. Using people as the measure, many NGOs, particularly trade unions and campaigning groups in the fields of human rights, women's rights, and the environment, have their membership measured in millions, whereas 40 of the 188 countries in the UN have populations of less than one million.[2] The differences also mean that there is great variation in the complexity and diversity of the economies and the societies of different countries and hence the extent to which they are each involved in transnational relations.

3. The problem of holism

Third, there is an underlying inconsistency in the **ontology** of supposing 'states' are located in an anarchical international system. Whether it means a legal unit, a country, or a government, the 'state' is seen as a **holistic entity**: it is considered to be a coherent unit, acting with common purpose and existing as something more than the sum of its parts (the individual people). At the same time, many advocates of the state-centric approach deny the possibility of holistic entities existing at the global level. The phrase, 'the international system', is used, but only to convey a loose assembly of 'states'. The reference to a **system** is not intended to carry its full technical meaning of a collectivity in which the component elements (the individual 'states') lose some of their independence. No philosophical argument has been put forward to explain the inconsistency in the assumptions made about the different levels of analysis. By exaggerating the coherence of 'states' and downplaying the coherence of global politics, both transnational relations and intergovernmental relations are underestimated.

4. The difference between state and nation

Fourth, there is a behavioural assumption that politics within 'states' is significantly different from politics between 'states'. This is based on the idea that people's loyalty to their **nation** is more intense than other loyalties. Clearly, it cannot be denied that nationalism and national identity invoke powerful emotions for most people, but various caveats must be made about their political relevance. Communal identities form a hierarchy from the local through the nation to wider groupings: a Yorkshire person may simultaneously be English and identify with the Commonwealth or with Europe. Thus, local communities and intergovernmental bodies, such as the European Community, can also make claims on a person's loyalty.

There has been a long-standing linguistic conjuring trick whereby national loyalty is made to appear as if it is focused on the '**nation-state**'. Both inter*national* relations and trans*national* relations cover relations across 'state' boundaries, although logically the words refer to relations between national groups, such as the Scots and the Welsh. In the real world, only a few countries, such as Iceland, Poland, and Japan, can make a reasonable claim that their people are from a single nation and in all such cases there are significant numbers of the national group resident in other countries, often in the USA. Most countries are multinational and many national groups are present in several countries. Thus national loyalty is actually quite different from loyalty to a country. National liberation movements, national cultural groups, and national minorities making political demands are transnational actors, which at times mount a significant challenge to governmental authority. Ironically, nationalism is one of the many sources of transnational relations.

Box 17.2 **Key concepts**

Ontology: concerned with our view of what is *real* and the nature of the types of entities that can or cannot exist.

A holistic entity: exists when a set of elements form a system that has distinct properties at the collective level. This is often expressed as 'the whole is more than the sum of the parts'. The clearest example is the way in which the parts of your body produce the properties of a living person. Similarly, people form social groups, organizations, societies, and nations that both reflect the individuals who make up the collective entity and affect the attitudes and behaviour of the individuals.

System: term commonly used to mean any set of elements that have a complex structure. This chapter uses the technical concept from Systems Science, which is limited to a holistic entity.

Key points

- The concept of the 'state' has three very different meanings: a legal person, a political community, and a government.

- The countries and governments around the world may be equal in law, but have few political similarities. Many governments control less resources than many transnational actors.

- It cannot be assumed that all country-based political systems are more coherent than global systems, particularly as national loyalties do not match country boundaries.

- By abandoning the language of 'states' and 'non-state' actors, we can admit the possibility of theorizing about many types of actors in global politics. By distinguishing government from society and nation from country, we can ask whether private voluntary groups, companies, and national minorities in each country engage in transnational relations.

- In summary, once 'states' are no longer described as homogeneous coherent entities, they must be analysed as open systems, having many channels for governmental and transnational connections to international systems.

Transnational companies as political actors

All companies that import or export are engaging in transnational economic activities. Often changes in health and safety standards, regulation of communication facilities, or the general economic policy of foreign governments will affect their ability to trade. If this is beneficial, they will not necessarily respond, but, if they expect to lose financially, they may well decide to lobby the foreign government. This can be done by four common routes:

1. indirectly by the company asking its own government to put pressure on the foreign government;

2. indirectly by raising a general policy question in an international organization;

3. directly at home via the diplomatic embassy; or

4. directly in the other country via the government ministries.

Several other routes to apply pressure, such as trade associations and more complex indirect routes, can also be used. Thus even a company that is based in a single country may be a significant transnational political actor.

The first companies that expanded beyond their home country to become **transnational companies** (TNCs), in the fullest sense, did so in the European empires or the quasi-empire of the United States in Latin America and Asia. The classic cases were companies in agriculture, mining, or oil. After decolon-

---

Box 17.3 **Key concepts**

Transnational company: in the most general sense any company based in one country that has dealings with the society or government in another country. However, the term, transnational company (TNC), is normally reserved for a company that has affiliates in a foreign country. The affiliates may be branches of the parent company, separately incorporated subsidiaries or associates, with large minority shareholdings.

Intra-firm trade: international trade from one branch of a TNC to an affiliate of the same company in a different country. In the case of bauxite all the trade is intra-firm and hence there is no such thing as a world market for bauxite.

Transfer price: the price set by a TNC for intra-firm trade of goods or services. For accounting purposes, a price must be set for exports, but it need not be related to any market price. Changes in the transfer price do not necessarily have any effect on the sales or the global pre-tax profits of the company.

Triangulation: occurs when trade between two countries is routed indirectly via a third country.

Arbitrage: the process of buying a product in one market and selling it in a different market, in order to make a profit from the difference between the prices in the two markets.

Regulatory arbitrage: in the world of banking, the process of moving funds or business activity from one country to another, in order to increase profits by escaping the constraints imposed by government regulations. By analogy the term can be applied to any transfer of economic activity by any company in response to government policy.

Extraterritoriality: arises when one government attempts to exercise its legal authority in the territory of another state. It mainly arises when the US federal government deliberately tries to use domestic law to control the global activities of TNCs.

ization the companies often had to be split up, so that the overseas branches became separate legal entities, but still under central control of the headquarters. From the 1960s there has been a massive expansion, with many of the major industrial manufacturers establishing overseas subsidiaries. Some financial services, like banking, had moved into the empires as the colonies began to develop, but from the 1970s onwards most of the service industries, including advertising, market research, auditing, and computing, also set up new operations around the world or formed global structures by mergers and acquisitions. Now transnational companies can be expected to operate in any major economic sector, except for products that are specific to particular cultures. The geographical spread has also widened, so industrialized countries that never had empires, such as Sweden and Canada, and also the larger developing countries have seen some of their companies expand transnationally. Among the 100 TNCs with the highest levels of assets outside their home country, 50 are from Western Europe, 27 from the USA, 17 from Japan, 3 from Canada and one each from Australia, Venezuela, and South Korea.

Through the globalization of companies, the nature of the transnational companies has changed. Originally there was a clear demarcation with production occurring at the headquarters and secondary activities occurring in the subsidiary branches. A TNC such as IBM could be regarded as an American company with many foreign branches. Now the companies can be truly global, with the headquarters merely being a convenient site for strategic decision-making. Global communications are so efficient and sales can be so widely spread that production does not need to be located at the headquarters. There are several indicators of a company moving from being a multinational federation to a unified global company. Production can be diversified so that different stages of production are located in different countries. Marketing can promote a uniform brand image in all countries. The management personnel may develop their careers across the whole company. Full globalization has occurred when the top management includes people from several countries, with no single country predominating, and when all managers have to speak a single language, usually English.

The growth in the number of TNCs, the scale of their activities, and the complexity of their transactions has had a major political impact. We will now see how TNCs have the ability to evade government attempts to control financial flows, to impose trade sanctions or to regulate production. TNCs also make intergovernmental relations more complicated. The **sovereignty** of most governments is significantly reduced.

Financial flows and loss of sovereignty

The consequences of the extensive transnationalization of major companies are profound. It is no longer possible to regard each country as having its own separate economy. Two of the most fundamental attributes of sovereignty, control over the currency and control over foreign trade have been substantially diminished. The two factors combined mean governments have lost control of financial flows. In the case of the currency, the successive crises since the early 1980s for the dollar, the pound, the French franc, and the yen have established that even the governments with the greatest financial resources are helpless against the transnational banks and other speculators.

The effects of trade on domestic and international finance are less obvious. When goods move physically across frontiers, it is usually seen as being trade between the relevant countries, but it may also be **intra-firm trade**. It has been estimated that intra-firm trade accounts for around one-third of all world trade in goods (UN 1995: 37), with the proportion reaching over a half in some high-technology manufacturing industries, (UN 1988: 91–2). As the logic of intra-firm trade is quite different from inter-country trade, governments cannot have clear expectations of the effects of their financial and fiscal policies on TNCs. In Box 17.4, a hypothetical illustration is given of a company setting **transfer prices** to reduce its taxes. Several other motives might induce a company to distort transfer prices, including evasion of controls on the cross-border movements of profits or capital.

Box 17.4 Transfer pricing for intra-firm trade

A very simple model illustrates how international intra-firm trade can be used to evade taxation. Consider a company in an industrialized country exporting semi-finished goods to a developing country, where they are finished and sold. Imagine that the government of the industrial country decides to reduce public expenditure and cut taxes, while the other government increases taxes to fund development.

The transfer price can be used by the company to determine the level of profits for each branch. By increasing the transfer price and declaring more of its profits in the low-tax industrial country, the company can avoid its global tax bill increasing. Then each government would find the effect on tax revenue is the opposite of its expectations.

TNCs may succeed in using artificial transfer prices either because the government does not know what a proper price would be or because the company fraudulently reports the volume or the quality of the goods.

Box 17.5 Can governments control transactions?

In April 1982 Argentina invaded the Falklands and until mid-June Argentina and Britain were at war. Both countries moved quickly to block economic transactions and the whole European Community banned imports from Argentina during the conflict.

Until February 1990, just before diplomatic relations were resumed, direct air connections were forbidden. Throughout this period it was still easy to fly between London and Buenos Aires. There was only a slight inconvenience: it was necessary to change planes in Rio de Janeiro or a European capital, such as Paris or Madrid.

The British government permitted Argentine imports from July 1985, but the Argentines did not lift restrictions until 1990. When trade was not supposed to be occurring, companies could still engage in 'triangulation', sending their exports via Brazil or Western Europe. Alternatively transnational companies could shift orders to a branch in a different country.

Triangulation of trade and loss of sovereignty

Governments have great difficulty regulating international transactions. If one government is antagonistic to another and wishes to impose a trade boycott, it is totally impossible for the government on its own to prevent movement of information or people for business purposes. Even the so-called 'superpower', the USA, was unable to prevent its citizens visiting communist Cuba during the cold war. It may be possible to prevent the *direct* import or export of goods. However, there is no guaranteed method of preventing *indirect* trade from one country to another. A simple example of evasion by **triangulation** is given in Box 17.5. Only if a UN Security Council resolution obliges all the countries of the world to impose sanctions is there a reasonable prospect of a determined government preventing TNCs from evading sanctions. However, in such a situation sovereignty over the relevant trade then lies with the Security Council and not with the individual governments.

Regulatory arbitrage and loss of sovereignty

It is difficult for governments to regulate the commercial activities of companies within their country, because companies may choose to engage in **regulatory arbitrage**. If a company objects to one government's policy, it may threaten to limit or close down its local production and increase production in another country. The government that imposes the least demanding health, safety, welfare, or environmental standards will offer competitive advantages to less socially responsible companies. It thus becomes difficult for any government to set high standards. In the case of banking the political dangers inherent in the risks of a bank collapsing through imprudent or criminal behaviour are so great that the major governments have set common capital standards. Under the Basle Committee rules all commercial banks must protect their viability by having capital to the value of 8 per cent of their outstanding loans. Similarly in the European Community the desire not to leave markets unregulated provides a political impetus towards harmonization of standards and creation of a joint social policy. While the Basle Committee and the EC are very effective, both these **international regimes** are limited by not covering all countries or all closely related activities. Nevertheless, whatever control is achieved does not represent the successful exercise of sovereignty over companies: it is the partial surrender of sovereignty to an intergovernmental body.

Extraterritoriality and sovereignty

In addition transnational companies generate clashes of sovereignty between different governments. Let us consider the example of a company that has its headquarters in the United States and a subsidiary company that it owns in the United Kingdom. Three lines of authority exist. The United States government can control the main company and the United Kingdom government can control the subsidiary. Each process would be the standard exercise of a government's sovereignty over its internal affairs. In addition, both governments would accept that the TNC can, within certain limits, control its own policies on purchasing, production, and sales. Under normal circumstances these three lines of authority can be exercised simultaneously and in harmony. However, when the US government decisions cover the global operations of the TNC, there can be a clash of sovereignty. Does the subsidiary obey the UK government or the orders of the US government issued via its headquarters? This problem of **extraterritoriality**, is inherent in the structure of all TNCs. An illustration of it producing a crisis is given in Box 17.6.

From domestic deregulation to global re-regulation

For most companies most of the time, their interests in expanding their production, increasing their market share, and maximizing their profits will be in accord with the government's policy of increasing employment and promoting economic growth. Conflicts will arise over the regulation of markets to

Box 17.6 The Siberian gas pipeline and extraterritoriality

During the crisis in 1979–80 over American diplomats being held hostage in the US embassy in Teheran, the British government was startled to find that US banks in London were being ordered to freeze Iranian assets. As a result of this and earlier conflicts over shipping and uranium mining, the Protection of Trading Interests Act was passed, so that the British government could overrule the obligation of TNCs to obey any decisions taken by other governments.

The Act was applied in 1982 during the crisis over Western responses to the declaration of martial law in Poland. The US government made strenuous efforts to prevent European participation in the building of a gas pipeline from Siberia to Western Europe. In this case, the attempt was made to exercise extraterritorial control not only within unified TNCs, but also in revoking the licensing arrangement for the use of high technology by independent British companies. For ten months the US government tried to rally its NATO allies on a cold war question, yet the result was a humiliating climb-down with the lifting of the extraterritorial sanctions in November 1982.

Contrary to the common perception of the US government and US companies dominating global politics, there was total failure to break the unity of the European governments and the other companies. Although the US President and Vice-President had ranked the question as their number one international priority and made it a matter of their personal prestige, they did not even gain a face-saving compromise.

avoid the risks of market failures or externalization of social and environmental costs of production, but often these conflicts will be negotiable. The most serious conflicts occur over the desire of companies to minimize their tax burden and the desire of governments to influence the patterns of trade and investment decisions. All these questions have been features of domestic politics in modern times. Globalization of economic activity has moved the questions from the domestic agendas of each country to the global political agenda. Domestic deregulation of the economy has become a global phenomenon.

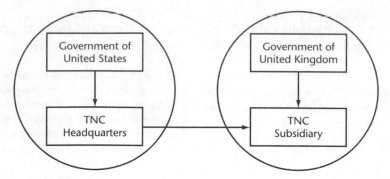

Fig. 17.2 Who controls the United Kingdom subsidiary of a United States TNC?

As there were many strong political pressures that led to regulation in the past, it is to be expected that reactions against deregulation will grow in strength after some years. However, the contemporary political process will be different. The examples of the International Baby Foods Action Network (IBFAN), the World Rainforest Movement and the Pesticides Action Network (PAN) indicate how the reaction against irresponsible behaviour by TNCs now is focused on the United Nations and its agencies. Re-regulation (governments again seeking to control markets) is more likely to be at the global level than within individual countries. One push towards the globalization of politics is that governments can only reassert control over transnational companies by acting collectively.

Key points

- All major companies, because of their involvement in international trade, are potential transnational political actors, but only those operating in more than one country are regarded as transnational companies.

- The ability of TNCs to change transfer prices means that they can evade taxation or government controls on their international financial transactions.

- The ability of TNCs to use triangulation means individual governments cannot control their country's international trade.

- The ability of TNCs to engage in regulatory arbitrage, by moving production from one country to another, means individual governments are constrained against regulating companies to promote high standards of social responsibility.

- The structure of authority over TNCs generates the potential for intense conflict between governments, when the legal authority of one government has extraterritorial impact on the sovereignty of another government.

- The four problems of sovereignty, discussed above, (unpredictable financial flows, trade triangulation, regulatory arbitrage, and extraterritoriality) weaken individual governments in relation to TNCs. In some areas of economic policy, sovereignty now has to be exercised through collective action rather than independently.

Non-legitimate groups and liberation movements as political actors

A variety of groups engage in violent and/or criminal behaviour on a transnational basis. A distinction can be made between activity that is considered criminal around the world, such as theft, fraud, haphazard violence, or drug trafficking, and activity that is claimed by those undertaking it to have legitimate political motives. In reality, the distinction may sometimes be blurred, when criminals claim political motives or political groups are responsible for acts such as torture or killing children. For all governments neither criminal activity nor political violence can be legitimate within their own jurisdiction. From the point of view of most governments most of the time, such activities are also to be condemned when they occur in other countries.

Transnational criminals and their political impact

Politically, the most important criminal industries are illicit trading in arms and in drugs. They have been estimated to be the two most valuable commodities in international trade. Trade in stolen goods generally is limited to high-value, easily transported goods, such as diamonds and computer chips. In addition, piracy of intellectual property, particularly of music, video films, and computer software, and trade in counterfeit goods is organized on a very large scale.

The same four sovereignty problems arise with tackling criminals as with regulating TNCs, but they take on a different significance. **First**, criminal financial flows can be massive and unpredictable. An additional problem of great complexity is that money-laundering threatens the integrity of banking and other financial institutions. **Second**, criminal trade has been so extensively diversified through triangulation that no government could confidently claim that their country is not a transit route for drug smuggling. In the arms trade, triangulation with false end-user certificates is also a common process.

Third, using the law against criminals produces a similar effect to movement by TNCs for regulatory arbitrage. Whereas governments do not want companies to close down, forcing criminals out of business would be a political victory. Nevertheless, well-organized gangs are more likely to be displaced to another country than to be jailed and disbanded, as has been shown by the shifting patterns of drugs production in Latin America. **Fourth**, extraterritoriality does occur with respect to jurisdiction over criminal behaviour. Various special cases, such as war criminals, hijackers, and miscreant diplomats, can be prosecuted in countries not directly affected by their offence. Illicit drugs, money-laundering, and terrorism involve transnational police activities that would be unthinkable in other fields. These examples contrast with the regulation of normal economic activity. Extraterritorial jurisdiction over the criminals is supported by the overwhelming majority of governments and is endorsed in a series of international treaties and UN resolutions.

As with TNCs, the global financial system, displacement, triangulation, and extraterritoriality, limit the effective exercise of sovereignty over criminals. The difference is that in some fields, where the threat is felt to be most severe, there have been strenuous efforts to re-establish control by surrender of sovereignty through international agreement.

Transnational guerrilla groups and gaining legitimacy

Political violence has been adopted by a variety of different groups. They range from broadly based nationalist movements and other groups with a clear political programme through alienated minorities, such as the militia in the USA or religious sects in several countries, to protest groups on specific issues. These groups are often called **terrorists** to express disapproval, **guerrillas** by those who are more neutral, or **national liberation movements** by their supporters. In general, nationalists are usually able to obtain some external support, from members of the same national group in other countries, from governments hostile to their own government or from other actors who consider nationalism to be legitimate. During the cold war, both communists and anti-communists gave support to violent groups taking their side in the ideological struggle, but this tended to be most effective when the ideology was allied to nationalism. Some violent groups may obtain support, by forming alliances with similar groups based in different countries.

Governments are very reluctant to accept the use of violence by transnational groups, even when the cause meets with their approval. Hijacking, hostage-taking, and deliberate bombing of civilian targets are so lacking in legitimacy in the intergovernmental world that governments will not seek to justify such acts, even when they have been actively involved in assisting the terrorists. Nevertheless, some groups do manage to move from the status of (bad) terrorists to (good) national liberation movements. Legitimacy in using violence is increased in *four* ways: (1) when a group appears to have widespread support within their constituency; (2) when political channels have been closed to them; (3) when the target government is exceptionally oppressive; and (4) when the

---

Box 17.7 Key concepts

Terrorists: a term of abuse generally used against groups who engage in violent behaviour, by people who oppose the goals of the group. It carries the connotation that suffering has been caused to children or other non-combatants in a conflict. The term might be more appropriately applied to those, including governments, who use indiscriminate violence for the purposes of political intimidation.

Guerrillas: a neutral term to cover all groups fighting for political goals, whether or not they adopt terrorist methods.

National liberation movement: a guerrilla group that is based upon one or more nations seeking liberation from domination by the government of a foreign nation. Use of the term conveys approval for the group and for its use of violence to pursue political goals.

---

violence is aimed at 'military targets' without civilian victims.

Groups such as the Republican and Loyalist paramilitaries in Northern Ireland or the Basque separatists, *Euzkadi to Askatasuna* (ETA) that fail to match these four characteristics only obtain very limited transnational support. Some other groups are able to gain legitimacy by winning respect on all four grounds. The African National Congress (ANC) and the South West African People's Organization (SWAPO) received widespread external support for their fight against the South African apartheid regime: they gained diplomatic status, money, and weapons supplies. The position of the Palestine Liberation Organization (PLO) was less clear cut, particularly in the 1970s, because of the fear generated by their hijacking of airliners and bombing of civilians.

Although there have been many guerrilla groups fighting as oppressed national minorities, only five groups have been significant diplomatic actors in the last two decades. In the mid-1970s, the PLO and SWAPO achieved membership of the Non-Aligned Movement and the Group of 77, along with observer status in the UN General Assembly and at all UN conferences. Three other groups the ANC, the Pan-African Congress (a smaller South African group), and the Patriotic Front of Zimbabwe, did not do so well, but they did obtain the right to attend UN conferences.

The significance of criminals and guerrillas

Criminals and guerrillas do not appear to present a challenge to orthodox state-centric theory. On the one hand, the drugs barons, smugglers, and thieves, along with militia, religious sects, and alienated minorities, seem to be marginal because they are not legitimate and are excluded from normal international transactions. On the other hand, the violent groups that do gain military, political, and diplomatic status on a transnational basis are generally nationalist groups, aspiring to govern a particular territory. Therefore they can be presented as endorsing the basic principles of a state-centric system.

Such an approach masks the way globalization has changed the nature of sovereignty and the processes of government. The operations of criminals and other non-legitimate groups have become more complex, spread over a wider geographical area and increased in scale, because the improvements in communications have made it so much easier to transfer people, money, weapons, and ideas on a transnational basis. Government attempts to control such activities have become correspondingly more difficult. Similarly, national liberation movements cannot be seen simply as part of a static inter-state system. They all start as small illegitimate groups and gain support by a process of mobilization, in which transnational legitimacy can sustain domestic legitimacy and vice versa. The legal concept of statehood may not be affected, but the practice of sovereignty has become significantly different. Now virtually every government feels it has to mobilize external support, to exercise 'domestic jurisdiction' over criminals or guerrilla groups.

Key points

- Effective action against transnational criminals by individual governments is difficult for the same reasons as control of TNCs is difficult.
- Extraterritoriality is accepted and sovereignty is surrendered, in order to tackle the most threatening criminals.
- Groups using violence to achieve political goals generally do not achieve legitimacy, but in exceptional circumstances they may be recognized as national liberation movements and take part in diplomacy.
- The transnational activities of criminals and guerrillas shift problems of the domestic policy of countries into the realm of global politics.

Non-governmental organizations as political actors

The politics of an individual country cannot be understood without knowing what groups lobby the government and what debate there has been in the media. Similarly, international diplomacy does not operate on some separate planet, cut off from global civil society. Analysts of British politics use two terms: interest group conveys a bias towards a group, such as a company or a trade union, seeking to influence economic policy; while pressure group invokes a wider range of groups promoting their values. In the United States the terms lobby group, public interest group, and private voluntary organization are used, with rather more normative connotations, to make similar distinctions. Because diplomats like to claim that they are pursuing 'the national interest' of a united society, they will not admit to relations with interest groups or pressure groups and they prefer the bland title, **non-governmental organizations** or simply NGOs. However, it must be emphasized that this established diplomatic jargon

does not cover all transnational actors. Although companies, criminals, and guerrillas are literally non-governmental, they are not NGOs.

Consultative status at the UN for NGOs

As a result of pressure, primarily from American groups, the draft United Nations Charter was amended to add an article providing for the Economic and Social Council (ECOSOC) to consult with NGOs (Article 71). In the early sessions the World Federation of Trade Unions took the lead to convert the vague general provision into a range of recognized rights of participation. After five years the Council formally codified the practice, in a resolution that effectively was a statute for NGOs. It recognized *three categories* of groups: (1) a small number of high-status NGOs, concerned with most of the

Box 17.8 Key concepts

Non-governmental organization (NGO): any group of people relating to each other regularly in some formal manner and engaging in collective action, provided that the activities are non-commercial, non-violent and are not on behalf of a government. NGOs based in a local community are rarely engaged in global politics. 'National NGOs', based in a single country, may engage in transnational activities, but usually only the largest and richest ones do so. International NGOs (INGOs) are a major influence upon all global diplomacy, (see also Box 17.12). At the UN, groups that challenge the legitimacy of specific governments or focus on human rights in one country will not be accepted as NGOs. People are often baffled by the dry, bland term, 'non-governmental organization'. Nevertheless, some of the international NGOs are better known than some of the smaller countries. They include

- Amnesty International

- Greenpeace

- Red Cross

- Save the Children

Many other international NGOs are not so well known, but are of major importance, such as economic bodies, e.g. International Chamber of Shipping; technical bodies e.g. International Organization for Standardization; or professional bodies, e.g. World Medical Association.

Network: any structure of communication for individuals and/or NGOs to exchange information, share experiences or discuss political goals and tactics. There is no clear boundary between a network and an NGO. A network is less likely than an NGO to become permanent, to have formal membership, to have identifiable leaders or to engage in collective action. The simplest type of network may be no more than an e-mail database, an Internet discussion group or a website. At the other end of the spectrum, a group calling itself a network may become institutionalized and gain recognition at the UN as an NGO.

Social movement: people with a diffuse sense of collective identity, solidarity and common purpose that usually leads to collective political behaviour. The concept covers all the different NGOs and networks, plus all their members and all the other individuals who share the common value(s). Thus, the women's movement and the environmental movement are much more than the specific NGOs who provide leadership and focus the desire for social change.

Council's work; (2) specialist NGOs, concerned with a few fields of activity and having a high reputation in those fields; and (3) a Roster of other NGOs that are expected to make occasional contributions to the Council.[3] Since then the term NGO has, for diplomats, been synonymous with a group that is eligible for ECOSOC consultative status.

The UN definition of an acceptable NGO

The ECOSOC statute and the way it has been applied embodies six principles:

1. An NGO should support the aims and the work of the UN. This has been interpreted so broadly as to place minimal restrictions on criticism of UN programmes. The case of Human Life Inter-

Box 17.9 Are you an NGO member?

You probably do not see yourself and your family as part of the global community of NGOs, but most well-known local organizations have global links. If you attend a church, a synagogue, or mosque; if you are in a trade union or a professional body; if you have joined a political party; if you attend a local family planning clinic; if you are in the Scouts, the Girl Guides, the Rotarians, or an automobile association; or if you have joined an environmental, development, human rights, or women's organization, you are very likely to be involved in the local branch of a global NGO that is represented at the United Nations.

national, an anti-abortion group, was a significant exception. Their campaign against American children raising money for UNICEF contributed

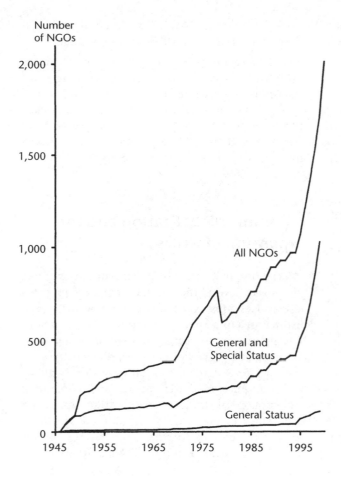

Fig. 17.3 The growth of NGOs at the UN
General Status: covering all continents and most ECOSOC fields
General and Special: global plus regional and/or specialist NGOs
All NGOs: including also the ECOSOC Roster

Table 17.1 The three levels of UN consultative status for NGOs

1946–50	1950–68	1968–96	1996–	Type of NGO
Category A	Category A	Category I	General Status	Global, large membership and work on many issues
Category B	Category B	Category II	Special Status	Regional and general *or* specialist and high status
Category C	Register	Roster	Roster	Small or highly specialist or work with UN agencies

to the ECOSOC decision to deny them consultative status.

2. An NGO should be a representative body, with identifiable headquarters, and officers, responsible to a democratic policy-making conference. In practice many highly prestigious NGOs, particularly development and environment NGOs, such as Oxfam and Greenpeace, do not have any internal democratic procedures. They are responsive to the general public rather than responsible to a membership.

3. An NGO cannot be a profit-making body. Indi-

vidual companies have no possibility of gaining formal consultative status, but this does not exclude them from the UN system. International trade federations have no problem in being recognized as NGOs.

4. An NGO cannot use or advocate violence. We have seen that a few guerrilla groups have been accepted as national liberation movements, but this is distinct from and of higher status than being an NGO.

5. An NGO must respect the norm of 'non-interference in the internal affairs of states'. This means an NGO cannot be a political party. However, like companies, parties can form international federations, which do gain consultative status. The principle was extended in 1968, by adding a new clause to the statute. NGOs concerned with human rights should not restrict their activities to a particular group, nationality, or country. (Exception was made with respect to anti-apartheid groups.)

6. An international NGO is one that is not established by intergovernmental agreement. This is a technical legal expression of the property of being non-governmental. It is explicitly stated that this does not exclude governmental bodies being members of an INGO. The significance of this blurring of the lines will be examined later.

Many NGO activists believe the UN should be more restrictive and only accept groups that are 'true' NGOs, contributing to 'progressive' **social movements**. Environmentalists are often upset that business federations are accepted and the whole NGO community at the UN agonized over the National Rifle Association being admitted to the Roster in November 1996.

Economic globalization and the expansion of NGOs

The creation of a complex global economy has had effects way beyond the international trade in goods and services. Most companies or employees, in each distinct area of activity, have formed organizations to facilitate communication, to harmonize standards and to manage adaptation to complex change. For example, air, sea, road, and rail transport, banking, telecommunications, the media, and computing could not operate transnationally without the necessary infrastructure, which includes the organizational structures of international NGOs. Cooperation is not essential to other companies, but they

---

Box 17.10 **International aviation organizations**

The airlines have come together in the International Air Transport Association (IATA) forming a global NGO to manage their commercial relations.

Governments are members of the International Civil Aviation Organization (ICAO), providing an effective regime for navigation and setting safety standards. Because of the importance of weather forecasts for flight safety, close co-operation is maintained with another intergovernmental organization, the World Meteorological Organization (WMO). Both ICAO and WMO are UN specialized agencies.

The people most affected by questions of air safety are the pilots. They put forward their views at ICAO through their professional body, the International Federation of Air Line Pilots Associations (IFALPA). In September 1969 they moved from safety 'into the political field', when they took the question of hijacking to the UN Secretary-General. Eventually IFALPA achieved a significant strengthening of the international law against hijacking.

ICAO has a less formal relationship with NGOs than does the UN. IATA and IFALPA have a permanent invitation to attend meetings. Other NGOs having strong working relationships include the trade unions through the International Transport Workers' Federation; a related commercial interest, the International Union of Aviation Insurers; a research forum, the Institute of Air Transport; scientists in the International Union of Geodesy and Geophysics; a sports body, the International Aeronautical Federation; and a standards body, the International Commission on Illumination.

find agreement on common standards and procedures is more efficient and hence cheaper. Equally the employees have found they face common problems in different countries and so trade unions and professional bodies have developed their own transnational links. Any form of **international regime** to formulate policy for an industry, whether it is non-governmental or intergovernmental, will encourage the strengthening of the global links among the NGOs concerned with its activities. An illustration is given in Box 17.10, with eight of the major NGOs involved in the commercial and safety regimes for aviation.

The globalization of communications

For most of the twentieth century any individual with enough money and enough time could travel in person or communicate in writing to most parts of the world, unless communications were disrupted by war. The technical revolution in the last fifty years lies in the increased density, the increased speed, and the reduced cost of communication. The political revolution lies in these changes bringing rapid global communication within the capabilities of most people. This includes even the poor, if they band together to fund a representative to articulate their case or gain access to the news media.

From the 1940s global radio broadcasting has been established, with small portable radio receivers appearing in the late 1950s; from the early 1960s cheap air services have linked all countries; from the early 1970s subscriber trunk dialling has provided transnational telephone connections; from the late 1980s the telephone networks have been used for facsimile transmissions; during the early 1990s satellites made possible both live television coverage of events anywhere in the world and transmission of global television services, such as CNN and the BBC; and finally in the mid-1990s the Internet took off as a facility for the instant exchange of massive volumes of information.

Together these changes in communications constitute a fundamental change in the structure of world politics. Governments have lost sovereignty

---

Box 17.11 The loss of sovereignty over transborder communications

Recent events have given dramatic illustrations of the extent to which governments have lost the ability to control transnational communications.

- The Tiananmen Square killings were shown directly on Western television, as they took place.
- Kuwaitis could put through calls on radio telephones to news agencies in London and Washington during the Iraqi occupation of 1990–1.
- Saudi dissidents could circulate accusations of corruption in the Saudi government by bombardment of the country with faxes from London.
- The Zapatista leader during a rebellion in southern Mexico could transmit press releases to the United States from his portable computer, while on the run from government troops

---

over the transnational relations of their citizens. They can choose from *three* options:

1. keep communication facilities open and lose all ability to control transnational transactions;

2. bear the heavy costs of maintaining an elaborate security apparatus in an unsuccessful attempt to monitor and control communications; or

3. close certain facilities to prevent normal economic transactions from occurring, but fail to inhibit the determined dissident.

Borders have never been completely impermeable, but now governments can only control a limited range of communications with limited success. Normal transnational communications do not have the dramatic qualities of the examples given in Box 17.11, but they still constitute a quiet revolution.

The news media as agents of globalization

The pattern of choices made by the news media in their coverage of events is at least part of the explanation of changing priorities on political agendas in most countries. Some of the similarities in political change in different countries are due to their separate responses to similar economic and social problems, but participation in the global system strengthens the similarities in the agenda for debate. Sometimes the media take the lead and sometimes they are being pushed by NGOs, TNCs, or governments, but their decisions are always important, particularly in the case of the biggest transnational press agencies and satellite television networks. The movement of ideas not only affects the agenda but also political outcomes. It is not a coincidence that individual human rights, women's rights, environmental concerns, monetarism, and privatization policies have gained increasing support in many countries around the same time. To make the illustrations more specific, the Chernobyl accident affected the politics of nuclear energy throughout the world, while the collapse of the Soviet system and of apartheid both strengthened the global process of democratization. It cannot be argued that the boundaries separating the political cultures and political systems of each country have been totally eroded, but it is the case that each country is a sub-system within the global political system.

The movement of NGOs from the local to the global

One effect of the globalization of communication is to make it physically and financially feasible for small groups of people to establish and to maintain co-operation, even though they may be based thousands of miles apart from each other. Thus it is very easy for NGOs to operate transnationally, but not all NGOs make this choice. They vary from local organizations solely operating in one small town to large global bureaucracies with a presence in most countries. The crucial factor in determining whether an NGO goes transnational is the nature of its goals.

- If the prime purpose is to offer a service to its own members, to pursue charitable activities locally or to campaign to change a particular law, then it may be decades before the question of establishing transnational links arises. Separate NGOs become well established in several countries before they decide to form an international NGO, as a loose federation, in order to exchange information and learn from each other's experience. Trade unions, women's organizations, charities for the elderly, and family-planning associations are examples.

- Campaigning NGOs in one country may only have the goal of affecting their own government's policy, but decide for tactical reasons to obtain support from foreign governments and NGOs. Environmental NGOs in developing countries have found support from transnational networks to be crucial.

- Sometimes campaigning NGOs decide from the start that they would be more effective as a transnational organization and they form sections simultaneously in several countries. Amnesty International and Friends of the Earth started in Britain and the United States respectively, but immediately appealed for support elsewhere.

- NGOs can be based in just one country, while defining their goals in transnational terms. For many years Oxfam in Britain and CARE in the USA raised funds to spend on disaster relief and development overseas, before they too joined international federations and then later gained sections in other countries.

- When regional or global intergovernmental organizations become the focus for policy-making, then NGOs seek to influence the proceedings. They use access to the international secretariat and the decision-making organs, as an indirect route to influence the policy of individual governments. As a result, the cities that host important IGOs also become centres for related international NGOs.

NGOs are so diverse in their goals and their tactics that the above list only indicates the main processes by which they move from local to global politics.

Key points

- Most transnational actors can expect to gain recognition as NGOs by the UN, provided they are not individual companies, criminals, or violent groups and they do not exist solely to oppose an individual government.

- While ECOSOC consultative status does not involve all transnational NGOs, its statute does provide an authoritative statement that NGOs have a legitimate place in international diplomacy.
- The creation of a global economy leads to the globalization of unions, commercial bodies, the professions, and scientists in international NGOs, which participate in the relevant international regimes.
- The technological revolution has globalized communications, both for individuals and for the news media. This has created a political revolution. Most governments have virtually no ability to control the flow of information across the borders of their country. A few authoritarian governments can impose some restrictions, but not without incurring very high political and economic costs.
- The improved communications make it more likely that NGOs will operate transnationally and make it very simple and cheap for them to do so.

International organizations as structures of global politics

International organizations provide the focus for global politics. The new physical infrastructure of global communications makes it easier for them to operate. In addition, when the sessions of the organizations take place, they become distinct structures for political communication. Face-to-face meetings produce different outcomes from telephone or written communications. Multilateral discussion produces different outcomes from interactions in networks of bilateral communications.

International organizations as systems

It was argued earlier that there is an ontological inconsistency in seeing 'states' as coherent entities, while asserting they remain independent sovereign units. We can be consistent by accepting the existence of systems at all levels of world politics. Governments, and groups making up civil society, from within countries, along with international organizations from the global level, all may have systemic properties. In the modern world, human groups are never so coherent that they are independent, closed systems (perhaps excepting monastic orders). Equally, once distinct organizational processes are established, they are never so open that the boundaries become insignificant. Thus international organizations of all types transcend country boundaries and have a major impact on the governmental actors and transnational actors composing them.

For a system to exist, there must be a sufficient density of interactions, involving each of its elements, at a sufficient intensity to result both in the emergence of properties for the system as a whole and in some consistent effect on the behaviour of the elements. In other words, systems make a difference or, as it is put in Systems Science, the whole is more than the sum of its parts. In some cases, such as the Commonwealth of Independent States and international NGO networks of people who never meet face to face, the interactions may be so weak that it could be argued the organizations are not systems. Generally, international organizations will have founding documents defining their goals, rules of procedure constraining the modes of behaviour, secretariats committed to the status and identity of the organization (or at least committed to their own careers), past decisions that provide norms for future policy, and interaction processes that socialize new participants. All these features at the systemic level will be part of the explanation of the behaviour of the members and thus the political outcomes will not be determined solely by the initial goals of the

---

Box 17.12 Key concepts

International organization: any institution with formal procedures and formal membership from three or more countries. The minimum number of countries is set at three rather than two, because multilateral relationships have significantly greater complexity than bilateral relationships.

Intergovernmental organization (IGO): an international organization in which full legal membership is officially solely open to states and the decision-making authority lies with representatives from governments. In practice many IGOs have also had a few colonial territories and/or national liberation movements as members.

International non-governmental organization (INGOs): an international organization in which membership is open to transnational actors. The major INGOs often mirror the world of diplomacy in being associations of 'national' NGOs that themselves group together many local NGOs from one country. For example, Amnesty International as a global INGO is composed of country-based sections, each having a structure of local groups. INGOs can also have companies or political parties as members. Another variant is to recruit individual people. There are even a few that themselves have INGOs as members and some have mixed membership structures.

Hybrid INGO: a third type of international organization. Just as governments form IGOs, and NGOs form INGOs, the two can form joint organizations in which they are each allowed to be members. The phenomenon goes largely unrecognized, because there is no standard English word to describe these organizations. On investigation it is possible to identify many such bodies and we may call them hybrids. (Logically they should be hybrid international organizations, but in diplomatic practic they are identified among the international NGOs and so hybrid-INGOs is perhaps a more appropriate term.)

International regime: a concept developed by Neo-Realists to analyse the paradox—for them—that international co-operation occurs in some issue areas, despite the struggle for power between states. They assume regimes are created and maintained by a dominant state and/or participation in a regime is the result of a rational cost-benefit calculation by each state. In contrast, Pluralists would also stress the independent impact of institutions, the importance of leadership, the involvement of transnational NGOs and companies, and processes of cognitive change, such as growing concern about human rights or the environment. For most, but not all writers, regimes are embodied in intergovernmental organizations. (See also Box 17.1 and Ch. 14.)

---

members. The statement that international organizations form systems is a statement that they are politically significant and that global politics cannot be reduced to 'inter-state' relations.

The intergovernmental versus non-governmental distinction

Normally a sharp distinction is made between **intergovernmental organizations** (IGOs) and **international non-governmental organizations** (INGOs). This conveys the impression that inter-state diplomacy and transnational relations are separate from each other. In practice governments do not rigidly maintain the separation. There is an overlapping pattern of relations in another category of international organizations, **hybrid INGOs**, in which governments work with NGOs. Among the most important hybrids are the International Red Cross, the World Conservation Union (IUCN), the International Council of Scientific Unions, the International Air Transport, Association and other economic bodies combining companies and governments.

In order to be regarded as a hybrid the organization must admit as full members *both* NGOs, parties, or companies *and* governments or governmental agencies. Both types of members must have full rights of participation in policy-making, including the right to vote on the final decisions. Voting may be with all members counted together, as in the International Conference of the Red Cross, or with separate majorities required in two categories of membership, as in the World Conservation Union. In the former case the principle of equality is maintained because one government's vote is equal to one Red Cross or Red Crescent society's vote. In the latter there is equality between the governments collectively and the NGOs collectively. In hybrid INGOs there is usually also a joint obligation to fund the activities of the organization. When the principle of formal equality of NGOs and governments is acknowledged by both sides in such a manner, the assumption that governments can dominate must be totally abandoned.

Relationships between international organizations

Once it is accepted that international organizations are politically significant in producing their own distinct policy, then the relations between the organizations also become important. The mutual recognition of IGOs, by granting each other observer status, and the existence of consultative status for INGOs are not simply obscure bureaucratic procedures. They are processes that legitimize political activity by international secretariats on behalf of their organizations. The systemic outputs of the organizations are then expressed as inputs to other systems. The density of these relationships, particularly in the United Nations, means that it is not possible to separate the intergovernmental world from the transnational world. Just as the hybrid INGOs break down the distinction in a fundamental way, by producing direct relations between governments, companies and NGOs, so also IGO relations with INGOs integrate, at a higher level of aggregation.

Key points

- International organizations are also structures for political communication. They are systems that constrain the behaviour of their members.
- Governments form intergovernmental organizations and transnational actors form international non-governmental organizations. In addition governments and transnational actors accord each other equal status by jointly creating hybrid international NGOs.

Issues and policy systems in global politics

One way state-centric writers accommodate transnational activity is by distinguishing the **high politics** of peace and security, taking place in military alliances and UN diplomacy, from the **low politics** of other policy questions, debated in specialist UN bodies, other IGOs and INGOs. Then, by asserting it is more important to analyse peace and war, actors in low politics are defined out of the analysis. In practice it is not so simple. Scientists, the Red Cross, religious groups, and other NGOs are involved in arms control negotiations; economic events may be treated as crises; social policy can concern matters of life and death; and heads of government do at times make the environment a top priority. It is useful to analyse global politics in terms of a variety of dimensions describing each **policy domain** and the actors within it, but the different dimensions do not correlate. A single high/low classification does not work.

The move from a state-centric to a Pluralist model, in which governments and transnational actors interact with each other bilaterally and multilaterally, depends on a shift from a static unidimensional concept of **power**. Actors enter a political process possessing resources and seeking particular goals: however, contrary to the Realist view, **capabilities** do not determine **influence**. Explaining outcomes requires examining whether the resources of actors are relevant to the goals being pursued, describing the degree of divergence between the goals of the different actors, and analysing how they are changed by the **interaction processes**.

Governments are usually characterized by having legal authority and control over military capabilities and economic resources. They may also have high status, possess specialist information, have access to communications and be able to articulate widely

---

Box 17.13 **Key concepts**

• The distinction between **high politics** and **low politics** is made by Realists but not by Pluralists. It is based on the following four dimensions.

	High politics	**Low politics**
(1) *Policy questions*	Peace and security	Economics, social questions, human rights, environment
(2) *Decision-makers*	Heads of government and senior ministers	Junior ministers or officials
(3) *Involvement of non-state actors*	Minimal, unless as agents of governments	Extensive activity by NGOs, TNCs, IGOs, and INGOs
(4) *Type of situation*	High priority or crises	Low priority, routine activity

Neo-realists would differ in moving major questions of trade and international finance from the low politics to the high politics category.

• **An issue** consists of a set of political questions that are seen as being related, because they all invoke the same value conflicts, e.g. the issue of human rights concerns questions that invoke freedom versus order.

• **A policy domain** consists of a set of political questions that have to be decided together because they are linked by the political processes in an international organization, e.g. financial policy is resolved in the IMF. A policy domain may cover several issues: financial policy includes development, environment, and gender issues.

Box 17.14 **Key concepts**

Power: in the most general sense, the ability of a political actor to achieve its goals. In the study of international relations, it is common to distinguish between capabilities and influence. In the Realist approach, it is assumed that possession of capabilities will result in influence, so the single word, power, is often used ambiguously to cover both. In the Pluralist approach, it is assumed that political interactions can modify the translation of capabilities into influence and therefore it is important to distinguish between the two.

Capabilities: the resources that are under an actor's direct control. Realist theorizing concentrates primarily on military capabilities and secondarily on economic resources. Pluralists also emphasize control of communication facilities (TV, radio, and telecommunications) and possession of information. By extension two abstract attributes of actors, legal authority and high status, can also be seen as capabilities.

Interaction processes: the flows of people, materials, energy, money, and information (including political ideas and proposals for policy), between the elements of a system. War is primarily determined by flows of people as soldiers and materials as weapons; economics by the exchange of money for all the other four types of flows; and politics by the flow of information. Thus, unless and until an issue involves armed conflict, structures of communication are the fundamental political structures.

Influence: the ability of one actor to change the values or the behaviour of another actor. Unwelcome change may be achieved as coercion by military threats, economic sanctions, or even by the possession of information, through blackmail. Acceptable change can be the result of a bargain in which the new behaviour is rewarded by military, economic, or political support. Influence may be regarded as being at its greatest when one actor uses political debate to change the political values of another actor, so that the new behaviour is adopted voluntarily.

---

shared values in support of their goals, but all these four capabilities can also be attributes of transnational actors and international organizations. In the process of political debate something else is crucial. It is the ability to communicate in a manner that commands the attention and respect of other actors. While this is enhanced by possession of status and resources, in a particular time and place—on the news media, in a speech before a public audience, during negotiations or when lobbying in private— the ability to communicate is a personal attribute of

the speaker. Some presidents and prime ministers fail to command respect, while some NGO activists are inspiring and cannot be ignored. If power is seen solely in military terms, governments are expected to be dominant. If power is seen solely in economic

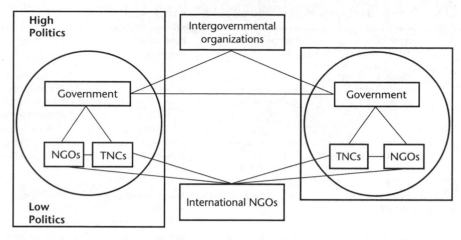

Fig. 17.4 The orthodox view of international relations.

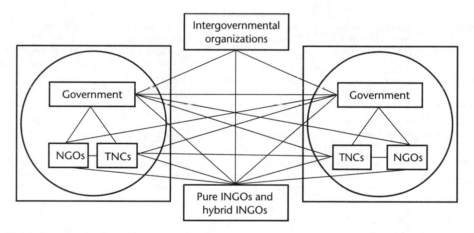

Fig. 17.5 The full range of international connections.

terms, TNCs are expected to be dominant. However, if power includes possession of status, information, and communication skills, then it is possible for NGOs and international organizations to mobilize support for their values and to exercise influence over governments. Most real-world situations will see a mix of different capabilities being brought to bear upon the policy debate.

The types of authority, status, resources, information, and skills that are relevant to political success are issue-specific. (They vary from one **issue** to another.) Thus the governments, the TNCs, the NGOs, the intergovernmental organizations, and the international NGOs that have the ability to exercise influence will vary according to the issues

invoked by a policy problem. Table 17.2 illustrates the point that there is not a single international system of nearly 200 'states', but a variety of **policy domains**, each involving their own distinct actors. Governments have a special role, linking the different domains, because membership of the UN obliges governments to form policy and vote on most issues. In practice, they are less central and cohesive than it appears in the UN, because different departments of government handle the different policy questions. The transnational actors and international organizations generally are more specialist and involved in a limited range of policy questions. Amnesty International rarely has significance in environmental politics and Greenpeace rarely is concerned with

Table 17.2 The variety of political actors involved in different policy domains

	Apartheid in South Africa	Human rights	Population planning	Environment
Main governments involved	South Africa, UK, USA versus African governments	Democratic versus authoritarian governments	All types of governments	Those who feel threatened by problems versus those who do not
Transnational companies	Wide range, but especially mining and oil	Any working with oppressive governments	Medical, pharmaceutical, and food	Mainly industrial, energy, and transport
Guerrillas	ANC, PAC and SWAPO	Any taking hostages	Any in control of territory	Generally not concerned
Grass-roots NGOs	Anti-Apartheid Movement	Human rights groups and the oppressed	Religious, women's, and health groups	Friends of the Earth, WWF, Greenpeace etc.
UN inter-governmental policy forum	Committee Against Apartheid and Security Council	Human Rights Commission	Commission on Population and Development	Commission on Sustainable Development
UN Secretariat	Centre Against Apartheid	Centre for Human Rights	UNICEF UN Pop. Fund	UNDP UNEP
Other IGOs	Organisation of African Unity	Council of Europe, OAS, and OAU	WHO World Bank	World Bank
International NGOs	Many involved, with a secondary concern	Amnesty International and others	International Planned Parenthood Federation	Environment Liaison Centre International and other networks
Hybrid INGOs	Those concerned with trade	None	None	World Conservation Union (IUCN)

human rights, but each is central to their own domain. Being a specialist actor is a weakness in relation to situations where issue linkages become important, but usually it is a great strength for NGOs and international secretariats. Being a specialist generates high status, achieves command over information, and enhances communication skills. These capabilities enable a challenge to be made to the governments that control military and economic resources.

Within both domestic and global politics, civil society is the source of change. Companies usually initiate economic change and NGOs are usually the source of new ideas for political action. At any one point in time, economics and politics may seem to

be relatively stable and under governmental control. Under the exceptional circumstances of war or under exceptional leadership, governments can generate change. However, NGOs generally provide the dynamics of politics. The European empires were dismembered by nationalist movements, with support from lawyers, journalists, unions, and the churches. Democracy and human rights have been extended by women's groups, ethnic minorities, and dissident groups. The environment has moved up the agenda in response to grassroots anger at the loss of natural beauty, protests against threats to health, and warnings from scientists about ecosystems being at risk of collapse. The right to have access to family planning supplies, sexual information, and reproductive health services has been established as a global norm. In some countries, notably the USA, this initially required women to go to jail to challenge repressive laws, but since 1953 the International Planned Parenthood Federation has grown to become the world's second largest NGO, even operating in virtually all Catholic and Islamic countries. The start of the cold war was not simply the formation of military alliances: it was a political struggle of communism as a transnational movement against the transnational appeal of democracy, the Catholic Church, and nationalism. The arms race and the process of *détente* included conflict between arms manufacturers and peace movements, with scientists being crucial to both sides. The end of the cold war was driven by economic failure within communist countries and the political failure in response to demands from unions, human rights dissidents, the churches, and environmentalists. The response to refugee crises produced by natural and human-made disasters has been dominated by the media, the UN, and NGOs. The shift from seeing development as increasing a country's GNP to meeting ordinary people's basic needs and using resources in a sustainable manner was driven by development NGOs and the environmental movement. The international relations of the twentieth century have all occurred within complex, pluralist political systems.

Key points

- The high politics, low politics, distinction is used to marginalize transnational actors. It is invalid because politics does not reduce to these two categories. All policy domains can be described by the type of issues, the status of the governmental decision-makers, and the degree of involvement of transnational actors and international organizations.

- A simple concept of power will not explain outcomes. Military and economic resources are not the only capabilities: communication facilities, information, authority, and status are also important political assets. In addition, an ability to use the interaction processes to mobilize support will contribute to influence over policy.

- Different policy domains contain different actors, depending upon the salience of the issues being debated.

- TNCs gain influence through the control of economic resources. NGOs gain influence through possessing information, gaining high status and communicating effectively. TNCs and NGOs have been the main source of economic and political change in global politics.

QUESTIONS

1 Outline three meanings of the concept of a 'state' and explain the implications of each for the study of transnational actors.

2 What are the five types of transnational actors? Give examples of each type.

3 What is a nation? What types of transnational actors can be based on national groups?

4 How do transnational companies affect the sovereignty of governments?

5 List all the NGOs that you, and your family, have joined. Assess from their newsletters how many are global organizations, how many are national, or local with global connections, and how many have no transnational relations.

6 What measures could you use to compare the size of countries, TNCs, NGOs, and international organizations? Are countries always larger than transnational actors?

7 How could a local women's group have a significant effect upon global politics?

8 What types of NGOs are, and what types are not, eligible to obtain consultative status with the Economic and Social Council of the United Nations?

9   Explain the expansion in the number of NGOs engaging in transnational activities.

10   What is a hybrid international NGO?

11   How is it possible for NGOs to exercise influence in global politics? (Note: this question can be answered both in theoretical terms and in practical empirical terms).

12   Explain the difference between analysing international relations as a single international system and as the global politics of many different policy domains.

GUIDE TO FURTHER READING

Case study materials

Keohane, R. O., and Nye, J. S. (eds.), *Transnational Relations and World Politics* (Cambridge, Mass.: Harvard University Press, 1972): the first major academic study of transnational relations, limited by the explicit decision to downplay non-economic actors.

Weiss, T. G., and Gordenker, L. (eds.), *NGOs, the UN and Global Governance* (Boulder, Colo.: Lynne Rienner, 1996): six studies of NGO activity and three chapters addressing cross-cutting themes, set within a Pluralist approach.

Willetts, P. (ed.), *Pressure Groups in the Global System: The Transnational Relations of Issue-Orientated Non-Governmental Organizations* (London: Pinter, 1982): in reaction against the omission of non-economic groups by Keohane and Nye, examines how pressure groups move from single-country to global activity.

Willetts, P. (ed.), *'The Conscience of the World'. The Influence of Non-Governmental Organizations in the UN System* (London: Hurst and Co., 1996): defines what is an NGO, gives the history of the League and the UN consultative arrangements and offers seven case-studies of the influence of NGOs in the UN system.

Risse-Kappen, T. (ed.), *Bringing Transnational Relations Back In* (Cambridge: Cambridge University Press, 1995): provides a set of six case-studies around the theme that transnational influence depends upon the structures of governance for an issue-area at both the domestic level and in international institutions.

Theoretical debate

Rosenau, J. N., *The Study of Global Interdependence: Essays on the Transnationalisation of World Affairs* (London: Pinter, 1980): a fruitful source of theoretical ideas for a Pluralist approach.

Willetts, P., 'Transactions, Networks and Systems', in A. J. R. Groom and P. Taylor, *Frameworks for International Co-operation* (London: Pinter, 1990), ch. 17: more detailed coverage of the development of International Relations theory on transnational and intergovernmental relations.

See also the editors' chapters in the case-study books.

UN materials

Kaul, I., *et al.*, *Human Development Report 1993* (New York: Oxford University Press, 1993): an official UN annual report, which in this edition concentrates on the contribution made by NGOs to development.

UNCTAD, Division on Transnational Corporations and Investment, *World Investment Report* (New York: UN, 1991 and each year thereafter): an official UN annual report, which assesses the scale of TNC participation in global production, investment and trade.

See also documents in the appendices to Willetts, *'The Conscience of the World'*.

WEB LINKS

www.un.org the United Nations home page, with separate links for the main organs and the major conferences. The site provides access to official documents and reports, but not any political analysis.

www.conferenceofngos.org Conference of Non-Governmental Organizations in Consultative Status with the Economic and Social Council of the United Nations.

www.oneworld.org a gateway to most of the active international NGOs. It can be used both to learn about particular organizations and to explore controversy about global issues.

NOTES

1. Data on transnational corporations is given in annual reports from the United Nations. The figures quoted come from *World Investment Report 1999*, (Geneva: UN, 1999), pp. 5–6. A parent TNC is defined as one that controls assets outside its home country and a foreign affiliate is defined as a subsidiary, a branch or an associate in which the parent has a stake of at least 10% of the equity (p. 465). The numbers of transnational and international organizations of different types are given in the statistical tables of the various editions of the UIA yearbook. The figures quoted come from *Yearbook of International Organizations 1999–2000* (Munich: K. G. Saur, for the Union of International Associations, 36th edn., 1999). In each case, the current author has rounded the figures. The total number of global actors has increased significantly compared to the data given in the first edition of this book: TNCs are up by 56%, their affiliates have more than doubled and INGOs are up by 24%. The number of intergovernmental organizations has dropped, because more than 15% of the regional IGOs have dissolved or become inactive. The UIA reports a minimal rise in the number of single-country NGOs that are internationally active (their categories G and N), but these categories are very difficult to define and to monitor.

2. Compare the *World Investment Report 1999*, which in Table III.1 lists 50 TNCs as having sales of more than $30 bn. in 1997, with the *World Bank Atlas, 2000* (Washington, DC: World Bank, 2000), 42–3, which gives GNP data for each country in 1998. Population data was taken from the *Human Development Report 1999* (New York: Oxford University Press, 1999), 198–200.

3. ECOSOC Resolution 288(X)B Arrangements for Consultation with Non-Governmental Organizations was passed in February 1950. It was amended and replaced by Resolution 1296(XLIV) in May 1968. A further process of review and amendment started in February 1993 and concluded in July 1996, with the passing of Resolution 1996/31. As specified in Table 17.1, the classifications were renamed in 1950, 1968, and 1996. The basic definition of an NGO has not changed since the 1950 resolution, but the details of their participation rights have been changed.

Part Four

International issues

In this section of the book we want to give you a wide-ranging overview of the main issues in contemporary world politics. The previous three sections have been designed to give you a comprehensive foundation for the study of contemporary international issues. As with the other sections, this one also has two aims: **first**, we want to give you an understanding of some of the more important pressing problems which appear every day in the media headlines and which, directly and indirectly, affect the lives of each of us. These issues are the stuff of globalization, and they take a number of different forms. Some, like the environment and nuclear proliferation pose dangers of global catastrophe. Others, like nationalism, cultural differences, and humanitarian intervention, together with regionalism and integration, raise important questions and dilemmas about the twin processes of fragmentation and unification which characterize the world in which we live. Yet other issues such as global trade and finance, gender, human rights, poverty, development, and hunger are fundamentally intertwined with globalization, whilst the development of the Internet represents a transformation of the ways in which people communicate and access information. Our **second** aim, of course, is that by providing overviews of these issues we are posing questions about the nature of globalization. Is it new? Is it beneficial? Is it unavoidable? Does it serve specific interests? Does it make it more or less easy to deal with the problems dealt with in these chapters? The picture that emerges from these chapters is that the process of globalization is a highly complex one, with major disagreements existing about its significance and its impact. Some contributors see opportunities for greater co-operation because of globalization whilst others see dangers of increased levels of conflict as the end of the century beckons. What do you think?

18 Environmental issues

Owen Greene

READER'S GUIDE

Environmental issues emerged in the late twentieth century as a major focus of international concern and activity. Understanding the causes and impacts of global environmental change is an urgent task. So too is improving knowledge of how to develop effective responses. Approaches and concepts developed within International Relations can contribute substantially to such understanding. At the same time, international environmental issues pose important challenges for International Relations theory. This chapter introduces these issues, and discusses some key characteristics of the causes and risks of global environmental change and responses to it. It outlines the historical development of international environmental politics and agreements, and then examines issues and phases in the development of environmental regimes (particularly the ozone regime), and the Earth Summit agreements and their outcomes.

Introduction: international environment issues

By the early twenty-first century, environmental issues had been high on the international agenda for a whole generation of political leaders, government officials, scientists, industrialists, and concerned citizens. Since the late 1960s, awareness of the risks and implications of a wide range of international environmental problems has increased greatly, and justifiably so.

Since that time, it has become clear that most of the world's seas and oceans are over-fished. Soil is being degraded and eroded on a large scale throughout the world. Natural habitats are being destroyed:

for example the area of tropical rainforest has reduced by over 50 per cent since 1950, and the process continues largely unabated. As a result, tens of thousands of species of plants and animals are probably becoming extinct each year. The dumping of waste products into the sea, air, and land means that pollution problems are ubiquitous. Huge quantities of waste, including hazardous chemicals, heavy metals, and radioactive materials, have been dumped at sea, either directly or carried by rivers. Together with sewage and oil spills, these have profoundly damaged sea environments, with lakes and semi-enclosed seas proving particularly vulnerable. Billions of people suffer daily air pollution. Acid rain, stratospheric ozone depletion, and climate change are major regional or global problems arising from atmospheric pollution.

Environmental problems are not new. Human societies have long had a major impact on their environment. Their tendency to exploit it as if it were an inexhaustible resource has repeatedly led to disaster, sometimes leading to the loss of entire human communities. Over much of human history, however, the environmental impacts of over-exploitation or pollution have typically been quite local. Communities could often escape the consequences of such activities by moving on to relatively unspoilt areas. Even if they could not, the local impoverishment did not necessarily affect the continued well-being of neighbouring societies. Widespread industrialization and rapid population growth changed this situation. Severe environmental damage and unsustainable exploitation occurred over whole regions of the world. By the late twentieth century, the impacts had become truly global.

This chapter examines the politics of **global environmental issues**. However, there are several senses in which the environment can be said to have become a global issue. First, some environmental problems are inherently global. CFCs (chlorofluorocarbons) released into the atmosphere contribute to the global problem of stratospheric ozone depletion irrespective of where they are emitted, just as carbon dioxide emissions contribute to global climate change. The effects are global, and the problems can only be tackled through co-operation on a global scale.

Second, some problems relate to the exploitation of **global commons**: resources shared by all members of the international community, such as the oceans, deep-sea bed, atmosphere, and outer space. Many argue that the world's genetic resources are a global resource, which should be preserved in the common interest.

Third, many environmental problems are intrinsically **transnational**, in that by their nature they cross state boundaries, even if they are not entirely global. For example, emissions of sulphur dioxide by one state will be carried by winds and deposited as acid rain on downwind countries. Wastes dumped into an enclosed or semi-enclosed sea affect all littoral states. Such transnational or regional problems exist in many parts of the world, and pose similar technical and political challenges to those of truly global problems. Moreover, states or non-state actors from outside the region may contribute to the problems or to efforts to tackle them.

Fourth, and following on from this, many processes of over-exploitation or environmental degradation are relatively local or national in scale, and yet they are experienced in such a large number of localities around the world that they can be considered to be global problems. Examples include unsustainable agricultural practices, soil degradation and erosion, deforestation, river pollution, and the many environmental problems associated with urbanization and industrial practices.

Finally, the processes leading to over-exploitation and environmental degradation are intimately linked to broader political and socio-economic processes, which themselves are part of a global political economy. Thus it is widely recognized that the causes of most environmental problems are closely related to the generation and distribution of wealth, knowledge, and power, and to patterns of energy consumption, industrialization, population growth, affluence, and poverty. In this respect, the processes of globalization and interdependence in the economic and other spheres of life, as discussed in Chapter 1, increasingly give all environmental issues a global dimension.

Thus, the phrase 'global environmental issues' encompasses a wide range of types of problems and issues, posing different challenges to those who wish to develop effective responses. Although they share some common characteristics, each issue is specific and needs to be analysed in its own right.

Key points

- International environmental issues emerged as a major focus for international politics and concern in the last three decades of the twentieth century.
- Although environmental problems are not new in themselves, industrialization and rapid population growth have greatly increased the scale and intensity of the over-exploitation of natural resources and environmental degradation, gener-

ating a wide range of urgent international and global problems.
- Environmental issues have become international and global in several senses. Many environmental problems are intrinsically transnational or global, or relate to global commons. Other local or national problems are experienced widely across the Earth. Finally, the processes generating most environmental problems are closely related to broader political or socio-economic processes, which are themselves part of an increasingly global system
- Global environmental issues exist in many different forms, and though they share some common characteristics, each needs specific examination in its own right.

Environmental issues on the international agenda: a historic outline

The early years

Environmental issues first emerged as a focus for international politics in the nineteenth century in the context of international agreements to manage resources. For example, the River Commissions for the Rhine and the Danube which are now deeply involved with environmental policy began life as arrangements to facilitate economic use of the rivers as waterways. The International Maritime Organization (IMO) was formed in 1948, more or less as a 'shipowners' club' to facilitate international shipping and navigation and promote safety. But in 1954 the IMO was given responsibility for implementing a landmark treaty on marine pollution: the Convention for the Prevention of Pollution of the Sea by Oil.

The first international treaty on flora, signed in Bern in 1889, was primarily concerned with preventing the spread of a disease (Phylloxera) which threatened to destroy European vineyards. This was followed by a series of global and regional agreements on flora in the 1920s and 1950s, which were all similarly concerned with maintaining healthy

stocks of cultivated plants or preventing disease. Likewise, the first agreement on fauna was the 1902 Convention for the Protection of Birds useful to Agriculture. In 1911 the USA, Canada, and Russia agreed a Convention for the Protection of Fur Seals, which were being unsustainably culled. In 1945, the UN Food and Agriculture Organization (FAO) was set up, with the conservation of natural resources included in its mandate. The 1946 International Whaling Convention essentially established a club of whaling nations to manage the 'harvesting' of whales.

Even at that time, however, there was emerging concern to protect wildlife for its own sake as well as an economic resource. Conventions were signed to protect birds, in large part due to public pressures mobilized by groups such as the Royal Society for the Protection of Birds. The first international efforts to establish wildlife parks and reserves began as early as 1900 (amongst the colonial powers in Africa), and were further advanced through a series of Conventions from the 1930s onwards.

It was in the 1960s, however, that international concern about pollution and the preservation of the natural environment began to develop rapidly, particularly in developed countries. Rachel Carson's book *Silent Spring* not only stimulated intense concern about the widespread use of DDT and other pesticides, but also helped to launch the modern environmental movement (Carson 1962). Wide awareness of the health risks posed by radioactive fall-out contributed to the pressures to conclude the ban on nuclear warhead tests in the atmosphere, agreed in 1963. Concern about sea pollution grew, stimulated by disasters such as the spill from the Torrey Canyon oil tanker in 1967, and the IMO became increasingly engaged with preventing oil pollution at sea. The problem of transboundary air pollution, and 'acid rain', attracted increasing attention, particularly in Scandinavia and Canada where damage to vulnerable forest and lake ecosystems was becoming manifest. In the mid-1960s, informal discussions began on the development of a new Law of the Sea to govern access to, and use of, the international seas and the seabed: the old regime was collapsing as unilateral claims were being made on transit rights and for economic control of waters up to 200 miles from coasts.

The Stockholm Conference

The **1972 UN Conference on the Human Environment** was organized in response to this dramatic increase in international environmental concern in the 1960s. The aim was to establish an international framework to promote a more co-ordinated approach to pollution and other environmental problems. The conference, which was held in Stockholm, marked a turning point in the development of international environmental politics. Some of the principles that were agreed, and the institutions and programmes that were established, had an enduring effect (see Box 18.1). Just as significantly, the debates at the conference established themes and practices that would remain central to international environmental politics for the next thirty years and beyond.

The importance of international environmental issues as a focus for international concern became institutionalized, along with the principle that states have a responsibility to co-operate with efforts to manage the global commons and reduce transboundary pollution. Developing countries insisted that they had less historical responsibility for global pollution and resource depletion than industrialized countries, and that actions to protect the environment had to be linked to efforts to promote their economic and social development—arguments that developed states accepted in principle. That is, the general relationship between **environment and development** in the context of North–South relations was for the first time formally elaborated at an intergovernmental meeting. At the same time, **environmental non-governmental organizations** (NGOs) from many countries gathered to monitor the entire proceedings of the Conference, to exert political pressure on the participants, and to network, thus establishing a practice that has continued ever since.

From Stockholm to Rio

In the 1970s and 1980s, dozens of international environmental agreements and programmes were established. For example, a series of conventions were set up to protect the environment of the Mediterranean, North Sea, Baltic Sea, and other regional seas, with UNEP playing an important leadership role. The 1972 London Dumping Convention established a framework for restricting the dumping of toxic wastes (including nuclear wastes) at sea. In 1973, an international convention was agreed to prevent intentional oil pollution from ships (the MARPOL Convention) which was further strengthened in 1978, after further public outcries about continuing oil spills. In 1979, European and North American countries set up the Long Range Transboundary Air Pollution (LRTAP) agreement to limit emissions of sulphur dioxide and other pollutants causing air pollution and acid rain. In 1985 the Vienna Convention for the Protection of the Ozone Layer was signed, followed two years later by the Montreal Protocol which imposed substantial limits on use of CFCs and other ozone depleting substances.

Largely as a result of sustained pressure by environmental NGOs, the Ramsar Convention to preserve wetland habitats of waterfowl was established in

Box 18.1 **The Stockholm Conference and its legacy**

The UN Conference on the Human Environment, held in Stockholm in 1972, was the UN's first major conference on international environmental issues. The Stockholm Conference attracted wide publicity, and many of the participants and observers no doubt learned a lot from the discussions of a wide range of specific environmental issues. The meeting agreed upon: a Declaration containing 26 principles concerning the environment and development; an Action Plan with 109 recommendations spanning six broad areas (human settlements, natural resource management, pollution, educational and social aspects of the environment, development and the environment, and international organizations); and a Resolution on various institutional and financial arrangements.

In following years dozens of international environmental agreements were achieved. However, apart from galvanizing public concern and educating governments, the most enduring specific contributions of the Stockholm Conference are widely believed to be the following.

First, some of the agreed principles significantly strengthened the framework for future environmental co-operation. They did not immediately command universal acceptance, not least because Soviet bloc countries boycotted the Stockholm Conference for broader foreign policy reasons. But over time they gained substantial international stature, and provided a basis for much subsequent environmental diplomacy. Principle 21 had particular significance, for example. It acknowledged states' sovereignty over their natural resources but stipulated that states have 'the responsibility to ensure that activities within their jurisdiction or control do not cause damage to the environment of other states or of areas beyond the limits of national jurisdiction'. Other principles established that: the international community should determine limits on the use and abuse of 'global commons'; resources identified as the '**Common Heritage of Mankind**' (such as the deep-sea bed) should be collectively managed, preserved or used to common benefit; measures to prevent pollution and protect the natural environment should be balanced against the economic and social goals; and that international agreements should take into account the different circumstances and responsibilities of developed and developing states.

Second, the Stockholm Conference led to the establishment of global and regional environmental monitoring networks, which have improved monitoring of environmental problems, such as marine pollution and ozone depletion, and have indirectly stimulated action to tackle them.

Third, the Conference led to the creation of the **UN Environment Programme (UNEP)**, which was tasked with co-ordinating the environment-related activities of other UN agencies and promoting the integration of environmental considerations into their work. In practice, UNEP subsequently played a key role in: raising political awareness of environmental problems; helping with the formation of scientific consensus on problems and responses to them; facilitating negotiations (particularly for the protection of regional seas and the ozone layer); and improving countries' environmental management capacities. Further, UNEP provided institutional frameworks through which broader agenda-setting activities could develop. For example, since the 1980s UNEP provided an important forum for raising awareness of the linkages between environmental degradation and women's lives, developing agendas to promote gender awareness in environmental projects and specific engagement environment and development institutions through the 1990s. Overall, the broader institutionalization of international environmental politics after the Stockholm Conference meant that the process acquired momentum to continue through periods when public and political concerns about the environment waned.

Finally, the Conference stimulated broader political and institutional changes. For example, many governments subsequently created Ministries for the Environment and national agencies for environmental monitoring or regulation. The development of international networks of environmental NGOs was stimulated. Moreover environmental NGOs, which at that time were primarily based in Europe or North America, began to engage more systematically with development issues and developing country groups.

1971, followed by the Convention on International Trade in Endangered Species (CITES) a year later. These were followed by a series of agreements to conserve habitats and animals including seals and polar bears. Furthermore, well-established resource-management regimes, such as the Antarctica Treaty and the International Whaling Convention were transformed into environmental protection agreements. Moratoriums on whaling and on the exploitation of Antarctic resources were established—marking a considerable departure from the original aims and priorities of these regimes.

It increasingly became the norm that non-governmental groups should have wide access to intergovernmental meetings on the environment, to an extent that would have shocked earlier generations of diplomats and is still unknown in some other spheres of international activity. Moreover, in many areas environmental NGOs came to command sufficient expertise and resources that they became substantial forces in international politics in their own right. Delegations from organizations such as Greenpeace, World Wildlife Fund, or Friends of the Earth at international meetings were frequently larger and more expert than those of all but the largest states, and through their access to the media and their expertise were able to shape international agendas. Industrial associations representing interested groups in the business community likewise became directly involved in seeking to shape international environmental regimes, rather than simply working through their governments.

However, the development agendas included in the Action Plan and Declaration of Principles agreed at Stockholm were never seriously followed up. Most of the international agreements listed above focused on environmental protection or pollution, without seriously integrating development concerns. Moreover, UNEP lacked the institutional weight seriously to co-ordinate other UN agencies, which typically vigorously protect their 'turf', and thus largely failed to achieve integration of environmental and development agendas in the UN system. This caused increasing international concern, particularly amongst developing countries.

The UN established a World Commission on Environment and Development, chaired by the then Prime Minister of Norway, Gro Harlem Brundtland, to propose ways forward. The 1987 **Brundtland Report** argued for priority to be given to achieving '**sustainable development**', and received wide international support (World Commission on Environment and Development, 1987). Though the Report discussed a variety of issues and institutional reforms, the exact meaning of the concept of 'sustainable development' remained contested or

---

Box 18.2 **Sustainable development**

The concept of 'sustainable development' was crystallized and popularized in the 1987 report of the UN World Commission on Environment and Development (the Brundtland Commission), which drew upon long established lines of thought that had developed substantially over the previous 20 years.

The Brundtland Commission's shorthand characterization of 'sustainable development' is development that meets the needs of the present without compromising the ability of future generations to meet their own needs. The prominence given to 'needs' reflects a concern to eradicate poverty and meet human basic needs, broadly understood.

The concept of sustainable development focused attention on finding strategies to promote economic and social development in ways that avoided environmental degradation, over-exploitation or pollution, and sidelined less productive debates about whether to prioritize development or the environment. A variety of important constituencies could support this concept. The emphasis on 'development' could be widely endorsed, and was particularly welcomed by developing country representatives, development agencies, and groups primarily concerned about poverty and social deprivation. The link with 'sustainability' satisfied a variety of environmental constituencies. It addressed those who were concerned that present patterns of economic and population growth would have to change because humankind was reaching the limits of the Earth's finite natural resources and 'carrying capacity', first popularized by the Club of Rome in the early 1970s (Meadows *et al.* 1972, 1992). It could also be welcomed by those who doubted this, and were more concerned about problems such as pollution, climate change, and threats to habitats and biodiversity.

unclear. Nevertheless, it was important because it developed an agenda which could attract strong support from a variety of important constituencies. As a result, the UN General Assembly decided in December 1989 to convene an '**Earth Summit**' as a twenty-year follow-up to the Stockholm Meeting, so that the international community could carry the sustainable development agenda forward. A **UN Conference on Environment and Development (UNCED)** was fixed to take place in Rio de Janeiro in June 1992.

Key points

- Environmental issues first emerged on the international agenda in the late nineteenth century.
- Environmental awareness and concern developed strongly after the 1960s, particularly in relation to pollution problems.
- The 1972 Stockholm Conference established a number of principles, institutions, and programmes which helped to provide a framework promoting the further development of international responses to transnational environmental problems.
- In the 1970s and 1980s, international environmental politics developed and matured. Green movements, environmental and industrial NGOs, and international organizations established themselves as key actors in international environmental politics alongside states.
- The Brundtland Commission promoted the concept of 'sustainable development', and preparations began for a 1992 UN Conference on Environment and Development.

Issues and challenges in international environmental politics

Some challenges for International Relations

As International Relations scholars came to study international environmental politics, they not surprisingly brought their established theoretical perspectives and prejudices with them. Such is the variety and complexity of the environmental issue area that advocates of each such perspective can find plenty of evidence that seems to support their case, be it 'realist', 'neo-realist', 'liberal', 'liberal institutionalist'; 'Marxist', 'social constructivist' or 'feminist'. Moreover, each perspective provides important insights into aspects of global environmental change or international environmental politics.

However, it is perhaps more interesting and important to note at the outset that international environmental issues pose particular challenges for some of the dominant approaches in International Relations. Theories and simplifying assumptions developed through other areas of study, such as security studies (Ch. 12) or international political economy (Ch. 13), should not be assumed to apply equally well to this area without careful examination of the evidence. In practice, they often require significant revision to take proper account of the particular characteristics of environmental issues.

One example relates to the significance and role of states. The dominant tradition within International Relations is state-centric, centred around concepts of state sovereignty and the belief that states are the primary actors in international affairs and that international politics is largely driven by states pursuing their interests (see Ch. 7). However, transnational environmental problems pose real problems for established notions about the nature and limits of state sovereignty. Moreover, international environmental problems are rarely caused by deliberate acts of national policy, but are rather unintended side-effects of broader socio-economic processes. A wide range and large number of non-state actors—including companies, local authorities, financial institutions, social groups, and individuals—are typically at least as important as states as actors in these processes.

It is true, however, that states retain a relatively privileged position in the international politics of responding to global environmental problems. Whereas states and their central governments do not generally directly control the economic, social, and environmental activities of concern, they do have sovereign authority to legislate within their territories and thus must play a central role in developing and implementing any environmental regulations. Thus, while the rise of environmental problems has brought state power and sovereignty into question, the responses to these problems may often extend and strengthen aspects of state authority and involvement in society. Moreover, to the extent that international agreements are important for co-operative responses to environmental problems, interstate diplomacy must come to the fore and states will be the legal parties to any treaties.

But, as already illustrated, even in relation to the politics of responding to international environmental problems, non-state actors typically also play a primary role. **Supranational organizations** such as the EU play a key international role alongside states, as well as being able to regulate activities within their member states. The EU is itself a party to several international environmental treaties. **International organizations**, international financial institutions, **transnational organizations** (such as industrial associations or environmental **non-governmental organizations** (NGOs)), social movements, womens groups, consumer groups, and scientists can all play a key role. Even in relation to international environmental negotiations and agreements, there are numerous examples of non-state actors playing central roles. Moreover, as states become enmeshed in international institutions or **regimes** established to tackle environmental problems, the policy process often acquires an important transnational or international dimension which in practice can substantially limit national autonomy.

Finally, implementing international environmental commitments typically has to involve a mixture of international institutions, states, and transnational and domestic organizations. Limiting atmospheric or sea pollution, for example, can rarely be directly carried out by government decision, like dismantling a missile or withdrawing a tank division in arms control. It involves a complex process of changing a variety of often well-established industrial or social activities, involving a wide range of non-governmental groups, local authorities, and individuals.

Just as studies of international environmental politics oblige us to take full account of a range of non-state actors, and to review the significance and role of states, they also raise questions about the relationship between the 'international' and 'domestic' spheres of political activity. Several strands of International Relations theory have been developed on the basis of there being a radical distinction between these two spheres. However, global environmental issues involve a range of connections between local, national, and international processes that raise questions about such distinctions. This is true not only for patterns of causation and impacts of environmental problems in an interdependent world, but also for responses to such problems. Transnational organizations and networks—for example, environmental NGOs, multinational companies, financial institutions, scientists—typically play a relatively important role, and these by definition cut across international/domestic boundaries. International organizations are sometimes directly involved in local projects with only nominal involvement of the national authorities. The relationship between international organizations and institutions, states, and non-state actors within countries is normally complex in this context, and particularly when it comes to implementing international programmes for environmental protection.

A third issue for International Relations raised particularly by studies of international environmental issues is the relationship between knowledge, power, and interests. Scientific or expert knowledge often plays an especially important role in environmental politics. Careful scientific monitoring and modelling of the environment is usually needed to identify and assess problems and to frame debates about possible responses. 'Knowledge' helps to set agendas, affects patterns of influence and power, and shapes assessments by key actors of their priorities and interests.

Typically, there is considerable scientific uncertainty—about the problems, impacts, and effective responses. Nevertheless, communities of scientists and experts can exert substantial influence. International environmental issues therefore provide an important area for exploring the ways in which power relations, patterns of interests, knowledge and learning processes, and values interact in determining outcomes. Attempts to explain the outcomes of international policy debates on environmental issues in terms of just one or two of these factors have normally failed.

The 'tragedy of the commons': an instructive parable

In 1968 Garrett Hardin proposed a particularly influential model to explain why communities may over-exploit shared environmental resources even where they know that they are doing so and are aware that it is against their long-term interests (Hardin 1968). This is known as the '**tragedy of the commons**'.

The notion of the 'tragedy of the commons' can be explained using a hypothetical example—or 'parable'—of the use of common fish resources (see Box 18.3). In brief, the notion shows how it is possible that 'rational' individual actions can lead to 'irrational' collective practices resulting in catastrophic over-exploitation of common resources. Where access to a common resource is open and unregulated, each user continues to have an individual interest in exploiting it to the maximum. Each user gains the full extra benefit of further resource extraction, while the cost of over-exploitation is shared by all of the communities that use the resource.

The 'tragedy of the commons' is that this depletion of 'open access' common resources can continue remorselessly to their destructive conclusion, even if each user involved is well intentioned, well informed, and exercising only its traditional and legal rights. Unilateral acts of public-spirited restraint are insufficient to tackle the problem. If the rest of the user community continues in its old ways, the public-spirited suffer along with the selfish

without even having benefited from the 'good times' in the meantime.

Many environmental problems of industrial society appear to have a similar structure. The owners of a factory have an interest in continuing to produce goods in the cheapest way, even if that involves dispersing untreated pollutants into the rivers or atmosphere. They gain most of the benefits of cheap production, while the pollution costs are uncertain and in any case shared by the whole 'downstream' community and other species of life. That is, the costs of pollution are **externalized**, since the polluter does not have to include them in its production costs. In this way some governments have been relatively tolerant of sulphur emissions from power

---

Box 18.3 **The 'tragedy of the commons': a parable**

Consider a sea or large lake on which many local fishing communities depend as a source of food and income. Each fisher has an immediate interest in making as large a catch of fish as s/he can sell or eat, in order to improve his or her standard of living. For centuries, this arrangement has worked satisfactorily. Human populations were sufficiently low, and fishing technologies were sufficiently primitive, that there was no over-fishing. Gradually, however, living conditions improved and human populations grew, increasing the number of people fishing and also the demand for fish. At the same time, fishing technologies improved. In recent years, the sea or lake has been fished at unsustainable levels, and the total fish stock is falling.

In spite of this, each individual fisher continues to have an interest in maintaining or improving their catch. Each fisher gains the full extra benefit of catching additional fish, but bears only a small part of the extra cost of fishing a depleted fish stock because this cost is shared throughout the whole community. Even concerned and environmentally aware fishers may be sorely tempted to continue to make large catches: they know that even if they desist, others are likely to continue to maximize their own catches while they can. The 'tragedy of the commons', in this parable, is that this process continues until fish stock are destroyed along with the fishing communities that depended on them.

stations in their territory, since the resulting acid rain was dispersed over a number of downwind states. Moreover, the damage caused by acid rain to buildings and forests typically does not appear in power-generation budgets, whereas the costs of cleaning the emissions would do so.

Preventing the over-exploitation of the commons

The notion of the 'tragedy of the commons' demonstrates the vulnerability of open access resources to over-exploitation. In principle, a range of types of responses to such over-exploitation are available. One traditional response is to '**exploit and move on**'. This has been the approach taken by 'slash and burn' agricultural communities in the tropical forests, cattle herdsmen in regions of Africa, and many international timber companies. Increasingly, however, this is no longer an option. The environment cannot recover (or is given insufficient time and space in which to do so), and there are fewer places to move on to.

Another type of response is '**privatization**'. Hardin himself drew the conclusion that the solution to 'tragedy of the commons' was a change in property rights, arguing that the problem of the commons is that they are 'owned' by everyone and that no one in particular had the authority or interest in managing them sustainably. Thus, in relation to the over-grazing of common land, for example, if ownership of the common grazing land were divided amongst the herd-keepers, each of these would have a direct interest in maintaining the value of his or her own land by grazing it at sustainable levels. Each would bear the full costs of any unsustainable practices, and each would have the ability to control how his or her land was managed.

In principle, the 'privatization' approach could play a significant role in improving resource management of the global commons. For example, the new UN Convention on the Law of the Sea, agreed in 1982, transferred effective ownership of much of the world's ocean resources to coastal states, with a broad obligation on these states to manage sustainably their Exclusive Economic Zones (EEZ) which

stretched 200 miles from their coasts. However, in general, in order for this approach to be effective the new 'owners' would have to have a clear interest in the long-term conservation and management of the resources under their control, and have the capacity and knowledge necessary for effectively carrying out their management role. In practice, such conditions would often not be met. For example, without regulation, it is not clear that owners of 'privatized' forest could be relied on to manage their forests sustainably rather than sell the timber and invest the proceeds in other businesses. Moreover, the approach would be difficult to apply to tackle resources or problems which by their nature do not respect artificial 'property' boundaries, such as atmospheric or sea pollution or migratory fish.

The third type of approach to promoting environmental conservation and sustainable management of the common is to establish systems of **governance** to prevent unsustainable or damaging practices. This approach tackles the problem by regulating access to shared resources rather than by changing patterns of ownership.

This third approach is in principle applicable to the widest range of problems. But it is clear that establishing any system of norms, rules, regulations, or taxes to tackle environmental problems is bound to be controversial, particularly when traditional rules of access have to be made more restrictive. Experience with attempts to prevent over-fishing, for example, has shown that some fishers can be expected to deny that there is an over-fishing problem. Others might dispute the maximum sustainable yield. Moreover, the ways in which fishing quotas or the burdens of implementing taxes or regulations are distributed amongst the community are also sure to be controversial. The benefits or costs of any environmental policy or regulation are bound to be distributed unevenly, leading to disputes about which regulations or policies to adopt and also to possible compliance problems in the future.

Such disputes and challenges are characteristic of all attempts to tackle environmental problems or to manage common resources. Nevertheless, the prospects for overcoming them and establishing effective management could be expected to be greatly improved if there is a strong hierarchical authority capable of taking decisions and enforcing them on dissenting groups. Thus most would agree that state regulation and control is a potentially effective approach to managing local or national resources within a well-developed state.

However, there is no world government with the power or authority to impose rules on the use of global commons. Authority for legislation and enforcement is dispersed amongst some 190 sovereign states, none of which can legally be obliged to obey an international law to which they do not subscribe. In this context, Hardin and many others have been deeply sceptical about the prospects for developing effective systems for **collective governance** of the global commons.

This focuses attention on the extent to which effective collective management systems can be developed and maintained. Such systems involve the development of collective institutions—in the form of sets of agreed principles, norms, rules, common understandings, organizations, consultation processes and such like—governing or shaping uses of the shared environmental resources. Ostrom and others examined the conditions for the successful formation of such institutions amongst local or regional communities in the absence of a central authority (Ostrom 1990). Perhaps unsurprisingly, they found them to be similar in character to the conditions conducive to the establishment of **international regimes**, particularly those identified by liberal institutionalists, as discussed in Chapters 9 and 14.

In practice, much of the international politics of responding to global environmental problems has been focused around the development, implementation, and effectiveness of international environmental regimes. In this context, an **international environmental regime** is an international agreement or social institution with (more or less) agreed-upon principles, norms, rules, decision-making procedures, and programmes that govern the activities and shape the expectations of actors in a specific environmental issue area.

Understandings of how international environmental regimes develop and operate, and what determines their effectiveness, remain contested. As discussed in Chapter 14 (International Regimes) for example, 'realists' and 'liberal institutionalists'

generally agree on the importance of the development of international rule-based behaviour, but differ between and amongst themselves on how to understand it. Realists tend to regard international regimes, including environmental regimes, as agreements that reflect particular patterns of power and interests of states, which are quite vulnerable to changes in such patterns. However, they accept that regimes may prove robust where participating states have strong interest in co-ordination, and where the regime enables them to operate on the so-called Pareto frontier of optimal co-ordination. Liberal institutionalists tend to see wider scope for developing robust environmental regimes, and emphasize their potential role in establishing collective environmental governance to tackle problems like the 'tragedy of the commons', involving collaboration amongst states that fear 'free-riding' or defection by competitors. Since the early 1990s, many analysts from the liberal tradition have emphasized the importance of seeing environmental regimes as international social institutions, through which ruled-based behaviour is induced not only through rational calculations of interest but also through the absorption of norms and values and through processes of social learning. In this way, environmental and other regimes may shape and transform governments' perceptions of state interests.

It is important to note that the above working definition of an environmental regime deliberately does not prejudge any of the above debates. It provides scope for environmental regimes to be an important focus not only for realist or liberal institutionalist investigations, but also for others including 'reflectivists' and 'social constructivists' (see Ch. 11). Environmental regimes from this perspective can provide an important framework for the interactions between a wide variety of international and domestic actors, and between power, interests, knowledge, and values.

An environmental regime provides a focus for the formulation and implementation of policies to tackle a particular international environmental problem, including the organization of relevant resource transfers and capacity-building activities. For many, however, regimes provide too restrictive and 'reformist' a framework for examining responses to global environmental change. Insufficient attention may be devoted to the activities and struggles of local groups around the world that do not explicitly engage with the regime politics or focus on particular environmental 'issue areas'. Similarly, environmental regimes have naturally tended to develop in issue areas where influential international actors perceive international co-operation to be most useful or essential. Nevertheless, as international environmental regimes and institutions have developed, and become interlinked, their forums and programmes have provided a focus for international efforts to promote awareness of such local issues, and also of broader concerns such as the importance of gender awareness in environmental programmes and the specific roles that women might play.

Finally, regimes are typically developed to shape and restrict the activities of relevant actors in order to tackle specific environmental problems, not to challenge or transform the socio-economic or political structures and processes that generate the global patterns of development, resource distribution, and environmental degradation. Thus an emphasis on regimes can be criticized by those who focus on 'world system' approaches or those for whom anything other than clearly transformatory agendas are inadequate. However, the scope of such agendas soon extends far beyond specifically environmental political issues.

Key Points

- Each of the main approaches within International Relations theory provide important insights into international environmental politics. At the same time, environmental issues pose major challenges, particularly relating to: the role and significance of states and the notion of sovereignty; the relationship between international and domestic spheres of political activity; and the relationship between knowledge, values, power, and interests in determining outcomes in international processes.

- The notion of the 'tragedy of the commons' provides an instructive model of how common resources can become over-exploited.

- The collective management of global commons in principle is more widely applicable than approaches focusing on 'privatization', though the development of international collective management regimes poses particular challenges.

- Much international environmental politics can be said to focus around the development and implementation of international environmental regimes.

The development and implementation of environmental regimes

By the year 2000, there were over 130 multilateral environmental agreements (and hundreds of bilateral ones). As indicated in Chapter 14 (International regimes), some of these must be regarded as 'dead letters'. Others are symbolic or weak, and have probably had little or no independent effect on the behaviour of relevant actors, or on the problem which they address. Nevertheless, case studies have shown that numerous environmental regimes have really been effective, in that they have changed behaviour in line with their aims and have

at least helped to tackle the problems for which they were established (Haas *et al.* 1993; Levy *et al.* 1995). The Montreal Protocol for the Protection of the Ozone Layer is a prime example. Such effective regimes are dynamic: they tend to develop and change over time, according to changing needs and opportunities and as the international context develops.

In this section we first outline the characteristic phases in the development of environmental regimes, and then illustrate some key issues through a short case-study of the regimes to protect the ozone layer. The processes of regime development can, in principle, be divided into several phases: agenda formation; negotiation and decision-making; implementation; and further development. In practice, these phases often overlap and interact—particularly as a dynamic regime becomes established.

The **agenda formation** stage includes the processes by which the problem becomes recognized, emerges onto the political stage, is framed for consideration and debate by the relevant policy communities, and rises high enough on the international political agenda to initiate negotiations and decision-making processes. For environmental issues, it can often be difficult even to secure recognition that there is a problem. Without careful scientific monitoring and assessment, problems such as pollution, depletion of fish stocks, decline in biodiversity, and climate change, may emerge slowly and not become clear until it is too late to prevent major impacts or even disaster. This is a major reason why science and 'knowledge production' processes are particularly important in environmental politics, as discussed above.

Such scientific findings are used in attempts to place the issue on the political agenda and to frame the debates about possible responses. However this process is by no means straightforward. The science enters a political arena with competing interest groups, and is in any case often uncertain. NGOs have typically been particularly important in agenda-setting, often in implicit coalitions with concerned scientific bodies, international secretariats, and sympathetic governments.

Vivid or dramatic events or discoveries have played an important role in mobilizing public concern and capturing political attention. Measures against oil pollution at sea were stimulated by oil tanker disasters, even though routine spillage had been posing at least as wide an environmental threat. Similarly, public concern in the UK about North Sea pollution was only mobilized sufficiently to persuade the government to support more stringent international action when it was linked to an epidemic amongst the (photogenic) seal population. In the 1970s, UNEP felt obliged to present the problem of desertification in terms of (scientifically dubious) images of desert sand-dunes advancing on farming areas in order stimulate international action.

The stage of **negotiating and agreeing commitments** takes a political process on an issue from the point where it becomes a priority item on the agenda of relevant policy-making or negotiating fora to the point where international decisions are made about which policies and rules will be adopted to address the issue. It is at this stage that choices are made about commitments, policies, and measures. In principle, there are normally a number of possible ways to respond to a given environmental problem. The ways in which the main policy response options are actually framed, considered, and assessed are a key part of environmental politics, and constitute another important dimension to the relationship between policy, science, and 'knowledge'. Some approaches may be assessed to be more effective in tackling the problem than others. In this context, transnational 'knowledge-based' communities of experts with shared understanding of the problem and preferred policy responses (i.e. '**epistemic communities**') have proved particularly influential.

Moreover, policies also differ in the ways they distribute the costs and benefits amongst different social groups and actors, and this also has a profound effect on the policy-making process and on final decisions. The problems of achieving agreement typically multiply as the number or participants and the variety of their interests increase.

Equity issues are generally central to the negotiation process. To be negotiable and have legitimacy, commitments generally need to be perceived to be reasonably fair and equitable. Sometimes it is possible to achieve agreement on a single principle to guide 'fair' distributions of burdens, such as the 'polluter pays' principle. In practice, however, many notions of equity are typically in play, including: equal quotas; equal percentage changes from the status quo; equality of burden in implementing commitments; burdens distributed according to historic responsibility for the problem, or according to capacity to pay; 'first come, first served; historic ('grandfathered') rights; and many others. Application of different principles would have very different implications for the distribution of costs and benefits from the agreement. Particularly in global negotiations, agreement on basic equity principles often cannot be achieved. In such cases, parties have to find ways to define commitments so that they at least appear 'arguably' equitable from a number of basic standpoints.

Successfully negotiating an effective environmental agreement typically requires **leadership**. When powerful states or groups of states, such as the United States or the EU, adopt a leading role, the prospects for achieving an agreement improve greatly. For example, US leadership in achieving a whaling moratorium in the IWC was critical. In any set of negotiations it is normally possible to identify 'leaders' that want an agreement and work hard to get one through a combination of active diplomacy, promoting the production and dissemination of relevant knowledge, or (informal or formal) sanctions or 'side payments'. In this way 'laggards'—states that are reluctant to achieve agreement or to agree to effective commitments—may be persuaded to sign. Further, co-ordination and persuasion can be achieved of the (often large number) of states that are willing in principle to join an agreement provided it is not too costly, but are not going to work hard to achieve one.

Naturally leader states aim to shape the commitments in line with their interests. But they usually have to compromise to get an agreement. Moreover, in any given issue area, there are likely to be 'veto states', without whose agreement and participation an effective regime cannot be established.

The **implementation** phase includes all of the activities involved in implementing the decisions and policies adopted in response to the problem. This can include: the incorporation of international commitments into domestic law; the development and operationalization of agreed programmes; and all other measures aimed at appropriately changing government, social, and economic practices in line with agreed rules and norms.

This stage is typically no less complex than the other two. On the contrary, experience shows that it is one thing to agree to international obligations, and quite another to bring them into operation and to achieve the desired effects on the behaviour of relevant actors. Those charged with implementing the decisions may lack necessary commitment or resources, and will typically interpret the decisions in their own ways. In practice, some countries tend to take legal obligations very seriously, whereas others tend to regard them as symbols of general intentions and a stage in an ongoing negotiation process, not to be interpreted too literally. Actors whose interests are substantially affected by the changes in policy can be expected to continue to try to influence the policy and the ways it is implemented. Compliance may leave much to be desired. In any case, the actual effects of decisions and rules can be very different to the expected ones.

Whether or not international agreements are implemented can depend greatly on the nature of the commitments themselves. Governments may not try hard to implement if they believe themselves to have been coerced into an unfair agreement, which is a reason why it is important that agreements should be regarded as legitimate and reasonably fair or in each participant's overall interest. This highlights the importance of equity and legitimacy for the implementation and effectiveness of regimes as well as for their negotiation.

The will to implement may be weak if parties suspect that others may not be complying, and attempting to 'free ride'. Thus whether or not the implementation and compliance of commitments can be monitored or verified may be an important factor. Similarly, international systems to review countries' progress in implementation can help, by increasing awareness of obligations and by identifying and facilitating timely responses to any emerging problems. Further, mechanisms to provide international aid can both increase countries' capacity to implement their commitments and increase their interest in doing so.

Finally, regimes usually need to **further develop** once they have been established in order to maintain or improve their effectiveness. Institutions and commitments may be strengthened and revised to adapt to changing circumstances, such as improved understandings of the problems and policy responses, or new political or economic challenges or opportunities. As outlined above and below, 'framework' conventions are explicitly designed to facilitate further development. More broadly, at least since the 1980s, such capacity to adapt has been widely regarded as a critical characteristic of effective agreements.

The development and implementation of the ozone regime

The Montreal Protocol, signed in 1987, stands at the centre of the regime to prevent the depletion of the ozone layer. It is widely regarded as one of the success stories in international environmental regimes.

Before it was signed, global consumption and production of the main ozone depleting substances (ODS) was increasing rapidly. By the mid-1990s, this trend had been halted and reversed, and most developed countries had virtually phased-out consumption of CFCs and halons (the most important ODS). Natural time-lags mean that the depletion of the ozone layer will nevertheless continue to get worse until after the first decade of the twenty-first

---

Box 18.4 Ozone depletion and the Montreal Protocol

Ozone is a molecule consisting of three oxygen atoms. It is relatively unstable and quite rare in the atmosphere. Most of it is found in the 'stratosphere' between 10 and 50 kilometres above the Earth's surface—the 'ozone layer'. There it absorbs nearly all of the high-energy ultraviolet radiation (UV-B) from the sun, protecting plants and animals from its damaging effects. The ozone layer is highly vulnerable to destruction by chlorine, fluorine, and bromine, which are highly reactive chemicals. However, until recently, it was relatively safe from these chemicals. Precisely because they were so reactive, their atmospheric lifetimes were too short for emissions from the Earth's surface to have time to drift up as high as the ozone layer.

Unfortunately, when humankind manufactured CFCs and halons, they created highly stable compounds containing chlorine, fluorine, or bromine. Indeed, they were so stable that they did not react in the lower atmosphere, allowing a proportion of them to drift gradually up to the ozone layer. There they were broken apart by the incoming ultraviolet radiation, releasing the chlorine and other chemicals to act as catalysts in destroying the ozone. Each atom of chlorine, for example, can destroy an average of about 100,000 ozone molecules before it is removed from the stratosphere.

For complex reasons, the losses of ozone are worst in the spring. By 1995, stratospheric ozone levels over Europe and North America, for example, were about 10 per cent lower than in the 1970s, and in places 20–50 per cent lower. Over the Antarctic, a particularly deep 'ozone hole' appeared annually, virtually wiping out all ozone in thick bands of the ozone layer. This led to substantial increases in the intensity of UV-B radiation at the Earth's surface. UV-B depresses immune systems, causes cataracts and skin cancers, damages the development of crops, and reduces the productivity of phytoplankton in the sea—undermining the marine food chain.

As awareness of the risks of ozone depletion grew in the 1970s, the USA, Canada, Sweden, and Norway unilaterally banned non-essential uses of CFCs. However it was not until 1985 that an international agreement was achieved: the Vienna Convention. This was a framework convention, which did not oblige parties to reduce their consumption of CFCs or other ODS. In 1987, the Montreal Protocol was agreed by 24 mainly industrialized states and the European Community. Parties to this protocol were obliged to cut their consumption of 5 types of CFCs by 50 per cent by 1999 and to freeze consumption of three halons.

Between 1987 and 2000, the Montreal Protocol was progressively strengthened: most importantly in London (1990), Copenhagen (1992), Vienna (1995), and Montreal (1997). The 1990 London Amendment committed developed countries to phase out an extended range of ODS (including the halons, methyl chloroform, carbon tetrachloride, and a longer list of 15 CFCs) by 2000. Developing countries were committed to phase out by 2010, with assistance from a new Multilateral Fund (MLF), created for the purpose. In 1992, the phase-out dates for developed states were brought forward to 1995, and new controls were agreed to phase-out HCFCs by 2030— which had been introduced as a less destructive substitute for CFCs—and to freeze use of methyl bromide. In 1995, developing countries also accepted some controls on HCFCs and methyl bromide. In 1997, more ozone-depleting chemicals were added to the list of restricted substances, and more stringent limits on methyl bromide and HCFCs were agreed. By 1999, 95 ozone-depleting chemicals were controlled under the Protocol, and worldwide CFC consumption had reduced from 1.1 million tonnes in 1986 to less than 150,000 tonnes per year. Moreover, the Montreal Protocol had become truly global, with over 160 parties.

century, but thereafter it is expected gradually to recover—returning to its pre-1970 levels by about 2060.

The agenda formation phase of the regime began in the early 1970s. In 1974, Rowland and Molina—two US-based scientists—published an analysis arguing that CFCs emitted into the atmosphere could lead to the destruction of stratospheric ozone (Molina and Rowland 1974). Coming at a time of intense debates in the United States about the risks that emissions from high-flying supersonic aircraft might pose to the upper atmosphere, this hypothesis immediately attracted public attention. CFCs were first invented in 1928, as a coolant for refrigeration, but since the 1960s production had increased rapidly as further uses were found in: air-conditioners; expanded foams for cushions and insulation; solvents to clean electronics; sterilants; and aerosol propellants. Halons—related chemicals including bromine—were also increasingly used as fire extinguishers and suppressants.

Environmental movements and the US Environmental Protection Agency (EPA) argued that at least non-essential uses of CFCs, as in aerosols, should be banned as a precautionary measure. DuPont and the other major chemical companies producing CFCs strongly disputed this, arguing that strong scientific evidence that the problem was real and serious should be required before any restrictions were introduced. The so-called 'spray can war' raged in the USA through the mid-1970s. After a US National Academy of Science report in 1976 judged that the risks were sufficiently large that precautionary measures would be justified, the balance of influence shifted towards the environmentalists and the EPA, and domestic legislation restricting CFC uses followed in 1978. These unilateral US actions had the effect of temporarily decreasing global CFC production, since the USA accounted for some 50 per cent of world consumption in the mid-1970s.

Internationally, the North American and Scandinavian countries became leaders in supporting UNEP's efforts to establish international restrictions on ozone depleting chemicals. However, initially the countries of the EU and Japan—the other major producers and consumers of CFCs at the time—were 'laggards': sceptical about the threat and supportive of their major chemical companies.

Thus began the international process of negotiating and decision-making. In the first half of the 1980s, progress was extremely slow. During the first Reagan Administration, the USA joined the sceptics and showed little enthusiasm for pressuring the EU and Japan on ozone issues. Under the charismatic leadership of Mostapha Tolba, UNEP played a key brokering role. In March 1985 the Vienna Convention for the Protection of the Ozone Layer was signed. However, this was a framework convention which obliged its signatories to do little more than to establish the principle that international action should be taken as necessary, carry out further research, exchange information, and periodically meet to review the adequacy of commitments.

Within two months, however, the discovery of a deep 'ozone hole' over the Antarctic was announced by scientists from the British Antarctic Survey. The political impact of this discovery provided a key illustration of the galvanizing effect of vivid or dramatic events in regime politics. The image of being exposed to UV radiation from space was already one that resonated with the general public. However, a surprise 'ozone hole' had much greater political impact than possible average depletion of 1–2 per cent per year, particularly when reinforced by NASA satellite images. Moreover, experiments in 1987 definitively showed the link between ozone depletion and the presence of chlorine: chanes in chlorine and ozone concentrations were measured while flying an aircraft across the edge of the ozone hole.

After this, DuPont, ICI, and other major CFC producers recognized that tough international restrictions on CFCs or other ODS had become virtually inevitable. Instead of continuing to oppose them, they focused on influencing any international agreement. In particular, they realized that stringent international controls on CFCs would create a market for substitutes, which they were in a better position to produce than their less sophisticated or wealthy competitors. By this time, Green parties and environmental movements were becoming powerful in most West European countries. In this context, governments that had previously vetoed stringent international controls had every interest in reversing their position. For example, the UK Prime Minister Mrs Thatcher removed her objections and declared her government to be a world leader in efforts to ban CFCs. The 1987 Montreal Protocol committed parties to cut their CFC consumption by 50 per cent by 1999, and within two years a consensus was emerging amongst developed western countries in favour of adopting a complete ban.

However, before a phase-out of CFCs and other ODS could be agreed, it was important to extend membership of the regime beyond developed Western states to include the Soviet bloc countries (as they were then) and developing countries. By the late 1980s production and consumption of CFCs in these countries were increasing rapidly, although still much smaller than in OECD states, and it was clear that countries like Russia, India, and China would have to join the regime if it was to be successful in the long term. The Soviet Union and its allies were persuaded to join (with some transitional concessions) at the end of the 1980s. However, developing countries refused to accept any commitments to phase-out CFCs and halons unless industrialized countries paid the 'incremental' costs they incurred in implementation. After much haggling, this was agreed in 1990. A Multilateral Fund (MLF) was established for this purpose, and developing countries agreed to phase out consumption of CFCs and halons by 2010.

From that stage, the processes of implementing and further developing the Montreal Protocol proceeded in tandem. Experience with implementing the Protocol's commitments, though complex, turned out to be easier and cheaper than many had feared. The chemical producers had a strong commercial incentive to develop substitutes quickly and also to monitor compliance amongst competitors. The Technology and Economic Assessement Panel (TEAP), established to advise on the availability and effectiveness of substitutes or alternatives for controlled substances, proved very effective in identifying opportunities and persuading users to accept them. Meanwhile the international Scientific Assessment Panel and the Environmental Impacts Panel produced authoritative reports on the need for ever more stringent commitments. UNEP continued to play a key role in brokering stringent agreements, supported by sympathetic states and environmental NGOs. In 1992, 1995, and 1997, the range of ODS controlled by the Montreal Protocol was widened,

and phase-out dates for CFCs and halons were brought forward to 1995 and 1994 respectively for industrialized countries.

Implementation of these phase-outs proceeded on time and reasonably effectively in Western developed states, though there were continuing problems with black-market trading of illicit CFCs in the mid-1990s. The process turned out to be much more difficult in the 'countries with economies in transition' (the former Soviet bloc countries). The profound social and economic transitions in these countries meant that several of them neglected their Montreal Protocol commitments. The ozone regime's systems for reporting and reviewing implementation picked this up in 1995, and co-ordinated international responses aimed at bringing the 'culprits' (primarily Russia, Ukraine, Belarus, and Bulgaria) into compliance as quickly as possible. This was done through a mixture of 'carrots and sticks', including conditional offers of international aid. Thus a crisis that could have substantially weakened the regime was averted, and the institutions of the regime played a key role in achieving this. As far as developing countries are concerned, the operation of the MLF was a continuing source of friction between them and donor countries. Nevertheless, after initial problems, many projects to phase out controlled substances in developing countries were underway by the mid-1990s, and in many cases these countries were on track to phase out significantly before their legal deadline. By 1999, over $900 million had been disbursed by the Multilateral Fund. Moreover, procedures for reviewing implementation of MLF-funded projects were developed in the mid-1990s to verify that such phase-outs actually took place. However, the ozone regime continues to adapt and develop, with major reviews every two to three years, and will probably have to do so for decades to come.

Key points

- The development of international environmental regimes can roughly be divided into four phases: agenda formation; negotiation and decision-making; implementation; and further development.

- The regime developed to limit and reverse ozone layer depletion illustrates each of these phases, and is justifiably regarded as an important and effective environmental regime.

The Rio Conference and its outcomes

As introduced above, in 1989 the UN General Assembly decided to convene an 'Earth Summit' in Rio in 1992 in order to promote and develop sustainable development.

Preparing for Rio

The agenda for the Rio Conference quickly developed. By the end of the 1980s, there was great international concern that anthropogenic emissions of 'greenhouse gases', such as carbon dioxide, methane, nitrous oxides, and CFCs, could be affecting the Earth's overall energy balance and causing rapid global warming and climate change. In 1988, an international panel of scientists (the Intergovernmental Panel on Climate Change (IPCC)) was set up under the auspices of UNEP and the World Meteorological Organization (WMO) to examine the risk of such climate change. On the basis of the IPCC's 1990 report (Houghton *et al.* 1990), representatives of 137 countries at the Second World Climate Conference in Geneva in November 1990 agreed that an international convention was urgently needed to address the problem. Negotiations began three months later, with a view to completing a Framework Convention on Climate Change (FCCC) in time for signing at the Rio Conference.

Similarly, there was also wide concern about the loss of natural habitats and the consequent rapid extinctions of many species of life. Between 1988 and 1990 UNEP had convened an group of experts to examine the issue, and negotiations for a Convention on Biological Diversity started in June 1991, working to the same timetable.

In addition, there was wide support in many industrialized countries for an international forestry convention to limit deforestation, particularly of tropical rainforests. However, this proposal was strongly opposed by some developing countries possessing such forests, such as Malaysia and Brazil, on the grounds that it was their sovereign right to use their forests as they chose—just as industrialized countries had done centuries before. In an effort to win African governments' support in this debate, Western governments agreed to support negotiations to establish a Convention to Combat Desertification. This was a priority issue for African countries, many of which suffered from land degradation in arid areas, and also one on which UNEP had campaigned since the mid-1970s.

In addition to these specific conventions, attention focused on preparing agreements to define and promote the goal of sustainable development. Negotiations centred on preparing two main documents for agreement at the Rio Conference. The first of these was a statement of agreed principles, which later emerged as the Rio Declaration. The second document was to be a detailed programme of action for sustainable development, which became known as Agenda 21.

The Rio Conference

The 1992 Rio Conference turned out to be one of the biggest summit meetings ever held. Some 150 states were represented, and at one stage 135 heads of state were present. About 45,000 people attended, including government delegations, over 10,000 press and media people, and representatives of 1,500 non-governmental organizations, including environment, development, and business organizations, a women's caucus, and indigenous peoples groups. Non-governmental organizations had their own parallel conference in Rio, but were also entitled to attend the intergovernmental meetings. The meet-

Box 18.5 The UNCED agreements

The Rio Declaration proclaims 27 general principles to guide action on environment and development. They include principles relating to: national responsibilities and international co-operation on environmental protection; the needs for development and eradication of poverty; and the roles and rights of citizens, women, and indigenous peoples. For example, Principle 7 affirms the 'common but differentiated responsibilities' of developed and developing states in environmental protection. Principle 10 states that environmental issues are best handled with the participation of all citizens, at the relevant level, and thus public education, participation, and access to information and redress should all be promoted. Principle 15 affirms that a precautionary approach should be adopted: 'lack of full scientific certainty shall not be used as a reason for postponing cost-effective measures to prevent environmental degradation'.

Agenda 21 is a 400-page document with 40 chapters aiming to provide a programme of action for sustainable development. The chapters cover a wide range of topics, such as: promoting sustainable urban development; combating deforestation; biotechnology management; managing fragile mountain ecosystems; and hazardous waste management. Several chapters are on strengthening the role of 'major groups', including local authorities, trade unions, business and industry, scientists, women, indigenous peoples, youth, and farmers. The last eight chapters address implementation issues, including financial mechanisms and institutional arrangements. The Global Environment Facility is to provide 'agreed incremental costs' to help developing countries implement aspects of the Agenda 21 programme. The Commission for Sustainable Development is established as part of the UN system, to promote and review progress on implementation and to help to co-ordinate activities of UN Agencies in this context.

The Framework Convention on Climate Change (FCCC) was signed by 153 states, and subsequently came into force within 18 months, on 21 March 1994. It is a **'framework convention'**, establishing principles, aims, institutions, and procedures which should subsequently be developed. The declared objective of the FCCC, as stated in Article 2, is to 'achieve stabilisation of greenhouse gas concentrations in the atmosphere at a level that would prevent dangerous anthropogenic interference with the climate system. Such a level should be achieved within a time frame sufficient to allow ecosystems to

adapt naturally to climate change, to ensure that food production is not threatened and to enable economic development to proceed in a sustainable manner'. Recognizing that developed states should take the lead, these states should as a first step 'individually or jointly return to their 1990 levels' of greenhouse gas emissions. However, this was not a legally binding obligation. The most important obligations in the FCCC are that parties must provide regular reports on: their national greenhouse gas emissions; their emissions projections; and their policies and measures to limit such emissions. These are then carefully reviewed and assessed internationally. This review process aims not only to stimulate negotiation of further commitments as required, but also to promote the development and implementation of national targets.

The Convention on Biological Diversity was signed by 155 states, and came into force on 29 December 1993. It is a framework convention, which aims to preserve the biological diversity of the Earth, through protection of species, ecosystems, and habitats, and to establish terms for the use of genetic resources and bio-technologies. Parties must develop plans to protect biodiversity, and to submit reports which will be internationally reviewed. The principles clarifying states' sovereign rights to genetic resources on their territory were highly contentious and thus vague and highly qualified: such rights were affirmed, provided that the fruits of such resources are shared in a fair and equitable way on terms to be mutually agreed.

The Forest Principles were the residue of the failed attempts to negotiate a forestry convention. It proclaims principles for forest protection and management while emphasizing that states have a sovereign right to exploit forests on their territory.

The Convention to Combat Desertification was not open for signature until June 1994, but it is nevertheless considered to be an UNCED agreement. It aims to promote co-ordinated international actions to address problems of 'land degradation in arid, semi-arid, and dry sub-humid areas resulting from various factors, including climatic variations and human activities'. It provides a code of good practices for the management of marginal lands, for governments of affected regions, and for donors. It aims to provide a framework for co-operation between local land-users, NGOs, governments, international organizations, funding agencies, and donor countries, but includes no binding obligations.

ing attracted great public attention, and received enormous media coverage.

The Rio Declaration, Agenda 21, and the Declaration of Forest Principles were all agreed, and the conventions on climate change and biodiversity were respectively signed by 154 and 150 governments. The Convention on Desertification was not ready in time, and was not agreed until June 1994. Nevertheless, it is customarily included amongst the Earth Summit agreements (see Box 18.5).

The implementation and development of the Rio conventions

The 1992 Rio Conference was widely regarded as an overall success. However, its real impact could only be judged according to how the Earth Summit agreements and conventions were subsequently developed and implemented.

It is worth noting that the conventions on climate change and biodiversity were 'framework conventions'. That is, they established basic aims, principles, norms, institutions, and procedures for co-ordinated international actions, including procedures for regularly reviewing commitments and for strengthening or revising them and developing other rules and institutions of the regime as deemed appropriate by the parties. However, the initial obligations on parties in the conventions were weak. Moreover, in order to achieve agreement in time for either of these conventions to be signed at Rio, it had proved necessary for many contentious or complex issues to be sidestepped or fudged. Thus many key rules, institutions, and procedures remained to be worked out before the convention could even begin to operate. Indeed, in the case of the Biodiversity Convention, even the aims and priorities of the agreement remained unclear. Thus, the Intergovernmental Negotiating Committees (INC) that were responsible for negotiating each agreement were immediately reconvened to sort out these issues before the conventions came into force.

Before they come into force, international treaties need to be **ratified** by a minimum number of parties (with this number being defined in the treaty). In the case of the climate convention, for example, ratification by fifty states was needed. The ratification process involves the relevant national legislature of each signatory state (such as the US Senate or the UK Parliament) confirming that the state will be legally bound by the treaty. It normally takes several years for enough countries to ratify a treaty for it to come into force (the new UN Law of the Sea, signed in 1982, did not come into force until 1994). However, the three Earth summit conventions came into force remarkably quickly: all within two years of being signed.

In many respects, the early progress in implementing commitments in the climate convention was striking. Developed country parties mostly prepared relatively detailed national reports on their national greenhouse gas emissions, their projected future emissions, and their policies and measures to reduce them. These reports were internationally reviewed in detail, in a way that established promising precedents for the future. However, the lack of legally binding commitments to limit emissions caused wide concern. The first CoP of the climate convention, meeting in Berlin in March 1995, decided immediately to begin negotiations to establish more stringent commitments on industrial countries to limit their emissions of greenhouse gases. The aim was to establish a new protocol, including legally binding limits on greenhouse gas emissions of industrialized states, at the December 1997 CoP due to take place in Kyoto, Japan. By 1995 almost all OECD countries and the EU had unilaterally pledged themselves to aim at least to stabilize their greenhouse gas emissions at 1990 levels by the year 2000, and some including Germany and the Netherlands had promised reductions by that time. However, it soon became clear that most developed countries were not on track to achieve such stabilization pledges.

In this context, negotiations for a **Kyoto Protocol** including more stringent commitments for industrial states were bound to be difficult, and so it proved. An Alliance of Small Island States (AOSIS), threatened as they were with inundation as a result of sea level rise, advocated a 20 per cent reduction in industrial country emissions by 2005. However, oil-exporting OPEC countries—their nominal allies in the G77 group of developing countries— campaigned strongly against any substantial commitments for developed countries, fearing that emission reduction measures would reduce demand for oil, and thus threaten their incomes. Similarly, the EU and some other West European states broadly supported emissions reduction targets of 5–10 per cent by 2010, but several other developed countries, including the USA, Japan, Australia, and Canada, were reluctant to support any obligations requiring emission reductions. Former communist countries in Eastern Europe and the former Soviet Union were typically suspicious of any obligations that could impede their economic recovery, and several did not think it fair that they should be classed as developed countries when relatively wealthy states such as South Korea, and Malaysia were classed as developing countries and thus under no immediate pressure to limit their emissions.

These debates highlight how complex equity issues rapidly become in global negotiations. The differences in circumstances of states within the groups of developed and developing states are in many ways as great as the differences between these groups. Even within Western developed countries, Southern European governments argued that their countries are comparatively poor and should not have to stabilize their emissions yet; Japan and others argued that they should not have to accept the same percentage cuts in emissions as the USA, for example, because they have already implemented energy efficiency measures. Moreover, elites within developing countries live 'first world' lifestyles, and in countries like Brazil, India, and China their number far exceed the populations of medium or small developed countries. Surely, some say, these elites should not be entirely exempt from pressure to adopt more 'climate friendly' lifestyles. However, negotiators were aware that any attempt in the name of equity to negotiate separate targets for each country, taking into account its individual circumstances, is a recipe for failure. Special pleading and complexity would bog the negotiations down.

In the event, the Kyoto Protocol was succesfully agreed in December 1997, and involved more stringent limits on most developed countries emissions than many had expected in the circumstances, as outlined in Box 18.6. This was a major achievement, but many challenges remain. Many technical issues needed to be resolved on which the effectiveness of

the Protocol depends; these were the subject of further negotiations between 1998–2001 and beyond. Moreover, there is the political challenge of achieving ratification of the Kyoto Protocol so that it comes legally into force. Particularly in United States, political opposition to the Kyoto Protocol (and to the emission reduction measures it implies) became highly mobilized in the late 1990s, raising questions about whether or when the US Senate would ratify it. Moreover, by the year 2001 it was clear that most industrialized countries needed to take much more active emissions reduction measures if they were to achieve their Kyoto Protocol commitments. This is a prerequisite to meeting the longer-term challenge of negotiating and establishing the further commitments, including commitments of developing countries to limit their increases in the greenhouse gas emissions as they industrialize, that are required to substantially reduce the risk of catastrophic climate change.

The challenges of making the Biodiversity Convention effective have proved to be at least as fundamental. Although in formal terms it also got off to a reasonably prompt start, fundamental disputes about its aims and priorities continued. Little progress was made on what many in the developed countries regarded as the primary objective: to protect natural habitats and thus the diversity of species of wildlife that depend upon them. Many developing countries had a wider agenda, including securing international financial and technology assistance and gaining a share of the economic benefits of biodiversity and bio-technology by securing intellectual property rights over any genetic resources from their territory and any products made from them. These were demands that most developed countries were reluctant to concede.

Some progress was achieved in implementing those parts of the Convention concerned with the development and reporting of national data on biodiversity and of national plans to protect and promote biodiversity in the future. However, after 1995, negotiating efforts soon focused on the elaboration of a protocol on 'biosafety', and particularly on regulating the movement of genetically engineered organisms across borders. After almost five years of difficult negotiations, the parties agreed on the **Cartegena Protocol on Biosafety** on 29 January 2000. It

Box 18.6 **The 1997 Kyoto Protocol to the framework convention on climate change**

At the core of the 1997 Kyoto Protocol are legally binding commitments by industrialized states to limit their greenhouse gas emissions. The EU, USA, and Japan respectively committed themselves to reduce their annual greenhouse gas emissions by 2008–12 to 8, 7, and 6 per cent less than 1990 levels. Prospective EU members such as Poland adopted EU targets, while Russia, Ukraine, and New Zealand agreed to stabilize their emissions at 1990 levels and Australia, Iceland, and Norway managed to negotiate limited increases in their permitted emissions. These commitments refer to net emissions, so that greenhouse gas emissions may be offset by absorption of such gases in sinks such as afforestation projects. Overall, these commitments would imply a 5 per cent reduction in greenhouse gas emissions in industrialized countries.

To achieve this agreement, a number of so-called flexibility mechanisms were established in the Protocol: Joint Implementation (allowing industrialized states to share the credit for emission reductions achieved in specific joint projects); Emissions Trading (allowing industrialized states to exchange part of their national emission allowances); and the Clean Development Mechanism (allowing industrialized states to obtain emission credits for financing approved climate-friendly projects in developing countries). Thus, for example, the USA is allowed to achieve its commitments not only by reducing net emissions from domestic sources, but also by buying spare emissions quotas from other industrialized parties such as Russia, and by getting credit for emission reductions achieved in approved Joint Implementation or Clean Development Mechanism projects which it supports in other countries. EU member states also had their own flexibility mechanism. They are permitted to distribute emissions targets amongst themselves, provided that their overall emissions reduced by 8 per cent. Within the EU Austria, Denmark, Germany, Luxembourg, and the UK agreed to achieve reductions of more than 8 per cent, enabling Southern European countries, France, and Ireland to be allocated much less stringent targets.

The agreement achieved in Kyoto in 1997 left many key issues open, requiring further negotiation. These included the design of each of the above flexiblity mechnisms, the rules for offsetting emissions with absorption by sinks, methodologies for calculating and reporting national emissions, and systems for assessing implementation and compliance and for responding to compliance problems. These were the focus for detailed negotiations between 1998 and 2000, with the aim of achieving agreements at the Amsterdam CoP in November 2000.

established a requirement for 'advanced informed agreement' before genetically modified organisms may be transferred. In view of the increasingly highly charged debates surrounding the use and trade in genetically modified organisms, particularly intended for use in agriculture, this protocol was a significant achievement. However, it will clearly do little to prevent loss of species or natural habitats. The effectiveness of the Biodiversity Convention in promoting these goals therefore remained in doubt at the turn of the century.

Similarly, although the Convention to Combat Desertification came into force by 1996, it was primarily designed to encourage donor countries to provide aid and assistance to developing countries in dry regions that are facing problems of land degradation. As such they are intimately linked with broader development programmes, and this is how most donor countries have preferred to approach the issue during a period when development aid budgets were generally declining. In practice, only slow progress was made in establishing specific multilateral funding mechanisms, and it proved difficult to attract additional donor interest.

Agenda 21: promoting sustainable development

The 1992 Rio Conference established several institutions to promote the overall implementation and further development of Agenda 21. The most significant of these were the Commission for Sustainable Development (CSD) and the Global Environment Facility (GEF), working in association with UNEP, UNDP, and other UN bodies. Clearly it was not expected that these institutions could directly implement Agenda 21, or force others to do so.

Rather the hope was that they could help to stimulate or shape broader international or domestic processes in a useful way.

The CSD consists of representatives of fifty–three states, elected for three-year terms in a way that ensures equitable geographical representation. It began its work in 1993, and has met annually since then to review progress on different aspects of Agenda 21, with numerous preparatory meetings. Ministerial participation in these meetings has been substantial, giving the process more political weight than some had feared. Moreover, non-governmental groups can participate in the proceedings, making each CSD meeting a sort of mini-Earth summit. Coalitions between environmental NGOs and sympathetic states have made the CSD a forum in which environmental agendas can be set and pursued.

Broadly, the CSD process has aimed to promote sustainable development in three ways. Its role in promoting co-ordinated approaches towards sustainable development by international agencies has had some real but modest successes. However, its second role of reviewing national reports on aspects of sustainable development may be of wider significance. The significance of the CSD process in simply stimulating governments to review their practices and prepare policies for inclusion in their national reports should not be underestimated. Moreover, the CSD has provided a forum where governments can be called to account, for the contents of their policies or for the gap between these and reality. The presence of NGOs has helped to make this process more substantial.

The third role of the CSD process has been to follow-up on unfinished business of UNCED and to promote the formation of new regimes where opportunities arise. For example, after discussions on deforestation at the CSD, an intergovernmental panel was established to review the issues. In 1996, this led to an agreement to begin international negotiations on a forestry convention: providing a second chance after the failure in the lead-up to UNCED.

Another aspect of follow-up to UNCED has been a series of follow-up summit meetings on particular issues such as population and development (Cairo 1994), social development (Copenhagen 1995), the role and rights of women (Beijing 1995), and urban development (Istanbul 1996). The significance of such summits is controversial, but they have helped to promote political awareness and concern, and to develop international networks of concerned experts, NGOs, citizens' groups, and local authorities, which can then hopefully become more effective in their local activities. Five years on, there were a number of follow-up conferences (labelled, for example, as 'Copenhagen + 5') to review and stimulate further progress in implementing and developing sustainable development in the relevant policy spheres.

Global Environment Facility (GEF) funds only amount to a few billion dollars ($3 billion was allocated for 1994–7), which is a tiny amount compared to the massive international flows of funds that take place through normal economic transactions, and also compared to the funds needed to implement sustainable development. However, numerous relatively small GEF grants to developing countries and to former communist states have contributed significantly to the preparation of national plans to promote sustainability. Moreover, in such countries, modest funds can contribute significantly to 'institutional capacity-building' where local expertise or resources are lacking. GEF funds for large-scale projects have been much slower to flow, and are a continual source of friction between recipients and donor countries.

Overall, therefore, the UNCED institutions to promote implementation of Agenda 21 have had some limited significance. But it is clear that they have had only a marginal impact on the broader economic and social processes that drive patterns of development.

At the end of the twentieth century, debates increasingly focused on the challenges of developing international mechanisms to shape broader patterns of trade and investment in line with environmental goals. Some believe that the norms and rules of the World Trade Organization (WTO), with their focus on removing constraints on international trade and investment, are inimical to efforts to promote environmental protection, sustainable development, and other social goals. Transnational NGO campaigns to challenge the dominance of WTO norms and rules proved resonant in 2000, for example, when they succeeded in disrupting the Seattle meeting of the WTO. In contrast, others believe that **trade and environment** regimes can be complementary and even mutually reinforcing (for example, by promoting international investment in modern, and more environmentally friendly, technologies). Principles have arguably been established whereby global environmental regimes, such as the ozone layer protection regime, may restrict trade in direct pursuit of its goals without falling foul of WTO rules. For example, the Montreal Protocol specifically includes provisions for restricting trade to non-parties or non-compliant parties, as well as restricting trade in goods containing ozone-depleting substances. However, the situation is much less clear when restrictions on trade for environmental purposes are imposed as part of national or regional measures that do not command wide support at the global level. In this context, tensions between environmental and trading regimes are likely to be a continuing source of friction. For example, in the mid-1990s international free trade rules were used to overturn measures by the USA to restrict imports of tuna in response to fishing methods that damage dolphin populations. In general, however, there is increasing international interest in designing the rules and mechanisms of international environmental regimes so that they work with the grain of globalized economic processes and market mechanisms, and seek to shape international patterns of trade and investment in line with environmental goals. The flexibility mechanisms agreed in the Kyoto Protocol to the framework Convention on Climate Change, discussed above, are just one illustration of this trend.

Key points

- Three new conventions were agreed at the Rio Conference, aimed at limiting climate change, preserving biodiversity, and combating desertification. Each of these came rapidly into force, but the process of making these conventions effective has proved a long-term task.

- The negotiations to develop further the climate change convention demonstrated the immense challenges involved in achieving a sufficient response to prevent substantial anthropogenic climate change, and also the complexity of equity issues in negotiations. The Kyoto Protocol agreed in 1997 established substantial legally binding commitments, but many challenges remain.

- There are still major disputes about the main aims and objectives of the Biodiversity Convention and means to achieve them.

- The institutions established to promote the implementation of Agenda 21 have stimulated the production of national plans for sustainable development and provided a forum where plans can be reviewed and where networks of non-governmental groups, government representatives, and international secretariats can develop and influence agendas. However, their influence on overall patterns of development has been small.

- The relationship between environment and trade regimes has emerged as a key issue.

Conclusion

Environmental issues emerged in the late twentieth century as a major focus of international concern and activity. They relate to globalization themes in several ways. Many environmental problems are intrinsically international or global, stimulating international political activities in response. Others, though local, are experienced across the world. Virtually all environmental issues are intimately linked to the dynamics of globalized political economic processes.

Awareness and concern about environmental issues grew substantially since the late 1960s. Since the 1970s, a wide range of agreements, institutions, and regimes for international environmental

Box 18.7 Key concepts for international environmental issues

agenda-formation: the processes by which an issue or problem becomes recognized, emerges onto the political stage, is framed for consideration and debate by the relevant policy communities, and rises high enough on the political agenda to initiate negotiations or decision-making processes.

collective governance: non-hierarchical (in the sense of the absence of a central coercive power) systems of management or governance.

environmental regime: an international regime addressing an environmental issue.

epistemic communities: knowledge-based transnational communities of experts with shared understandings of an issue or problem or preferred policy responses.

framework convention: an international convention establishing principles, norms, goals, organizations, and procedures for consultation, decision-making and review, with provision for flexible subsequent revision or development of rules or commitments.

global commons: resources open for use by the international community, and not under the jurisdiction of any state, such as: oceans, atmosphere, deep seabed, Antarctica.

international institutions: sets of internationally agreed principles, norms, rules, common understandings, organizations, and consultation and decision-making procedures that govern or shape activities in a particular area.

implementation: carrying out adopted decisions or policies.

over-exploitation: the unsustainable exploitation of a resource.

sustainable development: economic and social development that meets the needs of the present without compromising the ability of future generations to meet their own needs; programmes which maintain an appropriate balance between economic development, social development, and environmental protection. In practice, this is a contested concept, in that groups with differing political, economic, social, and environmental perspectives disagree about its exact meaning.

tragedy of the commons: the over-exploitation of open-access resources by users 'rationally' pursuing their individual interests.

transnational: cutting across national boundaries; linking the international and domestic sphere. Thus, for example, transnational processes are non-state processes that cut across national boundaries.

---

governance have developed. Much international political activity related to the environment has focused on the development and implementation of these regimes, involving a wide range of actors and processes. Since the late 1980s and particularly the UNCED summit in 1992, many international political processes have engaged with the linked issues of development and environment, and the contested notion of sustainable development. By the end of the 1990s, the relationship between the World Trade Organization regimes to promote and govern a globalized market economy and international environmental regimes was high on the political agenda, influencing the design of the rules of environmental regimes as well as providing a focus for political mobilization and dispute.

Although established perspectives within International Relations theory provide important

insights into the character and outcomes of such activities, international environmental issues nevertheless pose significant new challenges for students of International Relations. They raise questions about the significance and role of states in environmental politics, about the relationship between power and knowledge, and about the distinction between the 'international' and 'domestic' spheres of activity. Historical experience shows that, alongside many failures, some effective institutions for collective management—or regimes—have been developed to help to prevent the degradation of 'global commons' or to tackle other international environmental problems. Moreover, these systems for international governance are no longer isolated regimes dealing with narrow problems. At least since the 1990s they have formed a complex of interlinked institutions shaping the activities and expectations of all relevant actors across a wide range of activities. The primary challenge for the 1990s and beyond is to shape patterns of development to promote sustainability, including preserving biodiversity and preventing damaging climate change. The 1992 UNCED agreements continue to provide a framework for international efforts to promote and co-ordinate efforts to achieve this. But the challenges are immense.

QUESTIONS

1   In what ways has 'the environment' become a global issue in the late twentieth century?

2   What was the significance of the 1972 Stockholm Conference for international environmental politics?

3   What is meant by 'sustainable development', and why has this 'contested' concept become important in international environmental politics?

4   How does the study of international environmental issues pose particular challenges for International Relations theory?

5   What is the relevance of the notion the 'tragedy of the commons' to global environmental problems, and what approaches are available for preventing the over-exploitation of global commons such as the open seas, deep sea bed, atmosphere, and Antarctica?

6   'The nature of international society makes the prospects poor for developing collective institutions that can effectively tackle international environmental problems'. Discuss.

7   How effective has either the Montreal Protocol for the Protection of the Ozone Layer or the Climate Change Convention been?

8   What factors can contribute to (i) the formation and (ii) the implementation of international environmental regimes? Illustrate these factors with reference to the ozone layer and climate change regimes.

9   What are the key characteristics of a 'framework' convention. Illustrate these with reference to some existing framework conventions

10   How important was the 1992 UN Conference on Environment and Development (UNCED, or the 'Earth Summit') for environmental protection and the promotion of 'sustainable development'?

11   How have 'North–South' issues shaped international environmental politics?

12   Discuss the relationship between environment regimes and the rules of the World Trade Organization, and the challenges and opportunities that globalized trade and investment processes pose for those who want to promote sustainable development.

13   Assess the significance of non-governmental organizations in international environmental politics. How is their role affected by international environmental institutions and regimes?

GUIDE TO FURTHER READING

There are now many good books on international environmental issues and on the environment in international relations. For example, the following books provide good introductions, including historical reviews up to at least the mid-1990s: R. Blakemore and A. Reddish (eds.), *Global Environmental Issues*, 2nd edn. (London: Hodder and Stoughton, 1996); J. Vogler and M. Imber (eds.), *The Environment in International Relations* (London: Routledge, 1996); A. Blowers and P. Glasbergen (eds.), *Environmental Policy in an International Context, Vols. 1–4* (London: Arnold and New York: John Wiley and Son, 1996); J. Vogler, *The Global Commons: Environmental and Technological Governance*, 2nd edn. (Chichester, John Wiley and Sons, 2000); L. C. Hempel, *Environmental Governance: The Global Challenge* (Washington, DC: Island Press, 1996). L. Elliott, *The Global Politics of the Environment* (London: Macmillan Press, 1998); and S. Buck, *The Global Commons: An Introduction* (Washington, DC: Island Press, 1998).

There are a number of journals and yearbooks of particular value in this context. For example, *Environment* (Washington DC: Heldref Publications) is a monthly journal that provides detailed but accessible discussions of contemporary global environmental issues (broadly understood, as outlined above in this chapter). Useful annual yearbooks include: the World-Watch Institute's *State of the World* (London: Earthscan); the Fridtjof Nansen Institute's *Green Globe Yearbook* (Oxford: Oxford University Press) and VERTIC's *Verification: Arms Control and the Environment* (London: VERTIC). There are a number of more scholarly journals of direct relevance, such as *Environmental Politics* (Ilford, Frank Cass) and *The Journal of Environment and Development* (London, Sage Publications).

E. Ostrom, *Governing the Commons: The Evolution of Institutions for Collective Action* (Cambridge: Cambridge University Press, 1990) is an important text analysing collective governance of open-access commons. On the development and effectiveness of international environmental institutions, O. Young (ed.), *Global Governance: Drawing Insights from the Environmental Experience* (London: Cornell University Press, 1997); P. M. Haas, R. O. Keohane, and M. Levy (eds.), *Institutions for the Earth: Sources of Effective International Environmental Action* (London: MIT Press, 1993), and D. Victor, K. Raustiala, and G. Skolnikof (eds.), *The Effectiveness of International Environmental Agreements* (Cambridge, Mass.: MIT Press, 1998), provide good thematic and empirical examinations. Much of the best and most influential work on international environmental issues has focused on particular issues or regimes. For example, R. E. Benedick, *Ozone Diplomacy: New Directions in Safeguarding the Planet* (London: Harvard University Press, 1991) provides a readable 'insider's' story of the international negotiations to establish the Montreal Protocol, and I. Rowlands, *The Politics of Global Atmospheric Change* (Manchester: Manchester University Press, 1995) and E. Parson and O. Greene, 'The Complex Chemistry of Ozone Agreements', *Environment*, 37: 2 (1995), 16–20, 35–43, examine the subsequent development of the ozone regime. Similarly, there are many good books on the development of climate change politics and the development of the climate change regime, including: T. O'Riordan and J. Jager (eds.), *Politics of Climate Change: A European Perspective* (London: Routledge, 1996) and M. Grubb *et al.*, *The Kyoto Protocol: a Guide and Assessment* (London: Earthscan, 1999). For an examination of the Convention on Biological Diversity, see K. Raustiala and D. Victor, 'Biodiversity since Rio: the Future of the Convention on Biological Diversity', *Environment* (May 1996), 16–20, 37–45.

The UNCED agreements, including Agenda 21, are clearly outlined and examined by M. Grubb *et al.*, *The Earth Summit Agreements: A Guide and Assessment* (London: Earthscan, 1993). On sustainable development, the 'Brundtland' Report, or World Commission on Environment and Development, *Our Common Future* (Oxford: Oxford University Press, 1986), and the Agenda 21 document itself (*Agenda 21: The United Nations Programme of Action from Rio* (New York: United Nations, 1992) remain essential texts, but chapters in the WorldWatch Institute's annual *State of the World Report* are just one of many texts providing more recent detailed examinations. On the politics of environmental activism, see e.g. D. Pepper, *Modern Environmentalism: An Introduction* (London: Routledge, 1996), J. Dryzek, *The Politics of the Earth: Environmental Discourses* (Oxford: Oxford University Press, 1997), P. Wapner, *Environmental Activism and World Civic Politics* (New York: SUNY Press, 1997), and R. Lipshutz and J. Mayer, *Global Civil Society and Global Environmental Governance: Politics of Nature from Place to Planet* (New York: SUNY Press, 1996). M. Redclift and T. Benton (eds.), *Social Theory and the Global Environment* (London: Routledge, 1994) provides an excellent collection of articles on different social science perspectives on global environmental change issues.

WEB LINKS

There are many relevant websites. The International Institute for Sustainable Development maintains a site (at **www.iisd.ca**) that includes much detailed information, including Climate News and Earth Negotiations Bulletin (detailing on progress in international negotiations relating to the environment or sustainable development). Similarly, Global Change (**www.globalchange.org**) maintains a website with many useful links. Virtually every international institute, substantial non-governmental organization, and international secretariat associated with an environmental agreement now maintains a homepage, e.g. UN Environment Programme (**www. unep.org**), European Environment Agency (**www.eea.eu.int**), UN Framework Convention on Climate Change Secretariat (**www.unfccc.de**), The Biodiversity Convention (**www. biodiv.org**), Global Environmental Facility (**www.gefweb.org**), and World Wildlife Fund (**www. panda.org**).

19 Nuclear proliferation

Darryl Howlett

READER'S GUIDE

This chapter identifies those factors that have made nuclear proliferation a global phenomenon since 1945. Over this period, the nature of nuclear weapons has transformed military and political relationships, while the global diffusion of nuclear and ballistic missile technology has meant that more states are in a position both to manufacture a nuclear weapon and deliver it over longer distances. This chapter also reveals the complexities associated with the globalization of the nuclear proliferation issue and some of the theoretical aspects related to it. There are difficulties in determining both the motivations which lead to the acquisition of nuclear weapons and the capabilities that might be constructed once acquisition has occurred. This complexity has been made more acute as a result of novel and often unanticipated proliferation concerns, such as: the dissolution of the former Soviet Union in the early 1990s; the emergence of new nuclear-weapons capable states in South Asia; nuclear smuggling; and the suggestion that non-state actors might acquire a nuclear capability. To add a further dimension, there are those who argue that the spread of nuclear weapons is no bad thing as this may induce stability in conflictual regional situations. This contrasts with the traditional view which argues that further nuclear proliferation is likely to increase instability and the potential for conflict between states. Efforts have, therefore, focused primarily on measures designed to prevent the proliferation of nuclear weapons known, collectively, as the global nuclear non-proliferation regime.

Introduction

The issue of nuclear proliferation represents one of the more marked illustrations of the globalization of world politics. The advent of nuclear weapons and their unprecedented capacity for wreaking destruction across territorial boundaries has transformed the globe. Although only five states (China, France, Russia (formerly, Soviet Union), United Kingdom, and United States) are acknowledged by the Treaty on the Non-Proliferation of Nuclear Weapons (NPT) as possessing nuclear weapons, several others have the capability to construct nuclear devices at short notice and deliver them, if necessary, by increasingly sophisticated means. This latter aspect was emphasized in May 1998 when India and Pakistan, two states previously associated with having a 'threshold' or near-nuclear weapons position, made overt demonstrations of their respective capabilities by conducting a series of nuclear tests coupled with later high-profile ballistic missile launches. These events have also highlighted another aspect concerning the globalization of the nuclear proliferation issue: the potential emergence of a regionally differentiated world. While some regions have moved from a situation where nuclear weapons once had a high profile (or salience) in strategic thought and action to one where these weapons have assumed much lower salience, other regions appear to be moving in the opposite direction. In Latin America, South-East Asia, Africa, and Central Asia, the trend has been to establish and consolidate the region as a Nuclear-Weapon-Free Zone (NWFZ). In other regions, such as South Asia and possibly also the Middle East and North-East Asia, the contrasting trend appears to be towards a higher saliency for nuclear weapons. Developments such as these have consequently changed global politics radically since 1945 and created a situation where strategic nuclear interdependence has become a fact of life.

Concern about the proliferation of nuclear weapons has undoubtedly increased in significance on the global agenda since the end of the East–West cold war, yet many of the factors that have made it a global issue have been underway for several decades. Knowledge of the enormous destructive effects of nuclear weapons against human populations, for example, dates back more than five decades to the bombings of the Japanese cities Hiroshima and Nagasaki at the end of the Second World War. Similarly, the explosion that ripped apart the civil nuclear power plant at Chernobyl in the former Soviet Union in 1986 revealed the devastating effects of nuclear radiation and its potential for long-term damage across frontiers when carried on the prevailing winds.

Equally as significant, in 1945 only the United States possessed the capability to manufacture a nuclear weapon. Today, several states have acquired an infrastructure to construct at least crude nuclear devices, either as a direct result of a dedicated nuclear weapons programme or as a consequence of the global diffusion of nuclear technology. A similar diffusion of ballistic missile technology has also meant that the capacity to deliver nuclear weapons over considerable distances is no longer the preserve of the few.

Developments stemming from the dissolution of the former Soviet Union in the early 1990s have also raised novel problems concerning nuclear proliferation. This is the only case where a previously acknowledged nuclear-weapon state (NWS) has been subjected to political and territorial disintegration. At the time, there was little understanding of what the precise nuclear consequences would be from such a tumultuous state implosion and only in hindsight can we judge its full significance. That it was a period of unprecedented nuclear transformation, which ultimately called for long-term nuclear co-operation between previously hostile states, is not in doubt. Potentially less obvious is the observation that this period of transition was facilitated by the foresight of policymakers from both sides of the former cold war divide and by the framework of arms control and disarmament agreements that was in place at the time. Consequently, one judgement which could be made is that the maintenance of nuclear stability during this period would have been more difficult had it not been for policies such as the Co-operative Threat Reduction Programme, and agreements such as the multilateral NPT and the bilateral Strategic Arms Reduction Treaties (START), signed initially between the US and the former Soviet Union (and later between the US and Russia).

Another development that has gained in momentum during the 1990s has been the attention devoted both to theorizing why some states acquire nuclear weapons while others do not, and to the role of norms and taboos in this context. It is important to note, however, that aspects of these debates have been discussed in seminal texts, often decades before. When Hedley Bull published the first edition of *The Control of the Arms Race* in 1961, for example, the issue of why states might seek a nuclear weapons capability and the consequences of such an action was already exercising the minds of policymakers and strategic analysts. Nuclear proliferation at this time was often considered in the context of the 'Nth power problem', or as Bull expressed it (1961: 147):

the problem of preventing the expansion of the nuclear club, or of making adjustments to it, is a single one faced by international society as a whole (The Problem), and that it is one raised by any addition to the club's membership (Nth power).

Bull also noted the tension within this debate over how each state views their own possession of nuclear weapons and those of other possessors (that is, whether or not they are viewed as a threat); and the type of state possessing these weapons (1961: 147). This has resonance with later discussions concerning threat perceptions and the notion that some states may be viewed by others as 'outlaw or rogue' nuclear states. Another aspect of Bull's 1961 analysis is his reference to a US study that identified twenty six states, which to varying degrees depending on their economic and scientific resources, could develop a nuclear weapons capability within a relatively short time-span (1961: 150). It is therefore noteworthy that the number of states in possession of nuclear weapons has not reached the number suggested in the US study. Although today the number of states that could move relatively quickly to develop a nuclear capability has probably increased in the time since this initial US estimate was published.

One debate that has sparked diverging responses,

at least since the early 1980s, has been a thesis asserting that the gradual spread of nuclear weapons to additional states is to be welcomed rather than feared. This thesis is based on the proposition that just as nuclear deterrence maintained stability between East and West during the cold war, so can it induce similar stabilizing effects on other conflict situations. The assumptions underpinning this thesis have been challenged by those who hold that more will be worse not better and that measures to prevent nuclear proliferation represent the best way forward.

Efforts to prevent nuclear proliferation have embraced a wide range of unilateral, bilateral, regional, and global measures that are usually referred to collectively as the global nuclear non-proliferation regime. Advocates of this regime argue it is the evolution of these measures (which include arms control and disarmament treaties like the NPT, export controls, international monitoring procedures, nuclear supplier and trading agreements, and other standard setting arrangements) that has constrained the proliferation of nuclear weapons since the 1960s. Critics, on the other hand, contend that the nuclear non-proliferation regime is discriminatory because it continues to allow five states to possess nuclear weapons while all other parties must forego the acquisition of such a capability on signing the NPT. This aspect became a major factor in 1995 when the NPT was extended indefinitely and during debate at the Sixth five-yearly NPT Review Conference in April–May 2000. Significantly, at the latter Conference, the five NWS acknowledged by the Treaty reiterated, in a joint statement, their unequivocal intention to pursue the goal of the eventual elimination of their nuclear weapons. In the context of this discussion, emphasis was also placed on the need by all NPT parties to improve transparency, and for new measures to enhance verification and compliance. Attempts to prevent nuclear proliferation in the future will therefore depend on the capacity of the nuclear non-proliferation regime to deal with the range of demands for nuclear weapons that could emerge and on the ability of the five NWS to deliver on their collective statement of nuclear intent.

The nature of nuclear weapons and their effects

The technical basis of nuclear weapons

Unless a nuclear weapon or the key nuclear materials required for their manufacture can be obtained 'off the shelf' as a result of purchase or theft, a prospect that cannot be dismissed, the usual route for any state or non-state actor seeking to acquire a nuclear weapons capability would be via the development of the necessary technological infrastructure. The latter would include a range of nuclear, conventional, computational, and electronic technologies and individuals with key scientific and technical skills.

Nuclear reactors and nuclear weapons differ in their management of the nuclear chain reaction, and in the nature of the energy produced. Whereas in a reactor energy output is achieved through a sustained and regulated process, in a nuclear weapon the objective is to attain a large explosive yield by creating a critical mass of nuclear material as a result of an uncontrolled and rapid chain reaction (Gardner 1994: 6–7). Nuclear weapons consequently derive their explosive energy from either the splitting of atoms (so called fission weapons), or their combination (so-called thermonuclear or fusion weapons). Only atoms with a large mass, such as uranium or plutonium (the fissile materials), are capable of being split, while fusion can only occur in atoms with a very small mass, such as hydrogen (deuterium and tritium). A fission weapon consequently works through the creation of an uncontrolled nuclear reaction, which literally splits the atoms. A fusion weapon is often described as a fission weapon with a second fusion stage added. Fusion of the hydrogen atoms is achieved through the compression and heat generated by the initial or primary fission device.

In contrast, the process of energy production in a nuclear reactor involves a means for regulating the chain reaction, a moderator that surrounds the fissile core for maintaining the chain reaction, and a means for removing the heat produced from the reactor

---

Box 19.1 The technology of nuclear weapons

Separate processes are required to obtain the two fissile materials needed to construct a nuclear weapon. Uranium is found in nature and comprises 99.3% uranium 238 (U-238) and 0.7% uranium 235 (U-235). The U-235 has the same chemical properties as the U-238 but has a different atomic weight. It is the latter isotopic form that is used in a nuclear weapon. To produce the weapon, the amount of U-235 in a quantity of natural uranium is increased to weapons grade by a process called enrichment so that eventually it becomes 90%+ of the sample. Once a sufficient quantity of weapons grade U-235 has been accumulated to achieve a critical mass, defined by the International Atomic Energy Agency (IAEA) as 25 kilograms—although the amount could be smaller, then there is enough fissile material to construct one nuclear weapon.

Plutonium does not occur naturally. Rather, it is one of the end-products of the irradiation of natural or only very slightly enriched (2–3%) uranium in a nuclear reactor. Plutonium 239 (Pu-239) is thus the result of a controlled nuclear reaction process. Because the two are chemically different, it is possible to separate plutonium and uranium through a process known as reprocessing. Pu-239 is regarded as a very efficient fissile material because it has a smaller critical mass than U-235. The figure of 6 to 8 kilograms is usually the quantity quoted for one weapon although again some designs may use less than that.

---

core by the chain reaction, which can also provide the steam to drive turbines and generate electricity.

Nuclear weapons effects

The effects of nuclear weapons are considerable. Because of this, the United Nations Commission for Conventional Armaments in 1948 introduced a new category of 'weapons of mass destruction' (WMD) to distinguish nuclear weapons from conventional forms. As the Commission outlined the category, WMD included 'atomic explosive weapons, radio-active material weapons, lethal chemical and bio-logical weapons, and any weapons developed in the future which have characteristics comparable in destructive effect to those of the atomic bomb or other weapons mentioned above'.

Nuclear weapons produce their energy in three distinct forms: **blast**; **heat or thermal radiation**; and **nuclear radiation**. Experience of nuclear testing has also indicated another feature of a nuclear weapons explosion, the phenomenon known as electro-magnetic pulse (EMP). This can cause acute disruption to electronic equipment (Grace 1994: 1).

Extensive damage to human populations may result from a nuclear weapons detonation. Awareness of these effects stems from the two weapons dropped on Hiroshima and Nagasaki in 1945, which remain the only time nuclear weapons have been used. What is also known is the weapons that destroyed these Japanese cities were relatively small in comparison to the destructive forces generated by later testing of thermonuclear weapons. The largest weapon of this kind known to have been tested was estimated to be a 58 megaton (58 million tonnes of TNT) device produced by the Soviet Union during the height of the cold war. It has also been acknowledged that the Soviet Union stockpiled a 100 megaton weapon, although this device was never tested. One noticeable trend in recent years, however, has been a movement away from nuclear weapons with large explosive potential towards designs with much lower yields.

The long-term and widespread effects of nuclear radiation were also confirmed when, at 1.23 a.m. on 26 April 1986, a large explosion ripped the roof off the number four power unit at the Chernobyl nuclear complex in the former Soviet Union. The devastation caused by this explosion of an operating nuclear power plant shook the world. And while a much more serious nuclear accident was prevented by the bravery of those who dealt with the immediate aftermath, the long-term consequences were still profound. Nuclear radiation was carried on the pre-vailing winds across several borders, resulting in large numbers of animals having to be destroyed and humans well outside the initial blast area suffering varying degrees of radiation-induced illnesses.

The global diffusion of nuclear and ballistic missile technology

The diffusion of nuclear technology

Since 1945, nuclear technology for civil and military uses has disseminated on a global scale. In the immediate post-Second World War years, only the United States possessed the technological capability to manufacture a nuclear weapon. By 1964, four other states had crossed the nuclear weapons threshold, an event traditionally understood as the testing of a nuclear explosive device. As indicated earlier, these states were the former Soviet Union (1949), the United Kingdom (1952), France (1960), and China (1964). All five states have been defined by the NPT as NWS, referring to a state that 'has manufactured and exploded a nuclear weapon or other nuclear explosive device prior to 1 January 1967'.

Complications for this definition of a NWS, and for the NPT as a whole, have been raised by the detonation of nuclear devices by India and Pakistan in May 1998. Neither state was party to the NPT at the time (and both have remained outside the Treaty subsequently), so they were not in breach of any international legal obligation. Yet, their move from a presumed 'threshold' position to demonstrating an overt nuclear-weapons capability not only questioned the NPT's definition of a NWS, it also raised the issue of whether other states might also seek to follow the nuclear path trodden by India and Pakistan. If this were to occur, then it would potentially represent one of the greatest challenges to the future of the NPT as it is could involve defections among the Non-Nuclear-Weapon States (NNWS) currently party to the Treaty.

In addition to this development, there has also been a structural change in the civil nuclear trading market over the same period. For several years after the Second World War, the United States remained the pre-eminent nuclear supplier. By the 1970s, this position was challenged, first by European nuclear suppliers such as France and Germany, and then by Japan (Walker and Lönnròth 1983). Today, there are several nuclear suppliers with many more emerging, including China and former republics of the Soviet Union.

With many nuclear suppliers, and with the downturn in the global nuclear energy market seeming set to continue for the foreseeable future, there is concern that the guidelines for international nuclear trade will not be upheld and that it will become easier for nuclear proliferation to occur. Although, for the most part these concerns are unwarranted, in certain cases disagreements about the nuclear intentions of a state can create discord among suppliers.

The increasing sophistication of nuclear delivery

During the 1950s, nuclear weapons required large bomber aircraft designed specifically to carry these weapons to their target. Thereafter, as the technology developed for manufacturing ballistic missiles and for nuclear ordnance that was compact enough to be carried by these missiles, so the possibility increased that more states would seek to deliver nuclear weapons by this means.

Ballistic missiles consequently represent the most sophisticated method of nuclear delivery and were once restricted to a few technologically advanced states. But just as the diffusion of nuclear technology is a global phenomenon, so has the capability to deploy a ballistic missile become more commonplace. Should these programmes be linked to the delivery of nuclear ordnance, then more states will have the capacity to hit targets over longer distances

and, by implication, also widen their potential for political and strategic engagement. It is this aspect, probably more than any other, that increased the salience of the nuclear issue at the end of the 1990s and brought to the fore once more the debate over the merits of deploying defences against ballistic missiles.

Efforts to develop anti-ballistic missiles (ABM) that could intercept long-range missiles during their flight path date back to the 1950s. In the late 1960s, the issue of ABM deployments became a major factor in the strategic arms control talks between the United States and the Soviet Union. Negotiators took the view then that ABMs would undermine international stability and deterrence. This was because any state deploying these systems could theoretically be protected against the offensive strategic forces of the opponent. This was thought to be destabilizing in the context of the dominant conception of nuclear deterrence at the time, mutually assured destruction. As deterrence was thought to rest on the mutual vulnerability of each side to the other's strategic forces, defensive systems were viewed as a challenge to that. The ABM Treaty of 1972 thus limited the ABM deployments of the United States and the Soviet Union to two sites, one around each side's capital city, the other at an Inter-Continental Ballistic Missile (ICBM) site. In 1974, a Protocol to the ABM Treaty restricted such defensive deployments to one site.

In 1983, the United States embarked on a more ambitious plan to develop a system of ballistic missile defence intended to protect US territory from a potential Soviet attack. Known as the Strategic Defence Initiative (SDI), this involved research and development of a multi-tiered or astrodome defence system designed for the purpose of intercepting large numbers of ballistic missiles during various stages of their flight path. One complication for the SDI programme was the large technical requirement placed on it, as nothing less than the capacity to hit all incoming missiles was demanded.

With the ending of the cold war, the SDI programme was scaled down, but research on more limited ballistic missile defence systems continued. One variant was the Global Protection Against Limited Strikes (GPALS) idea, which was designed to offer protection against unauthorized launches and a limited missile attack. This system anticipated using early warning radars and sensors, together with large numbers of ground-based missiles and space-based or so-called 'brilliant pebbles' interceptors that would potentially be capable of dealing with missiles during different stages of their flight path and any satellite systems associated with them.

Interest has also been sparked in Theatre Missile Defence (TMD) systems that are designed to protect a given territory or specific combinations of military forces in a regional context. The 1991 Persian Gulf War gave renewed impetus to this debate when US interceptors were used to hit SCUD missiles fired by Iraq. Although there was much discussion over the success or otherwise of the interceptors in actually hitting the SCUDs, the episode nevertheless prompted further investment in defensive missile systems.

The debate entered a new phase, when the US Congress passed the National Missile Defense (NMD) Act in 1999. This Act proposed that the United States should develop the technical means to counter a possible small-scale ballistic missile attack on the US mainland. The timetable for the initial deployment of the NMD was set at 2005, although some commentators have suggested that a later date in the decade would be more likely if this particular defensive system goes ahead.

Since the announcement of the NMD proposal there have been a range of reactions both within the United States and from states elsewhere. Overall programme cost and technical feasibility have been a key element of the US domestic debate. For unlike the SDI proposal, which intended to use a range of technologies including nuclear explosions to hit incoming missiles, the NMD system would be based solely on kinetic energy to deal with such missiles: that is, the intention is to hit a missile with another missile during its flight. Such a system inevitably requires considerable early warning and computational capabilities, and a missile that is fast and manoeuvrable enough to hit a target potentially travelling at 7 kilometres per second.

International reaction to US missile defence proposals have met with concerns in Russia and China about its impact on stability if the ABM Treaty is eroded, while in Europe similar reservations have also been expressed. Some commentators have

therefore suggested that through a dialogue among the relevant parties it may be possible to reach a consensus on the way forward for these issues in the years ahead.

Key points

- The nature of nuclear weapons and the dissemination of the capabilities to manufacture them around the world since 1945 makes the issue of nuclear proliferation a good illustration of the globalization of world politics.

- The end of the cold war and the dissolution of the former Soviet Union has meant that new problems concerning nuclear proliferation have emerged.

- During the 1990s, greater attention has been paid to the theoretical aspects of nuclear proliferation and non-proliferation, although many of the key conceptual aspects were discussed in earlier seminal texts.

- A debate has emerged over the merits, for and against, the further proliferation/spread of nuclear weapons.

- The collection of measures put in place to prevent the proliferation of nuclear weapons are known as the global nuclear non-proliferation regime.

- A major element of the nuclear proliferation process is the acquisition of the key technologies to produce fissile materials to construct either a fission (nuclear) or fusion (thermo-nuclear) weapon.

- The effects of nuclear weapons are considerable and are manifest in the form of blast, heat, and nuclear radiation.

- Since 1945, the spread of nuclear technology for civil and military purposes has meant that several states beyond the five which have an acknowledged nuclear weapons capability now have the capacity to produce nuclear weapons at relatively short notice, if they have not already done so.

- Over the same period the structure of the civil nuclear trading market has also changed leading to concerns that nuclear proliferation could occur because there are now more nuclear suppliers around.

- The diffusion of ballistic missile and space-launch technology has also created a situation where several states have the capacity to deliver nuclear weapons over considerable distances if they choose to do so.

- A new debate has emerged over the merits of deploying defensive systems to counter emerging ballistic missile capabilities and the impact this might have on strategic stability

Theorizing nuclear proliferation and non-proliferation

Conceptual issues

Considerable attention has been paid to the theoretical and conceptual aspects of nuclear proliferation. One question that has provoked concerted interest is what constitutes nuclear proliferation: does it refer to a single decision to acquire a nuclear weapon or is it part of a process that may stretch over several years and consequently no one identifiable decision can be located? Research on what has been referred to as 'the proliferation puzzle' has thus embraced an increasingly complex array of variables and conceptual issues (Davis and Frankel: 1993, Lavoy: 1995, Ogilvie-White: 1996, Sagan: 1996). Similarly, while much literature remains wedded to the theoretical tenets of political realism, which asserts that in an anarchic international environment states will seek nuclear weapons to enhance their security, insights from other theoretical positions have become more commonplace in recent years. This has led to questions concerning what the appropriate 'level of analysis' should be in studying nuclear proliferation. Should the focus be on the individual, the organization, the cultural group, the state, the international system, or some combination of these? Similarly, in the context of fostering nuclear non-proliferation dialogues, some analysts have indicated the importance played by cultural and cross-cultural identity factors (Krause: 1998).

The argument has also been advanced by several writers that norms, taboos and epistemic communities have played an important role in the nuclear context (Adler: 1992; Price and Tannenwald: 1995). One viewpoint sees international norms as increasingly significant both as constraints on nuclear behaviour and in setting appropriate standards among a range of actors. In this context, a proposition often voiced is that a non-proliferation norm has evolved which has assisted in limiting the numbers of nuclear weapon states in existence, certainly from those expected by studies in the early 1960s.

Another issue with enduring resonance concerns the question of what can explain the now more than fifty years of nuclear 'non-use'? It is noteworthy that this debate started very early in the nuclear calendar. It has been observed that authors like Bernard Brodie, writing not long after the Second World War, argued that nuclear weapons were useful only in their non-use (Gray: 1996; Brodie: 1946). Over the years, the main explanation of non-use has centred on the notion of nuclear deterrence: states have been deterred from using nuclear weapons because of the concerns of retaliation in kind by adversaries.

In looking to alternative accounts of non-use, some have focused more on the nature of the weapon and the impact this has on normative judgements. Nina Tannenwald, for example, has challenged those arguments that rely on rational cost–benefit analysis relating to power, capabilities, and interests by exploring other non-material aspects, such as the constraining influence of what is termed the 'nuclear taboo' (1999). In identifying such a taboo, Barry Buzan and Eric Herring define it as 'a strategic cultural prohibition against the use of nuclear weapons ... an assumption that nuclear weapons should not be used rather than a conscious cost–benefit calculation' (1998: 165).

The role that 'epistemic communities' and other transnational and non-governmental organizations play in the debate over nuclear proliferation and arms control generally has also provoked interest. Some writers have consequently drawn attention to the importance of groups of individuals, often from different disciplines and countries (the 'epistemic community'), who operate as conduits for ideas and proposals on nuclear policy issues, particularly if the intergovernmental fora are in stalemate.

Nuclear motivations

Traditional analysis of the motivations for nuclear proliferation has tended to focus at the state and inter-state levels. For much of the post-Second World War period the pattern of nuclear weapon acquisition established by the five acknowledged NWS was considered to be the one most likely to be followed by any future proliferating state. Analysis of the motivational aspect of nuclear weapons acquisition consequently focused on the strategic, political, and prestige rationales that led these states to seek nuclear weapons. The **strategic motivation** focused on the role that nuclear weapons played in the context of the Second World War and its immediate aftermath when initially they were seen as war-fighting or war-winning weapons. Later, attention shifted to the role that nuclear weapons played in deterrence, leading to the assumption that one of the principal motivations for acquisition was the deterrence of other nuclear weapons-capable states. Similarly, the **political and prestige benefits** that nuclear weapons conferred on those states with the wherewithal to manufacture them were also deemed significant. Nuclear weapons were seen as the most modern form of weaponry and their custodians, by dint of their technological prowess, were automatically afforded a seat at the 'top table of international affairs'.

Inherent in traditional analysis of nuclear weapons acquisition was also a form of technological determinism, that once a state had acquired the necessary infrastructure it would automatically develop nuclear weapons. Supporting this assump-

tion was the view that these states would also tread the same acquisition path as the five NWS. Thus, it could be predicted that any new nuclear state would pursue a dedicated military nuclear programme, conduct an overt nuclear test, produce a stockpile of weapons, and finally, acquire an effective means for delivering the weapons to their target. While this explanation of the acquisition process and the motivations for embarking on a nuclear weapon programme is still relevant, over time, our understanding of the dynamics of nuclear proliferation have become more complex.

It is now more difficult to explain nuclear proliferation by focusing on a single variable. Increasingly analysts have argued it is necessary to consider a range of factors that may influence nuclear weapons acquisition. These may include: traditional technological factors, the availability of nuclear technology and a cadre of trained nuclear scientists encourages acquisition; domestic politics, imperatives within a political party or domestic political situation may propel a state towards nuclear weapons; diplomatic bargaining, that acquisition of a nuclear capability can be used to influence or bargain politically or economically with both perceived allies and enemies; and non-intervention, that a nuclear capability can deter or prevent intervention by other states.

Other features of the 'proliferation puzzle' that need to be understood are the instances of nuclear restraint, why some states abandon the nuclear weapons option, and nuclear reversal, why some states relinquish their nuclear capabilities (Reiss: 1995). One observation that can be made is that since 1945 developments have questioned the technological determinist argument. A number of factors have been identified to account for this. There may have been a change in strategic circumstances, such as the forging or the renegotiation of an alliance with a NWS. Similarly, technical difficulties encountered in the construction of the nuclear weapon, or the emergence of a perception that the acquisition of nuclear weapons would increase vulnerabilities, could create the necessary conditions for abandoning the nuclear option.

Further complexity is added when attention is focused at the **sub-state level** as the motivations of non-state actors may be different from those associated with states. In much traditional thinking, only states were considered to have the wherewithal to acquire nuclear capabilities. Nuclear commerce was conducted on a state-to-state basis, and it was states that entered into international arms control and disarmament treaties. Today, states are no longer the sole focus of attention as non-state actors have also featured.

Studies conducted during the 1970s and 1980s on **nuclear terrorism** indicated that there were risks associated with particular groups acquiring a nuclear device or threatening to attack civil or military nuclear installations. One study conducted by the International Task Force on Prevention of Nuclear Terrorism concluded that it was possible for a dedicated terrorist group to build a crude nuclear device provided it had sufficient quantities of chemical high-explosives and weapons-usable fissile materials. More significantly perhaps, in terms of thinking about the risks involved, it was also felt that such a group would be more interested in causing panic and social disruption by making a credible nuclear threat rather than actually detonating a nuclear device and causing mass killing and destruction (Leventhal and Alexander: 1987). More recent occurrences may have served to alter this latter judgement, though there is a view that the issue must still be kept in perspective. Events in the mid-1990s, such as the bombing of the International Trade Center in New York in 1993 and the attack against the US government building in Oklahoma in April 1995, revealed the extent of damage and loss of life that could be caused. While both these instances involved traditional methods of inflicting damage, the use of nerve agents (chemical weapons) in an underground train network in central Tokyo in March 1995 to cause both death and widespread panic has been viewed by some as representing a quantum change in methods. It has also been stressed, however, that although a WMD was used it was still not a nuclear weapon and this may be the telling point.

In addition to these factors, attention has focused on **nuclear smuggling** and the possibility that ethnic groups involved in civil conflict might seek a nuclear option to further their political or military objectives. Nuclear smuggling has been given heightened international media attention since the disconcerting discovery that materials suitable for making nuclear weapons may be being trafficked by several different groups. The problem here is that it is very difficult to determine the extent of the problem.

The fear that ethnic groups involved in civil conflict might resort to nuclear threats has also become a feature of the post-cold war security debate. The concern in this context is that the situations in which such threats might occur would be highly unpredictable. It would be very difficult to determine whether the leaders of these groups would act responsibly or predictably in situations where the political and military conditions were unstable. Moreover, the possession of a single or small number of nuclear devices might encourage usage or pre-emptive strategies because of fear of discovery.

Nuclear capabilities

Closely paralleling the problems of analysing the motivational aspect are those associated with determining whether a state actually possesses a nuclear capability: that is, whether nuclear proliferation has actually occurred.

In 1974, India complicated the issue by conducting an underground test of what its government termed was a peaceful nuclear explosion (PNE). The idea of using controlled nuclear explosions for civil, rather than military, purposes had gained credence during the early years of nuclear development. But it is precisely because the technologies involved in PNEs are indistinguishable from those used in military applications, as the India test made apparent, that it raises problems of determining nuclear weapon possession.

The case of South Africa also indicates the difficulties in this area. On 24 March 1993, the then President F. W. de Klerk announced that South Africa had produced six nuclear devices up until 1989 but had dismantled them prior to signing the NPT. While this announcement confirmed what many had previously speculated—that South Africa possessed a nuclear capability during the 1980s—it also confirmed that a state did not actually need to test a nuclear explosive device to be in possession of a nuclear stockpile.

During the 1970s and 1980s four other states were grouped together with India and South Africa as 'threshold' nuclear weapon-capable states. These were Argentina, Brazil, Israel, and Pakistan. These states were uniformly regarded as having made significant progress in nuclear technology but had not accepted nuclear inspection by the International Atomic Energy Agency (IAEA) on all the nuclear facilities and materials on their respective territories. Although the situation for three states has now changed—Argentina, Brazil, and South Africa have signed the NPT—the other three have remained outside the treaty.

What is also known is that during the 1950s, 1960s, and 1970s other states, in addition to the 'threshold' states, embarked on a nuclear explosive research programme before abandoning them. Sweden is perhaps the most documented of these states, but other cases have become public, such as the Republic of Korea's (RoK) contingency plans in the 1970s for a nuclear option if the US nuclear guarantee began to waver.

Both Sweden and the RoK are now NNWS parties to the NPT. In determining nuclear weapon capability, this is a significant factor. All NNWS that sign the Treaty have to subject their civil nuclear materials to IAEA safeguards. This means that their entire nuclear programme is continually being inspected and monitored. What these examples do indicate, though, is that around the world there are several other advanced industrialized states with large operating nuclear power programmes which could be used to produce quantities of fissile materials for military purposes if a political decision was taken to do so. The main barrier to nuclear weapon acquisition in such cases may therefore be political not technological.

One of the most significant developments concerning the issue of nuclear capabilities in recent years, however, has stemmed from the break-up of the former Soviet Union in 1991. Prior to its demise, the Soviet Union had deployed a vast nuclear weapon complex throughout its entire territory. This complex embraced a large nuclear weapons arsenal, which included several tactical and strategic systems and a sophisticated technical infrastructure involving around 100,000 personnel. The collapse of the Soviet Union therefore meant that both the nuclear arsenal and the technical infrastructure were spread around many of the now separate independent republics. Ensuring that this situation

does not create a further spur to nuclear proliferation has thus been an enduring task since the early 1990s.

Following the collapse, efforts were quickly undertaken to deal with the Soviet Union's nuclear weapons complex. In December 1991, the United States introduced its Soviet Threat Reduction Act, otherwise known as the Nunn–Lugar Safety, Security, Dismantlement (SSD) Programme. This Programme provided financial resources to assist in the denuclearization of Belarus, Kazakhstan, and Ukraine, three states which, in addition to Russia (acknowledged as the legal successor state to the Soviet Union), were left with strategic nuclear systems on their territory after the break-up.

Agreement was also reached to ensure that all the tactical nuclear weapon systems formerly spread throughout Soviet territory were transferred to Russia. However, there ensued a tense period between 1991 and 1994, during which a series of negotiations were held with the governments of Belarus, Kazakhstan, and Ukraine over the future dismantlement of the strategic systems located on their territories. This culminated in agreement by each of the three states, the last being Ukraine, to allow these nuclear systems to be transferred to Russia for dismantling and for the three states to become NNWS parties to the NPT.

Dealing with the former Soviet Union's technical nuclear infrastructure has added further complexity and raised novel questions such as, how to ensure secure employment for all the personnel involved in the weapons manufacturing process? Are the physical protection measures around the nuclear installations adequate? What should be done with any surplus nuclear materials? And are the export controls operating in the new republics adequate now that the Soviet Union's overarching system has disappeared?

In response to this situation, efforts have focused on improving the prospects of those formerly working in the nuclear weapons complex, strengthening export control procedures in Russia and the new republics, and introducing tighter security arrangements around storage sites where nuclear weapons or fissile nuclear materials are located.

All these schemes are thus part of a, so far successful, overall effort to reduce the risks of nuclear proliferation stemming from the break-up of the Soviet Union. However, until this task is complete, which will take several years and considerable resources, risks will remain.

Nuclear intentions

While being an NPT party may be a strong indication of nuclear intention, in a very few instances, such a commitment has been shown to be misleading.

Another NNWS party to the NPT that has challenged the IAEA's right to conduct inspections on its territory is the Democratic People's Republic of Korea (DPRK). The DPRK had signed the NPT in 1985 but did not sign a safeguards agreement with the IAEA until January 1992, although under the terms of the Treaty this document should have been concluded within 18 months of signature. As required by the document, the DPRK presented the IAEA with an inventory of all its nuclear facilities and materials.

Because of the problems which had arisen over Iraq, the IAEA wanted to ensure that the DPRK had declared the full extent of its nuclear operation and began a series of inspections to verify the DPRK inventory. By early 1993, the IAEA had identified discrepancies in the material inventory, which would need further investigation to ensure that no material existed on DPRK territory that had not been declared. In addition, information had also been provided to the IAEA indicating the existence of two undeclared sites that were suspected of being nuclear waste depositories. In an effort to clarify the situation, the IAEA decided to initiate a special inspection in the DPRK, but this was refused. In retaliation, the DPRK announced on 12 March 1993 its intention to withdraw from the NPT. By this stage speculation was rife that the DPRK had embarked on a clandestine nuclear weapon programme and the baulking at IAEA safeguards was because it had something to hide.

In the event, the DPRK did not withdraw from the NPT: but neither was the IAEA able to clarify the anomalies identified in its nuclear inventory or visit the suspected sites. For its part, the DPRK claimed the sites in question were military bases and therefore not subject to inspection.

Box 19.2 Iraq's non-compliance with the NPT

Following the Persian Gulf War of 1991, it was discovered that Iraq had developed a large-scale clandestine nuclear weapon programme, which had not been declared to the IAEA. Iraq, as an NPT party, had declared a small nuclear power programme to the IAEA and this had been subject to safeguards. No nuclear material had been diverted from the declared programme and so the IAEA had no cause to suspect any wrongdoing. Subsequently, the IAEA undertook a revision of its safeguards procedures so that any state embarking on an undeclared nuclear programme would stand a good chance of detection in the future. However, the critical factor is still that Iraq's clandestine nuclear programme would have remained undetected had its existence not been revealed following the Persian Gulf War. A United Nations Special Committee (UNSCOM) operating with the IAEA was subsequently established to determine the extent of Iraq's nuclear weapon effort, destroy it, and devise a long-term monitoring programme to ensure compliance in the future. But by the late 1990s, problems had emerged over access to particular sites in Iraq. This led to the withdrawal of UNSCOM inspectors and splits in the UN Security Council (UNSC) over how to respond. In December 1998, the United Kingdom and United States took military enforcement action against Iraq to get it to comply with UN Resolutions, while efforts thereafter have continued in the UNSC to find an acceptable plan for the resumption of inspections in that country.

In October 1994 an agreement was reached between the United States and the DPRK, which was seen as representing a compromise between the various positions. Known as the 'Agreed Framework', this has sought to ensure the DPRK's full compliance with the NPT by, among other things, providing it with Light-Water Reactors (LWRs) as an alternative to the graphite-moderated ('Magnox') reactors then in operation or under construction. The argument for this switch of technology was that LWRs are considered less proliferation sensitive than Magnox reactors because the former reactors are not regarded as good sources of weapon-grade plutonium.

Since October 1994 the 'Agreed Framework' has experienced several problems relating to implementation, which has resulted in continuing uncertainty concerning the DPRK's nuclear situation. This uncertainty was exacerbated when, in August 1998, the DPRK tested a ballistic missile whose trajectory took it over the territory of Japan and indicates the impact that emerging ballistic missiles capabilities can have on threat perceptions. One recent development that has been viewed as significant in potentially reducing tensions is the resumption of high-level talks between the two Koreas.

Another instance where the issue of nuclear intentions has caused difficulty concerns Iran, another NPT party. In the 1970s, German companies began constructing a nuclear power complex at Bushehr on the Persian Gulf coast. This complex was subsequently bombed during the Iran–Iraq war in the 1980s before it could be completed. In recent years, Iran has attempted either to have the damage to the Bushehr nuclear complex repaired or obtain alternative nuclear reactors. This attempt has met with a mixed reception from potential nuclear suppliers.

The United States has made clear its opposition to any nuclear assistance to Iran because of concerns that the technology will be used for military not civil purposes. By contrast, both China and Russia are prepared to trade with Iran and remain unconvinced by the protestations of the United States. The dispute over a nuclear supply agreement with Iran has thus soured relations between Russia and the United States and highlighted further the problem of determining nuclear intentions.

Key points

- Over time, the characterization of motivations for acquiring nuclear weapons has become more complex.

- There are also difficulties associated with determining whether nuclear proliferation has actually occurred due to technical ambiguities and the observation that a nuclear capability can be constructed without the need for a nuclear test.

- Six states beyond the five acknowledged NWS have acquired the technical capability to manufacture nuclear weapons, although three of these states have recently made commitments not to do so.

- Several other states have the capacity to manufacture nuclear weapons if they wanted, and a few actually embarked on military nuclear programmes before abandoning them.

- The potential role of non-state actors has added a further dimension to the nuclear proliferation issue in the post cold-war context.

- The dissolution of the former Soviet Union has raised unprecedented issues concerning nuclear proliferation.

- Efforts to ensure the safe custody of former Soviet nuclear forces have been implemented and new centres have been established to improve the prospects of personnel who formerly worked in the Soviet Union's nuclear weapon complex.

- The complexities surrounding compliance have been a feature of the debate since the early 1990s, especially in the context of Iraq and the DPRK.

- Some nuclear supply arrangements have raised difficult issues of nuclear transfers under the NPT.

Will more nuclear weapons be better or worse?

More will be better

One of the more provocative arguments concerning nuclear proliferation is the 'more may be better' thesis advanced by Kenneth N. Waltz in the early 1980s (Waltz: 1981). This thesis has been restated more recently to account for any changes brought about by the end of the cold war. Waltz advances an analysis of nuclear 'spread' (rather than, 'proliferation'), based on the assumptions of neo-realist theory. As many analysts of nuclear proliferation have pointed out, this analysis stresses the impact of structural causes on nuclear weapons acquisition. It means that the units, or states, in the international system have no option but to seek measures to preserve their own security. The upshot is that states will therefore seek nuclear weapons both to enhance their own security and to deter potential adversaries.

Waltz's initial thesis was advanced at a time when the East–West strategic relationship was still predominant and provoked debate because of the assertion that the spread of nuclear weapons should be viewed in positive rather than negative terms.

Although Waltz has restated this thesis to account for changes brought about by the end of the cold war, it has done little to change his underlying argument (Sagan and Waltz: 1995). Moreover, the assertion that the spread of nuclear weapons to additional states may result in greater stability has met with some support. Some analysts have argued, for example, that the acquisition of the capability to manufacture nuclear weapons by India and Pakistan has introduced a new cautionary factor in their decision-making and created a kind of strategic stability between these two neighbouring states. At the end of the cold war John Mearsheimer also adopted a similar approach to nuclear spread in certain contexts (Mearsheimer 1990). This view has been challenged by those advocating a 'more may be worse' assessment.

More will be worse

In a debate between Waltz and Scott D. Sagan, Sagan argues that Waltz and Mearsheimer are '**proliferation optimists**'. This is an outlook that he suggests 'flows easily from the logic of rational deterrence theory: the possession of nuclear weapons by two powers can reduce the likelihood of war precisely because it makes the costs of war so great' (Sagan and Waltz 1995: 48). Sagan offers an alternative position to the proliferation optimists, rooted in organization theory, which leads to a more pessimistic view of nuclear proliferation and the prospects for future stability.

Sagan concludes that it is therefore optimistic to expect a rational deterrence arrangement to operate between any future new nuclear weapon states in the

---

Box 19.3 The main arguments of the Waltz thesis

1. Nuclear weapons have spread rather than proliferated because these weapons have proliferated only vertically as the Nuclear Weapon States have increased their arsenals.

2. Nuclear weapons have spread horizontally to other states only slowly. However, this slowness of pace is fortunate as rapid changes in international conditions can be unsettling.

3. The gradual spread of nuclear weapons is better than either no spread or rapid spread.

4. New nuclear states will feel the constraints that nuclear weapons impose and this will induce a sense of responsibility on the part of their possessors and a strong element of caution on their use.

5. The likelihood of war decreases as deterrent and defensive capabilities increase and that nuclear weapons, responsibly used, make wars hard to start.

(Sagan and Waltz:1995)

Box 19.4 Sagan's 'proliferation pessimism' argument

1. Professional military organizations, because of common biases, inflexible routines, and parochial interests, display organization behaviours that are likely to lead to deterrence failures and deliberate or accidental war.

2. Because future nuclear-armed states are likely to have military-run or weak civilian governments, they will lack the positive constraining mechanisms of civilian control while military biases may serve to encourage nuclear weapons use, especially during crisis.

(Sagan and Waltz: 1995)

way that Waltz and others postulate. By contrast, Sagan argues that the most appropriate way forward is to encourage alternative arrangements which seek to reduce the demand for nuclear weapons and for strengthening the global nuclear non-proliferation regime, especially the NPT.

Key points

- A debate has emerged concerning the consequences of the further proliferation/spread of nuclear weapons.

- Kenneth N. Waltz asserts that the spread of nuclear weapons will induce greater stability since new nuclear states will use their weapons to deter other states from attacking them.

- A contrary position adopted by Scott D. Sagan argues that instability will result from more states acquiring nuclear weapons because of a greater potential for preventive nuclear wars and serious nuclear weapons accidents.

- Sagan, among others, has therefore argued in favour of measures to reduce the demand for nuclear weapons and for strengthening the global nuclear non-proliferation regime.

The evolution of the global nuclear non-proliferation regime

Early efforts to control nuclear weapons 1945–1970

Global efforts to constrain nuclear weapons acquisition began soon after the conclusion to the Second World War. In January 1946, the United Nations General Assembly passed a resolution establishing the UN Atomic Energy Commission (UNAEC). The remit of the UNAEC was to make proposals for the elimination of nuclear weapons and the use of nuclear energy for peaceful purposes under **international control**. On 14 June 1946, the United States submitted the so-called Baruch Plan as its proposal for meeting the Commissions objectives. The Soviet Union also proposed a similar scheme, but unlike the Baruch Plan, which envisaged inter-

national nuclear control arrangements, theirs was based on a national scheme for ownership and control of nuclear facilities. Neither plan was implemented, however, due to the radical differences between the United States and the Soviet Union over their respective methods for controlling atomic energy. During discussion of the plans, the United States moved to introduce unilateral legislation aimed at maintaining its monopoly over 'the use of atomic energy for the national defense'. The Atomic Energy Act (also known as the McMahon Act), passed on 1 August 1946, established the United States Atomic Energy Commission (USAEC) as the sole owner of all fissionable materials and facilities in the United States and prohibited all exchanges of nuclear information with other states.

The issue of international atomic energy control

was revisited following President Eisenhower's **'Atoms for Peace'** speech on 8 December 1953. It was stressed that Eisenhower's proposal was not a disarmament plan, but an initiative to open the benefits of atomic energy to the world community. There were elements of the proposal that did have arms control and security considerations, however. Negotiations to implement 'Atoms for Peace' culminated in a Conference on the Statute of the IAEA held at UN Headquarters in New York between September and October 1956. Following agreement at this Conference on the IAEA Statute, the Agency was inaugurated on 29 July 1957. But also contained in Eisenhower's 1953 proposal was the idea for a cut-off in the production of fissile nuclear materials. At the time of Eisenhower's speech, a major concern of the United States was that the Soviet Union would soon possess sufficient fissile material, and thus several nuclear weapons, to have a capability of delivering a surprise 'knock-out blow' on US military forces before they could be mobilized. One means for constraining the Soviet Union's ability to deliver such a blow was to restrict the amount of fissile material it had available for military explosive purposes. A key element of Eisenhower's speech was, therefore, a proposal that both the Soviet Union and the United States should transfer significant quantities of fissile material to the proposed IAEA for use in peaceful applications of atomic energy. This would have the consequence of reducing the fissile material available to the Soviet Union for military use.

The IAEA turned out to be a different organization to the one envisaged in the Baruch Plan or by President Eisenhower. From the outset, the IAEA was unable to fulfil the role of reducing the stockpiles of fissile material in the three then existing NWS (Soviet Union, United Kingdom, and United States). Due to opposition from the Soviet Union and India, it was not until after the mid-1960s that the IAEA was able to implement a comprehensive monitoring system (known as **safeguards**) to ensure peaceful nuclear energy use.

One safeguards system that did become operational at an early date was the one implemented by the European Atomic Energy Community (EURATOM), which came into being on 1 January 1958 as an organization of the European Community. EURATOM has since had the task of co-

ordinating nuclear energy development within the Community (now European Union) and implementing a regional safeguards system to ensure that nuclear materials are not diverted 'to purposes other than for those which they are intended'. The EURATOM safeguards system covers all civilian nuclear energy activities in the Member States, including those of France and the United Kingdom. Although the military programmes of the latter states are largely excluded from EURATOM safeguards coverage, efforts have been underway to introduce greater transparency and accountability into these programmes especially in the United Kingdom.

In the late 1950s, the United States introduced a more overt proposal for a total halt in the production of fissile materials for military purposes. This was viewed as part of a package of measures to freeze, and ultimately reverse, the 'nuclear arms race'. The idea was to start with a Comprehensive Test Ban Treaty (CTBT) and a fissile material cut-off, follow this by measures to halt the production of additional nuclear weapons, and finally, initiate a phased dismantling of national stockpiles. Given the United States' superiority in the number of weapons and in the size of its stockpile of fissile materials at this time, the proposals were greeted with little enthusiasm by the Soviet Union.

The negotiations on a CTBT occurred in the context of a Soviet Union–United Kingdom–United States moratorium on nuclear testing, from 1958 to 1961, and against a backdrop of calls for the three NWS to engage in nuclear disarmament. The negotiations did not result in an agreement, largely because the three states were unable to overcome differences concerning **verification**: namely, the provisions for a system of inspections and controls that could provide adequate assurance of detection of violation, especially for underground testing. However, in 1963, the Soviet Union, United Kingdom, and United States did agree the Partial Test Ban Treaty (PTBT). This prohibited nuclear testing in the atmosphere, in outer space, and underwater. It meant, in effect, that future testing by states party to the PTBT had to be conducted underground.

Since the late 1950s, attention has also focused on measures to prevent the nuclearization of specific environments and geographical areas (Goldblat

1993). The first such measure was the Antarctic Treaty of 1959, which included provisions for banning all nuclear explosions in the Antarctic and the disposal of radioactive waste. This Treaty served as a model for later measures because it seeks to limit the spread of nuclear weapons by preventing their introduction into specific areas (a 'non-armament' provision) and its explicit provisions for peaceful utilization of resources. The first NWFZ applied to a populated geographic region is the Treaty for the Prohibition of Nuclear Weapons in Latin America (the Tlatelolco Treaty), which was opened for signature in 1967.

Between 1958 and 1968 there was a greater focus on the dangers posed by additional states acquiring nuclear weapons. In 1961, the UN General Assembly adopted what became known as the **'Irish Resolution'**, which called for measures to limit the possibilities for additional states to acquire nuclear weapons and for all states to refrain from transfer or acquisition of such weapons. A breakthrough in the negotiation of a non-proliferation treaty came as a result of Resolution 2028 adopted by the UN General Assembly in 1965. This was followed by a period of intense negotiation to resolve differences over such issues as nuclear sharing arrangements in the NATO and Warsaw Pact alliances. Finally, on 11 March 1968 the Soviet Union and the United States tabled a joint draft NPT treaty. Following some further amendments, this draft was passed by the UN General Assembly on 12 June 1968, opened for signature on 1 July 1968, and the NPT formerly entered into force on 5 March 1970 (Shaker 1980).

During negotiation of the NPT, a major debate surfaced over the linkage between nuclear security assurances and nuclear proliferation. Because of the NPT's distinction between a NWS and NNWS some of the latter states were concerned that by signing the NPT they would not only be prohibited from acquiring nuclear weapons they might, at the same time, be threatened or actually attacked by a state in possession of such weapons. To allay these concerns the Soviet Union, the United Kingdom, and the United States agreed UN Security Council Resolution 255 on 19 June 1968. This Resolution contained positive security assurances, whereby the Security Council and 'above all its nuclear weapon State permanent members, would have to act immediately in accordance with their obligations under the United Nations Charter' in the event of a nuclear attack against a NNWS. However, this initiative did not go far enough for the states concerned and the matter has remained a source of contention within the context of the NPT.

Efforts to control nuclear weapons since 1970

Since 1970, the global nuclear non-proliferation regime has continued to evolve, strengthened by the international legal framework the Treaty provided. In March 1971, the IAEA negotiated its so-called INFCIRC/153 safeguards document which provides a model for all safeguards negotiated with parties to the NPT. Additional arrangements have also been established for the conduct of international nuclear trade. In 1971, the Zangger Committee adopted guidelines or a 'trigger list' pursuant to the NPT allowing for IAEA safeguards to be applied on nuclear transfers, especially those involving the equipment or material for the processing, use or production of special fissionable materials. But following the global expansion of nuclear power programmes, the increasing trade with non-NPT parties, and India's 'peaceful' nuclear explosion of 1974, it was decided by some nuclear suppliers that further export guidelines were necessary. The Nuclear Suppliers Group (NSG), formed in 1975 to respond to the new developments, agreed that additional conditions should be attached to sensitive nuclear exports, such as nuclear reprocessing plants.

At the First United Nations Special Session on Disarmament (UNSSOD–1) in 1978, China, France, the Soviet Union, the United Kingdom, and the United States all issued unilateral statements on so-called negative security assurances on the use or threat of use of nuclear weapons against NNWS. These assurances embraced specific qualifications related to each state's nuclear doctrine and security arrangements, but only China's was unconditional. China stated that it would not be the first to use nuclear weapons and undertook not to threaten to use nuclear weapons against any NNWS.

In 1987 seven missile technology exporters agreed to establish identical export guidelines to cover the sale of nuclear-capable ballistic or cruise missiles. Known as the Missile Technology Control Regime (MTCR), this supply arrangement seeks 'to limit the risks of nuclear proliferation by controlling transfers of technology which could make a contribution to nuclear weapons delivery systems other than manned aircraft' (Karp 1995). Over the years, membership of the MTCR has expanded to include many of the major missile producers and the guidelines have been modified to embrace missile systems capable of carrying chemical and biological payloads. Yet, concerns have still been expressed about the long-term viability of the MTCR. Many consider that while this arrangement has fulfilled its initial purpose in slowing down missile proliferation, new measures and agreements will be required in the future. Missile defences are one means for dealing with the problem, but other suggestions include a global ballistic test notification and monitoring centre, flight test bans at the regional level, establishing standards of responsible missile behaviour, and multilateral arms limitation measures for missiles with certain ranges.

The NPT also made provision for conferences to review the implementation of the Treaty to be held every five years. Since 1970, six review conferences have been held in 1975, 1980, 1985, 1990, 1995, and 2000. The review conference of 1995 also incorporated a new element, however. Article X.2 of the NPT had stated that 'twenty-five years after the entry into force of the Treaty, a conference shall be convened to decide whether the Treaty should be extended indefinitely, or for an additional fixed period or periods'. This meant that the 1995 Conference, held at UN headquarters in New York between 17 April and 12 May, was both a meeting to review the Treaty's implementation and to decide on its future duration.

Between the time of the indefinite extension of the NPT in 1995 and the convening of the Sixth NPT Review Conference in 2000, several issues emerged in the context of the nuclear non-proliferation regime. In 1995, expectations were high that the documents adopted by consensus would provide the foundation for strengthening this regime. Events afterwards indicated this assessment might be premature. In particular, strong differences surfaced between the parties over how the documents should

---

Box 19.5 The 1995 NPT review and extension conference

On 11 May 1995 the NPT Review and Extension Conference decided to extend the Treaty indefinitely without a vote. This extension decision was adopted in conjunction with two other documents and a resolution which established a set of principles and objectives for nuclear non-proliferation and disarmament; outlined new procedures for strengthening the Treaty review process; and called for the establishment of a Middle East zone free of nuclear weapons and other weapons of mass destruction within the context of the Middle East peace process. However, the parties were unable to agree a consolidated text on the review of the Treaty and, as in 1980 and 1990, the Conference concluded on 12 May without a final declaration. Even then, the outcome of the 1995 NPT Conference was still largely hailed as a success. This was because, as a result of decisions taken, the Treaty became permanent, new measures were established to strengthen future NPT review conferences and a plan of action for non-proliferation and disarmament was outlined. In particular, the Conference agreed to continue holding review conferences every five years and for the preparatory process in advance of these conferences to be strengthened.

---

be interpreted. The one associated with strengthening the Treaty review process, allowing for almost continual preparatory meetings of the parties beginning in 1997, fuelled discord because of disagreement over whether these sessions should deal with procedures related to the 2000 Conference or the substantive matters to be addressed, or some combination of the two.

Similar differences appeared over the other two documents. For many delegations, the main objective of the Principles and Objectives for Nuclear Non-Proliferation and Disarmament was to establish a programme of action in the lead up to the 2000 Conference. However, again difficulties emerged over interpretation. One noteworthy aspect of this debate was that the first part of the programme of action, to obtain agreement on the opening for signature of a CTBT by 1996, was achieved. Conversely, it has also been noted that the qualification for the entry into force provision of the CTBT is especially stringent: a group of 44 states (including the five NWS and states such as India, Pakistan, and the DPRK), are required to ratify it. This has meant that the success or otherwise of the Treaty is dependent on developments in several key states. Significantly, also, not everyone agrees that the CTBT is a worthwhile measure. Whereas proponents claim that the restriction on all nuclear testing will limit vertical and horizontal proliferation, critics argue the Treaty is unverifiable and will therefore be unable to constrain proliferation.

Problems have similarly been encountered over the next item in the Principles and Objectives document, a Fissile Material Cut-Off Treaty (FMCT). Here the principal issue has been whether the FMCT should prevent future production of fissile materials only or deal with this aspect in conjunction with an agreement to remove existing stockpiles. One feature of this debate that inevitably will demand innovative thinking is how, as safely and cost-effectively as possible, any excess fissile materials can be disposed of, given the large quantities involved.

Differences between the parties concerning the other document agreed in 1995 have also raised troubling issues. Tabled in 1995 by the Arab states party to the NPT, the Resolution on the Middle East calls on all states in the region to accede to the NPT. The debate over this Resolution has highlighted the problems associated with the attempt to ensure universal adherence to the Treaty. For although signatories to the NPT have increased to the point where 188 states are now party, four states have remained non-signatories: Cuba, Israel, India, and Pakistan. The key question, therefore, is how, if at all, can these states be brought into the Treaty?

It is against this background that the events in South Asia must be viewed. The nuclear tests by India and Pakistan have provoked an array of commentary, both on the consequences for the nuclear non-proliferation regime and for future stability in the region. As a challenge to the regime, the concerns have centred on whether the two states have weakened the norm on non-proliferation as a result of their demonstration of an overt nuclear weapons-capability.

The South Asian tests, combined with the difficulties encountered in other areas of nuclear non-proliferation and disarmament, seemed to indicate that the globalization of the nuclear proliferation issue was entering a new phase. Whereas the early-to-mid 1990s had witnessed a period of relative optimism that the non-proliferation regime was undergoing major strengthening and that nuclear weapons were increasingly becoming marginalized, the latter part of the decade gave way to an alternative observation of the future. In particular, a view emerged that a 'second nuclear age' was already upon us in which a key aspect is the potentially greater risks associated with this age than those experienced during the 'first nuclear age' between 1945 and 1989.

Yet, several aspects of this debate assumed a new guise as a range of complex questions emerged. Would the second nuclear age be characterized by a rapid or slow proliferation of new overt nuclear weapon capabilities? Would there be a greater propensity to resort to actual nuclear use? What sort of relationship existed between nuclear weapons and chemical and biological weapons, and could the former deter the latter? Would new precision-guided conventional and computer-generated capabilities, the so-called Revolution in Military Affairs (RMA), alter perceptions about the future role of nuclear weapons? And, would the nuclear non-proliferation regime prove robust enough if universality is not achieved, nuclear disarmament appears to be reversing and the five NWS are unable to meet their nuclear elimination commitment? These are questions that are likely to dominate the debate in the early decades of the twenty-first century (Gray 1999; Baylis and O'Neill 2000).

Key points

- The global nuclear non-proliferation regime has been evolving since the end of the Second World War when the Baruch Plan was submitted and later rejected at the United Nations.

- The IAEA and EURATOM have established both a regional and a global safeguards system.

- Attempts to negotiate a CTBT and a fissile material cut-off have gained new impetus since 1995 although these measures have been a perennial feature of negotiation since the 1950s.

A number of NWFZs have been negotiated, beginning with the Antarctic Treaty in 1959.

- The NPT has become the cornerstone of the global nuclear non-proliferation regime.

- Both positive and negative security assurances have been agreed but these have proven inadequate for many NNWS party to the NPT.

- Since 1987, the MTCR has been operating as an export control agreement among suppliers to constrain the proliferation of missile technology although many analysts now suggest that new measures are required in this area.

- In 1995, the NPT was extended indefinitely and review conferences have been held every five years since 1970, the latest being the Sixth Conference in April–May 2000.

- Since 1995, the global nuclear non-proliferation regime has encountered several new challenges related to new incidences of nuclear testing, attempts to achieve universality of the Treaty, disposal of fissile material, compliance and verification, and nuclear disarmament.

- It has been suggested that a 'second nuclear age' has emerged and this could raise new risks for nuclear proliferation in the future.

Conclusion

Since 1945, both the nature and the context of nuclear proliferation have altered markedly. At the end of the Second World War only the United States was in a position to build a nuclear weapon. Since then, knowledge of how to make nuclear weapons has diffused more widely. This has been coupled, throughout this period, by profound changes to global politics and epitomized by the momentous dislocation that occurred in the former Soviet Union following the end of the cold war.

As a result of these developments, nuclear proliferation has become a major issue on the global agenda. Yet, understanding the dimensions and complexity of this issue will represent a major challenge in the years ahead. However, in the 1990s greater theoretical attention has been paid to nuclear proliferation and non-proliferation, and insights from several areas have sought to add pieces to the 'puzzle'. Similarly, while aspects of traditional analyses of nuclear proliferation continue to have resonance, determining nuclear motivations, capabilities, and intentions is not straightforward. This is therefore an issue that is likely to receive increasing attention in the years ahead.

What can be done to reduce the dangers stemming from nuclear proliferation? Some analysts argue that the spread of nuclear weapons cannot be prevented so the most appropriate way forward is to try to manage the diffusion of nuclear capabilities to additional states so that stabilizing deterrent relationships can evolve. One feature of this strategy is that it assumes the process can be managed in all situations without breakdown and that the deterrent relationship will ultimately produce stability. The alternative view of nuclear spread suggests that this assumption is questionable.

Another strategy that evolved during the 1990s for dealing with nuclear proliferation is that of collective defence, or counter-proliferation as it is known. This strategy emphasizes the use of defensive measures for dealing with potential nuclear threats, which may in the future include ballistic missile defences. However, although it is prudent to consider the defensive measures that may be necessary for coping with nuclear proliferation, this strategy has its limitations and could represent only a partial remedy. A more comprehensive approach for dealing with the issue over the longer term would be to strengthen further the global nuclear non-proliferation regime. Today, this regime embodies measures aimed at the non-acquisition, the non-use, and eventual elimination of nuclear weapons globally. But for the latter to become a realizable goal, it is likely to require: attempts to resolve disputes and

Box 19.6 Chronology

1945   The United States detonates its, and the world's, first nuclear weapon

1946/7   The United States and the Soviet Union submit plans for the international control of atomic energy to the newly formed United Nations Atomic Energy Commission (UNAEC)

1949   The Soviet Union tests its first nuclear weapon

1952   The United Kingdom tests its first nuclear weapon

1953   President Eisenhower of the United States introduces his 'Atoms for Peace' proposal to the United Nations General Assembly

1957   The International Atomic Energy Agency (IAEA) was inaugurated

1958   The European Atomic Energy Community (EURATOM) begins its operation within the European Community

1960   France becomes the fourth state to test a nuclear weapon

1961   The United Nations General Assembly adopts the 'Irish Resolution' calling for measures to limit the spread of nuclear weapons to additional states

1963   The Partial Test Ban Treaty (PTBT) entered into force

1964   China becomes the fifth state to test a nuclear weapon

1967   The Treaty for the Prohibition of Nuclear Weapons in Latin America ('The Tlatelolco Treaty') was opened for signature

1968   The Treaty on the Non-Proliferation of Nuclear Weapons ('The NPT') was opened for signature

1969   The Tlatelolco Treaty entered into force

1970   The NPT entered into force

1971   The IAEA concludes the INFCIRC (Information Circular)/153 Safeguards Agreement and the Zangger Committee also

adopted a set of nuclear export guidelines pursuant to the NPT

1972   The Anti-Ballistic Missile (ABM) Treaty is signed between the United States and former Soviet Union

1974   India detonates a nuclear explosive device declared to be for peaceful purposes and the Nuclear Suppliers Group (NSG) is formed

1975   The First Review Conference of the NPT is held in Geneva, and by the end of the year 97 states had become party to the Treaty

1978   The First United Nations Special Session on Disarmament (UNSSOD–1) provides the forum for the five Nuclear Weapon States to issue unilateral statements on negative security assurances

1980   The Second NPT Review Conference is held in Geneva

1983   The United States announces its Strategic Defence Initiative (SDI)

1985   The Third NPT Review Conference is held in Geneva

1987   The Missile Technology Control Regime (MTCR) is established

1990   The Fourth NPT Review Conference is held in Geneva

1991   A United Nations Special Committee (UNSCOM) is established to oversee the dismantling of Iraq's undeclared nuclear weapon programme. The United States announces its Safety, Security, Dismantlement (SSD) Programme following the dissolution of the Soviet Union

1993   South Africa announces that it had produced six nuclear devices up until 1989 and then dismantled them prior to signing the NPT. The Democratic People's Republic of Korea announced its intention to withdraw from the NPT following allegations concerning its nuclear programme

---

Box 19.6 continued

1995	The Review and Extension Conference of the NPT is held in New York and the then 179 parties to the Treaty decide to extend the NPT indefinitely and also establish a new Treaty Review Process and a set of principles and objectives for non-proliferation and disarmament
1996	The Comprehensive Test Ban Treaty (CTBT) is opened for signature
1997	The first Preparatory Committee (PrepCom) for the new NPT Treaty Review process convenes in Geneva
1998	India and Pakistan conduct a series of nuclear and missile tests
1999	The United States announces its National Missile Defense (NMD) Act
2000	The Sixth NPT Review Conference is held in New York for the now 188 parties to the Treaty. The 5 NWS make an unequivocal undertaking 'to accomplish the total elimination of their nuclear arsenals'

---

build confidence at the bilateral and regional levels; the strengthening of international norms in this area; innovation in areas such as compliance, verification and fissile material disposal; the involvement of non-parties to the NPT; and continuing commitment by all parties to the Treaty to its objectives.

QUESTIONS

1 What properties make nuclear weapons different from conventional forms?

2 What are the implications of the global diffusion of nuclear and long-range delivery vehicle technology?

3 What role have norms, taboos, and epistemic communities played in the context of nuclear proliferation?

4 How have the motivations for acquiring nuclear weapons changed since 1945?

5 In what ways has it become more difficult to determine whether nuclear proliferation has actually occurred?

6 Does the non-state actor represent a new nuclear proliferation challenge?

7 What nuclear proliferation concerns have stemmed from the dissolution of the Soviet Union?

8 What are the main arguments for and against the proliferation/spread of nuclear weapons?

9 Were the early efforts to control nuclear weapons doomed to failure?

10 In what ways, if any, has the NPT made a contribution to preventing the proliferation of nuclear weapons?

GUIDE TO FURTHER READING

Theoretical aspects

Adler, Emmanuel, 'The Emergence of Cooperation: National Epistemic Communities and the International Evolution of the Idea of Nuclear Arms Control', *International Organization*, 50(1) (Winter 1996) 101–45.

Buzan, Barry, and Herring, Eric, *The Arms Dynamic in World Politics* (London: Lynne Rienner, 1998).

Davis, Zachary S., and Frankel, Benjamin (eds.), *The Proliferation Puzzle: Why Nuclear Weapons Spread and What Results* (London: Frank Cass, 1993).

Feaver, Peter D., 'Proliferation Optimism and Theories of Nuclear Operations', *Security Studies*, 2(3–4) (Spring/Summer 1993): 159–91.

Krause, Keith (ed.), *Culture and Security: Multilateral Arms Control and Security Building* (London: Frank Cass, 1999).

Lavoy, Peter, 'The Strategic Consequences of Nuclear Proliferation. A Review Essay', *Security Studies*, 4(4) (Summer 1995): 695–753.

Meyer, Stephen M., *The Dynamics of Nuclear Proliferation* (Chicago: University of Chicago Press, 1984).

Ogilvie-White, Tanya, 'Is There A Theory of Nuclear Proliferation?', *The Nonproliferation Review*, 4(1) (Fall 1996): 43–60.

Sagan, Scott D., and Waltz, Kenneth N., *The Spread of Nuclear Weapons. A Debate* (New York and London: Norton & Co., 1995).

Sagan, Scott D., 'Three Theories in Search of a Bomb', *International Security*, 21(3) (Winter 1996–97): 54–86.

On nuclear use and non-use

Gaddis, John Lewis, 'The Origins of Self-Deterrence: The United States and the Non-Use of Nuclear Weapons, 1945–1958', in John Lewis Gaddis, *The Long Peace: Inquiries into the History of the Cold War* (New York: Oxford University Press, 1987), 115–23.

Herring, Eric (ed.), *Preventing the Use of Weapons of Mass Destruction* (special issue), *Journal of Strategic Studies*, 23(1) (March 2000).

Lavoy, Peter, Sagan, Scott D., Wirtz, James J. (eds.), *Planning the Unthinkable: How New Powers Will Use Nuclear, Biological and Chemical Weapons*, (Ithaca, NY: Cornell University Press, 2000).

Paul, T. V., 'Nuclear Taboo and War Initiation in Regional Conflicts', *Journal of Conflict Resolution*, 39(4) (Dec. 1995): 696–718.

Price, Richard, and Tannenwald, Nina, 'Norms and Deterrence: The Nuclear and Chemical Weapons Taboos', in Peter J. Katzenstein (ed.), *The Culture of National Security: Norms and Identity in World Politics* (New York: Columbia University Press, 1996), 114–52.

Tannenwald, Nina, 'The Nuclear Taboo: The United States and the Normative Basis of Nuclear Non-Use', *International Organization*, 53(3) (Summer 1999) 433–68.

Nuclear proliferation after the cold war

Allison, Graham, Carter, Ashton B., Miller, Steven E., and Zelikow, Phillip (eds.), 'Cooperative Denuclearisation', *CSIA Studies in International Security*, no. 2 (Cambridge, Mass.: Harvard University Press, 1993).

Mearsheimer, John, 'Back to the Future: Instability in Europe After the Cold War', *International Security*, 15(1) (Summer 1990): 5 56.

Muller, Harald, 'Neither Hype Nor Complacency: WMD Proliferation after the Cold War', *The Nonproliferation Review*, 4(2) (Winter 1997): 62–71.

Ballistic missile proliferation and control issues

Bowen, Wyn, *The Politics of Ballistic Missile Nonproliferation* (London: Macmillan, 2000).

Karp, Aaron, *Ballistic Missile Proliferation: The Politics and Technics* (Oxford: Oxford University Press for SIPRI, 1996).

Karp, Aaron, 'The Spread of Ballistic Missiles and the Transformation of Global Security', *The Nonproliferation Review*, 7(3) (Fall-Winter 2000: 106–122.

Moltz, James C., 'The Impact of National Missile Defense on Nonproliferation Regimes', *The Nonproliferation Review*, 7(3) (Fall-Winter 2000): 61–74.

Historical context and background

Brodie, Bernard (ed.), *The Absolute Weapon: Atomic Power and World Order* (New York: 1946).

Bull, Hedley, *The Control of the Arms Race. Disarmament and Arms Control in the Missile Age* (London: International Institute for Strategic Studies, 1st edn. 1961).

Walker, William, 'Nuclear Order and Disorder', *International Affairs*, 76(4) 2000: 703–24.

Country case studies

Cohen, Avner, *Israel and the Bomb* (New York: Columbia University Press, 1998).

Frankel, Benjamin (ed.), *Opaque Nuclear Proliferation* (London: Frank Cass & Co., 1991).

Jones, Rodney W., and McDonough, Mark, with Dalton, T. and Koblentz, G. D., *Tracking Nuclear Proliferation 1998* (Washington, DC: Carnegie Endowment for International Peace, 1998).

Perkovitch, George, *India's Nuclear Bomb: The Impact on Global Proliferation* (Berkeley, Calif.: University of California Press, 1999).

Reiss, Mitchell, *Bridled Ambition—Why Countries Constrain their Nuclear Capabilities* (Washington, DC: Woodrow Wilson Center, 1995).

Long, William J., and Grillot, Suzette R., 'Ideas, Beliefs, and Nuclear Policies: The Cases of South Africa and Ukraine', *The Nonproliferation Review* (Spring 2000), 24–9.

Nuclear non-proliferation regime

Fischer, David A. V., *Stopping the Spread of Nuclear Weapons: The Past and the Prospects* (New York and London: Routledge, 1992).

Gardner, Gary T., *Nuclear Nonproliferation. A Primer* (London and Boulder, Colo.: Lynne Rienner, 1994).

Roberts, Brad, 'From Nonproliferation to Antiproliferation', *International Security*, 35(2) (Summer 1993): 3–30.

Scheinman, Lawrence, *The International Atomic Energy Agency and World Nuclear Order* (Washington, DC: Johns Hopkins University Press, 1987).

Schneider, Barry R., and Dowdy, William L. (eds.), *Pulling Back From The Nuclear Brink* (London: Frank Cass, 1998).

Shaker, Mohamed I., *The Nuclear Non-Proliferation Treaty*, vols. 1 and 2 (London: Oceana, 1980).

Simpson, John, and Howlett, Darryl (eds.), *The Future of the Non-Proliferation Treaty* (New York: St Martin's Press, 1995).

Spector, Leonard S., 'Neo-Nonproliferation', *Survival*, 37(1) (Spring 1995): 66–85.

Nuclear weapons technology

Grace, Charles S., *Nuclear Weapons: Principles, Effects and Survivability* (London: Brassey's, 1994).

Nuclear technology and trade

Potter, William C. (ed.), *International Nuclear Trade and Nonproliferation: The Challenge of the Emerging Suppliers* (Lexington Books, 1990).

Walker, William, and Lönnróth, Mans, *Nuclear Power Struggles: Industrial Competition and Proliferation Control* (London: Allen and Unwin, 1983).

Alternative nuclear futures

Baylis, John and O'Neill, Robert (eds.), *Alternative Nuclear Futures* (Oxford: Oxford University Press, 2000).

Gray, Colin S., 'The Second Nuclear Age: Insecurity, Proliferation, and the Control of Arms', in Williamson Murrey (ed.), *The Brassey's Mershon American Defense Annual, 1995–1996: The United States and the Emerging Strategic Environment*, (Washington, DC: Brassey's [US], 1995), 135–54.

Gray, Colin S., *The Second Nuclear Age* (Boulder, Colo. and London: Lynne Rienner, 1999).

Mazarr, Michael (ed.), *Nuclear Weapons in a Transformed World: The Challenge of Virtual Nuclear Arsenals* (London: Macmillan, 1997).

Rotblat, Joseph (ed.), *Nuclear Weapons: The Road to Zero* (Boulder, Colo.: Westview, 1998).

20 Nationalism

Fred Halliday

READER'S GUIDE

Nationalism, as a system of belief, an ideology, and as a political movement has been one of the formative processes in the creation of the contemporary world. It remains central to the process of globalization. As an ideology it provides a set of ideas about the organization of humanity into communities, about the appropriate political form for organizing these, and about how relations between states representing nations should be conducted. Nationalism has occasioned many disputes in social science in general, and in international relations in particular: some of these concern the explanation of why nationalism became such a worldwide phenomenon, others concern the difficulties of reconciling nationalist claims with the requirements of international order. Often regarded as a thing of the past, nationalism has been both resistant to, and in some ways promoted by, processes of globalization—migration, free trade, cultural transnationalism. It has also been a major source of conflict in the post-cold war era. The ultimate paradox of nationalism is that while, as an ideology, it stresses the distinct character of states and peoples, it is itself a result of a global process whereby all countries are incorporated into a single political and normative system.

Nationalism and globalization

Nationalism, as both ideology and social movement, has been one of the formative processes of the modern world. Yet until relatively recently, the topic of nationalism was not covered in most introductions to international relations. Nationalism was seen as a thing of the past, a cause of wars in Europe up to 1945, a relic of colonialism in the Third World, an irrational if necessary feature of international relations. It had been left behind as a result of the establishment of international peace between the great powers and the independence of former colonial countries. It was generally assumed that states would resort less and less to nationalism in dealings with each other and would, instead, use the new institutions of international order, be they the UN or the European Union, to promote greater co-operation. Globalization, seen as a form of closer integration of states and societies, was expected to further this process: differences mattered less between states, populations became more open to co-operation and trade, and even identities and loyalties, hitherto based on the nation state, were being affected. Indeed nothing could be seen as more contrary to the spirit of globalization than nationalism.

This approach is now no longer tenable, and there are many who would argue a contrary case. Nationalism, in both the developed and developing worlds, has been very much in evidence, be this in the demands of peoples for secession or greater autonomy within states, or in protests about migration and free trade. In relations between established states nationalism is invoked as a basis for disputes about economic advantage. In some earlier periods, the emphasis in domestic and international politics was on convergence, on universalization, even the creation of a single world community. There is now much more stress on the importance of what distinguishes people—on tradition, identity, authenticity, the politics of difference. In the post-communist world, the fall of authoritarian states has led to secession and ethnic conflict.

The implications of this for globalization are many. In the first place, it is clear that globalization sets in train different, often contradictory, processes.

By creating a world market and flows of goods, technology, and people between states it also provokes responses, and resistance, by those who feel their interests are threatened. This is as true in developed countries, for example in hostility to migration or free trade, as in Third World countries who feel they are being overwhelmed by the developed world. Nationalism can therefore, in the first instance, be seen as a *reaction against* globalization. But in another sense nationalism is also a *product of* globalization. On the one hand, the upsurge in nationalism of the 1980s and 1990s reflects the failure of other forms of state-building, above all in the former multi-ethnic countries of the communist world. After the collapse of Soviet communism in 1991 four states disintegrated along national lines—the USSR, Czechoslovakia, Yugoslavia, and Ethiopia. Twenty-two new states came into existence. A central reason for this process was the impact on the hitherto insulated communist world of social and economic pressures from the West. In a world of globalization, peoples began to demand not integration into larger states but **secession**, independence, and access to the world market on their own terms. On the other hand, the collapse of communism also led to another form of nationalist drive, that for **national unification**—evident in Germany, Yemen, China, Korea. The link between globalization and nationalism in the one case is **fragmentation**, through secession, while in the second case it was through unification, through fusion.

The argument on nationalism and globalization can, however, be taken back much further, to the very formation of the modern international system itself. Nationalism, as a doctrine, calls for the establishment of separate states. It invokes the distinct culture and history of peoples. It is, therefore, about how unique peoples are. But the doctrine itself has spread across the world over the past two centuries as a part of an international process: as a result of global changes, old forms of solidarity and loyalty have been broken down and a new idea has been promoted and diffused. This diffusion has itself been promoted by the transformation of the international

---

Box 20.1 Globalization and nationalism: contradictory processes

Factors opposing nationalism:

- shared prosperity
- economic integration
- migration
- travel and tourism
- employment abroad
- global threats
- world-wide communications
- end of belief in economic sovereignty

Factors promoting nationalism:

- loss of control to foreign investors
- hostility to immigration
- fears of unemployment
- resentment at supranational institutions
- dislike of alien cultures
- fears of terrorism and subversion
- hostility to global media
- attractions of secession

---

system: the increasing integration of the world market, the establishment of European colonial empires, the rise of movements of resistance to these empires, the world wars, and the spread of democracy. The paradox is, therefore, that nationalism, the doctrine that proclaims the separateness of peoples, has spread because of, and in reaction against, the international and globalizing trends of the past two hundred years.

This link between nationalism and the modern international system is, however, more than historical. It is also **normative**, that means concerned with values, with ideas of how people **should** live, and to whom they **owe obedience**. Nationalism has, through this spreading across the world, become the main justifying or legitimizing doctrine of the international system itself. Prior to the modern period, states were justified by reference to their rulers, their dynasties, and their religion. The spread of nationalism has removed this justification and produced instead a system in which states are justified on the grounds that **they represent their peoples**. From this we get the modern term '**nation-state**', which implies that all states can, and do, represent a people. We also get the principle of **national self-determination**, according to which every nation has the right to decide on its own fate, to be independent, or, if not, to choose freely to be part of a larger state. This has meant that all the principles of international order, law, legitimacy, derived originally from other bases, are now justified by reference to this principle. Nationalism has become the ethical, moral, basis of international relations so much so that the body grouping the states of the world is called the United Nations.

Key points

- Nationalism was only fully recognized as relevant by International Relations in the past two decades.
- Nationalism is both opposed to globalization and a product of it.
- The spread of nationalism is a result of the transformation of the international system over the past two centuries.
- Nationalism is now the moral basis of states and of the international system.

Nationalism as ideology

Nationalism, like many other terms in social science, such as 'democracy', 'revolution', 'liberalism', or 'socialism', is a broad one, and is used to describe two quite distinct things: a **political doctrine** or **ideology**, i.e. a set of political principles that movements and individuals espouse, and a **social and political movement**, a tendency that has, over the whole globe and for the past two centuries, affected all societies and transformed their politics. It is important, in this as in the other cases, to keep discussion of the two separate.

As an ideology nationalism has, like the other concepts mentioned above, many variants and permits of no easy one-line definition. This is all the more so because, unlike most other political doctrines, nationalism has no clear founding theorist, no classical text which others can refer to, or argue about. It is what philosophers sometimes call a 'cluster-concept' i.e. an idea with several elements usually attached. One of the major analysts of nationalism, Anthony Smith, has provided a clear set of seven themes which comprise the core doctrine, what we can term here 'the cluster', of nationalist ideology. Another writer, Ernest Gellner, has provided a notably succinct definition: 'Nationalism is primarily a political principle, which holds that the political and the national should be congruent' (Gellner 1983: 1). This can be said to mean that nationalism is above all a moral principle, which claims that nations do exist, that they should coincide with, i.e. cover the same people as, political communities and that they should be self-ruling. Nationalism as an ideology is, therefore, above all a moral or normative principle, a belief about how the world is and should be.

One of the claims of nationalism is that individual 'nations' and indeed the very sentiment of nationalism have existed throughout time or for at least hundreds of years. The invocation of history is very central to the whole nationalist view of the world: ideas of the 'ancient', the 'primordial', the 'traditional', the 'age-old' are commonly invoked. But the doctrine itself is of more recent origin, and is a result of changes in the international system during the

> ### Box 20.2 The core themes of nationalist ideology
>
> 1. Humanity is naturally divided into nations.
>
> 2. Each nation has its peculiar character.
>
> 3. The source of all political power is the nation, the whole collectivity.
>
> 4. For freedom and self-realization, men must identify with a nation.
>
> 5. Nations can only be fulfilled in their own states.
>
> 6. Loyalty to the nation-state overrides other loyalties.
>
> 7. The primary condition of global freedom and harmony is the strengthening of the nation-state.
>
> Anthony Smith, *Theories of Nationalism* 2nd edn. (London: Duckworth, 1983), 21.

latter part of the eighteenth and the first part of the nineteenth centuries. The word '**nation**', or equivalent words in other traditions, has existed for many centuries, variously describing what today would be called tribes, peoples, groups of subjects of a monarch, communities. Some idea of **community**, with its own history and identity, and often its own language or religion, has existed in all cultures. However, the contemporary usage of the word 'nation' and its associated doctrine 'nationalism' dates from the eighteenth century. It can be seen as having been created in three, separate but interlinked, phases.

The **first phase** is associated with the thinking of the **Enlightenment** and in particular with the principle of the self-determination of communities, i.e. the idea that a group of people have a certain set of shared interests and should be allowed to express their wishes on how these interests should best be promoted. Derived from the ancient Greek idea of the *polis*, or political community, this idea was most influentially expressed in the thinking of Jean-Jacques Rousseau. Rousseau laid the basis for modern ideas of democracy and the legitimacy of majority rule. Later democratic thinkers, notably John Stuart Mill, added to this with their stress on representative government as being the most desirable form of political system: once the idea of representative government is accepted, as a means of realizing in a collective form the principle of individual self-determination, then it is a short step to the idea of the self-determination of nations (see Ch. 7).

The **second phase** in the evolution of the idea of nationalism came with the French Revolution of 1789: the opponents of the monarch called themselves *la nation*, i.e. 'the nation', meaning by this the community of all French people irrespective of previous title or status. Here the concept 'nation' expressed above all the idea of a shared, common, equal citizenship, the unity of the people. The slogan of the French Revolution, 'Liberty, Equality, Fraternity', embodied this idea: perhaps the most common cry of the revolution was 'Vive la Nation', 'Long Live the Nation'. The concept of 'nation' was, therefore, tied to the principle of **equality** of all those living within states, to an early concept of democracy. This evolution in France was paralleled in the Americas, North and South: in the revolt against British rule in the North (1776–83), and in the later uprising against Spanish rule in the South (1820–8). Here the basis for revolt was political—i.e. rejection of rule from the imperial centres in Europe by a group of people, a settler elite, drawn from similar ethnic and linguistic backgrounds to those they were rejecting, but opposed to the denial of their political rights and of the self-determination of the community they represented.

This democratic and political conception of 'nation' was then joined by its **third**, and final, component, the German romantic idea of the *Volk* or people, a community based not so much on political identity but on history, tradition, and culture. In essence, the idea of the *Volk*, promoted by such thinkers as Herder and Fichte, argued that humanity was divided up into separate peoples whose distinctiveness and identity could be discovered through investigation. Just as scientists were mapping the plants, minerals, and animals of the world, and as linguists were mapping the different languages of the world, so it would be possible to identify the different peoples of the world, each with its own character.

Out of the combination of these three trends there emerged, by the early nineteenth century, the political doctrine we recognize today as nationalism. One of those who most vigorously expressed it was the Italian Giuseppe Mazzini. For Mazzini nations were a given, with their national territory, and should have independence. The Italian case involved the unification of hitherto fragmented entities. But Mazzini also espoused two other elements of what has come to be our modern concept of nationalism. One was the *moral* conception of the nation, according to which each individual not only belongs to a nation, but also owes the nation unquestioning obedience (see Box 20.2, point 6). In this way earlier concepts of loyalty, patriotism, identification with the community became part of the modern state system. The other idea which Mazzini promoted was the idea of a **'family of nations'**: if the world was divided up into nations, then they could, through identification and self-determination, be encouraged to acquire independence. The result would, he expected, be peace between nations, on this new basis. For the French writer Ernest Renan nationalism was 'a daily

---

Box 20.3 Mazzini on nationhood

' . . . the divine design will infallibly be fulfilled. Natural division, the innate spontaneous tendencies of the peoples will replace the arbitrary divisions sanctioned by bad governments. The map of Europe will be remade. The Countries of the People will rise, defined by the voice of the free, upon the ruins of the Countries of Kings and privileged castes. Between these Countries there will be harmony and brotherhood. And then the work of Humanity for the general amelioration, for the discovery and application of the real law of life, carried on in association and distributed according to local capacities, will be accomplished by peaceful and progressive development; then each of you, strong in the affections and in the aid of many millions of men speaking the same language, endowed with the same tendencies, and educated by the same historic tradition, may hope by your personal effort to benefit the whole of Humanity.'

J. Mazzini, *The Duties of Man* (London, 1907), as quoted in Evan Luard, *Basic Texts in International Relations* (London: Macmillan, 1992), 198–9.

plebiscite', a process by which a community, created by history, could constantly reaffirm, by its continued existence, its self-determination and its wishes.

Key points

• Nationalism as ideology is a normative idea; nations exist objectively and should have the right to self-determination.

• The modern idea of nationalism is a combination of (1) Enlightenment and liberal concepts of self-ruling community; (2) the French revolutionary idea of the community of equal citizens; (3) German conceptions of a people formed by history, tradition, and culture.

• Nationalism is both an idea of a history, a tradition, and one of obligation

Nationalism as a movement

From its origins in the late eighteenth century nationalism, evolving into the ideology we recognize today, has spread across the whole world. In the early nineteenth century, Europe saw the emergence of nationalism in Greece, Germany, Italy, and Ireland, and later in the multi-ethnic empires of Central and Eastern Europe—the Austro-Hungarian, Prussian, Russian, and Ottoman empires. Under pressure from within and without these empires gradually ceded to demands for independence until, in the cataclysm of World War I, all four empires foundered and a map of newly independent states was created. In Western Europe a fifth multi-national entity was forced to concede independence to one of its rebellious regions, when the British granted independence to Ireland in 1921.

World War I was the occasion on which the principle of **national self-determination**, hitherto confined to Europe and the white elites of the Americas, was now proclaimed as a universal principle, in radical revolutionary form by the Bolshevik Revolution in Russia (1917) and in liberal form by President Woodrow Wilson of the USA (1918). Prior to World War I many nationalists had argued that their rights could be realized short of secession—through the creation of federal or regional rights within states, or by forms of cultural autonomy: in some countries—Czechoslovakia, Belgium, Switzerland—this remained so. But after World War I self-determination came, increasingly, to be associated with full independence. It seemed that the era of

national self-determination and of the emergence of the 'family of nations' envisioned by Mazzini was at hand. But this was not to be, for three reasons.

In the **first** place, the European colonial powers refused to allow the subject peoples of Asia and Africa to attain independence: it was only after World War II, which weakened the victors as well as destroying the vanquished, that Britain, France, Holland, and Belgium became disposed to granting independence to their Third World colonies, a process that lasted through the 1950s and 1960s. In the **second** place, nationalism, where it did achieve fulfilment, led not to peace between states but to conflict, dictatorship, and in the end world war: if there was a 'family of nations' it was a very quarrelsome and unhappy family indeed. One reason for this was the fact that peoples, in the sense of communities with one language or religion, were often mixed up with each other, or had competing historical claims: there was no simple fit between national and territorial claims. Disputes over territory and communities led in the Balkans and elsewhere to inter-ethnic quarrels that no amount of mediation or redrawing of frontiers could resolve. The independence of Ireland, conceded by Britain but excluding six of the thirty-two counties of the island, led to similar rancour. More explosively still, the nationalism that came to dominate in two European countries, Germany and Italy, was one based on an idea of power aggrandisement, military expansion and, in the case of Germany, forceful revision of frontiers and the genocidal liquidation of Jews. All of this served to underline the dangers, as much as the benefits, of nationalism.

There was, however, a **third** reason for the failure of the 1918 hopes being realized—one that became more evident after World War II. This was that, even in states that were independent and where the issue of national identity and self-determination had supposedly been recognized, new tensions began to develop: there is no finality in the definition and formation of nations. This was at first evident in the developed world, in Western Europe and in the USA, where from the 1960s onwards new demands for national self-determination, or the recognition of ethnic diversity and rights within states, began to emerge: among the Basques in Spain, among the Catholic population in Northern Ireland, in Scotland, in Belgium, in Corsica. In the USA, meanwhile, a massive upsurge of protest, associated first with the issue of civil rights for blacks, and then with growing ethnic awareness amongst a wide range of non-white ethnic communities, began to develop. In Canada the French-speaking population of Quebec began to demand greater autonomy and, in many cases, independence. This revival of national and ethnic politics in Western Europe and North America was, for all its international implications, contained: in no case did states fragment.

The same was not so for the even more explosive development of nationalism in the communist countries of the East. Nationalism, i.e. hostility to Soviet rule and a desire to re-establish links with the pre-communist past, and linked to demands for economic improvement and for democracy, played an important part in the growing opposition to communism in Eastern Europe. It also, however, challenged the USSR itself: the Soviet Union had been created after World War I as a new multi-ethnic state. Once coercive control was relaxed, in 1991, the constituent states broke away to form fifteen independent states: in many cases this independence was carried out under the aegis of the local communist elites, who feared, as much as anything, the democratic trends emerging in Russia itself. The end result was, none the less, the greatest tide of secession and fragmentation of states—in the USSR and elsewhere—ever seen in the history of the modern international system. As we shall see later, even now the issue of nationalism's impact on the international system is far from resolved.

Key points

- Nationalism was evident first in Western Europe and in the Americas.

- After World War I, the collapse of the multi-ethnic empires in Eastern Europe, after World War II the end of the European empires in Asia and Africa.

- Decades of conflict followed the proclamation of self-determination by President Wilson in 1918.

Nationalism and international relations

The consequences of the emergence and spread of this doctrine for international relations are many, both at the level of the impact of nationalism on the international system and at the level of the problems—analytic and ethical—which nationalism poses for the study, and practice, of international relations.

In terms of **consequences**, four major ones can be identified. In the **first** place, nationalism has provided a new set of values, a new system of legitim-ation, for the system of states. Beyond justifications in terms of traditional understandings of sovereignty and its corollary, non-interference, represented in the **Westphalian System**, the states system can now claim to represent the interests of separate, individually legitimate, peoples. Hence the importance of the concept 'nation-state' and the implication, which many contest, that states do indeed represent nations. (The very term 'international' embodies this ambiguity: it was invented in 1780 by Jeremy

Box 20.4 **The UN Charter, article 1, section 2**

'2. To develop friendly relations among nations based on respect for the principle of equal rights and self-determination of peoples, and to take other appropriate measures to strengthen universal peace.'

Bentham, the English utilitarian political theorist, to denote the form of law existing between different Roman tribes. It has since come to mean 'inter-state', with the added implication that this is equivalent to 'inter-nation'.) Self-determination has come to be a universally accepted principle, and the supposed basis of the current international order. Both the Covenant of the League of Nations and the Charter of the United Nations rest on this assumption, and from it is derived the whole system of international law. States may or may not in practice represent their peoples but in the international system of today, in diplomacy and law, they are deemed to do so.

Second, nationalism has served as an important, essential, component of state-building and for the formation of a **common identity and consciousness** within societies. Pre-existing forms of loyalty certainly existed. Throughout history people have asserted that it is an individual's duty to die for his or her community. But the modern state, faced with the movement of large numbers of people into the cities, and with the need to mobilize resources against external competitors and threats, has been particularly keen to promote a sense of national identity and purpose. The means of doing so include education, conscription into national armies, the promoting of national histories, the making of patriotic films. All contribute to giving a people a sense of common identity and of promoting acceptance of the state. As such nationalism serves to consolidate support for elites and the established order. Writers on nationalism often argue that this promotion of nationalism is especially strong in former colonial countries where the very boundaries and identity of the state may be of a recent, externally imposed, character. Promotion of official nationalism undoubtedly has been part of this Third World, state-directed, nation-building. But it is by no means exclusive to the Third World: in developed countries—be it France, the USA, or Britain—the state has also sought to promote a sense of national identity and purpose, through education and the other means available to it. It has become part of the very formation of the link between state and society throughout the world, the indispensable domestic accompaniment of the consolidation of state power internationally. No state can survive and compete in the international arena without the promotion of a sense of national identity and purpose domestically. This top–down sense of identity is often reinforced by factors operating in society—the press, popular attitudes, educational and cultural trends.

Third, nationalism has provided a powerful impetus to the **drawing** and **redrawing** of the international map, i.e. to defining the territories of states and the frontiers between them. In theory this means that the map of the world reflects a pre-existing reality—the distribution of peoples across the globe. The map of states we see on an atlas today is supposed to be of pre-existing peoples, a reality like that of a geological survey or of the physical features of a part of the earth: but this is far from being the case. In practice it reflects where history has, often by accident, led the lines to be drawn—in Europe where armies grew tired of fighting, elsewhere in the world where colonial administrators and soldiers chose to draw them. Even such a settled frontier as that between the USA and Canada, or between Spain and Portugal, reflects haphazard history. However, the norm that the map of states should correspond to that of peoples has continued to push against these inherited frontiers. As already noted in the context of the collapse of communism, this challenge to the map has taken the form both of **fission** and **fusion**. Thus some nationalism has involved movements that aim to break up existing states, through secession or fragmentation of various forms. Other cases have involved the drive to unite parts previously divided: Italian and German unification in the nineteenth century, Irish, Arab, Korean, Somali, and many other nationalisms in the twentieth.

A **fourth** consequence of nationalism for the international system has been that it has been a source of **conflict**, and often of **war**. In the interwar period disputes over territorial division soured the belief that, once accepted, the principle of self-determination would produce peace between peoples. In the more recent past, frontier disputes and disputes where peoples are mixed together in multi-ethnic society have occasioned many conflicts: in the Arab–Israeli context, in former Yugoslavia, Kashmir, Sri Lanka to name but some. Even more catastrophically, nationalism has become a factor, both cause and pretext, in interstate wars, most dramatically of all in the drive of Germany to dominate Europe, and of Japan to dominate East Asia, through a combination of annexation and subjugation, in World War II. From the Nazi and Japanese imperial experiences we have derived the sense of nationalism as a destructive force. This hostility to nationalism is all the greater because, as in the German and Japanese cases, ferocious nationalism abroad is often combined with dictatorial and racist policies at home: nationalism is used by dictatorial regimes to crush dissent at home, even as it is deployed to mobilize support for aggression abroad.

Key points

- Nationalism for the past two centuries has been the moral, normative, basis for the system of states.
- Nationalism both legitimates states and has been promoted by states as part of nation-building.
- Nationalism has been the justification for secession and territorial claims.
- Nationalism closely relates to the incidence of war.

Four debates

The topic of nationalism is one that, at least as much as that of any other powerful ideological force, has provoked widespread controversy, in public political debate but also in the social sciences. The fact that, for many decades, only historians discussed it indicates that it presents difficulties: the lack of clear ideological definition, the apparent irrationality, the very denial of universal rational categories which it implies have all contributed to this. An important part of the difficulty has, however, been the controversy it has provoked within social science in general. Much of the debate about nationalism has taken place not in International Relations but in another social science, Sociology. But the sociological debates, and others in political theory, have important implications for International Relations and have affected or underlay much of the discussion about the subject. Here we shall look at four of these debates.

1. Justice versus order

The international system has rested on two principles—the sovereignty of states and the maintenance of peace between them. It has often been assumed that national self-determination and the expression of legitimate nationalist demands are compatible with these general principles. Often they are, and when disputes occur then there are mechanisms—arbitration, plebiscites, negotiated compromises—for securing peaceful and binding agreement. But one does not have to look far in the history of the international system over the past two centuries to see that there often is a conflict, and one that has led to conflict and injustice. In the first place, the principles of **balance of power** politics often conflict with those of self-determination: the maintenance of peace between great powers may involve carving out **spheres of influence** or agreeing to each having colonies. In the 1790s, for example, Russia and Prussia partitioned Poland, before that an independent kingdom, between them as part of the maintenance of the balance of power. In the late nineteenth and early twentieth centuries European states agreed to the creation of **colonies** and **spheres of influence** in Asia and Africa. During the cold war, and after, the Western world permitted Russia to exercise domination over peoples within Eastern Europe and within the USSR or Russia itself in order not to compromise broader considerations of stability and security. (To take two obvious examples: the Hungarian uprising of 1956, the Chechen rising of 1994 onwards. In both cases there was no Western official reaction to obvious denials of the right of peoples to self-determination.) In other parts of the world undoubtedly legitimate claims to independence have been ignored for reasons of regional security: from 1961, when war there began, the African states refused, until 1991, when it was a *fait accompli*, to recognize the right of Eritrea to independence from Ethiopia: equally no state in the world is prepared to grant the right of the over 20 million Kurds resident in Iran, Turkey, and Iraq to a separate state. When the communist system collapsed the international community was prepared to welcome the newly seceded states and recognize their independence: but this was done reluctantly, and the general consensus was that the process had to end as quickly as possible. No wonder that a meeting at the Royal Institute of International Affairs in London, in June 1993, the then British Foreign Secretary Douglas Hurd declared: 'I hope we do not see the creation of any more nation-states.'

Uncertainty on this issue underlay the confusion of Western policy-making on former Yugoslavia in the early 1990s: it was not clear how much support should be given for self-determination nor where this support should stop. But this case also raised another, related, problem. If one community was entitled to secede, then the issue of secession for minorities within that community's territory also arose: this concerned the Serbs of Bosnia and Croatia, but it is also posed in Northern Ireland, for Russians living in the Ukraine, for Arabs in Israel, as it was, earlier, for Germans living outside Hitler's Reich. No one can argue that every community in the world with a legitimate claim to its own identity should have its own state. There are, for example, up to ten thousand languages yet no one envisages ten thousand states. Even peoples of the same language can have separate states—as speakers of Arabic, Spanish, English, French, German, Malay, Persian do. The question is where to draw the line: for this, some **balance of justice and order** has to be found. The right to self-determination, conceived of as the right and need of peoples of one community to have an independent, single, state has always had to be set against other principles of international relations.

2. History versus modernity

Nationalism rests upon a claim of historical continuity—this people has existed for centuries, going back to some founding moment, real or imagined, or to the mists of time. The attainment of national independence and of statehood is the culmination of this history. Hence the use of words like 'reawakening' and 'rebirth', the interest in archaeology and ancestors. Claims derived from history are also used to settle arguments within a community about what is, or is not, 'authentic' and, with great consequences for international relations, what the historic, natural, sometimes 'God-given' extent of the national territory is. When people want to deny the legitimacy of another nation's claims it is common to claim that they are 'not really' a nation, or have not existed for long, or if they have then they existed somewhere else, or were, and may still be, agents of foreign powers. History in such a context is everything.

This approach to nationalism is the one common to all nationalist movements. It has been termed the **perennialist** approach. By contrast many social scientists adopted the view that nations are (*a*) arbitrary and (*b*) recent creations. This is generally held to be the **modernist** approach. In this view today's map of nations could have been very different from what it is, and reflects arbitrary and recent processes—the

---

Box 20.5 **A limit on self-determination**

'I hope we do not see the creation of any more nation-states.'

(Douglas Hurd, British Foreign Secretary, Royal Institute of International Affairs, London, June 1993)

drawing of colonial boundaries, accidents of war, the triumph of particular political groups claiming to represent peoples they then set about creating. Nationalism is not the working out of some historical destiny: it is a response to the breakdown of old forms of community, based on religion, dynastic rule, and rural life, and a way of giving the inhabitants of modern cities a sense of meaning and purpose. It creates a new sense of belonging—hence the term **imagined community**, coined by Benedict Anderson, to convey the idea of a group of people one knows one is part of, but all of whose members one can never meet. The past—tradition, history, language, folklore—is not what determines the present but is, rather, used to provide material, is used as a reserve, by political and intellectual leaders. Where the past is lacking, traditions are invented. There is not necessarily anything wrong with this, and, beyond its many benefits, nationalism may be unavoidable: but this **contingency** needs to be recognized. In the words of one modernist 'it is the magic of nationalism to turn chance into destiny' (Anderson 1992: 19).

In between these two positions there are other less extreme approaches. Some theorists argue that while nations and nationalism in the contemporary political sense are recent creations, they rest upon earlier cultural, linguistic, and political roots that mean they are more than just contingent creations. Thus, without accepting the perennialist case, it is possible to write a history of, say, the English, Russian, Chinese, Egyptian, or Italian peoples. This is the position of the well-known writer Anthony Smith, who focuses on symbolism (A. Smith 1991). Smith has, in particular, argued for the use of the concept *ethnie*, based on a French term for an ethnic group, to denote the communities which, in a pre-nationalist age, still form the basis for modern nations. Some writers have taken this approach to distinguish between different kinds of nations, those with a longer history derived from an ethnic basis— obvious candidates would be the Chinese or the Germans—and those which are more recent creations, a product of the European colonial system— the USA, Australia, and many countries in Latin America and Africa would be candidates. Here a distinction can be made between **ethnic** and **political** nationalisms, or 'historic' and 'newly created' forms, i.e. between cases where the state and its associated nationalism came to represent an already existing community, and ones where it was the state itself that created the nationalism and forged a sense of solidarity amongst the people. There may be some truth in such a distinction, but it may also understate the degree to which all states have promoted and to a considerable degree created modern nationalism: such states as the British, the French, the German, the Japanese have devoted considerable energy to instilling a particular sense of identity, history, language into their peoples and to tidying up what had hitherto been a much less packaged sense of national tradition.

3. Positive and negative

In discussions of the role of nationalism in international relations it has been common to counterpoise what are the positive, desirable functions of nationalism from those that are deemed to be negative and undesirable. On the positive side four arguments at least can be made. **First**, nationalism does provide a **principle of legitimacy** that underpins the modern state system. It suggests that states can, and should, represent their peoples and hence that they derive legitimacy from them: the Rousseau–Mill theme of representative government finds its international fulfilment in this way. **Second**, nationalism is a **realization of democratic principles**: nationalism is the means by which the Enlightenment principles of representative government should be realised in the international arena. **Third**, nationalism serves a very important **psychological function**: it provides a sense of belonging, of where one is coming from, of a past and a future, and of what the appropriate forms of cultural expression should be. Everyone has such needs and without them there would be chaos and despair: it is nationalism which answers those needs in modern conditions. **Fourth**, nationalism has been and remains one of the great sources of **human creativity and diversity**—the explosion of nationalism has had enormous consequences for art, literature, music, language, sport, and much else besides, not least gastronomy. It has enriched not only the individual peoples it has affected but the whole of humanity: the world would

---

Box 20.6 National symbols

(1) General

- Language
- Food and drink
- Clothing
- Commemorative holidays
- Military heroes
- Flags, colours, and anthems
- Terms of abuse for non-nationals

(2) 'Invented' traditions in the British Isles

- Christmas
- Morris dancing
- The kilt
- The shamrock
- The leek
- The ploughman's lunch

---

be a greyer, more boring, place without it. The explosion of multiculturalism, of cultural expression by ethnic groups living in larger communities, is the latest example of this.

There are also several powerful arguments on the negative side. The **first** is that nationalism is a cause of conflict, and war. By making unreconcilable claims to territory, and by raising the emotional temperature of national and international politics, nationalism has become the curse of the modern age, responsible for world wars, ethnic massacres, genocide, and unending low-level crises across the world. Nationalism may present itself as a reasonable, legitimate ideology but it very soon lapses into other forms of political thinking—**xenophobia**, hatred of foreigners, **chauvinism**, an aggressive approach to foreigners and foreign countries, **militarism**, the use of force to resolve problems, and **imperialism**, the desire to create empires that subject other peoples. **Second**, nationalism, even when it avoids military confrontation, may serve as an **obstacle to co-operation** on international issues—be this trade, migration, the environment, or any other issue in contemporary international politics. The world needs greater international co-operation and recognition not of separate, competing, national concerns but of common, global, interests: if this was always so it is all the more so in an era of potential nuclear proliferation or ecological challenge. **Third**, nationalism by promoting the **break-up of states** destroys viable political and economic units. Nothing is served by the fragmentation of larger

states: problems of political equity and resource allocation arise in any society but can be solved in other ways than by secession. **Fourth**, nationalism is undesirable on domestic grounds: it creates a climate within states of **intolerance and dictatorship**. This may take the form of a particular ruler using nationalism and arguments of security to justify their own holding of power. It may also involve the use of nationalism by one, majority group, to oppress, expel or in extreme cases exterminate those not considered part of that majority. Such a climate makes international pressure on human rights grounds all the easier to resist: states violating the rights of their peoples resort to standard defences—that all criticism is a form of interference in the nation's life, that critics are enemies of the nation, that the values of the critics are those of another nation. On the cultural level, nationalism provokes a smallmindedness, a mean, inward-looking, approach that is inimical to cultural exchange and which denies the rich interaction that has always characterized culture, religion, and language in the modern world. As long as there has been nationalism there has been criticism of it, by those who see and experience it as a tool of domination *within* societies.

4. Objects of primary loyalty

The moral claim underlying nationalism is one that raises issues central to political theory, but it is one that is also raised by the whole process of globalization. This is the claim that the individual, by dint of birth or subsequently acquired citizenship, owes loyalty first and foremost to the nation, and, in most circumstances, the nation as represented by the state. This is the basis upon which order within states and the legitimacy of the international states system has existed for the past two centuries or so.

The arguments for this claim are, as also noted, strong ones, but they are an answer to a question that allows, not least in an era of globalization, of other answers. In effect, an individual has *three* possible objects onto which to attach his or her primary loyalty: the nation-state, some community that is larger than or goes beyond the state (religion, the working class, humanity as a whole, Europe), or a grouping that is smaller than, contained within, the state (the family, tribe, local community, business enterprise). The choice as to which of these one owes primary loyalty is not a new one: prior to the rise of nationalism the choice was usually for some combination of the religious and the local or family unit. Many modern political or social movements—Communism, Catholicism, radical Islam, Feminism, Freemasonry, the Mafia—call on their supporters to have loyalty to something beyond the state. In some cases the decision to declare loyalty to one, minority or oppressed, nation means one rejects loyalty to a broader state-centred nation: this would be the case for a person of Scottish or Welsh nationalist orientation in Britain, or for someone belonging to any of the many ethnic groups in the USA. Many individuals have chosen to adhere primarily to one of the sub-groups. The writer E. M. Forster once said he would prefer to betray his country than betray a friend. Feminist writers have criticized the way in which the nation, defined and controlled by men, and used for the advantage of men, has served to oppress women. Virginia Woolf declared: 'As a woman I have no country.'

Such choices, as between the three possible categories of objects of loyalty, need not be absolute: most individuals owe some form of loyalty to all three and seek, usually without too much problem, in combining them. But the tension is always there, and in an era of globalization, when both broader international loyalties are invoked, and when the

---

Box 20.7 **Critics of nationalism**

Communist

'The working men have no country. We cannot take from them what they have not got . . . National differences, and antagonisms between peoples, are daily more and more vanishing, owing to the development of the bourgeoisie, to freedom of commerce, to the world market, to uniformity in the mode of production and in the conditions of life corresponding thereto.'

(Karl Marx and Friedrich Engels, *Manifesto of the Communist Party* in Karl Marx, *The Revolutions of 1848* (London: Penguin Books in association with *New Left Review*, 1973), 84–5)

Feminist

'Therefore you insist upon fighting to gratify a sex instinct which I cannot share; to procure benefits which I have not shared and probably will not share; but not to gratify my instincts, or to protect either myself or my country. "For", the outsider will say, "in fact, as a woman I have no country. As a woman I want no country. As a woman my country is the whole world." '

(Virginia Woolf, *A Room of One's Own. Three Guineas* (Oxford: Oxford University Press, 1992), 313).

---

weakening of the state in some areas of life allows of more local, small-scale, centres of legitimacy, the question is more present than is always the case: such processes as European integration, the growth of worldwide 'youth' and consumerist cultures, or employment in multinational enterprises may create complex shifts in loyalty. As with the other issues in debate concerning nationalism, however, there is no easy or quick answer to this question.

Key points

- Nationalism both underpins and challenges the security of states.

- Nationalism can be thought of as the fulfilment of a long historical development of peoples, or as a recent, modern, response to social change.

- There are strong arguments as to the benefits of

nationalism to the international system, and also as to the harm it causes relations between states.

• Nationalism is one among several answers to the question of loyalty and identity.

The effects of globalization: towards a post-nationalist age?

Nationalism is part of, not an alternative to, the increasing integration of the globe. Since the emergence of nationalism in the early nineteenth century, there have been those who have predicted, and wished, that it would decline, and be swept away in the tide of international processes that go beyond states and separate nations. Nineteenth-century liberals and communists believed the creation of the world market would sweep away differences between states. After World War I it was hoped that international law, the spread of democracy and the very triumph of self-determination could eliminate national conflict. Since the 1970s, first in the literature on **interdependence** and then in that on **globalization**, it has been argued that we are moving towards a more unified and cosmopolitan world, where national differences, and the nation state, will be less influential and less necessary.

Nationalism remains an enduring part of international relations, yet for all the persistence of nationalism and of problems associated with it, it can, in certain respects, be argued that there is nonetheless a changed situation as far as nationalism is concerned. We are not simply seeing a recurrence of the pattern of national conflict that has marked the world for the past two centuries. In the **first** place, and despite all the 'new' nationalisms that have arisen and will do so, the classical justification for nationalism and for demands for independence, namely rule by an alien, colonial, power has almost entirely gone. The collapse of the USSR and the other multi-ethnic communist states has ended that chapter of human history. So when claims for independence are made it will in the future be much harder for aspirant nationalisms to demand international recognition. There is the further constraint that following the end of European colonial rule and the

fragmentation of the communist world the international system has, with close on two hundred sovereign states, decided that that is basically enough: this is not based on considerations of justice, but rather on a tired, but widespread, belief that the world now has enough states and that adding large numbers of other ones will create disorder, overload and indecision. The argument of Mazzini and Woodrow Wilson has now been turned on its head: the general belief is that the creation of more states will promote disorder, and disharmony, rather than promote it. Taking Mazzini's metaphor, we can say that more children will make the family less, not more, happy.

Second, for all the nationalism evident in such states as the UK, USA, or Japan, the fate of relations between major powers depends to a considerable degree on the continuance of democracy: the argument that democratic states do not go to war with each other is a strong one, and would entail that, whatever their differences, including over economic ones, the major developed countries of the OECD will avoid war, and hence the worst consequences of nationalism (see Ch. 12). **Third**, we should not assume that the content, the political programme, of nationalism remains the same. While the 1980s and 1990s have seen a flowering of nationalisms of many kinds, not least in the former communist world, there is one respect in which the nationalist agenda has changed: as Eric Hobsbawm has argued, the old belief that national interest and greatness could be served by the promotion of a self-contained, 'national', economy has been substantially eroded to be replaced by another, also nationalist, idea, that separate statehood can provide the best means of negotiating a favourable position in the international market-place (Hobsbawm 1990).

Finally we come to the argument that is intrinsic to globalization itself, namely that the spread of links between societies—in trade, migration, tourism, communications—will erode national identities just as the growth of instruments and institutions of international and global governance, together with the globalization of markets, will erode the power of states. It is not necessary to adopt the most extreme variants of the globalization thesis, or to envisage or welcome the disappearance of the nation-state, to see that there could be some truth in this cosmopolitan argument (see Ch. 29). The counter-arguments have already been made: that integration produces a fragmenting counter-reaction, that much of what passes for globalization is the imposition of one country's values and interests on others. The process of globalization will, therefore, always be accompanied by centrifugal and separating trends as it has been throughout the history of the international system. As with nationalism, the very means and ideas of that separation may well be promoted by the international system itself. There may well, however, also be movement in the international direction, always capable of being undone, but nevertheless substantial: be this in European integration, or international co-operation to prevent and contain war, or in the growth of a cosmopolitan awareness and culture among younger generations. Nationalism in all its forms will in all probability remain part of the life of each people, and of the international system, yet as it is resisting and opposing the development of that system it is also being constrained and shaped by it. Nationalism is not an alternative to globalization, but an intrinsic part of it.

Key points

- Nationalism remains an important part of relations between states and also of the domestic politics of many countries.

- Expectations of a disappearance of nationalism, made over the past century and a half, were mistaken.

- Nationalism is a response to the new international context: in part benefiting from resentment at globalization, in part adjusting those parts of its programme that are no longer so relevant.

QUESTIONS

1   Why should students of international relations pay attention to nationalism?

2   What accounts for the spread of nationalism across the globe in the past two centuries?

3   Can nationalism be defined?

4   What have been the consequences for the international states system of the rise of nationalism?

5   Is nationalism a 'good thing'?

6   What has been the function of nationalism in the development of the modern state?

7   'Nations have always existed.' Discuss.

8   To what extent can the main theories of international relations provide an explanation for nationalism?

9   How has the international system dealt with demands for secession?

10   Can the world do without nationalism?

11   What is the relation of nationalism to the study of international political economy?

12   What are the implications for nationalism of globalization?

GUIDE TO FURTHER READING

A. Smith, *Nations and Nationalism in a Global Era* (Cambridge: Polity Press, 1995) assesses the relation of nationalism to globalization. J. Mayall, *Nationalism and International Society* (Cambridge: Cambridge University Press, 1990), F. H. Hinsley, *Nationalism and the International System* (London: Hodder and Stoughton, 1973), K. Deutsch, *Nationalism and Social Communication* (Cambridge, Mass.: MIT Press, 1996), and A. Heraclides, *The Self-Determination of Minorities in International Politics* (London: Cass, 1990) provide accounts of the impact of nationalism on international relations. M. Glenny, *The Balkans 1804–1999: Nationalism, War and the Great Powers* (London: Granta, 1999), gives a dramatic account of one recent case.

The debates on nationalism are analysed in U. Özkirimli, *Theories of Nationalism: A Critical Introduction* (London: Macmillan, 2000). B. Anderson, *Imagined Communities: Reflections on the Origin and Spread of Nationalism* (London: Verso, 1992), E. Gellner, *Nations and Nationalism* (Oxford: Blackwell, 1983), and E. Hobsbawm, *Nations and Nationalism Since 1780: Programme, Myth, Reality* (Cambridge: Cambridge University Press, 1990) give modernist accounts of nationalism as ideology and political movement, while A. Smith, *National Identity* (London: Penguin, 1991), offers an alternative, more historical, account.

21 Culture in world affairs

Simon Murden

READER'S GUIDE

The human experience is one of cultures. Culture and cultural differences have been at the heart of human behaviour throughout history. Indeed, at the end of the twentieth century, the significance of culture was highlighted in the rethinking of world politics that stemmed from the end of the cold war and the increasing pace of globalization. The shrinking of the globe brought different cultures into closer contact and represented a challenge to traditional patterns of culture and social order. All peoples faced the dilemma of what in their cultures could be maintained and what would be lost. Cultural change created friction. When people of one culture perceive those of another not just as alien but also as threatening conflict is likely. Long suppressed cultural conflicts reignited following the cold war. Peoples clashed at a local level, but there was also a broader tension between global and local forces. The culture of the West was the dominant force in globalization, and whilst Western culture seemed to be making the human experience more alike, it was also prompting cultural counter-reactions. New cultural suspicions created new frontiers of international security.

Culture in human affairs

Wherever human beings form communities, a culture comes into existence. Cultures may be constructed on a number of levels: in village or city locations, or across family, clan, ethnic, and national groups. All communities produce a linguistic, literary, and artistic genre, as well as beliefs and practices that characterize social life and indicate how society should be run. Culture transcends ideology, and is about the substance of identity for individuals in a society. An **awareness of a common language**, ethnicity, history, religion, and landscape repre- sent the building blocks of culture. Few cultures are completely insular or unchanging but, to be recognizable, totems of identity must enjoy some consensus and persistence within the community. Societies also define internal and external boundaries by inducing individuals and communities to believe in the value of their culture and the importance of its distinctiveness. Cultures almost always embody ideas and practices that support patterns of domin- ation or hegemony within and between societies.

Cultures refer to a variety of totems and boundar- ies, but religious affiliation has historically been amongst the most powerful of influences. Religions transmit values about the existence of god/gods, and how such knowledge must shape human life. Whilst some religions—Judaism, Hinduism, and Sikhism— define a limited community and have little appeal to outsiders, other religions—Christianity and Islam— offer universal values to the community of mankind. When claims are made in societies about 'cultural authenticity', they are most often made about religious totems, and by those priests, mullahs and gurus that claim to be qualified to transmit them.

The rational and scientific foundations of Western modernity have challenged all religious faiths since the eighteenth century. However, even at the start of the twenty-first century, religion retains a grip on the mind of humanity. The Islamic revival from the

1970s was one of the great phenomena of the cen- tury. In India, the secular foundations of the political system were challenged by the rise of the Hindu revivalist, *Bharatiya Janata Party* (BJP). In China, the relaxation of Communist totalitarianism allowed an explosion of local superstitions, most notably the Falun Gong movement, a cult inspired by a Chinese guru based in the United States that suddenly emerged with millions of followers. Across South- East Asia Islamic, Christian, and Buddhist revivalism was evident, as was increasing inter-communal con- flict. In Russia and Eastern Europe, Orthodox and other Christian sects retook a public space in former communist societies.

Culture is clearly important to human beings then, but using it as an analytical tool can be prob- lematic. Culture is such a multifaceted concept that it may only be possible to use in rather vague and intuitive ways. Deciding what culture is and isolat- ing its influence is the key problem. Cultures can never really be described in their entirety, partly because they are too complex and dynamic. In prac- tice, seeing through the cultural maze requires the identification of cultural totems: images, meanings, norms, values, and practices that seem particularly significant in determining what political or social life looks like. Thinking about culture in international relations is worthwhile. Whilst the dominant realist tradition of international relations suggests that all human behaviour is subsumed by the logic of power politics in the state system, it is difficult to look at the world and not see the significance of culture. Culture can help us understand why humans act in the way they do, and what similarities and differences exist amongst them. The world is divided into distinct communities, and a taxonomy of belonging and exclusion is the vital job that cultural analysis can undertake.

Culture writ large: the civilization

The broadest construction of cultural identity is the civilization. In the eighteenth and nineteenth cen- turies, the European notion of civilization was linked to social and intellectual accomplishment. The superiority of European civilization, with its Greek and Roman heritage and its modernity expressed in

---

Box 21.1 **Bhikhu Parekh on religion and the construction of identity**

Outlining why religion matters so much to the con- struction of individual identity and culture in many societies, Bhikhu Parekh observed that, 'however unworldly its orientation might be, every religion has a moral core, and an inescapable political dimension. If I am expected to be "my brother's keeper" or to "love my neighbour" or be an integral part of the *umma* (the universal Islamic community), or if I believe that everyone is created by God, it deeply matters to me how others live and are treated by their fellow humans and the state . . . Religious people sincerely wish to live out their beliefs and do not see this as an exclusively private or even personal matter'.

(Bhikhu Parekh, *Demos*, 11 (1997): 5)

the nation-state and science, was implicit in the term. Defining those outside civilization—**the Other**—made the idea more meaningful, and shaped the way in which areas and peoples of the world were regarded. Within Europe, 'civilized' rules were applicable; outside Europe, they were not. Europeans moved out to impose their culture by means of enslavement within colonial empires. Only by the mid-twentieth century did European beliefs about their superiority change, although the idea that the West represented a model of progress remained. Civilization has since been used as a term to categorize the broadest groups of people that are able to identify with a sufficiently coherent set of aesthetic, philosophic, historic, and social traditions.

Civilizations represent coherent traditions, but are dynamic over time and place. For instance, medieval Christendom drew on ancient and eastern civilizations for many of its philosophical and technological advances; subsequently, Christendom was remoulded into a European civilization based around the nation-state and, finally, was expanded and adapted in North America, and redesignated as Western civilization. The process embodied both physical and conceptual reformulation. The Western culture that we know at the beginning of the twenty-first century has come a long way. After bitter strug-

---

Box 21.2 The Western account of culture

There is the whole corpus of cultural and philosophical knowledge which provides the underpinning for the 'Western cultural account' . . . . Primarily this account emphasises the possibility of individual and social progress through the application of universal rationality and empirical science, goals which involve the mastery of nature for human ends. Then there is the status of the individual human being, who is at the ontological centre of the Western idea of modernity. The significance of the individual is reflected in debates about the sources or moral and political authority in the conceptions of free will versus determinism, and in accounts seeking to explain the dynamism of market societies by reference to the purposive behaviour of rational consumers.

(Barrie Axford, 1995: 2)

---

gles, monarchical, theocratic, and authoritarian principles of social governance were superseded by a tradition of human rights, democracy, and free markets. Individuals in the West assumed an unknown level of autonomy, although the dark side of Western society was the potential for social alienation and moral uncertainty.

Today, a number of civilizations clearly exist, notably the Western, Islamic, Indian, and Chinese. Other peoples are not so easily pigeonholed, either because they are not united around sufficiently distinct or powerful cultural totems, or because they are torn between different civilizations; in this respect, the location of peoples in South America, Africa, and Russia is problematic. However, no civilization is completely distinct from the influence of others and, in particular, all have been affected by the model of culture and modernity pioneered in the West.

The significance of cultures today

During the cold war, cultural differences ostensibly took a back seat to the global geopolitical struggle between the United States and Soviet Union. Differences were defined in ideological and economic terms, and superimposed upon world politics regardless of cultural characteristics. Both superpowers offered their model to the world for imitation, and alignment to one of the two great blocs defined the 'Other'.

The end of the cold war saw a radical reshaping of the forces underpinning world politics. The triumph of the West also furthered the technological revolution in communications underway. At what looked like the beginning of a new age of global capitalism, the changing patterns of global and local politics seemed to make understanding culture more relevant. Cultural analysis was central to a number of seminal texts that emerged in the post-cold war world, especially Francis Fukuyama's *End of History* (1992), Samuel Huntington's *Clash of Civilizations* (1996) and Benjamin Barber's *Jihad vs McWorld* (1996). Above all, culture offered a way of understanding the similarities and differences of the new age, where a globalized culture met a multicultural world, and where existing communities and cultures were in closer contact with each other.

The power of global capitalism and its consumer

culture looked immense. The United States, and its European and Japanese allies, had won the cold war, and their liberal-capitalism was now the dominant political and economic model. The emerging patterns of international hegemony were sophisticated. John Agnew and Stewart Corbridge perceived that a new 'deterritorialized' geopolitical order—**the hegemony of 'transnational liberalism'**—was emerging, and commented that 'a new ideology of the market (and of market access) [was] being embedded in and reproduced by a powerful constituency of liberal states, international institutions, and what might be called the "circuits of capital" themselves'. (Agnew and Corbridge, 1995: 166) Much of the world was brought into the world market economy. In most of the developing world, state-centred socialism was abandoned, and engagement with the West and its consumer culture sought. Francis Fukuyama certainly thought that the great debates about how societies should be run were basically over. What Fukuyama termed the **'liberal idea'**—the combination of liberal democracy and the market—had drawn a finishing line in the history of political and social development (Fukuyama 1992: 45).

The level of cultural penetration embodied in the new hegemony was unprecedented. The liberal politics of the West was translated into a wave of democratization across the world. Just as significant was the influence of what Benjamin Barber called McWorld: the inescapable experience of consumer icons, mostly American, such as Coca Cola, McDonalds, Disney, Nike, and Sony, and a landscape of shopping malls, cinemas, sports stadiums, and branded restaurants. Global culture drove the aspiration to work for money and to consume, and this had enormous social impact, not least the pressure to release women from the restrictions of traditional social structures. Globalization pressures were felt in all societies. The impact was most pronounced in the developing world, but Western societies also experienced rapid cultural change, although since modernity was forged in the West, its people were relatively familiar with the secularism and pluralism that makes adaptation easier.

The multiculturalism of globalization

Globalized culture itself was a multicultural one, and whilst it was developed in the West, it drew on many influences. In fact, the 'liberal idea' embraced a certain degree of multiculturalism. The never-ending quest of global and local capitalists to entertain and to sell did much to further cultural synthesis, most obviously in the realms of dress, art, film, television and food. One only has to think of the output of Disney to see how the stories and images of local cultures are absorbed into a globalized mainstream. Elsewhere, Western images and aspirations are mediated to the Middle East and Asian continent through India's Bollywood film industry. Chinese, Indian, and French cuisine coexist with McDonalds and Kentucky Fried Chicken almost everywhere on earth.

Globalization created common references, but the world was not about to become identical. Local ethnic and religious cultures survive alongside globalized culture and, as people and ideas increasingly flow around the world, exist in closer proximity to other cultures. The arenas for cultural mixing were the world's great cities—London, Paris, Berlin, New York, Los Angeles, Sydney, and Moscow—and living in such places meant embracing tolerance and multiculturalism, or it meant an urban nightmare of inter-communal suspicion and conflict. Today, Muslims, Christians, Jews, Hindus, Sikhs, Buddhists, and pagans from all races and sects do live side-by-side in varying degrees of conflict and co-operation. The consequences of cultural proximity are complex. Multicultural settings create multiple identities, and so challenge the totems of existing cultures as well as the interests of some of those within them. Above all, multiculturalism tends to undermine patriarchal culture. The uplifting of women in the West was the most significant social phenomenon of the twentieth century, and one that multiculturalism and globalization promises to extend everywhere.

Key points

- Culture defines the identity of society and the individual. A culture is composed of the customs, norms and genres that inform social life. Religion remains a key influence on cultures.

- Civilization is the broadest form of cultural identity, and represents a level of identity that may spread across nations and states.

- Cultural groups often define themselves by representing different cultures as alien, or as the 'Other'.

- The West has been the dominant civilization in the modern age, and all other civilizations have had to deal with its influence.

- The end of the cold war heightened the significance of cultural identity. The hegemony of the West and of its liberal-capitalism challenged the culture and social order of most societies. Globalization also fostered multicultural landscapes across the world.

The counter-revolutionaries of the global age

As globalized modernity challenged all societies, the forces of reaction gathered. A global-level theory of opposition to global markets and culture did not emerge, although resistance did tend to share hostility towards the West. The West was widely stereotyped for its arrogance, irresponsible individualism, and permissive sexual practices, and its liberal-capitalism denounced as exploitative and morally bankrupt. The opposition to globalization was largely parochial, reflected in the religious dimension of much of it. Across the world, societies clung to the familiar by remembering religion and its associated values. As ever, religion helped humans deal with uncertainty and fear. If religious doctrines were not taken on wholesale, then they were often translated into backward-looking moral prescriptions about such things as the role of women, the education of youth, the nature of personal responsibility, the punishment of deviancy, and the definition of the outsider. Wherever religious values made ground, it was clear that they could not be kept out of politics.

Popular culture was at the forefront of the cultural counter-revolution. In Saudi Arabia and Iran, the Islamic regimes sought to exclude news, films, music videos, and *Baywatch* by banning satellite television. The place of women in society, and especially the issue of veiling (the *hijab*), was the key totem for Islamists that sought to bolster the institutions of traditional culture and social control. In Asia, a debate about the importance of 'Asian values' got underway, with the state-business elite turning the 'liberal idea' on its head, and arguing that individualism and pluralism actually negated economic success. 'Asian values' in Malaysia and Singapore meant illiberal legislation to control the aspirations and behaviour of youth. Even in the United States, the voice of Protestant fundamentalists against the secular state, pop culture, liberal politics, abortion, and the teaching of evolution remained a force to be reckoned with.

Religious revivalism sometimes took the form of extreme literalism, often termed **fundamentalism**. The roots of fundamentalism varied. The charisma of messianic preachers has historically found an audience. More significantly, fundamentalism was a reaction to modernity, and to the insensitivity of the capitalist state and the market. Many fundamentalist groups were born in opposition to the secular state, as they sought to turn back the perceived evils of modernity's secularism, pluralism, social atomization and moral emptiness. Claiming the legitimacy of God, fundamentalists could formulate interpretations of their faith that allowed for political and social violence, and sometimes even looked forward to some apocalyptic final vision.

Fundamentalists often sought to purify society in the most extreme ways. Just as the Marxist-inspired

Box 21.3 Francis Fukuyama on Islam after the cold war

For Francis Fukuyama, the end of the cold war had left the 'liberal idea'—liberal democracy and market capitalism—as mankind's universal project. To Fukuyama, it seemed that there was 'no ideology with pretensions to universality that [was] in a position to challenge liberal-democracy, and no universal principle of legitimacy other than the sovereignty of the people'. Fukuyama could only see localized resistance to the liberal idea, notably in the form of Islam. Fukuyama thought that Islam represented:

a systematic and coherent ideology . . . with its own code of morality and doctrine of political and social justice. The appeal of Islam [was] potentially universal, reaching out to all men as men . . . And Islam has indeed defeated liberal democracy in many parts of the Islamic world, posing a grave threat to liberal practices even in countries where it has not achieved political power directly . . . Despite the power demonstrated by Islam in its current revival, however, it remains the case that this religion has virtually no appeal outside those areas that were culturally Islamic to begin with. The days of Islam's cultural conquests, it would seem, are over. It can win back lapsed adherents, but has no resonance for the young people of Berlin, Tokyo, or Moscow. And while nearly a billion are culturally Islamic—one-fifth of the world's population—they cannot challenge liberal-democracy on its own territory on the level of ideas. Indeed, the Islamic world would seem more vulnerable to liberal ideas in the long run than the reverse.

.(Fukuyama 1992: 45–6)

Box 21.4 Fundamentalism

Fundamentalism is more than a political protest against the West or the prevailing establishment. It also reflects deep-seated fear of modern institutions and has paranoid visions of demonic enemies everywhere. It is alarming that so many people in so many different parts are so pessimistic about the world that they can only find hope in fantasies of apocalyptic catastrophe. Fundamentalism shows a growing sense of grievance, resentment, displacement, disorientation, and anomie that any humane, enlightened government must attempt to address.

(Karen Armstrong, *Demos*, 11 (1997): 17)

in the 1990s, a group that sought to commit mass murder on the Tokyo underground with the use of nerve gas.

A clash of civilizations?

The significance of culture following the cold war was reflected in a debate that got underway in the West that was led by Harvard professor, Samuel Huntington. In an article entitled 'The Clash of Civilizations' (*Foreign Affairs*, 1993) and in a subsequent book, Huntington offered a new paradigm in which patterns of international conflict and cooperation were shaped by culture and, ultimately, by civilization. Huntington suggested that the civilizations that would determine international politics were the 'Western, Confucian, Japanese, Islamic, Hindu, Slavic-Orthodox, Latin American, and possibly African' (Huntington 1993: 25)

For Huntington, the clash of civilizations was an historic development. The history of the international system had been essentially about the struggles between monarchs, nations, and ideologies within Western civilization. The end of the cold war inaugurated a new period, where non-Westerners were no longer the helpless recipients of Western power, but now counted amongst the movers of history. The rise of civilizational politics intersected four long-run processes at play in the international system.

revolutionaries of the 1950s and 1960s disappeared, a new breed of religious militants became a principal cause of domestic insurgency and international terrorism in the world. Islamic fundamentalism led the way into violence. In Algeria and Egypt, Islamists proved themselves to God by committing terrible acts of brutality. In India, fundamentalist Muslim and Sikh secessionists fought pitched battles with the Indian Army, whilst Hindu extremists responded with growing force. Extremism could also be found in Christianity. In the United States, the Waco siege and the Oklahoma bombing were the most spectacular manifestations of violent paranoia against minorities, foreigners, and the federal government. Even eastern religion produced the Aum Shindri Kyo sect

1. The relative decline of the West.

2. The rise of the Asian economy and its associated 'cultural affirmation', with China poised to become the greatest power in human history.

3. A population explosion in the Muslim world, and the associated resurgence of Islam.

4. The impact of globalization, including the extraordinary expansion of transnational flows of commerce, information, and people.

The coincidence of these factors was forging a new international order.

Underpinning the new politics were cultural revivals on a grand scale. The world was becoming a smaller place, and this was raising human consciousness about cultural differences. Global economic changes had also weakened local and state loyalties. With Western-originated ideas widely seen to have failed, communities sought to recreate some rooted past. Socialism and nationalism gave way to 'Islamization, Hinduization, and Russianization'. The 'liberal idea' was presented as a new universal by the West, but its individualism, secularism, pluralism, democracy, and human rights had only superficial resonance in Islamic, Sinic, Hindu, Buddhist, and Orthodox cultures. In reality, the differences between civilizations ran deep: they were about man and God, man and woman, the individual and the state, and notions of rights, authority, obligation, and justice. Culture was about the basic perceptions of life that had been constructed over centuries.

For Huntington, culture worked at the level of motivation. States remained key actors, but civilizational politics became real when states and peoples identified with each other's cultural concerns or rallied around the 'core state' of a civilization. The Orthodox, Hindu, Sinic, and Japanese civilizations were clearly centred in powerful unitary states. The West had a closely linked core that included the United States, Germany, France, and Britain. Islam was without a clear core state, and for this reason experienced much more intra-civilizational conflict as a number of contenders—Turkey, Iran, Iraq, Egypt, Saudi Arabia—competed for influence. The fact that Islam was divided did not refute the idea that a pan-Islamic consciousness existed.

Cultural conflict could be found at a 'micro' and a 'macro' level. At the 'micro-level', groups from different civilizations were prone to conflict across local 'fault-lines', and by means of a 'kin-country syndrome' were liable to bring in their wider brethren. Huntington observed that Islam had particularly 'bloody borders', a situation that would continue until Muslim population growth slowed in the second or third decade of the twenty-first century. At the 'macro-level', a more general competition for capabilities and influence was evident, with the principal division between the 'West' and, to varying degrees, the 'Rest'. According to Huntington, the hegemony of the West was most contested by the two most forceful non-Western civilizations, the Sinic and Islamic. Resistance to the West was most evident over issues such as arms control and the promotion of Western political values. Western efforts to project their democracy and human rights were widely regarded as a form of neo-imperialism.

Huntington's thesis was highly contentious with critics pointing to conceptual and empirical problems (Murden, *Political Geography*, no. 18, 1999). The treatment of culture was brief, and the conclusions very pessimistic. Huntington failed to tell the stories of interaction and synthesis that have always gone on between civilizations. Having lost the Soviet Union as its Other, some thought Huntington was needlessly constructing new enemies for the West, and that the *Clash of Civilizations* could become a self-fulfilling prophecy. Much of the criticism was based on caricature, but some reflected the enduring difficulty of using culture to analyse. Unpacking the myriad of factors that cause conflicts with such an all-encompassing tool as the notion of civilization is problematic. Where Huntington could really be criticized, though, was in his downplaying of the power of global economics and its culture. Huntington failed to recognize the extent to which traditional cultures are moderated and synthesized by global society and markets, and how the belligerency of even the keenest of civilizational warriors is usually tempered by the imperatives of globalized life.

Notwithstanding the problems, Huntington initiated an important discussion about human motivations following the cold war, and about the emerging patterns of international conflict and cooperation. The civilization may be not a particularly coherent unit, but that did not mean that underlying cultural preferences do not exert specific and general influences. Huntington outlined the language and purpose of international conflict as the bipolar world became more multidimensional. The *Clash of Civilizations* may not have told the whole story of what was happening in the post-cold war world, but it told part of it.

Key points

- The advance of global culture and capitalism has met local resistance in some parts of the world

from those seeking to preserve their cultures from unbridled change. Religious revivalism has been a global phenomenon since the 1970s.

- Religious fundamentalism has become the most important cause of domestic insurgency and international terrorism in many parts of the world.

- As the cold war came to an end, a discourse was led by Samuel Huntington that suggested that a 'clash of civilizations' was about to become the principal cause of international conflict. Huntington highlighted the tension that existed between Western and Islamic culture.

The counter-revolution at the civilizational level: the case of Islam

In much of the post-cold war discourse on cultural conflict, it was Islam that came into the frame. Islam did seem to represent a particular source of conflict both as a homeland and as a diaspora. Certainly, Islamic peoples were locked in violent conflicts against adjoining civilizations and secular states across the Balkans, West and East Africa, the Middle East, the Caucasus, Central Asia, India, Indonesia, and the Philippines, with their efforts to promulgate Islamic law a particularly explosive issue. An Islamic consciousness that emphasized the corrupt character of Western modernity and liberal values had also been clear since the Iranian revolution of 1978–9.

Islamic culture in the modern age

The Islamic world represents an example *par excellence* of the experience of almost all non-Western cultures in the modern age. Islamic peoples have had to deal with the geopolitical and cultural hegemony of the West since the eighteenth century. The collapse of the Ottoman empire at the end of the First World War heralded a new era in which the secular, nationalist, and authoritarian state became the dominant form of organization. Modernizers argued that Islam was the cause of backwardness and

decline, and that modernization required the imitation of Western forms of culture and organization. In Turkey, the Ottoman Caliphate was abolished in 1924, and Western forms of law, script, and dress enforced. Women were forcibly unveiled. A similar model was adopted in Iran and the Arab world, although the attack on Islam was never quite so thoroughly pursued. Islam was divided by Turkish, Iranian, and Arab nationalism.

Secular nationalism as a culture and model of modernization was to be a failure in the Middle East. The secular state was too authoritarian and bureaucratic. In some places, notably Syria and Iraq, the state was used as an instrument of minority sectarian rule. Above all, Arab nationalism foundered on its demonstrable inability to take on Israel. The Six Day War of June 1967 was a shattering blow to the Arabs. Jerusalem was lost. The June War was a turning point, and although the notion of an Arab nation retained a grip on the Arab imagination, a new force was stirring: that force was revivalist Islam.

The Islamic revival of the 1970s grew in the Middle East, and would spread to the entire Muslim world. The storm had been gathering for some time. Muslim peoples saw themselves as assailed by the West, militarily through Israel, and culturally through everything from pop music to the thinking of

Islamic modernists. A deeper malaise within Islamic societies also drove the revival. According to Sohail Hashemi,

the Islamic revival [was] a complex mix of elements both unique to the Muslim world and shared with other post-colonial societies. The Islamic challenge is trivialised if explained as merely resentment of the power and wealth of the West. It derives its vitality and its appeal from a much more elemental factor: the widespread conviction that Islamic history has gone horribly astray, and that Muslim realities for centuries have been widely divergent from Islamic ethics. The fact today that Muslim countries are characterised by some of the most notoriously authoritarian regimes provides a powerful internal dynamic to the use of Islam as a revolutionary force. The fact that Muslim countries range in economic prosperity from the fabulously wealthy to the hopelessly impoverished provides a second powerful internal dynamic to the upsurge of religiously based calls for social justice. Muslim countries themselves contain ample domestic sources for the infusion of Islamic ideologies in the political arena. (Sohail Hashemi, *The Fletcher Forum*, 1996: 17)

The conservative Islamic monarchies of the Gulf promoted missionary (*da'wa*) activities, but the Islamic revival was really a mass social movement born in a crisis of modernization. Rapid population growth and rural–urban migration meant that urban life was characterized by poor housing, strained services, and widespread underemployment. The young urban poor had little hope of a better life, and could not look to the secular state for salvation. Islam filled the vacuum. Many young Muslims, especially those in the educated lower middle class, turned to Islam as a culture that gave the forgotten and the hopeless self-worth.

Key points

- The impact of the West has been the principal issue facing Islamic civilization since the eighteenth century. Muslim modernizers sought to imitate the West, and the secular nation-state was adopted. The secular state went on to fail in much of the Middle East.

- A deep crisis of modernization exists in many Muslim societies. Poor living conditions and few opportunities for improvement have created a young and frustrated urban population.

- Islam remains a powerful cultural force in the Muslim world, especially in the Middle East. When secular states faltered, Islam began to re-establish itself at the heart of political culture.

Islamic fundamentalism

Militant theology was a vehicle for political opposition. Sayyid Qutb in Egypt (d. 1966), Abu al-Ala al-Mawdudi in Pakistan (d. 1979), and Ruhollah Khomeini in Iran (d. 1989) led a militant Islamic discourse that struck a chord across the Muslim world. Most militants advocated a return to the basic texts of Islam—thus, the term **Islamic fundamentalists**—and the implementation of an Islamic state through Islamic law (the *sharia*). The militants spoke of striving for the faith in the language of *jihad* (Holy struggle) and martyrdom.

Militant Islam also stood in opposition to the West and its modernity. In the post-Enlightenment West, the idea of a better future is a central one, with human progress premised on individualism, secularism, and democracy. In militant Islam, Muslims look forward to a better past. The perfect Islamic polity had been established in the first years of Islam, and its eternal principles recorded in the Quran and other early scripts. The Quran and *sharia* represented the perfect constitution, in which sovereignty resided in God, not in human beings. Many Islamists recognized the validity of consultation (*shura*), but the idea of popular democracy was alien. Islamic injunctions—notably, a criminal law that still conducts public executions and amputations, and the archaic regulation of women and non-Muslims—were totems of an authentic Islamic community and could not be reformed.

The Muslim Brotherhood (*Ikhwan al-Muslimin*)—an organization originally founded in Egypt by Hasan al-Banna in 1928, and spread to Syria, Palestine, Jordan, and North Africa—organized the Islamic revival. Muslim Brotherhoods were both political organizations and benevolent social foundations. Much of the time, Muslim Brotherhoods focused on supporting Muslims in their communities, but on occasions members turned to politics and even to violence. In Egypt, the Muslim Brotherhood led a violent protest against the secular-socialist state led by Gamal Abdul Nasser. Sayyid Qutb, executed by Nasser's regime in 1966, became the icon of Sunni Muslim radicalism. Qutb argued that Islam was subject to a modern state of *jahiliyya*, a term referring to the condition of ignorance that existed before the Prophet Mohammed's time. Refusing to accept the idea or legitimacy of the state or nation, Qutb denounced Nasser as an infidel; it was a Muslim's duty to wage a *jihad* against such corruption.

Shia Muslims were moving in a separate but similar direction to militant Sunnis in the 1960s and 1970s. The driving force of Shia revivalism was Grand Ayatollah Ruhollah Khomeini. In his major work, *Islamic Government* (1971), Khomeini proposed a state dominated by religious scholars in which both **political and religious primacy** was vested in a supreme religious figure or council; the new system was termed the *velayet-e faqih* (the guardianship of the jurisconsult). The most senior Islamic expert would have the last word in ruling the state; it was a position that Khomeini was to fill himself. The Iranian Revolution that followed in 1978–9 would be about entrenching the *velayet-e faqih* in power, a process that was to take a number of years, and require the elimination of the Shia clergy's partners in the rebellion against the Shah's regime.

The Iranian Revolution itself provided great impetus to the Islamic revival. Whilst Iran's Revolution was of limited significance to Sunni radicals in theological terms, it was an example to emulate. A populist Islamic movement had overthrown a powerful secular state; what had seemed impossible had been done, and the language of *jihad* and martyrdom vindicated. An Islamic revolution was not about to sweep across the Arab world, but during the 1970s and 1980s, the Islamic revival exploded into violence. The crescendo of Islamic protest shook states of the Middle East, and on occasions represented a threat to the West.

Later, an 'international brigade' of Islamic militants would emerge from the war against Soviet forces in Afghanistan in the 1980s, and many went on to advocate new *jihad*s against other enemies of Islam, notably the United States. A dissident Saudi millionaire, Usama Bin Laden, was the best known of the new militants, leaving Saudi Arabia to find refuge in Sudan and the Taleban's Afghanistan. After attacks on US forces in Saudi Arabia, Bin Laden was linked to the huge bomb attacks on the US embassies in Kenya and Tanzania in August 1998 that killed 240 people, mostly Africans. The US responded by firing Cruise missiles at Sudan and Afghanistan, and a lengthy low-level war between the US and the Bin Laden militants had seemingly been engaged.

Most Islamic violence, however, remained directed into Muslim societies themselves. The conflict was characterized by a political dynamic evident across the Middle East. Whilst most Islamic revivalists broadly agreed over ends—an Islamic state and *sharia* law—they tended to differ over means. The most militant wanted a cultural and political revolution, but the majority were reluctant to engage in an all-out war with the state, society, or outside powers. Mainstream Islamists wanted to conduct a dialogue over gradually extending their values into societies. For most Arab governments, keeping the mainstream away from the extremists has been the central dynamic of politics since the 1970s. In Saudi Arabia, state and religion remained united under capitalism. In Jordan, the Muslim Brotherhood was brought into a democratization process quite successfully. In Egypt, the state struggled to keep the Muslim Brotherhood and violent secret societies apart. In Algeria, the army took decisions that brought mainstream and militants together in agreement over means, and produced a savage civil war. For the time being, the Islamic militants have met their match in the Middle Eastern state.

Key points

- Twentieth-century modernization produced widespread social alienation in the Muslim societies. Political Islam filled a political and social vacuum.

- Theological innovations allowed an Islamic revival in the 1970s that sought to enforce an Islamic state and a rigorous code of Islamic law (*sharia*).

- The Iranian Revolution of 1978–79 provided a powerful example to all Islamic revivalists.

- Revivalist Islam identified a cultural conflict with the West. A crescendo of Islamic violence appeared

Box 21.5 The crescendo of revivalist Islam from the late 1970s

- The Iranian Revolution (1978–9) talked of Western corruption, and of the United States as the 'Great Satan'. In November 1979, Iranian students took the US embassy in Tehran and held its staff hostage. The Revolution spilled over into the Middle East, prompting the Iran–Iraq war.

- The seizure of the Grand Mosque in Mecca on the first day of *Hijra* 1400 by the charismatic 'Islamic primitivist', Juhayman al-Utaiba. In the bitter fighting that followed in Nov.–Dec. 1979, hundreds were killed.

- The assassination of President Anwar Sadat at a public parade on 6 October 1981 by the Islamic militants in the Egyptian Army.

- The rise of Shia militancy in Lebanon after the Israeli invasion of 1982. Amal and Hizballah would wage a jihad against Israel and the West, notably with the bombing of the US Marine barracks in Beirut in 1983, the hijacking of a TWA airliner in 1985, and the kidnapping of Westerners in Beirut.

- The conflict over Salman Rushdie's book, *The Satanic Verses*. When the book that Muslims believed to be blasphemous led to anti-US riots in Pakistan in February 1989, Iran's Ayatollah Khomeini issued a *fatwa* condemning Rushdie to death. A $1 million bounty was put on Rushdie's life.

- The Algerian Civil War. When the *Front Islamique du Salut* (FIS) was denied office by the Algerian Army after they had won a general election in December 1991–January 1992, a civil war broke out in which tens of thousands were killed.

- The long-running campaign of Islamic terrorism in Egypt was directed not only at the regime of Husni Mubarak but also at foreign tourists.

- After the outbreak of the *intifadah* in 1987, the growth of HAMAS and Islamic Jihad re-energized the violence of the Palestinian struggle against Israel.

- After the *jihad* against Soviet and Soviet-backed forces in Afghanistan, militant Islamists descended into a civil war with conservative forces. Subsequently, Islamic 'students' formed an army, the Taleban, and seized most of the country to enforce a rigorous version of *sharia* law.

- In Bosnia, a travelling band of Islamic radicals assembled to fight for the mainly Muslim Bosnian government in its war against the Serbs. At the end of the 1990s, Albanian Muslim secessionism in Kosovo was suppressed by the Serbian state, prompting Western military intervention in 1999.

- After the Russian Republic of Chechenia seceded, Islamic fighters engaged in a bitter struggle with the Russian state. After achieving a brief period of independence in the mid-1990s, Russian troops returned in 1999–2000 to wage a war aimed at restoring Moscow's rule.

- The long-running dispute between India and Pakistan over Kashmir was given impetus in the 1990s by Islamic militants. In 1999, an invasion of Indian Kashmir by Islamic militants led to large-scale fighting, and threatened to escalate into a war between India and Pakistan.

- The violence of Islamic militants in Saudi Arabia, Egypt and North Africa was a continuing cause of instability. The Saudi dissident, Usama Bin Laden, symbolized the Islamic threat. Bin Laden organized terrorist bombings of US interests with the aim of compelling Western forces to leave the Arabian Peninsula. A low-level war between the United States and the Bin Laden militants began.

- From Nigeria to the Philippines, the effort of Muslims to assert Islamic principles and laws led to inter-communal fighting with Christians and secular states.

to substantiate the notion that there was a conflict between the West and Islam.

- The Islamic revival embodies different perspectives. Islamic revivalists are divided over the means to achieve an Islamic order.

The future of Islam in the global age

The Islamic revival was born in a crisis of twentieth-century modernization. The further exposure of the Middle East to the global economy since the 1970s deepened the crisis. In the 1950s and 1960s, secular elites had at least appealed to the masses with socialism and nationalism, but after the *infitah* (opening) model was initiated in Anwar Sadat's Egypt, the interests, values and lifestyles of Middle Eastern elites turned to the West. Secular elites essentially abandoned the masses, leaving Islam as the voice of opposition not only to ruling regimes, but also to the current practices of globalization, including the 'cultural invasion' that came with *infitah*.

Islamists did battle with the forces of secularism and the consequences of globalization, but the relationship between Islam and modernity is not straightforward. Islamists cannot escape practical politics and economics, and a coherent Islamic voice on the issue of globalization is not clear. Pragmatism has been a powerful impulse for Islamists whether in opposition or in power. The case of Iran is illuminating. The Revolution of 1978–9 promoted a missionary Islam that sought to take on all the forces of corruption on earth, notably the United States. For a time, the Islamic Republic quite simply ignored the sovereignty of other states and the niceties of diplomacy. The costs were unsustainable, and by the mid-1980s, the revolution had produced its 'pragmatists'. Fences were mended, and whilst the Islamic Republic continued to speak up for Muslim rights around the world, it was less prone to act on them.

The death of Ayatollah Khomeini in 1989 led to further reorganization in Iran. The Presidencies of Hashemi Rafsanjani and Mohammad Khatami speeded reform. Rafsanjani and Khatami sought to liberalize politics, give women more opportunities, embrace market principles and foreign capital, and foster relations with the West. The reformers realized that the stifling conformity and insularity of the original vision was untenable in the global age. The economy was not dynamic. The young, women, and the middle class also wanted more freedom, although there was a powerful conservative estab-lishment determined to stop them having it. The struggle within Iranian society would be prolonged, but the fundamentalism of 1978–9 was disappearing. Strangely, the Islamic Republic looked like becoming an agent of modernization and an important example of Islamic democratization.

The inescapable dilemma for Islamists was that they could not promote their values without political and economic pragmatism, yet engaging with the world opened the door to other influences and cultural synthesis. Finding the 'right path' was at the heart of contemporary Islamic discourse. The struggle for the body and soul of Muslim societies would be prolonged, and may have no clear outcome. What is certain is that the remorseless march of globalized economics and culture will change Islamic culture in the twenty-first century, although whether an open and inclusive Islam emerges remains to be seen. The global age demands a degree of conformity from all those engaged with it, but that does not mean that all traditional cultures will be tamed in the same way.

Key points

- The increasing engagement of Middle Eastern societies with the global economy since the 1970s deepened some of the social problems that produced the Islamic revival.

- Islamic movements have been suspicious of global culture and capitalism, but the pressures to be pragmatic are strong. The Iranian Revolution is a good example of how political and economic realities can force compromise on Islamists.

- Islam does not have a single voice. Muslims will meet the forces of globalization in different ways. Muslim societies will continue to change in the twenty-first century.

Conclusion

In the late twentieth century, all the societies and cultures of the world experienced an unknown level of interaction. Globalization brought a revolution in communications, a global culture of consumer icons and liberal values, and a multicultural landscape in the world's major cities. Existing societies absorbed new influences into their cultures, and a great deal of cultural synthesis was underway everywhere. A growing awareness of cultural identity was a global phenomenon, although whether this translated itself into a fundamental reorganization of world politics, as Samuel Huntington suggested, remained to be seen. A new degree of cultural identification, partisanship and conflict was evident following the end of the cold war, but the emergence of a 'clash of civilizations' overstated the case.

The cultural revivalism of the time was substantially related to the pressures created in societies by increasing levels of globalization and multiculturalism. A revival of religions was one of the most important manifestations of cultural and social insecurity: religion looked like a fixed cultural totem, even if it was not. To varying degrees, most societies and cultures adapted to the momentous changes brought by globalization, but the stresses did produce real resistance. Religious fundamentalism was the most significant form of resistance, and became the principal opposition to multiculturalism, to existing governments, and to the forces of globalization. Cultural revivals represented 'glocal moments' of reaction and resistance to the new globalized hegemony, although they seemed unlikely to halt the march of global capitalism and culture in the long run. Localized cultural rearguard actions would continue to be fought into the twenty-first century, but the imaginings of cultural authenticity were not only those of the parochial backwater, but were an impossible dream in the age of globalization.

QUESTIONS

1   What is culture?

2   How useful is the concept of culture when thinking about international relations?

3   How does religion influence cultural identity, and why has religion remained such a powerful influence in the world?

4   What significance do characterizations of the 'Other' have in cultural discourses?

5   Why did Samuel Huntington argue that differences between civilizations would become the principal cause of international conflict after the end of the cold war?

6   How did Middle Eastern peoples initially respond to the dominance of the West in the twentieth century?

7   What was the doctrinal basis of the Islamic revival of the 1970s?

8   How coherent is Islam as a civilization and as a political force?

9   How serious is the threat that Islam represents to the West, and vice versa?

10   What does the case of the Islamic Republic of Iran indicate about the future direction of Islamic cultures?

GUIDE TO FURTHER READING

Agnew, John, and Corbridge, Stuart, *Mastering Space: Hegemony, Territory, and International Political Economy* (London: Routledge, 1995). A study on hegemony and cultural discourse since the 19th century. The work argues that globalization has created a new 'deterritorialized' hegemony.

Axford, Barrie, *The Global System: Economics, Politics and Culture* (Cambridge: Polity Press, 1995). A study of Western modernity, and how it has been extended across the world.

Barber, Benjamin, *Jihad vs McWorld* (New York: Ballantine Books, 1996). An eloquent account of global culture and capitalism, and ways that it challenges local social systems and identities.

Bill, James, and Springborg, Robert, *Politics in the Middle East* (London: Scott, Foresman/Little, Brown, 1990). The basic text on the recent history of the Middle East.

Fukuyama, Francis, *The End of History and the Last Man* (London: Penguin Books, 1992). The book that explained the power of liberal democracy and capitalism, and proclaimed that political development had essentially reached an end. Liberal democracy was the best system that humankind could ever expect.

Huntington, Samuel, *The Clash of Civilizations and the Remaking of the World Order* (New York: Touchstone, 1996). The follow-up to his Foreign Affairs article (1993) that argued that civilizational references were becoming the driving force of international conflict and co-operation.

Said, Edward W., *Orientalism: Western Conceptions of the Orient* (London: Penguin, 1995, reprint with afterword). A landmark work that sought to explain the significance of cultural discourses, specifically how Oriental peoples had been negatively stereotyped in Western cultural discourses. Much of the work is an in-depth analysis of Western literature on the Orient over the past two centuries.

WEB LINKS

www.incore.ulst.ac.uk   The initiative on Conflict Resolution and Ethnicity (INCORE) is a joint project of the United Nations University and the University of Ulster. The web site contains research resources into ethnic conflicts around the world.

www.ceifo.su.se   The Centre for Research in International Migration and Ethnic Relations at the University of Stockholm has a web site detailing its research into migration, nationalism and ethnic relations.

www.lamp.ac.uk/cis/pathways   The Department of Theology, Religious and Islamic Studies at the University of Wales in Lampeter has an extensive list of Internet links related to the study of Islam.

www.irna.com   The Islamic Republic News Agency posts news, features and photographs on contemporary life and politics in Iran.

22 Humanitarian intervention and world politics

Nicholas J. Wheeler and Alex J. Bellamy

READER'S GUIDE

Non-intervention is the norm in international society, but should military intervention be legitimated in contravention of the sovereignty principle when governments massively violate the human rights of their citizens, or if states have collapsed into civil war and disorder? This is the guiding question addressed in this chapter. The society of states has outlawed war except for purposes of self-defence and the challenge posed by humanitarian intervention is whether it also should be exempted from the general ban on the use of force? This chapter examines the arguments for and against **forcible humanitarian intervention**, focusing on the tensions between considerations of power, order, and justice in world politics. This theoretical analysis is explored in relation to cold war and post-cold war cases of **forcible humanitarian intervention**. The final section of the chapter examines the claim that the traditional definition of humanitarian intervention should be broadened to include non-military forms of humanitarian intervention practised by states and non-state actors.

Introduction

Humanitarian intervention poses the hardest test for an international society built on principles of sovereignty, non-intervention, and non-use of force. The society of states has committed itself in the post-holocaust world to a 'human rights culture'[1] which outlaws genocide, torture, and massive human rights abuses, but these principles of humanitarianism can and do conflict with principles of sovereignty and non-intervention. Sovereign states are expected to act as guardians of their citizens' security, but what happens if states behave as gangsters towards their own people, treating sovereignty as a licence to kill? Should murderous[2] states be afforded protection of the norms of sovereignty and non-intervention, and what responsibilities do other states have to act as guardians of human rights in the society of states? Humanitarian intervention was not a legitimate practice during the cold war, but there has been a significant shift of attitudes since the early 1990s. This partly resulted from the growth in global interdependence and communication known as globalization. However, this shift is primarily confined to domestic publics within liberal states, and the wider legitimacy of humanitarian intervention is challenged by many non-Western states.

The early optimism associated with the international intervention to rescue the Kurds in northern Iraq in the immediate aftermath of the 1991 Gulf War gave way to a mood of pessimism and moral cynicism. This was the product of the UN's perceived failures in Bosnia and Somalia, and the appalling moral catastrophe of Rwanda where Western state leaders and publics watched genocide take place from the comfort of their living room chairs. Failures in Bosnia and Somalia led to a questioning of the efficacy of military force in promoting humanitarian ends. Some argued that what was needed in these cases was a greater willingness to employ military force in defence of humanitarian ends, but others contended that whilst governments and citizens have moral duties to go to the rescue of suffering humanity, these should be discharged by non-violent means since the use of force is always counter-productive. If there is debate over whether the use of force can promote humanitarian values and long-term reconstruction in **murderous** and/or **failed** states, then there is also the issue of whether states can be trusted with the responsibility to act as agents of **common humanity**. The abdication of moral responsibility on the part of the society of states in the face of the genocide in Rwanda—most crucially in the capitals of Western states—suggests that we should be cautious about investing too much faith in state leaders as guardians of human rights in world politics, and suspicious about their motivation when they do invoke human rights to legitimize military action. This was the lesson that many drew from NATO's use of force against the Federal Republic of Yugoslavia (FRY) in March 1999, but for others NATO's action represented a new-found willingness on the part of Western states to use force in defence of human rights. Nevertheless, even among those who supported the use of force against the Milosevic regime, there was considerable disquiet that the means chosen to save the Kosovars—a bombing campaign against targets in Kosovo and the FRY—contradicted the humanitarian rationale behind 'Operation Allied Force'. Scepticism that force can ever be a servant of humanitarian values leads some analysts to argue for a post-statist reconceptualization of humanitarian intervention, which they label non-forcible or non-violent humanitarian intervention (Ramsbotham and Woodhouse 1996).

This chapter is divided into six sections. The first part of the chapter sets up the traditional definition of humanitarian intervention. The second part identifies five key objections to the practice of forcible humanitarian advanced by realism (see Ch. 7) and **Pluralist international society theory**. Conversely, the third section examines the counter-arguments advanced by **Solidarist international society theory**. Next, we look at the legitimacy of humanitarian intervention in state practice during the cold war, focusing on two case-studies of intervention which led to the ending of genocidal practices: Tanzania's intervention against Idi Amin's Uganda and Vietnam's removal of the Pol Pot regime in Cambodia. The fifth part of the chapter focuses on international interventions in northern Iraq, Somalia, Rwanda, and Kosovo. The analysis here is subdivided into three key areas: the role of public opinion and the media in pressurizing state leaders to intervene; the legality and legitimacy of these interventions; and an evaluation of their success in promoting humanitarian outcomes. The final section of the chapter explores alternative conceptions of humanitarian intervention and considers the implications of globalization for practices of humanitarianism in world politics.

What is humanitarian intervention?

In his now classic definition in *Nonintervention and International Order*, R. J. Vincent defined intervention as set out in Box 22.1. Vincent was not writing specifically of humanitarian intervention but his definition sums up the traditional view. Humanitarian intervention is an act that seeks to intervene to stop a government murdering its own people. Traditionally, intervention has been defined in terms of a coercive breach of the walls of the castle of sovereignty. Such a breach violates the cardinal norm of sovereignty, and its logical corollary the principle of non-intervention, which is enshrined in customary international law and codified in Article 2 (7) of the UN Charter. This prohibits the UN from intervening in matters which are 'essentially within the domestic jurisdiction of any state'. Vincent's description of intervention does not offer a definitive judgement on its legality, and this is a very controversial issue in relation to humanitarian intervention. The majority of international lawyers, labelled **restrictionists**, argue that the prohibition on the use of force in Article 2 (4) of the UN Charter renders **forcible humanitarian intervention** illegal. The only legitimate exception to this general ban is the right of self-defence in Article 51 of the UN Charter. We will explore the reasoning behind this prohibition in the next section, but this position is contested by the '**counter-restrictionists**' who argue that there is a legal right of unilateral and collective humanitarian intervention in the society of states (this position is discussed in the fourth section of this chapter).

Conventionally, humanitarian intervention is defined in terms of intervention motivated by humanitarian considerations, but this raises the question as to what counts as humanitarian? The

> ## Box 22.1 R. J. Vincent's definition of intervention
>
> Activity undertaken by a state, a group within a state, a group of states or an international organization which interferes coercively in the domestic affairs of another state. It is a discrete event having a beginning and an end, and it is aimed at the authority structure of the target state. It is not necessarily lawful or unlawful, but it does break a conventional pattern of international relations.
>
> (Vincent 1974: 13)

International Committee of the Red Cross defines humanitarian acts as those that 'prevent and alleviate human suffering'. This definition of humanitarianism is claimed to be non-political and impartial in the sense that all human beings are included as worthy of concern irrespective of sex, race, and nationality. The problem with this definition is that it assumes that humanitarian acts are the same across time and space; that a capacity for humanitarianism naturally inheres in all humans by virtue of a common human nature. Critics of this position argue that what counts as human suffering changes from one historical epoch to another. There is nothing natural or inevitable about who gets defined as human/inhuman. Thus, slavery was regarded as perfectly natural in one century and identified as a scourge against humanity in the next. What this example illustrates is that '[o]ur conception of humanitarianism is culturally specific and has its own biases' (Parekh 1997).

Key points

- Traditionally, intervention has been defined as a forcible breach of sovereignty that interferes in a state's internal affairs.

- The legality of **forcible humanitarian interven-** **tion** is a matter of dispute between **restrictionists** and **counter-restrictionist**s.

- The expression of humanitarian sentiments in world politics is a product of changing historical and social processes.

Objections to legitimizing humanitarian intervention

There are five key objections to legitimizing a practice of **forcible humanitarian intervention** that have been advanced, at various times, by scholars, international lawyers, and policy-makers. These objections are not mutually exclusive and they can be found in the writings of both realists and liberals. For example, liberals recognize that principles of humanitarianism are often applied selectively, but in contrast to realists, they are optimistic that state practice can be changed. This liberal aspiration is embodied in **Solidarist international society theory** but the commitment of solidarism to legitimizing a practice of humanitarian intervention is challenged by pluralist international society theorists (see below).

States don't intervene for primarily humanitarian reasons

Bhikhu Parekh argues that humanitarian intervention 'is an act wholly or primarily guided by the sentiment of humanity, compassion or fellow-feeling, and is in that sense disinterested' (Parekh 1997: 54). Realism tells us that states only pursue their national interest (see Ch. 7) and thus humanitarian intervention is ruled out since states are motivated solely by what they judge to be their national interest.

States are not allowed to risk their soldiers' lives on humanitarian crusades

Realists not only argue that states do not intervene for humanitarian reasons, they are also asserting that states should not behave in this way. State leaders—those men and women who think and act in the name of states—do not have the moral right to shed blood on behalf of suffering humanity. Bhikhu Parekh expresses well the core postulates of the statist paradigm:[3] 'Citizens are the exclusive responsibility of their state, and their state is entirely their own business' (Parekh 1997: 56). Thus, if a civil authority has broken down or is behaving in an appalling way towards its citizens, this is the responsibility of that state's citizens and its political leaders. Outsiders have no moral duty to intervene even if they would be able to improve the situation and stop the killing.

The problem of abuse

This realist argument against humanitarian intervention contends that it should not be legitimated as an exception to the principle of the non-use of force because this will lead to **abuse**, a problem identified by Thomas Franck and Nigel Rodley. They contend that the prohibition on the use of force in Article 2 (4) of the UN Charter is already vulnerable to states abusing it in the name of self-defence without creating a new legal right of humanitarian intervention that would be equally open to **abuse.** In the absence of an impartial mechanism for deciding when humanitarian intervention was permissible, states might espouse humanitarian motives as a pretext to cover the pursuit of national self-interest (Franck and Rodley 1973: 275–305). The problem of **abuse** leads some to argue that humanitarian intervention will always be a weapon that the strong will use against the weak.

Selectivity of response

The argument here is that states will always apply principles of humanitarian intervention selectively, resulting in an inconsistency in policy. Because states will be governed by what they judge to be their national interest, they will intervene only when they deem this to be at stake. The problem of **selectivity** arises when an agreed moral principle is at stake in more than one situation, but national interest dictates a divergence of responses. A good recent example of the **selectivity** of response is the claim by critics of NATO that its intervention in Kosovo could not have been driven by humanitarian motives because the organization had done nothing to address the equally terrible plight of the Turkish Kurds, the Chechens, or the East Timorese. **Selectivity** of response is the problem of failing to treat like cases alike.

Disagreement on what principles should govern a right of humanitarian intervention

Pluralist[4] international society theory identifies an additional obstacle, namely, the problem of how to reach a consensus on what principles should underpin a doctrine of humanitarian intervention. Hedley Bull defined the pluralist conception as one in which states are capable of agreement only for certain minimum purposes, the most crucial being reciprocal recognition of sovereignty and the norm of non-intervention. The subject of humanitarian intervention is a difficult one for theorists of international society since it is the archetypal case where it might be expected that the society of states would agree to privilege individual justice over the norms of sovereignty and non-intervention. Bull was sensitive to considerations of individual justice, but argued that humanitarian intervention should not be permitted in the face of disagreement about what constitutes extreme human rights violations in international society. He was worried that in the absence of a consensus on what principles should govern a right of individual or collective humanitarian intervention, such a right would undermine international order. This moral defence of the non-intervention principle is based on what moral philosophers call **rule-consequentialism.** International order, and hence the general well-being of all individuals, is better served by upholding the principle of non-intervention than by allowing humanitarian intervention in the absence of a consensus on what considerations are to count as humanitarian. The basic difficulty is well summed up in the words of Chris Brown: 'The general problem here is that humanitarian intervention is always going to be based on the cultural predilections of those with the power to carry it out' (Brown 1992: 113).

Key points

- States will not intervene for primarily humanitarian reasons.

- States should not intervene for primarily humanitarian reasons as this violates the compact between state and citizens.

- States will abuse a right of humanitarian intervention using it as a cloak to promote national interests.

- States will apply principles of humanitarian intervention selectively.

- In the absence of a consensus on what principles should govern a right of individual or collective humanitarian intervention, such a right will undermine international order.

- Humanitarian intervention will always be based on the cultural preferences of the powerful.

The Solidarist case for humanitarian intervention

In contrast to **Pluralist international society theory**, **Solidarist international society theory** argues that states have both a legal right and a moral obligation to intervene in exceptional cases that offend against minimum standards of humanity. This section is divided into two parts. The **counter-restrictionist** case for a legal right of humanitarian intervention is explored in the first part, and in the second part we investigate the solidarist claim that whatever the legality of humanitarian intervention, there is a moral duty of forcible intervention in exceptional cases of human suffering. It was pointed out earlier that there is a dispute among international lawyers concerning the legality of humanitarian intervention. Anthony Clark Arend and Robert J. Beck argue that the **counter-restrictionist** case for a legal right of individual and collective humanitarian intervention rests on two key claims. First, that the UN Charter commits states to protecting fundamental human rights and second, that there is a right of humanitarian intervention in customary international law (Arend and Beck 1993: 132–7).

Protection of human rights

Counter-restrictionists challenge the view of **restrictionists** that the UN's primary purpose is to maintain international peace and security. They contend that the promotion of human rights should rank alongside the maintenance of international peace and security. Here, they point to the preamble to the UN Charter and Articles 1 (3), 55 and 56 of the Charter. Some **counter-restrictionists** are prepared to go even further, asserting that if the UN fails to take remedial action—as was so often the case during the cold war—individual states have a legal right to intervene with force to reduce human suffering. Michael Reisman and Mryes McDougal assert that the human rights provisions of the Charter—Articles 1 (3), 55 and 56—provide a legal basis for unilateral forcible intervention. They claim that were this not the case it 'would be suicidally destructive of the explicit purposes for which the United Nations was established' (quoted in Arend and Beck 1993: 133). As with the right to self-defence, humanitarian intervention is argued to be a legitimate exception to the non-use of force principle found in Article 2 (4) of the UN Charter.

A customary right of humanitarian intervention

An alternative grounding for a legal right of unilateral humanitarian intervention is found in the assertion that a customary legal right exists independently of the UN Charter. Customary international law is the law of state practice. If, over a period of time, states act in a certain way and come to regard that behaviour as required by the law, then a rule of customary international law has developed. Not only must states actually engage in the practice that is claimed to have the status of customary law, they must do so because they believe that this practice is permitted by the law. This is described in the language of international law as *opinio juris*. **Counter-restrictionists** contend that states were permitted to engage in humanitarian intervention under pre-Charter customary international law. However, this is a very controversial claim that is rejected by **restrictionists** like Franck and Rodley who argue that there is little or no support in state practice for a legal right of humanitarian intervention (Franck and Rodley 1973: 275–305). The legitimacy of humanitarian intervention in cold war state practice is the subject of the next section, but no discussion of the solidarist case would be complete without an examination of the claim that humanitarian intervention is sometimes morally required.

Is humanitarian intervention morally required?

Some lawyers argue that whatever the legality of humanitarian intervention, it might be morally required in those cases where the use of force is the only means of ending the slaughter. Thus, Franck and Rodley write that humanitarian intervention 'belongs in the realm not of law but of moral choice, which nations, like individuals must sometimes make' (Franck and Rodley 1973: 304). Their position is that this moral imperative cannot be legally recognized because of the dangers that such a legal right would be abused. The claim that humanitarian intervention is morally required is a much stronger one than the proposition that there is a legal right to engage in this practice because whilst the existence of a right enables action it does not determine it.

Even if an individual state or group of states feel sufficiently troubled by gross violations of human rights in another state to intervene, how should the society of states decide whether this action is legitimate? Put crudely, how many people have to die or be in imminent peril before the use of force is justified? **Solidarist international society theory** has not provided a satisfactory response to this question, but a pioneering attempt can be found in R. J. Vincent's discussion of this question as set out in Box 24.2.

Key points

- **Solidarist international society theory** is committed to developing consensual moral principles that would legitimate a practice of humanitarian intervention in international society.

- **Counter-restrictionists** argue for a legal right of **forcible humanitarian intervention** based on an interpretation of the human rights provisions in the UN Charter and the existence of customary international law.

- A legal right of humanitarian intervention enables intervention but it does not determine it. To

---

Box 22.2 R. J. Vincent's exceptions to the non-intervention principle

The international community has produced a number of conventions setting standards on human rights that go well beyond the proclamation of basic rights. The hard question is whether these standards legitimize action, either by international society as a whole or by states as its agents. Or, to put it another way, does a threat to life on the New York subway or in the Sahara desert trigger an international obligation to respond? Is intervention legitimate in these circumstances?

The answer is plainly no in these circumstances. Humanitarian intervention is, as Walzer puts it, reserved for extraordinary oppression, not the day-to-day variety. If the threat to life on the New York subway became the systematic killing of all commuters from New Jersey, or the threat to life in the Sahara desert reached famine proportions, in which local governments were implicated by failing to meet their responsibilities, *then* there might fall to the international community a duty of humanitarian intervention.

(Vincent 1986: 126–7)

Writing with Peter Wilson in a posthumous work, Vincent expressed his reservations with a 'morality of states' which requires that 'we have to act as if other states are legitimate, not because they are legitimate [in their upholding of plural conceptions of the good] but because to do otherwise would lead to chaos . . . states ought to satisfy certain basic requirements of decency before they qualify for the protection which the principle of non-intervention provides'

(Vincent and Wilson 1993: 124–5)

---

ensure intervention in cases where it is desperately needed states would have to recognize a duty or obligation to act.

State practice during the cold war

This section assesses the extent to which humanitarian intervention was a legitimate practice of states during the cold war. Here, we will focus upon two cases in the post-1945 period where interventionary action by a neighbouring state led to the ending of state sponsored mass murder: Vietnam's intervention in Cambodia in December 1978 and Tanzania's intervention in Uganda a few weeks later. Two key

Box 22.3 Summary of key concepts in the theory of humanitarian intervention

Abuse states cloak power political interests in the guise of humanitarianism.

Common humanity we all have human rights by virtue of our common humanity, and these rights generate correlative moral duties for individuals and state leaders.

Failed states states that have collapsed into civil war and disorder, and where the government of the state has ceased to exist inside the territorial borders of the state. Citizens find themselves in a quasi-state of nature.

Counter restrictionists international lawyers who argue that there is a legal right of humanitarian intervention in both UN Charter and customary international law.

Forcible humanitarian intervention military intervention which breaches the principle of state sovereignty where the primary purpose is to alleviate the human suffering of some or all within a state's borders.

Murderous states the sovereign government is massively abusing the human rights of its citizens, engaging in acts of mass murder and/or genocide.

Non-forcible/ non-violent intervention pacific intervention which can be either consensual (Red Cross) or non-consensual (Médecins Sans Frontières) and which is practised by states, international organizations and INGOs (international non-governmental organizations). It can be short-term (delivery of humanitarian aid) or long-term (conflict-resolution and reconstruction of political life within failed states).

Pluralist international society theory states are conscious of sharing common interests and common values, but these are limited to norms of sovereignty and non-intervention. Humanitarian intervention is illegitimate in the society of states.

Restrictionists international lawyers who argue that humanitarian intervention violates Article 2(4) of the UN Charter and is illegal under both UN Charter law and Customary international law.

Rule-consequentialism international order and hence general well-being is better served by a general prohibition against humanitarian intervention than by sanctioning humanitarian intervention in the absence of agreement on what principles should govern a right of unilateral humanitarian intervention.

Selectivity an agreed moral principle is at stake in more than one situation, but national interest dictates a divergence of response.

Solidarist international society theory international society is agreed or capable of agreeing on universal standards of justice and morality which would legitimize practices of humanitarian intervention.

Statism the moral claim that states only have duties to their own citizens, and that they should not risk their soldiers' lives on humanitarian crusades.

Chapter VII Article 39 of Chapter VII of the UN Charter authorizes the UN Security Council to 'decide what measures shall be taken in accordance with Articles 41 and 42, to maintain international peace and security'. Article 42 empowers the Security Council to 'take such action by air, sea, or land forces as may be necessary to maintain or restore international peace and security'.

issues will be explored in relation to these cases: first, the place of humanitarian motives in the decisions to intervene and the justifications offered by Tanzania and Vietnam for their actions; and second, the divergent responses of the society of states to these two cases.

The motives and official justifications of the Tanzanian and Vietnamese interventions

Gross human rights violations characterized Idi Amin's Ugandan Government from start to finish. Amnesty International estimated that up to 300,000 people had been killed during the eight years in which he had been in power. The record is even more appalling in the case of the Khmer Rouge which seized power in Cambodia in April 1975 and immediately embarked upon a course of domestic policies which involved some of the most appalling human rights abuses in the brutally long twentieth century. While accurate figures are difficult to obtain, there is broad agreement that of a population of about 7 million some 2–3 million people lost their lives during the three and a half years in which the Khmer Rouge were in power. Despite this level of human rights abuses, there was no collective intervention to remove these **murderous** regimes, and it was left to Tanzania and Vietnam to take the law into their own hands. But in neither case did the intervening state claim that its motives were humanitarian. Instead, both Tanzania and Vietnam argued that they were acting in self-defence—the legitimate right of all states under Article 51 of the UN Charter. They claimed with some legitimacy that they were the victims of armed aggression since both Cambodia, and especially Uganda, had undertaken cross-border incursions in the months prior to the invasions. At no time did the governments of Tanzania or Vietnam argue that they had a legal right to use force to remove a tyrannical government from power.

What explains the reluctance on the part of Tanzania and Vietnam to claim a right of humanitarian intervention? Three explanations have been advanced. First, it is argued that neither of them acted for primarily humanitarian reasons confirming the realist view that states don't risk their soldiers' lives unless vital interests are judged to be at stake. Gary Klintworth's study of these cases led him to conclude that, 'While saving human beings from being killed was an inevitable consequence of intervention by Vietnam and . . . Tanzania . . . it was always secondary to the overriding priority imposed by concern for vital security interests' (Klintworth

1989: 59). A further reason for the reluctance of the intervening states to claim a right of humanitarian intervention has been suggested by Adam Roberts. He writes, 'there was probably also a thought that to sanctify a doctrine of humanitarian intervention would be to store up trouble for themselves or their friends' (Roberts 1993: 434). The argument here is that states with dubious human rights records are fearful of setting precedents for a doctrine of humanitarian intervention because this might be employed against them at some future date. However, there is no evidence to substantiate the claim in relation to Vietnam, and in the case of Tanzania, President Julius Nyerere was a rare and outspoken exponent of humanitarian values. A final explanation is offered by Hedley Bull, who suggests that the society of states was sensitive to the risks involved in taking actions that eroded the principle of non-intervention. Writing in the mid-1980s, Bull stated:

There is no present tendency for states to claim, or for the international community to recognize, any such right [of humanitarian intervention] . . . The reluctance evident in the international community even to experiment with the conception of a right of humanitarian intervention reflects not only an unwillingness to jeopardise the rules of sovereignty and non-intervention by conceding such a right to individual states, but also the lack of any agreed doctrine as to what human rights are.   (Bull 1984a: 193)

The response of international society

Bull's judgement noted above reflected the fact that neither Vietnam nor Tanzania's actions were legitimated by wider international society as humanitarian exceptions to the rules of sovereignty, non-intervention and non-use of force. However, the international response that greeted the two interventions was radically different: Vietnam's use of force was almost universally condemned whereas Tanzania's intervention that breached the same rules as Vietnam's was treated much more leniently. What, then, explains this divergence of response? The international response was to a large degree conditioned by the political and strategic imperatives of the cold war. The case where armed intervention was arguably most justifiable on humanitarian grounds—Vietnam's intervention to overthrow the Pol Pot regime in Cambodia—received the greatest censure. Rather than legitimize the overthrow of the Pol Pot regime on humanitarian grounds, Vietnam was castigated and sanctioned by both the US-led Western bloc and China for acting as an agent of Soviet imperialism. In contrast, Tanzania's overthrow of Idi Amin received no public denunciation from the cold war protagonists, with the new Ugandan government rapidly receiving widespread recognition and financial aid from a number of foreign governments. Cold war geopolitics were not as strong a motivating influence in this case as they were with Cambodia, and Amin had almost totally alienated the Soviet Union, his superpower patron and only ally outside of Africa.

Turning to the regional reaction, with the exception of Nigeria and the outgoing chair of the Organization of African Unity (OAU) Sudan which roundly condemned Tanzania, the rest of the OAU reacted in a way which amounted to what Caroline Thomas calls 'almost tacit approval' (Thomas 1985: 122–3). This reflected the following considerations: the belief among most African leaders that Tanzania had

been the victim of a prior act of Ugandan aggression in late 1978 when Amin had seized the Kegara Salient; the perception that Tanzania as one of the poorest African countries was not a predatory state, and finally Amin's excesses at home and abroad had become an embarrassment to other African governments.

Key points

- Humanitarian considerations do not seem to have been decisive in the decisions of Vietnam and Tanzania to intervene.

- Vietnam and Tanzania justified their interventions in terms of the traditional norms of the society of states.

- The reluctance of the society of states to legitimize humanitarian intervention reflected fears about setting precedents which could erode the non-intervention principle.

- In the polarized world of the late 1970s, reactions to the Tanzanian and Vietnamese interventions were conditioned by cold war geopolitics.

Post-cold war humanitarian interventions

This section focuses on international interventions in northern Iraq, Somalia, Rwanda, and Kosovo. It is divided into three parts: first, the place of humanitarian impulses in state decisions to intervene; second, the legality and legitimacy of the interventions; and finally, the success of these military interventions.

The role of humanitarian sentiments in state decisions to intervene

In the cases of northern Iraq and Somalia, the principal force behind intervention was not state leaders taking the lead in persuading reluctant publics to respond to a humanitarian emergency. Rather, it was the media and domestic public opinion that pressur-

ized policy-makers into taking humanitarian actions. In the face of a massive refugee crisis caused by Saddam Hussein's oppression of the Kurds, US, British, French, and Dutch military forces intervened to create protected 'safe havens' for the Kurdish people. James Mayall argues that action was only taken to protect the Kurds 'because the attention devoted by the Western media to the plight of the Kurds along the Turkish border threatened the political dividends that Western governments had secured from their conduct of the war itself' (Mayall 1991: 426).

Similarly, the US military intervention in Somalia in December 1992 was a response to sentiments of compassion on the part of US citizens. However, this sense of solidarity disappeared once Americans saw the blood of their fellow countrymen being spilt on the streets of Mogadishu. The fact that the US pulled the plug on its Somali intervention after the loss of eighteen US Rangers in a fire-fight in October 1993 indicates how capricious public opinion is. Television pictures of starving and dying Somalis had persuaded the outgoing Bush administration to launch a humanitarian rescue mission, but once the US public saw the consequences of this in terms of dead Americans being dragged through the streets of Mogadishu, the Clinton administration was forced to announce a timetable for the withdrawal of all US forces from Somalia. What this case demonstrates is that the 'CNN factor' is a double-edged sword: it can pressurize governments into humanitarian intervention, yet with equal rapidity, pictures of casualties arriving home can lead to public disillusionment and calls for withdrawal.

In the cases of intervention in northern Iraq and Somalia, policy-makers primarily acted to appease the humanitarian sentiments of domestic publics. But whilst sensitivity to public opinion was probably the key factor, it would be churlish to deny that moral concerns played some part in leading Western governments to embark on these interventions. What these cases suggest is that even if there are no vital national interests at stake, liberal states will launch humanitarian rescue missions if sufficient public pressure is mobilized. Certainly, there is no evidence in either of these cases to support the realist claim that states cloak power political motives behind the guise of humanitarianism. Nevertheless, humanitarian interventions that are motivated by the primary concern of responding to pressures from domestic constituencies fail Bhikhu Parekh's definiton of humanitarian intervention as actions 'primarily guided by the sentiment of humanity, compassion or fellow-feeling'.

But if the motives driving the interventions in Somalia and northern Iraq fail Parekh's stringent criteria for a genuine humanitarian intervention, how much more so does the French intervention in Rwanda in July 1994 which seems to be an example of **Abuse**. The French government emphasized the strictly humanitarian character of the operation, but this interpretation lacks credibility given the evidence that they seem to have been covertly pursuing national self-interest behind the fig-leaf of humani-

tarianism. France had propped up the one-party Hutu state for twenty years, even providing troops when the Rwandan Patriotic Front (RPF), operating out of neighbouring Uganda, threatened to overrun the country in 1990 and 1993. The French President, François Mitterrand, was reportedly anxious to restore waning French credibility in Africa, and was fearful that an RPF victory in French-speaking Rwanda would result in the country coming under the influence of Anglophones. It seems, therefore, that French behaviour accords with the realist premise that states will only risk their soldiers in defence of the national interest. State leaders may have been partly motivated by humanitarian sentiments but this seems to be a case of a state abusing the concept of humanitarian intervention since the primary purpose of the intervention was to protect French national interests. This is the judgement of Bruce Jones who, on the basis of interviews with French diplomats, concludes that although humanitarian sentiment was not wholly absent, France's primary motives were non-humanitarian. The problem with this verdict, as Jones recognizes, is that for all of the criticisms made of the French intervention, it may be justified on the grounds that lives were saved (Jones 1996: 225–50).

According to Jones, the Rwandan case should lead us to broaden the traditional definition of humanitarian intervention, with its focus on the primacy of humanitarian motives, to encompass humanitarian outcomes. Figure 22.1 sets out Jones's matrix for judging the humanitarian character of interventions. For illustrative purposes, we have filled in three of the boxes with cases drawn from this chapter. Jones does not develop his understanding of humanitarian motives but it is helpful to think of the horizontal line of the matrix as a continuum with pure humanitarian motives at one end and the complete absence of humanitarian motives at the other. Humanitarian interventions launched to appease domestic publics are not examples where the humanitarian motive is primary, but they should be located nearer this end of the continuum than cases where state leaders espouse humanitarian motives to cloak the pursuit of national self-interest. Thus, in the cases of northern Iraq and Somalia, once the interventions were embarked upon, there is no evidence to suggest that the purpose of the intervention

Humanitarian outcomes

Humanitarian motives and outcomes: the international intervention in Northern Iraq in April 1991	**Non-humanitarian motives: humanitarian outcomes:** Vietnam's intervention in Cambodia in December 1978 and Tanzania's intervention in Uganda
Humanitarian motives, non-humanitarian outcomes: the UN intervention in Somalia from May 1993 to February 1995	**Non-humanitarian motives and outcomes:** Soviet intervention in Afghanistan in 1979

Humanitarian motivation (left side) · *Non-humanitarian motivation* (right side)

Non-humanitarian outcomes

Fig. 22.1 Matrix of humanitarian intervention—motivation and outcomes
Source: Adapted from a matrix in Bruce Jones (1996: 239)

was anything other than the promotion of humanitarian ends. By contrast, the securing of French national interests was the dominant factor shaping the purposes, execution, and character of French military intervention in Rwanda (Destexhe 1995: 51–5). The vertical line of the matrix indicates the success or failure of interventions in humanitarian terms, but this raises the question as to what counts as a successful humanitarian intervention. This is discussed later in the chapter.

The moral question raised by French intervention is why international society failed to intervene as soon as the genocide began in early April 1994. French intervention might have saved some lives but it came far too late to halt the genocide. The failure of international society to stop the genocide demonstrates the limits of states as guardians of human rights. It is some two decades since the 'killing fields' in Cambodia—the chilling description of Pol Pot's mass killing—but the response to Rwanda indicates that state leaders remain gripped by the mindset of **statism**. The expression of international solidarity in the face of genocide was limited to moral outrage and the provision of humanitarian aid to its victims.

If the French intervention in Rwanda can be criticized for being too little, too late, NATO's intervention in Kosovo in 1999 has been criticized for being too much, too soon. At the beginning of the war, NATO said it was intervening to prevent a humanitarian catastrophe. To do this, NATO aircraft were given two objectives, reduce Serbia's military capacity—especially its capacity to conduct internal repression, and coerce Milosevic into accepting the Rambouillet settlement, with the emphasis initially placed on the former. As George Robertson, the British Defence Minister, declared, 'our military objective—our clear, simple military objective—will be to reduce the Serbs' capacity to repress the Albanian population and thus to avert a humanitarian catastrophe'[5]. Three arguments were adduced to support NATO's claim that the resort to force was justifiable. First, it was argued that Serbian actions in Kosovo had created a supreme humanitarian emergency which breached a whole range of international legal commitments accepted by the FRY. Second, NATO governments pointed to the ad-hoc war crimes tribunal set up to deal with crimes committed in the wars in Croatia and Bosnia and argued that the Serbs were again committing crimes against humanity, possibly including genocide. Third, it was contended that the Milosevic regime's use of force against the Kosovar Albanians challenged global norms of **common humanity**, and that NATO had a moral obligation to act to stop such criminal actions as otherwise it would be complicit in Serb atrocities.

Closer analysis of the justifications articulated by Western leaders suggests that whilst humanitarianism may have provided the primary impulse for action, it was by no means the exclusive impulse, and as we will see, the complexity of the motives of the interveners coloured the character of the intervention. Whilst insisting that humanitarian need was the primary motive, Robin Cook argued that NATO credibility was also a key determinant, particularly as the previous twelve months of diplomacy with Milosevic had been underpinned by the supposed credible threat of force. The US was particularly concerned with the regional implications of continuing violence in Kosovo. Viewing the Dayton agreement, which brought peace to Bosnia in 1995, as an American diplomatic triumph, the administration's main interest in the region was Dayton's preservation. Thus, Clinton emphasized that the Kosovo tragedy was unfolding 'in the heart of Europe' and 'NATO's backyard' when he justified his policy to his electorate. Western states were also concerned that the massive flow of refugees in the southern Balkans could threaten the stability of the already weak states of Macedonia and Albania, and generate a massive inflow of asylum seekers in the West.

The initial, officially stated, objective of Operation Allied Force was to prevent the Serbs continuing their repression of Kosovar Albanians by destroying their capabilities. However, four years earlier, in Bosnia, the military commanders of 'Operation Deliberate Force' (aimed against the Bosnian Serbs) had soon realized that it was not possible to hit 'smoking gun' targets from the air. During Deliberate Force, targets around Sarajevo were engaged by British and French artillery based on Mount Igman, whilst NATO aircraft concentrated on destroying General Mladic's ability to control his army, by attacking weapons dumps, bridges, and communications installations. Not surprisingly, therefore, in the opening weeks of Operation Allied Force, ethnic cleansing and mass murder continued unabated.

Meanwhile, Western leaders subtly changed their objectives and justifications. The operation was no longer about 'preventing' a humanitarian catastrophe; it was now concerned with 'reversing' the effects of that catastrophe. When NATO failed to prevent the expulsion of over one million Kosovar Albanians and the deaths of thousands, it stated that its objective was 'Serbs out, NATO in, refugees home'.

The question that has to be asked is whether NATO employed the right means to secure its humanitarian ends? Or, did the use of bombing as the means of humanitarian intervention create the very humanitarian catastrophe that NATO claimed to be preventing by the use of force? The question that NATO spokespersons kept eluding during the conflict was how a campaign fought solely from the air could achieve the Alliance's humanitarian ends. Moreover as the campaign failed to deliver an early success, NATO planes switched from their largely unsuccessful targeting of Serb forces in Kosovo to attacks against a range of targets in the FRY that it was claimed had a military application. The number of Serb civilians killed is disputed with estimates varying between 500 and 2000. By employing state-of-the-art precision guided munitions, NATO was able to keep Serb civilian deaths to a minimum, but this aspect of the bombing campaign was highly controversial. During the campaign, the UN's human rights commissioner, Mary Robinson, criticized the Alliance for too permissive a definition of what counted as a legitimate military target, and in a report published several months after the conflict was concluded, the US based Human Rights Watch charged the Alliance with breaching the laws of war relating to the protection of civilians in armed conflicts. Critics of the bombing campaign argue that the best means for stopping the ethnic cleansing in Kosovo was the deployment of ground forces, but NATO governments ruled this out because it would have led to allied casualties. Ultimately, NATO's humanitarian commitment to protecting the Kosovars did not extend to risking soldiers' lives.

We showed earlier how the traditional focus on motives should be supplemented by studying humanitarian outcomes, and the Kosovo case highlights a further key issue in any discussion of humanitarian intervention, namely, the character of the means employed to defend humanitarian values. It is important that the means chosen to prosecute humanitarian interventions do not, as in the case of Kosovo, serve to undermine or even contradict the humanitarian purposes behind such actions. Selecting the appropriate means to achieve the humanitarian ends of an intervention is a crucial factor in securing both domestic and international legitimacy for an intervention.

How legal and legitimate were the interventions?

In contrast with state practice during the cold war, the interventions in northern Iraq, Somalia, Rwanda, and Kosovo were all legitimated in humanitarian terms by the intervening states. The norms of sovereignty and non-intervention remain the key foundations of order, but there is a growing sense—especially among Western states—that these principles should be overturned by the collectivity of states in cases of exceptional human suffering. However, if post-cold war international interventions suggest a growing willingness on the part of international society to legitimate humanitarian intervention inside state borders, then the key point to note is that none of these interventions have been legitimated by the UN Security Council solely on humanitarian grounds. **Chapter VII** of the Charter enables the Security Council to authorize military enforcement action only in cases where it finds a threat to 'international peace and security'. This attempt to justify humanitarian intervention on the grounds that human suffering constitutes a threat to international security was controversially employed in the case of northern Iraq.

Resolution 688 passed on 5 April 1991 identified the refugee crisis caused by Saddam Hussein's repression as constituting a threat to 'international peace and security'. The Resolution was not passed under **Chapter VII** and there was no explicit authorization of military enforcement action to defend the Kurds in northern Iraq. The reason for this was that Resolution 688 was highly controversial in the eyes of the Soviet Union, China, and a number of other non-Western states on the Council. These states were fearful that authorizing the use of force to protect

human rights would set a precedent for humanitarian intervention that might be employed against them and/or undermine the non-intervention norm in the society of states. The refusal of the UN Security Council to provide a military enforcement mandate for international intervention in northern Iraq forced the Western powers to justify their military intervention as authorized by Resolution 688. This attempt at securing legitimacy was not expressly endorsed by other states, but it was either tacitly legitimated or acquiesced in because no one wanted to challenge the legality of an intervention that was saving the lives of hundreds of thousands of Kurds.

In stark contrast to northern Iraq, the UN Security Council approved unanimously the US military intervention in Somalia to create a secure environment for the delivery of humanitarian aid. Resolution 794 passed under **Chapter VII** in December 1992 represented a sharp break in existing practice, for as Christopher Greenwood notes, 'it was the plight of the Somali people which was given as the reason for invoking **Chapter VII** of the Charter and authorizing intervention' (Greenwood 1993: 37). The direct relationship between the internal governance of Sub-Saharan states and the wider security of states and peoples in that region was affirmed in Resolution 794. However, this justification has to be seen in the context of a UN Security Council trying to accommodate new practices of humanitarian intervention in the society of states within the framework of the dominant restrictionist interpretation of UN Charter law (Roberts 1993: 440). The reason why the UN Security Council legitimated US military intervention in Somalia, in contrast to the position it had taken over intervention in northern Iraq, was because it did not conform to the classical model of intervention against a government's will. The Somali state had effectively collapsed and humanitarian intervention was legitimated because it was perceived as not undermining the principles of sovereignty and non-intervention (Roberts 1993: 429–49). Nevertheless, non-Western states were sufficiently sensitive to the dangers of being seen to legitimate exceptions to the non-intervention principle that they ensured that the drafting of Resolution 794 undermined its import as a case of humanitarian intervention. For example, immediately prior to noting the relationship between human suffering and threats to international peace and security, the resolution recognizes the 'unique character of the present situation in Somalia and mindful of its deteriorating, complex and extraordinary nature, requiring an immediate and exceptional response'. The use of terms such as 'unique', 'extraordinary', and 'exceptional' have to be seen as an attempt to differentiate the humanitarian crisis in Somalia from other cases of **failed states**, hence reducing the chance of setting a precedent for future humanitarian interventions. They seem to have been inserted specifically to appease the fears of states such as China which may otherwise have blocked a **Chapter VII** enforcement action.

More than any other case studied here, NATO's intervention in Kosovo raised the question of how international society should treat intervention where a state, or in this case a group of states, decides to use force to alleviate human suffering without the explicit authorization of the Security Council. A year before NATO's intervention, Britain tried to persuade Russia and China to agree to a **Chapter VII** resolution that would allow NATO to take military action if Milosevic did not stop his persecution and ethnic cleansing of Kosovar Albanians. Russia and China made it quite clear that they considered Kosovo to be an internal problem of the FRY and therefore not the legitimate concern of the Security Council. However, NATO did persuade them to agree to Resolution 1199. This was a **Chapter VII** resolution demanding that the FRY cease its actions against Kosovar Albanians, but it did not explicitly authorize the use of force. However, at the beginning of NATO's operation, Western governments argued that Resolution 1199 legitimated their actions because they were enforcing the will of the Security Council. Some lawyers, such as Christopher Greenwood, argued that when the Security Council makes demands but is unwilling to enforce those demands even when a state refuses to comply, there is a customary right, and indeed responsibility, for groups of states to act to fulfil the wishes of the Council. This argument was rejected by Russia, China, and India who insisted that no such customary right exists and that any such right would undermine the United Nations and threaten international order.

Although the UN did not expressly sanction NATO's use of force, the Security Council also chose not to condemn it. Immediately after NATO launched its first attacks against the FRY, Russia tabled a draft Security Council resolution condemning NATO's use of force and demanding an immediate halt to the bombing. Whilst the NATO members on the Council voted against the resolution, what was surprising was that only Russia, China, and Namibia voted in favour leading to a resounding defeat of the resolution.

After 78 days of bombing an agreement was reached which was legitimated in Resolution 1244, leading some to argue that international society tacitly legitimated NATO's intervention because it gave legal and moral validity to the outcome. But what is noteworthy about the Kosovo case is that international society chose not to explicitly engage with the relationship between sovereign rights and human rights. It refused to authorize a group of states to breach the sovereignty of the FRY to protect some of the citizens of that country, but it also refused to condemn or act against that same group of states for doing so. On the one hand, Kosovo may act as a precedent for other regional organizations to act to prevent human rights abuses within a state. Set against this, the society of states was explicit in Resolution 1244 that protecting the human rights of the Kosovars did not extend to recognizing their right to secede from the FRY. The principle of maintaining the territorial integrity of states remained sacrosanct.

The responses to two subsequent humanitarian emergencies in 1999 revealed just how limited the Kosovo precedent was. Although the Australian intervention in East Timor, authorized by Resolution 1264, was widely heralded as demonstrating the further consolidation of a norm of humanitarian intervention, the Australian Government was emphatic that it would only act with a mandate from the Security Council. China and Russia remained very sensitive about setting precedents that erode the rules of sovereignty and non-intervention, but were prepared to support Resolution 1264 because intervention in East Timor had the consent of the Indonesian government. The word consent in this context is something of a misnomer because Indonesia only agreed to the Australian intervention after severe financial pressure was applied against it by the US. The continuing influence of sovereignty-based norms was also evident in the international response to Russia's brutal suppression of the Chechens. Those Western states that had used force to protect human rights in Kosovo stood by and acquiesced in Russia's gross violation of the laws that protect civilians in armed conflict. Russia received a moral rebuke for its actions, but there was no attempt to try and influence Russian actions through the threat or use of economic sanctions.

What emerges from post-cold war state practice is that any normative shift on the question of humanitarian intervention is primarily confined to domestic publics within liberal democratic states, though in the case of Kosovo, the British and US governments placed the issue on the public agenda before there was a great clamour for action. Many non-Western states question Western (especially US) motives in advocating a new norm of humanitarian intervention, seeing it as a new form of 'imperialism' that will leave the weak vulnerable to the cultural preferences of the strong (Thomas 1993: 91–101). Non-Western state leaders may sincerely value the rules of sovereignty and non-intervention as a bulwark against Western military power, but they may also employ these legitimating principles to cover the fact that the human rights agenda of Western governments is a threat to their own power. Whilst the reaction of some Western states to recent humanitarian crises in northern Iraq and Somalia has been substantially influenced by the need to respond to domestic electorates, public opinion is not such a powerful force in those states which are hostile to the emerging human rights agenda of the post-cold war world.

The most powerful challengers to post-cold war Western-sponsored humanitarian interventions have been China and Russia. When issues of intervention have arisen, they have proved to be the most cautious of the Security Council's permanent members. Their concern over the erosion of the non-intervention principle stems less from a fear that, at some future date, they may themselves become the target of intervention. China and Russia are protected against such an eventuality by both their veto within the Security Council and a military capability that makes any form of coercive intervention wholly untenable. In the case of China, its experience at the hands of the colonial powers, a radically different conception of human rights, and its suspicion of Western motives in promoting humanitarian inter-

vention explain a normative position which places sovereignty and non-intervention at the pinnacle of a hierarchy of principles. A deep suspicion of Western motives and anxiety at what it sees as a growing unilateralism in US foreign policy seems to explain Russia's strident opposition to an emergent norm of humanitarian intervention. In the absence of a robust countervailing military capability that might deter US adventurism, Russia has a strong interest in strengthening the normative restraints on the use of force in the society of states.

In arguing that Western states are advancing a new norm of humanitarian intervention in international society, it is important to realize that this is confined to situations where the Security Council has either adopted a **Chapter VII** Resolution authorizing the use of force, or where there are existing **Chapter VII** resolutions demanding compliance but where the Council lacks the will to enforce its demands. The latter claim is heavily contested as the case of Kosovo shows, but what is not being argued for by Western states is a legal right of humanitarian intervention that could be invoked in the absence of any supporting **Chapter VII** resolutions.

Prior to French intervention in Rwanda, there were reports that it was considering intervention even without a Security Council mandate. However, French policy-makers, perhaps realizing the implications of being seen to claim a customary right of unilateral humanitarian intervention, were emphatic that their action was conditional on receiving a mandate from the UN Security Council. Nevertheless, there was suspicion on the part of many states on the Council that France was manipulating humanitarian sentiments to cover actions motivated primarily by national self-interest. This fear that France was abusing humanitarian claims was reflected in the fact that five Council members abstained on the vote on Resolution 929.

Whilst no Western state has expressly advanced a general customary right of humanitarian intervention, there is one case where a group of African states acted to stop a supreme humanitarian emergency in a context where there was no prior Security Council involvement. By contrast with NATO's legal defence over Kosovo, what distinguishes the ECOWAS (Economic Community of West-African States) intervention in Liberia in 1990 is that there were no existing

Security Council resolutions adopted under **Chapter VII** that could be invoked to justify the use of force. Although the UN did not authorize the intervention, it did subsequently adopt a resolution legitimating the action.

Ideally, humanitarian intervention will always operate with the flag of UN Security Council legitimacy. But as we have seen with the Tanzanian and Vietnamese interventions, cases have arisen where the UN Security Council has failed as a guardian of human rights, and local states have intervened without Security Council approval. The principal motivation in these cases was not humanitarian, but they produced positive humanitarian outcomes. Should Vietnam have been condemned by international society for breaching the principles of international order, even though its action ended Pol Pot's genocidal regime? The privileging of order over justice in the Cambodian case reflected the conviction among state leaders that legitimating unilateral humanitarian intervention would jeopardize the rules of sovereignty, non-intervention and non-use of force, leading to an erosion of the bases of international order. This advocacy of **Rule-Consequentialism** leads to the strong claim that even if it is calculated that military intervention could prevent or halt genocide, the absence of Security Council approval renders such an action not only illegal, but also illegitimate. A tension undeniably exists between the requirements of international order and the possibility that unilateral action may be the only way of stopping gross violations of human rights.

Were the interventions successful?

Does the record of post-cold war forcible interventions lend support to the proposition that the use of force can promote humanitarian values? We argued earlier that humanitarian outcomes are as significant as humanitarian motives in determining the humanitarian character of interventions. Humanitarian outcomes might usefully be divided into short and long-term ones. The former would refer to the immediate alleviation of human suffering through the termination of genocide or mass murder and/or the delivery of humanitarian aid to civilians trapped in war zones. Long-term humanitarian outcomes focus on how far intervention addresses the underlying causes of human suffering by facilitating conflict-resolution and the reconstruction of viable polities. Defining humanitarian outcomes in this manner is favoured by Bhikhu Parekh and Michael Walzer. Parekh argues that the delivery of aid in complex humanitarian emergencies is not humanitarian intervention which he defines as a political act 'intended to help create . . . a structure of civil authority acceptable to the people involved' (Parekh 1997: 55–6). His contention is that humanitarian intervention differs from other forms of intervention in aiming to ensure that new structures of government are evolved in consultation with local political actors, rather than being imposed from outside. This is also the argument of Walzer who challenges the traditional **counter-restrictionist** assumption that humanitarian interveners should conduct a quick military intervention and then withdrawal having removed the source of the human rights abuses (Arend and Beck 1993: 134). This might have been realistic in the cold war period where forcible intervention could end the human rights abuses of genocidal regimes (as in Tanzania's intervention in Uganda). However, Walzer argues that this type of intervention is not appropriate to post-cold war humanitarian crises where the sources of human suffering are often deeply rooted in the political, economic, and social structures of societies. Walzer contends that if intervention does not address the underlying roots of these conflicts, the withdrawal of the intervening force will simply lead to the resumption of violent conflict. He argues that the use of force in complex humanitarian emergencies should be employed as part of a long-term project of conflict-resolution and political, economic and social reconstruction (Walzer 1995: 35–6).

Given this conceptualization of short-term and long-term humanitarian outcomes, how should we evaluate the international interventions in northern Iraq, Somalia, and Kosovo? 'Operation Safe Haven' enjoyed initial success in dealing with the refugee problem in northern Iraq and clearly saved lives. However, as the media spotlight began to shift elsewhere and public interest waned, so did the commitment of Western governments to protect the Kurds. Whilst Western airforces continue to police a 'no-fly zone' over northern Iraq that extends some protection to the Kurds, the intervening states quickly handed over the running of the safe havens to what they knew was an ill-equipped and badly supported UN relief operation. This faces enormous problems given Iraq's enduring hostility towards its Kurdish minority. Despite its success in alleviating the immediate suffering of the Kurds, a decade later the intervention appears to have been little more than a short-term palliative which failed to address their long-term plight.

The initial US intervention in Somalia in the period between December 1992 and May 1993 is adduced by some as evidence of a successful humanitarian intervention. In terms of short-term success, the US arguably saved thousands of Somalis from starvation, but the mission eventually ended in disaster and withdrawal. This can be traced to the attempt by UNOSOM II (this UN force took over from the Americans in May 1993 but it was under a US commander and its military missions were principally controlled by the US) to go beyond the initial US mission of famine relief to the disarmament of the warring factions and the provision of law and order in Somali society. Suffering always has political causes, and the rationale behind the expanded mandate of UNOSOM II was to try and put in place a framework of political civility that would prevent a return to civil war and famine. However, this attempt to convert a short-term humanitarian outcome (famine relief) into the longer-term one of conflict-resolution and reconstruction proved a failure. The problem was that the UN's impartiality was more and more called into question as it tried to impose solutions upon the fragile 'clan' relations that underpin Somali society. Once the UN Security Council sanctioned the arrest of one of the warlords, General Aidid, after his forces had killed 23 UN peace-keepers in June 1993, UNOSOM II acted like an imperial power, relying on high-tech American weaponry to police the streets of Southern Mogadishu. Indeed, the shift from famine-relief to warmaking was graphically illustrated by the television footage of US helicopter gunships firing missiles into the urban areas of southern Mogadishu.

In Kosovo, NATO failed to achieve its primary objective—the prevention of a humanitarian catastrophe. Because it was unable to destroy Serbian air defences and was determined that no NATO pilots should be killed, it had to restrict its operations to medium altitude bombing (15,000 feet). Yet as General Wesley Clark who commanded NATO forces during the conflict pointed out at a press briefing during the conflict, the problem with this strategy was that 'air power alone cannot stop paramilitary action'.[6] Air power which initially had been the chosen instrument to prevent a humanitarian catastrophe now became the means to reverse the ethnic cleansing of the Kosovar Albanians. Indeed, it is generally accepted that the air campaign accelerated Serb ethnic cleansing in Kosovo by providing a cover that enabled Serb paramilitaries and regular forces to drive hundreds of thousands of Kosovars from their homes.

Having failed to prevent a humanitarian catastrophe, NATO governments changed the rationale for the bombing campaign to that of returning the refugees to their homes. The NATO-led force that went into Kosovo immediately after the air campaign (KFOR) did succeed in returning virtually all the refugees to their homes remarkably quickly. However, it is too early to judge the long-term success of the intervention. On the one hand, most of the Serbian population has fled Kosovo and those that are left live in fear of their lives in ghettos protected by KFOR troops. The grim truth is that the Kosovar Albanians who suffered at the hands of the Serbs through the 1990s are now inflicting their own brand of ethnic apartheid on those Serbs who continue to live in Kosovo. On the other hand, the majority people of Kosovo have their first opportunity to enjoy democratic and legitimate governance and projects such as the EU's Stability Pact offer the possibility of genuine post-war reconstruction.

Although dubbed the first 'humanitarian war', the post-war commitment of Western governments to reconstruction in Kosovo has not matched the demands of the situation. The failure to provide an adequate supply of well-trained police officers increased the vulnerability of the Serb minority and contributed to the criminality that is rife within Kosovo. If the overriding reason for intervening in Kosovo was to halt ethnic cleansing and promote democracy and human rights, then we could have expected to have seen a more concerted and better resourced post war reconstruction programme.

Is forcible intervention in humanitarian crises always condemned to be a short-term palliative? And if so, is it the most appropriate form of intervention? The problem in the cases studied here is that the initial determination to employ force in defence of humanitarian goals was not backed up by a long-term political, economic, and social commitment to the interventionary project. States that intervene militarily as agents of **common humanity** need to have a clear formulation of short-term and long-term objectives, which balances immediate responses to the humanitarian crisis with a sustained commitment to conflict-resolution and social reconstruction.

Key points

- Media images of human suffering have led Western publics to pressurize their leaders into post-cold war humanitarian interventions.

- Humanitarian intervention secures its greatest legitimation when it is done through the **Chapter VII** enforcement provisions of the Security Council, confirming the dominance of the **restrictionist** view of the illegality of non-Security Council authorized humanitarian intervention.

- Non-Western states, notably Russia and China, are suspicious of legitimating humanitarian intervention through the broadening of **Chapter VII**.

- Fears about **rule-consequentialism** and **Abuse** remain powerful barriers to legitimating humanitarian intervention outside of the Security Council.

- The humanitarian character of interventions should be judged in terms of motives, means and outcomes.

- Humanitarian outcomes should be conceptualized in terms of a continuum ranging from short-term (immediate relief of suffering) to long-term (addressing the underlying causes of suffering).

Globalization and non-forcible humanitarian intervention

As we have seen, the traditional approach to humanitarian intervention focuses on states and forcible intervention. Intervention is characterized by coercion, a breach of sovereignty, and is non-consensual. By contrast, **non-forcible humanitarian intervention** emphasizes the pacific activities of states, international organizations, and non-governmental organizations in delivering humanitarian aid and facilitating third party conflict-resolution and reconstruction. **Non-forcible humanitarian intervention** can be consensual or non-consensual. An example of the latter is the activities of Médecins Sans Frontières which frequently operates without the consent of host governments, but which works through non-violent methods to bring humanitarian relief. Consensual acts include the diplomacy of third party mediation and the practices of the International Committee of the Red Cross which normally only operates with the consent of sovereign governments. The weakness, then, of restricting humanitarian intervention to coercive/forcible acts is that such a definition provides no framework for accommodating the non-military humanitarian activities of states and non-state actors. The humanitarian interventions in northern Iraq and Somalia have shown the problems of holding too rigidly to the narrow definition, since in both these cases, military force was deployed in an effort to create a secure 'humanitarian space' within which the non-forcible arm of humanitarianism could operate (Ramsbotham and Woodhouse 1996).

The activities of humanitarian agencies in complex humanitarian emergencies reflect the growth of a global society in which humanitarian organizations operate transnationally. Globalization has generated many of the ills of contemporary life but it

Box 22.4 The mission of Médecins Sans Frontières

Médecins Sans Frontières (MSF) is the leading non-governmental organization for emergency medical aid. We provide independent medical relief to victims of war, disasters, and epidemics in 80 countries around the world. We strive to provide assistance to those who need it most, regardless of ethnic origin, religion, or political affiliation.

To get access to care for the most vulnerable, MSF must remain scrupulously independent of governments, as well as religious and economic powers. We rely on private individuals for the majority of our funding. In the field, we conduct our own assessments, manage projects directly and monitor the impact of our aid. We campaign locally and internationally for greater respect for humanitarian law and the right of civilians to impartial humanitarian assistance. We also campaign for fairer access to medicines and health care for the world's poorest people.[7]

has also created that growing sense of 'cosmopolitan moral awareness' (Bull 1984*b*: 12) which is beginning to make a reality of Kant's vision of a right's violation in one place being felt everywhere. Television represents images of humanity in peril that are beamed into living rooms across the globe, and it is this which, as we argued above, pressurized Western governments into raising new humanitarian claims to justify the use of force. It is simply no longer possible for state leaders and publics to isolate themselves and say that they do not know what is happening in places like Rwanda, Chechnya, and Sierra Leone. Rather, governments are required to justify their moral choices when confronted by other states and local agents committing crimes against humanity. The challenge for those individuals and organizations committed to the defence of minimum standards of humanity is to ensure that governments are held accountable for their moral choices when confronted by acts of genocide, mass murder, and ethnic cleansing. British Prime Minister, Tony Blair, showed awareness of how globalization was constructing new humanitarian sensibilities when he described his idea for a doctrine of international

community. Blair argued that despotic isolationism and brutal human rights abuses were no longer tolerable in a globalizing world and that, 'the principle of non-interference must be qualified in important respects'. When fundamental human values were at stake, argued Blair, it was no longer possible to hide behind the veil of sovereign inviolability.

The global human rights culture seeks to protect human rights and humanitarian values everywhere. This culture is a product of the post-holocaust world and it is embedded in the ideas and practices of international civil servants, media, local non-governmental organizations (NGOs) and a global network of humanitarian international non-governmental organizations (INGOs) that are sustained and supported by that transnational global citizenry committed to human rights and humanitarianism (Minear and Weiss 1995; Jones 1995). This community is anti-statist but not necessarily anti-state; governments often fail to act as local agents of **common humanity**, but a key challenge for those who want to deepen global moral solidarities is to harness state power to the purposes of global humanitarianism.

The global human rights culture is a unique and progressive feature of the globalization of world politics at the end of the millennium. Its existence reflects the growing recognition that the causes of human rights abuses and humanitarian crises are global ones that require global solutions. **Non-forcible humanitarian intervention** is usually defined in terms of the activities of non-state actors and third party mediators in complex humanitarian emergencies, but it also needs to encompass global interventionary strategies designed to address the underlying causes of human suffering in world politics.

The question of how and why human suffering gets constructed in the way it does is beyond the scope of this chapter. However, consider the following question posed by Parekh: Why, he asks, 'should suffering and death only become a matter of humanitarian intervention when they are caused by the breakdown of the state or by an outrageous abuse of its power?' (Parekh 1997). The answer to this question is that what counts as human suffering is a product of the ideological biases of global political and economic elites. It suits dominant elites to construct humanitarian intervention in terms of crisis management rather than developing the global political and economic policies to address the underlying structural causes of poverty and malnutrition. There is nothing natural or inevitable about the facts of global poverty; it is a product of the handiwork of individuals and social classes whose interactions have constructed global capitalism. These structures are deeply rooted, produce a global alienated underclass, and their transformation must be the objective of an emancipatory global politics of **non-forcible humanitarian intervention**.

Key points

- **Non-forcible humanitarian intervention** is characterized by the pacific activities of states, international organizations, and INGOs in the global humanitarian community.

- **Non-forcible humanitarian intervention** spans the crisis management activities of humanitarian INGOs and third party conflict-resolution by states and non-state actors.

- INGOs have succeeded in broadening the humanitarian agenda to include issues of development, the environment, and women's rights.

- Dominant Western political and economic elites encourage a crisis management approach to complex humanitarian emergencies which does nothing to tackle the underlying causes of these emergencies.

- Humanitarian crises like Somalia and Rwanda are the tip of the iceberg of human suffering. The slow death of millions through poverty and malnutrition are just as pressing cases for humanitarian intervention.

Conclusion

Humanitarian intervention remains a contested issue at the end of the cold war. Realism and **Pluralist international society theory** seek to interpret the cases we have discussed in this chapter as confirming their different theoretical positions. Realism purports to describe and explain the 'realities' of statecraft but the problem with this claim to objectivity is that it is the realist mindset that has constructed the very practices that realist theory seeks to explain. Realism identifies some important objections to the practice of humanitarian intervention, but this chapter has argued that **Pluralist international society theory** is essential to any understanding of why the society of states has proven so reluctant to legitimate humanitarian intervention. **Pluralist international society theory** reinforces the dominant practices of the society of states which continue to subordinate human rights concerns to state sovereignty. But crucially, there is nothing natural or inevitable about this hierarchy between order and justice. Indeed, changing values and norms

could lead to the growth of new solidarist sentiments which produce a just world order.

This chapter is sympathetic to **Solidarist international society theory**, but solidarism is a muted voice in contemporary global politics. Solidarism relies on states acting as trustees of **common humanity**, but what emerges from a study of state practice in the 1990s, is that it is not states but an emergent global civil society that is the principal agent promoting humanitarian values in global politics. Globalization is bringing nearer Kant's vision of moral interconnectedness, but as the Rwandan genocide so brutally demonstrates, this growth in 'cosmopolitan moral awareness' has not yet been translated into the solidarist project of **forcible humanitarian intervention**. Western publics living in the relatively secure sphere of global politics are increasingly sensitized to the human suffering of others, but this media nurtured sense of compassion is very selective in its response to human suffering. The media spotlight ensured that governments directed their humanitarian energies to the crises in northern Iraq, Somalia, and Bosnia, but during the same period millions perished in the brutal civil wars in Angola, Liberia, and Afghanistan.

A growing consciousness of **common humanity** permeates the emerging global civil society: but how can this society best promote humanitarianism? Is **forcible humanitarian intervention** sometimes the only way to respond to massive human rights abuses? Or, is the use of violence to stop even greater violence a strategy that can only result in a spiral of bloodletting to the detriment of humanitarian goals? Each case has to be judged on its merits but as the example of Somalia, and perhaps Kosovo demonstrate, interventions which begin with humanitarian credentials can all too easily degenerate into 'a range of policies and activities which go beyond, or even conflict with, the label "humanitarian"' (Roberts 1993: 448). A further fundamental problem with a strategy of **forcible humanitarian intervention** concerns the so-called 'body-bag' factor. Is domestic public opinion, especially in Western states, prepared to see their military personnel die in the cause of humanitarian intervention? The US withdrawal from Somalia after the killing of eighteen US Rangers and the reluctance to put air crews, and especially ground troops, in harms way in Kosovo suggests that liberal societies are not prepared to pay the human costs to save non-citizens in danger. Indeed, a striking feature of all post-cold war humanitarian interventions is that no Western government has yet chosen to risk its military personnel in defence of human rights in situations where there was a high risk of casualties from the outset.

This chapter has examined the case for **non-forcible humanitarian intervention**, which it has been argued, is a progressive manifestation of the globalization of world politics. The actors in this drama are frequently not states and the means employed are always non-violent. This type of intervention spans a continuum ranging from humanitarian crisis management to crisis prevention, and connects the subject of humanitarian intervention to broader issues of conflict resoluton and the role of third-party mediation. The unresolved question here concerns the issue of how far forcible intervention might have an important role to play in stimulating and supporting processes of conflict resolution in complex humanitarian emergencies. Beyond this, the non-forcible approach to humanitarian intervention opens up the normative question of what counts as human suffering at the end of the twentieth century? The 'loud emergencies' of genocide, ethnic cleansing, and famine receive media attention, and command the limited resources of the international donor community. This conception of humanitarianism is not rooted in objective facts; instead, it is the product of globally dominant beliefs and values which privilege the 'loud emergencies' and exclude the 'silent emergency' of slow death through poverty and malnutrition. The question for the future is why the eradication of global poverty is not as urgent a subject for humanitarian intervention as the deaths of those killed by men in uniform with machine guns? If humanitarianism is what we've made of it, we don't have to make it like this in our global future.

QUESTIONS

1 How far is the use of force the defining characteristic of a humanitarian intervention?

2 How important are motives, means, and outcomes in judging the humanitarian credentials of an intervention?

3 List the objections to humanitarian intervention.

4 How persuasive is the **counter-restrictionist** case for a legal right of humanitarian intervention?

5 Should considerations of international order always be privileged over concerns of individual justice in the society of states?

6 Why has the society of states failed to arrive at a collective consensus on what moral principles should underpin a right of humanitarian intervention?

7 Does the illegitimacy of humanitarian intervention in cold war state practice support the theoretical arguments of realists or pluralist international society theorists or both?

8 Is there a new legitimate practice of humanitarian intervention at the end of the cold war?

9 How far is military force an effective instrument for the promotion of humanitarian values?

10 What are the strengths and weaknesses of a strategy of **non-forcible humanitarian intervention**?

11 Are late twentieth-century conceptions of humanitarianism infused with the ideological biases and cultural preferences of the dominant Western states?

GUIDE TO FURTHER READING

Wheeler, N. J., *Saving Strangers: Humanitarian Intervention in International Society* (Oxford: Oxford University Press, 2000). Offers a new way of evaluating humanitarian interventions and considers a wide range of interventions in the cold war and post-cold war eras.

Ramsbotham, O., and Woodhouse, T., *Humanitarian Intervention in Contemporary Conflict* (Cambridge: Polity Press, 1996). Presents a powerful case for broadening humanitarian intervention to include non-forcible approaches. Also contains very good case-study material on Bosnia and Somalia.

Damrosch, L. F. (ed.), *Enforcing Restraint: Collective Intervention in Internal Conflicts* (New York: Council on Foreign Relations, 1993). Contains some very good theoretical chapters on the legality and legitimacy of humanitarian intervention, and excellent case-study material on the former Yugoslavia, northern Iraq, Somalia, Liberia, and Haiti.

Weiss, Thomas G., *Military-Civilian Interactions: Intervening in Humanitarian Crises* (Oxford: Rowman and Littlefield, 1999). Investigates the role that the military can play in supporting humanitarian agencies in complex humanitarian emergencies. Also provides excellent case studies of Iraq, Somalia, Bosnia, Haiti, and Rwanda.

Harriss, J. (ed.), *The Politics of Humanitarian Intervention* (London: Pinter, 1995). Very good at examining the role of the global humanitarian community in responding to complex humanitarian emergencies, and includes very good case-studies of northern Iraq and Somalia.

WEB LINKS

www.un.org The official website of the United Nations. Includes links to all the UN's major institutions and agencies concerned with humanitarian invention, including the Security Council and UNHCR.

www.nato.int/kosovo NATO website containing information on Operation Allied Force and the subsequent KFOR operation.

www.fco.gov.uk Home page of the British Foreign Office, containing speeches and briefing papers on the concept and practice of humanitarian intervention.

www.amnesty.org.uk   Provides details of Amnesty International's work and includes press briefings and links to detailed human rights reports.

www/isn.ethz.ch   Vast archive on all aspects of security and intervention, including many links to institutes working in the field.

www.osce.org   Home page of the OSCE, which has been at the forefront of several interventions in Europe and Central Asia.

www.usip.org   United States Institute for Peace. Research institute carrying out a lot of work in this area.

www.crisisweb.org   Home page of the International Crisis Group, a liberal advocacy group working throughout Africa and south-east Europe.

NOTES

1. The term is Eduardo Rabossi's and was discussed by Richard Rorty in his 1993 Amnesty International lecture, 'Sentimentality and Human Rights'.

2. The term is Stanley Hoffmann's. See his 'The Politics and Ethics of Military Intervention', *Survival*, 37: 4 (1995–6), 31.

3. We are following Tim Dunne and Brian Schmidt in this volume in conceptualizing **statism** as one of the common elements which make up the core of realism in world politics. They identify self-help and survival as the other two. For the purposes of this chapter, we define **statism** as the belief that states only have duties to their own citizens, and that they should not risk their soldiers' lives on humanitarian crusades.

4. The term pluralism here should not be confused with the idea of pluralism found in the literature on interdependence and transnationalism (see Ch. 8). Bull first used this term to refer to the debate within the international society tradition in his chapter on the 'The Grotian conception of international society, in Herbert Butterfield and Martin Wight (eds.), *Diplomatic Investigations* (London: Allen and Unwin, 1966).

5. George Robertson, House of Commons Select Committee on Defence, 24 March 1999, in answer to question 396.

6. 'Pentagon's revenge as NATO chief is told to go', The *Guardian*, 29 July 1999.

7. This quote is from the MSF pamphlet, 'Notes from the Field: The Work of the Médecins Sans Frontières', printed in London, 2000.

23 European and regional integration

Thomas Christiansen

READER'S GUIDE

This chapter discusses the dynamics of regional integration, with a special focus on the European Union. Charting the integration process from the beginnings in the post-war period, a distinction is drawn between supranational and intergovernmental features of the European Union. The role of the EU's central institutions is studied in some detail. The growing international role of the European Union, comprising external trade policies as well as efforts towards a common foreign and security policy, is viewed in the context of globalization. A further section looks beyond Europe to the efforts of regional co-operation in Asia, Africa, and the Americas and contrasts these developments with the more firmly institutionalized process of integration in Europe. The EU emerges as a post-sovereign polity that, despite its imperfections, has firmly established a new form of governance at an intermediate level between the global and the state.

The author is grateful for helpful comments on an earlier draft from Knud Erik Joergensen and Ben Tonra. The usual disclaimer applies.

Introduction

Since the Second World War, politics in Western Europe have been characterized by the emergence of a new political entity—the European Union (EU). In the course of a process of regional integration, the EU has gradually become an important factor in the domestic affairs of states as well as in the relations between them. Initially responsible for the regulation of specific sectors of the economy (coal, steel, agriculture), over time the European institutions have been entrusted with responsibility over an ever-increasing range of tasks. At the end of the century, these included monetary policy, military defence, and the protection of human rights, thus encroaching on what many regard as the core of state sovereignty. During the same period, the EU membership has grown from the six founding members to fifteen, with applications from a further twelve states under consideration (see Box 23.1).

In line with its growing role in economic and social regulation in Western Europe has come a greater weight in international affairs for the European Union. The EU's power to negotiate external trade agreements went hand-in-hand with the establishment of a Customs Union in the 1960s. But in the 1970s came first attempts to co-operate in foreign policy matters for the member states—an ambition that was upgraded to a 'Common Foreign and Security Policy' of the Union in the 1992 Maastricht Treaty. The same treaty also contained plans for a single European currency—the 'euro'—that was launched at the beginning of 1999.

Since the end of the cold war the perspectives for European integration have changed fundamentally. With the Iron Curtain gone, an originally *Western* European project has received a pan-European dimension. Central and East European states, as well as Malta, Cyprus, and Turkey, are seeking to join the EU, and the resulting prospect of a European Union of 25 or more states raises fundamental questions about the nature and direction of the integration process. In this chapter we will address some of these questions, having first looked at the evolution of the European Union, the workings of its main institutions, its relationship with the member states as well as with the wider world. Separate sections will also look at the relationship between the processes of integration and globalization and the emergence of regional co-operation in other parts of the globe.

The evolution of the European Union

After 1945 there was great expectation of a fundamental change in the nature of politics in Europe: after two decades of economic depression, totalitarian government, total war and holocaust, nation-states were widely regarded as failures. Even at best, states had not been able to provide citizens with welfare and security; at worst, they had been guilty of wilfully taking these away from their citizens. Consequently, many thinkers and activists were searching for an alternative form of political organization. One idea that had much support among dissidents and partisan leaders during the war was that of a **'federal union'**—a unification of the peoples of Europe under the umbrella of a federal government. In the immediate aftermath of 1945—in the face of a shattered continent—the time seemed indeed to have arrived for such a radical departure.

Among the organizations created in post-war Europe (see Box 23.2), the **Council of Europe** has been most closely associated with the aspirations of the federalist movement. But in the context of the cold war, the rapid rehabilitation—and rearmament—of European nation-states demonstrated the limitations of the federalist plans for radical, all-encompassing and pan-European union. The Council quickly turned into a disappointment for

Box 23.1 Current and prospective member states of the EU

Member States of the European Union (year of accession)	Candidate countries negotiating entry to the EU (year of application)	Countries participating in the Stability Pact for South-Eastern Europe[a]	Non-member states with strong bilateral or multilateral links with the European Union[b]
• Austria (1995)	• Bulgaria (1995)	• Bosnia and Herzegovina	• Iceland
• Belgium (1953)	• Cyprus (1990)	• Croatia	• Norway
• Denmark (1973)	• Czech Republic (1996)	• Federal Republic of Yugoslovia	• Switzerland
• Finland (1995)	• Estonia (1995)	• Macedonia	
• France (1953)	• Hungary (1994)	• Albania	
• Germany (1953)	• Latvia (1995)		
• Greece (1981)	• Lithuania (1995)		
• Ireland (1973)	• Malta (1990)		
• Italy (1952)	• Poland (1994)		
• Luxembourg (1953)	• Romania (1995)		
• Netherlands (1953)	• Slovakia (1995)		
• Portugal (1986)	• Slovenia (1996)		
• Spain (1986)	• Turkey (1987)[c]		
• Sweden (1995)			
• United Kingdom (1973)			

[a] The Stability Pact, launched in June 1999 in the wake of the Kosovo conflict, contains not only the promise of financial and economic assistance from the EU for the region, but also the prospect of eventual EU membership for the participating countries.

[b] Norway and Iceland are, together with the EU member states, participants in the European Economic Area (EEA) which provides for special access to the EU's Single European Market. After a negative referendum on the issue, Switzerland decided not to participate in the EEA, but instead maintains strong bilateral links with the European Union.

[c] Turkey's application for EU membership was accepted in 1999, but – in contrast to the other countries – accession negotiations have not yet begun as the EU is awaiting internal reforms in Turkey.

federalists, as once again governments, rather than the wider public, determined the next steps.

Considering the ambitions of federalists, the plan for a **European Coal and Steel Community** (ECSC), proposed by French Foreign Minister Robert Schuman in 1950, may not have seemed ambitious. But it was the ECSC rather than the Council of Europe that contained the seeds of subsequent developments in integrating Europe. Creating an institution charged with regulating the French and German coal and steel production—implying supranational control over these essential war industries—the Schuman Plan, drafted by the French economic planner, Jean Monnet, was a symbol of the Franco-German desire to make renewed war between the two countries impossible. (See Box 23.2 for details on key individuals involved in the integration process.)

But the historical significance of the Schuman Plan extended beyond this symbolic handshake between French and German statesmen—it established the pattern that would govern many of the subsequent developments in the evolution of the European Union (Urwin 1995). Crucially, it indicated the decision of a small number of countries to move ahead with supranational integration in a specific area, rather than seeking to include a larger number states or a move towards a much wider 'political union'. Both enlargement to new members and an eventual political union were not excluded—and did indeed follow later—but the key to achieving effective integration was seen to lie in a more gradualist strategy (see Box 23.4).

Recognizing the gradualist nature of the integration process is crucial in understanding the achievements, as well as the limitations, of the European Union. On the positive side, gradualism has given the

Box 23.2 International institutions in post-war Europe

Institution	Founded	Role
OECD (former OEEC)	1948	Co-operation in economic policy, economic forecasting, and the development of rules for corporate governance
Council of Europe	1949	Deliberation and co-operation in the areas of culture, human rights, and democratization
ECSC	1952	Regulating European coal and steel industries
West European Union	1954	Mutual defence guarantees among its members, limited co-operation in peace-making activities
EEC	1958	Creating a customs union and single market among its members
Euratom	1958	Co-operation and joint research in the area of nuclear energy and particle physics
EU (former EC)	1965	Arising from merger of ECSC, EEC, and Euratom, developing a common legal order and common policies in most aspects of economic and social life, providing for co-operation and joint action in home and justice affairs, foreign policy, and defence

Box 23.3 Key figures in the history of European integration

Altiero Spinelli	Italian Member of the European Parliament, one of the founders of the Federalist movement.
Robert Schuman	Foreign Minister of France 1948–53, proposed the creation of the European Coal and Steel Community (ECSC).
Konrad Adenauer	Chancellor of the Federal Republic of Germany 1949–1963, joined Schuman in supporting the creation of the ECSC.
Jean Monnet	French economic planner, driving force behind the Schuman Plan, first President of the High Authority of the ECSC.
Walter Hallstein	President of the Commission of the European Economic Community 1958–67.
Charles de Gaulle	President of France 1956–69, responsible for the protection of the national veto over important decisions and for delaying UK membership of the EEC.
Jacques Delors	President of the European Commission 1985–94, driving force behind the Single Market Programme and plans for a Single Currency.

Box 23.4 Aspects of gradualism in the process of European integration

- **Gradual expansion of competences**: the sectoral responsibilities of common institutions are gradually expanded to include ever-wider areas of socio-economic and political life.

- **Gradual expansion of membership**: rather than depending on a wider membership, the underlying dynamic has been for a smaller number of countries to forge ahead and be joined subsequently by new member states.

- **Gradual expansion of majority vote**: over time, an increasing number of decisions can be taken by 'qualified majority vote', i.e. national governments have agreed to give up their veto in more and more areas of policy-making.

- **Gradual expansion of parliamentary powers**: in line with national governments losing their veto, the European Parliament has acquired greater powers to scrutinize institutions and pass legislation.

member states the opportunity to continuously adapt and expand the common institutions in the light of changing needs and circumstances. On the other hand, any reform has had to work from the existing institutional layout, and as a result there has never been an occasion to 'start afresh'. Consequently, the European construction has turned out to be an odd compromise between innovation and inertia.

Key points

- The Second World War and its aftermath provided much impetus for a change in the nature of relations between the European states.

- Against the background of the cold war, designs for a federal union could not be realized.

- Sectoral integration, driven by a smaller core of six countries, led to the creation of the European Communities.

- Powers and competences of the European institutions were gradually expanded in a move from economic to political integration.

Conceptualizing European integration

Emphasizing the gradual nature of the integration process also allows us to distinguish between two different processes at work in the course of integration: the first of these is the reform of the treaties which first established ('Paris Treaty', 'Rome Treaties') or subsequently reformed the European Union ('Single European Act', 'Maastricht Treaty', 'Amsterdam Treaty', 'Nice Treaty') (see Box 23.5). These are the result of **Intergovernmental Conferences** (IGC), where representatives of national governments negotiate the legal framework within which the EU institutions operate. These treaty changes require ratification in each of the member states in order to come into force and—because of the significance of achieving agreement among all member states on what have usually been substantial reforms—can be considered as the 'grand bargains' in the evolution of the EU (Moravcsik 1993).

Within the framework of these treaties, which are referred to as the Union's 'primary legislation', a number of institutions operate that have more specific tasks and possess a degree of autonomy from the member states. They are responsible for running the day-to-day affairs of the Union, developing public policies, deciding on the annual budget and passing 'secondary' legislation such as EU directives and regulations (Wincott 1995).

It is important to recognize that the dynamics of decision-making differ significantly between the arenas of treaty reform and policy-making. Supranational institutions may have considerable autonomy in running the day-to-day affairs of the Union, but decisions about treaty change or substantial institutional reforms are dominated by national governments. In this respect, the existence of the **national** veto often leads to difficult

Box 23.5 Important events in the history of the European Union

Year	Treaty	Main subjects
1952	Paris Treaty	Regulation of coal and steel production in the member states, creation of supranational institutions.
1957	Rome Treaties	Plans for a common market and a customs union, agreement on the removal of all industrial tariffs on internal trade.
1985	Single European Act	Removal of all non-tariff barriers to the mobility of persons, goods, services, and capital (the '1992 programme'); foreign policy co-operation included in the treaty provisions.
1992	Maastricht Treaty	Economic and Monetary Union (the Euro), Political Union (incl. change of name from European Community to European Union), justice and home affairs included in the treaty; pillar structure of the EU treaties established.
1997	Amsterdam Treaty	Various institutional reforms, High Representative for CFSP, provisions for enhanced co-operation.
2000	Nice Treaty	Reform of Commission and Council (voting weights), expansion of majority voting; European Charter of Fundamental Rights.

and lengthy negotiations. The message here is that, in seeking to understand the integration process, we need to take account of the role played by both member states and supranational institutions. And **member states** are not just represented by national governments, as a host of state, non-state, and transnational actors participates in processes of domestic preference formation or in direct representation of interest in Brussels (Greenwood 1998). The relative openness of the European policy-process means that political groups or economic interests will try and influence EU decision-making if they feel that their position is not sufficiently represented by national governments. That is one reason why the EU is increasingly seen as a system of multilevel governance, involving a plurality of actors on different territorial levels: supranational, national, and subnational (Marks *et al.* 1996*a*)

One therefore needs to be clear about the issue one is talking about: whether, for example, it is possible to claim that the EU is 'imposing' a decision or a policy on a member state, or whether, on the other hand, a member state may be able to 'block' a decision, crucially depends on the decision-making mechanism that is applicable in any given situation.

The EU possesses a very complex institutional machinery, and general answers to such questions are not very meaningful.

This complexity, together with continuous change over time, has spawned a lively debate among integration theorists. Among the contributions to this debate are a variety of approaches, some of which are applications of more general theories of International Relations: the literature on both realism and interdependence has contributed to theorizing of integration (see Ch. 9). Other scholars have regarded the European Union as *sui generis*—in a category of its own—and therefore in need of the development of dedicated theories of integration (Rosamond 2000). The most prominent among these has been neo-functionalism, which sought to explain the evolution of integration in terms of 'spillover' from one sector to another as resources and loyalties of elites where being transferred to the European level (Haas 1958). More recently, as aspects of EU politics have come to resemble the domestic politics of states, scholars have turned to approaches drawn from Comparative Politics (Hix 1994).

However, while there have been these and other theoretical debates, it has been the exchange between 'supranational' and 'intergovernmental' approaches which has had the greatest impact on the study of European integration. **Supranational approaches** regard the emergence of supranational institutions in Europe as a distinct feature and turn these into the main object of analysis. Here, the politics *above* the level of states are regarded as the most significant, and consequently the political actors, institutions at the European level receive most attention (see Box 23.6). **Intergovernmentalist approaches**, on the other hand, continue to regard states as the most important aspect of the integration process and consequently concentrate on the study of politics *between* and *within* states (see Box 23.7). But whatever one's theoretical preferences, most scholars would agree that no analysis of the EU is complete without studying both the operation and evolution of the central institutions and the input from political actors in the member states. Furthermore, as we will see below, the process of European integration has been influenced by external forces, and by the wider trajectory of global politics.

Key points

- The development of integration theory originated as a branch of International Relations.

- Key debates in integration theory are between supranationalists, emphasizing the role of central institutions, and intergovernmentalists, arguing for the continued relevance of states, their resources and processes of domestic preference formation.

- Contending approaches emphasize different aspects of the integration process. Important distinctions in their focus are: institutional dynamics / state preferences; policy-making / treaty reform; long-term / short-term developments; and process / events.

Box 23.6 **Key arguments of supranational approaches to European integration**

- Integration as gradual process

- Supranational institutions are political actors in their own right

- Emergence of a new polity above the level of the state

- Integration process is to some extent driven by institutional dynamics

- Supranational laws provide constraints for member states

Box 23.7 **Key arguments of intergovernmentalist approaches to European integration**

- Integration as a series of 'bargains' among states

- Supranational institutions assist and facilitate negotiations among states

- EU as the framework for the execution of inter-state politics by different means

- Bargains reflect national interests of the member states

- Supranational laws reflect the interests of powerful states

---

- Greater theoretical pluralism, moving beyond the established debate, has developed in the course of the 1990s.

The role of the European institutions

'Brussels'—that is the commonly used shorthand for the European Union. It may be a handy term, given the location of most of the EU's institutions in the Belgian capital, but it also obscures the complexity of its institutional structure. Indeed, the frequent reference to 'Brussels' only emphasizes the difficulty most observers have in pointing to a dominant source of political authority in the EU. All the main institutions, as well as the individual member states, possess significant powers and the potential to influence decision-making (see Box 23.8).

The European Commission

It is the European Commission that usually has the highest profile among the institutions of the European Union. The Commission is much more than the secretariat of an international organization: it is a political actor in its own right and plays an important role in making and enforcing of European laws. There are **three core areas** of Commission activity:

- proposing legislation
- ensuring compliance with legislation
- managing the policies and the budget of the Union.

The Commission's most crucial role lies in proposing new legislation for the Union. In fact, in most areas of EU policy-making, the Commission has the monopoly to initiate the legislative process. Thus, even though other institutions ultimately pass new legislation, the Commission has a pivotal role in setting the agenda. It has been argued that in a number of fields—the environment and social policy, for example—the EU became active because the Commission, rather than the member states, sought to develop a new competence in the area (Cram 1994). Proposals for new legislation tend to reveal disagreements among the member states, and here it is the Commission that can help to mediate conflicts and assist the passage of its own proposals

On the whole, the nature of **EU legislation** requires the member states to administer the policies of the Union, but there is an obvious conflict of interests: member states may want to see European legislation on certain issues, yet may try to avoid applying these rules to their own industries, farmers or workers, who may therefore gain an unfair advantage. This is why the Commission is charged with overseeing the proper implementation of European rules in the member states. Finally, in addition to this monitoring role, the Commission has actually taken over the running of responsibilities like competition policy for which a single European-wide authority is deemed to be necessary.

The Commission may appear, at first sight, to be a primarily administrative body, a perception reinforced by frequent references to the 'bureaucrats' in Brussels. But the range and significance of the tasks that the Commission has to execute is testimony to the political weight of its actions—a weight that has increased over time. As a result, the Commission has come to be headed by senior politicians—twenty **Commissioners**—who are usually former ministers or prime ministers. They are appointed by national governments, with every country nominating at least one Commissioner. The Commission takes its decisions collectively but Commissioners also have their individual portfolios, much like ministers in national cabinets. The **President of the Commission** has a leadership role and is therefore the first among equals. Under the direction of the Commissioners, the detailed work on policy-planning and administration is done by some 17,000 officials. The number may appear large, but it is in fact a relatively small service, employing less staff than the administration of even a medium-sized European city. Consequently, in view of the Commission's wide range of responsibilities, its resources have often been stretched to the limit. The officials of the Commission, together with the employees of the other European institutions, form a 'European civil service' and are expected, like the Commissioners

Box 23.8 Institutions of the European Union

EU Institutions	Responsibilities	Location
European Commission	initiating, administrating, and overseeing the implementation of EU policies and legislation	Brussels and Luxembourg
European Parliament	directly elected representatives of EU citizens, scrutinizing the operation of the other institutions and, in certain areas, sharing with the Council the power to determine EU legislation	Strasbourg (plenary sessions) Brussels (MEP offices, committee meetings and some plenary sessions) Luxembourg (administration)
Council of Ministers	representing the views of national governments and determining, in many areas jointly with the EP, the ultimate shape of EU legislation	Brussels (some meetings in Luxembourg)
European Council	regular summits of Heads of State and Government, setting the EU's broad agenda and a forum of last resort to find agreement on divisive issues (NB: ≠ Council of Europe)	City in the member state holding the Presidency
European Court of Justice	the EU's highest court, ruling in disputes on matters of EU law between member states and EU institutions, as well as providing preliminary rulings on request from national courts in cases involving private persons (NB: ≠ European Court of Human Rights)	Luxembourg
European Central Bank	central bank responsible for setting the interest rates and controlling the money supply of the single European currency, the Euro	Frankfurt/M.
Committee of the Regions	advisory committee of 222 members representing the interests of local and regional authorities in the EU	Brussels
Economic and Social Committee	advisory committee of 222 members representing the interests of labour, employers', and consumer organizations in the EU	Brussels
Court of Auditors	the EU's audit office, responsible for auditing the revenues and the expenditure under the EU budget	Luxembourg

themselves, to be independent of any influence or interference from the member states. Recruited from across the member states, it is, by nature, a multinational, multilingual, and multicultural service, with all the opportunities and problems that this implies.

The European Parliament

The European Parliament (EP) started life as a parliamentary assembly and was initially composed of delegates from national parliaments. It was only in 1979 that the first direct elections to the parliament took place, and it was from then onwards that the EP could claim to be the only body in the EU with a direct mandate of the people.

In the course of subsequent enlargements, the size of the parliament has steadily grown. The number of **Members of the European Parliament** (MEPs) now stands at around 700. MEPs are elected on a national basis, with the voters in each member state electing a number of MEPs that is not quite proportional to their demographic share of the total electorate—the smaller member states send a disproportionally higher number of MEPs to the Parliament. But, once elected, MEPs constitute a number of party-political alliances that broadly reflect the 'European party families' (Christian-Democrats, Liberals, Socialists, etc.). Much of the EP's day-to-day work is done through its parliamentary committees, reflecting the various departments of the Commission from which the legislative proposals originate.

As far as the EP's role in the legislative process is concerned, the picture is a very complex one, as there are many different decision-making procedures. In principle, the EP shares with the Council of Ministers the power to approve, amend, or reject the legislative proposal submitted by the Commission, but the respective rights of either institution differ across policy-areas. In some areas, though, the EP is now the equal of national governments, and in these areas, its involvement in the policy-process has positively changed the nature of decision-making in these areas.

If the EP has over time acquired a greater legislative role, its members (MEPs) still lack some of the most elementary powers of parliaments: that of electing the government and proposing legislation. The EP does have a role in approving and dismissing the European Commission, but this is hardly the same as electing a government. Crucially, because the Commission is appointed by the member states, the election of the EP does *not* lead to the adoption of the specific party-political programme we know from domestic politics.

In the absence of powers to appoint the Commission or initiate legislation, the link between a parliamentary majority and the actual policies of the European Union is a tenuous one. As a result the EP has found it difficult to mobilize the electorate to its

five-yearly elections, and average turnout across the EU has remained below 50 per cent—a figure that is lower than most national elections in Europe, but higher than the participation in the local or regional elections of many European countries. More than the Commission, where French and English have established themselves as working languages, the EP also has to overcome the problem of working with the EU's eleven official languages. An even greater practical problem is the monthly ritual of all MEPs and their support staff travelling from Brussels, where they have their offices close to those of the Commission and the Council, to Strasbourg, where the plenary debates take place.

The European Court of Justice

Beside the Commission and the Parliament, the European Court of Justice (ECJ) is the third supranational institution of the Union. Sitting in Luxembourg, the Court is charged with the important task of guarding the treaties and maintaining the EU's legal order. It adjudicates in disputes among the member states, among the institutions and between a member state and one of the institutions. Private persons and businesses seeking redress under the EU law need to enter, in the first instance, the judicial process in the national courts. But in such cases, the European judges can provide national courts with preliminary rulings, advising them on request of their interpretation of EU laws—a practice which national courts have accepted as a source of authoritative guidance.

Through its judgements and preliminary rulings, the ECJ has made an enormous contribution to the integration process. The judges on the ECJ, whose impartiality is generally acknowledged, have helped to ensure that the European Union works as a system based on the rule of law. This, in itself, is already a substantive achievement, given the general weakness of law in relations between states. But more than simply upholding laws made by member states, the judges of the ECJ have made law themselves. Indeed, some of the most important legal principles governing the EU have been developed by the Court, rather than having been written into the treaties by the member states. Among these is the principle of supremacy of European law, which stipulates that EU laws override national laws if the two are in conflict. This principle—which has become accepted by national courts—has elevated the ECJ to what many now regard as a **quasi-constitutional court** of the Union. This demonstrates not only the significance of the Court, but is also an important statement about the nature of the European Union itself: for many observers, the existence, maintenance and expansion of a European legal order, watched over by a Court of Justice, is a key aspect of supranational governance in the EU (Weiler 1991*b*).

The European Central Bank

With the adoption of the single European currency, the Euro, as the official currency in eleven EU countries on 1 January 1999, a new European institution came into being: the European Central Bank (ECB) (see Box 23.9). The ECB has responsibility to run the **monetary policy** for these 'Euroland' countries, setting the interest rate for the Euro and controlling the money supply through a variety of other mechanisms. The day-to-day running of the ECB is in the hands of an executive board, headed by a President, but important decisions, such as changes to the interest rates, are made by the Governing Council, which is made up of the governors of national central banks.

The Council of Ministers

In terms of the theoretical debate referred to above, the Commission, Court, Parliament, and ECB are regarded as supranational institutions—they are expected to stand above the fray of competing national interests and execute their tasks in an impartial manner. National governments, as well as other political actors, interest groups, or foreign countries, may well try and exert informal influence, but formally these institutions are independent from the member states. The formal representation of member state interests is in the hands of a different set of institutions, most importantly the Council of Ministers. The Council is the forum through which national ministers and officials shape the policies of the EU. As mentioned above, it shares the legislative powers of the EU with the European Parliament, and in crucial areas of policy-making its vote takes precedence over that of the Parliament.

In terms of its organizational structure, we can distinguish between the Council's political and administrative levels. Politically, it is constituted by ministers from national governments. Initially, foreign ministers were the sole representatives of member states, but with the expansion of the EU's competences, an ever wider range of national ministries has become involved in the work of the Council. With the first meetings of EU defence ministers in the late 1990s, practically all government departments in the member states are now involved in regular Council meetings. However, foreign ministers, meeting as the General Affairs Council, have a special role to oversee the work of the other councils.

Before ministers meet in the Council, much preparatory work is done on the administrative level. A large number of committees and working groups will have worked on detailed aspects of European legislation, and often it is here, during the negotiations among officials from national administrations or the permanent representatives of the member states, that agreement on legislative proposals are reached. Only when officials are unable to agree or issues become highly political, will ministers get involved in the negotiations.

The section on the European Parliament already referred to the different decision-making processes. As far as the Council's participation in this process is concerned, the main distinction is between unanimity—the requirement for all governments to agree to legislative proposals—and **qualified majority voting** (QMV)—under which decisions can be taken with roughly 70 per cent of member states' weighted votes in the Council. However, the formal rules of decision-making only tell part of the story. EU negotiators will always seek to achieve the widest possible consensus, even if formally voting takes place under the rules of QMV. Consistently outvoting one or more of the member states is likely to damage the legitimacy of the EU in the affected

Box 23.9 Case study: Economic and monetary union and the Euro

A long-standing and fundamental aim of the EU has been the removal of all barriers to movement of goods, services, and capital between its member states. But the more tariff and non-tariff barriers were being dismantled in the 1960s, 1970s, and 1980s, the more the significance of fluctuating exchange rates in affecting intra-EU trade became evident. Flexible exchange rates produce uncertainty about the future cost of foreign supplies, the price of exported goods and the return on foreign direct investment (FDI), and this in turn acts as a major disincentive to trade and FDI—and therefore as a hidden barrier to trade in the EU.

In response to these problems, some European countries had begun in the 1970s to search for greater exchange rate stability. The European Monetary System—the EMS—was an agreement among participating central banks to ensure that their currencies would only fluctuate within certain bands. During the 1980s the EMS went some way to ameliorate the situation, but as the single market liberalized the movement of capital, it became increasingly difficult to maintain exchange rate stability based solely on agreements among central banks.

A first plan for a monetary union had already been launched in 1970, but had fallen victim to the economic turmoil that followed the wars in Vietnam and the Middle East. By the end of the 1980s, the European Union was ready to try again. A committee chaired by Commission President Jacques Delors was set up in 1988 and delivered a report in the following year. This 'Delors Report', which envisaged the achievement of Economic and Monetary Union (EMU) in three stages, was accepted by the great majority of governments as the basis for an Intergovernmental Conference which was launched in Rome in 1990.

The IGC resulted in the Maastricht Treaty and demonstrated that governments were willing to move ahead towards EMU and a single currency. Only the UK, later joined by Denmark and Sweden, opted out of this project and sought to maintain their own monetary policies, but agreed that the other member states could go ahead with the project, and utilize the EU institutions to do so. Despite some delays due to the problems of treaty ratification—in turn caused by substantial opposition to the project in some member states—and subsequent turbulence in the currency markets, the treaty was implemented, the exchange rates between participating currencies fixed and the Euro became a reality on 1 January 1999. Initially only a virtual currency used for bank transfers and electronic payments, Euro notes and coins will circulate and replace national currencies from January 2002.

The agreement at Maastricht is remarkable because monetary union is much more than a question of economic efficiency. The single currency does indeed provide greater certainty and transparency over prices within the single market, but it also incurs substantial 'political cost': by transferring monetary policy to a single European Central Bank (ECB), governments and national central banks not only accept the loss of important instruments of economic management, but in fact agree to run their economic and fiscal policies in a manner compliant with the 'stability criteria' set by the EU. This means that there are tight controls to ensure that state debt and public deficits are within the limits set by the EU—if states exceed these limits, they face reprimands and even fines from the European institutions.

The constraints imposed on states by the move to EMU have made the single currency highly controversial. One of these concerned the degree of independence of the ECB. The Maastricht Treaty, essentially exporting the German model of monetary policy-making, stipulated that the ECB must be sufficiently independent to pursue the aim of price stability without interference from governments. But both the independence of the ECB and the dominance of the price stability criterion in its decision-making have been contested, as some member states, in particular France, have sought an enhanced role for national governments in the setting of priorities. The weakness of the Euro after its launch—having lost by mid-2000 as much as a third of its value against the dollar—was a further bone of contention, as governments and institutions appeared divided on how to respond: while some seemed to welcome the boost the weak Euro gave to exports, others feared that it would result in a rise of inflation.

In the long term, what is bound to weigh heavier in the public debate is the political dimension of monetary union. For many critics and supporters alike the Euro is not just a functional tool which may assist trade and investment. EMU, though often presented in purely economic terms, is also seen as a mechanism which either creates a political union, or necessitates the creation of one. There is an expectation that a single currency threatens the continuation of national economic, tax, and social policies. Many therefore regard the Euro as a substantial loss of national sovereignty—a debate that is bound to continue for some time.

Box 23.9 continued

EMU exemplifies the underlying rationale of the wider integration project: the use of economic means towards political ends. Countries opting out of the Euro have refused to pay this 'political price' in return for the expected economic gains. There is an expectation that, as the economic and political cost of remaining outside the 'Eurozone' grows, they may reconsider their position. But even among, and within, the countries committed to EMU debate about the ultimate implications of creating a single currency have continued.

The single currency had been launched in the context of a favourable economic climate—more difficult economic conditions in the future are likely to provide more serious tests of the strength of the currency, the reliability of the decision-making procedures of EMU, and of its legitimacy in the public eye. In terms of its aims and methods, but also in terms of the difficult issues it raises, the Euro is closely tied to the wider integration project. Monetary union therefore remains an opportunity as well as a challenge for the future development of the European Union.

---

countries, and may also make implementation more difficult: it is the national administrations that have to put most EU rules and regulations into effect, and this is more likely to occur swiftly and effectively if the rules have been adopted with the support of all individual member states, rather than against the opposition of some.

Member states in the driving seat: Presidency, European Council, and Intergovernmental Conferences

A key feature in the work of the Council and of the EU generally is the institution of the **Presidency**: every six months, according to an agreed rota, one of the member states takes over the role of chairing the various working groups and Council meetings. This provides that country with an opportunity to identify the priorities for its term and to guide the setting of the agenda accordingly. At the same time, holding the Presidency implies a considerable responsibility, because a great deal of dynamism can be injected, or be lost, in those six months. The Presidency is therefore a balancing act between a member state's particular interests, which it may want to promote during its term, and the expectation that it will respect, and mediate between, the interests of all member states.

The most important event during any country's term is the **European Council**, a summit meeting of state leaders, which every Presidency will organize at least once during these six months. European Council meetings usually occur at the end of a country's Presidency and provide an opportunity for presidents and prime ministers to take stock, strike deals (where ministers have failed to reach agreement) and define the medium- and long-term priorities for the EU.

Intergovernmental Conferences (IGCs) are convened by the member states when changes or additions to the treaty are deemed necessary, and are conducted by government representatives over a period of about a year. The Commission and European Parliament also participate with delegated representatives, but ultimately only the member states decide on the changes to the treaty. The agreement of all member states is required and the signed treaty also needs to be ratified in each country. While most of the attention has usually focused on the negotiating phase—and the signing ceremony at the European Council—the aftermath of the Maastricht Treaty, where the negative outcome of a referendum in Denmark, judicial review *inter alia* in Germany, and controversial debates in some national parliaments emphasized the significance of the ratification stage.

Because of the importance of the issues being dealt with, and the length of time it takes to reach agreement on them, reforming the treaty is of particular significance in the politics of the EU. Intergovernmentalists regard IGCs rather than day-to-day decision-making as the defining aspect of the integration process, since it is here that member states agree—or refuse to agree—to hand over certain powers to European institutions. Whatever slippage may occur in the policy process, where the Commission or the Parliament may have an influence on the outcome, it is at the conference table of the IGC that member states are seen to rein in the institutions and make careful choices about areas to be governed jointly or left within the national domain.

Key points

- Supranational institutions are formally independent from member states and are able to make an autonomous contribution to the integration process.
- The European Commission is charged with proposing legislation and overseeing implementation and compliance. It can influence the EU agenda and acts as a mediator between member states, seeking to assist the search for a compromise between various national positions.
- The European Parliament is directly elected and shares a legislative function with the Council of Ministers. Initially only consulted on new proposals, its powers have expanded to include co-decision with the Council.
- Through its interpretations of the treaties, the European Court of Justice has become an important factor in the integration process, not only by

maintaining the rule of law in the European Union, but also by introducing fundamental principles of European law through its judgements.

- The European Central Bank is the independent monetary authority for those EU countries that participate in Economic and Monetary Union.
- The Council of Ministers, with a host of subsidiary committees and working groups, is the key institution though which member states represent their interests in the EU.
- Most decisions are now taken by qualified majority vote, but in certain areas member states still have a veto.
- Ministers meet along sectoral lines (agriculture, industry, transport, etc.) in different Councils, and heads of state and government meet 2–4 times a year as the European Council.
- Every six months, one country takes over the Presidency, thereby acquiring the opportunity—and responsibility—to chair meetings and guide the affairs of the EU.
- Member states seek to control the evolution through the convening of Intergovernmental Conferences (IGCs) in order to change or expand the treaty. The treaties, or treaty changes, resulting from IGCs need to be ratified in each member state according to its domestic process.

The EU in world politics

The original strategy underlying the integration process—to use economic means to achieve political integration—also meant that the EU's external relations only developed gradually. In fact, the explicit attempt to create a 'European Political Community' and a 'European Defence Community' failed in the mid-1950s. It was this failure that partially inspired the gradualist integration strategy adopted subsequently.

The EU and international trade

Even supposedly 'economic' integration quickly developed an external angle, as the creation of a Customs Union by definition requires a Common External Tariff, and therefore a common trade policy for all affected products. Consequently, the European institutions also acquired the exclusive responsibility to regulate the trade between member states and non-member states. This means that on behalf of the EU, the European Commission enters specific trade negotiations, either bilaterally or in the context of the World Trade Organization (WTO), with a brief based on a mandate from the Council of Ministers.

The EU has considerable weight in international trade, given that its share of global trade is about 20 per cent. Among its member states are some of the largest export economies of the world. The Single European Market and the adoption of the Euro by twelve of its member states also means that it constitutes the largest unified market in the world (Woolcock 2000). There is much at stake for the EU in terms of both exports and imports, and the EU has inevitably become a major player in international trade negotiations. It is a development which has, on occasion, led to disputes with the other main trading powers. In particular the EU and the US, notwithstanding their close security co-operation in the Atlantic Alliance, have often been at loggerheads in questions of international trade.

Such disputes, but also the efforts at settling these in the context of the WTO, demonstrate the degree to which the EU has become a single actor in the international trade regime. There are still areas in which member states have—and pursue—their separate interests, as there are different views on the common position the EU should be taking up in international trade negotiations. However, despite such internal differences the EU manages, by and large, to present a common front with respect to its external trade diplomacy. This unity of purpose may be an example of an effective policy produced by supranational governance, but it is also a sign of the way in which single market, single currency, and other common policies have led member states to share economic interests.

The development of a common foreign and security policy

Economically the Union may be speaking with one voice, but the same can hardly be said for political external relations. The EU's efforts at developing a Common Foreign and Security Policy (CFSP) began in the 1970s as co-operation between national for-

eign ministries. Since the Maastricht Treaty, they have been consigned to what is known as the 'second pillar' of the European Union. This means that foreign policy co-operation falls outside the rules for supranational governance that apply to economic integration. The European Parliament and the ECJ are excluded from decision-making in this area, while the Commission, though fully associated with CFSP, does not enjoy the sole right of initiative it possesses in the area of economic integration.

This is because the member states have been keen to preserve an intergovernmental mode of decision-making for the sensitive and symbolic area of foreign policy-making. Traditionally the emphasis has been on *co-operation* between, and *co-ordination* of, national foreign policies rather than supplanting these with a genuinely *European* foreign policy. In the past, the development of a common foreign policy for the EU also suffered from the requirement of unanimity. It is a provision that still applies to any foreign policy action with a military dimension, while in other areas decision-making has become more flexible through the introduction of QMV and new mechanisms like 'joint actions', 'common positions', or a 'constructive abstention'.

Of all EU policies, foreign policy co-operation has tended to confront member states with the starkest dilemma: both during and after the cold war, foreign policy has been an arena where the West European states faced an urgent need to unite and present a common front in order to have an impact on the decisions made by the superpowers. But foreign policy is also an area in which states have jealously guarded their particular interests and traditions. The development of a common European foreign policy is clearly difficult in the face of deep-seated differences between traditional foreign policies of EU member states. Any country's foreign policy is closely tied up with its own identity and self-perception, and the efforts of developing a common European foreign policy have progressed in a much more cautious manner than the economic integration which has led to the single market and the single currency.

Nevertheless, an impressive institutional structure for CFSP has developed over time. National foreign ministries are now co-operating intensively on all issues of foreign policy. There are close and frequent consultations at political as well as official level. Ministers meet frequently, and so do the political directors that are heading the administration of foreign ministries. Ministerial desk officers as well as embassy staff around the world co-operate regularly in order to establish a European dimension to foreign policy. Secure communications are channelled through a designated telex system, but officials also use telephone and email as a matter of course. The European Commission, with its network of 'delegations'—the EU's quasi-embassies across the globe—and its expertise in the EU's trade, development, and humanitarian aid policies, participates in this extensive multilateral exchange.

More recently member states have sought to utilize the Union's central institutions more systematically for the purposes of CFSP. In order to preserve the intergovernmental nature of this policy, these efforts have focused on the Council Secretariat rather than the Commission. The Council Secretariat is home to a CFSP secretariat and an 'early warning unit', and the Secretary-General also acts as the EU's High Representative for the Common Foreign and Security Policy. The creation of this post, in particular, was a response to the criticism that decision-making in the area of CFSP was too slow-moving and cumbersome, and that, all too often, the EU did not speak with one voice. In the 1970s the then US Secretary of State, Henry Kissinger, famously asked 'when I want to speak to Europe, who do I call?'—in 1998, the Amsterdam Treaty finally sought to provide the answer in creating the **High Representative**. The appointment of the former NATO Secretary-General, Javier Solana, as the first occupant of the post also established that this is a senior political rather than a mere administrative position.

These institutional innovations emphasize that in the past EU foreign policy often remained an ambition rather than effective action. EU foreign policy co-operation was more suited to the continuous and low-profile diplomacy of international conferences rather then the rapid and effective response to global or regional crises. In this respect, the break-up of the former Yugoslavia constituted a nadir for the EU's CFSP. In the eyes of many observers, the wars in Croatia, Bosnia, and in Kosovo appeared to demonstrate two things to the Europeans: **first**, that violent conflict, ethnic cleansing, and even genocide were not a thing of the distant past or of faraway places, but could actually occur right at the boundaries of the EU (see Ch. 22); **second**, that the EU was extremely ill-equipped to respond to these developments effectively. Despite a set of circumstances that was generally supportive of an EU role in crisis-management—geographical proximity, economic influence over the region, an obvious interest in maintaining stability at its own borders, and an ability to develop a common policy—the EU's efforts at achieving a peaceful resolution are often regarded as a failure. Eventually, Western diplomatic negotiation and military intervention relied on participation, even leadership, from the US rather than from the EU, and at times occurred in the face of disagreements among the European partners.

In the course of the 1990s, the EU states therefore also came to realize the significance of greater co-operation in defence matters. The developments in the former Yugoslavia, but also the increasingly felt need to be able to deploy troops outside the context of NATO, meant a search for a European solution to questions of 'humanitarian intervention' (see Ch. 22). Despite the great sensitivity of co-operation in defence matters, especially for Denmark (which has formally opted-out of defence discussions) and to a lesser extent the non-aligned member states (Sweden, Finland, Austria, and Ireland), the EU is now working towards establishing a 230,000-strong military force, which is to be co-ordinated by a newly created military staff within the Council Secretariat. The emerging institutional architecture within the Council Secretariat includes military, civilian crisis management, and political and security committees and is also linked to a partial transfer of tasks from the Western European Union. At the same time, mergers among European arms manufacturers—encouraged by national governments as well as by the dynamics of the integrating European market—have opened up new avenues for co-operation in the area of arms procurement. But, as in the past with co-operation in the non-military aspects of foreign and security policy, there is also the danger here that the EU will raise expectations—inside and outside its own borders—without possessing the capabilities to meet them (Hill 1993).

The EU has managed to establish itself as an increasingly self-confident actor in world politics, in particular in international trade diplomacy. It has developed unique mechanisms to allow its member states to co-operate in the area of foreign policy, and a co-ordinated European response to international crises and other global issues has become a matter of course. Nevertheless, member states have guarded national foreign policy positions even if they contradict a common position (to be) adopted in the context of the CFSP. A genuinely *common* foreign policy, alongside the EU's common trade policy, remains elusive, in particular in the context of further enlargements to the East and South in the near future. In terms of future developments, much will depend on whether future crises, perhaps requiring military intervention from the EU's military forces, will push the member states towards further integration in this field, or whether such tests will reveal continuing differences in their foreign policies.

Key points

- The EU member states have agreed on a common trade policy, represented by the European Commission in international trade negotiations.
- Efforts to agree on a common foreign and security policy have been hampered by the reluctance of member states to give up their independence in this area.
- The European Commission and Council Secretariat now have a part in projecting agreed positions of a common foreign policy towards the outside.
- There are ambitious plans for co-operation in military matters, in particular with respect to humanitarian co-operation, but—as with foreign policy in the past—these may raise expectations beyond the EU's capacity to deliver.

The global context to European integration

The early phase of European integration developed in the context of the cold war. Encouragement from the United States, the need to strengthen economic defences against a perceived Soviet threat, and the desire among some European countries to give some weight to European views in the emerging bipolar world all contributed to the speed of developments in that early phase of integration. In the same vein, external developments have been regarded as partially responsible for the **Eurosclerosis** of the 1970s and early 1980s: as successive oil crises led to economic recession in Europe, there was retrenchment within national boundaries. Keeping the integration project moving in the face of minimal or even negative economic growth became difficult, and thus the external environment has had a negative impact on the process.

The more recent phase of integration has occurred against the backdrop of globalization. Three dynamics of globalization, in particular, have been mirrored by developments in the EU. **First**, in terms of economic governance, European integration has fed on, and contributed to, the global trend towards neo-

liberal economic policy, with its emphasis on liberal trade, low inflation, deregulation, and tight fiscal budgets. To the extent to which this has shifted power from states to markets, the trend of 'marketization' is clearly visible in the EU. **Second**, the trend towards greater social and cultural exchange across national borders has also intensified in the European Union. Common policies and institutions in Europe are specifically designed to enhance possibilities of **greater mobility** across national borders, adding to secular trends on the global scale. As a matter of course, political parties, local and regional authorities, social movements, interest groups, and NGOs are now active, alongside national governments and supranational institutions, on a European scale. **Third**, despite the creation of an integrated market and the growth of trans-border economic, social and cultural exchange, the development of a transnational civil society has been limited by factors such as, for example, the diversity of languages. At the mass level, national and regional identities continue to take precedence over any emerging European identity. This lack of identification—the absence of a European *demos*—and the institutional limitations of the European Union hamper the democratization of supranational governance.

In the academic literature, attention has been drawn to the dual nature of the relationship between integration and globalization—with the EU acting both as a shelter from, and as an accelerator of, global processes (Wallace 2000). In the wider political and public debate, however, one or the other side of these aspects is being emphasized. In this respect, two very different interpretations of this interaction are on offer: European integration is regarded either as an expression of turbo-charged globalization or as a protective shield against the negative 'fall-out' from globalization. The following sections reproduce some of the arguments of this political debate, emphasizing that in their political interpretations observers often come to contrasting conclusions in their assessment of the integration process.

Integration as turbo-charged globalization?

In this perspective, the EU is little more than the local variant of the kind of the global trends mentioned above. If anything, globalization is being accelerated by the policies of the European Union. **Multinational corporations** benefit from the improved access to markets, and there is a general trend towards greater concentration of economic power in certain regions and large firms. States are abdicating their traditional welfare responsibilities in order to satisfy the demands of efficiency and price stability imposed by the single market and single currency. Supranational institutions have little to put in place instead, and the trend is towards an unevenly regulated market place. The development of a supranational legal order is based on the needs of economic integration, not the result of an explicit programme of political integration.

In the EU, there may be efforts to establish transnational social policies, citizenship rights, and environmental protection, but such attempts have been haphazard and have remained secondary to the overarching aim of market liberalization. The latter,

on the other hand, has been more effective and more far-reaching than elsewhere. Within the European Union, capital mobility and market access are hardly different from those within the nation-state, and as a result there are ever greater competitive pressures for firms as well as for public authorities.

In the face of the dynamic effects of economic integration, the political process at the European level remains imperfect. Supranational institutions have not been given effective tools to regulate economic exchange, as national governments and political parties maintain increasingly symbolic debates about the protection of 'national sovereignty'. Even to the extent to which these institutions can act, they are far removed from the citizens they are supposed to serve. Given the limitations alluded to earlier, the democratic process at the European level is hardly effective: EU decision-making lacks transparency, is complex and difficult to communicate, and as a result there is hardly any transnational debate on the priorities of European governance. The political process may function well at the national level—though even that is frequently questioned—but the setting of domestic preferences is hollowed out as individual countries have lost the capacity to act unilaterally.

Those who want to see political responses to these trends are faced with a dilemma: a more efficient EU, better able to respond to the challenges of globalization, is likely to be more centralized and even less responsive to the preferences of citizens and elected governments. Yet the 're-nationalization' of economic policy-making at the national level, where voters could directly register their influence, risks to reduce the effectiveness of political authority over internationalized markets even further. Nevertheless, the voters in countries such as Norway and Switzerland, who have opted to remain outside the EU, believe that the loss of autonomy implied by European integration is greater than the political control over the process gained by membership. The same logic applies to the choice of the UK, Denmark, and Sweden to remain outside the single currency when this was launched in 1999: like many other policies of the EU, the Euro is regarded as a reduction of national options in economic and fiscal policy and as being, not so much a European solution to the problems caused by globalization, but a further, even more damaging variety of these pressures (see Box 23.9).

Integration as protection against globalization?

Yet the advocates of the single currency, and of European integration generally, advertise it as precisely the opposite. In their view, integration provides nation-states and electorates in Europe with a mechanism to confront the challenges of globalization. There may be a dynamic process of economic integration, but the EU provides an institutional response to regulate this. Ultimately, the transnational market is regulated and political control is exercised, through the collaboration of supranational institutions and national governments (see Ch. 13). Individual citizens may have less influence on this process than they have on the traditional political process, but—similar to the move democratic theory made from the city-state to the nation-state—direct participation and representation must give way to the enhanced effectiveness of a greater polity (Dahl 1994).

Though uneven, there is the growth of such a supranational polity. Its development may have been led by the market, but eventually an effective legal order, a system of political rights and duties, and a political community have been established. Both states and firms are now subject to rules and regulations that go much further than anything that is available at the global scale. Indeed, global environmental and social regulation receives much impetus from the political consensus among the EU member states.

European integration has also helped to provide a **counterweight** to the economic interests of the US, the remaining superpower. It is difficult to see how individual states in Europe would respond to the demands for unregulated market access from US firms and the US administration. The EU, on the other hand, has regularly resisted such demands, often couched in complaints about protectionism, whether in response to preferential market access for developing countries, concerns over health or environmental safety, or simply because of the economic interests of the member states. In multilateral negotiations, the EU has permitted member states substantially to increase their voice and thus extend their influence in the international trade regime.

Supranational institutions, though distant from the individual citizen, have spawned an impressive network of transnational interests. Commission and Parliament provide the focus for political as well as economic interest representation, and a culture of political debate (and occasional conflict) is emerging in the wider public. Depending on the degree of integration in specific sectors, this reaches further in some areas than in others: farmers have consistently presented their case in Brussels, but other professions, less affected by EU decisions, may not have that high a profile. Even without a shift in loyalties or identity, there are the beginnings of a political community—not on a general, European-wide scale, but in certain areas and around certain issues.

Key points

- The process of integration has interacted with, and received much impetus from, developments at the global level.

- The relationship between processes of globalization and integration is contested: some see integration as a regional expression of globalization, accelerating the transnational nature of markets and thus further disenfranchising states and societies.

- However, the EU can also be regarded as a mechanism through which states and societies regain a degree of control over markets and are able to address trans-border issues such as environmental protection, health, migration, or international crime more effectively.

Beyond Europe: the global rise of regionalism

The interaction between processes of globalization and efforts to integrate regional economies is not limited to Europe alone. In fact, there has been a substantial increase in the regionally based institutionalized co-operation among states during the 1990s—to the extent that observers have termed this feature the **new regionalism** (Hettne, Inotai, and Sunkel 1999). This section will briefly scan developments in North America, Latin America, Asia, and Africa before comparing these to the experience of regional integration in Europe.

The critical point to be made at the outset of this discussion of the 'new regionalism' is the **dynamic relationship** between developments in different parts of the world. As countries in one continent agree to integrate their economies, creating free trade zones, customs unions, or more, the effects are felt elsewhere. Frequently, there has been a response 'in kind', i.e. the attempt to match the efforts of economic integration elsewhere. An important driving force for these processes has been the end of the cold war: the removal of superpower conflict with its repercussions in many parts of the world provided new opportunities for regions to co-operate in matters of trade and security (see Ch. 6). Further impetus came from the EU, both purposefully—the EU has a history of establishing and institutionalizing links with other regional groupings (Edwards and Regelsberger 1990)—and unintentionally through the competitive pressures exerted by the Single European Market. In North America and in South East Asia—regions which had been strongly competing with Western Europe in the preceding decade—there were concerns that the facilitation of easier market access within the European Community would lead to trade diversion and therefore be achieved at the expense of exports from overseas (Mattli 1999). This concern about the emergence of a **Fortress Europe** provided much of the impetus behind the dynamic development of the **North American Free Trade Agreement** (NAFTA), the **Association of South-East Asian States** (ASEAN) and the **Asia Pacific Economic Co-operation** (APEC), respectively. Regional groupings have also come to the fore in Latin America with the creation of **MERCOSUR**.

North America

The case of regionalism which is most frequently compared to the European Union is NAFTA which brings together the economies of Canada, Mexico, and the United States. NAFTA was based on an initial free trade agreement between the US and Canada which led, in 1992, to the conclusion of the wider, North American agreement including Mexico. It aims at abolishing barriers to the trade in goods and services between the three countries. To support this aim, the agreement provides for the progressive elimination of customs tariffs in many—though not all—areas of trade, and for a dispute settlement mechanism to deal with cases where disagreements between the partners arise. There is a small secretariat consisting of national offices in the three capitals, but essentially the administration of the agreement relies on national ministers—meeting in the Free Trade Commission—or by their appointed representatives in more specialized working groups and committees. NAFTA, being concerned with trade matters, does not provide for collective action in other areas. There are provisions for dispute settlement, but they imply the setting of arbitration panels when individual cases are raised rather than a permanent court. An agreement on labour co-operation was signed by the three countries in 1993 in order to provide a 'social dimension' to NAFTA, but it explicitly affirms each party's right to set their own labour standards and essentially provides for co-operation and consultation between national authorities, the exchange of information and the conduct of policy reviews rather than the setting of common standards for the region as a whole.

It is an important departure in global politics because it is the most far-reaching example of a regional co-operation project spanning the North–South divide. The diversity in the economic structures and levels of development between the participating countries makes the creation of a single free trade area among them a great challenge—one that was put to the test, in particular, when Mexico suffered a deep financial crisis in 1997 and had to rely on support from its larger neighbour. But NAFTA weathered the storm well—indeed it assisted the search for collaborative solutions to the crisis. NAFTA has led further proposals to conclude trade agreements also with the countries of South America (in particular the Free Trade Area of the Americas Treaty signed in Quebec City in 2001). The European Union also engaged with the United States in a series of transatlantic agreements, most recently through the Transatlantic Economic Partnership which was agreed in 1998.

Asia

The desire to liberalize trade, engage in regular economic co-operation, and thus create a greater degree of stability has also fed into efforts in the Pacific area, where a total of thirty-four countries have come together to form APEC. Again under leadership from the US, this highly diverse group of countries seeks to co-ordinate economic policies, reduce tariffs and duties, and enhance its negotiating position in global trade negotiations and within the WTO. There are annual summit meetings, but the more regular work is done in meetings of ministers and officials, co-ordinated by a secretariat based in Singapore. There is much emphasis on the role of non-state actors, especially business leaders, to contribute to APEC's goals of **enhancing trade**, **investment**, and a sense of **community** in the region. APEC's progress towards free trade has been severely limited, though, not only because of the great disparity among the economies of the region, but also because of the disturbances of the Asian financial crisis of the late 1990s (see Ch. 13). At the same time, the inclusiveness of APEC as a regional forum has been useful in order to discuss political and security issues among its members.

In terms of effective regional co-operation in South-East Asia, ASEAN, an older organization with a more limited membership, has probably been more significant. It dates back to an agreement among Indonesia, Malaysia, Thailand, Singapore, and the Philippines in the 1960s, but after successive enlargements in the 1980s and 1990s it now comprises also Brunei, Vietnam, Laos, Burma/Myanmar, and Cambodia. This membership bringing together neo-liberal and authoritarian **tiger economies** on the one hand, and socialist transition economies, on the other, is still highly diverse. What weighs more than similarities in size, common economic ties, and shared environmental and social problems is the external environment. ASEAN is a useful caucus for its members to agree negotiating positions vis-à-vis the larger economies of China, Japan, and South Korea and—occasionally together with these three—the United States and the European Union. Beyond trade, ASEAN serves as a useful forum to discuss security issues and, in the context of global debates about workers' and wider human rights issues, as the institutional support for arguments about 'Asian values'. But human rights, above all, have strained relations among members, given the continuing problems in Burma in this regard, and the resultant controversies surrounding its accession (see Ch. 23).

Latin America

In Latin America, again spurred by the developments in Europe and in North America, there has also been renewed dynamism in regional efforts to integrate economies more closely. Projects dating back to the early 1960s to create a Latin American Free Trade Association in the South and a Central American Common Market in the centre of the hemisphere floundered in the 1970s as they went against the grain of economic trends and political relations among their members. But plans for a **Common Market of the South**—known as MERCOSUR by its Spanish acronym—have taken off in the mid-1990s.

The aim of the contracting states of Argentina, Brazil, Paraguay, and Uruguay is to progressively abolish tariff barriers, establish a common external tariff, and thus enhance trade and investment between their economies. As with its counterpart in the North, the institutional framework is very thin, relying only on intergovernmental mechanisms for decision-making. There are ambitious aims to move integration further via the co-ordination of member states' economic policies, but at the end of the 1990s—some five years after the original deadline—

the customs union remained imperfect. Nevertheless, even these more modest advances have borne fruit, given that there have been substantial increases in the trade among MERCOSUR countries.

At the same time, the Rio Group has brought all the countries of South and Central America together in a looser framework. With an inclusive membership it has provided a forum for the exchange of views on a broad range of issues. These have included the search for peace and stability in the region, the fight against the drugs trade and against organized crime as well as more general economic co-operation. And just as the US has sought to establish permanent co-operation with Latin America via the FTAA, the EU has institutionalized its relationships with Latin America through regular summits and ministerial meetings with both the MERCOSUR and the Rio Group countries.

The organizations mentioned here are only the more prominent among the plethora of regional co-operation ventures across the world. In the context of a globalizing world, the end of the cold war and frequent economic and political instability there is greater need, and greater incentives, for countries to co-operate on a regional basis. As trade and other economic issues have become more salient in global politics, states increasingly seek to ally themselves with like-minded and similarly structured partners, and these are often neighbouring countries with whom there are already established trade patterns. Above all, a **domino effect** is at work: when countries in one region club together in order to pursue common economic interests, then other regions are bound to follow suit. This dynamic results not only from the need to counter the anticipated negative impact on the trade with other regions, but above all

---

Box 23.10 Differences between regional integration in Europe and regional co-operation in other continents

Parameters	Regional co-operation	European integration
Institutional characteristics	reliance on purely intergovernmental forms of decision-making	presence of autonomous supranational institutions that initiate and enforce common policies
Forms of decision-making	consensual decision-making (i.e. states have veto over decisions)	extensive use of qualified majority voting (i.e. states have no veto over decisions)
Degree of legal integration	arbitration and dispute settlement of individual cases	permanent court system developing a supranational legal order
Extent of political integration	concentration on economic co-operation among states	development of a political union with a system of economic, social and political rights for citizens
Range of issues covered	emphasis on trade, investment, and related economic issues	expansion of competences into much wider areas (single currency environment, culture, etc.)
Presence of democratic procedures	minimal, if any, involvement of parliaments	establishment of a democratic process, based on a directly elected parliament
Foreign policy co-operation	co-ordination of external relations limited to participation in multilateral trade negotiations	development of a common foreign, security and defence policy

in order to maintain a strong voice in multilateral and global trade negotiations. Thus the negotiations in the Uruguay Round and the ongoing discussions within the WTO have strongly encouraged the instances of regionalism discussed here (Fawcett and Hurrell 1995).

As a result, the 1990s witnessed the growth of 'new regionalism'—regional organizations in all parts of the world forming an integral part of the process of globalization. As we have seen, there are several similarities between these efforts at regional co-operation, which warrants its recognition as a global phenomenon. On the other hand, there are important distinctions between the established integration process in Europe and the more recent developments elsewhere (see Box 23.10). In any case, it is apparent that the rise of regional co-operation in the context of globalization is not a paradox—indeed the two processes are closely related to one another (see Ch. 30).

Key points

- Multilateral negotiations and global economic competition have provided powerful incentives for co-operation among states on a regional basis.

- Efforts to establish free trade areas and customs unions in Asia and in North and South America received a boost during the 1990s.

- On the whole, these forms of regionalism differ from European integration in only focusing on economic matters and relying on a very limited degree of institutionalization.

Conclusion

This chapter has illustrated the dynamics and dilemmas underlying the process of regional integration. In Europe, supranational institutions were created to oversee integration in a number of specific economic sectors. Gradually, their powers were extended, and ever wider areas of economic and social regulation became the responsibility of the European Union. With growing membership and expanding competences, member states progressively gave up their veto over decision-making in order to ensure efficient governance. The EU now takes decisions on a wide range of issues of direct relevance to the wider public, but citizens are only indirectly, and imperfectly, empowered to influence these. As a result, the legitimacy of the EU's institutional structure and of individual policies is fragile, and often under attack in the member states.

In other parts of the world, in particular in North America, South America, and Asia, there have also been intensifying efforts to co-operate on a regional basis. Here there has been more emphasis on encouraging free trade through progressive tariff reductions without the establishment of an exten-

sive central bureaucracy. Economically, this method of regional co-operation has shown itself to be effective, though politically such ventures remain close to established forms of inter-state relations.

The EU, in contrast, has made considerable advances towards the creation of a novel system of governance. This has been particularly effective in the economic realm, with a single market and a single currency creating a more competitive environment for business in Europe. Externally, economic integration has led to a common trade policy that has made the EU a key player in international trade negotiations. Political integration has somewhat lagged behind, and efforts at creating a common foreign and security policies have tended to promise more than they were able to deliver (see Ch. 12).

Much of what happens in the course of European integration is specific to its time and place, but at the same time we have seen that the EU receives the same dynamic effects from globalization as regional co-operation elsewhere. But the **end of sovereignty**, heralded by globalization, is more pronounced in the EU, where supranational institutions and national governments share political authority, and where market forces play an important role in the setting of standards and regulations. Yet while unilateral action has become all but unthinkable, **states are not at all withering away**. States continue to be an elementary part of the system, with much scope for affecting decisions and regulating their own affairs. Crucially, it is, on the whole, within states that electorates seek redress, citizens exercise their rights and communities share their identity—in this respect the European Union constitutes an addition to, not a replacement of, the nation-state.

Regional integration, more so than globalization, raises questions about transnational democracy, and the development of the European Parliament and the growth of transnational interest representation in Brussels demonstrate both the possibilities, and the limitations, of democracy beyond the nation-state (see Ch. 29). Most importantly, in the shadow of the often difficult institutional development of the EU social and economic mobility has increased substantially, transforming the nature of the regional economy and the way it is regulated. But this transformation has affected different countries, and different segments of society, unevenly. As a growing number of decisions affecting societies are taken on the European level, the tension between common rules and national diversity is bound to grow, something that will be further exacerbated when the EU receives new member states from Central and Eastern Europe.

Regional integration will continue to face such tensions and dilemmas. This has already led to greater flexibility, with some agreements applying only to some countries, or individual countries opting out of common policies. As the EU grows, such flexibility will become more important in order to allow the entire organization to function, but it will also make the institutional structure even more complex.

QUESTIONS

1 What have been the driving forces behind the process of European integration?

2 What are the main differences between supranationalist and intergovernmentalist approaches to the study of the EU?

3 What role do the supranational institutions play in the European policy process?

4 In which ways can member states influence decision-making in the EU?

5 How effective has the European Union been in the handling of its external affairs?

6 Has European integration improved or hindered the capacity of member states to respond to the challenges of globalization?

7 What are the main differences and similarities between the European Union and regional co-operation in other parts of the world?

8 What are the main challenges the European Union has to face in the coming years?

GUIDE TO FURTHER READING

Armstrong, K., and Bulmer, S., *The Governance of the Single European Market* (Manchester: Manchester University Press, 1997). Provides a thorough, theoretically grounded analysis of the way in which the Single Market is governed.

Fawcett, L., and Hurrell, A., *Regionalism in World Politics* (Oxford: Oxford University Press, 1995). Covers various forms of regional co-operation in different parts of the globe, looking at both the conceptual and the empirical issues arising from the revival of regionalism.

Hix, S., *The Political System of the European Union* (Basingstoke: Macmillan, 1999). This advanced textbook approaches the subject from a comparative politics angle, looking in detail at the executive, legislative, and judicial politics as well as at developments in various policy-areas.

Laffan., B., O'Donnell, R., and Smith, M., *Europe's Experimental Union* (London: Routledge, 1999). This co-authored volume puts the study of European integration into the context of world politics and the international political economy.

Marks, G. *et al.*, *Governance in the European Union* (London: Sage, 1996b). Brings together contributions to the theoretical debate from some of the leading scholars in the field.

Moravcsik, A., *The Choice for Europe: Social Purpose and State Power from Messina to Maastricht* (Ithaca, NY: Cornell University Press, 1998). This important text approaches the study of European integration from an intergovernmental angle. It provides an in-depth analysis of the key decisions in the history of the EU.

Neunreither, K. H., and Wiener, A. (eds.), *European Integration after Amsterdam* (Oxford: Oxford University Press, 2000). This edited volume contains chapters on the institutional dynamics, issues of democratic accountability and reform of the EU in preparation for enlargement.

Rosamond, B., *Theories of European Integration* (Basingstoke: Macmillan, 2000). This textbook provides a comprehensive overview and evaluation of efforts to theorize about the process of European integration.

Scharpf, F. W., *Governing in Europe* (Oxford: Oxford University Press, 1999). A study of the EU with approaches informed by rational choice and political economy. The author concentrates in particular on the tension between efficient decision-making and democratic legitimation in the EU.

Wallace, H., and Wallace, W. (eds.), *Policy-making in the European Union* (Oxford: Oxford University Press, 2000). This is a wide-ranging textbook that covers all major policies and also examines ways of studying the institutional setting and the dynamics of governance in the EU.

Weiler, J. H. H., *The Constitution of Europe* (Cambridge: Cambridge University Press, 1999). This collection of essays from a leading legal scholar of European integration provides important insights and original ideas regarding the interaction of law and politics in the EU.

WEB LINKS

www.europa.eu.int   This is the official website of the European Union, leading to separate sites of the EU institutions as well as links to the various policies. There is also a useful 'ABC' section providing basic information on the EU.

www.eurotext.ulst.ac.uk   Access to this website, providing full text copies of key documents as well as brief academic introductions to the main institutions and policies of the EU, is free for students at UK universities.

www.eiop.or.at/euroint   This website is an invaluable research resource, providing an extensive and well-organized collection of links to private and public websites with further information, debate, or publications about European integration.

24 Global trade and finance

Jan Aart Scholte

READER'S GUIDE

This chapter explores various economic aspects of contemporary globalization. It begins by distinguishing three general conceptions of economic globalization and highlights the third, geographical notion of increasing 'transborder' production, markets, and investment. This 'supraterritorial' dimension of contemporary world commerce is then described in more detail under headings of 'global trade' and 'global finance'. A fourth section of the chapter counters exaggerated claims about economic globalization by emphasizing some of its limits. Finally, globalization of commerce is linked to several major problems of injustice and insecurity in contemporary world politics.

Introduction

The globalization of world politics involves, among other things, a globalization of economics. As Ngaire Woods has emphasized elsewhere (Ch. 13), politics and economics are inseparable within social relations. Politics (the distribution and exercise of power) is integral to economics (the production, exchange, and consumption of resources). At the same time, and equally, economics is integral to politics, helping to determine where power lies and how it is exercised. Economics does not explain everything, but no account of world politics (and hence no analysis of globalization as a key issue of contemporary world history) is adequate if it does not explore the economic dimension.

Countless discussions of globalization have highlighted its economic aspects. For example, Milton Friedman, the Nobel Prize-winning economist, remarks that it has become possible 'to produce a product anywhere, using resources from anywhere, by a company located anywhere, to be sold anywhere' (cited in Naisbitt 1994: 19). Management consultants have ceaselessly extolled the virtues of global markets (e.g. Ohmae 1990). A senior researcher with American Express has described global financial integration of recent decades as marking 'the end of geography' (O'Brien 1992). Global governance bodies like the Bank for International Settlements (BIS), the Group of Seven (G7), the International Monetary Fund (IMF), the Organization of Economic Co-operation and Development (OECD), the United Nations Conference on Trade and Development (UNCTAD), the World Bank Group (WBG), and the World Trade Organization (WTO) have all put economic globalization high on their agendas. (On these and other institutions of global economic governance, see Box 24.1.) Usually these official circles have endorsed and encouraged the trend, as have most states. Meanwhile many social movements have focused their critiques of globalization on economic aspects of the process. Their analyses have depicted contemporary globalization of trade and finance as a major cause of high unemployment, a general decline in working standards, increased inequality, greater poverty for some, recurrent financial crises, and large-scale environmental degradation.

In their different ways, all of these assessments agree that the globalizing economy is a key development of contemporary history. True, the trend is often exaggerated. The sorts of qualifications made in Chapter 1 regarding globalization in general also apply to its economic aspects more particularly. However, it is just as wrong to argue, as some sceptics have done, that claims about a new globalizing economy rest on nothing but hype and myth. Instead—as in the case of most historical developments—economic globalization involves an intricate interplay of changes and continuities.

A globalizing economy

One key reason for disagreements over the extent and significance of economic globalization relates to the contrasting definitions that different analysts have applied to notions of globality. What, more precisely, is 'global' in global commerce? The following paragraphs distinguish three contrasting ways that the globalization of trade and finance has been broadly conceived, namely, in terms of: (a) the crossing of borders; (b) the opening of borders; and (c) the transcendence of borders. Although the three conceptions overlap to some extent, they involve important differences of emphasis. Most arguments concerning economic globalization have pitted sceptics who adopt the first perspective against enthusiasts who apply the second notion. However, to my mind the third conception of globality (already introduced in Chapter 1) offers a more distinctive and revealing approach. Later sections of the present chapter will therefore develop that alternative notion in relation to trade and finance.

Cross-border transactions

Scepticism about the significance of contemporary economic globalization has often arisen when analysts have conceived of the process in terms of **increased cross-border movements** between countries of people, goods, money, investments, messages, and ideas. From this perspective, globalization is seen as equivalent to **internationalization**. No significant distinction is drawn between global companies and international companies, between global trade and international trade, between global money and international money, between global finance and international finance.

When conceived in this way, economic globalization is nothing particularly new. Long-distance commerce has existed for centuries and in some cases even millennia. Ancient Babylon and the Roman Empire knew forms of long-distance lending and trade, for example. Shipments between Arabia and China via South and South-East Asia transpired

Box 24.1 Major public global governance agencies for trade and finance

BIS Bank for International Settlements. Established in 1930 with headquarters in Basle. Membership (1999) of 45 shareholding central banks, though some 120 public financial institutions use BIS facilities. Promotes co-operation among central banks and provides various services for global financial operations. For example, the Basle Committee on Banking Supervision, formed through the BIS in 1974, has spearheaded efforts at multilateral regulation of global banking. See further www.bis.org.

G7 Group of Seven. Established in 1975 as the G5 (France, Germany, Japan, UK, and USA); subsequently expanded to include Canada and Italy; now sometimes the G8 to include the Russian Federation. The G7 conducts semi-formal collaboration on world economic problems. Government leaders meet in annual G7 Summits, while finance ministers and/or their leading officials periodically hold other consultations.

GATT General Agreement on Tariffs and Trade. Established in 1947 with offices in Geneva. Membership had reached 122 states when it was absorbed into the WTO in 1995. The GATT co-ordinated eight 'rounds' of multilateral negotiations to reduce state restrictions on cross-border merchandise trade.

IMF International Monetary Fund. Established in 1945 with headquarters in Washington, DC. Membership (2001) of 183 states. The IMF monitors short-term cross-border payments and foreign exchange positions. When a country develops chronic imbalances in its external accounts, the IMF supports corrective policy reforms, often called 'structural adjustment programmes'. Since 1978 the IMF has undertaken comprehensive surveillance both of the economic performance of individual member states and of the world economy as a whole. The IMF also provides extensive technical assistance. In recent years the Fund has pursued various initiatives to promote efficiency and stability in global financial markets. See further www.imf.org.

IOSCO International Organization of Securities Commissions. Established in 1984 with headquarters in Montreal. Membership (1999) of 158 official securities regulators and (non-voting) trade associations and other agencies.

IOSCO aims to promote high standards of regulation in stock and bond markets, to establish effective surveillance of transborder securities transactions, and to foster collaboration between securities markets in the detection and punishment of offences. See further www.iosco.org/iosco.html.

OECD Organization of Economic Co-operation and Development. Founded in 1962 with headquarters in Paris. Membership (2000) of 29 states with advanced industrial economies. Provides a forum for multilateral intergovernmental consultations on a wide range of economic and social issues. OECD measures have especially addressed environmental questions, taxation, and transborder corporations. At regular intervals the OECD Secretariat produces an assessment of the macroeconomic performance of each member, including suggestions for policy changes. See further www.oecd.org.

UNCTAD United Nations Conference on Trade and Development. Established in 1964 with offices in Geneva. Membership (2000) of 188 states. UNCTAD monitors the effects of world trade on economic development, especially in the South. It provided a key forum in the 1970s for discussions of a New International Economic Order. See further www.unctad.org.

WBG World Bank Group. A collection of five agencies, the first established in 1945, with head offices in Washington, DC. The WBG promotes development in medium- and low-income countries with project loans, structural adjustment programmes and various advisory services. See further www.worldbank.org.

WTO World Trade Organization. Established in 1995 with headquarters in Geneva. Membership (2000) of 140 states. The WTO is a permanent instititution to replace the provisional GATT. It has a wider agenda, covering services, intellectual property, and investment issues as well as merchandise trade. The WTO also has greater powers of enforcement through its dispute settlement mechanism. The organization's Trade Policy Review Body conducts surveillance of members' commercial measures. See further www.wto.org.

with fair regularity more than a thousand years ago. Certain coins circulated widely around maritime South-East Asia in a prototypical 'international monetary regime' of the tenth century. Long-distance monies of the pre-modern Mediterranean world included the Byzantine *solidus* from the fifth century onwards and the Muslim *dinar* from the eighth to the thirteenth centuries. Banks based in Italian city-states maintained (temporary) offices along long-distance trade routes as early as the twelfth century. The Hanseatic League in the fourteenth century and companies based in Amsterdam, Copenhagen, London, and Paris in the seventeenth century operated overseas trading posts. The first brokerage houses with cross-border operations appeared in the eighteenth century with Amsterdam-based Hope & Co. and London-based Barings.

Indeed, on certain (though far from all) measures, cross-border economic activity reached similar levels in the late nineteenth century as it did a hundred years later. Relative to world population of the time, the magnitude of permanent migration was in fact considerably greater. When measured in relation to world output, cross-border investment in production facilities stood at roughly the same level on the eve of the First World War as it did in the early 1990s. International markets in loans and securities also flourished during the heyday of the **gold-sterling standard** between 1870 and 1914. Under this regime the British pound, fixed to a certain value in gold, served as a transworld currency and thereby greatly facilitated cross-border payments. Again citing proportional (rather than aggregate) statistics, several researchers (for example, Zevin 1992) have argued that these years witnessed larger capital flows between countries than in the late twentieth century. Meanwhile the volume of international trade grew at some 3.4 per cent per annum in the period 1870–1913, until its value was equivalent to 33 per cent of world output (Barraclough 1984: 256; Hirst and Thompson 1999: 21). By this particular calculation, cross-border trade was greater at the beginning than at the end of the twentieth century.

For the sceptics, then, the contemporary globalizing economy is nothing new. In their eyes recent decades have merely experienced a phase of increased cross-border trade and finance, much as occurred a hundred years before. Moreover, they note, just as growth of international interdependence in the late nineteenth century was substantially reversed with a forty-year wave of **protectionism** after 1914, so economic globalization of the present day may prove to be temporary. Governments can block cross-border flows if they wish, say the sceptics, and 'national interest' may well dictate that states once more tighten restrictions on international trade, travel, foreign exchange, and capital movements. Contemporary economic globalization gives little evidence, say these doubters, of an impending demise of the state, a weakening of national loyalties, and an end of war. Thus, for example, sceptics regularly point out that most so-called 'global' companies: (*a*) still conduct the majority of their business in their country of origin; (*b*) retain a strong national character and allegiances; and (*c*) remain heavily dependent on states for the success of their enterprises.

Open-border transactions

In contrast to the sceptics, enthusiasts for contemporary globalization of trade and finance generally define these developments as part of the long-term evolution towards a global society. In this second conception, globalization entails not an extension of internationalization, but the progressive removal of official restrictions on transfers of resources between countries. In the resultant world of **open borders**, global companies replace international companies, global trade replaces international trade, global money replaces international money, global finance replaces international finance. From this perspective, globalization is a function of **liberalization**, that is, the degree to which articles, communications, financial instruments, fixed assets, and people can circulate throughout the world economy free from state-imposed controls. Whereas sceptics generally back up their arguments of historical repetition with proportional data, globalists usually substantiate their claims of historical change with aggregate statistics, many of which do indeed appear quite staggering. (See Table 24.1.)

Table 24.1 Some indicators of contemporary economic globalization ($US billion)

Measure (worldwide figures)	Earlier level	Recent level
Foreign direct investment	$66 (1960)	$4,000 (1999)
Exports (1995 values)	$430 (1950)	$6,000 (1995)
Official foreign exchange reserves	$100 (1970)	$1,579 (1997)
Daily turnover on foreign exchange markets	$100 (1979)	$1,500 (1998)
Bank deposits by non-residents	$20 (1964)	$7,876 (1995)
Cross-border loan announcements	$9 (1972)	$957 (1999)
Cross-border bond issues	$1 (1960)	$1,157 (1999)
Euroequity issues	initiated 1984	$50 (1995)
Cross-border share dealing	$10 (1980)	$120 (1994)
Daily turnover of financial derivatives contracts	small before 1980	$1,162 (1995)

Sources: BIS, IMF, OECD, UNCTAD.

Globalists regard the forty-year interlude of protectionism (c.1910–50) as a temporary detour from a longer historical trend towards the construction of a single integrated world economy. In their eyes the tightening of border controls in the first half of the twentieth century was a major cause of economic depressions, authoritarian regimes, and international conflicts such as the world wars. In contrast, the emergent open world economy will (so runs the globalist promise) yield prosperity, liberty, democracy, and peace for all humanity. From this perspective—which is often termed **neoliberalism**—contemporary economic globalization continues the modern project launched several centuries ago.

Recent history has indeed witnessed considerable opening of borders in the world economy. For one thing, a succession of inter-state accords through the **General Agreement on Tariffs and Trade (GATT)** has since 1948 brought major reductions in customs duties, quotas, and other measures that previously inhibited cross-border movements of merchandise. Average tariffs on manufactures in countries of the North fell from over 40 per cent in the 1930s to less than 4 per cent by 1999. Following the Uruguay Round of multilateral trade negotiations (1986–94), the GATT was subsumed within the **World Trade Organization**. This successor agency has greater competences both to enforce existing trade agreements and to pursue new avenues of liberalization, for example, in respect of shipping, telecommunications, and investment flows. Meanwhile, as indicated in Chapter 23, regional frameworks in most areas of the world have (to varying degrees) removed official restrictions on trade between participating countries. Encouraged by such liberalization, cross-border trade expanded between 1950 and 1994 at an annual rate of just over 6 per cent: thus almost twice as fast as in the late nineteenth century. Total international trade multiplied fourteen-fold in real terms over this period, while expansion in respect of manufactures was even greater, with a twenty-six-fold increase (WTO 1995).

Borders have also opened considerably to money flows since 1950. A **gold–dollar standard** became fully operational through the **International Monetary Fund** in 1959. Under this regime major currencies—and especially the United States dollar—could circulate worldwide (though not in communist-ruled countries) and be converted to local monies at an official **fixed exchange rate**. The gold–dollar standard thereby broadly recreated the situation that prevailed under the gold–sterling standard in the late nineteenth century. Contrary to many expectations, the US government's termination of dollar–gold convertibility on demand in 1971 did not trigger new restrictions on cross-border payments. Instead, a regime of **floating exchange rates** developed: *de facto* from 1973 and formalized through the IMF in 1976. Moreover, from the mid-1970s onwards most states reduced or eliminated restrictions on the import and export of national currencies. In these circumstances foreign exchange trading burgeoned to historically unprecedented levels after 1980, reaching volumes of $1,500 billion per day in 1998.

Alongside liberalization of trade and money movements between countries, recent decades have also witnessed the widespread opening of borders to investment flows. These movements involve both direct investments (that is, fixed assets like research facilities and factories) and portfolio investments (that is, liquid assets like loans, bonds and shares).

Apart from a wave of expropriations in the South during the 1970s (many of them subsequently reversed), states have generally welcomed **foreign direct investment (FDI)** into their jurisdictions in contemporary history. Indeed, many governments have actively lured externally based business by lowering corporate tax rates, reducing restrictions on the repatriation of profits, relaxing labour and environmental standards, and so on. Since 1960 there has been a proliferation of what are variously called 'international', 'multinational', 'transnational', or 'global' corporations (hence the frequently encountered abbreviations **MNC** and **TNC**). The number of such companies grew from 3,500 in 1960 to 60,000 in 1999. The aggregate stock of FDI worldwide increased in tandem from $66 billion in 1960 to over $4,000 billion in 1999, as compared with only $14 billion in 1914 (UNCTAD 1996: ix, 4; UNCTAD 1999). In this world of more open borders, various globalists have described MNCs as 'footloose' and 'stateless'.

Substantial liberalization has also occurred since the 1970s in respect of cross-border portfolio investments. For example, many a state now permits non-residents to hold bank accounts within its jurisdiction. Other deregulation has removed legal restrictions on ownership and trading of stocks and bonds by non-resident investors. Further legislation has reduced controls on participation in a country's financial markets by externally based banks, brokers, and fund managers. As a result of such deregulation (for example, the City of London's so-called 'Big Bang' in 1986) financial institutions from all over the world have converged on **global cities** like Hong Kong, New York, Paris, and Tokyo. Levels of cross-border banking and securities business have risen markedly since the 1960s in tandem with such liberalization, as several statistics in Table 24.1 indicate. Corresponding indicators for the 1870–1914 period come nowhere close to these aggregate figures.

In sum, legal obstructions to economic transactions between countries have greatly diminished worldwide in contemporary history. At the same time, cross-border flows of merchandise, services, money, and investments have reached unprecedented levels, at least in aggregate terms. To this extent enthusiasts for globalization-as-liberalization can argue, against the sceptics, that borders have opened more than ever.

That said, significant official restrictions on cross-border economic activity persist. They include countless trade restrictions and continuing **capital controls** in many countries. While states have on the whole welcomed FDI, there is as yet no official regime to liberalize investment flows comparable to the GATT/WTO in respect of trade or the IMF in respect of money. (Negotiations for a **Multilateral Agreement on Investment** were abandoned at the end of 1998.) In addition, although many governments have loosened visa and travel restrictions in recent times, **immigration controls** are on the whole as tight as ever. Indeed, many have recently been reinforced. To this extent sceptics have grounds to affirm that international borders remain very much in place and can be opened or closed as states choose to do.

Transborder transactions

As mentioned earlier, most debates concerning economic globalization have unfolded between, on the one hand, globalists who see an inexorable trend towards an open world economy and, on the other hand, sceptics who regard the current situation as a limited and reversible expansion of cross-border transactions. However, these two most common positions do not exhaust the possible interpretations. Indeed, neither of these conventional perspectives requires a distinct concept of 'globalization'. Both views resurrect arguments that were elaborated using other vocabulary long before the word 'globalization' entered widespread circulation in the 1980s.

In a third conception, globalization refers to **processes whereby social relations acquire relatively distanceless and borderless qualities**, so that human lives are increasingly played out in the world as a single place (recall Ch. 1). In this usage, 'globalization' refers to a transformation of geography that occurs when a host of social conditions become less tied to territorial spaces.

On these lines a globalizing economy is one in which patterns of production, exchange, and consumption become increasingly delinked from a geography of territorial distances and territorial borders. 'Global' economic activity extends across widely dispersed terrestrial locations at the same time and moves between locations scattered across the world in effectively no time. While the patterns of 'international' economic interdependence are strongly influenced by territorial distances and national-state divisions, patterns of 'global' trade and finance often have little correspondence to distance and state boundaries. With air travel, satellite links, telecommunications, transworld organizations, global consciousness (that is, a mindset that conceives of the world as a single place) and more, much contemporary economic activity transcends borders. In this third sense globalization involves the growth of a **transborder** (as opposed to cross-border or open-border) economy.

This rise of **supraterritoriality** is reflected *inter alia* in increased transactions between countries. However, the geographical character of these **transworld** (as opposed to long-distance) movements is different from the territorial framework that has traditionally defined international interdependence. This qualitative shift means that contemporary statistics on international trade, money, and investment can only be crudely compared with figures relating to earlier times. Hence the issue is not so much the amount of trade between countries, but the way that much of this commerce forms part of transborder production processes and global marketing networks. The problem is not only the quantity of money that moves between countries, but also the instantaneity with which most funds are transferred. The question is not simply the number of international securities deals so much as the emergence of stock and bond issues that involve participants from multiple countries at the same time. In short, if one accepts this third conception of globalization, then both the sceptics and the enthusiasts are largely missing the crucial point. The next sections elaborate further.

Key points

- The 'globalization' of economic activity can be understood in several different ways.

- Sceptical interpretations emphasize that current levels of cross-border trade, money movements, and investment flows are neither new nor as great as some claim.

- Globalist interpretations argue that large-scale relaxations of border controls have taken international economic activity to unprecedented levels.

- Geographical interpretations highlight the proliferation of economic transactions in which territorial distance and borders present limited if any constraint.

Global trade

The distinctiveness of transborder, supraterritorial economic relations should become clearer with illustrations. Examples relating to global trade are given in the present section. Others concerning global finance follow in the next section. In each case it will be seen that, although the phenomena in question made some earlier appearances, their significance relates mainly to contemporary history.

Transborder production

Transborder production arises when a single process is spread across widely dispersed locations both within and between countries. Supraterritorial co-ordination links research centres, design units, procurement offices, materials processing installations, fabrication plants, finishing points, assembly lines, quality control operations, advertising and marketing bureaux, data-processing offices, after-sales service, and so on. Describing a global production operation, the head of Levi Strauss has noted that:

our company buys denim in North Carolina, ships it to France where it is sewn into jeans, launders these jeans in Belgium, and markets them in Germany using TV commercials developed in England   (R. D. Haas 1993: 103)

Transborder production can be contrasted with territorially centred production. In the latter instance, all stages of a given production process—from initial research to after-sales service—transpire within the same local or national unit. In global production, however, the stages are dispersed across different countries. Each of the various links in the transborder chain specializes in one or several functions, thereby creating economies of scale and/or exploiting cost differentials between locations. Through **global sourcing**, the company draws materials, components, machinery, finance, and services from anywhere in the world. Distance and borders figure only secondarily, if at all, in determining the sites. Indeed, a firm may relocate certain stages of production several times in short succession in search of profit maximization. In one striking example of **country-hopping**, athletic suppliers Nike during a five-year period opened or closed fifty-five factories in North America and East Asia in response to changes in relative costs of production (Abegglen 1994: 26).

What others have called **global factories** were unknown before the 1940s. They did not gain major prominence until the 1960s and have mainly spread since the 1970s. Supraterritorial production has developed mainly in the manufacture of textiles, garments, motor vehicles, leather goods, sports articles, toys, optical products, consumer electronics, semiconductors, aeroplanes, and construction equipment.

With the growth of global production, a large proportion of purportedly 'international' transfers of goods and services entails **intra-firm trade** within transborder companies. When the intermediate inputs and finished goods pass from one country to another they are officially counted as 'international' commerce; yet they primarily involve movements within a global company rather than between national economies. Conventional statistics do not measure intra-firm transfers, but estimates of the share of such exchanges in total cross-border trade have ranged from 25 to over 40 per cent.

Much (though far from all) transborder production has taken advantage of what are variously called special economic zones (SEZs), export processing zones (EPZs) or free production zones (FPZs). Within these enclaves the ruling national or provincial government exempts assembly plants and other facilities for transborder production from the usual import and export duties. The authorities may also grant other tax reductions, subsidies, and waivers of certain labour and environmental regulations. The first such zone was established in 1954 in Ireland, but most were created after 1970, mainly in Asia, the Caribbean, and the so-called *maquiladora* areas along the Mexican frontier with the USA. Nearly 850 EPZs were in place worldwide at the turn of the century (UNDP 1999: 86). Among other things, these manufacturing centres have been distinguished by their frequent heavy reliance on female labour.

Transborder products

Much of the output of both transborder and country-based production has acquired a **supraterritorial market** in the contemporary globalizing economy. Hence a considerable proportion of 'international' trade now involves the distribution and sale of **global goods**, often under a transworld brand name. Consumers dispersed across many corners of the planet purchase the same articles at the same time. The country location of a potential customer for, say, a Xerox photocopier, a Britney Spears CD, or Kellogg's corn flakes is of limited importance. Design, packaging, and advertising determine the market far more than territorial distance and borders.

Like other aspects of globalization, supraterritorial markets have a longer history than many contemporary observers appreciate. For example, Campbell Soup and Heinz began to become household names at widely dispersed locations across the world in the mid-1880s, following the introduction of automatic canning. From the outset Henry Ford regarded his first automobile, the Model T, as a world car. Coca-Cola was bottled in 27 countries and sold in 78 by 1929 (Pendergrast 1993: 174). On the whole, however, the numbers of goods, customers, and countries involved in these earlier global markets were relatively small.

In contrast, global goods pervade the contemporary world economy. They encompass a host of packaged foods, bottled beverages, tobacco products, designer clothes, household articles, music recordings, audio-visual productions, printed publications, interactive communications, office and hospital equipment, armaments, transport vehicles, and travel services. In all of these sectors and more, global products inject a touch of the familiar almost wherever on earth a person might visit. The countless examples include Nescafé (sold in 200 varieties worldwide), Heineken beer (drunk in 170 countries), Kiwi shoe polish (applied in 130 countries), Nokia mobile phones (used in 120 countries), Thomas Cook tourist bureaux (available in 140 countries), American International Group insurance policies (offered in 130 countries), television programmes by Globo of Brazil (distributed in 128 countries), and the *Financial Times* newspaper (read in 160 coun-

tries). Covering smokers in 170 lands, 'Marlboro Country' is a distinctly supraterritorial place.

Today many shops are mainly stocked with transborder articles. Moreover, since the 1970s a number of **retail chains** have gone global. Examples include Italy-based Benetton, Japan-based 7-Eleven, Sweden-based IKEA, UK-based Body Shop, and US-based Toys 'R' Us (Treadgold 1993). Owing largely to the various 'megabrands' and transborder stores, shopping

---

Box 24.2 Case study: Moscow in global markets

The current reach and power of global markets became acutely—and indeed somewhat painfully—apparent to me on a visit to Moscow at the turn of the year 1994–5. Less than a decade after the launch of perestroika, the city was flooded with global cigarettes, to the point that it had become nearly impossible to find a Russian brand. Dove Bars and Perrier were available for anyone who could pay, but it took me five days to find a sack of potatoes. Everywhere the eye turned, Nike was competing with Reebok, Pizza Hut with Burger King, Pepsi with Coke, Martini with Asti Spumanti, Wrigley's with Hershey, Pioneer with JVC, Philips with Bosch, Gold Star with TDK, Tide with Ajax, Wella with Flex, Cosmopolitan with Burda (each in Russian-language editions), Barbie with Cindy, Konica with Kodak, Casio with Rolex, Whiskas with Pedigree Chum. Moscow travel agents were beginning to flog fun-in-the-sun package holidays and time-share vacation homes, while US Global Health offered private medical insurance for the monied few. VDNH, once the communist Exhibition to the Achievements of the People's Economy, had been turned into a consumer playground. Its pavilions were now crammed with makeshift stalls selling global products, especially consumer electronics, many of them bought duty-free in the Persian Gulf region. In the north-west corner of the park, the large Cosmos hangar had been converted into a showroom for shiny Fords and Mercedes. Lenin's statue stared blandly as hordes of buyers scuttled past now-silent fountains with televisions, portable stereos, cordless telephones, and car alarms, while public loudspeakers pumped out strains of Brian Adams: 'Baby it's hard to believe, we're in heaven'. Comrades had become customers. (The situation on return visits to Moscow in 2000–2001 was broadly the same.)

centres of the twenty-first century are in good part global emporia. (See Box 24.2.)

Other supraterritorial markets have developed since the 1990s through **electronic commerce**. Today's global consumer can—equipped with a credit card and telephone, television, or Internet links—shop the world from home. Mail-order outlets and telesales units have undergone exponential growth, while optimistic projections estimate that e-commerce on the World Wide Web will expand from $2.6 billion in 1996 to over $300 billion in 2002 (Bacchetta *et al*. 1998: 23; UNDP 1999: 60).

Through transborder production and transworld products, global trade has become an integral part of everyday life for a notable proportion of the world's firms and consumers. Indeed, these developments could help to explain why the recessions of contemporary history have not, in spite of frequently expressed fears of 'trade wars', provoked a wave of protectionism. In previous prolonged periods of commercial instability and economic hardship (for example, during the 1870s–1890s and 1920s–1930s) most states responded by imposing major protectionist restrictions on cross-border trade. Reac-

tions to contemporary recession have been more complicated (cf. Milner 1988). While many territorial interests have pressed for protectionism, global commercial interests have generally resisted it. Thus many transborder companies actively promoted the Uruguay Round and have on the whole vigorously supported the new World Trade Organization.

Key points

- The second half of the twentieth century witnessed the development of transborder production and associated intra-firm trade in a number of industries.
- Many states have created special economic zones in order to attract so-called 'global factories'.
- Much contemporary commerce involves transborder marketing of global brand-name products.
- The growth of a substantial global dimension to world trade may have deterred protectionism.

Global finance

Finance has attracted some of the greatest attention in contemporary debates on globalization, especially following a string of crises in Latin America 1994–5, Asia 1997–8, Russia 1998, and Brazil 1999. The rise of supraterritoriality has affected both the forms that money takes and the ways that it is deployed in banking, securities, derivatives and (although not detailed below) insurance markets. (See Box 24.3 regarding terminology.) As international, cross-border activities, such dealings have quite a long history. However, as commerce that unfolds through telephone and computer networks that make the world a single place, global finance has experienced its greatest growth since the 1980s.

Supraterritorial money

The development of global production and the growth of global markets have each encouraged—and been facilitated by—the spread of global monies. It was noted earlier that the fixed and later floating exchange regimes operated through the IMF have allowed a number of 'national' currencies to enter transworld use. As familiar 'bureau de change' signs indicate, today retail outlets in scores of countries deal in multiple currencies on demand.

No national denomination has been more global in this context than the US dollar. About as many dollars circulate outside as inside the USA. Indeed, in certain financial crises this global money has displaced the locally issued currency in the everyday life of a national economy. Such 'dollarization' has

Box 24.3 A glossary of global finance

bond: a contractual obligation of a corporation, association, or governance agency to make payments of interest and repayments of principle on borrowed funds at certain fixed times.

derivative: a financial contract that 'derives' its value from an underlying asset, exchange rate, interest level, or market index.

equity: also called stock or share; a number of equal portions in the nominal capital of a company; the shareholder thereby owns part of the enterprise.

eurobond: a bond denominated in a currency that is alien to a substantial proportion of the underwriters through whom it is distributed and investors to whom it is sold; the borrower, the syndicate of managers, the investors, and the securities exchange on which the bond is listed are spread over a number of countries.

eurocurrency: national money in the hands of persons and institutions domiciled outside the currency's territorial 'home': hence 'eurodollar', 'eurozloty', etc.

euroequity: a share issue that is offered simultaneously in different stock markets, usually across several time zones; also called global equity.

merchant bank: also called an investment bank or securities house; a bank specializing in securities business, as opposed to a commercial bank engaged primarily in deposit and lending business. (That said, many major investment banks have in recent years become arms of global commercial banks: for example, Deutsche Morgan Grenfell and UBS Warburg.)

offshore finance centre: a site for financial business offering inducements such as tax reductions, regulation waivers, subsidies and rebates, secrecy guarantees, and so on; most are located in island and other mini-states, though offshore provisions also cover arrangements like International Banking Facilities in New York (since 1981), the Tokyo-based Japan Offshore Market (since 1986) and the Bangkok International Banking Facility (since 1993).

petrodollars: earnings from oil exports deposited outside the USA; they provided the largest single spur to growth in the euromarkets in the 1970s.

security: a contract with a claim to future payments in which (in contrast to bank credits) there is a direct and formally identified relationship between the investor and the borrower; also unlike bank loans, securities are traded in markets.

Special Drawing Right: the supraterritorial denomination issued since 1969 through the International Monetary Fund and used as its unit of account. As of March 2000, 21.4 billion SDRs were in circulation at a value of 1 SDR = US $1.34. A further allocation to double the amount of SDRs is pending.

Syndicated eurocredit: a loan provided in the euromarkets by an ad hoc association of a number of commercial banks.

---

occurred in parts of Latin America and much of Eastern Europe. Since the 1970s the German Mark (now to be superseded by the euro), Japanese yen, Swiss franc, and other major currencies have also acquired a substantial global character. Hence huge stocks of notionally 'national' money are now used in countless transactions that never touch the 'home' soil.

Foreign exchange dealing has become a thoroughly supraterritorial business. This round-the-clock, round-the-world market has no central meeting place. Many of the deals have nothing directly to do with the countries where the currencies involved are initially issued or eventually spent. The trading itself also transpires without distance. Transactions are generally concluded over the telephone and confirmed by telex or e-mail between buyers and sellers across whatever distance. Meanwhile shifts in exchange rates are flashed instantaneously and simultaneously on video monitors across the main dealing rooms worldwide.

Transborder money also takes other forms besides certain national currencies. Gold has already circulated across the planet for several centuries, although it moves cumbersomely through territorial space rather than instantly through telecommunication lines. A newer and more fully supraterritorial denomination is the **Special Drawing Right**, issued through the IMF since 1969. SDRs reside only in computer memories and not in pocketbooks for everyday transactions.

Meanwhile other supraterritorial money has entered daily use in plastic form. For example, many bank cards can extract local currency from automated teller machines (**ATMs**) worldwide. In addition, several types of **smart cards** (e.g. Mondex and the Clip card of Europay International) can simultaneously hold several currencies as digital cash on a microchip. Certain **credit cards** like Visa and MasterCard are accepted at several million venues the world over to make purchases in whatever local denomination.

In sum, then, contemporary globalization has—through the spread of transborder currencies, distinctly supraterritorial denominations, digital purses, and global credit and debit cards—significantly altered the shape of money. No longer is money restricted to the national-state-territorial form that prevailed from the nineteenth to the middle of the twentieth century.

Supraterritorial banking

Globalization has touched banking mainly in terms of: (*a*) the growth of transborder deposits; (*b*) the advent of transborder bank lending; (*c*) the expansion of transborder branch networks; and (*d*) the emergence of instantaneous transworld interbank fund transfers.

So-called **eurocurrency** deposits are bank assets denominated in a national money different from the official currency in the country where the funds are held. For instance, euroyen are 'Japanese' yen deposited in, say, Canada. Eurocurrency accounts first appeared in the 1950s, but mainly expanded after 1970, especially with the flood of so-called **petrodollars** that followed major rises of oil prices in 1973–4 and 1979–80. Eurocurrencies are supraterritorial: they do not attach neatly to any country's money supply; nor are they systematically regulated by the national central bank that issued them.

Globalization has also entered the lending side of banking. Credit creation from eurocurrency deposits first occurred in 1957, when 'American' dollars were borrowed through the 'British' office of a 'Soviet' bank. However, euroloans mainly proliferated after 1973 following the petrodollar deluge. Today it is common for a loan to be issued in one country, denominated in the currency of a second country (or perhaps a basket of currencies of several countries), for a borrower in a third country, by a bank or syndicate of banks in fourth and more countries.

Global banking transpires not only at age-old sites of world finance like London, New York, Tokyo, and Zurich, but also through multiple **offshore finance centres**. Much like EPZs in respect of manufacturing, offshore financial arrangements offer investors low levels of taxation and regulation. Although a few offshore centres including Luxembourg and Jersey predate the Second World War, most have emerged since 1960 and are now found in over forty countries. Most of the world's major banks now have branch networks across the principal 'onshore' (i.e. normally taxed and regulated) and offshore locations. For example, less than thirty years after passing relevant legislation in 1967, the Cayman Islands hosted over 500 offshore banks, with total deposits of $442 billion, none of them in the local currency (Roberts 1994; BIS 1996: 7).

The supraterritorial character of much contemporary banking also lies in the instantaneity of **interbank fund transfers**. Electronic messages have largely replaced territorial transfers by cheque or draft—and cost far less. The largest conduit for such movements is the Society for Worldwide Interbank Financial Telecommunications. Launched in 1977, SWIFT interconnected over 6,800 financial institutions in 189 countries by 1999, carrying payments with an average daily value of more than $5 trillion.

Supraterritorial securities

Alongside banking, globalization has also altered the shape of securities markets. First, some of the bonds and stocks themselves have become relatively detached from territorial space. Second, many investor portfolios have acquired a transborder character. Third, electronic interlinkage of trading sites has created conditions of anywhere/anytime securities dealing.

In regard to the first point, contemporary globalization has seen the emergence of several major securities instruments with a transborder character. These bonds and equities involve issuers, currencies, brokers, and/or exchanges across multiple countries at the same time. For example, a so-called **eurobond** is denominated in a currency that is alien to a substantial proportion of the parties involved: the borrower who issues it; the underwriters who distribute it; the investors who hold it; and/or the exchange(s) that list it. This transborder financial instrument is thereby different from a **foreign bond**, which is handled in one country for an external borrower. Cross-border bonds of the latter type have existed for several hundred years, but eurobonds first appeared in 1963. In that year the state highways authority in Italy issued bonds denominated in US dollars through managers in Belgium, Britain, Germany, and the Netherlands, with subsequent quotation on the London Stock Exchange. By the late 1980s eurobonds constituted the second largest bond market in the world, behind that for US domestic issues (Honeygold 1989: 19).

On a similar pattern, a **euroequity** issue involves a transborder syndicate of brokers selling a new share release for simultaneous listing on stock exchanges in several countries. This supraterritorial process contrasts with an international offer, where a company based in one country issues equity in a second country. Like foreign bonds, international share quotations have existed almost as long as stock markets themselves. However, the first transborder equity issue occurred in 1984, when 15 per cent of a privatization of British Telecommunications was offered on exchanges in Japan, North America, and Switzerland concurrently with the majority share release in the UK. Transworld placements of new shares have occurred less frequently than eurobond issues. However, it has become quite common for major transborder firms to list their equity on different stock exchanges across several time zones. For example, equity in Alcatel Alsthom is quoted on twelve exchanges, stock in Nestlé on eleven, and shares in Imperial Chemical Industries on nine.

Not only various securities instruments, but also many **investor portfolios** have become relatively de-linked from territory in the context of contemporary financial globalization. Thus, for example, an investor in one country may leave assets with a fund manager in a second country who in turn places those sums on markets in a collection of third countries. In other words, even when individual securities have a territorial character, they can be combined in a supraterritorial investment package. Indeed, a number of pension funds, insurance companies, and unit trusts have created explicitly designated 'global funds' whose component securities are drawn from multiple corners of the world. Many transborder institutional investors have furthermore registered offshore for tax and other cost advantages. For example, the Africa Emerging Markets Fund has its investments in Africa, its listing in Ireland, and its management base in the USA. As of 1995 Luxembourg hosted some $350 billion in offshore investment funds, largely outside the regulatory reach of the managers' home governments.

Finally, securities markets have gone global through the growing supraterritorial character of many exchanges since the 1970s. The open-outcry trading floors of old have largely given way to electronic transactions by telephone and computer networks. These telecommunications provide the infrastructure for distanceless deals (so-called **remote trading**), in which the brokers can in principle be located anywhere on earth. Most major investment banks (Daiwa Securities, Dresdner Kleinwort Benson, Merrill Lynch, etc.) now co-ordinate offices across several time zones in round-the-clock, round-the-world trading of bonds and shares. The first computerized order-routing system became operational in 1976, connecting brokers across the USA instantly to the trading floor of the New York Stock Exchange. Similar developments have since 1996 begun to link brokers anywhere in the European Union directly to its main exchanges. For its part the wholly computer-based National Association of Securities Dealers Automated Quotation system (Nasdaq) has since its launch in 1971 had no central meeting place at all. This transborder cyberspatial network has become the world's second largest stock market, listing over 5,000 companies with a total capitalization of $2.6 trillion at the end of 1998. The Europe-wide Easdaq system launched a similar screen-based market in 1996, although its proportions have thus far remained modest. Meanwhile, beginning with the Toronto and American Stock Exchanges in 1985, a number of securities markets have established electronic links to enable transborder dealing between them. This extensive growth of supraterritoriality in the securities markets helps to explain why, for example, the Wall Street crash of October 1987 triggered transworld reverberations within hours.

Much like global banking, transborder securities trading is mainly conducted through computerized clearing systems. The equivalents of SWIFT are the Euroclear network, established in 1968, and Cedel (now renamed Clearstream), launched in 1971. Between them these two global electronic bookkeeping operations handled a turnover of nearly $60 trillion in 1999.

Supraterritorial derivatives

A fourth area of finance suffused with globalization is the **derivatives** industry. A derivative product is a contract, the value of which depends on (hence is 'derived' from) the price of some underlying asset (for example, a raw material or an equity) or a particular reference rate (e.g. an interest level or stockmarket index). Derivatives connected to 'tangible' assets like raw minerals and land date from the middle of the nineteenth century, while derivatives based on financial indicators have proliferated since their introduction in 1972.

Derivatives contracts take two principal forms. The first type, called **futures** or **forwards**, oblige a buyer and seller to complete a transaction at a predetermined time in the future at a price agreed upon today. The second main type, called **options**, give parties a right (without obligation) to buy or sell at a specified price for a stipulated period of time up to the contract's expiry date. Other kinds of derivatives include 'swaps', 'warrants', and further—seemingly ever more obscure—financial instruments (Banks 1994).

Additional technical details and the various rationales relating to derivatives need not detain us here. It suffices for present purposes to emphasize the magnitude of this financial industry. Public derivatives exchanges have proliferated worldwide since 1982 along with even larger over-the-counter (OTC) markets. By 1995 the volume of trading on world derivatives markets totalled some $1.2 trillion per day. The value of outstanding OTC derivatives contracts alone reached $88 trillion at the end of 1999 (Sharpe 1996; BIS 1996: 27; BIS 2000: 26).

Like banking and securities, much derivatives business has become relatively distanceless and borderless. For example, a number of the contracts relate to supraterritorial indicators: e.g. the world price of copper; the interest rate on euroswiss franc deposits; and so on. In addition, much derivatives trading is undertaken through global securities houses and transworld telecommunications links. A number of derivatives instruments are traded simultaneously on several exchanges in a round-the-world, round-the-clock market. For example, contracts related to three-month eurodollar interest rates have been traded concurrently on the London International Financial Futures and Options Exchange (LIFFE), the New York Futures Exchange, the Sydney Futures Exchange, and the Singapore International Monetary Exchange (SIMEX). Starting with a connection between SIMEX and the Chicago Mercantile Exchange in 1984, electronic links have enabled distanceless, transborder trading between various market sites.

Owing to these tight global interconnections, major losses in the derivatives markets can have immediate world-wide repercussions. For example, deficits of $1.3 billion accumulated by the Singapore-based futures trader Nick Leeson triggered a transborder collapse of the venerable Barings investment bank in 1995. A succession of similarly huge losses in other quarters has caused some to worry that global derivatives trading could undermine the world financial system as a whole.

Key points

- Globalization has changed forms of money with the spread of transborder currencies, distinctly supraterritorial denominations, digital cash, and global credit cards.

- Globalization has reshaped banking with the growth of supraterritorial deposits, loans, branch networks, and fund transfers.

- Securities markets have gained a global dimension through the development of transborder bonds and stocks, transworld portfolios, and electronic round-the-world trading.

- Globalization has likewise affected the instruments and modes of trading on derivatives markets.

Limits to economic globalization

Having now reviewed the development of a supraterritorial dimension in the contemporary world economy (summarized chronologically in Box 24.4), and emphasized its significance, we must also recognize the limits of these changes. As noted in Chapter 1, and again earlier in the present chapter, many assessments of globalization are suffused with hype and exaggeration. However, one can appreciate the importance of globalization without slipping into such 'globalism'. Four main points are highlighted in this respect below: (*a*) the unevenness with which the globalization of trade and finance has spread; (*b*)

Box 24.4 Some key events in global trade and finance

1880s	development of first global products
1929	institution of the first offshore finance arrangements (in Luxembourg)
1944	Bretton Woods Conference drafts constitutions of the IMF and World Bank
1954	establishment of the first export processing zone (in Ireland)
1954	launch of the 'Marlboro cowboy' as a global commercial icon
1955	first McDonald's restaurant opened (operating in 119 countries 45 years later)
1957	issuance of the first eurocurrency loan
1959	gold-dollar standard enters into full operation
1963	issuance of the first eurobond
1965	start of the *maquiladora* programme in Mexico
1968	launch of Euroclear computerized transworld settlement of securities deals
1969	introduction of the Special Drawing Right
1971	establishment of the first wholly electronic stock exchange (Nasdaq)
1972	launch of markets in financial derivatives, starting with currency futures
1973	quadrupling of oil prices floods euromarkets with petrodollars
1974	formation of Basle Committee on Banking Supervision following the collapse of two banks heavily involved in foreign exchange dealing
1974	US government relaxes foreign exchange controls (other states follow in later years)
1976	IMF meeting in Jamaica formalizes the regime of floating exchange rates
1977	inauguration of the SWIFT system of electronic interbank fund transfers worldwide
1982	Mexico's threatened default on global loans triggers Third World debt crisis
1984	formation of the International Organization of Securities Commissions
1984	first transborder equity issue (by British Telecommunications)
1985	first transborder electronic link between stock exchanges
1987	stock-market crash on Wall Street reverberates worldwide within hours
1994	conclusion of the Uruguay Round of GATT
1995	inauguration of the World Trade Organization
1995	Leeson Affair highlights the volatility of global derivatives markets
1997–9	economic crises in Asia, Russia, and Brazil raise concerns about underregulated global finance

the continuing importance of territoriality in the contemporary globalizing economy; (c) the continuing key place of the state amidst these changes; and (d) the continuing significance of national attachments, and cultural diversity more generally, in the present era of economic globalization.

Irregular incidence

As already stressed in Chapter 1, globalization has not been experienced everywhere and by everyone to the same extent. In general, transborder trade and finance have developed furthest: (a) in East Asia, North America, and Western Europe; (b) in urban areas relative to rural districts worldwide; and (c) in wealthy and professional circles. On the other hand, few people and places are today completely untouched by economic globalization.

Supraterritorial trade and finance have transpired disproportionately in the so-called **North**, and then most especially in its **cities**. For example, in the 1990s over half of world manufacturing output and a third of merchandise exports were centred in just three countries: the USA, Japan, and Germany (Kidron and Segal 1995: 86–9). Usually only the labour-intensive assembly stage of a transborder production process has been located in the South. The sale of most global products has also been heavily concentrated in the North. For instance, although McDonald's fast food is dished up in 119 countries, the vast majority of these meals are consumed in a handful of those lands. In contrast to currencies issued in the North, the national denominations of countries in Africa have scarcely any mutual convertibility. At the time of writing, three-quarters and more of foreign direct investment, credit card transactions, stock market capitalization, derivatives trade, and transborder loans flowed within the North. In the light of such inequalities, a number of promoters as well as critics of globalization have worried that the trend is substantially bypassing the South.

This exclusion is far from complete, however. For instance, certain products originating in the South have figured significantly in global markets (for example, wines from Chile and package holidays in the Caribbean). Electronic banking has even reached parts of rural China. A number of offshore finance centres and large sums of transborder bank debt are found in the South. Global portfolios have figured strongly in the development of new securities markets in major cities of Africa, Asia, Eastern Europe, and Latin America since the mid-1980s. SIMEX and the São Paulo-based *Bolsa de Mercadorias & Futuros* (BM&F) have played a part in the burgeoning derivatives markets of recent decades.

Indeed, involvement in global trade and finance is often as much a function of **class** as the North-South divide. The vast majority of the world's population—including many in the North—have lacked the means to purchase most global products. Michael Porter of the Harvard Business School puts this point more euphemistically by noting that markets 'today seem based less on country differences and more on buyer differences that transcend country boundaries' (1986: 44). Likewise, placing investments in global financial markets depends on wealth, whose distribution does not always follow a North–South pattern. For example, petrodollars have been mostly owned by élites in the oil-exporting countries of Africa, Latin America, and the Middle East. Country comparisons have indicated that the populations of Brazil and Botswana have the world's largest income inequalities.

Space limitations do not permit full elaboration of the point here, but transborder markets and investments can be shown to have contributed significantly to **growing wealth gaps** within countries as well as between North and South (Scholte 2000: ch. 10). For example, the global mobility of capital, in particular to low-wage production sites and offshore finance centres, has encouraged most states to reduce upper-tax brackets and downgrade other public welfare measures. Such steps have contributed to growing inequality almost everywhere in the contemporary world. Increasingly, poverty has become connected as much to supraterritorial class, gender, and race structures as to country of domicile (see further Chs. 26 and 27).

The persistence of territory

On the other hand, the transcendence of territorial space in the contemporary world economy must not be overestimated. True, evidence presented in earlier sections of this chapter suggests that distance and borders have often lost the determining influence on economic geography that they once had. However, this is not to say that territoriality has lost all significance in the contemporary organization of production, exchange, and consumption. Robert Reich exaggerated when, shortly before joining the Clinton Administration, he declared that economic globalization yielded a situation of 'no *national* products or technologies, no national corporations, no national industries' (1991: 3, his emphasis).

On the contrary, after several decades of accelerated globalization a great deal of commercial activity still has only a secondary if any supraterritorial dimension. For example, although transborder manufacturing through global factories has affected a significant proportion of certain industries, it has involved but a small percentage of overall world production. Most processes have remained contained within one country, and only a tiny percentage of the world's workforce has so far been employed in EPZs. Even many global products (Boeing jets, Ceylon teas) are prepared within a single country although their distribution extends worldwide. While transborder products have generally been more prevalent than supraterritorial production, far from all sales items have acquired global circulation.

Many types of money, too, have remained restricted to a national or local domain. Likewise, the great bulk of retail banking has stayed territorial, as clients deal with their local branch offices. In spite of substantial growth since the 1980s, transborder share dealing remains a small fraction of total equity trading. Moreover, a large majority of turnover on most stock exchanges continues to involve shares of firms headquartered in the same country. The London Stock Exchange provides the only major case where externally based equity accounted for over half of business in the 1990s. Similarly, despite exponential expansion of the eurobond market, in 1995 the total value of outstanding transborder bonds ($2.8 trillion) was still dwarfed by the aggregate value of outstanding domestic issues ($23.9 trillion) (BIS 1996: 20).

Nor has most global commercial activity been wholly divorced from territorial geography. For example, local circumstances have strongly influenced corporate decisions regarding the location of transborder production facilities. In the foreign exchange markets dealers have mainly been clustered in half a dozen cities, even if their transactions are largely cyberspatial and can have immediate consequences anywhere in the world. It remains rare for a transborder company to issue a large proportion of its stock outside its country of origin. In the light of such qualifications Richard O'Brien has readily conceded the hyperbole in his depiction of global finance as 'the end of geography' (1992: 2).

Hence the importance of globalization is that it has ended the monopoly of territoriality in defining the spatial character of the world economy. This is not to say that the trend has eliminated territoriality altogether. The global dimension of contemporary world commerce has grown alongside, and in complex relations with, its territorial aspects. Globalization has been reconfiguring geography rather than obliterating territory.

The survival of the state

Similarly, as already seen in Chapter 1, globalization has repositioned the (territorial) state rather than signalled its demise. The expansion of transborder trade and finance has made claims of **sovereign statehood** obsolete, but the significance of states themselves remains. Through both unilateral decisions and multilaterally co-ordinated policies, states have done much to facilitate economic globalization and influence its course.

As already mentioned, states have encouraged the globalization of commerce *inter alia* through various policies of liberalization and the creation of special economic zones and offshore finance centres. At the same time, some governments have also slowed globalization within their jurisdiction by retaining certain restrictions on transborder activity. However, most states—including those still nominally 'communist'—have sooner or later responded to strong pressures to liberalize. Those retaining strict regulations have generally suffered capital flight abroad, especially offshore. In any case, governments have often lacked effective means fully to enforce their territorially bound controls on globally mobile capital. Only in respect of immigration restrictions have states largely sustained their borders against economic globalization, and even then substantial traffic in unregistered migrants has developed.

Yet states are by no means powerless in the face of economic globalization. Even the common claim that global finance lies beyond the state requires qualification. After all, governments and central banks continue to exert major influence on money supplies and interest rates, even if they no longer monopolize money creation and lack direct control over the euromarkets. Likewise, particularly through co-operative action, states can significantly shift exchange rates, even if they have lost the capacity to fix the conversion ratios and are sometimes overridden by currency dealers. Governments have also pursued collective regulation of transborder banking to some effect via the Basle Committee on Banking Supervision, set up through the BIS in 1974. The survival of offshore finance centres, too, depends to a considerable extent on the goodwill of governments, both the host regime and external authorities. Recent years have seen increased intergovernmental consultations to obtain tighter official oversight of offshore finance. Similarly, national regulators of securities markets have collaborated since 1984 through the International Organization of Securities Commissions (IOSCO). State oversight of derivatives trading may also intensify as those transactions become better understood.

In short, there is little sign that global commerce and the state are inherently antithetical. On the contrary, the two have shown considerable mutual dependence. States have provided much of the regulatory framework for global trade and finance, albeit that they have (as indicated in Ch. 1) shared these competences with substate and suprastate agencies.

The continuance of cultural diversity

Much evidence also confounds the common presumption that economic globalization is effecting **cultural homogenization** and a rise of cosmopolitan orientations over national identities. The growth of transborder production, the proliferation of global products, the multiplication of suprater-

ritorial monies and the expansion of transworld financial flows have shown little sign of heralding an end of difference in the world economy.

True, global trade and finance are moved by much more than national loyalties. Consumers have repeatedly ignored exhortations to 'buy British' and the like in favour of global products. Shareholders and managers have rarely put national sentiments ahead of the profit margin. For example, the global media magnate Rupert Murdoch happily traded Australian for US citizenship when it suited his commercial purposes. Foreign exchange dealers readily desert their national currency in order to reap financial gain.

However, in other respects national identities and solidarities have survived—and sometimes positively thrived—in the contemporary globalizing economy. Most transborder companies have retained a readily recognized national affiliation, even if the situation is in practice not always so clearcut. Most firms involved in global trade and finance have kept a mononational board of directors, and the operations of many of these enterprises continue to reflect a national style of business practice connected with the country of origin. Different national conventions have persisted in global finance as well. For instance, since equities have traditionally held a smaller place in German finance, globalization in that country has mainly involved banks and the bond markets.

Cultural diversity has also persisted in transborder marketing. Local peculiarities have often affected the way that a global product is sold and used in different places. Advertising has often been adjusted to local tastes to be more effective. New technologies like computer-aided design have moreover allowed companies to tailor some global products to local proclivities. In this vein Michael Porter has argued that 'national differences in character and culture, far from being threatened by global competition, prove integral to success in it' (1990: 30).

In sum, then, like globalization in general, its economic dimension has not had universal scope. Nor has the rise of global trade and finance marked the end of territorial space, the demise of the state, or full-scale cultural homogenization. However, recognition of these limitations does not entail a rejection of notions of globalization altogether, on the lines of the sceptics noted earlier. After discounting for exaggeration and non sequiturs, the growth of supraterritoriality remains a highly significant development in the contemporary world economy. The challenge for analysis is to tease out the interplay in economic globalization between territoriality and supraterritoriality, between territorial states and other governance arrangements, and between territorial identities and transborder affiliations.

Key points

- Global trade and finance have spread unevenly between different regions and different circles of people.

- Transborder commerce has to date often widened material inequalities within and between countries.

- Territorial geography continues to be important in the contemporary globalizing economy.

- Although lacking sovereign powers, states exercise significant influence in global trade and finance.

- While economic globalization has weakened cultural diversity and national attachments in some respects, it has promoted them in others.

Conclusion

The present chapter has shown that, among other things, the globalization of world politics is a deeply economic affair. The growth of global trade and finance has deeply shaped—and been shaped by—the developments in governance described in Chapter 1. Economic globalization has affected different places and people to different extents, and it has far from eliminated older core structures of world politics: territory, state, and nation. However, these developments have already shifted many contours of geography, governance, and community; and economic globalization seems likely to unfold further still in the future.

The preceding pages have only touched on the wide-ranging and deeply significant questions of global trade and finance. In particular, this discussion has but hinted at the substantial problems of human security, social justice, and democracy that contemporary economic globalization has raised. Chapter 26 by Caroline Thomas will address a number of these matters at greater length. For its part the present chapter will, I hope, have established the far-reaching importance of economic globalization when it is understood as the growth of a supraterritorial dimension in world commerce.

QUESTIONS

1 Distinguish different conceptions of economic globalization.

2 To what extent is economic globalization new to contemporary history?

3 How does transborder production differ from territorial production?

4 How has globalization been manifested in changed forms of money?

5 What makes financial dealings in the euromarkets 'supraterritorial'?

6 What is an offshore financial centre?

7 To what extent has contemporary economic globalization marked 'the end of geography'?

8 How has globalization of trade and finance affected state sovereignty?

9 Discuss the impact of global products on cultural diversity.

10 To what extent can it be said that global capital carries no flag?

11 Assess the relationship between globalization and income inequality.

12 In what ways might global commerce be reshaped to promote greater distributive justice?

GUIDE TO FURTHER READING

Barnet, R. J., and Cavanagh, J., *Global Dreams: Imperial Corporations and the New World Order* (New York: Simon and Schuster, 1994). A highly readable critical examination of transborder companies and global consumerism.

Brecher, J., and Costello, T., *Global Village or Global Pillage: Economic Reconstruction from the Bottom up* (Boston: South End, 1994). A denunciation of the globalization of trade as a worldwide 'race to the bottom' of labour and environmental standards.

Held, D. *et al.*, *Global Transformations: Politics, Economics and Culture* (Cambridge: Polity, 1999). Excellent on indicators and repercussions of economic globalization.

Hirst, P., and Thompson, G., *Globalization in Question: The International Economy and the Possibilities of Governance*, 2nd edn. (Cambridge: Polity Press, 1999). A critique of 'globalist' presumptions that economic globalization is new, irreversible, and wholly beyond state control.

Mittelman, J. H. (ed.), *Globalization: Critical Reflections* (Boulder, Colo.: Lynne Rienner, 1996). A collection of essays by leading researchers in the field of International Political Economy.

Ohmae, K., *The Borderless World: Power and Strategy in the Interlinked Economy* (London: Fontana, 1990). A management consultant's celebration of global business.

Peterson, V. S., and Runyan, A. S., *Global Gender Issues*, 2nd edn. (Boulder, Colo.: Westview Press, 1999). A critical examination of the impacts of globalization on, *inter alia*, women's employment and the feminization of poverty.

Porter, M. E. (ed.), *Competition in Global Industries* (Boston: Harvard Business School Press, 1986). A general discussion of global trade supplemented with numerous case studies from the Harvard Business School.

Scholte, J. A., *Globalization: A Critical Introduction* (Basingstoke: Palgrave, 2000). Elaborates the arguments presented in this chapter, including the implications of economic globalization for human security, social justice, and democracy.

Stubbs, R., and Underhill, G. R. D. (eds.), *Political Economy and the Changing Global Order*, 2nd edn. (Basingstoke: Palgrave, 2000). A textbook in International Political Economy with much concerning global trade and finance.

UNDP *Human Development Report* (New York: Oxford University Press, 1990–). This annual publication of the United Nations Development Programme includes much on the welfare consequences of economic globalization. See especially the 1999 edition.

WEB LINKS (see also Box 24.1)

www.iccwbo.org International Chamber of Commerce. Grouping member companies and associations from over 130 countries, the ICC is a strong business-sector proponent of economic globalization.

www.nasdaq.com Nasdaq Stock Market. Covers the history, organization and current trading activities of the world's largest completely screen-based stock exchange.

www.new-academy.ac.uk New Academy of Business. An education and research project, inspired by Body Shop founder Anita Roddick, to promote socially and environmentally responsible global companies.

www.oneworld.org Oneworld.Net—an online gateway to over 750 associations that campaign for reform of the global economy.

25 The communications and Internet revolution

Jonathan D. Aronson

READER'S GUIDE

During the 1990s the Internet and World Wide Web exploded onto the scene. Communications always was critical in the conduct of international relations, but it receives more attention today. After providing an historical backdrop, this chapter begins with an overview of the key changes globalizing communication and information. It then reviews the impact of the dramatic changes unleashed by the information revolution in three areas. First, it considers the impact on the key actors—countries, companies, non-governmental organizations, international institutions, and people—and their relative influence. Second, it suggests that path of the unfolding information revolution and the consequences for the future depend on four areas of policy which are driving the direction of globalization in the Internet age. Third, the chapter assesses the implications of the rise of global networks for international relations.

Introduction and historical backdrop

International Relations scholars and students long ignored the fundamental role of communications. By contrast communications is now at the forefront of globalization and international relations for three reasons. First, governments embraced new competitive and regulatory approaches for the communications sector, abandoning the traditional monopoly structure of communications. The impact of these national decisions was to promote competition and globalize communications. Second, competition and innovation fuelled fast-growing communications and information sectors that stimulated economic growth and created new jobs in industrial and many developing countries. Third, the sudden prominence of the Internet and the rise of the **World Wide Web** is changing the way international relations works and influences the path of globalization. Further, as Table 25.1 makes clear, the adoption of innovation associated with this information revolution is proceeding at record speed.

Communications and **information technology** firms now are at the core of a new world information economy. A critical, new component of globalization is that faster and cheaper communication tools including fax machines, mobile phones, computer-aided design, and Internet and electronic communications link many people, firms, and countries simultaneously. Food, shelter, health, and education

still are the most basic human needs. But, increasingly, access to efficient communications networks is widely accepted as critical to growth, innovation, higher productivity, and job creation. Further, instantaneous global communications empower non-state actors and may profoundly influence political and military relations as well as economic ones. Students of international relations have taken notice.

The source of these changes is the telecom and information technology sector that is growing and evolving on Internet time. (One Internet year is one calendar week.) The microprocessor and cheap memory revolutionized the communication industry in the 1980s. The Web did not exist in 1989 but during the 1990s the price of international telephone calls plummeted and the global networking of computers became nearly ubiquitous. In the coming decade the spread of wireless data communications could change everything yet again. As globalization proceeds, one central task is to understand the networks that tie everything together and why they matter.

Some historical background is helpful to set the context. National communications regimes almost all were based on the idea that telephone service could be most efficiently provided by government-owned or **government-controlled monopolies**. In most countries the monopoly telephone companies were slow to innovate because in return for their monopoly protection they were not allowed into new arenas such as television or satellites.

The international regime was built on two ideas. First, countries and companies agreed that there should be no competition in the provision of international calls, so international calls were extremely expensive and profitable for the companies. Second, standardized networks and equipment became the norm because global universal service required it. The scheme for managing international communications remained almost unchanged from the first telegraphic submarine cable until the mid-1970s. At its core was the International Telecommunication Union (ITU) that set technical standards and made

Table 25.1 The speed of change: years to penetrate 25 per cent of the US market

	Year invented	Years to penetrate
Household electricity	1873	46
Telephone	1876	35
Radio	1906	22
Television	1925	26
PC	1975	15
Cellular phone	1983	13
Internet	1991	7

Source: Federal Reserve Bank of Dallas, cited by Milken Instituite

> ## Box 25.1 Chronology of key communications events
>
> | | | | |
> |---|---|---|---|
> | 1843 | First telegraph message transmitted in Morse Code | 1956 | First transatlantic telephone cable |
> | 1876 | Invention of the telephone | 1965 | Invention of electronic mail |
> | 1894 | Marconi pioneers wireless telegraphy | 1974 | First personal computer—Altair 8800 |
> | 1900 | First voice broadcast by radio | 1981 | British Telecommunications Act of 1981 |
> | 1922 | First BBC radio transmissions for London | 1981 | Introduction of IBM PC |
> | 1934 | US Communications Act of 1934 establishes FCC | 1984 | AT&T broken up |
> | 1939 | Invention of the television | 1989 | Invention of the World Wide Web |
> | 1945 | First Electrical Computers (ENIAC) | 1990 | First World Wide Web browser/editor |

sure that they were compatible, allocated radio spectrum and made sure that they did not interfere with one another, provided technical assistance to poorer nations, and later gave out orbital slots. With the opening of space, the ITU was joined by Intelsat in 1964. Both the ITU and Intelsat served as virtual telephone cartels controlled by the national telephone monopolies in their member states.

The Thatcher–Reagan economic revolution at the start of the 1980s laid the groundwork for the transformation of global telecommunications. The British Telecommunications Act of 1981 separated telecommunications from the post office, began to privatize British Telecom and Cable & Wireless, and began to introduce competition in equipment and service provision. A new Office of Telecommunications (Oftel) was established as the new telecom regulator.

In the United States AT&T was broken up on 1 January 1984, by spinning off its local operating companies. In return, AT&T was permitted, for the first time, to compete to provide value-added and enhanced information services. This single action was the critical event that prompted countries around the world to re-examine their regulatory approaches and unleashed waves of competition and innovation. Many countries followed Britain and the United States to embrace greater telecom competition, privatization, and liberalization. Convergence became the watchword as boundaries

separating local and long-distance, voice and data, cable and telephone, and wireline and wireless services eroded. Service providers may now provide content and broadcasters, studios and other content providers may provide voice and data services. Energy utilities, railroads and other transportation companies, and water companies also migrated towards communications services. International partnerships and mergers proliferated. Box 25.1 provides a short chronology of key telecommunications and Internet developments since 1843.

Developing countries, like industrial countries, are moving towards **greater liberalization** and competition, but at a slower pace. As a result, the teledensity gap between middle income and the poorest countries is widening and unless investment increases substantially most poor countries will experience a 'digital divide' relative to the industrial world. An exception is China which, having passed Japan in early 2000, now has more mobile users than any country except the United States.

On the international level, the Uruguay Round of Trade Negotiations in the GATT that concluded in 1994, helped ensure that trade in new communications and information services would be liberalized. Persuading entrenched monopolists to cede their power so that ordinary telephone services would be provided competitively was more difficult.

Three major steps completed the transformation of the international communications regime. First,

Box 25.2 The WTO agreement on basic telecommunications services

During the WTO Negotiations on Basic Telecommunications, the United States offered to open its telecommunications markets if others opened their markets in exchange. On February 15 1997 negotiators concluded the agreement, an annex to the 1994 Uruguay Round agreement. The EU's strong offer attracted other offers to the table. Peru showed considerable courage and creativity and Brazil, a country usually associated with closed markets, showed resolve and ingenuity in showing that it was possible to table a credible offer in the midst of domestic reform. Hong Kong contributed to the work on regulatory principles, Japan and Korea showed flexibility on the same subject, and in the closing stages Singapore tabled a strong offer and pushed other ASEAN countries to do likewise. These efforts led to breakthroughs in Malaysia, Indonesia, the Philippines, and Pakistan.

Results came in four areas: market access, the adoption of regulatory principles, liberalization of foreign investment rules, and satellite offers. Market access soared. Fifty-nine countries agreed to adopt transparent, pro-competitive regulatory principles, representing 99 per cent of the WTO telecommunications market. Forty-four countries agreed to permit significant inward foreign investment. Fifty countries guaranteed market access for all domestic and international satellite services and facilities.

The results of the WTO negotiations exceeded expectations. Twenty-three of the twenty-five European and Eastern European countries made full offers in all four categories. Eleven of the twenty offers from the Americas were strong across the board. Australia, Japan, New Zealand, and Singapore were far ahead of the other twelve Asian countries fully in liberalizing their markets. None of the eight African and Middle Eastern countries made fully opening offers.

on Basic Telecommunications. Sixty-nine countries, which account for the vast majority of international telecommunications traffic, agreed, to varying degrees, to liberalize their telecommunications markets starting 1 January 1998. Many countries agreed to lower or remove domestic barriers to international competition in the provision of local, long-distance, and satellite services; pledged to adopt transparent regulatory principles to support competition; and agreed to make it possible for foreign firms to provide domestic satellite services. Box 25.2 summarizes the major accomplishments of this agreement. Third, the US Federal Communications Commission acted unilaterally to force a sharp reduction in international rates. Together, these three achievements completed the transformation of the global telecommunication regime from one dominated by monopolies to a much more competitive system for basic communications. This new regime, however, did not cover new information services.

Key points

- Communications and information technology firms are now at the core of a new world information economy.

- National monopolies provided telephone services in almost all countries for decades.

- National monopolies used the International Telecommunication Union, later supplemented by Intelsat, to prevent competition in the provision of international communications services.

- The Thatcher–Reagan regulatory revolution undermined monopolists, encouraged domestic and international communications competition in national and international communications, and unleashed significant technological innovation.

- During the 1990s there was significant progress at creating a competitive international regime for telephone services, but not for new information services.

the fifteen member countries of the European Union mandated competition in basic telephone services starting in 1998. Second, on 15 February 1997, negotiators successfully concluded the WTO Negotiations

The Internet and World Wide Web revolution

Competition pushed prices for long-distance and international calls down and unleashed innovation that stimulated tremendous investment in and growth of global communications. National firms partnered and merged, often across national borders, to achieve the scale and scope necessary to operate global networks. Competition and innovation also promoted three big developments that are reshaping the world information economy.

Competition, global networks, and global firms

The global telecom and information landscape is in flux. Consider telephone and cellular penetration. Table 25.2 shows, for 1998, the number of main telephone lines per 100 inhabitants and the percentage of all telephone subscribers who are cellular subscribers. Scandinavia and North America lead on installed telephone lines, with other major European countries lagging. Most EU member states have a higher percentage of cellular subscribers than the United States and all of them have a higher penetration rate than Canada. By contrast, **Internet penetration** is higher in the United States than in Europe.

Figures 25.1 and 25.2 illustrate the flows of telecommunications traffic between regions and within Europe in 1998. The United States is the lynchpin of interregional traffic flows. Combined traffic flows between Europe and Asia/Oceania was about a third of what passed between North America and the three main regions. Within Europe, Germany and the United Kingdom are the main hubs of international traffic flows with France in a strong third position. Europe generated 43.4 per cent of all outgoing international telecommunications flows in 1998, up from 41.4 per cent in 1996. North America originated 32.0 per cent of international traffic in 1998, down from 32.3 percent in 1996. With the economic downturn in Asia, the latter's share dropped from 17.0 per cent in 1996 to 15.5 per cent in 1998 while Latin America's share fell from 5.1 to 4.1 per cent.

Table 25.2 Telephone lines and cellular subscribers, 1998

Country	Main telephone lines (per 100 inhabitants)	Cellular subscribers (% of all phone subscribers)
Europe		
Switzerland	67.5	25.8
Sweden	67.4	40.8
Denmark	66.0	35.6
Norway	66.0	41.8
The Netherlands	59.3	26.4
France	57.0	24.8
Germany	56.7	23.0
United Kingdom	55.6	31.2
Finland	55.4	50.8
Greece	52.2	27.1
Belgium	50.0	25.6
Austria	49.1	33.7
Italy	45.1	44.1
Ireland	43.5	37.2
Portugal	41.4	42.8
Spain	41.4	30.2
Czech Republic	36.4	20.5
Hungary	33.6	23.8
Turkey	25.4	17.1
Poland	22.8	18.0
Russia	19.7	2.5
Americas		
United States	66.1	27.9
Canada	63.4	21.7
Chile	20.8	24.0
Argentina	20.3	27.8
Brazil	12.1	28.0
Mexico	10.4	25.2
Asia		
Singapore	56.2	38.1
Hong Kong	55.8	46.0
Taiwan	52.4	29.1
Australia	51.2	36.0
Japan	50.3	42.7

Table 25.2 continued

Country	Main telephone lines (per 100 inhabitants)	Cellular subscribers (% of all phone subscribers)
New Zealand	47.9	29.7
Korea	43.3	41.1
Malaysia	19.8	33.4
Thailand	8.4	28.0
China	7.0	21.4
Indonesia	2.7	16.1
India	2.2	5.2
Pakistan	1.0	6.8
Other		
Israel	47.1	43.2
United Arab Emirates	38.9	35.0
South Africa	11.5	33.0
Egypt	6.0	2.2

Source. International Telecommunication Union

Three revolutions: the Web, e-commerce, and wireless

While phone penetration and international voice traffic proceeds incrementally, three major trends are transforming global communications. **First**, the growth of data transmission is far outdistancing the growth of international voice traffic. Until late 1999 voice traffic flows exceeded data traffic flows. By the time you read these words there will be more than twice as much international data traffic as voice traffic and the gap will continue to widen. The **success of the Internet and the Web** explain this trend.

The Internet began in the 1960s as a US Defense Department's project to build a data network to connect researchers. Its growth became geometrical when its leadership was given to the US National Science Foundation during the 1980s. The World Wide Web has many parents, but precedence is usually given to Tim Berners-Lee, a British programmer working at CERN, the European Particle Physics

Laboratory, in the early 1990s. He envisioned the Web as a universal, all-encompassing space and provided the tools that allowed for almost instant navigation across its fast-expanding geography.

Table 25.3 provides a snapshot of the Web in 1999 and suggests its remarkable growth. Each day the number of pages increased nine times faster than world population. Worldwide, Internet users increased by more than a million each week. The number of Web hosts grew by almost 29 million during 1999, 13 million in the first half and 16 million in the second half. Web hosts grew from 1.31 million at the beginning of 1993, to 14.35 million at the start of 1996, to 29.67 million in January 1998, to 72.4 million in at the start of 2000. The number of unique Web sites grew by about 50 per cent during 1999. At the end of 1999 the United States accounted for 55 per cent of all public Web sites, almost ten times more than the runner-up, Germany. All indications, however, are that the US lead is eroding and the dominance of English on the Web is beginning to decline. By the end of 2000, as the graph in Fig. 25.3 shows, 38.3 per cent of the 353 million Internet users worldwide were located in the United States. Still, it is unclear whether firms and markets or governments and international institutions will dominate the rule-making process. It also is unclear who will be part of the information revolution and who will be excluded.

The **second** major trend involves **e-commerce**, the killer application (or simply 'killer app') of the Internet that will shape its future. Business-to-business e-commerce is growing much faster than business-to-consumer e-commerce. In 1997 the volume of transactions was about equal. By 1999 the value of business-to-business transactions was double the amount of business-to-consumer transactions. By 2001 the difference could be ten-to-one. As a result, e-commerce could climb from zero in the mid-1990s to 5 per cent or more of the GDP in many industrial economies a decade later. The United States leads this race, but Europe is close behind. Japan trails, but could leap into contention. Developing countries lag, but are making progress.

The **third** significant trend, **the wireless revolution**, is that wireless voice traffic and data transfer

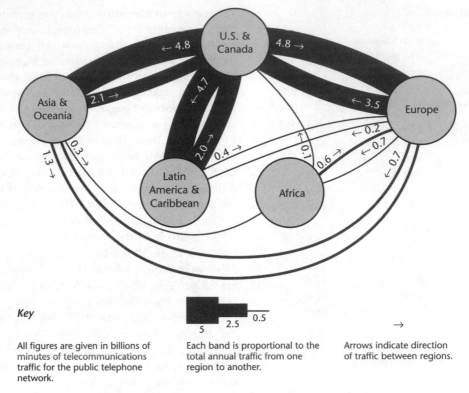

Key

All figures are given in billions of minutes of telecommunications traffic for the public telephone network.

Each band is proportional to the total annual traffic from one region to another.

Arrows indicate direction of traffic between regions.

Fig. 25.1 Interregional traffic flows, 1998
Source: TeleGeography, Inc. 1999

could shortly compete strongly with wireline voice and data transfer for dominance. Wireless voice traffic already exceeds wireline traffic in some countries, especially the poorest ones. At present there is only minimal wireless transfer of data. However, if the optimistic estimates in Fig. 25.4 are even close to the mark, the worldwide wireless Internet population could soar between 2000 and 2005. The early leaders are Japan and Finland, but the rest of Europe is expected grow quickly, with North America trailing. Wireless Internet holds the possibility of helping Europe achieve significant economic and competitive leverage vis-à-vis the United States in the struggle for economic innovation and leadership. Similarly, wireless business and consumer e-commerce revenue forecasts suggest that sales could rise more rapidly in Europe and the Asia-Pacific region than in the United States.

Table 25.3 A snapshot of the Web's size, 1999

Metric	1999 total	Estimated growth per day 1998–9
World population	6,000,000,000	213,000
Web pages	1,500,000,000	1,920,000
Devices accessing the Web	221,000,000	196,000
Worldwide Internet users	196,000,000	148,000
Internet hosts	72,400,000	80,000
Domain names	8,100,000	13,000
Unique Web sites	3,650,000	4,400

Source: *The Industry Standard*, 6 March, 2000, p. 174. Figures rounded by the author.

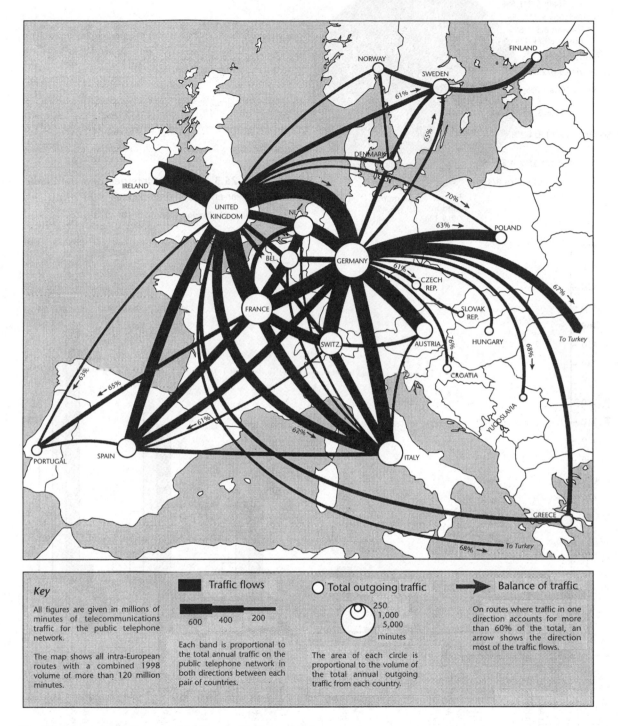

Fig. 25.2 European telecommunications traffic flows, 1998
Source: TeleGeography, Inc. 1999

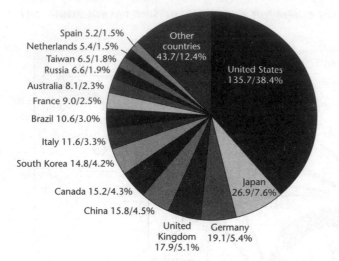

Spain 5.2/1.5%
Netherlands 5.4/1.5%
Taiwan 6.5/1.8%
Russia 6.6/1.9%
Australia 8.1/2.3%
France 9.0/2.5%
Brazil 10.6/3.0%
Italy 11.6/3.3%
South Korea 14.8/4.2%
Canada 15.2/4.3%
China 15.8/4.5%
United Kingdom 17.9/5.1%
Germany 19.1/5.4%
Japan 26.9/7.6%
United States 135.7/38.4%
Other countries 43.7/12.4%

Fig. 25.3 Number of Internet users worldwide at year-end 2000 (in millions)

Source: *Red Herring*, December 18, 2000, p. 55.

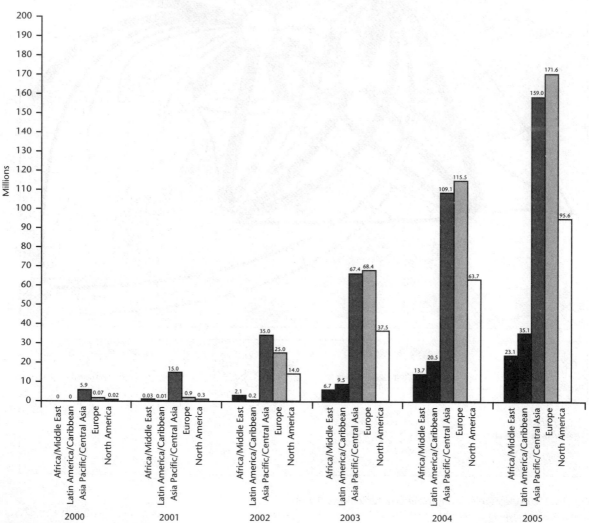

Fig. 25.4 Worldwide wireless Internet population forecast
Source: The Industry Standard, May 29, 2000, p. 202.

Key points

- Competition and innovation are forcing changes in the structure of firms. They are becoming as global as the structure of the world economy.
- The United States is the lynchpin of interregional telecommunications traffic, but European countries generate a third more international traffic flows than North America.
- Growth rates are higher in Europe, Latin America, Oceania, and Africa than in North America or Asia.

- International voice traffic is growing more slowly than international data traffic and shortly will be dwarfed by data traffic.
- e-commerce is likely to be the 'killer app' of the Internet, especially as business-to-business e-commerce surpasses business-to-consumer e-commerce.
- Wireless Internet connections could challenge wireline connections before 2007. This trend should favour Europe and Japan, more than North America.

The impact of the information revolution on actors

The information revolution is transforming the role various types of actors play in International Relations. The impact of the Thatcher–Reagan deregulatory push during the 1980s also tilted the balance of influence from government towards firms and markets. This section suggests how countries, companies, non-governmental actors (NGOs), international institutions and individuals have fared.

The impact on countries and their policymakers

The information revolution has altered the role and operation of governments and their policy-makers in four main ways. **First**, there is more information available to governments; indeed they may have access to **too much information**. Paralysis through information overload is a real danger so governments and policy-makers need to separate what is important from what is not. This problem is not new—US authorities intercepted messages about the Japanese plan to attack Pearl Harbor well before the incident.

Second, global networks mean that decision-making can be **centralized or decentralized**. Governments generally have centralized decision-making, reducing the importance of ambassadors and embassies who collect information to funnel

back to capitals while mostly attending to representational duties. Political leaders sometimes are tempted to micro-manage military situations and economic negotiations in distant parts because they can, not because they should. Firms, by contrast, appear likely to decentralize all but the most important decisions.

Third, global networks **erode the monopoly of information** in the hands of governments. Firms, journalists, and non-governmental organizations often have better, more timely information than governments. Policy-makers rely on the BBC and CNN for information and analysis, like everyone else. In one telling incident, a BBC correspondent seeking news of the storming of the Russian Duma had a senior official repeat her own story back to her.

Fourth, global networks provide **transparency to all** and thereby accentuate the problem of dealing with global issues such as global warming, making it difficult for countries unilaterally to take national policy decisions when the problem is global.

The impact on firms

Corporate talk of self-regulation illustrates the rise of private firms as political actors. These firms are much more outspoken in protecting what they see as their interests. Globalization and global networks are transforming business firms, altering their international influence. Global networks increasingly allow firms to think and act in terms of a global marketplace and grow through investment, partnerships, and acquisitions beyond their own borders. Global firms and the global movement of money and information to achieve global production strategies are difficult for national governments to regulate. As many governments liberalized their regulation of business, giant firms more and more shaped international relations, especially international economic and financial relations. By 2000 about half of the largest one hundred economic entities on the planet were corporations. In the absence of effective international regulation, these firms are gaining in influence.

The impact on Non-Governmental Organizations and international institutions

One consequence of global networks is the rise of Non-Governmental Organizations (NGOs) as powerful actors. The first beneficiaries were the giant media organizations like BBC, CNN, and News Corp that influence as well as report on the world events. More fundamentally globalization fostered the proliferation of NGOs everywhere. Global networks enable interested non-governmental parties to create, track, and disseminate information and to organize people and groups sympathetic to their goals to pursue specific policy outcomes. NGOs now are important in human rights advocacy, environmental protection, and women's rights (see Ch. 17).

The most striking example of the positive influence of NGOs was their major role in the negotiations to ban landmines that led to the wide-spread acceptance of the international landmine treaty and won the organizers a Nobel Peace Prize. NGO efforts to ban land mines are summarized in Box 25.3. In the Internet arena an example of a quasi-formal NGO seizing the lead on an issue is ICANN, the new group to oversee the distribution of domain names. ICANN is trying to manage the fair distribution of

domain names and minimize speculative hoarding of desirable domain names. An even more visible impact of NGOs came when environmental NGOs and labour unions joined to disrupt the attempt by governments to launch a WTO Trade Round in Seattle in November 1999 (see Ch. 15).

The information revolution requires policy-makers to take on new roles and develop new policies and governance institutions to cope with global networks. Ironically, international institutions like the WTO and the IMF are both more important and less effective international actors because of the rise of global networks. They are more important because in the absence of effective national policies to deal with globalization, these institutions are the logical venues through which to organize co-operative international policies. They are less effective because critics of such institutions who complain that they are neither democratic or even-handed have stymied their initiatives at major junctures.

Box 25.3 Fighting landmines

In 1997 the Nobel Peace Prize was awarded to the International Campaign to Ban Landmines (www.icbl.org/), a consortium of about 1,000 NGOs that helped mobilize public opinion and motivated governments. The cause was championed by Princess Diana, the International Committee of the Red Cross, and a handful of NGOs such as the Vietnam Veterans of America, which first advocated the ban. The Web allowed NGOs and individuals to organize support for the ban and assist sympathetic political leaders such as UN Secretary General Kofi Anan, Canadian Foreign Minister Lloyd Axworthy, and US Senator Patrick Leahy to move the process forward.

The December 1997 Mine Ban Treaty bans the use, production, stockpiling, and transfer of antipersonnel landmines. The treaty became international law on 1 March 1999, and by December 2000 had been ratified by 109 countries and signed by 139. However, as of December 2000 fifty-four countries, including major states such as the United States, Russia, China, India, Pakistan, the two Koreas, Egypt, Iran, Iraq, Israel, Turkey, Cuba, and Finland had not yet signed.

The impact on individuals

Global networks empower individuals and not just NGOs. Individual privacy may be threatened by these new technologies, but hackers now have the ability to infect the world with viruses that cripple networks or to post information about how to make bombs that incite terrorism or hate-mongering that can foment ethnic or religious conflict. Digital crime, from the theft of identities and creditworthiness to the money laundering of billions of dollars through unregulated enclaves is proliferating.

Key points
- The information revolution coupled with government deregulation to promote competition increased the influence of the market and of giant firms relative to governments.
- NGOs have increased in number and influence because global networks allow them access and the ability to easily share information across groups and borders.
- NGOs sometimes can promote positive changes, but also may stall initiatives that governments and firms launch through international institutions.
- Global networks make it more difficult to maintain individual privacy but also may empower individuals with positive or disruptive goals.

The information revolution and challenges for government policies

There is considerable debate about the impact of globalization on risk and uncertainty, growth and inequality, democracy and freedom, and family and social relationships. But globalization is a dynamic process that governments and other actors continuously influence. The information revolution caught policy-makers unprepared but, as it continues to unfold, the choices that governments (and other actors) make about policy do matter. So far governments and international institutions have no coherent plan about how or even whether they should guide the information revolution or about how to create an international regime for cyberspace. Here, four key challenges facing policy-makers with regard to cyberspace, which knows no geography, are considered.

The legal and policy areas most directly affected by the communication and Web revolution can be grouped into four main areas that impact (1) individuals, (2) the content that flows over global networks, (3) the global communication infrastructure, and (4) the global regulatory environment. Each of these areas requires attention because of the global nature of cyberspace, all of them may require global co-operation and co-ordination. The relative influence of the actors (governments, firms, NGOs and IGOs, and people) discussed above will be critical as the information revolution continues to unfold and globalization proceeds. Yet, the balance of influence among these actors varies from issue to issue.

Policies affecting individuals: privacy and secrecy

Privacy rights and data security concerns are heightened in cyberspace (including data security and encryption issues, sometimes referred to as the 'Balkans of the cyber age'). Data communications and especially electronic commerce transactions take place in a new form of 'space' in which much greater surveillance by governments, employers, or individuals is possible. How should the rights of individuals be protected and balanced against data security needs of governments and firms? Similarly, issues of censorship and the control of content are sensitive in many countries and are particularly controversial when what is permissible in one country is deemed inappropriate in another.

Policies affecting content: intellectual property

In a global digital age content that flows across global networks has great value. Intellectual property rules that protect the owners of content through copyright, patent, trademark and trade secrets are even more important now that perfect copies are easy and cheap to make. The potential for software or movie piracy in China or music piracy by students using Napster and other systems to download copyrighted materials is immense. Firms and innovators argue that investment and **research and development** will dry up if innovators are not fairly compensated for their inventions. By contrast, if intellectual property fees are so high that users, in developing countries, cannot afford to pay to license new technologies they face immense barriers to their development. Should, for example, Africans with AIDs who cannot afford to pay for expensive drug treatments be condemned to early death?

One of the most visible successes of the Uruguay Round trade negotiations was the 1994 TRIPs (Trade-Related Intellectual Property) agreement that strengthened international intellectual property protection and established new enforcement mechanisms and dispute settlement procedures. Critics in industrial and developing countries worry, however, that the TRIPs agreement and the similar arrangements agreed to by the United States, Canada, and Mexico negotiated under the NAFTA accord tilted the balance between the rights of innovators and of users too far towards the creators of intellectual property. Finding appropriate ways to balance and harmonize the rights of users and innovators across borders may prove a significant and ongoing challenge that governments, firms, and NGOs will need to negotiate.

Policies affecting the network: standard-setting

The global communications network is the largest single human creation. It is a logistical marvel that allows anyone anywhere to dial a few numbers on their phone or type a few strokes at a keyboard and be connected in moments to any other phone or computer in the world. Globalization depends on the smooth functioning of this global network. The computers in the network must be compatible with each other or nothing happens. Therefore, technical standards, set mainly by engineers, make global networking possible. For example, until all mobile phones support a single or compatible standard(s), phones that work in one country or locale will be useless in others.

Predictably those who control key standards get rich and powerful. Losers lag or vanish altogether. Therefore, countries and companies engage in ongoing **standards wars**. The outcome of these intense, but almost invisible battles, delineates the shape of networks, competition, and advantage in an era of globalization. Not surprisingly, governments and users want to encourage competition and discourage bottlenecks to promote efficient global networks. As a result, the regulation and setting of technical standards to ensure network interconnectivity and interoperability is important.

Policies affecting global competition: competition policy

Liberalization and the decline of micro-management is not the same as deregulation and free markets. To cope with global networks policymakers need to know when to act, and when not to act. They will need to understand how to act, and how not to act. They will need to balance domestic politics and national interests against international realities enhanced by globalization.

Specifically, there is growing attention being given to cross-national and international governance and rule-making in the face of claims by firms that self-governance will suffice. The pressures of determining jurisdiction and the limits of sovereignty is growing. Although the pendulum of influence may have swung towards markets and firms, government policy-makers and regulators will not go away. If they are savvy, they adapt to new circumstances and develop new tools. Competition is on the rise nationally and internationally, but, predictably, established incumbents continue to try to take advantage of their dominant position when they can. One consequence is that regulators nationally and internationally are concluding that competition policy (or antitrust policy as it is called in the United States) is trade policy. These **new-style regulators** are intent on promoting competition by curbing potential global monopolists.

Global networks operated by global firms are under increasing scrutiny. In Europe, the Competition Directorate of the European Commission has intervened to stop transborder mergers within Europe and has expressed strong concerns that caused mergers within the United States to be restructured or even abandoned. In the United States, the Anti-trust Bureau of the US Department of Justice acted against **Microsoft**'s dominance and anti-competitive practices, seeking its breakup. In mid-2000 objections on both sides of the Atlantic prevented Worldcom, which had previously purchased MCI, from acquiring Sprint. More generally,

as telecom and IT firms are transformed into global networking giants, regulators are trying to promote the efficient and affordable flow of information across national borders by ensuring that multiple carriers are positioned to compete to provide comparable services. Where they succeed in promoting competition, less regulation is needed.

Key points

- The nature of cyberspace impacts individuals, the content that flows over global networks, the communication infrastructure, and the global regulatory environment.

- A balance is needed between protecting the rights of individuals and the data security needs of governments and firms.

- A balance is needed between the rights of users of information and the creators of information. Therefore, valuing intellectual property on global networks is key.

- Whoever controls the winning standards wins. Therefore, 'standards wars' are fierce.

- Competition (antitrust) policy is becoming trade policy for the world information economy.

The impact of the information revolution on international relations

The information revolution is altering the way countries deal with each other. The question is: does more information available instantly translate into better policy decisions? Globalization and global networks change the conduct of diplomacy and military affairs, the economic relations among nations, and the role of NGOs and IGOs in international relations.

The impact on diplomatic and military affairs

Instant communication across global networks has produced a revolution in diplomatic and miliary affairs. This sea change can be divided into three components: the collection and analysis of information and intelligence, the process of decision-making, and the waging of war. However, these changes may not result in better policy-making and a more peaceful world.

First, global communication networks help

governments collect and analyse vast quantities of information to inform their decisions. The information collection capabilities of modern intelligence services was already evident in the 1980s after a Soviet fighter downed Korean Airlines 007. Within hours, President Reagan released the taped conversations between the Soviet pilot who shot down the plane and his ground base. It is less clear that more intelligence information translates into better policy. Even though the information exists, finding it in the data bases and archives can be challenging. Developing efficient search routines therefore becomes imperative in the conduct of **electronic espionage**, especially since cyber-terrorists have access to the same assets. Information overload may also leave less room for intuition, trust, and secret understandings that were traditional instruments of the process. In short, more information may be a blessing when bureaucrats and political leaders can manage, analyse, and synthesize the data. It can be a curse when abundant information overloads or dehumanizes the decision-making process to the detriment of creativity and flexibility.

Second, global communication networks may change who makes the decisions and how they decide. Global networks allows governments to centralize their decision-making apparatus, giving more influence to a narrow range of top-level leaders. The **centralization** of political decision-making authority does not automatically translate into sound, efficient choices emanating from capitals. Is it wise to allow the President sitting in Washington to dictate military strategy to field commanders halfway across the globe? Indeed, it may not be an accident that business, which usually is ahead of government, seems to be going in the opposite direction.

Third, global data communication networks and new information technologies are changing modern warfare. All modern military organizations are investing in information and communications technologies. Knowledge is the key to destruction as well as to production. Networked computers may soon outnumber guns in modern military forces. The potential power of information weapons was demonstrated in 1990 during the Gulf War. The military was bolstered by AWACS (Airborne Warning and Control System) which scanned the sky for enemy aircraft and missiles and sent targeting data to allied forces from modified Boeing 707s. In parallel, J-STARS (the Joint Surveillance and Target Attack System) helped detect, disrupt, and destroy Iraqi ground forces during Desert Storm with speed and precision. Similarly, the battle for Kosovo was fought from the air. Smart bombs were delivered by smart planes directed by smart computers. In this **virtual war** the attacking forces suffered no fatalities during the fighting. Apparently the Pentagon also considered launching cyber attacks on Serbian networks but decided not to proceed because of the uncertainties regarding cyber warfare's place amid the rules of armed conflict. However, there may be a danger in relying too much on new information technology: smart networks, smart planes, and smart bombs may not substitute for soldiers on the ground.

The impact on economic relations and international negotiations

International economic and financial relations are affected by the flow of information and funds across global networks. Predictably, given the centrality of

---

Box 25.4 **Cyberterrorism and cyberwar**

- In early 1999 hackers staged a sophisticated, coordinated assault on US Air Force computers in Texas through computer networks in Canada, Norway, and Thailand. Anyone with a computer is a potential enemy.

- 'It's not a matter of if America has an electronic Pearl Harbor—it's a matter of when' (Representative Curtis Weldon, Republican, Pennsylvania).

- Training soldiers in a 3-D virtual reality environment is an idea no longer confined to science fiction. A $45 million contract signed between the US Army and the University of Southern California in August 1999 created the Institute for Creative Technologies to provide realistic military training simulations— and better Hollywood special effects.

- 'The 21st Century Land Warriors are digitally enhanced, computer accessorized, and budgetarily gold-plated from the bottom of their combat boots to the top of their kevlars' (James Der Derian).

Box 25.5 **Key concepts**

Competition (anti-trust) policy: Policies that prohibit anti-competitive action and transactions by firms, especially monopolists, including state-owned enterprises.

Cyberwar: The use of digital networks and communications to attack enemies as an act of war or terrorism.

Deregulation: The removal of all regulation so that market forces not government policy control economic developments.

Digital divide: The division of digital haves and have-nots within and between countries with regard to access to advanced communications and information services.

e-commerce: Electronic commerce sold over the Web. Usually divided between business-to-business and business-to-consumer e-commerce.

Global network: Digital networks that span the globe allowing instant voice and data communication worldwide—the global information highway.

Intellectual property rights: Rules that protect the owners of content through copyright, patent, trademark and trade secrets.

Standards war: Conflict between countries or firms over which standards to adopt.

Wireless Internet: Communication data and voice traffic through microwave and satellite connections.

---

global networks, the content, software, standards, and infrastructure that allow global networks to work are the subject of international scrutiny and negotiations.

Global flows of information create transparency but undermine privacy. Global flows of funds may fuel growth and investment but also undermine national policies and facilitate crime and corruption. It is unclear, for example, whether national monetary authorities can control money supply or exchange rates in a globalized economy. This is especially true because billions of dollars and Euros are routinely 'laundered' by drug cartels and corrupt officials. In short, national governments cannot effectively manage global firms and markets (see Ch. 24). They have two choices. First, they can deregulate, step aside, and put their faith in the magic of markets. Unfortunately, in pursuit of power and profit large firms frequently distort markets. Over time firms may behave better and increasingly practise 'self-regulation' because their behaviour can and probably will be exposed globally, but the record of self-regulation is spotty at best.

Second, governments may try to work through international institutions like the WTO or IMF. Here too there is a problem. Activists and NGOs fear that international institutions are undemocratic and serve as puppets for rich firms and governments. Thus, although governments transformed the inter-

national telecommunications regime in a decade and half, between 1984 and 1999, the effort to create an **international regime** to govern the world information economy has not proceeded far (see Ch. 14). An opportunity was missed to establish international ground rules for the new information economy when the Seattle meeting of trade ministers collapsed amidst protests and confusion in late 1999. Any rules negotiated in a prolonged trade round will be out of date before they come into force. The only hope is if the rules are flexible enough to evolve along with the system. But that is so complicated that critics worry that if the wrong rules are negotiated too early, the impact could be negative. The challenge here is for policy-makers, sensitive to inputs from firms and NGOs, to figure out which rules are needed (and which are not) and how they should be structured, implemented and enforced.

Nobody has solved the challenge of managing global economies and information and financial flows in the absence of market forces or strong international agreements administered by trusted international institutions. Accepted regimes for the management of global networks, global firms, and global economies have not emerged. Therefore, when Trade Ministers launch the next trade round the task will be complex because there will be more 'players' at the table—developing countries, global firms, labour unions, and NGOs. Moreover, as the

Web powers the transition towards globalization, every country, large firm, and NGO will be actively engaged in the process because they realize that the agreements that are struck will determine whether they are winners or losers in the emerging world information economy. Their future is at stake.

Key points

- Global networks produced a revolution in diplomatic and military affairs related to the collection and analysis of information and intelligence, the process of decision-making, and the waging of war.

- National policies are not effective in managing global networks, global firms, and the global economy. Market forces also are an imperfect way to manage globalization and international institutions are not trusted.

- Global networks impact international economic and financial relations and are the subject of important international negotiations. The outcome of these negotiations will help determine which countries and firms are winners and losers in the future.

Conclusion

Global communications networks are a driving force propelling globalization and challenging policymakers to adapt to new international relations challenges. But it is not enough to say that global networks and the Web 'will change everything'. We also need to find out which changes are short-term fads driven by speedier delivery of more information and which constitute fundamental long-term shifts in the way people, organizations, and governments deal with one another. In the future international relations will involve more actors interacting about more issues on a transparent, but complex field of play. To succeed leaders will need to use the abundance of information at their disposal to help them decide what matters and how to achieve their goals. In that sense, all the forces that traditionally shaped international relations remain the same, but global networks have accelerated the intensity and speed of the interactions. The challenge will be to find ways for national governments, working alone or together, to guide globalization through its next phase.

QUESTIONS

1 Why did economists and countries traditionally decide that the monopoly provision of telecom services made more sense than competition in the provision of telecom services?

2 Why did policy-makers start to promote competition and reduce regulation in the provision of communication and information services during the 1980s and 1990s?

3 How are the Internet and World Wide Web connected to globalization?

4 What is new about e-commerce and why is it important?

5 How would easy, affordable wireless Internet connections change your life?

6 What is meant by the 'digital divide' and should policy-makers be concerned? How?

7 When the GATT/WTO got involved with trade in telecommunications services how do you expect that the ITU reacted to the trespassing on their turf?

8 If globalization is irreversible and national policies are increasingly ineffective, what should be done? Deregulate and get out of the way? Depend on international agreements and institutions? Something else?

GUIDE TO FURTHER READING

Berners-Lee, T., with Fischetti, M., *Weaving the Web: The Original Design and Ultimate Destiny of the World Wide Web by Its Inventor* (New York: Harper San Francisco, 1999). A first-hand account of the creation and evolution of the World Wide Web.

Brock, G. W., *Telecommunications Policy for the Information Age: From Monopoly to Competition* (Cambridge: Harvard University Press, 1994). Former FCC regulator's analysis of the challenges facing telecom regulators is even-handed.

Cairncross, F., *The Death of Distance: How the Communications Revolution Will Change Our Lives* (Boston: Harvard Business School Press, 1997). Senior editor at *The Economist* explores how communications revolution and the Internet will change everything.

Castells, M., *The Rise of Network Society*, 3 vols. (Oxford: Blackwell Publishers, 1996). Brilliant, dense, multilayered account of the economic and social dynamics of the information age. Castells sweeps across time and continents in an effort to formulate a systematic theory of the information society.

Computer Science and Telecommunications Board, National Research Council, *The Digital Dilemma: Intellectual Property in the Information Age* (Washington, DC: National Academy Press, 2000). Thoughtful report examines new intellectual property challenges in a digital age.

Cowhey, P., 'The International Telecommunications Regime: The Political Roots of Regimes for High Technology', *International Organization* 44:2 (Spring 1990), 169–99. The old regime as seen by an academic/policymaker who helped formulate the US international communications strategy in the late 1990s.

Ignatieff, M., *Virtual War: Kosovo and Beyond* (New York: Henry Holt, 2000). Journalist explores virtual and cyberwar in the Balkans and the future.

International Telecommunication Union, *World Telecommunication Development Report* (Geneva: ITU). The best available source of comparative data on communications. New reports are issued every year or so and also contain essays on specific issues, in 1998 it was universal access.

Lessig, L., *Code and Other Laws of Cyberspace* (New York: Basic Books, 1999). Stanford Law School Professor provides a lucid analysis of the relationship between law, cyberspace, and social organization. How the code is written determines who wins and loses.

Levy, B., and Spiller, P. T. (eds.), *Regulations, Institutions, and Commitment: Comparative Studies of Telecommunications* (New York: Cambridge University Press, 1996). Economists assess the impact of core political and social institutions on regulatory structures and performance in the telecommunications industry in Jamaica, the United Kingdom, Chile, Argentina, and the Philippines.

UNESCO, *World Culture Report: Culture, Creativity and Markets* (Paris: UNESCO, 1998). Excellent on the impact of communications on culture and society. Includes extensive comparative statistical tables on cultural indicators.

WEB LINKS

www.fcc.gov Federal Communications Commission (US). The first stop for those wanting to understand US domestic and international communications policy.

www.itu.int/indicators International Telecommunications Union. The best source on international communication statistics.

www.oftel.gov.uk Oftel (UK). The site of the British telecom regulatory authority.

www.telecompolicy.org and **www.camfordpublishing.com** *Telecommunications Policy* and *Info*, two of the leading journals that focus on international telecom and information policy and published in Europe.

www.totaltele.com A comprehensive site on international communications developments that includes *Communications Week International*.

www.open.gov.uk and **www.europa.eu.int** Wide-ranging British and European sites that include public sector information on the Internet.

www.sciencedirect.com/science/journal/03085961

26 Poverty, development, and hunger

Caroline Thomas

READER'S GUIDE

This chapter explores and illustrates the contested nature of a number of important concepts in International Relations. It examines the orthodox mainstream understanding of poverty, development, and hunger, and contrasts this with a critical alternative approach. Consideration is given to how successful the development orthodoxy has been in incorporating and thereby neutralizing the concerns of the critical alternative. The chapter then closes with an assessment of the likelihood of a globalization with a human face in the twenty-first century.

Introduction

Since 1945 we have witnessed over fifty years of unprecedented official development policies and impressive global economic growth. Yet global polarization is increasing, with the economic gap between rich and poor states and people growing.

Poverty, hunger, and disease remain widespread, and women and girls continue to comprise the majority of the world's poorest people. Moreover, this general situation is not confined to that part of

Table 26.1 Changing income ratios

Year	Income ratio of 20% global population in richest countries to 20% in poorest
1960	30:1
1990	60:1
1997	74:1

Source: Adapted from UNDP 1999: 3.

the world that we have traditionally termed the 'South' or the 'Third World'. Particularly during the 1980s and 1990s, the worldwide promotion of neo-liberal economic policies (the so-called Washington consensus) by global governance institutions has been accompanied by increasing inequalities within and between states. During this period the Second World countries of the former Eastern bloc were incorporated into the Third World grouping of states, and millions of people previously cushioned by the state were thrown into poverty with the transition to market economies. In the developed world, rising social inequalities characterized the social landscape of the 1980s and 1990s. Within the Third World countries, the adverse impact of globalization was felt acutely as countries were forced to adopt free market policies as a condition of debt rescheduling and in the hope of attracting new investment to spur development. Gendered outcomes of these neoliberal economic policies have been noted, though the global picture is very mixed with other factors such as class, race, and ethnicity contributing to local outcomes (Buvinic 1997: 39).

Traditionally, the discipline of International Relations focused on issues relating to inter-state conflict, and regarded security and development as separate areas. Practitioners and scholars neglected the less dramatic challenges presented to human well-being by the existence of global underdevelopment. At the beginning of the twenty-first century, with the challenges posed by the uneven impact of globalization, there is greater recognition that security and development are intimately interlinked. Indeed, Michel Camdessus, speaking as Managing Director of the IMF, has referred to poverty as 'the ultimate systemic threat' (Camdessus 2000).

The appalling statistics of global hunger and poverty, and the even more appalling reality that they represent in the daily lives of much of the world's population—particularly, women and girls—clearly point to the need for further investigation by those who are concerned with human welfare. This necessity should not be obviated by the fact that the global media, especially during the 1990s, has tended to direct attention away from the ever-present unvoiced crises that poverty and hunger represent. An analysis of broadcasting in the UK in the 1990s sponsored by a consortium of NGOs revealed that when non-Western parts of the world have been considered, the focus has been on soft travel and wildlife issues (Stone 2000).

The attempts of the majority of governments, intergovernmental organizations and non-governmental organizations (NGOs) since 1945 to address global hunger and poverty can be categorized into two very broad types, depending on the explanations they provide for the existence of these problems and the respective solutions that they prescribe. This can be illustrated by reference to the UN World Summit for Social Development in Copenhagen, March 1995, which was convened primarily to address the related matters of increasing global inequality and the continuation of widespread poverty and under- and unemployment. Various views were expressed at the formal Summit, and at the parallel Non-Governmental (NGO) Forum, as to why an estimated 2.6 billion people lack access to sanitation, and a billion cannot meet basic consumption requirements, and why 30 per cent of the global labour force are classified as under- or unemployed. Likewise, a variety of solutions were advocated. The different approaches evident in these various solutions could, broadly speaking, be said to mirror two fundamentally different interpretations of how and why the various development-related problems came into existence. These can be identified as the dominant **mainstream** or **orthodox approach**, which provides and values a particular body of developmental knowledge, and a **critical alternative approach**, which incorporates other more marginalized understandings of the development challenge and process. Most of this chapter will be devoted to an examination of the differences between these two approaches in relationship to the three related topics of poverty, development, and hunger, with particular emphasis being placed upon the topic of development. The chapter concludes with an assessment of whether the desperate conditions in which so many of the world's citizens find themselves today are likely to improve. Again, two contrasting approaches are outlined.

Poverty

Different conceptions of poverty underpin the mainstream and alternative views of development. There is basic agreement on the material aspect of poverty, such as lack of food, clean water, and sanitation, but disagreement on the importance of non-material aspects. Also, key differences emerge in regard to how material needs should be met, and hence about the goal of development: cash transactions in the market, or subsistence via community-regulated common resources such as land, water, and fodder.

Most governments, international organizations, citizens in the West and many elsewhere adhere to the orthodox conception of poverty. This refers to a situation where people do not have the money to buy adequate food or satisfy other basic needs, and are often classified as un- or underemployed. For example, the Report of the South Commission—an important statement on development in the 'South' drawn up by eminent persons of Southern origins—reflects an orthodox conception of poverty when it claims that a billion people in the developing countries 'are too poor to buy enough food to sustain their energy' (South Commission 1990: 84).

This mainstream understanding of poverty based on money has arisen as a result of the globalization of Western culture and the attendant expansion of the market. Thus a community which provides for itself outside of monetized cash transactions and wage labour, such as a hunter-gatherer pygmy group, is regarded as poor. Consequently it is increasingly common for people around the world to regard as poor those 'who provide for themselves rather than sell their crops and buy commercially produced food . . . wear handmade clothes rather than factory-made garments . . . build their own houses with the help of their neighbours rather than employing labourers . . . [and] whose children are educated by family and friends rather than by paid teachers' (The *Ecologist* 1993: 96).

In traditional subsistence methods, a common strategy for survival is provision for oneself and one's family via community-regulated access to common water, land, and fodder. However, mainstream development classifies this method of provision as outmoded and representative of poverty. Yet the autonomy characteristic of such methods may be highly valued by those who have traditionally practised them. Indeed some such methods have been sustained over thousands of years. For many people in the developing world the ability to provide for oneself and one's family may be preferable to dependence on an unpredictable market and/or an unreliable government.

Critical, alternative views of poverty exist in other cultures where the emphasis is not simply on money, but on spiritual values, community ties, and availability of common resources. Some would regard us in the West as deprived of the most basic human need of spiritual fulfilment. Similarly, others would consider us impoverished for our loss of the extended family and sense of community belonging. Critical views have emanated from within Western society also. For example, it has been asserted that our emphasis on monetary values has led to the creation of 'a system of production that ravishes nature and a society that mutilates man' (Schumacher 1973).

Since 1945, the meaning of poverty has been homogenized and almost universalized. Poverty is seen as an economic condition dependent on cash transactions in the market-place for its eradication. These transactions in turn are dependent on development defined as economic growth. An economic yardstick is used to measure and to judge all societies. Poverty has widely been regarded as characterizing the Third World, and it has a gendered face. An approach has developed whereby it is seen as incumbent upon the developed countries to 'help' the Third World eradicate 'poverty', and increasingly to address female poverty. James Wolfensohn, Managing Director of the World Bank, declared in February 2000 that 'The World Bank is committed to making gender equality central to its fight against poverty' (cited in World Bank 2000). The solution advocated is the further integration of the global economy (Thomas 2000) and of women into this process (Pearson 2000, Weber 2002). Increasingly however, poverty, defined in such economic terms is also coming to characterize significant sectors of population in advanced developed countries such as the USA (See Bello 1994, Thomas 2000).

Key points

- The monetary-based conception of poverty has been almost universalized among governments and international organizations since 1945.

- Poverty is interpreted as a condition suffered by people—the majority of whom are female—who do not earn enough money to satisfy their basic material requirements in the market place.

- Developed countries have regarded poverty as being something external to them and a defining feature of the Third World. This view has provided justification for the former to help 'develop' the latter by promoting their further integration into the global market.

- However, such poverty is increasingly endured by significant sectors of the population in the North, as well as the Third World, hence rendering traditional categories less useful.

- A critical alternative view of poverty places more emphasis on lack of access to community-regulated common resources, community ties and spiritual values.

Having considered the orthodox and critical alternative views of poverty, we will now turn to an examination of the important topic of development. This examination will be conducted in three main parts. The first part will start by examining the orthodox view of development and will then proceed to an assessment of its effect on post-war development in the Third World. The second part will examine the critical alternative view of development and its application to subjects such as empowerment and democracy. In the third part consideration will be given to the ways in which the orthodox approach to development has responded to some of the criticisms made of it by the critical alternative approach.

Development

When we consider the topic of development it is important to realize that all conceptions of development necessarily reflect a particular set of social and political values. Indeed, it is true to say that, 'Development can be conceived only within an ideological framework' (Roberts 1984: 7).

Since the Second World War the dominant understanding, favoured by the majority of governments and multilateral agencies, has seen development as synonymous with economic growth within the context of a free market international economy. Economic growth is identified as necessary for combating poverty, defined as the inability of people to meet their basic material needs through cash transactions. This is seen in the influential reports of the World Bank, where countries are categorized according to whether they are low-income, lower middle-income, upper middle-income, or high-income

countries. Those countries that have the lower national incomes per head of population are regarded as being less developed than those with higher incomes, and they are perceived as being in need of increased integration into the global market-place.

An alternative view of development has, however, emerged from the occasional government, UN agency, grass-roots movements, NGOs, and some academics. Their concerns have centred broadly on entitlement and distribution. Poverty is identified as the inability to provide for the material needs of oneself and one's family by subsistence or cash transactions, and by the absence of an environment conducive to human well-being broadly conceived in spiritual and community terms. These voices of opposition are growing significantly louder, as ideas polarize following the apparent universal triumph of economic liberalism. The language of opposition is

Box 26.1 The orthodox versus the alternative view of development

The orthodox view

Poverty: A situation suffered by people who do not have the *money to buy food* and satisfy other basic *material needs*.

Purpose: Transformation of traditional subsistence economies defined as 'backward' into industrial, commodified economies defined as 'modern'. Production of surplus. Individuals sell their labour for money, rather than producing to meet their family's needs.

Core ideas and assumptions: The possibility of unlimited economic growth in a free-market system. Economies would reach a 'take-off' point and thereafter wealth would trickle down to those at the bottom. Superiority of the 'Western' model and knowledge. Belief that the process would ultimately benefit everyone. Domination, exploitation of nature.

Measurement: Economic growth; Gross Domestic Product (GDP) per capita: industrialization, including of agriculture.

Process: Top-down; reliance on 'expert knowledge', usually Western and definitely external; large capital investments in large projects; advanced technology; expansion of the private sphere.

The alternative view

Poverty: A situation suffered by people who are not able to meet their *material and non-material needs* through their own effort.

Purpose: Creation of human well-being through sustainable societies in social, cultural, political, and economic terms.

Core ideas and assumptions: Sufficiency. The inherent value of nature, cultural diversity and the community-controlled commons (water, land, air, forest). Human activity in balance with nature. Self-reliance. Democratic inclusion, participation, for example, voice for marginalized groups e.g. women, indigenous groups. Local control.

Measurement: Fulfilment of basic material and non-material human needs of everyone; condition of the natural environment. Political empowerment of marginalized.

Process: Bottom-up; participatory; reliance on appropriate (often local) knowledge and technology; small investments in small-scale projects; protection of the commons.

changing to incorporate matters of democracy such as political empowerment, participation, meaningful self-determination for the majority and protection of the commons. The differences between the orthodox and the alternative views of development are summarized in Box 26.1. In the following two sections we will examine how the orthodox view of development has been applied at a global level and assess what measure of success it has achieved.

The development orthodoxy

Economic liberalism and the post-1945 international economic order

During the Second World War there was a strong belief amongst the allied powers that the protectionist trade policies of the 1930s had contributed sig-

nificantly to the outbreak of the War. Plans were drawn up by the US and the UK for the creation of a stable post-war international order with the United Nations (UN), its affiliates the International Monetary Fund (IMF) and the World Bank, plus the General Agreement on Tariffs and Trade (GATT) providing the institutional bases. The latter three provided the foundations of a liberal international economic order based on the pursuit of free trade, but allowing an appropriate role for state intervention in the market in support of national security and national and global stability (Rapley 1996). This has been called **embedded liberalism**. The decision-making procedures of these international economic institutions favoured a small group of developed Western states. Their relationship with the UN, which in the General Assembly has more democratic procedures, has not always been an easy one.

In the early post-war years, reconstruction of previously developed states took priority over assisting developing states. This reconstruction process really took off in the context of the cold war, with the transfer of huge sums of money from the United States to Europe in the form of bilateral aid from the Marshall Plan of 1947. In the 1950s and 1960s as decolonization progressed, the focus of the World Bank and the UN system generally shifted to the perceived needs of developing countries. The US was heavily involved as the most important funder of the World Bank and UN, and also in a bilateral capacity.

There was a widespread belief in the developed Western countries, amongst the managers of the major multilateral institutions, and throughout the UN system, that Third World states were economically backward and needed to be 'developed'. This process would require intervention in their economies. This attitude was widely shared by Western-educated elites in those countries. In the context of independence movements the development imperative came to be shared by many citizens in the Third World. The underlying assumption was that the Western lifestyle and mode of economic organization were superior and should be universally aspired to.

The cold war provided a context in which there was a competition between the West and the Eastern Bloc to win allies in the 'Third World'. The US believed that the path of liberal economic growth would result in development, and that development would result in hostility to socialist ideals. The USSR, by contrast, attempted to sell its economic system as the most rapid means for the newly independent states to achieve industrialization and development. The process of industrialization underpinned conceptions of development in both East and West, but whereas in the capitalist sphere the market was to be the engine of growth, in the socialist sphere central planning by the state was the preferred method. The majority of Third World states were born into and accepted a place within the Western, capitalist orbit, while a few either by choice or lack of options ended up in the socialist camp. Yet in the early post War and post colonial decades, all states, whether in the West, East, or Third World, favoured an important role for the state in development. Many Third World countries pursued a strategy of import substitution industrialization, in order to try to break out of the their dependent position in the world economy as peripheral producers of primary commodities for the core developed countries.

With the ending of the cold war and the collapse of the Eastern bloc post 1989, **neoliberal economic and political philosophy** came to dominate development thinking across the globe. This represented an important ideological shift. The championing of unadulterated liberal economic values played an important role in accelerating the globalization process. The 'embedded liberalism' of the early post War decades gave way to the unadulterated neo-classical economic policies which favoured a minimalist state and an enhanced role for the market . The belief was that global welfare would be maximized by the liberalization of trade, finance and investment, and by the restructuring of national economies to provide an enabling environment for capital. The former Eastern bloc countries were now seen to be in **transition** from centrally planned to market economies, and throughout the Third World the state was rolled back and the market given the role of major engine of growth and associated development. This approach was presented as common sense, with the attendant ideas that 'There is No Alternative' or TINA (Thomas 2000).

The achievements of the post-1945 international economic order

There have been major gains for developing countries since 1945 as measured by the orthodox criteria of economic growth, Gross Domestic Product (GDP) per capita and industrialization. The rates of total and per capita growth for developing countries in the periods 1960–70, 1970–80 and 1980–7 are shown in Fig. 26:1. With respect to economic growth, from 1950 to the end of the 1980s, the economies of developing countries grew on average at 4.9 per cent per year, compared with a growth of 3.5 per cent for developed economies (Adams 1993: 8). In countries with over 90 per cent of the population of the developing world, the annual average growth-rate of the GDP per capita remained positive over the period 1960–87. However, a striking feature of the per capita economic growth of developing countries revealed in Table 26.1 is its marked **regional diversity**, with some countries (largely in Asia and the Americas)

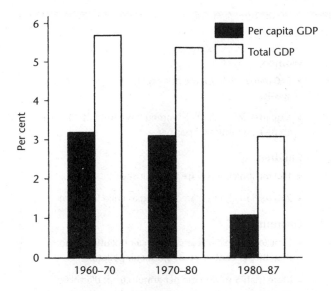

Fig. 26.1 Per capita and total GDP growth rates in the South between 1960 and 1987

Source: South Commission, 1990, p. 33 (based on UNCTAD data).

Table 26.2 Annual average rates of growth of per capita GDP of individual developing countries, 1960–1989

	<0%	0–2%	2–4%	>4%	Totals
No. of countries with growth rates falling within designed ranges	26	43	26	11	106
Breakdown of countries by major geographical regions:					
Americas	4	13	11	0	28
Africa	19	20	6	3	48
Asia	3	10	9	8	30
Share of total population* accounted for by countries in each growth range (%)	7.0	56.4	30.7	5.0	100

Source: Adams (1993: 12; based on UNCTAD data for 1989).   * Total population of those countries covered in the table.

achieving substantial growth rates, and others (largely in Africa) not doing so well.

In the 1990s, the picture was far less positive. The UNDP reports that: 'no fewer than 100 countries—all developing or in transition—have experienced serious economic decline over the past three decades. As a result, per capita income in these 100 countries is lower than it was 10, 20, even 30 years ago' (UNDP 1998: 37). Financial crises spread across the globe and indicated marked reversals in Mexico, the East Asian states, Brazil, and Russia. The African continent looked increasingly excluded from any economic benefits of globalization. By the end of the century, not a single former Second or Third world country had joined the ranks of the First World in a solid sense. Despite significant improvements in global social indicators such as adult literacy, access to safe water and infant mortality rates, global deprivation continues (UNDP 1997: 22). This is illustrated vividly in Box 26.2. Moreover, this situation continues despite the promise of the peace dividend that raised expectations that material inequalities would be ameliorated as resources freed up from the arms race would be devoted to development.

Having looked briefly at the broad achievements of the post-war international economic order, we will now proceed to an assessment of these achievements from, first of all, the perspective of the mainstream orthodox view of development, and then from the critical alternative view of development.

Box 26.2 Global deprivation, 1997

Health

- HIV/AIDS infections increased from less than 15 million in 1990 to more than 33 million in 1997

- 880 million people lack access to health services

- 2.6 billion lack access to sanitation

- 1.5 billion will not survive to the age 60

Education

- Over 850 million illiterate adults

- Over 260 million children are out of school at the primary and secondary levels

Nutrition

- 840 million people are malnourished

Poverty

- 1.3 billion live on less than US$1 per day

- 1 billion cannot meet basic consumption requirements

Women

- 340 million women are not expected to survive to the age 40

- A quarter to a half of all women have suffered physical abuse by an intimate partner

Children

- 160 million children are malnourished

- 250 million children are working as child labourers

Environment

- 3 million people a year die from air pollution—more than 80 per cent of them indoor air pollution

- More than 5 million die per annum from diarrhoeal diseases caused by water contamination

Security

- 12 million people are refugees

Source: Adapted from UNDP 1997: 22

The orthodox assessment of the post-war international economic order

Prior to the late 1970s, the rate of industrial growth was higher in the developing world as a whole than in the developed capitalist countries taken as a group. Many developing countries exhibited an impressive economic performance, and average per capita incomes in many developing states were rising. Following the first oil price shock of 1973, developing countries undertook large-scale borrowing of recycled petrodollars from Western commercial banks in an attempt to sustain their rates of economic growth. However, during the 1980s there was a serious regression in much of the developing world as a result of the rich countries' strategy for dealing with the second oil price hike in 1979, which resulted in massive rises in interest rates and steep falls in commodity prices in the early 1980s.

These changes precipitated the debt crisis. Once the debt crisis had come to a head in 1982, following

Mexico's threat to default, the Group of Seven leading developed Western countries decided to deal with the debt problem on a country-by-country basis, with the goal of avoiding the collapse of the international banking system by ensuring continued repayment of debt. In this regard, the IMF and the World Bank pursued a vigorous policy of **structural adjustment lending** throughout the developing world.

In applying the policy of structural adjustment lending, the Fund and Bank worked together in an unprecedented fashion to encourage developing countries to pursue market-oriented strategies based on rolling back the power of the state and opening Third World economies to foreign investment. Exports were promoted so that these countries would earn the foreign exchange necessary to keep up with their debt repayments. The strategy worked, in that debt repayments have largely been met, the exposure of Western banks has been very significantly reduced, and associated threat to the international financial system has receded. (It has since been replaced by other threats, such as the instability created by rapid capital liberalization in the 1990s). However, the anticipated influx of foreign investment into developing countries did not occur.

Despite the negative effects of the debt crisis upon many countries within the South, others among them enjoyed significant and sustained economic growth over the 1980s. China's economy grew at 9.4 per cent per annum, while India and South-East Asia averaged 5.5 per cent per annum. China and India benefited in this respect from their large size, the fact that they had negligible foreign debts at the beginning of the decade, and they were self-sufficient in food and capital goods. The East Asian Tigers, purportedly following a liberal development path (but in fact thriving on the policy of **state-assisted capitalism**) appeared to have broken out of the chains of economic dependence on the West and looked set to join the ranks of the developed countries.

The collapse of Communism in the late 1980s, represented for Francis Fukuyama 'the triumph of the West . . . an unabashed victory of economic and political liberalism . . . [and] the total exhaustion of viable systematic alternatives to Western [neo-] liberalism' (Fukuyama 1989: 3). The Western countries continued to advocate free market policies throughout the rest of the world. This strategy was pursued not just through the IMF and the World Bank, but very importantly, through the Uruguay Round of trade discussions carried out under the auspices of the GATT which resulted in the creation of the World Trade Organization. Importantly this expanded the private realm of the market into areas previously considered part of the public domain or subject to national regulation: for example, intellectual property rights, such as patents on seeds. It also created a rules-based institution to promote and oversee further integration of the global economy through trade liberalization.

The orthodox liberal assessment of the 1990s acknowledges that neoliberal economic policy has resulted in greater inequalities within and between states. However, it does not regard this as a problem so long as the social and political discontent which inequality engenders is not so extensive as to potentially derail implementation of the project itself. Indeed, the orthodox assessment regards these inequalities as desirable, as they may unleash entrepreneurial abilities that will contribute to maximizing wealth creation.

A critical alternative assessment of the post-war international economic order

Critics of the development orthodoxy do not believe that, on their own, statistical measurements of economic growth and per capita GDP give us an adequate picture of what is happening in developing countries, or indeed to human beings wherever they are located across the world. For example, Glyn Roberts points out that, 'GNP growth statistics might mean a good deal to an economist or to a maharajah, but they do not tell us a thing about the quality of life in a Third World fishing village' (Roberts 1984: 6). Those who advocate an alternative approach therefore place more emphasis on the pattern of distribution of gains within global society and within individual states. They believe that the economic liberalism which underpins the process of globalization has resulted, and continues to result, in increasing economic differentiation between and within countries.

As indicated above, there has been an explosive widening of the gap between the rich and the poor since 1945 compared with previous history, and more particularly in the 1990s (Adams 1993: vii; Thomas 2000). This trend has been evident over the very period when key global actors have been committed to promoting development worldwide, and indeed when there were fairly continuous world economic growth rates and positive rates of GDP growth per capita, at least until 1990 (Brown and Kane 1995).

The increasing gap between rich and poor was regarded as inevitable by dependency theorists such as André Gunder Frank (Frank 1967). Writing in the 1960s and 1970s, they stressed how the periphery, or Third World, was actively underdeveloped by activities which promoted the growth in wealth of the core Western countries, and of elites in the periphery. The periphery produced cheap primary products which were exported to the core. There, they were processed or converted into manufactured goods, then re-exported to the periphery with value added. Raul Prebisch of UNCTAD had argued that inevitably the periphery suffered from declining terms of trade, by which he meant that the selling-price of primary commodities relative to the buying-price of manufactured goods, tends to decline over the long term, and as a result conditions generally worsen in the periphery.

Informed by such concerns in the 1970s the developing countries campaigned unsuccessfully for a **New International Economic Order**. In fact they were calling for reforms of the existing order, and were especially concerned about declining terms of trade. They wanted the prevailing order to be made user-friendlier for the producers of primary commodities through such mechanisms as index-linking the prices of primary products to the prices of manufactured goods. They were also concerned to defend their right to exercise sovereignty over their natural resources and to form producer cartels. The success of OPEC had resulted in the illusion of commodity power, an illusion that was short-lived.

By the end of the 1970s it was clear that the orthodox conception of 'trickle-down' (the idea that overall economic growth as measured by increases in the GDP would automatically bring benefits for the poorer classes) had not worked. Despite impressive rates of growth in GDP per capita enjoyed by developing countries, this success was not reflected in their societies at large, and whilst a minority became substantially wealthier, the mass of the population saw no significant change. The South Commission concluded of this period that,

Inequalities tended to widen as the economy grew and became more industrialized . . . Increasingly, the rich and powerful in the countries of the South were able to enjoy the life-style and consumption patterns of developed countries of the North. But large segments of the population experienced no significant improvement in their standard of living, while being able to see the growing affluence of the few. (South Commission 1990: 38)

There was consequently a dawning recognition in some quarters that growth reduces poverty only if accompanied by specific economic and social policies directed to that end (Ibid. 36).

The 1980s have been described as the 'lost decade' for the majority of Southern states, with sub-Saharan Africa suffering the most. In the first half of the 1980s, over half of developing countries experienced a declining per capita GDP, whilst over the whole decade, developing countries as a group faced a 10 per cent decline in per capita GDP. As well as the stringent structural adjustment policies, they were faced with rising floating interest rates which increased their debt burden; commodity price fluctuations; declining terms of trade; uncertain markets for their goods as developed countries pursued protectionist policies whilst advocating free market policies for the rest of the world; and insufficient financial and technological transfers from the developed world. Not surprisingly therefore the international economic structure was perceived by developing states as being inherently unfair and disadvantageous to their interests. Moreover, increasingly it came to be seen by some groups as unfair in terms of gendered outcomes disadvantageous to women (UN 1999).

In 1987, UNICEF published a report entitled *Adjustment with A Human Face* (Cornia *et al.* 1987). This study highlighted the social cost of structural adjustment policies and argued for a redesign of structural adjustment to take these costs into account. Some authors took a more critical stance, arguing that adjustment amounted to economic genocide and was beyond reform (Chossudovsky 1997; Bello 1994). For the majority of debtor states and their populations the pursuit of SAPs in the context of an unsupportive external economic environment has resulted in increased debt, social hardship, political tension, and environmental degradation. As a group, debtor states entered the 1990s 61 per cent more indebted than in 1982, whilst sub-Saharan Africa's debt increased by 113 per cent over the same period (George 1992: xvi). Those paying the price are not the people who borrowed the money in the first place, nor the wealthy élites, but the poor. More specifically, poor women have been identified as losers in this process (Elson 1991; Tsikata 1995).

In 1990 the United Nations Development Programme (UNDP) developed the Human Development Index (HDI) to measure the development achievements of individual countries. Giving equal weight to life expectancy, adult literacy, and average local purchasing power, HDI results in a very different assessment of countries' achievements than does the traditional measurement of development based on per capita GDP (Thomas *et al.* 1994: 22). For example, China, Sri Lanka, Poland, and Cuba fare much better under HDI assessments, than they do under more orthodox assessments, whilst Saudi Arabia and Kuwait fare much worse. The HDI has been refined over the 1990s, and data for the HDI has been disaggregated in certain countries along racial, gender, regional, and ethnic groups. The Gender Empowerment Index (GEI) has been developed to monitor the relative position of women. However, the picture is very complex. As the UNDP Human Development Report 1996 shows, to disaggregate in India by gender is insufficient, for there may be disparities in female capabilities among regions, between ethnic groups, or urban and rural areas (UNDP 1996: 34). The promotion of the HDI reveals the contrasting approaches to development of some of the UN agencies on the one hand, and the IMF and World Bank on the other. It also reveals the complex and diverse nature of local situations on the ground.

Key points

- In 1945 the USA had *carte blanche* to set up a liberal international economic order, the institutional pillars of which were the IMF, the World Bank, and the GATT. Yet governments were responsive to the demands of national security, and embedded liberalism was the order of the day.

- The cold war stimulated competition between the West and the East to win allies in the developing world. Most of the latter were born into the Western international economy and saw their development within the context of that system i.e. based on growth within a free market, but also they stressed the role of the state in promoting development.

- Progress was achieved up to the 1980s according to the orthodox development criteria of GDP per capita, economic growth, and industrialization. Yet despite apparent success in conventional terms, there has been an explosive widening of the gap between the richest and poorest 20 per cent of the world's population, and the develop-

ing countries as a group entered the 1990s more indebted than the 1980s. Most of the countries of the former Eastern bloc or Second World, now known as the economies in transition from central-planning to free market, have suffered a rapid economic decline in the 1990s and effectively joined the Third World.

- Dependency theorists see the current predicament of the Third World as predictable, arguing that export-oriented, free-market development promoted in the Third World has increased the wealth of the West and of Southern elites.

- Trickle-down has been discredited, and it has been recognized that economic growth only reduces poverty if accompanied by specific economic and social policies.

- In recognition of the failure of economic growth-based indices of development, the UNDP Human Development Index was designed in 1990 to measure development in terms of longevity, education, and average purchasing power.

A critical alternative view of development

Since the early 1970s there have been numerous efforts to stimulate debate about development and to highlight its contested nature. Critical alternative ideas have been put forward that we can synthesize into an alternative approach. These have originated with various NGOs, grass-roots development organizations, individuals, UN organizations, and private foundations. Disparate social movements not directly related to the development agenda have contributed to the flourishing of the alternative viewpoints: for example, the women's movement, the peace movement, and movements for democracy and green movements (Thomas 2000). Noteworthy was the publication in 1975 by the Dag Hammarskjold Foundation of *What Now? Another Development*? This alternative conception of development (see Ekins 1992: 99) argued that the process of development should be:

1. need-oriented (material and non-material);

2. endogenous (coming from within a society);

3. self-reliant (in terms of human, natural and cultural resources);

4. ecologically sound; and

5. based on structural transformations (of economy, society, gender, power relations).

Since then various NGOs, such as the World Development Movement, have campaigned for a form of development that takes aspects of this alternative approach on board. Grass-roots movements have often grown up around specific issues, such as dams (Narmada in India) or access to common resources (the rubber tappers of the Brazilian Amazon; the Chipko movement, which began as a women's movement to secure trees in the Himalayas). Such campaigns received a great impetus in the 1980s with the growth of the green movement worldwide. The two-year preparatory process before the UN Conference on Environment and Development (UNCED) in Rio, June 1992, gave indigenous groups, women, children, and other previously voiceless groups a chance to express their views. This momentum was continued with the holding of an alternative NGO forum in Copenhagen, parallel to the UN Social Summit there in 1995, and the parallel conference in the same year at the Fourth World Conference on Women at Beijing.

Democracy, empowerment, and development

Democracy is at the heart of the alternative conception of development. The worldwide democratic transition over the the 1980s and 1990s was characterized more by the establishment of the formal institutions of Western democracy, such as regular multiparty elections, than by substantive changes in the power structure of societies and the associated entitlements of their members to resources (Gills *et al.* 1993). Thus the government may have changed from military to civilian, but its membership is often drawn from the same elite and shares similar values. The quality of life for the majority will have changed very little.

Grass-roots movements are playing an important role in challenging entrenched structures of power in formal democratic societies. In the face of increas-

ing globalization, with the further erosion of local community control over daily life and the further extension of the power of the market and transnational corporations, people are standing up for their rights as they define them. They are making a case for local control and local empowerment as the heart of development. They are protecting what they identify as the immediate source of their survival—water, forest, and land. They are rejecting the dominant agenda of private and public (government-controlled) spheres and setting an alternative one. Examples include the Chipkos in India, the Rubber Tappers in the Amazon, the Chiapas uprising in Mexico, and Indian peasant protests against foreign-owned seed factories. The protests at the WTO meeting in Seattle, November 1999, and at the IMF/World Bank Washington spring meeting in April 2000, were indicative of an increasingly widespread discontent with the process of globalization and with the distribution of its benefits. Such protests symbolize the struggle for substantive democracy which communities across the world are working for. In this context development is about facilitating a community's participation and lead role in deciding what sort of development is appropriate for it; it is not about assuming the desirability of the Western model and its associated values. This alternative conception of development therefore values diversity above universality, and is based on a different conception of rights.

The Alternative Declaration produced by the NGO Forum at the Copenhagen Summit enshrined principles of community participation and empowerment. It laid stress on equity, participation, self-reliance, and sustainability. The role of women and youth was singled out. With women comprising over half the global population, and with half of the world population under 15 years old by 2000, these groups are very important. The Alternative Declaration represents an alternative vision of past, present, and future that rejects the importance of the private sphere. It rejects the economic liberalism accepted by governments of North and South, seeing it as a path to aggravation rather than alleviation of the global social crisis. Moreover it identified trade liberalization and privatization as causes of the growing concentration of wealth globally. It called for immediate cancellation of all debt, improved terms of trade, transparency and accountability of the IMF and World Bank, and the regulation of multinationals. An alternative view of democracy was central to its conception of development. Similar ideas emanated from the parallel NGO fora, which accompanied all the UN global conferences in the 1990s. NGO statements have also been accompanied by follow-up. For example, the Women's Eyes on the Bank Campaign was launched at Beijing to keep up the pressure on the World Bank to mainstream gender concerns in its work.

Key points

- The last two decades of the twentieth century saw increasing debate about what constitutes development, with NGOs and grassroots activists playing a significant role.

- An alternative view of development emerged, based on the transformation of existing power structures which uphold the status quo. Such structures vary in scope from the global to the local, and these are often interlinked; for example, the global economy severely disadvantages the poorest 20 per cent of the global population, whilst at a local level access to common resources affects the ability of people to provide for themselves.

- Grass-roots organizations challenge entrenched power structures as people defend their rights, as they define them, seeking local control and empowerment. Development in this alternative view can be seen as facilitating a community's progress on its own terms. The Alternative Declarations of NGOs at global conferences have stressed community participation, empowerment, equity, self-reliance, and sustainability.

Now that we have looked at the critical alternative view of development, we will look at the way in which the orthodox view has attempted to respond to the criticisms of the alternative view.

The orthodoxy incorporates criticisms

In the mainstream debate the focus has shifted from growth to sustainable development. The concept was championed in the late 1980s by the influential Brundtland Commission (officially titled the World Commission on Environment and Development—see WCED 1987), and supported in the 1990s by a series of UN global conferences. Central to the concept of sustainable development is the idea that the pursuit of development by the present generation should not be at the expense of future generations. In other words, it stressed inter-generational equity as well as intra-generational equity. The importance of maintaining the environmental resource base was highlighted, and with this comes the idea that there are natural limits to growth. The Brundtland Report made clear, however, that further growth was essential; but it needed to be made environment-friendly. The Report did not address the belief, widespread amongst a sector of the NGO community, that the emphasis on growth had caused the environmental crisis in the first place. The World Bank took on board the concerns of the Report to some degree. When faced with an NGO spotlight on the adverse environmental implications of its projects, the Bank moved to introduce more rigorous environmental assessments of its funding activities. Similarly concerning gender, when faced with critical NGO voices, the World Bank eventually in 1994 came up with its Operational Policy 4.20 on gender. The latter aimed to 'reduce gender disparities and enhance women particularly in the economic development of their countries by integrating gender considerations in its country assistance programmes' (www.worldbank.org).

With the United Nations Conference on the Environment and Development (UNCED—sometimes referred to as the Rio Summit) in June 1992, the idea that the environment and development were inextricably interlinked was taken further. However, what came out of the official interstate process was legitimation of market-based development policies to further sustainable development. Official output from Rio, such as Agenda 21, however, recognized the huge importance of the sub-state level for addressing sustainability issues, and supported the involvement of marginalized groups. But while the groups had a role in the preparatory process, they have not been given an official role in the follow-up to UNCED. At the alternative summit where the largest selection of non-governmental views ever expressed was aired, the viability of this strategy was challenged. For example, the possibility of structural adjustment policies being made environment-friendly was seriously questioned.

The process of incorporation continued with the UN World Summit for Social Development held at Copenhagen in March, 1995. Three main issues were addressed: poverty reduction, social disintegration, and employment. There was a wide divergence of views between Northern and Southern governments in the run up to the Summit on matters such as debt, structural adjustment, multinational regulation, and reform of the Bretton Woods institutions dissipated at the Summit proper. Governments of developing countries accepted economic growth and the free-market strategy as the preferred route to development, but in many cases argued that this was insufficient to ensure social progress. Implicitly, countries like Malaysia were arguing for embedded liberalism such as that enjoyed by the developed countries since 1945. This would allow national needs to be taken into account. These differing views were largely dissipated at the Summit.

The intergovernmental Summit Declaration and Programme of Action contained only very watered-down references to debt, structural adjustment, and IMF/World Bank—UN dialogue, and no reference to the social responsibility of transnational corporations. Also whereas the UNCED had resulted in the creation of an organ (the Commission on Sustainable Development) to monitor progress on implementation of what had been agreed, no such monitoring machinery was put in place at Copenhagen. In line with the UK and US governments' position, the overall outcome of the Summit was to lend greater legitimacy to the pursuit of economic growth, free-market policies, and individual initiative as the best road to development. The traditional approach to development held sway, and the contribution of that method to the increasing global inequality was not on the agenda. The gendered outcomes of macroeconomic policies were ignored.

Interestingly, there was no discussion of, or commitment to, new transfers of finance from developed to developing countries. The North/South agenda had changed in the three years since the Rio Summit.

An appraisal of the responses of the orthodox approach to its critics

The terminology of alternative conceptions of development has been incorporated to a limited degree into the mainstream: 'sustainable development' or 'growth with a greener face' are the buzz words. The Fourth World Conference on Women at Beijing gave the appearance of the global mainstreaming of gender concerns. James Wolfensohn, President of the World Bank, declared at the conference: 'Despite progress over the last two decades, women are nonetheless more likely to be under-nourished, under-educated, over-worked and under-paid than their male partners . . . I need no persuading that women are absolutely central to sustainable development, economic advance and social justice' (Wolfensohn 1995). Yet the orthodox view of development remains largely unaltered, and the Washington consensus of the 1980s and 1990s remains largely intact. During 2000, a series of official ' + 5' mini-conferences were held, such as Rio + 5, Copenhagen + 5, and Beijing + 5, to assess progress in specific areas since the major UN conferences five years earlier. The assessments suggested that the international community had fallen short in its efforts to operationalize conference action plans and to mainstream these concerns in global politics. For example, a critical reading of Beijing suggests that the conference represented a continuation of the attempts of the 1970s and 1980s to integrate women into prevailing development practice (so-called 'WID'), in other words to increase their economic opportunities within the existing economic system. This stands in contrast to an attempt to fundamentally alter the social and economic power of women relative to men, which would require a transformation in prevailing development practice via the promotion of a gender and development ('GAD') approach (UN 2000: 7). The World

Bank's own assessment of its mainstreaming of gender, undertaken by the Social Development Task Force in 1996, concluded that gender concerns are not incorporated systematically into projects and are regarded by many as 'add-ons'. An even more critical evaluation of the World Bank was published by the Women's Eyes on the Bank and the Fifty Years is Enough Campaigns in 1997, which wanted the Bank to 'challenge women's subordination as the root cause of gender inequity' (Women's Eyes on the Bank 1997: 1).

Voices of criticism are few, though surprisingly they are growing in number and range. Even amongst supporters of the mainstream approach, voices of disquiet are heard as increasingly the maldistribution of the benefits of economic liberalism are seen to have been a threat to local, national, regional, and even global order. Moreover, the social protest which accompanies economic globalization is regarded by some as a potential obstacle to the neoliberal project. Thus supporters of globalization are keen to temper its most unpopular effects by modification of neoliberal policies. Small but nevertheless important changes are taking place. For example, the World Bank has guidelines on the treatment of indigenous peoples, on resettlement, and on the environmental impact of its projects. It has guidelines on gender, and on disclosure of information. It is implementing social safety nets when pursuing structural adjustment policies. It is promoting microcredit as a way to empower women. Indeed, Wolfensohn has claimed that 'The World Bank is committed to making gender equality central to its fight against poverty' (World Bank 2000: 7). With the IMF, it has developed a Heavily Indebted Poor Country Initiative to reduce the debt burden of the poorest states. The IMF has launched a Poverty Reduction with Growth Facility, which aims to reduce debt and free up more resources for education and healthcare. What is important however, is whether these guidelines and concerns inform policy, and whether these new policies and facilities result in practical outcomes that impact on the fundamental causes of poverty. The Bank has admitted that such changes have been incorporated largely due to the efforts of NGOs which have monitored its work closely and undertaken vigorous international campaigns to change the way the Bank

funds projects, and general operational processes. These campaigns continue, with the Bretton Woods Campaign and the Fifty Years is Enough Campaign being particularly significant in calling for open, transparent, and accountable decision-making by global economic institutions, and for local involvement in project planning and implementation. In addition to the NGO pressure for change, pressure is building within the institutional champions of the neoliberal development orthodoxy.

There is a tremendously long way to go in terms of gaining credence for the core values of the alternative model of development in the corridors of power nationally, and internationally. Nevertheless, the alternative view, marginal though it is, has had some noteworthy successes in modifying orthodox development. These may not be insignificant for those whose destinies have up till now been largely determined by the attempted universal application of a selective set of local, essentially Western values.

Key points

- The development orthodoxy remains essentially unchanged. However, the mainstream debate has shifted from growth to sustainable development—the view that current development should not be at the expense of future generations or the natural environment.

- The orthodox view asserts that sustainable development is to be achieved by further growth within a global free-market economy. This is the most effective way to maximize global wealth creation. Supporters believe that this will free up resources to care for the environment and to ensure social progress.

- This approach has been approved by the UNCED and the Copenhagen Summit, both of which legitimated further global integration via the free market. However, in the run up to Copenhagen, many developing countries advocated embedded liberalism rather than pure free market economics, as necessary to help meet the basic needs of their people and ensure political stability.

- Critical alternative views of development have been effectively neutralized by the formal incorporation of their language and concerns into the orthodox view. Nevertheless, the process of incorporation has resulted in some small positive changes in the implementation of the orthodox view, for example by the World Bank.

- Nevertheless, despite semantic changes, funda-

mental questions remain about the sustainability of the dominant model of development.

We have now concluded our examination of the topic of development from the orthodox and alternative approaches and will turn our attention to the topic of hunger.

Hunger

In addressing the topic of global hunger, it is necessary to face the paradox that whilst 'the production of food to meet the needs of a burgeoning population has been one of the outstanding global achievements of the post-war period', there are nevertheless around 800 million people in 46 countries who are malnourished, and 40,000 die every day from hunger-related causes (ICPF 1994: 104; 106). While famines may be exceptional phenomena, hunger is ongoing. Why is this so?

Broadly speaking there are two schools of thought with regard to hunger: the orthodox, nature-focused approach which identifies the problem largely as one of over-population, and the entitlement, society-focused approach, which sees the problem more in terms of distribution. Let us consider each of these two approaches in turn.

The orthodox, nature-focused explanation of hunger

The orthodox explanation of hunger, first mapped out in its essentials by Thomas Robert Malthus in his Essay on the Principle of Population in 1798, focuses on the relationship between human population growth and the food supply. It asserts that population growth naturally outstrips the growth in food production, so that a decrease in the per capita availability of food is inevitable, until eventually a point is reached at which starvation, or some other disaster, drastically reduces the human population to a level which can be sustained by the available food supply. This approach therefore places great stress on human over-population as being the cause of the

problem, and seeks for ways to reduce the fertility of the human race, or rather, that part of the human race which seems to breed faster than the rest—the poor of the 'Third World'. Recent supporters of this approach, such as Paul Ehrlich and Denis and Donella Meadows, argue that there are natural limits to population growth—principally that of the carrying capacity of the land—and that when these limits are exceeded disaster is inevitable.

The available data on the growth of the global human population indicates that it has quintupled since the early 1800s, and is expected to grow from 6 billion in 1999 to 10 billion in 2050. Over 50 per cent of this increase is expected to occur in seven countries: Bangladesh, Brazil, China, India, Indonesia, Nigeria, and Pakistan. Lately, population projections have had to be revised upwards because of a slowing down in the decline of fertility rates in some countries such as China, India, the Philippines, and Colombia. Unless this slow-down is arrested, population could increase to 23 billion by the end of the twenty-first century, as opposed to the current estimate of 11.3 billion. Tables 26.3 and 26.4 provide further data on population growth between the years 1950 and 1990, with projections to the year 2030. Table 26.3 focuses on the world population, whilst Table 26.4 focuses on the world's most populous countries. Table 26.3 shows that the world's population is likely to have tripled between 1950 and 2030, and that the rate of growth of the world's population is set to increase over the coming decades. Table 26.4 demonstrates that the world's most populous countries are located in the Third World and that only eleven of them account for over half of the world's population. Furthermore it shows that these eleven

Table 26.3 World population growth, 1950–1990, with projections to 2030

Year	Population (in billions)	Population growth (in billions)	Population growth per year (in millions)
1950	2.5		
1990	5.3	2.8	70
2030	8.9	3.6	90

Source: Brown and Kane (1995: 58).

countries are also likely to account for an increasing proportion of the world's population growth in the future. It is figures such as these that have convinced many adherents of the orthodox approach to hunger that it is essential that Third World countries adhere to strict family-planning policies which one way or another limit their population growth rates. Indeed, in the case of the World Bank, most women-related efforts until very recently were in the area of family planning.

The entitlement, society-focused explanation of hunger

Critics of the orthodox approach to hunger and its associated implications argue that it is too simplistic in its analysis of the situation and ignores the vital factor of food distribution. They point out that it fails to account for the paradox we observed at the beginning of this discussion on hunger: that despite the enormous increase in food production per capita that has occurred over the post-war period (largely due to the development of high-yielding seeds and industrial agricultural techniques), little impact has been made on the huge numbers of people in the world who experience chronic hunger. For example, the UN Food and Agriculture Organization estimates that although there is enough grain alone to provide everyone in the world with 3,600 calories a day (i.e. 1,200 more than the UN's recommended minimum daily intake), there are still over 800 million hungry people.

Furthermore critics note that the Third World, where the majority of starving people are found, produces much of the world's food, whilst those who consume most of it are located in the Western world. This latter point is supported by evidence such as that shown in Table 26.5, which demonstrates that the Third World countries of China and India, despite their enormous agricultural outputs, consume far less grain and livestock products per capita than do the two Western countries of Italy and the United States. Such evidence leads opponents of the orthodox approach to argue that we need to look much more closely at the social, political, and economic factors that determine how food is distributed and why access to food is achieved by some and denied to others.

A convincing alternative to the orthodox explanation of hunger was set forward in Amartya Sen's pioneering book, *Poverty and Famines: An Essay on Entitlement and Deprivation*, which was first published in 1981. From the results of his empirical research work on the causes of famines, Sen concluded that hunger is due to people not having enough to eat, rather than there not being enough to eat. He discovered that famines have frequently occurred when there has been no significant reduction in the level of per capita food availability and, furthermore, that some famines have occurred during years of peak food availability. For example, the Bangladesh Famine of 1974 occurred in a year of peak food availability, yet because floods wiped out the normal employment opportunities of rural labourers, the latter were left with no money to purchase the food which was readily available, and many of them starved.

Therefore, what determines whether a person starves or eats is not so much the amount of food available to them, but whether or not they can establish an entitlement to that food. For example, if there is plenty of food available in the shops, but a family does not have the money to purchase that food, and does not have the means of growing their own food, then they are likely to starve. The key

Table 26.4 Population growth, 1950–1990, with projections to 2030, for the most populous countries

Country	Population (in millions)			Population increase (in millions)	
	1950	1990	2030	1950–1990	1990–2030
Bangladesh	46	114	243	68	129
Brazil	53	153	252	100	99
China	563	1,134	1,624	571	490
Egypt	21	54	111	33	57
Ethiopia and Eritrea	21	51	157	30	106
India	369	853	1,443	484	590
Indonesia	83	189	307	106	118
Iran	16	57	183	41	126
Mexico	28	85	150	57	65
Nigeria	32	87	278	55	191
Pakistan	39	115	312	76	197
Total	1,271	2,892	5,060	1,621	2,168
Total as percentage of World Figure	50.8	54.6	56.8	57.9	60.2

Source: adapted from Brown and Kane (1995: 59).

Table 26.5 Annual per capita grain use and consumption of livestock products in selected countries, 1990

Country	Consumption (in kilograms)						
	Grain	Beef	Pork	Poultry	Lamb	Milk	Eggs
US	800	42	28	44	1	271	16
Italy	400	16	20	19	1	182	12
China	300	1	21	3	1	4	7
India	200	—	0.4	0.4	0.2	31	13

Source: Brown and Kane (1995; 64).

issue is not therefore per capita food availability, but the distribution of food as determined by the ability of people to establish entitlements to food. With the globalization of the market, and the associated curtailing of subsistence agriculture, the predominant method of establishing an entitlement to food has become that of the exercise of purchasing power, and consequently it is those without purchasing power who will go hungry amidst a world of plenty (Sen 1981; 1983).

Sen's focus on entitlement enables him to identify two groups who at the moment are particularly at risk of losing their access to food: landless rural labourers—such as in South Asia and Latin America—and pastoralists—such as in sub-Saharan Africa. The landless rural labourers are especially at risk because no arrangements are in place to protect their access to food. In the traditional peasant economy there is some security of land ownership, and therefore rural labourers have the possibility of growing their own food. However, this possibility is lost in the early stages of the transition to capitalist agriculture, when the labourers are obliged to sell their land and join the wage-based economy. Unlike in the developed countries of the West, no social security arrangements are in place to ensure that their access to food is maintained. In this context it is important to note that the IMF/World Bank austerity policies of the 1980s ensured that any little welfare arrangements that were previously enjoyed by vulnerable groups in developing countries were largely removed, and therefore these policies directly contributed to a higher risk of hunger in the Third World.

Building upon the work of Sen, the researcher Susan George in *The Hunger Machine* (Bennett and George 1987: 1–10) details how different groups of people experience unequal levels of access to food. She identifies six factors which are important in determining who goes hungry: the North/South divide between developed and developing countries; national policies on how wealth is shared; the rural/urban bias; social class; gender; and age. In addition, one could add to the list two other very important, and often neglected, factors determining hunger— that of race and disability. Consequently a person is more likely to experience hunger if they are disabled rather than able-bodied, black rather than white, a child rather than an adult, poor rather than wealthy, a rural-dweller rather than a town-dweller, a citizen of a non-welfare state rather than a welfare state, and an inhabitant of a developing country rather than a developed country.

Globalization and hunger

It is possible to explain the occurrence of hunger by reference to the process of globalization. Globalization means that events occurring in one part of the globe can affect, and be affected by, events occurring in other, distant parts of the globe. Often as individuals we remain unaware of our role in this process and its ramifications. When we drink a cup of tea or smoke a cigarette in the developed countries, we tend not to reflect on the changes experienced at the site of production of these cash crops in the developing world. However, it is possible to look at the effect of the establishment of a global, as opposed to a local, national, or regional system of food production. This has been done by David Goodman and Michael Redclift in their book, *Refashioning Nature: Food, Ecology and Culture* (1991), and the closing part of this discussion on hunger is largely based on their findings.

Since 1945 a global food regime has been established, and as we enter the twenty-first century we are witnessing an increasingly global organization of food provision and of access to food, with transnational corporations playing the major role. This has been based on the incorporation of local systems of food production into a global system of food production. In other words, local subsistence producers who traditionally have produced to meet the needs of their family and community may now be involved in cash-crop production for a distant market. Alternatively they may have left the land and become involved in the process of industrialization. The most important actor in the development and expansion of this global food regime has been the US, which, at the end of the Second World War, was producing large food surpluses. These surpluses became cheap food exports and initially were welcomed by the war-ravaged countries of Europe. They were also welcomed by many developing countries, for the model of development prevalent then depended on the creation of a pool of cheap wage labour to serve the industrialization process. Hence in order to encourage people off the land and away from subsistence production, the incentive to produce for oneself and one's family had to be removed. Cheap imported food provided this incentive, whilst the resulting low prices paid for domestic subsistence crops made them unattractive to grow; indeed, for those who continued to produce for the local market, such as in Sudan, the consequence has been the production of food at a loss (Bennett and George 1987: 78). Not surprisingly therefore the production of subsistence crops in the developing world for local consumption has drastically declined in the post-war period.

The post-war, US-dominated, global food regime has therefore had a number of unforeseen consequences. First, the domestic production of food staples in developing countries was disrupted. Secondly, consumer preferences in the importing countries changed in line with the cheap imports, and export markets for US-produced food were created. Effectively, a dependence on food aid was created (Goodman and Redclift 1991: 123). Third, there has been a stress on cash-crop production. The result has been the drive towards export-oriented, large-scale, intensively mechanized agriculture in the South. Technical progress resulted in the 'Green Revolution', with massively increased yields being produced from high-yield seeds and industrialized agricultural practices. This has in some respects been an important achievement. However the cost has been millions of peasants thrown off the land because their labour was no longer required, greater concentration of land in a smaller number of hands, and environmental damage from pesticides, fertilizers, and inappropriate irrigation techniques.

Since the early 1980s, the reform of national economies via SAPs has given a further boost to the undermining of the national organization of agriculture, and a further fillip to the activities of agribusiness. Also the aggressive pursuit of unilateralist trade policies by the US, such as the invocation of free trade to legitimize prising open the Korean agricultural market, has added to this. Global trade liberalization since the early 1980s, and especially the Uruguay Round's Agreement on Agriculture, and regional free trade agreements such as NAFTA, are further eroding local food security and throwing peasant producers and their families off the land. By the late 1980s the South produced well over 40 per cent of the world's food, but most of this was cash-crops for export. Production and marketing of these crops is controlled largely by transnational corporations such as Unilever. These large companies control food production and marketing from the seed to the supermarket shelf, and for them food is just another tradable commodity like diamonds or tin. The power of agribusiness is set to increase, as a result of the encouragement given to the globaliza-tion of food markets by the Uruguay Round. The effects of their policies are also likely to provide the focus for the formation of protest movements in the Third World; for example, in India disputes over intellectual property rights in regard to high-yielding crop-seeds has resulted in violent protest by peasant farmers at foreign-owned seed factories.

Key points

- In recent decades global food production has burgeoned, but paradoxically hunger and mal-nourishment remain widespread.

- The orthodox explanation for the continued exist-ence of hunger is that population growth outstrips food production.

- An alternative explanation for the continuance of hunger focuses on lack of access or entitlement to available food. Access and entitlement are affected by factors such as the North/South global divide; particular national policies; rural/urban divides; class; gender; and race.

- Globalization can simultaneously contribute to increased food production and increased hunger.

We have now concluded our discussion of the three topics of poverty, development, and hunger, and in the last part of this chapter we will assess the likeli-hood of globalization with a more human face.

Looking to the future: globalization with a human face?

As we enter the twenty-first century, we are faced with an awesome development challenge. The UN has set a target of a 50 per cent reduction in the number of absolute poor by 2015. All indications suggest that the target will not be met. The orthodox model of development is being held up for closer scrutiny, as we become more aware of the risks as well as the opportunities which globalization and the Washington consensus bring in their wake. Sur-prisingly, debate is flourishing even amongst con-cerned champions of the neoliberal development orthodoxy, prompted largely by the financial crises of the late 1990s that spread from East Asia to Russia and Brazil. The key question is: can globalization develop a human face?

Opinions differ. For Michel Camdessus, speaking as Head of the IMF, it is clear that a new paradigm of development is already emerging which entails the 'progressive humanization of basic economic concepts' (Camdessus 2000). However, more critical voices see in the reforms underway a complete failure to tackle fundamental issues of redistribution, which require valuing an economic system only if it works for people and the planet. Thus we can distinguish the contemporary evolution of a mainstream reformist development pathway, and a more critical alternative pathway.

The orthodox view argues that development as economic growth via the classical free market has been successful to date and that what is required now are minor reforms to dampen the worst excesses of globalization, and to ameliorate any opposition to the intensification of neoliberal development policy. Those who favour reform do so because their overriding goal is the extension of the neoliberal development agenda. Thus they seek to push the liberalization of trade, finance, and investment agendas further, to modify them around the edges and to increase ownership of them by reaching out to potential opponents, both civil society groups and states, and tying them into the project. Thus, for example, regarding investment, we see UN Secretary General Kofi Annan through the idea of a 'Global Compact' calling for partnerships between businesses, international organizations, governments and NGOs in order to attend to the adverse social and environmental effects of freer foreign investment. He does not advocate a mandatory global code of conduct for transnational corporations, but rather self-regulation through for example partnerships, company codes of conduct, guidelines on transnationals such as those of the OECD. Regarding trade liberalization, we see the WTO reaching out to civil society to explain the liberalization agenda, by hosting dialogue sessions with environmental and labour groups. Regarding finance, reformists want to go even further down the road to privatizing finance and reducing public finance in volume and proportion. Their suggested reforms include reducing the role of global economic institutions such as the IMF and the World Bank. They seek to expand ownership

of this financial liberalization agenda by bringing more countries into regular dialogue, such as through the G20. That grouping, which includes the G7 plus others such as India, China, Brazil, and Russia, has no decision-making power.

The critical alternative pathway emanating from some NGOs, a few Third World governments, and a handful of academics argues that the dominant model has clearly failed to maximize global welfare and moreover is resulting in increasing global economic instability. What is ideally needed is a radical new approach to defining development and a new development strategy which puts redistribution and human needs at the top of its agenda. However, since global revolution is not imminent, adherents of this alternative position are willing to work to tackle poverty and inequality in a more serious manner than that advocated by reformers, yet still working within the broad neoliberal framework. They reject further expansion of the liberalization agenda for trade, investment, and finance, and posit instead the centrality of the human experience. They want to see significant policy changes in favour of redistribution. They want to widen the participation of states in global economic governance, and introduce more substantive representation at the sub-state level. A return to embedded liberalism is their immediate aim, but a deeper and wider one than was experienced in the early post-Second World War decades, mindful for example of concerns of race, gender, and ecology. All this is a prelude to more far-reaching transformation. The sort of substantive policies advocated include: regulation of economic activity at the national and global levels in support of human needs; a tax on speculative movements of capital; the use of capital controls; a mandatory global code of conduct for transnationals; fair trade and ethical trade; and regional action such as an Asian Monetary Fund.

The current development orthodoxy is following the reformist pathway. History will reveal whether this pathway bears the seeds of its own destruction by delivering too little, too late to too few people.

QUESTIONS

1 What does poverty mean?

2 Explain the orthodox approach to development and outline the criteria by which it measures development.

3 Assess the critical alternative model of development.

4 How effectively has the orthodox model of development neutralized the critical, alternative view?

5 Compare and contrast the orthodox and alternative explanations of hunger.

6 What are the pros and cons of the global food regime established since World War Two?

7 Account for the increasing gap between rich and poor states and people after fifty years of official development policies.

8 Critically explore the gendered nature of poverty.

9 Which development pathway—the reformist or the alternative—do you regard as the more likely to contribute to global peace in the twenty-first century?

GUIDE TO FURTHER READING

General

Adams, N. B., *Worlds Apart: The North–South Divide and the International System* (London: Zed, 1993) presents an economic and political history of the North/South divide, and focuses on the role of the international economic system.

Rapley, J., *Understanding Development* (Boulder, Colo.: Lynne Rienner, 1996) analyses the theory and practice of development in the Third World post-Second World War in a straightforward, succinct manner.

Thomas, C., *Global Governance, Development and Human Security* (London: Pluto, 2000) examines the global development policies pursued by global governance institutions in the 1980s and 1990s. It assesses the impact of these policies on human security, and analyses different paths towards the achievement of human security for the twenty-first century.

Hunger

Dreze, J., Sen, A., Hussain, A. (eds.), *The Political Economy of Hunger* (Oxford: Clarendon Press, 1995) is an excellent collection on the political economy of hunger.

Sen, A., *Poverty and Families* (Oxford: Clarendon Press, 1981) provides a ground-breaking analysis of the causes of hunger which incorporates detailed studies of a number of famines and convincingly challenges the orthodox view of the causes of hunger.

WEB LINKS

www.oneworld.org   provides a very useful analysis by a number of Northern NGOs of broad development issues and global problems.

www.twnside.org   provides a view from the developing world. This site, arranged by the

Third World Network, Malaysia, provides an excellent range of papers and information on international political economy, development, environment, and human rights issues.

www.worldbank.org/gender   provides World Bank policy documents, speeches and research papers on development and gender issues.

www.unorg/gendernet   provides a UN database of materials on gender as well as access to many other sites.

27 Gender issues

Jan Jindy Pettman

READER'S GUIDE

This chapter asks why feminist scholarship and gender issues have come so late to the study of international politics, and suggests how asking feminist questions might make a difference. It then identifies different kinds of feminism, and traces the shifting debates about gender relations and sexual difference. The rest of the chapter explores a gender analysis of several aspects of globalization: deregulation and structural adjustment politics, the changing international division of labour and the 'export' of women workers; rising identity politics, and in particular the uses nationalisms make of women, and women's different responses to nationalism; and the ways women's transnational alliances and international conferences have globalized gender issues.

Introduction

International Relations has long been taught and theorized as if women were invisible: as if either there were no women in world politics, which was only men's business; or as if women and men were active in and affected by world politics in the same ways, in which case there would be no need to 'gender' the analysis. Now feminist scholarship is visible, if still marginal, and women's and gender issues are the focus of transnational politics. Both feminist understandings and women's organizing provide us with perspectives that contribute a more inclusive view of globalization.

Gendering international politics

Feminist international politics

Feminist scholarship is often strongly resisted by academic gatekeepers, for it reveals the partial and gendered nature of intellectual work which is built on (elite?) men's experiences. But feminism has come even later to International Relations, one of the most masculinist of the social sciences. Suggested explanations include that the discipline is male-dominated, and so more likely to reflect men's interests and fears; and that the way the discipline constructs its subject matter makes most people, including almost all women, disappear. Its focus on the 'high politics' of diplomacy, war, and statecraft called up a world of statesmen and soldiers, who were assumed to be male. Even when international political economy became a concern, this often took the form of analysis of relations between states and markets, or of structures of domination and exploitation. In either case, **gender relations** were rarely considered a necessary part of the analysis.

The intellectual field, or territory, further disguised women and gender relations through its distinction between the domestic or the inside of states, and the international or the in-between of states. In the process differences within states, including gender differences, were relegated away from its interest, and left to other disciplines like Political Science and Sociology. At the same time, world politics was often characterized in terms of conflict, competition, security (defined as military security), and power (demonstrated through the threat or use of force), drawing on a particular notion of human nature that was **gendered**, and also perhaps class and culture specific.

But many women have written on and thought about war and peace. The discipline of International Relations was established in 1919 in the wake of World War I, in the hope that there should never again be such a war. However, it ignored the critiques of women organizing for peace, including those who had held the Hague peace conference in 1915, in the midst of that war, and who opposed the punishing conditions imposed on Germany at its conclusion on the grounds that it would spread poverty, disease, and enmity through Europe, and generate further conflict (which it did). This is why feminists are concerned to ask whose experiences are being taken seriously? Whose understandings of politics, including international politics, become the material for theorizing about, and acting in, 'the world'?

Where are women in global politics?

Feminist questions unsettle assumptions which reflect only (some) men's experiences. In an early feminist intervention in the discipline, Cynthia Enloe asked the question: '**Where are the women?**' (1989). She found that women often were there, even where we might not expect them: keeping a military base going, for example, or as the majority of workers in export-processing zones.

Asking the question 'Where are the women?' can suggest different kinds of answers. For some, it leads to 'the famous few'—to name Indira Gandhi, Margaret Thatcher, or Golda Meir, for example. These particular women were strong leaders who showed no hesitation to use force in international conflicts. This led some to say that the only difference between men and women is that women are so rarely in power; if they are, they behave like men. Others argue that in national and world politics, only those who play the main game well will succeed. It may show more about contemporary politics as **masculinist**, than about whether women and men are 'different'. So, too, men who appear compassionate or seek to negotiate away from conflict may be accused of being wimps, 'women', or girls.

Others use the question 'Where are the women?' to identify places where women are not, because they are women. Until very recently, and still in many states, women were prohibited from combat roles, which in turn made it impossible for them to rise to commanding levels in their state's armed forces. But not just any man is seen as a soldier. The fierce debates over whether gay men should be allowed to serve are similar to those used against women soldiers: that they may break down under fire, or threaten group cohesion. Here military service is associated with men, and with certain kinds of **masculinity**.

Asking 'Where are the women?' reveals women in places where, otherwise, we might not look for them. Feminists take women seriously as knowledge-makers about the world. This means seeking to learn from their experiences of politics and global processes. Women are often under-represented in formal politics, as heads of state or parliamentary representatives or executive bureaucrats for example, though in the Scandinavian states, they are now close to equal (see Fig. 27.1). Women are more likely to organize in other politics, in social movements, and in non-governmental organizations (NGOs) for example. Through these politics, women were actors in global politics long before they were noticed in the study of International Relations.

Discovering gender

Asking 'Where are the women?' usually reveals women in different roles, for example, different relations to the military, or the market, compared with men. When we find women, we find gender relations. So war stories from very different states tell of brave soldier men, the protectors, and the women they protect, who wait, and weep, and have more sons for the killing (Elshtain 1987). These stories construct men as the agents of the state or nation, and women as passive, regardless of what actual men and women are doing. These constructions in turn place pressure on peaceful or unwilling men to fight, to protect 'womenandchildren'. They disguise some women's active support of or participation in wars, including as warriors. And they force conditions of dependence on women, who are expected to be grateful for this protection, even when they do not wish it.

The gendered war script is not an exception. The citizen is often presumed to be male, with public responsibilities, while women are relegated into the family, the domestic world. In foundation stories in political theory, women were also relegated away from the world of reason to one of emotions and passions, making them unreliable citizens, and even dangerous to men. The **public/private** split coincides with other splits, like reason/emotion, mind/body, and male/female. These are gendered divisions: they associate certain kinds of character or behaviour with a particular gender. The 'male' side of the dichotomy is usually given more value, and privileged, while the female side is devalued. In the process, 'gender' becomes both relational and a power relationship.

Feminism makes several very important strategic claims here. The first is that women's experiences are **systematically** different from men's, even from men of their own family or group. Another is that all social relations are gendered; so we experience our class, or race, for example, in gendered forms. We do not experience our gender alone, or in isolation from other social identities, including for example whether we are citizens, where we live, or our age. And gender is constitutive of other social relations. This reveals as partial those representations of social relations including global politics that appear gender-neutral, but on closer examination turn out to universalize (elite) men's experiences and knowledge.

Key points

- Gender analysis and feminism came late to International Relations.

- Women's experiences of and ideas about world politics were rarely admitted to the discipline.

- Asking the question 'Where are the women?' makes women visible in world politics.

- Making women visible also reveals gender relations as power relations.

- Feminism claims that women's experiences are systematically different from men's and that all social relations are gendered.

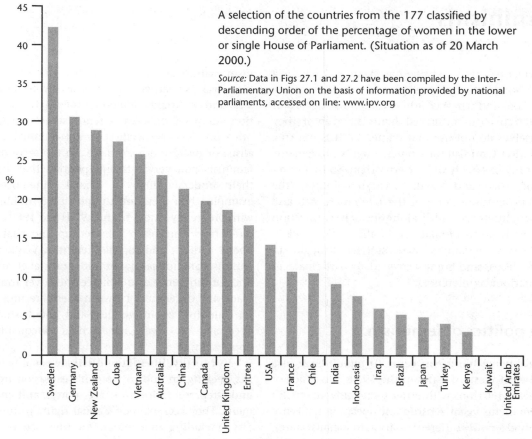

A selection of the countries from the 177 classified by descending order of the percentage of women in the lower or single House of Parliament. (Situation as of 20 March 2000.)

Source: Data in Figs 27.1 and 27.2 have been compiled by the Inter-Parliamentary Union on the basis of information provided by national parliaments, accessed on line: www.ipv.org

Women in national parliaments 1945–1995

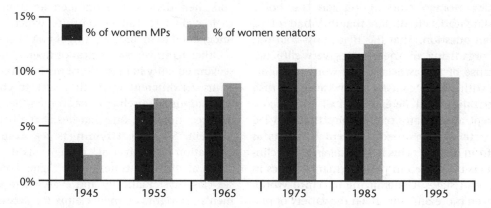

Fig. 27.1 Women's political participation

Sources: New Internationalist, April 1995, and *World Government Directory, 1994.*

Feminisms

Feminism is often identified as Western. There is a very complicated politics here about who names feminism, and whether other women's struggles for equal rights can be called feminist, even if they themselves do not use that name. But it is not true that either feminism or women's rights movements were only or largely of Western origin. So in a number of Asian and Middle Eastern colonies, 'the woman question' arose in the late nineteenth and early twentieth centuries, alongside or in connection with early anti-colonial nationalism. These early feminists were familiar with suffrage struggles in other places, and some travelled to participate in international conferences.

The politics of feminism

Second-wave feminism came to prominence in a number of Western states in the 1970s, alongside or in uneasy relations with other social movements for a more inclusive citizenship and social rights. Feminism had a rather different relation to socialist states, whose treatment of women as workers and their support for women working outside the home allowed state leaders to declare that they had solved the woman question. That has made post-cold war feminist organizing in these states very difficult, both because of the association of women's rights language with state socialism, and because the rush to marketization and deregulation of their economies swept away many of the gains that had led socialist state women to see Western feminists as 'coming from behind'. This helps explain the declining numbers of women in parliamentary politics in East European states. Generalizing to 'Third World' states is even more difficult, given the variety of pre-colonial, colonial, and post-colonial experiences to include.

We might describe feminism as a **political project** to understand and, therefore, to change women's inequality, exploitation, or oppression. But any generalizations about feminist politics globally are made even more difficult by the **differences** within feminism, within and between states. First-wave feminism was concerned with suffrage, with women's legal and civil rights, including their rights to education. Many of these early feminists were active in other politics—as socialists, or anti-colonial nationalists, or pacifists for example. So too second-wave feminists had very different politics, that affected their understanding of sexual difference, for example, their views on the possibility of alliances with progressive men. In the 1970s and 1980s, these differences were often summed up under labels of liberal, radical, and socialist feminist. While many feminists are not easily put under one label, and the lines of difference and alliance shift over time and place, the differences between them are important for thinking about gender, and about strategies necessary to overcome gender inequality or oppression.

Very broadly, **liberal feminists** are equality feminists, seeking an end to women's exclusion from or under-representation in office, power, and employment. They seek women's equal rights in the military, including in combat, for they see women's 'protection' as a way of keeping them from power, and their dependence on men as compromising their claims to full citizenship, which is usually understood to include fighting for one's country.

Other feminists are critical of liberal feminists as seeking equality in masculinist institutions on men's terms. In different ways, they seek to change the institutions themselves to be women-friendly. They disagree, however, on what lies at the heart of the problem. So **radical feminists** see women's subordination as universal, though taking different forms at different times. Some argue women are a sex-class, systematically and everywhere subject to men's sex-right, or their claims for access to their bodies, children, and labour. Violence against women is seen as key to keeping women resourceless and 'in their place'. They also draw attention to sexuality as politics.

Cultural feminists include those who see women as different from men, more nurturing and peaceable for example. They do not reject 'women's values', as liberal feminists do, but they argue that these values are just what world politics, and ecology, now need. Some cultural feminists are accused of essentialism, of representing these values as naturally women's, and so reinforcing the gendered stereotypes that underpin women's oppression. Others see women's values more as learned skills, as women are almost always those responsible for the care of children, health and community. They argue that men, too, can learn to nurture.

Socialist feminists put together class and gender, finding that a class analysis alone leaves out much that women experience. It cannot explain why women are those responsible for reproductive and family labour, why women are so over-represented among the poor, or why gender inequities, often reinforced by violence against women, continue even where women are integrated into the workforce.

These classic lines of difference in feminism are less clear these days, and are now supplemented by naming other feminisms. So in the 1980s **black** and **'Third World' feminists** accused white feminists of ignoring race, culture, and colonial relations as also affecting women. These locate white women in ambiguous ways, as oppressed in relation to gender and perhaps class, but privileged by their membership of the dominant race and/or culture, and by citizenship rights in rich countries. However, geographic location or social identity cannot predict a person's politics. Some Third World feminists are liberal feminists, seeking admission to their state or profession on equal terms with men, while others are socialist or left feminists who are concerned to build alliances across class lines between elite and poorer women, for example. Some white feminists also pursue anti-racist theories and politics.

Developments within feminism in recent years have shifted both theory and practical politics, for example, **post-modern feminists** have added to growing recognition of differences between women. These shifts have unsettled the category 'woman', raising issues about who speaks for 'women'. Whose experiences as women are not reflected in feminist knowledge-making and politicking? There is an ongoing tension in much feminism between equality and difference claims; between trying to build up the category woman for political purposes; while try-

ing to tear it down in the face of its use against women (Snitow 1989). This is made even more difficult in these times of growing right-wing and fundamentalist movements, which seek to discredit feminism and attack women's rights.

Sex and gender

Different feminisms, then, have different views on gender relations, and how to change them so they do not routinely count against women. The conversations and sometimes conflicts between these feminisms have taken us further in understanding gender relations and sexual difference. Jane Flax asks 'how do we think, or do not think or avoid thinking about gender' (1987). Just because gender is not made visible in many accounts of the world or our lives does not mean that it is absent. What then does a gender analysis contribute to our understanding of international and increasingly globalized politics?

Gender is often used as a code word for women. This does draw our attention to the ways in which dominant groups can normalize or naturalize their own identities—they name others while remaining themselves unnamed. But of course men have gender too, just as white people are also 'raced', and dominant culture members have culture.

An important early second-wave feminist intervention made a distinction between **sex and gender**. Sex was seen as biology: we are born male or female. Gender was seen as a social construction: what it means to be male or female in any particular place or time. This distinction was politically very important, for women have been badly done by biology, in its explanations of their inequality or extra burdens as natural, an inevitable extension of their childbearing difference. It built on the fact that while women's work appeared to be universal, just what that work involved, and how sexual difference was understood, varied from society to society, group to group, and over time (see Box 27.1). More recently, Men's Studies have explored the social construction of masculinities.

The distinction between sex and gender made room for a feminist project—for if gender is a social construction, it can be changed. It has also enabled us to explore different meanings of gender. Gender is

---

Box 27.1 Women's work

Much work in society goes unrecognized and unvalued—work in the household and in the community. And most of it is done by women.

Human Development Report 1995 estimated that, in addition to the $23 trillion in recorded world output in 1993, household and community work accounts for another $16 trillion. And women contribute $11 trillion of this invesible output.

In most countries women do more work than men. In Japan women's work burden is about 7% higher than men's, in Austria 11% higher and in Italy 28% higher. Women in developing countries tend to carry an even larger share of the workload than those in industrial countries—on average about 13% higher than men's share, and in rural areas 20% higher. In rural Kenya women do 35% more work than men.

In some countries women's work burden is extreme. Indian women work 69 hours a week, while men work 59. Nepalese women work about 77 hours, men 56. Moldova women work about 74 hours a week, and in Krygystan more than 76 hours.

Human Development Report, 1996.

---

a **personal identity**—how do I experience being a woman? a **social identity**—what do others expect of me, as a woman? and a **power relation**—why are women as a social category almost always under-represented in relations of power? Gender is political—it is contested, by men and women who regularly subvert, challenge, or bolster gender difference, at home or in other places, by feminists who seek women's liberation, and by anti-feminists, who seek to take back what women have won through struggle. Gender may be the basis for a **mobilized political identity**—of which 'feminist' is one. So too is the Australian anti-feminist women's group called Women Who Want to be Women.

Lately, some feminists have developed more fluid representations of gender. 'Doing gender', or gender as performance, suggests that we select and negotiate our ways through social possibilities and expectations. Gender as process reminds us that gender never just is, but rather that much work goes into its reproduction. Some feminists fault gender constructionists who continue to use the sex–gender distinction, for reinforcing yet another dichotomy nature and nurture—and for treating the body as a neutral 'thing' on which gender difference is written. They find it more productive to think about sexual difference, and stress embodiment—that our first place of location is our body. By drawing attention to bodies, they say, attention is inevitably drawn to sexual difference.

Women's politics and contests around gender, though still anchored often in local and particular sexual politics, are now increasingly globalized. These politics are a response to the gendered impact of **globalization**, and also take advantage of the opportunities for communication and organization transnationally that globalization offers. The rest of this chapter will pursue the changing international sexual division of labour, crises of the state in the face of globalization and restructuring, and rising identity conflicts. It will conclude by looking at women's politics, which are also being globalized.

Key points

- Feminism is not restricted to Western states.

- Contemporary feminisms are diverse in their understandings of the difference gender makes, and how to stop this difference from counting against women.

- Since the early 1980s, the issue of differences between women has become visible in feminist politics.

- Women's rights are not being progressively achieved. Today there is a global-wide backlash against women's rights.

Gender in the global political economy

Until recently, women and gender relations rarely appeared in studies of the international political economy (IPE). An exception was development studies (though these often remained separate from IPE). From 1970, feminist critiques and women's NGOs made visible the ways in which development planners overlooked women, including their roles as workers, owners, and entrepreneurs, as well as in subsistence and family production. They pointed out both that women were differently affected by development, often losing access to land and resources, and expected to take on additional work; and that the outcomes of development policies were affected by already existing gender relations, including local notions of what was women's work.

Women in development

The international **Decade for Women** (1976–85) generated a huge amount of material on women's lives, and the discriminations they faced. It also documented the gendered effects of development, and provided a base for the themes of peace, justice, development—which came out of the third women's conference in Nairobi in 1985. In the process, it supported a new field, known as **Women in Development** (WID).

There are very different approaches to WID, including between liberal feminists who seek to integrate women more equally into development, and other feminists who see development, currently defined, as damaging to women. They seek the empowerment of women, including through participation in development decisions that affect their own lives and choices.

Not all women are poor, in the 'Third World' or elsewhere. But no state treats its women as well as its men. Some years ago, it was said that women did one third of the paid work, two thirds of the productive work, for one tenth of the income and less than one hundredth of the property. Now it is likely that the figures are even more against women.

The Human Development Index (HDI) is based on three measures: life expectancy at birth, educational attainment, and standard of living. The Gender Development Index (GDI) measures these too, but adjusts for the disparity between women and men in each case. The Gender Empowerment Index (GEM) measures relative empowerment between men and women in political and economic spheres, and in terms of political representation.

A series of **global crises**, in terms of trade dependence, debt, and restructuring, have hit women especially hard. The conditions imposed on states in return for loans include structural adjustment policies, deregulating finance, liberalizing trade, favouring export industries and reducing social services and public support, including food subsidies.

These policies are not restricted to poorer 'Third World' states. They are evident in former and some

Table 27.1 Gender disparity—GEM, GDI, and HDI rankings (1999)

	GEM rank	GDI rank	HDI rank
Norway	1	2	2
Sweden	2	5	6
Denmark	3	14	15
Canada	4	1	1
Germany	5	15	14
United States	8	3	3
Australia	9	4	7
United Kingdom	16	11	10
South Africa	18	84	101
Cuba	21	53	58
Mexico	33	48	50
Japan	38	8	4
China	40	79	98
Indonesia	71	88	105
Kuwait	72	35	35
Bangladesh	83	123	150
Turkey	85	73	86
United Arab Emirates	96	45	43
Pakistan	101	116	138

Source: United Nations Human Development Report 1999

existing communist states, where marketization has similar effects, including removing state provision of many services that supported working women. They are reshaping Western states, too, as their governments give up on much economic regulation and cut back on social security and public enterprise.

These dramatic changes are part of the globalization of production and of 'the market'. Within states, they represent a dramatic shift from public to private expenditure, and from state to family, especially women's, responsibilities. We live in times of high unemployment, polarizing wealth within and between states, reducing state provision and growing impoverishment. These are gendered in their effects. **First**, cut-backs in state services like health, education, and social security especially affect women's employment opportunities. **Second**, women are everywhere overwhelmingly responsible for family and household maintenance, and must compensate through their own time and labour when (often inadequate) state support is reduced or removed. **Third**, the cost of globalization is not evenly spread: the 'feminization of poverty' refers to the growing proportion, as well as numbers, of women and their children living in poverty. This is in part a reflection of the worldwide trend, so that now between a third and a half of all families do not have a male breadwinner. The gendered effects of restructuring, then, amount to a massive crisis in reproduction. This has led UNICEF to identify an invisible adjustment, which is women's responsibility, largely unaided by those who allocate resources and wealth elsewhere.

The changing international division of labour

Fourth, the changing international division of labour is gendered. Transnational corporations go on the global prowl for cheap labour, which often means women's labour (Enloe 1992). Especially since the 1980s, increasingly competitive trading and labour deregulation in many states has accompanied the rise of a largely female marginalized workforce, with a core of skilled and professional workers who are mainly male.

Women are concentrated in poorly paid work, including part-time and outwork. This partly reflects many women's juggling between their domestic and their paid work. But it also reflects the construction of women workers as cheap labour—or, more accurately, as 'labour made cheap'. In many different cultures and states, women's labour is seen to be temporary, filling in before marriage, or supplementing husbands' income. At the same time, they are seen as 'naturally' good with their hands, patient and docile, and so particularly fitted to do work which men would not tolerate. Assumptions about women's work means that it is often classified as unskilled, even where, like sewing, it is seen as skilled if men do it. In these ways, particular constructions of femininity enter into the organization of work, and shape its status and rewards. So women are now the vast majority of workers on the global assembly line, in factories and in export processing zones, where their gender and often their youth help keep wages down.

The export of women

Women or girls come from rural areas into the towns or cities, into export processing zones or to military base servicing areas, or cross state borders in search of work. They may be their family's only income earner. This in turn unsettles gender relations, and gives those women experiences which range from liberating to extremely exploitative or downright dangerous.

Where once the labour migrant was presumed to be male (and often was), now about half of all those outside their country of birth are women. In some particular migrant labour flows, women are in the overwhelming majority. Many are domestic workers and child carers. They are part of a **global flow** of women from poorer states to wealthier ones, from Indonesia, Sri Lanka and the Philippines to Japan, Hong Kong, and oil-rich Middle East states (see Box 27.2), and from Central and South American states into the United States. This labour migration was largely unnoticed until the Gulf War revealed some 400,000 Asian women workers in Kuwait and a further 100,000 in Iraq. There are between 1 and 1.7 million women in the domestic worker trade from South and South-East Asia alone. This trade reinforces the assumption that it is women who are

Box 27.2 **The export of women from Indonesia**

- According to the International Labour Organization legal labour migration from Indonesia rose from 5,000 during the 1969–74 period to about 650,000 in the 1989–94 period. 62.8% went to Saudi Arabia, 19.4% went to Malaysia and 6.3% went to Singapore.

- Illegal labour migration is reliably thought to add at least another 500,000 to this number. Wages payable to illegal workers are estimated at one-half the wages payable to registered migrant workers.

- During the 1984–94 period two-thirds of these migrant workers were women working in domestic services. Women leave high rates of unemployment and poverty in rural Indonesia in search of wages to support themselves and their families.

- The Asian economic crisis of the late 1990s worsened the situation for Indonesian women as unemployment and lowered wages meant many had to seek work in the informal sector and many were forced into prostitution. In times of economic crisis women are often the first to lose work.

International Labour Organization, 1998, Emigration Pressures & Structural Change: Case Study of Indonesia.)

responsible for domestic labour, even where that labour is paid for and releases other women to go into paid work.

This **traffic in women** is big business. Recruitment agencies, banks, and airlines profit from it. So do the exporting states, in the form of remittances, for example, an estimated $3 billion per year to the Philippines. This trade contributes to those states' search for hard currency in the face of growing debt pressures, and relieves unemployment at home. It is therefore unlikely that the home state will act strongly in support of their citizens' rights when women are subject to abuse in other states; though another factor is their own poor record in labour and women's rights.

This trade in women reflects power and wealth relations globally. Those South-East Asian states exporting domestic workers had an average annual income in 1992 of $680, while those importing women had an average income of $10,376. It also has implications for states' standing, as some states become associated with servant status. In a further complication, the gendered representations of national difference reinforce earlier colonial and racist images of South-East Asian women as exotic and sexually available. In this way, the export of domestic workers is not so different from the international purchase of 'mail-order brides', and the international sex tourist industry. Women's organizations work transnationally to publicize the dangers in all these forms of trafficking in women, and to support the women caught up in these traffics.

Other forms of labour migration are not so obviously sexualized, though they may also involve exploitative working conditions and insecure rights in relation to both work and residence or citizenship. Many migrants move to and take up work in older industrial cities in Western states, and do work in clothing, textiles, electronics, and information services for example not so different from that which women do in some 'Third World' states. In conditions of urban decay, high unemployment, and cut backs in public expenditure and services, migrants can easily become scapegoats for other people's troubles. In this way, globalization and migration become targets in politics against 'outsiders'. **Racism** marks the boundaries of national belonging, and immigration and citizenship become major political issues. In these circumstances, those who are seen as different often organize in defence of their own rights, and may use their perceived difference as a basis for organizing. Instead of reducing differences between people, these aspects of globalization appear to heighten difference and intolerance.

Key points

- Feminist critiques, women's NGOs and the Decade for Women helped generate 'Women in Development' (WID).

- WID includes very different approaches to gender and development.

- Recent crises associated with intensifying globalization and restructuring impact on women in particular, generating a crisis in reproduction.

- The 'export of women' is big business, and also contributes significantly through remittances to poorer states' economies.

- Migrants and foreign workers are often scapegoated for rising unemployment and social distress.

Gender and nationalism

While we do now live in 'the world as a whole' for some purposes, we also live in a world where difference and particular political identities are as important as ever—perhaps more so. This can be seen in the resurgence of nationalisms and ethno-nationalisms and the rise of revivalist or fundamentalist religious politics globally. These identity politics usually call for a return to an imagined past. Women's roles and gender relations are a key element in the construction of the past and in the political mobilization of these identities.

Gendered nationalism

Since the end of the cold war, there has been an upsurge in identity conflicts. **Nationalism** is unsettling the presumed coincidence of nation and state. While in the past nationalism was more associated with progressive politics, for example in anti-colonial nationalism, nowadays it is often cast in exclusivist terms against 'the other'. In the process, women get caught up in nationalist politics in different ways, and identity politics come to impact on gender relations.

The language of nationalism is **familial language**—home, blood, kin. The state is often imagined as male, and the nation as female. The nation is often represented as a woman under threat of violation or domination, so that her citizen-sons must fight for her honour. The 'rape of Kuwait' told a typical story—of a feminized victim, with male villain and male hero fighting for her possession. These stories associate boundary transgression with sexual danger, and also associate proving manhood with nationalism and war. In these ways, regardless of what actual men and women are doing, men become the agents of nationalism and women passive or national possessions.

Where the nation is feminized, men are the responsible protectors. But women have obligations to the nation, too. Here we can trace a move from **nation-as-woman** to women as **mothers-of-the-nation**. This symbolic use of women and their confinement within roles as mothers can mean the policing of their bodies and behaviour, especially in wartime or in times of heightened identity conflicts.

Women and nationalism

Women are seen as the physical **reproducers** of the nation: they are 'nationalist wombs' (Enloe 1989). This makes it important that women have the right children, with the right men. They are also seen as social reproducers and cultural transmitters, bringing up their children as Palestinian for example, even—or especially—if they do not have a state of their own. Women are also seen as **signifiers of difference**, marking the boundaries of belonging. For this reason, much importance is attached to women's clothing and movements, especially their relations with those outside the nation. Beyond the symbolic uses made of them, women are also agents in or against nationalist politics in their own right.

It is easier for women to mobilize in support of nationalist causes, if this cause is in power in their state or region. Some women do organize in movements that are dangerous for others, including other women. So there are many women supporters and some leaders of the Indian right-wing Hindu movement, and some of these women participated in violence against Muslim women and children. Many Serbian women supported the Serbian nationalist project, which involved systematic violence against women as part of 'ethnic cleansing'.

Box 27.3 Women at the peace table

In conflict and war women bear great responsibility for the physical, educational, and economic well-being of their families, for caring for the wounded, for maintaining the national economy. They have also been increasingly targeted as weapons of war as they are raped, forced into marriage, abducted, and attacked. However women are not invited to the tense and delicate negotiations for peace. Indeed the culture of militarism so present during conflict tends to reinforce gender-based discrimination. In spite of resistance to their participation women are developing strategies for their voices to be heard at the peace-table. They form community groups and non-government organizations that campaign and lobby the peace process and international forums. Their strategies have been creative—in the Philippines women initiated peace zones to protect their children from recruitment by the militias and the army.

Women often take the lead in developing grass-roots movements to bring about peace because the men are away fighting, In Northern Ireland issues such as child-care, education, health, and micro-enterprise brought women together—Catholic and Protestant—to co-operate in resolving shared problems. It was from here that women came to launch a powerful campaign to bring about peace and be included in the peace process. The numerous grass-roots women's organizations came together to politicize and form the Northern Ireland Women's Coalition.

Sustaining peace requires commitment from people at the grass roots, it is they who must build lasting reconciliation and peace. The involvement of women in peace negotiations leads to ensuring a peace agreement that builds lasting peace at all levels.

(United Nations Development Fund for Women),
2000, *Women at the Peace Table.*

However, in some states women from dominant nationalist groups or states have organized in support for other women. Israeli **Women in Black** demonstrated in support of Palestinian women, and Belgrade feminists also demonstrated as Women in Black against Serbian nationalist aggression. These women have been subjected to much threat and sometimes violence, for their loyalty is supposed to be to their community, and not to women, or people more generally. At the same time, the idea of Women in Black has been taken up in many states experiencing nationalist violence, in expressions of solidarity with women across nationalist lines (see Box 27.3).

The high **symbolic** value attached to women in community conflicts makes them susceptible to attack from their own men, if they are seen as disloyal or rebellious. It also makes them especially vulnerable to attack from men on the other side, as a way of getting at their men. So mass rape in war and identity conflicts is not only war spoils. It is also a war strategy aimed at humiliating the enemy men by showing they are unable to protect their women.

War rape has a long history, though it is not usually regarded as political. So despite evidence of mass rape and of military sexual slavery in World War II, these were not prosecuted as war crimes. The recent visibility of sexual violence as part of war, especially in terms of the former Yugoslavia, but also of the Korean and other South-East Asian women forcibly recruited in to Japanese military brothels in World War II, is partly due to feminist work within states, to name rape and other violence against women as crimes against women, not against the honour of men. It is also a sign of globalizing gender issues, especially in the form of women's rights' claims.

Key points

- Nationalism is usually called up in gendered language.

- Women get caught up in nationalist politics in their construction as mothers of the nation and as markers of difference.

- Women also participate in or oppose nationalist politics.

- Women's symbolic significance in nationalism makes them vulnerable to violence, including war rape.

Globalizing gender issues

Women organizing in the face of global processes and documenting the impact on women become players in new global politics.

Naming **gender-specific violence** against women has been part of women's transnational politics. Violence against women in their homes is the most common crime in the world. It knows no boundaries, in terms of class, culture, or nationality. Other kinds of violence against women vary by region or take culture-specific forms. There has been an increase in dowry-burnings in India; in many states there are still 'honour' crimes which see husbands, fathers, and brothers exempt from punishment after killing women whose behaviour the family opposes; female genital mutilation maims and often kills girl children and women in some North African states.

Transnational women's movements

In some states, women are subjected to bodily violence through forced contraception or abortion, as in the China one-child policy. Many poor, racialized, and minority women in Western states face discrimination and lack of care in terms of health and social choices. There is now an **international women's health movement**, which struggles with different state policies and practices, and different views within women's NGOs and outside them, over how to secure women's sexuality and reproductive rights. 'Third World' women point out that these must go beyond individual rights, to ensure enabling conditions to access choice, including maternal and child health more generally. The 1994 international conference on population and development in Cairo was crucial in mobilizing women and building regional and global linkages. But even rhetorical gains are at risk in these backlash days. And there is no easy unity or single political position on these issues among women either.

International women's conferences

International conferences and preparations for them have been especially important in globalizing women's issues, networks, and alliances. The first two women's conferences in 1975 and 1980 (see Box 27.3) witnessed conflicting priorities between First World and Third World women. By the Nairobi conference in 1985 there were alliances across these divides, and more evident splits among women from the same state or region, especially between state-sponsored women's organizations and more radical dissident or exiled women. But Nairobi did place women's issues on the international agenda, and generated webs of connection between women's NGOs across state borders.

In recent years, women's activism has impacted on other kinds of international conferences. At the 1992 Earth Summit for example women named gender as shaping relations with the **environment**, including women's primary responsibilities for fuel and water in much of the world. They also identified militarism as the cause of much environmental degradation. The 1993 Human Rights conference was even more significant in highlighting **women's rights** claims internationally. In the lead-up to the conference, a series of preparatory committees and regional women's NGO meetings made their concerns visible. The Bangkok (Asia-Pacific) regional forum identified **five priority issues** to take to Vienna. These were violence against women, the international traffic in women, rising fundamentalisms (which usually target women's rights), military rape as a crime, and women's reproductive rights.

Women's global political campaigns helped win the adoption of the UN General Assembly Declaration against Violence against Women in 1993. This represents a significant advance in global gender issues. It recognizes violence as gender-based, supported by structural conditions which include women's subordination, and calls on states to punish perpetrators of violence whether in public or private places. It rejects religion or culture as excuses to abuse or discriminate against women. There are still

Box 27.4 Globalizing gender issues through the UN system

1946	The Commission on the Status of Women
1975	International Women's Year
1975	Mexico Women's Conference
1976–85	UN Decade for Women
1979	UN Convention on the Elimination of All Forms of Discrimination Against Women
1980	Copenhagen Women's Conference
1985	Nairobi Women's Conference
1993	Vienna Human Rights' Conference
1993	UN General Assembly Declaration on the Elimination of Violence Against Women
1994	Cairo International Conference on Population and Development
1995	Beijing Women's Conference

Box 27.5 Women's global political campaigns

Women's global political campaigns include a number of conferences that have been significant in pursuing justice and equality for women. Women have called governments to account for their actions, using benchmarks such as the United Nations Declaration for Human Rights and various conventions. They have also used these forums to establish commitments from governments regarding their performance on gender justice. The most recent was the 1995 Beijing International Women's Conference. This established a Platform for Action (PFA) that commits the 189 signatory governments to certain targets and as such it also represents a set of compromises. The commitments include: closing the gender gap in primary and secondary education by 2005; women should have at least a 30 per cent share of decision-making positions.

To date (early 2000), only six countries have achieved approximate gender equality in secondary school enrolment plus at least a 30 per cent share for women of seats in parliament or legislatures plus an approximate share of nearly 50 per cent paid employment in non-agricultural sector activities.

The targets from the conferences focus on closing gender inequality in education and health, however the conferences failed to endorse targets related to women's poverty and economic inequality. It is hoped that these issues will be addressed in the next Platform of Action to be developed.

(UNIFEM (United Nations Development Fund for Women), Biennial Report 2000 (preview), *Progress of the World's Women*.)

huge problems with implementation, but this declaration does politicize violence against women, and give states formal responsibility for the security of women.

Over 30,000 women attended the NGO forum at Huairoou, which ran parallel to the official fourth international women's conference in Beijing in 1995. In many states and in regional meetings, there was a process of consultation which culminated in the Platform for Action, which identified 12 crucial areas and strategies for pursuing them (see Fig. 27.2). The conference recognized the disproportionate costs to women of restructuring. It also witnessed reactions against women's rights which meant that much effort went into defending earlier gains. Of the themes of equality, development, and peace, the first took priority, though the NGO forum especially recognized the interconnections here.

Key points

- There are now different transnational women's movements, for example, for women's health and reproductive rights.

- International conferences, especially women's conferences, have been very important in building transnational women's networks, and in putting women's issues on the global agenda.

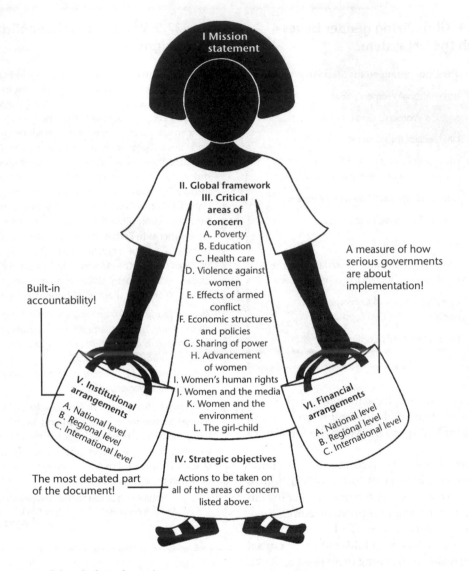

Fig. 27.2 Anatomy of the platform for action

Source: The *Tribune*, no. 54, August 1995.

- Recently, there has been a new visibility of women's rights claims.
- The Beijing conference is seen by some as an example of global feminism in action, while for others it illustrated the difficulties facing women's rights struggles globally.

Conclusion

Gender is a relevant category for analysis in global politics. Globalization affects women somewhat differently from men, though how it does so also depends on women's other identities and interests. In times of intensifying globalization which affects everyone, the state is no longer either willing or able to act in support of a global response. At the same time, both global restructuring and rising right-wing identity politics threaten hard-won gains, and in turn generate more women's activism. Now women are organizing transnationally, and gender issues are globalizing in the process.

QUESTIONS

1 Why did feminism come so late to International Relations?

2 What difference does it make to ask the question 'Where are the women?' about global politics?

3 What difference does it make being female, or male, in your experience?

4 What do you understand by gender?

5 What is feminism? What might different kinds of feminism contribute to our study of globalization?

6 What are the different approaches that are summed up under the label Women in Development?

7 What effects has globalization had on women, and on gender relations?

8 Why is there an increasing feminization of migrant labour, and of the global assembly line?

9 Are notions like the export of women, the global trade in women, or international traffic in women useful for tracking some global flows?

10 Discuss women's contradictory relations with nationalism.

11 Discuss the role of international conferences in putting women's rights on the global agenda.

12 Can we talk about global feminism, or transnational sisterhood?

GUIDE TO FURTHER READING

General

Beckman, P., and D'Amico, F. (eds.), *Women, Gender and World Politics: Perspectives, Policies and Prospects* (Westport, Conn.: Bergin & Gervey, 1994). This text pursues the question 'Does gender matter in world politics?' through the study of world politics and policies.

Enloe, C., *Bananas, Bases and Beaches: Making Feminist Sense of International Politics* (London, Pinter, 1989). This book asks 'Where are the women?' and reveals them in many different roles in international politics, in militaries, in export production, in prostitution and the sex trade, and in diplomacy.

Nelson, B., and Chowdhury, N. (eds.), *Women and Politics Worldwide* (Newhaven: Yale University Press, 1994). This useful resource book begins with overview chapters about women's different experiences of politics, and then has a number of chapters about women's participation in politics in different countries.

Peterson, V. S., and Runyan, A. S., *Global Gender Issues*, 2nd ed. (Boulder, Colo.: Westview Press, 1999). This text analyses gender in global politics, the gendered divisions of power, violence, and labour; and the politics of resistance, including women's politics.

Pettman, J. J., *Worlding Women: A Feminist International Politics* (London: Routledge, 1996). In this book, I explore aspects of global politics only briefly touched on in this chapter. It is organized in three sections: the gendered politics of identities, of war and peace, and of the international political economy.

Sen, G., and Grown, C., *Development, Crises and Alternative Visions: Third World Women's Perspectives* (New York: Monthly Review Press, 1987). This is a brief but broad-ranging review of the gendered impact of debt, dependence, and exploitation in Third World countries, and women's responses to these challenges.

Steans, J., *Gender and International Relations*, (Cambridge, Polity Press, 1998). An accessible exploration of feminist critique in International Relations, and gender analysis of nationalism, war, security, international political economy and development.

Tickner, A., *Gender in International Relations* (New York: Columbia University Press, 1992). A careful feminist critique of mainstream IR approaches to security, international political economy, and ecology.

WEB LINKS

www.unifem.undp.org   The United Nations Development Fund for Women (UNIFEM) works to ensure the participation of women in development planning and practice.

www.law-lib.utoronto.ca   International Human Rights Database (DINA) is a comprehensive database of electronic materials for human rights research.

www.un.org/womenwatch   Women Watch: an Internet gateway for the advancement and empowerment of women.

28 Human rights

Chris Brown

READER'S GUIDE

Over the last fifty years the growth of an international human rights regime based on the idea that human rights should be internationally protected has been striking, and seems a prime example of globalization. However, the record of compliance with human rights law is patchy, and states seem unwilling to give international action in support of human rights a high priority. Moreover there are serious conceptual problems involved in widening the notion of 'rights' to incorporate economic and collective rights. The Western origin of the doctrine of rights has also come to be seen as problematic in the postcolonial era, as the proponents of 'Asian Values' have stressed. It may be that in the next century only a limited notion of human rights will be defensible—or perhaps human rights will have to be defended in explicitly cultural terms.

Introduction

On the face of it, human rights are an ideal focus for a consideration of processes of globalization. Whereas it was once the case that rights were almost always associated with domestic legal and political systems, in the last half century a complex network of international law and practice (the 'international human rights regime') has grown up around the idea that individuals possess rights simply by virtue of being human, of sharing in a common humanity. The purpose of this chapter is to explain how this came about, but also, and in particular, to examine the many problems associated with the idea of universal human rights. This introduction will set the scene; the next section will examine some basic issues raised by rights language; the liberal position on human rights will then be examined, followed by discussion of the politics of international human rights protection as this has developed since 1945.

Many cultures and civilizations have developed ideas about the intrinsic worth and dignity of human beings, but the notion that humans are 'rights bearers' is specifically European. Medieval in origin, this notion was embodied in the positive law of a few countries in the early modern era—the US **'Bill of Rights'** of 1791 is the best example— and even before this latter date, in 1789, the French Revolution widened its scope with the **Declaration of the Rights of Man and of the Citizen**. Politics and thought in the revolutionary era of the 1790s also began tentatively to broaden the definition of Man by recognizing the rights of women, and, via campaigns against the slave trade, those of nonEuropeans, positions built upon in the nineteenth century. These preliminary moves set the scene for the globalization processes of the post-1945 era.

Here we have seen a number of global and regional treaties and declarations concerning human rights, and the emergence of non-governmental organizations (NGOs) such as Amnesty International dedicated to their enforcement. Moreover, governments such as that of the United States, and intergovernmental bodies (INGOs) such as the International Monetary Fund and the Commonwealth have increasingly (and controversially) seen it as part of their remit to promote human rights.

All of this amounts to an impressive body of international law and diplomatic practice, which has led to a further broadening and deepening of the idea of rights, often conceptualized in terms of three generations. Early statements concentrated on *First Generation* rights such as freedom of speech and assembly and 'the right to take part in the government of his (*sic*) country, directly or through freely chosen representatives' (**Universal Declaration, Article 21**). But the same declaration also recognized *Second Generation* rights to the 'economic, social and cultural rights indispensable for his dignity and the free development of his personality' (Article 22) and these economic and social rights feature very largely

---

> ## Box 28.1 **The International protection of human rights**
>
> The **Universal Declaration of Human Rights** adopted by the United Nations General Assembly in 1948:
>
> The **International Covenant on Civil and Political Rights** and the **International Covenant on Economic, Social and Cultural Rights** of 1966
>
> The **European Convention for the Protection of Human Rights and Fundamental Freedoms** of 1950
>
> The **American Convention on Human Rights** of 1969.
>
> The **African Charter on Human and Peoples' Rights** of 1981, usually referred to as the **Banjul Charter**
>
> The **Convention on the Prevention and punishment of the Crime of Genocide** of 1948
>
> The **International Convention on the Elimination of All Forms of Racial Discrimination** of 1965
>
> The **International Convention on the Elimination of Discrimination Against Women** of 1979.
>
> The **Vienna Declaration** and **Action Programme** of 1993

---

in later UN documents, especially, of course, the **International Covenant on Economic, Social, and Cultural Rights**. Both first and second generation rights are, in essence, possessed by individuals. *Third Generation* rights build on this collective dimension and concern the rights of 'peoples'; for example, under the **Banjul Charter** (see Box 28.1) peoples have the right to 'freely dispose of their wealth and natural resources' (**Article 21(1)**), while the individual has a duty 'to serve his natural community by placing his physical and intellectual abilities at its service' and to 'preserve and strengthen positive African cultural values in his relations with other members of the society . . . '(Article 29(2)&(7)).

This international human rights regime provides a

mixed and varied menu of items for discussion. There are *legal* issues concerning the ratification of these treaties, the interpretation of particular clauses and so on. These legal issues lead into *politico-legal* questions such as the vexed issue of 'compliance': there are clearly serious difficulties involved in making states live up to their legal obligations. This in turn raises *foreign policy* issues such as whether it is either practicable or prudent to make compliance with human rights law a touchstone of one's foreign relations. Clearly, there are straightforward *political* and *moral* issues here concerning the trade-off between particular values—is it worth risking a trading contract in order to make a point about a violation of human rights, or, putting the matter the other way round, should one overlook an obvious wrong in the interests of profit? The political problems posed by US trade policy towards the People's Republic of China over the last decade illustrate the difficulties here. Again, should foreign aid to poor countries be made dependent on the establishment of effective human rights? Finally, there are *conceptual*—perhaps *philosophical*—issues that cannot be avoided even by an account of human rights that tries to keep both feet firmly planted on the ground. For example, are first, second, and third generation rights compatible with each other? Indeed, are second or third generation 'rights', rights at all?

Each of these dimensions of human rights is worthy of discussion although the early items on this menu have been discussed so often that it is difficult to think that anything new (at least anything new and sensible) is likely to be said about them but nowadays the latter, philosophical, issues are increasingly coming to the fore. This is because of a general change of atmosphere in the late twentieth century, and especially after the end of the cold war. Until comparatively recently, few objected to the notion that human rights are universal; the *content* of human rights Declarations and Conventions was regarded by practical people as being rather less problematic than the issue of *compliance*. The key human rights problem was seen as one of forcing states to adhere to reasonably uncontroversial standards of behaviour.

Post-cold war, this problem has not gone away but some progress has been made: the establishment of International Tribunals after the Rwanda and Bosnia Conflicts, the Pinochet case in London, and the prospect of an International Criminal Court coming into being in the near future suggest that there is a spreading consensus that extreme human rights violations are a matter for the international community. However, this marginal but significant progress has been accompanied by the emergence of another set of issues putting in question the **universality** of human rights. Clearly one of the (third generation) rights of a '*people*' must be to be different from other people and could such difference be achieved other than at the expense of universal standards? In any event, does not the alleged universality of human rights hide the actual privileging of an essentially Western notion of politics, as is suggested by, among others, advocates of 'Asian Values'? Moreover, the 'masculinist' assumptions of human rights language have already been noted, and feminists have been critical of articles in the various Declarations and Covenants which assume traditional gender roles.

These new issues challenge, indeed reverse, the normal assumption of a process of globalization. The development of rights thinking from local and national to global and universal is usually seen as the great, albeit incomplete, achievement of the human rights movement—but from these perspectives this achievement is hollow and contestable.

Key points

- The International Human Rights Regime is an established feature of contemporary world society, and a good example of the processes of globalization.

- Modern thinking distinguishes between three generations of rights: first, broadly political; second, economic and social; third, the rights of peoples.

- One major set of contemporary problems concerns compliance and enforcement.

- More recently, the universal status of human rights has come to be challenged by critics who stress the western, masculine, intolerant nature of this universalism.

On rights in general

As we can no longer take the idea of rights for granted, we must now ask some fundamental questions—What kinds of rights might there be? Do rights necessarily imply **duties**? The standard legal answer to the first two questions is to distinguish different kinds of 'rights' some of which involve 'duties'; these same categories can be used in a wider political and moral context. On what **foundations** do rights rest? The answer in legal terms must be that they rest within a legal system, but what kind of legal system? Here we must return and reexamine the starting point of this chapter—the theory and practice of medieval European politics.

The *theory* of rights in the Middle Ages rested on the idea of **Natural Law**. Natural law theorists differed on many issues, but the central proposition is clear. Universal moral standards exist upon which the rights that individuals have are founded and there is a general duty to adhere to these standards. More will be said about this later, but for the

---

Box 28.2 Key concepts: kinds of rights

A standard analysis here, deriving from the American jurist Welsey Hofeld (Jones 1994 for a modern version) distinguishes four kinds of rights. **Claim-rights** are the most basic rights—the only true rights, Hofeld believed; the classic example of a claim-right is a right generated by a contract and accompanied by correlative duties. **Liberty-rights** occur when I have the right to do something in the sense that I have no obligation *not* to do it—for example, to dress as I please. Here there is no correlative duty, except perhaps the duty to let me do as I choose. Sometimes a right involves the exercise of a **power**. For example, to have the *right* to vote means to be *empowered* to vote, to be enfranchised. Finally, a right sometimes means an **immunity**, the essence of which is that others are disbarred from making claims under certain circumstances, for example, to be legally insane, or under age, is to be *immune* from criminal prosecution.

Box 28.3 Key concepts: natural law

The origin of Natural law thinking can be traced to the classical Greeks and early Christians, but in its modern form it is based on medieval Catholic Theology. The central idea is that human beings have an essential nature which dictates that certain kinds of human goods are always and everywhere desired; because of this there are common moral standards that govern all human relations and these common standards can be discerned by the application of reason to human affairs. For a modern defender of the traditional Catholic doctrine, see Finnis 1980.

---

moment it should be noted that the most important feature of this position is that it is not limited in application to any particular legal system, community, state, race, creed or civilization. In principle, *everyone* was subject to natural law and everyone was capable of discerning its contents and standards. Here is to be found the origin of much of the rhetoric of *universal* human rights.

Natural law provided the basis for a *theory* of rights in the Middle Ages; however, in the rougher world of medieval political *practice*, rights had rather different connotations. Here a right was a concession one extracted from a nominal superior, probably by force. The **Magna Carta** (1215) is a case in point. The Barons of England obliged King John to grant to them and their heirs in perpetuity a series of *liberties* which are, for the most part, very specific and related to particular grievances concerning, for example, the institutions of wardship and inheritance. From these clauses we can construct a list of practices by the King which were deplored by his subjects and which he was forced to abjure. His subjects obtained thereby a series of rights, liberties, powers, and immunities, while the Great Charter as a whole was based on the principle that the subjects of the King owe him duty only if he meets their claims. This is clearly a political bargain or contract.

There is no *necessary* incompatibility between the

Box 28.4 A jaundiced view of the Magna Carta

'the Barons compelled John to sign the Magna Charter which said:

1. That no one was to be put to death, save for some reason (except the common people).

2. That everyone should be free (except the common people).

3. That everything should be of the same weight and measure throughout the realm (except the common people).

4. That the Courts should be stationary, instead of following a very tiresome medieval official known as the *King's Person* all over the country.

5. That 'no person should be fined to his utter ruin' (except the King's Person).

6. That the Barons should not be tried except by a jury of other Barons who would understand.

Magna Charter was therefore the chief cause of Democracy in England, and thus a *Good Thing* for everyone (except the Common People).'

Walter Carruthers Sellar (*Aegrotat: Oxon*) and Robert Julian Yeatman (*Failed M.A. etc. Oxon*) *1066 and All That: A Memorable History of England* (London: Methuen, 1930)

---

rights established by political bargaining between monarch and subjects and the rights entailed by natural law (although, as Sellar and Yeatman observe, the liberties granted by the King do seem to have limited general applicability). However, it should not be forgotten that these two sources of the notion of rights are actually based not simply on different, but on *opposed* principles. Whereas rights based on **natural law** are derived from reason and the notion of human flourishing and are universal in time and space, '**Charter Rights**' simply describe in legal terms the result of a political bargain or contract and, by definition, are limited to the parties to the bargain, and thus restricted in time and space.

This potential opposition between a universal notion of rights based on a set of moral values, and a particularist notion based on positive law will come to be seen as having great significance for our contemporary international human rights regime.

Key points

- We need to establish the *status* of rights—what a right is, what kind of rights people have, whether rights imply duties, and why?

- The distinction between rights as claims, liberties, powers, and immunities helps to clarify these questions.

- The origin of thinking about rights can be traced to two features of medieval political and intellectual life, the doctrine of natural law and the political practice of extracting charters of liberties.

- Natural Law generates universal rights and duties, while a Charter confers local and particular liberties. The actual rights and liberties conveyed by Charters may be compatible with natural law, but this compatibility cannot be relied upon and a potential conflict exists between these two sources of the idea of rights.

The modern liberal synthesis on human rights

The complex language of medieval thinking on rights carried over into the modern period. Political philosophers such as **Hugo Grotius**, **Thomas Hobbes**, and **John Locke** continued to use notions of natural law, albeit in radically different ways from their predecessors. Political activists such as the Parliamentarians in the English Civil War drew on the rights and privileges they believed to have been granted to their forebears to sustain their notion of themselves as *'free-born Englishmen'*. Gradually, a synthesis emerged which can be termed the **Liberal Position on Rights**. This position is made up of two basic components:

1. Human beings possess rights to life, liberty, the secure possession of property, the exercise of freedom of speech, and so on which are inalienable —cannot be traded away—and unconditional— the only acceptable reason for constraining any one individual is to protect the rights of another.

2. The primary function of government is to protect these rights, political institutions are to be judged on their performance of this function, and political obligation rests on their success in this—in short, political life is based on a kind of implicit or explicit contract between people and government.

From a philosophical and conceptual point of view this position is easy to denigrate as a mish-mash of half-digested medieval ideas. As **G. W. F. Hegel** and many subsequent **communitarian** thinkers have pointed out, it assumes that individual rights, indeed individuals, predate society—and yet it is difficult to see how one could exist as an individual without being part of a society. For **Jeremy Bentham** the function of government was to promote the general good (which he called utility) and the idea that individuals might have the right to undermine this seemed to him madness, especially since no-one could tell him where these rights came from; the whole idea was 'nonsense upon stilts'. **Karl Marx**, on the other hand, and many subsequent radicals, pointed to the way in which the liberal position stresses property rights to the advantage of the rich and powerful.

All these points raise compelling questions, but they underestimate the powerful *rhetorical* appeal of the liberal position. Perhaps fortunately, most people are not political philosophers, and are less likely to be worried about the conceptual inadequacies associated with the liberal position on human rights than they are to be attracted by the obvious benefits of living in a political system based on or influenced by it. The plain fact is that the relatively few liberal democratic polities that have attempted to order their life along these lines have been the freest, safest, most congenial and civilized societies known to history—which, of course, is not to deny that these societies have also seen great and continuing injustices, injustices perhaps psychologically more difficult to bear because they exist in broadly just regimes.

The liberal position is a synthesis of the medieval *universalism* of natural law and the *particularism* of a contract between rulers and ruled; one of its uncertain features is the extent to which the rights it generates are considered to be universal. The **US Bill of Rights**, for example, is cast in quite general terms, but at crucial moments refers to the people in ways which make it clear that the people in question are the American people; the French Revolutionary **Declaration of the Rights of Man and of the Citizen** clearly by its very title is intended to be of universal scope, but even here the universalism of Article 1 *Men are born and remain free and equal in respect of rights* is soon followed by Article 3 *The nation is essentially the source of all sovereignty* . . . and when Revolutionary and Napoleonic France moved to bring the Rights of Man to the rest of Europe the end result looked to most contemporaries remarkably like a French Empire. The liberal position, while universal in principle, is particularistic in application and state boundaries are more or less taken for granted.

The humanitarianism and international standard-setting of the nineteenth and twentieth centuries brought these issues to the fore. The Congress of Vienna of 1815 saw the Great powers accept an obligation to end the slave trade, which was finally abolished by the Brussels Convention of 1890, while slavery itself was formally outlawed by the Slavery Convention of 1926. The **Hague Conventions** of 1907 and the **Geneva Conventions** of 1926 were designed to introduce humanitarian considerations into the conduct of war. The International Labour Office formed in 1901, and its successor the International Labour Organization attempted to set standards in the workplace via measures such as the Convention Concerning Forced or Compulsory Labour of 1930.

However, although these and other subsequent measures taken together do provide a quite elaborate framework for some kind of 'global governance', they exist within a context in which notions of sovereignty and nonintervention are taken for granted and only to be overridden with great reluctance; for example, abolishing *the slave trade*, which involves international transactions, was much easier than abolishing *slavery*, which concerns what states do to their own people—indeed, pockets of slavery survive to this day in parts of West Africa and the Middle East. Although the norms of international society condemned gross violations of human dignity, they did not support intervention under any less extreme circumstances.

All the while sovereignty remains a norm of the system, humanitarian impulses can only take the form of exhortation and standard-setting, and, for much of the nineteenth century, liberal supporters of human rights tended also to be supporters of the norm of sovereignty. In England, Manchester School radical liberals such as John Bright and Richard Cobden were bitterly critical of traditional diplomacy, but supported the norm of non-intervention on the grounds that their opponents—such as Britain's longstanding Foreign Secretary and Prime Minister Lord Palmerston—used moral arguments in support of interventions which were really engaged in for reasons of powerpolitics and general mischief-making. This is, of course, a familiar line of argument most likely in the late twentieth century to be directed at the American heirs of Britain's position in the world.

Cobden was a consistent anti-interventionist and anti-imperialist—other liberals were more selective; Gladstone's 1870s campaign to throw the Ottoman empire out of Europe bag and baggage was based on the more common view that different standards applied as between 'civilized' and 'uncivilized' peoples. In Gladstone's view the Ottoman empire—although, since 1856, a full member of international society—could not claim the rights of a sovereign state because its institutions did not come up to the requisite standards. Indeed this latter position was briefly established in international law in the notion of **standards of civilization** whereby non-European peoples such as the Chinese and Japanese could only achieve full sovereignty by adapting their ways to standards of good practice set in Europe. In the late twentieth century, this notion—and certainly talk of *civilization*—disturbs and unsettles, yet current conventional wisdom on human rights is based on quite similar ideas.

The willingness of liberals to extend their thinking on human rights in a more interventionist direction has been characteristic of the second half of the twentieth century. The horrors of the 1914–18 War

---

Box 28.5 **Key concepts: sovereignty and the standards of civilization**

When nineteenth-century Europeans travelled to China, Japan, and other non-European countries in pursuit of trade, they were reluctant to put themselves (and their property) under the jurisdiction of local legal systems, which often violated what Europeans regarded as basic principles of justice, for example, by allowing the aristocracy and military elite to dispense summary justice. However, a basic principle of International Society is the sovereignty of states, which required respect towards and non-interference with the institutions of the states which were its members. Where they had the power to do so, Europeans solved this problem by requiring that the countries concerned respected European legal conventions (the 'standards of civilization') before they were allowed full membership of International Society. In the meantime, special courts would be established by and for Europeans and those who dealt with them. These restrictions were bitterly resented as implying inferior status, and removing the regime of 'Capitulations'—as it was called—was a key nationalist demand everywhere in which they were set in place.

stimulated attempts to create a peace-system based on a form of international government, and although the **League of Nations** of 1919 (the inspiration of British and American liberal internationalists) had no explicit human rights provision, the underlying assumption was that its members would be states governed by the rule of law and respecting individual rights. The **Charter of the United Nations** of 1945 in the wake of the Second World War does have some explicit reference to human rights—a tribute to the impact on the general climate of thought of the horrors of that war, and, in particular of the murder of millions of Jews, Gypsies, and Slavs in the extermination camps of National Socialist Germany. In this context the need to assert a universal position was deeply felt, and the scene was set for the burst of international human rights legislation of the postwar era.

Key points

- From out of medieval theory and practice a synthesis emerged, the liberal position on human rights, which combines universal and particularist thinking—universal rights established by a contract between rulers and ruled.

- This position is conceptually suspect, but politically and rhetorically powerful.

- Nineteenth-century liberalism supported international humanitarian reform but within the limits of the norms of sovereignty and non-intervention.

- For some liberals these latter norms did not apply when the standards of civilization were in question. Twentieth-century thinking on human rights has been less restrictive, largely because of the horrors of the World Wars and the Holocaust.

1948 and the modern agenda

The post 1945 humanitarian impulse identified above led to the burst of lawmaking and standard-setting described in the introduction to this chapter. Although the 1966 Covenants now have the status of international law, and although the **European Convention** of 1950 has the most effective enforcement machinery via the **European Commission on Human Rights** and the **European Court of Human Rights**, nonetheless, for all its declamatory status and lack of teeth, the **Universal Declaration of Human Rights** by the UN General assembly in 1948 is, symbolically, central. This was the first time in history that the international community had attempted to define a comprehensive code for the internal government of its members. During the late 1940s the United Nations was dominated by the West, and the contents of the **Declaration** represented this fact, with its emphasis on political freedom. The voting was forty-eight for and none against. Eight states abstained, for interestingly different reasons:

South Africa abstained. The white-dominated

regime in South Africa denied political rights to the majority of its people and clearly could not accept that *all are born free and equal in dignity and rights* (Article 1). The South African government objected to the Declaration on the grounds that it violated the protection of the *domestic jurisdiction* of states guaranteed by Article 2(7) of the **United Nations Charter**. This is about as clear and uncomplicated a case of a first generation rights issue as one could imagine.

The Soviet Union and five Soviet Bloc countries abstained. Although Stalin's Russia was clearly a tyranny, the Soviet government did not officially object to the political freedoms set forth in the Declaration. After all, did not the Soviet Constitution of 1936 guarantee (on paper) exactly such freedoms? Instead the Soviet objection was to the absence of sufficient attention to social and economic rights by comparison to the detailed elaboration of 'bourgeois' freedoms and property rights. The Soviets saw the Declaration as a cold war document, designed to stigmatize socialist regimes—a not-wholly-inaccurate description of the motives of its promulgators. Here we see the first expression of second generation rights issues, which would later be taken up by more worthy proponents.

Saudi Arabia abstained. Saudi Arabia was one of the few non-Western members of the United Nations in 1948 and just about the only one whose system of government was not, in principle, based on some Western model. Saudi Arabia objected to the Declaration on religious grounds, specifically objecting to Article 18 which specifies the freedom to change and practise the religion of one's choice. These provisions did not simply contravene Saudi laws which, for example, forbade (and still forbid) the practice of the Christian religion in Saudi Arabia, they contravened the tenets of Islam which does not recognize a right of apostasy. Here, to complete the picture, we have an assertion of third generation rights and a denial of the universalism of the Declaration; different rules should apply to Saudi Arabia because Saudi Arabia is different from other countries (because the Saudi Ruler is the Custodian of the Holy Places of Islam).

Thus, the opening moment of the **Universal Human Rights Regime** sees the emergence of the themes which will make up the politics of human rights over the subsequent fifty years.

Key points

- The politics of the Universal Declaration of 1948 allow us to identify the three major human rights issues of the post 1945 era.

- First, there is the contest between the old norm of sovereignty and the new norm of universal domestic standards.

- Second, there is the contest between political and liberal and social and economic formulations of human rights.

- Finally, there is the assertion of the rights of peoples to be different.

The politics of human rights promotion

It is generally agreed that 'No one shall be subjected to torture or to cruel, inhuman or degrading treatment or punishment' [UN Declaration Article 5, Covenant on Civil and Political Rights Article 7, European Convention Article 3, American Convention Article 5(2)]. This is an *immunity* that is now so well established as to be part of customary international law. What in practice does this mean for someone faced with the prospect of such treatment?

If fortunate enough to live in a country governed by the rule of law, its **domestic courts** may well uphold an individual's immunity, and the international side of things will come into play only on the margins. Thus, a European dissatisfied with his or her treatment at home may be able to continue a legal dispute over a particular practice beyond his or her national courts to the **European Commission on Human Rights** and **European Court of Human**

Rights. In non-European countries governed by the rule of law no such direct remedy is available, but the existence of international standards may have an influence on the margin—although, for example, it should be said that the international consensus against the death penalty has had little effect on US practice. In any event, the international, universal side of human rights, at best, merely reinforces rights which are established elsewhere, in the domestic political order.

The more interesting case emerges if potential victims do not live in such a law-governed society, if, that is, 'their' government and courts are the problem and not a possible solution. What assistance have they the right to expect from the international community in such circumstances? What consequences will flow from their government's failure to live up to its obligations? Here, in circumstances where universal human rights are the first line of defence rather than a backup system problems can clearly be identified. Even in cases where violations are quite blatant it may be difficult to see what other states are able to actually do and, in any event, states rarely if ever act simply in terms of human rights considerations instead the whole range of relations between particular states will come into play.

Thus, during the cold war, the West regularly issued verbal condemnations of human rights violations by the Soviet Union and its associates, but rarely acted on these condemnations—the power of the Soviet Union made direct intervention imprudent, while even relatively minor sanctions would only be adopted if the general state of East–West relations suggested this would be appropriate. Conversely, violations by countries associated with the West were routinely overlooked or, in some cases, even justified. With the ending of the cold war it seemed possible that a more even-handed approach to human rights violations might emerge, and, as noted above, there has been some movement in the direction of holding governments responsible for their actions. However, expectations of major changes in attitude have not been met. In 1997, for example, the incoming Labour Government in Britain declared its determination to place human rights at the heart of its foreign policy. Unfortunately, but perhaps predictably, the actual policy of the new government has frequently been seen to be as determined by political and commercial considerations as in the past, and the 'ethical dimension' promised has not delivered much in the way of a new emphasis on human rights (Smith and Light 2001).

All told it seems unlikely that individuals ill-treated by non-constitutional regimes will find any real support from the international community unless their persecutors are weak, of no strategic significance, and commercially unimportant—and even then it is unlikely that effective action will be taken unless one further factor is present, namely the force of public opinion. This is the one positive factor that may goad states into action—the post-war growth of humanitarian non-governmental organizations has produced a context in which sometimes the force of public opinion can make itself felt, not necessarily in the oppressing regime, but in the

---

Box 28.6 Case study: The ending of apartheid in South Africa

White-dominated South Africa was commercially important to many Western businesses, and of some strategic importance in the cold war; initial attempts to boycott South African goods and stem the flow of investment to the country were unsuccessful. However, the impact of public opinion—reinforced in the United States by the power of the Black Congressional lobby, and African-American pressure groups—gradually made it commercially unwise to be associated with South Africa, while pressure in the United Nations and elsewhere produced a reasonably effective arms embargo. This international pressure certainly contributed to the decision of the South African regime to end *apartheid* and enter into negotiation with the African National Congress. However, this comparatively rare success story for the international human rights community may be a product of some of the peculiarities of the South African system. Although blatantly unjust, the old South Africa claimed to be preserving Western 'civilization', and did indeed have a freer judiciary and press than might have been expected. This made it more vulnerable to Western pressure than is the case with those repressive regimes who do not make this claim, or possess those institutions.

---

policy-formation processes of the potential providers of succour.

The situation with respect to *second generation* rights is more complicated, although equally depressing. Consider, for example, 'the right of everyone to an adequate standard of living for himself and his family, including adequate food, clothing and housing, and to the continuous improvement of living conditions' (**Covenant on Economic, Social and Cultural Rights, Article 11.1**), or the 'right of everyone to be free from hunger' (Article 11.2).

The Covenant makes the realization of these rights an obligation on its signatories, but this is a different kind of obligation to the obligation to refrain from, for example, 'cruel or degrading' punishments. In the latter case, as with other basically political rights, the remedy is clearly in the hands of national governments. The way to end torture is for states to stop torturing. The right not to be tortured is associated with a duty not to torture. The right to be free from hunger, on the other hand, is not simply a matter of a duty on the part of one's own and other states not to pursue policies that lead to starvation—it also involves a positive duty to 'ensure an equitable distribution of world food supplies in relation to need' (**Covenant on Economic, Social and Cultural Rights**, Article 11.2(b)). This is problematic.

First, it is by no means clear that, even assuming goodwill, these social and economic goals could always be met, and to think in terms of having a right to something that could not be achieved is to misuse language. In such circumstances a right simply means 'a generally desirable state of affairs'—and this weakening of the concept may have the effect of undermining more precise claims to rights which can be achieved (such as the right not to be tortured). **Second**, some states may seek to use economic and social rights more directly to undermine political rights. Thus, dictatorial regimes in poor countries quite frequently justify the curtailment of political rights in the alleged name of promoting economic growth, or economic equality. In fact, there is no reason to accept the general validity of this argument—Amartya Sen's work, for example, makes it clear that development and freedom go together (Sen 1999)—but it will still be made, and not always in bad faith. **Finally**, if it is accepted that all states have a positive duty to promote economic well-being and freedom from hunger everywhere, then the consequences go beyond the requirement of the rich to share with the poor, revolutionary though such a requirement would be. They also make *virtually all* national social and economic policies a matter for international regulation. Clearly rich states would have a duty to make economic and social policy with a view to its consequences on the poor, but so would poor states. The poor's right to assistance creates a duty on the rich to assist, but this in turn creates a right of the rich to insist that the poor have a duty not to worsen their plight—for example, by failing to restrict population growth or by inappropriate economic policies. Aid programmes promoted by the Commonwealth and World Bank, and the structural adjustment programmes of the IMF regularly include conditions of this kind. They are, however, widely resented because they contradict another widely supported economic and social right that 'All peoples have the right of self-determination. By virtue of that right they freely determine their political status and freely pursue their economic, social and cultural development' (**Covenant on Economic, Social and Cultural Rights**, Article 1.1). Even when applied in a well-meaning and consistent way—which cannot be guaranteed—external pressures to change policy are rarely popular, even with those they are intended to benefit.

In short, while all notions of human rights necessarily involve some restrictions in the exercise of state sovereignty, whereas political conceptions of human rights may still be just about compatible with the underlying norms of the existing international order, economic and social rights *if taken seriously as rights* are not.

Key points

- The politics of rights varies according to whether constitutional or non-constitutional regimes are involved.

- In any event, the international community rarely acts on human rights cases unless public opinion is engaged.

- Economic and social rights are conceptually different from political rights, and present a more basic challenge to existing norms of sovereignty and non-intervention.

Universalism challenged

The very idea of human rights implies limits to the range of variation in domestic regimes that is acceptable internationally. The **standards of civilization** of the last century implied such limits also, but post-1945 human rights law, if taken seriously and at face value, would create a situation where all states would be obliged to conform to a quite rigid template which dictated most aspects of their political, social, and economic structures and policies.

Conventional defenders of human rights argue that this would be a Good Thing—the universal spread of best practice in human rights matters is in the interest of all people. Others disagree. Does post-1945 law actually constitute best practice? The feminist critique of universal human rights is particularly apposite here. The universal documents all, in varying degrees, privilege a patriarchal view of the family as the basic unit of society, and, implicitly or explicitly, of the subordination of women within the family. Even such documents as the UN's **Declaration on Elimination of Discrimination against Women** of 1967, and the various **International Labour Organization** Conventions concerning women at work do no more than extend to women the standard liberal package of rights, and modern feminists debate whether this constitutes a genuine advance. (Peters and Wolper 1995)

More fundamentally, is the very idea of best practice sound? We have already met one objection to the idea in the Saudi abstention of 1948. The argument is simple: universalism is destructive not just of *undesirable* differences between societies but of *desirable and desired* differences. The human rights movement stresses the common humanity of the peoples of the world, but for many, the things that distinguish us from one another are as important as the things that unify us.

The movement towards establishing the *Rights of Peoples* partially reflects this perspective. The **Banjul Charter's** reference to the *duty* to strengthen '*African cultural values*', for example, conveys clearly the idea that Africans have rights and duties different from non-Africans. The **Declaration of Principles of Indigenous Rights** adopted in Panama in 1984 by a

---

Box 28.7 Key concepts: 'Asian values'

That Western states, INGOs and NGOs have sometimes taken it upon themselves to promote human rights has always been resented as hypocritical in the non-Western world, where the imperialist record of the West over the last four centuries has not been forgotten. In the 1990s, this resentment led a number of the leaders of the quasi-authoritarian newly industrializing nations of South-East Asia to assert the existence of 'Asian Values' that could be counterpoised to the (allegedly) Western values associated with the international human rights regime—in this they seemed to confirm the forthcoming 'clash of civilizations' forecast by Huntington (1996). Such thinking was partially reflected in the **Bangkok Declaration** of 1993, made by Asian ministers in the run-up to the **Vienna Conference** of that year (for text see Tang 1994). Western notions of human rights were seen as excessively individualistic, as opposed to the stress on the family of Asian societies, and insufficiently supportive of (if not downright hostile to) religion. Some, especially Prime Minister Matathir Mohammed of Malaysia, regarded the West as morally decadent because of the growth of gay rights and the relative success of the women's movement in combating gender discrimination. Critics accused Matathir and others of justifying their own authoritarian rule, although it should be noted that 'Asian Values' can only perform this task if the argument strikes a chord with ordinary people. More to the point, it may be doubted whether the conservative positions expressed by proponents of Asian values are in any genuine sense 'Asian'; many Western conservatives and fundamentalists share their critique of the West, while progressive Asian human rights activists are critical. Notions such as 'the West' or 'Asia' are unacceptably 'essentialist'— all cultures and civilizations contain different and often conflicting tendencies; the world of Islam, or of 'Confucian capitalism', is no more monolithic than is Christianity or Western secularism.

---

nongovernmental group, the **World Council of Indigenous Peoples**, lays out positions which are designed to preserve the traditions, customs, institutions and practices of indigenous peoples (many of which, it need hardly be said, contradict contemporary liberal norms).

However, a more basic challenge to universalism comes from advocates of 'Asian Values'. Here the case is not simply that Western governments, INGOs, NGOs, and journalists are engaging in a new form of imperialism by using universal human rights to attack various state practices in South-East Asia (and elsewhere) but also that these rights boil down to no more that a set of particular social choices which need not to be considered binding by those whose values (and hence social choices) are differently formed, for example, by Islam or Confucianism rather than by a secularized Christianity. The wording of the **Vienna Declaration on Human Rights** of 1993 which refers to the need to bear in mind 'the significance of national and regional particularities and various historical, cultural and religious backgrounds' when considering human rights partially reflects this viewpoint—and has been criticized for this by some human rights activists.

Returning to the history of rights, it is here that the distinction between rights grounded in natural law and rights grounded in a contract becomes crucial. As was noted above, it is only if rights are grounded in some account of human flourishing and reason that they are genuinely universal in scope. But is this position, as its adherents insist, free of cultural bias, a set of ideas that all rational beings must accept? It seems not, at least in so far as many apparently rational Muslims, Hindus, Buddhists, Atheists, Utilitarians, and so on clearly do not accept its doctrines! It seems that *either* the standards derived from natural law, or some such doctrine, are cast in such general terms that virtually any continuing social system will exemplify them—in which case the cutting edge of the doctrine is lost; *or*, if cast more specifically, the standards described are not in fact universally desired—in which case the claim that they are based on general features of human nature or the human condition is suspect.

Of course, we are under no obligation to accept all critiques of universalism at face value. Human rights may have first emerged in the West, but this does not in itself make rights thinking 'Western' (any more than, say, Darwinian theories of evolution are Eng-

lish because Darwin was an Englishman). It may be that an apparently principled rejection of universalism is, in fact, no more than a rationalization of tyranny. How do we know that the *inhabitants* of Saudi Arabia or Malaysia actually prefer not to live in a democratic system with Western liberal rights, as their governments assert? There is an obvious dilemma here: if we insist that we will only accept democratically validated regimes we will be imposing an alien test of legitimacy on these societies—yet what other form of validation is not open to the charge that it simply reflects the interests and values of the privileged?

In any event, does not the body of legal acts for the protection of universal human rights outlined in earlier sections of this chapter override local considerations? Should not the international community be given the last word? Again, defenders of difference will argue that international law is itself a Western, universalist, notion and that to pose the issue in these terms is to beg the question—in any event, they rightly note, the Western record of adherence to universal norms is not such as to justify any claim to moral superiority, pointing to the many crimes of the age of imperialism as well as to contemporary issues such as the treatment of asylum-seekers and refugees.

The general point is that there is no neutral language with which to discuss human rights—whatever way the question is posed reflects a particular viewpoint, and this is no accident, it is built into the nature of the discourse.

Key points

- The human rights template severely limits the degree of acceptable variation in social practices.

- This universalism can be challenged on feminist grounds as privileging patriarchy.

- More generally, the liberal position on rights privileges a particular account of human dignity.

- Cultural critics of universal rights such as proponents of 'Asian Values' can be seen as self-serving, but, by definition, no neutral criteria for assessing this criticism can exist.

Conclusion

It is difficult to see clearly the ways in which the international human rights regime might develop. Not only is it difficult to enforce compliance with universal standards, the very idea that there should be universal standards in the first place is under threat. On the other hand, many will be reluctant to give up on this idea—it is not only old-fashioned cultural imperialists who believe that it is good to live in a world where the rights of the individual—political, economic, and social—are taken seriously.

Is there any way in which the notion of universal rights can be saved from its critics? Two modern approaches seem fruitful. Even if we find it difficult to specify human rights, it may still be possible to talk of human wrongs—similarly, some have argued it is easier to specify what is *unjust* than what is *just*. To use Michael Walzer's terminology (1994*a*) there may be no thick moral code that is universally acceptable, to which all local codes conform, but there may be a thin code which at least can be used to de-legitimize some actions. Thus, to give two different kinds of example:

1. The **Genocide Convention** of 1948 seems a plausible example of a piece of international legislation that outlaws an obvious wrong—obvious in the sense that any moral code that did **not** condemn genocide would not be worthy of respect.

2. Whereas some local variations in the rights associated with gender may be unavoidable, it is still possible to say that practices such as **female genital mutilation** are simply **wrong**—again in the sense that any code which did not condemn such suffering would be unworthy of respect.

This may not take us as far as some would wish—essential to this approach is the notion that there are going to be some practices which many would condemn but which will have to be tolerated because the condemnation stems from a thick rather than a thin account of right and wrong—but it may be the most appropriate response to contemporary pluralism. It is noteworthy, for example, that most adherents of 'Asian Values' acknowledge the existence of a thin universal code concerning issues such as the abolition of torture or the right to a fair trial—it is the full human rights template to which they object.

An alternative approach is more supportive of universal ideas but on a non-foundationalist basis. This involves recognizing that human rights are based on a particular culture—Richard Rorty (in Shute and Hurley 1993) actually calls this the 'human rights culture'—and defending them *in these terms* rather than by reference to some universal cross-cultural code. This approach would involve abandoning the idea that it is possible to demonstrate that human rights exist; instead, it involves proselytizing on behalf of the sort of culture in which rights exist. The basic point is that human life is safer, pleasanter and more dignified when rights are acknowledged than when they are not.

This final point highlights what seems to be a central truth; whatever politicians and philosophers may say or do, it is on the strength of the *popular* support for universal human rights that the idea will flourish or die in the twenty-first century.

QUESTIONS

1 Can first, second, and third generation rights be distinguished?

2 Does a right always involve a correlative duty?

3 Are there such things as natural rights?

4 Can the promotion of human rights be a foreign policy goal of states? Are there moral as well as practical objections to such a policy?

5 In what sense can one speak of a right to an adequate standard of living?

6 Should peoples as well as individuals have rights? If so, do the rights in question include the right to override individual rights?

7 Are advocates of human rights necessarily cultural imperialists?

8 Is there a distinctively feminist approach to human rights?

9 How important is public opinion in mobilizing support for victims of human rights violations?

10 Is a democratic form of government a necessary pre-condition for the existence of human rights?

11 Are there specifically 'Asian Values' which provide the basis for a critique of universal human rights?

GUIDE TO FURTHER READING

Brownlie, I. (ed.), *Basic Instruments on Human Rights*, 4th edn. (Oxford: Clarendon Press, 1995) contains the texts of all the most important treaties and declarations.

Steiner, H. J. and Alston, P., *International Human Rights in Context: Law, Politics, Morals: Texts and Materials* (Oxford: Clarendon Press, 2000) contains abbreviated texts and a great deal of useful commentary in its 1,500 + pages! It is the single most useful book for the study of international human rights.

Jones, P., *Rights* (Basingstoke: Macmillan, 1994) is a good source for a discussion of the philosophical problems posed by the idea of rights.

Finnis, J., *Natural Law and Natural Rights* (Oxford: Clarendon Press, 1980) is more difficult, but the best introduction to modern natural law thinking.

On International Human Rights, the best introduction is a recent collection:

Dunne, T., and Wheeler, N. J. (eds.), *Human Rights in Global Politics* (Cambridge: Cambridge University Press, 1999).

Two older, but still useful studies are:

Vincent R. J., *Human Rights and International Relations* (Cambridge: Cambridge University Press, 1986), which links human rights protection to the theory of International Society, and, a good summary of the standard liberal position

Donnelly, J., *International Human Rights* (Boulder, Colo: Westview, 1993).

Smith, K. E. and Light, M. (eds.), *Ethics and Foreign Policy* (Cambridge: Cambridge University Press, forthcoming) sets out some of the problems involved in making human rights central to foreign policy.

Shue, H., *Basic Rights* (Princeton, Princeton University Press, 1983) is a very influential defence of second generation rights as genuine rights.

For third generation rights see:

Crawford, J. (ed.), *The Rights of Peoples* (Oxford: Clarendon Press, 1988).

So-called 'Asian values' are advocated in:

Mahathir Bin Mohamad, Shintaro Ishihara, *The Voice of Asia: Two Leaders Discuss the Coming Century* (Kodansha International Ltd., 1996), and discussed in

Tang, J. H. (ed.), *Human Rights and International Relations in the Asia-Pacific Region* (London: Pinter Press, 1994), and, most helpfully,

Bauer, J., and Bell, D. A. (eds.), *The East Asian Challenge for Human Rights* (Cambridge: Cambridge University Press, 1999).

The argument that development requires the curtailment of human rights is persuasively disposed of in:

Sen, A., *Development as Freedom* (Oxford: Oxford University Press, 1999).

A wider, but very controversial, context for these arguments is provided by:

Huntington, S., *The Clash of Civilisations and the Remaking of World Order* (New York: Simon and Schuster, 1996).

Walzer, M., *Thick and Thin: Moral Argument at Home and Abroad* (Notre Dame, Ind.: University of Notre Dame Press, 1994) makes the case for a 'thin' moral code that can operate cross-culturally.

Shute, S., and Hurley, S. (eds.), *On Human Rights* (New York: Basic Books, 1993) is an excellent collection of papers on the philosophy of human rights, including essays by

John Rawls, Richard Rorty, and Catherine Mackinnon. The latter offers one feminist view; for a good collection of others see:

Peters, J. S., and Wolper, A. (eds.) *Women's Rights, Human Rights: International Feminist Perspectives* (New York: Routledge).

The most useful journals in the field are: *Human Rights Quarterly: a Comparative and International Journal of the Social Sciences, Philosophy and Law* (Baltimore : John Hopkins University Press) and *The International Journal of Human Rights* (London: Frank Cass).

WEB LINKS

Some of the best web sites on human rights are associated with American Law Schools: the Project Diana Online Human Rights Archive at Yale Law School (named for a Yale librarian) is particularly good: **www.diana.law.yale.edu**; as is the University of Minnesota Human Rights Library at: **www1.umn.edu/humanrts**; while the Fletcher School of Diplomacy site offers the texts of treaties in easily downloadable form at: **www.tufts.edu/departments/fletcher/multi/humanRights.html**. The American Association for the Advancement of Science's Directory of Human Rights Resources on the Internet provides useful links to other sites: **www.shr.aaas.org/dhr.htm**. The University of Denver's Institute of International Human Rights at **www.du.edn/humanrights** is a valuable source.

UN sites such as: **www.un.org/rights** and, for the UN Commissioner for Human Rights: **www.unhchr.ch**, are also valuable resources. Amnesty International is served at **www.amnesty.org**. For individual country studies, the US State Department's Annual Individual Country Reports are invaluable: **www.state.gov/www/global/human_rights/hrp_reports_mainhp.html**.

Part Five

Globalization in the future

In this, final, part of the book we want to offer you some reflections on the impact of globalization for world politics in the new millennium. We thought long and hard about whether we, as editors, should write a conclusion to the second edition of this book given that some readers of the first edition wrote to us to suggest that there should be a concluding section to the book. But we eventually decided that it was impossible to do this given all the very different perspectives on globalization found in the preceding chapters. Our intention all along has been to show you that there are very distinct ways of looking at globalization, and writing a conclusion would have meant taking sides on which of these we preferred: we think that this is something that you, the reader, should do! Therefore we asked two scholars to contribute chapters in this section, and, although neither of them is intended as a conclusion, together they outline the main questions concerning the nature of world politics in the current world. Andrew Linklater's chapter examines the forms of political community that are emerging under globalization, whilst Ian Clark's chapter looks at the question of what kind of order exists in the post-cold war period. We have two main aims for this section of the book: **first**, we want to end the book by returning to world politics, rather than international politics, by asking about the relationship between political community and globalization; **second**, we want to summarize the main arguments about the nature of world politics since the cold war, to bring the historical story up to date, so to speak. Each of these chapters problematizes the traditional international politics notion of hermetically sealed states acting within a states-system. Above all, we want to leave you with a series of deep questions about the effect of globalization on both the state and on world politics. Is the form of political community found in the globalized world different to that found before? Is the state still the unit for political community or does globalization make cosmopolitan politics more possible? Is there order in the post-cold war world? Is there much difference between the form of order found in the contemporary period and that found in the cold war? Does globalization help or hinder the creation of a more just, or a more equal, world order? We hope that these two chapters will raise a series of questions that will allow you to come to judgements about the overall impact of globalization on politics in the world.

Part Five

Globalization in the future

29 Globalization and the transformation of political community

Andrew Linklater

READER'S GUIDE

Realist approaches to international relations focus on relations between independent polit-ical communities. They ask how far political communities—nation-states that wish to be sovereign or self-governing—can control the use of force and maintain order between themselves. In the main, those approaches assume that the human race will remain divided into separate political communities long into the future. They are right to emphasize the power of the state, but several challenges to traditional conceptions of political community now exist. Globalization has led many to doubt that the nation-state should be the dominant form of political community in an era of mounting global problems such as environmental devastation. Ethnic revolts occur because many groups believe they are second-class citizens in their states. Against the background of globalization and fragmen-tation, this chapter explains why the nation-state has been the dominant political community in the modern world. It analyses some of the new conceptions of political community and citizenship which have emerged in the most recent phase of globalization.

Introduction: what is a political community?

Many different forms of community exist in the modern world. They include local communities such as neighbourhood groups, national communities such as nation-states, transnational communities such as scientific associations or international non-governmental organizations, and 'virtual communities' which have arisen in conjunction with instant forms of communication in the recent phase of globalization. Each of these communities has its particular kind of solidarity and its distinctive pattern of co-operation.

Politics exist in all such communities because members rarely have identical views about the goals to pursue and the means of realizing them. In modern states, for example, there are differences of opinion about how far governments should be involved in redistributing wealth and how far markets should be left to allocate resources. Like states, religious communities have their politics but they may not be political communities according to the definition used in this chapter. The desire to worship with others is the key to religious community but it is the desire for **self-rule**—the desire to be free from the dominion of others—which turns a religious community, or any other community, into a **political** community (see Ch. 21).

In all forms of community, special ties exist between members who therefore prefer to co-operate with each other rather than with alien outsiders. References to a common past which usually includes the shared experience of suffering in war are frequently made to bind the community together. An example is the memory of the Battle of Britain in the Second World War and memories of wars of national liberation in the former colonies of Africa and Asia. The place of war in histories of the national past is a reminder that individuals have often been asked to die for the sake of their political community. Some religious communities have expected the same of their members. However, the duty to be prepared to die for the larger group has been a central theme in virtually all independent political communities.

Most human beings belong to several communities simultaneously—to national and religious groups, for example, as well as to the nation-state. Some political and religious communities have tried to persuade their members to forsake all other solidarities and loyalties. Totalitarian states such as Nazi Germany and Stalin's Russia demanded this of their citizens but they failed to achieve their aims because their populations valued their membership of communities which were not coterminous with the state. Many citizens of the Soviet Union, for example, attached more importance to their church or ethnic group than to the state. Liberal-democratic forms of political community recognize that citizens want to belong to various communities at any given time. These may be local communities, political parties, or international non-governmental associations such as Greenpeace and Amnesty International. Most of these states also believe they have moral duties to peoples elsewhere. Most believe that they should obey international law and most think they have a duty to promote respect for human rights in other parts of the world.

Nevertheless, war has had a huge impact on the evolution of modern political communities, and states have wanted to make sure that they could count on the loyalty of their citizens when the survival of the state was in question (see Smith ch. 11). States have tried to ensure that national loyalties are the most important political loyalties in the lives of their citizens, but not the only loyalties they have. But the importance of this theme has declined in those political communities which have been spared the ordeal of war in recent decades. The period since the end of the Second World War is the longest period of peace between the great powers since the Treaty of Westphalia in 1648. This is also the period in which globalization, the condition in which social relations are increasingly non-territorial (see Ch. 24), has been as important as the struggle between the great powers in shaping world politics. An intriguing question is what the declining role of great power rivalry and war, and the growing importance of globalization, mean for the future of political community. A crucial question is whether political communities will become less nationalistic because of globalization (see also Halliday ch. 20).

Key points

- The members of a political community are committed to self-rule, to governing themselves.

- Totalitarian states attempted to make the political community absolute but liberal-democratic states recognize that their citizens value their member-

ship of many communities in addition to the nation-state.

- Because they expected to be involved in major wars, states have tried to persuade their citizens to place obligations to the state ahead of duties to other communities, whether local or global.

- Globalization, and the declining significance of military competition between the great powers, raise the question of whether political communities will become less nationalistic.

Box 29.1 **Some political theorists on political community**

'Clearly then, as all associations aim at some good, that association which is most sovereign among them all and embraces all others will aim highest, i.e. at the most sovereign of all goods. This is the association which we call the state, the association which is "political".' (Aristotle)

'What makes a man a citizen (is) the mutual obligation between subject and sovereign.' (Jean Bodin)

'Individuals are so constituted that they could accomplish but little by themselves and could scarcely get on without the assistance of civil society and its laws. But as soon as a sufficient number have united under a government, they are able to provide for most of their needs, and they find the help of other political societies not so necessary to them as the State is itself to individuals.' (Emmerich de Vattel)

'It is through the small fatherland, which is the family, that we attach ourselves to the great fatherland; it is the good father, the good husband, the good son, who makes the good citizen.' (Jean-Jacques Rousseau)

'Do we want peoples to be virtuous? If so, let us begin by making them love their homeland. But how will they come to love it, if their homeland means nothing more to them than it does to foreigners, and if it grants to them

only what it cannot refuse to anyone?' (Jean-Jacques Rousseau)

'should we have been so slow to see that . . . each one of us being in the civil state as regards our fellow citizens, but in the state of nature as regards the rest of the world, we have taken all kinds of precautions against private wars only to kindle national wars a thousand times more terrible? And that in joining a particular group of men, we have really declared ourselves to be enemies of the whole race?' (Jean-Jacques Rousseau)

'War has the higher significance of (preserving) the ethical health of peoples.' (George Wilhelm Friedrich Hegel)

'I am a citizen of the world.' (Diogenes)

'I am not a citizen of the world . . . I am not even aware that there is a world such that one could be a citizen of it. No one has ever offered me citizenship, or described the naturalisation process, or enlisted me in the world's institutional structures, or given me an account of its decision procedures . . . or provided me with a list of the benefits and obligations of citizenship, or shown me the world's calendar and the common celebrations and commemorations of its citizens.' (Michael Walzer)

Nationalism and political community

The **nation-state** has been the dominant form of political community for two centuries but very different kinds of political community existed in other times. The first city-states of Mesopotamia and Ancient Greece, the early empires of Assyria, Persia and Rome, and the more recent Ottoman and Chinese empires were all political communities but they were not like modern nation-states. Ancient Greek city-states, for example, cherished their political independence but they had highly exclusionary conceptions of community compared with modern democratic states. In Greece, the right to participate in political life was restricted to adult males; women, resident aliens, and slaves were denied citizenship and were not full members of the community. Empires have been ruled by military elites and not by the people at large. Indeed, most forms of political community in human history have been hostile to the idea of popular rule. Imperial rulers certainly did not believe that states should represent nations or that each nation should have its own state. These are modern ideas. They have been influential ideas in politics for just over two centuries.

If we look at European states in the seventeenth century we will see that they were not nation-states at that time. They were **territorial states** governed by absolutist monarchs engaged in a struggle for security and survival. It is important to explain how territorial states differed from earlier states, how they were replaced by nation-states, and what these developments mean for the study of globalization.

Territorial states

Unlike earlier states which had a limited ability to direct the lives of their subjects, modern territorial states developed the capacity to regulate (if not control) most aspects of society, including the economy and relations within the family. Writing about this change, Michael Mann (1986: 7–10) argues that modern states have built up very high levels of 'intensive power': that is power that can be projected

deep into society. Unlike early states which had poorly defined frontiers and a limited ability to control groups at the frontier, the modern territorial state has clearly demarcated borders and the ability to impose its will right across its territory. Commenting on this second change, Mann (1986: 7–10) has argued that modern territorial states acquired a high level of 'extensive power', that is power that can be projected right across their territories. The fact that modern territorial states built overseas empires in the Americas and in Asia was a striking demonstration of their capacity to project power beyond their territorial borders. This is very important for understanding the history of globalization. Four centuries ago, when the Spanish and Portuguese colonized Central and South America, states were the main architects of globalization (Held *et al.* 1999).

From territorial states to nation-states

The territorial states which established these empires gradually turned into nation-states. There were two reasons for this: the rise of **capitalism** and **endemic warfare**. Benedict Anderson (1991) has argued that 'print capitalism' made the development of national consciousness possible. Books, pamphlets, and, in more recent times, national newspapers, radio, and television disseminated common national symbols and a shared sense of the past. Print capitalism meant that strangers who would never actually meet could identify with what Anderson had called the 'imagined community' of the nation. Ernest Gellner (1983) argued that industrialization was a principal reason for the emergence of national languages and cultures. The sheer number of commercial exchanges which are a feature of industrial societies simply could not take place unless strangers could communicate in the same language. A crucial point is that the world is not naturally divided into nations. States played a central role in creating national cultures not least by building national education systems which disseminated common values.

Modern territorial states emerged in the context of war and they were largely instruments for waging war. It has been said that in Europe in the sixteenth century these states were small enough to be governed from a central point and large enough to resist external threats (Mattingly 1955; see also Tilly 1992). War was just as important in the movement from territorial states to national states. Warring states wanted to be sure their citizens would fight in wars. They wanted to foster a strong sense of national loyalty. The turning-point in modern history was the **French Revolution** which created the idea of the 'nation in arms' along with national conscription. From the time of the French Revolution, nationalism has been the ideology that has had most impact on the evolution of political community.

It is important to remember then that warfare and industrialization led to the development of modern peoples with a strong sense of national consciousness. By claiming to represent the nation, states increased their ability to mobilize peoples in war and they were able to harness them for the purpose of building new overseas empires in the nineteenth century. At the end of that century, European states greatly expanded their worldwide empires by drawing non-European peoples into global economic, diplomatic, and military relations. Modern nation-states drove the process of integrating the human race. As with empires in the sixteenth century, states were the driving force behind globalization.

Nationalism, which is a European invention, was also exported to the rest of the world. Significantly, **nationalist movements** in the Third World used European ideas to replace alien government with self-rule. One consequence of the success of these movements was that the number of sovereign states more than tripled in the three decades following the Second World War but many of these new political communities failed to become nation-states. Frequently, ethnic rivalries meant that a sense of loyalty to the state did not develop, and in many regions, such as the Indian subcontinent, conflicting peoples dismembered the former colonial territories in the attempt to build their own nation-states. The

---

Box 29.2 **Key concepts**

Community: a human association in which members share common symbols and wish to cooperate to realize common objectives.

Political community: a community that wishes to govern itself and to be free from alien rule.

Territorial state: a state that has power over the population which resides on its territory but which does not seek to represent the nation or the people as a whole.

Nation-state: a political community in which the state claims legitimacy on the grounds that it represents the nation.

Capitalism: a system of production in which human labour and its products are commodities that are bought and sold in the marketplace.

Endemic warfare: the condition in which warfare is a recurrent feature of the relations between states not least because they regard it as inevitable.

Citizenship: the status of having the right to participate in and to be represented in politics.

Group rights: rights which are said to belong to groups such as minority nations or indigenous peoples rather than to individuals.

Quasi-state: a state which has 'negative sovereignty' because other states respect its sovereign independence but lacks 'positive sovereignty' because it does not have the resources or the will to satisfy the needs of its people.

Failed state: a state that has collapsed and cannot provide for its citizens without substantial external support.

Cosmopolitan democracy: a condition in which international organizations, transnational corporations, global markets, and so forth are accountable to the peoples of the world.

Neo-medievalism: a condition in which political power is dispersed between local, national, and supranational institutions none of which commands supreme loyalty.

separation of India and Pakistan, and of East Pakistan (Bangladesh) from West Pakistan, are famous illustrations of this point. Because of decolonization and the subsequent dismemberment of the old colonial territories, the modern state which is not indigenous to non-European societies became the dominant form of political community across the world. The globalization of separate states is one of the most important dimensions of globalization.

Key points

- Most forms of political community in human history have not represented the nation or the people.

- The idea that the state should represent the nation is a European development which has dominated politics for just over two hundred years.

- War and industrialization are the two most important reasons why the nation-state became the dominant form of political community.

- The extraordinary power of modern states—the growth of their 'intensive' and 'extensive' power—made global empires possible.

- States have been principal architects of globalization.

- The global spread of nationalism and the state are important examples of globalization.

Community and citizenship

We have seen that the modern political communities accumulated extraordinary powers, and that the existence of global empires clearly illustrates this point. It may seem odd that these political communities have also been the site for experiments in liberal-democratic forms of governance. But there is no paradox here. Nation-states created national peoples which they mobilized for war. But the peoples so formed resisted the ways in which the growth of state power impinged on their lives. They organized politically to win citizenship rights from the state. Demands for citizenship were first heard within the major European states but they are now a powerful theme in political communities in all parts of the world. These demands along with the spread of the language of universal human rights demonstrate that a globalized political culture has appeared in recent decades (see Ch. 28).

Citizenship and rights

We have to remember that territorial states in early modern Europe were governed by absolute monarchs who regarded the state as their property. In the eighteenth and nineteenth centuries, the commercial and industrial classes challenged monarchical power and sought **political rights** commensurate with their increasing economic power. The rising middle classes sought to destroy royal privileges and promote constitutional government. They demanded legal rights, especially the right to enjoy the **rule of law**, as well as the right to be represented in politics. They succeeded in winning democratic rights but they refused to grant the same rights to subordinate groups such as the working classes. The struggle to extend the suffrage to all adult men and women was a dominant theme in all modern industrial societies during the latter part of the nineteenth and the first part of the twentieth centuries. But it was not the only theme. Demands for welfare rights quickly followed.

The fundamental point here is that the labour movement and political parties on the Left argued that inequalities of power and wealth had increased under capitalism, the result being that the poor did not enjoy full membership of the political community. The argument was that legal and political rights do not mean very much unless individuals have the power to exercise them. (The claim that everyone is free to dine in the Ritz but not everyone can actually dine there captures the crucial point.)

Pressures therefore mounted to deepen the meaning of citizenship by adding social or **welfare rights** to the legal and political rights which had been won earlier. Early in the twentieth century many Western states introduced national health services, welfare provision for the poor, and more open educational systems as a result of these struggles for social justice and more inclusive political communities.

The most influential account of the evolution of citizenship, at least in the British context, is to be found in the writings of **T. H. Marshall** although later in this chapter we shall see that the struggle to deepen the meaning of citizenship has unfolded in ways that Marshall could not have anticipated. However, the key point to stress at this stage is that writers such as Marshall believed that political communities would enjoy greater legitimacy if they became more inclusive, and if their citizens came to enjoy the full range of legal, political, and social rights. There is no doubt that many governments in the industrialized West supported this package of citizenship rights in order to defuse social conflicts that threatened the survival of political community. Although it may seem extraordinary now, many writers in the 1950s and 1960s believed that 'the end of ideology' had arrived in societies such as the United States. What they meant was that Western liberal democracies had solved—or would shortly solve—the social conflicts which had threatened order and stability (see Ch. 8).

Many also argued that the new states in the Third World—Europe's former colonies in other words—would follow the same pattern of social and political development. Modernization theorists, as they were called, spoke about the modernization or development of traditional, non-Western societies (see Ch. 26). They thought that new states would emulate the states of Europe. They would repeat the process of nation-building which had started in the West. They would also undergo democratization, it was thought, and imitate the Western course of economic development.

The end of ideology thesis and modernization theory were seriously flawed. Civil rights movements, the student revolt, the conflict over the Vietnam war, feminism, and environmental movements revealed that the end of ideology thesis was

> ### Box 29.3 T. H. Marshall's analysis of citizenship in Britain
>
> T. H. Marshall identified three stages in the development of citizenship rights in Britain. In the eighteenth century the struggle for citizenship revolved around the quest for legal rights, specifically around the demand for the rule of law. In the nineteenth century, the emphasis shifted to political rights—to the right not only to be governed by law but to be represented in legislatures which make the law. In the twentieth century, the emphasis shifted again to social or welfare rights. The critical point here was that massive inequalities of wealth meant that the poor were not full members of the community. Significant transfers of wealth and more equal educational opportunities were essential if the poor were to be equal members of the political community.

mistaken. Ethnic conflict in many of the new states, the rise of military government as opposed to democratization, and economic stagnation rather than industrial development demonstrated that modernization theorists misunderstood the special forces affecting the types of political community that were emerging in the Third World. What was striking about modernization theory, though, was its belief that all societies were heading in the same direction, that all were following the Western path of economic and political development. Such views made an interesting claim about globalization which has resurfaced since the end of the bipolar world. It is that the liberal-democratic capitalist societies of the West will spread to most parts of the globe, just as nationalism and the idea of the modern state had spread to every part of the world in an earlier historical period.

Key points

- Demands for citizenship rights emerged in response to the growing power of the modern state.

- The demand to be treated as a citizen initially

centred on the enjoyment of legal and political rights but citizenship was redefined early in the twentieth century to include social or welfare rights.

- The stability of modern forms of political community has owed a great deal to the fact that citizens won these rights.

- Modernization theory argued that Western liberal-democracy had solved the social conflicts which had emerged in industrial societies.

- Modernization theory also assumed that non-Western societies would follow the Western path of economic and political development. Its exponents envisaged the globalization of Western forms of community and citizenship.

The changing nature of political community

One of the strange paradoxes of the modern world is that the globalization of economic and political life has increased dramatically in recent years with the result that the global influence of Western capitalist democracies has never been greater, and yet the national fragmentation of political communities has not declined. These two processes, **globalization** and **fragmentation**, are the two greatest influences on political communities at the present time (see also Ch. 20).

As we saw earlier, the national fragmentation of societies has always been especially pronounced in many regions of the Third World. The division of India and Pakistan in 1947, the civil war in Nigeria in the late 1960s, and the creation of the separate state of Bangladesh in 1970 were part of a much larger trend that included civil war in Ethiopia and the subsequent establishment of the new state of Eritrea in 1993. New approaches to precarious Third World states appeared in the early 1990s. The concept of the **quasi-state** was used to describe states which other states regarded as sovereign, states that were unable to satisfy the material needs of their peoples or which violated human rights (Jackson 1990). The notion of the **failed state** was used to describe states which could no longer govern their own societies and which desperately required significant international support (Helman and Ratner 1990).

New questions have been raised about whether liberal democratic societies have moral responsibilities to the peoples of failed states which include the right to intervene to try to prevent violations of human rights (see Ch. 22). But in an extraordinary and largely unforeseen development, the failed state is no longer a problem which is solely confined to the Third World. The disintegration of the former Yugoslavia is a striking example of a failed state in what was one of the most liberal and affluent socialist societies in Eastern Europe.

In this case, violent nationalism destroyed a multicultural political community which seemed to have found a way of maintaining harmony between different national groups. There is however a more general point to make which is illustrated by events in political communities such as Canada, Belgium, Italy, and the United Kingdom. It is that demands for greater respect for national or ethnic differences are a feature of virtually all of the most viable political communities. Now these are not unrelated developments unfolding within separate political communities. Rather they are part of a worldwide movement in which minority nations and indigenous peoples seek respect for their languages and cultures within the existing political communities. Although nationalist reactions to the influx of Western values are widespread in India and throughout the Muslim world, many of these demands for respect for cultural difference are not a challenge to globalization (see Ch. 21). They are in fact a manifestation of globalization, an expression of a globalizing political culture which attaches great value to national and cultural differences between peoples (see Ch. 28).

The politics of cultural difference

Another way of expressing the points made in the last paragraph is to suggest that traditional ideas about citizenship are being reconsidered across the world in the current phase of globalization. To understand exactly what is changing we need to return to the relationship between war and the evolution of modern political communities. States sought to create national cultures in modern Europe. More often than not what this meant was that the language and customs of a dominant culture were imposed on subordinate groups. Success in war went to states which succeeded in creating an overarching idea of the nation with its sense of national history and its national symbols such as flags, anthems, and so forth. In the case of Britain, the sense of Scottish or Welsh identity survived alongside efforts to create a wider British identity.

The desire to preserve local cultures, and the longing for some degree of political autonomy if not outright sovereign independence, persisted although these preferences rarely made much headway where political communities were repeatedly at war. But the 'long peace' between the great powers has provided new opportunities for movements that assert their national rights. Core industrial states no longer have the same need to mobilize their citizens for war and they are less able to wield national symbols effectively given that national cultures are more porous because of globalization. This may fundamentally alter the nature of political communities in the modern world.

Group rights

Claims for **group rights** exist in almost political communities across the modern world and they have produced a global shift in attitudes towards citizenship (Young 1990). The reality is that the earlier struggle for legal, political, and social rights usually assumed there were no significant cultural differences between citizens. Feminists have argued that the struggle for citizenship was gender-blind since no account was taken of the special needs of women (see Ch. 27). Consequently, exponents of new conceptions of citizenship have maintained that the differences between citizens—differences of culture and also gender—must be reflected in public policy. Minority nations throughout the world and the indigenous peoples in societies such as Australia, Canada, and New Zealand have spearheaded the claim that their group rights should be respected by the wider polity, most importantly by granting them significant self-government. These are not only major political actors in their respective societies; they participate in major international conferences and in transnational alliances which are struggling to advance the new global political culture that supports group rights.

The mass movement of peoples is one consequence of globalization that feeds into this process. Here too the argument is that traditional conceptions of citizenship have to be adapted to fit the increasingly multicultural nature of modern societies (see Ch. 21). In addition, no discussion of changing attitudes towards political community and national citizenship would be complete without noting how feminism has challenged dominant conceptions of the nation which have been shaped by the male experience of war (see Chs. 11 and 27). It is true that nationalist and racial responses to these

---

Box 29.4 Kymlicka on liberalism and group rights

Kymlicka (1989) maintains that in a liberal-democratic society the individual has the right to free movement, to own private property and to vote in elections. Traditional liberal thought does not recognize group rights, especially if these are in conflict with the fundamental rights of individuals. Kymlicka argues that indigenous cultures in societies such as Canada will not survive unless individual rights are curtailed. Indigenous cultures need to have a degree of self-government and for that to work limits have to be placed on the rights of members of the dominant culture. If members of the dominant culture have the right to purchase property in territories managed by individual peoples and the right to vote in their municipal elections then the indigenous culture will simply be overwhelmed. Respect for the rights of indigenous peoples entails the curtailment of certain individual rights which lie at the heart of the liberal-democratic polity.

challenges to traditional notions of political community do not seem likely to disappear. The same is true of patriarchal ideas and practices. Nevertheless, serious dissatisfaction with traditional forms of community is an important thread running though a global political culture.

Cosmopolitan democracy and transnational citizenship

One of the most intriguing dimensions of political communities is how they deal with differences of social class, gender, sexual identity, religion, race, and ethnicity; and one of the most interesting aspects of globalization is how subordinate groups have rejected claims that these differences justify the unequal distribution of rights and entitlements (see Ch. 1). Resistance to doctrines which claim that one race or nation has the right to dominate another, or that men are naturally entitled to more rights than women, is pronounced in most parts of the world.

Rethinking relations between citizens and aliens

Just as interesting is the matter of how political communities understand differences between citizens and aliens. There is also the question of whether globalization is changing one of the fundamental assumptions of modern political communities, namely that citizens have special duties to each other and fewer responsibilities to the rest of the human race. As already noted, the continuing strength of nationalist convictions in most regions of the world cannot be doubted. Indeed, globalization and the intrusion of alien values often trigger nationalist responses. But globalization unleashes other tendencies which question the idea that political communities should promote the interests of their citizens above all else. As an example, citizens in the more affluent societies are often disturbed by visual images of human suffering caused by state terror, civil conflict, natural disaster, and famine. Public support for humanitarian assistance for the vulnerable in Somalia and Kosovo followed images of suffering disseminated by the global media (although it is still true that national populations do not wish to endanger the lives of co-nationals for the sake of alien outsiders (see Ch. 22). Various global problems which states cannot hope to solve on their own—the problems of atmospheric pollution and global warming are familiar examples—have encouraged a rapid increase in the number of international non-governmental organizations concerned with the fate of the world as a whole. Globalization has encouraged the development of solidarities that cut across national borders and unite the citizens of different political communities. Many think that global civil society reveals the dawning of a new era of human co-operation, although sceptics point to the continuing appeal of nationalism and to the tenacity of the sovereign state (see Ch. 24).

Cosmopolitan democracy

There is no doubt though that globalization has led to a renewed interest in alternative forms of political community. **Cosmopolitan** approaches to political community are enjoying a renaissance at the present time. The idea of world citizenship is a concept that international non-governmental organizations use to support the development of a stronger sense of responsibility for the global environment and for the whole human species. Proponents of **cosmopolitan democracy** have argued that national democracies have little control over global markets and a limited ability to influence decisions taken by transnational corporations which affect currency values, levels of employment and so forth (see Ch. 24 and Held 1995). They maintain that democracy may not survive in any meaningful form if it remains limited to the nation-state. The task is to democratize international organizations such as the World Trade Organization and to make sure that transnational corporations are held accountable for decisions that harm vulnerable individuals and groups (see Ch. 26). One response to globalization then is to argue for new forms of **cosmopolitan political community** in which the members of different societies come together as **cosmopolitan citizens** to influence decisions that affect the whole world. The critics argue that notions of cosmopolitan democracy are fanciful. They maintain that democracy is unlikely to flourish at the global level where there is no counterpart to the nation, no political community with which individuals identify, and no community for

Box 29.5 Held on cosmopolitan democracy

David Held (1995) has developed a powerful argument in favour of cosmopolitan democracy. Some of the main steps in his argument are these:

'Territorial boundaries demarcate the basis on which individuals are included in and excluded from participation in decisions affecting their lives (however limited the participation might be), but the outcomes of these decisions often "stretch" beyond national frontiers.' (Held 1995: 18)

'both routine and extraordinary decisions taken by representatives of nations and nation-states profoundly affect citizens of other nation-states—who in all probability have had no opportunity to signal consent or lack of it—but . . . the international order is structured by agencies and forces over which citizens have minimum, if any, control, and in regard to which they have little basis to signal their (disagreement).' (Held 1995: 139)

'the problem for defenders and critics alike of modern democratic systems is that regional and global interconnectedness contests the traditional national resolutions of the key questions of democratic theory and practice. The very process of governance can escape the reach of the nation-state. National communities by no means exclusively make and determine decisions and policies for themselves, and governments by no means determine what is appropriate exclusively for their own citizens . . . The idea of a community which rightly governs itself and determines its own future—an idea at the very heart of the democratic polity itself—is, accordingly, deeply problematic.' (Held 1995: 16–17)

'Democratic political theory has to be rethought, and along with it the actual underlying principles and practices of democratic politics.' (Held 1995: x)

'A commitment to the principle of autonomy entails a duty to work towards the establishment of an international community of democratic states and societies committed to upholding democratic public law both within and across their boundaries: a cosmopolitan democratic community.' (Held 1995: 229)

Held recommends a number of short-term changes to promote the cosmopolitan ideal. They are:

1. Reform of the UN Security Council (to give developing countries a significant voice and effective decision-making capacity)

2. Creation of a UN Second Chamber (following an international constitutional convention)

3. Enhanced political regionalization (EU and beyond) and the use of transnational referenda.

4. Compulsory jurisdiction before the International Court. Creation of a new, international Human Rights Court.

5. Foundation of a new co-ordinating economic agency at regional and global levels

6. Establishment of an effective, accountable, international military force.

(Adapted from Held 1995: 279)

---

which they will make significant sacrifices (Miller 1999).

Neo-medievalist approaches

Neo-medievalism is a second and related vision of new forms of political community to attract attention in recent years. Neo-medievalism refers to an ideal political order in which individuals are governed by a number of overlapping authorities. This is how political community was organized in Europe in the Middle Ages prior to the rise of the modern states. The forces of globalization and fragmentation have renewed interest in the neo-medieval vision of

world order (Linklater 1998; Falk 2000). According to this model of world order, the state would transfer some powers to international institutions which would deal with global problems, and it would transfer other powers to the domestic regions where the sense of a distinctive cultural identity remains strong (see also Ch. 24). National governments would retain many powers in this vision of world order and citizens would remain loyal to their states, but the state would be only one tier of government, and loyalty to the state would coexist with loyalties to sub-state and transnational political authorities. None of these authorities would reign supreme; none of these

Box 29.6 Visions of new forms of community and citizenship

'The bourgeoisie has through its exploitation of the world-market given a cosmopolitan character to production and consumption in every country . . . All old-fashioned national industries have been destroyed or are daily being destroyed . . . In place of the old wants, satisfied by the productions of the country, we find new wants, requiring for their satisfaction the products of different lands and climes. In place of the old local and national seclusion and self-sufficiency, we have intercourse in every direction, universal interdependence of nations . . . The bourgeoisie, by the rapid improvement of all instruments of production, by the immensely facilitated means of communication, draws all, even the most barbarian nations, into civilisation. It compels all nations, on pain of extinction, to adopt the bourgeois mode of production . . . i.e. to become bourgeois themselves. In one word, it creates a world after its own image.' (Karl Marx)

'We have a system of national citizenship in a social context which requires a new theory of internationalism and universalistic citizenship.' (Bryan Turner)

'Every person holding the nationality of a Member State shall be a citizen of the Union.' (The Maastricht Treaty)

It is 'time to go higher in our search for citizenship, but also lower and wider. Higher to the world, lower to the locality . . . The citizen has been too puffed and too compressed.' (Andrew Wright)

'We may envisage a situation in which, say, a Scottish authority in Edinburgh, a British authority in London, and a European authority in Brussels were all actors in world politics and all enjoyed representations in world political organisations, together with rights and duties of various kinds in world law, but in which none of them claimed sovereignty or supremacy over the others, and a person living in Glasgow had no exclusive or overriding loyalty to any one of them. Such an outcome would take us truly "beyond the sovereign state" and is by no means implausible . . . '. (Hedley Bull)

'The preference of Western powers, especially the United States, for air strikes, despite the physical and psychological damage caused even with highly accurate munitions, arises from (the) privileging of nationals or Westerners. This type of national or statist thinking has not yet come to terms with the concept of a common human community . . . Whereas the soldier, as the traditional bearer of arms, had to be prepared to die for his country, the international soldier/policeman (would risk) his or her life for humanity.' (Mary Kaldor)

'Even if we still have a long way to go before fully achieving it, the cosmopolitan condition is no longer merely a mirage. State citizenship and world citizenship form a continuum whose contours, at least, are already becoming visible.' (Jurgen Habermas)

loyalties would be absolute. Whether this normative vision will ever appeal to all the peoples of the world is a moot point. Its best prospects may lie in those parts of Europe (such as the societies that belong to the European Union) in which we are witnessing the weakening of national sovereignty (see Ch. 23).

Key points

- Globalization and fragmentation are two phenomena which challenge traditional conceptions of political community and national citizenship.

- Ethnic fragmentation is one reason for the failed state in Europe as well as the Third World, but demands for the recognition of cultural differences exist in all political communities.

- Globalization theorists have argued for cosmopolitan democracy on the grounds that national democracies are less able to influence global forces which affect them.

- Globalization and fragmentation have renewed interest in neo-medieval visions of political community.

The dangers of new forms of political community?

In recent years, globalization and fragmentation have weakened or destroyed centralized nation-states as different as Indonesia, Ethiopia, Italy, the USSR, and Canada. Perhaps new forms of political community which are more respectful of cultural differences and more cosmopolitan than their predecessors will emerge in consequence. However, the disintegration of the former Yugoslavia reveals how impossible it is to generalize about such matters. Violent nationalism may triumph with the sudden collapse or steady erosion of the state.

As far as relations between the great powers are concerned, the apex of violent nationalism was reached in the first half of the twentieth century (see Ch. 3). In 1914 European governments led their populations into the most destructive war which had been fought in human history. Two decades later, a more destructive war took place following the rise of totalitarianism and nationalism in Europe. The desire not to return to major war was the main reason for the development of European international institutions such as the European Community in the aftermath of the Second World War (see Ch. 23). War no longer seems likely to engulf the continent and it is improbable that it will be waged between the core industrial powers in the foreseeable future. This may be a revolution in world politics although the realist approach to international relations insists that it is highly unlikely that peace between the great powers will survive indefinitely. It is impossible to predict whether the kind of nationalism which characterized international politics in the first half of the nineteenth century will return. But there is no doubt that globalization and fragmentation have reduced—at least for now—the modern state's willingness and capacity to wage the kinds of war which typified the last century (see Ch. 12).

Beyond realism and neo-realism

Recently, there have been several attempts to explain how globalization and fragmentation are transforming political communities, and there have been several efforts to develop visions of alternative forms of community and citizenship (Brown 1992; Linklater 1998). These are important developments in a discipline that has been powerfully influenced by realism and neo-realism. The latter focus on continuities rather than change in world politics. They have been concerned with patterns of international interaction which have endured across centuries (war, the balance of power, the rise and fall of the great powers, and so forth). The respects in which political communities may be changing or should change in future has not been one of their priorities. Recent approaches to international relations have been especially interested in how globalization and fragmentation may lead to new forms of political community. Three broad approaches deserve consideration: **cosmopolitanism**, **communitarianism**, and **post-modernism** (see Ch. 11).

Cosmopolitanism

Globalization may seem to create new opportunities for promoting the cosmopolitan idea that all human beings are equal. Cosmopolitans argue that solutions to global problems (such as environmental destruction) should promote the welfare of the species as a whole. Writers on the international law of war argue that the international community should defend the victims of war crimes wherever they may live. From this vantage-point, the establishment of an International Criminal Court is to be welcomed as an important step in promoting what Mary Kaldor (1999: 124 ff.) has called 'cosmopolitan law enforcement'. Many cosmopolitans applaud a recent House of Lords' ruling that leaders who are guilty of human rights violations should not be protected by the principle of sovereign immunity. (This ruling occurred following the legal claim that Pinochet should be extradited to Spain to be tried for human rights violations in Chile.) Following NATO's military action against Serbia in 1999, some cosmopolitans referred to the dawning of a new age of humanitarian war (Beck 1998). Opponents of NATO's action, and they included many equally good claims to be cosmopolitan, stressed the dangers associated with military action to defend human rights (see Ch. 22). Their concern is that the great powers will use cosmopolitanism to breach national sovereignty only when it is in their interests to do so.

Post-modernism

This takes us to post-modernism, and specifically to Foucault's claim that all forms of knowledge—including those that are designed to contribute to human freedom—are potentially dangerous. His point was that all forms of knowledge may lay the foundations for new forms of power and domination (see Ch. 11). This a telling criticism of Marxism which set out to liberate the human race from domination but became an instrument of totalitarian domination (see Ch. 10). Richard Ashley and R. B. J. Walker (1990) have argued that all political perspectives that claim to have uncovered universal truths contain this danger. Their point is that distinctions between those who possess the truth and those who live in ignorance are intrinsic to such perspectives, and therein lies the danger of domination. So in the case of cosmopolitanism, the distinction between those who think globally and those who remain wedded to particular communities may lead to a project of global domination. This argument resonates with claims that the universal human rights culture and support for humanitarian intervention may simply underpin Western power over the rest of the world. Similar themes are present in recent discussions about the dangers inherent in efforts to create a new international community in Europe. Jacques Derrida (1992) has argued that a Europe which weakens the nation-state and reduces its extraordinary powers is desirable. But movement in this direction is not risk-free. It is perfectly possible that efforts to promote close co-operation within Europe will engender dangerous distinctions between Europe and the rest of the world, and lead to stark contrasts between Europe and the Islamic world (see Ch. 21). The danger is that Europe might close in on itself, not least by creating tighter restrictions on access for migrants and refugees.

Communitarianism

The claim that cosmopolitans underestimate the role that separate communities play in the lives of human beings is a central theme in communitarianism. Communitarians such as Michael Walzer (1995a) maintain that individuals attach great importance to their membership of particular communities, and it is as members of particular communities that they come to have their fundamental rights and duties. This is not to deny that societies have obligations to one another; rather it is to argue that most human beings are not as moved by notions of humanity as they are by loyalties to their community. On this view, it is highly improbable that individuals will exchange their membership of particular societies and their special identities for membership of a cosmopolitan world order; and on this view it is a mistake to think that globalization will weaken particular communities so that human beings come to identify with humanity as a whole. To act on that assumption would be to endanger the most viable political communities in the modern world.

Walzer's critique of the idea of world citizenship is a good example of the communitarian critique of cosmopolitanism (Walzer 1994a). He argues that citizenship refers to a web of rights and duties (including the crucial right to take part in politics) which are only found within nation-states where a strong sense of community exists. It is highly unlikely in Walzer's view that any meaningful sense of citizenship which includes rights of involvement in politics and a willingness to make personal sacrifices for the good of the wider society will develop outside the nation-state. For this reason, the communitarian would argue, citizens of the member states of the European Union may be European citizens according to the Maastricht Treaty but this is a pale imitation of the forms of citizenship which have developed within separate political communities.

For most of the peoples of Europe and elsewhere, the communitarian would argue, citizenship is tied up with membership of national political communities.

This is a powerful line of argument but it is criticized by many post-modern thinkers and feminist writers. They have argued that communitarians often fail to recognize that the dominant conceptions of community in any place do not represent sections of the population. Members of minority nations and indigenous peoples fall into this category, and feminists have argued that large numbers of women belong to this category too (see Ch. 27). The main lesson to draw from this is that all communities include some human beings only to exclude others. This is why post-modern writers have been especially critical of the way in which the language of community can be used to marginalize, and even to oppress, subordinate groups (Ashley and Walker 1990). They argue that such dangers will remain whether peoples retain their attachments to sovereign states or try to build new forms of political community in response to globalization and fragmentation.

Key points

- The apex of nationalism in relations between the great powers occurred in the first half of the twentieth century.

- Nationalism remains a powerful force in the modern world but globalization and fragmentation encourage discussions about alternative forms of political community.

- Cosmopolitan approaches which envisage an international system in which all individuals are respected as equal have flourished in the contemporary phase of globalization.

- Communitarians argue that most peoples attach special importance to their membership of specific communities. Different peoples are unlikely to shift their loyalty to any political community other than the nation-state.

- Post-modern writers argue that all forms of community, whether local, national or international, are potentially dangerous because they can lead to the exclusion or domination of significant sections of society.

Conclusion

The study of international politics has been mainly concerned with understanding the relations between independent political communities and particularly relations between the great powers. Realists and neo-realists argue that all states are forced to compete for security and survival in the context of anarchy. They contend that separate states look to their own interests first and foremost. They maintain that the sense of community which exists between the citizens of particular states does not exist within the international political system at large. They further suggest that the level of co-operation is generally far greater within separate states than within the wider international system. Realists and neo-realists do not expect these circumstances to change while the anarchic condition survives.

There is no evidence to suggest that the inter-

national state-system is about to be replaced by some other form of world political organization. But there is clear evidence that globalization and fragmentation are transforming political communities across the world. It has always been important to examine the nature of political communities to understand international politics in any particular era, but arguably this is even more true today as globalization and fragmentation transform political communities. Under these conditions, the analysis of world politics cannot focus on relations between political communities without also looking at how these communities are being transformed by globalization and fragmentation.

The most recent phase in the development of globalization reopens old questions about the extent to which the forms of co-operation that one finds in stable political communities can develop in the relations between states. Optimists and pessimists give different answers to these questions. The optimist may choose to stress the existence of a global civil society which shows that transnational co-operation involving the members of different political communities is flourishing in this phase of globalization (see Ch. 24). The pessimist may choose to stress that it is the architects of a 'global business civilisation' with most to benefit from globalization that are often the strongest exponents of cosmopolitanism. In this context it is worth noting that inequalities between rich and poor which are often gendered in nature have increased with the expansion of the global economy (see Ch. 27; Ch. 26). There are reasons to doubt that privileged groups in the world economy will co-operate to protect the global poor, not least because the sense of obligation to the poorer members of national political communities declined in many Western industrial societies over the last two decades. Whether these trends will continue unchecked, and whether transnational co-operation will be strong enough to resist them, may turn out to be the most important questions of all to ask about the future of political community.

QUESTIONS

1   What is community, and what makes a community a political community?

2   Why has the modern state been the dominant form of political community?

3   What is the relationship between nationalism and political community?

4   What is the relationship between citizenship and political community?

5   What is the relationship between war and political community?

6   How are globalization and fragmentation affecting political community?

7   Is the idea of world citizenship a meaningful concept? Does it make sense to think of citizenship apart from the modern state?

8   What are the arguments for and against cosmopolitan democracy?

9   Do you think that separate political communities should use military force to prevent human rights violations in other countries?

10   What are the main differences between the cosmopolitan, communitarian, and post-modern approaches to political community?

GUIDE TO FURTHER READING

The main themes discussed in this chapter are considered in more detail in Linklater, A., *The Transformation of Political Community: Ethical Foundations of the Post-Westphalian Era* (Cambridge: Polity Press, 1998). For a more detailed account of the tension between communitarian and cosmopolitan approaches to political community, see Brown, C. J., *International Relations Theory: New Normative Approaches* (London: Harvester, 1992) and Cochran, M., *Normative Theory and International Relations* (Cambridge: Cambridge University Press, 1999). The latter volume also deals with post-modern thinking. Richard Devetak's essay on post-modernism in Burchill S., *et al.* (eds.), *Theories of International Relations* (London: Macmillan, 2001) is a good introduction to this subject. For a feminist critique of communitarianism, see Frazer E., and

Lacey, N., *The Politics of Community: A Feminist Critique of the Liberal-Communitarian Debate* (Hemel Hempstead: Harvester, 1993).

A vast literature exists on the rise of the modern European state. Tilly, C., *Coercion, Capital and European States: AD 990–1992* (Oxford: Blackwell, 1992) is an outstanding study of the rise of the modern state which also deals with the fate of the nation-state in Europe's former colonial territories. Giddens, A., *The Nation-State and Violence* (Cambridge: Polity Press, 1995) is also valuable. Mann, M., *Sources of Social Power*, vol. 1: *A History of Power from the Beginning to AD 1760* and vol. 2: *The Rise of Classes and Nation-States, 1760–1914* (Cambridge: Cambridge University Press, 1986 and 1994) contains a wealth of information about city-states and ancient empires as well as the modern state. In the first volume Mann sets out his conceptual framework which is indispensable for the historical analysis of political communities.

The literature on nationalism is vast. Anderson, B., *Imagined Communities: Reflections on the Origin and Spread of Nationalism* (London: Verso, 1983) is essential reading. The works by Giddens and Mann mentioned earlier contain useful sections on nationalism. Although it was published more than fifty years ago, E. H. Carr's slim volume, *Nationalism and After* (London: Macmillan, 1945) is a magisterial account of the development of the modern state and nationalism. See also Gellner, E., *Nations and Nationalism* (Oxford: Basil Blackwell, 1983). Marshall, T. H., *Class, Citizenship and Social Development* (Westport Conn.: Greenwood Press, 1973) contains the author's influential approach to the development of legal, political, and social rights. Kymlicka, W., *Liberalism, Community and Culture* (Oxford: Oxford University Press, 1989) is a pathbreaking study of the place of indigenous peoples and group rights in liberal-democratic societies.

Studies of possible alternatives to the nation-state are increasing in number. Tilly, C., 'The Futures of European States', *Social Research* (59) 1992, 705–17 is an inspiring short essay on possible developments in Europe. Strange, S., *The Retreat of the State: The Diffusion of Power in the World Economy* (Cambridge: Cambridge University Press, 1996) is an important statement from a political economy standpoint. Held, D., *Democracy and the Global Order: From the Modern State to Global Governance* (Cambridge: Polity Press, 1995) is the principal statement of cosmopolitan democracy. D. Held *et al.*, *Global Transformations: Politics, Economics and Culture* (Cambridge: Polity Press, 1999) is an important work on the varieties of, and consequences of, globalization. For a recent study of the arguments for and against the idea of world citizenship, see Hutchings K., and R. Danreuther (eds.), *Cosmopolitan Citizenship* (London: Macmillan, 1999).

WEB LINKS

www.arts.deakin.edu.au/IR/community   This website which has been specially created for this chapter contains some recent papers on political community, module handouts, information about further reading and information about other relevant websites.

30 Globalization and the post-cold war order

Ian Clark

READER'S GUIDE

This chapter explores the nature of the order that is developing in the period since the end of the cold war. It asks whether, and in which respects, that order is distinctive. It also asks whether globalization is the defining feature that sets it apart from earlier patterns of order. After distinguishing between various types of order—international, world, and global—the chapter sketches out the main ingredients of the contemporary order. These extend well beyond the traditional domain of international military security. The argument then addresses the forces that helped to bring the cold war to an end and asks if these remain as a point of continuity between the old and the new. The trend towards globalization is considered as one of these. It is accepted that globalization both contributed to the demise of the cold war and is a feature of the contemporary order. The chapter ends by suggesting that globalization is a condition that reflects changes in states, not just between them, and that what is distinctive about the present order is the continuation of a system of international order, the constituent units of which are globalized states.

Introduction

This chapter is concerned with two key questions. The first is whether or not there is now a discernible and distinctive pattern of **order** in the post-cold war world and, if so, what are its principal elements. The second is whether or not this order should be defined in terms of globalization.

A decade into the post-cold war era, it is timely to address the question whether there is, in fact, such a thing as a newly emergent order. Is there a pattern of international politics sufficiently distinctive to mark it off from that in existence prior to the end of the cold war? Implicit in this is the need to devise a description of the present period that tells us something substantive about how it functions. This goes beyond the indeterminate chronological label 'post-cold war' since that informs us merely that it followed on where the cold war left off. To understand our present period, we need to know more than that it was the phase that came after the cold war.

The second question directs attention to whether contemporary order can be captured by the imagery of globalization. There is, of course, intense debate as to the precise meaning, novelty and extent of globalization. But that some kind of transformation is underway is scarcely in doubt, even if commentators are unable to agree on the significance which should be attached to it, or on whether the changes are to be welcomed or not. But if some degree of globalization is occurring, is this simply one aspect amongst many others of the post-cold war order? Or is it so central to understanding the nature of the present order that we can define the order in terms of it? Is the contemporary order above all a globalized order and what might this mean in practice?

Serious study of the post-cold war order remains literally, and for obvious reasons, in its infancy. We are still too immersed in living it to have any real sense of perspective; because we do not know how it culminates (c.f. what we call 'the inter-war period'), it is not an 'enclosed' period with a determinate ending and we consequently find difficulty in assigning specific characteristics to it. While there have been studies aplenty of individual aspects of this present order (ethnicity, identity, peacekeeping, humanitarian intervention, globalization, regionalism, economic transition, democratization, integration, financial instability, etc.), we still lack the makings of a grand evaluation of its essential nature.

In analysing the contemporary order, we need to be mindful of how much greater are the demands upon, and the expectations about, the international order today than previously. In earlier periods, the interest in the **international order** was largely 'negative', and lay in ensuring that no threats were presented by it. Given present high levels of integration and interdependence, the interest is now 'positive' as well, as the international order is a much greater source and provider than hitherto of a range of social goods. The international order can deliver information, economic resources, human rights, intervention, access to global social movements and international non-governmental organizations, and permits the sharing of an abundance of cultural artefacts. Many of these 'goods' may be regarded as unwelcome intrusions, but they may also be desired by and useful to governments, and/or peoples, around the world.

Key points

- It is difficult to make out the characteristics of the contemporary order.

- Because we are in the middle of it, it is hard to get any sense of historical perspective.

- Our understanding of, say, the inter-war period is coloured by how it ended but we do not yet know how our present period will 'end'.

- We can see that international and transnational connections are a very important element of contemporary order because of currently high levels of interdependence.

Box 30.1 Elements of discontinuity and continuity between cold war and post-cold war orders

Cold war	Post-cold war
Discontinuity	
Soviet power in E. Europe	*dissolution of Soviet Union*
bipolar competition	*unipolar peacemaking*
rival ideologies	*supremacy of liberal capitalism*
global security integration	*greater regional autonomy*
military security as high politics	*national identity as high politics*

Continuity
Some security structures, e.g. NATO
economic globalization
human rights
reaction against secular state
multiple identities
environmental agendas
poverty in South

A typology of order

At the present moment, thinking about order is being pulled in a number of different directions. At the one end of the spectrum, it continues to be largely state-centred and to consider traditional models of order such as the structure of the balance of power, the polarity of the international system, and the current forms of collective security. At the other end is a widening agenda of order that encompasses the relationship between economic and political dimensions, new thinking about security, debates about the consequences of globalization, the role of human rights, the impact of environmentalism, and strategies for human emancipation. Clearly, in these various analyses, a number of differing, and potentially competing, conceptions of order are at work.

This was nicely illustrated in the early 1990s when then US President George Bush spoke about his vision of a New World Order. In an address to Congress on 11 September 1990, Bush outlined

A new era—freer from the threat of terror, stronger in pursuit of justice and more secure in quest for peace, an era in which

nations of the world . . . can prosper—a world where rule of law supplants the rule of the jungle, a world in which nations recognize the shared responsibility for freedom and justice, a world where the strong respect the rights of the weak.

Individually, these goals might all be highly desirable but the troublesome question is whether they all fit together into a consistent whole and, where some elements are in tension, what priority is to be assigned amongst them. Underlying the elements of this vision, we can distinguish competing conceptions of order. Some derive from traditional state-centric models and emphasize stability and peace amongst states. Others take the individual human being as the unit of account and construct order in terms of rights, justice, and prosperity.

This draws our attention to a number of semantic distinctions important to any assessment of the contemporary order. Are we to judge the degree and effectiveness of order solely as an aspect of the inter-state system and thus speak of international order? Or are we to widen the discussion and consider order in terms of its impact on individual human lives and

Box 30.2 **Key concepts (1)**

collectivization of security: the tendency for security to be organized on a multilateral basis, but without the institutional formality of a fully fledged collective security system.

concert: the directorial role played by a number of great powers, based on norms of mutual consent.

global governance: the loose framework of global regulation, both institutional and normative, that constrains conduct. It has many elements: international organizations and law; transnational organizations and frameworks; elements of global civil society; and shared normative principles.

globalized state: the notion of a particular kind of state that helps sustain globalization, as well as responding to its pressures. The distinctive feature of this concept is that the state is not 'in retreat' but simply behaving differently.

international order: the normative and the institutional pattern in the relationship between states. The elements of this might be thought to include such things as sovereignty, the forms of diplomacy, international law, the role of the great powers, and the codes circumscribing the use of force.

internationalization: this term is used to denote high levels of international interaction and interdependence, most commonly with regard to the world economy. In this context it refers to the volume of international trade and investment and to the organization of production. The term is often used to distinguish this condition from globalization as the latter implies that there are no longer distinct national economies in a position to interact.

liberal rights: the agenda of human rights that is driven largely from a Western perspective and derived from classical liberal positions.

Box 30.3 **Key concepts (2)**

minimum order: a view of international order that is concerned with peace and stability, rather than with the attainment of other values, such as justice.

multipolarity: a distribution of power among a number (at least three) of major powers or 'poles'.

multilateralism: the tendency for functional aspects of international relations (such as security, trade, or environmental management) to be organized around large numbers of states, or universally, rather than by unilateral state action.

order: this may denote any regular or discernible pattern of relationships that are stable over time, or may additionally refer to a condition that allows certain goals to be achieved.

primordialism: the belief that certain human or social characteristics, such as ethnicity, are deeply embedded in historical conditions.

state system: the regular patterns of interaction between states, but without implying any shared values between them. This is distinguished from the view of a 'society' of states.

triads: the three economic groupings (North America, Europe and East Asia).

unipolarity: a distribution of power internationally in which there is clearly only one dominant power or 'pole'. Some analysts argue that the international system became unipolar in the 1990s since there was no longer any rival to American power.

world order: this is a wider category of order than the 'international'. It takes as its units of order, not states, but individual human beings and assesses the degree of order on the basis of the delivery of certain kinds of goods (be it security, human rights, basic needs or justice) for humanity as a whole.

aspirations and thus talk of it as **world order**? Such a distinction is widely noted in the literature. But what are we to make of the introduction of the concept of globalization into the analysis? Does globalized order signify the same as world order or something different? An attempt will be made to answer that question in the final section of the chapter.

Theoretically, the result is that the search for the definitive elements of the contemporary order proceeds within quite separate frameworks. The first direction from which these issues have been approached is the broadly realist one. This concentrates upon the structure of the post-cold war system, especially upon the number of **Great Power** actors and the distribution of capabilities amongst them. It defines order largely in terms of the operative security structure within the system. It spawned a debate in the early 1990s about the polarity of the post-cold war system, and whether a return to **multipolarity** might herald the erosion of the stability generated by the cold war's bipolarity.

The second line is broadly liberal in derivation and focuses upon regimes and institutions towards one end of its spectrum, and a variety of norms and values towards the other. Its central claim is that patterns of integration and interdependence have become so deeply embedded in the cold war period, albeit for strategic and geopolitical reasons, that they now have a self-sustaining momentum that precludes any return to war and autarchy. Since complex systems of **global governance** have been spawned in the interim, these regimes will survive the collapse of the 'realist' conditions that gave rise to them in the first place.

A third line is the one that adjudges order in terms of its achievement of human emancipation. The evidence from either of the two former approaches is thereby deemed inadequate to the task. The mere facts of stability amongst the major powers, or the institutionalization of relations amongst the dominant groups of states, tells us little of importance about the quality of life for most inhabitants of the globe. If it is true, as writers like Ken Booth (1999)

argue, that governments are the main source of the abuse of human rights, we can scarcely learn anything about a human rights' order by studying their activities.

The fourth line of exploration is via the literature on globalization. This is not the place to rehearse the complex arguments about the nature of globalization in general (see Ch. 1). This chapter simply asks whether, or in what sense, globalization may be thought to constitute a form of order or not. Must we speak of globalization as a process without an end-state, or can we legitimately speak of a globalized world order as a distinctive political form? The latter view is clearly set forth, for instance, in the suggestion that the contemporary western state conglomerate, collectively, constitutes an 'emergent *global state*' (Shaw 1997: 503–4). Globalization, to this extent and with whatever qualifications, represents an incipient political order.

Key points

- When we speak of order, we need to specify order for whom—states, peoples, groups or individuals.

- International order focuses on stable and peaceful relations between states, often related to the balance of power. It is primarily about military security.

- World order is concerned with other values, such as justice, development, rights, and emancipation.

- A pattern of order may advance some values at the expense of others. There is often a tension, for example, between state-centred concepts of order and those that promote individual values. For instance, policies of the balance of power might lead to assistance being given to regimes with bad human rights' records.

- A key question about globalization is whether it supercedes all ideas of international order, or whether it can be incorporated into more traditional ideas.

Box 30.4 Typologies of order

	Units	Characteristics
Globalized	global system	end of national polities, societies, and economies
International	states	concern with agenda of sovereignty and stability
World	humanity	concern with agenda of rights, needs, and justice
Globalized international	globalized states	agenda of managing relations between states penetrated by global system but still distinguishable within it

---

The elements of contemporary order

The 'social-state' system

Initially, there is the basic nature of the contemporary **state system** itself. The state system is 'social', first, in the sense that states at the start of the century perform a range of social functions that distinguish them from earlier phases of the state system. The great revival in the political credibility of states, from its nadir in World War II, is attributable to the largely successful undertaking of this task. While states are not all equal in the ability to deliver these functions, most would now list responsibility for development and economic management, welfare and social planning as desirable roles for the state, even where effectiveness of delivery is variable.

It is 'social' also in the second sense that there are pressures for emulation within the system and this tends to reinforce common patterns of behaviour, and similar forms of state institutional structure. Historically, states have emulated each other in developing the social and economic infrastructures for generating military power. Now this task has broadened as states seek to adopt 'best practice' in terms of economic competitiveness and efficiency. They also face the social pressure to conform to certain standards of civil rights and this has permitted a measure of dilution and delegation of the state's exclusive jurisdiction over its own domestic affairs. In consequence, some of the key rules of the state system

(sovereignty, non-intervention) are undergoing considerable adaptation and this gives the contemporary state system many of its complex and ambivalent qualities.

Identity and the nation-state

A second feature is the multiplicity of issues about identity that have become prevalent in the 1990s. These revolve around contemporary forms of nationalism and are subject to contested assessments as to whether they represent a 'new' nationalism, or a reversion to a pre-existing **primordialism**. But the state is both challenged and reinforced by a welter of additional crises of identity—tendencies towards apparently new forms of political community driven by ethnic separatism, regional identities, new transnational projects, new social movements, and the return to culture/religion. Clearly, the key question here is the extent to which these are wholly new tendencies or represent some kind of historical atavism. The **politics of identity** at the turn of the millennium itself impacts on the social nature of the state as it raises explicit questions about the **nature of citizenship**—who is to count as a citizen, and what is the nature of the contract between state and citizen (see Ch. 29).

It must not, however, be imagined that all issues of

identity have emerged only in the aftermath of the cold war. For example, it could be said that there has been a widespread reaction in much of the developing world against what has been seen as the imposition of a modernizing, westernizing and secular form of state. The revolution in Iran in 1979 is a case in point and cautions us not to assume that 'identity politics' were invented only after the end of the cold war.

Polarity and the collectivization of security

A key area of concern remains the primary attributes of the contemporary security order. This addresses the debates about the present distribution of power, and whether that distribution should be assessed as being **unipolar**, bipolar, multipolar, or some kind of hybrid of them all. A key determinant of the present security order relates to the role of the United States and its willingness to become involved in general order-maintenance. The impression given during the past decade is that this is highly variable, with the US role in Kosovo standing in marked contrast to its unwillingness to become engaged in, say, Rwanda.

More generally, there are several general contemporary trends towards 'collectivization' of security (as distinct from collective security properly speaking). These cover the various forms of **multilateralism** in security, the role of coalitions, the rise and partial demise of peacekeeping and peace enforcement, and the trend to (as well as limits of) interventionism. There are analysts, such as Mary Kaldor (1999), who argue that fundamental restructuring in the nature of organized violence is taking place. Such conceptions are important as they link the discussion of violence to the other elements of order and treat it as a dynamic problem—rather than a static view that 'war is war is war'. Violence then becomes symptomatic of changes in other social spheres, rather than simply a structural constant produced by the 'anarchic' state system.

The organization of production and exchange

Another prominent dimension is the political economy of the present order. Central to the theme of order is our assessment of the degree of stability within the international trading and financial systems. The former remains beset by disputes between the world's three great trading groups or **'triads'**, while the latter shows periodic signs of undergoing meltdown, most recently during the financial turmoil that afflicted the East Asian economies towards the late 1990s. This economic order is partially managed by those elements of governance institutionalized in bodies such as the IMF, World Bank, and WTO. But the economic order penetrates more deeply than these obvious, and superficial, instances of it would indicate. The full effects of the '**internationalization**' of production can be appreciated only by taking into account cognate aspects, such as military production, environmentalism, social welfare, human (and specifically child) rights, and gender inequalities within the economy and in processes of development.

Multilateral management and governance

A remarkable aspect of the order is the highly dense and complex network of contemporary forms of international governance (regimes, international organizations and INGOs). These cover most aspects of life including developments in legal (human rights, war crimes), environmental, and economic regimes, as well as in the core peacekeeping activities of universal organizations like the UN. To what extent can we sensibly refer to the emergence of elements of international governance? What is its potential for further development? Are current regimes dependent on the underlying power structure of western dominance and reflective of western preferences, and how sustainable are they given the value and cultural diversity of the present world? These issues link the discussion directly to the next element of order, since much of this regime base is emerging at a regional level.

> **Box 30.5 Elements of order**
>
> **Structural elements**
>
> polarity
> multilateralism
> regionalism
> two worlds
>
> **Purposive elements**
>
> social-state
> identity
> economic order
> liberal rights

Regionalism

The development of contemporary regionalism is another key to understanding the emerging order (see Ch. 23). This takes various forms, including economic (trading regions), security (role of bodies such as NATO), and cultural. The intensification of regionalism is occasionally viewed as a refutation of trends towards globalization but is more plausibly regarded as an aspect of globalization, rather than evidence against it. The fact that a number of regions feel the need to develop regional institutions is itself a manifestation of globalization, in the same way that the universal spread of the nation-state, as the principal political form, was earlier a product of globalization. Nonetheless, there are interesting questions about the significance of regionalism for the post-cold war order, such as the seemingly greater degree of security autonomy 'enjoyed' by regions since the end of the cold war, and the role of regions in constituting new forms of identity. There is perhaps a paradox that, with the loss of cold war constraints, regions now have greater autonomy—while, at the same time, levels of interpenetration and globalization indicate diminished possibilities for regional insulation.

The liberal rights order

Arguably, this is the feature with the most striking continuities to the cold war period, and in contrast to the pre-1945 world. Human rights programmes have become a conspicuous feature of post-1945 international politics, largely in reaction to the catastrophic experiences of the period before 1945 (see Ch. 28). This theme was a paramount aspect of the cold war period itself and was again highlighted with the collapse of the Soviet bloc, since that event was portrayed as a major step forward in extending the liberal order. In this respect, the focus on **liberal rights** is another element of continuity between the two periods, rather than a concern that has materialized only since the demise of the cold war. Indeed, it is often argued that it was the growth of concern with rights in the former Eastern Europe that had a corrosive effect on the maintenance of authoritarian political systems within the region. However, and as commonly noted, the post-cold war order is paradoxically under pressure precisely because of its seemingly greater potential for universalism (which evokes forms of resistance).

This relates directly to wider questions about the future of democratization. This is of momentous import for the future stability of the international order and touches on a series of inter-related issues: about the status of democracy as a universal norm; the current experience with democratization; the pressures upon democracy arising from globalization (and hence the appeals for cosmopolitan forms of democracy); and the future of democracy as a source of inter-state peace and stability (see Ch. 29).

North–South and the two world orders

Any examination of the contemporary order must give a high profile to the apparent gulf within it, separating the experience of the industrialized North from the increasingly marginalized South. Some see the tensions to which this gives rise as undermining the prospects for longer-term stability (see Ch. 26). Are North–South relations more stable now than in the previous eras, or do they remain precariously rooted in inequalities of power, massive gaps in quality of life, and incompatibilities of cultural values? Does this divide threaten the durability of the post-cold war order or must we simply recognize it as a key component of that order, and for that reason understand it as an element of structural continuity with its predecessors?

As against this image of two monolithic blocs of North and South, other analysts insist that such a conception is now out-of-date. The impacts of globalization cut across states and not just between them, yielding complex patterns of stratification that defy easy classification into North and South. How accurate is it now to speak of two such orders, or is there much more diversity than such crude dichotomies tend to imply?

Key points

- Order is shaped by the changed nature of states and of the tasks they perform.
- There are complex questions about whether the end of the cold war has released a new agenda of nationalism and national identity or whether these issues have been present all along.

- Security is increasingly being dealt with on a multilateral basis even when this does not conform to classical 'collective security' models.

- The global economy is primarily shaped by relations between the three key groupings (North America, Western Europe and East Asia) and managed by a panoply of Western-dominated institutions.

- There are dense patterns of international institutions in all functional areas.

- There are strong trends towards regionalism but they take different forms in various regions.

- Matters to do with human rights have a much higher profile than in earlier historical periods.

- The gulf between rich and poor is wider than ever and this questions our ability to speak of a single order for all.

Is there a post-cold war order?

On the basis of the above assessment, is there then a discernible post-cold war order? That there is any such order has already received some vociferous denials. What is entailed by the concept of 'order' assumes, at the very least, some notion of an international system, even if its purview extends well beyond that. System is a necessary precondition for an order while by no means sufficient for it (Bull 1977). However, at least one historian has denied even the minimalist presence of an international system in the 1990s:

Thus, for the first time in two centuries, the world of the 1990s entirely lacked any international system or structure. The very fact that, after 1989, dozens of new territorial states appeared without any independent mechanism for determining their borders—without even third parties accepted as sufficiently impartial to act as general mediators—speaks for itself. Where was the consortium of great powers which had once established, or at least formally ratified disputed frontiers? (Hobsbawm 1994: 559)

Hobsbawm's judgement is made with reference to a traditional Great Power international system. Arguably, he goes beyond the requirements of a system *per se* and confuses this with an effective **Concert** of Great Powers, a particular form of system. The contention that there is no international system at all would otherwise appear extremely difficult to sustain.

Nonetheless, others share his scepticism, but base it upon the perceived absence of order, not just of system:

Despite the growing salience of the single term, globalization, to characterize much of our current 'post-cold war moment', the term refers to seemingly contrary processes, including integration and fragmentation; diffusion and concentration; and localization and transnationalization . . . The current relative thickness and diffuseness may indicate that it makes a lot less sense to talk now about any overarching international order. Instead, the possibility that a variety of orders are operating in different domains, regions, or even localities should be recognized. (Latham 1997: 205–6)

Any attempt to unravel these issues in the context of the present era confronts a complex of historical issues. Historically, the core problems relate to the elements of continuity and discontinuity embodied in the post-cold war world. The argument that the present order is distinctive relies implicitly upon an assumption of discontinuity: it is the break with the past that lends the period its unique qualities. However, any claim of this nature is highly problematic. It needs to be reconciled with the counter-argument that some of the very forces that eroded the salience

of the cold war remain as defining qualities in the world created in its wake. It would be naïve to imagine that the pressures which led to the collapse of the cold war structure would, in turn, have immediately dissipated when their work was done.

Key points

- Some commentators question whether there is any basis to the post-cold war international order

- Others suggest that there are many separate orders, rather than a single overarching one

- To resolve these issues, we need to determine how much changed with the end of the cold war. Are there important elements of continuity with the previous order?

Globalization and the end of the cold war

There is a tendency to regard the degree of globalization as a consequence of the end of the cold war. This is especially so with regard to the geographical extent of globalization. Areas of the world that were formerly excluded from the full force of global capitalism, global communications and global cultural intrusions are now more integrated into these networks than at any previous time. In that sense, the main effect of the end of the cold war has been precisely to break down the barriers that previously held globalization at bay, at least in so far as the 'second' or 'socialist' world was concerned.

Not surprisingly, many commentators see the 1990s as being characterized by the intensification of the processes of globalization, particularly with regard to financial integration. The global financial order is now virtually universal in its reach, as is the influence of its principal institutions such as the **World Bank** and the **International Monetary Fund**.

On this reasoning, it is the ending of the cold war that has allowed the further spread of globalization and we can therefore regard the scope of globalization as a point of difference between the cold war,

and post-cold war worlds. Unfortunately, there is a danger in such an analysis. The problem is that to regard globalization as simply the consequence of the end of the cold war is to neglect the extent to which globalization may also have served as a cause of its end. In this case, globalization may mark a point of continuity, rather than discontinuity, between the two periods.

In a wider sense, the danger with such a procedure is that it neglects other dimensions of continuity such as in the structure of power (Waltz 1993) or in American foreign policy (Cox 1995). But the prime example does relate to issues of globalization (Clark 1997) or more generally, to the construction of a liberal capitalist order (Ikenberry 1999). What is the historical evidence for this type of argument? Its principal element is the view that globalization grew out of the core of Western capitalist states that formed during the cold war, and became such a powerful force that it finally both weakened one of the cold war protagonists, namely the Soviet Union, but also made the point of the cold war increasingly irrelevant. As regards the Soviet Union, what damaged and eroded the effectiveness of the USSR as a military power was precisely the fact that it was not integrated into financial and technological sinews of global capitalism. As regards the logic of the cold war as a whole, the existence of a hostile Soviet bloc was a crucial element in the integration of the Western system. But by the 1980s, this system was effectively self-sustaining and no longer required an external enemy to provide its *raison d'être* or its dynamic for growth. In this sense, the Soviet Union had become redundant as far as the needs of the dominant western system itself were concerned.

If globalization was both an element of the pre-existing cold war system, but also continues now, in more intensive and extensive forms, as an element of the contemporary order, it needs to be seen as a point of continuity between the two periods. The logic of this, in turn, requires us to concede that the present order is not *sui generis* as it contains within it elements that were present also during the cold war. This suggests that the contemporary order should not be understood as wholly separate from that which preceded it. But if globalization is the element that binds both together, is it the key to understanding the present order? Is it the defining quality of today's world?

The claim that globalization defines the essential quality of the present order has been denied for a number of reasons. Most generally of all, if globalization is seen as a long-term historical trend—with various waves—then to interpret the present order in terms of globalization does not say enough about what is specific to it alone.

Beyond this, globalization has been described as the dystopic absence of order: negative qualities appear in abundance but without any seeming coherence. The clearest example is provided in Falk's description of globalization as 'a constellation of market, technological, ideological and civilizational developments that have nothing in common'. Moreover, he adds for good measure, 'there is little, or no, normative agency associated with this emergent world order: it is virtually designer-free, a partial dystopia that is being formed spontaneously' (1997: 125). Even at the most basic level, globalization seems not to constitute a **'minimum' order** of the kind that has traditionally underpinned international society (Bull 1977). It has no common

---

Box 30.6 Interpretations of globalization and the end of the cold war

'The end of the Cold War division into competing world orders marks a crucial substantive and symbolic transition to single-world economic, cultural and political orders.' (Shaw 1999: 194)

'America has ceased to be a superpower, because it has met its match: globalization—a globalization which, moreover, it helps to promote despite not managing to master totally its meaning.' (Laidi 1998: 170)

'Globalization is the most significant development and theme in contemporary life and social theory to emerge since the collapse of Marxist systems.' (Albrow 1996: 89)

'Globalization and globalism were thus the product of specific historical conditions in the last three decades of the twentieth century.' (Cox 1996: 34)

'Globalists continue to maintain that there are big, *fin-de-siècle* transformations under way in the world at large, which can be laid at the door of something called globalization. This new era—popularized as "a world without borders" and symbolized by the dismantling of the Berlin Wall—ostensibly came into its own where the cold war left off.' (Weiss 1999: 59)

---

institutions fulfilling minimally agreed societal functions. The essential point is made in the claim that globalization 'is a state; it is not a meaning' (Laidi 1998: 6).

Another version is the sociological appraisal of disorder resulting from the absence of overall control associated with globalization. The general claim is that 'no one seems now to be in control' (Bauman 1998: 58). 'Globalization is not about what we all . . . wish or hope *to do*', it has been said; 'It is about *what is happening to us all*' (Bauman 1998: 60). The present situation lacks order, on this reasoning, because it is devoid of human intention or agency.

All of these arguments suggest that globalization is inadequate as the conceptual basis for understanding the contemporary order because of what globalization *does*. It is too varied in its effects, and so lacking in purpose and goals, that we cannot visualize an order constructed on that basis. Indeed, the main theme of these writings on globalization is to draw attention to just how disorderly is the process of globalization. But a different form of argument can be made also on the basis of what globalization is, not just what it does. This will be set out in the next section.

Key points

- Globalization is often portrayed as an effect of the end of the cold war because this led to its further geographical spread.

- At the same time, globalization has to be understood as one of the factors that caused the end of the cold war. It was the Soviet Union's marginalization from processes of globalization that revealed its weaknesses.

- Accordingly, globalization is an element of continuity between the cold war and post-cold war orders and the latter cannot be regarded as wholly new.

- A variety of authors are sceptical about the claim that globalization is the hallmark of contemporary order.

- One of the reasons is that, as a long-term historical trend, globalization is not specific to the end of the twentieth century.

- Globalization embodies a range of often competing values.

- Globalization is too much outside our control to form an order. We are its objects rather than its subjects.

An international order of globalized states?

These are all plausible objections to globalization as the defining element in contemporary order. What they collectively miss, however, is that globalization by itself is unable to define the total condition of international order. Globalization could be taken to represent the mainstay of order only if it superseded all traditional elements of the international order itself. But if globalization is an addition, but not a substitute for, an international order, then it is scarcely surprising that it is not adequate to the task of providing us with the key quality of post-cold war order.

The point can be taken further. If it can be convincingly held that globalization is not some process over and above the activities of states, but is instead an element within **state transformation**, it is not unreasonable to develop on this basis a conception of the **globalized state**. Globalization does not make the state disappear but is a way of thinking about its present form. By extension of the same logic, globalization does not make redundant any notion of international order but instead requires us to think about a *globalized international order*. In short, what is required is a notion of international order that would be based on the emergence of the globalized state. Only when this has been set in place will we be able to assess the extent of the order that currently prevails.

Some of the confusion enters the debate about globalization by the tendency to see it as exclusively something pertaining to the environment in which states find themselves. Globalization is presented as a claim about the degree of interconnectedness between states, such that the significance of borders, and the reality of separate national actors, is called seriously into question. There is no denying that this is part of what globalization signifies. But what such a one-sided interpretation leaves out of account is the extent to which globalization also refers to a 'domestic' process of change within states. Thus regarded, globalization can equally be understood as an expression of the profound transformations in the nature of the state, and in state-society relations, that have developed in recent decades. These lead us to think in terms, not of the demise or retreat of the state, but about its changing functionality: states still

Fig. 30.1 Structural view of globalization as state form

exist but do different things, do some things less well than they used to, but also have taken on new responsibilities in exchange.

The extension of this argument is that, even in an age of globalization, there remain both states and a state system. While, as noted above, the idea of international order is more limited than that of world or global order, the suggestion that globalization refers (at least in part) to a condition of states invites us to develop a theory about the nature of international order appropriate for globalized states. We need to face the seeming paradox that there can indeed be an international order of globalized states. To be sure, this does not address all issues of order, but it still engages with a number of significant aspects of it. For example, one key respect in which states have become globalized is with regard to the provision of human rights, since they are by no means the sole providers of such rights. To the extent that this is the case, the recent attempts by the international community to articulate a modified practice of non-intervention, thereby to allow for some modest degree of intervention on behalf of human rights, can be understood as the quest for a set of ground rules—an international order—appropriate to the nature of the 'new' globalized states that form its membership. In a word, the principles of international order are not developed simply as rules governing the relations between anonymous 'billiard balls' but are a natural outgrowth of the kinds of creatures that states are in process of becoming. The mistake then is to imagine that globalization signifies the end of all projects for international order,

when what in fact is underway is the reconfiguration of the principles of international order to reflect the new realities of globalized states.

Key points

- Globalization is often thought of as an extreme form of interdependence. This sees it largely as a change in the external environment in which states find themselves.

- The implication of such analyses is that states are now much weaker as actors. They are in retreat or becoming obsolete.

- If this is the case, ideas of international order would be much less relevant to our concept of order

- But if globalization is considered as a transformation in the nature of states themselves, it suggests states are still central to the discussion of order: they are different but not obsolete. This leads to the idea of a globalized state as a state form.

- In this case, there is no contradiction between the norms and rules of a state system and the existence of globalized states.

- This international order will nonetheless have different norms in recognition of the new nature of states and their transformed functions. Rules of sovereignty and non-intervention are undergoing change as symptoms of this adaptation.

Conclusion

In short, we now face a **hybrid situation** in which states share a host of responsibilities with both intergovernmental organizations and a multiplicity of non-governmental and transnational actors. Formerly, the function of the international order was largely to cushion and protect the states so that they might go about their business as the principal providers of social goods to their citizens. This situation is now vastly more complex. Much of that provision (economic goods, monitoring of human rights, access to information, security, and so on) originates beyond the individual state itself, and indeed in non-state components that fall outside the jurisdiction of the international order narrowly conceived.

This does not, however, mean that the international order has become redundant. It means simply that it needs to be redesigned to take account of the new division of labour between states, global networks, and the rudimentary forms of global governance. As long as states persist as important sources of political agency, they will construct a state system with its own rules and norms. It is this that we regard as the essential basis of the international order. Currently, the identity of states is undergoing considerable change, to the extent that we can describe them as globalized states. But these globalized states still coexist within an international order, albeit one that now differs from its recent historical forms and is currently seeking to develop a set of principles to reflect this transformation. The quest for a post-cold war order is the expression of this uneasy search.

QUESTIONS

1 Is the post-cold war order still an international order?

2 How important an element in the contemporary order is the condition of globalization?

3 How would you distinguish between an international and a world order and which is the more important framework for assessing the contemporary situation?

4 In which respects are the 'identities' of states undergoing change?

5 How would you define the polarity of the contemporary international system?

6 Is global governance a significant element of today's order?

7 Is regionalism a contradiction of globalization?

8 Is the prominence of democracy and liberal rights convincing evidence of the impact of globalization?

9 Can globalization be considered the basis of the present order if its impact is so variable on different regions, states, and individuals?

10 Is the idea of an international order of globalized states contradictory?

GUIDE TO FURTHER READING

International order

Bull, H., *The Anarchical Society: A Study of Order in World Politics* (London: Macmillan, 1977), esp. Part 1, provides the standard introduction to this issue from an international society perspective.

Vincent, R. J., 'Order in International Politics', in J. D. B. Miller and R. J. Vincent (eds.), *Order and Violence* (Oxford: Oxford University Press, 1990) gives a useful commentary on Bull's position.

Cox, R., 'Social Forces, States, and World Orders: Beyond International Relations Theory', in R. Cox with T. J. Sinclair, *Approaches to World Order* (Cambridge: Cambridge University Press, 1996) is an alternative to the 'English School' approach and steps outside the state-centric framework.

Hall, J., *International Orders* (Cambridge: Polity Press, 1996) takes an historical overview of distinctive international orders.

New world orders and the post-cold war world

Clark, I., *The Post-Cold War Order: The Spoils of Peace* (Oxford: Oxford University Press, 2001). The most recent guide to the debates about the post-cold war period, viewing it as a kind of peace settlement.

Williams, A., *Failed Imagination? New World Orders of the Twentieth Century* (Manchester: Manchester University Press, 1998) discusses the historical precedents for new orders during the twentieth century

Leaver, R., and Richardson J. L., (eds.), *Charting the Post-Cold War Order* (Oxford: Westview Press, 1993). The material on the post-cold war order is voluminous but piecemeal. This is an early attempt at an overview.

Sellers, M., (ed.), *The New World Order: Sovereignty, Human Rights and the Self-Determination of Peoples* (Oxford: Berg, 1996) is a study around the theme of self-determination in the contemporary order.

Kaldor, M., *New and Old Wars: Organized Violence in a Global Era* (Cambridge: Polity Press, 1999) develops an argument about the changing nature of war in the new order.

Paul, T. V., and Hall J. A., (eds.), *International Order and the Future of World Politics* (Cambridge: Cambridge University Press, 1999) offers an up-to-date overview of the general issues of order after the cold war.

Globalization in the present order

Clark, I., *Globalization and International Relations Theory* (Oxford: Oxford University Press, 1999) develops a theoretical account of globalization in terms of state transformation.

—— *Globalization and Fragmentation: International Relations in the Twentieth Century* (Oxford: Oxford University Press, 1997) places the contemporary debates about globalization in historical perspective.

Held, D., McGrew, A., *et al.* (eds.), *Global Transformations* (Cambridge: Polity Press, 1999) is a detailed study of contemporary forms of globalization.

Holton, R. J., *Globalization and the Nation-State* (Houndmills: Macmillan, 1998) offers an accessible introduction to this general topic.

Weiss, L., *The Myth of the Powerless State: Governing the Economy in a Global Era* (Cambridge: Polity Press, 1998) is a sceptical portrayal of the economic aspects of globalization.

Archibugi, D., Held, D., and Kohler, M., (eds.), *Re-imagining Political Community: Studies in Cosmopolitan Democracy* (Cambridge: Polity Press, 1998) surveys the impact of globalization on democracy and ideas of community.

References

Abegglen, J. C. (1994), *Sea Change: Pacific Asia as the New World Industrial Center* (New York: Free Press).

Abu-Lughod, J. L. (1989), *Before European Hegemony: The World System AD 1250–1350* (Oxford: Oxford University Press).

Adams, N. B. (1993), *Worlds Apart: The North–South Divide and the International System* (London: Zed).

Adler, E. (1996), 'The Emergence of Cooperation: National Epistemic Communities and the International Evolution of the Idea of Nuclear Arms Control', *International Organization*, 50(1): 101–45.

—— and Barnett, M., (eds.) (1998), *Security Communities*, (Cambridge: Cambridge University Press).

Agnew, J., and Corbridge, S. (1995), *Mastering Space: Hegemony, Territory, and International Political-Economy* (London: Routledge).

Ahmed, A. S. (1992), *Post-Modernism and Islam: Predicament and Promise* (London: Routledge).

Albrow, M. (1990), 'Introduction', in M. Albrow and Elizabeth King (eds.), *Globalization, Knowledge and Society* (London: Sage).

—— (1996), *The Global Age* (Cambridge: Polity Press).

Allison, G., Carter, A. B., Miller, S. E., and Zelikow, P. (eds.) (1993), *Cooperative Denuclearisation*, CSIA Studies in International Security, 2, (Cambridge, Mass.: Harvard University Press).

Alperovitz, G. (1965), *Atomic Diplomacy: Hiroshima and Potsdam: The Use of the Atomic Bomb and the American Confrontation with Soviet Power* (New York: Simon and Schuster).

Anderson, B. (1991*), Imagined Communities: Reflections on the Origin and Spread of Nationalism* (London: Verso).

Anderson, P. (1974*a*), *Passages from Antiquity to Feudalism* (London: New Left Books).

—— (1974*b*), *Lineages of the Absolutist State* (London: New Left Books, 1974).

Angelo, S. (1969), *Machiavelli: A Dissection* (New York: Harcourt Brace).

Archibugi, D., and Held, D. (eds.) (1995), *Cosmopolitan Democracy: An Agenda for a New World Order* (Cambridge: Polity Press).

Arend, A. C., and Beck, R. J. (1993*), International Law and the Use of Force* (London: Routledge).

Ashley, R. K. (1981), 'Political Realism and Human Interests' *International Studies Quarterly*, 25(2): 204–36.

—— (1984), 'The Poverty of Neorealism', *International Organisation*, 38 (2), 225–86.

—— (1987), 'The Geopolitics of Geopolitical Space: Toward a Critical Social Theory of International Politics', *Alternatives*, 12 (4): 403–34.

—— (1988), 'Untying the Sovereign State: A Double Reading of the Anarchy Problematique', *Millennium*, 17 (2): 227–62.

—— and Walker, R. B. J. (1990), 'Reading Dissidence/Writing the Discipline: Crisis and the Question of Sovereignty in International Studies', *International Studies Quarterly*, 34: 367–416.

Axford, B. (1995), *The Global System: Economics, Politics, and Culture* (Cambridge: Polity Press).

Bacchetta, M. *et al.* (1998), *Electronic Commerce and the Role of the WTO* (Geneva: World Trade Organization).

Bailey, K. C. (1991), *Doomsday Weapons in the Hands of Many*, (Champaign, Ill.: Illinois Press).

Baldwin, D. (ed.) (1993), *Neorealism and Neoliberalism: The Contemporary Debate* (New York: Columbia University Press).

Banks, E. (1994), *Complex Derivatives: Understanding and Managing the Risks of Exotic Options, Complex Swaps, Warrants and Other Synthetic Derivatives* (Chicago: Probus).

Baran, P. (1957), *The Political Economy of Growth* (New York: Monthly Review Press).

Barber, P. (1979), *Diplomacy: The World of the Honest Spy* (London: The British Library).

Barker, D., and Mander, J. (1996), *Invisible Government: The World Trade Organization: Global Government For the Millennium?* (San Francisco, Calif.: International Forum on Globalization).

Barraclough, G. (ed.) (1984), *The Times Atlas of World History* (London: Times Books).

Barry, B. (1989), *Theories of Justice* (Hemel Hempstead: Harvester Wheatsheaf).

Barston, R. P. (1988), *Modern Diplomacy* (London: Longmans).

Bartelson, J. (1995), *A Genealogy of Sovereignty* (Cambridge: Cambridge University Press).

Bauman, Z. (1998), *Globalization: The Human Consequences* (Cambridge: Polity Press).

Baylis, J., and O'Neill, R. (eds.) (2000), *Alternative Nuclear Futures* (Oxford: Oxford University Press).

Beck, U. (1998) 'The Cosmopolitan Manifesto', *New Statesman*, 20 March.

Beitz, C. (1979), *Political Theory and International Relations* (Princeton: Princeton University Press).

—— (1994), 'Cosmopolitan Liberalism and the States System', in C. Brown (ed.), *Political Restructuring in Europe: Ethical Perspectives* (London: Routledge, 1994).

Bello, W. (1994), *Dark Victory: The United States, Structural Adjustment and Global Poverty* (London: Pluto Press).

Bennett, J., and George, S. (1987), *The Hunger Machine* (Cambridge: Polity Press).

Berners-Lee, T., with Fischetti, M. (1999), *Weaving the Web: The Original Design and Ultimate Destiny of the World Wide Web by Its Inventor* (New York: Harper San Francisco).

Berridge, G. R. (1995), *Diplomacy: Theory and Practice* (Hemel Hempstead: Harvester Wheatsheaf).

Bethell, L. (1970), *The Abolition of the Brazilian Slave Trade: Britain, Brazil and the Slave Trade Question 1807–1869* (Cambridge: Cambridge University Press).

Bhagwati, J. (1998), 'The Capital Myth: The Difference between Trade in Widgets and Trade in Dollars', *Foreign Affairs*, 73 (3).

Bialer, S. (1986), *The Soviet Paradox: External Expansion, Internal Decline* (New York: Knopf).

Bill, J., and Springborg, R. (1990), *Politics in the Middle East* (London: Scott, Foresman/Little, Brown Higher Education).

BIS (1996), *International Banking and Financial Market Developments* (Basle: Bank for International Settlements).

—— (2000), *Quarterly Review: International Banking and Financial Market Developments* (Basle: Bank for International Settlements).

Black, M. (1992), *A Cause for our Times: Oxfam, the First 50 Years* (Oxford: Oxford University Press).

Bonanate, L. (1995), 'Peace or Democracy', in D. Archibugi and D. Held (eds.), *Cosmopolitan Democracy* (Cambridge: Polity Press), 42–67.

Booth, J., and Walker, T. (1993), *Understanding Central America* (Boulder, Col.: Westview Press).

Booth, K. (1991), 'Security Emancipation', *Review of International Studies*, 17 (4): 313–26.

—— (1995a), 'Dare not to Know: International Relations Theory versus the Future', in Booth and Smith, (1995), 103–26.

—— (1995b), 'Human Wrongs and International Relations', *International Affairs*, 71 (1): 103–26.

—— (1999), 'Three Tyrannies', in T. Dunne and N. J. Wheeler (eds.), *Human Rights in Global Politics* (Cambridge: Cambridge University Press).

—— and Smith, S. (eds.) (1995), *International Relations Theory Today* (Cambridge: Polity Press).

—— and Dunne, T., 'Learning beyond Frontiers', in T. Dunne and N. J. Wheeler (eds.), *Human Rights in Global Politics* (Cambridge: Cambridge University Press, 1999), 303–28.

Bowker, M. (1997), *Russian Foreign Policy and the End of the Cold War* (Aldershot: Darmouth).

—— and Cameron, R. (eds.) (2000), *Russia after the Cold War* (London: Longman).

Boyer, R., and Drache, D. (eds.) (1996), *States against Markets: The Limits of Globalization* (New York: Routledge).

Braudel, F. (1975), *The Mediterranean and the Mediterranean World in the Age of Philip II*, 2 vols. (London: Fontana).

Brecher, M., and Wilkenfeld, J. (1991), 'International Crises and Global Instability: The Myth of the "Long Peace"', in C. Kegley (ed.), *The Long Postwar Peace: Contending Explanations and Projections* (New York: Harper Collins).

Brenner, R. (1977), 'The Origins of Capitalist Development: A Critique of Neo-Smithian Marxism', *New Left Review*, 104.

Bretherton, C., and Ponton, G. (eds.) (1996), *Global Politics: An Introduction* (Oxford: Blackwell).

Brewer, A. (1990), *Marxist Theories of Imperialism: A Critical Survey*, 2nd edn. (London: Routledge).

Brittan, A. (1989), *Masculinity and Power* (Oxford: Basil Blackwell).

Brock, G. W. (1994), *Telecommunications Policy for the Information Age: From Monopoly to Competition* (Cambridge: Harvard University Press).

Brodie, B. (ed.) (1946), *The Absolute Weapon: Atomic Power and World Order* (New York).

Brown, C. (1992), *International Relations Theory: New Normative Approaches* (Hemel Hempstead: Harvester Wheatsheaf).

—— (1999), 'History Ends, Worlds Collide', in Michael Cox, Ken Booth, and Tim Dunne (eds.), *The Interregnum: Controversies in World Politics 1989–1999* (Cambridge: Cambridge University Press), 41–57.

Brown, L. R. *et al.* (1990), *State of the World 1990* (London: Unwin)

—— and Kane, H. (1995), *Full House: Reassessing the Earth's Population Carrying Capacity* (London: Earthscan).

Brown, S. *et al.* (1977), *Regimes for the Ocean, Outer Space and the Weather* (Washington, DC: Brookings Institution).

Brownlie, I. (1971), (ed.), *Basic Documents on African Affairs* (Oxford: Clarendon).

—— (1979), *Principles of Public International Law* (Oxford: Clarendon).

Bruce, D. (1995), 'Intervention without Borders: Humanitarian Intervention in Rwanda, 1990–4', *Millennium*, 24 (2).

Buchbinder, D. (1994), *Masculinities and Identities* (Melbourne: Melbourne University Press).

Bukharin, O. (1994/5), 'Nuclear Safeguards and Security in the Former Soviet Union', *Survival*, 36 (4).

Bull, H. (1961), *The Control of the Arms Race: Disarmament and Arms Control in the Missile Age*, 1st edn. (London: International Institute for Strategic Studies).

—— (1977), *The Anarchical Society. A Study of Order in World Politics*, (London: Macmillan).

—— (ed.) (1984a), *Intervention in World Politics* (Oxford: Clarendon Press)

—— (1984b), *Justice in International Relations* (Ontario: Hagey Lectures, University of Waterloo).

—— and Watson, A. (1984), *The Expansion of International Society* (Oxford: Clarendon Press).

Burchill, S., Linklater, A., *et al.* (1996), *Theories of International Relations* (Basingstoke: Macmillan).

Burckhardt, J. (1958), *The Civilization of the Renaissance in Italy*, 1 (New York: Harper).

Burnham, P. (1991), 'Neo-Gramscian Hegemony and International Order', *Capital & Class* 45: 73–93.

—— (1994), 'Open Marxism and Vulgar International Political Economy', *Review of International Political Economy*, 1 (2).

—— (1999) 'The Politics of Economic Management', *New Political Economy*, 4 (1): 37–54

Burrows, W., and Windrem, R. (1994), *Critical Mass: The Dangerous Race for Superpowers in a Fragmented World* (New York: Simon and Schuster).

Burtless, G. *et al.* (1998), *Globalphobia: Confronting Fears About Open Trade* (Washington DC: Brookings Institution Press).

Burton, J. (1972), *World Society* (Cambridge: Cambridge University Press).

—— (1990), 'International Relations or World Society', in J. A. Vasquez (ed.), *Classics of International Relations* (Englewood Cliffs, NJ: Prentice Hall).

Butterfield, H. (1951), *History and Human Relations* (London: Collins).

Buvinic, M. (1997), 'Women in Poverty: A New Global Underclass', *Foreign Policy* (Fall), 38–53.

Buzan, B. (1983), *People, States and Fear* (London: Harvester Wheatsheaf).

—— and Herring, E. (1998), *The Arms Dynamic in World Politics* (London: Lynne Rienner).

Cable, V. (1994), *The World's New Fissures: The Politics of Identity* (London, Demos).

Cairncross, F. (1997), *The Death of Distance: How the Communications Revolution Will Change Our Lives* (Boston: Harvard Business School Press).

Callaghy, T. M. (1995), 'Africa and the World Political Economy: Still Caught between a Rock and a Hard Place', in J. W. Harbeson and D. Rothchild (eds.), *Africa in World Politics: Post-Cold War Challenges* (Oxford: Westview Press).

Calvert, P. (1994), *The International Politics of Latin America* (Manchester: Manchester University Press).

Camdessus, M., Address to the Tenth UNCTAD', *World Bank Development News* (Washington, DC: World Bank,).

Camilleri, J. A., and Falk, J. (1992), *The End of Sovereignty* (Aldershot: Edward Elgar).

Campbell, David (1992), *Writing Security: United States Foreign Policy and the Politics of Identity* (Manchester: Manchester University Press).

—— (1993), *Politics Without Principle: Sovereignty, Ethics and the Narratives of the Gulf War* (Boulder, Colo: Lynne Rienner).

—— (1998), *National Deconstruction: Violence, Identity, and Justice in Bosnia* (Minneapolis: University of Minnesota Press).

Caporaso, L. and Levine, D. (1992) *Theories of Political Economy* (New York: Cambridge University Press).

Cardoso, F. H., and Faletto, E. (1979), *Dependency and Development in Latin America* (Berkeley: University of California Press).

Carr, E. H. (1939; 2nd edn. 1946), *The Twenty Years' Crisis 1919–1939: An Introduction to the Study of International Relations* (London: Macmillan).

—— (1961), *What is History?* (Harmondsworth: Penguin).

Carson, R. (1962), *Silent Spring* (Harmondsworth: Penguin).

Carver, T. (1996) *Gender Is Not a Synonym for Women* (Boulder, Colo.: Lynne Rienner).

Castells, M. (1996), *The Rise of Network Society*, 3 Vols. (Oxford: Blackwell).

Cavanagh, J., Wysham, D., and Arruda, M. (eds.) (1994), *Beyond Bretton Woods, Alternatives to the Global Economic Order* (London: Pluto Press).

Cerny, P. (1993), 'Plurilateralism: Structural Differentiation and Functional Conflict in the Post-Cold War World Order', *Millenium*, 22 (1).

Chase-Dunn, C. (1989), *Global Formation: Structures of the World-Economy* (Oxford: Blackwell).

—— (1994), 'Technology and the Logic of World-Systems', in R. Palan and B. K. Gills (eds.), *Transcending the State–Global Divide: A Neostructuralist Agenda in International Relations* (Boulder, Colo.: Lynne Rienner), 84–105.

—— (1998), *Global Formation: Structures of the World-Economy*, updated edition (London : Rowman & Littlefield).

Chomsky, N. (1994), *World Orders, Old and New* (London: Pluto Press).

—— (1999), *The New Military Humanism: Lessons from Kosovo* (Monroe, Me.: Common Courage Press).

Chirot, D. (1982), Review of Wallerstein's 'The Modern World-System Vol. 2', *Journal of Social History*, 15 (3).

Chossudovsky, M., *The Globalization of Poverty* (London: Zed Press, 1997).

Clark, I. (1989), *The Hierarchy of States: Reform and Resistance in the International Order* (Cambridge: Cambridge University Press).

—— (1997), *Globalization and Fragmentation: International Relations in the Twentieth Century* (Oxford: Oxford University Press).

—— (1999), *Globalization and International Theory* (Oxford: Oxford University Press).

Claude, I. Jr. (1955), *National Minorities: An International Problem* (Cambridge, Mass.: Harvard University Press).

—— (1984), *Swords into Plowshares* (New York: Random House).

Cochran, Molly (1999), *Normative Theory in International Relations: A Pragmatic Approach* (Cambridge: Cambridge University Press).

Cohen, A. (1998), *Israel and the Bomb* (New York: Columbia University Press).

Cohen R., (1995), *Diplomacy 2000 B.C. – 2000 A.D.* Paper presented to the 20th Annual Conference of the British International Studies Association, Southampton, December.

Cohn, J. (1999) 'What Did Political Science Forget About Politics?', *The New Republic*, 25 Oct., 25–31.

Computer Science and Telecommunications Board, National Research Council, (2000), *The Digital Dilemma: Intellectual Property in the Information Age* (Washington, DC: National Academy Press).

Connell, R. W. (1995), *Masculinities* (London: Routledge).

Cooper, R. (1968), *The Economics of Interdependence* (New York: McGraw Hill).

Cornia, G. A. *et al.* (1987), *Adjustment with a Human Face* (Oxford: UNICEF/Clarendon Press).

Cowhey, P., 'The International Telecommunications Regime: The Political Roots of Regimes for High Technology,' *International Organization*, 44(2) 169–99.

Cox, M. (1994), 'Rethinking the End of the Cold War', *Review of International Studies*, 20 (20): 187 – 200.

—— (1995), *US Foreign Policy after the Cold War: Superpower Without a Mission?* (London: The Royal Institute of International Affairs).

—— (1998), 'Rebels Without A Cause? Radical Theorists and the World System after the Cold War', *New Political Economy*, 3 (3): 445–60.

—— Booth, K., and Dunne T. (eds.) (1999), *The Interregnum: Controversies in World Politics, 1989–1999* (Cambridge: Cambridge University Press).

—— Ikenberry, G. J., and Inoguchi, T. (eds.) (2000), *American Democracy Promotions: Impulses, Strategies, and Impacts* (Oxford: Oxford University Press).

Cox, R. (1981), 'Social Forces, States and World Orders: Beyond International Relations Theory', *Millennium Journal of International Studies*, 10 (2): 126–55

—— (1986), 'Social Forces, States and World Orders: Beyond International Relations Theory', in R. Keohane (ed.), *Neorealism and its Critics* (New York: Columbia University Press), 204–54.

—— (1992), 'Towards a Post-Hegemonic Conceptualization of World Order: Reflections on the Relevancy of Ibn Khaldun', in J. Rosenau, and E.-O. Czempiel, *Governance without Government: Order and Change in World Politics* (Cambridge: Cambridge University Press).

—— (1994), 'Multilateralism and the Democratization of World Order', Paper for International Symposium on Sources of Innovation in Multilateralism, 26–28 May, Lausanne.

—— (1996), 'A Perspective on Globalization', in J. H. Mittelman (ed), *Globalization: Critical Reflections* (Boulder, Col.: Lynne Rienner).

—— with Sinclair, T. (1996), *Approaches to World Order* (Cambridge: Cambridge University Press).

Cram, L. (1994), 'The European Commission as a Multi-Organization: Social Policy and IT Policy in the EU', *Journal of European Public Policy*, 1 (2), 194–217.

Crawford, J. (ed.) (1988), *The Rights of Peoples* (Oxford: Clarendon Press).

Crockatt, R. (1995), *The Fifty Years War: The United States and the Soviet Union in World Politics, 1941–1991* (London: Routledge).

Cumings, B. (1999), 'Still the American Century', *Review of International Studies*, 25, Dec. 271–99.

D'Amico, F., and Beckman, P. (eds.) (1995), *Women in World Politics* (Westport, Conn.: Bergin & Garvey).

Dahl, R., (1994), 'A Democratic Dilemma: System Effectiveness versus Citizen Participation', *Political Science Quarterly*, 109 (1), 23–32.

Damrosch, L. F. (ed.) (1993), *Enforcing Restraint: Collective Intervention in Internal Conflicts* (New York: Council on Foreign Relations).

Davis, Z. S., and Frankel, B. (eds.) (1993), *The Proliferation Puzzle: Why Nuclear Weapons Spread and What Results* (London: Frank Cass).

Dawisha, K. (1990), *Eastern Europe, Gorbachev and Reform: The Great Challenge* (Cambridge: Cambridge University Press).

Dehousse, R. (1995), 'Institutional Reform in the European Community: Are there Alternatives to the Majoritarian Avenue?', *West European Politics*, 18 (3).

—— *et al.*, (1992), *Europe after 1992: New Regulatory Strategies (EUI Working Paper LAW No. 92/31)* (Florence: European University Institute).

—— (ed.) (1997), *Europe: The Impossible Status Quo* (London: Macmillan).

Denemark, R. A., Freidman, J., Gills, B. K., and Modelski, G. (eds.) (2000), *World System History* (London: Routledge).

Derrida, J. (1976), *Of Grammatology* (Baltimore: Johns Hopkins University Press).

—— (1992), *The Other Heading: Reflections on Today's Europe*, (Bloomington: Indiana University Press, 1992).

Destexhe, A. (1995), *Rwanda and Genocide in the Twentieth Century* (London: Pluto Press).

Deutsch, K. W. (1968), *The Analysis of International Relations* (Englewood Cliffs, NJ: Prentice Hall).

—— (1996), *Nationalism and Social Communication* (Cambridge, Mass.: MIT Press).

Devetak, R. (1996a), 'Critical Theory', in Burchill, Linklater, *et al.*, 145–78.

—— (1996b), 'Postmodernism', in Burchill, Linklater, *et al.*, 179–209.

—— and Higgott, R. (1999), 'Justice Unbound? Globalisation, States and the Transformation of the Social Bond', *International Affairs*, 75 (3): 515–30.

Dibb, P. (1988), *The Soviet Union: The Incomplete Superpower* (London: International Institute for Strategic Studies/ Macmillan).

Dicken, P. (1992), *Global Shift: The Internationalisation of Economic Activity* (London: Paul Chapman).

Donelan, M. (1990), *Elements of International Political Theory* (Oxford: Clarendon Press).

Donnelly, J. (1993), *International Human Rights* (Boulder, Colo.: Westview).

Doyle, M. W. (1982), 'Kant, Liberal Legacies and Foreign Affairs', *Philosophy and Public Affairs*, 12, 205–35 and 323–53.

—— (1983a), 'Kant, Liberal Legacies, and Foreign Affairs, part 1', *Philosophy and Public Affairs*, 12 (3).

—— (1983b), 'Kant, Liberal Legacies, and Foreign Affairs, part 2', *Philosophy and Public Affairs*, 12 (4).

—— (1995a), 'On the Democratic Peace', *International Security*, 19 (4): 164–84.

—— (1995b), 'Liberalism and World Politics Revisited', in Charles W. Kegley (ed.), *Controversies in International Relations Theory: Realism and the Neoliberal Challenge* (New York: St Martin's Press), 83–105.

—— (1997), *Ways of War and Peace: Realism, Liberalism, and Socialism* (New York: W. W. Norton & Co.).

—— (1999), 'A Liberal View: Preserving and Expanding the Liberal Pacific Union', in T. V. Paul and John A. Hall, *International Order and the Future of World Politics* (Oxford: Oxford University Press, 1999), 41–66.

Dreze, J., Sen, A., and Hussain A. (eds.) (1995), *The Political Economy of Hunger* (Oxford: Clarendon Press).

Drower, G. (1992), *Britain's Dependent Territories* (Aldershot: Dartmouth).

Drucker, P. (1993), *Managing in Turbulent Times* (Oxford: Butterworth & Heinemann).

Dugard, J. (1987), *Recognition and the United Nations* (Cambridge: Grotius Publications Ltd).

Dunn, L. A. (1991), *Containing Nuclear Proliferation, Adelphi Papers, 263* (London: Brassey's for IISS).

Dunne, T. (1995), 'The Social Construction of International Society', *European Journal of International Relations* 1 (3).

—— (1998), *Inventing International Society* (London: Macmillan).

—— Hill, C., and Hanson, M. (2000), 'New Interventionism', in William T. Tow and Marianne Hanson (eds.), *International Relations in the New Century: An Australian Perspective* (Melbourne: Oxford University Press), 93–116.

Economides, S., and Taylor, P. (1996), 'Former Yugoslavia', in James Mayall (ed.), *The New Interventionism, 1991–1994* (Cambridge: Cambridge University Press).

Eden, L. (1991), 'Bringing the Firm back in: Multinationals and IPE', *Millennium: Journal of International Studies*, 20 (1) : 197–224.

Edwards, G., and Regelsberger, E. (1990), *Europe's Global Links* (London: Pinter).

Eichengreen, B. (1998), 'Dental Hygiene and Nuclear War: How International Relations Looks at Economics', *International Organization*, 52 (4): 993–1012.

Ekins, P. (1992), *A New World Order: Grassroots Movements for Global Change* (London: Routledge).

Elson, D., 'Structural Adjustment: Its Effects on Women', in Tina Wallace with Candida March (eds.), *Changing Peceptions* (Oxford: Oxfam, 1991).

Elshtain, J. B. (1987), *Women and War* (New York: Basic Books).

Enloe, C. (1989), *Bananas, Beaches and Bases: Making Feminist Sense of International Politics* (London: Pandora Books).

—— (1992), 'Silicon Tricks and the Two Dollar Woman', *New Internationalist*, July 1994.

—— (1993), *The Morning After: Sexual Politics at the End of the Cold War* (Berkeley: University of California Press).

—— (2000), *Maneuvers: The International Politics of Militarizing Women's Lives* (Berkeley: University of California Press).

Ertekun, N. M. (1984), *The Cyprus Dispute and the Birth of the Turkish Republic of Northern Cyprus* (Rustem and Brother).

Esposito, J. (ed.) (1983), *Voices of Resurgent Islam* (Oxford: Oxford University Press).

—— (1991), *The Straight Path* (Oxford: Oxford University Press).

—— and Piscatori, J. (1991), 'Democratization and Islam', *Middle East Journal*, Washington, 45 (3).

European Journal of International Relations, 1(3) 267–331.

Evans, G., and Grant, B. (1995), *Australia's Foreign Relations: In the World of the 1990s* (Melbourne: Melbourne University Press).

Falk, R. (1975), *A Study of Future Worlds* (New York: Free Press).

—— (1993), 'Global Apartheid: The Structure of the World Economy', *Third World Resurgence*, 37 (Nov.).

—— (1995a), 'Liberalism at the Global Level: The Last of the Independent Commissions', *Millennium Special Issue: The Globalization of Liberalism?* 24 (3), 563–76.

—— (1995b), *On Humane Governance: Toward a New Global Politics* (Cambridge: Polity Press).

—— (1997), 'State of Siege: Will Globalization Win Out?', *International Affairs*, 73 (1).

Falf, R., (2000), 'A "New Medievalism"?', in G. Fry and J. O'Hagan (eds.), *Contending Images of World Politics* (Basingstoke: Macmillan).

—— and Mendlovitz, S. (eds.) (1973), *Regional Politics and World Order* (San Francisco: W. H. Freeman).

Fawcett, L., and Hurrell, A. (1995), *Regionalism in World Politics* (Oxford: Oxford University Press).

Fine, B. (1998), 'The Triumph of Economics: "Rationality Can Be Dangerous To Your Reasoning"', in James G. Carrier and Daniel Miller (eds.), *Virtualism: A New Political Economy*, (New York: Berg).

Finnemore, M., and Sikkink, K., 'International Norms and Political Change', *International Organization*, 42 (4): 887–918

Finney, M. (1997), *The Origins of the Second World War* (London: Arnold).

Finnis, J. (1980), *Natural Law and Natural Rights* (Oxford: Clarendon Press).

Fischer, D. A. V. (1992), *Stopping the Spread of Nuclear Weapons: the Past and the Prospects* (New York and London: Routledge).

Fischer, F. (1961), *Griff Nach der Weltmacht* (Dusseldorf: Drosle Verlag).

Fishlow, A. (1994), 'Latin America and the United States in a Changing World Economy', in A. F. Lowenthal and G. F. Treverton (eds.), *Latin America in a New World* (Boulder, Colo.: Westview Press).

Flax, J. (1987), 'Postmodernism and Gender Relations in Feminist Theory', *Signs*.

Foot, R. and Walter, A. (1999), 'Whatever Happened to the Pacific Century?', *Review of International Studies*, 25 (Dec.): 245–69

Forde, S. (1992), 'Classical Realism', in T. Nardin and D. Mapel (eds.), *Traditions of International Ethics* (Cambridge: Cambridge University Press), 372–93.

Forsythe, D. P. (1988), 'The United Nations and Human Rights', in Lawrence S. Finkelstein (ed.), *Politics in the United Nations System* (Durham and London: Duke University Press).

Franck, T., and Rodley, N. (1973), 'After Bangladesh: The Law of Humanitarian Intervention by Force', *American Journal of International Law*, 67: 275–305.

Frank, A. G. (1979), *Dependent Accumulation and Underdevelopment* (New York: Monthly Review Press).

—— and Gills, B. (eds.) (1996), *The World System: Five Hundred Years or Five Thousand?* (London: Routledge).

Frank, A. J. (1967), *Capitalism and Underdevelopment in Latin America* (New York: Monthly Review Press).

Frankel, B. (ed.) (1991), *Opaque Nuclear Proliferation* (London: Frank Cass and Company).

Friedman, T. (1999), *The Lexus and the Olive Tree* (New York: Harper Collins).

Friori, G. (1990), *Antonio Gramsci: Life of a Revolutionary*, trans. Tom Nairn (London: Verso).

Frost, M. (1996), *Ethics in International Relations: A Constitutive Theory* (Cambridge: Cambridge University Press).

Fukuyama, F. (1989), 'The End of History', *The National Interest*, 16.

—— (1992), *The End of History and the Last Man* (London: Hamish Hamilton).

Gaddis, J. (1986), 'The Long Peace: Elements of Stability in the Postwar International System', *International Security* 10 (4): 99–142.

—— (1992), *The United States and the End of the Cold War: Implications, Reconsiderations, Provocations* (New York: Oxford University Press).

Galtung, J. (1971), 'A Structural Theory of Imperialism', *Journal of Peace Research*, 8 (1).

Gamble, A. (1999), 'Marxism after Communism: Beyond Realism and Historicism', *Review of International Studies*, Special Issue (Dec.): 127–44.

Gamble, C. (1994), *Timewalkers: The Prehistory of Global Colonization* (Cambridge, Mass.: Harvard University Press).

Gardner, G. T. (1994), *Nuclear Nonproliferation. A Primer* (London and Boulder, Colo.: Lynne Rienner).

Garthoff, R. (1994), *The Great Transition: American-Soviet Relations and the End of the Cold War* (Washington, DC: Brookings Institution).

Gati, C. (1990), *The Bloc that Failed: Soviet–East European Relations in Transition* (Bloomington: Indiana University Press).

Gellner, E. (1983), *Nations and Nationalism* (Oxford: Blackwell).

George, J. (1994), *Discourses of Global Politics: A Critical (Re)Introduction to International Relations* (Boulder, Col.: Lynne Rienner).

George, S. (1992), *The Debt Boomerang* (Boulder, Col.: Westview Press).

Germain, R (ed.) (1999), *Globalization and its Critics* (Basingstoke: Macmillan Press).

—— and Kenny, M. (1998), 'Engaging Gramsci: International Relations Theory and the New Gramscians', *Review of International Studies*, 24 (1): 3–21.

Giddens, A. (1990), *The Consequences of Modernity: Self and Society in the Late Modern Age* (Cambridge: Polity Press, and Stanford, Calif.: Stanford University Press).

Gierke, O. (1987), *Political Theories of the Middle Ages*, trans. F. W. Maitland (Cambridge: Cambridge University Press).

Gill, S. (ed.) (1993), *Gramsci, Historical Materialism and International Relations* (Cambridge: Cambridge University Press).

—— (1995) 'Globalization, Market Civilisation and Disciplinary Neoliberalism', *Millennium: A Journal of International Studies*, 24 (3): 399–423.

—— and Law, D. (1988), *The Global Political Economy: Perspectives, Problems and Policies* (Hemel Hempstead: Harvester Wheatsheaf).

Gills, B. K. *et al.* (eds.) (1993), *Low Intensity Democracy: Political Power in the New World Order* (London: Pluto Press).

Gilpin, R. (1981), *War and Change in World Politics* (New York: Cambridge University Press).

—— (1986), 'The Richness of the Tradition of Political Realism', in R. Keohane (ed.), *Neorealism and its Critics* (New York: Columbia University Press), 301–21.

—— (1987), *The Political Economy of International Relations* (Princeton: Princeton University Press).

Glaser, C. (1994/5), 'Realists as Optimists: Cooperation as Self-Help', *International Security*, 19 (3): 50–90.

Goldman, M. (1992), *What Went Wrong With Perestroika* (New York: Norton).

Goldstein, J. S. (1994), *International Relations* (New York: Harper Collins).

Goodman, D., and Redclift, M. (1991), *Refashioning Nature: Food, Ecology and Culture* (London: Routledge).

Gorbachev, M. (1988), *Perestroika: New Thinking for Our Country and the World* (London: Fontana).

Gowa, J. (1983), *Closing the Cold Window: Domestic Politics and the End of Bretton Woods* (Ithaca, NY: Cornell University Press).

Grace, C. S. (1994), *Nuclear Weapons. Principles, Effects and Survivability* (London: Brassey's).

Grant, R., and Newland, K. (eds.) (1989), *Gender and International Relations* (Milton Keynes: Open University Press).

Gray, C. S. (1996), 'The Second Nuclear Age: Insecurity, Proliferation, and the Control of Arms', in W. Murrey (ed.), *The Brassey's Mershon American Defense Annual, 1995–1996: The United States and the Emerging Strategic Environment* (Washington, DC: Brassey's), 135–54.

—— (1999), *The Second Nuclear Age* (Boulder, Colo. and London: Lynne Rienner).

Gray, J. (1995), *Enlightenment's Wake: Politics and Culture at the Close of the Modern Age* (London: Routledge).

Green, D. (1995), *Silent Revolution: The Rise of Market Economic in Latin America* (London: Latin America Bureau).

Greenwood, C. (1993), 'Is there a Right of Humanitarian Intervention?', *The World Today*, 49.

Greenwood, J., (1998), *Representing Interests in the European Union* (Basingstoke: Macmillan).

Grieco, J. (1988*a*), 'Anarchy and the Limits of Cooperation: A Realist Critique of the Newest Liberal Institution', *International Organization*, 42 (Aug.): 485–507.

—— (1988*b*), 'Realist Theory and the Problem of International Cooperation', *Journal of Politics*, 50 (Summer): 600–24.

—— (1997), 'Realist International Theory and the Study of World Politics', in M. Doyle and G. J. Ikenberry (eds), *New*

Thinking in International Relations Theory (Boulder Colo.: Westview Press), 163–201.

Grubb, M., Koch, M., Munson, A., Sullivan, F., and Thompson, K. (1993), *The Earth Summit Agreements: A Guide and Assessment* (London: Royal Institute for International Affairs).

Haas, E. (1958) *The Uniting of Europe* (Stanford, Calif.: Stanford University Press).

—— (1968), 'Technology, Pluralism, and the New Europe', in J. S. Nye (ed.), *International Regionalism* (Boston: Little, Brown).

Haas, P. M., Keohane, R. O., and Levy, M. (eds.) (1993), *Institutions for the Earth: Sources of Effective International Environmental Action* (London: MIT Press).

Haas, R. D. (1993), 'The Corporation without Boundaries', in M. Ray and A. Rinzler (eds.), *The New Paradigm in Business: Emerging Strategies for Leadership and Organizational Change* (New York: Tarcher/Perigee).

Halliday, F. (1983), *The Making of the Second Cold War* (London: Verso; 2nd edn. 1986).

—— (1994), *Rethinking International Relations* (London: Macmillan)

—— (1999), 'The Potentials of Enlightenment,' *Review of International Studies*, 25 (Dec.): 105–25.

Ham, P. van (1993), *Managing Non-Proliferation Regimes in the 1990s* (London: Royal Institute of International Affairs, Pinter Publishers).

Hamilton, K. and Langhorne, R., (1995), *The Practice of Diplomacy* (London: Routledge).

Hardin, G. (1968), 'The Tragedy of the Commons', *Science*, 162: 1243–8.

Harding, S. (1986), *The Science Question in Feminism* (Milton Keynes: Open University Press).

Harvey, D. (1987), 'The World Systems Theory Trap', *Studies in Comparative International Development*, 22 (1).

—— (1989), *The Condition of Postmodernity: An Enquiry into the Conditions of Cultural Change* (Oxford: Blackwell).

Hasenclever, A., Mayer, P., and Rittberger, V. (1997), *Theories of International Regimes* (Cambridge, Cambridge University Press).

—— —— —— (2000), 'Integrating theories of regimes', *Review of International Studies*, 26: 3–33

Hashemi, S. (1996), 'International Society and its Islamic Malcontents', *The Fletcher Forum of World Affairs*, 20 (2).

Heilbroner, R. and Milberg, (1995), *The Crisis of Vision in Modern Economic Thought* (Cambridge: Cambridge University Press).

Held, D. (1993), 'Democracy: From City-states to a Cosmopolitan Order?', in D. Held (ed.), *Prospects for Democracy: North, South, East, West* (Cambridge: Polity Press), 13–52.

Held, D., (1995), *Democracy and the Global Order: From the Modern State to Cosmopolitan Governance* (Cambridge: Polity Press).

—— Mcgrew, A., Goldblatt, D., and Perraton, J. (1999), *Global Transformations: Politics, Economics and Culture* (Cambridge: Polity Press).

Helleiner, E. (1995), 'Explaining the Globalization of Financial Markets: Bringing the State back in', *The Review of International Political Economy*, 2 (2): 315–41.

Helman, G. B., and Ratner, S. R. (1992/3), 'Saving Failed States', *Foreign Policy*, 89: 3–20.

Hempel, L. C. (1996), *Environmental Governance: The Global Challenge* (Washington, DC: Island Press).

Heraclides, A. (1990), *The Self-Determination of Minorities in International Politics* (London: Cass).

Hersh, S. M. (1983), *The Price of Power: Kissinger in the Nixon White House* (New York: Summit Books).

Hertz, J. H. (1962), *International Politics in the Atomic Age* (New York: Columbia University Press).

Herz, J. (1950), 'Idealist Internationalism and the Security Dilemma', *World Politics*, 2 (2)

—— (1981), 'Political Realism Revisited', *International Studies Quarterly*, 25: 182–97.

Hettne, B., Inotai, A., and Sunkel, O. (eds.) (1999), *Globalization and the New Regionalism* (Basingstoke: Macmillan).

Higgott, R. A., 'The Asian Economic Crisis: A Case Study in the Politics of Resentment', *New Political Economy*, 3 (3): 333–56.

—— (1999), 'Economics, Politics and (International) Political Economy: The Need for a Balanced Diet in an Era of Globalisation', *New Political Economy*, 4 (1) 23–36.

—— (2001), 'Taming Economics, Emboldening International Relations: The Theory and Practice of IPE 10 Years after the Cold War', in Stephanie Lawson (ed.), *After the Wall: International Relations after the Cold War* (Cambridge: Polity Press).

Hill, C. (1993), 'The Capability-Expectations Gap, or Conceptualizing Europe's International Role', *Journal of Common Market Studies*, (31)1: 305–28.

—— (1996), 'World Opinion and the Empire of Circumstance', *International Affairs*, 72 (1).

Hinsley F. H. (1967), *Power and the Pursuit of Peace* (Cambridge: Cambridge University Press).

—— (1973), *Nationalism and the International System* (London: Hodder and Stoughton).

Hirschmann, A. O. (1945), *National Power and the Structure of Foreign Trade* (Berkeley: University of California Press).

——(1977), *The Passions and the Interests* (Princeton: Princeton University Press).

—— (1986), 'Against Parsimony: Three Easy Ways of Complicating Some Categories of Economic Discourse', in Hirschmann (ed.), *Rival Views of Market Society and Other Recent Essays* (New York: Viking Books).

Hirst, J. (1996), 'In Defence of Appeasement: Indonesia and Australian Foreign Policy', *Quadrant*, 40 (4).

Hirst, P., and Thompson, G. (1996; 2nd edn. 1999), *Globalization in Question: The International Economy and the Possibilities of Governance* (Cambridge: Polity Press).

Hix, S. (1994), 'Approaches to the Study of the EC: The Challenge to Comparative Politics', *West European Politics*, 17 (1): 1–30.

Hobbes, T. (1991), *Leviathan*, ed. R. Tuck (Cambridge: Cambridge University Press).

Hobden, S. (1998), *International Relations and Historical Sociology: Breaking Down Boundaries* (London: Routledge).

Hobsbawm, E. (1990), *Nations and Nationalism Since 1780: Programme, Myth, Reality* (Cambridge: Cambridge University Press).

—— (1994), *Age of Extremes: The Short Twentieth Century, 1914–1991* (London: Michael Joseph).

—— (1995), 'Pax Americana: Bosnia is its First Success', *Independent*, 22 Nov.

Hobson, J. M. (2000), *The State and International Relations* (Cambridge: Cambridge University Press).

Hocking, B., (1999), *Foreign Ministries: Change and Adaptation* (Basingstoke: Macmillan).

—— and Smith, M. (1990), *World Politics: An Introduction to International Relations* (London: Harvester Wheatsheaf).

Hoffman, M. (1987), 'Critical Theory and the Inter-Paradigm Debate', *Millennium*, 16 (2): 231–49.

—— (1993), 'Agency, Identity and Intervention', in I. Forbes and M. Hoffman (eds.), *Political Theory, International Relations and the Ethics of Intervention* (Houndmills, Basingstoke: St Martin's Press).

Hoffmann, S. (1987), *Janus and Minerva: Essays on the Theory and Practice of International Politics* (Boulder, Colo.: Westview).

—— (1995), 'The Politics and Ethics of Military Intervention', *Survival*, 37 (4), 29–51.

Hogan, M. (ed.) (1992), *The End of the Cold War: Its Meaning and Implications* (Cambridge: Cambridge University Press).

Hollis, M., and Smith, S. (1990), *Explaining and Understanding International Relations* (Oxford: Clarendon Press).

Holsti, K. J. (1996), *War, the State, and the State of War* (Cambridge: Cambridge University Press).

Holt, P. M., Lambton, A., and Lewis, B. (1970), *The Cambridge History of Islam*, vols. 1 and 2 (Cambridge: Cambridge University Press).

Homer-Dixon, T. F. (1994), 'Environmental Scarcities and Violent Conflict: Evidence from Cases', *International Security* 19 (1): 5–40.

Honeygold, D. (1989), *International Financial Markets* (Cambridge: Woodhead-Faulkner).

Horsman, M., and Marshall, A. (1994), *After the Nation-State: Citizens, Tribalism and the New World Disorder* (New York: Harper Collins).

Hough, J. (1988), *Opening up the Soviet Economy* (Washington, DC: Brookings Institution).

Houghton, J., Jenkins, G., and Ephraums, J. (eds.) (1990), *Climate Change: The Ipcc Assessment* (Cambridge: Cambridge University Press).

Howlett, D., and Simpson, J. (1993), 'Nuclearisation and Denuclearisation in South Africa', *Survival*, 35 (3).

—— Leigh-Phippard, H., and Simpson, J. (1996), 'After the 1995 NPT Renewal Conference: Can the Treaty Survive the Outcome?', in John B. Poole and Richard Guthrie (eds.), *Verification Report 1996. Arms Control, Peacekeeping and the Environment* (Boulder, San Francisco, and Oxford: Westview Press).

Human Development Report 1999, United Nations Development Programme, www.undp.org

Humm, M. (1992), *Feminisms: A Reader* (New York: Harvester Wheatsheaf).

Hunger Project (1985), *Ending Hunger: An Idea whose Time has Come* (New York: Praeger).

Hunter, S. (ed.) (1988), *The Politics of Islamic Revivalism: Diversity and Unity* (Bloomington, Ind.: Indiana University Press).

Huntington, S. (1993), 'The Clash of Civilizations', *Foreign Affairs*, 72 (3): 22–169.

—— (1996), *The Clash of Civilizations and the Remaking of the World Order* (New York: Simon and Schuster).

Hurrell, A. (1994), 'Regionalism in the Americas', in A. Lowenthal and G. Treverton (eds.), *Latin America in a New World Order* (Boulder, Col.: Westview Press).

—— (1995), 'Explaining the Resurgence of Regionalism in World Politics', *Review of International Studies* 21 (4).

—— and Kingsbury B. (eds.) (1992), *The International Politics of the Environment: Actors, Interests and Institutions* (Oxford: Clarendon Press).

—— and Woods, N. (1995), 'Globalization and Inequality', *Millennium*, 24 (3): 447–70.

Hutton, W. (1995), *The State We're In* (London: Jonathan Cape).

ICPF (1994), *Uncommon Opportunities: An Agenda for Peace and Equitable Development* (London: Zed).

Ignatieff, M., 'The Show that Europe Missed', *Independent*, 22 Nov. 1995.

—— (2000), *Virtual War: Kosovo and Beyond* (New York: Henry Holt).

Ikenberry, G. John (1999), 'Liberal Hegemony and the Future of American Postwar Order', in T. V. Paul and J. A. Hall (eds.), *International Order and the Future of World Politics* (Cambridge: Cambridge University Press).

—— (2000), *After Victory: Institutions, Strategic Restraint, and the Rebuilding of Order after Major Wars* (Princeton: Princeton University Press).

International Affairs (2000), 'Europe: Where does it begin and where does it end? Special Issue, 76 (3): 437–574.

Jackson, B. (1990), *Poverty and the Planet* (London: Penguin).

Jackson, R. H. (1990), *Quasi-States: Sovereignty, International Relations and the Third World* (Cambridge: Cambridge University Press).

James, A. (1986), *Sovereign Statehood: The Basis of International Society* (London: Allen & Unwin).

—— (1993), 'System or Society?', *Review of International Studies*, 19 (3).

Jayawardena, K. (1986), *Feminism and Nationalism in the Third World* (London: Zed Books).

Jervis, R. (1983a), *The Illogic of American Nuclear Strategy* (Ithaca, NY: Cornell University Press).

—— (1983b), 'Security Regimes', in Krasner (1983)

—— (1999), 'Realism, Neoliberalism, and Cooperation: Understanding the Debate', *International Security*, 24 (Summer): 42–63.

John, I. M. W., and Garnett, J. (1972), 'International Politics at Aberystwyth 1919–1969', in B. Porter, *The Aberystwyth Papers: International Politics 1919–1969* (London: Oxford University Press), 86–102.

Jones, B. D. (1995), ' "Intervention Without Borders": Humanitarian Intervention in Rwanda, 1990–94', *Millennium: Journal of International Studies*, 24.

Jones, P. (1994), *Rights* (Basingstoke: Macmillan).

Jones R. W. , (1995), ' "Message in a Bottle"? Theory and Praxis in Critical Security Studies', *Contemporary Security Policy*, 16 (3)

—— (1999), *Security, Strategy and Critical Theory* (Boulder, Colo.: Lynne Rienner).

—— (ed.) (2000), *Critical Theory and World Politics* (Boulder, Colo.: Lynne Rienner).

Jørgensen, K. E. (1998), 'Sleeping Beauty is Awake!', *Studia Diplomatica*, 51 (1–2).

Kaldor, M. (1995), 'Who Killed the Cold War?', *The Bulletin of The Atomic Scientists*, July/Aug, 57–60.

—— (1999), *New and Old Wars: Organized Violence in a Global Era* (Cambridge: Polity Press).

Kant, I. (1991), *Political Writings*, ed. Hans Reiss (Cambridge: Cambridge University Press).

—— 'Perpetual Peace', in M. Forsyth, H. M. A. Keens-Soper, and P. Savigear (eds.), *The Theory of International Relations: Selected Texts from Gentili to Treitschke*, (London: Allen and Unwin, 1970).

Kanter, R. M. (1995), *World Class: Thriving Locally in the Global Economy* (New York: Simon and Schuster).

Kaplan, R. D. (1994), ' The Coming Anarchy', *The Atlantic Monthly*.

Karp, A. (1995), *Ballistic Missile Proliferation: The Politics and Technics* (Oxford: Oxford University Press for SIPRI).

Katzenstein, P. (ed.) (1996), *The Culture of National Security: Norms and Identity in World Politics* (New York: Columbia University Press).

—— Keohane, R. O., and Krasner, S (1998), 'International Organization and the Study of World Politics', *International Organization*, 52 (4): 463–85, 645–85.

Keck, M., and Sikkink, K. (1998), *Activists beyond Borders: Transnational Advocacy Networks in International Politics* (Ithaca, NY: Cornell University Press).

Kegley, C. (ed.) (1995), *Controversies in International Relations Theory: Realism and the Neoliberal Challenge* (New York: St Martin's).

—— and Wittkopf, E. (1999), *World Politics: Trend and Transformation*, 7th edn. (New York: St Martin's).

Kennan, G. (1992), 'The GOP Won the Cold War? Ridiculous', *New York Times*, 28 Oct.

Kennedy, P. (1998), *The Rise and Fall of Great Powers: Economic Change and Military Conflict from 1500–2000* (Harmondsworth: Penguin).

Keohane, R. (1984), *After Hegemony: Cooperation and Discord in the World Political Economy* (Princeton: Princeton University Press).

—— (ed.) (1989a), *International Institutions and State Power: Essays in International Relations Theory* (Boulder, Col.: Westview).

—— (1989b), 'Theory of World Politics: Structural Realism and Beyond', in Keohane (1989a).

—— and Martin, L. (1995), 'The Promise of Institutionalist Theory', *International Security*, 20 (1): 39–51.

—— and Nye, J. (eds.) (1971), *Transnational Relations and World Politics* (Cambridge, Mass.: Harvard University Press).

—— —— (1977), *Power and Interdependence: World Politics in Transition* (Boston: Little, Brown).

—— —— and Hoffmann, S. (eds.) (1993), *After the Cold War: International Institutions and State Strategies in Europe 1989–1991* (London: Harvard University Press).

Keylor, W. (1992), *The Twentieth Century World: An International History* (New York: Oxford University Press)

Keynes, J. M. (1919), *The Economic Consequences of the Peace* (London: Macmillan).

Khoman, T. (1992), 'ASEAN: Conception and Evolution', in Sandhu *et al.* (1992).

Khor, M. (1995), Remarks to the International Forum on Globalization (New York, November).

Kidron, M., and Segal, R. (1995), *The State of the World Atlas* (London: Penguin).

Kirkpatrick, J. (1979), 'Dictatorships and double Standards', *Commentary*, 68.

Kissinger, H. A. (1977), *American Foreign Policy*, 3rd edn. (New York: W. W. Norton).

Klintworth, G. (1989), *Vietnam's Intervention in Cambodia in International Law* (Canberra: AGPS Press).

Knox, P., and Agnew, J. (1994), *The Geography of the World Economy* (London: Edward Arnold).

Kohli, A. (1985), 'The Politics of Land Reform', in A. Gauhar (ed.), *Third World Affairs* (London: Third World Foundation).

Kolawoski, L. (1978), *The Main Currents of Marxism*. Vol. 1. *The Founders* Vol. 2. *The Golden Age* Vol. 3. *The Breakdown* (Oxford: Oxford University Press).

Kotschwar, B. R. (1995), 'South–South Economic Cooperation: Regional Trade Agreements among Developing Countries', *Cooperation South* (UN Development Programme).

Krasner, S. D. (ed.) (1983), *International Regimes* (Ithaca, NY: Cornell University Press).

—— (1985), *Structural Conflict: The Third World Against Global Liberalism* (Berkeley: University of California Press).

—— (1991), 'Global Communications and National Power: Life on the Pareto Frontier', *World Politics*, 43: 336–66

—— (1993), 'Sovereignty, Regimes and Human Rights' in Rittberger (1993).

Kratochwil, F. (1989), *Rules, Norms, and Decisions* (Cambridge: Cambridge University Press).

—— (1993), 'The Embarrassment of Changes: Neo-Realism as the Science of *Realpolitik* without Politics', *Review of International Studies*, 19(1): 63–80.

Krause, K. (ed.) (1999), *Culture and Security. Multilateral Arms Control and Security Building* (London: Frank Cass).

Krauthammer, C. (1990–1), 'The Unipolar Moment', *Foreign Affairs*, 70: 23–33.

—— (1992), 'In Bosnia, Partition Might Do', *International Herald Tribune*, 9 Sept.

Krugman, (1999), *The Return of Depression Economics* (London: Allen Lane, The Penguin Press).

Kupchan, C., and Kupchan, C. (1991), 'Concerts, Collective Security and the Future of Europe', *International Security*, 16 (1).

—— —— (1993), 'The Promise of Collective Security', *International Security* 20(1).

Laidi, Z (1998), *A World Without Meaning: The Crisis of Meaning in International Politics* (London: Routledge).

Lapid, Y. (1989), 'The Third Debate: On the Prospects of International Theory in a Post-Positivist Era', *International Studies Quarterly*, 33 (3): 235–25.

Latham, R. (1997), *The Liberal Moment: Modernity, Security, and the Making of Postwar International Order* (New York: Columbia University Press).

Lavoy, P. (1995), 'The Strategic Consequences of Nuclear Proliferation. A Review Essay', *Security Studies*, 4(4): 695–753.

Lawler, L. (1995), 'The Core Assumptions and Presumptions of "Cooperative Security"', in S. Lawson (ed.), *The New Agenda for Global Security: Cooperating for Peace and Beyond* (St Leonards).

Lebow, R., and Stein, J. (1994), 'Reagan and the Russians', *Atlantic Monthly*, 273 (2), Feb, 35–7.

Lenin, V. I. (1966), *Imperialism, the Highest Stage of Capitalism: A Popular Outline*, 13th edn. (Moscow: Progress Publishers).

Lessig, L. (1999), *Code and Other Laws of Cyberspace* (New York: Basic Books).

Leventhal, P., and Alexander, Y. (eds.) (1987), *Preventing Nuclear Terrorism* (Lexington, Mass., and Toronto: Lexington Books).

Levy, B., and Spiller, P. T. (eds.) (1996), *Regulations, Institutions, and Commitment: Comparative Studies of Telecommunications* (New York: Cambridge University Press).

Levy, M. A., Young, O. R., and Zurn, M. (1995), 'The Study of International Regimes', *European Journal of International Relations*, 1 (3): 267–330.

Linklater, A. (1990a), *Men and Citizens in the Theory of International Relations*, 2 edn.; 1 edn. 1982 (London: Macmillan).

—— (1990b), *Beyond Realism and Marxism: Critical Theory and International Relations* (London: Macmillan).

—— (1996), 'The Achievements of Critical Theory,' in S. Smith, K. Booth, and M. Zalewski (eds.), *International Theory: Positivism and Beyond* (Cambridge: Cambridge University Press), 279–98.

—— (1998), *The Transformation of Political Community: Ethical Foundations of the Post-Westphalian Era* (Cambridge: Polity).

Little, R. (1996), 'The Growing Relevance of Pluralism?', in S. Smith, K. Booth, and M. Zalewski (eds.), *International Theory: Positivism and Beyond* (Cambridge: Cambridge University Press), 66–86.

Long, D. (1996), 'The Harvard School of International Theory: A Case for Closure', *Millennium*, 24 (3): 489–506.

Luard, E. (ed.) (1992), *Basic Texts in International Relations* (London: Macmillan).

Luttwak, E. (1998), *Turbo Capitalism: Winners and Losers in the Global Economy*, London: Weidenfield and Nicolson.

Lynch, C. (1998), 'Social Movements and the Problem of Globalization', *Alternatives*, 23 (2): 149–73.

Lyons, G. M., and Mastanduno, M. (eds.) (1995), *Beyond Westphalia? State Sovereignty and International Intervention* (Baltimore and London: Johns Hopkins University Press).

Lyotard, J.-F. (1984), *The Postmodern Condition: A Report on Knowledge* (Manchester: Manchester University Press).

Machiavelli, N. (1965), *The Art of War*, ed. Neal Wood (New York: Da Capo Press).

—— (1988), *The Prince*, ed. Q. Skinner (Cambridge: Cambridge University Press).

McGrew, A. (2001), 'From Global Governance to Good Governance: Theories and Prospects of Democratizing the Global Polity', in Morten Ougaard and Richard Higgott (eds.), *The Global Polity* (London: Routledge, forthcoming).

—— Lewis, P., *et al*. (1992), *Global Politics* (Cambridge: Polity Press).

McLuhan, M. (1964), *Understanding Media* (London: Routledge).

McMichael, P. (1996), 'Globalization: Myths and Realities', *Rural Sociology*, 61 (1): 257–77.

Mann, M. (1986), *The Sources of Social Power*, Vol. 1. *A History of Power from the Beginning to A.D. 1760* (Cambridge: Cambridge University Press)

—— (1993), *The Sources of Social Power* Vol. 2. *The Rise of Classes and Nation States, 1760–1914* (Cambridge: Cambridge University Press).

Mansbach, R., Ferguson, Y., and Lampert, D. (1976), *The Web of World Politics* (Englewood Cliffs, NJ. Prentice-Hall).

Marks, G., *et al*. (1996a), 'European Integration from the 1980s: State-Centric v. Multilevel Governance', *Journal of Common Market Studies*, 34 (3) 341–79.

Marshall, J. (ed.) (1996), *The New Interventionism 1991–1994* (Cambridge: Cambridge University Press).

Martel, G. (1986) (ed.), *The Origins of the Second World War Reconsidered* (London: Allen & Unwin).

Marx, K. (1992), *Capital: Student Edition*, ed. C. J. Arthur (London: Lawrence & Wishart).

Mastanduno, M. (2000), 'Models, Markets and Power: Political Economy and the Asia-Pacific, 1989 – 1999', *Review of International Studies*, 26 (4): 493–508.

Mathews, J. T. (1997) 'Power Shift', *Foreign Affairs*, Jan./Feb.

Mattingly, G. (1995), *Renaissance Diplomacy* (Harmondsworth: Penguin).

Mattli, W. (1999), *The Logic of Regional Integration: Europe and Beyond* (Cambridge: Cambridge University Press).

Mayall, J. (1990), *Nationalism and International Society* (Cambridge: Cambridge University Press).

—— (1991), 'Non-Intervention, Self-Determination and the "New World Order"', *International Affairs*, 67.

—— (1996), *The Interventionism, 1991–1994* (Cambridge: Cambridge University Press).

Maynard, M. (1995), 'Beyond the "Big Three": The Development of Feminist Theory in the 1990s', *Women's History Review*, 4 (3).

Mazarr, M. (1995), 'Virtual Nuclear Arsenals', *Survival*, 37 (3).

Meadows, D. H., Meadows, D. L., and Randers, J. (1972), *The Limits to Growth* (London: Earth Island).

—— (1992), *Beyond the Limits: Global Collapse or a Sustainable Future* (London: Earthscan).

Mearsheimer, J. (1990), 'Back to the Future: Instability After the Cold War', *International Security*, 15 (1): 5–56.

—— (1994/5), 'The False Promise of International Institutions', *International Security* 19 (3); 5–49.

Meinecke, F. (1957), *Machiavellism: The Doctrine of 'Raison d'Etat' and Its Place in Modern History*, trans. D. Scott (London: Routledge).

Mendlovitz, S. (1975), *On the Creation of a Just World Order* (New York: Free Press).

Meyer, S. M. (1984), *The Dynamics of Nuclear Proliferation* (Chicago: University of Chicago Press).

Michalet, C.-A. (1982), 'From International Trade to World Economy: A New Paradigm', in H. Makler *et al.*, *The New International Economy* (London: Sage), 37–58.

Miller, D., (1999), 'Bounded Citizenship', in K. Hutchings and R. Danreuther (eds.), *Cosmopolitan Citizenship* (London: Macmillan.

Miller, J. (1993), 'The Challenge of Radical Islam', *Foreign Affairs*, 72.

Milner, H. V. (1988), *Resisting Protectionism: Global Industries and the Politics of International Trade* (Princeton: Princeton University Press).

Minear, L., and Weiss, T. G. (1995), *Mercy Under Fire: War and the Global Humanitarian Community* (Boulder, Col.: Westview Press).

Mitchell, R. (1995), *Bridled Ambition—Why Countries Constrain their Nuclear Capabilities* (Washington, DC: Woodrow Wilson Center).

Mitrany, D. (1943), *A Working Peace System* (London: RIIA).

Modelski, G. (1972), *Principles of World Politics* (New York: Free Press).

—— (1988), *Sea Power in Global Politics* 1494–1943 (Seattle: University of Washington Press).

Mohanty, C. *et al.* (eds.) (1991), *Third World Women and the Politics of Feminism* (Bloomington: Indiana University Press).

Molina, M. J., and Rowland, F. S. (1974), 'Stratospheric Sink for Chlorofluoromethanes: Chlorine Atom Catalysed Destruction of Ozone', *Nature*, 249: 810–14.

Moravcsik, A., (1993), 'Preferences and Power in the European Community: A Liberal Intergovernmentalist Approach', *Journal of Common Market Studies*, 31(4): 473–523.

Morgenthau, H. J. ([1948]1955), *Politics Among Nations: The Struggle for Power and Peace*, 2nd edn. (New York: Knopf).

—— (1978), *Politics Among Nations: The Struggle for Power and Peace* (New York: Knopf).

—— (1962), *Politics among Nations* (New York: A. Knopf).

Morse, E. (1976), *Modernization and the Transformation of International Relations* (New York: Free Press).

Morton, A. (1999), 'On Gramsci', *Politics*, 19 (1): 1–8.

Munting, R. (1982), *The Economic Development of the USSR* (London: Macmillan).

Murphy, C. N. (1994), *International Organization and Industrial Change* (Cambridge: Polity Press).

Naisbitt, J. (1994), *Global Paradox: The Bigger the World Economy, the More Powerful its Smallest Players* (London: Brealey).

Nardin, T. (1983), *Law, Morality and the Relations of States* (Princeton: Princeton University Press).

Naya, S., and Imada, P. (1992), 'Implementing AFTA, 1992–2007', in Sandhu (1992).

Nicolson, H. (1954), *The Evolution of Diplomatic Method* (London: Constable).

Nye, J. S. (ed.) (1968), *International Regionalism: Readings* (Boston: Little, Brown).

O'Brien, P. (1984), 'Europe in the World Economy', in H. Bull and A. Watson (eds.), *The Expansion of International Society* (Oxford: Clarendon Press).

O'Brien, R. (1992), *Global Financial Integration: The End of Geography* (London: Pinter).

Oberdorfer, D. (1992), *The Turn: From the Cold War to a New Era* (New York: Touchstone Books).

Ogilvie-White, T. (1996), 'Is There A Theory of Nuclear Proliferation?', *The Nonproliferation Review*, 4(1): 43–60.

Ohmae, K. (1990), *The Borderless World: Power and Strategy in the Interlinked Economy* (London: Fontana).

—— (1995), *The End of the Nation State: The Rise of Regional Economies* (New York: Free Press).

Olson, M. (1965), *The Logic of Collective Action* (Cambridge: Harvard University Press).

Onuf, N. (1989), *A World of our Making: Rules and Rule in Social Theory and International Relations* (Columbia: University of South Carolina Press).

O'Rourke, K. H. and Williamson, J. J. (1999), *Globalization and History: The Evolution of the Nineteenth-Century Atlantic Economy* (Cambridge, Mass: MIT Press).

Ostrom, E. (1990), *Governing the Commons: Evolution of Institutions for Collective Action* (Cambridge: Cambridge University Press).

Owen, R. (1992), *State, Power and Politics in the Making of the Modern Middle East* (London: Routledge).

Oye, K. A. (ed.) (1986), *Cooperation Under Anarchy* (Princeton: Princeton University Press).

Panagariya, A. (1994), 'East Asia; A New Trading Bloc?' *Finance and Development*, March.

Parekh, B. (1997), 'Rethinking Humanitarian Intervention', *International Political Science Review*, 18(1): 49–70.

Pauly. L., and Reich, S. (1997) 'National Structures and Multinational Corporate Behavior: Enduring Differences in the Age of Globalization', *International Organisation*, 51 (1): 1–30.

Pearson, R. (2000), 'Rethinking Gender Matters in Development', in T. Allen, and A. Thomas (eds.), *Poverty and Development into the Twenty-first Century* (Oxford: University Press), 383–402.

Pendergrast, M. (1993), *For God, Country and Coca-Cola: The Unauthorized History of the Great American Soft Drink and the Company that Makes It* (London: Weidenfeld and Nicolson).

Peterson, V. S. (1990), 'Whose Rights? A Critique of the "Givens" in Human Rights Discourse', *Alternatives*, 15.

—— (1992), 'Security and Sovereign States: What is at Stake in Taking Feminism Seriously', in Peterson (ed.), *Gendered States: Feminist (Re)Visions of International Relations Theory* (London: Lynne Rienner)

—— (1994), 'Gendered Nationalism', *Peace Review*, 6.

Petrella, R. (1996), 'Globalization and Internationalization: The Dynamics of the Emerging World Order', in Boyer and Drache (1996).

Pettman, J. J. (1996), *Worlding Women: A Feminist International Politics* (St Leonards: Allen and Unwin).

Phillips, A. (2000), 'The Political Economy of Russia: Transition or Condition?', in Bowker and Ross, eds, (2000): 121–34.

Pipes, R. (1992), Letter to the Editor, *New York Times*, 6 Nov.

Piscatori, J. (1992), 'Islam and World Politics', in John Baylis and N. J. Rengger (eds.), *Dilemmas of World Politics; International Issues in a Changing World* (Oxford: Oxford University Press).

Pope Atkins, G. (1995), *Latin America in the International Political System* (Oxford, Westview Press).

Porter, G., and Brown, J. W. (1991), *Global Environmental Politics* (Boulder, Colo.: Westview Press).

Porter, M. E. (ed.) (1986), *Competition in Global Industries* (Boston: Harvard Business School Press).

—— (1990), *The Competitive Advantage of Nations* (London: Macmillan).

Potter, W. (1995), 'Before the Deluge? Assessing the Threat of Nuclear Leakage From the Post-Soviet States', *Arms Control Today*, Oct.

Prebisch, R. (1963), *Towards a Dynamic Development Policy in Latin America* (New York, United Nations).

—— (1964), *Towards a New Trade Policy for Development* (New York: United Nations).

Price, R., and Tannenwald, N. (1996), 'Norms and Deterrence: The Nuclear and Chemical Weapons Taboos', in P. J.

Katzenstein (ed.), *The Culture of National Security: Norms and Identity in World Politics* (New York: Columbia University Press), 114–152.

Raffety, F. W. (1928), *The Works of the Right Honourable Edmund Burke*, vol. 6 (Oxford: Oxford University Press).

Ramsbotham, O., and Woodhouse, T. (1996), *Humanitarian Intervention in Contemporary Conflict* (Cambridge: Polity Press,).

Rapley, J. (1996), *Understanding Development* (Boulder, Colo.: Lynne Rienner).

Rawls, J. (1971), *A Theory of Justice* (Oxford: Oxford University Press).

Reich, R. B. (1991), *The Work of Nations: Preparing Ourselves for 21st-Century Capitalism* (New York: Simon & Schuster).

Reinecke, W. (1988), *Global Public Policy: Governing without Government* (Washington DC: Brookings Institution).

Reiser, O. L., and Davies, B. (1944), *Planetary Democracy: An Introduction to Scientific Humanism and Applied Semantics* (New York: Creative Age Press).

Reiss, H. (ed.) (1989), *Kant's Political Writings* (Cambridge: Cambridge University Press).

Reiss, M. (1995), *Bridled Ambition—Why Countries Constrain Their Nuclear Capabilities* (published by the Woodrow Wilson Center Press, Washington, DC: and distributed by the Johns Hopkins University Press, Baltimore).

—— and Lutwak, R. (eds.) (1994), *Nuclear Proliferation After the Cold War*, (Washington, DC: Woodrow Wilson Center Press).

Rengger, N. (1992), 'Culture, Society and Order in World Politics', in John Baylis and N. J. Rengger (eds.), *Dilemmas of World Politics: International Issues in a Changing World* (Oxford: Oxford University Press).

—— (2000), *International Relations, Political Theory and the Problem of Order: Beyond International Relations Theory?* (London: Routledge).

Review of International Studies (2000), Special Section on 'The Asian-Pacific Crisis', 26(3): 359–428.

Richardson, J. L. (1994), *Crisis Diplomacy: The Great Powers since the Mid-Nineteenth Century* (Cambridge: Cambridge University Press).

Rittberger, V. (ed.) (1993), *Regime Theory and International Relations* (Oxford: Clarendon Press).

Roberts, A. (1993), 'Humanitarian War: Military Intervention and Human Rights', *International Affairs*, 69.

—— (1996), 'The United Nations: Variants of Collective Security', in Ngaire Woods, *Explaining International Relations Since 1945* (Oxford: Oxford University Press) 309–36.

—— and Kingsbury, B. (1993), 'Introduction: The UN's Roles in International Society since 1945', in Roberts and Kingsbury (eds.), *United Nations, Divided World* (Oxford: Clarendon Press).

Roberts, G. (1984), *Questioning Development* (London: Returned Volunteer Action).

Roberts, S. (1994), 'Fictitious Capital, Fictitious Spaces: The Geography of Offshore Financial Flows', in S. Corbridge *et al.* (eds.), *Money, Power and Space* (Oxford: Blackwell).

Robertson, E. M. (ed.) (1971), *The Origins of the Second World War: Historical Interpretations* (London: Macmillan).

Robertson, R. (1992), *Globalization: Social Theory and Global Culture* (London: Sage).

Rodley, N. S. (ed.) (1992), *To Loose the Bands of Wickedness: International Intervention in Defence of Human Rights* (London: Brasseys).

Rodney, W. (1972), *How Europe Underdeveloped Africa* (London: Bogle-L'Ouverture).

Rodrik, D. (1998) *Has Globalization Gone Too Far?* (Washington DC: Institute for International Economics).

—— (1999), *The New Global Economy and Developing Countries: Making Openness Work* (Washington, DC: Overseas Development Council), 148.

Rorty, R. (1993), 'Sentimentality and Human Rights', in S. Shute and S. Hurley (eds.), *On Human Rights* (New York: Basic Books).

Rosamond, B. (2000), *Theories of European Integration* (Basingstoke: Macmillan).

Rosenau, J. N. (1990), *Turbulence in World Politics* (Princeton: Princeton University Press).

—— (1997), 'The Dynamics of Globalization: Toward an Operational Formula', *Security Dialogue*, 27 (3): 247–62.

—— and Czempiel, E.-O. (1992), *Governance without Government: Order and Change in World Politics* (Cambridge: Cambridge University Press).

Rosenberg, J. (1994), *The Empire of Civil Society: A Critique of the Realist Theory of International Relations* (London: Verso).

Rostow, W. (1960), *The Stages of Economic Growth: A Non-Communist Manifesto* (London: Cambridge University Press).

Rotblat, J. (ed.) (1998), *Nuclear Weapons. The Road to Zero* (Boulder, Colo.: Westview).

Rousseau, J.-J. (1991), 'The State of War', in S. Hoffmann and D. P. Fidler (eds.), *Rousseau on International Relations* (Oxford: Clarendon Press).

Roxburgh, A. (1991), *The Second Russian Revolution* (London: BBC Publications).

Ruggie, J. G. (1982), 'International Regimes, Transactions and Change: Embedded Liberalism in the Post-War Economic Order', *International Organisation*, 36 (2).

—— (1995), 'At Home Abroad, Abroad at Home: International Liberalisation and Domestic Stability in the New World Economy', *Millennium: Journal of International Studies*, 24 (3): 507–26.

—— (1998), *Constructing the World Polity: Essays on International Institutionalization* (London: Routledge).

Rupert, M. (1995), *Producing Hegemony: The Politics of Mass Production and American Global Power* (Cambridge: Cambridge University Press).

Rusi, A (1997), *Dangerous Peace: New Rivalry in World Politics* (Boulder, Col: Westview Press).

Russett, B. (1993), *Grasping the Democratic Peace: Principles for a Post-Cold War World* (Princeton: Princeton University Press).

—— (1995), 'The Democratic Peace', *International Security* 19 (4): 164–84.

Sagan, S. D. (1996/7), 'Three Theories in Search of a Bomb', *International Security*, 21(3): 54–86.

—— (1993), *The Limits of Safety: Organisations, Accidents and Nuclear Weapons* (Princeton: Princeton University Press).

—— and Waltz, K. N. (1995), *The Spread of Nuclear Weapons: A Debate* (New York and London: W. W. Norton and Co.).

Said, E. W. (1993), *Culture and Imperialism* (London: Chatto and Windus).

—— (1995), *Orientalism: Western Conceptions of the Orient* (London: Penguin Books).

Sandhu, K. S. (ed.) (1992), *The ASEAN Reader* (Singapore: Institute of South East Asian Studies).

Scharpf, F. W., (1996), 'Positive and Negative Integration in the Political Economy of European Welfare States', in G. Marks *et al.*, *Governance in the European Union* (London: Sage).

Scheinman, L. (1987), *The International Atomic Energy Agency and World Nuclear Order* (Washington, DC: Johns Hopkins University Press).

Schelling, T. C. (1960), *The Strategy of Conflict* (Oxford: Oxford University Press).

Schlesinger, P. R. (1994), 'Europe's Contradictory Communicative Space', *Daedalus* 123(2).

Schmidt, B. C. (1998), *The Political Discourse of Anarchy: A Disciplinary History of International Relations* (Albany, NY: SUNY Press).

Schmitter, P. (1992), 'Representation and the Future Euro-Polity', *Staatswissenschaften und Staatspraxis*, 2(3).

Scholte, J. A. (1993), *International Relations of Social Change* (Buckingham: Open University Press)

—— (1996), 'Globalisation and Collective Identities', in J. Krause and N. Renwick (eds.), *Identities in International Relations* (London: Macmillan).

—— (1997a), *Globalisation: A Critical Introduction* (London: Macmillan).

—— (1997b), 'Global Capitalism and the State', *International Affairs*, 73 (3): 427–52.

—— (2000), *Globalization: A Critical Introduction* (Basingstoke: Macmillan).

Schumacher, E. F. (1973), *Small is Beautiful: Economics as if People Mattered* (New York: Harper and Row).

Seaman, J. (1996), 'The International System of Humanitarian Relief in the "New World Order" ', in John Harriss (ed.), *The Politics of Humanitarian Intervention* (London: Pinter), 17–32..

Seidler, V. (1989), *Rediscovering Masculinity: Reason, Language and Sexuality* (London: Routledge).

Sen, A. (1981), *Poverty and Famines* (Oxford: Clarendon Press).

—— (1983), 'The Food Problem: Theory and Policy', in A. Gauhar (ed.), *South–South Strategy* (London: Zed).

—— (1997), 'Rational Fools: A Critique of the Behavioural Foundations of Economic Theory', *Philosophy and Public Affairs*, 6 (4): 713–44.

Shaker, M. I. (1980), *The Nuclear Non-Proliferation Treaty*, Vols. 1–2 (London: Oceana).

Shannon T. R. (1989 and 1996), *An Introduction to the World-System Perspective* (Boulder, Colo.: Westview Press).

Sharpe, A. (1996), 'Exotic Derivatives "Less Favoured" ', *Financial Times*, 12 Feb. 8.

Shaw. M. (1994), *Global Society and International Relations* (Cambridge: Polity Press).

—— (1997), 'The State of Globalization: Towards a Theory of State Transformation', *Review of International Political Economy*, 4 (3).

—— (1999), 'The Global Revolution and the Twenty-first Century: From International Relations to Global Politics', in S. Chan and J. Wiener (eds.), *Twentieth Century International History* (London: I. B. Tauris).

Shue, H. (1980), *Basic Rights* (Princeton: Princeton University Press).

Shute, S., and Hurley, S. (eds.) (1993), *On Human Rights* (New York: Basic Books).

Simpson, J., and Howlett, D. (eds.) (1995), *The Future of the Non-Proliferation Treaty* (New York: St Martin's Press).

Sinclair, T. J. (1994), 'Passing Judgement: Credit Rating Processes as Regulatory Mechanisms of Governance in the Emerging World Order', *Review of International Political Economy*, 1 (Spring).

Singer, H., and Roy, S. (1993), *Economic Progress and Prospects in the Third World* (Aldershot: Edward Elgar).

Singer, M., and Wildavsky, A. (1993), *The Real World Order: Zones of Peace/Zones of Turmoil* (New Jersey: Chatham House Publishers).

Singer, P. (1985), *Marx* (Oxford: Oxford University Press).

Sivan, E. (1989), 'Sunni Radicalism in the Middle East and the Iranian Revolution', *International Journal of Middle Eastern Studies*, 21 (1).

Skinner, Q. (1988), 'Meaning and Understanding in the History of Ideas', in J. Tully (ed.), *Meaning and Context: Quentin Skinner and his Critics* (Cambridge: Polity Press), 29–67.

Skocpol, T. (1977), 'Wallerstein's World Capitalist System: A Theoretical and Historical Critique', *American Journal of Sociology*, 82 (5).

Smith, A. (1991), *National Identity* (London: Penguin).

Smith, D. (1991), *The Rise of Historical Sociology* (Cambridge: Polity Press).

Smith, M. (1986), *Realist Thought from Weber to Kissinger* (Baton Rouge: Louisiana State University Press).

Smith, S. (2000), 'Wendt's World', *Review of International Studies*, Vol. 26 (1): 151–63.

—— Booth, K., and Zalewski, M. (eds.) (1996), *International Theory: Positivism and Beyond* (Cambridge: Cambridge University Press).

Snitow, A. (1989), 'Pages from a Gender Diary: Basic Divisions in Feminism', *Dissent*, 36: 205–24.

Snyder, J. (1991), *Myths of Empire: Domestic Politics and International Ambition* (Ithaca, NY: Cornell University Press).

Soros, G. (1998) *The Crisis of Global Capitalism* (London: Little, Brown & Company).

South Commission (1990), *The Challenge to the South* (Oxford: Oxford University Press).

Spector, L., McDonough, M., with Medeiros, E. (1995), *Tracking Nuclear Proliferation: A Guide to Maps and Charts*, (Washington, DC: Carnegie Endowment for International Peace).

Spero, J. (1981), *The Politics of International Economic Relations* (New York: St Martin's Press).

Staar, H. (1999), *Anarchy, Order, and Integration: How to Manage Interdependence* (The University of Michigan Press).

Steans, J. (1998), *Gender and International Relations: An Introduction* (Cambridge: Polity Press).

Stein, A. (1982), 'Coordination and Collaboration in an Anarchic World', *International Organization*, 36 (2): 299–324.

—— (1983), 'Coordination and Collaboration in an Anarchic World', in Krasner (1983), 115–40.

Stiglitz, J. (1998), 'Towards a New Paradigm for Development: Strategies, Policies and Processes', *The Prebisch Lecture* (Geneva, UNCTAD, 19 Oct.). To be found at http://.www.worldbank.org/html/etme/jssp101998.htm.

Stopford, J., and Strange, S. (1991), *Rival States, Rival Firms: Competition for World Market Shares* (Cambridge: Cambridge University Press).

Strange, S. (1970), 'International Relations and International Economics: A Case of Mutual Neglect', *International Affairs*, 46 (2): 304–15

—— (1988), *States and Markets* (London: Pinter).

—— (1994a), 'Wake up, Krasner! The world HAS changed', *Review of International Political Economy*, 1 (2).

—— (1994b), *States and Markets*, 2nd edn. (London: Pinter).

Suganami, H. (1989), *The Domestic Analogy and World Order Proposals* (Cambridge: Cambridge University Press).

Sylvester, C. (1994), *Feminist Theory and International Relations in a Postmodern Era* (Cambridge: Cambridge University Press).

Tannenwald, N. (1999), 'The Nuclear Taboo: The United States and the Normative Basis of Nuclear Non-Use', *International Organization*, 53(3): 433–68.

Taylor, A. J. P. (1983), *A Personal History* (London: Hamish Hamilton).

Taylor, P. (1995), *International Organization in the Modern World* (London: Pinter).

—— (1996a), *The European Union since the 1990s* (Oxford: Oxford University Press).

—— (1996b), 'Options for the Reform of the International System for Humanitarian Assistance', in J. Harriss (ed.), *The Politics of Humanitarian Intervention* (London: Pinter).

—— and Groom, A. J. R. (eds.) (1989), *Global Issues in the United Nations Framework* (Basingstoke: Macmillan).

—— —— (1992), *The United Nations and the Gulf War, 1990–91*, RIIS discussion paper no. 38.

The *Ecologist* (1993), 'Whose Common Future? Reclaiming the Commons' (London: Earthscan).

Thomas, A. *et al.* (1994), *Third World Atlas*, 2nd edn. (Milton Keynes: Open University Press).

Thomas, C. (1985), *New States, Sovereignty and Intervention* (Aldershot: Gower).

—— (1993), 'The Pragmatic Case Against Intervention', in I. Forbes and M. Hoffmann (eds.), *Political Theory, International Relations and the Ethics of Intervention* (Basingstoke: St Martin's Press).

—— (1999) 'Where is the Third World Now?', *Review of International Studies*, December, special millennium edn.

—— (2000), *Global Governance, Development and Human Security* (London: Pluto).

Thomas, Sir J., and Tickell, Sir C. (1993), *The Expanding Role of the United Nations and its Implications . . .* (London: HMSO).

Thompson, E. (1990), 'The Ends of Cold War', *New Left Review*, 182, July/Aug, 139–46.

Thucydides (1954), *History of the Peloponnesian War*, trans. R. Warner (London: Penguin).

Tickner, J. A. (1988), 'Hans Morgenthau's Principles of Political Realism: A Feminist Reformulation', *Millennium*, 17 (3): 429–40

Tilly, C. (1990), *Coercion, Capital, and European States, AD 990–1990* (Oxford: Blackwell).

Tocqueville, A. (1933), *De Tocqueville's Ancien Regime*, trans. M. W. Patterson(Oxford: Basil Blackwell).

Treadgold, A. (1993), 'Cross-Border Retailing in Europe: Present Status and Future Prospects', in H. Cox *et al.* (eds.), *The Growth of Global Business* (London: Routledge).

Tsikata, D. (1995), 'Effects of Structural Adjustment on Women and the Poor', *Third World Resurgence*, no. 61/2, 56–9.

Tucker, R. W. (1977), *The Inequality of Nations* (New York: Basic Books).

UN Centre on Transnational Corporations (1988), *Transnational Corporations in World Development. Trends and Prospects* (New York: United Nations).

UN Conference on Environment and Development (1992), *Nations of the Earth* (New York: United Nations).

UN Conference on Trade and Development, Division on Transnational Corporations and Investment (1995), *World Investment Report 1995* (New York: United Nations).

UN (1999), *1999 World Survey on the Role of Women in Development: Globalization, Gender and Work* (New York: UN).

UNCTAD (1996), *Transnational Corporations and World Development* (London: International Thomson Business Press).

UNCTAD (1999), *World Investment Report 1999: Foreign Direct Investment and the Challenge of Development*. Geneva: United Nations Conference on Trade and Development.

UNDP (1994–), *Human Development Report 1994* (New York: Oxford University Press).

UNESCO, (1998), *World Culture Report: Culture, Creativity and Markets* (Paris: UNESCO).

UNFPA/Myers, N. (1991), *Population, Resources and the Environment* (NewYork: UNFPA).

Urwin, D. (1995), *The Community of Europe : A History of European Integration Since 1945 (The Postwar World)* (London: Addison-Wesley Longman, 1995).

Van der Wee, H. (1987), *Prosperity and Upheaval: The World Economy 1945–1980* (Harmondsworth: Penguin).

Vasquez, J. A. (1983), *The Power of Power Politics: A Critique* (London: Pinter).

—— (1993), *The War Puzzle* (Cambridge: Cambridge University Press).

—— (1998), *The Power of Power Politics: From Classical Realism to Neotraditionalism* (Cambridge: Cambridge University Press).

Vincent, R. J. (1974), *Nonintervention and International Order* (Princeton: Princeton University Press).

—— (1981), 'The Hobbesian Tradition in Twentieth Century International Thought', *Millennium*, 10 (2).

—— (1982), 'Realpolitik', in James Mayall (ed.), *The Community of States* (London: George Allen & Unwin).

—— (1986), *Human Rights and International Relations* (Cambridge: Cambridge University Press).

Viner, J. (1948), 'Power versus Plenty as Objectives of Foreign Policy in the Seventeenth and Eighteenth Centuries', *World Politics*, 1 (1): 1–29.

Viotti, P. R., and Kauppi, M. V. (1993), *International Relations*

Theory: Realism, Pluralism, Globalism (New York: Macmillan).

—— —— (eds.) (1999), *International Relations Theory: Realism, Pluralism, Globalism and Beyond* (Boston, Mass.: Allyn and Bacon).

Wade, R. (1996), 'Globalization and its Limits: Reports of the Death of the National Economy are Greatly Exaggerated', in Suzanne Berger and Ronald Dore (eds.), *National Diversity and Global Capitalism* (Ithaca, NY: Cornell University Press).

Waever, O. (1996), 'The Rise and Fall of the Inter-Paradigm Debate', in Smith *et al.* (1996): 149–85.

—— Buzan, B., Kelstrup, M., and Lemaitre, P. (1993), *Identity, Migration and the New Security Agenda in Europe* (London: Pinter).

Walker, R. B. J. (1993), *Inside/Outside: International Relations as Political Theory* (Cambridge: Cambridge University Press).

Wallace, H. (2000), 'The Policy Process', in H. Wallace and W. Wallace (eds.), *Policy-making in the European Union* (Oxford: Oxford University Press).

Wallace, W. (ed.) (1990), *The Dynamics of European Integration* (London: Pinter).

Wallerstein, I. (1974), *The Modern World-System*. Vol. 1. *Capitalist Agriculture and the Origins of the European World-Economy in the Sixteenth Century* (San Diego: Academic Press).

—— (1979), *The Capitalist World-Economy* (Cambridge: Cambridge University Press).

—— (1980), *The Modern World-System*. Vol. 2. *Mercantilism and the Consolidation of the European World-Economy, 1600–1750* (San Diego: Academic Press).

—— (1984), *The Politics of the World Economy: The States, the Movements, and the Civilisations* (Cambridge: Cambridge University Press).

—— (1989), *The Modern World-System*. Vol. 3. *The Second Era of Great Expansion of the Capitalist World-Economy* (San Diego: Academic Press).

—— (1991*a*), *Unthinking Social Science: The Limits of Nineteenth-Century Paradigms* (Cambridge: Polity Press).

—— (1991*b*), *Geopolitics and Geoculture: Essays on the Changing World-System* (Cambridge: Cambridge University Press).

—— (1994), 'The Agonies of Liberalism—What Hope Progress?', *New Left Review*, 204.

—— (1995), *After Liberalism* (New York: New Press).

—— (1996), 'The Inter-State Structure of the Modern World-System', in Smith, Booth, and Zalewski (1996).

Walt, S. (1998), 'International Relations: One World, Many Theories', *Foreign Policy*, 110: 29–46.

Waltz, K. (1959), *Man, the State and War* (New York: Columbia University Press).

—— (1979), *Theory of International Politics* (Reading, Mass.: Addison-Wesley).

—— (1981), *The Spread of Nuclear Weapons: More May Be Better*, Adelphi Paper 171 (London: International Institute for Strategic Studies).

—— (2000), 'Globalization and American Power', *The National Interest*, 59 (Spring): 46–56.

Walzer, M. (1977), *Just And Unjust Wars: A Moral Argument with Historical Illustration* (Harmondsworth: Penguin, and New York: Basic Books).

—— (1994*a*), *Thick and Thin: Moral Argument at Home and Abroad* (Notre Dame: University of Notre Dame Press).

—— (1994*b*) 'Spheres of Affection', *Boston Review*, 19 (5): 29.

—— (1995*a*) *The Spheres of Justice: A Defence of Pluralism and Equality*, (Oxford: Blackwell).

—— (1995*b*), 'The Politics of Rescue', *Dissent* (Winter).

Warren, B. (1980), *Imperialism: Pioneer of Capitalism* (London: New Left Books).

Washbrook, D. (1990), 'South Asia, The World System and World Capitalism', *Journal of Asian Studies*, 49 (3).

Waters, M. (1995), *Globalization* (London: Routledge).

Watson, A. (1982), *Diplomacy: The Dialogue Between States* (London: Methuen)

—— (1992), *The Evolution of International Society* (London: Routledge).

Weber, C. (1995), *Simulating Sovereignty: Intervention, the State and Symbolic Exchange* (Cambridge: Cambridge University Press).

Weber, H. (2001), *The Politics of Microcredit: Global Governance and Poverty Reduction* (London: Pluto).

Webster (1961), *Webster's Third New International Dictionary of the English Language Unabridged* (Springfield, Mass.: Merriam).

Wedgwood, C. V. (1992), *The Thirty Years War* (London: Pimlico).

Weiler, J. (1991*a*), 'Problems of Legitimacy in Post-1992 Europe', *Aussenwirtschaft*, 46 (3–4).

—— (1991*b*), 'The Transformation of Europe', *Yale Law Journal*, 100(8): 2403–83.

Weiss, L. (1998) *The Myth of the Powerless State*, Ithaca, NY: Cornell University Press.

—— (1999), 'Globalization and Governance', *Review of International Studies*, 25 (Special Issue).

Weiss, T. G. *et al.* (1994), *The United Nations and Changing World Politics*. (Boulder, Colo.: Westview).

Wendt, A. (1992), 'Anarchy is What States Make of It: The Social Construction of Power Politics', *International Organisation*, 46 (2): 391–425.

—— (1994), 'Collective Identity Formation and the International State', *American Political Science Review*, 88 (2): 384–96.

—— (1995), 'Constructing International Politics', *International Security* 20(1).

Wendt, A. (1999), *Social Theory of International Politics* (Cambridge: Cambridge University Press).

Wheeler, N. J. (1996), 'Guardian Angel or Global Gangster? A Review of the Ethical Claims of the Society of States', *Political Studies*, 44 (2).

—— (2000), *Saving Strangers: Humanitarian Intervention in International Society* (Oxford: Oxford University Press).

—— and Booth, K. (1992), 'The Security Dilemma', in J. Baylis and N. J. Rengger (eds.), *Dilemmas of World Politics: International Issues in a Changing World* (Oxford: Oxford University Press).

Wheen, F. (1999), *Karl Marx* (London: Fourth Estate).

White, S. (1990), *Gorbachev in Power* (Cambridge: Cambridge University Press).

Whitworth, S. (1989), 'Gender and the Inter Paradigm Debate', *Millennium*.

Wight, M. (1977), *Systems of States* (Leicester: Leicester University Press).

—— (1986), *Power Politics*, 2nd edn. (London: Penguin).

Willetts, P. (ed.) (1996), *The Conscience of the World* (London: Hurst and Co.).

Williams, M. (1994), *International Economic Institutions and the Third World* (London: Harvester Wheatsheaf).

Williams, P., and Black, S. (1994), 'Transnational Threats: Drug Trafficking and Weapons Proliferation', *Contemporary Security Policy*, 15 (1).

Williamson, J. (1990), 'What Washington Means by Policy Reform', in John Williamson (ed.), *Latin American Adjustment, How Much Has Happened?* (Washington, Institute for International Economics).

Wilson, P. (1998) 'The Myth of the "First Great Debate"', *Review of International Studies*, 24 (Special Issue).

Wincott, D. (1995), 'Institutional Interaction and European Integration: Towards an Everyday Critique of Liberal Intergovernmentalism', *Journal of Common Market Studies*, 33(4): 597–610.

Winham, G. (1977), 'Negotiation as a Management Process', *World Politics*, 30 (1) (Oct.) as reprinted in F. S. Sondermann, D. S. McClellan, and W. C. Olsen, *The Theory and Practice of International Relations* (Englewood Cliffs, NJ: Prentice-Hall)

Wolfensohn, J., 'President Wolfensohn's speech at the 1995 Beijing conference', www.worldbank.org/gender/how/policy.htm

Wolin, S. (1960), *Politics and Vision* (Boston: Little, Brown).

Women's Eyes on the World Bank-US Chapter and 50 Years Campaign (1997), *Gender Equity and the World Bank Group: A Post-Beijing Assessment* (Washington, DC).

Woolcock, S. (2000), 'European Trade Policy', H. Wallace and W. Wallace (eds.), *Policy-making in the European Union* (Oxford: Oxford University Press), 373–400.

World Bank (2000), *Addressing Gender Equity: World Bank Action Since Beijing* (Washington: World Bank), also available on World Bank web site.

World Commission on Environment and Development (1987), *Our Common Future* (*The Brundtland Report*) (Oxford: Oxford University Press).

World Trade Organization (WTO) (1995), *International Trade: Trends and Statistics* (Geneva: WTO).

Worsley, P. (1980), 'One World or Three? A Critique of the World-System Theory of Immanuel Wallerstein', *Socialist Register* (London: Merlin Press).

Wyatt-Walter, A. (1996), 'Adam Smith and the Liberal Tradition in International Relations', *Review of International Studies*, 22 (1), 142–172.

Young, I. M. (1990), *Justice and the Politics of Difference* (Princeton: Princeton University Press).

Young, O. (1997), *Global Governance* (Cambridge, Mass.: MIT Press).

Yuval-Davis, N., and Anthias, F. (eds.) (1989), *Woman Nation State* (London: Macmillan).

Zacher, M. W., with Sutton, B. A. (1996), *Governing Global Networks: International Regimes for Transportation and Communications* (Cambridge: Cambridge University Press).

Zalewski, M. (1993a), 'Feminist Standpoint Theory Meets International Relations Theory: A Feminist Version of David and Goliath', *The Fletcher Forum of World Affairs*, 17 (2).

—— (1993b), 'Feminist Theory and International Relations', in M. Bowker and R. Brown (eds.), *From Cold War to Collapse: Theory and World Politics in the 1980s* (Cambridge: Cambridge University Press).

—— and Enloe, C. (1995), 'Questions of Identity in International Relations', in K. Booth and S. Smith (eds.), *International Relations Theory Today* (Cambridge: Polity Press).

Zartman, I. W. (1995), *Collapsed States* (Boulder and London: Lynne Rienner).

Zevin, R. (1992), 'Are World Financial Markets More Open? If So, Why and With What Effects?', in T. Banuri and J. B. Schor (eds.), *Financial Openness and National Autonomy: Opportunities and Constraints* (Oxford: Clarendon Press).

Index

V